GEOMETRIC TOOLS FOR COMPUTER GRAPHICS

The Morgan Kaufmann Series in Computer Graphics and Geometric Modeling

Series Editor: Brian A. Barsky, University of California, Berkeley

GEOMETRIC TOOLS FOR COMPUTER GRAPHICS

PHILIP J. SCHNEIDER

DAVID H. EBERLY

MORGAN KAUFMANN PUBLISHERS

AN IMPRINT OF ELSEVIER SCIENCE

AMSTERDAM   BOSTON   LONDON   NEW YORK
OXFORD   PARIS   SAN DIEGO   SAN FRANCISCO
SINGAPORE   SYDNEY   TOKYO

Publishing Director   Diane Cerra
Publishing Services Manager   Edward Wade
Senior Developmental Editor   Belinda Breyer
Project Management   Elisabeth Beller
Cover Design   Ross Carron Design
Cover Image   Getty/Spencer Jones
Text Design   Rebecca Evans & Associates
Composition   Windfall Software, using ZzTEX
Technical Illustration and Figure Revision   Dartmouth Publishing, Inc.
Copyeditor   Ken DellaPenta
Proofreader   Jennifer McClain
Indexer   Steve Rath
Printer   The Maple-Vail Book Manufacturing Group

Designations used by companies to distinguish their products are often claimed as trademarks or registered trademarks. In all instances in which Morgan Kaufmann Publishers is aware of a claim, the product names appear in initial capital or all capital letters. Readers, however, should contact the appropriate companies for more complete information regarding trademarks and registration.

Morgan Kaufmann Publishers
An imprint of Elsevier Science
340 Pine Street, Sixth Floor
San Francisco, CA 94104-3205
www.mkp.com

Printed and bound in the United Kingdom
Transferred to Digital Printing, 2010

Library of Congress Control Number: 2002107242
ISBN: 1-55860-594-0

This book is printed on acid-free paper.

To my wife, Suzanne, and my sons, Dakota and Jordan   —PS

To my wife, Shelly, for her patience through yet another book   —DE

FOREWORD

Eric Haines

On my shelf is an old book called *A Programmer's Geometry,* by Bowyer and Woodwark. It was published in 1983, reprinted twice in 1984 and 1985, but then discontinued. Over the years I have guarded my copy, keeping careful track of who borrowed it. Checking on the Web today, I found six used copies ranging in price from $50 to $100. This is a high price range for a paperback book only 140 pages in length. The reason the book is worth this much is that it describes how to program various operations related to 2D geometry. It does not just present geometric formulae; it also describes efficient ways to accomplish tasks and gives code snippets (in FORTRAN).

Now, almost two decades later, we have a worthy successor to that slim volume. The book before you distills a huge amount of literature on geometry into that which is most useful to programmers. The field of computer graphics has evolved considerably since 1983, and this volume reflects those advances. Due to the continuing improvement in computer processor performance, operations that once were only part of offline analysis packages are now commonly done in interactive programs. Polygon triangulation, collision detection and response, and surface modelling and modification are now possible at real-time rates. This book gives solid explanations and code to perform these and many other algorithms.

Beyond providing a solid reference for a wide range of geometry-related tasks, this volume also presents the underpinnings of the theory behind the algorithms. Rather than employ a pure cookbook approach, which can leave the reader with runnable code and no comprehension of how it works, the authors explain key concepts. This approach makes each algorithm a tool that, further on, can be recombined with other tools.

The dynamic nature of computer graphics makes it a particularly interesting area of study. Research and implementation of rendering methods respond to changes in the underlying hardware. For example, in the field of interactive rendering, the emerging programmable nature of the graphics accelerator has changed the relative costs of different techniques. On a broader scale, the evolution of the CPU has made memory access and caching rise in importance, compared to the older practice of minimizing the number of operations (e.g., counting multiplies and adds). However, the underlying theory and algorithms for, say, finding the convex hull of an object are considerably more long-lasting, less affected by changes. Of course, more efficient algorithms are found over time, and hardware influences which method currently is considered the fastest, but the basic principles remain the same. Years after you have shed your books on DirectX 9 or Intel's 64-bit Itanium architecture, you are likely to have some edition of this book on your shelf.

Another reason this book will have increased staying power is the Internet. I am the archivist for the "Graphics Gems" series code repository. The code for this series of books, including code by Philip Schneider, was wisely made free for reuse when the series was published in the early 1990s. Over the years readers have sent in bug fixes and improvements to the code base, so benefiting all. Similarly, Dave Eberly has carefully maintained his "Magic Software" Web site (*www.magic-software.com*), which includes working versions of many of the algorithms presented in this volume. Called "a national treasure" by a leading researcher in computer graphics, this site allows addenda and corrigenda to be made available instantly whenever they are needed. Code does not rust; it improves with age when properly supported. This is particularly true for algorithms in this book as they are not tied to particular hardware, network protocols, or other transient objects.

Over the years I and many others have used algorithms and code by the authors in products and research projects. An hour of a programmer's time often costs more than the price of a book. By this measure, you hold a volume potentially worth thousands of dollars. That it can be purchased for a fraction of this cost I consider a modern miracle. The amount of information crammed into this book is incredible. The mathematics may be slow going at times, but the alternative would be to include wordier and less precise descriptions of fewer algorithms. If you are looking for a lightweight text you can read through and check off your list, keep searching. This book sometimes requires effort and struggle to fully comprehend but then, so do most of the worthwhile things in the world.

CONTENTS

CHAPTER

4

MATRICES, VECTOR ALGEBRA, AND TRANSFORMATIONS

CHAPTER

7

INTERSECTION IN 2D 241

CHAPTER

10

DISTANCE IN 3D   365

CHAPTER
11

INTERSECTION IN 3D   481

CHAPTER

12

MISCELLANEOUS 3D PROBLEMS   663

CHAPTER

13

APPENDIX

A

NUMERICAL METHODS   827

APPENDIX
C

BASIC FORMULAS FOR GEOMETRIC PRIMITIVES   949

FIGURES

TABLES

PREFACE

The advent of fast and inexpensive consumer graphics hardware has led to an increased demand for knowledge of how to program various geometric tasks for applications including computer games, scientific visualization, medical image analysis, simulation, and virtual worlds. The types of applications are themselves evolving to take advantage of the technology (Crawford 2002) and even include 3D environments for the purposes of code analysis and visual debugging, and analysis of coalition formation of political parties by representing the party beliefs as convex objects whose intersections indicate a potential coalition.

It is possible to find much of the graphics knowledge in resources that are scattered about, whether it be books, Web sites, newsgroups, journal articles, or trade magazines. Sometimes the resources are easy to comprehend, but just as often not. Sometimes they are presented with enough detail to illustrate underlying principles, sometimes not. Sometimes a concept is presented with an eye toward numerical issues that arise when using floating-point arithmetic, yet in other cases the concept is presented only in its full theoretical glory. Correctness of the presentation can even be an issue, especially with online articles. The time spent in locating the resources; evaluating their relevance, effectiveness, and correctness; and adapting them to your own needs is time better spent on other tasks. The book is designed with this in mind. It provides you with a comprehensive collection of many of the two- and three-dimensional geometric algorithms that you will encounter in practical applications. We call these *geometric tools* since, after all, the algorithms and concepts really are tools that allow you to accomplish your application's goals.

The level of difficulty of the topics in this book falls within a wide range. The problem can be as simple as computing the distance from a point to a line segment, or it can be as complicated as computing the intersection of two nonconvex, simple, closed polyhedra. Some of the tools require only a few simple concepts from vector algebra. Others require more advanced concepts from calculus such as derivatives of functions, level sets, or constrained minimization using Lagrange multipliers. Generally a book will focus on one end of the spectrum; ours does not. We intend that this book will be used by newcomers to the field of graphics and by experienced practitioners. For those readers who require a refresher on vector and matrix algebra, we have provided three gentle chapters on the topics. Various appendices are available, including one summarizing basic formulas from trigonometry and one covering various numerical methods that are used by the tools.

xliii

The book may be used in two ways. The first use is as a teaching tool. The material is presented in a manner to convey the important ideas in the algorithms, thus making the book suitable for a textbook in a college course on geometric algorithms for graphics. Although the book comes without exercises at the end of the sections, it does come with a lot of pseudocode. An appropriate set of assignments for the course could very well be to implement the pseudocode in a real programming language. To quote a famous phrase: the proof is in the pudding.

The second use for the book is as a reference guide. The algorithms chapters are organized by dimension, the two-dimensional material occurring first, the three-dimensional second. The chapter on computational geometry is a mixture of dimensions, but is better grouped that way as a single chapter. The organization makes it easy to locate an algorithm of interest. The attempt at separation by dimension comes at a slight cost. Some of the discussions that can normally be written once and apply to arbitrary dimensions are duplicated. For example, distance from a point to a line segment can be described in a dimensionless and coordinate-free manner, but we have chosen to discuss the problem both in two dimensions and in three dimensions. We believe this choice makes the sections relatively self-contained, thereby avoiding the usual reader's syndrome of having multiple pieces of paper or pens stuck in various locations in a book just to be able to navigate quickly to all the sections relevant to the problem at hand!

Inclusion of working source code in a computer science book has become common practice in the industry. In most cases, the code to illustrate the book concepts can be written in a reasonable amount of time. For a book of this magnitude that covers an enormous collection of algorithms, a full set of code to illustrate all the algorithms is simply not feasible. This is a difficult task even for a commercial venture. As an alternative, we have tried to add as much pseudocode as possible. The bibliography contains many references to Web sites (valid links as of the first printing of the book) that have implementations of algorithms or links to implementations. One site that has many of the algorithms implemented is *www.magic-software.com*, hosted by Magic Software, Inc. and maintained by Dave Eberly. The source code from this site may be freely downloaded. This site also hosts a Web page for the book, *www.magic-software.com/GeometricTools.html*, that contains information about the book, book corrections, and an update history with notifications about new source code and about bug fixes to old source code. Resources associated with the book are also available at *www.mkp.com/gtcg*.

We want to thank the book reviewers, Tomas Akenine-Möller (Chalmers University of Technology), Ian Ashdown (byHeart Consultants Limited), Eric Haines (Autodesk, Inc.), George Innis (Magic Software, Inc.), Peter Lipson (Toys for Bob, Inc.), John Stone (University of Illinois), Dan Sunday (Johns Hopkins University), and Dennis Wenzel (True Matrix Software), and the technical editor, Parveen Kaler (Simon Fraser University). A book of this size and scope is difficult to review, but their diligence paid off. The reviewers' comments and criticisms have helped to improve many aspects of the book. The input from Peter and Dennis is especially appreciated since they took on the formidable task of reading the entire book and provided detailed comments about nearly every aspect of the book, both at a low and a high level. David M. Eberle (Walt Disney Feature Animation) provided much of the pseudocode for several chapters and some additional technical reviewing; his help is greatly appreciated. We also want to thank our editor, Diane Cerra, and her assistant, Belinda Breyer, for the time they spent in helping us to assemble such a large tome and for their patience in understanding that authors need frequent encouragement to complete a work of this magnitude. The success of this book is due to the efforts of all these folks as well to ours. Enjoy!

C H A P T E R 1
INTRODUCTION

1.1 How to Use This Book

This book has many facets. An initial glance at the table of contents shows that the book is about two- and three-dimensional geometric algorithms that are applicable in computer graphics and in other fields as well. The sections have been organized to make it easy to locate an algorithm of interest and have been written with the goal of making them as self-contained as possible. In this guise the book is well suited as a reference for the experienced practitioner who requires a specific algorithm for the application at hand.

But the book is more than just a reference. A careful study of the material will reveal that many of the concepts used to analyze a geometric query are common to many of the queries. For example, consider the three-dimensional geometric queries of computing the distance between pairs of objects that are points, line segments, triangles, rectangles, tetrahedra, or boxes. The query for each pair of objects can be analyzed using specific knowledge about the form of the object. The common theme that unifies the analysis of the queries is that the objects can be parameterized by zero (point), one (segment), two (triangle, rectangle), or three (tetrahedra, box) parameters. The squared distance between any two points, one from each object, is a quadratic polynomial of the appropriate parameters. The squared distance between the two objects is the minimum of the quadratic polynomial. A search of the domain of the function will lead to the parameters that correspond to the closest points on the objects and, consequently, the minimum squared distance between the objects. This idea of searching the parameter domain is the foundation of the GJK distance algorithm that is used for computing the distance between two convex polyhedra. The common ideas in the various queries form the basis for a set of analytical tools that any practitioner in computer graphics should have readily available for solving new problems. Thus, this book is also well suited as a learning tool for someone wishing

1

to practice the science of computer graphics, and we believe that it is a good choice for a textbook in a course on geometric algorithms for computer graphics.

For the reader who, before jumping into the analyses of the geometric algorithms, wishes to obtain a moderate exposure to the basic mathematical tools necessary to understand the analyses, we have provided three chapters that summarize vector and matrix algebra. The appendices include a review of trigonometric formulas and a summary of many of the numerical methods that are used in the algorithms. Our intent is that the book contain enough of the basics and of the advanced material that a reader will have a very good understanding of the algorithms. However, some of the peripheral concepts may require additional study to comprehend fully what an implementation of the algorithm requires. For example, some algorithms require solving a system of polynomial equations. There are a few methods available for solving a system, some more numerically suited to the particular algorithm than others. Of course we encourage all readers to study as many peripheral topics as possible to have as much knowledge at hand to address the problems that arise in applications. The more depth of knowledge you have, the easier it will be to solve these problems.

1.2 ISSUES OF NUMERICAL COMPUTATION

We believe the book satisfies the needs of a wide audience of readers. Regardless of where in the spectrum a reader is, one inescapable dilemma for computer programming is having to deal with the problems of computation in the presence of a floating-point number system. Certainly at the highest level, a solid understanding of the theoretical issues for an algorithm is essential before attempting an implementation. But a theoretical understanding is not enough. Those programmers who are familiar with floating-point number systems know that they take on a life of their own and find more ways than you can imagine to show you that your program logic is not quite adequate!

1.2.1 LOW-LEVEL ISSUES

The theoretical formulation of geometric algorithms is usually in terms of real numbers. The immediate problem when coding the algorithms in a floating-point system is that not all real numbers are represented as floating-point numbers. If r is a real number, let $f(r)$ denote its floating-point representation. In most cases, f is chosen to round r to the nearest floating-point number or to truncate r. Regardless of method, the round-off error in representing r is $|f(r) - r|$. This is an absolute error measurement. The relative error is $|f(r) - r|/|r|$, assuming $r \neq 0$.

Arithmetic operations on floating-point numbers also can introduce numerical errors. If r and s are real numbers, the four basic arithmetic operations are addition, $r + s$; subtraction, $r - s$; multiplication, $r \times s$; and division, r/s. Let $\oplus$, $\ominus$, $\otimes$, and $\oslash$ denote the equivalent arithmetic operations for floating-point numbers. The sum $r + s$ is approximated by $f(r) \oplus f(s)$, the difference $r - s$ by $f(r) \ominus f(s)$, the product $r \times s$ by $f(r) \otimes f(s)$, and the quotient r/s by $f(r) \oslash f(s)$. The usual properties of arithmetic for real-valued numbers do not always hold for floating-point numbers. For example, if $s \neq 0$, then $r + s \neq r$. However, it is possible that $f(r) \oplus f(s) = f(r)$, in particular when $f(r)$ is much larger in magnitude than $f(s)$. Real-valued addition is associative and commutative. It does not matter in which order you add the numbers. The order for floating-point addition does matter. Suppose that you have numbers r, s, and t to be added. It is the case that $(r + s) + t = r + (s + t)$. In floating-point arithmetic, it is not necessarily true that $(f(r) \oplus f(s)) \oplus f(t) = f(r) \oplus (f(s) \oplus f(t))$. For example, suppose that $f(r)$ is so much larger in magnitude than $f(s)$ and $f(t)$ that $f(r) \oplus f(s) = f(r)$ and $f(r) \oplus f(t) = f(r)$. Then $(f(r) \oplus f(s)) \oplus f(t) = f(r) \oplus f(t) = f(r)$. It is possible to construct an example where $f(s) \oplus f(t)$ is sufficiently large so that $f(r) \oplus (f(s) \oplus f(t)) \neq f(r)$, thereby producing an example where associativity does not apply. Generally, the sum of nonnegative floating-point numbers should be done from smallest to largest to avoid the large terms overshadowing the small terms. If r_1 through r_n are the numbers to add, they should be ordered as $r_{i_1} \leq \cdots \leq r_{i_n}$ and added, in floating point, as $(((f(r_{i_1}) \oplus f(r_{i_2})) \oplus f(r_{i_3})) \oplus \cdots \oplus f(r_{i_n}))$.

Other floating-point issues to be concerned about are cancellation of significant digits by subtraction of two numbers nearly equal in magnitude and division by numbers close to zero, both cases resulting in unacceptable numerical round-off errors. A classic example illustrating remedies to both issues is solving the quadratic equation $ax^2 + bx + c = 0$ for $a \neq 0$. The theoretical roots are

$$x_1 = \frac{-b + \sqrt{b^2 - 4ac}}{2a} \quad \text{and} \quad x_2 = \frac{-b - \sqrt{b^2 - 4ac}}{2a}$$

Suppose that $b > 0$ and that b^2 is much larger in magnitude than $4ac$. In this case, $\sqrt{b^2 - 4ac}$ is approximately b, so the numerator of x_1 involves subtraction of two numbers of nearly equal magnitudes, leading to a loss of significant digits. Observe that x_2 does not suffer from this problem since its numerator has no cancellation. A remedy is to observe that the formula for x_1 is equivalent to

$$x_1 = \frac{-2c}{b + \sqrt{b^2 - 4ac}}$$

The denominator is a sum of two positive numbers of the same magnitude, so the subtractive cancellation is not an issue here. However, observe that

$$x_2 = \frac{-2c}{b - \sqrt{b^2 - 4ac}}$$

so in this formulation x_2 now suffers from subtractive cancellation and the division is by a number close to zero. Clearly it is not enough to choose one formulation of the roots over the other. To be completely robust, you should look at the magnitudes of b and $\sqrt{b^2 - 4ac}$ and select the appropriate formula for x_1 and for x_2.

Even if the numerical errors are within reason, this example shows another problem to deal with. An analysis might show that theoretically $b^2 - 4ac \geq 0$, so the quadratic equation has only real-valued roots. Numerical round-off errors might very well lead to a floating-point representation of $b^2 - 4ac$ that is just slightly negative, in which case the square root operation would fail (typically with a silent NaN [Not a Number]). If you know theoretically that $b^2 - 4ac \geq 0$, a safe way to calculate the square root is as $\sqrt{|b^2 - 4ac|}$ or $\sqrt{\max\{0, b^2 - 4ac\}}$.

1.2.2 HIGH-LEVEL ISSUES

One of the main traps in floating-point number systems that the mathematical mind falls into is related to the *Law of the Excluded Middle*. Simply stated, a proposition is either true or false. In symbolic terms, if S is a Boolean statement (its value is either true or false), then the Boolean statement S *or not* S is always true. Code tends to be implemented assuming the Law of the Excluded Middle always holds. Not so in floating-point arithmetic.

EXAMPLE   Consider a convex quadrilateral with counterclockwise-ordered vertices V_i for $0 \leq i \leq 3$ and a point P that is contained by the interior of the quadrilateral; that is, P is inside but not on any of the four edges. Exactly one of the following three statements must be true when all points are represented by real numbers:

- P lies in the interior of triangle $\langle V_0, V_1, V_3 \rangle$.
- P lies in the interior of triangle $\langle V_1, V_2, V_3 \rangle$.
- P lies in the interior of the common edge $\langle V_1, V_3 \rangle$.

In a floating-point number system where the containment test is based on computing barycentric coordinates, it is possible for all statements to be false! The problem is that P is nearly on the common edge $\langle V_1, V_3 \rangle$. One of the barycentric coordinates for the triangle containing P is theoretically a small positive number. Floating-point round-off errors can cause this coordinate to be a small negative number. If so, P is tagged as being outside that triangle. If also outside the other triangle, the three Boolean conditions are all false. This problem may occur when attempting to determine which triangle in a mesh of triangles contains a specified point, for example, during incremental construction of a Delaunay triangulation. ∎

EXAMPLE   Consider again a convex quadrilateral. Any set of three vertices forms a triangle. The circumscribed circle of that triangle might or might not contain the fourth vertex. When all points are represented as real numbers, theoretically it must be the case that at least one of the circumscribed circles must contain the fourth vertex.

In the presence of a floating-point number system, it is possible that floating-point round-off errors lead to tests that show none of the circumscribed circles contain the respective fourth vertices. This problem may occur when attempting to compute the minimum area circle that contains a finite set of points. ∎

EXAMPLE Theoretically, the intersection of a convex polyhedron and a plane is either a point, a line segment, or a convex polygon. In the presence of a floating-point number system, it is possible that the computed intersection may consist of a convex polygon with one or more line segments attached to the vertices. For example, the intersection could contain four points V_i, $0 \leq i \leq 3$, a triangle $\langle V_0, V_1, V_2 \rangle$, and an edge $\langle V_2, V_3 \rangle$. Your program logic for constructing the polygon of intersection must handle such aberrant cases. ∎

Numerous such examples may occur in nearly any implementation involving floating-point numbers, so you should always be aware not to rely solely on your mathematical reasoning when constructing the program logic.

A high-level issue in many computational geometry algorithms is the occurrence of collinear, coplanar, or cocircular points. Theoretical discussions about the algorithms tend to include assumptions that preclude these occurrences, just to make the analysis simpler. For example, in a Delaunay triangulation of a collection of points, if no four points are cocircular, the triangulation is unique. An incremental algorithm for constructing the triangulation is simple to construct. However, an implementation must be prepared to make the decision between one of two possible configurations when four cocircular points do occur (or nearly occur relative to the floating-point system; see the earlier example in the low-level issues). Construction of convex hulls is also plagued by issues of collinearity and coplanarity of points.

Certain algorithms involving the construction of intersection points require careful implementation because of floating-point problems. Consider computing the points of intersection of two ellipses. As you will see later, this is equivalent to computing the roots of a fourth-degree polynomial of a single variable. Numerical algorithms for locating roots may be applied to this polynomial equation, but beware when the coefficient of the fourth-degree term is zero or nearly zero. Root finders may go astray in this situation. Geometrically this occurs when the ellipses are circles or nearly circular. Even if the leading coefficient is sufficiently large, another type of numerical problem might occur, that of roots of even multiplicity. If r is a root of odd multiplicity for a function $f(x)$, then $f(r) = 0$, but f is negative on one side of the root and positive on the other side of the root (at least for x sufficiently close to r). If r is a root of even multiplicity, the sign of f is the same on both sides of the root (for x sufficiently close to r). The classic examples are $f(x) = x$ where $r = 0$ is a root of odd multiplicity (1) and $f(x) = x^2$ where $r = 0$ is a root of even multiplicity (2). The bisection root-finding method *requires* that the root be of odd multiplicity, so roots of $f(x) = x^2$ cannot be found with that method. The standard presentation of Newton's method for finding roots is done so for roots of multiplicity 1, although more advanced presentations will discuss modifications to the method to handle roots of larger multiplicity.

The numerical problems with finding roots might be viewed simply as a side effect of using floating-point numbers, one that does not occur frequently. However, sometimes the problems occur because of the very nature of the geometric query! Consider the problem of detecting when two moving ellipses intersect for the first time. Assuming the ellipses have different axis lengths, at the first time of contact the intersection consists of a single point. Moreover, at that time the fourth-degree polynomial that must be solved to produce the root has, *by the construction*, a root of even multiplicity. Therefore, your root finder absolutely must be able to handle even multiplicity roots. When dealing with intersection of objects, the concepts of odd and even multiplicity are related to *transversality* and *tangency*. If one curve intersects another and the respective tangent lines of the curves at the point of intersection are not parallel, the intersection is transverse. Any polynomial equation related to the intersection will have a root of odd multiplicity corresponding to that intersection. If the tangent lines are parallel, the contact is tangential and the polynomial equation will have a root of even multiplicity. Tangential contact is important in many applications, especially in collision detection of moving objects.

Finally, a phenomenon that is less frequently considered when implementing an algorithm is *order-dependence of the input parameters*. For example, if you implement a function `TestIntersection(Segment,Segment)` that tests if two line segments intersect (the return value is either `true` or `false`), it is desirable that `TestIntersection(S0,S1)` and `TestIntersection(S1,S0)` produce the same result for any pair of inputs S0 and S1. If the function fails to satisfy this constraint, it could be due to a poor algorithmic design, but more likely it is due to incorrect handling of floating-point issues in the implementation.

1.3 A SUMMARY OF THE CHAPTERS

For those readers wishing to review the basic concepts in vector and matrix algebra, we have provided three chapters (2, 3, and 4). A summary of many of the numerical methods used in the algorithms in the book is provided in Appendix A. Formulas from trigonometry may be found in Appendix B. Appendix C is a quick reference for basic formulas for some of the geometric primitives encountered in the book.

Chapter 5 provides the definitions for the various two-dimensional objects to which the geometric queries apply. These include lines, rays, line segments, polygons, conic sections (curves defined by quadratic equations), and polynomial curves. The main geometric queries are distance measurements, discussed in Chapter 6, and intersection queries, discussed in Chapter 7. Miscellaneous queries of interest are provided in Chapter 8.

Chapter 9 provides the definitions for the various three-dimensional objects to which the geometric queries apply. These include lines, rays, line segments, planes and planar objects (two-dimensional objects embedded in a plane in three dimensions), polyhedra and polygon meshes, quadric surfaces (surfaces defined by quadratic equations), polynomial curves, polynomial surfaces, rational curves, and rational surfaces. The main geometric queries are distance measurements, discussed in Chapter 10, and intersection queries, discussed in Chapter 11. Miscellaneous queries of interest are provided in Chapter 12.

An extensive amount of material on topics in computational geometry is provided in Chapter 13. The topics include binary space-partitioning trees, Boolean operations on polygons and polyhedra, point-in-polygon and point-in-polyhedron tests, construction of convex hulls of point sets, Delaunay triangulation of point sets, triangulation of polygons and decomposition of polygons into convex pieces, and minimum area and volume bounding containers for point sets. A section is also included on area calculations for polygons, whether in two or three dimensions, and on volume calculations for polyhedra.

CHAPTER 2

MATRICES AND LINEAR SYSTEMS

2.1 INTRODUCTION

One of the purposes of this book is to provide a large set of "recipes" for solving many commonly encountered geometric problems in computer graphics. While it is our intention to provide some explanation of *how* these recipes work, we'd also like to go a step further. There is an old proverb that states "Give a man a fish, he will eat for a day. Teach a man to fish, he will eat for a lifetime." To that end, we've included several chapters that attempt to impart an understanding of *why* and *how* many of the basic tools of geometry in computer graphics work. When you encounter a new problem of the type addressed in this book, you can develop solutions based not only on adapting the recipes we have provided, but also based on a true understanding of the concepts, principles, and techniques upon which our recipes are built.

2.1.1 MOTIVATION

Most books covering some aspect of computer graphics include a chapter or appendix addressing the basic background for computing with points, vectors, and matrices; this book is no different in that respect. However, we part company beyond that point. Many computer graphics texts covering the mathematical analysis employed in computer graphics begin with a coordinate-based, matrix-oriented approach. This approach is also commonly used in the interface of many graphics libraries that have been in commercial or research use.

Coordinate-based methods emphasize analysis based on the relationship of geometric entities relative to some specific coordinate system. This approach is useful in some situations—for example, if we have a hierarchically defined model and we wish to find the distance between two points that are defined in different parts of the hierarchy, we need to transform the coordinates of one of the points into the space of the other point and determine the Euclidean distance in the usual fashion.

However, even in this simple example, you can see some shortcomings of this approach. Consider an example given by DeRose (1989) of simply showing the code for a matrix-based transformation. In the absence of any "contextual" information, the real nature of the computation is ambiguous. Consider a few lines of C-like code for transforming a 2D point:

```
float P[2];
float PPrime[2];
float M[2][2];


P[0] = x;
P[1] = y;

M[0][0] = 3; M[0][1] = 0;
M[1][0] = 0; M[1][1] = 2;

PPrime[0] = P[0] * M[0][0] + P[1] * M[1][0];
PPrime[1] = P[0] * M[0][1] + P[1] * M[1][1];
```

This code fragment can be interpreted in any of three ways:

1. As a change of coordinates, which leaves the point unchanged geometrically, but changes the coordinate system (see Figure 2.1(a)).
2. As a transformation of the coordinate plane onto itself, which moves the point but leaves the coordinate system itself unchanged (see Figure 2.1(b)).
3. As a transformation from one plane to another (see Figure 2.1(c)).

As DeRose points out, these interpretations are not interchangeable: in the first interpretation, lengths and angles don't change, but they can in the second and third.

A further complication, which can be seen in this example, is that the representation of P yields no clue as to whether it represents a point or a vector. Thus, code written and conceptualized in this fashion can perform what Ron Goldman (1985) calls "illicit" operations such as adding two points together.

Such arguments may perhaps be viewed by some as being technically correct, but so long as the job gets done, what's the harm? It turns out that excessive dependence on a strictly coordinate-based approach not only makes for ambiguous implementations and offers many opportunities for illicit operations, but also can make a problem that is relatively simple conceptually into a nightmare of implementation. An excellent example, provided by Miller (1999a, 1999b) is as follows: Suppose we have two vectors $\vec{u}$ and $\vec{v}$, and we want a transformation matrix that rotates $\vec{u}$ onto $\vec{v}$ (note that there are infinitely many ways to rotate one vector onto another; here, we con-

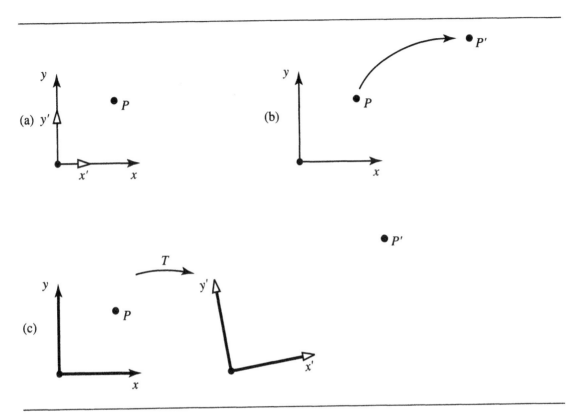

Figure 2.1   Various ways of interpreting the example ambiguous transformation: (a) change of coordinates; (b) transformation of plane onto itself; and (c) transformation from one plane to another.

sider a rotation in the plane containing the two vectors, with the smallest possible angle). In a strictly coordinate-based approach, you would have to do the following:

Step 1. Determine the series of transformations that would map each vector onto, say, the z-axis.

Step 2. Concatenate the transformations for $\vec{u}$ with the inverse of those for $\vec{v}$.

If we just look at, as Miller suggests, a small part of this sequence of computations such as that of transforming $\vec{u}$ onto the z-axis by following the development in Foley et al. (1996), we get a matrix that is the product of

$$\begin{bmatrix} 1 & 0 & 0 \\ 0 & \dfrac{\sqrt{u_x^2+u_z^2}}{\|\vec{u}\|} & \dfrac{-u_y}{\|\vec{u}\|} \\ 0 & \dfrac{u_y}{\|\vec{u}\|} & \dfrac{\sqrt{u_x^2+u_z^2}}{\|\vec{u}\|} \end{bmatrix} \begin{bmatrix} \dfrac{u_x}{\sqrt{u_x^2+u_z^2}} & 0 & \dfrac{u_z}{\sqrt{u_x^2+u_z^2}} \\ 0 & 1 & 1 \\ \dfrac{-u_z}{\sqrt{u_x^2+u_z^2}} & 0 & \dfrac{u_x}{\sqrt{u_x^2+u_z^2}} \end{bmatrix}$$

Miller points out several difficulties with this approach (aside from the obvious ugliness of the above derivation): The denominators, particularly in the second matrix, may be zero or nearly zero. This would require the implementation to carefully range-check these values before using them. This situation would arise if $\vec{u}$ happened to be parallel (or nearly so) to the y-axis, a condition that is otherwise irrelevant geometrically to the problem at hand. This problem exists with the analogous matrices for the $\vec{v}$ vector's transformations as well. Finally, it is also necessary to invert both the matrices for $\vec{v}$, which tends to introduce numerical imprecision.

An alternative vector-based approach would start by noting that the problem can be viewed as computing the transformation matrix $\mathbf{M}$ that rotates about a vector $\vec{w} = \vec{u} \times \vec{v}$. We start by computing the sine and cosine of θ, the angle between $\vec{u}$ and $\vec{v}$:

$$\sin \theta = \frac{\|\vec{u} \times \vec{v}\|}{\|\vec{u}\|\|\vec{v}\|}$$

$$\cos \theta = \frac{\vec{u} \cdot \vec{v}}{\|\vec{u}\|\|\vec{v}\|}$$

According to Goldman (1990b) such a transformation can be constructed using the following formula:

$$\mathbf{M} = \cos \theta \mathbf{I} + (1 - \cos \theta)\hat{w} \otimes \hat{w} + \sin \theta \mathbf{W}$$

where

$$\hat{w} = \frac{\vec{w}}{\|\vec{w}\|}$$

$$\mathbf{W} = \begin{bmatrix} 0 & -w_z & w_y \\ w_z & 0 & -w_x \\ -w_y & w_x & 0 \end{bmatrix}$$

I is the identity matrix, and $\otimes$ is the tensor product operator (see Section 4.4.3).

In contrast to the coordinate-based approach is the *vector geometric* approach, an example of which we just saw. Rather than being concerned from the start with components of points (and vectors), and rather than starting out thinking of transformations as 3×3 or 4×4 matrices, this alternative approach instead emphasizes thinking about points and vectors as *abstract* geometric entities, which are manipulated by (again, abstract) geometric operators (transformations, cross products, etc.). In short, we're talking about a *geometric algebra*. DeRose (1989) and Goldman (1987) refer to this approach as *coordinate-free geometry* to point up the difference between this and the coordinate-based approach that is commonly used.

Many of the sections in the next chapter attempt to build up the fundamentals of this geometric algebra. There are several motivations for doing so. First, the algorithms presented in this book can only be well understood if the reader has a firm grasp on what's really going on (for example, what *does* a cross product really do, and why is it formulated as it is?). Second, a good understanding of these basic principles will allow readers themselves to construct correct and robust algorithms for new problems they encounter. Finally, this approach is, in the authors' opinions, much more intuitive, and it serves the graphics community to help counter the usual approach to the subject, which generally consists of introducing points and vectors as arrays of real numbers, and various operations (dot products, cross products, transformations) as apparently arbitrary arithmetic combinations of the members of these arrays.

Finally, the discussions and explanations in this book are, as much as possible, given in terms of this vector geometry approach, and accordingly, we attempt to make as clear as possible the distinction between points and vectors. Supporting this distinction are notational conventions that reflect widespread usage in the computer graphics literature:

- Points are represented in equations as uppercase Times italic characters, generally using the letters P, Q, R, and so on, or in the case of sequences or sets of points, subscripted versions of this notation: P_1, P_2, and so on.

- Vectors are represented as lowercase Times italic letters, with a diacritical arrow above them, generally using the letters $\vec{u}$, $\vec{v}$, $\vec{w}$, or subscripted versions in the case of sets, sequences, or arrays of them: $\vec{v}_1$, $\vec{v}_2$, and so on. Unit-length vectors are denoted with a "hat" instead of a diacritical arrow: $\hat{u}$, $\hat{v}$, $\hat{w}$.

This notation allows for the maximum visual distinction and reflects an approach best justified by Ron Goldman (1985):

> The coordinate approach to vector geometry—where both points and vectors are represented as 3 rectangular coordinates—is the source of much confusion. If we fix a coordinate origin, then there is a natural 1–1 correspondence between points and vectors. Thus the point P can be represented by the vector OP where O is the origin of the coordinate system, but this subtle distinction is generally ignored. Even so, it is not correct to write $P = OP$; an elephant is not a banana, and a point is not a vector.

2.1.2 ORGANIZATION

Most books covering geometry in computer graphics tend to mix the discussion of points, vectors, transformations, and matrices all into one explanation; we're going to take a different approach.

In spite of our comments in the previous section regarding the coordinate-based approach, an understanding of matrices and linear algebra is still important. One reason is that one component of affine spaces (which we'll discuss in the next chapter) is a vector space, which has a close involvement with linear systems. Another reason is that matrix operations can be (and are, generally) used to implement vector geometric operations. This chapter, then, is a presentation of matrices and linear algebra principles that are relevant to the succeeding presentations of vector algebra and the use of matrices in implementing vector algebra. Readers who are highly familiar with linear algebra may wish to jump directly to the next chapter. We have included this material in the body of the book for those readers who would like "the whole picture" and to provide a better narrative flow of the ideas linking matrices, linear algebra, and vector algebra.

Chapter 3 shifts gears entirely and covers vector algebra from a completely coordinate-free approach. Much of this material directly "overlaps" the linear-algebra-based presentation of this chapter, and readers will certainly be able to see this; for example, this chapter covers vector space from an abstract linear algebra perspective, while the next chapter explains a vector space from the more concrete, visual perspective of directed line segments. It turns out, of course, that these are the *same* vector spaces.

Chapter 4 explictly brings together vector algebra, linear algebra, and matrices. Other treatments of these interrelationships have either simply mixed them all together, which obscures the intuitive, vector-algebra-based concepts, or taken the position that the vector algebra is "merely" a geometric *interpretation* of linear algebra. Our contention is that the ideas of location, direction, distance, and angle are the more fundamental, and that linear algebra and matrices are simply a way of representing and manipulating them. This difference may be a bit of a "religious" or philosophical issue that is essentially unresolvable, but in any case it's certainly true that the coordinate-free vector algebra approach has many advantages in terms of fostering intuition. For example, if you start with the linear algebra definition of a dot product, it is extremely difficult to understand why this apparently arbitrary sequence of arithmetic operations on the elements of an array has any relationship at all to the angle between vectors; however, if you understand the dot product in terms of what its geometrical definition is and are then shown how this is implemented in terms of matrix operations, you understand what the dot product really means and how you might make use of it when you try to deal with new geometry problems.

2.1.3   Notational Conventions

This book contains a rather large number of equations, diagrams, code, and pseudocode; in order to help readability, we employ a consistent set of notational conventions, which are outlined in Table 2.1.

2.2   Tuples

Before we get into matrices themselves, we'll back up a level of abstraction and talk about *tuples*. Conceptually, a tuple is an ordered list of elements; however, because this book is about geometry in computer graphics, we're going to restrict our discussions to real numbers. Nevertheless, it should be remembered that tuples and ma-

Table 2.1   Mathematical notation used in this book.

Entity	Math Notation	Pseudocode
Set	$\{a, b, c\}$	
Scalar	$\alpha, \beta, \gamma, a, b, c$	`float alpha, a;`
Angle	θ, ϕ	`float theta, phi;`
Point	P, Q, R, P_1, P_2	`Point2D p, q, r1;Point3D p1, p2;`
Vector	$\vec{u}, \vec{v}, \vec{w}$	`Vector2D u, v; Vector3D w;`
Unit vector	$\hat{u}, \hat{v}, \hat{w}$	`Vector2D uHat, vHat; Vector3D wHat;`
Perpendicular vector	$\vec{u}_\perp, \vec{v}_\perp$	`Vector2D uPerp, vPerp;`
Parallel vector	$\vec{u}_\parallel, \vec{v}_\parallel$	`Vector2D uPar, vPar;`
Vector length	$\|\vec{u}\|$	
Matrix	$\mathbf{M}, \mathbf{N}, \mathbf{M}_1, \mathbf{M}_2$	`Matrix3x3 m, m; Matrix4x4 m1, m2;`
Matrix transpose	$\mathbf{M}^T, \mathbf{N}^T$	`Matrix3x3 mTrans, nTrans;`
Matrix inverse	$\mathbf{M}^{-1}, \mathbf{N}^{-1}$	`Matrix3x3 mInv, nInv;`
Tuple	$\mathbf{a} = (a_1, a_2, \ldots, a_n)$	
Determinant	$|\mathbf{M}|$ or $\det(\mathbf{M})$	`Det(m)`
Space (linear, etc.)	$\mathcal{V}, S^2$	
Space (reals)	$\mathbb{R}, \mathbb{R}^2, \mathbb{R}^3$	
Dot (inner) product	$a = \vec{u} \cdot \vec{v}$	`a = Dot(u, v);`
Cross product	$\vec{w} = \vec{u} \times \vec{v}$	`w = Cross(u, v);`
Tensor (outer) product	$\vec{w} = \vec{u} \otimes \vec{v}$	`w = Outer(u, v);`

trices may (conceptually) be composed of complex numbers, or any arbitrary type, and that much of what is discussed (in terms of properties, in particular) applies to arbitrary element types.

2.2.1 DEFINITION

A single real number is commonly referred to as a *scalar*; for example, 6.5, 42, or π. If we have two scalars and wish to group them together in such a way as to give meaning to order, we call them an *ordered pair*; a group of three is an *ordered triple*; a group of four is an *ordered quadruple*; and so on. The general term for such lists is *tuple*. For the time being, we'll notate them with lowercase Roman boldface and show the elements as parentheses-delimited lists; for example:

$$\mathbf{a} = (6.5, 42)$$

$$\mathbf{b} = (\pi, 3.75, 8, 15)$$

Generically, we refer to a tuple of n elements as an *n-tuple* and use subscript notation for it: $\mathbf{a} = (a_1, a_2, \ldots, a_n)$.

2.2.2 ARITHMETIC OPERATIONS

The tuples we're interested in are composed of real numbers, and it's natural to inquire into arithmetic using tuples.

Addition (and subtraction) of tuples is meaningful if each tuple has the same number of elements and the elements represent "corresponding" quantities. In this case, we can simply add (subtract) two tuples by adding (subtracting) their elements pairwise:

$$\mathbf{a} = \left(a_1, a_2, \cdots, a_n\right)$$

$$\mathbf{b} = \left(b_1, b_2, \cdots, b_n\right)$$

$$\mathbf{a} + \mathbf{b} = \left(a_1 + b_1, a_2 + b_2, \cdots, a_n + b_n\right)$$

$$\mathbf{a} - \mathbf{b} = \left(a_1 - b_1, a_2 - b_2, \cdots, a_n - b_n\right)$$

For example, $(6, 3, 7) + (1, -2, 4) = (7, 1, 11)$.

Multiplication and division of tuples by scalars is defined as simply applying the multiplication (division) to each element of the tuple:

$$k\mathbf{a} = \left(ka_1, ka_2, \cdots, ka_n\right)$$

$$\frac{\mathbf{a}}{k} = \left(\frac{a_1}{k}, \frac{a_2}{k}, \cdots, \frac{a_n}{k}\right)$$

For example, $2 \times (6, 3, 7) = (12, 6, 14)$, and $(6, 3, 7) / 2 = (3, 1.5, 3.5)$.

What about multiplication of two tuples? This is a natural question, but the answer is not so direct as it is for addition/subtraction and scalar multiplication/division. It turns out there are two different types of tuple/tuple multiplication, but we're going to hold off on this until we can put it into more context.

Given this idea of tuples, it's natural to consider collections of tuples, which together have some meaning or function (in the general and specific meanings of that term). The type of organization of tuples of interest to us here is a matrix, whose representation, properties, and application are the subject of the rest of this chapter.

2.3 MATRICES

At its most basic level, a matrix is simply a rectangular array of items; these elements are real numbers, or symbols representing them. In computer graphics books, matrices are often discussed at a rather "mechanistic" level—a "bag" of numbers, and rules for operating on them, that can be used for representing and manipulating graphical objects. This treatment, however, fails to convey *why* matrices work, and it is the intention of the next few chapters to try to bring together linear algebra, matrices, and computer graphics geometry in a more intuitive fashion. To that end, you are encouraged to try to think of matrices as lists of tuples, or perhaps better as "tuples of tuples," whose order has some deeper meaning than "that's just the way it works."

For many reasons, a list (or tuple) of tuples can be most advantageously represented by writing them as a top-to-bottom stack of horizontally oriented individual tuples, or as a left-to-right grouping of vertically oriented individual tuples.

Conventional notation is to bracket a matrix on the left and right with some sort of delimiter—in this book, we'll use square brackets, for example:

$$\begin{bmatrix} 3.2 & 7 \end{bmatrix} \qquad \begin{bmatrix} a \\ b \\ c \end{bmatrix} \qquad \begin{bmatrix} 4 & 7 & 93.5 \\ 5 & 9 & 12 \end{bmatrix}$$

2.3.1 NOTATION AND TERMINOLOGY

We denote a matrix with boldface uppercase letters like this: $\mathbf{M}$ or $\mathbf{A}$. Each of the items in a matrix is called an *element*. The horizontal and vertical arrays of elements (that is, tuples) are called *rows* and *columns*, respectively. The numbers of rows and columns are typically denoted by m and n, respectively, and the *size* of a matrix is given as "m by n," notated $m \times n$. If $m = n$, the matrix is said to be *square*.

If we want to refer to a matrix's elements generically, we will be using a common convention:

$$\mathbf{M} = \begin{bmatrix} a_{1,1} & a_{1,2} & \cdots & a_{1,n} \\ a_{2,1} & a_{2,2} & \cdots & a_{2,n} \\ \vdots & \vdots & \ddots & \vdots \\ a_{m,1} & a_{m,2} & \cdots & a_{m,n} \end{bmatrix}$$

Note that the subscripts are in (*row, column*) order.

If we wish to refer to a matrix even more generically, the notation we'll use will be like this: $\mathbf{A} = [a_{i,j}]$, to indicate we have a matrix $\mathbf{A}$ whose elements are specified as in the above example.

2.3.2 TRANSPOSITION

The *transpose* of an $m \times n$ matrix $\mathbf{M}$ is formed by taking the m rows of $\mathbf{M}$ and making them (in order) the columns of a new matrix (which of course makes the columns of $\mathbf{M}$ become the rows). You can also think about it in terms of rotating the matrix about a line going diagonally from the upper left to the lower right. The resulting transpose of $\mathbf{M}$ is notated $\mathbf{M}^T$ and will of course be $n \times m$ in size. Let's transpose the matrices we gave as our initial examples:

$$\mathbf{M}_1 = [\, 3.2 \quad 7 \,] \qquad\qquad \mathbf{M}_1^T = \begin{bmatrix} 3.2 \\ 7 \end{bmatrix}$$

$$\mathbf{M}_2 = \begin{bmatrix} a \\ b \\ c \end{bmatrix} \qquad\qquad \mathbf{M}_2^T = [\, a \quad b \quad c \,]$$

$$\mathbf{M}_3 = \begin{bmatrix} 4 & 5 & 93.5 \\ 5 & 9 & 12 \end{bmatrix} \qquad \mathbf{M}_3^T = \begin{bmatrix} 4 & 5 \\ 5 & 9 \\ 93.5 & 12 \end{bmatrix}$$

In general, if we have a matrix

$$\mathbf{M} = \begin{bmatrix} a_{1,1} & a_{1,2} & \cdots & a_{1,n} \\ a_{2,1} & a_{2,2} & \cdots & a_{2,n} \\ \vdots & \vdots & \ddots & \vdots \\ a_{m,1} & a_{m,2} & \cdots & a_{m,n} \end{bmatrix}$$

then its transpose is

$$\mathbf{M}^T = \begin{bmatrix} a_{1,1} & a_{2,1} & \cdots & a_{m,1} \\ a_{1,2} & a_{2,2} & \cdots & a_{m,2} \\ \vdots & \vdots & \ddots & \vdots \\ a_{1,n} & a_{2,n} & \cdots & a_{m,n} \end{bmatrix}$$

Matrix transposition has several properties worth mentioning:

i. $(\mathbf{AB})^T = \mathbf{B}^T\mathbf{A}^T$

ii. $(\mathbf{A}^T)^T = \mathbf{A}$

iii. $(\mathbf{A} + \mathbf{B})^T = \mathbf{A}^T + \mathbf{B}^T$

iv. $(k\mathbf{A})^T = k(\mathbf{A}^T)$

2.3.3 ARITHMETIC OPERATIONS

Addition and subtraction of matrices, and multiplication and division of a matrix by a scalar, follow naturally from these same operations on scalars and tuples. Furthermore, the properties of these operations (commutativity, associativity, etc.) are shared with scalars and tuples.

Addition and Subtraction

Addition of two matrices is the natural extension of tuple addition: if we have two matrices $\mathbf{A} = [a_{i,j}]$ and $\mathbf{B} = [b_{i,j}]$, then their sum is computed by simply summing the elements of each tuple (row):

$$\mathbf{A} + \mathbf{B} = \begin{bmatrix} a_{1,1} & a_{1,2} & \cdots & a_{1,n} \\ a_{2,1} & a_{2,2} & \cdots & a_{2,n} \\ \vdots & \vdots & \ddots & \vdots \\ a_{m,1} & a_{m,2} & \cdots & a_{m,n} \end{bmatrix} + \begin{bmatrix} b_{1,1} & b_{1,2} & \cdots & b_{1,n} \\ b_{2,1} & b_{2,2} & \cdots & b_{2,n} \\ \vdots & \vdots & \ddots & \vdots \\ b_{m,1} & b_{m,2} & \cdots & b_{m,n} \end{bmatrix}$$

$$= \begin{bmatrix} a_{1,1} + b_{1,1} & a_{1,2} + b_{1,2} & \cdots & a_{1,n} + b_{1,n} \\ a_{2,1} + b_{2,1} & a_{2,2} + b_{2,2} & \cdots & a_{2,n} + b_{2,n} \\ \vdots & \vdots & \ddots & \vdots \\ a_{m,1} + b_{m,1} & a_{m,2} + b_{m,2} & \cdots & a_{m,n} + b_{m,n} \end{bmatrix}$$

Scalar Multiplication and Division

Multiplication of a matrix by a scalar is defined analogously to multiplication of a tuple by a scalar: each element is simply multiplied by the scalar. Thus, if we have a scalar k and a matrix $\mathbf{A}$, we define $k\mathbf{A}$ as

$$k\mathbf{A} = \begin{bmatrix} ka_{1,1} & ka_{1,2} & \cdots & ka_{1,n} \\ ka_{2,1} & ka_{2,2} & \cdots & ka_{2,n} \\ \vdots & \vdots & \ddots & \vdots \\ ka_{m,1} & ka_{m,2} & \cdots & ka_{m,n} \end{bmatrix}$$

Division by a scalar is analogous.

The Zero Matrix

As we mentioned previously, matrix addition exhibits many of the properties of normal (scalar) addition. One of these properties is that there exists an *additive identity* element: that is, there is an $m \times n$ matrix, called the $\mathbf{0}$ matrix, with the property such that $\mathbf{M} + \mathbf{0} = \mathbf{M}$, for any matrix $\mathbf{M}$. This zero matrix also has the property that $\mathbf{M0} = \mathbf{0}$, and so it acts like the number 0 for scalar multiplication. An $m \times n$ zero matrix simply has all its elements as 0 and is sometimes notated as $\mathbf{0}_{m \times n}$:

$$\mathbf{0}_{2 \times 3} = \begin{bmatrix} 0 & 0 & 0 \\ 0 & 0 & 0 \end{bmatrix} \qquad \mathbf{0}_{3 \times 2} = \begin{bmatrix} 0 & 0 \\ 0 & 0 \\ 0 & 0 \end{bmatrix}$$

Properties of Arithmetic Operations

Because we've defined these arithmetic operations on matrices in terms of operations on their tuples, and because the operations on tuples were defined in terms of arithmetic operations on their scalar elements, it should be unsurprising that the properties of operations on matrices are the same as those for scalars:

i. Commutativity of addition: $\mathbf{A} + \mathbf{B} = \mathbf{B} + \mathbf{A}$.

ii. Associativity of addition: $\mathbf{A} + (\mathbf{B} + \mathbf{C}) = (\mathbf{A} + \mathbf{B}) + \mathbf{C}$.

iii. Associativity of scalar multiplication: $k\,(l\mathbf{A}) = (kl)\,\mathbf{A}$.

iv. Distributivity of scalar multiplication over addition: $k\,(\mathbf{A} + \mathbf{B}) = k\mathbf{A} + k\mathbf{B}$.

v. Distributivity of scalar addition over multiplication $(k_1 + k_2)\,\mathbf{A} = k_1\mathbf{A} + k_2\mathbf{A}$.

vi. Additive inverse: $\mathbf{A} + (-\mathbf{A}) = \mathbf{0}$.

vii. Additive identity: $\mathbf{A} + \mathbf{0} = \mathbf{A}$.

viii. Scalar multiplicative identity: $1 \cdot \mathbf{A} = \mathbf{A}$.

ix. Zero element: $0 \cdot \mathbf{A} = \mathbf{0}$.

We'll save the multiplicative identity and multiplicative inverse for the next section.

2.3.4 MATRIX MULTIPLICATION

Multiplication of matrices is not quite as straightforward an extension of multiplication of scalars as, say, matrix addition was an extension of scalar addition.

Tuple Multiplication

Just as we defined matrix addition in terms of addition of tuples, so too we define matrix multiplication in terms of multiplication of tuples. But what does this mean? Let's begin with a real-world example. Say we have a tuple $\mathbf{a} = (2, 3, 2)$ that lists the volumes of three different items (say, gravel, sand, and cement, the ingredients for concrete), and a tuple $\mathbf{b} = (20, 15, 10)$ that lists the weight of each ingredient per unit volume. What's the total weight? Obviously, you just multiply the volumes and weights together pairwise and sum them:

$$\mathbf{ab} = (2 \times 20) + (3 \times 15) + (2 \times 10) = 105$$

This is known as the *scalar product* or, because it's conventionally notated $\mathbf{a} \cdot \mathbf{b}$, the *dot product*. In general, if we have two n-tuples $\mathbf{a} = (a_1, a_2, \cdots, a_n)$ and

$\mathbf{b} = \left(b_1, b_2, \cdots, b_n\right)$, their product is computed as

$$\mathbf{a} \cdot \mathbf{b} = a_1 b_1 + a_2 b_2 + \cdots + a_n b_n$$

Properties of Tuple Multiplication

Because tuple multiplication is defined simply in terms of scalar addition and multiplication, it again should be unsurprising that tuple multiplication follows the same rules as scalar multiplication:

  i. Commutativity: $\mathbf{a} \cdot \mathbf{b} = \mathbf{b} \cdot \mathbf{a}$.
 ii. Associativity: $(k\mathbf{a}) \cdot \mathbf{b} = k\left(\mathbf{a} \cdot \mathbf{b}\right)$.
iii. Distributivity: $\mathbf{a} \cdot \left(\mathbf{b} + \mathbf{c}\right) = (\mathbf{a} \cdot \mathbf{b}) + (\mathbf{a} \cdot \mathbf{c})$.

Multiplying Matrices by Matrices

As we'll see in the rest of the book, the operation of multiplying a matrix by a matrix is one of the most important uses of matrices. As you might expect, matrix multiplication is an extension of tuple multiplication, just as matrix addition and scalar multiplication of a matrix were extensions of tuple addition and scalar tuple multiplication.

There is, however, an important aspect of matrix multiplication that is not necessarily intuitive or obvious. We'll start off by looking at multiplying matrices consisting each of a single n-tuple. A matrix of one n-tuple may be written as an $n \times 1$ matrix (a single column), or as a $1 \times n$ matrix (a single row). If we have two matrices $\mathbf{A}$ and $\mathbf{B}$, each consisting of an n-tuple $\mathbf{a}$ or $\mathbf{b}$, respectively, we can multiply them if $\mathbf{A}$ is written as a row matrix and $\mathbf{B}$ is a column matrix, and they are multiplied in that order:

$$\mathbf{AB} = \begin{bmatrix} a_1 & a_2 & \cdots & a_n \end{bmatrix} \begin{bmatrix} b_1 \\ b_2 \\ \vdots \\ b_n \end{bmatrix} = a_1 b_1 + a_2 b_2 + \cdots + a_n b_n \qquad (2.1)$$

We can see here that multiplying a row by a column produces a *single* real number. So, if we have two matrices with several rows and columns, we would of course compute several real numbers.

By definition, general matrix multiplication works this way: given an $m \times n$ matrix $\mathbf{A}$ and an $n \times r$ matrix $\mathbf{B}$, the product $\mathbf{AB}$ is a matrix $\mathbf{C}$ of size $m \times r$; its elements $c_{i,j}$ are the dot product of the ith row of $\mathbf{A}$ and the jth column of $\mathbf{B}$:

$$
AB = \begin{bmatrix} a_{1,1} & a_{1,2} & \cdots & a_{1,n} \\ a_{2,1} & a_{2,2} & \cdots & a_{2,n} \\ \vdots & \vdots & \ddots & \vdots \\ a_{m,1} & a_{m,2} & \cdots & a_{m,n} \end{bmatrix} \begin{bmatrix} b_{1,1} & b_{1,2} & \cdots & b_{1,r} \\ b_{2,1} & b_{2,2} & \cdots & b_{2,r} \\ \vdots & \vdots & \ddots & \vdots \\ b_{n,1} & b_{n,2} & \cdots & b_{n,r} \end{bmatrix}
$$

$$
= \begin{bmatrix} a_{1,1}b_{1,1} + a_{1,2}b_{2,1} + \cdots + a_{1,n}b_{n,1} & a_{1,1}b_{1,2} + a_{1,2}b_{2,2} + \cdots + a_{1,n}b_{n,2} & \cdots & a_{1,1}b_{1,r} + a_{1,2}b_{2,r} + \cdots + a_{1,n}b_{n,r} \\ a_{2,1}b_{1,1} + a_{2,2}b_{2,1} + \cdots + a_{2,n}b_{n,1} & a_{2,1}b_{1,2} + a_{2,2}b_{2,2} + \cdots + a_{2,n}b_{n,2} & \cdots & a_{2,1}b_{1,r} + a_{2,2}b_{2,r} + \cdots + a_{2,n}b_{n,r} \\ \vdots & \vdots & \ddots & \vdots \\ a_{m,1}b_{1,1} + a_{m,2}b_{2,1} + \cdots + a_{m,n}b_{n,1} & a_{m,1}b_{1,2} + a_{m,2}b_{2,2} + \cdots + a_{m,n}b_{n,2} & \cdots & a_{m,1}b_{1,r} + a_{m,2}b_{2,r} + \cdots + a_{m,n}b_{n,r} \end{bmatrix}
$$

For example, if

$$
A = \begin{bmatrix} 2 & 3 \\ 9 & 1 \end{bmatrix}
$$

and

$$
B = \begin{bmatrix} 1 & 7 & 5 \\ 4 & 6 & 8 \end{bmatrix}
$$

then

$$
C = AB
$$

$$
= \begin{bmatrix} 2 & 3 \\ 9 & 1 \end{bmatrix} \begin{bmatrix} 1 & 7 & 5 \\ 4 & 6 & 8 \end{bmatrix}
$$

$$
= \begin{bmatrix} 2 \times 1 + 3 \times 4 & 2 \times 7 + 3 \times 6 & 2 \times 5 + 3 \times 8 \\ 9 \times 1 + 1 \times 4 & 9 \times 7 + 1 \times 6 & 9 \times 5 + 1 \times 8 \end{bmatrix}
$$

$$
= \begin{bmatrix} 14 & 32 & 34 \\ 13 & 69 & 53 \end{bmatrix}
$$

Properties of Matrix Multiplication

Unlike scalar multiplication and addition of matrices, matrix multiplication does *not* share all the properties of real number multiplication.

i. Commutativity: This does *not* hold. If we are to multiply matrices **A** and **B** in that order, we saw that the number of columns in **A** must equal the number of rows in **B**, but the number of rows in **A** and number of columns in **B** may be arbitrarily different. Thus, if we try to multiply **B** by **A**, we may fail due to a size mismatch. Even if this were not the case, the result is not necessarily the same.

ii. Associativity: If we have A (BC), then (AB) C is defined and is equivalent.

iii. Associativity of scalar multiplication: If AB is a legal operation, then $(k\text{A}) \text{B} = k (\text{AB})$.

iv. Distributivity of multiplication over addition: If A is $m \times n$ and B and C are $n \times r$, then A (B + C) = AB + AC. Note that because commutativity does not hold, we have (B + C) A = BA + CA, which is a different result.

Multiplying Row or Column Tuples by General Matrices

In computer graphics, two of the most common operations involving matrices are the multiplication of two square matrices (as described in the previous section) and the multiplication of a row or column matrix by a square matrix.

We've just defined tuple multiplication and the rule for computing element c_{ij}. If we take these two together, we see that the matrix representation of tuple-tuple multiplication *must* be in the order shown in Equation 2.1—the row tuple must be on the left and the column tuple on the right. Consider a pair of two-element tuples and their product:

$$\mathbf{a} = (a_1, a_2)$$

$$\mathbf{b} = (b_1, b_2)$$

$$\mathbf{ab} = a_1 b_1 + a_2 b_2$$

If we were to multiply them as a column matrix by row matrix, in that order, we'd have

$$\begin{bmatrix} a_1 \\ a_2 \end{bmatrix} [\, b_1 \quad b_2 \,] = \begin{bmatrix} a_1 b_1 & a_1 b_2 \\ a_2 b_1 & a_2 b_2 \end{bmatrix}$$

if we follow the rule for matrix multiplication, but the result conflicts with the definition of tuple multiplication.

This result extends to the case where one of A or B is a general matrix. The result of this is that multiplication of a single tuple by a matrix must have the single tuple either as a row matrix on the left *or* as a column matrix on the right. However, we can't simply reorder the multiplication because matrix multiplication isn't commutative.

The first property of matrix transposition (see Section 2.3.2) tells us that the transposition of a matrix product is equivalent to the product of the transposition of each matrix, with the order of multiplication reversed: $(\text{AB})^{\text{T}} = \text{B}^{\text{T}} \text{A}^{\text{T}}$. This means that the two following representations of multiplying a tuple a by a general matrix B are equivalent:

$$\begin{bmatrix} a & b \end{bmatrix} \begin{bmatrix} c & d \\ e & f \end{bmatrix} = \begin{bmatrix} ac + be & ad + bf \end{bmatrix}$$

$$\begin{bmatrix} c & e \\ d & f \end{bmatrix} \begin{bmatrix} a \\ b \end{bmatrix} = \begin{bmatrix} ca + eb \\ da + fb \end{bmatrix}$$

We'll see later that computation of a function of a tuple is conveniently implemented as a multiplication of the tuple by a matrix. Given the preceding discussion, it should be clear that we could represent tuples as row *or* column matrices, and simply use the matrix or its transpose, respectively. In computer graphics literature, you see both conventions being used, and this book also uses both conventions. When reading any book or article, take care to notice which convention an author is using. Fortunately, converting between conventions is trivial: simply reverse the order of the matrices and vectors, and use instead the transpose of each. For example:

$$\vec{u}\mathbf{M} = \begin{bmatrix} u_1 & u_2 & u_3 \end{bmatrix} \begin{bmatrix} m_{1,1} & m_{1,2} & m_{1,3} \\ m_{2,1} & m_{2,2} & m_{2,3} \\ m_{3,1} & m_{3,2} & m_{3,3} \end{bmatrix}$$

$$\equiv \begin{bmatrix} m_{1,1} & m_{2,1} & m_{3,1} \\ m_{1,2} & m_{2,2} & m_{3,2} \\ m_{1,3} & m_{2,3} & m_{3,3} \end{bmatrix} \begin{bmatrix} u_1 \\ u_2 \\ u_3 \end{bmatrix} = \mathbf{M}^\mathrm{T}\vec{u}^\mathrm{T}$$

2.4 LINEAR SYSTEMS

Linear systems are an important part of linear algebra because many important problems in linear algebra can be dealt with as problems of operating on linear systems. Linear systems can be thought of rather abstractly, with equations over real numbers, complex numbers, or indeed any arbitrary field. For the purposes of this book, however, we'll restrict ourselves to the real field $\mathbb{R}$.

2.4.1 LINEAR EQUATIONS

Linear equations are those whose terms are each linear (the product of a real number and the first power of a variable) or constant (just a real number). For example:

$$5x + 3 = 7$$

$$2x_1 + 4 = 12 + 17x_2 - 5x_2$$

$$6 - 12x_1 + 3x_2 = 42x_3 + 9 - 7x_1$$

The mathematical notation convention is to collect all terms involving like variables (unknowns) and to refer to the equations in terms of the number of unknowns. The preceding equations would thus be rewritten as

$$5x = 4$$

$$2x_1 - 12x_2 = 8$$

$$-5x_1 + 3x_2 - 42x_3 = 3$$

and referred to, respectively, as linear equations of one, two, and three unknowns. The *standard forms* for linear equations in one, two, and n unknowns, respectively, are

$$ax = c$$

$$a_1x_1 + a_2x_2 = c$$

$$a_1x_1 + a_2x_2 + \cdots + a_nx_n = c$$

where the as are (given) real number *coefficients* and the xs are the unknowns.

Solving linear equations in one unknown is trivial. If we have an equation $ax = c$, we can solve for x by dividing each side by a: $x = c/a$ (provided $a \neq 0$).

Linear equations with two unknowns are a bit different: a solution consists of a pair of numbers (x_1, x_2) that satisfies the equation

$$a_1x_1 + a_2x_2 = c$$

We can find a solution by assigning any arbitrary value for x_1 or x_2 (thus reducing it to an equation of one unknown) and solve it as we did for the one-unknown case. For example, if we have the equation

$$3x_1 + 2x_2 = 6$$

we could substitute $x_1 = 2$ in the equation, giving us

$$3(2) + 2x_2 = 6$$

$$6 + 2x_2 = 6$$

$$2x_2 = 0$$

$$x_2 = 0$$

So, $(2, 0)$ is a solution. But, if we substitute $x_1 = 6$, we get

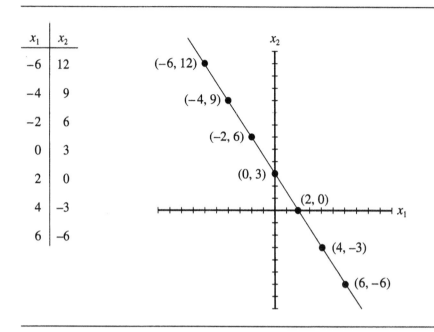

Figure 2.2   The solutions of the linear equation $3x_1 + 2x_2 = 6$.

$$3(6) + 2x_2 = 6$$

$$18 + 2x_2 = 6$$

$$2x_2 = -12$$

$$x_2 = -6$$

yielding another solution $u = (6, -6)$. Indeed, there are an infinite number of solutions. At this point, we can introduce some geometric intuition: if we consider the variables x_1 and x_2 to correspond to the x-axis and y-axis of a 2D Cartesian coordinate system, the individual solutions consist of points in the plane. Let's list a few solutions and plot them (Figure 2.2).

The set of all solutions to a linear equation of two unknowns consists of a line; hence the name "linear equation."

2.4.2 Linear Systems in Two Unknowns

Much more interesting and useful are *linear systems*—a set of two or more linear equations. We'll start off with systems of two equations with two unknowns, which have the form

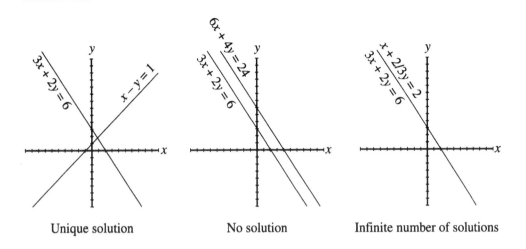

Figure 2.3 Three possible two-equation linear system solutions.

$$a_{1,1}x + a_{1,2}y = c_1$$

$$a_{2,1}x + a_{2,2}y = c_2$$

Recall from our previous discussion that a two-unknown linear equation's solution can be viewed as representing a line in 2D space, and thus a two-equation linear system in two unknowns represents two lines. Even before going on, it's easy to see that there are three cases to consider:

i. The lines intersect at one point.

ii. The lines do not intersect—they're parallel.

iii. The lines coincide.

Recalling that a solution to a single linear equation in two unknowns represents a point on a line, the first case means that there is one $u = (k_1, k_2)$ point that is a solution for both equations. In the second case, there are no points that are on both lines; there is no solution to the system. In the third case, there are an infinite number of solutions because any point on the line described by the first equation also satisfies the second equation (see Figure 2.3). The second and third cases occur when the coefficients in the two linear equations are proportional:

$$\frac{a_{1,1}}{a_{2,1}} = \frac{a_{1,2}}{a_{2,2}}$$

What distinguishes the two cases is whether or not the constant terms are proportional to the coefficients. The system has an infinite number of solutions (the two lines are the same) if the coefficients and the constant terms are all proportional:

$$\frac{a_{1,1}}{a_{2,1}} = \frac{a_{1,2}}{a_{2,2}} = \frac{c_1}{c_2}$$

but no solutions (the lines are parallel) if the coefficients are proportional, but the constants are not:

$$\frac{a_{1,1}}{a_{2,1}} = \frac{a_{1,2}}{a_{2,2}} \neq \frac{c_1}{c_2}$$

If there *is* a solution, it may be found by a process known as *elimination*:

Step 1. Multiply the two equations by two numbers so that the coefficients of one of the variables are negatives of one another.

Step 2. Add the resulting equations. This eliminates one unknown, leaving a single linear equation in one unknown.

Step 3. Solve this single linear equation for the one unknown.

Step 4. Substitute the solution back into one of the original equations, resulting in a new single-unknown equation.

Step 5. Solve for the (other) unknown.

EXAMPLE   Given

$$
\begin{array}{rll}
(1) & 3x + 2y & = & 6 \\
(2) & x - y & = & 1
\end{array}
$$

we can multiply (1) by 1 and (2) by -3 and then add them:

$$
\begin{array}{lrll}
1 \times (1): & 3x + 2y & = & 6 \\
-3 \times (2): & -3x + 3y & = & -3 \\
\hline
\text{Sum:} & 5y & = & 3
\end{array}
$$

which we solve trivially: $y = 3/5$. If we substitute this back into (1) we get

$$3x + 2\left(\frac{3}{5}\right) = 6$$

$$3x + \frac{6}{5} = 6$$

$$3x = \frac{24}{5}$$

$$x = \frac{8}{5}$$

Thus $(8/5, 3/5)$ is the solution, which corresponds to the point of intersection. ■

2.4.3 GENERAL LINEAR SYSTEMS

The general form of an $m \times n$ system of linear equations is

$$a_{1,1}x_1 + a_{1,2}x_2 + \cdots + a_{1,n}x_n = c_1$$

$$a_{2,1}x_1 + a_{2,2}x_2 + \cdots + a_{2,n}x_n = c_2$$

$$\vdots$$

$$a_{m,1}x_1 + a_{m,2}x_2 + \cdots + a_{m,n}x_n = c_m$$

A system in which $c_1 = c_2 = \cdots = c_m = 0$ is known as a *homogeneous* system. Frequently, linear systems are written in matrix form:

$$\mathbf{AX} = \mathbf{C}$$

$$\begin{bmatrix} a_{1,1} & a_{1,2} & \cdots & a_{1,n} \\ a_{2,1} & a_{2,2} & \cdots & a_{2,n} \\ & & \vdots & \\ a_{m,1} & a_{m,2} & \cdots & a_{m,n} \end{bmatrix} \begin{bmatrix} x_1 \\ x_2 \\ \vdots \\ x_n \end{bmatrix} = \begin{bmatrix} c_1 \\ c_2 \\ \vdots \\ c_m \end{bmatrix}$$

The matrix $\mathbf{A}$ is referred to as the *coefficient matrix*, and the matrix

$$\begin{bmatrix} a_{1,1} & a_{1,2} & \cdots & a_{1,n} & c_1 \\ a_{2,1} & a_{2,2} & \cdots & a_{2,n} & c_2 \\ & & \vdots & & \\ a_{m,1} & a_{m,2} & \cdots & a_{m,n} & c_m \end{bmatrix}$$

is known as the *augmented matrix*.

Methods for solving general linear systems abound, varying in generality, complexity, efficiency, and stability. One of the most commonly used is called *Gaussian elimination*—it's the generalization of the elimination scheme described in the previous section. Full details of the Gaussian elimination algorithm can be found in Section A.1 in Appendix A.

2.4.4   ROW REDUCTIONS, ECHELON FORM, AND RANK

We can look back at the example of the use of the technique of elimination for solving a linear system and represent it in augmented matrix form:

$$\begin{bmatrix} 3 & 2 & 6 \\ 1 & -1 & 1 \end{bmatrix}$$

We then multiplied the second row by -3, yielding an equivalent pair of equations, whose matrix representation is

$$\begin{bmatrix} 3 & 2 & 6 \\ -3 & 3 & -3 \end{bmatrix}$$

The next step was to add the two equations together and replace one of the equations with their sum:

$$\begin{bmatrix} 3 & 2 & 6 \\ 0 & 1 & \frac{3}{5} \end{bmatrix}$$

We then took a "shortcut" by substituting $\frac{3}{5}$ into the first row and solving directly.

Note that the lower left-hand corner element of the matrix is 0, which of course resulted from our choosing the multiplier for the second row in a way that the sum of the first row and the "scaled" second row eliminated that element.

So, it's clear we can apply these operations—multiplying a row by a scalar and replacing a row by the sum of it and another row—without affecting the solution(s).

Another operation we can do on a system of linear equations (and hence the matrices representing them) is to interchange rows, without affecting the solution(s) to the system; clearly, from a mathematical standpoint, the order is not significant.

If we take these two ideas together, we essentially have described one of the basic ideas of Gaussian elimination (see Section A.1): by successively eliminating the leading elements of the rows, we end up with a system we can solve via back substitution. What is important for the discussion here, though, is the form of the system we end up with (just prior to the back-substitution phase); our system of equations that starts out like this:

$$a_{1,1}x_1 + a_{1,2}x_2 + a_{1,3}x_3 + \cdots + a_{1,n}x_n = c_1$$

$$a_{2,1}x_1 + a_{2,2}x_2 + a_{2,3}x_3 + \cdots + a_{2,n}x_n = c_2$$

$$\vdots$$

$$a_{m,1}x_1 + a_{m,2}x_2 + a_{m,3}x_3 + \cdots + a_{m,n}x_n = c_m$$

ends up in upper triangular form, like this:

$$b_{1,1}x_1 + b_{1,2}x_2 + b_{1,3}x_3 + \cdots + b_{1,n}x_n = d_1$$

$$b_{2,k_2}x_{k_2} + b_{2,k_3}x_3 + \cdots + b_{2,n}x_n = d_2$$

$$\vdots$$

$$b_{r,k_r}x_{k_r} + \cdots + b_{r,n}x_n = d_r$$

Notice that the subscripts of the last equation no longer involve m, but rather $r <= m$, because this process may eliminate some equations: the process might sometimes produce equations of the form

$$0x_1 + 0x_2 + \cdots + 0x_n = c_i$$

If $c_i = 0$, then the equation can be eliminated entirely, without affecting the results; if $c_i \neq 0$, then the system is inconsistent (has no solution), and we can stop at that point. The result is that successive applications of these operations on rows will tend to make the system smaller.

Several other important statements can be made about the number r:

- If $r = n$, then the system has a unique solution.

- If $r < n$, then there are more unknowns than equations, which implies that there are many solutions to the system.

In general, we call these operations *elementary row operations*—these are operations that can be applied to a linear system (and its matrix representation) that do not change the solution set, and they may be codified as follows:

- Exchanging two rows.

- Multiplying a row by a (nonzero) constant.

- Replacing a row by the sum of it and another row.

Combinations of operations that result in the elimination of at least one nonzero row element are called *row reductions*.

As the operations are applied to the various equations, we can represent this as a series of transformations on the matrix representation of the system; a system of equations, and the matrix representation of it, is in *echelon form* as a result of this process (that is, once row reduction is complete, and the matrix cannot be further reduced). The number of equations r of such a "completely reduced" matrix is known as the *rank* of the matrix; thus, it may be said that the rank is an inherent property of the matrix that's only apparent once row reduction is complete.

The rank of a matrix is related to the concepts of basis, dimension, and linear independence in the following way: the rank is the number of linearly independent row (or column) vectors of the matrix, and if the rank is equal to the dimension, then the rows of the matrix can be seen as a basis for a space defined by the matrix.

The preceding claim equating the rank with the number of linearly independent rows of an echelon-form matrix follows from the fact that if two row vectors were *not* linearly independent, that is,

$$a_1 \vec{v}_i + a_2 \vec{v}_j = 0$$

for some $a_1, a_2 \in \mathbb{R}$, then we could have properly applied a row reduction operation to them, which would mean that the matrix was, contrary to our assumption, *not* in echelon form.

2.5   Square Matrices

Within the general realm of linear algebra, square matrices are particularly significant; this is in great part due to their role in representing, manipulating, and solving linear systems. We'll see in the next chapters that this significance extends to their role in representing geometric information and their involvement in geometric transformations. We'll start by going over some specific types of square matrices.

2.5.1   Diagonal Matrices

Diagonal matrices are those with 0 elements everywhere but along the diagonal:

$$\mathbf{M} = \begin{bmatrix} a_{1,1} & 0 & \cdots & 0 \\ 0 & a_{2,2} & \cdots & 0 \\ \vdots & \vdots & \ddots & \vdots \\ 0 & 0 & \cdots & a_{n,n} \end{bmatrix}$$

Diagonal matrices have some properties that can be usefully exploited:

i. If **A** and **B** are diagonal, then **C** = **AB** is diagonal. Further, **C** can be computed more efficiently than naively doing a full matrix multiplication: $c_{ii} = a_{ii}b_{ii}$, and all other entries are 0.

ii. Multiplication of diagonal matrices is commutative: if **A** and **B** are diagonal, then **C** = **AB** = **BA**.

iii. If **A** is diagonal, and **B** is a general matrix, and **C** = **AB**, then the ith row of **C** is a_{ii} times the ith row of **B**; if **C** = **BA**, then the ith column of **C** is a_{ii} times the ith column of **B**.

Scalar Matrices

Scalar matrices are a special class of diagonal matrices whose elements along the diagonal are all the same:

$$\mathbf{M} = \begin{bmatrix} \alpha & 0 & \cdots & 0 \\ 0 & \alpha & \cdots & 0 \\ \vdots & \vdots & \ddots & \vdots \\ 0 & 0 & \cdots & \alpha \end{bmatrix}$$

Identity Matrices

Just as the zero matrix is the additive identity, there is a type of matrix that is the multiplicative identity, and it is normally simply called **I**. So, for any matrix **M**, we have **IM** = **MI** = **M**. Note that *unlike* the zero matrix, the identity matrix cannot be of arbitrary dimension; it must be square, and thus is sometimes notated $\mathbf{I}_n$. For an $m \times n$ matrix **M**, we have $\mathbf{I}_m\mathbf{M} = \mathbf{M}\mathbf{I}_n = \mathbf{M}$. The identity matrix is one whose elements are all 0s, except the top-left to bottom-right diagonal, which is all 1s; for example:

$$\mathbf{I}_2 = \begin{bmatrix} 1 & 0 \\ 0 & 1 \end{bmatrix} \qquad \mathbf{I}_3 = \begin{bmatrix} 1 & 0 & 0 \\ 0 & 1 & 0 \\ 0 & 0 & 1 \end{bmatrix}$$

In general, the form of an identity matrix is

$$\mathbf{I}_n = \begin{bmatrix} 1 & 0 & \cdots & 0 \\ 0 & 1 & \cdots & 0 \\ \vdots & \vdots & \ddots & \vdots \\ 0 & 0 & \cdots & 1 \end{bmatrix}$$

A scalar matrix can be viewed as a scalar multiple of an identity matrix, that is, $\alpha\mathbf{I}$. Note that multiplication by the identity matrix is equivalent to (scalar) multiplication by 1, and that multiplication by a scalar matrix $\alpha \mathbf{I}$ is equivalent to multiplication by the scalar α.

2.5.2 TRIANGULAR MATRICES

Two particularly important types of triangular matrices are termed *upper triangular* and *lower triangular*—these are matrices that have, respectively, all 0 elements below and above the diagonal:

$$\mathbf{M} = \begin{bmatrix} a_{1,1} & a_{1,2} & \cdots & a_{1,n} \\ 0 & a_{2,2} & \cdots & a_{2,n} \\ \vdots & \vdots & \ddots & \vdots \\ 0 & 0 & \cdots & a_{n,n} \end{bmatrix}$$

$$\mathbf{M} = \begin{bmatrix} a_{1,1} & 0 & \cdots & 0 \\ a_{2,1} & a_{2,2} & \cdots & 0 \\ \vdots & \vdots & \ddots & \vdots \\ a_{n,1} & a_{n,2} & \cdots & a_{n,n} \end{bmatrix}$$

Triangular matrices have some useful properties as well:

i. If $\mathbf{A}$ and $\mathbf{B}$ are lower triangular, then $\mathbf{C} = \mathbf{AB}$ is lower triangular, and similarly for upper triangular.

ii. If $\mathbf{A}$ and $\mathbf{B}$ are lower triangular, then $\mathbf{C} = \mathbf{A} + \mathbf{B}$ is lower triangular, and similarly for upper triangular.

iii. If $\mathbf{A}$ is an invertible lower triangular matrix, its inverse $\mathbf{A}^{-1}$ is lower triangular, and similarly for upper triangular (Section 2.5.4 covers the inverse of a matrix).

Triangular matrices are particularly important in the representation and solution of linear systems, as can be seen in Sections 2.4.4 and A.1.

2.5.3 THE DETERMINANT

The determinant of a square matrix (it's not defined for nonsquare matrices) is a real number, which can be computed in a variety of ways. For 2×2 and 3×3 matrices, there are some reasonably intuitive interpretations/uses of the determinant (see Sections 3.3.2 and 4.4.4), but in the general case, the various definitions and computation schemes seem rather arbitrary. In 2D, a matrix $\mathbf{M}$ maps a unit square with vertices $\vec{0}, \vec{\imath}, \vec{\jmath}, \vec{\imath} + \vec{\jmath}$ to a parallelogram with vertices $\vec{0}, \vec{\imath}\,\mathbf{M}, \vec{\jmath}\,\mathbf{M}, (\vec{\imath} + \vec{\jmath})\mathbf{M}$. The area of the parallelogram is $|\det(\mathbf{M})|$. If $\det(\mathbf{M}) > 0$, then the counterclockwise ordering of the square's vertices is preserved by $\mathbf{M}$ (that is, the parallelogram's vertices are also ordered counterclockwise); if det(M) < 0, then the corresponding parallelogram's vertices are ordered clockwise. In 3D, a matrix M with nonzero determinant maps the unit cube to a parallelepiped, whose volume is |det(M)|. Vertex ordering preservation is analogous to the 2D case.

Terminology

We'll start with some terminology: given a matrix M, the determinant of M is notated as det(M) or |M|. The "vertical bar" notation is frequently applied to the matrices as well; for example, if we have

$$\mathbf{M} = \begin{bmatrix} a_{1,1} & a_{1,2} \\ a_{2,1} & a_{2,2} \end{bmatrix}$$

we can write det(M) as

$$|\mathbf{M}| = \begin{vmatrix} a_{1,1} & a_{1,2} \\ a_{2,1} & a_{2,2} \end{vmatrix}$$

Special Solutions for 2×2 and 3×3 Matrices

Because they're so common, here are the formulas for the 2×2 and 3×3 cases:

$$\begin{vmatrix} a_{1,1} & a_{1,2} \\ a_{2,1} & a_{2,2} \end{vmatrix} = a_{1,1}a_{2,2} - a_{2,1}a_{1,2}$$

$$\begin{vmatrix} a_{1,1} & a_{1,2} & a_{1,3} \\ a_{2,1} & a_{2,2} & a_{2,3} \\ a_{3,1} & a_{3,2} & a_{3,3} \end{vmatrix} = \begin{matrix} a_{1,1}a_{2,2}a_{3,3} + a_{1,2}a_{2,3}a_{3,1} + \\ a_{1,3}a_{2,1}a_{3,2} - a_{3,1}a_{2,2}a_{1,3} - \\ a_{3,2}a_{2,3}a_{1,1} - a_{3,3}a_{2,1}a_{1,2} \end{matrix}$$

And, by definition, for the 1×1 case:

$$|a_{1,1}| = a_{1,1}$$

In fact, these are so frequently encountered that it's quite useful to have the formulas memorized. For the 1×1 and 2×2 cases, this isn't too tough, but for the 3×3 case, there's a convenient trick: write out the matrix, then write out another copy of the first two columns just to the right of the matrix. Next, multiply together the elements along each diagonal, and add the results of the upper-left to lower-right diagonals, and subtract the results of the lower-left to upper-right diagonals:

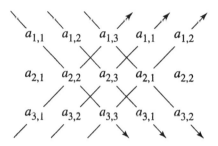

Note that this also works for the 2 × 2 case as well, but not for anything larger than 3 × 3.

General Determinant Solution

A more general appproach to computing det(M) is known as *determinant expansion by minors* or *Laplacian expansion*. To understand this, we need to define the terms *submatrix*, *minor*, and *cofactor*.

A *submatrix* is simply a matrix formed by deleting one or more rows and/or columns from a matrix. For example, if we have a matrix

$$M = \begin{bmatrix} 3 & 9 & 2 & 5 \\ 2 & 7 & 1 & 3 \\ 8 & 4 & 6 & 1 \\ 9 & 5 & 2 & 6 \end{bmatrix}$$

we can form a submatrix by deleting the third column and fourth row of M:

$$M'_{4,3} = \begin{bmatrix} 3 & 9 & 5 \\ 2 & 7 & 3 \\ 8 & 4 & 1 \end{bmatrix}$$

A *minor* is a determinant of a submatrix; specifically, for an element $a_{i,j}$ of M, its minor is the determinant of the matrix M'_{ij}, which is formed by deleting the ith row and jth column of M.

A *cofactor* $c_{i,j}$ of an element $a_{i,j}$ of M is the minor for that element, or its negation, as defined by

$$c_{i,j} = (-1)^{i+j} \left| M'_{i,j} \right|$$

(Note that these cofactors are frequently taken together as a matrix of cofactors, often denoted C.) An example can make this clear. If we have a 3 × 3 matrix, we can use this cofactor-based method to compute the determinant as follows:

$$
\begin{vmatrix} a_{1,1} & a_{1,2} & a_{1,3} \\ a_{2,1} & a_{2,2} & a_{2,3} \\ a_{3,1} & a_{3,2} & a_{3,3} \end{vmatrix} = a_{1,1} \begin{vmatrix} a_{2,2} & a_{2,3} \\ a_{3,2} & a_{3,3} \end{vmatrix} - a_{1,2} \begin{vmatrix} a_{2,1} & a_{2,3} \\ a_{3,1} & a_{3,3} \end{vmatrix} + a_{1,3} \begin{vmatrix} a_{2,1} & a_{2,2} \\ a_{3,1} & a_{3,2} \end{vmatrix}
$$

In general, a determinant of an $n \times n$ matrix gets "reduced" to a sum of scaled $(n-1) \times (n-1)$ determinants, which we can solve individually by applying the same approach, and so on until we have a single scalar (of course, in the above example, we get 2×2 minors, which we could solve using the direct method described earlier).

Properties of the Determinant

Like the other operations on matrices, the determinant possesses a number of interesting and useful properties:

i. The determinant of a matrix is equal to the determinant of its transpose: $|\mathbf{M}| = \left|\mathbf{M}^{\mathrm{T}}\right|$.

ii. The determinant of the product of two matrices is equal to the product of the determinants: $\left|\mathbf{M}\mathbf{M}_1\right| = |\mathbf{M}| \left|\mathbf{M}_1\right|$.

iii. The determinant of the inverse of a matrix is equivalent to the multiplicative inverse of the determinant of the matrix: $\left|\mathbf{M}^{-1}\right| = 1/ |\mathbf{M}|$.

iv. The determinant of the identity matrix is 1: $|\mathbf{I}| = 1$.

v. The determinant of a scalar multiple of a matrix is the product of the scalar, raised to the size of the matrix, times the determinant of the matrix: $|\alpha\mathbf{M}| = \alpha^n |\mathbf{M}|$. The n shows up because $\mathbf{M}$ is an $n \times n$ matrix.

vi. Interchanging any two rows (or columns) of $\mathbf{M}$ changes the sign of $|\mathbf{M}|$.

vii. If all the elements of one row (or column) of $\mathbf{M}$ are multiplied by a constant α, then the determinant is $\alpha |\mathbf{M}|$.

viii. If two rows (or columns) of $\mathbf{M}$ are identical, then $|\mathbf{M}| = 0$.

ix. The determinant of a triangular matrix is equal to the product of the diagonal elements:

$$
\begin{vmatrix} a_{1,1} & a_{1,2} & \cdots & a_{1,n} \\ 0 & a_{2,2} & \cdots & a_{2,n} \\ \vdots & \vdots & \ddots & \vdots \\ 0 & 0 & \cdots & a_{n,n} \end{vmatrix} = \begin{vmatrix} a_{1,1} & 0 & \cdots & 0 \\ a_{2,1} & a_{2,2} & \cdots & 0 \\ \vdots & \vdots & \ddots & \vdots \\ a_{n,1} & a_{n,2} & \cdots & a_{n,n} \end{vmatrix} = a_{1,1}a_{2,2} \cdots a_{n,n}
$$

2.5.4 INVERSE

We've seen that many of the properties of scalar multiplication apply to matrices. One useful property is the multiplicative inverse: for any real $\alpha \neq 0$, there is a number β such that $\alpha\beta = 1$, and of course $\beta = 1/\alpha$. It would be quite useful to have this property apply to matrices as well, as we just saw in the previous section. Recalling that the identity element for matrices is I, the identity matrix, for a given matrix M_1 we would like to find a matrix M_2, if possible, such that $M_1 M_2 = I$. If there is such a matrix, it is called the *inverse* of M_1 and is denoted $M_2 = M_1^{-1}$.

Now the question is, how can you *compute* M_1^{-1}, and when is it possible to do so? Recall that multiplying a matrix M_1 by M_2 is accomplished by computing each element i, j of the result by multiplying the ith row of M_1 by the jth column of M_2. If we employ the notational scheme of writing each $n \times 1$ column of M_2 as $v_1, v_2, \cdots, v_n$, the product $M_1 M_2$ can be computed column-by-column by multiplying each row of M_1 by column v_i of M_2: $M_1 v_i$. If we then consider each column of the identity matrix I to consist of the $n \times 1$ vector e_i, which consists of all zero elements save the i, which is 1, we can rewrite the product $M_1 M_2 = I$ as

$$M_1 [\, v_1 \quad v_2 \quad \cdots \quad v_n \,] = [\, e_1 \quad e_2 \quad \cdots \quad e_n \,]$$

This can be interpreted as a series of n linear systems:

$$M_1 v_1 = e_1$$
$$M_1 v_2 = e_2$$
$$\vdots$$
$$M_1 v_n = e_n$$

If we then solve *each* of these n linear systems, we'll be solving for each *column* of M_2, and since the product is I, we'll have computed M_1^{-1}. Because these are just linear systems, we can solve them using any of the general techniques, such as Gaussian elimination (see Section A.1) or LU decomposition (Press et al. 1988).

Another approach to computing the inverse of a matrix can be found by looking at a formal definition of the inverse of a matrix: if we have a square matrix M, if it has an inverse M^{-1}, then element $a_{i,j}^{-1}$ of M^{-1} is defined as

$$a_{i,j}^{-1} = \frac{(-1)^{i+j} \left| M'_{j,i} \right|}{|M|}$$

Recall that the expression in the numerator is just a cofactor, and so we can then write

$$\mathbf{M}^{-1} = \frac{\mathbf{C}^T}{|\mathbf{M}|}$$

Note that the transposition is the result of the subscript ordering j, i in the previous equation; the matrix $\mathbf{C}^T$ is also known as the *adjoint* of $\mathbf{M}$.

To see how this works, we'll show a simple example with a 2×2 matrix. Let

$$\mathbf{M} = \begin{bmatrix} 1 & 2 \\ 3 & 4 \end{bmatrix}$$

with determinant $|\mathbf{M}| = 1 \times 4 - 3 \times 2 = -2$. We then compute the cofactors

$$c_{11} = (-1)^{1+1}|\mathbf{M}'_{11}| \quad = |4| = 4$$

$$c_{12} = (-1)^{1+2}|\mathbf{M}'_{12}| = -|3| = -3$$

$$c_{21} = (-1)^{2+1}|\mathbf{M}'_{21}| = -|2| = -2$$

$$c_{22} = (-1)^{2+2}|\mathbf{M}'_{22}| \quad = |1| = 1$$

giving us

$$\mathbf{C} = \begin{bmatrix} 4 & -3 \\ -2 & 1 \end{bmatrix}$$

The inverse then is

$$\mathbf{M}^{-1} = \frac{\mathbf{C}^T}{|\mathbf{M}|}$$

$$= \frac{\begin{bmatrix} 4 & -2 \\ -3 & 1 \end{bmatrix}}{-2}$$

$$= \begin{bmatrix} -2 & 1 \\ 3/2 & -1/2 \end{bmatrix}$$

Verifying, we see

$$\begin{bmatrix} 1 & 2 \\ 3 & 4 \end{bmatrix} \begin{bmatrix} -2 & 1 \\ 3/2 & -1/2 \end{bmatrix} = \begin{bmatrix} 1 & 0 \\ 0 & 1 \end{bmatrix} = \mathbf{I}$$

Properties of the Inverse

There are a number of useful properties of the matrix inverse (assuming the inverses exist):

   i. If $MM^{-1} = I$, then $M^{-1}M = I$

  ii. $(M_1 M_2)^{-1} = M_2^{-1} M_1^{-1}$

 iii. $(M^{-1})^{-1} = M$

 iv. $(\alpha M)^{-1} = (1/\alpha)\, M^{-1}$ (with $\alpha \neq 0$)

When Does the Inverse Exist?

The previous sections have hinted that the inverse does not always exist for a square matrix, and this is indeed the case. So, the question is how to determine whether an inverse exists for a given $n \times n$ matrix M. There are several (equivalent) ways to put this:

   i. It is of rank n.

  ii. It is *nonsingular*.

 iii. $|M| \neq 0$.

 iv. Its rows (columns) are linearly independent.

  v. Considered as a transformation, it does not reduce dimensionality.

Singular Matrices

A matrix M is defined to be *nonsingular* if it is square ($n \times n$) and its determinant is nonzero ($|M| \neq 0$). Any matrix failing to meet either of these conditions is called *singular*. Nonsingularity is an important property of a matrix, as can be seen by this list of equivalent if-and-only-if criteria for an $n \times n$ matrix M being nonsingular:

   i. $|M| \neq 0$.

  ii. The rank of M is n.

 iii. The matrix M^{-1} exists.

 iv. The homogeneous system $MX = 0$ has only the trivial solution $X = 0$.

This last definition is particularly significant—because that property and the first are if-and-only-if conditions, it follows that a homogeneous system $MX = 0$ has a nontrivial solution ($X \neq 0$) if and only if $|M| = 0$.

2.6 LINEAR SPACES

In this section, we'll introduce the concept of a linear (or *vector*) space and discuss the representation of vector spaces, and operations on linear spaces, in terms of matrices and matrix operations. Unlike some treatments of this subject, we're going to forgo references to any sort of geometrical interpretation of such spaces for the time being; a subsequent chapter will address these issues explicitly, after we've covered geometrical vectors themselves in an abstract fashion.

2.6.1 FIELDS

Before formally defining a linear space, we need to define the term *field*. A field is "an algebraic system of elements in which the operations of addition, subtraction, multiplication, and division (except by zero) may be performed without leaving the system, and the associative, commutative, and distributive rules hold" (*www.wikipedia.com/ wiki/Field*). Formally, a *field* F consists of a set and two binary operators "+" and "*" (addition and multiplication) with the following properties:

i. Closure of F under addition and multiplication: $\forall a, b \in F$, both $(a + b) \in F$ and $(a * b) \in F$.

ii. Associativity of addition and multiplication: $\forall a, b, c \in F$, both $a + (b + c) = (a + b) + c$ and $a * (b * c) = (a * b) * c$.

iii. Commutativity of addition and multiplication: $\forall a, b \in F$, $a + b = b + a$ and $a * b = b * a$.

iv. Distributivity of multiplication over addition: $\forall a, b, c \in F$, both $a * (b + c) = (a * b) + (a * c)$ and $(b + c) * a = (b * a) + (c * a)$.

v. Existence of additive identity element: $\exists 0 \in F$ such that $\forall a \in F$, $a + 0 = a$ and $0 + a = a$.

vi. Existence of multiplicative identity element: $\exists 1 \in F$ such that $\forall a \in F$, $a * 1 = a$ and $1 * a = 1$.

vii. Additive inverse: $\forall a \in F$, $\exists -a \in F$ such that $a + (-a) = 0$ and $(-a) + a = 0$.

viii. Multiplicative inverse: $\forall a \neq 0 \in F$, $\exists a^{-1} \in F$ such that $a * a^{-1} = 1$ and $a^{-1} * a = 1$.

A field is also known as a *commutative ring* or *commutative division algebra*. Examples of fields are

- the rational numbers $\mathbb{Q} = \{\frac{a}{b} | a, b \in \mathbb{Z}, b \neq 0\}$, where $\mathbb{Z}$ denotes the integers
- the real numbers $\mathbb{R}$
- the complex numbers $\mathbb{C}$

Note that the integers do *not* form a field, but only a *ring* (there is no multiplicative inverse for integers).

2.6.2 DEFINITION AND PROPERTIES

Informally, a linear space consists of a collection of objects (called *vectors*), real numbers (*scalars*), and two operations (adding vectors and multiplying vectors by scalars), which are required to have certain properties. Rather than sticking to the lowercase boldface generic tuple notation, we're going to use a notation that makes explicit the fact that we're dealing with vectors—vectors will be notated as lowercase italic letters with a diacritical arrow. Typically, we use $\vec{u}$, $\vec{v}$, and $\vec{w}$, or $\vec{v}_1, \vec{v}_2, \ldots, \vec{v}_n$ for lists of vectors. Formally, suppose we have the following:

- A field K (which, for us, will be $\mathbb{R}$).

- A (nonempty) set of vectors $\mathcal{V}$.

- An addition operator "+" defined on elements $\vec{u}, \vec{v} \in \mathcal{V}$.

- A multiplication operator "$*$" defined on scalars $k \in K$ and $\vec{v} \in \mathcal{V}$ (often, the "$*$" is omitted and concatenation used, as in $\vec{v} = k\vec{u}$).

- The addition and multiplication operations exhibit the rules listed below.

Properties:

i. Closure under multiplication: $\forall k \in K$ and $\forall \vec{v} \in \mathcal{V}, k\vec{v} \in \mathcal{V}$.

ii. Closure under addition: $\forall \vec{u}, \vec{v} \in \mathcal{V}, \vec{u} + \vec{v} \in \mathcal{V}$.

iii. Associativity of addition: $\forall \vec{u}, \vec{v}, \vec{w} \in \mathcal{V}, \vec{u} + (\vec{v} + \vec{w}) = (\vec{u} + \vec{v}) + \vec{w}$.

iv. Existence of additive identity element: $\forall \vec{v} \in \mathcal{V}, \exists$ a vector $\vec{0} \in \mathcal{V}$ called the zero vector, such that $\vec{v} + \vec{0} = \vec{v}$.

v. Existence of additive inverse: $\forall \vec{v} \in \mathcal{V}, \exists$ a vector $-\vec{v}$, such that $\vec{v} + (-\vec{v}) = \vec{0}$.

vi. Commutativity of addition: $\forall \vec{u}, \vec{v} \in \mathcal{V}, \vec{u} + \vec{v} = \vec{v} + \vec{u}$.

vii. Distributivity of multiplication over addition: $\forall k \in K$ and $\forall \vec{u}, \vec{v} \in \mathcal{V}, k(\vec{u} + \vec{v}) = k\vec{u} + k\vec{v}$.

viii. Distributivity of addition over multiplication: $\forall k_1, k_2 \in K$ and $\forall \vec{v} \in \mathcal{V}, (k_1 + k_2)\vec{v} = k_1\vec{v} + k_2\vec{v}$.

ix. Associativity of multiplication: $\forall k_1, k_2 \in K$, and $\forall \vec{v} \in \mathcal{V}, (k_1 k_2)\vec{v} = k_1(k_2\vec{v})$.

x. Existence of multiplicative identity: $\forall \vec{v} \in \mathcal{V}, 1 * \vec{v} = \vec{v}$.

As we stated earlier, our concern here is with computer graphics, and as a result the field K is just the real numbers $\mathbb{R}$, and the vectors in $\mathcal{V}$ are tuples of real numbers: $\mathbf{a} = (a_1, a_2, \ldots, a_n)$. In later chapters, once we've established the relationship between geometrical vectors, vector spaces, and matrices, we'll switch from this rather abstract tuple-oriented notation for vectors to one that reflects the geometrical interpretation of tuples in $\mathbb{R}^n$ (the set of all such n-tuples).

2.6.3 SUBSPACES

Given a linear space $\mathcal{V}$ over $\mathbb{R}$, let S be a subset of $\mathcal{V}$, and let the operations of S and $\mathcal{V}$ be the same. If S is also a linear space over $\mathbb{R}$, then S is a *subspace* of $\mathcal{V}$.

While the above seems rather obvious, its subtlety is revealed by pointing out that a subset of a linear space may or may not *itself* be a linear space. An example from Agnew and Knapp (1978) shows this rather nicely: Consider a subset S_1 of $\mathbb{R}^3$ consisting of all 3-tuples of the form $(a_1, a_2, 0)$. A quick check of this against all the rules defining a linear space shows that this is, indeed, a linear space. However, if we have a subspace S_2 consisting of 3-tuples of the form $(a_1, a_2, 1)$, and check if all the rules for a linear space apply to it, we see that it fails on several of them:

i. Closure under addition: $(a_1, a_2, 1) + (b_1, b_2, 1) = (a_1 + b_1, a_2 + b_2, 2)$, which is not in S_2.

ii. Closure under multiplication: $(a_1, a_2, 1) \in S_2$, but $k(a_1, a_2, 1) = (ka_1, ka_2, k) \notin S_2$ for $k \neq 1$.

iii. Existence of identity element: $(0, 0, 0) \notin S_2$.

iv. Existence of additive inverse: $(a_1, a_2, 1) \in S_2$, but $(-a_1, -a_2, -1) \notin S_2$.

v. Closure under multiplication: $(a_1, a_2, 1) \in S_2$, but $k(a_1, a_2, 1) = (ka_1, ka_2, k) \notin S_2$ for $k \neq 1$.

It is interesting to note that this example is not simply arbitrary, and its significance will become apparent later.

2.6.4 LINEAR COMBINATIONS AND SPAN

A *linear combination* of a set of items is constructed by forming a sum of scalar multiples of the items. Suppose we have a vector set $\mathcal{A}$ whose elements are a set of vectors (tuples) in $\mathbb{R}^n : \{\vec{a}_1, \vec{a}_2, \ldots, \vec{a}_n\}$. You can form a vector $\vec{u} = k_1\vec{a}_1 + k_2\vec{a}_2 + \cdots + k_n\vec{a}_n$. This vector $\vec{u}$ is of course itself a vector because each $k_i\vec{a}_i$ is a vector and the sum of each of these vectors is itself a vector.

Given a set of vectors (tuples) $\{\vec{v}_1, \vec{v}_2, \ldots, \vec{v}_n\}$ defining a linear space $\mathcal{V}$, the set S of all linear combinations of the vectors is itself a linear space, and this space is the space *spanned* by $\{\vec{v}_1, \vec{v}_2, \ldots, \vec{v}_n\}$. The set $\{\vec{v}_1, \vec{v}_2, \ldots, \vec{v}_n\}$ is called the *spanning set* for S. The significance of this idea of a spanning set is that any vector $\vec{w} \in S$ can be written in terms of $\{\vec{v}_1, \vec{v}_2, \ldots, \vec{v}_n\}$, by simply finding the scalars $k_1, k_2, \ldots, k_n$ for which $\vec{w} = k_1\vec{v}_1 + k_2\vec{v}_2 + \cdots + k_n\vec{v}_n$.

2.6.5 LINEAR INDEPENDENCE, DIMENSION, AND BASIS

The concept of linear combination arises frequently in linear algebra and is particularly important in understanding linear independence and basis—two critical points to an intuitive understanding of linear algebra.

Linear Independence

Suppose we have a vector space $\mathcal{V}$. Given any set of vectors $\{\vec{v}_1, \vec{v}_2, \ldots, \vec{v}_n\}$, we can classify them as either (linearly) *independent* or *dependent*. By definition, a set of vectors is linearly dependent if there exist constants $c_1, c_2, \ldots, c_n$, not all 0, such that

$$c_1\vec{v}_1 + c_2\vec{v}_2 + \cdots + c_n\vec{v}_n = \vec{0}$$

and linearly independent if

$$c_1\vec{v}_1 + c_2\vec{v}_2 + \cdots + c_n\vec{v}_n = \vec{0}$$

only when *all* the constants are 0.

An example of a linearly dependent set of vectors would be $\vec{v}_1 = (2, 5, 3)$, $\vec{v}_2 = (1, 4, 0)$, and $\vec{v}_3 = (7, 22, 6)$ because the set of constants $\{2, 3, -1\}$ leads to

$$2\vec{v}_1 + 3\vec{v}_3 + -1\vec{v}_3 = 2(2, 5, 3) + 3(1, 4, 0) + -1(7, 22, 6)$$

$$= (4, 10, 6) + (3, 12, 0) + (-7, -22, -6)$$

$$= \vec{0}$$

The preceding definition of linear dependence is fairly standard, but perhaps is not the most intuitive, particularly for our purposes (which will become apparent in a subsequent chapter). (Nonzero) vectors in a set $\{\vec{v}_1, \vec{v}_2, \ldots, \vec{v}_n\}$ are linearly independent if and only if none of the vectors is a linear combination of the others. In the preceding example $\vec{v}_3$ was a linear combination of $\vec{v}_1$ and $\vec{v}_2$, with coefficients 2 and 3, respectively. In fact, a somewhat stronger definition may be made: (Nonzero) vectors in a set $\{\vec{v}_1, \vec{v}_2, \ldots, \vec{v}_n\}$ are linearly dependent if and only if one of them, say, $\vec{v}_i$, is a linear combination of the *preceding* vectors:

$$c_1\vec{v}_1 + c_2\vec{v}_2 + \cdots + c_{i-1}\vec{v}_{i-1} = \vec{v}_i$$

Basis and Dimension

The concept of linear independence is important in defining the dimension of a space. By definition, if we have a set of vectors $\{\vec{v}_1, \vec{v}_2, \ldots, \vec{v}_n\}$, they are said to form a *basis* for a linear space $\mathcal{V}$ if and only if they are both linearly independent and span the space. The *dimension* of $\mathcal{V}$ is n, the number of such linearly independent vectors.

Several facts follow from this definition:

- Any set of linearly independent vectors in $\mathcal{V}$ with fewer than n vectors fails to span $\mathcal{V}$.

- Any set of vectors in $\mathcal{V}$ with greater than n vectors must be linearly dependent.

- There is no unique basis for a space $\mathcal{V}$ of dimension n; there are an infinite number of such sets of basis vectors having n elements.

The concepts of subspace, span, linear combinations, and dimension are related in the following way: let $\mathcal{V}$ be a vector space of dimension n spanned by, and defined as all linear combinations of, basis vectors $\mathbf{V} = \{\vec{v}_1, \vec{v}_2, \ldots, \vec{v}_n\}$; then, if we select a set of linearly independent vectors $\mathbf{W} = \{\vec{w}_1, \vec{w}_2, \ldots, \vec{w}_m\} \in \mathcal{V}$, where $m < n$, then the set of all vectors that are linear combinations of $\mathbf{W}$ form a subspace $\mathcal{W}$ of $\mathcal{V}$, having dimension m.

2.7 LINEAR MAPPINGS

In this section, we begin by reviewing the concept of mapping in general as a way of leading into linear mappings, which are functions from one linear space to another. We then show how matrices are used to represent linear mappings.

2.7.1 MAPPINGS IN GENERAL

The basic idea of a function is a rule that associates members of one set with members in another set. The terms *mapping*, *function*, and *transformation* are all synonyms for a particular type of such pairing of elements.

DEFINITION   Let $\mathcal{A}$ and $\mathcal{B}$ be two sets with elements $\{a_1, a_2, \ldots, a_m\}$ and $\{b_1, b_2, \ldots, b_n\}$, respectively. A *function T* from $\mathcal{A}$ to $\mathcal{B}$, written

$$T : \mathcal{A} \longrightarrow \mathcal{B}$$

is a set of pairs (a, b) such that $a \in \mathcal{A}$ and $b \in \mathcal{B}$. Every pair in the set is unique, and every element $a \in \mathcal{A}$ appears in exactly one pair in the set. The set $\mathcal{A}$ is called the *domain* of the function, and the set $\mathcal{B}$ is called the *range* or *co-domain*. A function can be displayed schematically as in Figure 2.4. ∎

For any element $a \in \mathcal{A}$, the value in $\mathcal{B}$ that the function associates with a is denoted $T(a)$ or aT and called the *image* of a. If an element $b \in \mathcal{B}$ is the image of some $a \in \mathcal{A}$, then that a is called the *preimage* of b. It is important to understand that while every element $a \in \mathcal{A}$ appears in the set of pairs, it is not necessarily true

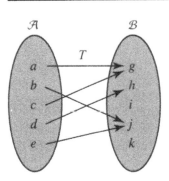

Figure 2.4   Schematic diagram of a function.

that every element $b \in \mathcal{B}$ appears. Indeed, a trivial function may map *every* element in $\mathcal{A}$ to just a single element in $\mathcal{B}$.

The domain and range of a function may be *any* sets of objects, whose elements may be of the same type, or not. We can map real numbers to real numbers: for example, T may be defined as mapping a real number to its square root: $x \mapsto \sqrt{x}$.

Composition of Mappings

Suppose we have two functions: $T : \mathcal{A} \longrightarrow \mathcal{B}$ and $U : \mathcal{B} \longrightarrow C$. By definition, for every $a \in \mathcal{A}$, there is some $b \in \mathcal{B}$ such that $T(a) = b$. Of course, the function U maps that element b (the image of a) to some element $c \in C$. The application of the two functions T and U to a is called the *composition* of T and U and is denoted as

$$(U \circ T)(a) = U(T(a))$$

(or $a(T \circ U) = aTU$ using the other convention), and we say

$$a \mapsto U(T(a))$$

Composition of mappings is associative. Suppose we have three functions: $T : \mathcal{A} \longrightarrow \mathcal{B}$, $U : \mathcal{B} \longrightarrow C$, and $V : C \longrightarrow \mathcal{D}$. Then $(V \circ U) \circ T = V \circ (U \circ T)$. A schematic of a composition of two functions is shown in Figure 2.5.

Special Types of Mappings

Three important classes of mappings are *one-to-one*, *onto*, and *isomorphic* (both one-to-one and onto). These are shown schematically in Figure 2.6. A one-to-one mapping $T : \mathcal{A} \longrightarrow \mathcal{B}$ is one in which every $a \in \mathcal{A}$ is associated with a unique $b \in \mathcal{B}$.

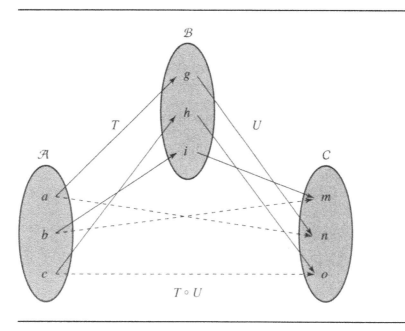

Figure 2.5   Composition of two functions.

An onto mapping $T : \mathcal{A} \longrightarrow \mathcal{B}$ is one in which every $b \in \mathcal{B}$ is the image of some $a \in \mathcal{A}$ (or several). Examples of these functions are $T(x) = 2^x$ and $T(x) = x^2$ for $\mathcal{A}$ being the set of real numbers and $\mathcal{B}$ being the set of positive real numbers in the first case, and $\mathcal{B}$ being the set of nonnegative real numbers in the second case (see Figure 2.7).

Inverse Mappings

Given a mapping $T : \mathcal{A} \longrightarrow \mathcal{B}$, it's natural to consider the mapping that *inverts* (reverses) T. Formally, a linear mapping T is invertible if there exists a mapping $T^{-1} : \mathcal{B} \longrightarrow \mathcal{A}$ such that $TT^{-1} = I$, where I is the identity mapping. As T^{-1} *is* a mapping, it must by definition have the entirety of $\mathcal{B}$ as its domain; further, every element $a \in \mathcal{A}$ must be in T^{-1}'s range. These two facts show that a mapping must be both one-to-one and onto for it to be invertible. See Figure 2.8.

2.7.2 LINEAR MAPPINGS

Of course what we're really interested in here are *linear* mappings; that is, mappings relating linear spaces. Given two linear spaces $\mathcal{A}$ and $\mathcal{B}$, a linear mapping $T : \mathcal{A} \longrightarrow \mathcal{B}$ is a function that *preserves vector addition and scalar multiplication*:

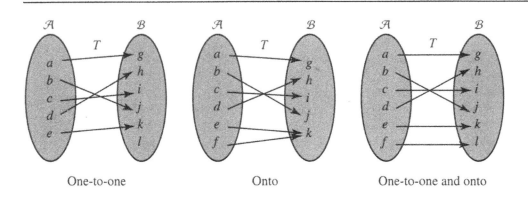

Figure 2.6   One-to-one, onto, and isomorphic maps.

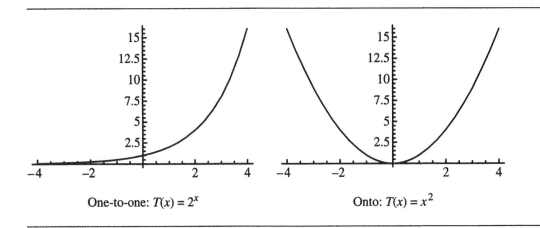

Figure 2.7   One-to-one and onto functions.

i. $\forall \vec{u}, \vec{v} \in \mathcal{A}, T(\vec{u} + \vec{v}) = T(\vec{u}) + T(\vec{v})$.

ii. $\forall \alpha \in \mathbb{R}$ and $\forall \vec{v} \in \mathcal{A}, T(\alpha \vec{v}) = \alpha T(\vec{v})$.

An important implication of this is that a linear mapping preserves linear combinations: that is, $T(\alpha \vec{u} + \beta \vec{v}) = \alpha T(\vec{u}) + \beta T(\vec{v})$.

We discussed in the previous section that a mapping may be one-to-one or onto. A linear function $T : \mathcal{A} \longrightarrow \mathcal{B}$ is said to be an *isomorphism* if it is one-to-one and maps $\mathcal{A}$ onto $\mathcal{B}$.

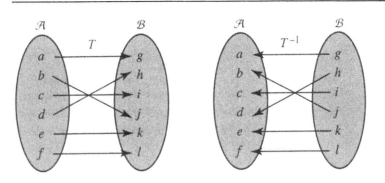

Figure 2.8   An invertible mapping.

An important aspect of linear mappings is that they are completely determined by how they transform the basis vectors; this can be understood by recalling that any vector $\vec{v} \in \mathcal{V}$ can be represented as a linear combination of the basis vectors, and that linear mappings preserve linear combinations.

2.7.3   MATRIX REPRESENTATION OF LINEAR MAPPINGS

Linear mappings from $\mathbb{R}^m$ to $\mathbb{R}^n$ may be represented by matrices; that is, we can use a matrix to specify how a vector in $\mathcal{A}$ is mapped to a vector in $\mathcal{B}$. We saw earlier that a linear mapping is completely determined by its effects on the basis vectors, and it is this fact that shows us how a matrix can be used to define (or implement) a linear mapping.

Suppose we have linear spaces $\mathcal{A}$ and $\mathcal{B}$ with basis vectors $\vec{u}_1, \vec{u}_2, \ldots, \vec{u}_m$ and $\vec{v}_1, \vec{v}_2, \ldots, \vec{v}_n$ and a linear mapping $T : \mathcal{A} \longrightarrow \mathcal{B}$. The transformed basis vectors $T(\vec{u}_1), T(\vec{u}_2), \ldots, T(\vec{u}_m)$ are elements in $\mathcal{B}$, and therefore can be represented as some linear combination of $\mathcal{B}$'s basis vectors $\vec{v}_1, \vec{v}_2, \ldots, \vec{v}_n$:

$$T(\vec{u}_1) = a_{1,1}\vec{v}_1 + a_{1,2}\vec{v}_2 + \cdots + a_{1,n}\vec{v}_n$$

$$T(\vec{u}_2) = a_{2,1}\vec{v}_1 + a_{2,2}\vec{v}_2 + \cdots + a_{2,n}\vec{v}_n$$

$$\vdots$$

$$T(\vec{u}_m) = a_{m,1}\vec{v}_1 + a_{m,2}\vec{v}_2 + \cdots + a_{m,n}\vec{v}_n$$

We can form the matrix T of coefficients for the above; this is the matrix representation of T relative to the bases of $\mathcal{A}$ and $\mathcal{B}$:

$$T = \begin{bmatrix} a_{1,1} & a_{1,2} & \cdots & a_{1,n} \\ a_{2,1} & a_{2,2} & \cdots & a_{2,n} \\ \vdots & \vdots & \ddots & \vdots \\ a_{m,1} & a_{m,2} & \cdots & a_{m,n} \end{bmatrix}$$

This result leads to two important facts:

1. The (row) matrix representation of *any* vector in $\mathcal{A}$ can be transformed into the space $\mathcal{B}$ by multiplying it by T:

$$T(\vec{x}) = \begin{bmatrix} x_1 & x_2 & \cdots & x_m \end{bmatrix} \begin{bmatrix} a_{1,1} & a_{1,2} & \cdots & a_{1,n} \\ a_{2,1} & a_{2,2} & \cdots & a_{2,n} \\ \vdots & \vdots & \ddots & \vdots \\ a_{m,1} & a_{m,2} & \cdots & a_{m,n} \end{bmatrix}$$

2. The matrix representation of a composition of two linear mappings is the concatenation of the matrices representing each of the mappings: let $a_1, a_2, \ldots, a_m$, $b_1, b_2, \ldots, b_n$, and $c_1, c_2, \ldots, c_l$ be the bases for linear spaces $\mathcal{A}$, $\mathcal{B}$, and C, respectively, and let $T : \mathcal{A} \longrightarrow \mathcal{B}$ and $S : \mathcal{B} \longrightarrow C$ be linear mappings with matrix representations T and S, respectively. Then, $R : \mathcal{A} \longrightarrow C$, the composition of T and S, is represented by

$$S(T(\vec{v})) = \vec{v} \, \text{TS}.$$

2.7.4 CRAMER'S RULE

Cramer's rule is a method for directly computing the solution to a system of linear equations, provided one exists. To motivate this, let's consider the case of a linear system in two variables:

$$a_{1,1}x_1 + a_{1,2}x_2 = c_1$$

$$a_{2,1}x_1 + a_{2,2}x_2 = c_2$$

If we take the approach of using elimination, we multiply the first equation by $a_{2,1}$ and the second equation by $a_{1,1}$ and subtract, and we get

$$
\begin{array}{rcl}
a_{2,1}a_{1,1}x_1 + a_{2,1}a_{1,2}x_2 & = & a_{2,1}c_1 \\
a_{1,1}a_{2,1}x_1 + a_{1,1}a_{2,2}x_2 & = & a_{1,1}c_2 \\
\hline
a_{2,1}a_{1,2}x_2 - a_{1,1}a_{2,2}x_2 & = & a_{2,1}c_1 - a_{1,1}c_2,
\end{array}
$$

giving us

$$x_2 = \frac{a_{1,1}c_2 - a_{2,1}c_1}{a_{1,1}a_{2,2} - a_{2,1}a_{1,2}}$$

provided $a_{1,1}a_{2,2} - a_{2,1}a_{1,2} \neq 0$. Substituting this value for x_2 back in the first equation yields

$$a_{1,1}x_1 + a_{1,2}x_2 = c_1$$

$$a_{1,1}x_1 + a_{1,2}\left(\frac{a_{1,1}c_2 - a_{2,1}c_1}{a_{1,1}a_{2,2} - a_{2,1}a_{1,2}}\right) = c_1$$

$$a_{1,1}x_1 = c_1 - \frac{a_{1,2}a_{1,1}c_2 - a_{1,2}a_{2,1}c_1}{a_{1,1}a_{2,2} - a_{1,2}a_{2,1}}$$

$$= \frac{a_{1,1}a_{2,2}c_1 - a_{1,2}a_{1,1}c_2}{a_{1,1}a_{2,2} - a_{1,2}a_{2,1}}$$

$$x_1 = \frac{c_1 a_{2,2} - c_2 a_{1,2}}{a_{1,1}a_{2,2} - a_{1,2}a_{2,1}}$$

provided $a_{1,1}a_{2,2} - a_{2,1}a_{1,2} \neq 0$. The numerators and denominators of both x_1 and x_2 can be expressed as determinants:

$$x_1 = \frac{\begin{vmatrix} c_1 & a_{1,2} \\ c_2 & a_{2,2} \end{vmatrix}}{\begin{vmatrix} a_{1,1} & a_{1,2} \\ a_{2,1} & a_{2,2} \end{vmatrix}}, \quad x_2 = \frac{\begin{vmatrix} a_{1,1} & c_1 \\ a_{2,1} & c_2 \end{vmatrix}}{\begin{vmatrix} a_{1,1} & a_{1,2} \\ a_{2,1} & a_{2,2} \end{vmatrix}}$$

We can solve the example of Section 2.4.2 using Cramer's rule. We have

$$3x + 2y = 6$$

$$x - y = 1$$

for which Cramer's rule has

$$x_1 = \frac{\begin{vmatrix} 6 & 2 \\ 1 & -1 \end{vmatrix}}{\begin{vmatrix} 3 & 2 \\ 1 & -1 \end{vmatrix}} = \frac{8}{5}$$

$$x_2 = \frac{\begin{vmatrix} 3 & 6 \\ 1 & 1 \end{vmatrix}}{\begin{vmatrix} 3 & 2 \\ 1 & -1 \end{vmatrix}} = \frac{3}{5}$$

In its general form, Cramer's rule is as follows: Let A denote the matrix of coefficients

$$\mathbf{A} = [\, a_{i,j} \,]$$

and let $\mathbf{B}_i$ be the matrix formed by taking $\mathbf{A}$ and replacing column i by the column of constants $c_1, c_2, \cdots, c_n$. Then, if $|\mathbf{A}| \neq 0$, there is a unique solution

$$\vec{u} = \left(\frac{|\mathbf{B}_1|}{|\mathbf{A}|}, \frac{|\mathbf{B}_2|}{|\mathbf{A}|}, \cdots, \frac{|\mathbf{B}_n|}{|\mathbf{A}|} \right)$$

It should be noted that Cramer's rule can be unstable if the determinant of the matrix is nearly zero, just as with other methods. There are two issues with respect to Cramer's rule for larger systems: first, efficiency—for an $n \times n$ system, Cramer's rule is $O(n!)$, while Gaussian elimination is $O(n^3)$; second, subtractive cancellation, which in Gaussian elimination is handled with full pivoting.

2.8 EIGENVALUES AND EIGENVECTORS

Recall that we call $n \times 1$ and $1 \times n$ matrices *vectors*; without too much elaboration at this point (we'll discuss the geometric implications of linear algebra and vectors in a subsequent chapter), you can think of a vector as specifying a direction and distance in some "space" (such as Cartesian 2D space). Multiplying a vector by a matrix then can be considered as transforming the direction and/or length of a vector. (Note that we're restricting our discussion to square matrices again).

We can represent this multiplication of vector $\vec{v}$ by the matrix $\mathbf{M}$ in the usual fashion:

$$\vec{v}' = \vec{v}\mathbf{M}$$

For some special vector $\vec{v}$, we can find a constant λ such that

$$\vec{v}' = \lambda\vec{v}$$

and thus

$$\vec{v}\mathbf{M} = \lambda\vec{v}$$

A vector $\vec{v}$ for which we can find such a value λ is known as an *eigenvector* of $\mathbf{M}$, and the value λ is called an *eigenvalue*. Notice that since λ is a scalar, the value $\lambda\vec{v}$ is simply a scaled version of $\vec{v}$, and thus whatever the multiplication by $\mathbf{M}$ does to an arbitrary vector, it simply scales its eigenvectors.

The question now arises: how do we *find* the eigenvalues for a particular matrix M? Let's do a little manipulation of the definition:

$$\vec{v}M = \lambda\vec{v} \tag{2.2}$$

$$\vec{v}\,(\lambda I - M)\ = \vec{0} \tag{2.3}$$

So long as $\vec{v}$ isn't the $\vec{0}$ vector, it must be the case that

$$|\lambda I - M| = 0$$

which is known as the *characteristic polynomial*.

Here's an example: let

$$M = \begin{bmatrix} 6 & 4 \\ 2 & 4 \end{bmatrix}$$

We're looking for scalar λ such that $\vec{v}M = \lambda\vec{v}$:

$$[\, v_1 \quad v_2\,] \begin{bmatrix} 6 & 4 \\ 2 & 4 \end{bmatrix} = \lambda\, [\, v_1 \quad v_2\,]$$

This corresponds to the linear system

$$6v_1 + 2v_2 = \lambda v_1 \tag{2.4}$$

$$4v_1 + 4v_2 = \lambda v_2 \tag{2.5}$$

which can be rewritten as the homogeneous system

$$(\lambda - 6)v_1 - 2v_2 = 0$$

$$-4v_1 + (\lambda - 4)v_2 = 0$$

The determinant of the matrix of coefficients for this system is zero if and only if the linear system has a nonzero solution, so

$$\begin{vmatrix} \lambda - 6 & -2 \\ -4 & \lambda - 4 \end{vmatrix} = \lambda^2 - 10\lambda + 16 = (\lambda - 8)(\lambda - 2) = 0$$

and so the eigenvalues for M are $\lambda_1 = 8$ and $\lambda_2 = 2$.

If we substitute $\lambda = 8$ into Equation 2.4, we get

$$2v_1 - 2v_2 = 0$$

$$-4v_1 + 4v_2 = 0$$

which gives us $\vec{v} = [\, 1 \quad 1 \,]$ as an eigenvector for eigenvalue $\lambda = 8$. Similarly, if we substitute $\lambda = 2$, we get

$$-4v_1 - 2v_2 = 0$$

$$-4v_1 - 2v_2 = 0$$

which gives us $\vec{v} = [\, 1 \quad -2 \,]$ as an eigenvector for eigenvalue $\lambda = 2$. Note that any scalar multiples of these eigenvectors are also eigenvectors for their associated eigenvalues.

This naturally extends to $n \times n$ arrays, whose characteristic equations are nth-degree polynomials. Just as with any polynomial, there may be no, one, or up to n real roots, and you should be aware that for $n > 4$, no general closed-form solutions exist. Fortunately, we most often deal with matrices of 4×4 and smaller in computer graphics.

2.9 EUCLIDEAN SPACE

From the standpoint of computer graphics, the particular subclass of linear spaces called *Euclidean* space is the most important. Our earlier discussions of linear spaces didn't include mention of "length" or "orthogonality," instead focusing on vector spaces in general.

2.9.1 INNER PRODUCT SPACES

We begin with a definition: Let $\mathcal{V}$ be a vector space over $\mathbb{R}^n$. Let $\mathcal{V}^2$ denote the set of all pairs $(\vec{u}, \vec{v})$ where $\vec{u}, \vec{v} \in \mathcal{V}$. An *inner product* is a function from $\mathcal{V}^2$ to $\mathbb{R}$, denoted $\langle \vec{u}, \vec{v} \rangle$, that satisfies the following conditions:

i. Distributivity: $\langle a_1 \vec{u}_1 + a_2 \vec{u}_2, \vec{v} \rangle = a_1 \langle \vec{u}_1, \vec{v} \rangle + a_2 \langle \vec{u}_2, \vec{v} \rangle$.

ii. Commutativity: $\langle \vec{u}, \vec{v} \rangle = \langle \vec{v}, \vec{u} \rangle$.

iii. Positive definiteness: $\langle \vec{u}, \vec{u} \rangle \geq 0$, and $\langle \vec{u}, \vec{u} \rangle = 0 \iff \vec{u} = \vec{0}$.

Then, the space $\mathcal{V}$ is an *inner product* space. As suggested earlier, a vector space in general may have elements of arbitrary type, but as we're concerned with tuples of real numbers, the remainder of this discussion makes this assumption.

Norm, Length, and Distance

There are infinitely many inner products of $\mathbb{R}^n$—that is, you can specify any arbitrary function on such tuples that satisfy the conditions just described. The dot product we first introduced in Section 2.3.4 is one particular choice of inner product; it has properties that make it particularly useful. The third condition for the inner product is involved with the definition of length; from it, we know that any nonzero vector has a positive value as the inner product with itself. The square root of this inner product is called the *norm* and is notated as

$$\|\vec{u}\| = \sqrt{\langle \vec{u}, \vec{u} \rangle}$$

As we'll see later, the geometric "interpretation" of Euclidean space allows us to view the norm as the *length* of a vector.

If the norm of a vector is 1, that is, $\|\vec{u}\| = 1$, then we say that the vector is *normalized*. Any (nonzero) vector $\vec{u} \in \mathcal{V}$ can be normalized by multiplying it by $1/\|\vec{u}\|$. The *distance* between two vectors $\vec{u}, \vec{v} \in \mathcal{V}$ is defined as $\|\vec{v} - \vec{u}\|$. An inner product space over $\mathbb{R}^n$ whose inner product is the dot product is defined as a Euclidean space.

2.9.2 ORTHOGONALITY AND ORTHONORMAL SETS

Given a Euclidean space $\mathcal{V}$, an inner product equal to 0 has particular significance: if $\langle \vec{u}, \vec{v} \rangle = 0$, then they are called *orthogonal*.

Orthogonality has a particularly important role, relative to the concept of basis vectors. Let $\mathbf{V} = \{\vec{v}_1, \vec{v}_2, \ldots, \vec{v}_n\}$ be a set of basis vectors for a vector space $\mathcal{V}$. If we have $\langle \vec{v}_i, \vec{v}_k \rangle = 0, \forall \vec{v}_i, \vec{v}_k \in \mathbf{V}, i \neq k$, then the set $\mathbf{V}$ is itself called an *orthogonal set*.

If $\mathbf{V}$ is an orthogonal set of basis vectors, and $\|\vec{v}_i\| = 1, \forall \vec{v}_i \in \mathbf{V}$, then $\mathbf{V}$ is further defined to be *orthonormal*. A Euclidean space with a standard orthonormal frame is known as *Cartesian* space.

Any Euclidean space has an infinite number of sets of basis vectors that define the space. Any set of basis vectors may be orthogonal, orthonormal, or neither of these. However, any set of basis vectors may be converted into an orthonormal set by means of the *Gram-Schmidt orthogonalization* process.

Before we go into the orthogonalization process itself, we must understand a property of orthonormal sets of basis vectors: an orthonormal set of vectors $\mathbf{V}' = \{\vec{v}_1, \vec{v}_2, \ldots, \vec{v}_k\}$, with $k < n$ (the dimension of $\mathcal{V}$) because it is a subset of some set of basis vectors, must be linearly independent; further, for any $\vec{u} \in \mathcal{V}$, the vector

$$\vec{w} = \vec{u} - \langle \vec{u}, \vec{v}_1 \rangle \vec{v}_1 - \langle \vec{u}, \vec{v}_2 \rangle \vec{v}_2 - \cdots - \langle \vec{u}, \vec{v}_k \rangle \vec{v}_k \qquad (2.6)$$

is orthogonal to each $\vec{v}_i \in \mathbf{V}'$.

Let $\mathcal{V}$ be an inner product space, and $\mathbf{V} = \{\vec{v}_1, \vec{v}_2, \ldots, \vec{v}_n\}$ be a basis for it. We can construct an orthonormal basis $\mathbf{U} = \{\vec{u}_1, \vec{u}_2, \ldots, \vec{u}_n\}$ using the Gram-Schmidt orthogonalization process:

Step 1. Set $\vec{u}_1 = \frac{\vec{v}_1}{\|\vec{v}_1\|}$. Note that this makes $\vec{u}_1$ unit length.

Step 2. Set $\vec{u}_2 = \frac{\vec{v}_2 - \langle \vec{v}_2, \vec{u}_1 \rangle \vec{u}_1}{\|\vec{v}_2 - \langle \vec{v}_2, \vec{u}_1 \rangle \vec{u}_1\|}$. Note that $\vec{u}_2$ is of unit length and (by Equation 2.6) is orthogonal to $\vec{u}_1$. This makes the set $\{\vec{u}_1, \vec{u}_2\}$ orthonormal.

Step 3. Set $\vec{u}_3 = \frac{\vec{v}_3 - \langle \vec{v}_3, \vec{u}_1 \rangle \vec{u}_1 - \langle \vec{v}_3, \vec{u}_2 \rangle \vec{u}_2}{\|\vec{v}_3 - \langle \vec{v}_3, \vec{u}_1 \rangle \vec{u}_1 - \langle \vec{v}_3, \vec{u}_2 \rangle \vec{u}_2\|}$. Again, $\vec{u}_3$ is unit length and (by Equation 2.6) is orthogonal to $\vec{u}_1$ *and* $\vec{u}_2$. Hence, the set $\{\vec{u}_1, \vec{u}_2, \vec{u}_3\}$ is orthonormal.

Step 4. Repeat the previous step for the rest of the $\vec{u}_i$.

At the end of this process, we have an orthonormal basis for $\mathcal{V}$.

2.10 Least Squares

The clever reader may have noted that all our linear systems so far have conveniently had exactly as many equations as unknowns. So, as long as there exists a unique solution, we can use one of several techniques to solve it. However, often situations arise in which there are more equations than unknowns.

Consider a simple example: if we have two points and wish to determine the equation of a line that passes through the points, we can set up a linear system to solve; this system will have two equations and two unknowns, and so long as the points are not coincident, a solution can be computed. For example, suppose we have two points:

$$P_1 = \begin{pmatrix} p_{1,1} & p_{1,2} \end{pmatrix}$$

$$P_2 = \begin{pmatrix} p_{2,1} & p_{2,2} \end{pmatrix}$$

Of course, these define a line, which may be expressed as $x_2 = mx_1 + b$. We can solve for the coefficients m and b by representing the points as a linear system and applying, say, Cramer's rule. Our points must be on the line, and therefore satisfy the line equation, and so we can write the linear system as

$$p_{1,1}m + b = p_{1,2}$$

$$p_{2,1}m + b = p_{2,2}$$

which in matrix form is

$$\begin{bmatrix} p_{1,1} & 1 \\ p_{2,1} & 1 \end{bmatrix} \begin{bmatrix} m \\ b \end{bmatrix} = \begin{bmatrix} p_{1,2} \\ p_{2,2} \end{bmatrix}$$

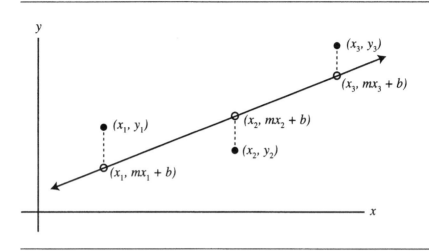

Figure 2.9   Least squares example.

Cramer's rule has the solution as

$$m = \frac{\begin{vmatrix} p_{1,2} & 1 \\ p_{2,2} & 1 \end{vmatrix}}{\begin{vmatrix} p_{1,1} & 1 \\ p_{2,1} & 1 \end{vmatrix}} = \frac{p_{1,2} - p_{2,2}}{p_{1,1} - p_{2,1}}$$

$$b = \frac{\begin{vmatrix} p_{1,1} & p_{1,2} \\ p_{2,1} & p_{2,2} \end{vmatrix}}{\begin{vmatrix} p_{1,1} & 1 \\ p_{2,1} & 1 \end{vmatrix}} = \frac{p_{1,1}p_{2,2} - p_{2,1}p_{1,2}}{p_{1,1} - p_{2,1}}$$

However, consider if we have more than two points we wish to fit a line to; in general, any three points in the plane will not be all on a line. In this case, we'd like to have a line that minimizes the (vertical) distance between it and each of the points. The line can be considered as a function f returning the y-value for a given x-value (specifically, $f(x) = mx + b$). See Figure 2.9. We can represent this particular example as a linear system:

$$p_{1,1}m + b = p_{1,2}$$

$$p_{2,1}m + b = p_{2,2}$$

$$p_{3,1}m + b = p_{3,2}$$

which in matrix form is

$$\begin{bmatrix} p_{1,1} & 1 \\ p_{2,1} & 1 \\ p_{3,1} & 1 \end{bmatrix} \begin{bmatrix} m \\ b \end{bmatrix} = \begin{bmatrix} p_{1,2} \\ p_{2,2} \\ p_{3,2} \end{bmatrix}$$

Note that we now have three equations, but only two unknowns; this is what's called an *overdetermined* system, and for these sorts of systems, the best we can generally hope for is some sort of approximate solution, which satisfies some objective criteria.

The vertical distance D_1, then, between a point (x_1, y_1) and the line is $|f(x_1) - y_1|$. For various reasons, we want to actually look at the sum of the squares of the distances between the points and the line:

$$D^2 = \left(f(x_1) - y_1\right)^2 + \left(f(x_2) - y_2\right)^2 + \cdots + \left(f(x_n) - y_n\right)^2$$

So, we want to choose the function (line) f so that D^2 is minimized. That is, we need to choose m and b in an approximate way so that our objective criterion is met (the minimization of D^2). This is the reason this is called a *least squares* solution.

To understand how we go about solving this, you have to kind of stand on your head for a while. Imagine a space $\mathcal{R}^n$ of n dimensions, where n is the number of points to fit (equations in the system). We can view the components of the coordinates of a location y in this n-dimensional space as consisting of the y-values of the points we're trying to fit (that is, $y = (y_1, y_2, \cdots, y_n)$). Another location $T(f)$ in this n-dimensional space can be considered to have coordinates consisting of the y-values of the points on the fitted line corresponding to each point we're trying to fit; that is, $T(f) = (f(x_1), f(x_2), \cdots, f(x_n))$. The total distance D^2 between the points and the fitted line is thus the square of the distance (in the n-dimensional space $\mathcal{R}^n$) of the vector $T(f) - y$.

In the case of our example of fitting a line to three points, the transformation T corresponds to a matrix

$$\mathbf{M} = \begin{bmatrix} 1 & x_1 \\ 1 & x_2 \\ 1 & x_3 \end{bmatrix}$$

We need to find f (that is, m and b) such that we minimize D^2 (that is, $\|T(f) - y\|$). If we represent this in matrix form, we get

$$\mathbf{M}[f] - [y] = \mathbf{M}\begin{bmatrix} b \\ m \end{bmatrix} - [y]$$

$$= \begin{bmatrix} 1 & x_1 \\ 1 & x_2 \\ 1 & x_3 \end{bmatrix} \begin{bmatrix} b \\ m \end{bmatrix} - [y]$$

$$= \begin{bmatrix} b + mx_1 - y_1 \\ b + mx_2 - y_2 \\ b + mx_3 - y_3 \end{bmatrix}$$

Recall that we need to minimize D^2, which we wrote earlier as

$$D^2 = \left(f(x_1) - y_1\right)^2 + \left(f(x_2) - y_2\right)^2 + \cdots + \left(f(x_n) - y_n\right)^2$$

in general, or specifically for our case

$$D^2 = \left(b + mx_1 - y_1\right)^2 + \left(b + mx_2 - y_2\right)^2 + \left(b + mx_3 - y_n\right)^2$$

Since this is just a function, we know that the minimum occurs exactly when the partial derivatives of D^2 with respect to b and m, respectively, are zero. This leads to the system we need to solve:

$$\left(b + mx_1 - y_1\right) + \left(b + mx_2 - y_2\right) + \left(b + mx_3 - y_3\right) = 0$$

$$x_1\left(b + mx_1 - y_1\right) + x_2\left(b + mx_2 - y_2\right) + x_3\left(b + mx_3 - y_3\right) = 0$$

If we rewrite this in matrix form we get

$$\begin{bmatrix} 1 & 1 & 1 \\ x_1 & x_2 & x_3 \end{bmatrix} \begin{bmatrix} b + mx_1 - y_1 \\ b + mx_2 - y_2 \\ b + mx_3 - y_3 \end{bmatrix}$$

We can, for clarity, rewrite this as

$$\begin{bmatrix} 1 & 1 & 1 \\ x_1 & x_2 & x_3 \end{bmatrix} \left(\begin{bmatrix} 1 & x_1 \\ 1 & x_2 \\ 1 & x_3 \end{bmatrix} \begin{bmatrix} b \\ m \end{bmatrix} - \begin{bmatrix} y_1 \\ y_2 \\ y_3 \end{bmatrix} \right) = \begin{bmatrix} 0 \\ 0 \end{bmatrix}$$

In this form, we can see that it incorporates our matrix **M** in various forms:

$$\mathbf{M}^{\mathrm{T}}\left(\mathbf{M}\begin{bmatrix} b \\ m \end{bmatrix} - \begin{bmatrix} y_1 \\ y_2 \\ y_3 \end{bmatrix}\right) = \begin{bmatrix} 0 \\ 0 \end{bmatrix}$$

$$\mathbf{M}^{\mathrm{T}}\left(\mathbf{M}\,[\,f\,] - [\,y\,]\right) = \mathbf{0}$$

$$\mathbf{M}^{\mathrm{T}}\mathbf{M}\,[\,f\,] - \mathbf{M}^{\mathrm{T}}\,[\,y\,] = \mathbf{0}$$

Rearranging,

$$\mathbf{M}^{\mathrm{T}}\mathbf{M}\,[\,f\,] = \mathbf{M}^{\mathrm{T}}\,[\,y\,]$$

$$[\,f\,] = \left(\mathbf{M}^{\mathrm{T}}\mathbf{M}\right)^{-1}\mathbf{M}^{\mathrm{T}}\,[\,y\,]$$

The astute reader may have noticed that the final manipulation to isolate $[\,f\,]$ involved an operation that may not necessarily be justifiable—specifically, we've assumed that we can invert the matrix $\mathbf{M}^{\mathrm{T}}\mathbf{M}$. Certainly it's square, and it can be shown that if the values x_1, x_2, and x_3 are distinct, the matrix can be inverted.

RECOMMENDED READING

There are an enormous number of books on linear algebra; a recent search for the string "linear algebra" on an Internet bookseller's site yielded 465 entries. Particularly appropriate are undergraduate texts in linear algebra, such as

Jeanne Agnew and Robert C. Knapp, *Linear Algebra with Applications*, Brooks/Cole, Monterey, CA, 1978.

Howard Anton, *Elementary Linear Algebra*, John Wiley and Sons, New York, 2000.

Also quite useful and accessible is

Seymour Lipschutz, *Schaum's Outline of Theory and Problems of Linear Algebra*, McGraw-Hill, New York, 1968.

In the area of computer graphics, the following contain much of interest related to linear algebra:

M. E. Mortenson, *Mathematics for Computer Graphics Applications*, Industrial Press, New York, 1999 (Chapters 1–3).

James D. Foley, Andries van Dam, Steven K. Feiner, and John F. Hughes, *Computer Graphics: Principles and Practice*, 2nd ed., Addison-Wesley, Reading, MA, 1996 (Appendix: Mathematics for Computer Graphics).

Gerald Farin and Dianne Hansford, *The Geometry Toolbox for Graphics and Modeling*, A. K. Peters, Natick, MA, 1998.

VECTOR ALGEBRA

3.1 Vector Basics

Before talking about vector spaces, let's go back to basic principles. To keep things concrete, we'll talk physics. One fundamental class of physical properties and phenomena can be described by a single value; for example, mass, volume, distance, or temperature. However, a second class of properties or phenomena cannot be so described; rather, they are by nature *multiple-valued*. One example of this class is motion of an object, which has two components—speed and direction (as, say, kilometers per hour and compass heading). The first class of properties can be called *scalar-valued*, and the second class of properties can be called *vector-valued*. Vector-valued entities may also be referred to as *multidimensional*, and the individual values making up the entity are known as its *components*.

Later on, we'll discuss some of the mathematics underlying these vector-valued numbers, but for now let's stick to a particular subclass defined by distance and direction, which we'll simply call *vectors*. To visualize this class of entities—these vectors—we'll draw them as arrows (directed line segments), as shown in Figure 3.1. The direction is indicated by the orientation of these arrows, while distance is indicated by their relative lengths.

3.1.1 Vector Equivalence

One of the most important characteristics of vectors is that of *equivalence*—what does it mean to say that two vectors are equal or not? Recall that the components of a vector are its direction and length; "position" is not part of the definition. In Figure 3.1, vectors $\vec{u}$ and $\vec{t}$ have different directions and lengths, and are thus different

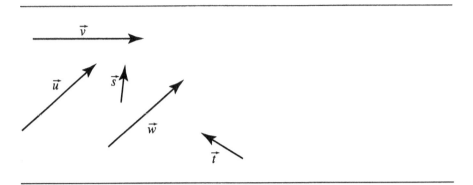

Figure 3.1   Vectors as directed line segments.

vectors. However, vectors $\vec{u}$ and $\vec{w}$ have the same direction and length, and are thus equivalent, even though they are drawn at different locations in the figure. If this seems to be counterintuitive, think of it this way: if you start off at your house and walk three kilometers due east, the relative path is the same as if you had started your trip at your neighbor's house.

3.1.2   VECTOR ADDITION

With this direction-and-distance interpretation in place, we're now in position to talk about operations on vectors. First, let's talk about addition—what does it mean to add two (or more) vectors? Going back to our "taking a walk" intuitive hook, this would correspond to walking a particular distance in a particular direction (one vector) and then immediately walking in some other direction for some distance. Of course, you could have walked directly to your final destination; this would correspond to yet another vector, which is defined as the sum of the first two.

For example, say we had two vectors $\vec{u}$ and $\vec{v}$, as seen in Figure 3.2, that represented a two-stage journey. Remembering that the positions of the vectors aren't significant, we can redraw them as in Figure 3.3. That more direct path from the journey's start to its finish is the sum of the two vectors and can be drawn "head-to-tail" as shown in Figure 3.4, which makes it more obvious that their sum is the vector $\vec{w}$. This can be mathematically represented as $\vec{u} + \vec{v} = \vec{w}$.

Because adding two vectors always gives us another vector, we can extend this idea to "chains" of vector addition, as shown in Figure 3.5, which represents the vector sum $\vec{s} + \vec{t} + \vec{u} + \vec{v} = \vec{w}$.

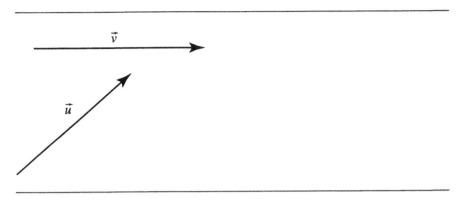

Figure 3.2   Two vectors.

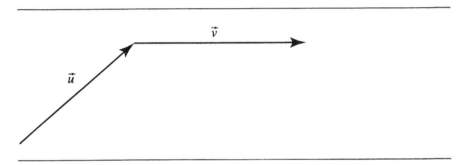

Figure 3.3   Two vectors drawn head-to-tail.

3.1.3 VECTOR SUBTRACTION

We can also *subtract* one vector from another. Intuitively, this is equivalent to taking a journey of some distance in a particular direction, and then going in the reverse of some other direction for another distance. This is shown in Figure 3.6.

3.1.4 VECTOR SCALING

Another fundamental operation on vectors is that of *scalar multiplication* or *scaling*. This simply means changing the length of a vector without changing its direction. In Figure 3.7 we can see that the vector $\vec{v}$ has exactly the same orientation as $\vec{u}$, but is twice the length. This is represented mathematically as $\vec{v} = 2\vec{u}$.

In general, scalar multiplication is $\vec{v} = \alpha\vec{u}$, where α is *any* real number. In the previous example, we had $\alpha = 2$, but we could just as easily have a negative α value.

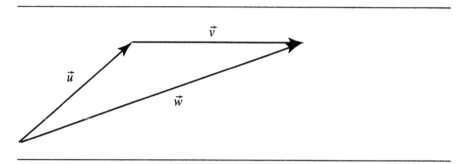

Figure 3.4   Vector addition.

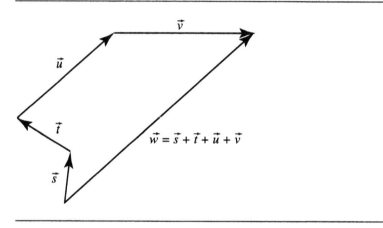

Figure 3.5   Vector addition chain.

Figure 3.8 shows a scaling of $\vec{u}$ by $\alpha = -1$ (which can be called, for obvious reasons, vector *negation*).

3.1.5   PROPERTIES OF VECTOR ADDITION AND SCALAR MULTIPLICATION

Now, given these two operations of vector addition and scalar multiplication, you might wonder if the rules for combining these two operations follow what you know about ordinary addition and multiplication of simple (i.e., real) numbers.

Let's look at some of the usual properties:

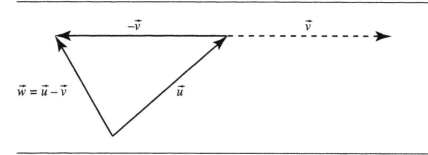

Figure 3.6   Vector subtraction.

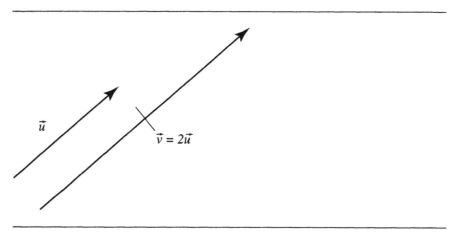

Figure 3.7   Vector multiplication.

    i. Commutativity: $\vec{u} + \vec{v} = \vec{v} + \vec{u}$. From Figure 3.9, we can see that the sum is the same irrespective of the order of the terms.

    ii. Associativity: $\vec{u} + (\vec{v} + \vec{w}) = (\vec{u} + \vec{v}) + \vec{w}$. From Figure 3.10, we can see that the sum is the same irrespective of the grouping of the terms.

    iii. Distributivity of addition over multiplication: $(\alpha + \beta)\vec{u} = \alpha\vec{u} + \beta\vec{u}$. See Figure 3.11.

    iv. Distributivity of multiplication over addition: $\alpha(\vec{u} + \vec{v}) = \alpha\vec{u} + \alpha\vec{v}$. From Figure 3.12, we can see that the sum is the same irrespective of the grouping of the terms.

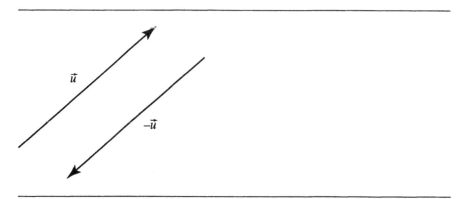

Figure 3.8   Vector negation.

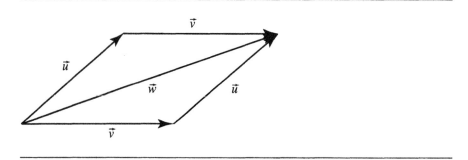

Figure 3.9   Commutativity of vector addition.

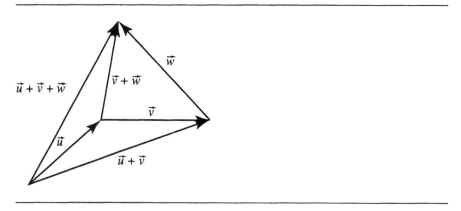

Figure 3.10   Associativity of vector addition.

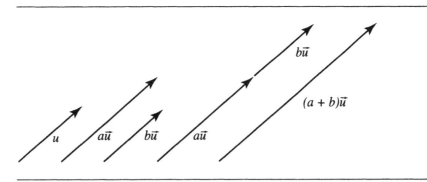

Figure 3.11   Distributivity of addition over multiplication.

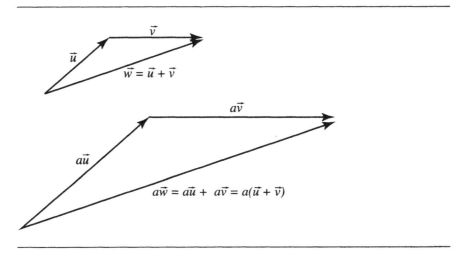

Figure 3.12   Distributivity of multiplication over addition.

3.2 VECTOR SPACE

Although we've been talking about vectors as "directed line segments," the abstract concept of a *vector space* can be formalized as follows: a vector space (over real numbers) consists of a set $\mathcal{V}$, whose elements are called "vectors," and which has these properties:

   i. Addition (and subtraction) of vectors is defined, and the result of addition or subtraction is another vector.

    ii. The set $\mathcal{V}$ is closed under linear combinations: if we have $\vec{u}, \vec{v} \in \mathcal{V}$, and $\alpha, \beta \in \mathbb{R}$, then $\alpha\vec{u} + \beta\vec{v} \in \mathcal{V}$ as well.

    iii. There exists a unique vector $\vec{0} \in \mathcal{V}$, called the *zero vector*, such that the following properties hold:

        a. $\forall \vec{v} \in \mathcal{V}, 0 \cdot \vec{v} = \vec{0}$, where $0 \in \mathbb{R}$.

        b. $\forall \vec{v} \in \mathcal{V}, \vec{0} + \vec{v} = \vec{v}$.

(Note that these all work intuitively for our "directed line segments" version of vectors, except that we haven't yet talked about multiplication of vectors by vectors. Also, note that the "closed under linear combinations" includes multiplication of a single vector by a scalar, which we already discussed.)

3.2.1   SPAN

Given a set of vectors $\{\vec{v}_1, \vec{v}_2, \cdots, \vec{v}_n\} \in \mathcal{V}$, the set S of all linear combinations of these vectors is an (infinite) set of vectors comprising another vector space, and this space is called the space *spanned* by $\{\vec{v}_1, \vec{v}_2, \cdots, \vec{v}_n\}$. That is, any vector $\vec{w} \in S$ can be written as $\vec{w} = \lambda_1\vec{v}_1 + \lambda_2\vec{v}_2 + \cdots + \lambda_n\vec{v}_n$, for $\lambda_i \in \mathbb{R}$. The set $\{\vec{v}_1, \vec{v}_2, \cdots, \vec{v}_n\}$ is called the *spanning set* for S.

    Here's an example to make this more clear: if we have two (nonparallel) vectors $\vec{u}$ and $\vec{v}$ that are directed line segments existing in three-dimensional space, then the space spanned by these two vectors consists of *all* vectors lying within the plane defined by $\vec{u}$ and $\vec{v}$ (see Figure 3.13).

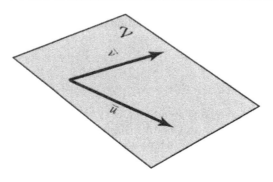

Figure 3.13   The span of two vectors in 3D space is a plane.

3.2.2   LINEAR INDEPENDENCE

Suppose we have a set of vectors $\vec{u}$ and $\vec{v}$ that span some space S. Notice that in the example diagrammed in Figure 3.13, we stipulated that the vectors $\vec{u}$ and $\vec{v}$ must not be parallel. Intuitively, you can see that if they *were* parallel, we wouldn't be defining a plane with them; we'd be defining a line. Consider the case where we have three vectors $\vec{u}$, $\vec{v}$, and $\vec{w}$, but with $\vec{w} = \alpha\vec{u}$. We'd still be defining a plane, and the three vectors would span the same set S. So, either $\vec{u}$ or $\vec{w}$ could be considered redundant.

This intuition can be formalized in the definition of *linear independence*: the set $\{\vec{v}_1, \vec{v}_2, \cdots, \vec{v}_n\} \in \mathcal{V}$ is *linearly dependent* if there exist scalars $\lambda_1, \lambda_2, \cdots, \lambda_n$, not all zero, such that

$$\lambda_1\vec{v}_1 + \lambda_2\vec{v}_2 + \cdots + \lambda_n\vec{v}_n = \vec{0}$$

and *linearly independent* if

$$\lambda_1\vec{v}_1 + \lambda_2\vec{v}_2 + \cdots + \lambda_n\vec{v}_n = \vec{0}$$

only if $\lambda_1 = 0, \lambda_2 = 0, \cdots, \lambda_n = 0$. More intuitively speaking, this means that a set of vectors is linearly independent if and only if no $\vec{v}_i$ is a linear combination of the other vectors in the set.

3.2.3   BASIS, SUBSPACES, AND DIMENSION

If we have a vector space S, then a set $\{\vec{v}_1, \vec{v}_2, \cdots, \vec{v}_n\}$ is a *basis* for S if

  i. $\{\vec{v}_1, \vec{v}_2, \cdots, \vec{v}_n\}$ are linearly independent
  ii. $\{\vec{v}_1, \vec{v}_2, \cdots, \vec{v}_n\}$ is a spanning set for S

If we have a vector space $\mathcal{V}$, and some set of basis vectors $\mathbf{V} = \{\vec{v}_1, \vec{v}_2, \cdots, \vec{v}_n\} \in \mathcal{V}$, then the space S spanned by $\mathbf{V}$ is called a *subspace* of $\mathcal{V}$. The *dimension n* of S is defined as the maximum number of linearly independent vectors in S.

To make this more concrete, the example we showed in Figure 3.13 has as the vector space all directed line segments in three-dimensional space (i.e., $\mathcal{V} = \mathbb{R}^3$), the basis vectors are the two directed line segments (i.e., $\mathbf{V} = \{\vec{u}, \vec{v}\}$), and the space S spanned by $\mathbf{V}$ is the plane in which those two vectors lie. The dimension of S is 2.

It is important to note that, for any given subspace S of $\mathcal{V}$, there are infinitely many spanning sets. Going back to our example, any two nonparallel directed line segments in the plane constitute a basis for that planar subset of three-dimensional space.

Suppose we have a set of vectors $\mathbf{V} = \{\vec{v}_1, \vec{v}_2, \cdots, \vec{v}_n\} \in \mathcal{V}$, which are linearly independent as described earlier. Any other vector $\vec{w}$ that is in the space spanned by

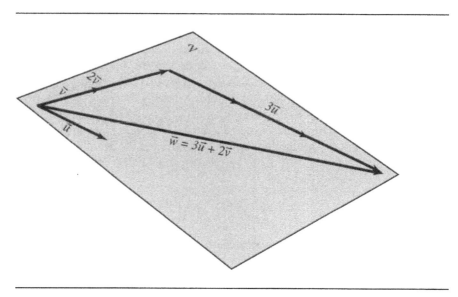

Figure 3.14   A vector as the linear combination of basis vectors.

V can be described as a linear combination of **V**:

$$\vec{w} = x_1\vec{v}_1 + x_2\vec{v}_2 + \cdots + x_n\vec{v}_n, \qquad x_i \in \mathbb{R}$$

It's important to note that the factors x_i are unique for a given $\vec{w}$ (otherwise, the vectors $\vec{v}_i$ would not be linearly independent). We then define a set of vectors **V** = $\{\vec{v}_1, \vec{v}_2, \cdots, \vec{v}_n\} \in \mathcal{V}$ that are linearly independent as forming a *basis* of (or for) $\mathcal{V}$. We call the elements $x_i\vec{v}_i$ the *components* of $\vec{w}$, and the coefficients x_i the *coordinates* of $\vec{w}$.

An example should make this more clear. Figure 3.14 shows the same two vectors $\vec{u}$ and $\vec{v}$ from Figure 3.13. Because they're linearly independent (i.e., not parallel and neither is the $\vec{0}$ vector), they form a basis.

The vector $\vec{w}$, which lies in the space $\mathcal{V}$ spanned by $\vec{u}$ and $\vec{v}$, can be described as a linear combination of the basis vectors (specifically, $\vec{w} = 3\vec{u} + 2\vec{v}$). You can see, intuitively, that the coefficients (coordinates) of $\vec{w}$ can only be $x_1 = 3$, $x_2 = 2$ ("proof by diagram"); assume that x_1 is *not* 3, and note that *no possible* value of x_2 could give you the vector $\vec{w}$.

A formal proof of the claim that the linear combination is unique requires that we state and prove a simpler proposition: Let **V** = $\{\vec{v}_1, \vec{v}_2, \cdots, \vec{v}_n\}$ be a basis in $\mathcal{V}$. Then, $\sum c_i\vec{v}_i = 0 \Leftrightarrow c_1 = c_2 = \cdots = c_n = 0$.

PROOF   We need to prove both directions. Let's do the easy one first: if $c_1 = c_2 = \cdots = c_n = 0$, then certainly $\sum c_i\vec{v}_i = 0$ by the definitions of addition and multiplication. To prove the other direction, suppose that $\sum c_i \vec{v}_i = 0$, and $c_j \neq 0$ for some j. Then,

$$\vec{v}_j = \sum_{i \neq j} \frac{-c_i}{c_j} \vec{v}_i$$

which contradicts the assumption of linear independence, and therefore $c_1 = c_2 = \cdots = c_n = 0$. ∎

(This proposition can be stated more intuitively: the zero vector can only be described as a linear combination of the basis vectors with all the constants equal to zero, and conversely, if all the constants in a linear combination are zero, the only thing that it defines is the zero vector.)

Now, on to the proof that the linear combination is unique. Stated more formally, let $\mathbf{V} = \{\vec{v}_1, \vec{v}_2, \cdots, \vec{v}_n\}$ be a basis in $\mathcal{V}$. Then every vector in $\mathcal{V}$ can be written as a unique linear combination of $\vec{v}_1, \vec{v}_2, \cdots, \vec{v}_n$.

PROOF   Suppose we have $\vec{w} \in \mathcal{V}$. Then there exist $c_1, c_2, \ldots, c_n \in \mathbb{R}$ such that

$$\vec{w} = c_1 \vec{v}_1 + c_2 \vec{v}_2 + \cdots + c_n \vec{v}_n$$

Suppose that these constants are *not* unique, that is,

$$\vec{w} = d_1 \vec{v}_1 + d_2 \vec{v}_2 + \cdots + d_n \vec{v}_n$$

where some $c_i \neq d_i$. But if that were true, then

$$\vec{0} = (d_1 - c_1)\vec{v}_1 + (d_2 - c_2)\vec{v}_2 + \cdots + (d_n - c_n)\vec{v}_n$$

Recall from the previous proposition that the coefficients of the linear combination producing the zero vector $\vec{0}$ are all zero; this means that $d_i = c_i, \forall i \in 1 \ldots n$. This proves that every vector $\vec{w} \in \mathcal{V}$ can be defined as a unique linear combination of the basis vectors. ∎

3.2.4 ORIENTATION

Suppose we have two linearly independent vectors $\vec{u}$ and $\vec{v}$. As we have seen, these can be considered to define a plane, or if the vectors are three-dimensional, a plane in 3-space. Figure 3.15 shows these vectors $\vec{u}$ and $\vec{v}$ and the angle $\theta_{\vec{u}\vec{v}}$ between them. Note that we're "exploiting" some unstated conventions here. We've mentioned the vectors in lexicographic order ($\vec{u}$ *then* $\vec{v}$) and spoken of the angle between them in that order ($\theta_{\vec{u}\vec{v}}$), and the angle arrow in Figure 3.15 goes *from* $\vec{u}$ *to* $\vec{v}$, suggesting that the angle is positive. The angle direction is, in common parlance, "counterclockwise"—it increases as you go in that standard direction. But, all of these conventions are based on an assumption that's so obvious, you're probably not even thinking about it: all of

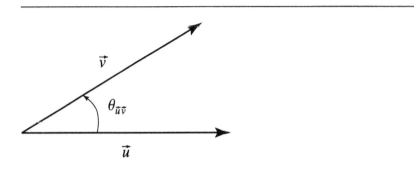

Figure 3.15   Angle between vectors.

these drawings are done on a page, which has a built-in third dimension, but which also has a well-defined third direction—that being what "out of the page" means (the page has thickness, the ink on the diagram is on one of the surfaces, and we consider that surface to be the "front" as opposed to the "back," and so counterclockwise is well defined).

What if we look at Figure 3.15 as what it really defines—an infinitely thin plane—and look at it from the other side? Then, our notion of "in" or "out" of the page reverses the sense of what's counterclockwise (i.e., the orientation). So, in reality we can't distinguish the orientation. We've just been "cheating" by exploiting well-established conventions for printing diagrams on a page, in particular the idea of "out of the page" as opposed to "into the page." That last observation suggests that it's really this idea of a third direction that allows us to define orientation and gives us a way out of the ambiguity.

Now, suppose we have, in addition to the basis vectors $\vec{u}$ and $\vec{v}$, a third (linearly independent) vector $\vec{w}$; we can think of $\vec{w}$ as giving us that "out of the page" direction. Of course, $\vec{v}$ can serve the same role with respect to $\vec{u}$ and $\vec{w}$, and so on. This (finally) allows us to define the orientation, or *sign*, for a basis as follows:

$$\mathrm{sgn}\left(\vec{u}, \vec{v}, \vec{w}\right) = \mathrm{sgn}\left(\theta_{\vec{u}\vec{v}}\right)$$

If we refer back to Figure 3.15, we'd have $\vec{w}$ pointing in or out of the page, depending on how we chose our convention. It seems a bit more "natural" to choose $\vec{w}$ to be out of the page, as that corresponds to our idea of a front and back of a sheet of paper. This convention is known as the "right-hand rule" because if we take our right hand and curl our fingers in the direction of positive rotation, that orientation-defining direction corresponds to the direction our thumb is pointing, as shown in Figure 3.16. If the sign of a basis is positive, we use the notation

$$\mathrm{sgn}\left(\vec{u}, \vec{v}, \vec{w}\right) = +1$$

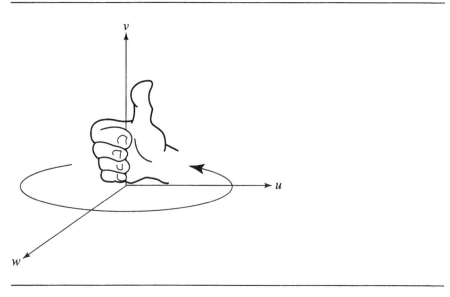

Figure 3.16   The right-hand rule for orientation.

3.2.5 CHANGE OF BASIS

We just showed that every vector in a particular space is a unique linear combination of a particular set of basis vectors. However, this doesn't mean that every vector has a unique linear combination representation. For any given vector space $\mathcal{V}$ of dimension n, there are an infinite number of linearly independent n-ary subsets of $\mathcal{V}$. That is, any vector $\vec{w} \in \mathcal{V}$ can be represented as a linear combination of any arbitrarily chosen set of basis vectors. The vector $\vec{w} = 3\vec{u} + 2\vec{v}$ in Figure 3.14 can also be represented as $\vec{w} = 3\vec{s} + \vec{t}$, as shown in Figure 3.17.

How this can be true is fairly obvious, intuitively. A formal explanation of how this works might be useful: Suppose we have two sets of basis vectors $\vec{a}_1, \vec{a}_2, \ldots, \vec{a}_n$ and $\vec{b}_1, \vec{b}_2, \ldots, \vec{b}_n$ for $\mathcal{V}$. We know that any vector in $\mathcal{V}$ can be represented in terms of any basis, and of course this is true for vectors that themselves make up another set of basis vectors. That is, each of the $\vec{a}$'s can be represented in the basis formed by the $\vec{b}$'s:

$$\vec{a}_k = c_{1,k}\vec{b}_1 + c_{2,k}\vec{b}_2 + \cdots + c_{n,k}\vec{b}_n \tag{3.1}$$

If we have a vector $\vec{w} \in \mathcal{V}$, we can represent it as a linear combination of $\vec{a}_1, \vec{a}_2, \ldots, \vec{a}_n$ and substitute the $\vec{a}_k$ equations (3.1) in that combination to obtain

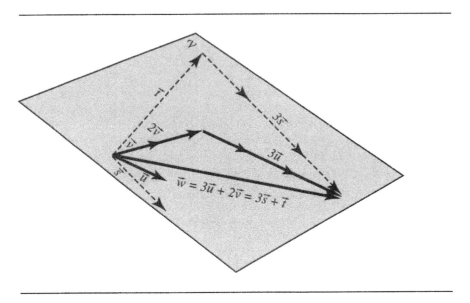

Figure 3.17 A vector as the linear combination of two different sets of basis vectors.

$$\vec{w} = d_1\vec{a}_1 + d_2\vec{a}_2 + \cdots + d_n\vec{a}_n$$

$$= d_1(c_{1,1}\vec{b}_1 + c_{2,1}\vec{b}_2 + \cdots + c_{n,1}\vec{b}_n)$$

$$+ d_2(c_{1,2}\vec{b}_1 + c_{2,2}\vec{b}_2 + \cdots + c_{n,2}\vec{b}_n)$$

$$+ \cdots + d_n(c_{1,n}\vec{b}_1 + c_{2,n}\vec{b}_2 + \cdots + c_{n,n}\vec{b}_n)$$

$$= (d_1 c_{1,1} + d_2 c_{1,2} + \cdots + d_n c_{1,n})\vec{b}_1$$

$$+ (d_1 c_{2,1} + d_2 c_{2,2} + \cdots + d_n c_{2,n})\vec{b}_2$$

$$+ \cdots + (d_1 c_{n,1} + d_2 c_{n,2} + \cdots + d_n c_{n,n})\vec{b}_n$$

We'll see in the next chapter that this laborious-looking computation can be accomplished trivially by using matrix multiplication.

3.2.6 LINEAR TRANSFORMATIONS

Before we delve into this directly, let's review a little precalculus. If we have two sets $\mathcal{D}$ and $\mathcal{R}$, we can define an operation that associates each element in $\mathcal{D}$ with exactly one element in $\mathcal{R}$. If we apply this operation to all elements of $\mathcal{D}$, then we can

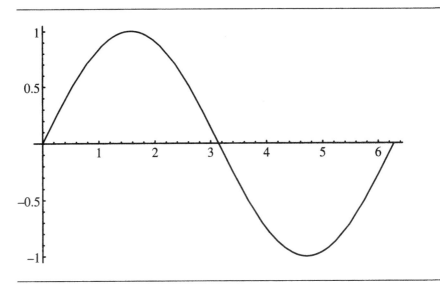

Figure 3.18   The sine function.

view the results as a set of pairs of elements (a, b), $a \in \mathcal{D}$, $b \in \mathcal{R}$. Formally, we call this operation of associating elements of the two sets a *function, transformation,* or *mapping* (all of which are equivalent and interchangeable terms); the set $\mathcal{D}$ is known as the *domain*, and the set $\mathcal{R}$ is known as the *range* of the function. It is important to note that either or both the domain and range may be infinite or finite. Further, the function may be continuous or discontinuous. Many values in the domain may be mapped to the same value in the range, but each value in the domain may be mapped to only one value in the range.

Frequently, a function is depicted as some sort of a graph, with the domain along the horizontal axis, the range along the vertical axis, and the values of the function shown as a line or curve, or as bars. Formally the set $\{(x, f(x)) : x \in \mathcal{D}\} \subset \mathcal{D} \times \mathcal{R}$ is defined to be the *graph of a function*. A canonical example of a function is the trigonometric function sine. The domain consists of all real numbers; the range is all real numbers between -1 and 1 (see Figure 3.18).

What we're interested in talking about here are what we call *linear transformations*, which are mappings from one linear (vector) space to another. Formally, a linear transformation between two vector spaces $\mathcal{U}$ and $\mathcal{V}$ is a map $T : \mathcal{U} \rightarrow \mathcal{V}$ such that

   i. $T\left(\vec{u} + \vec{v}\right) = T\left(\vec{u}\right) + T(\vec{v})$ for any vectors $\vec{u}, \vec{v} \in \mathcal{V}$

   ii. $T\left(\alpha\vec{u}\right) = \alpha T\left(\vec{u}\right)$ for any $\alpha \in \mathbb{R}$ and any $\vec{u} \in \mathcal{V}$

Frequently, a linear transformation is said to *preserve linear combinations*. Recall that a linear combination of vectors is defined as $x_1\vec{v}_1 + x_2\vec{v}_2 + \cdots + x_n\vec{v}_n$, $x_i \in \mathbb{R}$,

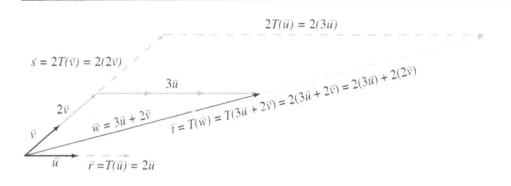

Figure 3.19   Linear transformation "scale by two."

which can be decomposed into the two operations specified above, and you can see how these are equivalent requirements. Linear transformations always map lines to lines (or to zero), and it is always the case that $T(\vec{0}) = \vec{0}$. Figure 3.19 should give you an intuition for this. In this case, the transformation is "scale by a factor of two." You can see directly that the linear combination is preserved:

$$\vec{t} = T\left(\vec{w}\right)$$

$$= 2\left(3\vec{u} + 2\vec{v}\right)$$

$$= 2\left(3\vec{u}\right) + 2\left(2\vec{v}\right)$$

Because linear transformations preserve linear combinations, and all vectors $\vec{u}_i \in \mathcal{V}$ can be written as a linear combination of some set of basis vectors $\{\vec{v}_1, \vec{v}_2, \ldots, \vec{v}_n\}$, a linear transformation can be characterized by what it does to the basis vectors. We can understand what sorts of operations linear transformations can perform by considering what transformations we can perform on a vector: changing its length (scaling) or direction (rotation). The transformation shown in Figure 3.19 was a *uniform scaling*, as the basis vectors were both scaled by the same value; however, it is certainly permissible to scale each vector by a *different* value, in which case we get a *nonuniform scaling* (Figure 3.20 shows the results of scaling one basis vector by 2 and the other by 1.5). If we rotate the basis vectors in the same way, we effect a rotation (by the same amount) in all vectors that are linear combinations of those basis vectors (Figure 3.21). Finally, a shear transform scales only one component of a basis vector (Figure 3.22).

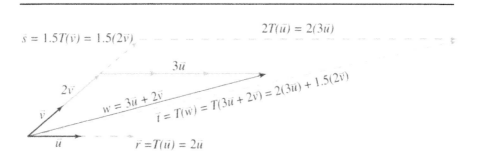

Figure 3.20 Nonuniform scale linear transformation.

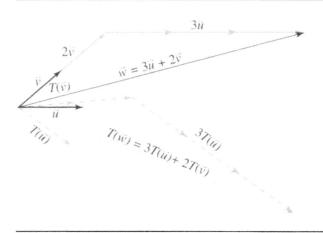

Figure 3.21 Rotation transformation.

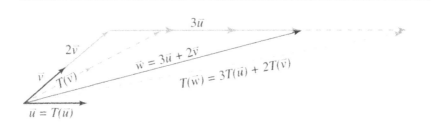

Figure 3.22 Shear transformation.

3.3 AFFINE SPACES

So far, all we've talked about are vectors—what they are, what you can do with them, and so on. But what about *points*? The world can be viewed as a space of points (locations). How can we relate these points to the vectors we've been talking about? The rather obvious intuition is that if we have a point, we can "attach" a vector to it, and at the end of that vector we have another point. Further, if we have two points, there is a vector pointing from one to the other, and vice versa.

So, we have this clear functional distinction between points and vectors. In order to make it very clear which we're talking about, we've adopted a common convention for our notation: a vector always appears with either a diacritical arrow over it ($\vec{u}, \vec{v}$) or a "hat" ($\hat{u}, \hat{v}$) in the case of unit-length vectors and is generally lowercase; points are written without the arrow and are uppercase (P, Q). Since we can have a vector between two points, occasionally we'll use a notation that makes this explicit—$\vec{pq}$ is a vector from P to Q.

Formally, an *affine space* $\mathcal{A}$ consists of a set of points $\mathcal{P}$ and a set of vectors $\mathcal{V}$, which are a vector space spanned by some basis or bases of $\mathcal{V}$. The dimension n of $\mathcal{A}$ is the dimension of $\mathcal{V}$. We refer to the points in $\mathcal{A}$ as $\mathcal{A}.\mathcal{P}$ and the vectors as $\mathcal{A}.\mathcal{V}$.

The relationship between the point space and *underlying* vector space of an affine space was intuitively explained above. More formally, the relationship is determined by the axioms defining subtraction of pairs of points and the so-called *Head-to-Tail Axiom*:

i. $\forall P, Q \in \mathcal{A}.\mathcal{P}, \exists$ a unique vector $\vec{v} \in \mathcal{A}.\mathcal{V}$ such that $\vec{v} = P - Q$.

ii. $\forall Q \in \mathcal{A}.\mathcal{P}, \forall \vec{v} \in \mathcal{A}.\mathcal{V}, \exists$ a unique point P such that $P - Q = \vec{v}$.

iii. $\forall P, Q, R \in \mathcal{A}.\mathcal{P}, (P - Q) + (Q - R) = P - R$.

Note that condition (i) above can be rewritten as $P = Q + \vec{v}$ and also implies that $P = P + \vec{0}$. Figure 3.23 shows the first two axioms. The Head-to-Tail Axiom is depicted graphically in Figure 3.24.

Finally, we have another axiom (what DeRose calls the *Coordinate Axiom*), defining two important multiplicative operations on points:

$$\forall P \in \mathcal{A}.\mathcal{P}, 1 \cdot P = P \text{ and } 0 \cdot P = \vec{0}$$

which simply tells us that multiplying a point by 1 gives us back the point, and multiplying a point by 0 gives us back the zero vector for $\mathcal{A}.\mathcal{V}$.

A number of identities are worth listing (DeRose 1992):

i. $Q - Q = \vec{0}$

PROOF   If we set $Q = R$, then the Head-to-Tail Axiom can be rewritten as $(P - Q) + (Q - Q) = P - Q$, which means that $(Q - Q) = \vec{0}$. ∎

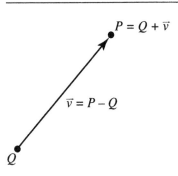

Figure 3.23   Definition of point subtraction.

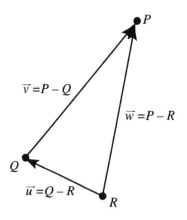

Figure 3.24   The Head-to-Tail axiom.

ii. $R - Q = -(Q - R)$

PROOF   If we set $P = R$, then the Head-to-Tail Axiom can be rewritten as $(R - Q) + (Q - R) = R - R$. Since $R - R = \vec{0}$, this implies that $(R - Q) = -(Q - R)$. ∎

iii. $\vec{v} + (Q - R) = (Q + \vec{v}) - R$

PROOF   Let $\vec{v} = P - Q$. Substituting this into the Head-to-Tail Axiom gives us $\vec{v} + (Q - R) = P - R$. Substituting $Q + \vec{v}$ then gives us the result. ∎

iv. $Q - (R + \vec{v}) = (Q - R) - \vec{v}$

PROOF   Follows from the above by multiplying by -1. ∎

v. $P = Q + (P - Q)$

PROOF   We can rewrite the Head-to-Tail Axiom, by invoking the definition of addition, as $P = R + (P - Q) + (Q - R)$. If we then substitute $Q = R$, we get $P = Q + (P - Q) + (Q - Q)$. Since $(Q - Q) = \vec{0}$, we have the desired result. ∎

vi. $(Q + \vec{v}) - (R + \vec{w}) = (Q - R) + (\vec{v} - \vec{w})$.

PROOF

$$(Q + \vec{v}) - (R + \vec{w})$$

$$
\begin{aligned}
&= \left[(Q + \vec{v}) - R\right] + \left[R - (R + \vec{w})\right] && \text{by Head-to-Tail Axiom} \\
&= \left[(Q + \vec{v}) - R\right] + \left[(R - R) - \vec{w}\right] && \text{by part (iv)} \\
&= \left[(Q + \vec{v}) - R\right] - \vec{w} && \text{by part (i)} \\
&= \left[(Q + \vec{v}) - Q\right] + [Q - R] - \vec{w} && \text{by Head-to-Tail Axiom} \\
&= \left[\vec{v} + (Q - Q)\right] + [Q - R] - \vec{w} && \text{by part (iii)} \\
&= (Q - R) + (\vec{v} - \vec{w}) && \text{by part (i)} \quad ∎
\end{aligned}
$$

Affine Combinations

Recall that we can do the following:

- Add two vectors together, yielding a third
- Multiply a vector by a scalar, yielding a vector
- Add a vector to a point, yielding another point
- Subtract two points, yielding a vector

Note that we haven't talked about the following:

- Multiplying a point by a scalar
- Adding two points together

The first has no sensible interpretation whatsoever in an affine space—what would it mean to *scale* a location? Remember that we have no distinguished origin. The second operation has no sensible interpretation either.

However, there is an operation that is *sort of* like adding two points together, and it's called an *affine combination*. In an affine combination, we effectively add together fractions of points. Before you object too strongly to this as being even more bizarre than adding or scaling points, consider the situation where we have two points P and Q. We know now that these points can be considered to differ by a vector $\vec{v} = Q - P$. There are, of course, an infinite number of points along the way from P to Q, each some fraction of the way along $\vec{v}$. Consider an arbitrary point R somewhere between

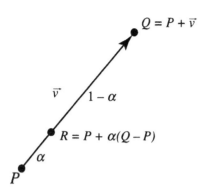

$Q = P + \vec{v}$

$\vec{v}$

$1 - \alpha$

$R = P + \alpha(Q - P)$

α

P

Figure 3.25   Affine combination of two points.

P and Q. It divides the vector between them by some ratio, say, $\alpha : 1 - \alpha$. We then can write

$$R = P + \alpha \, (Q - P)$$

which is depicted graphically in Figure 3.25. Let's pretend for a minute we're just doing algebra. We could then rewrite the above as

$$R = (1 - \alpha) \, P + \alpha Q$$

or as

$$R = \alpha_1 P + \alpha_2 Q$$

where $\alpha_1 + \alpha_2 = 1$. We've just done two "forbidden" operations on points—scaling by a vector and directly adding them. But, what we've just done is "clean up" the original affine combination, so we've done nothing technically wrong. However, this notation is so convenient, it's become common practice to employ it whenever we know what we "really mean." Let's just "define our way out of the problem" by stating the following: Wherever the expression

$$\alpha_1 P + \alpha_2 Q$$

appears, if $\alpha_1 + \alpha_2 = 1$, then it's defined to mean the point

$$P + \alpha_2 \, (Q - P)$$

This form is generally used when the term *affine combination* is used and is quite a convenient notation.

It should be clear that if we set α between 0 and 1, the point R will be between P and Q; if this is the case, then we call this a *convex combination*. However, our definition of affine combination doesn't really preclude us from setting α outside this range, in which case the resulting R will be somewhere on the (infinite) line defined by P and Q.

We can extend the affine combination, as you may have suspected, to involve more than just two points: Given n points $P_1, P_2, \ldots, P_n$, and n real numbers $\alpha_1, \alpha_2, \ldots, \alpha_n$ whose sum is 1, we can define an affine combination to be

$$P_1 + \alpha_2 \left(P_2 - P_1\right) + \alpha_3 \left(P_3 - P_2\right) + \cdots + \alpha_n \left(P_n - P_1\right)$$

and again rewrite this as

$$\alpha_1 P_1 + \alpha_2 P_2 + \cdots + \alpha_n P_n$$

An example is shown in the top of Figure 3.26, in which $\alpha_1 = \alpha_2 = \alpha_3 = \alpha_4 = 0.25$. The careful reader may have noticed that α_1 does not appear in the original affine combination, yet it does appear in the rewritten form below it. Why are P_1 and α_1 "special"? Actually, they are not. We can interchange the roles of P_1 and any of the other points, compute the affine combination using the same coefficients, and produce the same point. The lower diagram in Figure 3.26 shows what happens when we interchange P_1 and P_2—we get the same Q as an affine combination.

3.3.1 EUCLIDEAN GEOMETRY

You should have noticed several things missing from all of these discussions of affine geometry:

- There has been no mention of any concept of an *origin* in an affine space.

- We've only really talked about angle in a rather general sense, but not specified *how* we define or compute angles.

- While it's clear that two points in affine space are separated by some distance, we've not discussed it beyond that.

These have not been accidental omissions. In fact, affine space by definition has no origin (there is no special point distinct from all others) and does not include any mechanism for defining length or angle (remember, affine space itself consists of points, and thus the questions "What is the angle between two points?" and "What is the length of a point?" are meaningless).

The lack of a predefined origin to an affine space shouldn't really bother us, though: typically, in computer graphics and geometric design, models (in the sense of

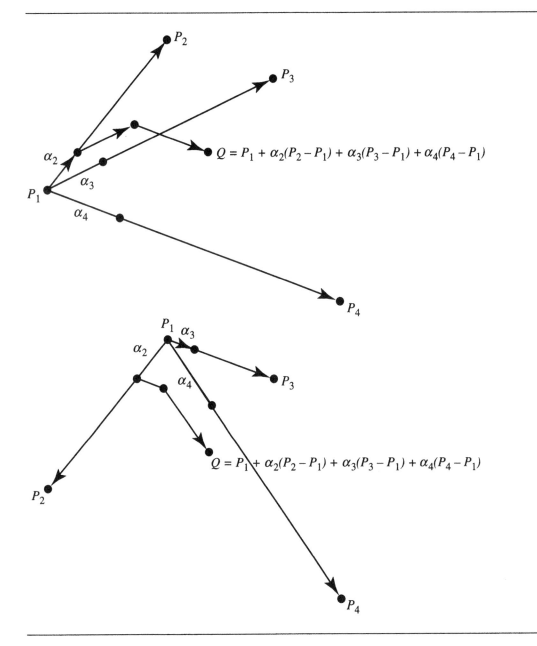

Figure 3.26   Affine combination of several points.

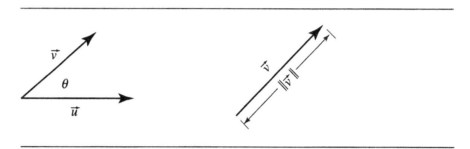

Figure 3.27   Angle between vectors and vector length.

cars, etc. or virtual worlds) are defined by hierarchies of components, each of which is created in its own space, and then its space is located inside the "next higher level's" space, and so no point really is distinguished—only the relative relationships between points matter. We'll get to the problem of origins of spaces in a later section.

For now, let's concentrate on length, distance, and angle. These aren't omitted from affine space because they're not useful concepts—of course they're essential. It's just that these properties are properly part of what's called *Euclidean space*, which can be considered to be affine space with the addition of this "metric" information. Euclidean space can then be considered a specialization of, or a subset of, affine space; all of the principles and properties we've discussed about affine space apply to Euclidean space, plus these new metric properties.

We've seen how to add and subtract vectors, and how to multiply them by scalars, and also how these two sorts of operations interact. There are two other fundamental vector operations, both of which are forms of multiplying two vectors together; these are the *scalar product*, so called because it produces a single-valued (i.e., scalar) result, and the *vector product*, so called because it produces another vector.

The scalar product is related to the questions "What is the angle between two vectors?" and "What is the length of a vector?" (Figure 3.27), while the vector product is related to the area of the parallelogram formed by two vectors placed tail-to-tail, as when we diagram the additive operation (Figure 3.28).

Scalar Product

The scalar product is commonly known as the *dot product*, a special case of an *inner product*. Before continuing, there are a few symbols we need to define:

- Length: The length of a vector $\vec{u}$ is written as $\|\vec{u}\|$.
- Direction: The direction of a vector $\vec{u}$ is written as $\mathrm{dir}(\vec{u})$.
- Sign: The sign of a scalar is written as $\mathrm{sgn}(\alpha)$.

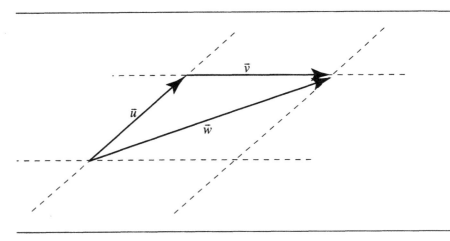

Figure 3.28   Parallelogram rule for vector addition.

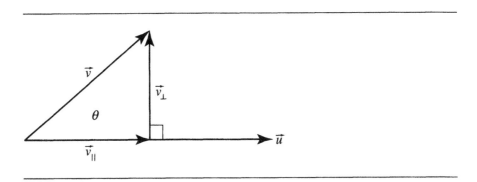

Figure 3.29   Vector projection.

- Perpendicular: A vector $\vec{u}$ perpendicular to a vector $\vec{v}$ is written as $\vec{u} \perp \vec{v}$.
- Parallel: A vector $\vec{u}$ parallel to a vector $\vec{v}$ is written as $\vec{u} \parallel \vec{v}$.

Before discussing the scalar product, we need to step back a little and discuss *projection* of vectors, in order to provide some intuition as to why the scalar product is useful and why it is so defined.

Suppose we have two vectors $\vec{u}$ and $\vec{v}$ and draw them as shown in Figure 3.29, so that the angle between them is θ. The vector $\vec{v}$ can be decomposed into two components relative to $\vec{u}$:

- $\vec{v}_\perp$ (perpendicular to $\vec{u}$)
- $\vec{v}_\parallel$ (parallel to $\vec{u}$)

Note also that $\vec{v}_\parallel + \vec{v}_\perp = \vec{v}$. By convention $\vec{v}_\perp$ is called the *normal component* of $\vec{v}$ with respect to $\vec{u}$, and $\vec{v}_\parallel$ is called the *orthogonal projection* of $\vec{v}$ on $\vec{u}$ ("orthogonal" because it's projected in a direction perpendicular to $\vec{u}$).

What we're interested in here are the relationships between $\vec{v}_\parallel$, $\vec{v}_\perp$, and the angle θ. First let's apply a little trigonometry and look at the lengths of $\vec{v}_\perp$ and $\vec{v}_\parallel$, and observe that (by definition of sine and cosine, respectively)

$$\|\vec{v}_\perp\| = \|\vec{v}\| \, |\sin \theta| \tag{3.2}$$

and

$$\|\vec{v}_\parallel\| = \|\vec{v}\| \, |\cos \theta| \tag{3.3}$$

Now, what about the vectors themselves? This takes a bit more explanation than just appealing to the definitions of fundamental trigonometric relationships. The first claim is that

$$\vec{v}_\parallel = \|\vec{v}\| \cos \theta \hat{u}$$

where $\hat{u} = \frac{\vec{u}}{\|\vec{u}\|}$ is a unit (length $= 1$) vector having the same direction as $\vec{u}$. That is, $\vec{v}_\parallel$ is obtained by scaling $\vec{u}$ by the ratio of the length of $\vec{v}$ to $\vec{u}$ multiplied by the cosine of the angle between them. To show that this is the case, we have to show that these two vectors ($\vec{v}_\parallel$ and $\frac{\|\vec{v}\|}{\|\vec{u}\|} \cos \theta \vec{u}$) are the same; we have to show that they have the same direction and length. Taking length first:

$$\|\vec{v}_\parallel\| = \|\vec{v} \cos \theta \hat{u}\|$$

$$\|\vec{v}_\parallel\| = \|\vec{v}\| \, |\cos \theta| \, \|\hat{u}\|$$

but $\|\hat{u}\| = 1$ because it is by definition a unit vector, so we have

$$\|\vec{v}_\parallel\| = \|\vec{v}\| \, |\cos \theta|$$

which proves the vectors have the same length.

To show equivalent direction, we have to consider two cases:

i. $\cos \theta$ is positive (as in Figure 3.29).

ii. $\cos \theta$ is negative (as in Figure 3.30).

In the former

$$\text{dir}\left(\|\vec{v}\| \cos \theta \hat{u}\right) = \text{dir}\left(\hat{u}\right) \iff \cos \theta > 0$$

$$\text{dir}\left(\|\vec{v}\| \cos \theta \hat{u}\right) = -\,\text{dir}\left(\hat{u}\right) \iff \cos \theta < 0$$

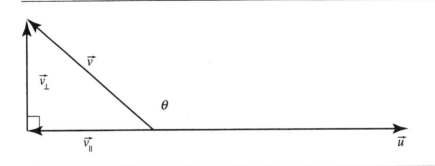

Figure 3.30 $\cos\theta$ negative.

So for $\cos\theta < 0$ and $\cos\theta > 0$, we have

$$\text{dir}\left(\|\vec{v}\|\cos\theta\hat{u}\right) = \text{dir}\left(\vec{v}_{\|}\right) \tag{3.4}$$

Note that if $\cos\theta = 0$ ($\theta = 90°$ or $\theta = 270°$), both $\|\vec{v}\|\cos\theta\hat{u}$ and $\vec{v}_{\|}$ become the $\vec{0}$ vector, and the relationship still holds.

To show that $\|\vec{v}_{\perp}\| = \|\vec{v}\|\,|\sin\theta|$, we can simply note that

$$\vec{v} = \vec{v}_{\perp} + \vec{v}_{\|}$$

which we can rearrange as

$$\vec{v}_{\perp} = \vec{v} - \vec{v}_{\|}$$

and the desired result follows directly.

So, we have in the orthogonal projection $(\vec{v}_{\|})$ an entity that is related to the angle θ between two vectors.[1] If you look at the relations we just proved, and the figures that go with them, you'll notice that the length and direction of $\vec{v}$, and the direction of $\vec{u}$, affect the length and direction of $\vec{v}_{\|}$, but the length of $\vec{u}$ has no effect! Furthermore, $\vec{v}_{\|}$ is a *vector,* and it would be preferable to have a *scalar*—a single value—to characterize the angle while simultaneously taking into account the lengths of the two vectors.

The foregoing is the long way around to justifying the otherwise seemingly arbitrary definition of the dot (scalar) product of two vectors; formally, the dot product is defined as follows: if $\vec{u}$ and $\vec{v}$ are vectors and θ is the angle between $\vec{u}$ and $\vec{v}$, then the *dot product* $\vec{u} \cdot \vec{v}$ is defined by

---

1. We can just arbitrarily focus on $\vec{v}_{\|}$ because if we know $\vec{v}$ and $\vec{v}_{\|}$, $\vec{v}_{\perp}$ can be computed with a simple vector subtraction.

$$\vec{u} \cdot \vec{v} = \begin{cases} \|\vec{u}\| \|\vec{v}\| \cos \theta, & \text{if } \vec{u} \neq \vec{0} \text{ and } \vec{v} \neq \vec{0} \\ 0, & \text{if } \vec{u} = \vec{0} \text{ or } \vec{v} - \vec{0} \end{cases} \tag{3.5}$$

which of course implies that, for nonzero vectors $\vec{u}$ and $\vec{v}$,

$$\cos \theta = \frac{\vec{u} \cdot \vec{v}}{\|\vec{u}\| \|\vec{v}\|} \tag{3.6}$$

and

$$\theta = \cos^{-1} \frac{\vec{u} \cdot \vec{v}}{\|\vec{u}\| \|\vec{v}\|} \tag{3.7}$$

The dot product has a number of important properties:

i. Definition: $\vec{u} \cdot \vec{v} = \|\vec{u}\| \|\vec{v}\| \cos \theta$.

ii. Bilinearity: $\forall \alpha, \beta \in \mathbb{R}$, and $\forall \vec{u}, \vec{v}, \vec{w} \in \mathcal{A}.\mathcal{V}$,

    a. $\left(\alpha \vec{u} + \beta \vec{v} \right) \cdot \vec{w} = \alpha \left(\vec{u} \cdot \vec{w} \right) + \beta \left(\vec{v} \cdot \vec{w} \right)$.

    b. $\vec{u} \cdot \left(\alpha \vec{v} + \beta \vec{w} \right) = \alpha \left(\vec{u} \cdot \vec{v} \right) + \beta \left(\vec{u} \cdot \vec{w} \right)$.

iii. Positive definiteness:

    a. $\forall \vec{u} \in \mathcal{A}.\mathcal{V}, \vec{u} \neq \vec{0}, \vec{u} \cdot \vec{u} > 0$.

    b. $\vec{0} \cdot \vec{0} = 0$.

iv. Commutativity: $\vec{u} \cdot \vec{v} = \vec{v} \cdot \vec{u}$.

PROOF
$$\vec{u} \cdot \vec{v} = \|\vec{u}\| \|\vec{v}\| \cos \theta$$
$$= \|\vec{u}\| \|\vec{v}\| \cos(-\theta)$$
$$= \vec{v} \cdot \vec{u} \quad \blacksquare$$

v. Distributivity of the dot product over vector addition: $\vec{u} \cdot \left(\vec{v} + \vec{w} \right) = \left(\vec{u} \cdot \vec{v} \right) + \left(\vec{u} \cdot \vec{w} \right)$ First, we must prove a simple relationship: $\vec{u} \cdot \vec{v}_{\|} = \vec{u} \cdot \vec{v}$. The angle α between $\vec{v}_{\|}$ and $\vec{u}$ is either $0°$ or $180°$, depending on whether θ is less than $90°$. So, $\cos(\alpha)$ is either 1 or -1, respectively; this may be restated as saying that $\cos(\alpha) = \text{sgn}(\cos \theta)$. Thus, we have

$$\vec{u} \cdot \vec{v}_{\|} = \|\vec{u}\| \|\vec{v}_{\|}\| \cos \alpha \tag{3.8}$$

$$= \|\vec{u}\| \|\vec{v}\| |\cos \theta| \, \text{sgn}(\cos \theta) \tag{3.9}$$

$$= \|\vec{u}\| \|\vec{v}\| \cos \theta \tag{3.10}$$

$$= \vec{u} \cdot \vec{v} \tag{3.11}$$

PROOF Let γ be the angle between $\vec{v}_\parallel + \vec{w}_\parallel$ and $\vec{u}$. By Equation 3.8, we have

$$\vec{u} \cdot (\vec{v} + \vec{w}) = \vec{u} \cdot (\vec{v} + \vec{w})_\parallel$$

$$= \vec{u} \cdot (\vec{v}_\parallel + \vec{w}_\parallel)$$

$$= \|\vec{u}\| \|\vec{v}_\parallel + \vec{w}_\parallel\| \cos \gamma$$

There are now two cases, depending on whether $\vec{v}_\parallel$ and $\vec{w}_\parallel$ point in the same or opposite directions. In each case, we may have $\cos \gamma = 1$ or $\cos \gamma = -1$. The proof handles both situations, in each case.

a. $\vec{v}_\parallel$ and $\vec{w}_\parallel$ point in the same direction

$$\vec{u} \cdot (\vec{v} + \vec{w}) = \|\vec{u}\| \|\vec{v}_\parallel + \vec{w}_\parallel\| \cos \gamma$$

$$= \|\vec{u}\| \left(\|\vec{v}_\parallel\| + \|\vec{w}_\parallel\| \right) \cos \gamma$$

$$= \|\vec{u}\| \|v_\parallel\| \cos \gamma + \|\vec{u}\| \|\vec{w}_\parallel\| \cos \gamma$$

$$= \vec{u} \cdot \vec{v}_\parallel + \vec{u} \cdot \vec{w}_\parallel$$

$$= \vec{u} \cdot \vec{v} + \vec{u} \cdot \vec{w}$$

b. $\vec{v}_\parallel$ and $\vec{w}_\parallel$ point in opposite directions

$$\vec{u} \cdot (\vec{v} + \vec{w}) = \|\vec{u}\| \|\vec{v}_\parallel + \vec{w}_\parallel\| \cos \gamma$$

$$= \|\vec{u}\| (\|\vec{v}_\parallel\| - \|\vec{w}_\parallel\|)$$

$$= \|\vec{u}\| \|\vec{v}_\parallel\| - \|\vec{u}\| \|\vec{w}_\parallel\|$$

$$= \vec{u} \cdot \vec{v}_\parallel + \vec{u} \cdot \vec{w}_\parallel$$

$$= \vec{u} \cdot \vec{v} + \vec{u} \cdot \vec{w} \quad \blacksquare$$

vi. Distributivity of vector addition over the dot product: $(\vec{u} + \vec{v}) \cdot \vec{w} = \vec{u} \cdot \vec{w} + \vec{v} \cdot \vec{w}$.

PROOF
$$(\vec{u} + \vec{v}) \cdot \vec{w} = \vec{w} \cdot (\vec{u} + \vec{v}) \qquad \text{by commutativity}$$

$$= \vec{w} \cdot \vec{u} + \vec{w} \cdot \vec{v} \qquad \text{by distributivity}$$

$$= \vec{u} \cdot \vec{w} + \vec{v} \cdot \vec{w} \qquad \text{by commutativity} \quad \blacksquare$$

So we have

i. Squared length: $\vec{u} \cdot \vec{u} = \|\vec{u}\|^2$

ii. Angle: $\theta = \cos^{-1} \frac{\vec{u} \cdot \vec{v}}{\|\vec{u}\| \|\vec{v}\|}$

iii. Projection: $\vec{v}_\parallel = \frac{(\vec{u} \cdot \vec{v}) \vec{u}}{\vec{u} \cdot \vec{u}}$

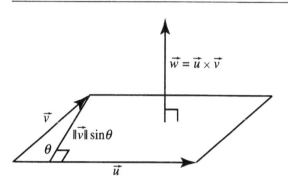

Figure 3.31 The vector product.

iv. Normal: $\vec{v}_\perp = \vec{u} - \frac{(\vec{u}\cdot\vec{v})\vec{u}}{\vec{u}\cdot\vec{u}}$

v. Perpendicular: $\vec{u} \cdot \vec{v} = 0 \iff \vec{u} \perp \vec{v}$

In the discussion of affine combinations earlier in this section, we explained a "notational abuse," in which we allowed ourselves to multiply a point by a scalar. In the case of dot products, we also will occasionally abuse the notation and allow ourselves to take the dot product of a vector with a point. For example, in Section 5.1.1, we describe the implicit form of a line as $\vec{n} \cdot X = d$. Of course, dot products involving points are not strictly "legal"; however, as with the case of the affine combinations, we'll define our way out of the problem by just stating the following: wherever an expression like $\vec{n} \cdot X$ appears, what we really mean is $\vec{n} \cdot (X - \mathcal{O})$, where $\mathcal{O}$ is the origin of the affine frame.

Vector Product

The other vector multiplication operation, the *vector product*, is also known as the *cross product*. The scalar product was discussed in an n-dimensional setting, but here, we restrict the discussion of the cross product to three dimensions; the extension of cross products to higher dimensions only works for some dimensions. Like the dot product, the cross product is related to the angle between two vectors, but can also be understood as defining the area of the parallelogram formed by two vectors placed tail-to-tail (see Figure 3.31).

Another useful way of motivating the idea of the cross product is this: if we have two (nonparallel) vectors $\vec{u}$ and $\vec{v}$, we can consider them to define a (two-dimensional) plane. If you think about this plane as "floating about in space," rather than "on the page," then the dot product can help us find the angle between the vectors, but says nothing about the orientation of the plane in space.

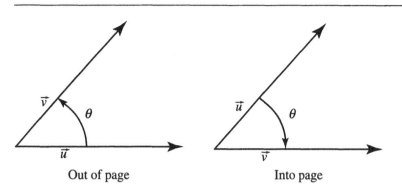

Figure 3.32   The right-hand rule.

We can go about defining the cross product of two vectors $\vec{u}$ and $\vec{v}$ as another vector $\vec{w}$ that is perpendicular to the plane containing $\vec{u}$ and $\vec{v}$, and whose length is related to the angle between these two vectors. We use the $\times$ symbol to indicate the cross product. The defining properties are the following:

i. The cross product of two vectors $\vec{w} = \vec{u} \times \vec{v}$ is a vector.

ii. The cross product of two vectors is perpendicular to those two vectors: $\mathrm{dir}(\vec{u} \times \vec{v}) \perp \vec{u}, \vec{v}$

iii. The length of the cross product of two vectors is equal to the area of the parallelogram formed by $\vec{u}$ and $\vec{v}$: $\|\vec{u} \times \vec{v}\| = \mathrm{Area}\left(\vec{u}, \vec{v}\right) = \|\vec{u}\|\|\vec{v}\| \sin\theta$

Note that if $\theta > 0$, the area is positive, and if $\theta < 0$, then the area is negative; if the unsigned area is desired, then the absolute value of $\sin\theta$ should be used instead.

The astute reader may have noted that there are *two* vectors perpendicular to the plane defined by $\vec{u}$ and $\vec{v}$—one points "outward" or "up," and the other is its opposite, pointing "inward" or "down." By convention, we use the right-hand rule we introduced earlier: if the angle θ between $\vec{u}$ and $\vec{v}$ is positive, then the cross product vector points "out of the page," and conversely if θ is negative (see Figure 3.32).

Other properties of the vector product:

i. Anticommutativity: $\vec{u} \times \vec{v} \neq \vec{v} \times \vec{u}$.

ii. Distributivity: $\vec{u} \times \left(\vec{v} + \vec{w}\right) = \left(\vec{u} \times \vec{v}\right) + \left(\vec{u} \times \vec{w}\right)$.

iii. Distributivity: $\left(\alpha\vec{u}\right) \times \vec{v} = \vec{u} \times \left(\alpha\vec{v}\right) = \alpha\left(\vec{u} \times \vec{v}\right)$.

iv. Parallelism: $\vec{u} \parallel \vec{v} \Longleftrightarrow \vec{u} \times \vec{v} = \vec{0}$.

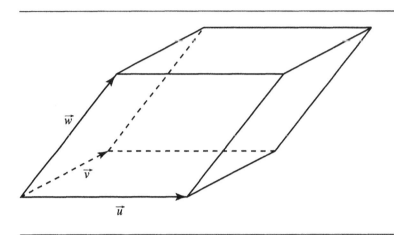

Figure 3.33   Parallelepiped defined by three vectors.

3.3.2 VOLUME, THE DETERMINANT, AND THE SCALAR TRIPLE PRODUCT

It's natural to assume, because we have operations defining length and area, that we also can define volume using vector operations. Naturally, the volumetric equivalent to the parallelogram we used in the cross product is the parallelepiped (Figure 3.33). First, let's introduce a notation for volume: if we have a parallelepiped defined by three linearly independent vectors $\vec{u}$, $\vec{v}$, and $\vec{w}$, its volume is

$$\text{Vol}\left(\vec{u}, \vec{v}, \vec{w}\right)$$

Note that the order of this isn't significant:

$$\text{Vol}\left(\vec{u}, \vec{v}, \vec{w}\right) = \text{Vol}\left(\vec{v}, \vec{w}, \vec{u}\right) = \cdots = \text{Vol}\left(\vec{w}, \vec{v}, \vec{u}\right)$$

because they all describe the same parallelepiped.

Now, given we have these three (basis) vectors, how do we determine Vol $(\vec{u}, \vec{v}, \vec{w})$? Look at Figure 3.34.

$$
\begin{aligned}
\text{Vol}\left(\vec{u}, \vec{v}, \vec{w}\right) \quad &= \text{base} \,\times\, \text{height} && \text{by definition} \\
&= \|\vec{u}\|\|\vec{v}\|\sin\psi\,\|\vec{w}\|\,|\cos\theta| && \text{by trigonometry} \\
&= \|\vec{u}\|\|\vec{v}\|\sin\psi\,\|\vec{w}_\parallel\| && \text{definition of } \vec{w}_\parallel \\
&= \|\vec{u}\times\vec{v}\|\|\vec{w}_\parallel\| && \text{definition of cross product} \\
&= \|\vec{u}\times\vec{v}\cdot\vec{w}_\parallel\| && \text{see explanation following} \\
&= \|\vec{u}\times\vec{v}\cdot\vec{w}\|
\end{aligned}
$$

The fifth step requires some explanation: since $\vec{u}\times\vec{v}$ and $\vec{w}_\parallel$ are parallel, the angle α between them is 0 radians. So, since $\cos\alpha = 1$,

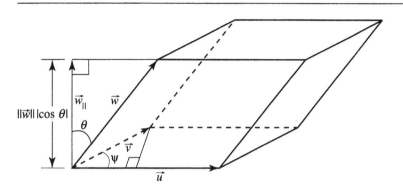

Figure 3.34   The scalar triple product.

$$(\vec{u} \times \vec{v}) = \|\vec{u} \times \vec{v}\| \, \|\vec{w}_{\|}\| \cos \alpha$$

$$= \|\vec{u} \times \vec{v}\| \, \|\vec{w}_{\|}\|$$

But, you say, what about orientation? From the above, we can make two observations:

$$\text{Vol}\left(\vec{u}, \vec{v}, \vec{w}\right) = \begin{cases} \left(\vec{u} \times \vec{v}\right) \cdot \vec{w} & \Longleftrightarrow \vec{w}_{\|} \text{ is in the same direction as } \vec{u} \times \vec{v} \\ -\left(\vec{u} \times \vec{v}\right) \cdot \vec{w} & \Longleftrightarrow \vec{w}_{\|} \text{ is in the same direction as } -\vec{u} \times \vec{v} \end{cases}$$

By the right-hand rule,

$$\text{sgn}\left(\vec{u}, \vec{v}, \vec{w}\right) = \text{sgn}\left(\vec{u}, \vec{v}, \vec{w}_{\|}\right) = \begin{cases} +1 & \Longleftrightarrow \vec{w}_{\|} \text{ is in the same direction as } \vec{u} \times \vec{v} \\ -1 & \Longleftrightarrow \vec{w}_{\|} \text{ is in the same direction as } -\vec{u} \times \vec{v} \end{cases}$$

So, we can conclude that

$$\text{Vol}\left(\vec{u}, \vec{v}, \vec{w}\right) = \text{sgn}\left(\vec{u}, \vec{v}, \vec{w}\right)\left(\left(\vec{u} \times \vec{v}\right) \cdot \vec{w}\right). \tag{3.12}$$

The expression

$$\left(\vec{u} \times \vec{v}\right) \cdot \vec{w} \tag{3.13}$$

is commonly referred to as the *scalar triple product* and is the determinant of a matrix whose ordered rows (or columns) are $\vec{u}, \vec{v}, \vec{w}$, which we notate as

$$\det\left(\vec{u}, \vec{v}, \vec{w}\right)$$

In the preceding discussion, we separated the sign to emphasize that the determinant is the signed volume.

Note that the definition of the determinant (Equation 3.13) is a subexpression of Equation 3.12; that is, the determinant is the *signed* volume:

$$\mathrm{Vol}\left(\vec{u}, \vec{v}, \vec{w}\right) = \mid \det\left(\vec{u}, \vec{v}, \vec{w}\right)\mid = \mathrm{sgn}(\vec{u}, \vec{v}, \vec{w})\det\left(\vec{u}, \vec{v}, \vec{w}\right)$$

Other properties relating to the determinant, scalar triple product, and volume are as follows (Goldman 1987):

i. The determinant $\det(\vec{u}, \vec{v}, \vec{w})$ is nonzero if and only if the set $\{\vec{u}, \vec{v}, \vec{w}\}$ forms a basis. In three-dimensional space, for example, if three vectors don't form a basis, then they must span only a plane or a line, neither of which has volume.

ii. The determinant $\det(\vec{u}, \vec{v}, \vec{w})$ is positive if and only if the sign of $\{\vec{u}, \vec{v}, \vec{w}\}$ is positive.

iii. Cyclic permutations of the vectors don't change their determinant:

$$\det(\vec{u}, \vec{v}, \vec{w}) = \det(\vec{w}, \vec{u}, \vec{v}) = \det(\vec{v}, \vec{w}, \vec{u})$$

iv. Reversing the order of the vectors changes the sign, but not the magnitude of the determinant:

$$\det(\vec{u}, \vec{v}, \vec{w}) = -\det(\vec{w}, \vec{v}, \vec{u}) = -\det(\vec{v}, \vec{u}, \vec{w}) = -\det(\vec{u}, \vec{w}, \vec{v})$$

v. Negating any one of the vectors changes the sign of the determinant:

$$\det(\vec{u}, \vec{v}, \vec{w}) = -\det(-\vec{u}, \vec{v}, \vec{w}) = -\det(\vec{u}, -\vec{v}, \vec{w}) = -\det(\vec{u}, \vec{v}, -\vec{w})$$

vi. Scaling the vectors directly scales the determinant:

$$\det(c\vec{u}, \vec{v}, \vec{w}) = \det(\vec{u}, c\vec{v}, \vec{w}) = \det(\vec{u}, \vec{v}, c\vec{w}) = c\det(\vec{u}, \vec{v}, \vec{w})$$

vii. The basis vectors of a right-handed orthonormal space have a unit determinant.

3.3.3 FRAMES

We're now ready to talk about coordinates with respect to affine spaces. Recall that an affine space $\mathcal{A}$ is defined as a set (space) of points $\mathcal{P}$ (a *point space*) plus an associated or underlying vector space $\mathcal{V}$, each having the same dimension n. If we pick an arbitrary point $\mathcal{O} \in \mathcal{P}$ and a basis $\vec{v}_1, \vec{v}_2, \ldots, \vec{v}_n \in \mathcal{V}$, this forms what we call a *frame*[2] for $\mathcal{A}$. We can write this frame as

---

2. Following DeRose (1989), we eschew the common practice of using the term "space" or "coordinate space" because this use is technically incorrect, or at least, inaccurate and misleading:

$$\mathcal{F} = \left(\vec{v}_1, \vec{v}_2, \ldots, \vec{v}_n, \mathcal{O} \right)^{\mathrm{T}}$$

Recall that, in a vector space, any vector can be written as a linear combination of a set of basis vectors (Section 3.2.3). Any $\vec{u} \in \mathcal{V}$ can be written as

$$\vec{u} = a_1 \vec{v}_1 + a_2 \vec{v}_2 + \cdots + a_n \vec{v}_n$$

The $a_1, a_2, \ldots, a_n$ are the *coordinates* of $\vec{u}$, relative to the basis $\vec{v}_1, \vec{v}_2, \ldots, \vec{v}_n$.

What about the points in $\mathcal{P}$? Here is where the vector and point spaces come together. Recall that if we have any point P and any vector $\vec{u}$, there is a unique point $Q = P + \vec{u}$. If we choose the point $\mathcal{O}$ from $\mathcal{F}$ as P, then any point $Q \in \mathcal{P}$ can be defined in terms of some unique vector $\vec{u} = a_1 \vec{v}_1 + a_2 \vec{v}_2 + \cdots + a_n \vec{v}_n$ added to $\mathcal{O}$:

$$Q = \vec{u} + \mathcal{O}$$

$$= a_1 \vec{v}_1 + a_2 \vec{v}_2 + \cdots + a_n \vec{v}_n + \mathcal{O}$$

and so again the coordinates of Q are $a_1, a_2, \ldots, a_n$. Figure 3.35 shows an affine space $\mathcal{A} = \left(\mathcal{P}. \mathcal{V} \right)$ with frame $\mathcal{F} = \left(\vec{v}_1, \vec{v}_2, \mathcal{O} \right)^{\mathrm{T}}$; the point Q is $\mathcal{O} + \vec{w}$ and has coordinates $(3, 2)$.

Cartesian Frames

Note that we've now mentioned coordinates, and at least the hint of a relative origin in the (otherwise arbitrary) choice of $\mathcal{O}$. However, so far all we've required for frames and their underlying basis vectors is that they be linearly independent. Up until we introduced the dot product, we had no way of formally defining or describing angles or lengths. We now exploit the angle- and length-defining properties of the dot product to define a special subclass of Euclidean spaces.

Every vector $\vec{v}$ has associated with it what's known as a *unit vector*, denoted $\hat{v}$, which specifies the same direction as $\vec{v}$, but has a length of 1:

$$\hat{v} = \frac{\vec{v}}{\| \vec{v} \|}$$

That is, we just scale $\vec{v}$ by dividing by its own length.

---

there may be different frames within the same coordinate space, but if you use the common terminology, you'd have to say that there were different coordinate spaces within the same coordinate space. This sort of statement makes it clear that common usage is overloading the term "space" with two distinct meanings.

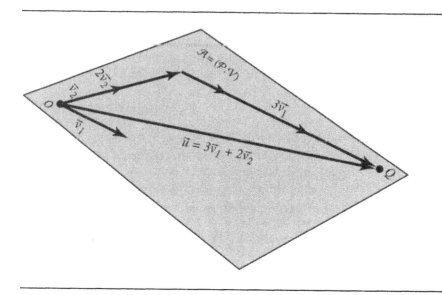

Figure 3.35   Coordinates of an affine point, relative to an arbitrary frame.

As we can now measure and define angles, we can now ensure that basis vectors are *perpendicular* or *orthogonal* by requiring that $\vec{v}_1 \cdot \vec{v}_2 = 0$. If we have a three-dimensional space, and the three basis vectors are mutually perpendicular, then it will also be the case that each vector will be the cross product of the other two (taken in order—$\vec{v}_1 \times \vec{v}_2 = \vec{v}_3$, $\vec{v}_2 \times \vec{v}_3 = \vec{v}_1$, and $\vec{v}_3 \times \vec{v}_1 = \vec{v}_2$ for a right-handed system).

With these tools in hand, we can define a special type of frame for a Euclidean space—the *Cartesian* frame—which has basis vectors of unit length, which are mutually perpendicular. Such a basis is also referred to as *orthonormal*.

3.4 AFFINE TRANSFORMATIONS

An *affine transformation* is a map taking points and vectors in one affine space to points and vectors, respectively, in another affine space. In general we say $T : \mathcal{A}^n \mapsto \mathcal{B}^m$ is an affine transformation if it preserves affine combinations:

$$T\left(a_1 P_1 + a_2 P_2 + \cdots + a_n P_n\right) = a_1 T\left(P_1\right) + a_2 T\left(P_2\right) + \cdots + a_n T\left(P_n\right) \quad (3.14)$$

with $P_i \in \mathcal{A}$ and $\sum_{i=1}^{n} a_i = 1$. Note that the dimensions n and m need not be the same, but $m \leq n$.

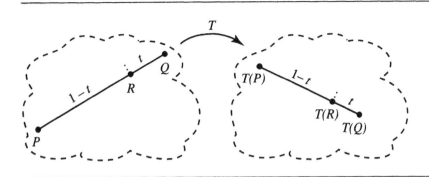

Figure 3.36   Affine maps preserve relative ratios.

Because an affine transformation maps points to points, it also maps line segments to line segments, planes to planes, and so on. We can show this more directly: Recall that we can write a point R on a line as an affine combination of two other (noncoincident) points P and Q on the line:

$$R = (1 - \alpha)\, P + \alpha Q$$

for some α. If we apply the affine map T, we get

$$T(R) = T((1 - \alpha)\, P + \alpha Q)$$
$$= (1 - \alpha)\, T(P) + \alpha T(Q)$$

This is very closely related to writing out the equation of a line in parametric form:

$$R(t) = (1 - t)\, P + t Q$$

to which the map T can be applied:

$$T(R(t)) = T((1 - t)\, P + t Q)$$
$$= (1 - t)\, T(P) + t T(Q)$$

This is just the parametric equation for the line defined by P and Q. Although this is fairly obvious, it is important to point out that the constants in the above equations are not affected by the transformation T—t and $1 - t$ do not change. Put another way, R has the same *relative* distances between it and P and Q. Formally, we say that affine maps *preserve relative ratios* (see Figure 3.36).

An affine space, as you recall, is a set of points *plus* a set of vectors. So, naturally the question arises as to what effect an affine transformation has on vectors. Suppose we have an affine map T that operates on the points of an affine space $\mathcal{A}$. Given two points $P, Q \in \mathcal{A}$, we can take their difference to find a vector

$$\vec{v} = Q - P$$

because this operation defines the relationship between points and vectors in an affine space. Now, what happens if we apply the affine map? We get

$$T(\vec{v}) = T(Q - P)$$
$$= T(Q) - T(P)$$

So, the transformed vector is just the one between the transformed points. Recall, however, that the vectors that underlie an affine space are elements of a vector space, and that in a vector space, *location* of a vector is meaningless. There are *infinitely many* other pairs of points in $T(\mathcal{A})$ whose difference is $T(\vec{v})$; if you draw a directed line segment between each of these pairs of points, you just get "copies" of $T(\vec{v})$ that have the same direction and magnitude, but which are merely offset or translated from one another.

We can go even further than this, though: formally, we say that affine maps *preserve parallelism*. To see this, suppose we have two pairs of points $\{P_1, P_2\}$ and $\{Q_1, Q_2\}$. Each pair of points defines a line:

$$\mathcal{L}_1 = P_1 + \alpha(P_2 - P_1)$$
$$\mathcal{L}_2 = Q_1 + \beta(Q_2 - Q_1)$$

These lines are parallel if $P_2 - P_1 = \gamma(Q_2 - Q_1)$ (that is, these vectors differ only in length by a relative ratio of γ and are in the same direction). An affine map then maps these vectors to scaled versions of the same vector, and so affine maps preserve parallelism.

We'll use this observation to characterize affine transformations, in conjunction with the following: an affine map T is a linear transformation with respect to the vectors of an affine space $\mathcal{A}$. In Section 3.2.6, we defined a linear transformation as one that preserves linear combinations. A linear combination of vectors is defined as

$$\vec{w} = x_1\vec{v}_1 + x_2\vec{v}_2 + \cdots + x_n\vec{v}_n, x_i \in \mathbb{R}$$

for a set of linearly independent vectors $\vec{v}_i \in \mathcal{V}$. To say that a linear map preserves linear combinations requires that

$$T(\vec{w}) = T\left(\vec{v}_1x_1 + \vec{v}_2x_2 + \cdots + \vec{v}_nx_n\right) \tag{3.15}$$

$$= T\left(\vec{v}_1x_1\right) + T\left(\vec{v}_2x_2\right) + \cdots + T\left(\vec{v}_nx_n\right) \tag{3.16}$$

$$= x_1T\left(\vec{v}_1\right) + x_2T\left(\vec{v}_2\right) + \cdots + x_nT\left(\vec{v}_n\right) \tag{3.17}$$

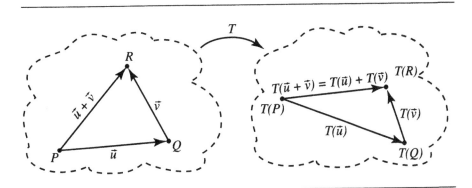

Figure 3.37   Vector sum.

$\forall x_1, x_2, \ldots, x_n \in \mathbb{R}, \forall \vec{v}_1, \vec{v}_2, \ldots, \vec{v}_n \in \mathcal{V}$. Equation 3.15 above was broken down into Equations 3.16 and 3.17 separately in order to show the two aspects to preservation of linear combinations, and accordingly, we must show that both conditions hold. We can do this for a two-dimensional affine space and extend it to higher dimensions by induction on the number of basis vectors. First, we have to show

$$T(\vec{u} + \vec{v}) = T(\vec{u}) + T(\vec{v}) \tag{3.18}$$

Suppose we have two vectors $\vec{u}$ and $\vec{v}$, as shown in Figure 3.37. The proof is trivial:

$$\begin{aligned} T(\vec{u} + \vec{v}) &= T(R - P) \\ &= T(R) + (T(Q) - T(Q)) - T(P) \\ &= (T(R) - T(Q)) + (T(Q) - T(P)) \\ &= T(\vec{v}) + T(\vec{u}) \\ &= T(\vec{u}) + T(\vec{v}) \end{aligned}$$

We must also show now that

$$T(\alpha \vec{v}) = \alpha T(\vec{v})$$

As shown in Figure 3.38, we can rewrite $\alpha \vec{v}$ as $((1 - \alpha)P + \alpha Q) - P$. If the "proof by diagram" isn't sufficient, consider the following:

$$\begin{aligned} T(\alpha \vec{v}) &= T(((1 - \alpha)P + \alpha Q) - P) & \text{by substitution} \\ &= T((1 - \alpha)P + \alpha Q) - T(P) & \text{by Equation 3.18} \\ &= (1 - \alpha)T(P) + \alpha T(Q) - T(P) & \text{by Equation 3.18} \\ &= \alpha T(\vec{v}) & \text{by definition of affine combination} \end{aligned}$$

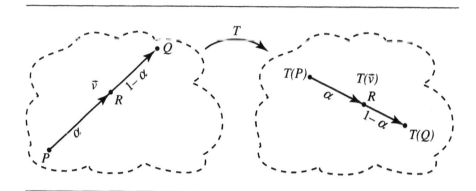

Figure 3.38   Vector scale.

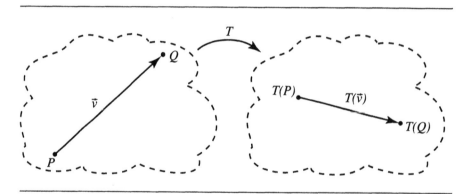

Figure 3.39   Sum of point and vector.

Finally, an affine map also preserves addition of vectors to points:

$$T(P + \vec{v}) = T(P) + T(\vec{v})$$

Referring to Figure 3.39, we can see the usual definition of a point as the sum of a point and a vector: $Q = P + \vec{v}$, or $\vec{v} = Q - P$. This leads to the following proof (DeRose 1992):

$$
\begin{aligned}
T(P + \vec{v}) &= T(P + (Q - P)) && \text{by definition of subtraction of points} \\
&= T(P) + T(Q) - T(P) && \text{by definition of transformation} \\
&= T(P) + (T(Q) - T(P)) && \text{by associativity of vector addition} \\
&= T(P) + T(\vec{v}) && \text{by definition of subtraction of points}
\end{aligned}
$$

Together, these properties show that an affine transformation T preserves affine coordinates:

$$T\left(\alpha_1\vec{v}_1 + \alpha_2\vec{v}_2 + \cdots + \alpha_n\vec{v}_n + \mathcal{O}\right) = \alpha_1 T(\vec{v}_1) + \alpha_2 T(\vec{v}_2) + \cdots + \alpha_n T(\vec{v}_n) + T(\mathcal{O})$$

The above was written as a general statement, but notice that the notation is that of an affine frame. So, an affine transformation is completely and uniquely defined by its action on a frame, or on a simplex.

3.4.1 TYPES OF AFFINE MAPS

As shown in the previous section, an affine map's operation on the vectors of an affine space $\mathcal{A}$ is that of a linear map; this allows for rotations and scales (both uniform and nonuniform). Because vectors (even those of $\mathcal{A}.\mathcal{V}$) carry no positional information, this excludes any operation that is related to position (such as translation).

As affine maps operate on both $\mathcal{A}.\mathcal{P}$ and $\mathcal{A}.\mathcal{V}$, mapping points to points and so on, they are able to represent transformations involving relative positions:

- Translations
- Mirror or reflection about an arbitrary line or plane
- Parallel projection
- Rotation about an arbitrary point
- Shearing relative to arbitrary lines or planes

These transformations will be covered in more detail in Section 4.7.

3.4.2 COMPOSITION OF AFFINE MAPS

In Section 2.7.1, we discussed maps in a general sense, and how you can compose maps by using the output (the range) of a function T as the domain of another function U. Affine maps, of course, are no different in this regard; we can build up a complex series of transformations by simply applying one affine map after another. The characteristics of affine maps, as described in the previous sections, ensure that we never leave affine space, and thus we can consider the composition of any number of affine maps to be just another single affine map, albeit a more complex one. A rather obvious example of this is a series of rotations (about the same point) of α, β, and γ degrees; clearly this is the same as a single rotation of $\alpha + \beta + \gamma$ (Figure 3.40).

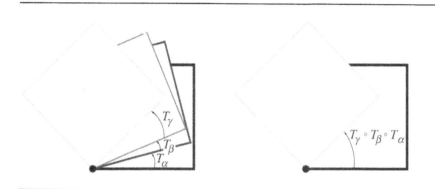

Figure 3.40   Composition of affine maps (rotation).

3.5 BARYCENTRIC COORDINATES AND SIMPLEXES

We saw that the coordinates of points in an affine space can be defined in terms of the basis vectors of the underlying vector space, relative to the point $\mathcal{O}$ of $\mathcal{F}$:

$$Q = \vec{u} + \mathcal{O}$$

$$= a_1\vec{v}_1 + a_2\vec{v}_2 + \cdots + a_n\vec{v}_n + \mathcal{O}$$

An alternative is to use what we might call "basis points": $P_0 = \mathcal{O}$, $P_1 = \mathcal{O} + \vec{v}_1$, $P_2 = \mathcal{O} + \vec{v}_2, \ldots, P_n = \mathcal{O} + \vec{v}_n$ (that is, a set of points consisting of $\mathcal{O}$ and the points generated by adding the basis vectors to $\mathcal{O}$).

We can then represent a point $Q \in \mathcal{A}$, relative to $\mathcal{F}$ as

$$Q = P_0 \left(1 - a_1 - a_2 - \cdots - a_n\right) + P_1 a_1 + P_2 a_2 + \cdots + P_n a_n$$

or

$$Q = P_0 a_0 + P_1 a_1 + \cdots + P_n a_n$$

where a_0 is defined by

$$1 = a_0 + a_1 + \cdots + a_n$$

This last identity is particularly important—the coefficients sum to 1.

This should be recognizable as an affine combination, and the values a_0, $a_1, \ldots, a_n$ are called the *barycentric coordinates* of Q with respect to $\mathcal{F}$. Figure 3.41 shows both the standard frame coordinates and the barycentric coordinates.

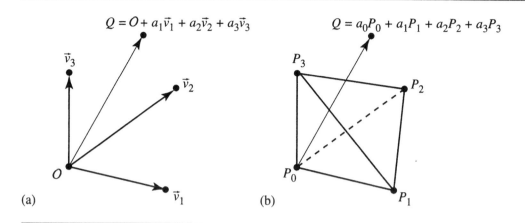

Figure 3.41   Affine (a) and barycentric (b) coordinates.

You might expect, due to the fundamental relationship between points and vectors in an affine space, that vectors themselves can also be represented using barycentric coordinates; this is indeed the case. Recall that we can write any vector as

$$\vec{u} = a_1\vec{v}_1 + a_2\vec{v}_2 + \cdots + a_n\vec{v}_n$$

If we let $a_0 = -\left(a_1 + a_2 + \cdots + a_n\right)$, then we can rewrite the vector as

$$\vec{u} = a_0P_0 + a_1P_1 + \cdots + a_nP_n$$

Note that

$$a_0 + a_1 + \cdots + a_n = -\left(a_1 + a_2 + \cdots + a_n\right) + a_1 + a_2 + \cdots + a_n$$
$$= 0$$

That is, the coefficients sum to 0, not 1 as we have for points. The "basis points" are generally referred to as a *simplex*, just as the distinguished point plus basis vectors are called a *frame*.

An affine map's preservation of relative ratios applies to barycentric coordinates for higher-order simplexes as well as to lines (see Section 3.4). Let's take this reasoning a step further. A basis point K of a simplex is simply that point for which the barycentric coordinates are of the form $\left(a_0 = 0, a_1 = 0, \ldots, a_k = 1, \ldots, a_n = 0\right)$. So, if the basis points are transformed, we get another set of basis points defining another simplex, affine combinations of which are equivalent to points to which the affine map has been applied. So, an affine map can be completely and uniquely described by its operation on a simplex. However, it turns out that an affine map is even more general than that. It may transform an n-simplex into a set of n points that is *not* a simplex; this is what happens when the map is a projection.

3.5.1   BARYCENTRIC COORDINATES AND SUBSPACES

Just as we can have subspaces of linear (vector) spaces, so too can we have affine subspaces, and barycentric coordinates can be discussed in terms of these. Suppose we have an n-dimensional affine space $\mathcal{A}$ as defined by a simplex $S = (P_0, P_1, \ldots, P_n)$. We can then define an m-dimensional subspace $\mathcal{B} \subset \mathcal{A}$, as specified by a simplex $\mathcal{T} = (Q_0, Q_1, \ldots, Q_m)$. Any point $R \in \mathcal{B}$ can be represented as

$$R = b_0 Q_0 + b_1 Q_1 + \cdots + b_m Q_m$$

with the usual definition of $1 = b_0 + b_1 + \cdots + b_m$. Of course, since the Q_i are representable in terms of $\mathcal{A}$, we could rewrite R in terms of $\mathcal{A}$.

Each n-simplex is composed of $n + 1$ points, so a 1-simplex is a line segment, a 2-simplex is a triangle (defining a plane), and a 3-simplex is a tetrahedron (defining a volume), as shown in Figure 3.42. This figure also illustrates the relationship between barycentric and frame coordinates. Consider the 2-simplex in the middle of the figure: the point R can be defined as described above in terms of barycentric coordinates; however, emanating from Q_0 is a line segment that intersects the opposite side of the simplex at a point $c\,(Q_2 - Q_1)$ (and similarly for the other two basis points), and we can consider any of the Q_i to be $\mathcal{O}$ and the vectors from that point to its two neighbors as defining an affine frame. It's particularly interesting to note that any two of these interior, intersecting line segments are sufficient to determine R. This also suggests that only two of the simplicial coefficients are sufficient to specify a point; the reason this "works" is due to the fact that these coefficients sum to 1, and so if we know two coefficients, the third value is implied.

3.5.2   AFFINE INDEPENDENCE

For an affine frame, the basis vectors must be linearly independent. Considering that an affine frame or simplex can be used to define an affine space, it's logical to assume there's an analogous independence criterion for simplexes.

Recall that linear independence of vectors means that none of them are parallel. Intuitively, the analogous characteristic for basis points is that none of them are coincident, and that no more than two are collinear. That is, none are an affine combination of the others. Formally, we can say that a set of basis points are affinely independent if their simplicial coordinates are linearly independent (in the same way that vectors in a vector space are linearly independent).

Let $P_0, P_1, \ldots, P_n$ be the $n + 1$ points defining an n-simplex, and $\vec{v}_i = P_i - P_0$ (recall that we're using the convention that $P_0 = \mathcal{O}$). If the n vectors $\vec{v}_1, \vec{v}_2, \ldots, \vec{v}_n$ are linearly independent, then the points $P_0, P_1, \ldots, P_n$ are *affinely independent*. This

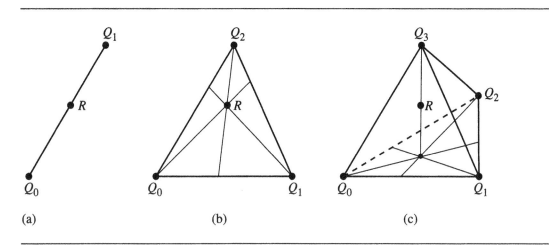

Figure 3.42   The first three simplexes: a line (a), a triangle (b), and a tetrahedron (c).

can be observed by looking at Figure 3.42: the two points defining the 1-simplex cannot be coincident; the three points defining the 2-simplex cannot be all collinear; the four points defining the 3-simplex cannot be all coplanar. Note that if we "degenerate" any of these simplexes in that way, we get a space whose dimension is 1 less, which corresponds to the "next smallest" simplex.

C H A P T E R 4

MATRICES, VECTOR ALGEBRA, AND TRANSFORMATIONS

4.1 INTRODUCTION

The point of the preceding chapter was to introduce the concepts and principles of geometry in a coordinate-free fashion. For example, most treatments of the dot product simply describe it in terms of how you perform arithmetic on row and column matrices, without providing much in the way of an intuitive understanding or justification, whereas our approach was purely geometrical.

DeRose (1989,1992) and Goldman (1985, 1987) strongly advocate this coordinate-free approach. DeRose describes a coordinate-free API, and an implementation is available. Such an approach has much to recommend it, especially in contrast to the more usual scheme of requiring programmers to explicitly multiply matrices, invert them, generally keep track of "what space they're in," and perform all operations on coordinates.

On the other hand, the reality is that most graphics software is not so constructed, and the programmer needs to deal with matrices and operations on them; further, even a coordinate-free library would likely involve matrices in its implementation.

The goal of this chapter is to bring together the concepts and techniques introduced in the previous chapter and the matrices introduced in the chapter before that.

In Chapter 2 we covered matrices as a rather abstract tool, rather divorced from their relationship to the vector algebra described in Chapter 3. However, we've dropped a few clues along the way, such as our calling $1 \times n$ matrices "row vectors," or discussing coordinates in the context of affine transformations; readers who have been taught about transformations, spaces, and matrices would have seen this as rather obvious, and readers for whom this sort of presentation of the topics is new were probably making the connections as well.

Now, we bring together all these concepts and show explicitly how matrices are used to represent points, vectors, and transformations, but from the point of view of the "vector algebra" approach. This differs from the more typical treatment as found, for example, in Rogers and Adams (1990) or Newman and Sproull (1979), which generally start off by describing points and vectors in terms of x-, y-, and z-coordinates, dot products as unintuitive and seemingly arbitrary operations on the coordinates, and transformations as multiplications of magically constructed matrices multiplied by the coordinates of a point or vector.

4.2   MATRIX REPRESENTATION OF POINTS AND VECTORS

In Section 3.3.3, we showed that an affine frame $\mathcal{F}$ can be represented as a set of basis vectors and an origin

$$\mathcal{F} = \left(\vec{v}_1, \vec{v}_2, \ldots, \vec{v}_n, \mathcal{O} \right)^{\mathrm{T}}$$

that any $\vec{u} \in \mathcal{V}$, where $\mathcal{V}$ is a vector space, can be written as

$$\vec{u} = a_1 \vec{v}_1 + a_2 \vec{v}_2 + \cdots + a_n \vec{v}_n \qquad (4.1)$$

and that any point $P \in \mathcal{P}$ (the set of points related to the associated vector space for the frame) can be expressed as

$$P = a_1 \vec{v}_1 + a_2 \vec{v}_2 + \cdots + a_n \vec{v}_n + \mathcal{O} \qquad (4.2)$$

Recall that the Coordinate Axiom defined in Section 3.3 says that a point multiplied by 0 yields the zero vector, so we can write $0 \cdot \mathcal{O} = \vec{0}$. If we also recall the definition of tuple multiplication (Section 2.3.4) and the matrix notation associated with it, we can rewrite Equation 4.1 in matrix notation:

$$\vec{u} = a_1\vec{v}_1 + a_2\vec{v}_2 + \cdots + a_n\vec{v}_n$$

$$= a_1\vec{v}_1 + a_2\vec{v}_2 + \cdots + a_n\vec{v}_n + (0 \cdot \mathcal{O})$$

$$= [\, a_1 \quad a_2 \quad \ldots \quad a_n \quad 0 \,][\, \vec{v}_1 \quad \vec{v}_2 \quad \ldots \quad \vec{v}_n \quad \mathcal{O}\,]^{\mathrm{T}}$$

$$= [\, a_1 \quad a_2 \quad \cdots \quad a_n \quad 0\,] \begin{bmatrix} \vec{v}_1 \\ \vec{v}_2 \\ \vdots \\ \vec{v}_n \\ \mathcal{O} \end{bmatrix} \tag{4.3}$$

$$= [\, a_1 \quad a_2 \quad \cdots \quad a_n \quad 0\,] \begin{bmatrix} v_{1,1} & v_{1,2} & \cdots & v_{1,n} \\ v_{2,1} & v_{2,2} & \cdots & v_{2,n} \\ \vdots & \vdots & \ddots & \vdots \\ v_{n,1} & v_{n,2} & \cdots & v_{n,n} \\ \mathcal{O}_1 & \mathcal{O}_2 & \cdots & \mathcal{O}_n \end{bmatrix}$$

So, we can represent a vector as a row matrix whose first n elements are the coefficients of the affine coordinates and whose last element is 0. If the affine frame is clear from context, we will use the shorthand notation $\vec{u} = [\, a_1 \quad a_2 \quad \cdots \quad a_n \quad 0 \,]$. Be aware that this notation is for convenience in identifying a vector $\vec{u}$ and its representation in the frame, but the equality is really in the sense of that shown in Equation 4.3.

We can apply the same argument for points. Again invoking the Coordinate Axiom, we can rewrite Equation 4.2 in matrix notation:

$$P = a_1\vec{v}_1 + a_2\vec{v}_2 + \cdots + a_n\vec{v}_n + \mathcal{O}$$

$$= a_1\vec{v}_1 + a_2\vec{v}_2 + \cdots + a_n\vec{v}_n + (1 \cdot \mathcal{O})$$

$$= [\, a_1 \quad a_2 \quad \ldots \quad a_n \quad 1\,][\, \vec{v}_1 \quad \vec{v}_2 \quad \ldots \quad \vec{v}_n \quad \mathcal{O}\,]^{\mathrm{T}}$$

$$= [\, a_1 \quad a_2 \quad \cdots \quad a_n \quad 1\,] \begin{bmatrix} \vec{v}_1 \\ \vec{v}_2 \\ \vdots \\ \vec{v}_n \\ \mathcal{O} \end{bmatrix} \tag{4.4}$$

$$= [\, a_1 \quad a_2 \quad \cdots \quad a_n \quad 1\,] \begin{bmatrix} v_{1,1} & v_{1,2} & \cdots & v_{1,n} \\ v_{2,1} & v_{2,2} & \cdots & v_{2,n} \\ \vdots & \vdots & \ddots & \vdots \\ v_{n,1} & v_{n,2} & \cdots & v_{n,n} \\ \mathcal{O}_1 & \mathcal{O}_2 & \cdots & \mathcal{O}_n \end{bmatrix}$$

So, we can represent a point as a row matrix whose first n elements are the coefficients of the affine coordinates and whose last element is 1. If the affine frame is clear from context, we will use the shorthand notation $P = [\, a_1 \quad a_2 \quad \cdots \quad a_n \quad 1 \,]$. Be aware that this notation is for convenience in identifying a point P and its representation in the frame, but the equality is really in the sense of that shown in Equation 4.4.

Of course, the basis vectors and origin for an affine frame $\mathcal{F}$ are no different than any other vectors and points in an affine space, and so we can rewrite the matrix representing them as

$$
\begin{bmatrix}
v_{1,1} & v_{1,2} & \cdots & v_{1,n} & 0 \\
v_{2,1} & v_{2,2} & \cdots & v_{2,n} & 0 \\
\vdots & \vdots & \ddots & \vdots & \vdots \\
v_{n,1} & v_{n,2} & \cdots & v_{n,n} & 0 \\
\mathcal{O}_1 & \mathcal{O}_2 & \cdots & \mathcal{O}_n & 1
\end{bmatrix}
\tag{4.5}
$$

which is, as you can see, a square $(n+1) \times (n+1)$ matrix. This will come in handy, as you'll see in the subsequent discussions.

Readers who have had any sort of experience programming two- or three-dimensional graphics applications may well be objecting at this point that you typically use only the coordinates to represent a point or vector. A bit of explanation is in order: Typically, representations of individual objects and entire scenes are implemented as some sort of hierarchy. Parts of, say, a car are grouped, and each part consists of subparts, and so on. Subparts are often defined in their own "local" frame, which is then transformed into the space of its "parent," which itself is transformed into the space of *its* parent, and so on upward in the hierarchy toward the root, which is generally defined to be in "world space."

At each level, there is a local frame. This frame has as its origin the point $[\,0 \quad 0 \quad 1\,]$ or $[\,0 \quad 0 \quad 0 \quad 1\,]$, depending on whether it's a two-dimensional or three-dimensional system, respectively. Further, the frame has as its set of basis vectors what is referred to as the *usual basis* (or more formally, the *standard Euclidean basis*). The basis is orthonormal, follows the right-hand rule, and is ordered as follows: vector $\vec{v}_i$ has a 1 in the ith position and 0 elsewhere. Conventionally, these are called the x-, y-, and z-axes, respectively. The coefficients of a point or vector—its coordinates—are also referred to as the x-, y-, and z-components, respectively. Thus, the matrix seen in Equation 4.5 is, in a three-dimensional system,

$$
\begin{bmatrix}
1 & 0 & 0 & 0 \\
0 & 1 & 0 & 0 \\
0 & 0 & 1 & 0 \\
0 & 0 & 0 & 1
\end{bmatrix}
$$

and similarly for two-dimensional systems. Obviously, these are just identity matrices, and so we can write the last line of Equation 4.4 as simply

$$P = [\, a_1 \quad a_2 \quad \cdots \quad a_n \quad 1 \,]$$

It was shown in Section 2.9.2 that we can construct an orthonormal basis from any other (linearly independent) basis; thus, we can conventionally use these usual bases for all local frames ("coordinate systems"), with no loss of representational power. The usual bases have obvious advantages in terms of intuitive appeal and computation. The rest of this chapter assumes the use of usual bases.

4.3 ADDITION, SUBTRACTION, AND MULTIPLICATION

In Section 4.2, we showed how points and vectors were represented in matrix form. Here, we show formally how addition, subtraction, and scalar multiplication of points and/or vectors are defined in terms of their coordinate/matrix representation.

In all our previous discussions of affine spaces, we've been (intentionally) quite general: basis vectors have been given names like $\vec{u}$, $\vec{v}$, and so on, and their coordinates been given names like a_1, a_2, and so on. By convention, in two- and three-dimensional space, the basis vectors are generally referred to as the x-, y-, and z-axes, and the coordinates are generally referred to directly as the x-, y-, and z coordinates. However, to avoid confusion in the following sections, we're going to refer to the basis vectors using a convention, often observed in calculus texts, which calls the basis vectors i, j, and k. We'll call the origin $\mathcal{O}$ as before (Figures 4.1 and 4.2 show this notation).

4.3.1 VECTOR ADDITION AND SUBTRACTION

Suppose we have two vectors $\vec{u} = u_1\vec{i} + u_2\vec{j} + u_3\vec{k}$ and $\vec{v} = v_1\vec{i} + v_2\vec{j} + v_3\vec{k}$, and we wish to add or subtract them in their matrix representations:

$$\vec{u} + \vec{v} = [\, u_1 \quad u_2 \quad u_3 \quad 0 \,] + [\, v_1 \quad v_2 \quad v_3 \quad 0 \,]$$

$$= u_1\vec{i} + u_2\vec{j} + u_3\vec{k} + v_1\vec{i} + v_2\vec{j} + v_3\vec{k}$$

$$= (u_1 + v_1)\vec{i} + (u_2 + v_2)\vec{j} + (u_3 + v_3)\vec{k}$$

$$= [\, u_1 + v_1 \quad u_2 + v_2 \quad u_3 + v_3 \quad 0 \,]$$

The proof for subtraction is analogous.

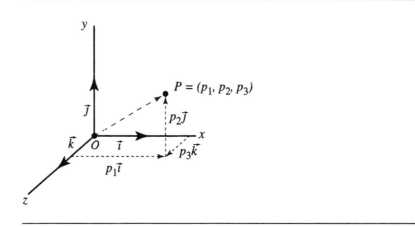

Figure 4.1 $P = p_1\vec{i} + p_2\vec{j} + p_3\vec{k} + \mathcal{O} = [p_1 \quad p_2 \quad p_3 \quad 1]$.

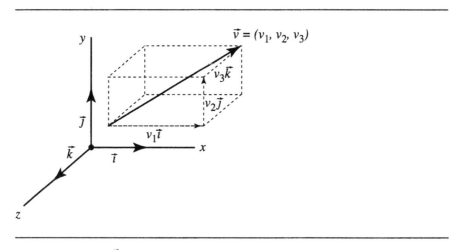

Figure 4.2 $\vec{v} = v_1\vec{i} + v_2\vec{j} + v_3\vec{k} = [v_1 \quad v_2 \quad v_3 \quad 0]$.

4.3.2 POINT AND VECTOR ADDITION AND SUBTRACTION

Adding or subtracting a point and vector is similar to vector/vector addition and subtraction: Suppose we have a point $P = p_1\vec{i} + p_2\vec{j} + p_3\vec{k} + \mathcal{O}$ and vector $\vec{v} = v_1\vec{i} + v_2\vec{j} + v_3\vec{k}$. To add their matrix representations:

$$P + \vec{v} = [\, p_1 \quad p_2 \quad p_3 \quad 1\,] + [\, v_1 \quad v_2 \quad v_3 \quad 0\,]$$

$$= p_1\vec{i} + p_2\vec{j} + p_3\vec{k} + \mathcal{O} + v_1\vec{i} + v_2\vec{j} + v_3\vec{k}$$

$$= (p_1 + v_1)\vec{i} + (p_2 + v_2)\vec{j} + (p_3 + v_3)\vec{k} + \mathcal{O}$$

$$= [\, p_1 + v_1 \quad p_2 + v_2 \quad p_3 + v_3 \quad 1\,]$$

Again the proof for subtraction is similar.

4.3.3 SUBTRACTION OF POINTS

Suppose we have two points $P = p_1\vec{i} + p_2\vec{j} + p_3\vec{k} + \mathcal{O}$ and $Q = q_1\vec{i} + q_2\vec{j} + q_3\vec{k} + \mathcal{O}$, and we wish to subtract them in their matrix representations:

$$P - Q = [\, p_1 \quad p_2 \quad p_3 \quad 1\,] - [\, q_1 \quad q_2 \quad q_3 \quad 1\,]$$

$$= (p_1\vec{i} + p_2\vec{j} + p_3\vec{k} + \mathcal{O}) - (q_1\vec{i} + q_2\vec{j} + q_3\vec{k} + \mathcal{O})$$

$$= (p_1 - q_1)\vec{i} + (p_2 - q_2)\vec{j} + (p_3 - q_3)\vec{k}$$

$$= [\, p_1 - q_1 \quad p_2 - q_2 \quad p_3 - q_3 \quad 0\,]$$

4.3.4 SCALAR MULTIPLICATION

Suppose we have a vector $\vec{v} = v_1\vec{i} + v_2\vec{j} + v_3\vec{k}$, which we wish to multiply by a scalar α. In terms of the matrix representation we have

$$\alpha\vec{v} = \alpha\,[\, v_1 \quad v_2 \quad v_3 \quad 0\,]$$

$$= \alpha(v_1\vec{i} + v_2\vec{j} + v_3\vec{k})$$

$$= (\alpha v_1)\vec{i} + (\alpha v_2)\vec{j} + (\alpha v_3)\vec{k} \tag{4.6}$$

$$= [\, \alpha v_1 \quad \alpha v_2 \quad \alpha v_3 \quad 0\,]$$

4.4 PRODUCTS OF VECTORS

While the preceding proofs of addition, subtraction, and multiplication were trivial and obvious, we'll see in the following sections that the approach taken will be of great benefit in assisting our understanding of the componentwise operations involved in the computation of the dot and cross products. Generally, texts discussing these operations simply present the formula; our intention is to show *why* these operations work.

4.4.1 DOT PRODUCT

In Section 3.3.1, we discussed the scalar (or *dot*) product of two vectors as an abstract, coordinate-free operation. We also discussed, in Section 2.3.4, an inner (specifically, the *dot*) product of a $1 \times n$ matrix ("row vector") and an $n \times 1$ matrix ("column vector"). The perceptive reader may have noted that both of these operations were called the *dot product*, and of course this is no coincidence. Specifically, we have

$$\vec{u} \cdot \vec{v} = [\, u_1 \quad u_2 \quad \cdots \quad u_n \,] \begin{bmatrix} v_1 \\ v_2 \\ \vdots \\ v_n \end{bmatrix}$$

That is, the scalar/dot product of two vectors is represented in terms of matrix operations as the inner/dot product of their matrix representations.

Of course, the interesting point here is *why* this is so; it's not directly obvious why multiplying the individual coordinate components, and then summing them, yields a value related to the angle between the vectors. To understand this, it's better to go the other direction: assume the coordinate-free definition of the dot product, and then show how this leads to the matrix inner product. The approach is again similar to that used to prove addition and subtraction of points and vectors.

Suppose we have two vectors $\vec{u}$ and $\vec{v}$. By definition their dot product is

$$\vec{u} \cdot \vec{v} = \|\vec{u}\| \|\vec{v}\| \cos \theta$$

If we apply this definition to the basis vectors, we get

$$\vec{\imath} \cdot \vec{\imath} = \|\vec{\imath}\| \|\vec{\imath}\| \cos \theta = 1 \cdot 1 \cdot 1 = 1$$

$$\vec{\jmath} \cdot \vec{\jmath} = \|\vec{\jmath}\| \|\vec{\jmath}\| \cos \theta = 1 \cdot 1 \cdot 1 = 1$$

$$\vec{k} \cdot \vec{k} = \|\vec{k}\| \|\vec{k}\| \cos \theta = 1 \cdot 1 \cdot 1 = 1$$

because the angle between any vector and itself is 0, whose cosine is 1.

Applying the dot product defintion to the basis vectors pairwise yields

$$\vec{\imath} \cdot \vec{\jmath} = \|\vec{\imath}\| \|\vec{\jmath}\| \cos \theta = 1 \cdot 1 \cdot 0 = 0$$

$$\vec{\imath} \cdot \vec{k} = \|\vec{\imath}\| \|\vec{k}\| \cos \theta = 1 \cdot 1 \cdot 0 = 0$$

$$\vec{\jmath} \cdot \vec{k} = \|\vec{\jmath}\| \|\vec{k}\| \cos \theta = 1 \cdot 1 \cdot 0 = 0$$

because the basis vectors are of unit length, and the angle between them is $\pi/2$, whose cosine is 0.

If we have vectors $\vec{u} = u_1\vec{i} + u_2\vec{j} + u_3\vec{k}$ and $\vec{v} = v_1\vec{i} + v_2\vec{j} + v_3\vec{k}$, we can compute their dot product as

$$\begin{aligned}
\vec{u} \cdot \vec{v} &= [\, u_1 \quad u_2 \quad u_3 \quad 0\,] \cdot [\, v_1 \quad v_2 \quad v_3 \quad 0\,] \\
&= (u_1\vec{i} + u_2\vec{j} + u_3\vec{k}) \cdot (v_1\vec{i} + v_2\vec{j} + v_3\vec{k}) \\
&= u_1v_1(\vec{i} \cdot \vec{i}) + u_1v_2(\vec{i} \cdot \vec{j}) + u_1v_3(\vec{i} \cdot \vec{k}) \\
&\quad + u_2v_1(\vec{j} \cdot \vec{i}) + u_2v_2(\vec{j} \cdot \vec{j}) + u_2v_3(\vec{j} \cdot \vec{k}) \\
&\quad + u_3v_1(\vec{k} \cdot \vec{i}) + u_3v_2(\vec{k} \cdot \vec{j}) + u_3v_3(\vec{k} \cdot \vec{k}) \\
&= u_1v_1 + u_2v_2 + u_3v_3
\end{aligned}$$

4.4.2 CROSS PRODUCT

While the matrix representation of the dot product was almost painfully obvious, the same cannot be said for the cross product. The definition for the cross product (see Section 3.3.1) is relatively straightforward, but it wasn't given in terms of a single matrix operation; that is, if we see an expression like

$$\vec{w} = \vec{u} \times \vec{v} \qquad (4.7)$$

how do we implement this in terms of matrix arithmetic?

There are actually two ways of dealing with this:

- If we simply want to compute a cross product itself, how do we do so directly?
- Can we construct a matrix that can be used to compute a cross product? If we have a sequence of operations involving dot products, cross products, scaling, and so on, then such a matrix would allow us to implement them consistently—as a sequence of matrix operations.

We'll deal with both of these approaches, in that order.

Direct Cross Product Computation

As with the discussion of the dot product, we start by recalling the definition of the cross product: if we have two vectors $\vec{u} = u_1\vec{i} + u_2\vec{j} + u_3\vec{k}$ and $\vec{v} = v_1\vec{i} + v_2\vec{j} + v_3\vec{k}$, their cross product is defined by three properties:

i. Length:

$$\|\vec{u} \times \vec{v}\| = \|\vec{u}\|\|\vec{v}\| |\sin\theta|$$

If we apply this to each of the basis vectors we have the following:

$$\vec{\imath} \times \vec{\imath} = \vec{0}$$
$$\vec{\jmath} \times \vec{\jmath} = \vec{0}$$
$$\vec{k} \times \vec{k} = \vec{0}$$

because the angle between any basis vector and itself is 0, and the sine of 0 is 0.

ii. Orthogonality:

$$\vec{u} \times \vec{v} \perp \vec{u}$$
$$\vec{u} \times \vec{v} \perp \vec{v}$$

iii. Orientation: The right-hand rule determines the direction of the cross product (see Section 3.2.4). This, together with the second property, can be applied to the basis vectors to yield the following:

$$\vec{\imath} \times \vec{\jmath} = \vec{k}$$
$$\vec{\jmath} \times \vec{\imath} = -\vec{k}$$
$$\vec{\jmath} \times \vec{k} = \vec{\imath}$$
$$\vec{k} \times \vec{\jmath} = -\vec{\imath}$$
$$\vec{k} \times \vec{\imath} = \vec{\jmath}$$
$$\vec{\imath} \times \vec{k} = -\vec{\jmath}$$

because the basis vectors are mutually perpendicular and follow the (arbitrarily chosen) right-hand rule.

With all of this in hand, we can now go on to prove the formula for the cross product:

$$\vec{u} \times \vec{v} = [\, u_1 \quad u_2 \quad u_3 \quad 0\,] \times [\, v_1 \quad v_2 \quad v_3 \quad 0\,]$$

$$= (u_1\vec{i} + u_2\vec{j} + u_3\vec{k}) \times (v_1\vec{i} + v_2\vec{j} + v_3\vec{k})$$

$$= (u_1v_1)(\vec{i} \times \vec{i}) + (u_1v_2)(\vec{i} \times \vec{j}) + (u_1v_3)(\vec{i} \times \vec{k})$$

$$+ (u_2v_1)(\vec{j} \times \vec{i}) + (u_2v_2)(\vec{j} \times \vec{j}) + (u_2v_3)(\vec{j} \times \vec{k})$$

$$+ (u_3v_1)(\vec{k} \times \vec{i}) + (u_3v_2)(\vec{k} \times \vec{j}) + (u_3v_3)(\vec{k} \times \vec{k})$$

$$= (u_1v_1)\vec{0} + (u_1v_2)\vec{k} + (u_1v_3)(-\vec{j})$$

$$+ (u_2v_1)(-\vec{k}) + (u_2v_2)\vec{0} + (u_2v_3)\vec{i}$$

$$+ (u_3v_1)\vec{j} + (u_3v_2)(-\vec{i}) + (u_3v_3)\vec{0}$$

$$= (u_2v_3 - u_3v_2)\vec{i} + (u_3v_1 - u_1v_3)\vec{j} + (u_1v_2 - u_2v_1)\vec{k} + \vec{0}$$

$$= [\, u_2v_3 - u_3v_2 \quad u_3v_1 - u_1v_3 \quad u_1v_2 - u_2v_1 \quad 0\,]$$

Cross Product as Matrix Multiplication

Perhaps it would be best to show an example and then go on to *why* this works. Given an expression like Equation 4.7, we'd like to look at it in this way:

$$\vec{w} = \vec{u} \times \vec{v}$$

$$= [\, u_1 \quad u_2 \quad u_3\,] \begin{bmatrix} & & \\ & ? & \\ & & \end{bmatrix}$$

Recall that the definition of cross product is

$$\vec{w} = \vec{u} \times \vec{v}$$

$$= \left(u_2v_3 - u_3v_2, u_3v_1 - u_1v_3, u_1v_2 - u_2v_1 \right)$$

Using the definition of matrix multiplication, we can then reverse-engineer the desired matrix, a "skew symmetric matrix," and we use the notation $\tilde{v}$:

$$\tilde{v} = \begin{bmatrix} 0 & -v_3 & v_2 \\ v_3 & 0 & -v_1 \\ -v_2 & v_1 & 0 \end{bmatrix}$$

Taking all this together, we get

$$\vec{w} = \vec{u} \times \vec{v}$$

$$= [\, u_1 \quad u_2 \quad u_3 \,]\, \tilde{v}$$

$$= [\, u_1 \quad u_2 \quad u_3 \,] \begin{bmatrix} 0 & -v_3 & v_2 \\ v_3 & 0 & -v_1 \\ -v_2 & v_1 & 0 \end{bmatrix}$$

Depending on the context of the computations, we might wish to instead reverse which vector is represented by a matrix. Because the cross product is not commutative, we can't simply take $\tilde{v}$ and replace the vs with us. Recall, however, that the cross product is antisymmetric

$$\vec{u} \times \vec{v} = -(\vec{v} \times \vec{u})$$

and recall that in Section 2.3.4, we showed that we could reverse the order of matrix multiplication by transposing the matrices.

Thus, if we want to compute $\vec{w} = \vec{v} \times \vec{u}$ (with, as before, $\vec{u}$ retaining its usual matrix representation), we have

$$\tilde{v} = \begin{bmatrix} 0 & v_3 & -v_2 \\ -v_3 & 0 & v_1 \\ v_2 & -v_1 & 0 \end{bmatrix}$$

resulting in

$$\vec{w} = \vec{v} \times \vec{u}$$

$$= \tilde{v}\vec{u}$$

$$\begin{bmatrix} w_1 \\ w_2 \\ w_3 \end{bmatrix} = \begin{bmatrix} 0 & v_3 & -v_2 \\ -v_3 & 0 & v_1 \\ v_2 & -v_1 & 0 \end{bmatrix} \begin{bmatrix} u_1 \\ u_2 \\ u_3 \end{bmatrix}$$

4.4.3 TENSOR PRODUCT

Another common expression that arises in vector algebra is of this form:

$$\vec{t} = (\vec{u} \cdot \vec{v})\, \vec{w} \tag{4.8}$$

We'd like to express this in terms of matrix arithmetic on $\vec{u}$, in order to have operations of the form

$$[\,t_1 \quad t_2 \quad t_3\,] = [\,u_1 \quad u_2 \quad u_3\,][\quad ? \quad]$$

Recall from Section 4.4.1 the definition of a dot product (yielding a scalar), and from Section 4.3.4 the definition of multiplication of a vector by a scalar (yielding a vector). We can use these to reverse-engineer the needed matrix, which is a *tensor product* of two vectors and is noted as $\vec{v} \otimes \vec{w}$, and so we have

$$\vec{t} = (\vec{u} \cdot \vec{v})\,\vec{w}$$

$$= [\,u_1 \quad u_2 \quad u_3\,] \begin{bmatrix} v_1 w_1 & v_1 w_2 & v_1 w_3 \\ v_2 w_1 & v_2 w_2 & v_2 w_3 \\ v_3 w_1 & v_3 w_2 & v_3 w_3 \end{bmatrix}$$

If you multiply this out, you'll see that the operations are, indeed, the same as those specified in Equation 4.8. This also reveals the nature of this operation; it transforms the vector $\vec{u}$ into one that is parallel to $\vec{w}$:

$$\vec{t} = [\,(u_1 v_1 + u_2 v_2 + u_3 v_3)w_1 \quad (u_1 v_1 + u_2 v_2 + u_3 v_3)w_2 \quad (u_1 v_1 + u_2 v_2 + u_3 v_3)w_3\,]$$

This operation is a linear transformation of $\vec{u}$ for the two vectors $\vec{v}$ and $\vec{w}$ because it transforms vectors to vectors and preserves linear combinations; its usefulness will be seen in Section 4.7. It is also important to note that the order of the vectors is important: generally, $(\vec{w} \otimes \vec{v})^{\mathrm{T}} = \vec{v} \otimes \vec{w}$.

4.4.4 THE "PERP" OPERATOR AND THE "PERP" DOT PRODUCT

The perp dot product is a surprisingly useful, but perhaps underused, operation on vectors. In this section, we describe the perp operator and its properties and then go on to show how this can be used to define the perp dot operation and describe its properties.

The Perp Operator

We made use of the $\perp$ (pronounced "perp") operator earlier, without much in the way of explanation. If we have a vector $\vec{v}$, then $\vec{v}^{\perp}$ is a vector perpendicular to it (see Figure 4.3). Of course, in 2D there are actually *two* perpendicular vectors (of the same length), one at 90° clockwise and one at 90° counterclockwise. However, since we have adopted a right-handed convention, it makes sense to choose the perpendicular vector 90° counterclockwise, as shown in the figure.

Perpendicular vectors arise frequently in 2D geometry algorithms, and so it makes sense to adopt this convenient notation. In terms of vectors, the operation is intuitive and rather obvious. But what about the matrix representation? The vector

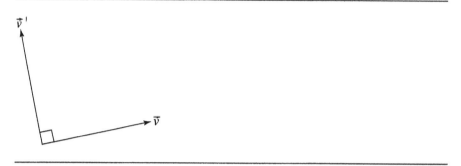

Figure 4.3   The "perp" operator.

$\vec{v}$ in Figure 4.3 is approximately $[\,1 \quad 0.2\,]$. Intuitively, the "trick" is to exchange the vector's two components and then negate the first. In matrix terms, we have

$$\vec{v}^{\perp} = [\,1 \quad 0.2\,]\begin{bmatrix} 0 & 1 \\ -1 & 0 \end{bmatrix}$$

$$= [\,-0.2 \quad 1\,]$$

In 3D, there are an infinite number of vectors that are perpendicular to, and the same length as, a given vector (defining a "disk" perpendicular to the vector). It is not possible to define a consistent rule for forming a unique, distinguished "perp" in 3D for all vectors, which seems to limit the applicability of the perp operator for 3D; we therefore concentrate on 2D for the remainder of the discussion.

Properties

Hill (1994) gives us some useful properties of the perp operator:

i. $\vec{v}^{\perp} \perp \vec{v}$.

ii. Linearity:

    a. $(\vec{u} + \vec{v})^{\perp} = \vec{u}^{\perp} + \vec{v}^{\perp}$.

    b. $(k\vec{v})^{\perp} = k(\vec{v}^{\perp}), \forall k \in \mathbb{R}$.

iii. $\|\vec{v}^{\perp}\| = \|\vec{v}\|$.

iv. $\vec{v}^{\perp\perp} = (\vec{v}^{\perp})^{\perp} = -\vec{v}$.

v. $\vec{v}^{\perp}$ is 90° counterclockwise rotation from $\vec{v}$.

PROOF   i. $\vec{v}^{\perp} \cdot \vec{v} = [\,-v_y \quad v_x\,] \cdot [\,v_x \quad v_y\,] = -v_y \cdot v_x + v_x \cdot v_y = 0$. Since the dot product is zero, the two vectors are perpendicular.

ii. a.
$$(\vec{u} + \vec{v})^{\perp} = \vec{u}^{\perp} + \vec{v}^{\perp}$$

$$([\,u_x \quad u_y\,] + [\,v_x \quad v_y\,])^{\perp} = [\,-u_y \quad u_x\,] + [\,-v_y \quad v_x\,]$$

$$[\,u_x + v_x \quad u_y + v_y\,]^{\perp} = [\,-(u_y + v_y) \quad u_x + v_x\,]$$

$$[\,-(u_y + v_y) \quad u_x + v_x\,] = [\,-(u_y + v_y) \quad u_x + v_x\,]$$

  b.
$$(k\vec{v})^{\perp} = k(\vec{v}^{\perp})$$

$$(k\,[\,v_x \quad v_y\,])^{\perp} = k\,[\,v_x \quad v_y\,]^{\perp}$$

$$[\,kv_x \quad kv_y\,]^{\perp} = k\,[\,-v_y \quad v_x\,]$$

$$[\,-kv_y \quad kv_x\,] = [\,-kv_y \quad kv_x\,]$$

iii.
$$\sqrt{(-v_y)^2 + (v_x)^2} = \sqrt{(v_x)^2 + (v_y)^2}$$

iv.
$$
\begin{array}{ccccc}
\vec{v}^{\perp\perp} & = & (\vec{v}^{\perp})^{\perp} & = & -\vec{v} \\
[\,v_x \quad v_y\,]^{\perp\perp} & = & ([\,v_x \quad v_y\,]^{\perp})^{\perp} & = & -[\,v_x \quad v_y\,] \\
[\,-v_y \quad v_x\,]^{\perp} & = & [\,-v_y \quad v_x\,]^{\perp} & = & [\,-v_x \quad -v_y\,] \\
[\,-v_x \quad -v_y\,] & = & [\,-v_x \quad -v_y\,] & = & [\,-v_x \quad -v_y\,]
\end{array}
$$

v. If we have a complex number $x_a + y_a \cdot i$ and multiply it by the complex number i, we get a complex number that is 90° counterclockwise from a: $-y_a + x_a \cdot i$. A vector $\vec{v}$ can be considered to be the point $v_x + v_y \cdot i$ in the complex plane, and $\vec{v}^{\perp}$ can be considered to be the point $-v_y + v_x \cdot i$. ∎

The Perp Dot Operation

Hill's excellent article provides a variety of applications of the perp dot operation, and you are encouraged to study them in order to understand how widely useful that operation is. So, here we will be content just to briefly summarize the operation and its significance.

The perp dot operation is simply the application of the usual dot product of two vectors, the first of which has been "perped": $\vec{u}^{\perp} \cdot \vec{v}$. Before identifying and proving various properties of the perp dot product, let's analyze its geometric properties.

Geometric Interpretation

There are two important geometrical properties to consider. Let's first recall the relationship of the standard dot product of two vectors to the angle between them. Given two vectors $\vec{u}$ and $\vec{v}$, we have

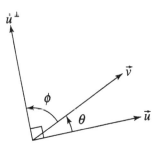

Figure 4.4   The perp dot product reflects the signed angle between vectors.

$$\cos \theta = \frac{\vec{u} \cdot \vec{v}}{\|\vec{u}\|\|\vec{v}\|} \tag{4.9}$$

(see Section 3.3.1). So, if we consider the relationship between $\vec{u}^{\perp}$ and $\vec{v}$ in terms of the angle between them (as shown in Figure 4.4), we can see that

$$\cos \phi = \frac{\vec{u}^{\perp} \cdot \vec{v}}{\|\vec{u}^{\perp}\|\|\vec{v}\|}$$

As we proved earlier, $\|\vec{u}^{\perp}\| = \|\vec{u}\|$, so the above can be rewritten as

$$\cos \phi = \frac{\vec{u}^{\perp} \cdot \vec{v}}{\|\vec{u}\|\|\vec{v}\|} \tag{4.10}$$

or

$$\vec{u}^{\perp} \cdot \vec{v} = \|\vec{u}\|\|\vec{v}\| \cos \phi \tag{4.11}$$

To carry this further, we note that if $\theta + \phi = \pi/2$, then $\sin \theta = \cos \phi$ (we encourage you to break out your copy of your preferred symbolic math application program to verify this). We can see directly from the figure that indeed $\theta + \phi = \pi/2$, and so Equation 4.10 can be rewritten as

$$\vec{u}^{\perp} \cdot \vec{v} = \|\vec{u}\|\|\vec{v}\| \sin \theta$$

It may help if you suppose that the two vectors are normalized, in which case

$$\hat{u}^{\perp} \cdot \hat{v} = \sin \theta \tag{4.12}$$

This makes it completely obvious that the perp dot product reflects not only the angle between two vectors but the *direction* (that is, the sign) of the angle between

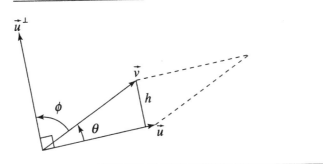

Figure 4.5   The perp dot product is related to the signed area of the triangle formed by two vectors.

them. Let $\vec{u} = (u_1, u_2)$ and $\vec{v} = (v_1, v_2)$. Then $\vec{u}^\perp = (-u_2, u_1)$ and $\vec{u}^\perp \cdot \vec{v} = u_1 v_2 - u_2 v_1$. Write $\vec{u}$ and $\vec{v}$ as vectors in 3D, say, $\vec{u}' = (u_1, u_2, 0)$ and $\vec{v}' = (v_1, v_2, 0)$. Then $\vec{u}' \times \vec{v}' = (0, 0, u_1 v_2 - u_2 v_1) = (0, 0, \vec{u}^\perp \cdot \vec{v})$. If you reverse the roles of $\vec{u}$ and $\vec{v}$, then $\vec{v}^\perp \cdot \vec{u} = -\vec{u}^\perp \cdot \vec{v}$ and $\vec{v}' \times \vec{u}' = (0, 0, \vec{v}^\perp \cdot \vec{u})$. The "sign of the angle" is a reference to measuring a counterclockwise (positive) or clockwise (negative) angle between two vectors when you cross the two using the right-hand rule. Contrast this with the relationship between the (usual) dot product of two vectors and their angle, as shown in Equation 4.9, which indicates the angle between the vectors, but fails to discriminate the orientation of the angle (i.e., the signed angle).

The second geometric property of the perp dot product can be seen by observing Figure 4.5. By definition, $\sin\theta = h/\|\vec{v}\|$, so the height of the parallelogram defined by $\vec{u}$ and $\vec{v}$ is $h = \|\vec{v}\| \sin\theta$. Its base is, of course, $\|\vec{u}\|$, so we have

$$\text{Area} = \|\vec{u}\| \|\vec{v}\| \sin\theta$$

Note that the right-hand side of this equation is the same as that of Equation 4.12, from which we can conclude that the perp dot product of two vectors is equal to twice the signed area of the triangle defined by the two vectors.

Recall from Section 3.3.1 that the cross product of two vectors (in 3-space) is related to the area of the parallelogram, so we can now see, as Hill (1994) pointed out, that the perp dot product can be viewed as the 2D analog of the 3D cross product.

Another way of arriving at this is to simply write out the perp dot product in terms of its components:

$$\vec{u}^\perp \cdot \vec{v} = -u_y v_x + u_x v_y$$

$$= u_x v_y - u_y v_x$$

$$= \begin{vmatrix} u_x & u_y \\ v_x & v_y \end{vmatrix}$$

If we consider $\vec{u}$ and $\vec{v}$ to be 3D vectors that are embedded in the $z = 0$ plane, then the above can be seen to be exactly the triple scalar product $(\vec{u} \times \vec{v}) \cdot [0 \quad 0 \quad 1]$. As shown in Equation 3.13 in Section 3.3.1, the triple scalar product is related to the determinant formed by the three vectors as rows of a matrix, which defines the volume of the parallelepiped. As the height in our case is 1, this is also related to the area.

Properties

We conclude by enumerating and proving several properties of the perp dot product where they differ from the usual dot product properties:

i. $\vec{u}^{\perp} \cdot \vec{v} = -\vec{v}^{\perp} \cdot \vec{u}$. The usual dot product rule is $\vec{u} \cdot \vec{v} = \vec{v} \cdot \vec{u}$.

ii. $\vec{v}^{\perp} \cdot \vec{v} = 0$. The usual dot product rule is $\vec{v} \cdot \vec{v} = \|\vec{v}\|^2$.

iii. $\vec{u}^{\perp} \cdot \vec{v} = \|\vec{u}\|\|\vec{v}\| \sin \theta$. The usual dot product rule is $\vec{u} \cdot \vec{v} = \|\vec{u}\|\|\vec{v}\| \cos \theta$.

4.5 MATRIX REPRESENTATION OF AFFINE TRANSFORMATIONS

In Section 2.1.1, we showed that a matrix multiplication can be interpreted in any one of several fashions—as a change of coordinates, a transformation of a plane onto itself, or as transformation from one plane to another. In Section 4.6 we discuss how, in general, we can construct a matrix that performs a change-of-basis transformation. In this section, we discuss how to construct a matrix that performs an affine transformation on points and vectors.

Suppose we have two affine spaces $\mathcal{A}$ and $\mathcal{B}$, and with each we have arbitrarily chosen frames $\mathcal{F}_{\mathcal{A}}(\vec{v}_1, \vec{v}_2, \ldots, \vec{v}_n, \mathcal{O}_{\mathcal{A}})$ and $\mathcal{F}_{\mathcal{B}}(\vec{w}_1, \vec{w}_2, \ldots, \vec{w}_n, \mathcal{O}_{\mathcal{B}})$, respectively. If we have an arbitrarily chosen point P, we can describe its position in terms of $(\vec{v}_1, \vec{v}_2, \ldots, \vec{v}_n, \mathcal{O}_{\mathcal{A}})$ as $[a_1 \quad a_2 \quad \ldots \quad a_n \quad 1]$. If we have an affine transformation T that maps $\mathcal{A}$ to $\mathcal{B}$, then we use the notation $T(P)$ to refer to the point resulting from applying that transformation to the point. This is all very abstract and coordinate-free, but as we're now discussing matrix representations (and hence coordinates), we'd like to be able to find the coordinates of $T(P)$ relative to $(\vec{w}_1, \vec{w}_2, \ldots, \vec{w}_n, \mathcal{O}_{\mathcal{B}})$, respectively.

We showed in Section 4.2 how to represent a point (or vector) in matrix terms, so we can expand $T(P)$ as

$$T\left(a_1\vec{v}_1 + a_2\vec{v}_2 + \cdots + a_n\vec{v}_n + \mathcal{O}_{\mathcal{A}}\right) \tag{4.13}$$

We can invoke the property of preservation of affine combinations (Equation 3.14) to rewrite Equation 4.13 as

$$a_1 T\left(\vec{v}_1\right) + a_2 T\left(\vec{v}_2\right) + \cdots + a_n T\left(\vec{v}_n\right) + T\left(\mathcal{O}_{\mathcal{A}}\right)$$

affect them. This can be shown formally:

$$
\begin{aligned}
T(\vec{w}) &= T(Q - P) && \text{by definition of } \vec{w} \\
&= T(Q) - T(P) && \text{since } T \text{ is an affine transformation} \\
&= (P + \vec{w}) - P && \text{applying the definition of } T \\
&= (P - P) + \vec{w} && \text{by identity iii on page 81} \\
&= \vec{O} + \vec{w} && \text{by identity i on page 80} \\
&= \vec{w} && \vec{O} \text{ is the additive identity for vectors}
\end{aligned}
$$

Translation doesn't modify orientation or length of vectors, and of course this includes the basis vectors; that is, the first n rows of the matrix representation of T are just the coefficients that yield the original basis vectors. If the coordinates of point P are $[p_1 \ p_2 \ \cdots \ p_n]$, we have

$$
T(P) = [\, p_1 \quad p_2 \quad \cdots \quad p_n \quad 1 \,]
\begin{bmatrix}
T\left(\vec{v}_1\right) \\
T\left(\vec{v}_2\right) \\
\vdots \\
T\left(\vec{v}_n\right) \\
T\left(\mathcal{O}\right)
\end{bmatrix}
$$

$$
= [\, p_1 \quad p_2 \quad \cdots \quad p_n \quad 1 \,]
\begin{bmatrix}
\vec{v}_1 \\
\vec{v}_2 \\
\vdots \\
\vec{v}_n \\
\mathcal{O} + \vec{u}
\end{bmatrix}
$$

$$
= [\, p_1 \quad p_2 \quad \cdots \quad p_n \quad 1 \,]\, \mathrm{T}
\begin{bmatrix}
\vec{v}_1 \\
\vec{v}_2 \\
\vdots \\
\vec{v}_n \\
\mathcal{O}
\end{bmatrix}
$$

Using the definition of matrix multiplication, we can see that

$$
\mathrm{T} =
\begin{bmatrix}
1 & 0 & \cdots & 0 & 0 \\
0 & 1 & \cdots & 0 & 0 \\
\vdots & 0 & 1 & 0 & 0 \\
0 & 0 & \cdots & 1 & 0 \\
u_1 & u_2 & \cdots & u_n & 1
\end{bmatrix}
$$

$$
=
\begin{bmatrix}
\mathbf{I} & \vec{0}^{\mathrm{T}} \\
\vec{u} & 1
\end{bmatrix}
$$

which can be seen diagrammatically in Figure 4.10.

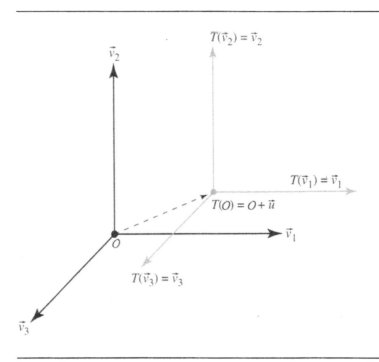

Figure 4.10   Translation of a frame.

4.7.3 ROTATION

Rotation in 3D is frequently treated only as rotation about one of the coordinate axes with general rotation treated as a reduction to this simpler case (using translation). Here we describe the simple case but then go on to show how the general case can be solved directly and more efficiently.

Simple Cases

The most general specification for a rotation is given by an arbitrary center of rotation, an arbitrary axis, and an angle. However, we'll wait to address this until we describe the simplest form: the frame's origin is the center of rotation, and the axis of rotation is one of the frame's basis vectors ("rotation about a coordinate axis"). Building up a matrix for this can be done directly, using only vector algebra principles (Figure 4.11). We'll describe how to build the matrix $\mathbf{T}$ for a rotation about the z-axis by the angle θ. For the 3D case we'll be discussing, the notation for the elements of $\mathbf{T}$ is as follows:

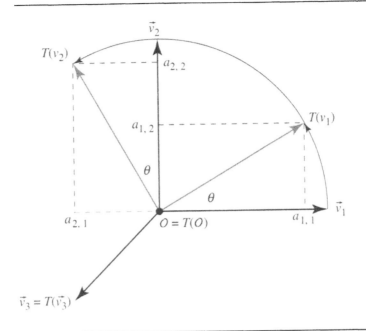

Figure 4.11   Simple rotation of a frame.

$$
\mathbf{T} = \begin{bmatrix} a_{1,1} & a_{1,2} & a_{1,3} & 0 \\ a_{2,1} & a_{2,2} & a_{2,3} & 0 \\ a_{3,1} & a_{3,2} & a_{3,3} & 0 \\ 0 & 0 & 0 & 1 \end{bmatrix}
$$

First, consider the effect of the transformation on the x-axis; that is, $\vec{v}_1$. We know from our discussion of the dot product (Section 3.3.1) that $T(\vec{v}_1)$ can be decomposed into $T(\vec{v}_1)_{\parallel}$ and $T(\vec{v}_1)_{\perp}$ (relative to $\vec{v}_1$). Using the definition of the dot product (Equations 3.5, 3.6, and 3.7), we have

$$
\cos\theta = \frac{T(\vec{v}_1) \cdot \vec{v}_1}{\|T(\vec{v}_1)\| \|\vec{v}_1\|}
$$

but $\|T(\vec{v}_1)\| = 1$ and $\|\vec{v}_1\| = 1$, so we have

$$
\cos\theta = T(\vec{v}_1) \cdot \vec{v}_1
$$

Recalling that the dot product projects $T(\vec{v}_1)$ onto $\vec{v}_1$, we can conclude that $a_{1,1} = \cos\theta$.

We can compute $a_{1,2}$ similarly: the angle between $T(\vec{v}_1)$ and $\vec{v}_2$ (the y-axis) is $\pi/2 - \theta$. If we apply the same reasoning as we just used for the x-axis, we see that $a_{1,2} = \cos(\pi/2 - \theta)$. From trigonometry we know that $\cos(\pi/2 - \theta) = \sin \theta$, so we can conclude that $a_{1,2} = \sin \theta$. Thus, we have the transformed coordinates of basis vector $\vec{v}_1$:

$$T(\vec{v}_1) = [\,\cos\theta \quad \sin\theta \quad 0 \quad 0\,]$$

We can follow the same sort of reasoning for computing $a_{2,1}$ and $a_{2,2}$, the coordinates of $T(\vec{v}_2)$ (the image of the y-axis under the rotation transformation T). The projection of $T(\vec{v}_2)$ onto $\vec{v}_1$ is $-\cos(\pi/2 - \theta)$ (negative because it points in the opposite direction as $\vec{v}_1$; see Equation 3.4), and so we can conclude that $a_{2,1} = -\sin\theta$. The projection (dot product) of $T(\vec{v}_2)$ onto $\vec{v}_2$ gives us $a_{2,2} = \cos\theta$, and so we have the transformed coordinates of basis vector $\vec{v}_2$:

$$T(\vec{v}_2) = [\,-\sin\theta \quad \cos\theta \quad 0 \quad 0\,]$$

Next, we consider what the matrix must do to the z-axis; again, nothing:

$$T(\vec{v}_3) = \vec{v}_3$$

$$= [\,0 \quad 0 \quad 1 \quad 0\,]$$

Finally, consider what the transformation must do to the origin; that is, nothing:

$$T(\mathcal{O}) = \mathcal{O}$$

$$= [\,0 \quad 0 \quad 0 \quad 1\,]$$

So, our matrix for the rotation is formed by simply taking the images of the basis vectors and origin under T as the rows:

$$\mathbf{T}_z(\theta) = \begin{bmatrix} \cos\theta & \sin\theta & 0 & 0 \\ -\sin\theta & \cos\theta & 0 & 0 \\ 0 & 0 & 1 & 0 \\ 0 & 0 & 0 & 1 \end{bmatrix}$$

For rotation about the x- or y-axis, the same sort of reasoning will produce the following simple rotation matrices:

$$\mathbf{T}_x(\theta) = \begin{bmatrix} 1 & 0 & 0 & 0 \\ 0 & \cos\theta & \sin\theta & 0 \\ 0 & -\sin\theta & \cos\theta & 0 \\ 0 & 0 & 0 & 1 \end{bmatrix}$$

and

$$\mathbf{T}_y(\theta) = \begin{bmatrix} \cos\theta & 0 & -\sin\theta & 0 \\ 0 & 1 & 0 & 0 \\ \sin\theta & 0 & \cos\theta & 0 \\ 0 & 0 & 0 & 1 \end{bmatrix}$$

Of course, these values can be arrived at via purely trigonometric reasoning, also exploiting the fact that the basis vectors are orthonormal.

General Rotation

While individual rotations of points about the basis vectors (the "coordinate axes") may be a part of any graphics application, the general case is for a rotation by some angle about an arbitrarily oriented axis. That being the case, most graphics texts then go on to explain how you construct the matrix for a general rotation by decomposing it (in a rather complex fashion) into a sequence of individual steps—translation of a point on the rotation axis to the origin, determination of the three different angles of rotation about each coordinate axis, and translation to "undo" the first translation. The matrix for each of these steps is computed, and the final matrix representing the general rotation is created by multiplying all of these matrices together.

This conventional approach can be shown to "work," in that you can be convinced that the matrix "does the right thing," but the process is quite complex and results in a matrix that's essentially a "black box" from an intuitive standpoint—that is, there is provided no understanding of the properties or characteristics of the rotation matrix.

In this section, we'll show how a general rotation can be defined in terms of (coordinate-free) vector algebra and how this approach allows us to construct a rotation matrix directly (i.e., as opposed to breaking it down into a sequence of translations and Euler rotations), in a way that we hope will leave you with an intuitive understanding of the structure and properties of a rotation matrix. In short, we wish to show *why* a general rotation matrix is the way it is, rather than just *how* you can construct one using ad hoc trigonometric operations.

Figure 4.12 shows the general case of rotation of points and vectors about an arbitrary axis. That figure, and the one following it, are a bit complex, so here are the definitions of the symbols:

$Q, \hat{u}$	point and unit vector defining the axis of rotation
θ	angle of rotation
P	point to be rotated
$T(P)$	rotated point
$\vec{v}$	vector to be rotated

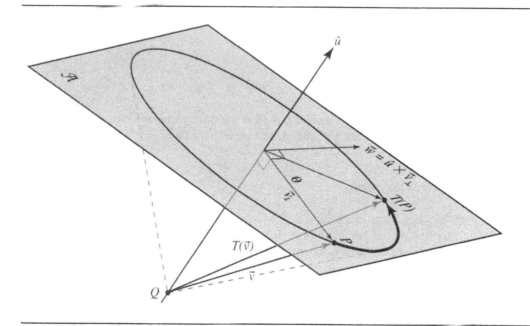

Figure 4.12   General rotation.

$T(\vec{v})$	rotated vector
$\mathcal{A}$	plane perpendicular to $\hat{u}$
$\vec{v}_\perp$	projection of $\vec{v}$ on $\mathcal{A}$

We're considering a rotation about a (unit) vector $\hat{u}$, defining, along with Q, an axis of rotation, and an angle θ defining a (right-hand rule) counterclockwise rotation about it. For convenience, select vector $\vec{v}$ as $P - Q$ so we can use one diagram for discussion of rotation of points and rotation of vectors. Recall our discussion in Section 3.3.1, where we showed that a vector can be broken down into its parallel and perpendicular components, relative to another vector; here we project $\vec{v}$ onto $\hat{u}$, yielding us $\vec{v}_\parallel$ and $\vec{v}_\perp$. Note that we can draw $\vec{v}$ as originating at Q on the rotation axis because vectors are position independent, and drawing it there makes the diagrams easier to understand.

To make the rest of this easier to see, refer to Figure 4.13, which shows the plane $\mathcal{A}$ perpendicular to $\hat{u}$ and containing $P = Q + \vec{v}$. With this in hand, we can make the following assertions:

$$
\begin{aligned}
T\left(\vec{v}_\perp\right) &= T\left(\vec{v}\right)_\perp \\
&= (\cos\theta)\vec{v}_\perp + (\sin\theta)\hat{u} \times \vec{v}_\perp
\end{aligned}
$$

$$(4.25)$$

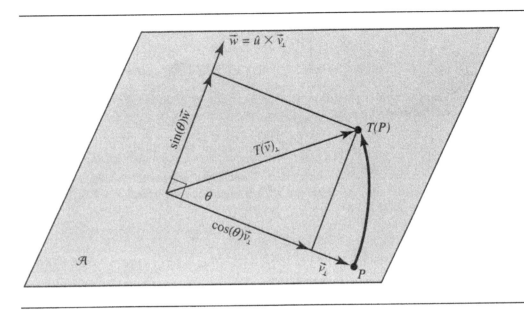

Figure 4.13   General rotation shown in the plane $\mathcal{A}$ perpendicular to $\hat{u}$ and containing P.

and

$$T\left(\vec{v}_{\parallel}\right) = T\left(\vec{v}\right)_{\parallel}$$

$$= \vec{v}_{\parallel}$$

(4.26)

Because $\vec{v} = \vec{v}_{\parallel} + \vec{v}_{\perp}$ and T is a linear transformation, we have

$$T\left(\vec{v}\right) = T(\vec{v}_{\parallel}) + T(\vec{v}_{\perp})$$

We can substitute Equations 4.25 and 4.26 and expand these using the definitions of parallel and perpendicular vector components (identities iii and iv on pages 91–92), and we get

$$T\left(\vec{v}\right) = (\vec{v} \cdot \hat{u})\hat{u} + (\cos\theta)(\vec{v} - (\vec{v} \cdot \hat{u})\hat{u}) + (\sin\theta)(\hat{u} \times (\vec{v} - (\vec{v} \cdot \hat{u})\hat{u}))$$

$$= (\cos\theta)\vec{v} + (1 - \cos\theta)(\vec{v} \cdot \hat{u})\hat{u} + (\sin\theta)(\hat{u} \times \vec{v})$$

This formulation is variously known as the *rotation formula* or *Rodriguez's formula* (Hecker 1997).

Finally, we can use this formula, along with the definition of adding points and vectors, to find the formula for rotation of a point:

$$T(P) = Q + T(P - Q)$$

$$= Q + T(\vec{v})$$

$$= Q + (\cos\theta)\vec{v} + (1 - \cos\theta)(\vec{v} \cdot \hat{u})\hat{u} + (\sin\theta)(\hat{u} \times \vec{v})$$

Now, if we want the matrix representation of this, recall that we're going to be "pulling out" the vector from these equations. Let

$$\mathbf{T}_{\tilde{u},\theta} = (\cos\theta)\mathbf{I} + (1 - \cos\theta)\vec{u} \otimes \vec{u} + (\sin\theta)\tilde{u}$$

be the upper left-hand submatrix of **T** (recall that $\tilde{u}$ is the skew-symmetric matrix for the cross product operation involving $\hat{u}$, as discussed in Section 4.4.2). Then, our total transform is now

$$\mathbf{T} = \begin{bmatrix} \mathbf{T}_{\tilde{u},\theta} & \vec{0}^{\mathrm{T}} \\ Q - Q\mathbf{T}_{\tilde{u},\theta} & 1 \end{bmatrix}$$

The submatrix $\mathbf{T}_{\tilde{u},\theta}$ should be easy to understand: it's just the (linear) transform of the vector $\vec{v}$. The bottom row, however, may require a little explanation. First, observe that this bottom row only affects the transformation of points because the last component of the matrix representation of a vector is 0. Clearly, vectors will be properly transformed by T because $\mathbf{T}_{\tilde{u},\theta}$, which represents the linear transformation component of the rotation, affects the calculation, but the bottom row does not. This is tantamount to assuming the point Q is at the origin. Thus, if Q is *not* at the origin, then we must translate by the difference between Q and its rotated counterpart.

4.7.4 SCALING

We're going to treat scaling as two separate cases: uniform versus nonuniform. Recall that earlier (Section 3.3), we claimed that certain operations on points are somewhat "illegitimate"; scaling a point seems to be one of these operations. As we pointed out, scaling only means something when it's relative to some frame of reference. We could, then, define scaling points relative to the affine frame's origin; however, a more general approach could be to define scaling relative to an arbitrary origin and scaling vector (a vector whose components are the scaling factor in each dimension).

Simple Scaling

The simplest form of scaling is to use the frame's origin as the center of scaling. Scaling may be uniform or nonuniform: in the uniform case, a single scaling parameter is applied to each of the basis vectors, or separate scaling parameters for each basis vector.

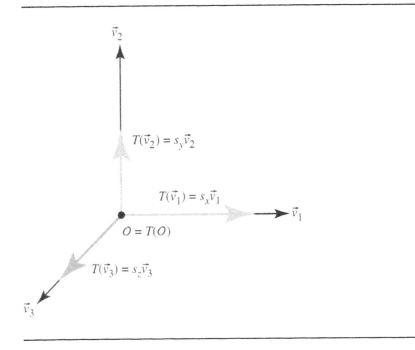

Figure 4.14   Scaling a frame.

Again, we proceed by considering in turn what the scaling transformation T does to each of the basis vectors (Figure 4.14). We'll assume a separate scaling parameter for each, noting that a uniform scale simply has each of these specified with the same value. For $\vec{v}_1$ (the x-axis) we apply Equation 4.6 to the matrix representation of the x-axis:

$$T(\vec{v}_1) = s_x \vec{v}_1$$
$$= s_x \begin{bmatrix} 1 & 0 & 0 & 0 \end{bmatrix}$$
$$= \begin{bmatrix} s_x & 0 & 0 & 0 \end{bmatrix}$$

and similarly for the y-axis:

$$T(\vec{v}_2) = s_y \vec{v}_2$$
$$= s_y \begin{bmatrix} 0 & 1 & 0 & 0 \end{bmatrix}$$
$$= \begin{bmatrix} 0 & s_y & 0 & 0 \end{bmatrix}$$

and the z-axis:

$$T(\vec{v}_3) = s_z \vec{v}_3$$

$$= s_z \begin{bmatrix} 0 & 0 & 1 & 0 \end{bmatrix}$$

$$= \begin{bmatrix} 0 & 0 & s_z & 0 \end{bmatrix}$$

As for the origin $\mathcal{O}$, it remains unchanged, as it is the center of scaling:

$$T(\mathcal{O}) = \mathcal{O}$$

$$= \begin{bmatrix} 0 & 0 & 0 & 1 \end{bmatrix}$$

We then construct a matrix whose rows consist of the transformed basis vectors and origin, which implements this simple scaling about the origin:

$$T_{s_x,s_y,s_z} = \begin{bmatrix} T(\vec{v}_1) \\ T(\vec{v}_2) \\ T(\vec{v}_3) \\ T(\mathcal{O}) \end{bmatrix}$$

$$= \begin{bmatrix} s_x & 0 & 0 & 0 \\ 0 & s_y & 0 & 0 \\ 0 & 0 & s_z & 0 \\ 0 & 0 & 0 & 1 \end{bmatrix}$$

In this approach, uniform scaling about a point Q *other* than the origin requires three steps:

Step 1. Translation to the origin (i.e., by $(\begin{bmatrix} 0 & 0 & 0 \end{bmatrix} - Q)$).

Step 2. Apply the scaling about the origin, as above.

Step 3. Translation back by the inverse of step 1.

Note that this sequence of operations (the two "extra" translations) is something we explicitly sought to avoid in our discussion of rotations. We present this simple approach because it is frequently the case that scaling is done about the origin. We mention the necessity of the three-step scheme for scaling about a point other than the origin in order to motivate the next section, in which we describe a more general method.

General Scaling

The more general approach to scaling allows for scaling about an arbitrary point, along a direction specified by an arbitrary vector, and by a specified (scalar) factor.

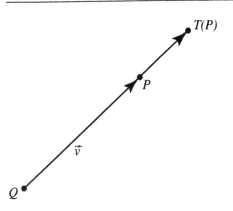

Figure 4.15   Uniform scale.

Here, we describe separate approaches for uniform and nonuniform scaling, due to Goldman (1987).

Uniform Scaling

The case of uniform scaling, as shown in Figure 4.15, is defined in terms of a *scaling origin Q* and *scaling factor s*. Vector scaling, as you recall from Section 4.3.4, is simply multiplying the vector by the scalar, which in the case of the matrix representation means multiplying each of the vector's components by the scaling factor:

$$T(\vec{v}) = s\vec{v} \qquad (4.27)$$

Scaling of points is almost as trivial, and follows directly from the definitions of vector scaling and addition and subtraction of points and vectors:

$$
\begin{aligned}
T(P) &= Q + T(\vec{v}) \\
&= Q + s\vec{v} \\
&= Q + s(P - Q) \\
&= sP + (1 - s)Q
\end{aligned}
\qquad (4.28)
$$

Converting these vector algebra equations into a matrix is straightforward, and the development is similar to that for the rotation matrix. If we have a vector we wish to scale, obviously we need only concern ourselves with Equation 4.27, and so we need to fill in the upper left-hand $n \times n$ submatrix to scale each of the components:

$$\mathbf{T}_s = s\mathbf{I}$$

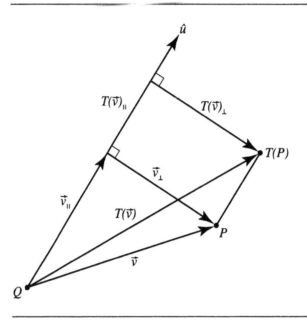

Figure 4.16   Nonuniform scale.

For scaling points, we need to fill in the bottom row—the translational part of the matrix—with the rightmost term in Equation 4.28, so our resulting matrix is

$$\mathbf{T}_{s,Q} = \begin{bmatrix} \mathbf{T}_s & \vec{0}^{\mathrm{T}} \\ (1-s)Q & 1 \end{bmatrix}$$

Nonuniform Scaling

The general case for nonuniform scaling is a bit more complex. Like the case for uniform scaling, we have a scaling origin Q and scaling factor s, but in addition we specify a scaling direction by means of a (unit) vector $\hat{u}$, as shown in Figure 4.16.

To see how we scale a vector $\vec{v}$, project it down onto $\hat{u}$, yielding the perpendicular and parallel components $\vec{v}_\perp$ and $\vec{v}_\parallel$, respectively. As is obvious from the diagram, we have

$$T(\vec{v}_\perp) = \vec{v}_\perp$$

$$T(\vec{v}_\parallel) = s\vec{v}_\parallel$$

By definition of addition of vectors, and by substituting the above equations, we then have

$$T(\vec{v}) = T(\vec{v}_\perp) + T(\vec{v}_\parallel)$$

$$= \vec{v}_\perp + s\vec{v}_\parallel$$

If we then substitute the definitions of the perpendicular and parallel components (in terms of operations on $\vec{v}$ and $\hat{u}$), we have

$$T(\vec{v}) = \vec{v}_\perp + s\vec{v}_\parallel$$

$$= \vec{v} - (\vec{v} \cdot \hat{u})\hat{u} + s(\vec{v} \cdot \hat{u})\hat{u} \tag{4.29}$$

$$= \vec{v} + (s - 1)(\vec{v} \cdot \hat{u})\hat{u}$$

Now that we have this, we can exploit the definition of point and vector addition and substitute the above:

$$T(P) = Q + T(\vec{v})$$

$$= Q + T(P - Q) \tag{4.30}$$

$$= P + (s - 1)((P - Q) \cdot \hat{u})\hat{u}$$

Again, we deal first with the upper left-hand $n \times n$ submatrix that implements the linear transformation by simply extracting the $\vec{v}$ from Equation 4.29:

$$\mathbf{T}_{s,\hat{u}} = \mathbf{I} - (1 - s)(\hat{u} \otimes \hat{u})$$

For the case of points, we can extract the P from Equation 4.30, yielding our desired matrix:

$$\mathbf{T}_{s,Q,\hat{u}} = \begin{bmatrix} \mathbf{T}_{s,\hat{u}} & \vec{0}^{\mathrm{T}} \\ (1 - s)(Q \cdot \hat{u})\hat{u} & 1 \end{bmatrix} \tag{4.31}$$

The term "nonuniform scaling" may be suggestive of "simple scaling" where $s_x, s_y,$ and s_z are not all the same value, and the construction presented here may not directly lead you to a different interpretation. Consider if our scaling vector $\hat{u} = [\,1 \quad 0 \quad 0\,]$. In this case, we have

$$\mathbf{T}_{s,\hat{u}} = \mathbf{I} - (1 - s)(\hat{u} \otimes \hat{u})$$

$$= \begin{bmatrix} 1 & 0 & 0 \\ 0 & 1 & 0 \\ 0 & 0 & 1 \end{bmatrix} - (1 - s) \begin{bmatrix} 1 & 0 & 0 \\ 0 & 0 & 0 \\ 0 & 0 & 0 \end{bmatrix}$$

$$= \begin{bmatrix} s & 0 & 0 \\ 0 & 1 & 0 \\ 0 & 0 & 1 \end{bmatrix}$$

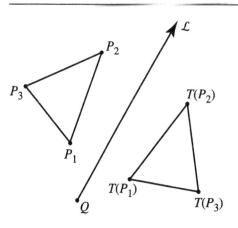

Figure 4.17   Mirror image.

However, consider if our scaling direction is $\vec{u} = [\,1 \quad 1 \quad 0\,]$, which normalized is $\hat{u} = [\,\frac{1}{\sqrt{2}} \quad \frac{1}{\sqrt{2}} \quad 0\,]$. In this case we have

$$\mathbf{T}_{s,\hat{u}} = \mathbf{I} - (1 - s)(\hat{u} \otimes \hat{u})$$

$$= \begin{bmatrix} 1 & 0 & 0 \\ 0 & 1 & 0 \\ 0 & 0 & 1 \end{bmatrix} - (1-s) \begin{bmatrix} \frac{1}{2} & \frac{1}{2} & 0 \\ \frac{1}{2} & \frac{1}{2} & 0 \\ 0 & 0 & 0 \end{bmatrix}$$

$$= \begin{bmatrix} 1 + \frac{-1+s}{2} & \frac{-1+s}{2} & 0 \\ \frac{-1+s}{2} & 1 + \frac{-1+s}{2} & 0 \\ 0 & 0 & 1 \end{bmatrix}$$

This shows clearly that this nonuniform scaling is indeed more general than "simple scaling."

4.7.5 REFLECTION

Reflection is a transformation that mirrors a point across a line (in two dimensions) or across a plane (in three dimensions); the two-dimensional case is shown in Figure 4.17. One particularly important aspect of reflection is that it reverses orientation, as can be seen in the figure.

Simple Reflection

The simplest case of reflection is to reflect about a line through the origin, in the direction of one of the basis vectors (in two dimensions) or about a plane through the origin and defined by two of the three basis vectors (i.e., the xy-, xz-, or yz-plane). We show the case for two dimensions for purposes of clarity and describe how this extends to three dimensions.

We assume reflection about the y-axis. Again, we consider in turn what the transformation does to each basis vector and to the origin, and construct our matrix by making the transformed vectors and point be the rows.

Reflection about the y-axis doesn't affect basis vector $\vec{v}_2$, so we have

$$T(\vec{v}_2) = \vec{v}_2$$
$$= \begin{bmatrix} 0 & 1 & 0 \end{bmatrix}$$

Basis vector $\vec{v}_1$, however, is affected by T; the operation is simply to reverse its direction, so we have

$$T(\vec{v}_1) = -\vec{v}_1$$
$$= \begin{bmatrix} -1 & 0 & 0 \end{bmatrix}$$

Finally, T clearly has no effect on the origin $\mathcal{O}$, so we have

$$T(\mathcal{O}) = \mathcal{O}$$
$$= \begin{bmatrix} 0 & 0 & 1 \end{bmatrix}$$

and thus our transformation matrix is

$$\mathbf{T} = \begin{bmatrix} T(\vec{v}_1) \\ T(\vec{v}_2) \\ T(\mathcal{O}) \end{bmatrix}$$

$$= \begin{bmatrix} -\vec{v}_1 \\ \vec{v}_2 \\ \mathcal{O} \end{bmatrix}$$

$$= \begin{bmatrix} -1 & 0 & 0 \\ 0 & 1 & 0 \\ 0 & 0 & 1 \end{bmatrix}$$

as shown in Figure 4.18.

The extension to simple 3D reflection should be obvious. Instead of simply reflecting about a single basis vector, we reflect about a pair of basis vectors; this pair

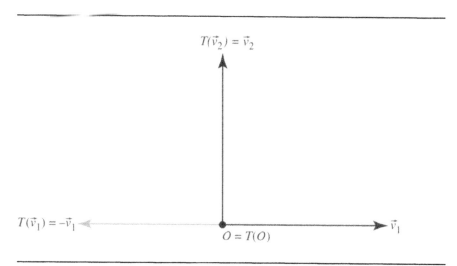

$T(\vec{v}_2) = \vec{v}_2$

$T(\vec{v}_1) = -\vec{v}_1$

$O = T(O)$

$\vec{v}_1$

Figure 4.18   Simple reflection in 2D.

of basis vectors defines a plane going through the origin—either the xy-, xz-, or yz-plane. In the example of 2D reflection about $\vec{v}_2$ (the y-axis), we saw that the reflection transformation T had no effect on basis vector $\vec{v}_2$, but reversed $\vec{v}_1$; in 3D, reflection about the xz-plane (see Figure 4.19) would have no effect on either $\vec{v}_1$ or $\vec{v}_3$, but would reverse $\vec{v}_2$ (the y-axis), giving us a transformation matrix

$$\mathbf{T} = \begin{bmatrix} T(\vec{v}_1) \\ T(\vec{v}_2) \\ T(\vec{v}_3) \\ T(\mathcal{O}) \end{bmatrix}$$

$$= \begin{bmatrix} \vec{v}_1 \\ -\vec{v}_2 \\ \vec{v}_3 \\ \mathcal{O} \end{bmatrix}$$

General Reflection

The general reflection transformation is defined in terms of reflecting points and vectors across an arbitrary line (in 2D) or plane (in 3D). For our purposes, we define a 2D reflection line $\mathcal{L}$ by a point Q on the line and a vector $\vec{d}$, as shown in Figure 4.17,

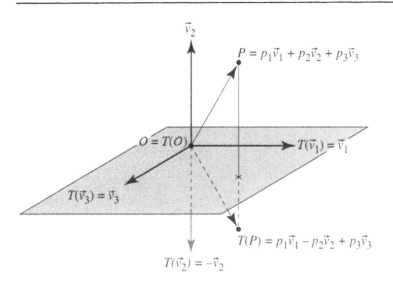

Figure 4.19   Simple reflection in 3D.

and a 3D reflection plane $\mathcal{M}$ by a point Q lying on it and a normal vector $\hat{n}$, as shown in Figure 4.20.

The 2D case is shown in Figure 4.21. We're reflecting about an arbitrarily oriented line defined by an origin point Q and a direction vector $\hat{d}$.

As usual, we'll look at reflection of a vector first. If we project $\vec{v}$ onto $\hat{d}^{\perp}$, we get the perpendicular and parallel components $\vec{v}_{\perp}$ and $\vec{v}_{\parallel}$, respectively.[1] By observing that $\vec{v}_{\perp}$ is parallel to $\hat{d}$, and that $\vec{v}_{\parallel}$ lies along $\hat{d}^{\perp}$, which is by definition perpendicular to $\hat{d}$, we can easily conclude

$$T(\vec{v}_{\perp}) = \vec{v}_{\perp}$$

$$T(\vec{v}_{\parallel}) = -\vec{v}_{\parallel}$$

By definition of addition of vectors, substituting these two equations, and applying the definition of vector projection, we then can conclude that

---

1. Note the distinction between the usage of the $\perp$ operator: as a superscript, it indicates a vector perpendicular to the given vector; as a subscript, it indicates the perpendicular component of a projection of that vector onto another vector.

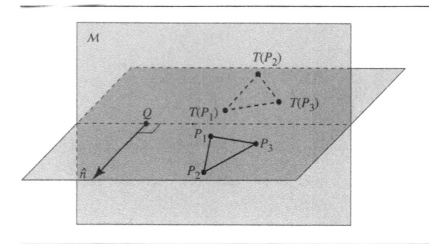

Figure 4.20   General reflection in 3D.

$$T(\vec{v}) = T(\vec{v}_\perp) + T(\vec{v}_\parallel)$$

$$= \vec{v}_\perp - \vec{v}_\parallel$$

$$= \vec{v} - 2\vec{v}_\parallel \tag{4.32}$$

$$= \vec{v} - 2(\vec{v} \cdot \hat{d}^\perp)\hat{d}^\perp$$

As before, we can exploit the definition of addition of points and vectors, and see that we can transform points as follows:

$$T(P) = Q + T(\vec{v})$$

$$= Q + T(P - Q)$$

$$= P - 2((P - Q) \cdot \hat{d}^\perp)\hat{d}^\perp$$

Again, we deal first with the upper left-hand $n \times n$ submatrix that implements the linear transformation by simply extracting the $\vec{v}$ from Equation 4.32:

$$\mathbf{T}_{\hat{d}} = [\, \mathbf{I} - 2(\hat{d}^\perp \otimes \hat{d}^\perp) \,]$$

The translational portion of the matrix can be computed as before, yielding a complete reflection matrix:

$$\mathbf{T}_{\hat{d},Q} = \begin{bmatrix} \mathbf{T}_{\hat{d}} & \vec{0}^{\mathrm{T}} \\ 2(Q \cdot \hat{d}^\perp)\hat{d}^\perp & 1 \end{bmatrix}$$

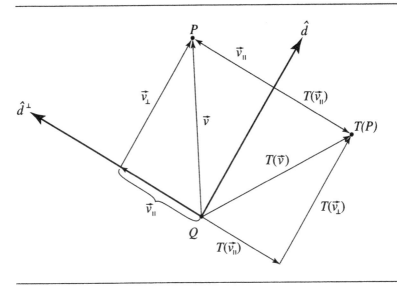

Figure 4.21   Mirror image in 2D.

You may wonder why we chose to project the vector $\vec{v}$ onto $\hat{d}^\perp$ rather than $\hat{d}$. The reason is that we can directly extend this to 3D if the plane about which we reflect is represented by a point Q on the plane and a normal $\hat{n}$ to the plane, as shown in Figure 4.22.

Following the same construction as we had for the 2D case, the resulting matrix is

$$T_{\hat{n},Q} = \begin{bmatrix} T_{\hat{n}} & \vec{0}^T \\ 2(Q \cdot \hat{n})\hat{n} & 1 \end{bmatrix}$$

4.7.6   SHEARING

The shear transformation is one of the more interesting affine transforms. Figure 4.23 shows two different examples of this in 2D—shearing relative to each of the basis vectors (coordinate axes). Shearing is less commonly used than are the other affine transformations, but you see an example of it quite frequently in typography—italic fonts are created by the sort of shear in the right-hand side of Figure 4.23 (although with perhaps a bit smaller angle).

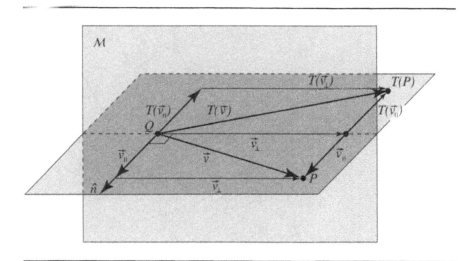

Figure 4.22   Mirror image in 3D.

Simple Shearing

Shearing, in general, may be done along any line (in 2D) or orthogonally to any plane (in 3D), but as with the other transforms, we'll discuss the simple cases first. The simple shears are done along the basis vectors and through the origin. Shears, as can be seen in Figure 4.23, transform rectangles into parallelograms; these parallelograms, however, must have the same area as the original rectangle. As any parallelogram has its area as *base* × *height*, it should be clear why the simple shears preserve either the base or height of an axis-aligned rectangle.

There are numerous options for specifying a simple shear. The one we'll use here specifies the axis along which the shearing takes place and the shearing angle; other books, such as Möller and Haines (1999), specify a shearing scale rather than an angle.

Again we'll construct a transformation matrix by considering in turn what the transformation must do to the basis vectors and origin of our frame. We'll show a shear along the x-axis (the right-hand image in Figure 4.23); we'll refer to this as $T_{xy,\theta}$ (the reason for the subscript being xy rather than just x will be more clear when we cover 3D shearing).

First, let's consider the image of $\vec{v}_1$—the x-axis, under $T_{xy,\theta}$. As can be seen in Figure 4.24, the x-axis remains unchanged:

$$T_{xy,\theta}(\vec{v}_1) = \vec{v}_1$$

$$= [\, 1 \quad 0 \quad 0 \,]$$

less than n dimensions (generally, $n - 1$). The most significant use of projection in computer graphics is in the rendering pipeline of graphics display systems and libraries, where three-dimensional objects are projected onto a plane before being rasterized and displayed on a terminal screen.

The class of projective transformations contains two subclasses that are of particular interest in computer graphics: parallel and perspective. A projection can be defined as the result of taking the intersection of a line connected to each point on a geometric object with a plane. In parallel projection, all of these *projectors* are parallel, while in perspective projection, the projectors meet at a common point, referred to as the *center of projection*. As pointed out in Foley et al. (1996, Section 6.1), you can justifiably consider the center of projection in a parallel projection to be a point at infinity.

In the following sections, we'll show how orthographic and perspective projection transformation matrices can be constructed using only vector algebra techniques. For a thorough treatment of the various subclasses of parallel projections, and the construction of parallel and perspective projection transformation matrices for the purposes of creating viewing transformations, see Foley et al. (1996, Chapter 6).

4.8.1 ORTHOGRAPHIC

Orthographic projection (also called *orthogonal*) is the simplest type of projection we'll discuss: it consists of merely projecting points and vectors in a perpendicular fashion onto a plane, as shown in Figure 4.26. As in the case of the mirror transform, we define the plane $\mathcal{M}$ by a point Q on the plane and (unit) normal vector $\hat{u}$.

Orthographic projection of a vector $\vec{v}$ is simply the usual sort of projection we've been using all along: we project $\vec{v}$ onto $\hat{u}$ to get the parallel and perpendicular components, and note that since $\vec{v}_\perp$ is position independent, the relative location of Q is not considered. Thus, we have

$$\begin{aligned} T(\vec{v}) &= \vec{v}_\perp \\ &= \vec{v} - (\vec{v} \cdot \hat{u})\hat{u} \end{aligned} \tag{4.33}$$

The transformation of a point P is similarly trivial:

$$\begin{aligned} T(P) &= Q + T(\vec{v}) \\ &= Q + T(P - Q) \\ &= P - ((P - Q) \cdot \hat{u})\hat{u} \end{aligned} \tag{4.34}$$

The matrix representation of this is accomplished by factoring out $\vec{v}$ from Equation 4.33 to give the upper left-hand $n \times n$ submatrix:

$$\mathbf{T}_{\hat{u}} = \mathbf{I} - (\hat{u} \otimes \hat{u})$$

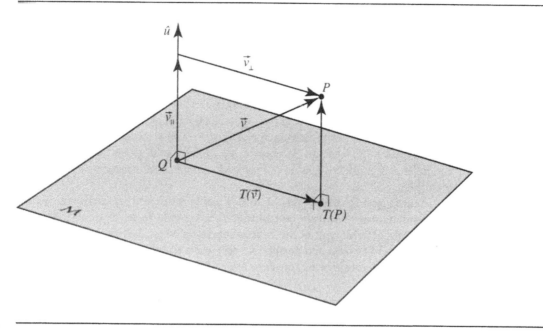

Figure 4.26 Orthographic (orthogonal) projection.

The bottom row is computed as usual by factoring out the above and the point P from Equation 4.34:

$$T_{\hat{u},Q} = \begin{bmatrix} T_{\hat{u}} & \vec{0}^T \\ (Q \cdot \hat{u})\hat{u} & 1 \end{bmatrix}$$

4.8.2 OBLIQUE

Oblique (or *parallel*) projection is simply a generalization of orthographic projection—the projection is parallel, but the plane need not be perpendicular to the projection "rays." Again, the projection plane $\mathcal{M}$ is defined by a point Q on it and a normal vector $\hat{u}$, but since $\hat{u}$ no longer also defines the direction of projection, we need to specify another (unit) vector $\hat{w}$ as the projection direction, as shown in Figure 4.27.

An edge-on diagram of this (Figure 4.28) will help us explain how to determine the transformation of vectors. We can start out by observing that

$$\vec{v} = T(\vec{v}) + \alpha \hat{w}$$

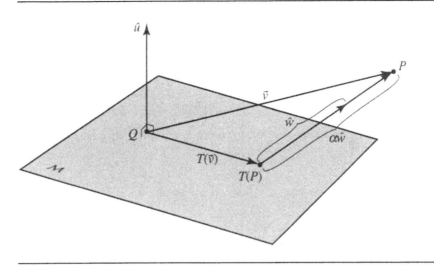

Figure 4.27   Oblique projection.

which we can rearrange as

$$T(\vec{v}) = \vec{v} - \alpha\hat{w} \qquad (4.35)$$

Obviously, what we need to compute is α, but this is relatively straightforward, if we realize that

$$\|\vec{v}_{\parallel}\| = \|(\alpha\hat{w})_{\parallel}\|$$

We can exploit this as follows:

$$\frac{\|\vec{v}_{\parallel}\|}{\|\hat{w}_{\parallel}\|} = \frac{\|(\alpha\hat{w})_{\parallel}\|}{\|\hat{w}_{\parallel}\|}$$

$$= \alpha$$

which we can rewrite using the definition of the dot product:

$$\alpha = \frac{\vec{v} \cdot \hat{u}}{\hat{w} \cdot \hat{u}} \qquad (4.36)$$

We then can substitute Equation 4.36 into Equation 4.35 to get the transformation for vectors:

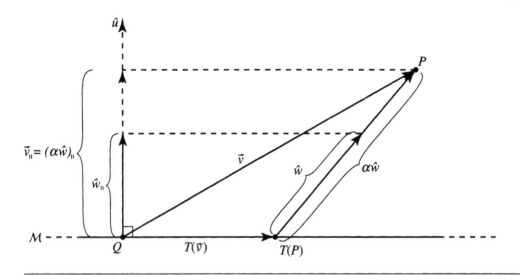

Figure 4.28   Edge-on view of oblique projection.

$$T(\vec{v}) = \vec{v} - \frac{\vec{v} \cdot \hat{u}}{\hat{w} \cdot \hat{u}} \hat{w} \tag{4.37}$$

We can then, as usual, employ the definition of point and vector addition and subtraction to obtain the formula for transforming a point:

$$
\begin{aligned}
T(P) &= Q + T(\vec{v}) \\
&= Q + T(P - Q) \\
&= P - \frac{((P - Q) \cdot \hat{u})\hat{w}}{\hat{w} \cdot \hat{u}}
\end{aligned}
\tag{4.38}
$$

To convert this to matrix representation, we apply the usual technique of extracting $\vec{v}$ from Equation 4.37 to compute the upper left-hand $n \times n$ submatrix:

$$\mathrm{T}_{\hat{u},\hat{w}} = \mathrm{I} - \frac{(\hat{u} \otimes \hat{w})}{\hat{w} \cdot \hat{u}}$$

To compute the bottom row of the transformation matrix, we extract that and the P from Equation 4.38, and the complete matrix looks like this:

$$
\mathrm{T}_{\hat{u},Q,\hat{w}} =
\begin{bmatrix}
\mathrm{T}_{\hat{u},\hat{w}} & \vec{0}^{\mathrm{T}} \\
\frac{Q \cdot \hat{u}}{\hat{w} \cdot \hat{u}} \hat{w} & 1
\end{bmatrix}
$$

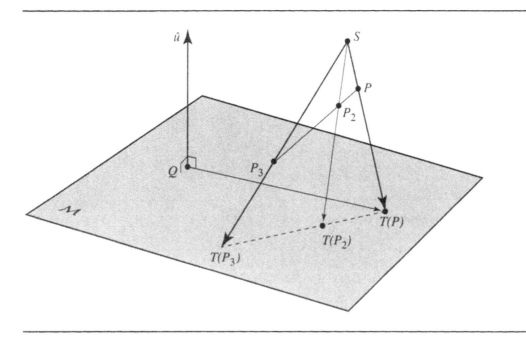

Figure 4.29   Perspective projection.

4.8.3 PERSPECTIVE

Perspective projection is *not* an affine transformation; it does not map parallel lines to parallel lines, for instance. Unlike the orthographic and parallel projections, the projection vectors are not uniform for all points and vectors; rather, there is a *projection point* or *perspective point*, and the line of projection is defined by the vector between each point and the perspective point, as shown in Figure 4.29.

Perspective projection does, however, preserve something called *cross-ratios*. Recall that affine maps preserve ratios: given three collinear points P, R, and Q, the ratio of the distance between P and R (which we notate as $\overline{PR}$) to $\overline{RQ}$ is the same as the ratio of $\overline{T(P)T(R)}$ to $\overline{T(R)T(Q)}$ (see Figure 3.36).

The cross-ratio is defined as follows: given four collinear points P, R_1, R_2, and Q, the cross-ratio is

$$\mathrm{CrossRatio}(P, R_1, R_2, Q) = \frac{\overline{PR_1}/\overline{R_1Q}}{\overline{PR_2}/\overline{R_2Q}}$$

as shown on the left side of Figure 4.30. Preservation of cross-ratio means that the following holds:

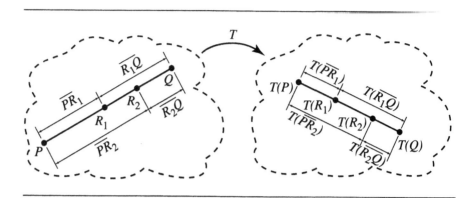

Figure 4.30   Cross-ratio.

$$\text{CrossRatio}(P, R_1, R_2, Q) = \text{CrossRatio}(T(P), T(R_1), T(R_2), T(Q))$$

as shown in Figure 4.30. A more thorough treatment of the cross-ratio can be found in Farin (1990) or DeRose (1992).

It is important to understand that perspective projection of vectors is ill defined. If we take any two sets of points whose difference is a given vector, the vector between the parallel projections of each set of points will be the same. This is not true with the perspective projection; consider Figure 4.31, where we have two such pairs of points, (P_1, P_2) and (P_3, P_4), each of which differ by the vector $\vec{v}_1 = \vec{v}_2$. However, if we look at the vectors between the projections of these pairs of points ($T(\vec{v}_1) = T(P_2) - T(P_1)$ and $T(\vec{v}_2) = T(P_4) - T(P_3)$, respectively), it's clear that these vectors are *not* equivalent.

However, perspective projection *is* well defined for points. Clearly, $T(P)$ is a point at the end of a scaled version of the vector between P and S:

$$T(P) = P + \alpha(S - P) \qquad (4.39)$$

Another way of looking at this is to note that

$$T(P) - Q = (P - Q) + \alpha(S - P)$$

which must also be perpendicular to the plane normal, so we have

$$0 = \hat{u} \cdot ((P - Q) + \alpha(S - P))$$
$$= \hat{u} \cdot (P - Q) + \alpha \hat{u} \cdot (S - P)$$

If we solve the above for α, we get

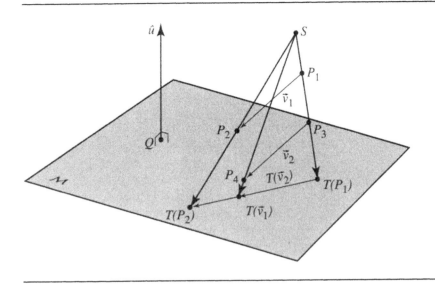

Figure 4.31   Perspective map for vectors.

$$\alpha = \frac{\hat{u} \cdot (Q - P)}{\hat{u} \cdot (S - P)} \tag{4.40}$$

We can now substitute Equation 4.40 into Equation 4.39 and do a little vector arithmetic to yield the final formula:

$$T(P) = P + \frac{(Q - P) \cdot \hat{u}}{(S - P) \cdot \hat{u}}(S - P)$$

$$= \frac{((S - Q) \cdot \hat{u})P + ((Q - P) \cdot \hat{u})S}{(S - P) \cdot \hat{u}}$$

The transformation matrix for this, then, is

$$\mathbf{T}_{\vec{u},Q,S} = \begin{bmatrix} ((S - Q) \cdot \hat{u})\mathbf{I} - \hat{u} \otimes S & -\hat{u}^{\mathrm{T}} \\ (Q \cdot \hat{u})S & S \cdot \hat{u} \end{bmatrix}$$

4.9 TRANSFORMING NORMAL VECTORS

Vectors, as we saw, can be transformed by matrix multiplication in the same way as points. A natural-seeming application of this principle would be to treat surface normal vectors in this way, but it turns out this is (in general) incorrect. As this may

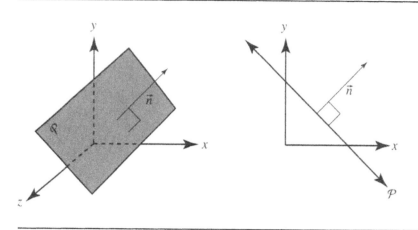

Figure 4.32   The plane $x + y = k$.

seem initially counterintuitive, a bit of explanation as to *why* this is wrong may be useful, before we explain the correct method.

The culprit here is nonuniform scaling. An example by Eric Haines (1987) shows this quite nicely: Consider a plane in three-dimensional space. If we look down the z-axis, this would appear as a line with a 45° angle, as shown in Figure 4.32. The normal to this plane is $\vec{n} = [\, 1 \quad 1 \quad 0 \,]$. Suppose we have a nonuniform scale transform T where only x is scaled by a factor of two. This gives us a transformation matrix

$$T = \begin{bmatrix} 2 & 0 & 0 & 0 \\ 0 & 1 & 0 & 0 \\ 0 & 0 & 1 & 0 \\ 0 & 0 & 0 & 1 \end{bmatrix}$$

If we apply this transformation to the plane and the normal, we get the plane stretched as expected. However, consider the transformation on the normal

$$T(\vec{n}) = \vec{n}T = [\, 1 \quad 1 \quad 0 \,] \begin{bmatrix} 2 & 0 & 0 & 0 \\ 0 & 1 & 0 & 0 \\ 0 & 0 & 1 & 0 \\ 0 & 0 & 0 & 1 \end{bmatrix} = [\, 2 \quad 1 \quad 0 \,]$$

as shown in Figure 4.33. Clearly, this is incorrect. What's going on? The problem is that a normal vector isn't really a vector in the usual sense. Rather, a normal to a surface is actually the cross product of two (linearly independent) vectors that are tangent to the surface

$$\vec{n} = \vec{u} \times \vec{v}$$

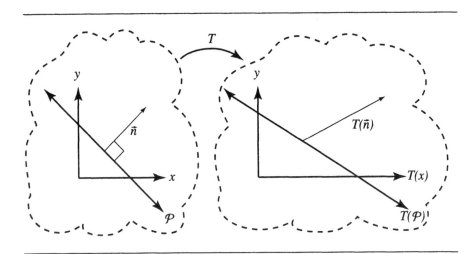

Figure 4.33   Incorrectly transformed normal.

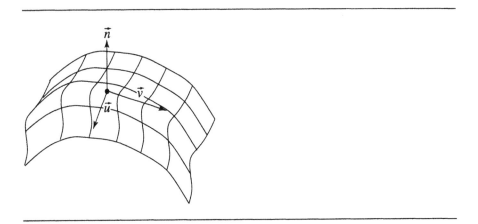

Figure 4.34   Normal as cross product of surface tangents.

as shown in Figure 4.34. If T is a linear transform of the space containing the surface, then the transformed tangents are $T(\vec{u})$ and $T(\vec{v})$, both tangent to the transformed surface. A normal to the transformed surface can be chosen as $\vec{m} = T(\vec{u}) \times T(\vec{v})$. But $\vec{m}$ (as we have seen) is not necessarily the transformed normal $T(\vec{n})$; $T(\vec{u} \times \vec{v}) \neq T(\vec{u}) \times T(\vec{v})$, and more generally $T(\vec{u} \times \vec{v})$ is not necessarily parallel to $T(\vec{u}) \times T(\vec{v})$.

Perpendicularity of $\vec{n}$ with respect to any tangent vector $\vec{u}$ can be expressed as

$$\vec{u} \cdot \vec{n} = \vec{u}\vec{n}^{\mathrm{T}} = 0$$

We want the transformed normal to be perpendicular to the transformed tangent(s):

$$T(\vec{u}) \cdot \vec{m} = 0$$

If we just crunch through the math, we get

$$0 = \vec{u}\vec{n}^{\mathrm{T}}$$
$$= \vec{u}\mathrm{T}\mathrm{T}^{-1}\vec{n}^{\mathrm{T}}$$
$$= (\vec{u}\mathrm{T})(\vec{n}(\mathrm{T}^{-1})^{\mathrm{T}})^{\mathrm{T}}$$
$$= T(\vec{u}) \cdot (\vec{n}(\mathrm{T}^{-1})^{\mathrm{T}})$$

Therefore, a normal vector to the transformed surface is $\vec{m} = \vec{n}(\mathrm{T}^{-1})^{\mathrm{T}}$, where $\vec{n}$ is a normal vector to the surface. The matrix $(\mathrm{T}^{-1})^{\mathrm{T}}$ is called the *inverse transpose* of T. You should be aware that even if $\vec{n}$ is unit length, the vector $\vec{m} = \vec{n}(\mathrm{T}^{-1})^{\mathrm{T}}$ is *not* necessarily unit length, so for applications requiring unit-length normals, $\vec{m}$ needs to be normalized.

RECOMMENDED READING

A thorough and deep understanding of vector algebra is a powerful tool for the computer graphics programmer. Unfortunately, good coverage is rare in the more widely read graphics literature, and courses covering it are rare in computer science programs. Programmers with an academic background in mechanical engineering or physics are more likely to have been exposed to this type of material, although it is probably possible to get through some undergraduate mathematics programs without an explicit course in vector analysis. This may be more the case now than in the past, considering the very large number of textbooks with "Vector Analysis" in their title (or *as* their title) that are notated as "out of print" in book search databases. Goldman (1987) cites the following two books:

E.B. Wilson, *Vector Analysis*, Yale University Press, New Haven, CT, 1958.

A. P. Wills, *Vector Analysis with an Introduction to Tensor Analysis*, Dover Publications, New York, 1958.

Several other useful mathematically oriented sources are

Murray Spiegel, *Schaum's Outline of Theory and Problems of Vector Analysis, and an Introduction to Tensor Analysis*, McGraw-Hill, New York, 1959.

Banesh Hoffman, *About Vectors*, Dover, Mineola, NY, 1966, 1975.

Harry Davis and Arthur Snider, *Introduction to Vector Analysis*, McGraw-Hill, New York, 1995.

More related to computer graphics are

Ronald Goldman, "Vector Geometry: A Coordinate-Free Approach," in *1987 SIGGRAPH Course Notes 19: Geometry for Computer Graphics and Computer Aided Design*, ACM, New York, 1987.

Ronald Goldman, "Illicit Expressions in Vector Algebra," in *ACM Transactions on Graphics*, Vol. 4, No. 3, July 1985.

Tony D. DeRose, "A Coordinate-Free Approach to Geometric Programming," *Math for SIGGRAPH: Course Notes 23, SIGGRAPH '89*, pages 55–115, July 1989.

Tony D. DeRose, *Three-Dimensional Computer Graphics: A Coordinate-Free Approach*. Unpublished manuscript, University of Washington, 1992 (*www.cs .washington.edu*).

James R. Miller, "Vector Geometry for Computer Graphics," *IEEE Computer Graphics and Applications*, Vol. 19, No. 3, May 1999.

James R. Miller, "Applications of Vector Geometry for Robustness and Speed," *IEEE Computer Graphics and Applications*, Vol. 19, No. 4, July 1999.

C H A P T E R **5**

GEOMETRIC
PRIMITIVES IN 2D

This chapter contains the definitions for various two-dimensional geometric primitives that are commonly used in applications. Some of the primitives have multiple representations. A geometric query involving an object might be more effectively formulated with one representation than another. The discussion about a query will indicate which representation is more appropriate.

In geometric queries with objects such as polygons, the object can be treated as a one-dimensional or a two-dimensional object. For example, the triangle as a one-dimensional object is just the closed polyline perimeter. As a two-dimensional object, the triangle refers to its polyline perimeter and the region that it bounds. Some objects have distinct names for the two possibilities. For example, *circle* refers to the one-dimensional curve, and *disk* refers to the curve and the region it bounds. When necessary, the distinction will be made clear. In the absence of distinct names, the word *solid* will be used. For example, the method for computing distance between a point and a triangle treats the triangle as a solid. If a point is inside the triangle boundary, then the distance is zero.

5.1 LINEAR COMPONENTS

Linear components may be represented either implicitly or parametrically. In the case of lines, both representations have equal expressive power, but as we shall see, the parametric form is convenient for representing rays and segments.

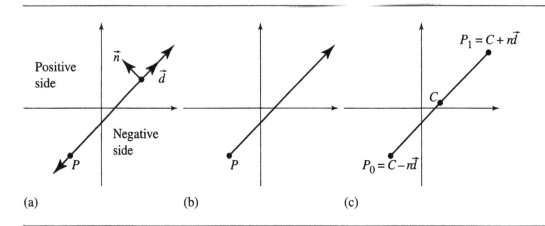

Figure 5.1   Examples of (a) a line, (b) a ray, and (c) a segment.

5.1.1 IMPLICIT FORM

A *line* is defined by $\vec{n} \cdot X = d$. A normal vector to the line is $\vec{n} = (n_0, n_1)$, and points on the line are represented by the variable $X = (x_0, x_1)$. If P is a specific point on the line, then the equation for the line is $\vec{n} \cdot (X - P) = 0 = \vec{n} \cdot X - d$, where $\vec{n} \cdot P = d$. This definition for a line is called the *normal form*. A direction vector for the line is $\vec{d} = (d_0, d_1) = (n_1, -n_0)$. Figure 5.1(a) illustrates a typical line in the plane. Of course we cannot draw a line having infinite extent in both directions. The arrowheads are meant to imply that what is drawn in fact does extend infinitely in both directions. A line partitions the plane into two half-planes. The half-plane on the side of the line to which the normal points is called the *positive side of the line* and is represented algebraically by $\vec{n} \cdot X - d > 0$. The other half-plane is called the *negative side of the line* and is represented algebraically by $\vec{n} \cdot X - d < 0$.

Although $\vec{n}$ is not required to be a unit-length vector, it is convenient in many geometric queries if it is unit length. In this case $\hat{d}$ is also unit length. The point P and the unit-length vectors $\hat{d}$ and $\hat{n}$ form a right-handed coordinate system where P is the origin and the unit-length vectors are the directions of the coordinate axes. See Section 3.3.3 for a discussion of coordinate systems. Any point X can be represented by $X = P + y_0\hat{d} + y_1\hat{n}$, where $y_0 = \hat{d} \cdot (X - P)$ and $y_1 = \hat{n} \cdot (X - P)$. The positive side of the line is characterized by $y_1 > 0$, the negative side of the line is characterized by $y_1 < 0$, and $y_1 = 0$ represents the line itself.

Another commonly seen representation of a line is the implicit form

$$ax + by + c = 0$$

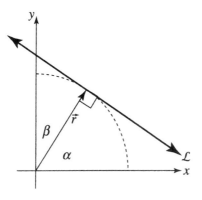

Figure 5.2   Implicit definition of a line.

This can be seen to be equivalent to the previous definition if we let $\hat{n} = [\,a \quad b\,]$, $X = [\,x \quad y\,]$, and $d = -c$. If $a^2 + b^2 = 1$, then the line equation is said to be *normalized*; a nonnormalized equation can be normalized by multiplying through by

$$\frac{1}{\sqrt{a^2 + b^2}}$$

This, of course, is equivalent in the other representation as $\|\hat{n}\| = 1$. With the equation so normalized, we can more easily gain an intuition of the coefficients:

$$a = \cos\alpha$$
$$b = \cos\beta$$
$$c = \|\vec{r}\|$$

In other words, a and b are the x- and y-components of a vector perpendicular to the line (that is, $\hat{n}$), and c is the minimum (signed) distance from the line to the origin, as can be seen in Figure 5.2.

5.1.2 PARAMETRIC FORM

The *parametric form* of the line is $X(t) = P + t\vec{d}$ for $t \in \mathbb{R}$. A *ray* is a line with the parametric restriction $t \geq 0$. The *origin* of the ray is P. Figure 5.1(b) illustrates a ray in the plane. As with drawing a line, it is not possible to draw a ray with infinite extent, so we use an arrowhead to imply that the ray continues infinitely in the specified direction. A *line segment*, or simply *segment*, is a line with the parametric restriction $t \in [t_0, t_1]$. If P_0 and P_1 are end points of the segment, the *standard form* for the segment is $X(t) = (1 - t)P_0 + tP_1$ for $t \in [0, 1]$. This form is converted to the parametric form by setting $\vec{d} = P_1 - P_0$. The *symmetric form* for a segment consists of a center point C, a unit-length direction vector $\hat{d}$, and a radius r. The parameterization is $X(t) = C + t\hat{d}$ for $|t| \le r$. The length of a segment is $\| P_1 - P_0 \|$ for the standard form and $2r$ for the symmetric form. Figure 5.1(c) illustrates a segment in the plane. It is sometimes convenient to use the notation $\langle P_0, P_1 \rangle$ for a line segment.

Throughout this book, the term *linear component* is used to denote a line, a ray, or a line segment.

5.1.3   CONVERTING BETWEEN REPRESENTATIONS

Some algorithms in this book utilize the implicit form, while others utilize the parametric form. Usually the choice is not arbitrary—some problems are more easily solved with one representation than the other. Here we show how you can convert between the two so you can take advantage of the benefits of the most appropriate choice.

Parametric to Implicit

Given a line in parametric form

$$x = P_x + td_x$$
$$y = P_y + td_y$$

its implicit equivalent is

$$-d_y x + d_x y + (P_x d_y - P_y d_x) = 0$$

Implicit to Parametric

Given a line in implicit form

$$ax + by + c = 0$$

the parametric equivalent is

$$P = \left[\frac{-ac}{a^2 + b^2} \quad \frac{-bc}{a^2 + b^2} \right]$$

$$\vec{d} = [\, -b \quad a \,]$$

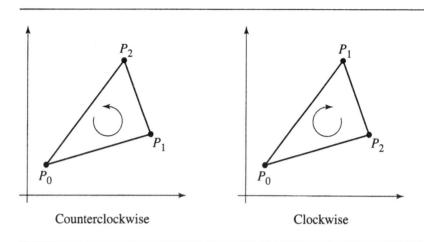

Counterclockwise   Clockwise

Figure 5.3   The two possible orderings for a triangle.

5.2 TRIANGLES

A *triangle* is determined by three noncollinear points P_0, P_1, and P_2. If P_0 is considered to be the origin point, the triangle has edge vectors $\vec{e}_0 = P_1 - P_0$ and $\vec{e}_1 = P_2 - P_0$. Each point is called a *vertex* of the triangle (plural *vertices*). The order in which the vertices occur is important in most applications. The order is either *counterclockwise* if P_2 is on the left side of the line with direction $P_1 - P_0$, or *clockwise* if P_2 is on the right side of the line with direction $P_1 - P_0$. If $P_i = (x_i, y_i)$, define

$$\delta = \det \begin{bmatrix} 1 & 1 & 1 \\ x_0 & x_1 & x_2 \\ y_0 & y_1 & y_2 \end{bmatrix}$$

The triangle is counterclockwise ordered if $\delta > 0$ and clockwise ordered if $\delta < 0$. If $\delta = 0$, the triangle is degenerate since the three vertices are collinear. Figure 5.3 shows two triangles with different orderings. In this book triangles will use the counterclockwise ordering. Observe that as you walk counterclockwise around the triangle, the bounded region is always to your left. The three-point representation of a triangle is called the *vertex form*.

The *parametric form* of the triangle is $X(t_0, t_1) = P_0 + t_0\vec{e}_0 + t_1\vec{e}_1$ for $t_0 \in [0, 1]$, $t_1 \in [0, 1]$, and $0 \leq t_0 + t_1 \leq 1$. The *barycentric form* of the triangle is $X(c_0, c_1, c_2) = c_0 P_0 + c_1 P_1 + c_2 P_2$ for $c_i \in [0, 1]$ for all i and $c_0 + c_1 + c_2 = 1$. The parametric form is a function $X : D \subset \mathbb{R}^2 \to \mathbb{R}^2$ whose domain D is a right isosceles triangle in the plane and whose range is the triangle with the three specified vertices. Figure 5.4 shows the domain and range triangles and the correspondence between the vertices. The

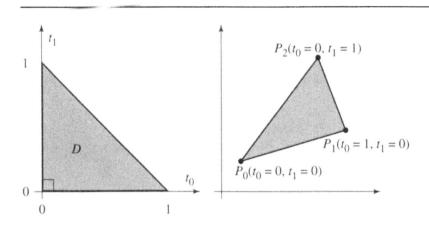

Figure 5.4   The domain and range of the parametric form of a triangle.

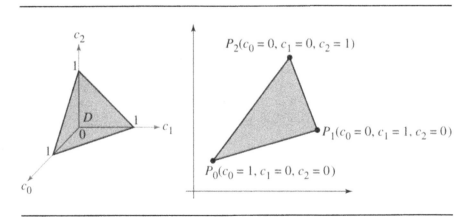

Figure 5.5   The domain and range of the barycentric form of a triangle.

barycentric form is a function $X : D \subset \mathbb{R}^3 \to \mathbb{R}^2$ whose domain D is an equilateral triangle in space and whose range is the triangle with the three specified vertices. Figure 5.5 shows the domain and range triangles and the correspondence between the vertices.

If $P_i = (x_i, y_i)$ for $0 \le i \le 2$, then $\vec{e}_0 = (x_1 - x_0, y_1 - y_0)$ and $\vec{e}_1 = (x_2 - x_0, y_2 - y_0)$. The signed area of a triangle is just the determinant mentioned earlier that relates the sign to vertex ordering:

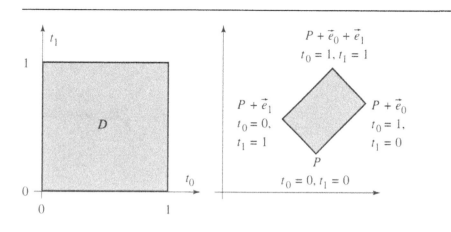

Figure 5.6   The domain and range for the parametric form of a rectangle.

$$\text{Area}(P_0, P_1, P_2) = \frac{1}{2} \det \begin{bmatrix} 1 & 1 & 1 \\ x_0 & x_1 & x_2 \\ y_0 & y_1 & y_2 \end{bmatrix} = \frac{1}{2}((x_1 - x_0)(y_2 - y_0) - (x_2 - x_0)(y_1 - y_0))$$

5.3 RECTANGLES

A *rectangle* is defined by a point P and two edge vectors $\vec{e}_0$ and $\vec{e}_1$ that are perpendicular. This form is called the *vertex-edge form*. The *parametric form* for a rectangle is $X(t_0, t_1) = P + t_0\vec{e}_0 + t_1\vec{e}_1$ for $t_0 \in [0, 1]$ and $t_1 \in [0, 1]$. The rectangle is said to be *axis aligned* if the edge vectors are parallel to the coordinate axes. Although all rectangles can be said to be *oriented*, this term is typically used to emphasize that the rectangles under consideration are not necessarily axis aligned. The *symmetric form* for a rectangle consists of a centerpoint C, two unit-length vectors $\hat{u}_0$ and $\hat{u}_1$ that are perpendicular, and two extents $e_0 > 0$ and $e_1 > 0$. The parameterization is $X(t_0, t_1) = C + t_0\hat{u}_0 + t_1\hat{u}_1$ for $|t_0| \le e_0$ and $|t_1| \le e_1$. The area of a rectangle is $\|\vec{e}_0\| \, \|\vec{e}_1\|$ for the parametric form and $4e_0e_1$ for the symmetric form. Figure 5.6 shows the domain square, range rectangle, and the correspondence between the vertices for the parametric form. Figure 5.7 shows the symmetric form for a rectangle.

5.4 POLYLINES AND POLYGONS

A *polyline* consists of a finite number of line segments $\langle P_i, P_{i+1} \rangle$ for $0 \le i < n$. Adjacent line segments share an end point. Although not common in applications,

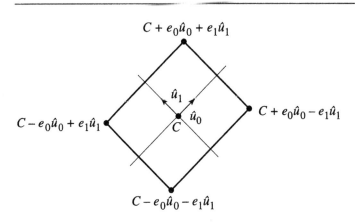

Figure 5.7   The symmetric form of a rectangle.

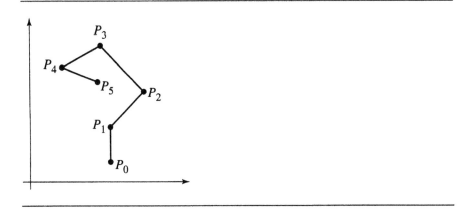

Figure 5.8   A typical polyline.

the definition can be extended to allow polylines to include rays and lines. An example is a polyline that consists of the line segment with end points $(0, 0)$ and $(0, 1)$, a ray with origin $(0, 0)$ and direction vector $(1, 0)$, and a ray with origin $(0, 1)$ and direction vector $(-1, 0)$. Figure 5.8 shows a typical polyline in the plane. The polyline is *closed* if the last point of the line is connected to the first by a line segment. The convention in this book is to specify an additional point $P_n = P_0$ for indexing purposes. A polyline that is not closed is said to be *open*.

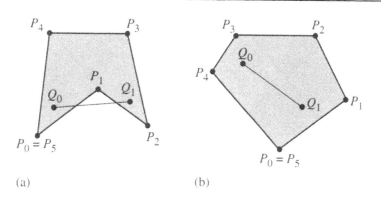

Figure 5.9 Examples of (a) a simple concave polygon and (b) a simple convex polygon.

A *polygon* is a closed polyline. Each point P_i is called a *vertex* of the polygon. Each line segment is called an *edge* of the polygon. The polygon is said to be *simple* if non-adjacent line segments do not intersect. A simple polygon bounds a simply connected region in the plane. The points in this region are said to be *inside* the polygon. The vertices of a simple polygon can be ordered as clockwise or counterclockwise, just as for triangles. The vertices are counterclockwise ordered if a traversal of the vertices keeps the bounded region to the left. A simple polygon is *convex* if for any two points inside the polygon, the line segment connecting the two points is also inside the polygon. Special cases of convex polygons are triangles, rectangles, parallelograms (four-sided with two pairs of parallel sides), and convex quadrilaterals (four-sided with each point outside the triangle formed by the other three points). A polygon that is not convex is said to be *concave*.

Figure 5.9 shows two simple polygons. The polygon in Figure 5.9(a) is concave since the line segment connecting two interior points Q_0 and Q_1 is not fully inside the polygon. The polygon in Figure 5.9(b) is convex since, regardless of how Q_0 and Q_1 are chosen inside the polygon, the line segment connecting them is always fully inside the polygon. Figure 5.10 shows two nonsimple polygons. The polygon in Figure 5.10(a) has nonadjacent line segments $\langle P_1, P_2 \rangle$ and $\langle P_3, P_4 \rangle$ that intersect. The intersection point is not a vertex of the polygon. The polygon in Figure 5.10(b) is the same polygon with the intersection point included as a vertex. But the polygon is still nonsimple since it has multiple nonadjacent line segments that intersect at P_2. Polygons of this latter type are referred to as *polysolids* (Maynard and Tavernini 1984).

A *polygonal chain* is an open polyline for which nonadjacent line segments do not intersect. A polygonal chain C is *strictly monotonic* with respect to a line $\mathcal{L}$ if every line orthogonal to $\mathcal{L}$ intersects C in at most one point. The chain is *monotonic*

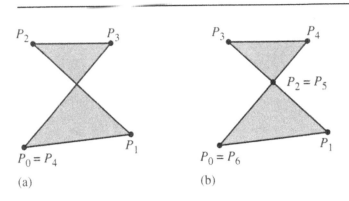

Figure 5.10 Examples of nonsimple polygons. (a) The intersection is not a vertex. (b) The intersection is a vertex. The polygon is a polysolid.

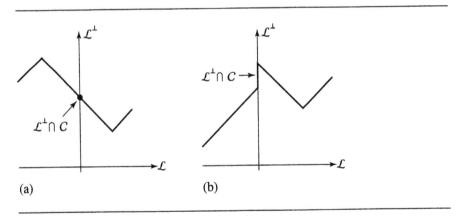

Figure 5.11 Examples of polygonal chains: (a) strictly monotonic; (b) monotonic, but not strict.

if the intersection of C and any line orthogonal to $\mathcal{L}$ is empty, a single point, or a single line segment. A simple polygon cannot be a monotonic polygonal chain. A *monotone* polygon is a simple polygon that can be split into two monotonic polygonal chains. Figure 5.11 shows a strictly monotonic polygonal chain and a monotonic chain. Figure 5.12 shows a monotone polygon.

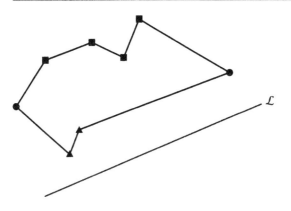

Figure 5.12   A monotone polygon. The squares are the vertices of one chain. The triangles are the vertices of the other chain. The circles are those vertices on both chains.

5.5 QUADRATIC CURVES

Quadratic curves are determined implicitly by the general quadratic equation in two variables

$$a_{00}x_0^2 + 2a_{01}x_0x_1 + a_{11}x_1^2 + b_0x_0 + b_1x_1 + c = 0 \tag{5.1}$$

Let $A = [a_{ij}]$ be a symmetric 2×2 matrix and let $B = [b_i]$ and $X = [x_i]$ be 2×1 vectors. The matrix form for the quadratic equation is

$$X^{\mathrm{T}}AX + B^{\mathrm{T}}X + c = 0 \tag{5.2}$$

A quadratic equation can define a point, a line, a circle, an ellipse, a parabola, or a hyperbola. It is also possible that the equation has no solution.

The type of object that Equation 5.2 defines is more easily determined by factoring A and making a change of variables. Since A is a symmetric matrix, it can be factored into $A = R^{\mathrm{T}}DR$, where R is a rotation matrix whose rows are the eigenvectors of A, and D is a diagonal matrix whose diagonal entries are eigenvalues of A. To factor A, see the eigendecomposition subsection of Section A.3. Define $E = RB$ and $Y = RX$. Equation 5.2 is transformed to

$$Y^{\mathrm{T}}DY + E^{\mathrm{T}}Y + c = d_0y_0^2 + d_1y_1^2 + e_0y_0 + e_1y_1 + c = 0 \tag{5.3}$$

The classification is based on the diagonal entries of **D**. If a diagonal entry d_i is not zero, then the corresponding terms for y_i and y_i^2 in Equation 5.3 can be factored by completing the square. For example, if $d_0 \neq 0$, then

$$d_0 y_0^2 + e_0 y_0 = d_0 \left(y_0^2 + \frac{e_0}{d_0} y_0 \right)$$

$$= d_0 \left(y_0^2 + \frac{e_0}{d_0} y_0 + \frac{e_0^2}{4d_0^2} - \frac{e_0^2}{4d_0^2} \right)$$

$$= d_0 \left(y_0 + \frac{e_0}{2d_0} \right)^2 - \left(\frac{e_0}{2d_0} \right)^2$$

CASE $d_0 \neq 0$ AND $d_1 \neq 0$. The equation factors into

$$d_0 \left(y_0 + \frac{e_0}{2d_0} \right)^2 + d_1 \left(y_1 + \frac{e_1}{2d_1} \right)^2 = \frac{e_0^2}{4d_0} + \frac{e_1^2}{4d_1} - c =: r$$

Suppose $d_0 d_1 > 0$. There is no real-valued solution when $d_0 r < 0$. The solution is a single point when $r = 0$. Otherwise $d_0 r > 0$, and the solution is an ellipse when $d_0 \neq d_1$ or a circle when $d_0 = d_1$. Now suppose $d_0 d_1 < 0$. If $r \neq 0$, the solution is a hyperbola. If $r = 0$, the solution is two intersecting lines, the 2D equivalent of a 3D cone. Figure 5.13 shows the possibilities. ■

CASE $d_0 \neq 0$ AND $d_1 = 0$. The equation factors into

$$d_0 \left(y_0 + \frac{e_0}{2d_0} \right)^2 + e_1 y_1 = \frac{e_0^2}{4d_0} - c =: r$$

If $e_1 = 0$, there are three cases. There is no real-valued solution when $d_0 r < 0$. The solution is a line when $r = 0$. Otherwise $d_0 r > 0$ and the solution is two parallel lines, the 2D equivalent of a 3D cylinder. If $e_1 \neq 0$, the solution is a parabola. Figure 5.14 shows the possibilities. ■

CASE $d_0 = 0$ AND $d_1 \neq 0$. This case is symmetric to that of $d_0 \neq 0$ and $d_1 = 0$. ■

CASE $d_0 = 0$ AND $d_1 = 0$. The equation is

$$e_0 y_0 + e_1 y_1 + c = 0$$

If $e_0 = e_1 = 0$, then there is no solution when $c \neq 0$, and the original equation is the tautology $0 = 0$ when $c = 0$. If $e_0 \neq 0$ or $e_1 \neq 0$, then the solution is a line. ■

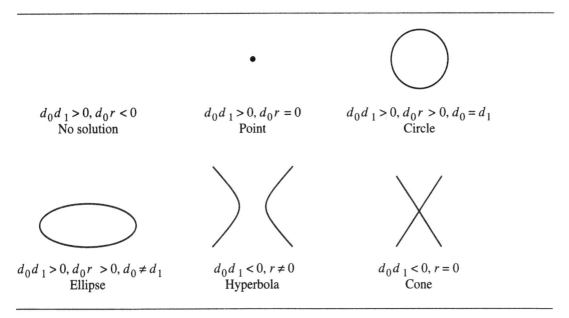

$d_0d_1 > 0, d_0r < 0$
No solution

$d_0d_1 > 0, d_0r = 0$
Point

$d_0d_1 > 0, d_0r > 0, d_0 = d_1$
Circle

$d_0d_1 > 0, d_0r > 0, d_0 \neq d_1$
Ellipse

$d_0d_1 < 0, r \neq 0$
Hyperbola

$d_0d_1 < 0, r = 0$
Cone

Figure 5.13   Solutions to the quadratic equation depending on the values for $d_0 \neq 0$, $d_1 \neq 0$, and r.

5.5.1 CIRCLES

A *circle* consists of a center C and a radius $r > 0$. The *distance form* of the circle is $\|X - C\| = r$. The *parametric form* is $X(t) = C + r\hat{u}(t)$, where $\hat{u}(t) = (\cos t, \sin t)$ for $t \in [0, 2\pi)$. To verify, observe that $\|X(t) - C\| = \|r\hat{u}(t)\| = r\|\hat{u}(t)\| = r$, where the last equality is true since $\hat{u}(t)$ is a unit-length vector. Figure 5.15 shows the (implicit) distance form and the parametric form. The *quadratic form* is $X^TIX + B \cdot X + c = 0$, where I is the 2×2 identity matrix. In the quadratic form, the coefficients are related to the center and radius by $B = -2C$ and $c = C^TC - r^2$.

The area of a circle is πr^2 for the distance and parametric forms and $\pi(B^TB/4 - c)$ for the quadratic form.

5.5.2 ELLIPSES

An *ellipse* consists of a center C, axis half-lengths $\ell_0 > 0$ and $\ell_1 > 0$, and an orientation angle θ about its center and measured counterclockwise with respect to the x-axis, as shown in Figure 5.16. Let $D = \text{Diag}(1/\ell_0^2, 1/\ell_1^2)$ and let $R = R(\theta)$ be the rotation matrix corresponding to the specified angle. The *factored form* of the ellipse is $(X - C)^TR^TDR(X - C) = 1$. The *parametric form* of the ellipse is $X(t) = C + R^TD^{-1/2}\hat{u}(t)$, where $\hat{u}(t) = (\cos t, \sin t)$ for $t \in [0, 2\pi)$. To verify, observe that

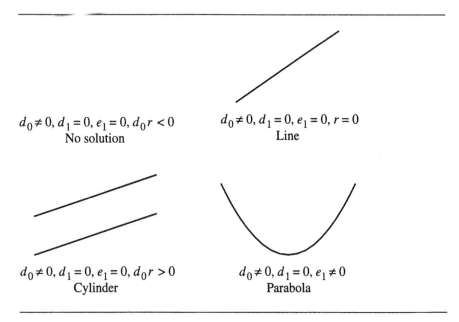

$d_0 \neq 0, d_1 = 0, e_1 = 0, d_0 r < 0$
No solution

$d_0 \neq 0, d_1 = 0, e_1 = 0, r = 0$
Line

$d_0 \neq 0, d_1 = 0, e_1 = 0, d_0 r > 0$
Cylinder

$d_0 \neq 0, d_1 = 0, e_1 \neq 0$
Parabola

Figure 5.14   Solutions to the quadratic equation depending on the values for $d_0 \neq 0$, $d_1 = 0$, e_1, and r.

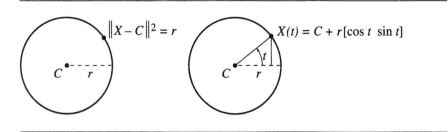

$\|X - C\|^2 = r$

$X(t) = C + r[\cos t \ \sin t]$

Figure 5.15   Circles defined in distance (implicit) and parametric forms.

the factored form states that $\|\mathbf{D}^{1/2}\mathbf{R}(X - C)\| = 1$. The vector whose length is indicated here must be unit length, so $\mathbf{D}^{1/2}\mathbf{R}(X - C) = \hat{u}(t)$ is a valid choice. Solving for X produces the parametric form. The *quadratic form* is $X^T\mathbf{A}X + B \cdot X + c = 0$, where $\mathbf{A}$ is a 2×2 matrix whose diagonal entries are positive and whose determinant is positive. Moreover, $C = -\mathbf{A}^{-1}B/2$ and $\mathbf{R}^T\mathbf{D}\mathbf{R} = \mathbf{A}/(B^T\mathbf{A}^{-1}B/4 - c)$.

The area of an ellipse is $\pi \ell_0 \ell_1$ for the factored and parametric forms and $\pi(B^T\mathbf{A}^{-1}B/4 - c)/\sqrt{\det(\mathbf{A})}$ for the quadratic form.

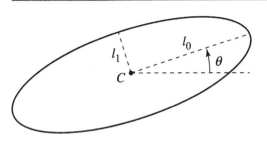

Figure 5.16   Definition of an ellipse.

5.6 POLYNOMIAL CURVES

A *polynomial curve* in the plane is a vector-valued function $X : D \subset \mathbb{R} \to R \subset \mathbb{R}^2$, say, $X(t)$, and has domain D and range R. The components $X_i(t)$ of $X(t)$ are each a polynomial in the specified parameter

$$X_i(t) = \sum_{j=0}^{n_i} a_{ij} t^j$$

where n_i is the degree of the polynomial. In most applications the degrees of the components are the same, in which case the curve is written as $X(t) = \sum_{j=0}^{n} A_j t^j$ for known points $A_j \in \mathbb{R}^2$. Even if the degrees are different, we can still use the vector notation by selecting $n = \max_i n_i$ and setting coefficients $a_{ij} = 0$ for $n_i < j \le n$. The domain D in the applications is typically either $\mathbb{R}$ or $[0, 1]$. A *rational polynomial curve* is a vector-valued function $X(t)$ whose components $X_i(t)$ are ratios of polynomials

$$X_i(t) = \frac{\sum_{j=0}^{n_i} a_{ij} t^j}{\sum_{j=0}^{m_i} b_{ij} t^j}$$

where n_i and m_i are the degrees of the numerator and denominator polynomials.

A few common types of curves that occur in computer graphics are Bézier curves, B-spline curves, and nonuniform rational B-spline (NURBS) curves. Only the definitions for these curves are given here. Various properties of interest may be found in other texts on curves and surfaces (Bartels, Beatty, and Barsky 1987; Cohen, Riesenfeld, and Elber 2001; Farin 1990, 1995; Rogers 2001; Yamaguchi 1988).

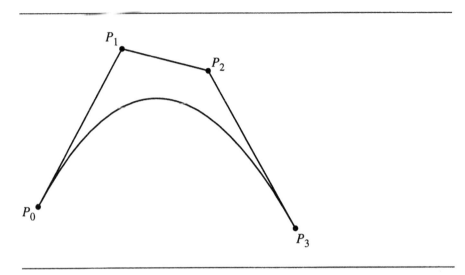

Figure 5.17   A cubic Bézier curve.

5.6.1 BÉZIER CURVES

A planar *Bézier curve* is constructed from a set of points $P_i \in \mathbb{R}^2$ for $0 \leq i \leq n$, called *control points*, by

$$X(t) = \sum_{i=0}^{n} \binom{n}{i} t^i (1-t)^{n-i} P_i = \sum_{i=0}^{n} B_i(t) P_i, \quad t \in [0,1]$$

where

$$\binom{n}{i} = \frac{n!}{i!(n-i)!}$$

is the number of combinations of i items chosen from a set of n items. The real-valued polynomials $B_i(t)$ are called the Bernstein polynomials, each of degree n. The polynomial components of $X(t)$ are therefore also of degree n. Figure 5.17 shows a cubic Bézier curve, along with the control points and control polygon.

5.6.2 B-SPLINE CURVES

A planar *B-spline curve of degree j* is constructed from a set of points $P_i \in \mathbb{R}^2$, called *control points*, and a monotone set of parameters t_i (i.e., $t_i \leq t_{i+1}$), called *knots*, for $0 \leq i \leq n$, by

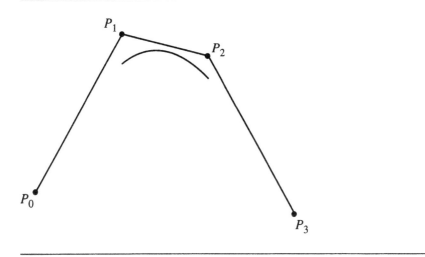

Figure 5.18   A cubic B-spline curve.

$$X(t) = \sum_{i=0}^{n} B_{i,j}(t) P_i$$

where $t \in [t_0, t_n]$ and $1 \leq j \leq n$. The vector $(t_0, \ldots, t_n)$ is called a *knot vector*. The real-valued polynomials $B_{i,j}(t)$ are of degree j and defined by the Cox–de Boor recursion formulas

$$B_{i,0}(t) = \begin{cases} 1, & t_i \leq t < t_{i+1} \\ 0, & \text{otherwise} \end{cases}$$

and

$$B_{i,j}(t) = \frac{(t - t_i) B_{i,j-1}(t)}{t_{i+j-1} - t_i} + \frac{(t_{i+j} - t) B_{i+1,j-1}(t)}{t_{i+j} - t_{i+1}}$$

for $1 \leq j \leq n$. The polynomial components of $X(t)$ are actually defined piecewise on the intervals $[t_i, t_{i+1}]$. On each interval the polynomial is of degree j. The knot values are not required to be evenly spaced. In this case the curve is said to be a *nonuniform B-spline curve*. If the knot values are equally spaced, then the curve is called a *uniform B-spline curve*. Figure 5.18 shows a uniform cubic B-spline curve, along with the control points and control polygon.

5.6.3 NURBS CURVES

A planar *nonuniform rational B-spline curve* or *NURBS curve* is obtained from a nonuniform B-spline polynomial curve in three dimensions. The control points are $(P_i, 1) \in \mathbb{R}^3$ for $0 \leq i \leq n$, with weights $w_i > 0$, and the polynomial curve is

$$(Y(t), w(t)) = \sum_{i=0}^{n} B_{i,j}(t) w_i (P_i, 1)$$

where $B_{i,j}(t)$ is the same polynomial defined in the previous subsection. The NURBS curve is obtained by treating $(Y(t), w(t))$ as a homogeneous vector and dividing through by the last component (often referred to as the *weight*) to obtain a projection in three dimensions

$$X(t) = \frac{Y(t)}{w(t)} = \sum_{i=0}^{n} R_{i,j}(t) P_i$$

where

$$R_{i,j}(t) = \frac{w_i B_{i,j}(t)}{\sum_{k=0}^{n} w_k B_{k,j}(t)}$$

CHAPTER 6
DISTANCE IN 2D

This chapter contains information on computing distance between geometric primitives in 2D. An application might not want to pay the price for an expensive square root calculation, so many of the algorithms in this chapter provide a construction for squared distance. Of course, fundamental to any distance algorithm is the squared distance between two points $X = (x_0, x_1)$ and $Y = (y_0, y_1)$

$$\text{Distance}^2(X, Y) = \|X - Y\|^2 = (x_0 - x_1)^2 + (y_0 - y_1)^2 \qquad (6.1)$$

We will discuss algorithms for computing the distance between a point and another object first; other combinations are discussed later in the chapter. When both objects are convex with polyline or polygonal boundaries, including the degenerate case when one is a linear component, the distance algorithms can be implemented by applying a derivativeless numerical minimizer using the point-object formulas. For example, the distance between a line segment and a triangle can be computed as a minimization of a one-dimensional function. If $F(X, T)$ is the squared distance between the point X and the triangle T, then the squared distance between a line segment $X(t) = P_0 + t(P_1 - P_0)$, $t \in [0, 1]$, and the triangle is $G(t) = F(X(t), T)$. A numerical minimizer can be applied to $G(t)$ for $t \in [0, 1]$. Such an iterative approach certainly can produce a reasonable numerical estimate for the squared distance, but typically the approach takes more time to find the estimate than a method that computes the squared distance using a noniterative method. The trade-off is ease of implementation versus time efficiency of the algorithm.

189

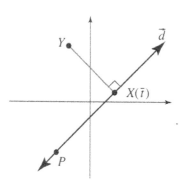

Figure 6.1   Closest point $X(\bar{t})$ on a line to a specified point Y.

6.1 POINT TO LINEAR COMPONENT

This section covers the distance algorithms for the three combinations of points with lines, rays, or line segments: point-line, point-ray, and point-segment.

6.1.1 POINT TO LINE

Given a point Y and a line $\mathcal{L}$ parameterized as $X(t) = P + t\vec{d}$, the closest point on the line to Y is the projection $X(\bar{t})$ of Y onto the line for some parameter value $\bar{t}$. Figure 6.1 illustrates the relationship. As shown in the figure, the vector $Y - X(\bar{t})$ must be perpendicular to the line direction $\vec{d}$. Thus,

$$0 = \vec{d} \cdot (Y - X(\bar{t})) = \vec{d} \cdot (Y - P - \bar{t}\vec{d}) = \vec{d} \cdot (Y - P) - \bar{t}\|\vec{d}\|^2$$

and the parameter of the projection is $\bar{t} = \vec{d} \cdot (Y - P)/\|\vec{d}\|^2$. The squared distance is $\|Y - P - \bar{t}\vec{d}\|^2$. Some algebra leads to

$$\text{Distance}^2(Y, \mathcal{L}) = \|Y - P\|^2 - \frac{\left(\vec{d} \cdot (Y - P)\right)^2}{\|\vec{d}\|^2} \qquad (6.2)$$

If $\vec{d}$ is already unit length, then the equation is slightly simplified in that $\|\hat{d}\| = 1$ and no division is required to compute the squared distance.

If the line is represented as $\vec{n} \cdot X = c$, the closest point K on the line satisfies the relationship $Y = K + s\vec{n}$ for some s. Dotting with $\vec{n}$ yields $\vec{n} \cdot Y = \vec{n} \cdot K + s\|\vec{n}\|^2 = c + s\|\vec{n}\|^2$, so $s = (\vec{n} \cdot Y - c)/\|\vec{n}\|^2$. The distance between the point and the line is $\|Y - K\| = |s|\|\vec{n}\|$, or

$$\text{Distance}\left(Y, \mathcal{L}\right) = \frac{|\vec{n} \cdot Y - c|}{\|\vec{n}\|} \tag{6.3}$$

If $\vec{n}$ is unit length, then the equation is slightly simplified in that $\|\hat{n}\| = 1$ and no division is required to compute the distance.

Equation 6.3 looks a lot simpler than Equation 6.2 and is less expensive to compute. The relationship between the two equations is clear from the following identity with the assumption that $\hat{d}$ and $\hat{n}$ are unit length:

$$
\begin{aligned}
\|Y - P\|^2 &= (Y - P)^{\mathrm{T}}(Y - P) \\
&= (Y - P)^{\mathrm{T}} \mathrm{I}(Y - P) \\
&= (Y - P)^{\mathrm{T}}(\hat{d}\hat{d}^{\mathrm{T}} + \hat{n}\hat{n}^{\mathrm{T}})(Y - P) \\
&= \left(\hat{d} \cdot (Y - P)\right)^2 + \left(\hat{n} \cdot (Y - P)\right)^2 \\
&= \left(\hat{d} \cdot (Y - P)\right)^2 + \left(\hat{n} \cdot Y - c\right)^2
\end{aligned}
$$

The key identity in the construction is $\mathrm{I} = \hat{d}\hat{d}^{\mathrm{T}} + \hat{n}\hat{n}^{\mathrm{T}}$, where I is the 2×2 identity matrix. This identity is true for any pair of orthonormal vectors. The proof relies on the fact that $\{\hat{d}, \hat{n}\}$ is an orthonormal basis for $\mathbb{R}^2$, so every vector can be represented as

$$\mathrm{I}X = X = (\hat{d}^{\mathrm{T}}X)\hat{d} + (\hat{n}^{\mathrm{T}}X)\hat{n} = (\hat{d}\hat{d}^{\mathrm{T}})X + (\hat{n}\hat{n}^{\mathrm{T}})X = (\hat{d}\hat{d}^{\mathrm{T}} + \hat{n}\hat{n}^{\mathrm{T}})X$$

Since this is true for all X, it must be that $\mathrm{I} = \hat{d}\hat{d}^{\mathrm{T}} + \hat{n}\hat{n}^{\mathrm{T}}$. Observe that the term $\hat{d}\hat{d}^{\mathrm{T}}$ is not to be confused with the dot product $\hat{d}^{\mathrm{T}}\hat{d}$. The vector $\hat{d}$ is a 2×1 vector, so $\hat{d}^{\mathrm{T}}$ is a 1×2 vector and the product $\hat{d}\hat{d}^{\mathrm{T}}$ is a 2×2 matrix.

6.1.2 POINT TO RAY

The construction is similar to that of point to line. The difference is that in some cases the projection of Y onto the line containing the ray $\mathcal{R}$ might not be a point on the ray. In a sense, Y is behind the ray. Figure 6.2 shows the two possibilities. Figure 6.2(a) shows the case when the projection is onto the ray. In this case $\bar{t} \geq 0$, and Equations 6.2 and 6.3 apply. Figure 6.2(b) shows the case when the projection is not onto the ray. In this case $\bar{t} < 0$, and the closest point to Y is the ray origin P. The squared distance is

$$\text{Distance}^2\left(Y, \mathcal{R}\right) = \begin{cases} \|Y - P\|^2 - \dfrac{\left(\vec{d} \cdot (Y - P)\right)^2}{\|\vec{d}\|^2}, & \vec{d} \cdot (Y - P) > 0 \\ \|Y - P\|^2, & \vec{d} \cdot (Y - P) \leq 0 \end{cases} \tag{6.4}$$

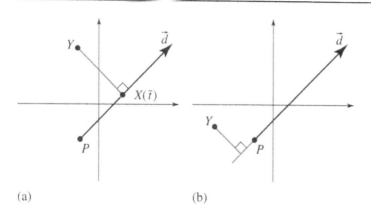

(a)   (b)

Figure 6.2   Closest point on a ray to a given point: (a) $X(\bar{t})$ closest to Y; (b) P closest to Y.

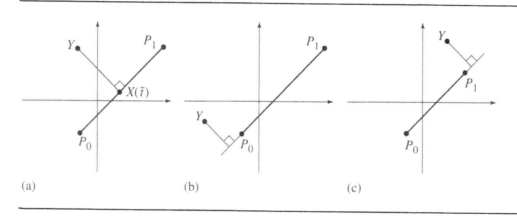

(a)   (b)   (c)

Figure 6.3   Closest point on a segment to a given point: (a) $X(\bar{t})$ closest to Y; (b) P_0 closest to Y; (c) P_1 closest to Y.

6.1.3 POINT TO SEGMENT

The construction is also similar to that of point to line. The difference now is that the projection of Y onto the line might not lie on the line segment S. The projection could lie behind the initial point or ahead of the final point of the segment. Figure 6.3 shows the three possibilities. The direction vector is $\vec{d} = P_1 - P_0$, the difference of end points for the line segment. The parameter interval is $[0, 1]$. The value $\bar{t}$ is computed, just as for the line, but then it is tested against the parameter interval $[0, 1]$ for the segment. The squared distance is

$$\text{Distance}^2 (Y, S) = \begin{cases} \|Y - P_0\|^2, & \bar{t} \leq 0 \\ \|Y - (P_0 + \bar{t}\vec{d})\|^2, & \bar{t} \in (0, 1) \\ \|Y - P_1\|^2, & \bar{t} \geq 1 \end{cases} \tag{6.5}$$

where $\bar{t} = \vec{d} \cdot (Y - P_0)/\|\vec{d}\|^2$. For the symmetric form (see Section 5.1.2), the squared distance is

$$\text{Distance}^2(Y, S) = \begin{cases} \|Y - (C - r\vec{d})\|^2, & \bar{t} \leq -r \\ \|Y - (C + \bar{t}\vec{d})\|^2, & |\bar{t}| < r \\ \|Y - (C + r\vec{d})\|^2, & \bar{t} \geq r \end{cases} \tag{6.6}$$

where $\bar{t} = \vec{d} \cdot (Y - C)$.

For applications that compute a large number of distances, it might be important to make the squared distance calculations as fast as possible. If the direction vector $\vec{d}$ is not unit length, then a division occurs in the formulas. A space-time trade-off can be made to avoid the division. If memory permits, whether in the parametric or standard form, the quantity $1/\|\vec{d}\|^2$ can be precomputed and stored with the line segment. If memory is not readily available, then the division can be deferred until absolutely needed. For example, in the standard form the algorithm to defer the division is

```
float SquaredDistance(Point Y, Segment S)
{
    Point D = S.P1 - S.P0;
    Point YmP0 = Y - S.P0;
    float t = Dot(D, YmP0);

    if (t <= 0) {
        // P0 is closest to Y
        return Dot(YmP0, YmP0);
    }

    float DdD = Dot(D, D);
    if (t >= DdD) {
        // P1 is closest to Y
        Point YmP1 = Y - S.P1;
        return Dot(YmP1, YmP1);
    }

    // closest point is interior to segment
    return Dot(YmP0, YmP0) - t * t / DdD;
}
```

6.2 POINT TO POLYLINE

For calculating the distance between a point Y and a polyline $\mathcal{L}$ with vertices P_0 through P_n and line segments S_i, $0 \le i < n$, whose end points are P_i and P_{i+1}, the straightforward algorithm is to calculate the minimum of the distances between the point and the line segments of the polyline:

$$\text{Distance}^2(Y, \mathcal{L}) = \min_{0 \le i < n} \text{Distance}^2(Y, S_i) \qquad (6.7)$$

Iterating blindly over the line segments can potentially be expensive for polylines with a large number of segments or for an application with a large number of polylines for which the distance calculations must be made frequently.

A variation is to use rejection methods that determine that a line segment is not sufficiently close enough to the test point that it could replace the currently known minimum distance, μ. The savings in time occurs by avoiding the potential division that occurs when the closest point to Y on a line segment is interior to that segment. Let $Y = (a, b)$. As long as μ remains the current minimum, any line segment that is outside the circle with center Y and radius μ is farther away from Y than μ, so that segment cannot cause an update of μ. Figure 6.4 illustrates this. The segments S_1 and S_2 are rejected for the full calculation of distance because both are outside the circle of radius μ centered at Y. The segment S_3 is not rejected since it intersects the circle. However, this begs the question since the rejection tests require computing the distances from the segments to Y, exactly the tests we are trying to avoid!

A faster, but coarser, rejection test uses axis-aligned infinite strips that contain the circle. Let $S_i = \langle (x_i, y_i), (x_{i+1}, y_{i+1}) \rangle$ be the next segment to be tested. If S_i is outside the infinite strip $|x - a| \le \mu$, then it cannot intersect the circle. The rejection test is therefore

$$|x_i - a| \ge \mu \quad \text{and} \quad |x_{i+1} - a| \ge \mu \quad \text{and} \quad (x_i - a)(x_{i+1} - a) > 0$$

The first two conditions guarantee each segment end point is outside the strip. The last condition guarantees that the end points are on the same side of the strip. Similarly, if S_i is outside the infinite strip $|y - b| \le \mu$, then it cannot intersect the circle. The rejection test is

$$|y_i - b| \ge \mu \quad \text{and} \quad |y_{i+1} - b| \ge \mu \quad \text{and} \quad (y_i - b)(y_{i+1} - b) > 0$$

Figure 6.4 illustrates this. The segment S_1, although outside the circle, is not rejected because it partly lies in each infinite strip. However, S_2 is rejected because it is outside the vertical strip.

Since square roots should be avoided in the intermediate calculations, an implementation maintains the squared-distance μ^2 instead of μ. The rejection test must be restructured accordingly to use μ^2:

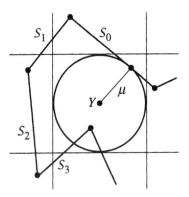

Figure 6.4   The segment S_0 generated the current minimum distance μ between the polyline and Y. S_1 and S_2 cannot cause μ to be updated because they are outside the circle of radius μ centered at Y. Segment S_3 does cause an update since it intersects the circle. The infinite-strip test does not reject S_1 and S_3 since they lie partly in both infinite strips, but S_2 is rejected since it is outside the vertical strip. The rectangle test rejects S_1 and S_2 since both are outside the rectangle containing the circle, but does not reject S_3.

$$|x_i - a|^2 \geq \mu^2 \quad \text{and} \quad |x_{i+1} - a|^2 \geq \mu^2 \quad \text{and} \quad (x_i - a)(x_{i+1} - a) > 0$$

or

$$|y_i - b|^2 \geq \mu^2 \quad \text{and} \quad |y_{i+1} - b|^2 \geq \mu^2 \quad \text{and} \quad (y_i - b)(y_{i+1} - b) > 0$$

The quantities in the rejection test are also used in the squared-distance calculation, so these can be temporarily saved in case they are needed later to avoid redundant calculations. Also, the quantities $x_{i+1} - a$ and $y_{i+1} - b$ in the current rejection test become the $x_i - a$ and $y_i - b$ values in the next rejection test, so these should be saved in temporary variables and used later when needed, again to avoid redundant calculations.

A modification of the rejection test involves testing for intersection between a segment and the axis-aligned rectangle that contains the circle of radius μ centered at Y. We can use the method of separating axes discussed in Section 7.7. The improvement is illustrated by Figure 6.4. The segment S_1 was not rejected by the previous method because it lies partly in both infinite strips. However, S_1 is rejected by the current method because it does not intersect the axis-aligned rectangle.

If the segments of the polyline are stored using the symmetric form $C + t\hat{u}$, where C is the center of the segment, $\hat{u}$ is a unit-length vector, and $|t| \leq r$, then the rejection test is as follows. Define $\vec{\Delta} = C - Y = (\Delta_0, \Delta_1)$ and $\hat{u} = (u_0, u_1)$. The segment is rejected (and is outside the box) if any of the tests are true:

$$|\Delta_0| \geq \mu + r|u_0|$$
$$|\Delta_1| \geq \mu + r|u_1|$$
$$|\Delta_0 u_1 - \Delta_1 u_0| \geq r\mu(|u_0| + |u_1|)$$

Since the square root is being avoided by tracking the value of μ^2, the three tests must be slightly revised to use μ^2:

$$|\Delta_0| - r|u_0| \geq 0 \quad \text{and} \quad (|\Delta_0| - r|u_0|)^2 \geq \mu^2$$
$$|\Delta_1| - r|u_1| \geq 0 \quad \text{and} \quad (|\Delta_1| - r|u_1|)^2 \geq \mu^2$$
$$|\Delta_0 u_1 - \Delta_1 u_0|^2 \geq r^2 \mu^2 (|u_0| + |u_1|)^2$$

Finally, if an application has specific knowledge of the form of its polylines, it might be possible to organize the polyline with a data structure that helps localize the calculations. These algorithms, of course, will be specific to the application and might not work as general tools.

6.3 POINT TO POLYGON

The only difference between measuring distance from a point to a polygon and measuring distance between a point and a polyline is that the polygon is treated as a solid object. If the point is inside the polygon, then the distance is zero. If the point is outside, then for a nonconvex simple polygon without any preprocessing, the point-to-polyline distance algorithms are applied. See Section 13.3 for the point-in-polygon containment query.

Some special cases are handled here. We consider the special cases of computing the distance between a point and a triangle, a rectangle, and an orthogonal frustum, all polygons being convex. We also mention a couple of methods for computing distance from a point to a convex polygon.

6.3.1 POINT TO TRIANGLE

Let Y be the test point, and let the triangle have vertices P_i, $0 \leq i \leq 2$, that are counterclockwise ordered. If Y is inside the solid triangle, then the distance is defined to be zero. If Y is outside the solid triangle, then the problem reduces to finding the closest point on the triangle (as a polyline). The algorithm localizes the search for the closest point by determining where Y is relative to the triangle. This is more efficient than just computing distances from the test point to all three triangle edges and selecting the minimum. Figure 6.5 illustrates a few configurations. Figure 6.5(a) shows a point that is zero distance from the triangle since it is contained in the triangle. Figure 6.5(b) shows a point that is closest to an edge of the triangle. Figure 6.5(c) shows a point that is closest to a vertex of the triangle. The solid lines indicate the lines that contain the edges of the triangles. The dotted lines indicate the perpendicular directions to the edges. Figure 6.5(d) shows a point that is closest to an edge of the triangle,

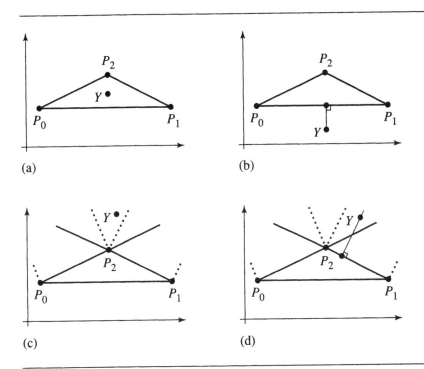

Figure 6.5   Closest point on a triangle to a given point: (a) $\mathrm{Dist}(Y, \mathcal{T}) = 0$; (b) $\mathrm{Dist}(Y, \mathcal{T}) = \mathrm{Dist}(Y, < P_0, P_1 >)$; (c) $\mathrm{Dist}(Y, \mathcal{T}) = \mathrm{Dist}(Y, P_2)$; (d) $\mathrm{Dist}(Y, \mathcal{T}) = \mathrm{Dist}(Y, < P_1, P_2 >)$.

but is in the wedge formed by the two (solid) edge-rays with common origin at the vertex. This example shows that the closest point on the triangle to a Y is determined by the location of Y in the plane as partitioned by the edge-perpendicular lines at the vertices, not the edge-lines themselves. In particular, the difference shows up at an obtuse angle of the triangle.

We present two methods of searching for the closest point. The first method effectively searches the triangle interior first and the edges second. Its main goal is to allow at most one division and to do that division only if absolutely necessary. The trade-off for avoiding the expensive division is more floating-point comparisons. On current architectures where floating-point addition and multiplication are now faster than floating-point comparisons, this could be an issue if the application has a large number of point-triangle distance queries. The second method effectively does the search in the reverse order, edges first and triangle interior second. Its main goal is to hope that the closest point is a vertex and is found quickly.

Interior-to-Edge Search for a Closest Point

The algorithm uses the parameterized form of the triangle. Let $\vec{d}_0 = P_1 - P_0$ and $\vec{d}_1 = P_2 - P_0$. The triangle points are $X(t_0, t_1) = P_0 + t_0\vec{d}_0 + t_1\vec{d}_1$ for $t_0 \geq 0$, $t_1 \geq 0$, and $t_0 + t_1 \leq 1$. The squared distance between the test point Y and a point $X(t_0, t_1)$ on the triangle is the quadratic function

$$F(t_0, t_1) = \|X(t_0, t_1) - Y\|^2 = \|P_0 + t_0\vec{d}_0 + t_1\vec{d}_1 - Y\|^2$$

$$= a_{00}t_0^2 + 2a_{01}t_0t_1 + a_{11}t_1^2 - 2b_0t_0 - 2b_1t_1 + c$$

where $a_{00} = \|\vec{d}_0\|^2$, $a_{01} = \vec{d}_0 \cdot \vec{d}_1$, $a_{11} = \|\vec{d}_1\|^2$, $b_0 = \vec{d}_0 \cdot (Y - P_0)$, $b_1 = \vec{d}_1 \cdot (Y - P_0)$, and $c = \|Y - P_0\|^2$. Although the parameters t_0 and t_1 are subject to the previously mentioned constraints for the triangle, we consider $F(t_0, t_1)$ as a function for all values of t_0, t_1. The set of all pairs (t_0, t_1) is referred to as the *parameter plane*. The global minimum of F occurs when

$$(0, 0) = \vec{\nabla}F = 2\left(a_{00}t_0 + a_{01}t_1 - b_0, a_{01}t_0 + a_{11}t_1 - b_1\right)$$

The solution to this system of equations is

$$\bar{t}_0 = \frac{a_{11}b_0 - a_{01}b_1}{a_{00}a_{11} - a_{01}^2} \quad \text{and} \quad \bar{t}_1 = \frac{a_{00}b_1 - a_{01}b_0}{a_{00}a_{11} - a_{01}^2}$$

The closest triangle point to Y depends on where $(\bar{t}_0, \bar{t}_1)$ lies in the parameter plane. Figure 6.6 shows the partition of the parameter plane into seven regions by the lines that contain the triangle edges. If $(\bar{t}_0, \bar{t}_1)$ is in region 0, then Y is inside the triangle and the distance is zero. For the other regions, notice that the level curves defined by $F(t_0, t_1) = \lambda > 0$ are ellipses. (For a definition and discussion of level curves, see Section A.9.1.) If $(\bar{t}_0, \bar{t}_1)$ is in region 1, then the closest triangle point is on the edge where $t_0 + t_1 = 1$. If there is a value $\lambda_0 > 0$ so that the corresponding level curve is tangent to the edge, then the point of intersection $(\hat{t}_0, \hat{t}_1)$ yields the closest point to Y. It is possible that no level curve is tangent to the edge. In this case, the closest point to Y must correspond to an end point of the edge. Figure 6.7 illustrates these two cases. The same argument applies when $(\bar{t}_0, \bar{t}_1)$ lies in region 3 or region 5. Figure 6.7(a) shows tangential contact with an edge. Figure 6.7(b) shows contact with a vertex.

If $(\bar{t}_0, \bar{t}_1)$ is in region 2, three possibilities arise. If there is a $\lambda_0 > 0$ so that the corresponding level curve is tangent to the edge contained by $t_0 + t_1 = 1$, then the point of intersection $(\hat{t}_0, \hat{t}_1)$ yields the closest point to Y. If there is no level curve tangent to that edge, there might be one that is tangent to the edge contained by $t_0 = 0$. The point of intersection $(0, \hat{t}_1)$ yields the closest point to Y. If no level curves are tangent to the two edges, then the closest point Y is the triangle vertex corresponding to

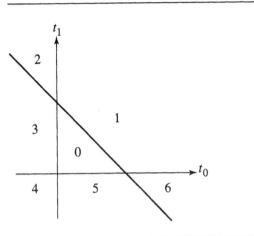

Figure 6.6   Partitioning of the parameter plane into seven regions.

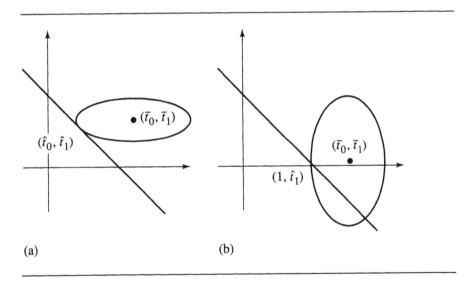

Figure 6.7   Contact points of level curves of $F(t_0, t_1)$ with the triangle: (a) contact with an edge; (b) contact with a vertex.

the parameter pair $(0, 1)$. Figure 6.8 illustrates these three cases. The same argument applies when $(\bar{t}_0, \bar{t}_1)$ lies in region 4 or region 6. Figure 6.8(a) shows tangential contact with one edge. Figure 6.8(b) shows tangential contact with another edge. Figure 6.8(c) shows contact with a vertex.

The following code fragment is structured so that at most one division occurs.

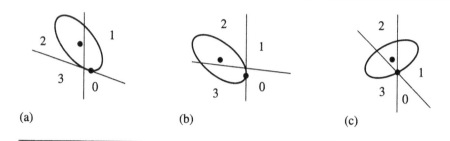

(a)   (b)   (c)

Figure 6.8   Contact points of level curves of $F(t_0, t_1)$ with the triangle: (a) contact with an edge; (b) contact with another edge; (c) contact with a vertex.

```
float SquaredDistance(Point Y, Triangle T)
{
    // coefficients of F(t0, t1), calculation of c is deferred until needed
    Point D0 = T.P1 - T.P0, D1 = T.P2 - T.P0, Delta = Y - T.P0;
    float a00 = Dot(D0, D0), a01 = Dot(D0, D1), a11 = Dot(D1, D1);
    float b0 = Dot(D0, Delta), b1 = Dot(D1, Delta);

    // Grad F(t0, t1) = (0, 0) at (t0, t1) = (n0 / d, n1 / d)
    float n0 = a11 * b0 - a01 * b1;
    float n1 = a00 * b1 - a01 * b0;
    float d  = a00 * a11 - a01 * a01;  // theoretically positive

    if (n0 + n1 <= d) {
        if (n0 >= 0) {
            if (n1 >= 0) {
                region 0
            } else {
                region 5
            }
        } else if (n1 >= 0) {
            region 3
        } else {
            region 4
        }
    } else if (n0 < 0) {
        region 2
    } else if (n1 < 0) {
        region 6
    } else {
        region 1
    }
}
```

The code block for region 0 just returns zero since Y is inside the triangle and the squared distance is zero.

```
// Region 0.  Point is inside the triangle, squared distance is zero.
return 0;
```

If $(\bar{t}_0, \bar{t}_1)$ is in region 5, then the squared-distance function reduces to

$$G(t_0) = F(t_0, 0) = a_{00}t_0^2 - 2b_0t_0 + c$$

The problem now is to compute $\hat{t}_0$ to minimize $G(t_0)$ for $t_0 \in [0, 1]$. This is effectively the same problem as minimizing F, but in one less dimension. The minimum occurs either at a value where $G' = 0$ or at one of the end points of the interval. The solution to $G' = 2(a_{00}t_0 - b_0) = 0$ is $t_0 = b_0/a_{00}$. If $t_0 \in (0, 1)$, then $\hat{t}_0 = b_0/a_{00}$. If $t_0 \le 0$, then $\hat{t}_0 = 0$. Otherwise $t_0 \ge 1$ and $\hat{t}_0 = 1$. The code block for region 5 is

```
// Region 5.  Minimize G(t0) = F(t0, 0) for t0 in [0, 1].  G'(t0) = 0 at
// t0 = b0 / a00.

float c = Dot(Delta, Delta);
if (b0 > 0) {
    if (b0 < a00) {
        // closest point is interior to the edge
        return c - b0 * b0 / a00;   // F(b0 / a00, 0)
    } else {
        // closest point is end point (t0, t1) = (1, 0)
        return a00 - 2 * b0 + c;   // F(1, 0)
    }
} else {
    // closest point is end point (t0, t1) = (0, 0)
    return c;   // F(0, 0)
}
```

A similar reduction in dimension applies for region 3. The code block is

```
// Region 3.  Minimize G(t1) = F(0, t1) for t1 in [0, 1].  G'(t1) = 0 at
// t1 = b1 / a11.

float c = Dot(Delta, Delta);
if (b1 > 0) {
    if (b1 < a11) {
        // closest point is interior to the edge
        return c - b1 * b1 / a11;  // F(0, b1 / a11)
    } else {
        // closest point is end point (t0, t1) = (0, 1)
```

```
        return a11 - 2 * b1 ı c;   // F(0, 1)
    }
} else {
    // closest point is end point (t0, t1) = (0, 0)
    return c;   // F(0, 0)
}
```

A similar reduction in dimension also applies for region 1, but the algebra is slightly more complicated. The function to minimize is

$$G(t_0) = F(t_0, 1 - t_0) = (a_{00} - 2a_{01} + a_{11})t_0^2 + 2(a_{01} - a_{11} - b_0 + b_1)t_0$$

$$+ (a_{11} - 2b_1 + c)$$

The solution to $G' = 0$ is $t_0 = (a_{11} - a_{01} + b_0 - b_1)/(a_{00} - 2a_{01} + a_{11})$. Theoretically the denominator is positive.

```
// Region 1. Minimize G(t0) = F(t0, 1 - t0) for t0 in [0, 1]. G'(t0) = 0 at
// t0 = (a11 - a01 + b0 - b1) / (a00 - 2 * a01 + a11).

float c = Dot(Delta, Delta);
float n = a11 - a01 + b0 - b1, d = a00 - 2 * a01 + a11;
if (n > 0) {
    if (n < d) {
        // closest point is interior to the edge
        return (a11 - 2 * b1 + c) - n * n / d;   // F(n / d, 1 - n / d)
    } else {
        // closest point is end point (t0, t1) = (1, 0)
        return a00 - 2 * b0 + c;   // F(1, 0)
    }
} else {
    // closest point is end point (t0, t1) = (0, 1)
    return a11 - 2 * b1 + c;   // F(0, 1)
}
```

Region 2 is more complex to analyze, as shown earlier, since the closest point can be on one of two edges of the triangle. The pseudocode tests if the closest point is an interior point of the edge $t_0 = 0$. If so, the distance is calculated and the function returns. If not, the closest point on the other edge $t_0 + t_1 = 1$ is found, the distance calculated, and the function returns.

```
// Region 2.  Minimize G(t1) = F(0, t1) for t1 in [0, 1].  If t1 < 1, the
// parameter pair (0, max{0, t1}) produces the closest point.  If t1 = 1,
// then minimize H(t0) = F(t0, 1 - t0) for t0 in [0, 1].  G'(t1) = 0 at
```

```
// t1 = b1 / a11.  H'(t0) = 0 at t0 = (a11 - a01 + b0 - b1) / (a00 - 2 * a01
// + a11).

float c = Dot(Delta, Delta);

// minimize on edge t0 = 0
if (b1 > 0) {
    if (b1 < a11) {
        // closest point is interior to the edge
        return c - b1 * b1 / a11;  // F(0, b1 / a11)
    } else {
        // minimize on the edge t0 + t1 = 1
        float n = a11 - a01 + b0 - b1 d = a00 - 2 * a01 + a11;
        if (n > 0) {
            if (n < d) {
                // closest point is interior to the edge
                return (a11 - 2 * b1 + c) - n * n / d;  // F(n / d, 1 - n / d)
            } else {
                // closest point is end point (t0, t1) = (1, 0)
                return a00 - 2 * b0 + c;  // F(1, 0)
            }
        } else {
            // closest point is end point (t0, t1) = (0, 1)
            return a11 - 2 * b1 + c;  // F(0, 1)
        }
    }
} else {
    // closest point is end point (t0, t1) = (0, 0)
    return c;  // F(0, 0)
}
```

The pseudocode for region 6 has a similar implementation:

```
// Region 6.  Minimize G(t0) = F(t0, 0) for t0 in [0, 1].  If t0 < 1, the
// parameter pair (max{0, t0}, 0) produces the closest point.  If t0 = 1,
// then minimize H(t1) = F(t1, 1 - t1) for t1 in [0, 1].  G'(t0) = 0 at
// t0 = b0 / a00.  H'(t1) = 0 at t1 = (a11 - a01 + b0 - b1) / (a00 - 2 * a01
// + a11).

float c = Dot(Delta, Delta);

// minimize on edge t1 = 0
if (b0 > 0) {
    if (b0 < a00) {
```

```
                // closest point is interior to the edge
                return c - b0 * b0 / a00;  // F(b0 / a00, 0)
        } else {
            // minimize on the edge t0 + t1 = 1
            float n = a11 - a01 + b0 - b1, d = a00 - 2 * a01 + a11;
            if (n > 0) {
                if (n < d) {
                    // closest point is interior to the edge
                    return (a11 - 2 * b1 + c) - n * n / d;  // F(n / d, 1 - n / d)
                } else {
                    // closest point is end point (t0, t1) = (1, 0)
                    return a00 - 2 * b0 + c;  // F(1, 0)
                }
            } else
                // closest point is end point (t0, t1) = (0, 1)
                return a11 - 2 * b1 + c;  // F(0, 1)
        }
    }
} else {
    // closest point is end point (t0, t1) = (0, 0)
    return c;  // F(0, 0)
}
```

Finally, the pseudocode for region 4 is

```
// Region 4.  Minimize G(t0) = F(t0, 0) for t0 in [0, 1].  If t0 > 1, the
// parameter pair (min{1, t0}, 0) produces the closest point.  If t0 = 0,
// then minimize H(t1) = F(0, t1) for t1 in [0, 1].  G'(t0) = 0 at
// t0 = b0 / a00.  H'(t1) = 0 at t1 = b1 / a11.

float c = Dot(Delta, Delta);

// minimize on edge t1 = 0
if (b0 < a00) {
    if (b0 > 0) {
        // closest point is interior to edge
        return c - b0 * b0 / a00;  // F(b0 / a00, 0)
    } else {
        // minimize on edge t0 = 0
        if (b1 < a11) {
            if (b1 > 0) {
                // closest point is interior to edge
                return c - b1 * b1 / a11;  // F(0, b1 / a11)
```

```
            } else {
                // closest point is end point (t0, t1) = (0, 0)
                return c;   // F(0, 0)
            }
        } else {
            // closest point is end point (t0, t1) = (0, 1)
            return a11 - 2 * b1 + c;   // F(0, 1)
        }
    }
} else {
    // closest point is end point (t0, t1) = (1, 0)
    return a00 - 2 * b0 + c;   // F(1, 0)
}
```

Interior-to-Edge Search Time Analysis

The operation counts for the pseudocode are presented here to provide best-case and worst-case performance of the code. We count additions A; multiplications M; divisions D; comparisons of two floating-point numbers C_T, neither known to be zero; and comparisons of a floating-point number to zero C_Z. The comparisons are partitioned this way because floating-point libraries tend to support a test of the sign bit of a number that is faster than a general floating-point comparison.

The block of code in SquaredDistance that occurs before the set of conditional statements, but including the sum in the first conditional, requires 15 additions and 16 multiplications. Each region block incurs the cost of these operations. Table 6.1 shows the best-case and worst-case operation counts for the various regions. As expected because of the design, the best case for region 0 requires the least amount of time per point. The worst case for region 6 requires the most amount of time per point.

Edge-to-Interior Search for a Closest Point

This method, proposed by Gino van den Bergen in a post to the newsgroup *comp.graphics.algorithms*, is an attempted speedup by computing distance to edges first and hoping that a common vertex for two edges is the closest point. The argument in that post is that intuitively this method should perform better than the previous one when Y is far from the triangle. The basis is that if you were to select a large bounding box for the triangle, and if the test points are uniformly distributed in that box, the probability that a vertex is closest to a test point is much larger than the probability that an edge point is closest to a test point or that the test point is interior to the triangle. To motivate this, consider a triangle with vertices $(0, 0)$, $(1, 0)$, and

Table 6.1 Operation counts for point-to-triangle distance calculation using the interior-to-edge approach.

Region/count	A	M	D	C_T	C_Z
0, best	15	16	0	1	2
0, worst	15	16	0	1	2
1, best	23	20	0	1	3
1, worst	24	21	1	2	3
2, best	16	18	0	1	2
2, worst	24	21	1	3	3
3, best	16	18	0	1	3
3, worst	17	19	1	2	3
4, best	18	19	0	2	2
4, worst	17	19	1	3	4
5, best	16	18	0	1	3
5, worst	17	19	1	2	3
6, best	16	18	0	1	3
6, worst	24	21	1	3	4

$(0, 1)$ and a bounding box $[-r, r]^2$, where $r \geq 1$. Figure 6.9 illustrates these and shows the regions of points closest to vertices and to edges.

Regions V_0, V_1, and V_2 are the sets of points closest to $(0, 0)$, $(1, 0)$, and $(0, 1)$, respectively. Regions E_0, E_1, and E_2 are the sets of points closest to edges $\langle (0, 0), (1, 0) \rangle$, $\langle (1, 0), (0, 1) \rangle$, and $\langle (0, 1), (0, 0) \rangle$, respectively. Region T is the triangle interior. The area of T is $A_T = 1/2$. The total area of the edge regions is $A_E = 4r - 3/2$. The total area of the vertex regions is $A_V = 4r^2 - 4r + 1$. Clearly $A_V > A_E$ for sufficiently large r since A_V is quadratic in r, but A_E is only linear in r. Therefore, for sufficiently large r, a randomly selected point in the rectangle has the largest probability of being in a vertex region. It makes sense in this case to have an algorithm that tests vertices first for closeness to a test point.

However, now consider small r. If $r = 1$, the only vertex region with positive area is V_0 and has area $A_V = 1$. The edge region area is $A_E = 5/2 > A_V$. In general $A_E \geq A_V$ for $1 \leq r \leq 1 + \sqrt{6}/4 \doteq 1.612$. For this range of r values, a randomly selected point in the rectangle has the largest probability of being in an edge region. The chances that the actual distribution of the test points in an application are uniformly distributed in the sense mentioned above is small, so the method for measuring distance from a point to a triangle is best determined by testing your own data with these algorithms.

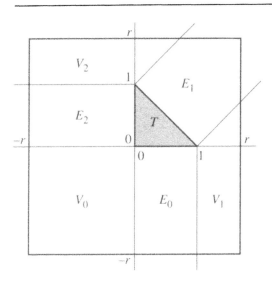

Figure 6.9   A triangle, a bounding box of the triangle, and the regions of points closest to vertices and to edges.

The pseudocode for the current algorithm is listed below. The code indicates that the closest triangle point to the test point is returned. The distance to the test point can be calculated from this.

```
float SquaredDistance (Point Y, Triangle T)
{
    // triangle vertices V0, V1, V2,  edges E0=<V0, V1>,  E1=<V1, V2>, E2=<V2, V0>

    // closest point on E0 to P is K0 = V0 + t0 * (V1 - V0) for some t0 in [0, 1]
    float t0 = ParameterOfClosestEdgePoint(P, E0);

    // closest point on E1 to P is K1 = V1 + t1 * (V2 - V1) for some t1 in [0, 1]
    float t1 = ParameterOfClosestEdgePoint(P, E1);

    if (t0 == 0 and t1 == 0)  // closest point is vertex V1
        return SquaredLength(Y - V1);

    // closest point on E2 to P is K2 = V2 + t2 * (V0 - V2) for some t2 in [0, 1]
    float t2 = ParameterOfClosestEdgePoint(P, E2);

    if (t1 == 0 and t2 == 0)  // closest point is vertex V2
        return SquaredLength(Y - V2);
```

```
    if (t0 == 0 and t2 == 0)  // closest point is vertex V0
        return SquaredLength(Y - V0);

    // Y = c0 * V0 + c1 * V1 + c2 * V2 for c0 + c1 + c2 = 1
    GetBarycentricCoordinates(Y, V0, V1, V2, c0, c1, c2);

    if (c0 < 0)  // closest point is K1 on edge E1
        return SquaredLength(Y - (V1 + t1 * (V2 - V1)));

    if (c1 < 0)  // closest point is K2 on edge E2
        return SquaredLength(Y - (V2 + t2 * (V0 - V2)));

    if (c2 < 0)  // closest point is K0 on edge E0
        return SquaredLength(Y - (V0 + t0 * (V1 - V0)));

    return 0;  // Y is inside triangle
}
```

The function `ParameterOfClosestEdgePoint(P,E)` effectively is what is used in computing distance from a point to a line segment. The projection of P onto the line containing the edge $\langle V_0, V_1 \rangle$ is $K = V_0 + t(V_1 - V_0)$, where $t = (P - V_0)/\|V_1 - V_0\|^2$. If $t < 0$, it is clamped to $t = 0$ and the closest point to P is V_0. If $t > 1$, it is clamped to $t = 1$ and the closest point is V_1. Otherwise, $t \in [0, 1]$ and the closest point is K. The aforementioned function returns the t value. If the function were to be implemented as described, it involves a division by the squared length of the edge. At least two calls are made to this function, so the distance calculator would require a minimum of two divisions, an expensive proposition. A smarter implementation does not do the division, but computes the numerator n and denominator d of t. If $n < 0$, t is clamped to 0. If $n > d$, t is clamped to 1. The numerators and denominators should be stored as local variables at the scope of the function body for use later in the barycentric coordinate calculations. If the function returns any of the three vertices, the division n/d for any of the t-values is never performed.

The function `GetBarycentricCoordinates` computes $P = \sum_{i=0}^{2} c_i V_i$, where $\sum_{i=0}^{2} c_i = 1$. Once c_1 and c_2 are known, we can solve $c_0 = 1 - c_1 - c_2$. The equation for P is equivalent to $P - V_0 = c_1(V_1 - V_0) + c_2(V_2 - V_0)$. The vector equation represents two linear equations in the two unknowns c_1 and c_2, a system that can be solved in the usual manner. The solution, if implemented in a straightforward manner, requires a division by the determinant of the coefficient matrix. The division is not necessary to perform. The barycentric calculator can return the coordinates as three rational numbers $c_i = n_i/d$ having the same denominator. The numerators and denominator are returned in separate storage. The sign test $c_0 < 0$ is equivalent to $n_0 d < 0$, so the division is replaced by a multiplication. The conditional test is a sign test, so the conventional floating-point comparison can be replaced by a (typically faster) test of the sign bit of the floating-point number. Even better would be to avoid the multiplications $n_i d$ and have a conditional statement that tests the sign bit of d. Each clause of the test has three conditionals testing the sign bits of n_i.

If $c_0 < 0$, the closest point is on the edge E_1 and is $K_1 = V_1 + t_1(V_2 - V_1)$. The actual value of t_1 is needed. If the division n_1/d_1 is deferred by the call to ParameterOfClosestEdgePoint, it must now be calculated in order to compute K_1. Similar arguments apply for the conditional statements for c_1 and c_2.

More detailed pseudocode that uses the deferred division and avoids the division in the barycentric calculator is listed below. The return statements are marked for reference by the section on the time analysis of the pseudocode.

```
float SquaredDistance (Point Y, Triangle T)
{
    // T has vertices V0, V1, V2

    // t0 = n0/d0 = Dot(Y - V0, V1 - V0) / Dot(V1 - V0, V1 - V0)
    Point D0 = Y - V0, E0 = V1 - V0;
    float n0 = Dot(D0, E0);

    // t1 = n1/d1 = Dot(Y - V1, V2 - V1) / Dot(V2 - V1, V2 - V1)
    Point D1 = Y - V1,  E1 = V2 - V1;
    float n1 = Dot(D1, E1);

    if (n0 <= 0 and n1 <= 0)  // closest point is V1
        return Dot(D1, D1);  // RETURN 0

    // t2 = n2/d2 = Dot(Y - V2, V0 - V2) / Dot(V0 - V2, V0 - V2);
    Point D2 = Y - V2,  E2 = V0 - V2;
    float n2 = Dot(D2, E2);

    if (n1 <= 0 and n2 == 0)  // closest point is V2
        return Dot(D2, D2);  // RETURN 1

    if (n0 <= 0 and n2 <= 0)  // closest point is V0
        return Dot(D0, D0);  // RETURN 2

    // D0 = Y - V0 = V0 + c1 * (V1 - V0) + c2 * (V2 - V0) = V0 + c1
    // * E1 - c2 * E2 for
    // c0 + c1 + c2 = 1, c0 = m0 / d, c1 = m1 / d, c2 = m2 / d
    float e00 = Dot(E0, E0), e02 = Dot(E0, E2), e22 = Dot(E2, E2);
    float d = e02 * e02 - e00 * e22;
    float a = Dot(D0, E2);
    float m1 = e02 * a - e22 * n0;
    float m0, m2;
    Point D;
```

```
if (d > 0) {
    if (m1 < 0) {  // closest point is V2 + t2 * E2
        t2 = n2 / e22;
        D = Y - (V2 + t2 * E2);
        return Dot(D, D);  // RETURN 3a
    }

    m2 = e00 * a - e02 * n0;
    if (m2 < 0) { // closest point is V0 + t0 * E0
        t0 = n0 / e00;
        D = Y - (V0 + t0 * E0);
        return Dot(D, D);  // RETURN 4a
    }

    m0 = d - m1 - m2;
    if (m0 < 0) { // closest point is V1 + t1 * E1
        t1 = n1/Dot(E1, E1);
        D = Y - (V1 + t1 * E1);
        return Dot(D, D);  // RETURN 5a
    }
} else {
    if (m1 > 0) {  // closest point is V2 + t2 * E2
        t2 = n2 / e22;
        D = Y - (V2 + t2 * E2);
        return Dot(D, D);  // RETURN 3b
    }

    m2 = e00 * a - e02 * n0;
    if (m2 > 0) { // closest point is V0 + t0 * E0
        t0 = n0 / e00;
        D = Y - (V0 + t0 * E0);
        return Dot(D, D);  // RETURN 4b
    }

    m0 = d - m1 - m2;
    if (m0 > 0) { // closest point is V1 + t1 * E1
        t1 = n1 / Dot(E1, E1);
        D = Y - (V1 + t1 * E1);
        return Dot(D, D);  // RETURN 5b
    }
}

return 0;  // Y is inside triangle, RETURN 6
}
```

Table 6.2   Operation counts for point-to-triangle distance calculation using the edge-to-interior approach.

Return/count	A	M	D	C_Z
0	11	6	0	2
1	17	10	0	4
2	18	12	0	6
3a, 3b	29	28	1	8
4a, 4b	30	30	1	9
5a, 5b	33	32	1	10
6	27	26	0	10

Edge-to-Interior Search Time Analysis

The operation counts for the pseudocode are presented here to provide best-case and worst-case performance of the code. We count additions A, multiplications M, divisions D, and comparisons of a floating-point number to zero C_Z. No general comparisons occur in this pseudocode, so C_T as defined for the previous algorithm is always zero. Table 6.2 shows the operation counts for each of the return statements in the pseudocode. The worst case is assumed for the pair of conditions for the first three return blocks; that is, both sign tests occur with the second one false so that the return is skipped. The best case is that the condition fails because the first sign test in each condition is false and the return is skipped. The best case is when the function terminates at the very first return statement marked RETURN 0. The worst case occurs at the return statements marked RETURN 5a and RETURN 5b.

Comparing this to the results of the other algorithm whose operation counts are summarized in Table 6.1, we see that the best case for the edge-to-interior algorithm ($11A, 6M, 0D, 2C_Z$) is faster than the best case for the interior-to-edge algorithm ($15A, 16M, 0D, 1C_T, 2C_Z$). However, the worst case for the edge-to-interior algorithm ($33A, 32M, 1D, 10C_Z$) is slower than the worst case for the interior-to-edge algorithm ($24A, 21M, 1D, 3C_T, 4C_Z$). To decide which algorithm is the best one for your application will require either some type of amortized analysis or actual experiments that compute the execution time.

6.3.2   POINT TO RECTANGLE

Calculating the distance between a point and a rectangle is less complicated than that between a point and a triangle. The fact that the polygon has all right angles greatly simplifies the problem. Within the coordinate system whose axes are aligned

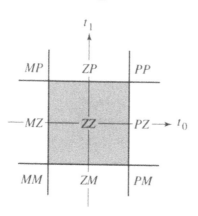

Figure 6.10   Partitioning of the plane by a rectangle.

with the rectangle sides, the problem decomposes into distance calculations in each dimension.

Let the test point be Y. The symmetric form for the rectangle is $X(t_0, t_1) = C + t_0 \hat{u}_0 + t_1 \hat{u}_1$ for $|t_0| \le e_0$ and $|t_1| \le e_1$. The vectors $\hat{u}_i$ are unit length, and C is the center of the rectangle. This form is used to avoid any divisions at all. The test point can be transformed to $Y = C + s_0 \hat{u}_0 + s_1 \hat{u}_1$. Setting $\vec{\Delta} = Y - C$, we have $s_0 = \hat{u}_0 \cdot \vec{\Delta}$ and $s_1 = \hat{u}_1 \cdot \vec{\Delta}$. The closest point on the rectangle to Y depends on which of the nine regions contains (s_0, s_1) in the (t_0, t_1) parameter plane. Figure 6.10 illustrates these regions. If (s_0, s_1) is in region ZZ, then Y is inside the rectangle and the distance is zero. If (s_0, s_1) is in one of regions PZ, ZP, MZ, or ZM, then the closest point is the projection onto the corresponding edge of the rectangle. Otherwise (s_0, s_1) is in one of regions PP, PM, MP, or MM. The closest point is the corresponding vertex of the rectangle.

The skeleton of the pseudocode could be set up to have nested conditional statements, each clause corresponding to one of the nine regions in the partition of the parameter plane. However, this is not necessary because of the orthogonality of the rectangle edges. The skeleton is set up to handle each dimension separately.

```
float SquaredDistance(Point Y, Rectangle R)
{
    Point Delta = Y - R.C;
    float s0 = Dot(R.U0, Delta), s1 = Dot(R.U1, Delta), sqrDist = 0;

    float s0pe0 = s0 + R.e0;
    if (s0pe0 < 0) {
        sqrDist += s0pe0 * s0pe0;
```

```
    } else {
        float s0me0 = s0 - R.e0;
        if (s0me0 > 0)
            sqrDist += s0me0 * s0me0;
    }

    float s1pe1 = s1 + R.e1;
    if (s1pe1 < 0) {
        sqrDist += s1pe1 * s1pe1;
    } else {
        float s1me1 = s1 - R.e1;
        if (s1me1 > 0)
            sqrDist += s1me1 * s1me1;
    }

    return sqrDist;
}
```

6.3.3 POINT TO ORTHOGONAL FRUSTUM

A *single cone* is defined as the set of points whose boundary consists of two rays with a common origin, called the *vertex of the cone*. Let the vertex be denoted V. Let the rays have unit-length directions $\hat{d}_0$ and $\hat{d}_1$. The *axis of the cone* is the bisector ray. Let $\hat{a}$ be the unit-length direction of the axis. The *angle of the cone* is the angle $\theta \in (0, \pi)$ between $\hat{a}$ and either ray direction vector. In this section we restrict our attention to cones for which $\theta < \pi/2$. Figure 6.11(a) shows a single cone.

If two parallel lines are specified that transversely intersect the cone, the convex quadrilateral that is bounded by the cone and the lines is called a *frustum* of the cone. Figure 6.11(b) shows such a frustum. If the lines are perpendicular to the cone axis, the frustum is said to be an *orthogonal frustum*. Figure 6.11(c) shows an orthogonal frustum.

A point X is inside a cone if the angle between $X - V$ and $\hat{a}$ is smaller than θ. We can write this constraint in terms of dot products as $\hat{a} \cdot (X - V) \geq \cos(\theta)$. A frustum has additional constraints. If the parallel line closest to the vertex contains the point P and has a unit-length normal $\hat{n}$ that points inside the frustum, the line equation is $\hat{n} \cdot (X - P) = 0$. The other line contains a point $P + s\hat{n}$ for some $s > 0$. The line equation is $\hat{n} \cdot (X - P) = s$. The extra constraints for X to be inside the frustum are $0 \leq \hat{n} \cdot (X - P) \leq s$. If the frustum is orthogonal, $\hat{n} = \hat{a}$.

An orthogonal frustum in two dimensions is the analog of the view frustum that is used in three dimensions when the camera model is based on perspective projection. In two dimensions, V plays the role of the eye point, the two parallel lines play the role of the near and far planes, and the two bounding rays play the role of the left and right extents of the view frustum. This section provides an algorithm for computing

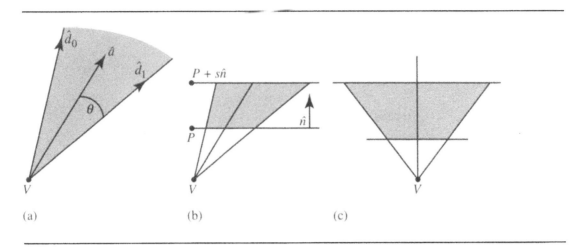

Figure 6.11   (a) An example of a single cone. (b) A frustum of a cone. (c) An orthogonal frustum.

the distance from a point to an orthogonal frustum. The idea is to motivate the same problem in three dimensions. A distance query for point to frustum is useful for visibility testing, in particular when the point represents the center of a bounding sphere for a drawable mesh. If the bounding sphere is outside the frustum, then the mesh is *culled*—it does not have to be sent to the renderer for drawing. The bounding sphere is outside whenever the distance from the sphere center to the frustum is larger than the sphere radius. Observe that in three dimensions, if the world is constructed on the xy-plane and if the camera movement is restricted to translation in the xy-plane and to rotation only about its up-vector, then visibility testing of a bounding sphere against the left or right frustum planes can be done in 2D by projection onto the xy-plane. The problem is reduced to testing if a circle is outside a 2D orthogonal frustum.

The algorithm for computing the distance from a point to an orthogonal frustum is based on determining the Voronoi regions for the edges and vertices of the frustum. The region containing the point is computed. The nearest point on the frustum in that region is also computed. From this the distance can be calculated. The concepts in 2D generalize in a straightforward manner to 3D and are discussed later in this book.

The orthogonal frustum has origin E, unit-length direction vector $\hat{d}$, and perpendicular unit-length vector $\hat{l}$. The near line has normal $\hat{d}$ and contains the point $E + n\hat{d}$ for some $n > 0$. The far line has normal $\hat{d}$ and contains the point $E + f\hat{d}$ for some $f > n$. The four vertices of the frustum are $E + n\hat{d} \pm \ell\hat{l}$ for some $\ell > 0$, and $E + (f/n)(n\hat{d} \pm \ell\hat{l})$. Let P be the point whose distance to the frustum is required. The point can be written in the frustum coordinate system as

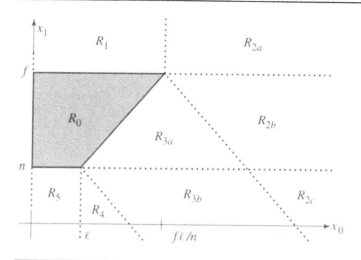

Figure 6.12 Portion of frustum in first quadrant.

$$P = E + x_0\hat{l} + x_1\hat{d}$$

so $x_0 = \hat{l} \cdot (P - E)$ and $x_1 = \hat{d} \cdot (P - E)$. It is sufficient to demonstrate the construction for $x_0 \geq 0$. For if $x_0 < 0$, a reflection can be made by changing the sign on x_0, the closest point can be calculated, then a reflection on that point yields the closest point to the original. Figure 6.12 shows the portion of the frustum in the first quadrant.

The Voronoi region boundaries are dotted. Region R_0 contains those points inside the frustum. Region R_1 contains those points closest to the top edge of the frustum. Region R_2 contains those points closest to the vertex $(f\ell/n,\, f)$ of the frustum. That region is split into three subregions based on $\hat{d}$ component being larger than f, between n and f, or smaller than n. Region R_3 contains those points closest to the slanted edge of the frustum. That region is split into two subregions based on $\hat{d}$ component being between n and f or smaller than n. Region R_4 contains those points closest to the vertex (ℓ, n) of the frustum. Finally, region R_5 contains those points closest to the bottom edge of the frustum.

The pseudocode for determining the Voronoi region for (x_0, x_1) is

```
if (x1 >= f) {
    if (x0 <= f * 1 / n)
        point in R1;
    else
        point in R2a;
} else if (x1 >= n) {
```

```
            t = Dot((n, -1), (x0, x1));
            if (t <= 0)
                point in R0;
            else {
                t = Dot((1, n), (x0, x1));
                if (t <= Dot((1, n), (f * 1 / n,f)))
                    point in R3a;
                else
                    point in R2b;
            }
        } else {
            if (x0 <= 1 )
                point in R5;
            else  {
                t = Dot((1, n), (x0, x1));
                if (t <= Dot((1, n), (1, n)))
                    point in R4;
                else if (t <= Dot((1, n), (f * 1 / n, f)))
                    point in R3b;
                else
                    point in R2c;
            }
        }
    }
```

The closest point to (x_0, x_1) in R_1 is (x_0, f). The closest point in R_2 is $(f\ell/n, f)$. The closest point in R_4 is (ℓ, n). The closest point in R_5 is (x_0, n). Region R_3 requires projecting out the $(n, -\ell)$ component from (x_0, x_1). The closest point is $(x_0, x_1) - [(nx_0 - \ell x_1)/(\ell^2 + n^2)](n, -\ell)$.

6.3.4 POINT TO CONVEX POLYGON

In the special case of a convex polygon, not all point-to-segment tests need to be made while searching for the minimum distance between the point and edges of the polygon. Only those edges that are visible to the point X must be considered. Figure 6.13 illustrates the idea.

Assuming that each edge $\langle P_i, P_{i+1} \rangle$ has an associated normal vector $\vec{n}_i$ that points to the interior of the polygon, an edge is visible only if $\vec{n}_i \cdot (X - P_i) \geq 0$. By testing this dot product first, and if negative, the potential division that occurs in the point-to-segment distance calculation is avoided. Moreover, a further reduction in calculations is attained by checking if the next point-to-segment distance is larger than the current one. If the distance to the current edge is smaller or equal to the distance from the two neighboring edges, then the current distance is the minimum distance to the polygon boundary.

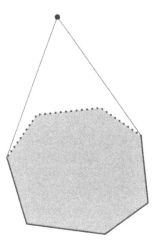

Figure 6.13   Only those edges visible to the test point must be searched for the closest point to
the test point. The three visible edges are dotted. The invisible edges are drawn in
black. The visible edges are in a cone with vertex at the test point and whose sides are
tangent to the convex polygon.

Finally, given a point and a convex polygon, the GJK algorithm described in
Section 6.10 provides a viable alternative to a boundary search algorithm that looks
for a closest feature. The method extends to higher dimensions and to arbitrary
convex objects, not necessarily polygons or polyhedra.

6.4 POINT TO QUADRATIC CURVE

The general quadratic equation is

$$Q(X) = X^{\mathrm{T}}\mathbf{A}X + B^{\mathrm{T}}X + c = 0$$

where $\mathbf{A}$ is a symmetric 2×2 matrix, but not necessarily invertible, B is a 2×1 vector,
and c is a scalar. The parameter is X, a 2×1 vector. Given the curve $Q(X) = 0$ and
a point Y, we need an algorithm for computing the closest point on the curve to Y.
Geometrically, the closest point X must satisfy the condition that $Y - X$ is normal
to the curve. Figure 6.14 illustrates this. Since the gradient $\vec{\nabla}Q(X)$ is normal to the
curve, $Y - X$ and $\vec{\nabla}Q(X)$ must be parallel and the algebraic condition for the closest
point is therefore

$$Y - X = t\vec{\nabla}Q(X) = t(2\mathbf{A}X + B)$$

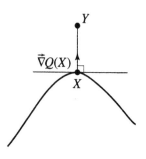

Figure 6.14   Closest point on a quadratic curve to a given point.

for some scalar t. Therefore,

$$X = (\mathbf{I} + 2t\mathbf{A})^{-1}(Y - tB)$$

where $\mathbf{I}$ is the identity matrix. This equation for X can be replaced into the general quadratic equation to obtain a polynomial in t of at most fourth degree.

Instead of immediately replacing X in the quadratic equation, we can reduce the problem to something simpler to implement. Factor $\mathbf{A}$ using an eigendecomposition to obtain $\mathbf{A} = \mathbf{RDR}^T$, where $\mathbf{R}$ is an orthonormal matrix whose columns are eigenvectors of $\mathbf{A}$ and where $\mathbf{D} = \text{Diag}\{d_0, d_1\}$ is a diagonal matrix whose diagonal entries are the eigenvalues of $\mathbf{A}$ (see Section A.3). Then

$$
\begin{aligned}
X &= (\mathbf{I} + 2t A)^{-1}(Y - tB) \\
&= (\mathbf{RR}^T + 2t\mathbf{RDR}^T)^{-1}(Y - tB) \\
&= [\mathbf{R}(\mathbf{I} + 2t D)\mathbf{R}^T]^{-1}(Y - tB) \\
&= \mathbf{R}(\mathbf{I} + 2t D)^{-1}\mathbf{R}^T(Y - tB) \\
&= \mathbf{R}(\mathbf{I} + 2t D)^{-1}(\vec{\alpha} - t\vec{\beta})
\end{aligned}
$$

where $\vec{\alpha} = (\alpha_0, \alpha_1) = \mathbf{R}^T Y$ and $\vec{\beta} = (\beta_0, \beta_1) = \mathbf{R}^T B$. Replacing X in the quadratic equation and simplifying yields

$$0 = (\vec{\alpha} - t\vec{\beta})^T (\mathbf{I} + 2t D)^{-1} \mathbf{D}(\mathbf{I} + 2t D)^{-1}(\vec{\alpha} - t\vec{\beta}) + \vec{\beta}^T(\mathbf{I} + 2t D)^{-1}(\vec{\alpha} - t\vec{\beta}) + c$$

The inverse diagonal matrix is $(\mathbf{I} + 2t D)^{-1} = \text{Diag}\{1/(1 + 2td_0), 1/(1 + 2td_1)\}$. Multiplying through by $((1 + 2td_0)(1 + 2td_1))^2$ leads to a polynomial of at most fourth degree, $p(t) = p_0 + p_1 t + p_2 t^2 + p_3 t^3 + p_4 t^4$, with

$$p_0 = c + \alpha_0 \beta_0 + \alpha_1 \beta_1 + \alpha_0^2 d_0 + \alpha_1^2 d_1$$

$$p_1 = 4[c(d_0 + d_1) + \alpha_0 d_1(\beta_0 + \alpha_0 d_0) + \alpha_1 d_0(\beta_1 + \alpha_1 d_1)] - (\beta_0^2 + \beta_1^2)$$

$$p_2 = 4[c((d_0 + d_1)^2 + 2 d_0 d_1) + \alpha_0 d_1^2(\beta_0 + \alpha_0 d_0) + \alpha_1 d_0^2(\beta_1 + \alpha_1 d_1)]$$
$$- \beta_0^2(4d_1 + d_0) - \beta_1^2(4d_0 + d_1)$$

$$p_3 = 4(d_0 + d_1)[4c d_0 d_1 - (\beta_1^2 d_0 + \beta_0^2 d_1)]$$

$$p_4 = 4 d_0 d_1 [4 c d_0 d_1 - (\beta_1^2 d_0 + \beta_0^2 d_1)]$$

The roots of $p(t)$ are computed and $X = (I + 2t A)^{-1}(Y - t B)$ is computed for each root t. The minimum squared distance is selected from the set of values $\|X(t) - Y\|^2$ for all roots t.

Numerical concerns are warranted with this algorithm. If the curve is a parabola, then $d_0 d_1 = 0$, in which case $p_4 = 0$. If $d_0 d_1$ is nearly zero, then the curve is not a parabola, but p_4 is nearly zero itself. A numerical polynomial root finder must be robust enough to handle such a situation. If the curve is a circle and Y is the center of the circle, then all points on the circle attain minimum distance to Y. The coefficients of the polynomial are identically zero. If the curve is an ellipse that is nearly circular in shape, then the leading coefficient of the polynomial could be sufficiently close to zero to cause problems with a root finder.

6.5 POINT TO POLYNOMIAL CURVE

We consider the case of a curve $X(t) = \sum_{i=0}^{n} \vec{A}_i t^i$, where $\vec{A}_n \neq \vec{0}$. Let Y be the test point. Just as in the case of quadratic curves, the closest point $X(t)$ must satisfy the condition that $Y - X(t)$ is normal to the curve, but only when t is an interior point of the domain of the function. It is possible that the closest point is an end point of the curve; distance to end points can be computed separately. Equivalently for the closest interior point, $Y - X(t)$ must be perpendicular to the curve tangent $\vec{X}'(t)$. Figure 6.15 illustrates this. The interior point condition and end point testing follow from a direct application of calculus to minimizing the squared-distance function $F(t) = \|X(t) - Y\|^2$ for $t \in I$, where I is the domain interval for the curve. The global minimum of F must occur either where $F'(t) = 0$ or at an end point of I (if any exist). Since $F(t) = (X(t) - Y) \cdot (X(t) - Y)$, half the derivative is $F'(t)/2 = (X(t) - Y) \cdot \vec{X}'(t)$. The right-hand side is the dot product of two vector-valued polynomials. The result is a scalar-valued polynomial of degree $2n - 1$. The problem of computing the minimum distance is reduced to finding the roots of a polynomial.

Specifically, define $\vec{B}_0 = \vec{A}_0 - Y$ and $\vec{B}_i = \vec{A}_i$ for $i \geq 1$. The derivative of the curve function is $\vec{X}'(t) = \sum_{j=0}^{n-1} (j + 1) \vec{B}_{j+1} t^j$. Define $\vec{C}_{i,j} = (j + 1) \vec{B}_i \cdot \vec{B}_{j+1}$ for the appropriate values of i and j; then

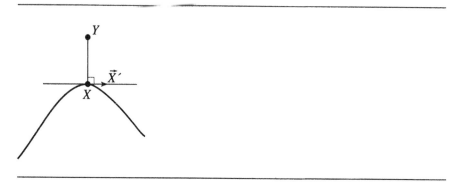

Figure 6.15 Closest point on a polynomial curve to a given point.

$$F'(t)/2 = (X(t) - Y) \cdot \vec{X}'(t)$$

$$= \sum_{i=0}^{n} \sum_{j=0}^{n-1} (j+1)\vec{B}_i \cdot \vec{B}_{j+1} t^{i+j}$$

$$= \sum_{k=0}^{2n-1} \sum_{m=\max\{0,k-n\}}^{k} C_{k-m,m} t^k \qquad (6.8)$$

$$= \sum_{k=0}^{2n-1} D_k t^k$$

where the last equality defines the D_k terms. The candidates for minimum distance are those t such that $F'(t) = 0$, or equivalently, those t that are solutions to $\sum_{k=0}^{2n-1} D_k t^k = 0$.

For large degrees, numerical polynomial root finders can be ill conditioned. An alternative to solving the problem uses a numerical minimizer for $F(t)$. The minimizer can use derivative information since $\vec{X}'(t)$ is readily computed (for example, Brent's method, discussed in Section A.6) or can use just $X(t)$ itself (for example, Powell's direction set method, also discussed in Section A.6).

Another alternative is to subdivide the curve to approximate it by a polyline (see Section A.8), then compute the distance from Y to the polyline as an attempt to approximate the distance or to localize the search for the closest point. In the latter case, the numerical minimizer may be applied on the curve parameter intervals corresponding to the line segments that yielded the smallest distances among all line segments.

After subdivision, the squared distances are calculated between Y and the polyline of the subdivision. On a final subinterval $[t_0, t_1]$ in the subdivision, the derivative of the squared-distance polynomial $P(t)$ in Equation 6.8 can be tested for roots on

$[t_0, t_1]$ (see the subsection in Section A.5 on Sturm sequences for polynomials). If there are no roots, then $P(t)$ is monotonic on the interval, and the minimum and maximum distances occur at t_0 and t_1. If the subinterval is an interior one, then the minimum distance is not attained on the subinterval. If t_0 or t_1 are end points of the original parameter interval, then the squared distances at those points must be compared to any interior local minima that are calculated. If $P'(t)$ has one root on the subinterval, then a robust method such as bisection can be applied to locate the root. If $P'(t)$ has multiple roots on the subinterval, further subdivision should be applied to obtain only intervals that have at most one root.

6.6 LINEAR COMPONENTS

This section covers the distance algorithms for the six combinations of lines, rays, or line segments: line-line, line-ray, line-segment, ray-ray, ray-segment, and segment-segment.

6.6.1 LINE TO LINE

Let the lines be represented by normal forms $\vec{n}_i \cdot X = c_i$ for $i = 0, 1$. If the two lines intersect, the distance is zero. Otherwise the lines are parallel, and the distance between the lines is positive if the lines are disjoint or zero if the lines are the same. Figure 6.16 illustrates the possibilities. In the case of parallel lines, the distance is attained at a point P_0 on the first line and a point $P_1 = P_0 + t\vec{n}_0$ on the second line. The distance itself is $\|t\vec{n}_0\|$. The value of t is determined by $c_1 = \vec{n}_1 \cdot P_1 = \vec{n}_1 \cdot P_0 + t\vec{n}_1 \cdot \vec{n}_0$, in which case $t = (c_1 - \vec{n}_1 \cdot P_0)/(\vec{n}_1 \cdot \vec{n}_0)$. A point on the first line is $P_0 = c_0\vec{n}_0/\|\vec{n}_0\|^2$. Replacing this in the equation for t, substituting that into $\|t\vec{n}_0\|$, and rearranging some terms leads to the distance formula

$$\text{Distance}\,(\mathcal{L}_0, \mathcal{L}_1) = \begin{cases} 0, & \vec{n}_0 \cdot \vec{n}_1^\perp \neq 0 \\ \frac{|(\vec{n}_0 \cdot \vec{n}_0)c_1 - (\vec{n}_0 \cdot \vec{n}_1)c_0|}{\|\vec{n}_0\||\vec{n}_0 \cdot \vec{n}_1|}, & \vec{n}_0 \cdot \vec{n}_1^\perp = 0 \end{cases} \quad (6.9)$$

If $\|\vec{n}_0\| = \|\vec{n}_1\|$, the second portion of the distance formula reduces to $|c_1 - \sigma c_0|/\|\vec{n}_0\|$, where $\sigma = \text{Sign}(\vec{n}_0 \cdot \vec{n}_1)$. The division is avoided if additionally $\|\vec{n}_0\| = 1$.

The equivalent formula for the parametric representations $P_i + t_i\vec{d}_i$, $i = 0, 1$, is

$$\text{Distance}\,(\mathcal{L}_0, \mathcal{L}_1) = \begin{cases} 0, & \vec{d}_0 \cdot \vec{d}_1^\perp \neq 0 \\ \frac{|\vec{d}_0^\perp \cdot \vec{\Delta}|}{\|\vec{d}_0\|}, & \vec{d}_0 \cdot \vec{d}_1^\perp = 0 \end{cases} \quad (6.10)$$

where $\vec{\Delta} = P_1 - P_0$. The second portion of the formula is the length of the projection of $\vec{\Delta}$ onto a normal line that is perpendicular to the two given lines.

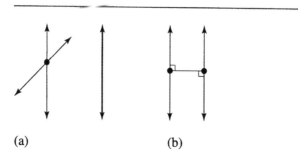

(a)   (b)

Figure 6.16   Various line-line configurations: (a) zero distance; (b) positive distance.

6.6.2   LINE TO RAY

The distance calculations are similar to the case for line versus line. The only difference is that if the line $\mathcal{L}$ and ray $\mathcal{R}$ are not parallel, the ray might not intersect the line. Figure 6.17 shows the possibilities. Let the normal representation for the line be $\vec{n}_0 \cdot X = c_0$. Let the ray be represented parametrically as $P_1 + t\vec{d}_1$ for $t \geq 0$. If P_1 is on the side of the line to which $\vec{n}_0$ points, then the line and ray intersect if the ray points toward the line, that is, if $\vec{n}_0 \cdot \vec{d}_1 < 0$. In this case the distance between the line and the ray is zero. Otherwise, the ray points away from the line and the distance is attained at P_1 on the ray and its projection onto the line; call this point P_0. Similarly, if P_1 is on the opposite side of the line to which $\vec{n}_0$ points, then the line and ray intersect if the ray points toward the line, that is, if $\vec{n}_0 \cdot \vec{d}_1 > 0$. Otherwise, the ray points away from the line, and the distance is attained at P_1 and its projection onto the line, P_0. In the nonintersection case, if $\vec{\Delta} = P_1 - P_0$, then the distance between the line and the ray is $|\vec{n}_0 \cdot \vec{\Delta}|/\|\vec{n}_0\| = |\vec{n}_0 \cdot P_1 - c_0|/\|\vec{n}_0\|$. Thus, it is not necessary to actually compute P_0 when computing the distance. The distance is summarized by

$$\text{Distance}\,(\mathcal{L}, \mathcal{R}) = \begin{cases} 0, & (\vec{n}_0 \cdot \vec{d}_1)(\vec{n}_0 \cdot P_1 - c_0) < 0 \\ \frac{|\vec{n}_0 \cdot P_1 - c_0|}{\|\vec{n}_0\|}, & (\vec{n}_0 \cdot \vec{d}_1)(\vec{n}_0 \cdot P_1 - c_0) \geq 0 \end{cases} \qquad (6.11)$$

The equivalent formula for the parametric line $P_0 + t_0\vec{d}_0$, $t_0 \in \mathbb{R}$, and the parametric ray $P_1 + t_1\vec{d}_1$, $t_1 \geq 0$, is

$$\text{Distance}\,(\mathcal{L}, \mathcal{R}) = \begin{cases} 0, & (\vec{d}_0^{\perp} \cdot \vec{d}_1)(\vec{d}_0^{\perp} \cdot \vec{\Delta}) < 0 \\ \frac{|\vec{d}_0^{\perp} \cdot \vec{\Delta}|}{\|\vec{d}_0\|}, & (\vec{d}_0^{\perp} \cdot \vec{d}_1)(\vec{d}_0^{\perp} \cdot \vec{\Delta}) \geq 0 \end{cases} \qquad (6.12)$$

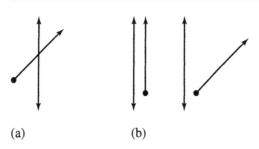

(a)   (b)

Figure 6.17   Various line-ray configurations: (a) zero distance; (b) positive distance.

where $\vec{\Delta} = P_1 - P_0$ and $(x, y)^{\perp} = (y, -x)$. The second portion of the formula is the length of the projection of $\vec{\Delta}$ onto a normal line that is perpendicular to the two given lines.

6.6.3 LINE TO SEGMENT

Given a line $\mathcal{L}$ represented by $\vec{n} \cdot X = c$ and a line segment S with end points Q_0 and Q_1, either they intersect, in which case the distance between them is zero, or they do not intersect, in which case the distance between them is attained by the closer of the two line segment end points. Figure 6.18 shows the possibilities. The distance is

$$\text{Distance}\,(\mathcal{L}, S) = \begin{cases} 0, & (\vec{n} \cdot Q_0 - c)(\vec{n} \cdot Q_1 - c) < 0 \\ \min\left(\frac{|\vec{n}\cdot Q_0 - c|}{\|\vec{n}\|}, \frac{|\vec{n}\cdot Q_1 - c|}{\|\vec{n}\|}\right), & (\vec{n} \cdot Q_0 - c)(\vec{n} \cdot Q_1 - c) \geq 0 \end{cases}$$

(6.13)

The equivalent formula for the parametric line $P_0 + t_0 \vec{d}_0$, $t_0 \in \mathbb{R}$, and the parametric segment $P_1 + t_1 \vec{d}_1$, $t_1 \in [0, T_1]$, is

$$\text{Distance}\,(\mathcal{L}, S) = \begin{cases} 0, & (\vec{d}_0^{\perp} \cdot \vec{\Delta})(\vec{d}_0^{\perp} \cdot (\vec{\Delta} + T_1 \vec{d}_1)) < 0 \\ \min\left(\frac{|\vec{d}_0^{\perp}\cdot \vec{\Delta}|}{\|\vec{d}_0\|}, \frac{|\vec{d}_0^{\perp}\cdot (\vec{\Delta}+T_1\vec{d}_1)|}{\|\vec{d}_0\|}\right), & (\vec{d}_0^{\perp} \cdot \vec{\Delta})(\vec{d}_0^{\perp} \cdot (\vec{\Delta} + T_1 \vec{d}_1)) \geq 0 \end{cases}$$

(6.14)

where $\vec{\Delta} = P_1 - P_0$.

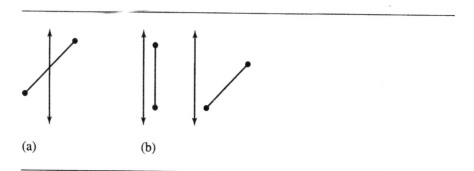

Figure 6.18 Various line-segment configurations: (a) zero distance; (b) positive distance.

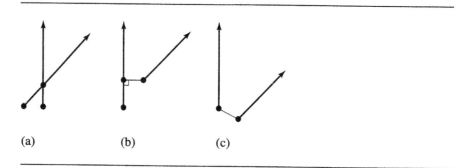

Figure 6.19 Various nonparallel ray-ray configurations: (a) zero distance; (b) positive distance from end point to interior point; (c) positive distance from end point to end point.

6.6.4 RAY TO RAY

Let the rays be $P_i + t_i \vec{d}_i$ for $i = 0, 1$ and for $t_i \geq 0$. If the rays intersect, the distance is zero. If the rays do not intersect, then the minimum distance is attained at either (1) an end point of one ray and an interior point of the other ray or (2) end points of both the rays. First consider the case when the rays are not parallel. Figure 6.19 illustrates the various possibilities. Figure 6.19(a) shows intersecting rays where zero distance is attained at an interior point on each ray. Figure 6.19(b) shows a positive distance that is attained at an end point of one ray and an interior point of the other ray. Figure 6.19(c) shows a positive distance that is attained at the end points on both rays.

Define $\vec{\Delta} = P_0 - P_1$. The squared distance between any points $P_0 + t_0 \vec{d}_0$ and $P_1 + t_1 \vec{d}_1$ is

$$F(t_0, t_1) = \|t_0 \vec{d}_0 - t_1 \vec{d}_1 + \vec{\Delta}\|^2 = a_{00}t_0^2 - 2a_{01}t_0t_1 + a_{11}t_1^2 + 2b_0t_0 - 2b_1t_1 + c \quad (6.15)$$

where $a_{ij} = \vec{d}_i \cdot \vec{d}_j$, $b_i = \vec{d}_i \cdot \vec{\Delta}$, and $c = \vec{\Delta} \cdot \vec{\Delta}$. F is a quadratic polynomial that is nonnegative. If the lines are not parallel, they must intersect at a point, and the squared distance between the two lines is zero since that point is common to both lines. That is, there are parameters $(\bar{t}_0, \bar{t}_1)$ for which $F(\bar{t}_0, \bar{t}_1) = 0$. Also observe that zero is the global minimum for F, so the gradient must be zero at the minimum:

$$(0, 0) = \vec{\nabla} F(\bar{t}_0, \bar{t}_1) = \left(2(\bar{t}_0 \vec{d}_0 - \bar{t}_1 \vec{d}_1 + \vec{\Delta}) \cdot \vec{d}_0, -2(\bar{t}_0 \vec{d}_0 - \bar{t}_1 \vec{d}_1 + \vec{\Delta}) \cdot \vec{d}_1 \right) \quad (6.16)$$

Although this is a linear system of two equations in two unknowns that can be solved by standard means, a less expensive solution may be calculated based on the following observation. Since the lines are not parallel, the vectors $\vec{d}_0$ and $\vec{d}_1$ are linearly independent. Equation 6.16 states that $\bar{t}_0 \vec{d}_0 - \bar{t}_1 \vec{d}_1 + \vec{\Delta}$ is a vector perpendicular to both $\vec{d}_0$ and $\vec{d}_1$. The only way a vector can be perpendicular to two linearly independent vectors in the plane is if that vector is the zero vector. Thus, $\bar{t}_0 \vec{d}_0 - \bar{t}_1 \vec{d}_1 + \vec{\Delta} = \vec{0}$. Dotting the equation with $\vec{d}_0^{\perp}$ and $\vec{d}_1^{\perp}$ leads to the solution

$$(\bar{t}_0, \bar{t}_1) = \frac{(\vec{d}_1^{\perp} \cdot \vec{\Delta}, \vec{d}_0^{\perp} \cdot \vec{\Delta})}{\vec{d}_1^{\perp} \cdot \vec{d}_0} \quad (6.17)$$

The level curves of F are ellipses with centers at $(\bar{t}_0, \bar{t}_1)$. If the lines are parallel, then F is constant for any t_0, so F is minimized along an entire line where $\partial F / \partial t_0 = 0$,

$$(\bar{t}_0, \bar{t}_1) = \left(\frac{a_{01}\bar{t}_1 - b_0}{a_{00}}, \bar{t}_1 \right) \quad (6.18)$$

The level curves of F are lines parallel to this line. The minimization of F on its domain $[0, \infty)^2$ is based on analyzing the relationship between the level curves of F and its domain.

First consider nonparallel rays. If $\bar{t}_0 > 0$ and $\bar{t}_1 > 0$, then the two rays intersect at interior points. If $\bar{t}_0 > 0$ and $\bar{t}_1 \leq 0$, then the minimum of F must occur at $(\max\{\hat{t}_0, 0\}, 0)$, where $\partial F(\hat{t}_0, 0) / \partial t_0 = 2(a_{00}\hat{t}_0 + b_0) = 0$. This is clear by considering the level curve of F that just touches the t_0-axis. Figure 6.20 illustrates this. Note that $\hat{t}_0 = -b_0/a_{00}$ and $F(\hat{t}_0, 0) = c - b_0^2/a_{00} = (\vec{d}_0^{\perp} \cdot \vec{\Delta})^2 / \|\vec{d}_0\|^2$. Similarly, if $\bar{t}_0 \leq 0$ and $\bar{t}_1 > 0$, then the minimum of F must occur at $(0, \max\{\hat{t}_1, 0\})$, where $\partial F(0, \hat{t}_1) / \partial t_1 = 2(a_{11}\hat{t}_1 - b_1) = 0$. Note that $\hat{t}_1 = b_1/a_{11}$ and $F(0, \hat{t}_1) = c - b_1^2/a_{00} = (\vec{d}_1^{\perp} \cdot \vec{\Delta}) / \|\vec{d}_1\|^2$. If $\bar{t}_0 \leq 0$ and $\bar{t}_1 \leq 0$, the minimum of F can occur on either boundary of the parameter domain, depending on how the level curves of F are located relative to the boundary. However, it is not possible for $\partial F(\hat{t}_0, 0) / \partial t_0 = 0$ and $\partial F(0, \hat{t}_1) / \partial t_1 = 0$ in this situation, so it is enough to check each location separately. The distance formula is given

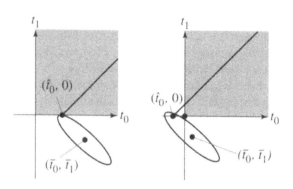

Figure 6.20 Relationship of level curves of F to boundary minimum at $(\hat{t}_0, 0)$ or $(0, 0)$.

below. It is assumed that the last term is used for the distance only if the Boolean expressions for the other terms have already been checked.

$$\text{Distance}\left(\mathcal{R}_0, \mathcal{R}_1\right) = \begin{cases} 0, & \bar{t}_0 > 0 \quad \text{and} \quad \bar{t}_1 > 0 \\ |\vec{d}_0^{\perp} \cdot \vec{\Delta}|/\|\vec{d}_0\|, & \hat{t}_0 > 0 \quad \text{and} \quad \bar{t}_1 \leq 0 \\ |\vec{d}_1^{\perp} \cdot \vec{\Delta}|/\|\vec{d}_1\|, & \hat{t}_1 > 0 \quad \text{and} \quad \bar{t}_0 \leq 0 \\ \|\vec{\Delta}\|, & \text{otherwise} \end{cases} \quad (6.19)$$

Now consider the case when the rays are parallel. Figure 6.21 shows the various configurations. Figure 6.21(a) shows rays pointing in the same direction. The minimum distance is attained at an end point of one ray and an interior point of the other ray. Figure 6.21(b) shows rays pointing in opposite directions with one ray overlapping the other (if projected onto each other). Again, the minimum distance is attained at an end point of one ray and an interior point of the other ray. Figure 6.21(c) shows rays pointing in opposite directions, but with no projected overlap. The minimum distance is attained at the end points of the rays. The distance is

$$\text{Distance}\left(\mathcal{R}_0, \mathcal{R}_1\right) = \begin{cases} \|\vec{\Delta}\|, & \vec{d}_0 \cdot \vec{d}_1 < 0 \quad \text{and} \quad \vec{d}_0 \cdot \vec{\Delta} \geq 0 \\ |\vec{d}_0^{\perp} \cdot \vec{\Delta}|/\|\vec{d}_0\|, & \text{otherwise} \end{cases} \quad (6.20)$$

6.6.5 RAY TO SEGMENT

Let the ray be $P_0 + t_0 \vec{d}_0$ for $t_0 \geq 0$, and let the segment be $P_1 + t_1 \vec{d}_1$ for $t_1 \in [0, T_1]$. The construction is similar to that for two rays where we analyzed how the level curves of F on all of $\mathbb{R}^2$ interact with its domain for the specific problem. The boundary

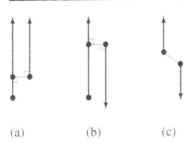

(a)   (b)   (c)

Figure 6.21   Various parallel ray-ray configurations: (a) rays pointing in the same direction; (b) rays pointing in opposite directions with overlap; (c) rays pointing in opposite directions with no overlap.

points of interest for two rays were $(\hat{t}_0, 0)$ and $(0, \hat{t}_1)$, points for which a partial derivative of F is zero. For the ray-segment problem, an additional point to consider is $(\tilde{t}_0, T_1)$, where $\partial F(\tilde{t}_0, T_1)/\partial t_0 = 0$. The solution is $\tilde{t}_0 = (a_{01} T_1 - b_0)/a_{00}$. Observe that $F(\tilde{t}_0, T_1) = a_{11} T_1^2 - 2b_1 T_1 + c - (a_{01} T_1 - b_0)^2/a_{00} = (\vec{d}_0^{\perp} \cdot (\vec{\Delta} - T_1\vec{d}_1))^2/\|\vec{d}_0\|^2$. The last equality just states that we are computing the squared distance between the ray and the line segment end point $P_1 + T_1\vec{d}_1$.

For the nonparallel case, if $(\bar{t}_0, \bar{t}_1) \in (0, \infty) \times (0, T_1)$, then the ray and segment intersect at interior points. Otherwise, it must be determined where the elliptical level curves centered at $(\bar{t}_0, \bar{t}_1)$ first meet the boundary of the domain. The distance formula is given below. It is assumed that the last two terms are used for the distance only if the Boolean expressions for the other terms have already been checked.

$$\text{Distance}\,(\mathcal{R}, \mathcal{S}) = \begin{cases} 0, & \bar{t}_0 > 0 \quad \text{and} \quad \bar{t}_1 \in (0, T_1) \\ |\vec{d}_0^{\perp} \cdot \vec{\Delta}|/\|\vec{d}_0\|, & \hat{t}_0 > 0 \quad \text{and} \quad \bar{t}_1 \leq 0 \\ |\vec{d}_0^{\perp} \cdot (\vec{\Delta} - T_1\vec{d}_1)|/\|\vec{d}_0\|, & \bar{t}_0 > 0 \quad \text{and} \quad \bar{t}_1 \geq T_1 \\ |\vec{d}_1^{\perp} \cdot \vec{\Delta}|/\|\vec{d}_1\|, & \hat{t}_1 \in (0, T_1) \quad \text{and} \quad \bar{t}_0 \leq 0 \\ \|\vec{\Delta}\|, & \hat{t}_0 \leq 0 \quad \text{and} \quad \hat{t}_1 \leq 0 \\ \|\vec{\Delta} - T_1\vec{d}_1\|, & \hat{t}_0 \leq 0 \quad \text{and} \quad \hat{t}_1 \geq T_1 \end{cases} \tag{6.21}$$

The first equation occurs when the ray intersects the line segment so that the distance is zero. The second equation occurs when the line segment end point P_1 and an interior ray point are closest. The third equation occurs when the line segment end point $P_1 + T_1\vec{d}_1$ and an interior ray point are closest. The fourth equation occurs when the ray origin P_0 and an interior line segment point are closest. The fifth equation occurs when the ray origin P_0 and the line segment end point P_1 are closest. The sixth equation occurs when the ray origin P_0 and the line segment end point $P_1 + T_1\vec{d}_1$ are closest.

For the parallel case the distance is

$$\text{Distance}\,(\mathcal{R}, S) = \begin{cases} \|\vec{\Delta}\|, & \vec{d}_0 \cdot \vec{d}_1 < 0 \quad \text{and} \quad \vec{d}_0 \cdot \vec{\Delta} \geq 0 \\ \|\vec{\Delta} - T_1\vec{d}_1\|, & \vec{d}_0 \cdot \vec{d}_1 > 0 \quad \text{and} \quad \vec{d}_0 \cdot (\vec{\Delta} - T_1\vec{d}_1) \geq 0 \\ |\vec{d}_0^{\perp} \cdot \vec{\Delta}|/\|\vec{d}_0\|, & \text{otherwise} \end{cases}$$

$$(6.22)$$

The first equation occurs when the ray and line segment have opposite directions and the projection of the line segment onto the line of the ray is disjoint from the ray. The second equation occurs when the ray and line segment have the same directions and the projection of the line segment onto the line of the ray is disjoint from the ray. The third equation occurs when the projection of the line segment onto the line of the ray intersects the ray itself.

6.6.6 SEGMENT TO SEGMENT

Let the segments be $P_i + t_i\vec{d}_i$ for $t_i \in [0, T_i]$. The construction is similar to that for a ray and a segment. Yet one more boundary point of interest is $(T_0, \tilde{t}_1)$, where $\partial F/\partial t_1 = 0$. The solution is $\tilde{t}_1 = (a_{01}T_0 + b_1)/a_{11}$. Observe that $F(T_0, \tilde{t}_1) = a_{00}T_0^2 + 2b_0T_0 + c - (a_{01}T_0 + b_1)^2/a_{11} = (\vec{d}_1^{\perp} \cdot (\vec{\Delta} + T_0\vec{d}_0))^2/\|\vec{d}_1\|^2$.

For the nonparallel case, if $(\bar{t}_0, \bar{t}_1) \in (0, T_0) \times (0, T_1)$, then the segments intersect at interior points. Otherwise, it must be determined where the elliptical level curves centered at $(\bar{t}_0, \bar{t}_1)$ first meet the boundary of the domain. The distance formula is given below. It is assumed that the last four terms are used for the distance only if the Boolean expressions for the other terms have already been checked.

$$\text{Distance}\,(S_0, S_1) = \begin{cases} 0, & \bar{t}_0 \in (0, T_0) \quad \text{and} \quad \bar{t}_1 \in (0, T_1) \\ |\vec{d}_0^{\perp} \cdot \vec{\Delta}|/\|\vec{d}_0\|, & \hat{t}_0 \in (0, T_0) \quad \text{and} \quad \bar{t}_1 \leq 0 \\ |\vec{d}_0^{\perp} \cdot (\vec{\Delta} - T_1\vec{d}_1)|/\|\vec{d}_0\|, & \hat{t}_0 \in (0, T_0) \quad \text{and} \quad \bar{t}_1 \geq T_1 \\ |\vec{d}_1^{\perp} \cdot \vec{\Delta}|/\|\vec{d}_1\|, & \hat{t}_1 \in (0, T_1) \quad \text{and} \quad \bar{t}_0 \leq 0 \\ |\vec{d}_1^{\perp} \cdot (\vec{\Delta} + T_0\vec{d}_0)|/\|\vec{d}_1\|, & \hat{t}_1 \in (0, T_1) \quad \text{and} \quad \bar{t}_0 \geq T_0 \\ \|\vec{\Delta}\|, & \hat{t}_0 \leq 0 \quad \text{and} \quad \hat{t}_1 \leq 0 \\ \|\vec{\Delta} + T_0\vec{d}_0\|, & \hat{t}_0 \geq T_0 \quad \text{and} \quad \hat{t}_1 \leq 0 \\ \|\vec{\Delta} - T_1\vec{d}_1\|, & \hat{t}_0 \leq 0 \quad \text{and} \quad \hat{t}_1 \geq T_1 \\ \|\vec{\Delta} + T_0\vec{d}_0 - T_1\vec{d}_1\|, & \hat{t}_0 \geq T_0 \quad \text{and} \quad \hat{t}_1 \geq T_1 \end{cases}$$

$$(6.23)$$

The first equation occurs when the line segments intersect and the distance is zero. The second equation occurs when an interior point of the first segment and the end point P_1 of the second segment are closest. The third equation occurs when an interior point of the first segment and the end point $P_1 + T_1\vec{d}_1$ of the second segment are closest. The fourth equation occurs when an interior point of the second segment and the end point P_0 of the first segment are closest. The fifth equation occurs when an interior point of the second segment and the end point $P_0 + T_0\vec{d}_0$ of the first segment are closest. The sixth equation occurs when the two end points P_0 and P_1 are closest. The seventh equation occurs when the two end points $P_0 + T_0\vec{d}_0$ and P_1 are closest. The eighth equation occurs when the two end points P_0 and $P_1 + T_1\vec{d}_1$ are closest. The ninth equation occurs when the two end points $P_0 + T_0\vec{d}_0$ and $P_1 + T_1\vec{d}_1$ are closest.

For the parallel case the distance is

$$
\text{Distance}\,(S_0, S_1) =
\begin{cases}
\|\vec{\Delta}\|, & \vec{d}_0 \cdot \vec{d}_1 < 0 \quad \text{and} \quad \vec{d}_0 \cdot \vec{\Delta} \geq 0 \\
\|\vec{\Delta} + T_0\vec{d}_0\|, & \vec{d}_0 \cdot \vec{d}_1 > 0 \quad \text{and} \quad \vec{d}_0 \cdot (\vec{\Delta} + T_0\vec{d}_0) \geq 0 \\
\|\vec{\Delta} - T_1\vec{d}_1\|, & \vec{d}_0 \cdot \vec{d}_1 > 0 \quad \text{and} \quad \vec{d}_0 \cdot (\vec{\Delta} - T_1\vec{d}_1) \geq 0 \\
\|\vec{\Delta} + T_0\vec{d}_0 - T_1\vec{d}_1\|, & \vec{d}_0 \cdot \vec{d}_1 < 0 \quad \text{and} \quad \vec{d}_0 \cdot (\vec{\Delta} + T_0\vec{d}_0 - T_1\vec{d}_1) \geq 0 \\
|\vec{d}_0^{\perp} \cdot \vec{\Delta}| / \|\vec{d}_0\|, & \text{otherwise}
\end{cases}
$$

$$(6.24)$$

The first four equations occur in the same manner as the last four equations of Equation 6.23 based on which pair of end points are closest. The fifth equation occurs when the projection of one segment onto the line of the other segment intersects that segment.

6.7 LINEAR COMPONENT TO POLYLINE OR POLYGON

The distance between a line and polygonal objects or polylines can be handled with the same algorithm. If the line does not intersect the object, the distance between them is positive and must be attained by a vertex of the object. It is enough to analyze the distances from the vertices to the line. Let the vertices be P_i for $0 \leq i < n$. Let the line be represented by $\hat{n} \cdot X = c$ for unit length $\hat{n}$. If all $\hat{n} \cdot P_i - c > 0$ or if all $\hat{n} \cdot P_i - c < 0$, the object lies completely on one side of the line, in which case the distance is $\min_i |\hat{n} \cdot P_i - c|$. Otherwise there must be two consecutive points, P_i and P_{i+1}, for which $(\hat{n} \cdot P_i - c)(\hat{n} \cdot P_{i+1} - c) \leq 0$ and the object intersects the line. In this case the distance between the line and the object is zero.

Given an open polyline or a closed polyline that is not assumed to be the boundary for a region, the distance between a ray or segment and the polyline can be calculated in the standard exhaustive manner by computing the distance between the ray or segment and each segment of the polyline, then selecting the minimum from that set of numbers.

The distance between a ray and a solid polygon can also be computed with the exhaustive algorithm where the distance between the ray and each edge of the polygon is computed and the minimum distance is selected. A slight modification allows a

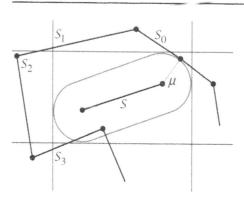

Figure 6.22   The configuration for the segment S attaining current minimum distance μ that is the analogy of Figure 6.4 for the point Y attaining current minimum distance.

potential early exit from the algorithm. A point-in-polygon test (see Section 13.3) can be applied to the ray origin. If that point is inside the polygon, then the distance between the ray and the solid polygon is zero. If the point is outside, then we resort to the exhaustive comparisons.

The exhaustive comparisons are not sufficient for computing the distance between a line segment and a solid polygon. The problem occurs when the line segment is fully inside the polygon. The distance from the segment to any polygon edge is positive, but the distance between the segment and the solid polygon is zero since the segment is contained by the polygon. However, we can apply point-in-polygon tests to the end points of the segment. If either point is inside, the distance is zero. If both points are outside, then the exhaustive comparisons are done.

Inexpensive rejection tests similar to those for point-to-polyline distance are possible for rejection of polyline edges during a segment-to-polyline distance calculation, but slightly more complicated. The point-to-polyline rejections were based on culling of segments outside infinite axis-aligned strips containing a circle centered at the test point or outside an axis-aligned rectangle containing the circle. The test object in the current discussion is a line segment S, not a point. If μ is the current minimum distance from S to the already processed polyline segments, then another polyline segment cannot cause μ to be updated if it is outside the *capsule* of radius μ that is generated by S. Just as the circle was the set of points of distance μ from the test point Y, the capsule is the set of points of distance μ from the test segment S. This object is a rectangle with hemicircular caps. Figure 6.22 shows the configuration for S that is the analogy of Figure 6.4 for Y. Infinite axis-aligned strips or an axis-aligned bounding rectangle can be constructed and used for culling purposes, just as in the case of point-to-polyline distance calculation.

6.8 LINEAR COMPONENT TO QUADRATIC CURVE

First consider the case of computing distance between a line and a quadratic curve. If the line intersects the quadratic curve, then the distance between the two is zero. The intersection can be tested using the parametric form for the line, $X(t) = P + t\vec{d}$. The quadratic curve is implicitly defined by $Q(X) = X^{\mathrm{T}} A X + B^{\mathrm{T}} X + c = 0$. Replacing the line equation into the quadratic equation produces the polynomial equation

$$(\vec{d}^{\mathrm{T}} A \vec{d}) t^2 + \vec{d}^{\mathrm{T}} (2 A P + B) t + (P^{\mathrm{T}} A P + B^{\mathrm{T}} P + C) = e_2 t^2 + e_1 t + e_0 = 0$$

This equation has real-valued solutions whenever $e_1^2 - 4 e_0 e_2 \geq 0$, in which case the distance between the line and the curve is zero.

If the equation has only complex-valued solutions, then the line and curve do not intersect and the distance between them is positive. In this case we use the line equation $\hat{n} \cdot X = c$, $\|\hat{n}\| = 1$, for the analysis. The squared distance between any point X and the line is $F(X) = (\hat{n} \cdot X - c)^2$. The problem is to find a point X on the quadratic curve that minimizes $F(X)$. This is a constrained minimization problem that is solved using the method of Lagrange multipliers (see Section A.9.3). Define

$$G(X, s) = (\hat{n} \cdot X - c)^2 + s Q(X)$$

The minimum of G occurs when $\vec{\nabla} G = \vec{0}$ and $\partial G / \partial s = 0$. The first equation is $2 (\hat{n} \cdot X - c) \hat{n} + s \vec{\nabla} Q = \vec{0}$, and the second equation just reproduces the constraint $Q = 0$. Dotting the first equation with $\vec{d} = \hat{n}^{\perp}$ yields the condition

$$L(X) := \vec{d} \cdot \vec{\nabla} Q(X) = \vec{d} \cdot (2 A \vec{X} + B) = 0$$

a linear equation in X. Geometrically, the condition $\vec{d} \cdot \vec{\nabla} Q = 0$ means that when the minimum distance is positive, the line segment connecting the two closest points must be perpendicular to both the line and the quadratic curve. Figure 6.23 illustrates this.

All that remains is to solve the two polynomial equations $L(X) = 0$ and $Q(X) = 0$ for X. The linear equation is degenerate when $A \vec{d} = \vec{0}$. This happens in particular when the quadratic equation only represents a line or point. It can also happen, though, when the quadratic is a parabola or hyperbola. For example, this happens for the parabola defined by $y = x^2$ and the line $x = 0$, but the intersection test between line and quadratic would have already ruled out this possibility. It is possible that the line defined by the degenerate quadratic equation and the test line are disjoint and parallel. In this case $\vec{d} \cdot B = 0$ in addition to $A \vec{d} = \vec{0}$ and $L(X) = 0$ is a tautology, so distance should be measured using the algorithm for two lines.

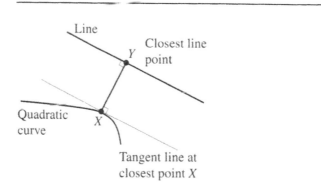

Figure 6.23   Segment connecting closest points is perpendicular to both objects.

When $A\vec{d} \neq \vec{0}$, the linear equation can be solved for one of its variables, and that variable substituted into the quadratic curve equation to obtain a quadratic polynomial of one variable. This equation is easily solved; see Section A.2. The resulting solution X is used to calculate the distance $|\hat{n} \cdot X - c|$.

An alternative approach to computing the distance between the line and the quadratic curve is to use a numerical minimizer. If the line is $X(t) = P + t\vec{d}$ for $t \in \mathbb{R}$ and the distance between a point X and the quadratic curve is $F(X)$, the distance between the line point $X(t)$ and the quadratic curve is $G(t) = F(P + t\vec{d})$. A numerical minimizer can be implemented that searches the t-domain $\mathbb{R}$ for those values of t that produce the minimum for $G(t)$. The trade-offs to be considered are twofold. The approach that sets up a system of polynomial equations has potential numerical problems if variables are eliminated to produce a single polynomial equation of large degree. Both the elimination process and the root finding are susceptible to numerical errors due to nearly zero coefficients. The approach that sets up a function to minimize might be more stable numerically, but convergence to a minimum is subject to the problem of slowness if an initial guess is not close to the minimum point, or the problem of the iterates trapped at a local minimum that is not a global minimum.

The previous discussion involved a line and a curve. If the linear component is a ray, a slight addition must be made to the algorithm. First, the distance is calculated between the line containing the ray and the curve. Suppose Y is the closest point on the line to the curve; then $Y = P + t\vec{d}$ for some t. If $t \geq 0$, then Y is on the ray itself, and the distance between the ray and the curve is the same as the distance between the line and the curve. However, if $t < 0$, then the closest point on the line is not on the ray. In this case the distance from the ray origin P to the curve must be calculated using the method shown in Section 6.4; call it Distance(P, C), where C denotes the curve. The distance from the ray to the curve is Distance(P, C).

If the linear component is a segment, the distance is first calculated between the line of the segment and the curve. If Y is the closest point on the line to the curve, then $Y = P + t\vec{d}$ for some t. If $t \in [0, 1]$, then Y is already on the segment, and the distance from the segment to the curve is Distance(Y, C). However, if $t < 0$, the distance between the segment and the curve is Distance(P, C). If $t > 1$, the distance between the segment and the curve is Distance($P + \vec{d}, C$).

6.9 LINEAR COMPONENT TO POLYNOMIAL CURVE

First consider the case of computing the distance between a line and a polynomial curve. Let the line be represented by $\hat{n} \cdot X = c$, where $\hat{n}$ is unit length. The distance between the line and the polynomial curve $X(t)$ for $t \in [t_0, t_1]$ occurs at a t for which the function $F(t) = (\hat{n} \cdot X(t) - c)^2$ is minimized. A numerical minimizer can be directly applied to $F(t)$, or a calculus approach can be used to compute the solutions to $F'(t) = 0$ as potential places where the minimum occurs. In the latter case, $F'(t) = 2(\hat{n} \cdot X(t) - c)(\hat{n} \cdot \vec{X}'(t))$, a polynomial of degree $2n - 1$, where the degree of $X(t)$ is n. A polynomial root finder can be applied to solve this equation. Localization of the roots can be accomplished using subdivision by variation, just as was done in computing the distance between a point and a polynomial curve.

If the linear component is a ray, a slight addition must be made to the algorithm. First, the distance is calculated between the line containing the ray and the curve. Suppose Y is the closest point on the line to the curve; then $Y = P + t\vec{d}$ for some t. If $t \geq 0$, then Y is on the ray itself, and the distance between the ray and the curve is the same as the distance between the line and the curve. However, if $t < 0$, then the closest point on the line is not on the ray. In this case the distance from the ray origin P to the curve must be calculated using the method shown in Section 6.5; call it Distance(P, C), where C denotes the curve. The distance between the ray and the curve is Distance(P, C).

If the linear component is a segment, the distance is first calculated between the line of the segment and the curve. If Y is the closest point on the line to the curve, then $Y = P + t\vec{d}$ for some t. If $t \in [0, 1]$, then Y is already on the segment, and the distance from the segment to the curve is Distance(Y, C). However, if $t < 0$, the distance between the segment and the curve is Distance(P, C). If $t > 1$, the distance between the segment and the curve is Distance($P + \vec{d}, C$).

6.10 GJK ALGORITHM

We now discuss an effective method for computing the distance between two convex polygons in 2D. The original idea was developed by E. G. Gilbert, D. W. Johnson, and S. S. Keerthi (1988) for convex polyhedra in 3D, but the ideas apply in any dimension to the generalization of convex polyhedra in that dimension. The algorithm has become known as the *GJK algorithm,* where the acronym is just the initial letters of the last names of the authors of the paper. The algorithm was later extended to handle convex objects in general (Gilbert and Foo 1990). An enhancement of the algorithm was also developed that computes penetration distances when the polyhedra are intersecting (Cameron 1997).

6.10.1 SET OPERATIONS

The *Minkowski sum* of two sets A and B is defined as the set of all sums of vector pairs, one from each set. Formally, the set is $A + B = \{X + Y : X \in A,\ Y \in B\}$. The *negation* of a set B is $-B = \{-X : X \in B\}$. The *Minkowski difference* of the sets is $A - B = \{X - Y : X \in A,\ Y \in B\}$. Observe that $A - B = A + (-B)$. If the sets A and B are both convex, then $A + B$, $-B$, and $A - B$ are all convex sets. If A is a convex polygon with n vertices and B is a convex polygon with m vertices, in the worst case the sum $A + B$ has $n + m$ vertices. Figure 6.24 illustrates where A is the triangle $\langle U_0, U_1, U_2 \rangle = \langle (0,0), (2,0), (0,2) \rangle$ and B is the triangle $\langle V_0, V_1, V_2 \rangle = \langle (2,2), (4,1), (3,4) \rangle$. The origin $(0,0)$ is marked as a black dot.

Figure 6.24(a) shows the original triangles. Figure 6.24(b) shows $-B$. Figure 6.24(c) shows $A + B$. To provide some geometric intuition on the sum, the figure shows three triangles, with black edges corresponding to triangle A translated by each of the three vertices of triangle B. Triangle B itself is shown with gray edges. Imagine painting the hexagon interior by the translated triangle A where you move $U_0 + V_0$ within triangle B. The same geometric intuition is illustrated in the drawing of $A - B$ (Figure 6.24(d)).

The distance between any two sets A and B is formally

$$\text{Distance}(A, B) = \min\{\|X - Y\| : X \in A,\ Y \in B\} = \min\{\|Z\| : Z \in A - B\}$$

The latter equation shows that the Minkowski difference can play an important role in distance calculations. The minimum distance is attained by a point in $A - B$ that is closest to the origin. Figure 6.24(d) illustrates this for two triangles. The closest point to the origin is the dark gray dot at the point $(-1, -1) \in A - B$. That point is generated by $(1, 1) \in A$ and $(2, 2) \in B$, so the distance between A and B is $\sqrt{2}$ and is attained by the aforementioned points.

The heart of the distance calculation is how to efficiently search $A - B$ for the closest point to the origin. A straightforward algorithm is to compute $A - B$ directly, then iterate over the edges and compute the distance from each edge to the origin. The minimum such distance is the distance between A and B. However, this approach is not efficient in that it can take significant time to compute $A - B$ as the convex hull of the set of points $U - V$, where U is a vertex of A and V is a vertex of B. Moreover, an exhaustive search of the edges will process edges that are not even visible to the origin. The approach is $O(nm)$ where A has n vertices and B has m vertices since the convex hull can have nm vertices. The GJK algorithm is an iterative method designed

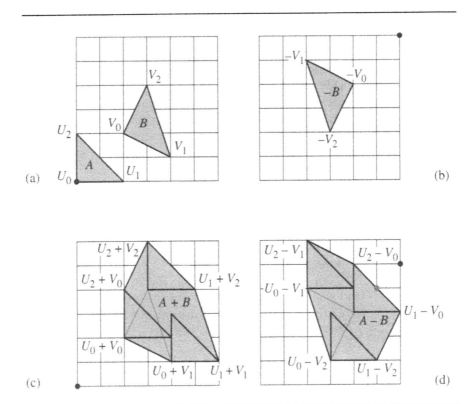

Figure 6.24   (a) Triangles A and B; (b) set $-B$; (c) set $A + B$; (d) set $A - B$, where the gray point is the closest point in $A - B$ to the origin. The black dots are the origin $(0, 0)$.

to avoid the direct convex hull calculation and to localize the search to edges near the origin.

6.10.2 OVERVIEW OF THE ALGORITHM

The discussion here is for the general n-dimensional problem for convex objects A and B. Let $C = A - B$, where A and B are convex sets. As noted earlier, C itself is a convex set. If $0 \in C$, then the original sets intersect and the distance between them is zero. Otherwise, let $Z \in C$ be the closest point to the origin. It is geometrically clear that only one such point exists and must lie on the boundary of C. However, there can be many $X \in A$ and $Y \in B$ such that $X - Y = Z$. For example, this happens for two disjoint convex polygons in 2D whose closest features are a pair of parallel edges, one from each polygon.

The GJK algorithm is effectively a descent method that constructs a sequence of points on the boundary of C, each point having smaller distance to the origin than the previous point in the sequence. In fact, the algorithm generates a sequence of simplices with vertices in C (triangles in 2D, tetrahedra in 3D), each simplex having smaller distance to the origin than the previous simplex. Let S_k denote the simplex vertices at the kth step, and let $\bar{S}_k$ denote the simplex itself. The point $V_k \in \bar{S}_k$ is selected to be the closest point in $\bar{S}_k$ to the origin. Initially, $S_0 = \emptyset$ (the empty set) and V_0 is an arbitrary point in C. The set C is projected onto the line through 0 with direction V_0, the resulting projection being a closed and bounded interval on the line. The interval end point that is farthest left on the projection line is generated by a point $W_0 \in C$. The next set of simplex vertices is $S_1 = \{W_0\}$. Figure 6.25 illustrates this step.

Since S_1 is a singleton point set, $\bar{S}_1 = S_1$ and $V_1 = W_0$ is the closest point in $\bar{S}_1$ to the origin. The set C is now projected onto the line containing 0 with direction V_1. The interval end point that is farthest left on the projection line is generated by a point $W_1 \in C$. The next set of simplex vertices is $S_2 = \{W_0, W_1\}$. Figure 6.26 illustrates this step.

The set $\bar{S}_2$ is the line segment $\langle W_0, W_1 \rangle$. The closest point in $\bar{S}_2$ to the origin is an edge-interior point V_2. The set C is projected onto the line containing 0 with direction V_2. The interval end point that is farthest left on the projection line is generated by a point $W_2 \in C$. The next set of simplex vertices is $S_3 = \{W_0, W_1, W_2\}$. Figure 6.27 illustrates this step.

The set $\bar{S}_3$ is the triangle $\langle W_0, W_1, W_2 \rangle$. The closest point in $\bar{S}_3$ to the origin is a point V_3 on the edge $\langle W_0, W_2 \rangle$. The next simplex vertex that is generated is W_3. The next set of simplex vertices is $S_4 = \langle W_0, W_2, W_3 \rangle$. The old simplex vertex W_1 is discarded. Figure 6.28 illustrates this step. The simplex $\bar{S}_3$ is shown in dark gray.

Generally, V_{k+1} is chosen to be the closest point to the origin in the convex hull of $S_k \cup \{W_k\}$. The next set of simplex vertices S_{k+1} is chosen to be set $M \subseteq S_k \cup \{W_k\}$ with the fewest number of elements such that V_{k+1} is in the convex hull of M. Such a set M must exist and is unique. Figure 6.29(a) shows the convex hull of $S_3 \cup \{W_3\}$, a quadrilateral. The next iterate V_4 is shown on that hull. Figure 6.29(b) shows the simplex $\bar{S}_4$ that was generated by $M = \{W_0, W_2, W_3\}$.

We state without proof that the sequence of iterates is monotonically decreasing in length, $\|V_{k+1}\| \leq \|V_k\|$. In fact, equality can only occur if $V_k = Z$, the closest point. For convex faceted objects, the closest point is reached in a finite number of steps. For general convex objects, the sequence can be infinite, but must converge to Z. If the GJK algorithm is implemented for such objects, some type of termination criterion must be used. Numerical issues also arise when the algorithm is implemented in a floating-point number system. A discussion of the pitfalls is given by van den Bergen (1997, 1999, 2001a), and the ideas are implemented in a 3D collision detection system called SOLID (Software Library for Interference Detection) (van den Bergen 2001b). The main concern is that the simplices eventually become flat in one or more dimensions.

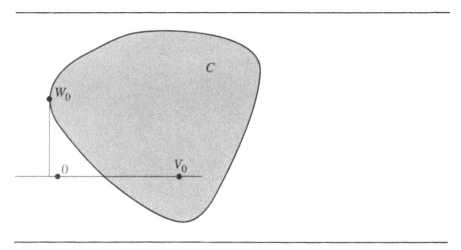

Figure 6.25   The first iteration in the GJK algorithm.

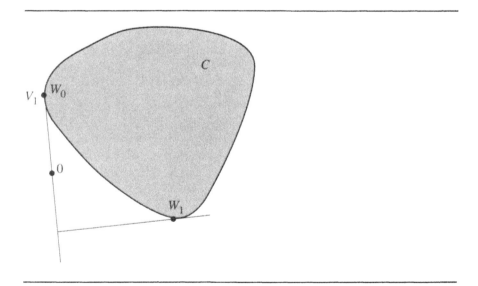

Figure 6.26   The second iteration in the GJK algorithm.

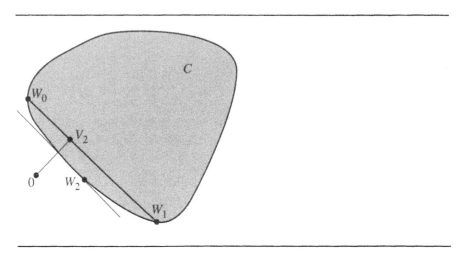

Figure 6.27   The third iteration in the GJK algorithm.

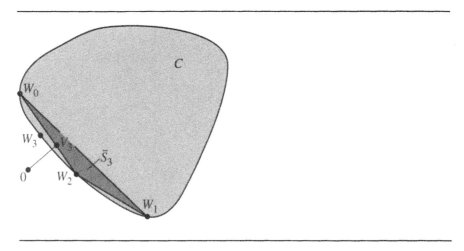

Figure 6.28   The fourth iteration in the GJK algorithm.

6.10.3 ALTERNATIVES TO GJK

The GJK algorithm is by no means the only algorithm for computing distance between convex polygons or convex polyhedra, but good, robust implementations are publicly available (van den Bergen 2001b). The distance between two nonintersecting convex polygons can be computed using the method of rotating calipers (Pirzadeh 1999). This powerful method is useful for solving many other types of problems in

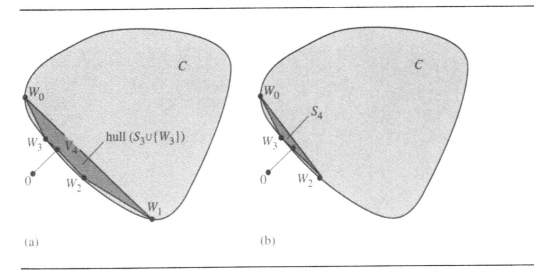

Figure 6.29   (a) Construction of V_{k+1} in the convex hull of $S_k \cup \{W_k\}$. (b) The new simplex $\bar{S}_{k+1}$ generated from $M = \{W_0, W_2, W_3\}$.

computational geometry. Assuming both polyhedra have $O(n)$ vertices, an $O(n^2)$ algorithm, both in space and in time, for computing the distance is given by Cameron and Culley (1986). An asymptotically better algorithm is given by Dobkin and Kirkpatrick (1990) and is $O(n)$ in space and $O(\log^2 n)$ in time. However, no implementation appears to be publicly available. The method is based on constructing a hierarchical representation of a polyhedron that is useful for solving other queries, for example, in rapid determination of an extreme point of a polyhedron for a specified direction. In more recent times, the Lin-Canny algorithm (Lin and Canny 1991) is $O(n)$ in space, empirically $O(n)$ in time, but maintains the closest pair of features to exploit frame coherence. After computing the distance in one frame, the polyhedra move slightly, and the distance must be recalculated in the next frame. The incremental update is $O(1)$ in time. Implementations based on this method are I-Collide (Cohen et al. 1995) and V-Clip (Mirtich 1997).

INTERSECTION IN 2D 7

This chapter contains information on computing the intersection of geometric primitives in 2D. The simplest object combinations to analyze are those for which one of the objects is a linear component (line, ray, segment). These combinations are covered in the first four sections. Section 7.5 covers the intersection of a pair of quadratic curves; Section 7.6 covers the problem of intersection of a pair of polynomial curves. The last section is about the method of separating axes, a very powerful technique for dealing with intersections of convex objects.

7.1 LINEAR COMPONENTS

Recall from Chapter 5 the definitions for lines, rays, and segments. A *line* in 2D is parameterized as $P + t\vec{d}$, where $\vec{d}$ is a nonzero vector and where $t \in \mathbb{R}$. A *ray* is parameterized the same way except that $t \in [0, \infty)$. The point P is the origin of the ray. A *segment* is also parameterized the same way except that $t \in [0, 1]$. The points P and $P + \vec{d}$ are the end points of the segment. A *linear component* is the general term for a line, a ray, or a segment.

Given two lines $P_0 + s\vec{d}_0$ and $P_1 + t\vec{d}_1$ for $s, t \in \mathbb{R}$, they are either intersecting, nonintersecting and parallel, or the same line. To help determine which of these cases occurs, define for two input 2D vectors the scalar-valued operation $\text{Kross}((x_0, y_0), (x_1, y_1)) = x_0 y_1 - x_1 y_0$. The operation is related to the cross product in 3D given by $(x_0, y_0, 0) \times (x_1, y_1, 0) = (0, 0, \text{Kross}((x_0, y_0), (x_1, y_1)))$. The operation has the property that $\text{Kross}(\vec{u}, \vec{v}) = -\text{Kross}(\vec{v}, \vec{u})$.

A point of intersection, if any, can be found by solving the two equations in two unknowns implied by setting $P_0 + s\vec{d}_0 = P_1 + t\vec{d}_1$. Rearranging terms yields $s\vec{d}_0 - t\vec{d}_1 = P_1 - P_0$. Setting $\vec{\Delta} = P_1 - P_0$ and applying the Kross operation yields

$\text{Kross}(\vec{d}_0, \vec{d}_1)\, s = \text{Kross}(\vec{\Delta}, \vec{d}_1)$ and $\text{Kross}(\vec{d}_0, \vec{d}_1)\, t = \text{Kross}(\vec{\Delta}, \vec{d}_0)$. If $\text{Kross}(\vec{d}_0, \vec{d}_1) \neq 0$, then the lines intersect in a single point determined by $s = \text{Kross}(\vec{\Delta}, \vec{d}_1)/\text{Kross}(\vec{d}_0, \vec{d}_1)$ or $t = \text{Kross}(\vec{\Delta}, \vec{d}_0)/\text{Kross}(\vec{d}_0, \vec{d}_1)$. If $\text{Kross}(\vec{d}_0, \vec{d}_1) = 0$, then the lines are either nonintersecting and parallel or the same line. If the Kross operation of the direction vectors is zero, then the previous equations in s and t reduce to a single equation $\text{Kross}(\vec{\Delta}, \vec{d}_0) = 0$ since $\vec{d}_1$ is a scalar multiple of $\vec{d}_0$. The lines are the same if this equation is true; otherwise, the lines are nonintersecting and parallel.

If using floating-point arithmetic, distinguishing the nonparallel from the parallel case can be tricky when $\text{Kross}(\vec{d}_0, \vec{d}_1)$ is nearly zero. Using the relationship of Kross to the 3D cross product, a standard identity for the cross product in terms of Kross is $\|\text{Kross}(\vec{d}_0, \vec{d}_1)\| = \|\vec{d}_0\|\|\vec{d}_1\||\sin\theta|$, where θ is the angle between $\vec{d}_0$ and $\vec{d}_1$. For the right-hand side of the last equation to be nearly zero, one or more of its three terms must be nearly zero. A test for parallelism using an absolute error comparison $\|\text{Kross}(\vec{d}_0, \vec{d}_1)\| \leq \varepsilon$ for some small tolerance $\varepsilon > 0$ may not be suitable for some applications. For example, two perpendicular direction vectors that have very small length can cause the test to report that the lines are parallel when in fact they are perpendicular. If possible, the application should require that the line directions be unit-length vectors. The absolute error test then becomes a test on the sine of the angle between the directions: $\|\text{Kross}(\vec{d}_0, \vec{d}_1)\| = |\sin\theta| \leq \varepsilon$. For small enough angles, the test is effectively a threshold on the angle itself since $\sin\theta \doteq \theta$ for small angles. If the application cannot require that the line directions be unit length, then the test for parallelism should be based on relative error:

$$\frac{\|\text{Kross}(\vec{d}_0, \vec{d}_1)\|}{\|\vec{d}_0\|\|\vec{d}_1\|} = |\sin\theta| \leq \varepsilon$$

The square root calculations for the two lengths and the division can be avoided by using instead the equivalent inequality

$$\|\text{Kross}(\vec{d}_0, \vec{d}_1)\|^2 \leq \varepsilon^2\|\vec{d}_0\|^2\|\vec{d}_1\|^2$$

If the two linear components are a line ($s \in \mathbb{R}$) and a ray ($t \geq 0$), the point of intersection, if it exists, is determined by solving for s and t as shown previously. However, it must be verified that $t \geq 0$. If $t < 0$, the first line intersects the line containing the ray, but not at a ray point. Computing the solution t as specified earlier involves a division. An implementation can avoid the cost of the division when testing $t \geq 0$ by observing that $t = \text{Kross}(\vec{\Delta}, \vec{d}_0)\text{Kross}(\vec{d}_0, \vec{d}_1)/(\text{Kross}(\vec{d}_0, \vec{d}_1))^2$ and using the equivalent test $\text{Kross}(\vec{\Delta}, \vec{d}_0)\text{Kross}(\vec{d}_0, \vec{d}_1) \geq 0$. If in fact the equivalent test shows that $t \geq 0$ and if the application needs to know the corresponding point of intersection, only then should t be directly computed, thus deferring a division until it is needed. Similar tests on s and t may be applied when either linear component is a ray or a segment.

Finally, if the two linear components are on the same line, the linear components intersect in a t-interval, possibly empty, bounded, semi-infinite, or infinite. Computing the interval of intersection is somewhat tedious, but not complicated. As an example, consider the case when both linear components are line segments, so $s \in [0, 1]$ and $t \in [0, 1]$. We need to compute the s-interval of the second line segment that corresponds to the t-interval $[0, 1]$. The first end point is represented as $P_1 = P_0 + s_0 \vec{d}_0$; the second is represented as $P_1 + \vec{d}_1 = P_0 + s_1 \vec{d}_0$. If $\vec{\Delta} = P_1 - P_0$, then $s_0 = \vec{d}_0 \cdot \vec{\Delta} / \|\vec{d}_0\|^2$ and $s_1 = s_0 + \vec{d}_0 \cdot \vec{d}_1 / \|\vec{d}_0\|^2$. The s-interval is $[s_{\min}, s_{\max}] = [\min(s_0, s_1), \max(s_0, s_1)]$. The parameter interval of intersection is $[0, 1] \cap [s_{\min}, s_{\max}]$, possibly the empty set. The 2D points of intersection for the line segment of intersection can be computed from the interval of intersection by using the interval end points in the representation $P_0 + s \vec{d}_0$.

The pseudocode for the intersection of two lines is presented below. The return value of the function is 0 if there is no intersection, 1 if there is a unique intersection, and 2 if the two lines are the same line. The returned point I is valid only when the function returns 1.

```
int FindIntersection(Point P0, Point D0, Point P1, Point D1, Point& I)
{
    // Use a relative error test to test for parallelism.  This effectively
    // is a threshold on the angle between D0 and D1.  The threshold
    // parameter 'sqrEpsilon' can be defined in this function or be
    // available globally.

    Point E = P1 - P0;
    float kross = D0.x * D1.y - D0.y * D1.x;
    float sqrKross = kross * kross;
    float sqrLen0 = D0.x * D0.x + D0.y * D0.y;
    float sqrLen1 = D1.x * D1.x + D1.y * D1.y;
    if (sqrKross > sqrEpsilon * sqrLen0 * sqrLen1) {
        // lines are not parallel
        float s = (E.x * D1.y - E.y *D1.x) / kross;
        I = P0 + s * D0;
        return 1;
    }

    // lines are parallel
    float sqrLenE = E.x * E.x + E.y * E.y;
    kross = E.x * D0.y - E.y * D0.x;
    sqrKross = kross * kross;
    if (sqrKross > sqrEpsilon * sqrLen0 * sqrLenE) {
        // lines are different
        return 0;
    }
```

```
    // lines are the same
    return 2;
}
```

The pseudocode for the intersection of two line segments is presented below. The return value of the function is 0 if there is no intersection, 1 if there is a unique intersection, and 2 if the two segments overlap and the intersection set is a segment itself. The return value is the number of valid entries in the array I[2] that is passed to the function. Relative error tests are used in the same way as they were in the previous function.

```
int FindIntersection(Point P0, Point D0, Point P1, Point D1, Point2 I[2])
{
    // segments P0 + s * D0 for s in [0, 1], P1 + t * D1 for t in [0,1]

    Point E = P1 - P0;
    float kross = D0.x * D1.y - D0.y * D1.x;
    float sqrKross = kross * kross;
    float sqrLen0 = D0.x * D0.x + D0.y * D0.y;
    float sqrLen1 = D1.x * D1.x + D1.y * D1.y;
    if (sqrKross > sqrEpsilon * sqrLen0 * sqrLen1) {
        // lines of the segments are not parallel
        float s = (E.x * D1.y - E.y * D1.x) / kross;
        if (s < 0 or s > 1) {
            // intersection of lines is not a point on segment P0 + s * D0
            return 0;
        }

        float t = (E.x * D0.y - E.y * D0.x) / kross;
        if (t < 0 or t > 1) {
            // intersection of lines is not a point on segment P1 + t * D1
            return 0;
        }

        // intersection of lines is a point on each segment
        I[0] = P0 + s * D0;
        return 1;
    }

    // lines of the segments are parallel
    float sqrLenE = E.x * E.x + E.y * E.y;
    kross = E.x * D0.y - E.y * D0.x;
    sqrKross = kross * kross;
    if (sqrKross > sqrEpsilon * sqrLen0 * sqrLenE) {
```

```
        // lines of the segments are different
        return 0;
    }

    // Lines of the segments are the same.  Need to test for overlap of
    // segments.
    float s0 = Dot(D0, E) / sqrLen0, s1 = s0 + Dot(D0, D1) / sqrLen0, w[2];
    float smin = min(s0, s1), smax = max(s0, s1);
    int imax = FindIntersection(0.0, 1.0, smin, smax, w);
    for (i = 0; i < imax; i++)
        I[i] = P0 + w[i] * D0;
    return imax;
}
```

The intersection of two intervals $[u_0, u_1]$ and $[v_0, v_1]$, where $u_0 < u_1$ and $v_0 < v_1$, is computed by the function shown below. The return value is 0 if the intervals do not intersect; 1 if they intersect at a single point, in which case w[0] contains that point; or 2 if they intersect in an interval whose end points are stored in w[0] and w[1].

```
int FindIntersection(float u0, float u1, float v0, float v1, float w[2])
{
    if (u1 < v0 || u0 > v1)
        return 0;

    if (u1 > v0) {
        if (u0 < v1) {
            if (u0 < v0) w[0] = v0; else w[0] = u0;
            if (u1 > v1) w[1] = v1; else w[1] = u1;
            return 2;
        } else {
            // u0 == v1
            w[0] = u0;
            return 1;
        }
    } else {
        // u1 == v0
        w[0] = u1;
        return 1;
    }
}
```

7.2 Linear Components and Polylines

The simplest algorithm for computing the intersection of a linear component and a polyline is to iterate through the edges of the polyline and apply an intersection test for linear component against line segment. If the goal of the application is to determine if the linear component intersects the polyline without finding where intersections occur, then an early out occurs once a polyline edge is found that intersects the linear component.

If the polyline is in fact a polygon and the geometric query treats the polygon as a solid, then an iteration over the polygon edges and applying the intersection test for a line or a ray against polygon edges is sufficient to determine intersection. If the linear component is a line segment itself, the iteration is not enough. The problem is that the line segment might be fully contained in the polygon. Additional tests need to be made, specifically point-in-polygon tests applied to the end points of the line segment. If either end point is inside the polygon, the segment and polygon intersect. If both end points are outside, then an iteration over the polygon edges is made and segment-segment intersection tests are performed.

If the intersection query is going to be performed often for a single polyline but with multiple linear components, then some preprocessing can help reduce the computational time that is incurred by the exhaustive edge search. One such algorithm for preprocessing involves *binary space partitioning* (BSP) *trees,* discussed in Section 13.1. In that section there is some material on intersection of a line segment with a polygon that is already represented as a BSP tree. The exhaustive search of n polygon edges is an $O(n)$ process. The search through a BSP tree is an $O(\log n)$ process. Intuitively, if the line segment being compared to the polygon is on one side of a partitioning line corresponding to an edge of the polygon, then that line segment need not be tested for intersection with any polygon edges on the opposite side of the partition. Of course, there is the preprocessing cost of $O(n \log n)$ to build the tree.

Another possibility for reducing the costs is to attempt to rapidly cull out segments of the polyline so they are not used in intersection tests with the linear component. The culling idea in Section 6.7 may be used with this goal.

7.3 Linear Components and Quadratic Curves

We discuss in this section how to test or find the intersection points between a linear component and a quadratic curve. The method for an implicitly defined quadratic curve is presented first. The special case for intersections of a linear component and a circle or arc are presented second.

7.3.1   LINEAR COMPONENTS AND GENERAL QUADRATIC CURVES

A quadratic curve is represented implicitly by the quadratic equation $X^{\mathrm{T}}AX + B^{\mathrm{T}}X + c = 0$, where A is a 2×2 symmetric matrix, B is a 2×1 vector, c is a scalar, and X is the 2×1 variable representing points on the curve.

The intersection of a line $X(t) = P + t\vec{d}$ for $t \in \mathbb{R}$ and a quadratic curve is computed by substituting the line equation into the quadratic equation to obtain

$$0 = X(t)^{\mathrm{T}}AX(t) + B^{\mathrm{T}}X(t) + c$$

$$= \left(\vec{d}^{\mathrm{T}}A\vec{d}\right)t^2 + \vec{d}^{\mathrm{T}}(2AP + B)t + \left(P^{\mathrm{T}}AP + B^{\mathrm{T}}P + c\right)$$

$$=: e_2 t^2 + e_1 t + e_0$$

This quadratic equation can be solved using the quadratic formula, but attention must be paid to numerical issues, for example, when e_2 is nearly zero or when the discriminant $e_1^2 - 4e_0 e_2$ is nearly zero. If the equation has two distinct real roots, the line intersects the curve in two points. Each root $\bar{t}$ is used to compute the actual point of intersection $X(\bar{t}) = P + \bar{t}\vec{d}$. If the equation has a repeated real root, then the line intersects the curve in a single point and is tangent at that point. If the equation has no real-valued roots, the line does not intersect the curve.

If the linear component is a ray with $t \geq 0$, an additional test must be made to see if a root $\bar{t}$ to the quadratic equation is nonnegative. It is possible that the line containing the ray intersects the quadratic curve, but the ray itself does not. Similarly, if the linear component is a line segment with $t \in [0, 1]$, additional tests must be made to see if a root $\bar{t}$ to the quadratic equation is also in $[0, 1]$.

If the application's goal is to determine only if the linear component and quadratic curve intersect, but does not care about where the intersections occur, then the root finding for $q(t) = e_2 t^2 + e_1 t + e_0 = 0$ can be skipped to avoid the expensive square root and division that occur in the quadratic formula. Instead we only need to know if $q(t)$ has a real-valued root in $\mathbb{R}$ for a line, in $[0, \infty)$ for a ray, or in $[0, 1]$ for a line segment. This can be done using Sturm sequences, as described in Section A.5. This method uses only floating-point additions, subtractions, and multiplications to count the number of real-valued roots for $q(t)$ on the specified interval.

7.3.2   LINEAR COMPONENTS AND CIRCULAR COMPONENTS

A *circle* in 2D is represented by $\|X - C\|^2 = r^2$, where C is the center and $r > 0$ is the radius of the circle. The circle can be parameterized by $X(\theta) = C + r\hat{u}(\theta)$, where $\hat{u}(\theta) = (\cos\theta, \sin\theta)$ and where $\theta \in [0, 2\pi)$. An *arc* is parameterized the same way except that $\theta \in [\theta_0, \theta_1]$ with $\theta_0 \in [0, 2\pi)$, $\theta_0 < \theta_1$, and $\theta_1 - \theta_0 < 2\pi$. It is also possible to represent an arc by center C, radius r, and two end points A and B that correspond to angles θ_0 and θ_1, respectively. The term *circular component* is used to refer to a circle or an arc.

Consider first a parameterized line $X(t) = P + t\vec{d}$ and a circle $\|X - C\|^2 = r^2$. Substitute the line equation into the circle equation, define $\vec{\Delta} = P - C$, and obtain the quadratic equation in t:

$$\|\vec{d}\|^2 t^2 + 2\vec{d} \cdot \vec{\Delta} t + \|\vec{\Delta}\|^2 - r^2 = 0$$

The formal roots of the equation are

$$t = \frac{-\vec{d} \cdot \vec{\Delta} \pm \sqrt{(\vec{d} \cdot \vec{\Delta})^2 - \|\vec{d}\|^2 (\|\vec{\Delta}\|^2 - r^2)}}{\|\vec{d}\|^2}$$

Define $\delta = (\vec{d} \cdot \vec{\Delta})^2 - \|\vec{d}\|^2 (\|\vec{\Delta}\|^2 - r^2)$. If $\delta < 0$, the line does not intersect the circle. If $\delta = 0$, the line is tangent to the circle in a single point of intersection. If $\delta > 0$, the line intersects the circle in two points.

If the linear component is a ray, and if $\bar{t}$ is a real-valued root of the quadratic equation, then the corresponding point of intersection between line and circle is a point of intersection between ray and circle if $\bar{t} \geq 0$. Similarly, if the linear component is a segment, the line-circle point of intersection is also one for the segment and circle if $\bar{t} \in [0, 1]$.

If the circular component is an arc, the points of intersection between the linear component and circle must be tested to see if they are on the arc. Let the arc have end points A and B, where the arc is that portion of the circle obtained by traversing the circle counterclockwise from A to B. Notice that the line containing A and B separates the arc from the remainder of the circle. Figure 7.1 illustrates this. If P is a point on the circle, it is on the arc if and only if it is on the same side of that line as the arc. The algebraic condition for the circle point P to be on the arc is $\mathrm{Kross}(P - A, B - A) \geq 0$, where $\mathrm{Kross}((x_0, y_0), (x_1, y_1)) = x_0 y_1 - x_1 y_0$.

7.4 LINEAR COMPONENTS AND POLYNOMIAL CURVES

Consider a line $P + t\vec{d}$ for $t \in \mathbb{R}$ and a polynomial curve $X(s) = \sum_{i=0}^{n} \vec{A}_i s^i$, where $\vec{A}_n \neq \vec{0}$. Let the parameter domain be $[s_{\min}, s_{\max}]$. This section discusses how to compute points of intersection between the line and curve from both an algebraic and geometric perspective.

7.4.1 ALGEBRAIC METHOD

Intersections of the line and curve, if any, can be found by equating $X(s) = P + t\vec{d}$ and solving for s by eliminating the t-term using the Kross operator:

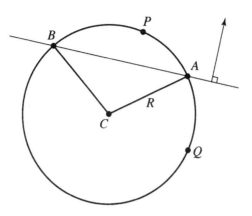

Figure 7.1   An arc of a circle spanned counterclockwise from A to B. The line containing A and B separates the circle into the arc itself and the remainder of the circle. Point P is on the arc since it is on the same side of the line as the arc. Point Q is not on the arc since it is on the opposite side of the line.

$$\sum_{i=0}^{n} \left(\mathrm{Kross}(\vec{d}, \vec{A}_i)\right) s^i = \mathrm{Kross}(\vec{d}, X(s)) = \mathrm{Kross}(\vec{d}, P + t\vec{d}) = \mathrm{Kross}(\vec{d}, P)$$

Setting $c_0 = \mathrm{Kross}(\vec{d}, \vec{A}_0 - P)$ and $c_i = \mathrm{Kross}(\vec{d}, \vec{A}_i)$ for $i \geq 1$, the previous equation is reformulated as the polynomial equation $q(s) = \sum_{i=0}^{n} c_i s^i = 0$. A numerical root finder can be applied to this equation, but beware of c_n being zero (or nearly zero) when $\vec{d}$ and $\vec{A}_n$ are parallel (or nearly parallel). Any $\bar{s}$ for which $q(\bar{s}) = 0$ must be tested for inclusion in the parameter domain $[s_{\min}, s_{\max}]$. If so, a point of intersection has been found.

EXAMPLE   Let the line be $(0, 1/2) + t(2, -1)$ and the polynomial curve be $X(s) = (0, 0) + s(1, 2) + s^2(0, -3) + s^3(0, 1)$ for $s \in [0, 1]$. The curve is unimodal and has x-range $[0, 1]$ and y-range $[0, 3/8]$. The polynomial equation is $q(s) = 2s^3 - 6s^2 + 5s - 1 = 0$. The roots are $s = 1, 1 \pm \sqrt{2}/2$. Only the roots 1 and $1 - \sqrt{2}/2$ are in $[0, 1]$. Figure 7.2 shows the line, curve, and points of intersection $\vec{I}_0$ and $\vec{I}_1$. ∎

The numerical root finders might have problems finding roots of even multiplicity or at a root where $q(s)$ does not have a large derivative. Geometrically these cases happen when the line and tangent line at the point of intersection form an angle that is nearly zero.

Just as in the problem of computing intersections of linear components with quadratic curves, if the application's goal is to determine only if the linear component and polynomial curve intersect, but does not care about where the intersections

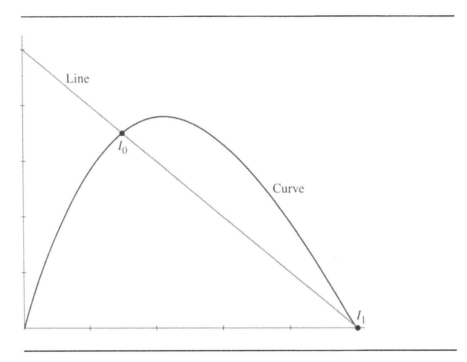

Figure 7.2   Intersection of a line and a cubic curve.

occur, then the root finding for $q(s) = 0$ can be skipped and Sturm sequences used (Section A.5) to count the number of real-valued roots in the domain $[s_{min}, s_{max}]$ for the curve $X(s)$. If the count is zero, then the line and polynomial curve do not intersect.

EXAMPLE   Using the same example as the previous one, we only want to know the number of real-valued roots for $q(s) = 0$ in $[0, 1]$. The Sturm sequence is $q_0(s) = 2s^3 - 6s^2 + 5s - 1, q_1(s) = 6s^2 - 12s + 5, q_2(s) = 2(s - 1)/3,$ and $q_3(s) = 1$. We have $q_0(0) = -1, q_1(0) = 5, q_2(0) = -2/3,$ and $q_3(0) = 1$ for a total of 3 sign changes. We also have $q_0(1) = 0, q_1(1) = -1, q_2(1) = 0,$ and $q_3(1) = 1$ for a total of 1 sign change. The difference in sign changes is 2, so $q(s) = 0$ has two real-valued roots on $[0, 1]$, which means the line intersects the curve. ∎

7.4.2 POLYLINE APPROXIMATION

The root finding of the algebraic method can be computationally expensive. An attempt at reducing the time complexity is to approximate the curve by a polyline and find intersections of the line with the polyline. The curve polyline is obtained by subdivision (see Section A.8). The line-polyline tests that were discussed earlier in this chapter can be applied. Any intersections that are found can be used as approximations to line-curve intersections if the application is willing to accept that the polyline is a suitable approximation to the curve. However, the points of intersection might be used as an attempt to localize the search for actual points of intersection on the curve. For example, if a line-polyline intersection occurred on the segment $\langle X(s_i), X(s_{i+1})\rangle$, the next step could be to search for a root of $q(s) = 0$ in the interval $[s_i, s_{i+1})$.

7.4.3 HIERARCHICAL BOUNDING

The algebraic method mentioned earlier always incurs the cost of root finding for a polynomial equation. Presumably the worst case is that after spending the computer time to find any real-valued roots of $q(s) = 0$, there are none; the line and polynomial curve do not intersect. An application might want to reduce the cost for determining there is no intersection by providing coarser-level tests in hopes of an "early out" from the intersection testing. Perhaps more important is that if the application will perform a large number of line-curve intersection tests with different lines, but the same curve, the total cost of polynomial root finding can be prohibitive. Some type of curve preprocessing certainly can help to reduce the costs.

One coarse-level test involves maintaining a bounding polygon for the curve. In particular, if the curve is built from control points and the curve lies in the convex hull of the control points, an intersection test is first applied to the line and the convex hull (a convex polygon). If they do not intersect, then the line and curve do not intersect. If the line and polygon do intersect, then the application proceeds to the more expensive line-curve test.

An alternative is to use an axis-aligned bounding rectangle for the curve. The line-rectangle intersection test is quite inexpensive and is discussed in Section 7.7 on separating axes. If the application is willing to allow a few more cycles in hopes of an early-out no-intersection test, a variation of the algorithm is to construct a hierarchy of bounding boxes, each level providing a better fit (in some sense) than the previous level. Moreover, if the line does not intersect a bounding box at some level, then there is no point in processing further levels below the node of that box since the line cannot intersect the curve in that localized region. Figure 7.3 illustrates the idea. A curve is shown with a two-level hierarchy. The line intersects the top-level box, so the next level of the hierarchy must be analyzed. The line intersects the left child box at the next level, so further intersection tests are needed using either line-box or line-curve tests. The line does not intersect the right child box at the next level, so the line cannot intersect the curve contained in that box. No further processing of that subtree of the hierarchy is needed.

The main question, of course, is how do you construct an axis-aligned bounding box for a curve? For special classes of curves, specifically Bézier curves, this is not difficult. An axis-aligned bounding box for the curve that is not usually of smallest area is constructed for the control points of the curve. A hierarchy of boxes can be built by subdividing the curve and fitting boxes to the control points that correspond to each

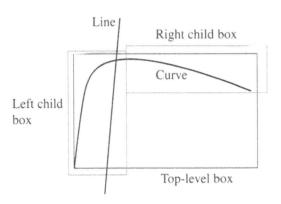

Figure 7.3   Line-curve intersection testing using a hierarchy of bounding boxes.

subcurve. For polynomial curves in general, finding the smallest-area axis-aligned bounding box appears to be as complicated as the algorithm for finding intersections of the line and the curve. The extent of the box in the x-direction is determined by the x-extreme points on the curve. The x-extreme points are characterized by having vertical tangents to the curve. Mathematically, $(x(t), y(t))$ has a vertical tangent if $x'(t) = 0$. Similarly, the y-extreme points are characterized by having horizontal tangents to the curve where $y'(t) = 0$. Each derivative equation is a polynomial equation that can be solved by numerical methods, but proceeding this way invalidates the goal of using a bounding box to avoid expensive root finding in regions where the line does not intersect the curve. This might not be an issue if the original curve is cubic, in which case the derivative equations can be solved using the quadratic formula. This is also not an issue if the application plans on testing for intersections between multiple lines and a single curve. The preprocessing costs for computing a bounding box are negligible compared to the total costs of root finding for the line-curve intersection tests.

7.4.4   MONOTONE DECOMPOSITION

Now suppose that $x'(t) \neq 0$ for any $t \in [t_{min}, t_{max}]$. The curve is monotonic in x, either strictly increasing or strictly decreasing. In this special case, the x-extents for the axis-aligned bounding box correspond to $x(t_{min})$ and $x(t_{max})$. A similar argument applies if $y'(t) \neq 0$ on the curve domain. Generally, if $x'(t) \neq 0$ and $y'(t) \neq 0$ for $t \in [a, b] \subseteq [t_{min}, t_{max}]$, then the curve segment is monotonic and the axis-aligned bounding box is determined by the points $(x(a), y(a))$ and $(x(b), y(b))$. Determining that a derivative equation does not have roots is an application of Sturm sequences, as discussed in Section A.5.

The idea now is to subdivide the curve using a simple bisection on the parameter interval with the goal of finding monotonic curve segments. If $[a, b]$ is a subinterval in the bisection for which the curve is monotonic, no further subdivision occurs; the axis-aligned bounding box is known for that segment. Ideally, after a few levels of bisection we obtain a small number of monotonic segments and their corresponding bounding boxes. The line-box intersection tests can be applied between the line and each box in order to cull out monotone segments that do not intersect the line, but if the number of boxes is large, you can always build a hierarchy from the bottom up by treating the original boxes as leaf nodes of a tree, then grouping a few boxes at a time to construct parent nodes. The bounding box of a parent node can be computed to contain the bounding boxes of its children. The parents themselves can be grouped, the process eventually leading to the root node of the tree with a single bounding box. The method of intersection illustrated in Figure 7.3 may be applied to this tree.

A recursive subdivision may be applied to find monotone segments. The recursion requires a stopping condition that should be chosen carefully. If the derivative equations $x'(t) = 0$ and $y'(t) = 0$ both indicate zero root counts on the current interval, then the curve is monotonic on that interval and the recursion terminates. If one of the equations has a single root on the current interval and the other does not, a subdivision is applied. It is possible that the subdivision t-value is the root itself, in which case both subintervals will report a root when there is only a single root. For example, consider $(x(t), y(t)) = (t, t^2)$ for $t \in [-1, 1]$. The derivative equation $x'(t) = 0$ has no solution since $x'(t) = 1$ for all t, but $y'(t) = 2t = 0$ has one root on the interval. The subdivision value is $t = 0$. The equation $y'(t) = 0$ has one root on the subinterval $[-1, 0]$ and one root on the subinterval $[0, 1]$, but these are the same root. The end points of subintervals should be checked to avoid deeper recursions than necessary. The typical case, though, is that a root of a subinterval occurs in the interior of the interval. Once a subinterval that has a single interior root is found, a robust bisection can be applied to find the root and subdivide the subinterval at the root. The recursion terminates for that subinterval.

In an application that will perform intersection queries with multiple lines but only one curve, the monotone segments can be found as a preprocessing step by solving $x'(t) = 0$ and $y'(t) = 0$ using numerical root finders.

7.4.5 RASTERIZATION

A raster approach may be used, even though it is potentially quite expensive to execute. An axis-aligned bounding box $[x_{min}, x_{max}] \times [y_{min}, y_{max}]$ is constructed to contain the curve. An $N \times M$ raster is built to represent the box region. The grid points are uniformly chosen as (x_i, y_j) for $0 \le i < N$ and $0 \le j < M$. That is, $x_i = x_{min} + (x_{max} - x_{min})i/(N - 1)$ and $y_j = y_{min} + (y_{max} - y_{min})j/(M - 1)$. Both the line and the curve are drawn into the raster. The step size for the parameter of the curve should be chosen to be small enough so that as the curve is sampled you generate adjacent raster values, potentially with a raster cell drawn multiple times

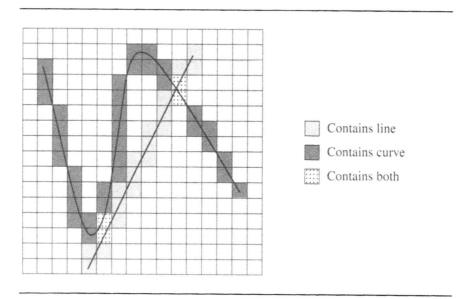

Figure 7.4   A line and a curve rasterized on a grid that is initially zero. The line is rasterized by or-ing the grid with the mask 1 (light gray). The curve is rasterized by or-ing the grid with the mask 2 (dark gray). Grid cells that contain both the line and the curve have a value 3 (dotted).

because multiple curve samples fall inside that cell. The overdraw can be reduced by sampling the curve based on arc length rather than the curve parameter. If the raster is initialized with 0, the line is drawn by or-ing the pixels with 1, and the curve is drawn by or-ing the pixels with 2. The pixels that are associated with line-curve intersections are those with a final value of 3. Figure 7.4 illustrates this.

The effectiveness of this method depends on how well the grid cell size is chosen. If it is chosen to be too large, the line and curve can pass through the same pixel, yet not intersect. The rasterization method reports an intersection when there is none. This situation is shown in Figure 7.4 in the lower-left portion of the grid. If the cell size is chosen to be too small, a lot of time is consumed in rasterizing the curve, especially in pixels that the line does not intersect.

Just as in the polyline approach, the application can choose to accept the pixel values as approximations to the actual line-curve intersections. If more accuracy is desired, the pixels tagged as 3 (and possibly immediate neighbors) can be used as a localization of where the intersections occur. If a contiguous block of pixels is tagged, such as is shown in the upper right of the grid in Figure 7.4, and if the application chooses to believe the block occurs because of a single intersection of curves, a suitable choice for the approximation is the average of pixel locations. If the application chooses not to accept the pixel values as approximations, then it can store the original line and curve parameters for samples occurring in a pixel with that pixel. Those parameter values can be used to start a search for intersections using a numerical root finder or a numerical distance calculator.

7.5 QUADRATIC CURVES

We present a general algebraic method for computing intersection points between two curves defined implicitly by quadratic curves. The special case of circular components is also presented because it handles intersection between circular arcs. Variations on computing intersection points of two ellipses are also presented here as an illustration of how you might go about handling the more general problem of intersection between two curves, each defined as a level curve for a particular function.

7.5.1 GENERAL QUADRATIC CURVES

Given two curves implicitly defined by the quadratic equations $F(x, y) = \alpha_{00} + \alpha_{10}x + \alpha_{01}y + \alpha_{20}x^2 + \alpha_{11}xy + \alpha_{02}y^2 = 0$ and $G(x, y) = \beta_{00} + \beta_{10}x + \beta_{01}y + \beta_{20}x^2 + \beta_{11}xy + \beta_{02}y^2 = 0$, the points of intersection can be computed by eliminating y to obtain a fourth-degree polynomial equation $H(x) = 0$. During the elimination process, y is related to x via a rational polynomial equation, $y = R(x)$. Each root $\bar{x}$ of $H(x) = 0$ is used to compute $\bar{y} = R(\bar{x})$. The pair $(\bar{x}, \bar{y})$ is an intersection point of the two original curves.

EXAMPLE   The equation $x^2 + 6y^2 - 1 = 0$ defines an ellipse whose center is at the origin. The equation $2(x - 2y)^2 - (x + y) = 0$ determines a parabola whose vertex is the origin. Figure 7.5 shows the plots of the two curves. The ellipse equation is rewritten as $y^2 = (1 - x^2)/6$. Substituting this in the parabola equation produces

$$0 = 2x^2 - 8xy + 8y^2 - x - y = 2x^2 - 8xy + 8(1 - x^2)/6 - x - y$$

$$= -(8x + 1)y + (2x^2 - 3x + 4)/3$$

This may be solved for

$$y = \frac{2x^2 - 3x + 4}{3(8x + 1)} =: R(x)$$

Replacing this in the ellipse equation produces

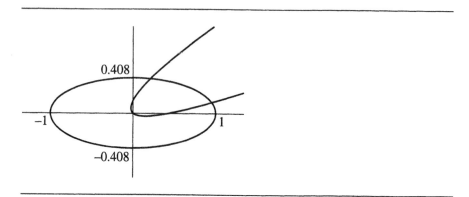

Figure 7.5   Intersections of an ellipse and a parabola.

$$0 = x^2 + 6y^2 - 1$$

$$= x^2 + 6\left(\frac{2x^2 - 3x + 4}{3(8x + 1)}\right)^2 - 1$$

$$= \frac{9(8x + 1)^2(x^2 - 1) + 6(2x^2 - 3x + 4)^2}{9(8x + 1)^2}$$

$$= \frac{200x^4 + 24x^3 - 139x^2 - 96x + 29}{3(8x + 1)^2}$$

Therefore, it is necessary that

$$0 = 200x^4 + 24x^3 - 139x^2 - 96x + 29 =: H(x) \quad \blacksquare$$

The polynomial equation $H(x) = 0$ has two real-valued roots, $x_0 \doteq 0.232856$ and $x_1 \doteq 0.960387$. Replacing these in the rational polynomial for y produces $y_0 = R(x_0) \doteq 0.397026$ and $y_1 = R(x_1) \doteq 0.113766$. The points (x_0, y_0) and (x_1, y_1) are the intersection points for the ellipse and parabola.

The general method of solution of two polynomial equations is discussed in detail in Section A.2.

As with any root finder, numerical problems can arise when a root has even multiplicity or the derivative of the function near the root is small in magnitude. These problems tend to arise geometrically when the two curves have an intersection point for which the angle between tangent lines to the curves at the point is nearly zero. If you need extreme accuracy and do not want to miss intersection points, you will need your root finder to be quite robust at the expense of some extra computational time.

If the application only needs to know if the curves intersect, but not where, then the method of Sturm sequences for root counting can be applied to $H(x) = 0$. The method is discussed in Section A.5.

7.5.2 CIRCULAR COMPONENTS

Let the two circles be represented by $\|X - C_i\|^2 = r_i^2$ for $i = 0, 1$. The points of intersection, if any, are determined by the following construction. Define $\vec{u} = C_1 - C_0 = (u_0, u_1)$. Define $\vec{v} = (u_1, -u_0)$. Note that $\|\vec{u}\|^2 = \|\vec{v}\|^2 = \|C_1 - C_0\|^2$ and $\vec{u} \cdot \vec{v} = 0$. The intersection points can be written in the form

$$X = C_0 + s\vec{u} + t\vec{v} \tag{7.1}$$

or

$$X = C_1 + (s - 1)\vec{u} + t\vec{v} \tag{7.2}$$

where s and t are constructed by the following argument. Substituting Equation 7.1 into $\|X - C_0\|^2 = r_0^2$ yields

$$(s^2 + t^2)\|\vec{u}\|^2 = r_0^2 \tag{7.3}$$

Substituting Equation 7.2 into $\|X - C_1\|^2 = r_1^2$ yields

$$((s - 1)^2 + t^2)\|\vec{u}\|^2 = r_1^2 \tag{7.4}$$

Subtracting Equations 7.3 and 7.4 and solving for s yields

$$s = \frac{1}{2}\left(\frac{r_0^2 - r_1^2}{\|\vec{u}\|^2} + 1\right) \tag{7.5}$$

Replacing Equation 7.5 into Equation 7.3 and solving for t^2 yields

$$
\begin{aligned}
t^2 &= \frac{r_0^2}{\|\vec{u}\|^2} - s^2 = \frac{r_0^2}{\|\vec{u}\|^2} - \frac{1}{4}\left(\frac{r_0^2 - r_1^2}{\|\vec{u}\|^2} + 1\right)^2 \\
&= -\frac{(\|\vec{u}\|^2 - (r_0 + r_1)^2)(\|\vec{u}\|^2 - (r_0 - r_1)^2)}{4\|\vec{u}\|^4}
\end{aligned}
\tag{7.6}
$$

In order for there to be solutions, the right-hand side of Equation 7.6 must be non-negative. Therefore, the numerator is negative:

$$(\|\vec{u}\|^2 - (r_0 + r_1)^2)(\|\vec{u}\|^2 - (r_0 - r_1)^2) \le 0 \tag{7.7}$$

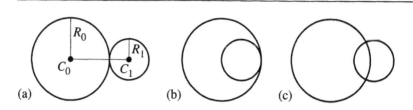

Figure 7.6   Relationship of two circles, $\vec{u} = C_1 - C_0$: (a) $\|\vec{u}\| = |r_0 + r_1|$; (b) $\|\vec{u}\| = |r_0 - r_1|$; (c) $|r_0 - r_1| < \|\vec{u}\| < |r_0 + r_1|$.

If $w = \|\vec{u}\|$, the left-hand side of Inequality 7.7 defines a quadratic function of w, the graph being a parabola that opens upwards. The roots are $w = |r_0 - r_1|$ and $w = |r_0 + r_1|$. For the quadratic function to be negative, only values of w between the two roots are allowed. Inequality 7.7 is therefore equivalent to

$$|r_0 - r_1| \le \|\vec{u}\| \le |r_0 + r_1| \tag{7.8}$$

If $\|\vec{u}\| = |r_0 + r_1|$, each circle is outside the other circle, but just tangent. The point of intersection is $C_0 + (r_0/(r_0 + r_1))\vec{u}$. If $\|\vec{u}\| = |r_0 - r_1|$, the circles are nested and just tangent. The circles are the same if $\|\vec{u}\| = 0$ and $r_0 = r_1$; otherwise the point of intersection is $C_0 + (r_0/(r_0 - r_1))\vec{u}$. If $|r_0 - r_1| < \|\vec{u}\| < |r_0 + r_1|$, then the two circles intersect in two points. The s-value from Equation 7.5 and the t-values from taking the square root in Equation 7.6 can be used to compute the intersection points as $C_0 + s\vec{u} + t\vec{v}$. Figure 7.6 shows the various relationships for the two circles.

If either or both circular components are arcs, the circle-circle points of intersection must be tested if they are on the arc (or arcs) using the circular-point-on-arc test described earlier in this chapter.

7.5.3   ELLIPSES

The algebraic method discussed earlier for testing/finding points of intersection applies, of course, to ellipses since they are implicitly defined by quadratic equations. In some applications, more information is needed other than just knowing points of intersection. Specifically, if the ellipses are used as bounding regions, it might be important to know if one ellipse is fully contained in another. This information is not provided by the algebraic method applied to the two quadratic equations defining the ellipses. The more precise queries for ellipses $\mathcal{E}_0$ and $\mathcal{E}_1$ are

- Do $\mathcal{E}_0$ and $\mathcal{E}_1$ intersect?

- Are $\mathcal{E}_0$ and $\mathcal{E}_1$ separated? That is, does there exist a line for which the ellipses are on opposite sides?

- Is $\mathcal{E}_0$ properly contained in $\mathcal{E}_1$, or is $\mathcal{E}_1$ properly contained in $\mathcal{E}_0$?

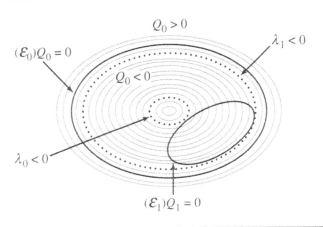

$Q_0 > 0$

$(\mathcal{E}_0)Q_0 = 0$

$\lambda_1 < 0$

$Q_0 < 0$

$\lambda_0 < 0$

$(\mathcal{E}_1)Q_1 = 0$

Figure 7.7 $\mathcal{E}_1$ is contained in $\mathcal{E}_0$. The maximum $\mathcal{E}_0$ level curve value λ_1 for $\mathcal{E}_1$ is negative.

Let the ellipse $\mathcal{E}_i$ be defined by the quadratic equation $Q_i(X) = X^T A_i X + B_i^T X + c_i$ for $i = 0, 1$. It is assumed that the A_i are positive definite. In this case, $Q_i(X) < 0$ defines the inside of the ellipse, and $Q_i(X) > 0$ defines the outside.

The discussion focuses on level curves of the quadratic functions. Section A.9.1 provides a discussion of level sets of functions. All level curves defined by $Q_0(x, y) = \lambda$ are ellipses, except for the minimum (negative) value λ for which the equation defines a single point, the center of every level curve ellipse. The ellipse defined by $Q_1(x, y) = 0$ is a curve that generally intersects many level curves of Q_0. The problem is to find the minimum level value λ_0 and maximum level value λ_1 attained by any (x, y) on the ellipse $\mathcal{E}_1$. If $\lambda_1 < 0$, then $\mathcal{E}_1$ is properly contained in $\mathcal{E}_0$. If $\lambda_0 > 0$, then $\mathcal{E}_0$ and $\mathcal{E}_1$ are separated or $\mathcal{E}_1$ contains $\mathcal{E}_0$. Otherwise, $0 \in [\lambda_0, \lambda_1]$ and the two ellipses intersect. Figures 7.7, 7.8, and 7.9 illustrate the three possibilities. The figures show the relationship of one ellipse $\mathcal{E}_1$ to the level curves of another ellipse $\mathcal{E}_0$.

This can be formulated as a constrained optimization that can be solved by the method of Lagrange multipliers (see Section A.9.3): Optimize $Q_0(X)$ subject to the constraint $Q_1(X) = 0$. Define $F(X, t) = Q_0(X) + t Q_1(X)$. Differentiating with respect to the components of X yields $\vec{\nabla} F = \vec{\nabla} Q_0 + t \vec{\nabla} Q_1$. Differentiating with respect to t yields $\partial F / \partial t = Q_1$. Setting the t-derivative equal to zero reproduces the constraint $Q_1 = 0$. Setting the X-derivative equal to zero yields $\vec{\nabla} Q_0 + t \vec{\nabla} Q_1 = \vec{0}$ for some t. Geometrically this means that the gradients are parallel.

Note that $\vec{\nabla} Q_i = 2A_i X + B_i$, so

$$\vec{0} = \vec{\nabla} Q_0 + t \vec{\nabla} Q_1 = 2(A_0 + t A_1)X + (B_0 + t B_1)$$

Formally solving for X yields

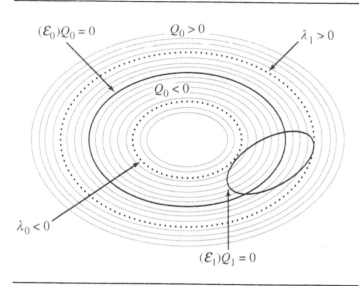

Figure 7.8 $\mathcal{E}_1$ transversely intersects $\mathcal{E}_0$. The minimum $\mathcal{E}_0$ level curve value λ_0 for $\mathcal{E}_1$ is negative; the maximum value λ_1 is positive.

$$X = -\frac{1}{2}(A_0 + tA_1)^{-1}(B_0 + tB_1) = \frac{1}{\delta(t)}\vec{Y}(t)$$

where $A_0 + tA_1$ is a matrix of linear polynomials in t and $\delta(t)$ is its determinant, a quadratic polynomial. The components of $\vec{Y}(t)$ are quadratic polynomials in t. Replacing this in $Q_1(X) = 0$ yields

$$p(t) := \vec{Y}(t)^T A_1 \vec{Y}(t) + \delta(t)B_1^T \vec{Y}(t) + \delta(t)^2 C_1 = 0 \qquad (7.9)$$

a quartic polynomial in t. The roots can be computed, the corresponding values of X computed, and $Q_0(X)$ evaluated. The minimum and maximum values are stored as λ_0 and λ_1, and the earlier comparisons with zero are applied.

This method leads to a quartic polynomial, just as the original algebraic method for finding intersection points did. But the current style of query does answer questions about the relative positions of the ellipses (separated or proper containment) whereas the original method does not.

EXAMPLE   Consider $Q_0(x, y) = x^2 + 6y^2 - 1$ and $Q_1(x, y) = 52x^2 - 72xy + 73y^2 - 32x - 74y + 28$. Figure 7.10 shows the plots of the two ellipses. The various parameters are

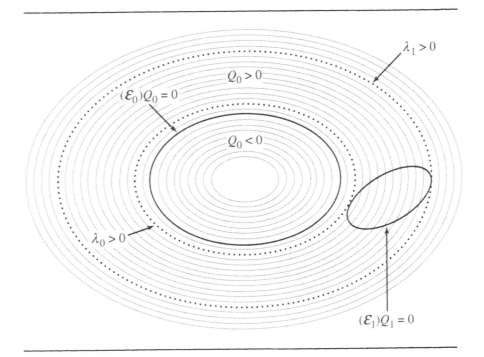

Figure 7.9 $\mathcal{E}_1$ is separated from $\mathcal{E}_0$. The minimum $\mathcal{E}_0$ level curve value λ_0 for $\mathcal{E}_1$ is positive.

$$\mathbf{A}_0 = \begin{bmatrix} 1 & 0 \\ 0 & 6 \end{bmatrix}, \quad \mathbf{B}_0 = \begin{bmatrix} 0 \\ 0 \end{bmatrix}, \quad C_0 = -1, \quad \mathbf{A}_1 = \begin{bmatrix} 52 & -36 \\ -36 & 73 \end{bmatrix},$$

$$\mathbf{B}_1 = \begin{bmatrix} -32 \\ -74 \end{bmatrix}, \quad C_1 = 28$$

From these are derived

$$\vec{Y}(t) = \begin{bmatrix} 4t(625t + 24) \\ t(2500t + 37) \end{bmatrix}, \quad \delta(t) = 2500t^2 + 385t + 6$$

The polynomial of Equation 7.9 is $p(t) = -156250000t^4 - 48125000t^3 + 1486875t^2 + 94500t + 1008$. The two real-valued roots are $t_0 \doteq -0.331386$ and $t_1 \doteq 0.0589504$. The corresponding $X(t)$ values are $X(t_0) = (x_0, y_0) \doteq (1.5869, 1.71472)$ and $X(t_1) = (x_1, y_1) \doteq (0.383779, 0.290742)$. The axis-aligned ellipse level values at these points are $Q_0(x_0, y_0) = -0.345528$ and $Q_0(x_1, y_1) = 19.1598$. Since $Q_0(x_0, y_0) < 0 < Q_0(x_1, y_1)$, the ellipses intersect. Figure 7.10 shows the two points on $Q_1 = 0$ that have extreme Q_0 values. ∎

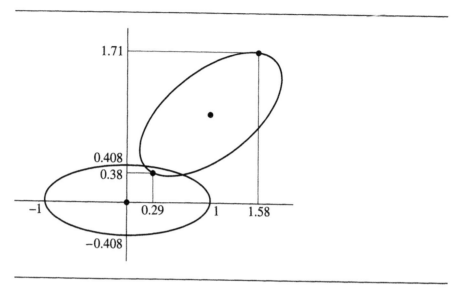

Figure 7.10   Intersection of two ellipses.

7.6 Polynomial Curves

Consider two polynomial curves, $X(s) = \sum_{i=0}^{n} \vec{A}_i s^i$, where $\vec{A}_n \neq \vec{0}$ and $s \in [s_{\min}, s_{\max}]$, and $Y(t) = \sum_{j=0}^{m} \vec{B}_j t^j$, where $\vec{B}_m \neq \vec{0}$ and $t \in [t_{\min}, t_{\max}]$. This section discusses how to compute points of intersection between the curves from both an algebraic and geometric perspective.

7.6.1 Algebraic Method

The straightforward algebraic method is to equate $X(s) = Y(t)$ and solve for the parameters s and t. Observe that the vector equation yields two polynomial equations of degree $\max\{n, m\}$ in the two unknowns s and t. The method of elimination may be used to obtain a single polynomial equation in one variable, $q(s) = 0$. The method of solution is a simple extension to what was shown in the section on intersection finding for lines and polynomial curves, except that the degree of $q(s)$ will be larger than in that case (for the line, $m = 1$; for curves, we generally have $m > 1$).

7.6.2 Polyline Approximation

The root finding of the algebraic method can be computationally expensive. Similar to Section 7.4 for line-curve intersection testing, the time complexity is reduced by approximating both curves by polylines and finding intersections of the two polylines. The polylines are obtained by subdivision, described in Section A.8. Any intersections between the polylines can be used as approximations to curve-curve intersections if the application is willing to accept that the polylines are suitable approximations to the curves. However, the points of intersection might be used as an attempt to localize the search for actual points of intersection.

7.6.3   HIERARCHICAL BOUNDING

In Section 7.4 we discussed using coarse-level testing using bounding polygons, bounding boxes, or hierarchies of bounding boxes to allow for an early out when the two underlying objects do not intersect. The same ideas apply to curve-curve intersection testing. If the curves are defined by control points and have the convex hull property, then an early-out algorithm would test first to see if the convex polygons containing the curves intersect. If not, then the curves do not intersect. If so, a finer-level test is used, perhaps directly the algebraic method described earlier.

A hierarchical approach using box trees can also be used. Each curve has a box hierarchy constructed for it. To localize the intersection testing, pairs of boxes, one from each tree, must be compared. This is effectively the 3D-oriented bounding box approach used by Gottschalk, Lin, and Manocha (1996), but in 2D and applied to curve segments instead of polylines. One issue is to perform an amortized analysis to determine at what point the box-box intersection tests become more expensive than the algebraic method for curve-curve intersection tests. At that point the simplicity of box-box intersection tests is outweighed by its excessive cost. A lot of the cost is strongly dependent on how deep the box hierarchies are. Another issue is construction of axis-aligned bounding boxes for curves. This was discussed in Section 7.4.

7.6.4   RASTERIZATION

Finally, a raster approach may be used, even though it is potentially quite expensive to execute. An axis-aligned bounding box $[x_{min}, x_{max}] \times [y_{min}, y_{max}]$ is constructed to contain both curves. An $N \times M$ raster is built to represent the box region. The grid points are uniformly chosen as (x_i, y_j) for $0 \le i < N$ and $0 \le j < M$. That is, $x_i = x_{min} + (x_{max} - x_{min})i/(N-1)$ and $y_j = y_{min} + (y_{max} - y_{min})j/(M-1)$. Each curve is drawn into the raster. The step size for the parameter of the curve should be chosen to be small enough so that as the curve is sampled you generate adjacent raster values, potentially with a raster cell drawn multiple times because multiple curve samples fall inside that cell. The overdraw can be minimized by sampling the curve based on arc length rather than the curve parameter. If the raster is initialized with 0, the first curve drawn by or-ing the pixels with 1, and the second curve drawn by

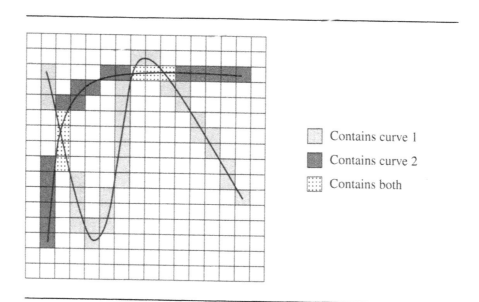

Figure 7.11   Two curves rasterized on a grid that is initially zero. The first curve is rasterized by or-ing the grid with the mask 1 (light gray). The second curve is rasterized by or-ing the grid with the mask 2 (dark gray). Grid cells that contain both curves have a value 3 (dotted).

or-ing the pixels with 2, the pixels that are associated with curve-curve intersections are those with a final value of 3 (see Figure 7.11).

Notice that the leftmost block of pixels (dotted cells) make it uncertain where the curves might intersect, if at all. The problem generally is that two curves can be near each other, yet not intersect, and be rasterized into the same pixels. The solution is to increase the number of cells while reducing the cell size to get a finer-resolution grid. How small a cell size should be to properly detect intersections and not produce false positives is usually information that is not known ahead of time.

Just as in the polyline approach, the application can choose to accept the pixel values as approximations to the actual curve-curve intersections. If more accuracy is desired, the pixels tagged as 3 (and possibly immediate neighbors) can be used as a localization of where the intersections occur. If a contiguous block of pixels is tagged, such as is shown in the left of the grid in Figure 7.11, and if the application chooses to believe the block occurs because of a single intersection of curves, a suitable choice for the approximation is the average of pixel locations. If the application chooses not to accept the pixel values as approximations, then it can store the original curve parameters for samples occurring in a pixel with that pixel. Those parameter values can be used to start a search for intersections using a numerical root finder or a numerical distance calculator.

7.7   THE METHOD OF SEPARATING AXES

A set S is *convex* if given any two points P and Q in S, the line segment $(1 - t)P + tQ$ for $t \in [0, 1]$ is also in S. This section describes the *method of separating axes* in 2D—a method for determining whether or not two stationary convex objects are intersecting. The ideas extend to moving convex objects and are useful for predicting collisions of the objects by computing the first time of contact and for computing the contact set. Two types of geometric queries are considered. The first is a *test-intersection* query that just indicates whether or not an intersection exists for stationary objects or will occur for moving objects. The second is a *find-intersections* query that involves computing the set of intersections for two stationary objects or for two moving objects at the time of first contact. This section describes both types of queries for convex polygons in 2D.

The following notation is used throughout this section. Let C_j for $j = 0, 1$ be the convex polygons with vertices $\{V_i^{(j)}\}_{i=0}^{N_j - 1}$ that are counterclockwise ordered. The edges of the polygons are $\vec{e}_i^{(j)} = V_{i+1}^{(j)} - V_i^{(j)}$ for $0 \le i < N_j$ and where $V_{N_j}^{(j)} = V_0^{(j)}$. Outward pointing normal vectors to the edges are $\vec{d}_i^{(j)} = \mathrm{Perp}\left(\vec{e}_i^{(j)}\right)$, where $\mathrm{Perp}(x, y) = (y, -x)$.

7.7.1   SEPARATION BY PROJECTION ONTO A LINE

A test for nonintersection of two convex objects is simply stated: if there exists a line for which the intervals of projection of the two objects onto that line do not intersect, then the objects do not intersect. Such a line is called a *separating line* or, more commonly, a *separating axis* (see Figure 7.12). The translation of a separating line is also a separating line, so it is sufficient to consider lines that contain the origin. Given a line containing the origin and with unit-length direction $\vec{d}$, the projection of a convex set C onto the line is the interval

$$I = [\lambda_{\min}(\vec{d}), \lambda_{\max}(\vec{d})] = [\min\{\vec{d} \cdot \vec{X} : \vec{X} \in C\}, \max\{\vec{d} \cdot \vec{X} : \vec{X} \in C\}]$$

where possibly $\lambda_{\min}(\vec{d}) = -\infty$ or $\lambda_{\max}(\vec{d}) = +\infty$; these cases arise when the convex set is unbounded. Two convex sets C_0 and C_1 are *separated* if there exists a direction $\vec{d}$ such that the projection intervals I_0 and I_1 do not intersect. Specifically they do not intersect when

$$\lambda_{\min}^{(0)}(\vec{d}) > \lambda_{\max}^{(1)}(\vec{d}) \quad \text{or} \quad \lambda_{\max}^{(0)}(\vec{d}) < \lambda_{\min}^{(1)}(\vec{d}) \tag{7.10}$$

The superscript corresponds to the index of the convex set. Although the comparisons are made where $\vec{d}$ is unit length, the comparison results are invariant to changes in length of the vector. This follows from $\lambda_{\min}(t\vec{d}) = t\lambda_{\min}(\vec{d})$ and $\lambda_{\max}(t\vec{d}) = t\lambda_{\max}(\vec{d})$ for $t > 0$. The Boolean value of the pair of comparisons is also invariant

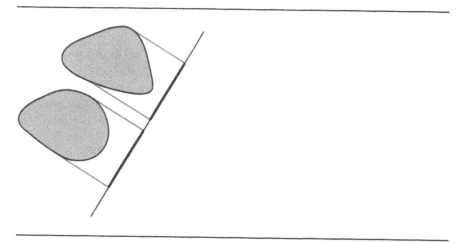

Figure 7.12   Nonintersecting convex objects and a separating line for them.

when $\vec{d}$ is replaced by the opposite direction $-\vec{d}$. This follows from $\lambda_{\min}(-\vec{d}) = -\lambda_{\max}(\vec{d})$ and $\lambda_{\max}(-\vec{d}) = -\lambda_{\min}(\vec{d})$. When $\vec{d}$ is not unit length, the intervals obtained for the separating line tests are not the projections of the object onto the line; rather they are scaled versions of the projection intervals. We make no distinction between the scaled projection and regular projection. We will also use the terminology that the direction vector for a separating line is called a *separating direction*, a direction that is not necessarily unit length.

Please note that in two dimensions, the terminology for separating line or axis is potentially confusing. The separating line separates the *projections* of the objects on that line. The separating line does *not* partition the plane into two regions, each containing an object. In three dimensions, the terminology should not be confusing since a plane would need to be specified to partition space into two regions, each containing an object. No real sense can be made for partitioning space by a line.

7.7.2   SEPARATION OF STATIONARY CONVEX POLYGONS

For a pair of convex polygons, only a finite set S of direction vectors needs to be considered for separation tests. That set contains only the normal vectors to the edges of the polygons. Figure 7.13(a) shows two nonintersecting polygons that are separated along a direction determined by the normal to an edge of one polygon. Figure 7.13(b) shows two polygons that intersect; there are no separating directions.

The intuition for why only edge normals must be tested is based on having two convex polygons just touching with no interpenetration. Figure 7.14 shows the three possible configurations: edge-edge contact, vertex-edge contact, and vertex-vertex

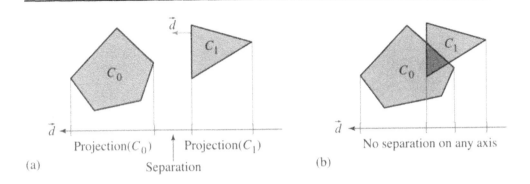

(a) Projection(C_0)   Projection(C_1)

Separation

(b) No separation on any axis

Figure 7.13   (a) Nonintersecting convex polygons. (b) Intersecting convex polygons.

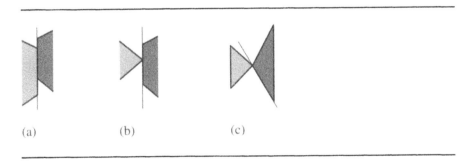

(a)   (b)   (c)

Figure 7.14   (a) Edge-edge contact, (b) vertex-edge contact, and (c) vertex-vertex contact.

contact. The lines between the polygons are perpendicular to the separation lines that would occur for one object translated away from the other by an infinitesimal distance.

The mathematical proof that S contains only edge normals is based on showing that if $\vec{d}$ is a separating direction that is not normal to an edge of either convex polygon, then there must be an edge normal that is also a separating direction. Let $\vec{d} = (\cos\theta, \sin\theta)$ be a separating direction that is not normal to an edge. For the sake of argument, assume that the projection of C_0 onto the separating line is on the left of the projection of C_1. A similar argument directly applies if it were on the right. Since $\vec{d}$ is not an edge normal, only one vertex V_0 of C_0 maps to $\lambda_{max}^{(0)}$, and only one vertex V_1 of C_1 maps to $\lambda_{min}^{(1)}$. Let θ_0 be the largest angle smaller than θ so that $\vec{d}_0 = (\cos\theta_0, \sin\theta_0)$ is an edge normal, but $\vec{d}(\phi) = (\cos\phi, \sin\phi)$ is not an edge normal for all $\phi \in (\theta_0, \theta]$. Similarly, let θ_1 be the smallest angle larger than θ so that $\vec{d}_1 =$

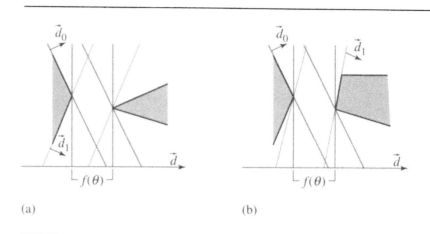

(a)   (b)

Figure 7.15   The edge normals closest to a non-edge-normal separation direction: (a) from the same triangle and (b) from different triangles.

$(\cos \theta_1, \sin \theta_1)$ is an edge normal, but $\vec{d}(\phi)$ is not an edge normal for all $\phi \in [\theta, \theta_1)$. For all directions $\vec{d}(\phi)$ with $\phi \in (\theta_0, \theta_1)$, V_0 is the unique vertex that maps to $\lambda_{max}^{(0)}$ and V_1 is the unique vertex that maps to $\lambda_{min}^{(1)}$. The separation between the intervals is the continuous function $f(\phi) = (\cos \phi, \sin \phi) \cdot (V_1 - V_0) = A \cos(\phi + \psi)$, where A is a constant amplitude and ψ is a constant phase angle. Also, $f(\theta) > 0$ since $\vec{d}$ is a separating direction.

If $f(\theta_0) > 0$, then the edge normal $\vec{d}_0$ is also a separating direction. If $f(\theta_1) > 0$, then the edge normal $\vec{d}_1$ is also a separating direction. Suppose that $f(\theta_0) \leq 0$ and $f(\theta_1) \leq 0$. Since $f(\theta) > 0$, there must exist two zeros of f on $[\theta_0, \theta_1]$, one smaller than θ and one larger than θ. The zeros of f are separated by π radians. This forces $\theta_1 - \theta_0 \geq \pi$, in which case the angle between the consecutive edge normals $\vec{d}_0$ and $\vec{d}_1$ is at least π radians. This happens only if the angle is exactly π, the two edges sharing V_0 are parallel to $\vec{d}$, and the two edges sharing V_1 are parallel to $\vec{d}$, a contradiction to the angles at those vertices being strictly positive. Therefore, it is impossible that both $f(\theta_0) \leq 0$ and $f(\theta_1) \leq 0$. In summary, if $f(\theta) > 0$, then either $f(\theta_0) > 0$, in which case $\vec{d}_0$ is a separating edge normal, or $f(\theta_1) > 0$, in which case $\vec{d}_1$ is a separating edge normal.

Figure 7.15 illustrates what $\vec{d}_0$ and $\vec{d}_1$ mean. Figure 7.15(a) shows the case where both nearest edge normals are from the same triangle. Figure 7.15(b) shows the case where the nearest edge normals are from different triangles.

The Direct Implementation

The direct implementation for a separation test for direction $\vec{d}$ just computes the extreme values of the projection and compares them. That is, compute $\lambda_{\min}^{(j)}(\vec{d}) = \min_{0 \le i < N_0}\{\vec{d} \cdot V_i^{(j)}\}$ and $\lambda_{\max}^{(j)}(\vec{d}) = \max_{0 \le i < N_1}\{\vec{d} \cdot V_i^{(j)}\}$ and test the inequalities in Equation 7.10. The pseudocode is listed below.

```
bool TestIntersection(ConvexPolygon C0, ConvexPolygon C1)
{
    // test edge normals of C0 for separation
    for (i0 = 0, i1 = C0.N-1; i0 < C0.N; i1 = i0, i0++) {
        D = Perp(C0.E(i1));   // C0.E(i1) = C0.V(i0) - C0.V(i1)
        ComputeInterval(C0, D, min0, max0);
        ComputeInterval(C1, D, min1, max1);
        if (max1 < min0 || max0 < min1)
            return false;
    }

    // test edge normals of C1 for separation
    for (i0 = 0, i1 = C1.N - 1; i0 < C1.N; i1 = i0, i0++) {
        D = Perp(C1.E(i1));   // C1.E(i1) = C1.V(i0) - C1.V(i1));
        ComputeInterval(C0, D, min0, max0);
        ComputeInterval(C1, D, min1, max1);
        if (max1 < min0 || max0 < min1)
            return false;
    }

    return true;
}

void ComputeInterval(ConvexPolygon C, Point D, float& min, float& max)
{
    min = max = Dot(D, C.V(0));
    for (i = 1; i < C.N; i++) {
        value = Dot(D, C.V(i));
        if (value < min)
            min = value;
        else if (value > max)
            max = value;
    }
}
```

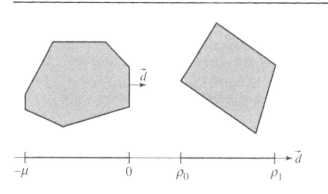

Figure 7.16   Two polygons separated by an edge-normal direction of the first polygon.

Observe that the implementation always processes potential separating lines that contain the origin. When polygons are relatively far from the origin, a variation on the implementation to deal with floating-point errors would involve choosing a potential separating line that contains a polygon vertex, thereby hoping to keep intermediate floating-point values relatively small.

An Alternative Implementation

An alternative algorithm avoids projecting all the vertices for the polygons by only testing for separation using the maximum of the interval for the first polygon and the minimum of the interval for the second polygon. If $\vec{d}$ is an outward pointing normal for the edge $V_{i+1} - V_i$ of the first polygon, then the projection of the first polygon onto the separating line $V_i + t\vec{d}$ is $[-\mu, 0]$, where $\mu > 0$. If the projection of the second polygon onto this line is $[\rho_0, \rho_1]$, then the reduced separation test is $\rho_0 > 0$. Figure 7.16 illustrates two separated polygons using this scheme. The value μ is irrelevant since we only need to compare ρ_0 to 0. Consequently, there is no need to project the vertices of the first polygon to calculate μ. Moreover, the vertices of the second polygon are projected one at a time until either the projected value is negative, in which case $\vec{d}$ is no longer considered for separation, or until all projected values are positive, in which case $\vec{d}$ is a separating direction.

```
bool TestIntersection(ConvexPolygon C0, ConvexPolygon C1)
{
    // Test edges of C0 for separation.  Because of the counterclockwise ordering,
    // the projection interval for C0 is [m,0] where m <= 0.  Only try to determine
    // if C1 is on the 'positive' side of the line.
```

```
for (i0 = 0, i1 = C0.N - 1; i0 < C0.N; i1 = i0, i0++) {
    D = Perp(C0.E(i1));   // C0.E(i1) = C0.V(i0) - C0.V(i1));
    if (WhichSide(C1.V, C0.V(i0), D) > 0) {
        // C1 is entirely on 'positive' side of line C0.V(i0) + t * D
        return false;
    }
}

// Test edges of C1 for separation.  Because of the counterclockwise ordering,
// the projection interval for C1 is [m,0] where m <= 0.  Only try to determine
// if C0 is on the 'positive' side of the line.
for (i0 = 0, i1 = C1.N - 1; i0 < C1.N; i1 = i0, i0++) {
    D = Perp(C1.E(i1));   // C1.E(i1) = C1.V(i0) - C1.V(i1));
    if (WhichSide(C0.V, C1.V(i0), D) > 0) {
        // C0 is entirely on 'positive' side of line C1.V(i0) + t * D
        return false;
    }
}

return true;
}

int WhichSide(PointSet S, Point P, Point D)
{
    // S vertices are projected to the form P + t * D.  Return value is +1 if all t > 0,
    // -1 if all t < 0, 0 otherwise (in which case the line splits the polygon).

    positive = 0; negative = 0; zero = 0;
    for (i = 0; i < C.N; i++) {
        t = Dot(D, S.V(i) - P);
        if (t > 0) positive++; else if (t < 0) negative++; else zero++;
        if (positive && negative || zero) return 0;
    }
    return positive ? 1 : -1;
}
```

An Asymptotically Better Alternative

Although the alternative implementation is roughly twice as fast as the direct implementation, both are of order $O(NM)$, where N and M are the number of vertices for the convex polygons. An asymptotically better alternative uses a form of bisection to find an extreme point of the projection of the polygon (O'Rourke 1998). The bisection effectively narrows in on sign changes of the dot product of edges with the specified direction vector. For a polygon of N vertices, the bisection is of order $O(\log N)$, so the total algorithm is $O(\max\{N \log M, M \log N\})$.

Given two vertex indices i_0 and i_1 of a polygon with N vertices, the *middle index* of the indices is described by the following pseudocode:

```
int GetMiddleIndex(int i0, int i1, int N)
{
    if (i0 < i1)
        return (i0 + i1) / 2;
    else
        return (i0 + i1 + N) / 2 % N);
}
```

The division of two integers returns the largest integer smaller than the real-value ratio, and the percent sign indicates modulo arithmetic. Observe that if $i_0 = i_1 = 0$, the function returns a valid index. The condition when $i_0 < i_1$ has an obvious result: the returned index is the average of the input indices, certainly supporting the name of the function. For example, if the polygon has $N = 5$ vertices, inputs $i_0 = 0$ and $i_1 = 2$ lead to a returned index of 1. The other condition handles wraparound of the indices. If $i_0 = 2$ and $i_1 = 0$, the implied set of ordered indices is $\{2, 3, 4, 0\}$. The middle index is selected as 3 since $3 = (2 + 0 + 5)/2 \pmod 5$.

The bisection algorithm to find the extreme value of the projection is

```
int GetExtremeIndex(ConvexPolygon C, Point D)
{
    i0 = 0; i1 = 0;
    while (true) {
        mid = GetMiddleIndex(i0,i1);
        next = (mid + 1) % C.N;
            E = C.V(next) - C.V(mid);
        if (Dot(D, E) > 0)  {
            if (mid != i0) i0 = mid; else return i1;
        } else  {
            prev = (mid + C.N - 1) % C.N;
                E = C.V(mid) - C.V(prev);
            if (Dot(D, E) < 0) i1 = mid; else return mid;
        }
    }
}
```

Using the bisection method, the intersection testing pseudocode is

```
bool TestIntersection(ConvexPolygon C0, ConvexPolygon C1)
{
    // Test edges of C0 for separation.  Because of the counterclockwise ordering,
    // the projection interval for C0 is [m, 0] where m <= 0.  Only try to determine
    // if C1 is on the 'positive' side of the line.
    for (i0 = 0, i1 = C0.N - 1; i0 < C0.N; i1 = i0, i0++)  {
        D = Perp(C0.E(i1)); // C0.E(i1) = C0.V(i0) - C0.V(i1));
        min = GetExtremeIndex(C1, -D);
        diff = C1.V(min) - C0.V(i0);
        if (Dot(D, diff) > 0) {
            // C1 is entirely on 'positive' side of line C0.V(i0) + t * D
            return false;
        }
    }

    // Test edges of C1 for separation.  Because of the counterclockwise ordering,
    // the projection interval for C1 is [m, 0] where m <= 0.  Only try to determine
    // if C0 is on the 'positive' side of the line.
    for (i0 = 0, i1 = C1.N - 1; i0 < C1.N; i1 = i0, i0++) {
        D = Perp(C1.E(i1));  // C1.E(i1) = C1.V(i0) - C1.V(i1));
        min = GetExtremeIndex(C0, -D);
        diff = C0.V(min) - C1.V(i0);
        if (Dot(D,diff) > 0) {
            // C0 is entirely on 'positive' side of line C1.V(i0) + t * D
            return false;
        }
    }

    return true;
}
```

7.7.3 SEPARATION OF MOVING CONVEX POLYGONS

The method of separating axes extends to convex polygons moving with constant velocity. The algorithm is attributed to Ron Levine in a post to the GD algorithms mailing list (Levine 2000). If C_0 and C_1 are convex polygons with velocities $\vec{w}_0$ and $\vec{w}_1$, it can be determined via projections if the polygons will intersect for some time $T \geq 0$. If they do intersect, the first time of contact can be computed. It is enough to work with a stationary polygon C_0 and a moving polygon C_1 with velocity $\vec{w}$ since we can always use $\vec{w} = \vec{w}_1 - \vec{w}_0$ to perform the calculations as if C_0 were not moving.

If C_0 and C_1 are initially intersecting, then the first time of contact is $T = 0$. Otherwise the convex polygons are initially disjoint. The projection of C_1 onto a line with direction $\vec{d}$ not perpendicular to $\vec{w}$ is itself moving. The speed of the projection along the line is $\omega = (\vec{w} \cdot \vec{d})/\|\vec{d}\|^2$. If the projection interval of C_1 moves away from the projection interval of C_0, then the two polygons will never intersect. The cases when intersection might happen are those when the projection intervals for C_1 move toward those of C_0.

The intuition for how to predict an intersection is much like that for selecting the potential separating directions in the first place. If the two convex polygons intersect at a first time $T_{\text{first}} > 0$, then their projections are not separated along any line at that time. An instant before first contact, the polygons are separated. Consequently there must be at least one separating direction for the polygons at time $T_{\text{first}} - \varepsilon$ for small $\varepsilon > 0$. Similarly, if the two convex polygons intersect at a last time $T_{\text{last}} > 0$, then their projections are also not separated at that time along any line, but an instant after last contact, the polygons are separated. Consequently there must be at least one separating direction for the polygons at time $T_{\text{last}} + \varepsilon$ for small $\varepsilon > 0$. Both T_{first} and T_{last} can be tracked as each potential separating axis is processed. After all directions are processed, if $T_{\text{first}} \leq T_{\text{last}}$, then the two polygons do intersect with first contact time T_{first}. It is also possible that $T_{\text{first}} > T_{\text{last}}$, in which case the two polygons cannot intersect.

Pseudocode for testing for intersection of two moving convex polygons is given below. The time interval over which the event is of interest is $[0, T_{\text{max}}]$. If knowing an intersection at *any* future time is desired, then set $T_{\text{max}} = \infty$. Otherwise, T_{max} is finite. The function is implemented to indicate there is no intersection on $[0, T_{\text{max}}]$, even though there might be an intersection at some time $T > T_{\text{max}}$.

```
bool TestIntersection(ConvexPolygon C0, Point W0, ConvexPolygon C1, Point W1,
    float tmax, float& tfirst, float& tlast)
{
    W = W1 - W0;  // process as if C0 is stationary, C1 is moving
    tfirst = 0;  tlast = INFINITY;

    // test edges of C0 for separation
    for (i0 = 0, i1 = C0.N - 1; i0 < C0.N; i1 = i0, i0++) {
        D = Perp(C0.E(i1));  // C0.E(i1) = C0.V(i0) - C0.V(i1));
        ComputeInterval(C0, D, min0, max0);
        ComputeInterval(C1, D, min1, max1);
        speed = Dot(D, W);
        if (NoIntersect(tmax, speed, min0, max0, min1, max1, tfirst, tlast))
            return false;
    }

    // test edges of C1 for separation
    for (i0 = 0, i1 = C1.N - 1; i0 < C1.N; i1 = i0, i0++) {
```

```
            D = Perp(C1.E(i1)); // C1.E(i1) = C1.V(i0) - C1.V(i1));
            ComputeInterval(C0, D, min0, max0);
            ComputeInterval(C1, D, min1, max1);
            speed = Dot(D, W);
            if (NoIntersect(tmax, speed, min0, max0, min1, max1, tfirst, tlast))
                return false;
        }
        return true;
    }


    bool NoIntersect(float tmax, float speed, float min0, float max0,
        float min1, float max1, float& tfirst, float& tlast)
    {
        if (max1 < min0) {
            // interval(C1) initially on 'left' of interval(C0)
            if (speed <= 0) return true;   // intervals moving apart
            t = (min0 - max1) / speed;  if (t > tfirst) tfirst = t;
            if (tfirst > tmax) return true;
            t = (max0 - min1) /speed;  if (t < tlast) tlast = t;
            if (tfirst > tlast) return true;
        } else if (max0 < min1) {
            // interval(C1) initially on 'right' of interval(C0)
            if (speed >= 0) return true;   // intervals moving apart
            t = (max0 - min1)/speed;  if ( t > tfirst ) tfirst = t;
            if (tfirst > tmax) return true;
            t = (min0 - max1)/speed;  if ( t < tlast ) tlast = t;
            if (tfirst > tlast) return true;
        }  else {
            // interval(C0) and interval(C1) overlap
            if (speed > 0) {
                t = (max0 - min1) / speed;  if (t < tlast) tlast = t;
                if (tfirst > tlast) return true;
            } else if (speed < 0) {
                t = (min0 - max1) / speed;  if (t < tlast) tlast = t;
                if (tfirst > tlast) return true;
            }
        }
        return false;
    }
```

The following example illustrates the ideas. The first box is the unit cube $0 \leq x \leq 1$ and $0 \leq y \leq 1$ and is stationary. The second box is initially $0 \leq x \leq 1$ and $1 + \delta \leq y \leq 2 + \delta$ for some $\delta > 0$. Let its velocity be $(1, -1)$. Whether or not the second box intersects the first box depends on the value of δ. The only potential separating

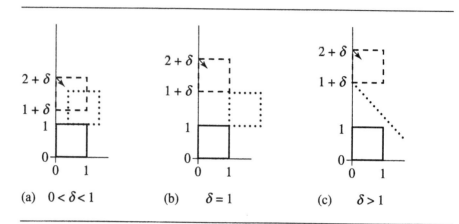

(a) $0 < \delta < 1$ (b) $\delta = 1$ (c) $\delta > 1$

Figure 7.17   (a) Edge-edge intersection predicted. (b) Vertex-vertex intersection predicted. (c) No intersection predicted.

axes are $(1, 0)$ and $(0, 1)$. Figure 7.17 shows the initial configuration for three values of δ, one where there will be an edge-edge intersection, one where there will be a vertex-vertex intersection, and one where there is no intersection. The black box is stationary. The dashed box is moving. The black vector indicates the direction of motion. The dotted boxes indicate where the moving box first touches the stationary box. In Figure 7.17(c) the dotted line indicates that the moving box will miss the stationary box. For $\vec{d} = (1, 0)$, the pseudocode produces min0 = 0, max0 = 1, min1 = 0, max1 = 1, and speed = 1. The projected intervals are initially overlapping. Since the speed is positive, T = (max0 - min1)/speed = 1 < TLast = INFINITY and TLast is updated to 1. For $\vec{d} = (0, 1)$, the pseudocode produces min0 = 0, max0 = 1, min1 = 1 + delta, max1 = 2 + delta, and speed = -1. The moving projected interval is initially on the right of the stationary projected interval. Since the speed is negative, T = (max0 - min1)/speed = delta > TFirst = 0 and TFirst is updated to delta. The next block of code sets T = (min0 - max1)/speed = 2 + delta. The value TLast is not updated since $2 + \delta < 1$ cannot happen for $\delta > 0$. On exit from the loop over potential separating directions, $T_{\text{First}} = \delta$ and $T_{\text{last}} = 1$. The objects intersect if and only if $T_{\text{first}} \le T_{\text{last}}$, or $\delta \le 1$. This condition is consistent with Figure 7.17. Figure 7.17(a) has $\delta < 1$, and Figure 7.17(b) has $\delta = 1$; intersections occur in both cases. Figure 7.17(c) has $\delta > 1$, and no intersection occurs.

7.7.4   INTERSECTION SET FOR STATIONARY CONVEX POLYGONS

The find-intersection query for two stationary convex polygons is a special example of Boolean operations on polygons. Section 13.5 provides a general discussion for computing Boolean operations. In particular there is a discussion on linear time computation for the intersection of convex polgons. That is, if the two polygons have N and M vertices, the order of the intersection algorithm is $O(N + M)$. A less efficient algorithm, but one perhaps easier to understand, clips the edges of each polygon against the other polygon. The order of this algorithm is $O(NM)$. Of course the asymptotic analysis applies to large N and M, so the latter algorithm is potentially a good choice for triangles and rectangles.

7.7.5 CONTACT SET FOR MOVING CONVEX POLYGONS

Given two moving convex objects C_0 and C_1, initially not intersecting and with velocities $\vec{w}_0$ and $\vec{w}_1$, we showed earlier how to compute the first time of contact T, if it exists. Assuming it does, the sets $C_0 + T\vec{w}_0 = \{X + T\vec{w}_0 : X \in C_0\}$ and $C_1 + T\vec{w}_1 = \{X + T\vec{w}_1 : X \in C_1\}$ are just touching with no interpenetration. Figure 7.14 shows the various configurations.

The TestIntersection function can be modified to keep track of which vertices or edges are projected to the end points of the projection interval. At the first time of contact, this information is used to determine how the two objects are oriented with respect to each other. If the contact is vertex-edge or vertex-vertex, then the contact set is a single point, a vertex. If the contact is edge-edge, the contact set is a line segment that contains at least one vertex. Each end point of the projection interval is either generated by a vertex or an edge. A two-character label is associated with each polygon to indicate the projection type. The single-character labels are V for a vertex projection and E for an edge projection. The four two-character labels are VV, VE, EV, and EE. The first letter corresponds to the minimum of the interval, and the second letter corresponds to the maximum of the interval. It is also necessary to store the projection interval and the vertex or edge indices of the components that project to the interval extremes. A convenient data structure is

```
Configuration
{
    float min, max;
    int index[2];
    char type[2];
};
```

where the projection interval is [min, max]. For example, if the projection type is EV, index[0] is the index of the edge that projects to the minimum, and index[1] is the index of the vertex that projects to the maximum.

Two configuration objects are declared, Cfg0 for polygon C_0 and Cfg1 for polygon C_1. In the first loop in TestIntersection, the projection of C_0 onto the line containing vertex V_{i_0} and having direction perpendicular to $\vec{e}_{i_1} = V_{i_0} - V_{i_1}$ produces a projection type whose second index is E since the outer pointing edge normal is used. The first index can be either V or E depending on the polygon. The pseudocode is

```
void ProjectNormal(ConvexPolygon C, Point D, int edgeindex, Configuration Cfg)
{
    Cfg.max = Dot(D, C.V(edgeindex));    // = Dot(D, C.V((edgeindex + 1) % C.N))
        Cfg.index[1] = edgeindex;
    Cfg.type[0] = 'V';
    Cfg.type[1] = 'E';

    Cfg.min = Cfg.max;
    for (i = 1, j = (edgeindex + 2) % C.N; i < C.N; i++, j = (j + 1) % C.N) {
            value = Dot(D, C.V(j));
        if (value < Cfg.min) {
            Cfg.min = value;
            Cfg.index[0] = j;
        } else if (value == Cfg.min) {
            // Found an edge parallel to initial projected edge.  The
            // remaining vertices can only project to values larger than
            // the minimum.  Keep the index of the first visited end point.
            Cfg.type[0] = 'E';
            return;
        } else { // value > Cfg.min
            // You have already found the minimum of projection, so when
            // the dot product becomes larger than the minimum, you are
            // walking back towards the initial edge.  No point in
            // wasting time to do this, just return since you now know
            // the projection.
            return;
        }
    }
}
```

The projection of C_1 onto an edge normal line of C_0 can lead to any projection type. The pseudocode is

```
void ProjectGeneral(ConvexPolygon C, Point D, Configuration Cfg)
{
    Cfg.min = Cfg.max = Dot(D, C.V(0));
    Cfg.index[0] = Cfg.index[1] = 0;

    for (i = 1; i < C.N; i++) {
        value = Dot(D, C.V(i));
        if (value < Cfg.min)  {
            Cfg.min = value;
            Cfg.index[0] = i;
        } else if (value > Cfg.max) {
```

```
            Cfg.max = value;
            Cfg.index[1] = i;
        }
    }

    Cfg.type[0] = Cfg.type[1] = 'V';
    for (i = 0; i < 2; i++) {
        if (Dot(D, C.E(Cfg.index[i] - 1)) == 0) {
            Cfg.index[i] = Cfg.index[i] - 1;
            Cfg.type[i] = 'E';
        } else if (Dot(D, C.E(Cfg.index[i] + 1)) == 0) {
            Cfg.type[i] = 'E';
        }
    }
}
```

The index arithmetic for the edges of C is performed modulo C.N so that the resulting index is within range.

The NoIntersect function accepted as input the projection intervals for the two polygons. Now those intervals are stored in the configuration objects, so NoIntersect must be modified to reflect this. In the event that there will be an intersection between the moving polygons, it is necessary that the configuration information be saved for later use in determining the contact set. As a result, NoIntersect must keep track of the configuration objects corresponding to the current first time of contact. Finally, the contact set calculation will require knowledge of the order of the projection intervals. NoIntersect will set a flag with value $+1$ if the intervals intersect at the maximum of the C_0 interval and the minimum of the C_1 interval or with value -1 if the intervals intersect at the minimum of the C_0 interval and the maximum of the C_1 interval. The modified pseudocode is

```
bool NoIntersect(float tmax, float speed, Configuration Cfg0,
    Configuration Cfg1, Configuration& Curr0, Configuration& Curr1,
    int& side, float& tfirst, float& tlast)
{
    if (Cfg1.max < Cfg0.min) {
        if (speed <= 0) return true;
        t = (Cfg0.min - Cfg1.max) / speed;
        if (t > tfirst) {
            tfirst = t;  side = -1;  Curr0 = Cfg0;  Curr1 = Cfg1;
        }
        if (tfirst > tmax  return true;
        t = (Cfg0.max - Cfg1.min) / speed;  if (t < tlast) tlast = t;
        if (tfirst > tlast) return true;
    } else if (Cfg0.max < Cfg1.min) {
```

```
            if (speed >= 0) return true;
            t = (Cfg0.max - Cfg1.min) / speed;
            if (t > tfirst) {
                tfirst = t;  side = +1;  Curr0 = Cfg0;  Curr1 = Cfg1;
            }
            if (tfirst > tmax) return true;
            t = (Cfg0.min - Cfg1.max) / speed;  if (t < tlast) tlast = t;
            if (tfirst > tlast) return true;
        } else {
            if (speed > 0) {
                t = (Cfg0.max - Cfg1.min) / speed;  if (t < tlast) tlast = t;
                if (tfirst > tlast) return true;
            } else if (speed < 0) {
                t = (Cfg0.min - Cfg1.max) / speed;  if (t < tlast) tlast = t;
                if (tfirst > tlast) return true;
            }
        }
    }
    return false;
}
```

With the indicated modifications, TestIntersection has the equivalent formulation:

```
bool TestIntersection(ConvexPolygon C0, Point W0, ConvexPolygon C1, Point W1,
                      float tmax, float& tfirst, float& tlast)
{
    W = W1 - W0;  // process as if C0 stationary and C1 moving
    tfirst = 0;   tlast = INFINITY;

    // process edges of C0
    for (i0 = 0, i1 = C0.N - 1; i0 < C0.N; i1 = i0, i0++) {
        D = Perp(C0.E(i1)); // = C0.V(i0) - C0.V(i1));
        ProjectNormal(C0, D, i1, Cfg0);
        ProjectGeneral(C1, D, Cfg1);
        speed = Dot(D, W);
        if (NoIntersect(tmax, speed, Cfg0, Cfg1, Curr0, Curr1, side, tfirst,
                        tlast))
            return false;
    }

    // process edges of C1
    for (i0 = 0, i1 = C1.N - 1; i0 < C1.N; i1 = i0, i0++) {
        D = Perp(C1.E(i1)); // = C1.V(i0) - C1.V(i1));
        ProjectNormal(C1, D, i1, Cfg1);
```

```
        ProjectGeneral(C0, D, Cfg0);
        speed = Dot(D, W);
        if (NoIntersect(tmax, speed, Cfg0, Cfg1, Curr0, Curr1, side, tfirst,
                        tlast))
            return false;
    }

    return true;
}
```

The FindIntersection pseudocode has exactly the same implementation as Test-Intersection, but with one additional block of code after the two loops that is reached if there will be an intersection. When the polygons will intersect at time T, they are effectively moved with their respective velocities and the contact set is calculated. Let $U_i^{(j)} = V_i^{(j)} + T\vec{w}^{(j)}$ represent the polygon vertices after motion. In the case of edge-edge contact, for the sake of argument suppose that the contact edges are $\vec{e}_0^{(0)}$ and $\vec{e}_0^{(1)}$. Figure 7.18 illustrates the configurations for two triangles: Because of the counterclockwise ordering of the polygons, observe that the two edge directions are parallel, but in opposite directions. The edge of the first polygon is parameterized as $U_0^{(0)} + s\vec{e}_0^{(0)}$ for $s \in [0, 1]$. The edge of the second polygon has the same parametric form, but with $s \in [s_0, s_1]$ where

$$s_0 = \frac{\vec{e}_0^{(0)} \cdot \left(U_1^{(1)} - U_0^{(0)}\right)}{||\vec{e}_0||^2} \quad \text{and} \quad s_1 = \frac{\vec{e}_0^{(0)} \cdot \left(U_0^{(1)} - U_0^{(0)}\right)}{||\vec{e}_0||^2}$$

The overlap of the two edges occurs for $\bar{s} \in I = [0, 1] \cap [s_0, s_1] \neq \emptyset$. The corresponding points in the contact set are $V_0^{(0)} + T\vec{w}^{(0)} + \bar{s}\vec{e}_0^{(0)}$.

In the event the two polygons are initially overlapping, the contact set is more expensive to construct. This set can be constructed by standard methods involving Boolean operations on polygons.

The pseudocode is shown below. The intersection is a convex polygon and is returned in the last two arguments of the function. If the intersection set is nonempty, the return value of the function is true. The set must itself be convex. The number of vertices in the set is stored in quantity, and the vertices in counterclockwise order are stored in the array I[]. If the return value is false, the last two arguments of the function are invalid and should not be used.

```
bool FindIntersection(ConvexPolygon C0, Point W0, ConvexPolygon C1, Point W1,
        float tmax, float& tfirst, float& tlast, int& quantity, Point I[])
{
    W = W1 - W0;  // process as if C0 stationary and C1 moving
    tfirst = 0;  tlast = INFINITY;
```

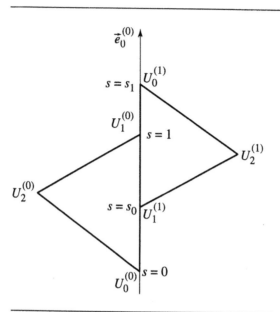

Figure 7.18 Edge-edge contact for two moving triangles.

```
// process edges of C0
for (i0 = 0, i1 = C0.N - 1; i0 < C0.N; i1 = i0, i0++) {
    D = Perp(C0.E(i1)); // C0.E(i1) = C0.V(i0) - C0.V(i1));
    ProjectNormal(C0, D, i1, Cfg0);
    ProjectGeneral(C1, D, Cfg1);
    speed = Dot(D, W);
    if (NoIntersect(tmax, speed, Cfg0, Cfg1, Curr0, Curr1, side, tfirst,
                    tlast))
        return false;
}

// process edges of C1
for (i0 = 0, i1 = C1.N - 1; i0 < C1.N; i1 = i0, i0++) {
    D = Perp(C1.E(i1)); // C1.E(i1) = C1.V(i0) - C1.V(i1));
    ProjectNormal(C1, D, i1, Cfg1);
    ProjectGeneral(C0, D, Cfg0);
    speed = Dot(D, W);
    if (NoIntersect(tmax, speed, Cfg0, Cfg1, Curr0, Curr1, side, tfirst,
                    tlast))
        return false;
}
```

```
        // compute the contact set
        GetIntersection(C0, W0, C1, W1, Curr0, Curr1, side, tfirst, quantity, I);
        return true;
}
```

The intersection calculator pseudocode is shown below. Observe how the projection types are used to determine if the contact is vertex-vertex, edge-vertex, or edge-edge.

```
void GetIntersection(ConvexPolygon C0, Point W0, ConvexPolygon C1, Point W1,
    Configuration Cfg0, Configuration Cfg1, int side, float tfirst,
    int& quantity, Point I[])
{
    if (side == 1) {   // C0-max meets C1-min
        if (Cfg0.type[1] == 'V') {
            // vertex-vertex or vertex-edge intersection
            quantity = 1;
            I[0] = C0.V(Cfg0.index[1]) + tfirst * W0;
        } else if (Cfg1.type[0] == 'V') {
            // vertex-vertex or edge-vertex intersection
            quantity = 1;
            I[0] = C1.V(Cfg1.index[0]) + tfirst * W1;
        } else {   // Cfg0.type[1] == 'E' && Cfg1.type[0] == 'E'
            // edge-edge intersection
            P = C0.V(Cfg0.index[1]) + tfirst * W0;
            E = C0.E(Cfg0.index[1]);
            U0 = C1.V(Cfg1.index[0]);
            U1 = C1.V((Cfg1.index[0]+ 1) % C1.N);
            s0 = Dot(E, U1 - P) / Dot(E, E);
            s1 = Dot(E,U0 - P) / Dot(E, E);
            FindIntervalIntersection(0, 1, s0, s1, quantity, interval);
            for (i = 0; i < quantity; i++)
                I[i] = P + interval[i] * E;
        }
    } else if (side == -1) { // C1-max meets C0-min
        if (Cfg1.type[1] == 'V') {
            // vertex-vertex or vertex-edge intersection
            quantity = 1;
            I[0] = C1.V(Cfg1.index[1]) + tfirst * W1;
        } else if (Cfg0.type[0] == 'V') {
            // vertex-vertex or edge-vertex intersection
            quantity = 1;
            I[0] = C0.V(Cfg0.index[0]) + tfirst * W0;
        } else { // Cfg1.type[1] == 'E' && Cfg0.type[0] == 'E'
```

```
            // edge-edge intersection
            P = C1.V(Cfg1.index[1]) + tfirst * W1;
            E = C1.E(Cfg1.index[1]);
            U0 = C0.V(Cfg0.index[0]);
            U1 = C0.V((Cfg0.index[0] + 1) % C0.N);
            s0 = Dot(E, U1 - P) / Dot(E, E);
            s1 = Dot(E, U0 - P) / Dot(E, E);
            FindIntervalIntersection(0, 1, s0, s1, quantity, interval);
            for (i = 0; i < quantity; i++)
                I[i] = P + interval[i] * E;
        }
    } else { // polygons were initially intersecting
        ConvexPolygon C0Moved = C0 + tfirst * W0;
        ConvexPolygon C1Moved = C1 + tfirst * W1;
        FindPolygonIntersection(C0Moved, C1Moved, quantity, I);
    }
}
```

The final case occurs when the two polygons were initially overlapping, so the first time of contact is $T = 0$. FindPolygonIntersection is a general routine for computing the intersection of two polygons.

CHAPTER 8

MISCELLANEOUS 2D PROBLEMS

This chapter includes a variety of problems involving lines, circles, and triangles. Most of these are commonly (or at least occasionally) encountered problems, while others, although less commonly encountered, serve to show how various techniques may be brought to bear on new problems.

8.1 CIRCLE THROUGH THREE POINTS

Suppose we have three points P_0, P_1, and P_2. These three points define a unique circle $C : \{C, r\}$, as shown in Figure 8.1. This problem is equivalent to finding the circumscribed circle of the triangle formed by the three vertices, the solution to which can be found in Section 13.10.

8.2 CIRCLE TANGENT TO THREE LINES

Suppose we have three lines $\mathcal{L}_0$, $\mathcal{L}_1$, and $\mathcal{L}_2$. If none of these lines are parallel, then a unique circle $C : \{C, r\}$ can be found that is tangent to all three lines, as shown in Figure 8.2.

The intersections of the three lines form a triangle, and so this problem is equivalent to finding what is known as the *inscribed circle* or *incircle* of a triangle. If we first compute these intersections, our problem is then equivalent to finding the inscribed circle of the triangle so formed, the solution to which can be found in Section 13.10.

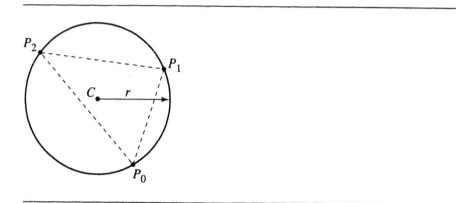

Figure 8.1   Circle through three points.

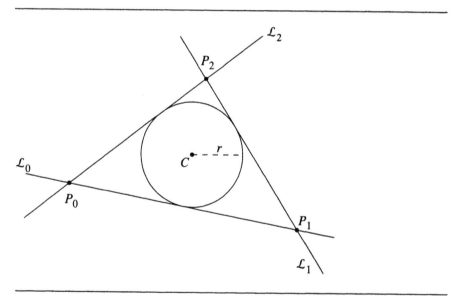

Figure 8.2   Circle tangent to three lines.

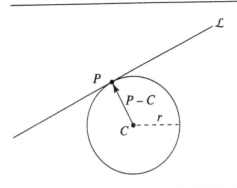

Figure 8.3   Line tangent to a circle at a given point.

8.3 LINE TANGENT TO A CIRCLE AT A GIVEN POINT

Figure 8.3 shows the construction of a line through a given point on a circle and tangent to it. Computation of the line in parametric form is trivial

$$\mathcal{L}:\{P, (P-C)^{\perp}\}$$

or in coordinate terms

$$x = P_x - t(P_y - C_y)$$
$$y = P_y + t(P_x - C_x)$$

The implicit form is equally trivial to compute:

$$\mathcal{L}:\{P-C, -((P-C)\cdot P)\}$$

The pseudocode is

```
void LineTangentToCircleAtGivenPoint(Line2D line, Point2D c, Point2D p)
{
    Vector2D v = p - c;
    line.direction.x = -v.y;
    line.direction.y = v.x;
    line.origin = p;
}
```

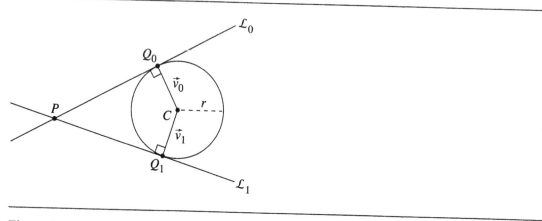

Figure 8.4   Line through point, tangent to a circle.

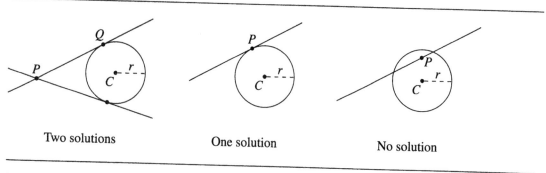

Two solutions   One solution   No solution

Figure 8.5   In general, there are two tangents, but there may be one or none.

8.4 LINE TANGENT TO A CIRCLE THROUGH A GIVEN POINT

Suppose we have a circle C, defined by its center C and radius r, and a point P, and we wish to compute the lines $\mathcal{L}_0$ and $\mathcal{L}_1$ through P and tangent to C, as shown in Figure 8.4. Note that for an arbitrary point P and circle C, there may be one, two, or no tangents, as can be seen in Figure 8.5.

The key to the solution here is in noting that the direction vector of $\mathcal{L}_0$ ($\mathcal{L}_1$) is perpendicular to vectors $\vec{v}_0$ ($\vec{v}_1$) between the center of C and point(s) Q_0 (Q_1) on C. Consider the angle θ between $\vec{v}$ (either one) and $\vec{u} = P - C$: using the definition of the dot product, we know that

$$\cos \theta = \frac{\vec{u} \cdot \vec{v}}{\|\vec{u}\| \|\vec{v}\|}$$

But we also know by trigonometry that

$$\cos \theta = \frac{r}{\|\vec{u}\|}$$

If we equate these, we get

$$\frac{\vec{v} \cdot \vec{u}}{\|\vec{u}\| \|\vec{v}\|} = \frac{r}{\|\vec{u}\|}$$

If we note that $\|\vec{v}\| = r$, we can simplify this as follows:

$$\frac{\vec{u} \cdot \vec{v}}{\|\vec{u}\| \|\vec{v}\|} = \frac{r}{\|\vec{u}\|}$$

$$\frac{\vec{u} \cdot \vec{v}}{r\|\vec{u}\|} = \frac{r}{\|\vec{u}\|}$$

$$\vec{u} \cdot \vec{v} = r^2$$

We now have two equations

$$\vec{u} \cdot \vec{v} = r^2$$

$$\|\vec{v}\| = r$$

where $\vec{u}$ and r are known and $\vec{v}$ comprises two unknowns. In component form, we have

$$u_x v_x + u_y v_y = r^2$$

$$\sqrt{v_x v_x + v_y v_y} = r$$

which we can solve for the two unknowns v_x and v_y:

$$v_x = \frac{r^2 - \frac{r^2 u_y^2}{u_x^2 + u_y^2} \mp \frac{u_y \sqrt{-(r^4 u_x^2) + r^2 u_x^4 + r^2 u_x^2 u_y^2}}{u_x^2 + u_y^2}}{u_x}$$

$$v_y = \frac{r^2 u_y \pm \sqrt{-(r^4 u_x^2) + r^2 u_x^4 + r^2 u_x^2 u_y^2}}{u_x^2 + u_y^2}$$

The two vectors $\vec{v}_0$ and $\vec{v}_1$ can be obtained by computing both combinations of the $+/-$ and $-/+$ appearing in the equation above. The tangent lines are perpendicular to $\vec{v}_0$ and $\vec{v}_1$, and so we have the two tangents:

$$\mathcal{L}_0(t) = P + t\vec{v}_0^{\perp}$$

$$\mathcal{L}_1(t) = P - t\vec{v}_1^{\perp}$$

The pseudocode is

```
int TangentLineToCircleThroughPoint(
    Point2D p,
    float   radius,
    Point2D center,
    Line    solution[2])
{
    int   numSoln;
    float distanceCP;

    distanceCP = dist2D(center,p);

    Vector2D u, v0, v1;

    if (distanceCP < radius) {
        numSoln = 0;
    } else if (distanceCP == radius) {
        numSoln = 1;
        u = p - center;
        solution[0].setDir(-u.y, u.x);
        solution[0].setPoint(p.x, p.y);
    } else if (distanceCP > radius) {
        numSoln = 2;
        u = p - center;
        float ux2 = u.x * u.x;
        float ux4 = ux2 * ux2;
        float uy2 = u.y * u.y;
        float r2  = radius * radius;
        float r4  = r2 * r2;
        float num = r2 * uy2;
        float denom = ux2 + uy2;
        float rad = sqrt(-(r4 * ux2) + r2 * ux4 + r2 * ux2 * uy2);

        v0.x = (r2 - (num + u.y * rad)/denom)/u.x
        v0.y = (r2 * u.y) + rad)/ denom;
```

```
v1.x = (r2 - (num - u.y * rad)/denom)/u.x
v1.y = (r2 * u.y) - rad)/ denom;

solution[0].setDir(-v0.y, v.x);
solution[0].setPoint(p.x, p.y);

solution[1].setDir(v1.y, -v1.x)
solution[1].setPoint(p);

// Note: may wish to normalize line directions
// before returning, depending on application
}
return numSoln;
}
```

8.5 LINES TANGENT TO TWO CIRCLES

Given two circles, we wish to find a line tangent to both circles, as shown in Figure 8.6. The circles are defined by their respective centers and radii: $\{C_0, r_0\}$ and $\{C_1, r_1\}$. As can be seen in Figure 8.7, in general there can be four, two, one, none, or an infinite number of tangents. In our solution, we'll assume that the two circles neither contain nor intersect one another; this condition is satisfied if $\|C_1 - C_0\| > r_0 + r_1$.

We'll solve for the lines in parametric form, $\mathcal{L} : X(t) = P + t\hat{d}$, and assume that $r_0 \geq r_1$. A line intersecting the first circle satisfies

$$r_0^2 = \|X(t) - C_0\|^2 = t^2 + 2(\hat{d} \cdot (P - C_0))t + \|P - C_0\|^2 \qquad (8.1)$$

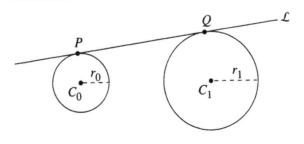

Figure 8.6   Line tangent to two circles.

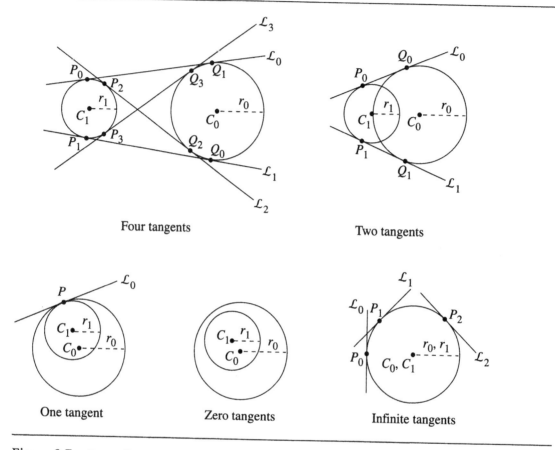

Figure 8.7   Depending on the relative sizes and positions of the circles, the number of tangents between them will vary.

For the line to be tangent at the point of intersection, the line must also satisfy

$$0 = \hat{d} \cdot (X(t) - C_0) = t + \hat{d} \cdot (P - C_0) \tag{8.2}$$

If we solve for t in Equation 8.2, and substitute it back into Equation 8.1, we get

$$r_0^2 = \|P - C_0\|^2 - (\hat{d} \cdot (P - C_0))^2 \tag{8.3}$$

For the second circle, we can apply the same steps and get

$$r_1^2 = \|P - C_1\|^2 - (\hat{d} \cdot (P - C_1))^2 \tag{8.4}$$

The point P can be chosen on the line containing C_0 and C_1, the centers of the circle. Let $P = (1 - s)C_0 + sC_1$, for some s, and let $\vec{w} = C_1 - C_0$. Then

$$P - C_0 = s\vec{w}$$

$$P - C_1 = (s - 1)\vec{w}$$

If we substitute these back into Equations 8.3 and 8.4 we get

$$r_0^2 = s^2(\|\vec{w}\|^2 - (\hat{d} \cdot \vec{w})^2)$$

$$r_1^2 = (s - 1)^2(\|\vec{w}\|^2 - (\hat{d} \cdot \vec{w})^2)$$

So $r_0^2/s^2 = r_1^2/(s - 1)^2$, or

$$(r_1^2 - r_0^2)s^2 + 2r_0^2 s - r_0^2 = 0$$

If the two circles have the same radius (that is, $r_0 = r_1$), then $s = 1/2$, and thus P is the midpoint of the line segment between C_0 and C_1, the centers of the circles. Moreover

$$(\hat{d} \cdot \vec{w})^2 = \|\vec{w}\|^2 - 4r_0^2 = a^2 > 0$$

and so $\hat{d} \cdot \vec{w} = a$ (of course, we could use $-a$ as the root, but this just leads to a direction vector with the opposite sign). If we let $\hat{d} = (d_0, d_1)$, then $\hat{d} \cdot \vec{w} = a$ is the equation for a line. The constraint $\|\hat{d}\|^2 = 1$ corresponds to a circle. The two together represent the intersection of a line with a circle. Either solution will do.

Let $\vec{w} = (w_0, w_1)$. Then $w_0 d_0 + w_1 d_1 = a$ and $d_0^2 + d_1^2 = 1$. If $|w_0| \geq |w_1|$, then $d_0 = (a - w_1 d_1)/w_0$ and

$$(w_0^2 + w_1^2)d_1^2 - 2aw_1 d_1 + a^2 - w_0^2 = 0$$

If $|w_1| \geq |w_0|$, then $d_1 = (a - w_0 d_0)/w_1$ and

$$(w_0^2 + w_1^2)d_0^2 - 2aw_0 d_0 + a^2 - w_1^2 = 0$$

In either case, the two roots lead to two direction vectors for the tangent lines.

If $r_0 > r_1$, the quadratic in s has two real-valued solutions. From the geometry, one of the values must satisfy $0 < s < 1$ and produces the two tangents that intersect each other between the two circles ($\mathcal{L}_2$ and $\mathcal{L}_3$ in the "Four tangents" case in Figure 8.7). The other root cannot be $s = 0$ (otherwise P would be at a circle center, which is not possible).

For each root s, the same idea as in the case $r_1 = r_0$ works. The quadratic to solve is

$$(\hat{d} \cdot \vec{w})^2 = \|\vec{w}\|^2 - r_0^2/s_2 = a^2 > 0$$

Also,

$$(\hat{d} \cdot \vec{w})^2 = \|\vec{w}\|^2 - r_1^2/(s-1)^2 = a^2 > 0$$

The first equation should be used when $s^2 \geq (s-1)^2$; otherwise, use the second one. The same quadratics may be set up for d_0 or d_1 (a has a different value, though) and solved.

The pseudocode is

```
void GetDirections(
    Vector2D  w,
    double    a,
    Vector2D& dir0,
    Vector2D& dir1)
{
    double aSqr = a * a;
    double wxSqr = w.x * w.x;
    double wySqr = w.y * w.y;
    double c2 = wxSqr + wySqr, invc2 = 1.0 / c2;
    double c0, c1, discr, invwx, invwy;

    if (fabs(w.x) >= fabs(w.y)) {
        c0 = aSqr - wxSqr;
        c1 = -2.0 * a * w.y;
        discr = sqrt(fabs(c1 * c1 - 4.0 * c0 * c2));
        invwx = 1.0 / w.x;
        dir0.y = -0.5 * (c1 + discr) * invc2;
        dir0.x = (a - w.y * dir0.y) * invwx;
        dir1.y = -0.5 * (c1 - discr) * invc2;
        dir1.x = (a - w.y * dir1.y) * invwx;
    } else {
        c0 = aSqr -w ySqr;
        c1 = -2.0 * a * w.x;
        discr = sqrt(fabs(c1 * c1 - 4.0 * c0 * c2));
        invwy = 1.0 / w.y;
        dir0.x = -0.5 * (c1 + discr) * invc2;
        dir0.y = (a - w.x * dir0.x) * invwy;
        dir1.x = -0.5 * (c1 - discr) * invc2;
        dir1.y = (a - w.x * dir1.x) * invwy;
    }
}

int LinesTangentToTwoCircles(
    Circle2D circle0,
```

```
        Circle2D circle1,
        Line2D line[4])
{
    Vector2D w = { circle1.center.x - circle0.center.x,
                   circle1.center.y - circle0.center.y };
    double wLenSqr = w.x * w.x + w.y * w.y;
    double rSum = circle0.radius + circle1.radius;
    if (wLenSqr <= rSum * rSum) {
        return 0;  // circles are either intersecting or nested
    }

    double epsilon = 1e-06;
    double rDiff = circle1.radius - circle0.radius;
    if (fabs(rDiff) >= epsilon) {
        // solve (R1^2-R0^2)*s^2 + 2*R0^2*s - R0^2 = 0.
        double R0sqr = circle0.radius * circle0.radius;
        double R1sqr = circle1.radius * circle1.radius;
        double c0 = -R0sqr;
        double c1 = 2.0 * R0sqr;
        double c2 = circle1.radius * circle1.radius - R0sqr, invc2 = 1.0 / c2;
        double discr = sqrt(fabs(c1 * c1 - 4.0 * c0 * c2));
        double s, oms, a;

        // first root
        s = -0.5 * (c1 + discr) * invc2;
        line[0].p.x = circle0.center.x + s * w.x;
        line[0].p.y = circle0.center.y + s * w.y;
        line[1].p.x = line[0].p.x;
        line[1].p.y = line[0].p.y;
        if (s >= 0.5) {
            a = sqrt(fabs(wLenSqr - R0sqr / (s * s)));
        } else {
            oms = 1.0-s;
            a = sqrt(fabs(wLenSqr - R1sqr / (oms * oms)));
        }
        GetDirections(w, a, line[0].direction, line[1].direction);

        // second root
        s = -0.5 * (c1 - discr) * invc2;
        line[2].p.x = circle0.center.x + s * w.x;
        line[2].p.y = circle0.center.y + s * w.y;
        line[3].p.x = line[2].p.x;
        line[3].p.y = line[2].p.y;
        if (s >= 0.5) {
```

```
                a = sqrt(fabs(wLenSqr - R0sqr / (s * s)));
            } else {
                oms = 1.0 - s;
                a = sqrt(fabs(wLenSqr - R1sqr / (oms * oms)));
            }
            GetDirections(w, a, line[2].direction, line[3].direction);
        } else {
            // circles effectively have same radius

            // midpoint of circle centers
            Point2 mid =
            {
                0.5 * (circle0.center.x + circle1.center.x),
                0.5 * (circle0.center.y + circle1.center.y)
            };

            // tangent lines passing through midpoint
            double a = sqrt(fabs(wLenSqr - 4.0 * circle0.radius * circle0.radius));
            GetDirections(w, a, line[0].direction, line[1].direction);
            line[0].p.x = mid.x;
            line[0].p.y = mid.y;
            line[1].p.x = mid.x;
            line[1].p.y = mid.y;

            // unitize w
            double invwlen = 1.0 / sqrt(wLenSqr);
            w.x *= invwlen;
            w.y *= invwlen;

            // tangent lines parallel to unitized w
            //   1.  D = w
            //   2.  a. P = mid + R0 * perp(w), perp(a, b) = (b, -a)
            //       b. P = mid - R0 * perp(w)
            line[2].p.x = mid.x + circle0.radius * w.y;
            line[2].p.y = mid.y - circle0.radius * w.x;
            line[2].direction.x = w.x;
            line[2].direction.y = w.y;
            line[3].p.x = mid.x - circle0.radius * w.y;
            line[3].p.y = mid.y + circle0.radius * w.x;
            line[3].direction.x = w.x;
            line[3].direction.y = w.y;
        }

        return 1;
    }
```

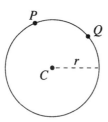

Figure 8.8   Circle through two points with a given radius.

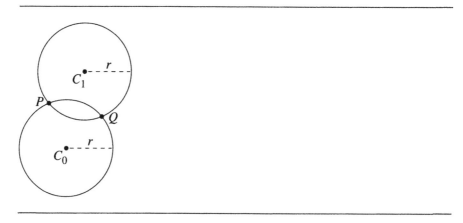

Figure 8.9   Both possible circles through two points with a given radius.

8.6 CIRCLE THROUGH TWO POINTS WITH A GIVEN RADIUS

Given two points P and Q, not coincident, we'd like to find a circle passing through both points. Of course, there are actually an infinite number of such circles, so we must specify a desired radius r, as shown in Figure 8.8. As usual, there is more than one solution to this—there are actually two such possible circles, as shown in Figure 8.9.

The insight for this problem is to note that the desired circle's center is at the intersection of two circles of radius r, centered at P and Q, respectively, as can be seen in Figure 8.10. That is, we simply create two circles of radius r, centered at P and Q, respectively, and compute their intersections—these intersections will be the

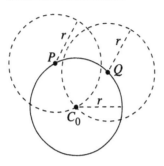

Figure 8.10   Insight for computing circle of given radius through two points.

centers of two circles of radius r that pass through P and Q. The solution to the problem of intersecting two circles can be found in Section 7.5.2.

The pseudocode is

```
CircleThrough2PointsGivenR(Point2D p1, Point2D p2, float radius,
                           Point2D centers[2])
{
    // See Section 7.5.2
    FindIntersectionOf2DCircles(p1, p2, radius, radius, centers);
}
```

8.7 CIRCLE THROUGH A POINT AND TANGENT TO A LINE WITH A GIVEN RADIUS

Suppose we have a line $\mathcal{L}$ and a point P. The problem is to find a circle C with a given radius r that is tangent to the line and passes through the point, as shown in Figure 8.11. Of course, there are actually two (potential) such circles, as we can see in Figure 8.12.

Other possible configurations are to have the point P lying on the line, or to have P lying at a distance from $\mathcal{L}$ greater than $2r$. In the first case, there are two solutions, but they lie on either side of the line; in the second case, there are no solutions, as seen in Figure 8.13.

The insight for this problem comes from the observation that the center C of C must be at a distance r from $\mathcal{L}$. Furthermore, aside from the case where P lies *on* $\mathcal{L}$, C must be on the same side of the line as P.

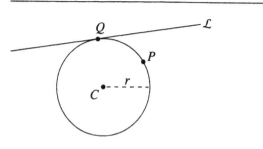

Figure 8.11   Circle through a point and tangent to a line with a given radius.

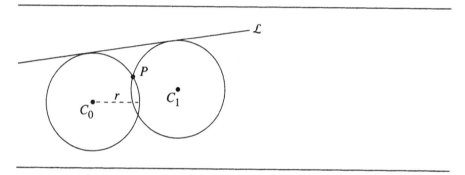

Figure 8.12   In general, there are two distinct circles through the given point.

If the line is given in implicit form $\mathcal{L}: ax + by + c = 0$, then the (signed) distance from P to $\mathcal{L}$ is

$$r = \frac{aC_x + bC_y + c}{\sqrt{a^2 + b^2}}$$

We also know that the circle must pass through P, and so that point must satisfy the circle's equation:

$$(C_x - P_x)^2 + (C_y - P_y)^2 = r^2$$

This gives us, generally speaking, two equations in two unknowns. It is certainly possible to simply solve these two equations for $\{C_x, C_y\}$, but this yields

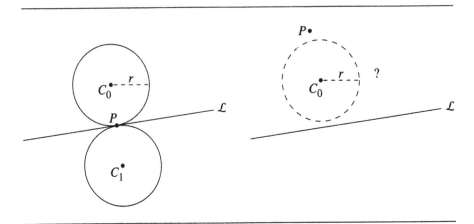

Figure 8.13   If P lies on the line, the circles are mirrored across the line; if P is further from the line than the diameter of the circle, there are no solutions.

$$C_x = \frac{1}{a(a^2 + b^2)^{\frac{3}{2}}} a^4 r + ab^2\sqrt{a^2 + b^2} P_x$$

$$-b\sqrt{a^2 + b^2}\sqrt{-\left(a^2\left(c + aP_x + bP_y\right)\left(c - 2\sqrt{a^2 + b^2}r + aP_x + bP_y\right)\right)}$$

$$-a^2\left(\sqrt{a^2 + b^2}c + b\left(-(br) + \sqrt{a^2 + b^2}P_y\right)\right) \tag{8.5}$$

$$C_y = \frac{-\left(b\left(c - \sqrt{a^2 + b^2}r + aP_x\right)\right) + a^2 P_y + \sqrt{-\left(a^2\left(c + aP_x + bP_y\right)\left(c - 2\sqrt{a^2 + b^2}r + aP_x + bP_y\right)\right)}}{a^2 + b^2} \tag{8.6}$$

There are several ways to approach solving this (see Chasen 1978 and Bowyer and Woodwark 1983). Following Bowyer and Woodwark (1983), we translate the entire system so that P is at the origin; this of course doesn't change the a and b coefficients of $\mathcal{L}$, but only the constant c:

$$c' = c + aP_x + bP_y$$

Then, we check the sign of c'. If it is negative, we multiply the equation through (entirely) by -1 (we could have arbitrarily preferred a negative value for c and compensated in the subsequent equations). If $\mathcal{L}$ is normalized, Equations 8.5 and 8.6 simplify to

$$C_x = -a(c' - r) \pm b\sqrt{-c'^2 + 2c'r}$$

$$C_y = -b(c' - r) \mp a\sqrt{-c'^2 + 2c'r}$$

The pseudocode is

```
int CircleThroughPointTangentToLineGivenRadius(
    Point2D point,
    Line2D  line,
    float   radius,
    Point2D center[2])
{
    // Returns number of solutions

    //  Translate line so point is at origin
    float cPrime = line.c + line.a * point.x + line.b * point.y;

    //  Check if point lies on, or nearly on, the line
    if (Abs(cPrime) < epsilon) {
        Vector2D tmp = { line.a, line.b };
        center[0] = point + tmp * r;
        center[1] = point - tmp * r;
        return 2;
    }
    float a;
    float b;
    float c;
    if (cPrime < 0) {
        //  Reverse line
        a = -line.a;
        b = -line.b;
        c = -line.c;
    } else {
        a = line.a;
        b = line.b;
        c = line.c;
    }

    float tmp1 = cPrime - radius;
    float tmp2 = r * r + tmp1 * tmp1;
    if (tmp2 < -epsilon) {
        //  No solutions - point further away from
```

```
        //  line than radius.
        return 0;
    }

    if (tmp2 < epsilon) {
        //  One solution only
        center[0].x = point.x - a * tmp1;
        center[0].y = point.y - b * tmp1;
        return 1;
    }

    //  Otherwise, two solutions
    tmp2 = Sqrt(tmp2);
    Point2D tmpPt = { point.x - a * tmp1, point.y - b * tmp1 };
    center[0] = { tmpPt + b * tmp2, tmpPt - a * tmp2 };
    center[1] = { tmpPt - b * tmp2, tmpPt + a * tmp2 };
    return 2;
}
```

8.8 CIRCLES TANGENT TO TWO LINES WITH A GIVEN RADIUS

Suppose we have two nonparallel lines $\mathcal{L}_0$ and $\mathcal{L}_1$. A circle C with a given radius r can be constructed so that it is tangent to both lines, as shown in Figure 8.14. Of course, there are actually *four* such circles, as shown in Figure 8.15.

Given the two lines $\mathcal{L}_0$ and $\mathcal{L}_1$, and the radius r, our problem is to find the circles' centers C_0, C_1, C_2, and C_3. The insight here begins with the observation that each of C_i is at a distance r from both $\mathcal{L}_0$ and $\mathcal{L}_1$. If C_i is to be at a distance r from $\mathcal{L}_0$, then it must be somewhere on a line that is *parallel* to $\mathcal{L}_0$ and is separated by a distance r; if C_i is to be at a distance r from $\mathcal{L}_1$, then it must be somewhere on a line that is *parallel* to $\mathcal{L}_1$ and is separated by a distance r as well.

Thus, the circle center C_i must be at the intersection of these two lines that are parallel to, and at a distance r from, $\mathcal{L}_0$ and $\mathcal{L}_1$, respectively, as shown in Figure 8.16 for one of the four circles. All four possible tangential circles are constructed by considering all pairs of intersections between the two lines parallel to $\mathcal{L}_0$ and the two lines parallel to $\mathcal{L}_1$.

If the two lines are defined implicitly

$$\mathcal{L}_0 : a_0 x + b_0 y + c_0 = 0$$

$$\mathcal{L}_1 : a_1 x + b_1 y + c_1 = 0$$

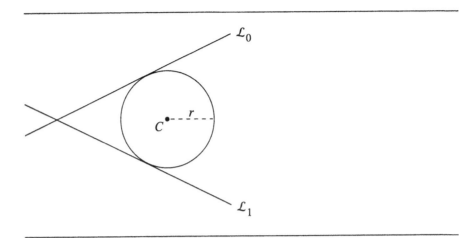

Figure 8.14   Circles tangent to two lines with a given radius.

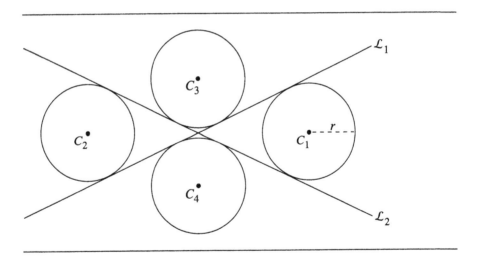

Figure 8.15   In general, there are four circles of a given radius tangent to two lines.

then the two lines parallel to these, at a distance r from each, are

$$\mathcal{L}_0 : a_0 x + b_0 y + c_0 \pm \sqrt{a_0^2 + b_0^2}\, r = 0$$

$$\mathcal{L}_1 : a_1 x + b_1 y + c_1 \pm \sqrt{a_1^2 + b_1^2}\, r = 0$$

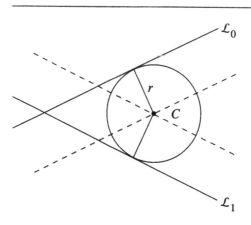

Figure 8.16   Constructive approach for circle tangent to two lines.

If we solve for x and y, we'll have the circles' centers:

$$x = -\frac{b_1\left(c_0 \pm \sqrt{a_0^2 + b_0^2}\,r\right) - b_0\left(c_1 \pm \sqrt{a_1^2 + b_1^2}\,r\right)}{-a_1 b_0 + a_0 b_1}$$

$$y = -\frac{-a_1\left(c_0 \pm \sqrt{a_0^2 + b_0^2}\,r\right) + a_0\left(c_1 \pm \sqrt{a_1^2 + b_1^2}\,r\right)}{-a_1 b_0 + a_0 b_1}$$

The pseudocode is

```
void CircleTangentToLinesGivenR(Line2D l0, Line2D l1, float radius, Point2D center[4])
{
    float discrm0 = sqrt(l0.a * l0.a + l0.b * l0.b) * radius;
    float discrm1 = sqrt(l1.a * l1.a + l1.b * l1.b) * radius;
    float invDenom = 1.0 / (-l1.a * l0.b + l0.a * l1.b);

    center[0].x = -(l1.b * (l0.c + discrm0) - l0.b * (l1.c + discrm1)) * invDenom;
    center[0].y = -(-l1.a * (l0.c + discrm0) + l0.a * (l1.c + discrm1)) * invDenom;

    center[1].x = -(l1.b * (l0.c + discrm0) - l0.b * (l1.c - discrm1)) * invDenom;
    center[1].y = -(-l1.a * (l0.c + discrm0) + l0.a * (l1.c - discrm1)) * invDenom;

    center[2].x = -(l1.b * (l0.c - discrm0) - l0.b * (l1.c + discrm1)) * invDenom;
    center[2].y = -(-l1.a * (l0.c - discrm0) + l0.a * (l1.c + discrm1)) * invDenom;
```

```
center[3].x = -(11.b * (10.c - discrm0) - 10.b * (11.c - discrm1)) * invDenom;
center[3].y = -(-11.a * (10.c - discrm0) + 10.a * (11.c - discrm1)) * invDenom;
}
```

8.9 CIRCLES THROUGH A POINT AND TANGENT TO A CIRCLE WITH A GIVEN RADIUS

Given a circle $C_0 : \{C_0, r_0\}$ and a point P, the problem is to find a circle $C_1 : \{C_1, r_1\}$, with a given radius, that passes through the point and is tangent to the given circle (see Figure 8.17). As is typical with problems involving tangents, there are, in general, two solutions. If P is further from C_0 than $r_0 + 2r$, or closer than $r_0 - 2r$, then no solution is possible. Depending on the relative sizes of the circles, and the placement of P, one of the circles may be contained within the other—and of course, there may be four solutions, two solutions, or no solutions (see Figure 8.18). This particular problem is interesting because it can be solved in (at least) two entirely different ways—one more analytical and one more constructive.

The more analytical approach is based on the fact that we know the lengths of the sides of the triangle (P, C_0, C_1) (see Figure 8.19). Clearly, if circle C_0 is tangent to C_1, then $\|C_1 - C_0\| = r_0 + r_1$. The given point P is on the circle, and so $\|P - C_1\| = r_1$. Finally, both P and C_0 are given. Note that this approach works even when P is actually *on* circle C_0, in which case the triangle degenerates to a line.

To reduce calls to the square root function, we can instead consider the squared distances. To further simplify the equations, we can translate the system so that one of the points is at the origin, then solve it, and translate the solution back; we arbitrarily choose to translate P to the origin. This yields a system of two equations in two unknowns $\{C_{1,x}, C_{1,y}\}$

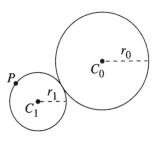

Figure 8.17   Circles through a point and tangent to a circle with a given radius.

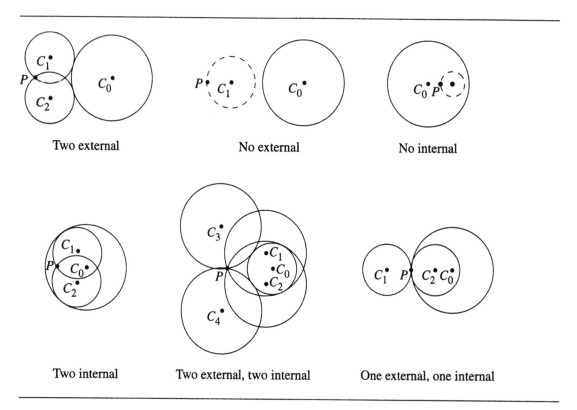

Figure 8.18   Depending on the relative positions and radii of the circle, there may be four, two, or no solutions.

$$(-C_{0,x} + C_{1,x})^2 + (-C_{0,y} + C_{1,y})^2 = (r_0 + r_1)^2$$
$$C_{1,x}^2 + C_{1,y}^2 = r_1^2 \tag{8.7}$$

whose solution (with the translation put back in) is

$$C_{1,x} = P_x + \frac{-\left(r_0^2 C_{0,x}^2\right) - 2r_0 r_1 C_{0,x}^2 + C_{0,x}^4 + C_{0,x}^2 C_{0,y}^2 \mp C_{0,y} k}{2C_{0,x}\left(C_{0,x}^2 + C_{0,y}^2\right)}$$

$$C_{1,y} = P_y + \frac{-\left(r_0^2 C_{0,y}\right) - 2r_0 r_1 C_{0,y} + C_{0,x}^2 C_{0,y} + C_{0,y}^3 \pm k}{2\left(C_{0,x}^2 + C_{0,y}^2\right)} \tag{8.8}$$

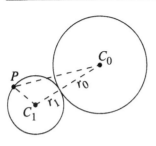

Figure 8.19   Insight for solving problem.

where

$$k = \sqrt{ - \left(C_{0,x}^2 \left(-r_0^2 + C_{0,x}^2 + C_{0,y}^2\right)\left(-r_0^2 - 4r_0r_1 - 4r_1^2 + C_{0,x}^2 + C_{0,y}^2\right)\right)}$$

The pseudocode is

```
int CircleThroughPTangentToC(Point2D p, Circle2D cIn, float r1, Circle2D cOut[4]
{
    float distanceCPS = Distance2D(p, cIn.center);
    int numSoln;
    if (distanceCP > cIn.radius + 2 * r1) {
        numSoln = 0;
    } else if (distanceCP < cIn.radius - 2 * r1) {
        numSoln = 0;
    } else {
        numSoln = 4;
        float k = sqrt(-(cIn.x^2 * (-cIn.radius^2 + cIn.x^2 + cIn.y^2)) *
            (-cIn.radius^2 - 4 * cIn.radius * r1 - 4 * r1^2 + cIn.x^2 + cIn.y^2));
        float invDenom = 1.0 / (2 * (cIn.x * cIn.x + cIn.y * cIn.y));

        float temp1 = -(cIn.radius^2 * cIn.x^2 ) -2 * cIn.radius * r1 * cIn.x ^2
                    + cIn.x^4 + cIn.x^2 * cIn.y^2;

        float temp2 = -(cIn.radius^2 * cIn.y) -2 * cIn.radius * r1 * cIn.y
                    + cIn.x^2 cIn.y + cIn.y^3;

        cOut[0].x = (p.x + (temp1 - cIn.y * k) * invDenom) / cIn.x;
        cOut[0].y = (p.y + (temp2 + k) * invDenom);
```

```
            cOut[1].x = (p.x + (temp1 + cIn.y * k) * invDenom) / cIn.x;
            cOut[1].y = (p.y + (temp2 - k) * invDenom);

            k = -k;

            cOut[2].x = (p.x + (temp1 - cIn.y * k) * invDenom) / cIn.x;
            cOut[2].y = (p.y + (temp2 + k) * invDenom);

            cOut[3].x = (p.x + (temp1 + cIn.y * k) * invDenom) / cIn.x;
            cOut[3].y = (p.y + (temp2 - k) * invDenom);
        }

    // Note: all solutions not necessarily unique - calling routine
    // should check...
    return numSoln;
}
```

The more "constructive" approach is based on the same observation as the more "analytic" approach—$\|C_1 - C_0\| = r_0 + r_1$ and $\|P - C_1\| = r_1$. Consider Figure 8.20. If we draw a circle of radius r_1, centered at P, it will clearly include C_1. If we also draw a circle centered at C_0, of radius $r_0 + r_1$, it will also clearly include C_1. So, C_1 is located at the intersection of the two circles so constructed (and the second solution is centered at the other intersection).

This is very nearly as simple as it appears. The problem is recast as simply finding the intersections of the two "auxiliary" circles. The only complication is that you must consider if P is actually *inside* C_0; in this case, the "auxiliary" circle we draw centered at C_0 must have the radius $r_0 - r_1$ (see Figure 8.21). The two cases—P being inside or outside of C_0—can be relatively inexpensively distinguished: if we compare the squared distance from P and C_0 to r_0^2, we can avoid an unnecessary square root.

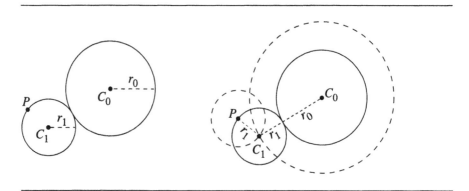

Figure 8.20   Constructive approach to solving problem.

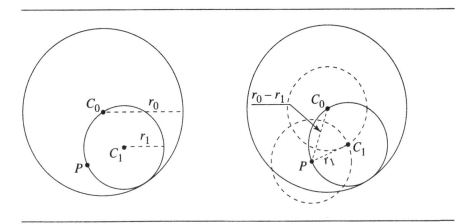

Figure 8.21   Special case for constructive approach.

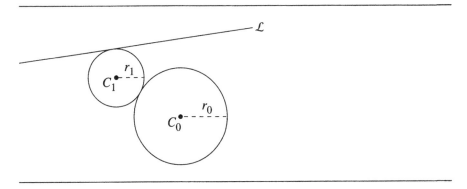

Figure 8.22   Circles tangent to a line and a circle with a given radius.

8.10 CIRCLES TANGENT TO A LINE AND A CIRCLE WITH A GIVEN RADIUS

Suppose we have a circle $C_0 : \{C_0, r_0\}$ and a line $\mathcal{L} : ax + by + c = 0$, and we wish to find the circle(s) tangent to both the line and the circle with a given radius, as shown in Figure 8.22. Of course, there is more than one possible solution; in fact, there are as many as eight distinct circles, as can be seen in Figure 8.23, or there may be no solutions, in the case when the distance between C_0 and $\mathcal{L}$ is greater than $2r_1 + r_0$, as in Figure 8.24.

The insight here is to note that C_1 is at a distance r_1 from $\mathcal{L}$ if it is tangent to it, and thus is located somewhere along a line $\mathcal{L}'$ that is parallel to $\mathcal{L}$ and at a distance r_1

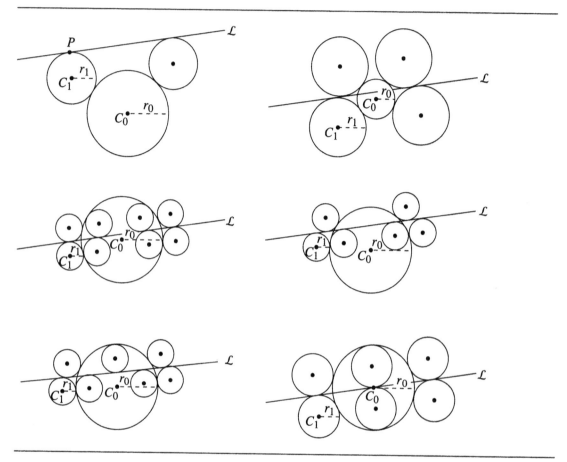

Figure 8.23 The number of distinct solutions varies depending on the relative positions of the line and circle, and the circle's radius.

from it, as can be seen in Figure 8.25. Further, C_1 must be at a distance $r_0 + r_1$ from C_0 if it is tangent to C. Put another way, C_1 must be on a circle $C' : \{C_0, r_0 + r_1\}$. Circles simultaneously tangent to $\mathcal{L}$ and C must then be centered at the intersection of $\mathcal{L}'$ and C' (see Figure 8.26).

In order to account for all eight possible tangent circles seen in Figure 8.23, we need to be able to generate the circles that are "externally" tangent to C_0 as well as "internally" tangent. The internally tangent circles are those whose centers are at the intersection of $\mathcal{L}'$ and the circle centered at C_0 and have the radius $r_0 - r_1$.

All of this might seem like it would yield some very complex calculations. However, if we employ the "trick" described by Bowyer and Woodwark (1983) consisting of translating the entire thing so that P_0 is at the origin, it can be much simplified.

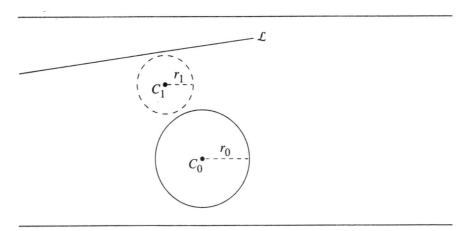

Figure 8.24   No solutions if given radius is too small.

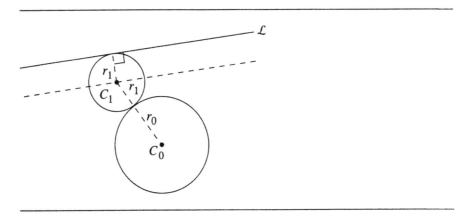

Figure 8.25   Insight for finding circle of given radius.

We then solve for the center of the desired circles and translate their centers back. Translating C is trivial—we add its center back into the equation

$$(x - C_{0,x} + C_{0,x})^2 + (y - C_{0,y} + C_{0,y})^2 + c = r_0^2$$

which is simply

$$x^2 + y^2 = r_0^2$$

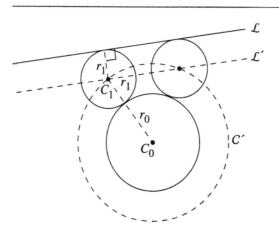

Figure 8.26   Schematic for the solution.

If our line is in implicit form $ax + by + c = 0$, the translated line of course has the same a and b coefficients, and the new c coefficient is simply

$$c' = c + aC_{0,x} + bC_{0,y}$$

If $c' < 0$, then we multiply the entire equation through by -1.
The resulting equations for the center of C_1 are

$$C_{1,x} = C_{0,x} + \frac{a(c' - r_1) \pm b\sqrt{(a^2 + b^2)(r_1 \pm r_0)^2 - (c' - r_1)^2}}{a^2 + b^2}$$

$$C_{1,y} = C_{0,y} + \frac{b(c' - r_1) \mp a\sqrt{(a^2 + b^2)(r_1 \pm r_0)^2 - (c' - r_1)^2}}{a^2 + b^2}$$

The pseudocode is

```
int CirclesTangentToLineAndCircleGivenRadius(
    Line2D    l,
    Circle2D  c,
    float     radius,
    Circle2D  soln[8])
{
    if (l.distanceToPoint(c.center) > 2 * radius + c.radius){
        return 0;
```

```
} else {
    // Some of these solutions may be duplicates.
    // It is up to the application to deal with this.
    float a, b, c;
    l.getImplicitCoeffs(a,b,c);

    for (i = 0 ; i < 8 ; i++){
        soln.radius = radius;
    }
    float apbSqr = a^2 + b^2;
    float cp = c + a * c.center.x + b * c.center.y;

    float discrm1 = sqrt(apbSqr * (radius + c.radius)^2 - (cp - radius)^2);
    float discrm2 = sqrt(apbSqr * (radius - c.radius)^2 - (cp - radius)^2);
    float cpminusr = cp - radius;

    soln[0].center.x = c.center.x + (b * cpminusr + b * discrm1) / apbSqr;
    soln[0].center.y = c.center.y + (a * cpminusr - a * discrm1) / apbSqr;

    soln[1].center.x = c.center.x + (b * cpminusr - b * discrm2) / apbSqr;
    soln[1].center.y = c.center.y + (a * cpminusr + a * discrm2) / apbSqr;

    soln[2].center.x = c.center.x + (b * cpminusr + b * discrm2) / apbSqr;
    soln[2].center.y = c.center.y + (a * cpminusr + a * discrm2) / apbSqr;

    soln[3].center.x = c.center.x + (b * cpminusr - b * discrm2) / apbSqr;
    soln[3].center.y = c.center.y + (a * cpminusr - a * discrm2) / apbSqr;

    soln[4].center.x = c.center.x + (b * cpminusr + b * discrm1) / apbSqr;
    soln[4].center.y = c.center.y + (a * cpminusr + a * discrm1) / apbSqr;

    soln[5].center.x = c.center.x + (b * cpminusr - b * discrm1) / apbSqr;
    soln[5].center.y = c.center.y + (a * cpminusr - a * discrm1) / apbSqr;

    soln[6].center.x = c.center.x + (b * cpminusr + b * discrm2) / apbSqr;
    soln[6].center.y = c.center.y + (a * cpminusr - a * discrm2) / apbSqr;

    soln[7].center.x = c.center.x + (b * cpminusr - b * discrm1) / apbSqr;
    soln[7].center.y = c.center.y + (a * cpminusr + a * discrm1) / apbSqr;
    return 8;
}
}
```

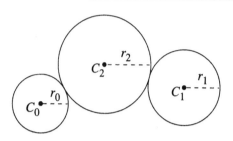

Figure 8.27   Circles tangent to two circles with a given radius.

8.11   Circles Tangent to Two Circles with a Given Radius

Suppose we have two circles, $C_0 : \{C_0, r_0\}$ and $C_1 : \{C_1, r_1\}$, and we wish to find a circle tangent to these two circles and having a given radius, as shown in Figure 8.27. There are, of course, a variety of possible solutions, depending on the relative positions of the circles, their radii, and the radius specified for the other circle, as shown in Figure 8.28.

Our third circle $C_2 : \{C_2, r_2\}$ has a known radius; it is our problem to compute its center. This circle must be tangent to C_0 and C_1, which means that its center must be $r_0 + r_2$ from C_0 and $r_1 + r_2$ from C_1. The insight here leading to a solution is to note that this is equivalent to finding the intersection of two circles centered at C_0 and C_1, having radii $r_0 + r_2$ and $r_1 + r_2$, respectively, as shown in Figure 8.29. If our original circles are

$$C_0: \quad (x - C_{0,x})^2 + (y - C_{0,y})^2 = r_0^2$$

$$C_1: \quad (x - C_{1,x})^2 + (y - C_{1,y})^2 = r_1^2$$

then they have the equations

$$C_0': \quad (x - C_{0,x})^2 + (y - C_{0,y})^2 = (r_0 + r_2)^2$$

$$C_1': \quad (x - C_{1,x})^2 + (y - C_{1,y})^2 = (r_1 + r_2)^2$$

If we compute the intersection of C_0' and C_1', we'll have the origins of the circles tangent to them. The intersection of two circles is covered in Section 7.5.2.

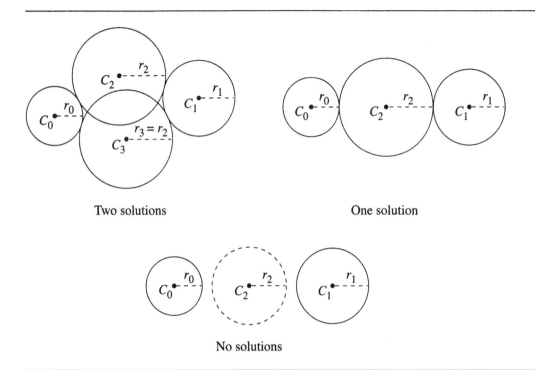

Two solutions   One solution

No solutions

Figure 8.28   In general there are two solutions, but the number of distinct solutions varies with the relative sizes and positions of the given circles.

The pseudocode is

```
int CircleTangentToCirclesGivenRadius(
    Circle2D c1,
    Circle2D c2,
    float radius,
    Circle2D c[2])
{
    Vector2D v = c2.center - c1.center;
    float dprod =  Dot(v, v);
    float dSqr = dprod - (c1.radius + c2.radius)^2;
    if (dSqr > radius^2) {
        // No solution
        return 0;
    } else if (dSqr == radius^2) {
        float distance = sqrt(dprod);
        c.center.x = c1.center.x + (c1.radius + radius) * v.x / distance;
        c.center.y = c1.center.y + (c1.radius + radius) * v.y / distance;
```

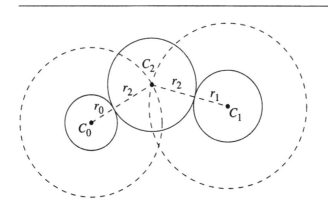

Figure 8.29   Construction for a circle tangent to two circles.

```
            c.radius = radius;
            return 1;
        } else {
            Circle2D cp1;
            Circle2D cp2;
            cp1.center.x = c1.center.x;
            cp1.center.y = c1.center.y;
            cp1.center.radius = c1.radius + radius;
            cp2.center.x = c2.center.x;
            cp2.center.y = c2.center.y;
            cp2.center.radius = c2.radius + radius;
            // Section 7.5.2
            findIntersectionOf2DCircles(c1, c2, c);
            c[0].radius = radius;
            c[1].radius = radius;
            return 2;
        }
    }
```

8.12 LINE PERPENDICULAR TO A GIVEN LINE THROUGH A GIVEN POINT

Suppose we have a line $\mathcal{L}_0$ and a point Q. Our problem is to find a line $\mathcal{L}_1$ that is perpendicular to $\mathcal{L}_0$ and passes through Q, as shown in Figure 8.30. If $\mathcal{L}_0$ is in implicit form, $a_0 x + b_0 y + c_0 = 0$, then the equation for $\mathcal{L}_1$ is

$$b_0 x - a_0 y + (a_0 Q_y - b_0 Q_x) = 0 \qquad (8.9)$$

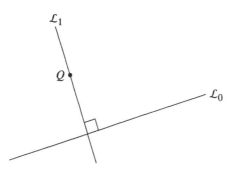

Figure 8.30   Line normal to a given line and through a given point.

If the line is in parametric form, $\mathcal{L}_0(t) = P_0 + t\vec{d}$, then the equation for $\mathcal{L}_1$ is

$$\mathcal{L}_1(t) = Q + t\vec{d}^{\perp}$$

The pseudocode is

```
LineNormaltoLineThroughPoint(Line2D l0, Point2D q, Line2D& lOut)
{
    lOut.origin = q;
    Vector2D dPerp;
    dPerp.x = -l0.y;
    dPerp.y = l0.x;
    lOut.direction = dPerp;
}
```

8.13 LINE BETWEEN AND EQUIDISTANT TO TWO POINTS

Suppose we have two points Q_0 and Q_1, not coincident, and we wish to find the line that runs between them and is at an equal distance from them (see Figure 8.31). Of course, any line passing through a point midway between Q_0 and Q_1 satisfies the criterion of being an equal distance from them, but by "between" here we mean that the line should be perpendicular to the vector $Q_1 - Q_0$; thus, this problem can be thought of as finding the perpendicular bisector of the line segment defined by the two points.

The parametric representation requires a point and a direction; clearly, the point $P = Q_0 + \frac{(Q_1 - Q_0)}{2}$ is on the line. As $\vec{d}$ is simply $(Q_1 - Q_0)^{\perp}$, we have

$$\mathcal{L}(t) = Q_0 + \frac{(Q_1 - Q_0)}{2} + t(Q_1 - Q_0)^{\perp} \qquad (8.10)$$

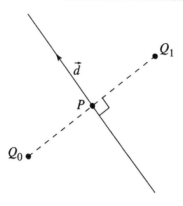

Figure 8.31   Line between and equidistant to two points.

The implicit form can be computed just as easily:

$$(Q_{1,x} - Q_{0,x})x + (Q_{1,y} - Q_{0,y})y - \frac{(Q_{1,x}^2 + Q_{1,y}^2) - (Q_{0,x}^2 + Q_{0,y}^2)}{2}$$

The pseudocode is

```
LineBetweenAndEquidistantTo2Points(Point2D q0, Point2D q1, Line2D& line)
{
    line.origin.x = q0.x + (q1.x - q0.x) / 2;
    line.origin.y = q0.y + (q1.y - q0.y) / 2;
    line.direction.x = (q0.y - q1.y);
    line.direction.y = (q1.x - q0.x);
}
```

8.14   LINE PARALLEL TO A GIVEN LINE AT A GIVEN DISTANCE

Suppose we have a line $\mathcal{L}_0$ and wish to construct another line $\mathcal{L}_1$ parallel to it at a given distance d, as shown in Figure 8.32. If the line is in parametric form $\mathcal{L}_0(t) = P_0 + t\vec{d}_0$, then a line parallel to it clearly has the same direction vector. By noting that the origin of $\mathcal{L}_1$ must be on a line perpendicular to $\vec{d}_0$, it's easy to see that

$$P_1 = P_0 + \frac{d\vec{d}_0^{\perp}}{\|\vec{d}_0\|}$$

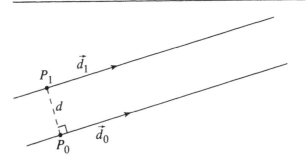

Figure 8.32   Line parallel to a given line at a distance d.

This gives us

$$\mathcal{L}_1(t) = P_0 + \frac{d\vec{d}_0^{\perp}}{\|\vec{d}_0\|} + t\vec{d}_0$$

or

$$\mathcal{L}_1(t) = P_0 + \frac{d\vec{d}_0^{\perp}}{\|\vec{d}_0\|} + t\vec{d}_0$$

or simply

$$\mathcal{L}_1(t) = P_0 + d\hat{d}_0^{\perp}$$

if $\mathcal{L}_0$ is normalized.

If the line is in implicit form $ax + by + c = 0$, then we have

$$d = \begin{cases} \dfrac{\pm(ax+by+c)}{-\sqrt{a^2+b^2}} & b \geq 0 \\[2ex] \dfrac{\pm(ax+by+c)}{\sqrt{a^2+b^2}} & b < 0 \end{cases}$$

The plus sign in the numerator is used if we want the line *above* the given line, and the negative sign is used if we want the line *below* the given line. If we plug in the desired distance and simplify, we get the equation for the desired line.

For example, if we have a line $\mathcal{L} : 5x - \sqrt{11}y - 7 = 0$ and want the line 8 units above it, we'd have

$$8 = \frac{5x - \sqrt{11}y - 7}{-\sqrt{5^2 + (-\sqrt{11})^2}}$$

which simplifies to

$$5x - \sqrt{11}y + 39 = 0$$

The pseudocode is

```
LineParallelToGivenLineAtGivenDistance(Line2D l1, Line2D& lOut, float distance)
{
    // Assumes l1 is not normalized
    lOut.direction = l1.direction;
    Vector2D dPerp;
    // Chose the perpendicular vector direction
    // Two answers are possible though.
    dPerp.x = -l1.direction.y;
    dPerp.y = l1.direction.x;
    float length = dPerp.length();
    lOut.origin = l1.origin + distance * dPerp / length;
}
```

8.15 Line Parallel to a Given Line at a Given Vertical (Horizontal) Distance

Suppose we have a given line $\mathcal{L}(t) = P + t\vec{d}$ and wish to find the line at a given vertical distance v or given horizontal distance h from $\mathcal{L}$, as shown in Figure 8.33. If we can compute the perpendicular distance d from h (or v), then this reduces to the previous problem. Using simple trigonometry, we have

$$\cos\theta = \frac{d}{v}$$

or

$$\cos\theta = \frac{d}{h}$$

for the vertical and horizontal cases, respectively. We can solve these for d

$$v\cos\theta = d$$

or

$$h\cos\theta = d$$

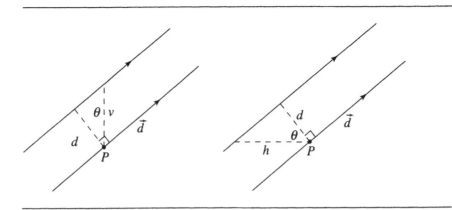

Figure 8.33   Line parallel to a given line at a vertical or horizontal distance d.

respectively. The cosine of the angle θ is easy to compute:

$$\cos \theta = \frac{\vec{d}^{\perp} \cdot [0 \quad 1]}{\|\vec{d}\|}$$

or

$$\cos \theta = \frac{\vec{d}^{\perp} \cdot [1 \quad 0]}{\|\vec{d}\|}$$

The pseudocode is

```
LineParallelToGivenLineAtVorHDistance(Line2D l1, Line2D lOut, float distance,
                                      int vOrH)
{
    float cosTheta;
    float scalar, length;
    Vector2D dPerp;

    // Again there is another possible
    // perpendicular vector to the one chosen
    dPerp.x = -l1.y;
    dPerp.y = l1.x;

    length = l1.d.length();

    if (vOrH) {
        // vertical case
```

```
        cosTheta = dPerp.y / length;
    } else {
        // horizontal case
        cosTheta = dPerp.x / length;
    }

    scalar = distance * cosTheta;
    lOut.origin = l1.p + scalar * dPerp / length;
    lOut.direction = l1.direction;
}
```

8.16 LINES TANGENT TO A GIVEN CIRCLE AND NORMAL TO A GIVEN LINE

Suppose we have a circle C and line $\mathcal{L}_0$ and we wish to find the lines $\mathcal{L}_1$ and $\mathcal{L}_2$, tangent to C and normal (perpendicular) to $\mathcal{L}_0$, as shown in Figure 8.34.

If the equation of the line is $\mathcal{L}_0 : ax + by + c = 0$, and the equation of the circle is $C : (x - x_C) + (y - y_C) - r = 0$, then the equations of the lines are

$$\mathcal{L}_0 : -\frac{b}{\sqrt{a^2+b^2}}x + \frac{a}{\sqrt{a^2+b^2}}y + r + \frac{b}{\sqrt{a^2+b^2}}C_x - \frac{a}{\sqrt{a^2+b^2}}C_y = 0$$

$$\mathcal{L}_1 : \frac{b}{\sqrt{a^2+b^2}}x - \frac{a}{\sqrt{a^2+b^2}}y + r - \frac{b}{\sqrt{a^2+b^2}}C_x + \frac{a}{\sqrt{a^2+b^2}}C_y = 0$$

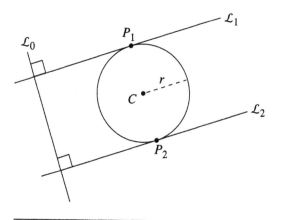

Figure 8.34   Lines tangent to a given circle and normal to a given line.

The pseudocode is

```
LinesTangentToCircleNormalToLine(Circle2D cir, Line2D l1, Line2D lOut[2])
{
    float discrm = sqrt(l1.a * l1.a + l1.b * l1.b);

    lOut[0].a = -l1.b / discrm;
    lOut[0].b =  l1.a / discrm;
    lOut[0].c =  cir.radius + ((b * cir.center.x) - (a * cir.center.y)) / discrm;

    lOut[1].a =  l1.b / discrm;
    lOut[1].b = -l1.a / discrm;
    lOut[1].c =  cir.radius + ((-b * cir.center.x) + (a * cir.center.y)) / discrm;
}
```

If our line is given in normalized parametric form $\mathcal{L}(t) = P_0 + t\hat{d}$, our two new lines are simply

$$\mathcal{L}_1(t) = (C + r\hat{d}) + t\hat{d}^\perp$$

$$\mathcal{L}_2(t) = (C - r\hat{d}) + t\hat{d}^\perp$$

However, if $\mathcal{L}_0$ is not normalized, we have

$$\mathcal{L}_1(t) = \left(C + r\frac{\vec{d}}{\|\vec{d}\|}\right) + t\vec{d}^\perp$$

$$\mathcal{L}_2(t) = \left(C - r\frac{\vec{d}}{\|\vec{d}\|}\right) + t\vec{d}^\perp$$

The pseudocode is

```
LinesTangentToCircleNormalToLine(Circle2D cir, Line2D l1, Line2D lOut[2])
{
    Vector2D dPerp;
    dPerp.x = -l1.direction.y;
    dPerp.y = l1.direction.x;

    if (l1.isNormalized()) {
        lOut[0].origin.x = cir.center.x + cir.radius * l1.direction.x;
        lOut[0].origin.y = cir.center.y + cir.radius * l1.direction.y;
        lOut[0].direction.x = dPerp.x;
        lOut[0].direction.y = dPerp.y;
```

```
            1Out[1].origin.x = cir.center.x - cir.radius * 11.direction.x;
            1Out[1].origin.y = cir.center.y - cir.radius * 11.direction.y;
            1Out[1].direction.x = dPerp.x;
            1Out[1].direction.y = dPerp.y;
        } else {
            float invLength = 1.0/11.direction.length();
            1Out[0].origin.x = cir.center.x + cir.radius * 11.direction.x * invLength;
            1Out[0].origin.y = cir.center.y + cir.radius * 11.direction.y * invLength;
            1Out[0].direction.x = dPerp.x;
            1Out[0].direction.y = dPerp.y;

            1Out[1].origin.x = cir.center.x - cir.radius * 11.direction.x * invLength;
            1Out[1].origin.y = cir.center.y - cir.radius * 11.direction.y * invLength;
            1Out[1].direction.x = dPerp.x;
            1Out[1].direction.y = dPerp.y;
        }
    }
```

C H A P T E R **9**

GEOMETRIC PRIMITIVES IN 3D

This chapter contains the definitions for various three-dimensional geometric primitives that are commonly used in applications. Some of the primitives have multiple representations. A geometric query involving an object might be more effectively formulated with one representation than another. The discussion about a query will indicate which representation is more appropriate.

In geometric queries with objects such as polyhedra, the object can be treated as a two-dimensional or a three-dimensional object. For example, the tetrahedron as a two-dimensional object is just the collection of four triangle faces. As a three-dimensional object, the tetrahedron refers to its faces and the region that it bounds. Some objects have distinct names for the two possibilities. For example, *sphere* refers to the two-dimensional surface and *ball* refers to the sphere and the region it bounds. When necessary, the distinction will be made clear. In the absence of distinct names, the word *solid* will be used. For example, the method for computing the distance between a point and a tetrahedron treats the tetrahedron as a solid. If a point is inside the tetrahedron boundary, then the distance is zero.

9.1 LINEAR COMPONENTS

The simplest form to work with for a *line* in 3D is the *parametric form*, $X(t) = P + t\vec{d}$ for $t \in \mathbb{R}$, P a point on the line, and $\vec{d} \neq \vec{0}$ a direction for the line. A *ray* is a line with the restriction on the parametric form that $t \geq 0$. The *origin* of the ray is P. A *line segment*, or simply *segment*, is a line with the restriction on the parametric form that $t \in [t_0, t_1]$. If P_0 and P_1 are end points of the segment, the *standard form* for the segment is $X(t) = (1 - t)P_0 + tP_1$ for $t \in [0, 1]$. This form is converted to the parametric form by setting $\vec{d} = P_1 - P_0$. The *symmetric form* for a segment consists of a centerpoint C, a unit-length direction vector $\hat{d}$, and a radius r. The parameterization is $X(t) = C + t\hat{d}$ for $|t| \leq r$. The length of a segment is $\|P_1 - P_0\|$ for the standard form and $2r$ for the symmetric form.

Lines in 2D were equivalently defined as the set of points satisfying the algebraic equation $\vec{n} \cdot X = c$, where $\vec{n} \neq \vec{0}$ is a normal vector to the line. The geometric analogy in 3D is that a line is the set of intersection of two algebraic equations $\vec{n}_0 \cdot X = c_0$ and $\vec{n}_1 \cdot X = c_1$, where $\vec{n}_0$ and $\vec{n}_1$ are linearly independent. The two linear equations have three unknowns, the components of X, so we expect that there is a single free variable in the solution. This variable corresponds to the parameter of the line in the parametric form. The formulation in terms of the intersection of two planes is called the *normal form* for the line.

A parametric form for the line can be derived from the normal form. The cross product $\vec{n}_0 \times \vec{n}_1$ is perpendicular to both linearly independent vectors $\vec{n}_0$ and $\vec{n}_1$, so the three vectors form a linearly independent set. Any point can be written as a linear combination of the vectors. In particular, $P = d_0\vec{n}_0 + d_1\vec{n}_1 + t\vec{n}_0 \times \vec{n}_1$. Define $e_{ij} = \vec{n}_i \cdot \vec{n}_j$. Taking dot products of the equation for P with the normal vectors, we arrive at two equations $c_0 = \vec{n}_0 \cdot P = e_{00}d_0 + e_{01}d_1$ and $c_1 = \vec{n}_1 \cdot P = e_{01}d_0 + e_{11}d_1$. The two equations in the two unknowns d_0 and d_1 can be solved in the usual manner. The parametric form for the line is

$$X(t) = \frac{e_{11}c_0 - e_{01}c_1}{e_{00}e_{11} - e_{01}^2}\vec{n}_0 + \frac{e_{00}c_1 - e_{01}c_0}{e_{00}e_{11} - e_{01}^2}\vec{n}_1 + t\vec{n}_0 \times \vec{n}_1$$

Throughout this book, the term *linear component* is used to denote a line, ray, or segment.

9.2   PLANAR COMPONENTS

Various definitions for planes are provided in this section. In many applications, standard 2D objects are manipulated within a 3D environment. These objects must be manipulated in a 3D coordinate system, even though they are naturally defined in a 2D coordinate system. The process of constructing the 3D representations of planar 2D objects is described here. Planes and any objects defined in a plane are collectively referred to as *planar components*.

9.2.1   PLANES

A *plane* is defined by the algebraic equation $\vec{n} \cdot (X - P) = 0$, where $\vec{n} \neq \vec{0}$ is a normal to the plane and where P is a point on the plane, as shown in Figure 9.1. This form

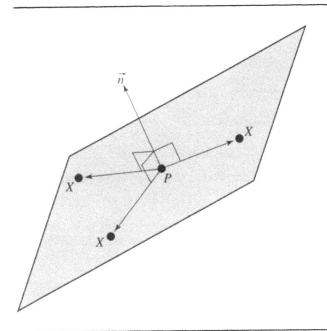

Figure 9.1   A plane is defined as the set of all points X satisfying $\vec{n} \cdot (X - P) = 0$.

is referred to as the *normal-point form*. A similar definition is $\vec{n} \cdot X = c$ for some constant c. This form is referred to as the *normal-constant form*. To construct a point on the plane using the normal-constant form, choose $P = d\vec{n}$ for some scalar d. Replacing this in the formula yields $c = \vec{n} \cdot (d\vec{n}) = d\|\vec{n}\|^2$. Thus, $d = c/\|\vec{n}\|^2$. Going in the other direction, given the normal-point form, the constant c in the normal-constant form is $c = \vec{n} \cdot P$.

If we let $X = [\, x \quad y \quad z \,]$, we can rewrite the vector $X - P$ in terms of its components, yielding

$$X - P = [\, x - P_x \quad y - P_y \quad z - P_z \,]$$

If we let $\vec{n} = [\, a \quad b \quad c \,]$, then we can rewrite the normal-point form of the plane equation as

$$ax + by + cz + d = 0 \tag{9.1}$$

where a, b, and c are constants, not all zero, and $d = -\vec{n} \cdot P$. This is known as the *implicit form* of a plane equation—simply a slightly different rendering of the normal-constant form—that is frequently seen in the literature.

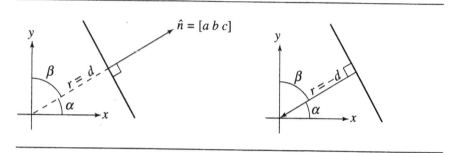

Figure 9.2   Geometric interpretation of plane equation coefficients.

If $a^2 + b^2 + c^2 = 1$ (or, equivalently, if $\|\vec{n}\| = 1$), then the plane equation is said to be *normalized*. A nonnormalized representation can be converted by multiplying the coefficients through by

$$\frac{1}{\sqrt{a^2 + b^2 + c^2}}$$

While it is not necessary, in the abstract, to use a normalized representation, many algorithms involving planes can be made somewhat less computationally expensive if a normalized representation is maintained; this is because the square root and division can be done once "up front" and then avoided in various intersection or distance computations.

The normalized form allows for a more intuitive geometric interpretation of the coefficients. Looking at Figure 9.2, we see a "cross section" of a plane that is perpendicular to the page. Simple trigonometry shows us that

$$a = \cos \alpha$$
$$b = \cos \beta$$
$$c = \cos \theta$$

where θ is the angle formed with the positive z-axis.

More significantly (at least for intuition) is the following: if the distance from the origin to the plane is r, then $|d| = r$; further, the sign of d is negative if $\hat{n}$ points away from the origin and positive if it points toward the origin.

The *parametric form* for a plane is $X(s,t) = P + s\hat{u} + t\hat{v}$ for $s \in \mathbb{R}$ and $t \in \mathbb{R}$. The point P is on the plane. The directions $\hat{u} \neq \vec{0}$ and $\hat{v} \neq \vec{0}$ must be linearly independent vectors (see Figure 9.3).

To convert from parametric form to normal-point form, just use P as the point on the plane. The normal vector must be perpendicular to both direction vectors, so $\hat{n} = \hat{u} \times \hat{v}$. To convert from normal-point form to parametric form, again use P as is. We must choose two linearly independent vectors $\hat{u}$ and $\hat{v}$ that are perpen-

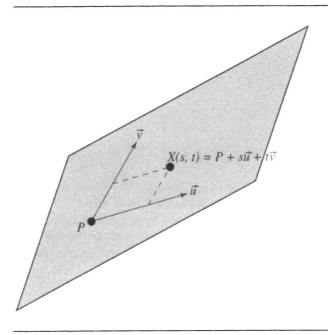

Figure 9.3   The parametric representation of a plane.

dicular to $\hat{n}$. There are infinitely many choices, but here is one that allows a robust numerical implementation. The idea is to choose a unit-length vector $\hat{u} = (u_0, u_1, u_2)$ perpendicular to $\hat{n} = (n_0, n_1, n_2)$ so that $\hat{u}$ has a zero component. You cannot safely choose any component to be zero. For example, if you choose $\hat{u} = (u_0, u_1, 0)$, then $0 = \vec{n} \cdot \hat{u} = n_0 u_0 + n_1 u_1$. A formal solution is $\hat{u} = (n_1, -n_0, 0)/\sqrt{n_0^2 + n_1^2}$, but clearly there is an algebraic problem when $n_0 = n_1 = 0$ and numerical problems when n_0 and n_1 are both nearly zero. Better is to choose a component of $\hat{u}$ to be zero based on information about $\hat{n}$.

The pseudocode is

```
Vector N = nonzero plane normal;
Vector U, V;

if (|N.x| >= |N.y|) {
    // N.x or N.z is the largest magnitude component, swap them
    U.x = +N.z;
    U.y = 0;
    U.z = -N.x;
} else {
```

```
        // N.y or N.z is the largest magnitude component, swap them
        U.x = 0;
        U.y = +N.z;
        U.z = -N.y;
    }

    V = Cross(N, U);
```

9.2.2 COORDINATE SYSTEM RELATIVE TO A PLANE

Given a plane with normal $\vec{n}$ and point P, sometimes it is convenient to have a full orthonormal coordinate system for $\mathbb{R}^3$ with origin at P, $\vec{n}$ as one of the coordinate axis directions, and two other coordinate axes in the plane itself. In this case, $\vec{n}$ is first normalized so that it is a unit-length vector. The vector $\hat{u}$ created in the pseudocode of the last subsection is also normalized to unit length. The cross product $\hat{v} = \hat{n} \times \hat{u}$ is automatically unit length.

The pseudocode is

```
Vector N = unit-length plane normal;
Vector U, V;

if (|N.x| >= |N.y|) {
    // N.x or N.z is the largest magnitude component
    invLength = 1 / sqrt(N.x * N.x + N.z * N.z);
    U.x = +N.z * invLength;
    U.y = 0;
    U.z = -N.x * invLength;
} else {
    // N.y or N.z is the largest magnitude component
    invLength = 1 / sqrt(N.y * N.y + N.z * N.z);
    U.x = 0;
    U.y = +N.z * invLength;
    U.z = -N.y * invLength;
}

V = Cross(N, U);   // automatically unit length
```

Any point $X \in \mathbb{R}^3$ can be written in the implied coordinate system as

$$X = P + y_0\hat{u} + y_1\hat{v} + y_2\hat{n} = P + \mathbf{R}\vec{y}$$

where $\mathbf{R}$ is a rotation matrix whose columns are $\hat{u}$, $\hat{v}$, and $\hat{n}$ (in that order) and where $\vec{y} = (y_0, y_1, y_2)$ is a 3×1 vector.

9.2.3 2D Objects in a Plane

Consider a set $S \subset \mathbb{R}^2$ in the xy-plane that represents a 2D object. Abstractly,

$$S = \{(x, y) \in \mathbb{R}^2 : (x, y) \text{ satisfies some constraints}\}$$

This object can be embedded in a 2D plane in 3D. Let the plane contain the point P and have a unit-length normal $\hat{n}$. If $\hat{u}$ and $\hat{v}$ are vectors in the plane so that $\hat{u}$, $\hat{v}$, and $\hat{n}$ form an orthonormal set, then the (x, y) pairs for the object in 2D can be used as the coordinates of $\hat{u}$ and $\hat{v}$ as a method for embedding the 2D object in the plane in 3D, the embedded set labeled $S' \subset \mathbb{R}^3$. This set is defined by

$$S' = \{P + x\hat{u} + y\hat{v} \in \mathbb{R}^3 : (x, y) \in S\}$$

Observe that there are infinitely many planes in which the 2D object can be embedded. Within each plane there are infinitely many ways to choose the vectors $\hat{u}$ and $\hat{v}$.

In many applications the problem is the reverse one—start with the object that lives in a specific plane in 3D and obtain a congruent object in the xy-plane. The term "congruent" refers to obtaining one object from the other by applying a rigid motion. If S' is a set of points on a plane $\hat{n} \cdot (X - P) = 0$, any point $Q \in S'$ can be converted to a point in the xy-plane by solving $Q = P + x\hat{u} + y\hat{v}$ for x and y. It is assumed that $\{\hat{u}, \hat{v}, \hat{n}\}$ is an orthonormal set. The solution is simple: $x = \hat{u} \cdot (Q - P)$ and $y = \hat{v} \cdot (Q - P)$. Since Q is on the plane, $\hat{n} \cdot (Q - P) = 0$. To see that the two triangles are congruent, the three equations can be written in vector form as

$$\begin{bmatrix} x \\ y \\ 0 \end{bmatrix} = \begin{bmatrix} \hat{u} \cdot (Q - P) \\ \hat{v} \cdot (Q - P) \\ \hat{n} \cdot (Q - P) \end{bmatrix} = R(Q - P)$$

where R is a rotation matrix whose rows are $\hat{u}$, $\hat{v}$, and $\hat{n}$. Thus, points $(x, y, 0)$ in the xy-plane are obtained from points in the plane $\hat{n} \cdot (X - P) = 0$ by a translation followed by a rotation, in total a rigid motion.

EXAMPLE   Given a 2D triangle with vertices (x_i, y_i) for $i = 0, 1, 2$, and given a plane $\hat{n} \cdot (X - P) = 0$ in which the triangle should live, a simple choice for vertices of the triangle in 3D is $V_i = P + x_i\hat{u} + y_i\hat{v}$ for $i = 0, 1, 2$. Given vertices W_i for $i = 0, 1, 2$, construct a triangle in the xy-plane that is congruent to the original triangle. To solve this problem, construct a plane containing the original triangle. Define the plane origin to be $P = W_0$. Define the edge vectors $\vec{e}_0 = W_1 - W_0$ and $\vec{e}_1 = W_2 - W_0$. A unit-length normal vector to the plane of the triangle is $\hat{n} = (\vec{e}_0 \times \vec{e}_1)/\|\vec{e}_0 \times \vec{e}_1\|$. Construct $\hat{u}$ and $\hat{v}$ as described earlier. Determine the coefficients d_{ij} in the representations $\vec{e}_0 = d_{00}\hat{u} + d_{01}\hat{v}$ and $\vec{e}_1 = d_{10}\hat{u} + d_{11}\hat{v}$. The coefficients are easily computed using dot products, $d_{00} = \vec{e}_0 \cdot \hat{u}$, $d_{01} = \vec{e}_0 \cdot \hat{v}$, $d_{10} = \vec{e}_1 \cdot \hat{u}$, and $d_{11} = \vec{e}_1 \cdot \hat{v}$. The representations lead to $W_1 = W_0 + \vec{e}_0 = P + d_{00}\hat{u} + d_{01}\hat{v}$ and $W_2 = W_1 + \vec{e}_1 = P + d_{10}\hat{u} + d_{11}\hat{v}$.

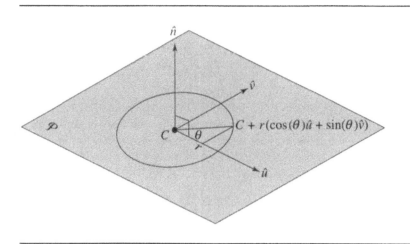

Figure 9.4   The parametric representation of a circle in 3D.

The vertices of the triangle as a 2D object are $(0, 0)$, (d_{00}, d_{01}), and (d_{10}, d_{11}) and correspond to W_0, W_1, and W_2, respectively. ■

EXAMPLE   Suppose you want to have a formula for working with a circle in 3D whose center is $C \in \mathbb{R}^3$ and whose radius is r. The plane containing the circle is specified to have a unit-length normal $\hat{n}$. The center of the circle must lie in the plane, so an equation for the plane is $\hat{n} \cdot (X - C) = 0$. The circle points X must be equidistant from the center C, so another constraint is $\|X - C\| = r$. This algebraic equation defined on all of $\mathbb{R}^3$ produces a sphere centered at C and of radius r. However, only points on the plane are desired, so the circle can be viewed as the set of intersection of the plane and sphere. In 2D, a circle centered at the origin and having radius r is parameterized by $x = r \cos \theta$ and $y = r \sin \theta$ for $\theta \in [0, 2\pi)$ (see Figure 5.15). Formally, the circle in 2D is the set $S = \{(r \cos \theta, r \sin \theta) \in \mathbb{R}^2 : \theta \in [0, 2\pi)\}$. In 3D, the circle embedded in the plane is the set $S' = \{C + (r \cos \theta)\hat{u} + (r \sin \theta)\hat{v} : \theta \in [0, 2\pi)\}$ (see Figure 9.4). If we define a vector-valued function $\hat{w}(\theta) = \cos \theta \hat{u} + \sin \theta \hat{v}$, then the parametric 3D circle definition can be written more compactly as

$$P = C + r\hat{w}(\theta)$$

It is simple to verify the constraints on $X = C + (r \cos \theta)\hat{u} + (r \sin \theta)\hat{v}$. First,

$$\hat{n} \cdot (X - C) = \hat{n} \cdot ((r \cos \theta)\hat{u} + (r \sin \theta)\hat{v})$$

$$= (r \cos \theta)\hat{n} \cdot \hat{u} + (r \sin \theta)\hat{n} \cdot \hat{v}$$

$$= (r \cos \theta)0 + (r \sin \theta)0, \quad \hat{n} \text{ is orthogonal to } \hat{u} \text{ and } \hat{v}$$

$$= 0$$

Second,

$$\|X - C\|^2 = \|(r \cos \theta)\hat{u} + (r \sin \theta)\hat{v}\|^2$$

$$= (r^2 \cos^2 \theta)\|\hat{u}\|^2 + (2r^2 \sin \theta \cos \theta)\hat{u} \cdot \hat{v} + (r^2 \sin^2 \theta)\|\hat{v}\|^2$$

$$= (r^2 \cos^2 \theta)1 + (2r^2 \sin \theta \cos \theta)0 + (r^2 \sin^2 \theta)1,$$

$$\hat{u} \text{ and } \hat{v} \text{ are orthonormal}$$

$$= r^2 \cos^2 \theta + r^2 \sin^2 \theta$$

$$= r^2$$

Similar constructions apply to other quadratic curves in the plane. ∎

Another quite useful method for obtaining a 2D representation of a planar object S' in 3D is described below. The method uses projection, so the two objects are not congruent. If the plane normal is $\hat{n} = (n_0, n_1, n_2)$, and if $n_2 \neq 0$, the projection of a point $Q = (q_0, q_1, q_2) \in S'$ onto the xy-plane is $Q' = (q_0, q_1)$. The condition that $n_2 \neq 0$ is important. If it were zero, the plane of the object projects onto a straight line, thereby losing much information about the original object. If in fact $n_2 = 0$, the projection can be made onto the xz-plane if $n_1 \neq 0$ or onto the yz-plane if $n_0 \neq 0$. In practice, the largest magnitude normal component is used to identify the coordinate plane of projection. This makes the projected object as large as possible compared to its projections on the other coordinate planes. A typical application where this type of construction is useful is in triangulation of a planar polygon in 3D. The congruent mapping requires computing $(x, y) = (\hat{u} \cdot (Q - P), \hat{v} \cdot (Q - P))$ for all polygon vertices Q. The difference $Q - P$ requires 3 subtractions, and each dot product requires 2 multiplications and 1 addition. The total operation count for n vertices is $9n$. The projection mapping requires identifying a nonzero normal component and extracting the two components for the coordinate plane of projection. Finding the normal component is the only computational expense and requires a couple of floating-point comparisons, clearly much cheaper than the congruent mapping. The triangulation in the xy-plane produces triples of vertex indices that represent the triangles. These triples are just as valid for the original polygon in 3D. Another application is in computing the area of a planar polygon in 3D; Section 13.12 has more detail on the construction.

9.3 POLYMESHES, POLYHEDRA, AND POLYTOPES

In this section are definitions for objects that consist of three types of geometric components: *vertices*, *edges*, and *faces*. Vertices are, of course, just single points. Edges are line segments whose end points are vertices. Faces are convex polygons that live in 3D. Many applications support only triangular faces because of their simplicity in storage and their ease of use in operations applied to collections of

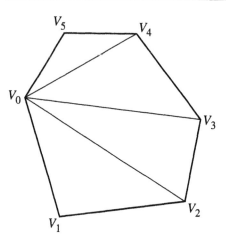

Figure 9.5   A convex polygon and its decomposition into a triangle fan.

the faces. It is possible to allow nonconvex polygon faces, but this only complicates the implementation and manipulation of the objects. If triangles are required by an application and the faces are convex polygons, the faces can be *fanned* into triangles. If the n vertices of the face are ordered as V_0 through V_{n-1}, the $n-2$ triangles whose union is the face are $\langle V_0, V_i, V_{i+1} \rangle$ for $1 \leq i \leq n-2$. Figure 9.5 shows a convex face and its decomposition into a triangle fan. If a face is a simple polygon that is not convex, it can be decomposed into triangles by any of the triangulation methods discussed in Section 13.9. Figure 9.6 shows a nonconvex face and its decomposition into triangles. Triangulation is generally an expense that an application using meshes should not have to deal with at run time; hence the common restriction that the faces be triangles themselves or, in the worst case, convex polygons.

A finite collection of vertices, edges, and faces is called a *polygonal mesh*, or in short a *polymesh*, as long as the components satisfy the following conditions:

- Each vertex must be shared by at least one edge. (No isolated vertices are allowed.)
- Each edge must be shared by at least one face. (No isolated edges or polylines allowed.)
- If two faces intersect, the vertex or edge of intersection must be a component in the mesh. (No interpenetration of faces is allowed. An edge of one face may not live in the interior of another face.)

If all the faces are triangles, the object is called a *triangle mesh*, or in short a *trimesh*.

Figure 9.7 shows a triangle mesh. Figure 9.8 shows a collection of vertices, edges, and triangles that fails the first condition—a vertex is isolated and not used by a triangle. Figure 9.9 shows a collection of vertices, edges, and triangles that fails the

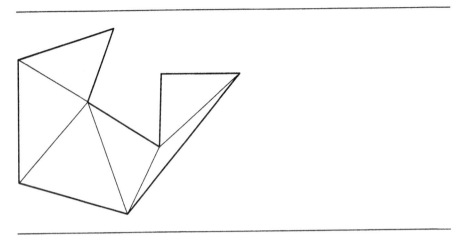

Figure 9.6   A nonconvex polygon and its decomposition into triangles.

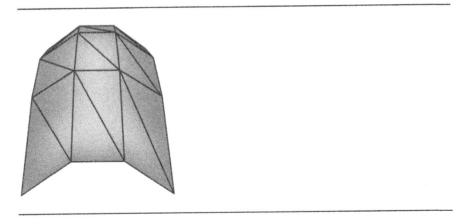

Figure 9.7   A triangle mesh.

second condition—an edge is not an edge of the triangle, even though an end point is a vertex of a triangle. Figure 9.10 shows a collection of vertices, edges, and triangles that fails the third condition—two triangles are interpenetrating, so they intersect at some points that are not in the original collection of vertices, edges, and triangles.

A *polyhedron* (plural: *polyhedra*) is a polymesh that has additional constraints. The intuitive idea is that a polyhedron encloses a bounded region of space and that it has no unnecessary edge junctions. The simplest example is a *tetrahedron*, a polymesh that has four vertices, six edges, and four triangular faces. The standard tetrahedron has vertices $V_0 = (0, 0, 0)$, $V_1 = (1, 0, 0)$, $V_2 = (0, 1, 0)$, and $V_3 = (0, 0, 1)$.

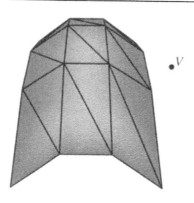

Figure 9.8   Vertices, edges, and triangles are not a mesh since a vertex is isolated.

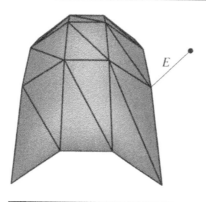

Figure 9.9   Vertices, edges, and triangles are not a mesh since an edge is isolated.

The edges are $E_{01} = \langle V_0, V_1 \rangle$, $E_{02} = \langle V_0, V_2 \rangle$, $E_{03} = \langle V_0, V_3 \rangle$, $E_{12} = \langle V_1, V_2 \rangle$, $E_{23} = \langle V_2, V_3 \rangle$, and $E_{13} = \langle V_1, V_3 \rangle$. The faces are $T_{012} = \langle V_0, V_1, V_2 \rangle$, $T_{013} = \langle V_0, V_1, V_3 \rangle$, $T_{023} = \langle V_0, V_2, V_3 \rangle$, and $T_{123} = \langle V_1, V_2, V_3 \rangle$. The additional constraints for a polymesh to be a polyhedron are as follows:

- The mesh is connected when viewed as a graph whose nodes are the faces and whose arcs are the edges shared by adjacent faces. Intuitively, a mesh is connected if you can reach a destination face from any source face by following a path of pairwise adjacent faces from the source to the destination.

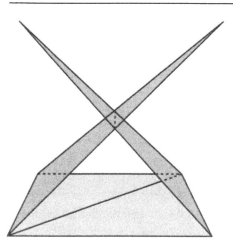

Figure 9.10   Vertices, edges, and triangles are not a mesh since two triangles interpenetrate.

- Each edge is shared by exactly two faces. This condition forces the mesh to be a closed and bounded surface.

Figure 9.11 shows a polyhedron. Figure 9.12 is a polymesh, but not a polyhedron since it is not connected. Observe that the tetrahedron and the rectangle mesh share a vertex, but the connectivity has to do with triangles sharing edges, not sharing singleton vertices. Figure 9.13 is a polymesh, but not a polyhedron since an edge is shared by three faces.

A *polytope* is a polyhedron that encloses a convex region R. That is, given any two points X and Y in R, the line segment $(1 - t)X + tY$ is also in R for any $t \in [0, 1]$. Figure 9.14 shows a polytope.

9.3.1 VERTEX-EDGE-FACE TABLES

An implementation of a polymesh requires some type of data structure for representing the components and their adjacencies. A simple data structure is a *vertex-edge-face table*. The N unique vertices are stored in an array, Vertex[0] through Vertex[N-1], so vertices can be referred to by their indices into the array.

Edges are represented by pairs of vertex indices, and faces are represented by ordered lists of vertex indices. The table is defined by the grammar:

```
VertexIndex = 0 through N - 1;
VertexIndexList = EMPTY or { VertexIndex V; VertexIndexList VList; }
EdgeList = EMPTY or { Edge E; EdgeList EList; }
```

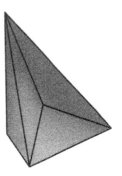

Figure 9.11   A polyhedron that consists of a tetrahedron, but an additional vertex was added to form a depression in the centered face.

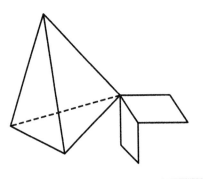

Figure 9.12   A polymesh that is not a polyhedron since it is not connected. The fact that the tetrahedron and rectangle mesh share a common vertex does not make them connected in the sense of edge-triangle connectivity.

```
FaceList = EMPTY or { Face F; FaceList FList; }
Vertex = { VertexIndex V; EdgeList EList; FaceList FList; }
Edge = { VertexIndex V[2]; FaceList FList; }
Face = { VertexIndexList VList; }
```

The edge list EList in the Vertex object is a list of all edges that have an end point corresponding to the vertex indexed by V. The face list FList in the Vertex object is a list of all faces that have a vertex corresponding to the vertex indexed by V. The face list FList in the Edge object is a list of all faces that share the specified edge. An Edge object does not directly know about edges sharing either of its vertices. A Face object

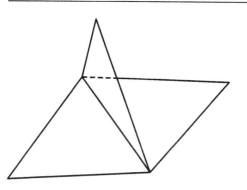

Figure 9.13   A polymesh that is not a polyhedron since an edge is shared by three faces.

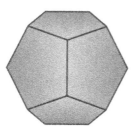

Figure 9.14   A polytope, a regular dodecahedron.

does not know about vertices or edges that share the face's vertices. This information can be indirectly obtained by various queries applied to the subobjects of either Edge or Face.

By the definition of a polymesh, the face list in Edge cannot be empty since any edge in the collection must be part of at least one face in the collection. Similarly, the edge and face lists in Vertex must both be nonempty. If both were empty, the vertex would be isolated. If the edge list were not empty and the face list were empty, the vertex would be part of an isolated polyline, and the immediately adjacent edges have no faces containing them.

The edges can be classified according to the number of faces sharing them. An edge is a *boundary edge* if it has exactly one face using it. Otherwise, the edge is an *interior edge*. If an interior edge has exactly two faces sharing it, it is called a *manifold edge*. All edges of a polyhedron are required to be of this type. If an interior edge has three or more faces sharing it, it is called a *junction edge*.

9.3.2 CONNECTED MESHES

A direct application of depth-first search to the mesh allows us to construct the *connected components* of the mesh. Initially all faces are marked as unvisited. Starting with an unvisited face, the face is marked as visited. For each unvisited face adjacent to the initial face, a traversal is made to that face and the process is applied recursively. When all adjacent faces of the initial face have been traversed, a check is made on all faces to see if they have all been visited. If so, the mesh is said to be *connected*. If not, the mesh has multiple connected submeshes, each called a connected component. Each of the remaining components can be found by starting a recursive traversal with any unvisited face. The pseudocode below illustrates the process, but with a stack-based approach rather than one using a recursive function call.

```
MeshList GetComponents(Mesh mesh)
{
    MeshList componentList;

    // initially all faces are unvisited
    Face f;
    for (each face f in mesh)
        f.visited = false;

    // find the connected component of an unvisited face
    while (mesh.HasUnvisitedFaces()) {
        Stack faceStack;
        f = mesh.GetUnvisitedFace();
        faceStack.Push(f);
        f.visited = true;

        // traverse the connected component of the starting face
        Mesh component;
        while (not faceStack.empty()) {
            // start at the current face
            faceStack.Pop(f);
            component.InsertFace(f);

            for (int i = 0; i < f.numEdges; i++) {
                // visit faces sharing an edge of f
                Edge e = f.edge[i];

                // visit each adjacent face
                for (int j = 0; j < e.numFaces; j++) {
                    Face a = e.face[j];
                    if (not a.visited) {
```

```
                             // this face not yet visited
                             faceStack.Push(a);
                             a.visited = true;
                         }
                     }
                 }
             }
         componentList.Insert(component);
     }

     return componentList;
 }
```

If all that is required is determining if a mesh is connected, the following pseudocode is a minor variation of the previous code that does the trick:

```
bool IsConnected(Mesh mesh)
{
    // initially all faces are unvisited
    Face f;
    for (each face f in mesh)
        f.visited = false;

    // start the traversal at any face
    Stack faceStack;
    f = mesh.GetUnvisitedFace();
    faceStack.Push(f);
    f.visited = true;

    while (not faceStack.empty()) {
        // start at the current face
        faceStack.Pop(f);
        for (int i = 0; i < f.numEdges; i++) {
            // visit faces sharing an edge of f
            Edge e = f.edge[i];

            // visit each adjacent face
            for (int j = 0; j < e.numFaces; j++) {
                Face a = e.face[j];
                if (not a.visited) {
                    // this face not yet visited
                    faceStack.Push(a);
                    a.visited = true;
                }
```

```
                }
            }
        }

        // check if any face has not been visited
        for (each face f in mesh) {
            if (f.visited == false)
                return false;
        }

        // all faces were visited, the mesh is connected
        return true;
}
```

9.3.3   MANIFOLD MESHES

A connected mesh is said to be a *manifold mesh* if each edge in the mesh is shared by at most two faces. The topology of manifold face meshes is potentially more complicated than for meshes in the plane. The problem is one of *orientability*. Although there is a formal mathematical definition for orientable surfaces, we will use a definition for manifold meshes that hints at a test itself for orientability. A manifold mesh is *orientable* if the vertex orderings for the faces can be chosen so that adjacent faces have *consistent orderings*. Let F_0 and F_1 be adjacent faces sharing the edge $\langle V_0, V_1 \rangle$. If V_0 and V_1 occur in this order for F_0, then they must occur in F_1 in the order V_1 followed by V_0. The prototypical case is for a mesh of two triangles that share an edge. Figure 9.15 shows the four possible configurations.

A Möbius strip is an example of a nonorientable surface. Figure 9.16 shows this. Two parallel edges of a rectangle in 3D can be joined together to form a cylindrical strip that is orientable. However, if the rectangle is twisted so that the edges join in reversed order, a Möbius strip is obtained, a nonorientable surface.

In nearly all graphics applications, meshes are required to be orientable. Observe that the definition for manifold mesh is topological in the sense that only vertex orderings and connectivity information are mentioned in the definition, not vertex, edge, or face locations. The definition does not rule out self-intersections, a geometrical property. Usually applications also require a mesh to be non-self-intersecting.

9.3.4   CLOSED MESHES

A connected mesh is said to be a *closed mesh* if it is manifold with each edge shared by exactly two faces and is non-self-intersecting. The typical example of a closed mesh is a triangle mesh that tessellates a sphere. If a mesh is not closed, it is said to be an *open mesh*. For example, a triangle mesh that tessellates a hemisphere is open.

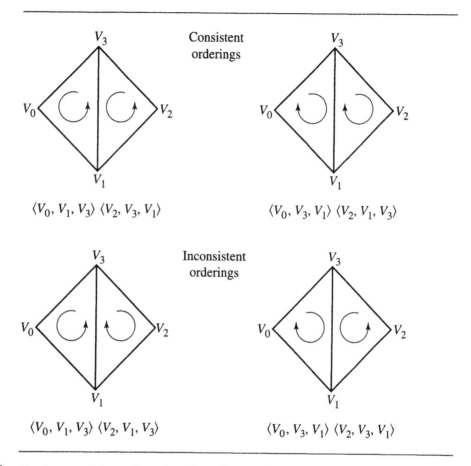

Figure 9.15   The four possible configurations for ordering of two adjacent triangles.

9.3.5 CONSISTENT ORDERING

The condition of orientability for a manifold mesh is very important in computer graphics applications. By implication, a manifold mesh has two consistent orderings of its faces. Each ordering provides a set of face normals. In the two-triangle example of Figure 9.15, an open manifold mesh, the top images show the two consistent orderings for the mesh. The normal vectors for the ordering on the left are $\vec{n}_0 = (V_1 - V_0) \times (V_3 - V_0)$ and $\vec{n}_1 = (V_3 - V_2) \times (V_1 - V_2)$. Both normals point out of the plane of the page of the image. The normal vectors for the ordering on the right are just $-\vec{n}_0$ and $-\vec{n}_1$. Generally, the set of normal vectors for one consistent ordering of a mesh is obtained from the set of normal vectors for the other consistent ordering by negating all the normals from the first set.

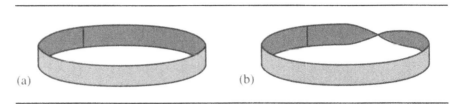

(a)   (b)

Figure 9.16   A rectangle has two parallel edges joined together forming (a) a cylindrical strip (orientable) or (b) a Möbius strip (nonorientable).

An application has to decide which of the two consistent orderings it will use for meshes. The typical choice is based on visibility of the mesh from an eye point (camera location). The ordering is chosen so that mesh faces that are visible (ignoring self-occlusion for the sake of the argument) have normal vectors that are directed toward the eye point. That is, if a mesh face is in a plane $\vec{n} \cdot (X - P) = 0$, and if the eye point is E, the face is visible when $\vec{n} \cdot (E - P) > 0$. Such faces are said to be *front-facing*. The vertices, when viewed from the eye point, are counterclockwise ordered in the plane of the face. The faces for which $\vec{n} \cdot (E - P) \leq 0$ are said to be *back-facing*. In a standard graphics rendering system, back-facing faces can be discarded immediately and not transformed or lit, thereby saving a lot of time in rendering. For a scene with a lot of closed meshes, the intuition is that approximately half of the faces are back-facing. Not drawing them leads to a signicant increase in performance.

Using the same convention for selecting the consistent ordering, the normals of a closed mesh point outside the region bounded by the mesh. This is important for visibility and lighting as mentioned earlier, but it is also important for geometric queries. For example, a point-in-polytope query might depend on the fact that all normals are outward pointing. Of course, if all normals are inward pointing, the test can still be correctly implemented. What is important is that a consistent ordering be chosen and the various systems that manipulate meshes adhere to that ordering.

Toward that goal, sometimes applications can construct a connected manifold mesh that is orientable, but the face orderings are not consistent. The classic example is extraction of a level surface from a 3D voxel data set as a mesh of triangles. Each voxel is processed independently of the others, and a collection of triangles that approximate the level surface is constructed. The triangles are specified as triples of indices into an array of vertices that lie on the level surface. The full set of triangles forms an orientable mesh (level surfaces are always orientable), but the triangle orderings might not be consistent because of the independent processing. It is desirable to reorder some of the triples of indices to produce a consistent ordering for the mesh. If the mesh is stored in a vertex-edge-face table, a depth-first search of the abstract graph represented by the table can be used to obtain the consistency. An initial face is selected. All faces in the mesh will be reordered to be consistent with that initial face. The reordering is purely topological and has only to do with the order of vertices, not with any geometric properties of the faces. As such, you get a consistent ordering, but for a closed mesh, you might get all inward-pointing normals when in fact you wanted outward-pointing ones. If the desired ordering is known in advance, additional information must be supplied to order the initial face as desired, perhaps by some visibility test from an eye point. The initial face is marked as visited. If an adjacent face has a consistent ordering with the initial face, then nothing is done to the adjacent face. Otherwise, the ordering is inconsistent, and the adjacent triangle is reordered to make it consistent. The adjacent triangle is then marked as visited, and the search is applied recursively to its unvisited adjacent faces. The pseudocode is listed below.

```
void MakeConsistent(Mesh mesh)
{
    // assert: mesh is a connected manifold

    // initially all faces are unvisited
    Face f;
    for (each face f in mesh)
        f.visited = false;

    // start the traversal at any face
    Stack faceStack;
    f = mesh.GetUnvisitedFace();
    faceStack.Push(f);
    f.visited = true;

    // traverse the connected component of the starting triangle
    while (not faceStack.empty()) {
        // start at the current face
        faceStack.Pop(f);
        for (int i = 0; i < f.numEdges; i++) {
            // visit faces sharing an edge of f
            Edge e = f.edge[i];
            if (f has an adjacent face a to edge e) {
                if (not a.visited) {
                    if (a.ContainsOrderedEdge(e.V(0), e.V(1))) {
                        // f and a have inconsistent orders
                        a.ReorderVertices();
                    }
                    faceStack.Push(a);
                    a.visited = true;
                }
            }
        }
    }
}
```

Figure 9.17   The five Platonic solids. Left to right: tetrahedron, hexahedron, octahedron, dodecahedron, icosahedron.

9.3.6 PLATONIC SOLIDS

A *regular polygon* is a convex polygon whose edge lengths are all the same and whose angles between edges are all the same. For a specifed $n \geq 3$, the vertices of a regular polygon inscribed in a unit circle are constructed by $(x_k, y_k) = (\cos(2\pi k/n), \sin(2\pi k/n))$ for $0 \leq k < n$. A *regular polyhedron* is a convex polyhedron whose faces are congruent regular polygons and for which the number of faces sharing each vertex is the same at each vertex. As it turns out, only five such polyhedra are possible, but the proof is not given here. These polyhedra are called the *Platonic solids*. In particular, the solids are a *tetrahedron*, a cube or *hexahedron*, an *octahedron*, a *dodecahedron*, and an *icosahedron*. Figure 9.17 illustrates the five solids. Provided here are relationships between various quantities for a Platonic solid. A vertex-face table can be constructed for each solid inscribed in the unit sphere; the tables are useful for rendering the solids or for providing an initial polyhedron that is to be subdivided for purposes of tessellating the sphere.

Let v, e, and f denote the number of vertices, edges, and faces, respectively, for the solid. Euler's formula relating these quantities is $v - e + f = 2$. Let p denote the number of edges in a face, and let q denote the number of edges at each vertex. The common edge length is denoted by L. The angle between two adjacent faces is called a *dihedral angle* (literally *di* for "two" and *hedra* for "faces") and is denoted A. The radius of the circumscribed sphere is denoted by R, and the radius of the inscribed sphere is denoted by r. The surface area is denoted by S, and the volume is denoted by V. All these quantites are interrelated by the equations

$$\sin(A/2) = \cos(\pi/q)/\sin(\pi/p) \qquad R/L = \tan(\pi/q)\tan(A/2)/2$$

$$r/L = \cot(\pi/p)\tan(A/2)/2 \qquad R/r = \tan(\pi/p)\tan(\pi/q)$$

$$S/L^2 = fp\cot(\pi/p)/4 \qquad\qquad V = rS/3$$

Table 9.1 summarizes the relationships for the Platonic solids.

Table 9.1   Various relationships for Platonic solids.

	v	e	f	p	q
Tetrahedron	4	6	4	3	3
Hexahedron	8	12	6	4	3
Octahedron	6	12	8	3	4
Dodecahedron	20	30	12	5	3
Icosahedron	12	30	20	3	5

	$\sin(A)$	$\cos(A)$	R/L	r/L	S/L^2	V/L^3
Tetrahedron	$\frac{\sqrt{8}}{3}$	$\frac{1}{3}$	$\frac{\sqrt{6}}{4}$	$\frac{\sqrt{6}}{12}$	$\sqrt{3}$	$\frac{\sqrt{2}}{12}$
Hexahedron	1	0	$\frac{\sqrt{3}}{2}$	$\frac{1}{2}$	6	1
Octahedron	$\frac{\sqrt{8}}{3}$	$-\frac{1}{3}$	$\frac{\sqrt{2}}{2}$	$\frac{\sqrt{6}}{6}$	$2\sqrt{3}$	$\frac{\sqrt{2}}{3}$
Dodecahedron	$\frac{2}{\sqrt{5}}$	$-\frac{1}{\sqrt{5}}$	$\frac{\sqrt{3}(\sqrt{5}+1)}{4}$	$\frac{\sqrt{250+110\sqrt{5}}}{20}$	$3\sqrt{25+10\sqrt{5}}$	$\frac{15+7\sqrt{5}}{4}$
Icosahedron	$\frac{2}{3}$	$-\frac{\sqrt{5}}{3}$	$\frac{\sqrt{10+2\sqrt{5}}}{4}$	$\frac{\sqrt{42+18\sqrt{5}}}{12}$	$5\sqrt{3}$	$\frac{5(3+\sqrt{5})}{12}$

The following subsections provide vertex-face tables for the Platonic solids. The polyhedron is centered at the origin and the vertices are all unit length. The face connectivity is provided as a list of indices into the vertex array. The vertices of a face are counterclockwise ordered as you look at the face from outside the polyhedron. The faces for the tetrahedron, octahedron, and icosahedron are already triangles. The faces for the hexahedron are squares, and the faces for the dodecahedron are pentagons. In these two cases, a vertex-triangle table is also provided for those renderers that support only triangle faces.

Tetrahedron

The vertices are

$$V_0 = (0, 0, 1) \qquad V_2 = (-\sqrt{2}/3, \sqrt{6}/3, -1/3)$$

$$V_1 = (2\sqrt{2}/3, 0, -1/3) \quad V_3 = (-\sqrt{2}/3, -\sqrt{6}/3, -1/3)$$

The triangle connectivity is

$$T_0 = \langle 0, 1, 2 \rangle \quad T_2 = \langle 0, 3, 1 \rangle$$

$$T_1 = \langle 0, 2, 3 \rangle \quad T_3 = \langle 1, 3, 2 \rangle$$

Hexahedron

The vertices are

$$V_0 = (-1, -1, -1)/\sqrt{3} \quad V_4 = (-1, -1, 1)/\sqrt{3}$$
$$V_1 = (1, -1, -1)/\sqrt{3} \quad V_5 = (1, -1, 1)/\sqrt{3}$$
$$V_2 = (1, 1, -1)/\sqrt{3} \quad V_6 = (1, 1, 1)/\sqrt{3}$$
$$V_3 = (-1, 1, -1)/\sqrt{3} \quad V_7 = (-1, 1, 1)/\sqrt{3}$$

The face connectivity is

$$F_0 = \langle 0, 3, 2, 1 \rangle \quad F_3 = \langle 6, 5, 1, 2 \rangle$$
$$F_1 = \langle 0, 1, 5, 4 \rangle \quad F_4 = \langle 6, 2, 3, 7 \rangle$$
$$F_2 = \langle 0, 4, 7, 3 \rangle \quad F_5 = \langle 6, 7, 4, 5 \rangle$$

The triangle connectivity is

$$T_0 = \langle 0, 3, 2 \rangle \quad T_6 = \langle 6, 5, 1 \rangle$$
$$T_1 = \langle 0, 2, 1 \rangle \quad T_7 = \langle 6, 1, 2 \rangle$$
$$T_2 = \langle 0, 1, 5 \rangle \quad T_8 = \langle 6, 2, 3 \rangle$$
$$T_3 = \langle 0, 5, 4 \rangle \quad T_9 = \langle 6, 3, 7 \rangle$$
$$T_4 = \langle 0, 4, 7 \rangle \quad T_{10} = \langle 6, 7, 4 \rangle$$
$$T_5 = \langle 0, 7, 3 \rangle \quad T_{11} = \langle 6, 4, 5 \rangle$$

Octahedron

The vertices are

$$V_0 = (1, 0, 0) \quad V_3 = (0, -1, 0)$$
$$V_1 = (-1, 0, 0) \quad V_4 = (0, 0, 1)$$
$$V_2 = (0, 1, 0) \quad V_5 = (0, 0, -1)$$

The triangle connectivity is

$$T_0 = \langle 4, 0, 2 \rangle \quad T_4 = \langle 5, 2, 0 \rangle$$
$$T_1 = \langle 4, 2, 1 \rangle \quad T_5 = \langle 5, 1, 2 \rangle$$
$$T_2 = \langle 4, 1, 3 \rangle \quad T_6 = \langle 5, 3, 1 \rangle$$
$$T_3 = \langle 4, 3, 0 \rangle \quad T_7 = \langle 5, 0, 3 \rangle$$

Dodecahedron

The vertices are constructed using the following intermediate terms: $a = 1/\sqrt{3}$, $b = \sqrt{(3 - \sqrt{5})/6}$, and $c = \sqrt{(3 + \sqrt{5})/6}$. The vertices are

$$V_0 = (a, a, a) \quad\quad V_{10} = (b, -c, 0)$$
$$V_1 = (a, a, -a) \quad\quad V_{11} = (-b, -c, 0)$$
$$V_2 = (a, -a, a) \quad\quad V_{12} = (c, 0, b)$$
$$V_3 = (a, -a, -a) \quad\quad V_{13} = (c, 0, -b)$$
$$V_4 = (-a, a, a) \quad\quad V_{14} = (-c, 0, b)$$
$$V_5 = (-a, a, -a) \quad\quad V_{15} = (-c, 0, -b)$$
$$V_6 = (-a, -a, a) \quad\quad V_{16} = (0, b, c)$$
$$V_7 = (-a, -a, -a) \quad V_{17} = (0, -b, c)$$
$$V_8 = (b, c, 0) \quad\quad V_{18} = (0, b, -c)$$
$$V_9 = (-b, c, 0) \quad\quad V_{19} = (0, -b, -c)$$

The face connectivity is

$$F_0 = \langle 0, 8, 9, 4, 16 \rangle \quad\quad F_6 = \langle 0, 12, 13, 1, 8 \rangle$$
$$F_1 = \langle 0, 16, 17, 2, 12 \rangle \quad F_7 = \langle 8, 1, 18, 5, 9 \rangle$$
$$F_2 = \langle 12, 2, 10, 3, 13 \rangle \quad F_8 = \langle 16, 4, 14, 6, 17 \rangle$$
$$F_3 = \langle 9, 5, 15, 14, 4 \rangle \quad\quad F_9 = \langle 6, 11, 10, 2, 17 \rangle$$
$$F_4 = \langle 3, 19, 18, 1, 13 \rangle \quad F_{10} = \langle 7, 15, 5, 18, 19 \rangle$$
$$F_5 = \langle 7, 11, 6, 14, 15 \rangle \quad F_{11} = \langle 7, 19, 3, 10, 11 \rangle$$

The triangle connectivity is

$$
\begin{array}{lll}
T_0 = \langle 0, 8, 9 \rangle & T_{12} = \langle 0, 9, 4 \rangle & T_{24} = \langle 0, 4, 16 \rangle \\
T_1 = \langle 0, 12, 13 \rangle & T_{13} = \langle 0, 13, 1 \rangle & T_{25} = \langle 0, 1, 8 \rangle \\
T_2 = \langle 0, 16, 17 \rangle & T_{14} = \langle 0, 17, 2 \rangle & T_{26} = \langle 0, 2, 12 \rangle \\
T_3 = \langle 8, 1, 18 \rangle & T_{15} = \langle 8, 18, 5 \rangle & T_{27} = \langle 8, 5, 9 \rangle \\
T_4 = \langle 12, 2, 10 \rangle & T_{16} = \langle 12, 10, 3 \rangle & T_{28} = \langle 12, 3, 13 \rangle \\
T_5 = \langle 16, 4, 14 \rangle & T_{17} = \langle 16, 14, 6 \rangle & T_{29} = \langle 16, 6, 17 \rangle \\
T_6 = \langle 9, 5, 15 \rangle & T_{18} = \langle 9, 15, 14 \rangle & T_{30} = \langle 9, 14, 4 \rangle \\
T_7 = \langle 6, 11, 10 \rangle & T_{19} = \langle 6, 10, 2 \rangle & T_{31} = \langle 6, 2, 17 \rangle \\
T_8 = \langle 3, 19, 18 \rangle & T_{20} = \langle 3, 18, 1 \rangle & T_{32} = \langle 3, 1, 13 \rangle \\
T_9 = \langle 7, 15, 5 \rangle & T_{21} = \langle 7, 5, 18 \rangle & T_{33} = \langle 7, 18, 19 \rangle \\
T_{10} = \langle 7, 11, 6 \rangle & T_{22} = \langle 7, 6, 14 \rangle & T_{34} = \langle 7, 14, 15 \rangle \\
T_{11} = \langle 7, 19, 3 \rangle & T_{23} = \langle 7, 3, 10 \rangle & T_{35} = \langle 7, 10, 11 \rangle
\end{array}
$$

Icosahedron

Let $t = (1 + \sqrt{5})/2$. The vertices are

$$
\begin{array}{ll}
V_0 = (t, 1, 0)/\sqrt{1 + t^2} & V_6 = (-1, 0, t)/\sqrt{1 + t^2} \\
V_1 = (-t, 1, 0)/\sqrt{1 + t^2} & V_7 = (-1, 0, -t)/\sqrt{1 + t^2} \\
V_2 = (t, -1, 0)/\sqrt{1 + t^2} & V_8 = (0, t, 1)/\sqrt{1 + t^2} \\
V_3 = (-t, -1, 0)/\sqrt{1 + t^2} & V_9 = (0, -t, 1)/\sqrt{1 + t^2} \\
V_4 = (1, 0, t)/\sqrt{1 + t^2} & V_{10} = (0, t, -1)/\sqrt{1 + t^2} \\
V_5 = (1, 0, -t)/\sqrt{1 + t^2} & V_{11} = (0, -t, -1)/\sqrt{1 + t^2}
\end{array}
$$

The triangle connectivity is

$$
\begin{aligned}
T_0 &= \langle 0, 8, 4 \rangle & T_{10} &= \langle 2, 9, 11 \rangle \\
T_1 &= \langle 0, 5, 10 \rangle & T_{11} &= \langle 3, 11, 9 \rangle \\
T_2 &= \langle 2, 4, 9 \rangle & T_{12} &= \langle 4, 2, 0 \rangle \\
T_3 &= \langle 2, 11, 5 \rangle & T_{13} &= \langle 5, 0, 2 \rangle \\
T_4 &= \langle 1, 6, 8 \rangle & T_{14} &= \langle 6, 1, 3 \rangle \\
T_5 &= \langle 1, 10, 7 \rangle & T_{15} &= \langle 7, 3, 1 \rangle \\
T_6 &= \langle 3, 9, 6 \rangle & T_{16} &= \langle 8, 6, 4 \rangle \\
T_7 &= \langle 3, 7, 11 \rangle & T_{17} &= \langle 9, 4, 6 \rangle \\
T_8 &= \langle 0, 10, 8 \rangle & T_{18} &= \langle 10, 5, 7 \rangle \\
T_9 &= \langle 1, 8, 10 \rangle & T_{19} &= \langle 11, 7, 5 \rangle
\end{aligned}
$$

9.4 QUADRIC SURFACES

An excellent discussion of quadric surfaces is in Finney and Thomas (1996), but considers all equations in axis-aligned form. The discussion here involves the general quadratic equation and relies on an eigendecomposition of a matrix to characterize the surfaces. The algorithm for eigendecomposition is discussed in Section A.3.

The general quadratic equation is $X^{\mathrm{T}}AX + B^{\mathrm{T}}X + c = 0$, where A is a 3×3 nonzero symmetric matrix, B is a 3×1 vector, and c is a scalar. The 3×1 vector X represents the variable quantities. Since A is symmetric, it can be factored as $A = R^{\mathrm{T}}DR$, where D is a diagonal matrix whose diagonal entries are the eigenvalues of A and R is a rotational matrix whose rows are corresponding eigenvectors. Setting $Y = RX$ and $E = RB$, the quadratic equation is $Y^{\mathrm{T}}DY + E^{\mathrm{T}}Y + c = 0$. The quadratic equation can be factored by completing the square on terms. This allows us to characterize the surface type or determine that the solution is degenerate (point, line, plane). Let $D = \mathrm{Diag}(d_0, d_1, d_2)$ and $E = (e_0, e_1, e_2)$.

9.4.1 THREE NONZERO EIGENVALUES

The factored equation is

$$
d_0 \left(y_0 + \frac{e_0}{2d_0} \right)^2 + d_1 \left(y_1 + \frac{e_1}{2d_1} \right)^2 + d_2 \left(y_2 + \frac{e_2}{2d_2} \right)^2 + c - \frac{e_0^2}{4d_0} - \frac{e_1^2}{4d_1} - \frac{e_2^2}{4d_2} = 0
$$

Define $\gamma_i = -e_i/(2d_i)$ for $i = 0, 1, 2$, and define $f = e_0^2/4d_0 + e_1^2/4d_1 + e_2^2/4d_2 - c$. The equation is $d_0(y_0 - \gamma_0)^2 + d_1(y_1 - \gamma_1)^2 + d_2(y_2 - \gamma_2)^2 = f$.

Suppose $f = 0$. If all eigenvalues are positive or all are negative, then the equation represents a *point* $(\gamma_0, \gamma_1, \gamma_2)$. If at least one eigenvalue is positive and one eigenvalue is negative, reorder terms and possibly multiply by -1 so that $d_0 > 0$, $d_1 > 0$, and $d_2 < 0$. The equation is $(y_2 - \gamma_2)^2 = (-d_0/d_2)(y_0 - \gamma_0)^2 + (-d_1/d_2)(y_1 - \gamma_1)^2$ and represents an *elliptic cone* (circular cone if $d_0 = d_1$).

Suppose $f > 0$; otherwise multiply the equation so that f is positive. If all eigenvalues are negative, then the equation has no solutions. If all the eigenvalues are positive, the equation represents an *ellipsoid*. The center is $(\gamma_0, \gamma_1, \gamma_2)$ and the semi-axis lengths are $\sqrt{f/d_i}$ for $i = 0, 1, 2$. If at least one eigenvalue is positive and one eigenvalue is negative, then the equation represents a *hyperboloid* (one or two sheets depending on number of positive eigenvalues). Figure 9.18 shows these quadrics, along with their standard (axis-aligned) equations.

9.4.2   TWO NONZERO EIGENVALUES

Without loss of generality, assume that $d_2 = 0$. The factored equation is

$$d_0\left(y_0 + \frac{e_0}{2d_0}\right)^2 + d_1\left(y_1 + \frac{e_1}{2d_1}\right)^2 + e_2 y_2 + c - \frac{e_0^2}{4d_0} - \frac{e_1^2}{4d_1} = 0$$

Define $\gamma_i = -e_i/(2d_i)$ for $i = 0, 1$, and define $f = e_0^2/4d_0 + e_1^2/4d_1 - c$. The equation is $d_0(y_0 - \gamma_0)^2 + d_1(y_1 - \gamma_1)^2 + e_2 y_2 = f$.

Suppose $e_2 = 0$ and $f = 0$. If d_0 and d_1 are both positive or both negative, then the equation represents a *line* containing $(\gamma_0, \gamma_1, 0)$ and having direction $(0, 0, 1)$. Otherwise the eigenvalues have opposite signs, and the equation represents the *union of two planes*, $y_1 - \gamma_1 = \pm\sqrt{-d_0/d_1}(y_0 - \gamma_0)$.

Suppose $e_2 = 0$ and $f > 0$ (if $f < 0$, multiply the equation by -1). If d_0 and d_1 are both negative, then the equation has no solution. If both are positive, then the equation represents an *elliptic cylinder* (a circular cylinder if $d_0 = d_1$). Otherwise d_0 and d_1 have opposite signs, and the equation represents a *hyperbolic cylinder*.

Suppose $e_2 \neq 0$. Define $\gamma_2 = f/e_q$. The equation is $d_0(y_0 - \gamma_0)^2 + d_1(y_1 - \gamma_1)^4 + e_2(y_2 - \gamma_2) = 0$. If d_0 and d_1 have the same sign, the equation represents an *elliptic paraboloid* (circular paraboloid if $d_0 = d_1$). Otherwise d_0 and d_1 have opposite signs, and the equation represents a *hyperbolic paraboloid*. Figure 9.19 shows these quadrics.

9.4.3   ONE NONZERO EIGENVALUE

The factored equation is

$$d_0\left(y_0 + \frac{e_0}{2d_0}\right)^2 + e_1 y_1 + e_2 y_2 + c - \frac{e_0^2}{4d_0} = 0$$

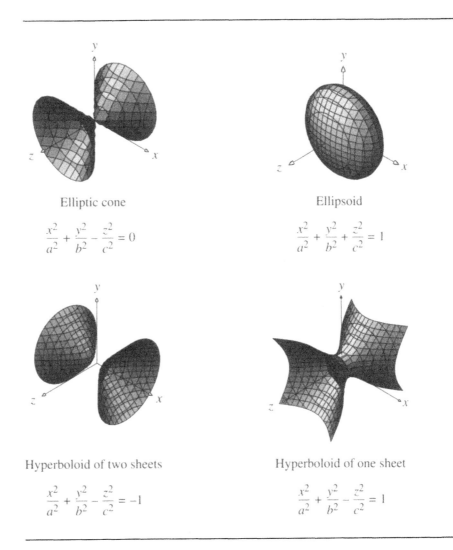

Figure 9.18   Quadrics having three nonzero eigenvalues.

If $e_1 = e_2 = 0$, then the equation is degenerate (either no solution, or y_0 is constant, in which case the solution is a *plane*). Otherwise, define $L = \sqrt{e_1^2 + e_2^2} \neq 0$ and divide the equation by L. Define $\alpha = d_0/L$, $\beta = (c - e_0^2/(4d_0))/L$, and make the rigid change of variables $z_0 = y_0 + e_0/(2d_0)$, $z_1 = -(e_1 y_1 + e_2 y_2)/L$, and $z_2 = (-e_2 y_1 + e_1 y_2)/L$. The equation in the new coordinate system is $z_1 = \alpha z_0^2 + \beta$, so the surface is a *parabolic cylinder*. Figure 9.20 shows these quadrics.

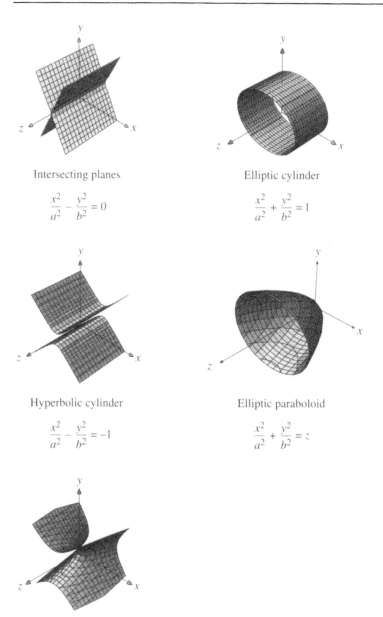

Intersecting planes

$$\frac{x^2}{a^2} - \frac{y^2}{b^2} = 0$$

Elliptic cylinder

$$\frac{x^2}{a^2} + \frac{y^2}{b^2} = 1$$

Hyperbolic cylinder

$$\frac{x^2}{a^2} - \frac{y^2}{b^2} = -1$$

Elliptic paraboloid

$$\frac{x^2}{a^2} + \frac{y^2}{b^2} = z$$

Hyperbolic paraboloid

$$\frac{y^2}{b^2} - \frac{x^2}{a^2} = z$$

Figure 9.19   Quadrics having two nonzero eigenvalues.

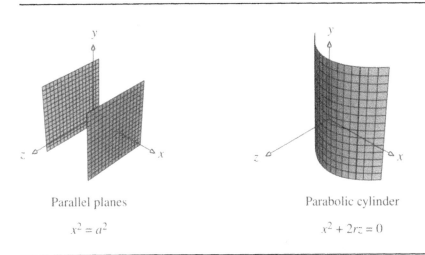

Parallel planes

$$x^2 = a^2$$

Parabolic cylinder

$$x^2 + 2rz = 0$$

Figure 9.20   Quadrics having one nonzero eigenvalue.

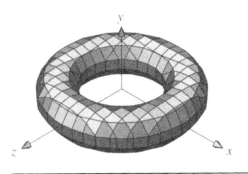

Figure 9.21   A standard "ring" torus.

9.5 TORUS

A torus in 3D is a quartic (degree 4) surface, having (in its most common range of proportions) the shape commonly known as a "doughnut," as shown in Figure 9.21.

A torus may be considered to be defined by rotating a circle about an axis lying in the plane of the circle, or by taking a rectangular sheet and pasting the opposite edges together (so that no twists form). Several alternative representations are possible: two different implicit definitions

$$x^4 + y^4 + z^4 + x^2 y^2 + 2x^2 z^2 + 2y^2 z^2 - 2(r_0^2 + r_1^2)x^2 + 2(r_0^2 - r_1^2)y^2$$

$$- 2(r_0^2 + r_1^2)z^2 + (r_0^2 - r_1^2)^2 = 0$$

and

$$(r_0 - \sqrt{x^2 + y^2})^2 + z^2 = r_1^2,$$

and a parametric definition

$$x = (r_0 + r_1 \cos v) \cos u$$

$$y = (r_0 + r_1 \cos v) \sin u$$

$$z = r_1 \sin v$$

where r_0 is the radius from the center of the torus to the center of the "tube" of the torus (the *major radius*) and r_1 is the radius of the "tube" itself (the *minor radius*). Generally, the major radius is greater than the minor radius ($r_0 > r_1$); this corresponds to a *ring torus*, one of the three standard tori; the other two are the *horn torus* ($r_0 = r_1$) and the *self-intersecting spindle torus* ($r_0 < r_1$) (Weisstein 1999).

The surface area S and volume V of a ring torus can be easily computed (Weisstein 1999). Recalling that the circumference and area of a circle with radius r are $2\pi r$ and πr^2, respectively, and that a torus can be considered to be the surface resulting from rotating a circle around an axis parallel to the plane in which it lies, it can be seen directly that

$$S = (2\pi r_1)(2\pi r_0)$$

$$= 4\pi^2 r_1 r_0$$

and

$$V = (2\pi r_1^2)(2\pi r_0)$$

$$= 2\pi^2 r_1^2 r_0$$

9.6 POLYNOMIAL CURVES

A *polynomial curve* in space is a vector-valued function $X : D \subset \mathbb{R} \to R \subset \mathbb{R}^3$, say, $X(t)$, and has domain D and range R. The components $X_i(t)$ of $X(t)$ are each a polynomial in the specified parameter

$$X_i(t) = \sum_{j=0}^{n_i} a_{ij} t^j$$

where n_i is the degree of the polynomial. In most applications the degrees of the components are the same, in which case the curve is written as $X(t) = \sum_{j=0}^{n} A_j t^j$ for known points $A_j \in \mathbb{R}^3$. The domain D is typically either $\mathbb{R}$ or $[0, 1]$. A *rational polynomial curve* is a vector-valued function $X(t)$ whose components $X_i(t)$ are ratios of polynomials

$$X_i(t) = \frac{\sum_{j=0}^{n_i} a_{ij} t^j}{\sum_{j=0}^{m_i} b_{ij} t^j}$$

where n_i and m_i are the degrees of the numerator and denominator polynomials.

A few common types of curves that occur in computer graphics are Bézier curves, B-spline curves, and nonuniform rational B-spline (NURBS) curves. Only the definitions for these curves are given here. Various properties of interest may be found in other texts (Bartels, Beatty, and Barsky 1987; Cohen, Riesenfeld, and Elber 2001; Farin 1990, 1995; Rogers 2001; Yamaguchi 1988).

9.6.1 BÉZIER CURVES

A spatial *Bézier curve* is constructed from a set of points $P_i \in \mathbb{R}^3$ for $0 \le i \le n$, called *control points*, by

$$X(t) = \sum_{i=0}^{n} \binom{n}{i} t^i (1-t)^{n-1} P_i = \sum_{i=0}^{n} B_i(t) P_i$$

where $t \in [0, 1]$. The real-valued polynomials $B_i(t)$ are called the Bernstein polynomials, each of degree n. The polynomial components of $X(t)$ are therefore also of degree n. Figure 9.22 shows a cubic Bézier curve, along with the control points and control polygon.

9.6.2 B-SPLINE CURVES

A spatial *B-spline curve of degree j* is constructed from a set of points $P_i \in \mathbb{R}^3$, called *control points*, and a monotone set of parameters t_i (i.e., $t_i \le t_{i+1}$), called *knots*, for $0 \le i \le n$, by

$$X(t) = \sum_{i=0}^{n} B_{i,j}(t) P_i$$

where $t \in [t_0, t_n]$ and $1 \le j \le n$. The vector $(t_0, \ldots, t_n)$ is called a *knot vector*. The real-valued polynomials $B_{i,j}(t)$ are of degree j and defined by the Cox–de Boor recursion formulas

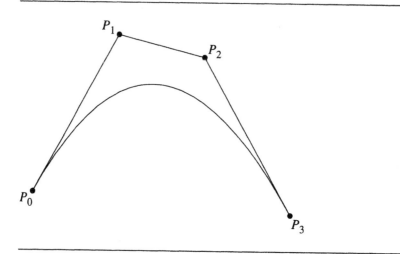

Figure 9.22   A cubic Bézier curve.

$$B_{i,0}(t) = \begin{cases} 1, & t_i \le t < t_{i+1} \\ 0, & \text{otherwise} \end{cases}$$

$$B_{i,j}(t) = \frac{(t - t_i)B_{i,j-1}(t)}{t_{i+j-1} - t_i} + \frac{(t_{i+j} - t)B_{i+1,j-1}(t)}{t_{i+j} - t_{i+1}}$$

for $1 \le j \le n$. The polynomial components of $X(t)$ are actually defined piecewise on the intervals $[t_i, t_{i+1}]$. On each interval the polynomial is of degree j. The knot values are not required to be evenly spaced. In this case the curve is said to be a *nonuniform B-spline curve*. If the knot values are equally spaced, then the curve is called a *uniform B-spline curve*. Figure 9.23 shows a uniform cubic B-spline curve, along with the control points and control polygon.

9.6.3   NURBS Curves

A spatial *nonuniform rational B-spline curve* or *NURBS curve* is obtained from a nonuniform B-spline polynomial curve in three dimensions. The control points are $(P_i, 1) \in \mathbb{R}^4$ for $0 \le i \le n$, with weights $w_i > 0$, and the polynomial curve is

$$(Y(t), w(t)) = \sum_{i=0}^{n} B_{i,j}(t)w_i(P_i, 1)$$

where $B_{i,j}(t)$ is the same polynomial defined in the previous subsection. The NURBS curve is obtained by treating $(Y(t), w(t))$ as a homogeneous vector and dividing

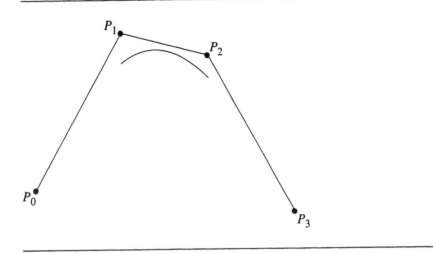

Figure 9.23   A cubic B-spline curve.

through by the last component to obtain a projection in three dimensions

$$X(t) = \frac{Y(t)}{w(t)} = \sum_{i=0}^{n} R_{i,j}(t) P_i$$

where

$$R_{i,j}(t) = \frac{w_i B_{i,j}(t)}{\sum_{i=0}^{n} w_i B_{i,j}(t)}$$

9.7 POLYNOMIAL SURFACES

A *polynomial surface* is a vector-valued function $X : D \subset \mathbb{R}^2 \to \mathbb{R}^3$, say, $X(s,t)$, whose domain is D and range is R. The components $X_i(s,t)$ of $X(s,t)$ are each a polynomial in the specified parameters

$$X_i(s,t) = \sum_{j=0}^{n_i} \sum_{k=0}^{m_i} a_{ijk} s^j t^k$$

where $n_i + m_i$ is the degree of the polynomial. The domain D is typically either $\mathbb{R}^2$ or $[0, 1]^2$. A *rational polynomial surface* is a vector-valued function $X(s,t)$ whose components $X_i(s,t)$ are ratios of polynomials

$$X_i(s, t) = \frac{\sum_{j=0}^{n_i} \sum_{k=0}^{m_i} a_{ijk} s^j t^k}{\sum_{j=0}^{p_i} \sum_{k=0}^{q_i} b_{ijk} s^j t^k}$$

where $n_i + m_i$ is the degree of the numerator polynomial and $p_i + q_i$ is the degree of the denominator polynomial.

A few common types of surfaces that occur in computer graphics are Bézier surfaces, B-spline surfaces, and nonuniform rational B-spline (NURBS) surfaces. Only the definitions for these surfaces are given here. Various properties of interest may be found in other texts (Bartels, Beatty, and Barsky 1987; Cohen, Riesenfeld, and Elber 2001; Farin 1990, 1995; Rogers 2001; Yamaguchi 1988).

9.7.1 BÉZIER SURFACES

The two types of surfaces defined here are Bézier rectangle patches and Bézier triangle patches.

Bézier Rectangle Patches

Given a rectangular lattice of three-dimensional control points P_{i_0,i_1} for $0 \leq i_0 \leq n_0$ and $0 \leq i_1 \leq n_1$, the Bézier rectangle patch for the points is

$$X(s, t) = \sum_{i_0=0}^{n_0} \sum_{i_1=0}^{n_1} B_{n_0,i_0}(s) B_{n_1,i_1}(t)\, P_{i_0,i_1}, \quad (s, t) \in [0, 1]^2$$

where

$$\binom{n}{i} = \frac{n!}{i!(n-i)!}$$

is the number of combinations of i items chosen from a set of n items. The coefficients are products of the Bernstein polynomials

$$B_{n,i}(z) = \binom{n}{i} z^i (1-z)^{n-i}$$

The patch is called a rectangle patch because the domain $[0, 1]^2$ is a rectangle in the st-plane. Figure 9.24 shows a bicubic Bézier surface, along with the control points and control polygon.

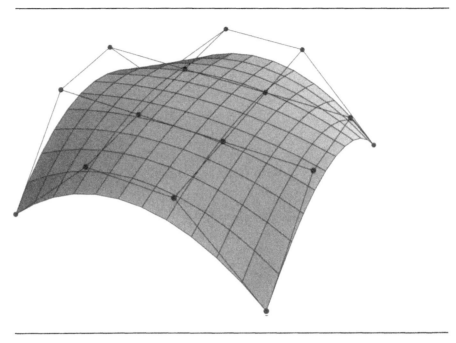

Figure 9.24   A bicubic Bézier surface.

Bézier Triangle Patches

Given a triangle lattice of three-dimensional control points P_{i_0,i_1,i_2} for $i_0 \geq 0$, $i_1 \geq 0$, $i_2 \geq 0$, and $i_0 + i_1 + i_2 = n$, the Bézier triangle patch for the points is

$$X(u, v, w) = \sum_{|I|=n} B_{n,I}(u, v, w)\, P_I$$

where $I = (i_0, i_1, i_2)$, $|I| = i_0 + i_1 + i_2$, $u \geq 0$, $v \geq 0$, $w \geq 0$, and $u + v + w = 1$. The summation involves $(n + 1)(n + 2)/2$ terms. The Bernstein polynomial coefficients are

$$B_{n,I}(u, v, w) = \binom{n}{i_0, i_1, i_2} u^{i_0} v^{i_1} w^{i_2} = \frac{n!}{i_0! i_1! i_2!} u^{i_0} v^{i_1} w^{i_2}$$

Although the patch has three variables u, v, and w, the fact that $w = 1 - u - v$ really shows that X depends only on u and v. The patch is called a triangle patch because the domain $u \geq 0$, $v \geq 0$, $w \geq 0$, and $u + v + w = 1$ is an equilateral triangle

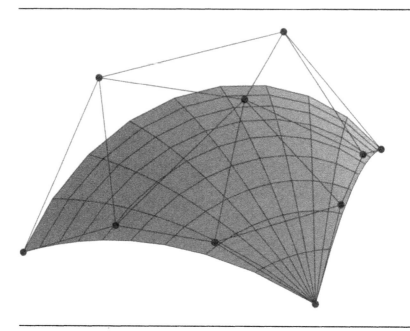

Figure 9.25   A cubic triangular Bézier surface.

in uvw-space with vertices at $(1, 0, 0)$, $(0, 1, 0)$, and $(0, 0, 1)$. Figure 9.25 shows a cubic triangular Bézier surface, along with the control points and control polygon.

9.7.2 B-SPLINE SURFACES

We only consider one type of B-spline surface, a B-spline rectangle patch. The concept of B-spline triangle patches does exist (Dahmen, Micchelli, and Seidel 1992), but is not considered in this book.

Let $\{s_i\}_{i=0}^{n_0}$ be a monotone set, that is, $s_i \leq s_{i+1}$ for all i. The elements are called *knots*, and the vector $(s_0, \ldots, s_{n_0})$ is called a *knot vector*. Similarly, let $\{t_i\}_{i=0}^{n_1}$ be a monotone set using the same terminology. Given a rectangular lattice of three-dimensional *control points* P_{i_0,i_1} for $0 \leq i_0 \leq n_0$ and $0 \leq i_1 \leq n_1$, a B-spline rectangle patch is

$$X(s, t) = \sum_{i_0=0}^{n_0} \sum_{i_1=0}^{n_1} B_{i_0,j_0}^{(0)}(s) B_{i_1,j_1}^{(1)}(t) \, P_{i_0,i_1}$$

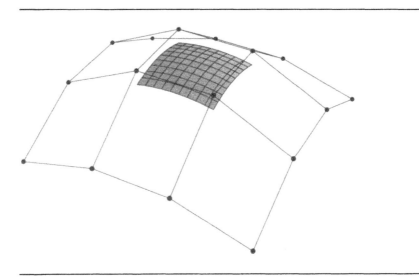

Figure 9.26 A uniform bicubic B-spline surface.

where $s \in [s_0, s_{n_0}]$, $t \in [t_0, t_{n_1}]$, $1 \le j_0 \le n_0$, $1 \le j_1 \le n_1$, and the polynomials in the expression satisfy the Cox–de Boor formulas

$$B_{i,0}^{(0)}(s) = \begin{cases} 1, & s_i \le s < s_{i+1} \\ 0, & \text{otherwise} \end{cases}$$

$$B_{i,j}^{(0)}(s) = \frac{(s - s_i) B_{i,j-1}^{(0)}(s)}{s_{i+j-1} - s_i} + \frac{(s_{i+j} - s) B_{i+1,j-1}^{(0)}(s)}{s_{i+j} - s_{i+1}}$$

and

$$B_{i,0}^{(1)}(t) = \begin{cases} 1, & t_i \le t < t_{i+1} \\ 0, & \text{otherwise} \end{cases}$$

$$B_{i,j}^{(1)}(t) = \frac{(t - t_i) B_{i,j-1}^{(1)}(t)}{t_{i+j-1} - t_i} + \frac{(t_{i+j} - t) B_{i+1,j-1}^{(1)}(t)}{t_{i+j} - t_{i+1}}$$

The polynomial components of $X(s, t)$ are actually defined piecewise on the sets $[s_i, s_{i+1}] \times [t_j, t_{j+1}]$. On each such set the polynomial is of degree $i + j$. The knot values are not required to be evenly spaced. In this case the surface is said to be a *nonuniform B-spline surface*. If the knot values are equally spaced, then the surface is called a *uniform B-spline surface*. Figure 9.26 shows a uniform bicubic B-spline surface, along with the control points and control polygon.

9.7.3 NURBS SURFACES

A *nonuniform rational B-spline surface* or *NURBS surface* is obtained from a nonuniform B-spline polynomial surface in four dimensions. The control points are $(P_{i_0,i_1}, 1) \in \mathbb{R}^4$ for $0 \le i_0 \le n_0$ and $0 \le i_1 \le n_1$, with weights $w_{i_0,i_1} > 0$, and the polynomial surface is

$$(Y(s,t), w(s,t)) = \sum_{i_0=0}^{n_0} \sum_{i_1=0}^{n_1} B_{i_0,j_0}^{(0)}(s) B_{i_1,j_1}^{(1)}(t)\, w_{i_0,i_1}(P_{i_0,i_1}, 1)$$

where $B_{i,j}^{(0)}(s)$ and $B_{i,j}^{(1)}(s)$ are the polynomials defined in the previous subsection. The NURBS surface is obtained by treating $(Y(s,t), w(s,t))$ as a homogeneous vector and dividing through by the last component to obtain a projection in three dimensions

$$X(s,t) = \frac{Y(s,t)}{w(s,t)} = \sum_{i_0=0}^{n_0} \sum_{i_1=0}^{n_1} R_{i_0,i_1,j_0,j_1}(s,t)\, P_{i_0,i_1}$$

where

$$R_{i_0,i_1,j_0,j_1}(s,t) = \frac{w_{i_0,i_1} B_{i_0,j_0}^{(0)}(s) B_{i_1,j_1}^{(1)}(t)}{\sum_{k_0=0}^{n_0} \sum_{k_1=0}^{n_1} w_{k_0,k_1} B_{k_0,j_0}^{(0)}(s) B_{k_1,j_1}^{(1)}(t)}$$

C H A P T E R

Distance in 3D 10

10.1 Introduction

Suppose we have two geometric objects $\mathcal{A}$ and $\mathcal{B}$, and we wish to compute the distance between them. If we consider each object to be represented by parametric functions $A(\vec{s})$ and $B(\vec{t})$ with $\vec{s} \in S \subset \mathbb{R}^m$ and $\vec{t} \in \mathcal{T} \subset \mathbb{R}^n$, then there is a general method for computing the distance. This method consists of finding a point on $\mathcal{A}$ and a point on $\mathcal{B}$ whose squared distance is the minimum of all squared distances between all possible pairs of points on the objects. Expressed as a function, we have $Q(\vec{s}, \vec{t}) = \|A(\vec{s}) - B(\vec{t})\|^2$, for $(\vec{s}, \vec{t}) \in S \times \mathcal{T} \subset \mathbb{R}^m \times \mathbb{R}^n$. The solution is the minimum of this function—either it occurs at an interior point of $S \times \mathcal{T}$, in which case $\nabla(Q) = \vec{0}$, or it occurs at a boundary point of $S \times \mathcal{T}$, in which case the solution consists of minimizing a quadratic function. Besides this general solution, we also provide solutions for certain specific cases, often exploiting geometric properties of the primitives involved in the problem.

10.2 Point to Linear Component

Suppose we have a point Q and a line $\mathcal{L}(t) = P + t\vec{d}$, and we wish to find the minimum distance between Q and $\mathcal{L}$, as shown in Figure 10.1. If we look at the point on $\mathcal{L}$ closest to Q and consider the line segment joining those two points, we see that the line segment is perpendicular to $\mathcal{L}$. This observation suggests the use of a dot product, and that indeed is the case—the closest point Q' is the projection of Q on $\mathcal{L}$ (see Figure 10.2). The parametric value of Q' is

$$t_0 = \frac{\vec{d} \cdot (Q - P)}{\vec{d} \cdot \vec{d}} \tag{10.1}$$

365

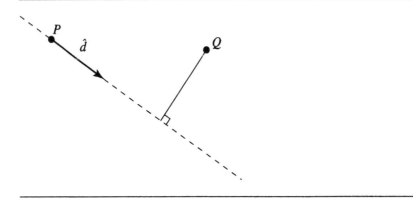

Figure 10.1   Distance between a line and a point.

and of course

$$Q' = P + t_0 \vec{d}$$

The distance from Q to $\mathcal{L}$ is then

$$d = \|Q - Q'\|$$
$$= \|Q - (P + t_0\vec{d})\|$$

Note that if the direction $\vec{d}$ of $\mathcal{L}$ is normalized, we have $\|\hat{d}\| = 1$, so Equation 10.1 becomes

$$t_0 = \hat{d} \cdot (Q - P)$$

and the necessity of a division is eliminated.

The pseudocode is

```
float PointLineDistanceSquared3D(Point q, Line l, bool normalized, float& t)
{
    float distanceSquared;

    t = Dot(l.direction, VectorSubtract(q, l.origin));
    if (!normalized) {
        t /= Dot(l.direction, l.direction);
    }
    Point3D qPrime;

    qPrime = l.origin + t * l.direction;
```

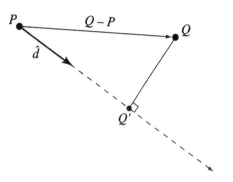

Figure 10.2   The projection of Q on $\mathcal{L}$.

```
Vector3D vec = Q - qPrime;
distanceSquared = Dot(vec, vec);

return distanceSquared;
}
```

10.2.1 POINT TO RAY OR LINE SEGMENT

If $\mathcal{L}$ is a line, then the solution is as described above. If $\mathcal{L}$ is a ray, we restrict the solution to only nonnegative values of t_0; if $t_0 < 0$, then the distance from Q to $\mathcal{L}$ is $\|Q - P\|$:

$$d = \begin{cases} \|Q - P\| & t_0 \leq 0 \\ \|Q - (Q + t_0\vec{d})\| & t_0 > 0 \end{cases}$$

If $\mathcal{L}$ is a line segment defined by its two end points P_0 and P_1, then the direction vector is defined by

$$\vec{d} = P_1 - P_0$$

Note that this makes $P_0 = \mathcal{L}(0)$ and $P_1 = \mathcal{L}(1)$, and so we have

$$d = \begin{cases} \|Q - P_0\| & t_0 \leq 0 \\ \|Q - (P_0 + t_0\vec{d})\| & 0 < t_0 < 1 \\ \|Q - (P_0 + \vec{d})\| & t_0 \geq 1 \end{cases}$$

(see Figure 10.3).

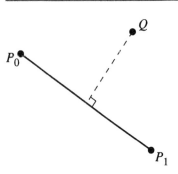

Figure 10.3   Distance between a line segment and a point.

The pseudocode for the case of the ray is

```
float PointRayDistanceSquared3D(Point q, ray r, bool normalized, float& t)
{
    float distanceSquared;

    // Get distance to line - may have t < 0
    distanceSquared = PointLineDistanceSquared3D(q, r, normalized, &t);

    if (t < 0) {
        t = 0;
        // Get distance to ray origin instead
        Vector3D vec = q - r.origin;
        distanceSquared = Dot(vec, vec);
    }

    return distanceSquared;
}
```

The pseudocode for the line segment case is

```
float PointLineSegDistanceSquared3D(Point3D q, Segment3D s, bool normalized,
                                    float& t)
{
    float distanceSquared;

    // Get distance to line - may have t < 0 or t > 1
    distanceSquared = PointLineDistanceSquared3D(q, s, normalized, &t);
```

```
    if (t < 0) {
        t = 0;
        // Get distance to segment origin instead
        Vector3D vec = q - s.p0;
        distanceSquared = Dot(vec, vec);
    } else if (t > 1) {
        t = 1;
        // Get distance to segment terminus instead
        Vector3D vec = q - s.p1;
        distanceSquared = Dot(vec, vec);
    }

    return distanceSquared;
}
```

10.2.2 POINT TO POLYLINE

For calculating the distance between a point P and a polyline $\mathcal{L}$ with vertices V_0 through V_n and line segments S_i, $0 \leq i < n - 1$, whose end points are V_i and V_{i+1}, the straightforward algorithm is to calculate the minimum of the distances between the point and the line segments of the polyline

$$\text{Distance}^2 (P, \mathcal{L}) = \min_{0 \leq i < n-1} \text{Distance}^2 (P, S_i) \qquad (10.2)$$

Iterating blindly over the line segments can potentially be expensive for polylines with a large number of segments or for an application with a large number of polylines for which the distance calculations must be made frequently.

We could instead use a 3D extension of the suggested technique for computing the distance between a 2D point and a polyline, as described in Section 6.2. The approach is to iterate over the polyline's segments and do a relatively cheap rejection on segments that we know cannot possibly be closer than the current closest segment's distance. If the current closest segment S_c is at a distance d to the point P, we can consider a sphere with center $P = (a, b, c)$ and radius d. Any segment that does not intersect the sphere cannot be closer than d; however, as pointed out in Section 6.2, computing this distance would entail just the sort of calculation that we wish to avoid. In the 2D case, the alternative is to instead consider infinite strips bounding the circle (see Figure 6.4) and reject polyline segments having both vertices contained within one of the strips. The 3D analog to this is to consider instead the slabs that bound the sphere, as shown in Figure 10.4.

Let $S_i = \langle (x_i, y_i, z_i), (x_{i+1}, y_{i+1}, z_{i+1}) \rangle$ be the next segment to be tested. If S_i is outside the infinite slab $|x - a| \leq d$, then it cannot intersect the circle. The rejection test is therefore

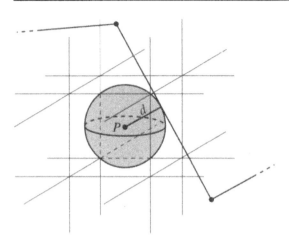

Figure 10.4   Utilizing half-spaces to speed up point/polyline distance tests.

$$|x_i - a| \geq d \quad \text{and} \quad |x_{i+1} - a| \geq d \quad \text{and} \quad (x_i - a)(x_{i+1} - a) > 0$$

The first two conditions guarantee each segment end point is outside the slab. The last condition guarantees that the end points are on the same side of the slab. Similarly, if S_i is outside the infinite slab $|y - b| \leq d$, then it cannot intersect the circle. The rejection test is

$$|y_i - b| \geq d \quad \text{and} \quad |y_{i+1} - b| \geq d \quad \text{and} \quad (y_i - b)(y_{i+1} - b) > 0$$

Finally, if S_i is outside the infinite slab $|z - c| \leq d$, then it cannot intersect the circle. The rejection test is

$$|z_i - c| \geq d \quad \text{and} \quad |z_{i+1} - c| \geq d \quad \text{and} \quad (z_i - c)(z_{i+1} - c) > 0$$

Figure 10.5 illustrates this. The segment S_0 generated the current minimum distance d between the polyline and the point P. The segment S_1, although outside the circle, is not rejected because it partly lies in each infinite slab. However, S_2 is rejected because it is outside the vertical slab (for purposes of clarity in the illustration, the z-planes are not shown).

Since square roots should be avoided in the intermediate calculations, an implementation maintains the squared distance d^2 instead of d. The rejection test must be restructured accordingly to use d^2:

$$|x_i - a|^2 \geq d^2 \quad \text{and} \quad |x_{i+1} - a|^2 \geq d^2 \quad \text{and} \quad (x_i - a)(x_{i+1} - a) > 0$$

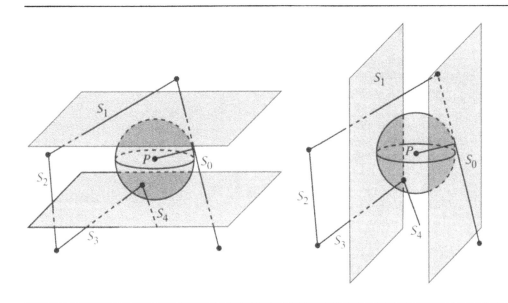

Figure 10.5   Rejection example for point/polyline distance.

or

$$|y_i - b|^2 \ge d^2 \quad \text{and} \quad |y_{i+1} - b|^2 \ge d^2 \quad \text{and} \quad (y_i - b)(y_{i+1} - b) > 0$$

or

$$|z_i - c|^2 \ge d^2 \quad \text{and} \quad |z_{i+1} - c|^2 \ge d^2 \quad \text{and} \quad (z_i - c)(z_{i+1} - c) > 0$$

The quantities in the rejection test are also used in the squared-distance calculation, so these can be temporarily saved in case they are needed later to avoid redundant calculations. Also, the quantities $x_{i+1} - a$, $y_{i+1} - b$, and $z_{i+1} - c$ in the current rejection test become the $x_i - a$, $y_i - b$, and $z_i - c$ values in the next rejection test, so these should be saved in temporary variables and used later when needed, again to avoid redundant calculations.

The pseudocode is

```
float PointPolylineDistanceSquared3D(Point p, Point vertices[],
                                     int nSegments)
{
    float dSq = INFINITY;
    float xMinusA, yMinusB, zMinusC;
    float xNextMinusA, yNextMinusB, zNextMinusC;
```

```
float xMinusASq, yMinusBSq, zMinusCSq;
float xNextMinusASq, yNextMinusBSq, zNextMinusCSq;

xMinusA = vertices[0].x - p.x;
yMinusB = vertices[0].y - p.y;
zMinusC = vertices[0].z - p.z;

xMinusASq = xMinusA * xMinusA;
yMinusBSq = yMinusB * yMinusB;
zMinusCSq = zMinusC * zMinusC;

xNextMinusA = vertices[1].x - p.x;
yNextMinusB = vertices[1].y - p.y;
zNextMinusC = vertices[1].z - p.z;

xNextMinusASq = xNextMinusA * xMNextinusA;
yNextMinusBSq = yNextMinusB * yNextMinusB;
zNextMinusCSq = zNextMinusC * zNextMinusC;

// Compute distance to first segment
Line l = { vertices[i], vertices[i+1] - vertices[i] };
float t;
dSq = PointLineDistanceSquared3D(p, l, FALSE, t)

// If closest point not on segment, check appropriate end point
if (t < 0) {
    dSq = MIN(dsq, xMinusASq + yMinusBSq + zMinusCSq);
} else if (t > 1) {
    dSq = MIN(dsq, xNextMinusASq + yNextMinusBSq + zNextMinusCSq);
}

// Go through each successive segment, rejecting if possible,
// and computing the distance squared if not rejected.
for (i = 1; i < nSegments - 1; i++) {
    // Rejection test
    if (((Abs(xMinusASq) > dSq) && (Abs(xNextMinusASq) <= dSq)
                            && (xMinusA * xNextMinusA > 0)) ||
        ((Abs(yMinusBSq) > dSq) && (Abs(yNextMinusBSq) <= dSq)
                            && (yMinusB * yNextMinusB > 0)) ||
        ((Abs(zMinusCSq) > dSq) && (Abs(zNextMinusCSq) <= dSq)
                            && (zMinusC * zNextMinusC > 0))) {

            if (i != nSegments - 2) {
```

```
                    xMinusA = xNextMinusA;
                    yMinusB = yNextMinusB;
                    zMinusC = zNextMinusC;

                    xNextMinusA = vertices[i + 2].x - p.x;
                    yNextMinusB = vertices[i + 2].y - p.y;
                    zNextMinusC = vertices[i + 2].z - p.z;
                }

            continue;
        }
        // Rejection test failed - check distance to line
        Line  l = { vertices[i], vertices[i+1] - vertices[i] };
        float t;
        dSq = PointLineDistanceSquared3D(p, l, FALSE, t)

        // If closest point not on segment, check appropriate end point
        if (t < 0) {
            dSq = MIN(dsq, xMinusASq + yMinusBSq + zMinusCSq);
        } else if (t > 1) {
            dSq = MIN(dsq, xNextMinusASq + yNextMinusBSq + zNextMinusCSq);
        }

        if (i != nSegments - 2) {
            xMinusA = xNextMinusA;
            yMinusB = yNextMinusB;
            zMinusC = zNextMinusC;

            xNextMinusA = vertices[i + 2].x - p.x;
            yNextMinusB = vertices[i + 2].y - p.y;
            zNextMinusC = vertices[i + 2].z - p.z;
        }
    }

    return dSq;
}
```

A modification of the rejection test involves testing for intersection between a segment and the axis-aligned box that contains the circle of radius d centered at P. We can use the method of separating axes discussed in Section 11.11. The improvement is illustrated by Figure 10.5. The segment S_1 was not rejected by the previous method because it lies partly in both infinite strips. However, S_1 is rejected by the current method because it does not intersect the axis-aligned rectangle.

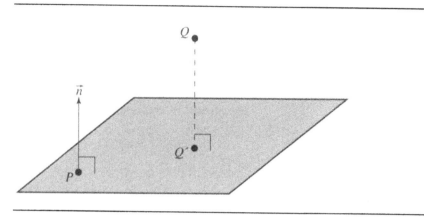

Figure 10.6   Distance between a point and a plane.

10.3   POINT TO PLANAR COMPONENT

In this section, we discuss the problem of computing the distance between a point and planar components—planes, triangles, rectangles, polygons, circles, and disks.

10.3.1   POINT TO PLANE

In this section, we consider the distance from a point Q to a plane $\mathcal{P} : \{P, \vec{n}\}$, where $\vec{n}$ is a normal vector of the plane and P is a point on $\mathcal{P}$ (Section 9.2.1); see Figure 10.6. The point on the plane $\mathcal{P}$ closest to Q is denoted Q'. Note that the vector between Q and Q' is perpendicular to $\mathcal{P}$ (that is, parallel to $\vec{n}$), and we can exploit this fact in determining the distance from Q to $\mathcal{P}$.

Figure 10.7 shows an edge-on view of plane $\mathcal{P}$. From trigonometry, we can observe that

$$\cos\theta = \frac{\|Q - Q'\|}{\|Q - P\|}$$

So we have

$$
\begin{aligned}
d &= \|Q - Q'\| \\
  &= \|Q - P\| \cos\theta
\end{aligned}
\tag{10.3}
$$

By definition, $\vec{u} \cdot \vec{v} = \|\vec{u}\|\|\vec{v}\| \cos\theta$, so we can rewrite Equation 10.3 as

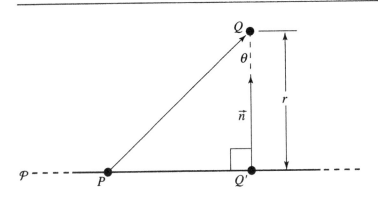

Figure 10.7   Edge-on view of plane $\mathcal{P}$.

$$d = \|Q - P\| \cos \theta$$

$$= \|Q - P\| \frac{-k\vec{n} \cdot -(Q - P)}{\|k\vec{n}\| \|Q - P\|}$$

$$= \frac{|\vec{n} \cdot (Q - P)|}{\|\vec{n}\|}$$

If the plane's normal is unit length, then the denominator is 1, and no division is required.

In some situations, the side of a plane that a point is on may be important. In this case, the signed distance (the sign being relative to the plane normal) may be required. A simple algorithm (Georgiades 1992) exists for finding this signed distance if the plane equation is normalized. If we have a plane $\mathcal{P}$ in the "vector version" of the implicit form

$$P \cdot \hat{n} + d = 0$$

and a point Q, then the line connecting the projection Q' of Q onto $\mathcal{P}$ is parallel to $\hat{n}$. If the plane normal is normalized, then $\|Q - Q'\|$ is a scalar multiple of $\hat{n}$; that is, that scalar multiple is the distance.

Following Georgiades (1992), the derivation is as follows: Let $r = \|Q - Q'\|$; then

$$Q = r\hat{n} + Q'$$

If we multiply both sides by $\hat{n}$, we have

$$\hat{n} \cdot Q = r\hat{n} \cdot \hat{n} + \hat{n} \cdot Q' \tag{10.4}$$

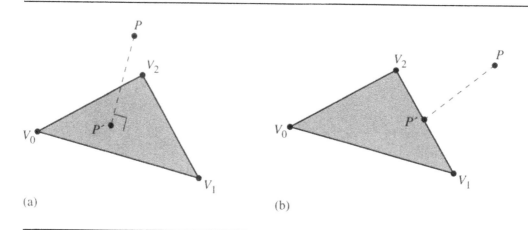

(a)   (b)

Figure 10.8   Distance between a point and a triangle. The closest point may be on the interior of the triangle (a), on an edge (b), or be one of the vertices.

However, $\|\hat{n}\| = 1$ because of the assumption of normalization. Further, $\hat{n} \cdot Q' = -d$ because Q' is on the plane by definition. If we substitute these back into Equation 10.4, we get

$$r = \hat{n} \cdot Q + d$$

Thus, the distance from Q to plane $\mathcal{P}$ is r, and the sign of r is positive if Q is on the side of $\mathcal{P}$ toward which the normal points and negative if it is on the other side.

10.3.2   POINT TO TRIANGLE

In this section, we discuss the problem of finding the distance between a point P and a triangle, as shown in Figure 10.8. For the purposes of this section, we define a triangle $\mathcal{T}$ with vertices $\{V_0, V_1, V_2\}$ parametrically

$$\mathcal{T}(s, t) = B + s\vec{e}_0 + t\vec{e}_1$$

for $(s, t) \in D = \{(s, t) : s \in [0, 1], t \in [0, 1], s + t \le 1\}$, $B = V_0$, $\vec{e}_0 = V_1 - V_0$, and $\vec{e}_1 = V_2 - V_0$. The minimum distance is computed by locating the values $(\bar{s}, \bar{t}) \in D$ corresponding to the point P', the closest point on the triangle to P.

The distance from any point on the triangle to P is

$$\|\mathcal{T}(s, t) - P\|$$

but we use instead the squared-distance function

$$Q(s,t) = \|\mathcal{T}(s,t) - P\|^2$$

for $(s,t) \in D$. If we expand the terms and multiply them out, we can see that this function is quadratic in s and t:

$$Q(s,t) = as^2 + 2bst + ct^2 + 2ds + 2et + f$$

where

$$a = \vec{e}_0 \cdot \vec{e}_0$$

$$b = \vec{e}_0 \cdot \vec{e}_1$$

$$c = \vec{e}_1 \cdot \vec{e}_1$$

$$d = \vec{e}_0 \cdot (B - P)$$

$$e = -\vec{e}_1 \cdot (B - P)$$

$$f = (B - P) \cdot (B - P)$$

Quadratics are classified by the sign of $ac - b^2$. For Q

$$ac - b^2 = (\vec{e}_0 \cdot \vec{e}_0)(\vec{e}_1 \cdot \vec{e}_1) - (\vec{e}_0 \cdot \vec{e}_1)^2$$

$$= \|\vec{e}_0 \times \vec{e}_1\|^2$$

$$> 0$$

This value is positive because we assume that the two edges $\vec{e}_0$ and $\vec{d}_1$ of the triangle are linearly independent (that is, not parallel and neither having zero length). Thus, their cross product is a nonzero vector.

In calculus terms, the goal is to minimize $Q(s,t)$ over the domain D. Since Q is a continuously differentiable function, the minimum occurs either at an interior point of D where the gradient $\nabla Q = 2(as + bt + d, bs + ct + e) = (0,0)$ (that is, inside the triangle) or at a point on the boundary of D.

The gradient of Q is zero only when

$$\bar{s} = \frac{be - cd}{ac - b^2}$$

and

$$\bar{t} = \frac{bd - ad}{ac - b^2}$$

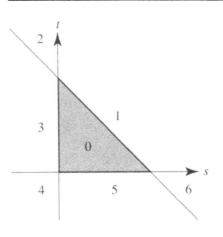

Figure 10.9   Partition of the *st*-plane by triangle domain *D*.

If $(\bar{s}, \bar{t}) \in D$, then we have found the minimum of Q. Otherwise, the minimum must occur on the boundary of the triangle. To find the correct boundary, consider Figure 10.9. The central triangle labeled 0 is the domain of Q, $(s, t) \in D$. If $(\bar{s}, \bar{t})$ is in region 0, then P', the point on the triangle closest to P, is on the interior of the triangle.

Suppose $(\bar{s}, \bar{t})$ is in region 1. The level curves of Q are those in the *st*-plane for which Q is a constant. Since the graph of Q is a paraboloid, the level curves are ellipses (see Section A.9.1). At the point where $\nabla Q = (0, 0)$, the level curve degenerates to a single point $(\bar{s}, \bar{t})$. The global minimum of Q occurs there; call it $V_{\min}$. As the level values V increase from $V_{\min}$, the corresponding ellipses are increasingly further away from $(\bar{s}, \bar{t})$. There is a smallest level value V_0 for which the corresponding ellipse (implicitly defined by $Q = V_0$) just touches the triangle domain edge $s + t = 1$ at a value $s = s_0 \in [0, 1]$, $t_0 = 1 - s_0$. For level values $V < V_0$, the corresponding ellipses do not intersect D. For level values $V > V_0$, portions of D lie inside the corresponding ellipses. In particular, any points of intersection of such an ellipse with the edge must have a level value $V > V_0$. Therefore, $Q(s, 1 - s) > Q(s_0, t_0)$ for $s \in [0, 1]$ and $s \neq s_0$. The point (s_0, t_0) provides the minimum squared distance between P and the triangle. The triangle point is an edge point. Figure 10.10 illustrates the idea by showing various level curves.

An alternative way of visualizing where the minimum distance point occurs on the boundary is to intersect the graph of Q, which lives in (s, t, Q) space, with the plane $s + t = 1$. The curve of intersection is a parabola and is the graph of $F(s) = Q(s, 1 - s)$ for $s \in [0, 1]$. Now the problem has been reduced by one dimension to minimizing a function $F(s)$ for $s \in [0, 1]$. The minimum of F occurs either at an

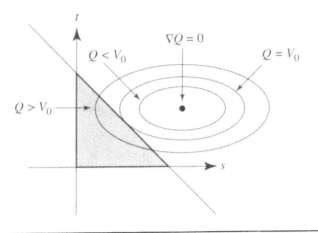

Figure 10.10   Various level curves $Q(s, t) = V$.

interior point of $[0, 1]$, in which case $F'(s) = 0$ at that point, or at an end point $s = 0$
or $s = 1$. Figure 10.10 shows the case when the minimum occurs at an interior point.
At that point the ellipse is tangent to the line $s + t = 1$. In the end point cases, the
ellipse may just touch one of the vertices of D, but not necessarily tangentially.

To distinguish between the interior point and end point cases, the same partitioning idea applies in the one-dimensional case. The interval $[0, 1]$ partitions the real line
into three intervals: $s < 0$, $s \in [0, 1]$, and $s > 1$. Let $F'(\hat{s}) = 0$. If $\hat{s} < 0$, then $F(s)$ is
an increasing function for $s \in [0, 1]$. The minimum restricted to $[0, 1]$ must occur at
$s = 0$, in which case Q attains its minimum at $(s, t) = (0, 1)$. If $\hat{(s)} > 1$, then $F(s)$
is a decreasing function for $s \in [0, 1]$. The minimum for F occurs at $s = 1$, and the
minimum for Q occurs at $(s, t) = (1, 0)$. Otherwise, $\hat{s} \in [0, 1]$, F attains its minimum
at $\hat{s}$, and Q attains its minimum at $(s, t) = (\hat{s}, 1 - \hat{s})$.

The occurrence of $(\bar{s}, \bar{t})$ in region 3 or region 5 is handled in the same way as when
the global minimum is in region 0. If $(\bar{s}, \bar{t})$ is in region 3, then the minimum occurs
at $(s_0, 0)$ for some $s_0 \in [0, 1]$. Determining if the first contact point is at an interior or
end point of the appropriate interval is handled the same as discussed earlier.

If $(\bar{s}, \bar{t})$ is in region 2, it is possible the level curve of Q that provides first contact
with the unit square touches either $s + t = 1$ or edge $s = 0$. Because the global minimum occurs in region 2, and because the level sets of Q are ellipses, at least one of
the directional derivatives $(0, -1) \cdot \nabla Q(0, 1)$ and $(1, -1) \cdot \nabla Q(0, 1)$ must be positive.
The two vectors $(0, -1)$ and $(1, -1)$ are directions for the edges $s = 0$ and $s + t = 1$,
respectively. The choice of edges $s + t = 1$ or $s = 0$ can be made based on the signs of
$(0, -1) \cdot \nabla Q(0, 1)$ and $(1, -1) \cdot \nabla Q(0, 1)$.

The same type of argument applies in region 6. In region 4, the two quantities whose signs determine which edge contains the minimum are $(1, 0) \cdot \nabla Q(0, 0)$ and $(0, 1) \cdot \nabla Q(0, 0)$.

The implementation of the algorithm is designed so that at most one floating-point division is used when computing the minimum distance and corresponding closest points. Moreover, the division is deferred until it is needed. In some cases, no division is required.

Quantities that are used throughout the code are computed first. In particular, the values computed are

$$\vec{d} = B - P$$

$$a = \vec{e}_0 \cdot \vec{e}_0$$

$$b = \vec{e}_0 \cdot \vec{e}_1$$

$$c = \vec{e}_1 \cdot \vec{e}_1$$

$$d = \vec{e}_0 \cdot \vec{d}$$

$$e = \vec{e}_1 \cdot \vec{d}$$

$$f = \vec{d} \cdot \vec{d}$$

The code actually computes $\sigma = |ac - b^2|$ since it is possible for small edge lengths that some floating-point round-off errors lead to a small negative quantity.

In the theoretical development, we compute $\bar{s} = (be - cd)/\sigma$ and $\bar{t} = (bd - ae)/\sigma$ so that $\nabla Q(\bar{s}, \bar{t}) = (0, 0)$. The location of the global minimum is then tested to see if it is in the triangle domain D. If so, then we have already determined what we need to compute the minimum distance. If not, then the boundary of D must be tested. To defer the division by σ, the code instead computes $\bar{s} = be - dc$ and $\bar{t} = bd - ae$ and tests for containment in a scaled domain: $s \in [0, \sigma], t \in [0, \sigma]$, and $s + t \leq \sigma$. If in that set, then the divisions are performed. If not, then the boundary of the unit square is tested. The general outline of the conditionals for determining which region contains $(\bar{s}, \bar{t})$ is

```
det = a*c - b*b;  s = b*e - c*d;  t = b*d - a*e;
if (s + t <= det) {
    if (s < 0) {
        if (t < 0) {
            region 4
        } else {
            region 3
        }
    }
} else {
```

```
    if (s < 0) {
        region 2
    } else if (t < 0) {
        region 6
    } else {
        region 1
    }
}
```

The block of code for handling region 0 is

```
invDet = 1 / det;
s *= invDet;
t *= invDet;
```

and requires a single division.

The block of code for region 1 is

```
//  F(s) = Q(s, 1 - s) = (a - 2b + c)s^2 + 2(b - c + d - e)s + (c + 2e + f)
//  F'(s)/2 = (a - 2b + c)s + (b - c + d - e)
//  F'(s} = 0 when s = (c + e - b - d)/a - 2b + c)
//  a - 2b + c = |e0 - e1|^2 > 0,
//  so only the sign of c + e - b - d need be considered

numer = c + d - b - d;

if (numer <= 0) {
    s = 0;
} else {
    denom = a - 2 * b + c;  // positive quantity
    s = (numer >= denom ? 1: numer/denom);
}
t = 1 - s;
```

The block of code for region 3 is given below. The block for region 5 is similar.

```
//  F(t) = Q(0, t) = ct^2 + et + f
//  F'(t)/2 = ct + e
//  F'(t) = 0 when t = -e/c

s = 0;
t = (e >= 0 ? 0 : (-e >= c ? 1: -e/c));
```

The block of code for region 2 is given below. Blocks for regions 4 and 6 are similar.

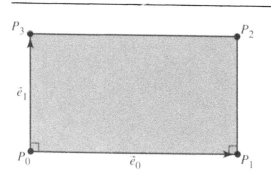

Figure 10.11   Alternative definition of a rectangle.

```
//  Grad{Q} = 2(as + bt + d, bs + ct + e)
//  (0, -1) * Grad(Q(0, 1)) = (0, -1) * (b + d, c + e) = -(c + e)
//  (1, -1) * Grad(Q(0, 1)) = (1, -1) * (b + d, c + e) = (b + d) - (c + e)
//  min on edge s + t = 1 if (1, -1) * Grad(Q(0, 1)) < 0)
//  min on edge s = 0 otherwise

tmp0 = b + d;
tmp1 = c + e;
if (tmp1 > tmp0) {  //  min on edge s + t = 1
    numer = tmp1 - tmp0;
    denom = a - 2 * b + c;
    s = (numer >= denom? 1 : numer / denom);
    t = 1 - s;
} else {
    s = 0;
    t = (tmp1 <= 0 ? 1 : (e >= 0 ? 0 : -e / c));
}
```

10.3.3 POINT TO RECTANGLE

Typically, a rectangle is defined by a list of four vertices P_0, P_1, P_2, and P_3. However, if we let $P = P_0$ and define $\vec{e}_0 = P_1 - P$ and $\vec{e}_1 = P_3 - P$, then a rectangle can be equivalently defined as $\mathcal{R}(s, t) = P + s\vec{e}_0 + t\vec{e}_1$ for $(s, t) \in [0, 1]^2$, as shown in Figure 10.11.

Given a point Q and a rectangle $\mathcal{R}$, we wish to find the distance from Q to Q', the closest point of $\mathcal{R}$ to Q, as shown in Figure 10.12. The closest point on the rectangle

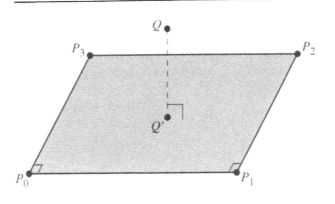

Figure 10.12 Distance between a point and a rectangle.

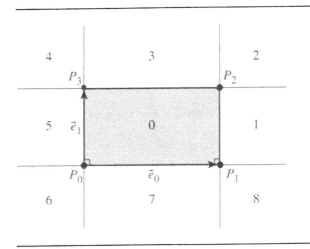

Figure 10.13 Partition of the plane by a rectangle.

to Q is obtained by projecting Q onto the plane containing $\mathcal{R}$, and then analyzing the relationship of Q' to the vertices and edges of $\mathcal{R}$. If Q' is in the interior of $\mathcal{R}$, then that is the closest point; however, if Q' is on the exterior of $\mathcal{R}$, then the closest point is instead either a vertex of $\mathcal{R}$ or a point on an edge of $\mathcal{R}$. The vectors $\vec{e}_0$ and $\vec{e}_1$ are orthogonal and, if extended outside the range $[0, 1]$, can be seen to divide the plane into nine regions, as shown in Figure 10.13.

If the projected point is in region 0, then that projected point is the closest to Q. If it instead is in any one of regions 2, 4, 6, or 8, then the closest point is P_2, P_3, P_0, or P_1, respectively. Finally, if it is in any one of regions 1, 3, 5, or 7, then the closest point is the projection of *that* point onto edge P_1P_2, P_2P_3, P_3P_0, or P_0P_1, respectively.

The projection of Q onto the plane containing $\mathcal{R}$ is

$$Q' = Q + s\vec{e}_0 + t\vec{e}_1$$

where

$$s = (Q - P) \cdot \vec{e}_0 \tag{10.5}$$

$$t = (Q - P) \cdot \vec{e}_1 \tag{10.6}$$

The pseudocode is

```
float PointRectangleDistanceSquared3D(Point q, Rectangle rectangle)
{
    float d = q - rectangle.p;

    float s = Dot(rectangle.e0, d);
    if (s > 0) {
        float dot0 = Dot(rectangle.e0, rectangle.e0);
        if (s < dot0) {
            d = d - (s / dot0) * rectangle.e0;
        } else {
            d = d - rectangle.e0;
        }

    }

    float t = Dot (rectangle.e1, d);
    if (t > 0) {
        float dot1 = Dot(rectangle.e1, rectangle.e1);
        if (t < dot1) {
            d = d - (t / dot1) * rectangle.e1;
        } else {
            d = d - rectangle.e1;
        }
    }

    return Dot(d, d);
}
```

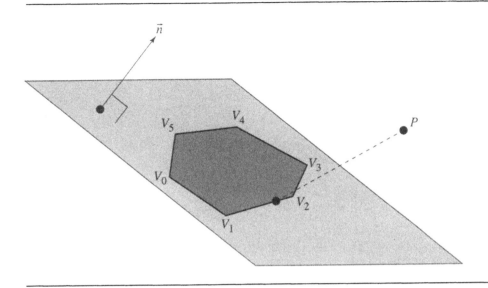

Figure 10.14   Distance from a point to a polygon.

10.3.4 POINT TO POLYGON

In this section we address the problem of finding the distance from a point to a polygon in 3D, as shown in Figure 10.14. A polygon is defined as a list of n vertices: $V_0, V_1, \ldots, V_{n-1}$. The plane in which these points lie can be computed by finding three noncollinear and noncoincident points $V_i, V_j, V_k, i < j < k$, by taking the cross product $(V_j - V_i) \times (V_k - V_i)$ as the normal to the plane and any of $V_i, 0 \le i \le n - 1$, as a point on the plane. Given floating-point imprecision and the actual computation involved in determining noncollinearity, it may be wise to instead use Newell's method (Tampieri 1992), described in Section A.7.4.

Let the plane of the polygon $\mathcal{P}$ be defined as $ax + by + cz + d =$. The projection of the point P onto $\mathcal{P}$ is

$$P' = P - \frac{P \cdot \vec{n} + d}{\vec{n} \cdot \vec{n}} \vec{n}$$

Then if we project the V_i and P' onto one of the XY, XZ, or YZ planes (typically, we project along the axis that the points of the polygon differ least in), we can compute Q', the point on the (projected) polygon closest to P'', using the 2D point-polygon distance algorithm found in Section 6.3.4. The point Q on the unprojected polygon closest to P can be computed by plugging in the coordinates of Q' that

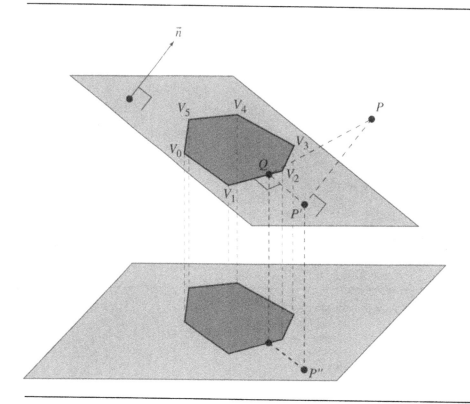

Figure 10.15   Solving the 3D point-polygon distance test by projecting to 2D.

did not correspond to the axis of projection into the plane equation of the polygon. The distance between P and Q is then the distance from P to the polygon (see Figure 10.15).

The pseudocode is

```
float PointPolygonDistanceSquared3D(Point p, Polygon poly)
{
    // Get plane equation for polygon
    float a, b, c, d;
    PolygonPlaneEquation(poly, a, b, c, d);
    Vector n = { a, b, c };

    // Project point onto plane of polygon
    Point pPrime;
```

```
pPrime = p - ((Dot(p, n) - d) / Dot(n, n)) * n;

// Determine plane to project polygon onto
if (MAX(n.x, MAX(n.y, n.z)) == n.x) {
    projectionPlane = YZ_PLANE;
} else if (MAX(n.x, MAX(n.y, n.z)) == n.y) {
    projectionPlane = XZ_PLANE;
} else {
    projectionPlane = XY_PLANE;
}

//  Project poly and pPrime onto plane
Point pPrimePrime = pPrime;
if (projectionPlane == YZ_PLANE) {
    pPrimePrime.x = 0;
} else if (projectionPlane == XZ_PLANE) {
    pPrimePrime.y = 0;
} else {
    pPrimePrime.z = 0;
}

Polygon2D poly2D;
for (i = 0; i < poly.nVertices; i++) {
    poly2D.vertices[i] = poly.vertices[i];
    if (projectionPlane == YZ_PLANE) {
        poly2D.vertices[i].x = 0;
    } else if (projectionPlane == XZ_PLANE) {
        poly2D.vertices[i].y = 0;
    } else {
        poly2D.vertices[i].z = 0;
    }
}

//  Find closest point in 2D
Point qPrime;
float dist2D;
dist2D = PointPolygonDistance2D(pPrimePrime, poly2D, qPrime);

//  Compute q, the closest point on the 3D polygon's plane
q = qPrime;
if (projectionPlane == YZ_PLANE) {
    qPrime.x = (-b * qPrime.y - c * qPrime.z - d) / a;
} else if (projectionPlane == XZ_PLANE) {
```

```
        qPrime.y = (-a * qPrime.x - c * qPrime.z - d) / b;
    } else {
        qPrime.z = (-a * qPrime.x - b * qPrime.y - d) / c;
    }


    // Finally, compute distance (squared)
    Vector3D d = p - qPrime;
    return Dot(d, d);
}
```

10.3.5 POINT TO CIRCLE OR DISK

A circle in 3D is represented by a center C, a radius r, and a plane containing the circle, $\hat{n} \cdot (X - C) = 0$, where $\hat{n}$ is a unit-length normal to the plane. If $\hat{u}$ and $\hat{v}$ are also unit-length vectors so that $\hat{u}$, $\hat{v}$, and $\hat{n}$ form a right-handed orthonormal coordinate system (the matrix with these vectors as columns is orthonormal with determinant 1), then the circle is parameterized as

$$X = C + r(\cos(\theta)\hat{u} + \sin(\theta)\hat{v}) =: C + r\hat{w}(\theta)$$

for angles $\theta \in [0, 2\pi)$. Note that $\|X - C\| = r$, so the X values are all equidistant from C. Moreover, $\hat{n} \cdot (X - C) = 0$ since $\hat{u}$ and $\hat{v}$ are perpendicular to $\hat{n}$, so the X lie in the plane.

For each angle $\theta \in [0, 2\pi)$, the squared distance from a specified point P to the corresponding circle point is

$$F(\theta) = \|C + r\hat{w}(\theta) - P\|^2 = r^2 + \|C - P\|^2 + 2r(C - P) \cdot \hat{w}$$

The problem is to minimize $F(\theta)$ by finding θ_0 such that $F(\theta_0) \leq F(\theta)$ for all $\theta \in [0, 2\pi)$. Since F is a periodic and differentiable function, the minimum must occur when $F'(\theta) = 0$. Also, note that $(C - P) \cdot \hat{w}$ should be negative and as large in magnitude as possible to reduce the right-hand side in the definition of F. The derivative is

$$F'(\theta) = 2r(C - P) \cdot \hat{w}'(\theta)$$

where $\hat{w} \cdot \hat{w}' = 0$ since $\hat{w} \cdot \hat{w} = 1$ for all θ. The vector $\hat{w}'$ is a unit-length vector since $\hat{w}'' = -\hat{w}$ and $0 = \hat{w} \cdot \hat{w}'$ implies $0 = \hat{w} \cdot \hat{w}'' + \hat{w}' \cdot \hat{w}' = -1 + \hat{w}' \cdot \hat{w}'$. Finally, $\hat{w}'$ is perpendicular to $\hat{n}$ since $\hat{n} \cdot \hat{w} = 0$ implies $0 = \hat{n} \cdot \hat{w}'$. All conditions imply that $\hat{w}$ is parallel to the projection of $P - C$ onto the plane and points in the same direction.

Let Q be the projection of P onto the plane. Then

$$Q - C = P - C - \left(\hat{n} \cdot (P - C)\right)\hat{n}$$

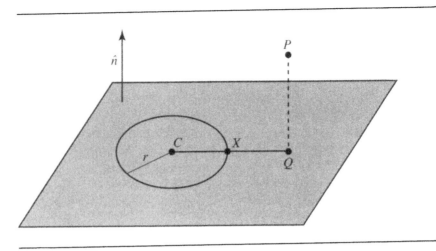

Figure 10.16   Typical case, closest point to circle.

The vector $\hat{w}(\theta)$ must be the unitized projection $(Q - C)/\|Q - C\|$. The closest point on the circle to P is

$$X = C + r\frac{Q - C}{\|Q - C\|}$$

assuming that $Q \neq C$. The distance from point to circle is then $\|P - X\|$.

If the projection of P is exactly the circle center C, then all points on the circle are equidistant from C. The distance from point to circle is the length of the hypotenuse of any triangle whose vertices are C, P, and any circle point. The lengths of the adjacent and opposite triangle sides are r and $\|P - C\|$, so the distance from point to circle is $\sqrt{r^2 + \|P - C\|^2}$.

The typical case where P does not project to the circle center is shown in Figure 10.16. The case where P does project to the circle center is shown in Figure 10.17.

Point to Disk

Finding the distance from a point to a disk requires a minor modification of the point and circle algorithm. The disk is the set of all points $X = C + \rho\hat{w}(\theta)$, where $0 \leq \rho \leq r$. If the projection of P is contained in the disk, then the projection is already the closest point to P. If the projection is outside the disk, then the closest point to P is the closest point on the disk boundary, a circle. Figure 10.18 shows the case when P projects inside the disk. Figure 10.19 shows the case when P projects outside the disk.

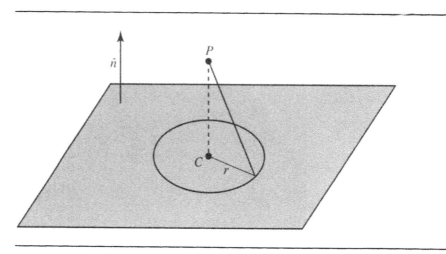

Figure 10.17   Closest point is circle center.

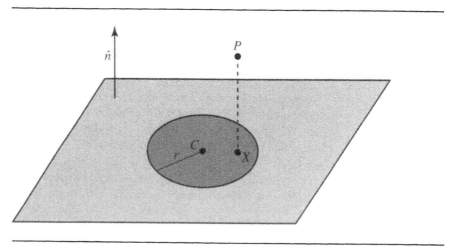

Figure 10.1ᴜ   Closest point when *P* projects inside the disk.

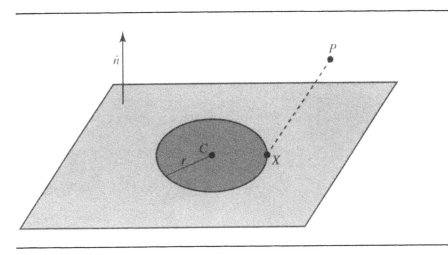

Figure 10.19   Closest point when P projects outside the disk.

10.4 POINT TO POLYHEDRON

In this section, we address the problem of finding the distance from a point to a polyhedron. We first consider the general case and then address two commonly encountered specific instances—oriented bounding boxes (OBBs) and orthogonal frustums.

10.4.1 GENERAL PROBLEM

In this section we consider the distance between a point and a polyhedron. We present three algorithms—one for tetrahedra, one for strictly convex polyhedra, and one for simply convex and concave polyhedra.

Point to Tetrahedron

We take the tetrahedron to be a special case of this problem, as we can exploit its properties in finding its distance to a point. Consider a point P and a tetrahedron with noncoplanar vertices V_i for $0 \leq i \leq 3$, as shown in Figure 10.20. The point may be closest to an edge, to the interior of a face, or to one of the vertices (or it may be on the interior of the tetrahedron, in which case the distance is 0). To simplify the discussions, we assume that the vertices are ordered so that the 3×3 matrix $\mathbf{M}$ whose columns are $V_i - V_0$ for $0 \leq i \leq 2$, in that order, has a positive determinant. The canonical tetrahedron with this ordering is

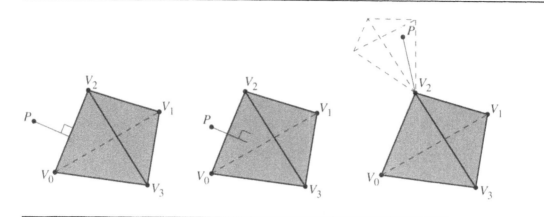

Figure 10.20   Distance from a point to a polyhedron (tetrahedron).

$$V_0 = (0, 0, 0)$$
$$V_1 = (1, 0, 0)$$
$$V_2 = (0, 1, 0)$$
$$V_3 = (0, 0, 1)$$

Outward-pointing normal vectors for the triangular faces are

$$\vec{n}_0 = (V_1 - V_3) \times (V_2 - V_3)$$
$$\vec{n}_1 = (V_0 - V_2) \times (V_3 - V_2)$$
$$\vec{n}_2 = (V_3 - V_1) \times (V_0 - V_1)$$
$$\vec{n}_3 = (V_2 - V_0) \times (V_1 - V_0)$$

The face to which $\vec{n}_i$ is normal is the one opposite vertex V_i and contains the vertex V_{3-i}.

The point P is inside the tetrahedron if it is on the negative side of each face plane; that is, when $\vec{n}_i \cdot (P - V_{3-i}) < 0$ for all i. In this case the distance will be zero. It is possible that P is on the tetrahedron boundary itself, in which case $\vec{n}_i \cdot (P - V_{3-i}) \leq 0$ for all i with equality for at least one i. If an equality occurs once, the point is on a face, but not on an edge or at a vertex. If two equalities occur, the point is on an edge, but not at a vertex. If three equalities occur, the point is at a vertex. It is not possible for equality to occur four times.

We know that if P is *not* contained within the tetrahedron, then it will have a nonnegative distance to one, two, or three faces. Thus, we can calculate the dot product

$$\vec{n}_i \cdot (P - V_{3-i})$$

for $i = 0, 1, 2, 3$. By looking at the signs of all four dot products, we can determine which (if any) faces the point is outside of; we then can compute the distance to each face for which the dot product is nonnegative, and take the minimum of these distances to be our final solution.

Point to Convex Polyhedron

If the convex polyhedron is strictly convex (no faces share a plane), then an approach can be taken that is analogous to that taken for the tetrahedron. Let the faces be contained in the planes $\vec{n}_i \cdot (X - V_i) = 0$, where V_i is a vertex on the face and $\vec{n}_i$ is an outer normal vector to the face. The point P is inside the polyhedron when $\vec{n}_i \cdot (P - V_i) < 0$ for all i. The point is outside if $\vec{n}_i \cdot (P - V_i) > 0$ for some i. The point is on the polyhedron boundary itself if $\vec{n}_i \cdot (P - V_i) \leq 0$ for all i with equality occurring for at least one i. If one equality occurs, the point is interior to a face. If two equalities occur, the point is interior to an edge. If three or more equalities occur, the point is a vertex. In this latter case, the number of equalities is the number of faces sharing that vertex.

In any case, if we examine each face $i = 0, 1, 2, \ldots, n - 1$ in turn, and find that all the dot products have a negative value, then P is inside the polyhedron, and the distance is zero. Otherwise, we find one or more faces whose signed distance is nonnegative, and we then must compute the distance between P and each such face, and the distance is the minimum of such distances so calculated. If the faces are triangular, then the algorithm of Section 10.3.2 can be used; otherwise, the more general algorithm of Section 10.3.4 must be used.

Point to General Polyhedron

We start by noting that a point that is contained within a polyhedron is considered to be at zero distance from the polyhedron. Thus, in general we can first test the point for containment inside the polyhedron using the algorithm described in Section 13.4.3 for general polyhedra. If the point is in the polyhedron, then its distance is zero, and no further tests need be done. Otherwise, we must then apply a method analogous to that used in the previous section for convex polyhedra—for each face, if the point P is on the outside of the face, find the distance from P to that face using the algorithm of either Section 10.3.2 or Section 10.3.4 if the face is triangular or nontriangular, respectively.

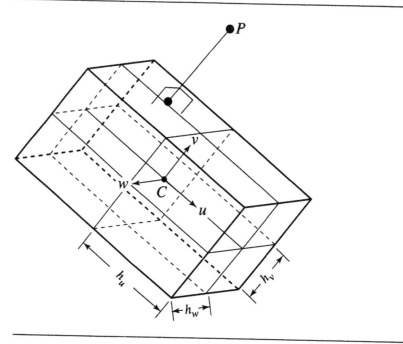

Figure 10.21   Distance from a point to an oriented bounding box.

10.4.2 POINT TO ORIENTED BOUNDING BOX

In this section we address the problem of computing the distance from a point to an oriented bounding box (OBB). An OBB is defined as a centerpoint C; three unit vectors $\hat{u}$, $\hat{v}$, and $\hat{w}$ forming a right-handed orthornormal basis; and three scalars h_u, h_v, and h_w representing half the dimension in each of the u, v, and w directions. This can be seen in Figure 10.21.

We could, of course, consider that an OBB consists of six rectangles, and simply compute the distance from the point to each rectangle, and take the minimum; however, this is inefficient.

The OBB's centerpoint C and $\hat{u}$, $\hat{v}$, and $\hat{w}$ define a frame. Observe that, relative to that frame, the OBB is an axis-aligned box centered at the origin, whose sides lie in one of the XY, XZ, or YZ planes. If we compute the position of a point P in this frame, then we can exploit this axis-aligned, origin-centered nature of the OBB and compute the closest point, and the distance to it, quite trivially.

Given the OBB's center C and $\hat{u}$, $\hat{v}$, and $\hat{w}$, a point P's coordinates in that frame can be computed as

$$P' = [\,(P - C) \cdot \hat{u} \quad (P - C) \cdot \hat{v} \quad (P - C) \cdot \hat{w}\,]$$

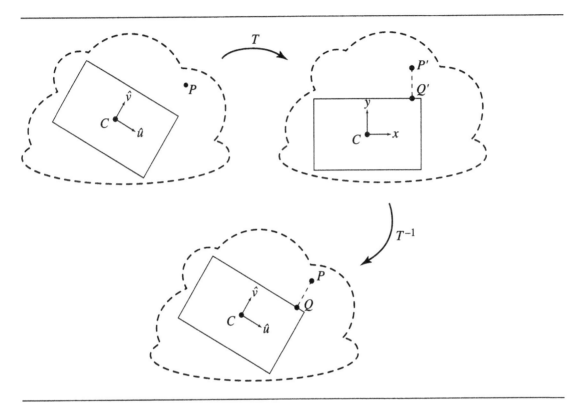

Figure 10.22 Computing the distance between a point and an OBB.

That is, we simply project the vector between the P and C onto each of the OBB's basis vectors. Note that this is functionally equivalent to creating a transform T from global space into the local space of the OBB with matrix

$$\mathbf{T} = \begin{bmatrix} \hat{u}^{\mathrm{T}} & \hat{v}^{\mathrm{T}} & \hat{w}^{\mathrm{T}} & \vec{0}^{\mathrm{T}} \\ & -C & & 1 \end{bmatrix}$$

and multiplying by P, but is more efficient.

We can then simply project P' onto the box—this yields a point Q' closest to P'—and trivially find the distance between them, which is also the distance between the original point P and the box. If we want the coordinates of the closest point in global space, we simply transform Q' by the $\mathbf{T}^{-1}$, yielding the point Q closest to P. An example of this, shown in 2D for ease of illustration, appears in Figure 10.22.

The pseudocode is below (note we compute the distance squared and return the nearest point Q only if asked):

```
float PointOBBDistanceSquared(Point p, OBB box, boolean computePoint,
                              Point& q)
{
    // Transform p into box's coordinate frame
    Vector offset = p - box.center();
    Point  pPrime(Dot(offset, box.u), Dot(offset, box.v), Dot(offset, box.w));

    // Project pPrime onto box
    float distanceSquared = 0;
    float d;

    if (pPrime.x < -box.uHalf) {
        d = pPrime.x + box.uHalf;
        distanceSquared += d * d;
        qPrime.x = -box.uHalf;
    } else if (pPrime.x > box.uHalf) {
        d = pPrime.x - box.uHalf;
        distanceSquared += d * d;
        qPrime.x = box.uHalf;
    } else {
        qPrime.x = pPrime.x;
    }

    if (pPrime.y < -box.vHalf ) {
        d = pPrime.y + box.v;
        distanceSquared += d * d;
        qPrime.y = -box.vHalf;
    } else if (pPrime.y > box.vHalf) {
        d = pPrime.y - box.vHalf;
        distanceSquared += d * d;
        qPrime.y = box.vHalf;
    } else {
        qPrime.y = pPrime.y;
    }

    if (pPrime.z < -box.wHalf) {
        d = pPrime.z + box.wHalf;
        distanceSquared += d * d;
        qPrime.z = -box.wHalf;
    } else if (pPrime.z > box.wHalf) {
        d = pPrime.z - box.wHalf;
        distanceSquared += d * d;
        qPrime.z = box.wHalf;
    } else {
```

```
        qPrime.z = pPrime.z;
    }


    //  If requested, compute the nearest point in global space (T^{-1})
    if (computePoint) {
        q.x = qPrime.x * box.u.x + qPrime.y * box.v.x + qPrime.z * box.w.x;
        q.y = qPrime.x * box.u.y + qPrime.y * box.v.y + qPrime.z * box.w.y;
        q.x = qPrime.x * box.u.z + qPrime.y * box.v.z + qPrime.z * box.w.z;

        q += box.center;
    }


    return distanceSquared;
}
```

10.4.3 POINT TO ORTHOGONAL FRUSTUM

The material in this section is motivated in two dimensions in Section 6.3.3. The algorithm for computing the distance from a point to an orthogonal frustum is based on determining the *Voronoi regions* for the faces, edges, and vertices of the frustum. Given a set of objects, the Voronoi region for a single object is the set of all points that are closer to that object than to any other object. The Voronoi region containing the point is computed. The nearest point on the frustum in that region is also computed. From this the distance can be calculated.

The *orthogonal view frustum* has origin E. Its coordinate axes are determined by left vector $\hat{l}$, up-vector $\hat{u}$, and direction vector $\hat{d}$. The vectors in that order form a right-handed orthonormal system. The extent of the frustum in the $\hat{d}$ direction is $[n, f]$, where $0 < n < f$. The four corners of the frustum in the near plane are $E \pm \ell\hat{l} \pm \mu\hat{u} + n\hat{d}$. The four corners of the frustum in the far plane are $E + (f/n)(\pm\ell\hat{l} \pm \mu\hat{u} + n\hat{d})$. The frustum axis is the ray with origin E and direction $\hat{d}$. The frustum is orthogonal in the sense that its axis is perpendicular to the near and far faces.

Let P be the point whose distance to the frustum is required. The point can be written in the frustum coordinate system as

$$P = E + x_0\hat{l} + x_1\hat{u} + x_2\hat{d}$$

so $x_0 = \hat{l} \cdot (P - E)$, $x_1 = \hat{u} \cdot (P - E)$, and $x_2 = \hat{d} \cdot (P - E)$. It is sufficient to demonstrate the construction for $x_0 \geq 0$ and $x_1 \geq 0$. The idea is the same as in the 2D case: reflect the x_0 and x_1 components, find the closest point, then reflect its x_0 and x_1 components back to the original quadrant.

The naming conventions for the frustum components are N for near, F for far, U for up, and L for left. The top face of the frustum is labeled the F-face. It has two edges: the UF-edge that is in the direction of $\hat{l}$ and the LF-edge that is in the direction

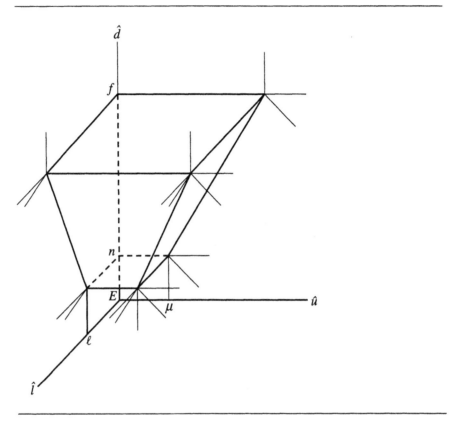

Figure 10.23   The portion of the frustum in the first octant.

of $\hat{u}$. It also has a vertex: the *LUF*-vertex at $(f\ell/n, f\mu/n, f)$. The bottom face of the frustum is labeled the N-face. It has two edges: the UN-edge that is in the direction of $\hat{l}$ and the LN-edge that is in the direction of $\hat{u}$. It also has a vertex: the *LUN*-vertex at (ℓ, μ, n). The remaining two faces are the L-face whose normal is $(n, 0, -\ell)$ and the U-face whose normal is $(0, n, -\mu)$. Finally there is the LU-edge that is shared by the L-face and the U-face. Figure 10.23 illustrates the Voronoi region boundaries. The thin black lines indicate the near and far planes that split some of the Voronoi regions.

The pseudocode for determining the Voronoi region for (x_0, x_1, x_2) is given below.

```
if (x2 >= f) {
    if (x0 <= f * 1 / n) {
        if (x1 <= f * u / n)
```

```
                    F-face is closest;
            else
                UF-edge is closest;
    } else {
        if (x1 <= f * u / n)
            LF-edge is closest;
        else
            LUF-vertex is closest;
    }
} else if (x2 <= n) {
    if (x0 <= 1) {
        if (x1 <= u)
            N-face is closest;
        else {
            t = u * x1 + n * x2;
            if (t >= (f / n) * (u * u + n * n))
                UF-edge is closest;
            else if (t >= u * u + n * n)
                U-face is closest;
            else
                UN-edge is closest;
        }
    } else {
        if (x1 <= u) {
            t = 1 * x0 + n * x2;
            if (t >= (f / n) * (1 * 1 + n * n))
                LF-edge is closest;
            else if (t >= 1 * 1 + n * n)
                L-face is closest;
            else
                LN-edge is closest;
        } else {
            r = 1 * x0 + u * x1 + n * x2;
            s = u * r - (1 * 1 + u * u + n * n) * x1;
            if (s >= 0.0) {
                t = 1 * x0 + n * x2;
                if (t >= (f / n) * (1 * 1 + n * n))
                    LF-edge is closest;
                else if (t >= 1 * 1 + n * n)
                    L-face is closest;
                else
                    LN-edge is closest;
            } else {
                s = 1 * r - (1 * 1 + u * u + n * n) * x0;
```

```
                    if (s >= 0.0) {
                        t = u * x1 + n * x2;
                        if (t >= (f / n) * (u * u + n * n))
                            UF-edge is closest;
                        else if (t >= u * u + n * n)
                            U-face is closest;
                        else
                            UN-edge is closest;
                    } else {
                        if (r >= (f / n)(1 * 1 + u * u + n * n))
                            LUF-vertex is closest;
                        else if (r >= 1 * 1 + u * u + n * n)
                            LU-edge is closest;
                        else
                            LUN-vertex is closest;
                    }
                }
            }
        }
    } else {
        s = n * x0 - 1 * x2;
        t = n * x1 - u * x2;
        if (s <= 0) {
            if (t <= 0)
                point inside frustum;
            else {
                t = u * x1 + n * x2;
                if (t >= (f / n) * (u * u + n * n))
                    UF-edge is closest;
                else
                    U-face is closest;
            }
        } else {
            if (t <= 0) {
                t = 1 * x0 + n * x2;
                if (t >= (f / n) * (1 * 1 + n * n))
                    LF-edge is closest;
                else
                    L-face is closest;
            } else {
                r = 1 * x0 + u * x1 + n * x2;
                s = u * r - (1 * 1 + u * u + n * n) * x1;
                if (s >= 0) {
                    t = 1 * x0 + n * x2;
```

```
                if (t >= (f / n) * (l * l + n * n))
                    LF-edge is closest;
                else
                    L-face is closest;
            } else {
                t = l * r - (l * l + u * u + n * n) * x0;
                if (t >= 0) {
                    t = u * x1 + n * x2;
                    if (t >= (f / n) * (u * u + n * n))
                        UF-edge is closest;
                    else
                        U-face is closest;
                } else {
                    if (r >= l * l + u * u + n * n)
                        LUF-vertex is closest;
                    else
                        LU-edge is closest;
                }
            }
        }
    }
}
```

The closest point in each region is obtained by projection onto that component.

10.5 POINT TO QUADRIC SURFACE

In this section we address the problem of computing the distance from a point to a quadric surface. As we shall see, the general case involves solving a sixth-degree equation: all the roots must be computed, and their associated distances compared, in order to find the actual minimum distance. We can exploit the geometry of specific types of quadrics and obtain a somewhat less expensive algorithm; the example we give is for an ellipsoid.

10.5.1 POINT TO GENERAL QUADRIC SURFACE

This section describes an algorithm for computing the distance from a point to a quadric surface. The general quadratic equation is

$$Q(X) = X^{\mathrm{T}}\mathbf{A}X + B^{\mathrm{T}}X + c = 0$$

where A is a symmetric 3×3 matrix, not necessarily invertible (for example, in the case of a cylinder or paraboloid), B is a 3×1 vector, and c is a scalar. The parameter is X, a 3×1 vector. Given the surface defined implicitly by $Q(X) = 0$ and a point Y, find the distance from Y to the surface and compute a closest point X.

Geometrically, the closest point X on the surface to Y must satisfy the condition that $Y - X$ is normal to the surface. Since the surface gradient $\nabla Q(X)$ is normal to the surface, the algebraic condition for the closest point is

$$Y - X = t \nabla Q(X) = t(2AX + B)$$

for some scalar t. Therefore,

$$X = (I + 2tA)^{-1}(Y - tB)$$

where I is the identity matrix. We could replace this equation for X into the general quadratic equation to obtain a polynomial in t of at most sixth degree.

Instead of immediately replacing X in the quadratic equation, we can reduce the problem to something simpler to code. Factor A using an eigendecomposition to obtain $A = RDR^T$, where R is an orthonormal matrix whose columns are eigenvectors of A and where D is a diagonal matrix whose diagonal entries are the eigenvalues of A. Then

$$\begin{aligned}
X &= (I + 2tA)^{-1}(Y - tB) \\
&= (RR^T + 2tRDR^T)^{-1}(Y - tB) \\
&= [R(I + 2tD)R^T]^{-1}(Y - tB) \\
&= R(I + 2tD)^{-1}R^T(Y - tB) \\
&= R(I + 2tD)^{-1}(\vec{\alpha} - t\vec{\beta})
\end{aligned}$$

where the last equation defines $\vec{\alpha}$ and $\vec{\beta}$. Replacing in the quadratic equation and simplifying yields

$$0 = (\vec{\alpha} - t\vec{\beta})^T(I + 2tD)^{-1}D(I + 2tD)^{-1}(\vec{\alpha} - t\vec{\beta}) + \vec{\beta}^T(I + 2tD)^{-1}(\vec{\alpha} - t\vec{\beta}) + C$$

The inverse diagonal matrix is

$$(I + 2tD)^{-1} = \text{Diag}\{1/(1 + 2td_0), 1/(1 + 2td_1), 1/(1 + 2td_2)\}$$

Multiplying through by $((1 + 2td_0)(1 + 2td_1)(1 + 2td_2))^2$ leads to a polynomial equation of at most sixth degree.

The roots of the polynomial are computed and $X = (I + 2tA)^{-1}(Y - tB)$ is computed for each root t. The distances between X and Y are computed, and the minimum distance is selected from that set.

10.5.2 POINT TO ELLIPSOID

The previous section discussed a general solution to the problem of the distance from a point to a quadric surface. The equation of the intersection can be as much as a sixth-degree equation; solutions for such equations exist, but they can be relatively expensive.

For a specific type of quadric surface, simplifications can be made by exploiting the geometry of the object. We'll look at the ellipsoid as an example. The equation of an ellipsoid is

$$q(\mathbf{x}) = \frac{x^2}{a^2} + \frac{y^2}{b^2} + \frac{z^2}{c^2} - 1 = 0 \tag{10.7}$$

Let P be the point from which we wish to compute the distance. The closest point on the ellipsoid can be viewed as being connected by a line that is normal to P; that is,

$$P - \mathbf{x} = \nabla q(\mathbf{x}) \tag{10.8}$$

where $\mathbf{x}$ is the point on the surface and $\nabla q(\mathbf{x})$ is the normal to the ellipsoid at $\mathbf{x}$.

The normal to a point on the surface of the ellipsoid is

$$\nabla q(X) = (\frac{\partial q}{\partial x}, \frac{\partial q}{\partial y}, \frac{\partial q}{\partial z})$$
$$= 2(\frac{x}{a^2}, \frac{y}{b^2}, \frac{z}{c^2}) \tag{10.9}$$

Substituting Equation 10.9 into Equation 10.8 and then substituting the results into Equation 10.7 will give us the equation we need to solve to find the closest point:

$$a^2(\lambda + b^2)^2(\lambda + c^2)^2 P_x^2 + b^2(\lambda + a^2)^2(\lambda + c^2)^2 P_y^2 + c^2(\lambda + a^2)^2(\lambda + b^2)^2 P_z^2$$

$$- (\lambda + a^2)^2(\lambda + b^2)^2(\lambda + c^2)^2 = 0$$

To see that this is a sixth-degree equation, consider eliminating λ and then using two of the equations to solve for, say, x and y in terms of the constants and z. This yields this unpleasant equation:

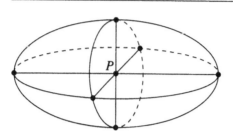

Figure 10.24   Six possible "closest points" on an ellipsoid's surface.

$$z^6(b-c)^2(b+c)^2(a-c)^2(a+c)^2 + z^5 2c^2 P_z(b-c)(b+c)(a-c)(a+c)(b^2+a^2-2c^2)$$

$$+ z^4 - c^2(-2a^4b^2c^2 - 6c^6 P_z^2 + 6c^4 P_z^2 b^2 + a^4b^4 - a^4c^2 P_z^2 + c^4b^4$$

$$- 2c^6b^2 - 2a^2c^2b^4 - 4c^2a^2 P_z^2 b^2 - 2a^2c^6 + 6c^4a^2 P_z^2 + c^8 + a^4c^4$$

$$+ 4a^2c^4b^2 + 2c^2a^2 P_x^2 b^2 - c^4 P_y^2 b^2 - a^4 P_y^2 b^2 - c^2 P_z^2 b^4 - b^4 P_x^2 a^2$$

$$- c^4a^2 P_x^2 + 2c^2b^2 P_y^2 a^2) + z^3 - 2c^4 P_z(-c^2b^4 + c^2 P_y^2 b^2 + 2c^4 P_z^2$$

$$- 4a^2b^2c^2 + 3b^2c^4 - 2c^6 - c^2 P_z^2 b^2 - b^2 P_x^2 a^2 + 3c^4a^2 - a^2 P_y^2 b^2$$

$$+ b^2a^4 - a^4c^2 - c^2a^2 P_z^2 + c^2a^2 P_x^2 + b^4a^2) + z^2 - c^6 P_z^2(4a^2b^2$$

$$- 6a^2c^2 - c^2 P_z^2 - 6b^2c^2 - P_y^2 b^2 - P_x^2 a^2 + 6c^4 + a^4 + b^4)$$

$$+ z^1 - 2c^8 P_z^3(b^2+a^2-2c^2) + z^0 - c^{10}P_z^4 = 0$$

Alternatively, consider if P is at the center of the ellipsoid, as shown in Figure 10.24; there are six candidates at which we must look, at least two of which will have minimal distance.

In any case, Hart (1994) makes several observations:

- The graph of λ has a decreasing slope beyond the largest root. This suggests that the expensive sixth-degree numerical root finder can be avoided, in favor of, say, Newton iteration; in that case, providing a "sufficiently large" initial estimate will result in quick convergence.

- If P is (exactly) on the surface, or inside the ellipsoid, an initial guess of $\lambda = 0$ will work because the maximum root will be less than or equal to zero.

- If P is outside the ellipsoid, then a starting value of

$$\lambda = \| P - \mathcal{O} \| \max\{a, b, c\}$$

is "sufficiently large" ($\mathcal{O}$ is the origin).

10.6 POINT TO POLYNOMIAL CURVE

In this section we address the problem of computing the distance from a point to a polynomial curve in 3D. Without loss of generality, we assume that our curve is a parametric polynomial curve (e.g., a Bézier curve), which may be piecewise (e.g., a NURBS curve).

Given a parametric curve $Q(t)$ and a point P, we want to find the point on Q closest to P. That is, we wish to find the parameter t such that the distance from $Q(t)$ to P is a minimum. Our approach begins with the geometric observation that the line segment (whose length we wish to minimize) from P to $Q(t)$ is perpendicular to the tangent of the curve at $Q(t_0)$, as shown in Figure 10.25. The equation we wish to solve for t is

$$(Q(t) - P) \cdot Q'(t) = 0 \tag{10.10}$$

If the degree of $Q(t)$ is d, then $Q'(t)$ is of degree $d - 1$, so Equation 10.10 is of degree $2d - 1$. So, for any curve of degree higher than two, no closed-form solution is available, and some numerical root finder must be used. One choice is to use Newton iteration; however, this requires a reasonable first guess. An approach suggested by

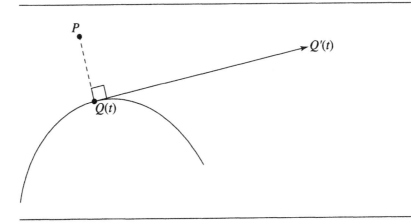

Figure 10.25   Distance from an arbitrary point to a parametric curve.

Piegl and Tiller (1995) is to evaluate curve points at n equally spaced parameter values (or at n equally spaced parameter values in the case of a piecewise polynomial curve) and compute the distance (squared) from each point to P. The parameter value of the closest evaluated point can be used as the initial guess for the Newton iteration.

Assume we have an initial guess t_0. Call t_i the parameter obtained at the ith Newton iteration. The Newton step is then

$$t_{i+1} = t_i - \frac{(Q(t) - P) \cdot Q'(t)}{((Q(t) - P) \cdot Q'(t))'}$$

$$= t_i - \frac{(Q(t) - P) \cdot Q'(t)}{(Q(t) - P) \cdot Q''(t_i) + \|Q'(t_i)\|^2} \qquad (10.11)$$

Newton iteration is, in general, discontinued when some criteria are met. In Piegl and Tiller (1995), two zero tolerances are used:

- ϵ_1: a Euclidean distance measure
- ϵ_2: a zero cosine measure

They check the following criteria in this order:

1. Point coincidence:

$$\|Q(t_i) - P\| \leq \epsilon_1$$

2. Zero cosine (angle between $Q(t_i) - P$ and $Q'(t)$ is sufficiently close to 90°):

$$\frac{\|(Q(t) - P) \cdot Q'(t)\|}{\|Q(t) - P\| \|Q'(t)\|} \leq \epsilon_2$$

If either of these criteria are not yet met, then a Newton step is taken. Then, two more conditions are checked:

3. Whether the parameter stays within range $a \leq t_i \leq b$ by clamping it
4. Whether the parameter doesn't change significantly:

$$\|(t_{i+1} - t_i) Q'(t_i)\| \leq \epsilon_1$$

If the final criterion is satisfied, then Newton iteration is discontinued. The current parameter value t_{i+1} is considered to be the desired root, the closest point to P is $Q(t_{i+1})$, and the distance from P to the curve $Q(t)$ is $\|(Q(t_{i+1}) - P)\|$.

An alternative, which avoids the necessity of computing a number of points on $Q(t)$ required to get a reasonable initial guess for the Newton iteration, is to convert the curve to Bézier form and use the Bézier-based root finder described in Schneider (1990); this approach is particularly efficient if the curve is already in Bézier form.

10.7 POINT TO POLYNOMIAL SURFACE

In this section we address the problem of computing the distance from a point to a polynomial surface. Without loss of generality, we assume that our surface is a parametric polynomial surface (e.g., a Bézier surface), which may be piecewise (e.g., a NURBS surface).

Given a parametric surface $S(u, v)$ and a point P, we want to find the point on S closest to P. That is, we wish to find the parameters (u, v) such that the distance from $S(u, v)$ to P is a minimum. Our approach begins with the geometric observation that the line segment (whose length we wish to minimize) from P to $Q(t)$ is perpendicular to the tangent plane of the surface at $S(u_0, v_0)$, as shown in Figure 10.26.

The vector between the surface and the arbitrary point can be expressed as a function of the parameters of the surface:

$$r(u, v) = S(u, v) - P$$

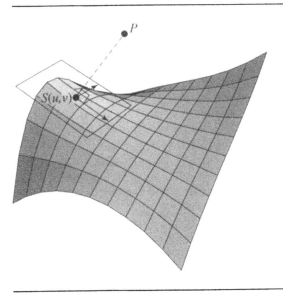

Figure 10.26   Distance from an arbitrary point to a parametric surface.

and the condition for the line $S(u, v) - P$ to be perpendicular to the tangent plane can be expressed as two conditions—the line must be perpendicular to the partial derivatives $(S_u(u, v)$ and $S_v(u, v))$ in each direction:

$$f(u, v) = r(u, v) \cdot S_u(u, v)$$

$$= 0$$

$$g(u, v) = r(u, v) \cdot S_v(u, v)$$

$$= 0$$

and so in order to find the closest point, we must solve this system of equations. As with the case of the problem of finding the distance from a point to a polynomial curve, we use Newton iteration. Again, we can find an initial guess by evaluating the surface at $n \times n$ regularly spaced points, computing the distance (squared) of each point to P, and using the (u, v) parameters of the closest point as an initial guess for the Newton iteration.

Let

$$\sigma_i = \begin{bmatrix} \delta u \\ \delta v \end{bmatrix}$$

$$= \begin{bmatrix} u_{i+1} - u_i \\ v_{i+1} - v_i \end{bmatrix}$$

$$J_i = \begin{bmatrix} f_u(u_i, v_i) & f_v(u_i, v_i) \\ g_u(u_i, v_i) & g_v(u_i, v_i) \end{bmatrix}$$

$$= \begin{bmatrix} \|S_u(u_i, v_i)\|^2 + r(u_i, v_i) \cdot S_{uu}(u_i, v_i) & S_u(u_i, v_i) \cdot S_v(u_i, v_i) + r(u_i, v_i) \cdot S_{uv}(u_i, v_i) \\ S_u(u_i, v_i) \cdot S_v(u_i, v_i) + r(u_i, v_i) \cdot S_{vu}(u_i, v_i) & \|S_v(u_i, v_i)\|^2 + r(u_i, v_i) \cdot S_{vv}(u_i, v_i) \end{bmatrix}$$

$$\kappa_i = -\begin{bmatrix} f(u_i, v_i) \\ g(u_i, v_i) \end{bmatrix}$$

Assume we have an initial guess of (u_0, v_0). At the ith Newton iteration, solve the 2×2 system of equations in σ_i:

$$J_i \sigma_i = \kappa_i$$

and compute the next parameter values as

$$u_{i+1} = \delta u + u_i$$

$$v_{i+1} = \delta v + v_i$$

Newton iteration is, in general, discontinued when some criteria are met. In Piegl and Tiller (1995), two zero tolerances are used:

- ϵ_1: a Euclidean distance measure
- ϵ_2: a zero cosine measure

They check the following criteria in this order:

1. Point coincidence:

$$\|S(u_i, v_i) - P\| \le \epsilon_1$$

2. Zero cosine ((angle between $S(u_i, v_i) - P$ and $S_u(u_i, v_i)$ is sufficiently close to 90°, and similarly for $S_v(u_i, v_i)$):

$$\frac{\|S_u(u_i, v_i) \cdot (S(u_i, v_i) - P)\|}{\|S_u(u_i, v_i)\| \|S(u_i, v_i) - P\|} \le \epsilon_2$$

$$\frac{\|S_v(u_i, v_i) \cdot (S(u_i, v_i) - P)\|}{\|S_v(u_i, v_i)\| \|S(u_i, v_i) - P\|} \le \epsilon_2$$

If either of these criteria are not yet met, then a Newton step is taken. Then, two more conditions are checked:

3. Whether the parameters stay within range $a \le u_i \le b$ and $c \le v_i \le d$ by clamping them

4. Whether the parameters don't change significantly:

$$\|(u_{i+1} - u_i S_u(u_i, v_i)) + (v_{i+1} - v_i S_u(u_i, v_i))\| \le \epsilon_2$$

10.8 Linear Components

In this section, we discuss the problem of computing the distance between linear components—lines, segments, and rays—in all combinations.

10.8.1 Lines and Lines

Suppose we have two lines $\mathcal{L}_0(s) = P_0 + s\vec{d}_0$ and $\mathcal{L}_1(t) = P_1 + t\vec{d}_1$, and we wish to find the minimum distance between them. Let $Q_0 = P_0 + s_c\vec{d}_0$ and $Q_1 = P_1 + t_c\vec{d}_1$ be the points on $\mathcal{P}_0$ and $\mathcal{P}_1$, respectively, such that the distance between them is a minimum, and let $\vec{v} = Q_0 - Q_1$ (see Figure 10.27).

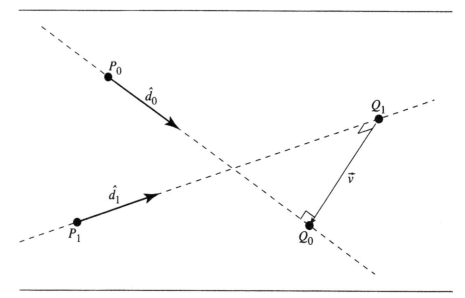

Figure 10.27   Distance between two lines.

The key to solving the problem of finding s_c and t_c (and thereby computing the minimum distance) is to note that $\vec{v}$ is perpendicular to *both* $\mathcal{L}_0$ and $\mathcal{L}_1$ only when $\|\vec{v}\|$ is minimized. In mathematical terms,

$$\vec{d}_0 \cdot \vec{v} = 0 \tag{10.12}$$

$$\vec{d}_1 \cdot \vec{v} = 0 \tag{10.13}$$

must both be satisfied. If we expand the definition of $\vec{v}$:

$$\vec{v} = Q_0 - Q_1$$

$$= (P_0 + s_c \vec{d}_0) - (P_1 + t_c \vec{d}_1)$$

and then substitute this back into Equations 10.12 and 10.13, we get

$$(\vec{d}_0 \cdot \vec{d}_0)s_c - (\vec{d}_0 \cdot \vec{d}_1)t_c = -\vec{d}_0 \cdot (P_0 - P_1)$$

$$(\vec{d}_1 \cdot \vec{d}_0)s_c - (\vec{d}_1 \cdot \vec{d}_1)t_c = -\vec{d}_1 \cdot (P_0 - P_1)$$

Let $a = \vec{d}_0 \cdot \vec{d}_0$, $b = \vec{d}_0 \cdot \vec{d}_1$, $c = \vec{d}_1 \cdot \vec{d}_1$, $d = \vec{d}_0 \cdot (P_0 - P_1)$, $e = \vec{d}_1 \cdot (P_0 - P_1)$, and $f = (P_0 - P_1) \cdot (P_0 - P_1)$. We now have two equations in two unknowns, whose solution is

$$s_c = \frac{be - cd}{ac - b^2}$$

$$t_c = \frac{ae - bd}{ac - b^2}$$

If the denominator $ac - b^2 < \epsilon$, then $\mathcal{L}_0$ and $\mathcal{L}_1$ are parallel. In this case, we can arbitrarily choose t_c to be anything we like and solve for s_c. We can minimize the computations by setting $t_c = 0$, in which case the calculation reduces to $s_c = -d/a$.

Finally, once we have computed the parameter values of the closest points, we can compute the distance between $\mathcal{L}_0$ and $\mathcal{L}_1$:

$$\|\mathcal{L}_0(s_c) - \mathcal{L}_1(t_c)\| = \|(P_0 - P_1) + \frac{(be - cd)\vec{d}_0 - (ae - bd)\vec{d}_1}{ac - b^2}\|$$

The pseudocode is

```
float LineLineDistanceSquared(Line line0, Line line1)
{
    u = line0.base - line1.base;
    a = Dot(line0.direction, line0.direction);
    b = Dot(line0.direction, line1.direction);
    c = Dot(line1.direction, line1,direction);
    d = Dot(line0.direction, u);
    e = Dot(line1.direction, u);
    f = Dot(u, u);
    det = a * c - b * b;

    // Check for (near) parallelism
    if (det < epsilon) {
        // Choose largest denominator to minimize floating-point problems
        if (b > c) {
            t = d / b;
        } else {
            t = e / c;
        }
        return -e * t + f;
    } else {
        // Nonparallel lines
        invDet = 1 / det;
        s = (b * e - c * d) * invDet;
```

```
        t = (a * e - b * d) * invDet;

        return s * (a * s - b * t + 2 * d) + t * (-b * s + c * t - 2 * e) + f;
    }
}
```

10.8.2   SEGMENT/SEGMENT, LINE/RAY, LINE/SEGMENT, RAY/RAY, RAY/SEGMENT

There are three different linear components—lines, rays, and segments—yielding six different combinations (segment/segment, line/ray, line/segment, ray/ray, ray/segment, and line/line) for distance tests.

Let's step back a bit and reconsider the mathematics of the problem at hand. Trying to find the distance between two lines, as we just saw, is equivalent to computing s and t such that the length of vector $\vec{v} = Q_1 - Q_0$ is a minimum. We can rewrite this as

$$\|\vec{v}\|^2 = \vec{v} \cdot \vec{v}$$

$$= ((P_0 - P_1) + s\vec{d}_0 - t\vec{d}_1) \cdot ((P_0 - P_1) + s\vec{d}_0 - t\vec{d}_1)$$

This is a quadratic function in s and t; that is, it is a function $f(s, t)$ whose shape is a paraboloid. For the case of lines, the domain of s and t is unrestricted, and the solution $\{s_c, t_c\}$ corresponds to the point where f is minimized (that is, the "bottom" of the paraboloid).

However, if either of the linear components is a ray or line segment, then the domain of s and/or t is restricted—in the case of a ray, s (or t) must be nonnegative, and in the case of a line segment, $0 \leq s \leq 1$ (and similarly for t). We can create a table of all the possible combinations of domain restrictions (see Figure 10.28).

In general, the global minimum of the quadratic function may not be *within* the restricted domain; in such cases, the minimum will be at some point *along* one of the boundary edges of the domain. The partitioning of the domain resulting from the restriction of the parameter values for either linear component can be used to generate an algorithm that classifies the location of (s_c, t_c), and then applies a "custom" set of operations to determine the actual closest points and their distance (Section 10.8.3 shows this approach for the intersection of two line segments). However, a somewhat simpler scheme due to Dan Sunday (2001b) can also be employed.

Analogous to the approach of categorizing the region in which (s_c, t_c) lies, this approach considers which edges of the bounded domain are "visible" to (s_c, t_c). For example, in the case of segment/segment distance, the domain is restricted to $[0, 1] \times [0, 1]$. Figure 10.29 shows two of the possible visibility conditions for a solution: on the left, only the boundary $t = 1$ is visible, and on the right, both $s = 1$ and $t = 1$ are visible.

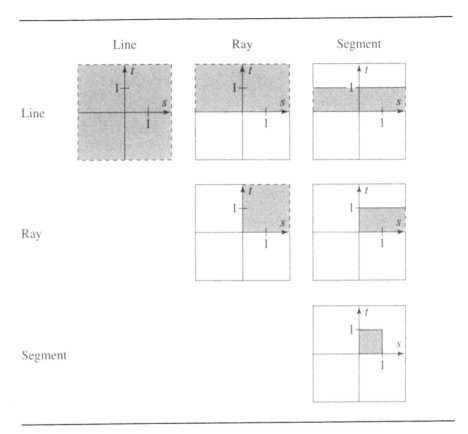

Figure 10.28   Domains for each possible combination of linear component distance calculation.

By simply comparing the values of s_c and t_c, we can easily determine which domain boundary edges are visible. For each visible boundary edge, we can compute the point on it closest to (s_c, t_c). If only one boundary edge is visible, then that closest solution point will be in the range $[0, 1]$; otherwise, the closest solution point will be outside that range, and thus we need to check the other visible edge.

The basic idea is to first compute the closest points of the infinite lines on which the ray(s) or segment(s) lie—that is, s_c and t_c. If both of these values are within the domain of the parameters s and t, respectively, of the linear components, then we are done. However, if one or both the linear components are not infinite lines and are instead a ray(s) or segment(s), then the domains of s and/or t are restricted, and we must find the points that minimize the squared-distance function over the restricted domains; these points will have parameter values that correspond to points on the boundary.

In Sunday (2001b), we see that we can easily compute the closest points on the boundary edges by employing a little calculus. For the case of the edge $s = 0$, we have

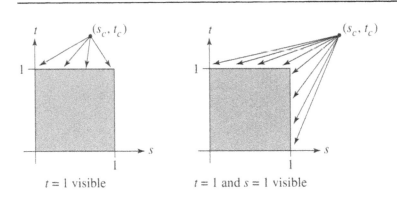

Figure 10.29   Definition of visibility of domain boundaries.

$\|\vec{v}\|^2 = (\vec{u} - t\vec{d}_1) \cdot (\vec{u} - t\vec{d}_1)$, where $\vec{u} = P_0 - P_1$. The derivative of this with respect to t gives us

$$0 = \frac{d}{dt}\|\vec{v}|^2$$

$$= -2\vec{d}_1 \cdot (\vec{u} - t\vec{d}_1)$$

giving us a minimum at

$$t' = \frac{\vec{d}_1 \cdot \vec{u}}{\vec{d}_1 \cdot \vec{d}_1}$$

If $0 \leq t' \leq 1$, then this is the actual solution; otherwise, the actual solution is 1 if $t' > 1$ or 0 if $t' < 0$.

The case for the edge $t = 0$ is exactly analogous: In this case we have $\|\vec{v}\|^2 = (-\vec{u} - s\vec{d}_0) \cdot (-\vec{u} - s\vec{d}_0)$. The derivative of this with respect to s gives us

$$0 = \frac{d}{ds}\|\vec{v}|^2$$

$$= -2\vec{d}_0 \cdot (-\vec{u} - s\vec{d}_0)$$

giving us a minimum at

$$s' = \frac{-\vec{d}_0 \cdot \vec{u}}{\vec{d}_0 \cdot \vec{d}_0}$$

If $0 \le s' \le 1$, then this is the actual solution; otherwise, the actual solution is 1 if $s' > 1$ or 0 if $s' < 0$.

In the case of edge $s = 1$, we have $\|\vec{v}\|^2 = (\vec{u} + \vec{d}_0 - t\vec{d}_1) \cdot (\vec{u} + \vec{d}_0 - t\vec{d}_1)$. Taking the derivative with respect to t gives us

$$0 = \frac{d}{dt}\|\vec{v}\|^2$$

$$= -2\vec{d}_1(\vec{u} - t\vec{d}_1 + \vec{d}_0)$$

giving us a minimum at

$$t' = \frac{\vec{d}_1 \cdot \vec{u} + \vec{d}_0 \cdot \vec{d}_1}{\vec{d}_1 \cdot \vec{d}_1}$$

If $0 \le t' \le 1$, then this is the actual solution; otherwise, the actual solution is 1 if $t' > 1$ or 0 if $t' < 0$.

In the case of edge $t = 1$, we have $\|\vec{v}\|^2 = (-\vec{u} + \vec{d}_1 - s\vec{d}_0) \cdot (-\vec{u} + \vec{d}_1 - s\vec{d}_0)$. Taking the derivative with respect to s gives us

$$0 = \frac{d}{ds}\|\vec{v}\|^2$$

$$= -2\vec{d}_0(-\vec{u} - s\vec{d}_0 + \vec{d}_1)$$

giving us a minimum at

$$s' = \frac{-\vec{d}_0 \cdot \vec{u} + \vec{d}_1 \cdot \vec{d}_0}{\vec{d}_0 \cdot \vec{d}_0}$$

If $0 \le s' \le 1$, then this is the actual solution; otherwise, the actual solution is 1 if $s' > 1$ or 0 if $s' < 0$.

Figure 10.30 should make this more clear, but note that the figures are intended to be schematic. It is not necessary that the two linear components be perpendicular.

Segment to Segment

Figure 10.31 shows two line segments we want to find the distance between, and the restricted domain for the solution. In this case, the domain of the solution is restricted to $[0, 1] \times [0, 1]$; the domain is bounded on all four sides: $s = 0, s = 1, t = 0$, and $t = 1$. If *either* s_c or t_c lies outside this region, we have to find the point on the boundary edge of the domain that is closest to the solution point (s_c, t_c). The domain

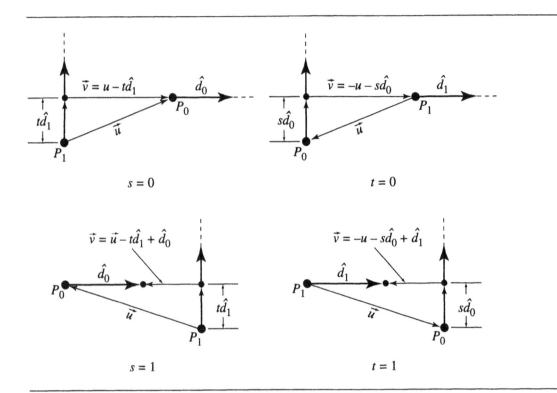

Figure 10.30   Cases for the four edges of the domain.

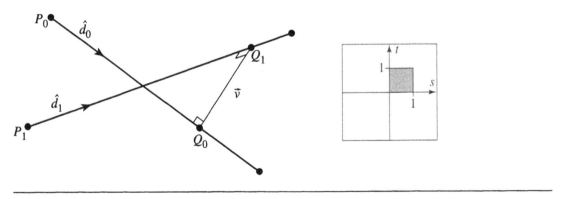

Figure 10.31   Distance between two line segments.

is bounded on all four sides, but clearly we need only to find the boundary point on at most two of the edges.

The pseudocode is

```
float SegmentSegmentDistance3D(Segment seg0, Segment seg1)
{
    u = seg0.base - seg1.base;
    a = Dot(seg0.direction, seg0.direction);
    b = Dot(seg0.direction, seg1.direction);
    c = Dot(seg1.direction, seg1.direction);
    d = Dot(seg0.direction, u);
    e = Dot(seg1.direction, u);
    det = a * c - b * b;

    // Check for (near) parallelism
    if (det < epsilon) {
        // Arbitrary choice
        sNum = 0;
        tNum = e;
        tDenom = c;
        sDenom = det;
    } else {
        // Find parameter values of closest points
        // on each segment's infinite line. Denominator
        // assumed at this point to be ''det'',
        // which is always positive. We can check
        // value of numerators to see if we're outside
        // the [0, 1] x [0, 1] domain.
        sNum = b * e - c * d;
        tNum = a * e - b * d;
    }

    // Check s
    sDenom = det;
    if (sNum < 0) {
        sNum = 0;
        tNum = e;
        tDenom = c;
    } else if (sNum > det) {
        sNum = det;
        tNum = e + b;
        tDenom = c;
    } else {
```

```
        tDenom = det;
    }

    //  Check t
    if (tNum < 0) {
        tNum = 0;
        if (-d < 0) {
            sNum = 0;
        } else if (-d > a) {
            sNum = sDenom;
        } else {
            sNum = -d;
            sDenom = a;
        }
    } else if (tNum > tDenom) {
        tNum = tDenom;
        if ((-d + b) < 0) {
            sNum = 0;
        } else if ((-d + b) > a) {
            sNum = sDenom;
        } else {
            sNum = -d + b;
            sDenom = a;
        }
    }

    //  Parameters of nearest points on restricted domain
    s = sNum / sDenom;
    t = tNum / tDenom;

    //  Dot product of vector between points is squared distance
    //  between segments
    v = seg0.base + (s * seg0.direction) - seg1.base + (t * seg1.direction);
    return Dot(v,v);
}
```

Line to Ray

Figure 10.32 shows two line segments we want to find the distance between, and the restricted domain for the solution. In the case of a line/ray distance test, the domain of the distance function is $[-\infty, \infty] \times [0, \infty]$ (or vice versa); the domain is bounded on one side only, corresponding to either $s = 0$ or $t = 0$. If the parameter of the closest point on the ray's infinite line is less than 0, then we need only compute the nearest point along that one edge.

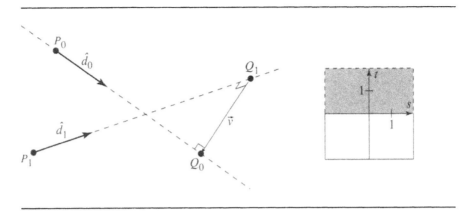

Figure 10.32   Distance between a line and a ray.

The pseudocode is

```
float LineRayDistance3D(Line line, Ray ray)
{
    u = line.base - ray.base;
    a = Dot(line.direction, line.direction);
    b = Dot(line.direction, ray.direction);
    c = Dot(line.direction, ray.direction);
    d = Dot(line.direction, u);
    e = Dot(ray.direction, u);
    det = a * c - b * b;
    sDenom = det;

    // Check for (near) parallelism
    if (det < epsilon) {
        // Arbitrary choice
        sNum = 0;
        tNum = e;
        tDenom = c;
    } else {
        // Find parameter values of closest points
        // on each segment's infinite line. Denominator
        // assumed at this point to be ''det'',
        // which is always positive. We can check
        // value of numerators to see if we're outside
        // the (-inf, inf) x [0, inf) domain.
        sNum = b * e - c * d;
        tNum = a * e - b * d;
    }
```

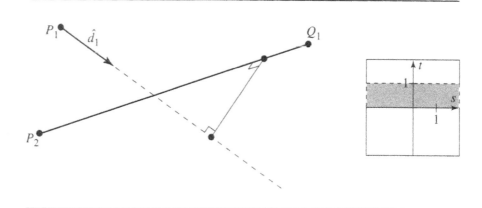

Figure 10.33   Distance between a line and a line segment.

```
// Check t
if (tNum < 0) {
    tNum = 0;
    sNum = -d;
    sDenom = a;
}

// Parameters of nearest points on restricted domain
s = sNum / sDenom;
t = tNum / tDenom;

// Dot product of vector between points is squared distance
// between segments
v = line.base + (s * line.direction) - s1.base + (t * ray.direction);
return Dot(v,v);
}
```

Line to Segment

Figure 10.33 shows two line segments we want to find the distance between, and the restricted domain for the solution. In the case of a line/segment distance test, the domain of the distance function is $[-\infty, \infty] \times [0, 1]$ (or vice versa); the domain is bounded on opposite sides, corresponding to either $s = 0$ and $s = 1$, or $t = 0$ and $t = 1$. If the parameter of the closest point on the segment's infinite line is less than 0 or greater than 1, then we need to compute the nearest point along one of those two edges.

The pseudocode is

```
float LineSegmentDistance3D(Line line, Segment s)
{
    u = line.base - seg.base;
    a = Dot(line.direction, line.direction);
    b = Dot(line.direction, seg.direction);
    c = Dot(seg.direction, seg.direction);
    d = Dot(line.direction, u);
    e = Dot(seg.direction, u);
    det = a * c - b * b;
    sDenom = det;

    // Check for (near) parallelism
    if (det < epsilon) {
        // Arbitrary choice
        sNum = 0;
        tNum = e;
        tDenom = c;
    } else {
        // Find parameter values of closest points
        // on each segment's infinite line. Denominator
        // assumed at this point to be ''det'',
        // which is always positive. We can check
        // value of numerators to see if we're outside
        // the [0,1] x [0,1] domain.
        sNum = b * e - c * d;
        tNum = a * e - b * d;
    }

    // Check t
    if (tNum < 0) {
        tNum = 0;
        sNum = -d;
        sDenom = a;
    } else if (tNum > tDenom) {
        tNum = tDenom;
        sNum = -d + b;
        sDenom = a;
    }

    // Parameters of nearest points on restricted domain
    s = sNum / sDenom;
    t = tNum / tDenom;
```

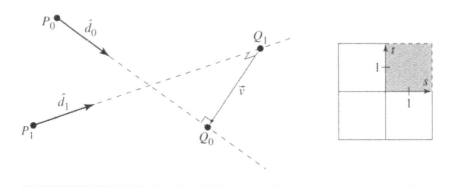

Figure 10.34   Distance between two rays.

```
    // Dot product of vector between points is squared distance
    // between segments
    v = line.base + (s * line.direction) - seg.base + (t * seg.direction);
    return Dot(v,v);
}
```

Ray to Ray

Figure 10.34 shows two line segments we want to find the distance between, and the restricted domain for the solution. In the case of a ray/ray distance test, the domain of the distance function is $[0, \infty] \times [0, \infty]$; the domain is bounded on two adjacent sides, corresponding to $s = 0$ and $t = 0$. If the parameter of the closest point on either ray's infinite line is less than 0, then we need to compute the nearest points on either or both of the $s = 0$ and $t = 0$ edges.

The pseudocode is

```
float RayRayDistance3D(Ray ray0, Ray ray1)
{
    u = ray0.base - ray1.base;
    a = Dot(ray0.direction, ray0.direction);
    b = Dot(ray0.direction, ray1.direction);
    c = Dot(ray1.direction, ray1.direction);
    d = Dot(ray0.direction, u);
    e = Dot(ray1.direction, u);
    det = a * c - b * b;

    // Check for (near) parallelism
```

```
    if (det < epsilon) {
        // Arbitrary choice
        sNum = 0;
        tNum = e;
        tDenom = c;
        sDenom = det;
    } else {
        // Find parameter values of closest points
        // on each segment's infinite line. Denominator
        // assumed at this point to be ''det'',
        // which is always positive. We can check
        // value of numerators to see if we're outside
        // the [0, inf) x [0, inf) domain.
        sNum = b * e - c * d;
        tNum = a * e - b * d;
    }

    // Check s
    sDenom = det;
    if (sNum < 0) {
        sNum = 0;
        tNum = e;
        tDenom = c;
    }

    // Check t
    if (tNum < 0) {
        tNum = 0;
        if (-d < 0) {
            sNum = 0;
        } else {
            sNum = -d;
            sDenom = a;
        }
    }

    // Parameters of nearest points on restricted domain
    s = sNum / sDenom;
    t = tNum / tDenom;

    // Dot product of vector between points is squared distance
    // between segments
    v = ray0.base + (s * ray0.direction) - ray1.base + (t * ray1.direction);
    return Dot(v,v);
}
```

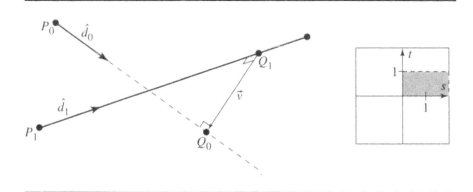

Figure 10.35   Distance between a ray and a line segment.

Ray to Segment

Figure 10.35 shows two line segments we want to find the distance between, and the restricted domain for the solution. In the case of a ray/segment distance test, the domain of the distance function is $[0, \infty] \times [0, 1]$ (or vice versa); the domain is bounded on three sides: either $s = 0, s = 1$, and $t = 0$, or $t = 0, t = 1$, and $s = 0$. If the parameter of the closest point on the ray's infinite line is less than 0, or if the parameter of the closest point on the segment's infinite line is less than 0 or greater than 1, then we need to compute the nearest point on at most two of those edges.

The pseudocode is

```
float RaySegmentDistance3D(Ray ray, Segment seg)
{
    u = ray.base - seg.base;
    a = Dot(ray.direction, ray.direction);
    b = Dot(ray.direction, seg.direction);
    c = Dot(seg.direction, seg.direction);
    d = Dot(ray.direction, u);
    e = Dot(seg.direction, u);
    det = a * c - b * b;

    // Check for (near) parallelism
    if (det < epsilon) {
        // Arbitrary choice
        sNum = 0;
        tNum = e;
        tDenom = c;
```

```
        sDenom = det;
    } else {
        //  Find parameter values of closest points
        //  on each segment's infinite line. Denominator
        //  assumed at this point to be ''det'',
        //  which is always positive. We can check
        //  value of numerators to see if we're outside
        //  the [0, inf) x [0,1] domain.
        sNum = b * e - c * d;
        tNum = a * e - b * d;
    }

    //  Check s
    sDenom = det;
    if (sNum < 0) {
        sNum = 0;
        tNum = e;
        tDenom = c;
    } else {
        tDenom = det;
    }

    //  Check t
    if (tNum < 0) {
        tNum = 0;
        if (-d < 0) {
            sNum = 0;
        } else {
            sNum = -d;
            sDenom = a;
        }
    } else if (tNum > tDenom) {
        tNum = tDenom;
        if ((-d + b) < 0) {
            sNum = 0;
        } else {
            sNum = -d + b;
            sDenom = a;
        }
    }

    //  Parameters of nearest points on restricted domain
    s = sNum / sDenom;
    t = tNum / tDenom;
```

```
    // Dot product of vector between points is squared distance
    // between segments
    v = ray.base + (s * ray.direction) - seg.base + (t * seg.direction);
    return Dot(v,v);
}
```

10.8.3   SEGMENT TO SEGMENT, ALTERNATIVE APPROACH

The problem is to compute the minimum distance between points on two line segments $\mathcal{L}_0(s) = B_0 + s\vec{m}_0$ for $s \in [0, 1]$ and $\mathcal{L}_1(t) = B_1 + t\vec{m}_1$ for $t \in [0, 1]$. The minimum distance is computed by locating the values $\bar{s} \in [0, 1]$ and $\bar{t} \in [0, 1]$ corresponding to the two closest points on the line segments.

The squared-distance function for any two points on the line segments is $Q(s, t) = \|\mathcal{L}_0(s) - \mathcal{L}_1(t)\|^2$ for $(s, t) \in [0, 1]^2$. The function is quadratic in s and t

$$Q(s, t) = as^2 + 2bst + ct^2 + 2ds + 2et + f$$

where $a = \vec{m}_0 \cdot \vec{m}_0, b = -\vec{m}_0 \cdot \vec{m}_1, c = \vec{m}_1 \cdot \vec{m}_1, d = \vec{m}_0 \cdot (B_0 - B_1), e = -\vec{m}_1 \cdot (B_0 - B_1)$, and $f = (B_0 - B_1) \cdot (B_0 - B_1)$. Quadratics are classified by the sign of $ac - b^2$. For function Q,

$$ac - b^2 = (\vec{m}_0 \cdot \vec{m}_0)(\vec{m}_1 \cdot \vec{m}_1) - (\vec{m}_0 \cdot \vec{m}_1)^2 = \|\vec{m}_0 \times \vec{m}_1\|^2 \geq 0$$

If $ac - b^2 > 0$, then the two line segments are not parallel and the graph of Q is a paraboloid. If $ac - b^2 = 0$, then the two line segments are parallel and the graph of Q is a parabolic cylinder.

In calculus terms, the goal is to minimize $Q(s, t)$ over the unit square $[0, 1]^2$. Since Q is a continuously differentiable function, the minimum occurs either at an interior point of the square where the gradient $\nabla Q = 2(as + bt + d, bs + ct + e) = (0, 0)$ or at a point on the boundary of the square.

Nonparallel Line Segments

When $ac - b^2 > 0$ the line segments are not parallel. The gradient of Q is zero only when $\bar{s} = (be - cd)/(ac - b^2)$ and $\bar{t} = (bd - ae)/(ac - b^2)$. If $(\bar{s}, \bar{t}) \in [0, 1]^2$, then we have found the minimum of Q. Otherwise, the minimum must occur on the boundary of the square. To find the correct boundary, consider Figure 10.36. The central square labeled region 0 is the domain of Q, $(s, t) \in [0, 1]^2$. If $(\bar{s}, \bar{t})$ is in region 0, then the two closest points on the 3D line segments are interior points of those segments.

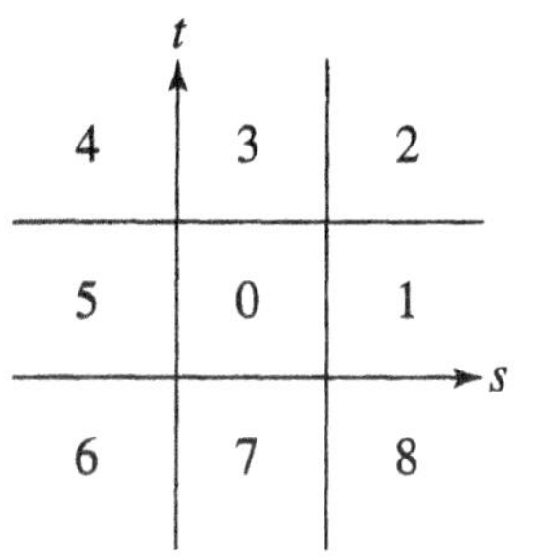

Figure 10.36   Partitioning of the st-plane by the unit square.

Suppose $(\bar{s}, \bar{t})$ is in region 1. The level curves of Q are those curves in the st-plane for which Q is a constant. Since the graph of Q is a paraboloid, the level curves are ellipses. At the point where $\nabla Q = (0, 0)$, the level curve degenerates to a single point $(\bar{s}, \bar{t})$. The global minimum of Q occurs there; call it $V_{\min}$. As the level values V increase from $V_{\min}$, the corresponding ellipses are increasingly further away from $(\bar{s}, \bar{t})$. There is a smallest level value V_0 for which the corresponding ellipse (implicitly defined by $Q = V_0$) just touches the unit square edge $s = 1$ at a value $t = t_0 \in [0, 1]$. For level values $V < V_0$, the corresponding ellipses do not intersect the unit square. For level values $V > V_0$, portions of the unit square lie inside the corresponding ellipses. In particular any points of intersection of such an ellipse with the edge must have a level value $V > V_0$. Therefore, $Q(1, t) > Q(1, t_0)$ for $t \in [0, 1]$ and $t \neq t_0$. The point $(1, t_0)$ provides the minimum squared distance between two points on the 3D line segments. The point on the first line segment is an end point, and the point on the second line segment is interior to that segment. Figure 10.37 illustrates the idea by showing various level curves.

An alternative way of visualizing where the minimum distance point occurs on the boundary is to intersect the graph of Q with the plane $s = 1$. The curve of intersection is a parabola and is the graph of $F(t) = Q(1, t)$ for $t \in [0, 1]$. Now the problem has been reduced by one dimension to minimizing a function $F(t)$ for $t \in [0, 1]$. The minimum of $F(t)$ occurs either at an interior point of $[0, 1]$, in which case $F'(t) = 0$ at that point, or at an end point $t = 0$ or $t = 1$. Figure 10.37 shows the case when the minimum occurs at an interior point. At that point the ellipse is tangent to the line $s = 1$. In the end point cases, the ellipse may just touch one of the corners of the unit square, but not necessarily tangentially.

To distinguish between the interior point and end point cases, the same partitioning idea applies in the one-dimensional case. The interval $[0, 1]$ partitions the real line into three intervals, $t < 0$, $t \in [0, 1]$, and $t > 1$. Let $F'(\hat{t}) = 0$. If $\hat{t} < 0$, then $F(t)$

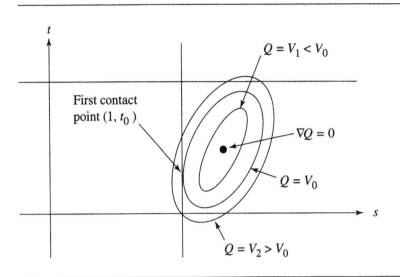

Figure 10.37   Various level curves $Q(s, t) = V$.

is an increasing function for $t \in [0, 1]$. The minimum restricted to $[0, 1]$ must occur at $t = 0$, in which case Q attains its minimum at $(s, t) = (1, 0)$. If $\hat{t} > 1$, then $F(t)$ is a decreasing function for $t \in [0, 1]$. The minimum for F occurs at $t = 1$, and the minimum for Q occurs at $(s, t) = (1, 1)$. Otherwise, $\hat{t} \in [0, 1]$, F attains its minimum at $\hat{t}$, and Q attains its minimum at $(s, t) = (1, \hat{t})$.

The occurrence of $(\bar{s}, \bar{t})$ in region 3, 5, or 7 is handled in a similar fashion as when the global minimum is in region 0. If $(\bar{s}, \bar{t})$ is in region 3, then the minimum occurs at $(s_0, 1)$ for some $s_0 \in [0, 1]$. If $(\bar{s}, \bar{t})$ is in region 5, then the minimum occurs at $(0, t_0)$ for some $t \in [0, 1]$. Finally, if $(\bar{s}, \bar{t})$ is in region 7, then the minimum occurs at $(s_0, 0)$ for some $s_0 \in [0, 1]$. Determining if the first contact point is at an interior or end point of the appropriate interval is handled the same as discussed earlier.

If $(\bar{s}, \bar{t})$ is in region 2, it is possible the level curve of Q that provides first contact with the unit square touches either edge $s = 1$ or edge $t = 1$. Because the global minimum occurs in region 2, the gradient at the corner $(1, 1)$ cannot point inside the unit square. If $\nabla Q = (Q_s, Q_t)$, where Q_s and Q_t are the partial derivatives of Q, it must be that the partial derivatives cannot both be negative. The choice of edge $s = 1$ or $t = 1$ can be made based on the signs of $Q_s(1, 1)$ and $Q_t(1, 1)$. If $Q_s(1, 1) > 0$, then the minimum must occur on edge $t = 1$ since $Q(s, 1) < Q(1, 1)$ for $s < 1$ but close to 1. Similarly, if $Q_t(1, 1) > 0$, then the minimum must occur on edge $s = 1$. Determining whether the minimum is interior to the edge or at an end point is handled as in the case of region 1. The occurrence of $(\bar{s}, \bar{t})$ in regions 4, 6, and 8 is handled similarly.

Parallel Line Segments

When $ac - b^2 = 0$, the gradient of Q is zero on an entire st-line, $s = -(bt + d)/a$ for all $t \in \mathbb{R}$. If any pair (s, t) satisfying this equation is in $[0, 1]$, then that pair leads to two points on the 3D lines that are closest. Otherwise, the minimum must occur on the boundary of the square. Rather than solving the problem using minimization, we take advantage of the fact that the line segments lie on parallel lines.

The origin of the first line is assumed to be B_0, and the line direction is $\vec{m}_0$. The first line segment is parameterized as $B_0 + s\vec{m}_0$ for $s \in [0, 1]$. The second line segment can be projected onto the first line. The end point B_1 can be represented as

$$B_1 = B_0 + \sigma_0 \vec{m}_0 + \vec{u}_0$$

where $\vec{u}_0$ is a vector orthogonal to $\vec{m}_0$. The coefficient of $\vec{m}_0$ is

$$\sigma_0 = \frac{\vec{m}_0 \cdot (B_1 - B_0)}{\vec{m}_0 \cdot \vec{m}_0} = -\frac{d}{a}$$

where a and d are some coefficients of $Q(s, t)$ defined earlier. The other end point $B_1 + \vec{m}_1$ can be represented as

$$B_1 + \vec{m}_1 = B_0 + \sigma_1 \vec{m}_0 + \vec{u}_1$$

where $\vec{u}_1$ is a vector orthogonal to $\vec{m}_0$. The coefficient of $\vec{m}_0$ is

$$\sigma_1 = \frac{\vec{m}_0 \cdot (\vec{m}_1 + B_1 - B_0)}{\vec{m}_0 \cdot \vec{m}_0} = -\frac{b + d}{a}$$

where b is also a coefficient of $Q(s, t)$. The problem now reduces to determining the relative position of $[\min(\sigma_0, \sigma_1), \max(\sigma_0, \sigma_1)]$ with respect to $[0, 1]$. If the two intervals are disjoint, then the minimum distance occurs at end points of the two 3D line segments. If the two intervals overlap, then there are many pairs of points at which the minimum distance is attained. In this case the implementation returns a pair of points, an end point of one line and an interior point of the other line.

Implementation

The implementation of the algorithm is designed so that at most one floating-point division is used when computing the minimum distance and corresponding closest points. Moreover, the division is deferred until it is needed. In some cases no division is needed.

Quantities that are used throughout the code are computed first. In particular, the values computed are $\vec{d} = B_0 - B_1$, $a = \vec{m}_0 \cdot \vec{m}_0$, $b = -\vec{m}_0 \cdot \vec{m}_1$, $c = \vec{m}_1 \cdot \vec{m}_1$,

$d = \vec{m}_0 \cdot \vec{d}$, $e = -\vec{m}_1 \cdot \vec{d}$, and $f = \vec{d} \cdot \vec{d}$. We also need to determine immediately whether or not the two line segments are parallel. The quadratic classifier is $\delta = ac - b^2$ and is also computed initially. The code actually computes $\delta = |ac - b^2|$ since it is possible for nearly parallel lines that some floating-point round-off errors lead to a small negative quantity. Finally, δ is compared to a floating-point tolerance value. If larger, the two line segments are nonparallel, and the code for that case is processed. If smaller, the two line segments are assumed to be parallel, and the code for that case is processed.

Nonparallel Line Segments

In the theoretical development, we computed $\bar{s} = (be - cd)/\delta$ and $(bd - ae)/\delta$ so that $\nabla Q(\bar{s}, \bar{t}) = (0, 0)$. The location of the global minimum is then tested to see if it is in the unit square $[0, 1]$. If so, then we have already determined what we need to compute minimum distance. If not, then the boundary of the unit square must be tested. To defer the division by δ, the code instead computes $\bar{s} = be - cd$ and $\bar{t} = bd - ae$ and tests for containment in $[0, \delta]^2$. If in that set, then the divisions are performed. If not, then the boundary of the unit square is tested.

The general outline of the conditionals for determining which region contains $(\bar{s}, \bar{t})$ is

```
det = a * c - b * b;  s = b * e - c * d;  t = b * d - a * e;
if (s >= 0) {
    if (s <= det) {
        if (t >= 0) {
            if (t <= det) {
                region 0
            } else {
                region 3
            }
        } else {
            region 7
        }
    } else {
        if (t >= 0) {
            if (t <= det) {
                region 1
            } else {
                region 2
            }
        } else {
            region 8
        }
    }
}
```

```
} else {
    if (t >= 0) {
        if (t <= det) {
            region 5
        } else {
            region 4
        }
    } else {
        region 6
    }
}
```

The block of code for handling region 0 is

```
invDet = 1 / det;
s *= invDet;
t *= invDet;
```

and requires a single division.

The block of code for handling region 1 is

```
// F(t) = Q(1, t) = (a + 2 * d + f) + 2 * (b + e) * t + (c) * t^2
// F'(t) = 2 * ((b + e) + c * t)
// F'(T) = 0 when T = -(b + e) / c
s = 1;
tmp = b + e;
if (tmp > 0)   // T < 0, so minimum at t = 0
    t = 0;
else if (-tmp > c)   // T > 1, so minimum at t = 1
    t = 1;
else   // 0 <= T <= 1, so minimum at t = T
    t = -tmp / c;
```

Notice that at most one division occurs in this block during run time. Code blocks for regions 3, 5, and 7 are similar.

The block of code for handling region 2 is

```
// Q_s(1, 1) / 2 = a + b + d,  Q_t(1, 1) / 2 = b + c + e
tmp = b + d;
if (-tmp < a)   // Q_s(1, 1) > 0
{
    // F(s) = Q(s, 1) = (c + 2 * e + f) + 2 * (b + d) * s + (a) * s^2
    // F'(s) = 2 * ((b + d) + a * s), F'(S) = 0 when S = -(b + d) / a < 1
    t = 1;
```

```
        if (tmp > 0)  // S < 0, so minimum at s = 0
            s = 0;
        else  // 0 <= S < 1, so minimum at s = S
            s = -tmp / a;
    } else {
        // Q_s(1,1) <= 0
        s = 1;
        tmp = b + e;
        if (-tmp < c) {
            // Q_t(1,1) > 0
            // F(t) = Q(1,t) = (a + 2 * d + f) + 2 * (b + e) * t + (c) * t^2
            // F'(t) = 2 * ((b + e) + c * t), F'(T) = 0 when T = -(b + e) / c < 1
            if (tmp > 0)  // T < 0, so minimum at t = 0
                t = 0
            else  // 0 <= T < 1, so minimum at t = T
                t = -tmp / c;
        } else {
            // Q_t(1,1) <= 0, gradient points to region 2, so minimum at t = 1
            t = 1;
        }
    }
}
```

Notice that at most one division occurs in this block during run time. Code blocks for regions 4, 6, and 8 are similar.

Parallel Line Segments

The first information to be computed is the ordering of $\sigma_0 = -d/a$ and $\sigma_1 = -(b + d)/a$. Once the ordering is known, we can compare the two s-intervals to determine minimum distance. Note that $-d/a$ corresponds to $t = 0$ and $-(b + d)/a$ corresponds to $t = 1$.

```
if (b > 0) {
    // compare intervals [-(b + d) / a, -d / a] to [0, 1]
    if (d >= 0)
        // -d / a <= 0, so minimum is at s = 0, t = 0
    else if (-d <= a)
        // 0 < -d / a <= 1, so minimum is at s = -d / a, t = 0
    else
        // minimum occurs at s = 1, need to determine t (see below)
} else {
    // compare intervals [-d / a, -(b + d) / a] to [0, 1]
    if (-d >= a)
        // 1 <= -d / a, so minimum is at s = 1, t = 0
```

```
        else if (d <= 0)
            // 0 <= -d / a < 1, so minimum is at s = -d / a, t = 0
        else
            // minimum occurs at s = 0, need to determine t (see below)
}
```

When $b > 0$, the remaining problem is to determine on which side of $s = 1$ is the quantity $-(b + d)/a$. We do so by first finding that value of t for which $-(bt + d)/a \in [-(b + d)/a, -d/a]$ corresponds to $s = 1$. Simply set $-(bt + d)/a = 1$ and solve for $t = -(a + d)/b$. By the time we get to this case at run time, we know $a + d < 0$, so $t > 0$. If $t \leq 1$, then we can use it as is. But if $t > 1$, then we clip to $t = 1$. The block of code is

```
tmp = a + d;
if (-tmp >= b) t = 1; else t = -tmp / b;
```

Again note that the division is deferred until actually needed.

When $b < 0$, the remaining problem is to determine on which side of $s = 0$ is the quantity $-(b + d)/a$. Set $-(bt + d)/a = 0$ and solve for $t = -d/b$. By the time we get to this case at run time, we know $d > 0$, so $t > 0$. If $t \leq 1$, then we can use it as is. But if $t > 1$, then we clip to $t = 1$. The block of code is

```
if (d >= -b) t = 1; else t = -d / b;
```

10.9 LINEAR COMPONENT TO TRIANGLE, RECTANGLE, TETRAHEDRON, ORIENTED BOX

In this section, we discuss the problem of computing the distance between linear components and two planar components—triangles and rectangles—and two particular polyhedra—tetrahedra and oriented bounding boxes.

10.9.1 LINEAR COMPONENT TO TRIANGLE

In this section, we consider the problem of computing the distance between a linear component and a triangle, as shown in Figure 10.38. For this problem, we represent the linear component parametrically: the line is defined by a point and a direction vector

$$\mathcal{L}(t) = P + t\vec{d}, \quad t \in D_{\mathcal{L}}$$

where $-\infty \leq t \leq \infty$ for a line, $0 \leq t \leq \infty$ for a ray, and $0 \leq t \leq 1$ for a segment (where P_0 and P_1 are the end points of the segment and $\vec{d} = P_1 - P_0$). Triangles

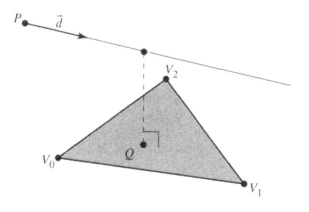

Figure 10.38   Distance between a line and a triangle.

are typically represented as three vertices V_0, V_1, and V_2. For the purposes of this problem, however, we use a parametric representation:

$$\mathcal{T}(u, v) = V + u\vec{e}_0 + v\vec{e}_1$$

where V is a vertex of the triangle, say, V_0, and $\vec{e}_0 = V_1 - V_0$ and $\vec{e}_1 = V_2 - V_0$. Any point in the triangle can then be described in terms of the two parameters u and v, with $0 \leq u, v \leq 1$, and $u + v \leq 1$ (see Figure 10.39). Computing the distance between the linear component and the triangle means that we must find the values of t, u, and v that minimize the (squared) distance function

$$Q(u, v, t) = \|\mathcal{T}(u, v) - \mathcal{L}(t)\|^2$$

Expanding terms and multiplying, we get

$$
\begin{aligned}
Q(u, v, t) ={}& \|\mathcal{T}(u, v) - \mathcal{L}(t)\|^2 \\
={}& (\vec{e}_0 \cdot \vec{e}_0)u^2 + (\vec{e}_1 \cdot \vec{e}_1)v^2 + (\vec{d} \cdot \vec{d})t^2 \\
& + 2(\vec{e}_0 \cdot \vec{e}_1)uv + 2(-\vec{e}_0 \cdot \vec{d})ut + 2(-\vec{e}_1 \cdot \vec{d})vt \\
& + 2(\vec{e}_0 \cdot (V - P))u + 2(\vec{e}_1 \cdot (V - P))v + 2(-\vec{d} \cdot (V - P))t \\
& + (V - P) \cdot (V - P)
\end{aligned}
$$

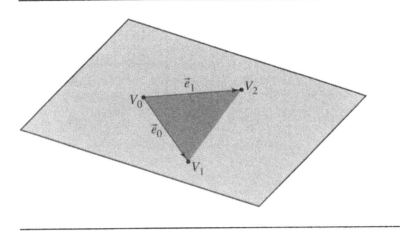

Figure 10.39   Parametric representation of a triangle.

or, more compactly

$$Q(u, v, t) = a_{00}u^2 + a_{11}v^2 + a_{22}t^2 + 2a_{01}uv + 2a_{02}ut + 2a_{12}vt + 2b_0u$$
$$+ 2b_1v + 2b_2t + c \qquad (10.14)$$

where

$$a_{00} = \vec{e}_0 \cdot \vec{e}_0$$
$$a_{11} = \vec{e}_1 \cdot \vec{e}_1$$
$$a_{22} = \vec{d} \cdot \vec{d}$$
$$a_{01} = \vec{e}_0 \cdot \vec{e}_1$$
$$a_{02} = -\vec{e}_0 \cdot \vec{d}$$
$$a_{12} = -\vec{e}_1 \cdot \vec{d}$$
$$b_0 = \vec{e}_0 \cdot (V - P)$$
$$b_1 = \vec{e}_1 \cdot (V - P)$$
$$b_2 = -\vec{d} \cdot (V - P)$$
$$c = (V - P) \cdot (V - P)$$

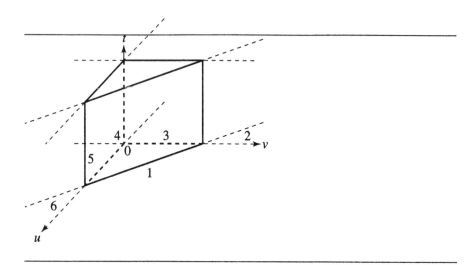

Figure 10.40   Possible partitionings of the solution space for the linear component/triangle distance problem.

As the solution to this consists of three values (u_0, v_0, t_0), we can think of the solution space as three spatial dimensions (not to be confused with the 3D space in which the linear component and the triangle lie). This is analogous to the partitioning of the two-dimensional solution space domain in the point-triangle distance test shown in Figure 10.9, except that we now have a third dimension corresponding to the parameter t of the linear component. For linear components, we have three possible domains, and so there are three possible partitionings of the solution space:

■ Line: an infinite triangular prism

■ Line segment: a finite triangular prism

■ Ray: a semi-infinite triangular prism

The case for a line segment is shown in Figure 10.40.

If the configuration of the triangle and linear component are such that the point on the plane containing the triangle that is nearest to the linear component actually lies within the triangle, and the point on the linear segment nearest the triangle is within the bounds (if any) of the linear segment, then the solution $(\bar{u}, \bar{v}, \bar{t})$ will lie within region 0 of the solution domain's triangular prism; the distance between the linear segment and the triangle will be $\| \mathcal{T}(\bar{u}, \bar{v}, \bar{t}) - \mathcal{L}(t) \|$. Otherwise, the minimum of $\nabla Q = (\bar{u}, \bar{v}, \bar{t})$ will be on a face separating the regions (and where it lies on a face may be along an edge or vertex of the boundaries between regions).

The first step in the algorithm is to find the values of u, v, and t that minimize the squared-distance function of Equation 10.14. Formally, we must find where the gradient $\nabla Q = 0$; this can be expressed as finding the solution to the system of equations

$$\begin{bmatrix} a_{00} & a_{01} & a_{02} \\ a_{10} & a_{11} & a_{12} \\ a_{20} & a_{21} & a_{22} \end{bmatrix} \begin{bmatrix} b_0 \\ b_1 \\ b_2 \end{bmatrix} = \begin{bmatrix} u \\ v \\ t \end{bmatrix}$$

which can be done by inverting the 3×3 matrix. As noted in Section 2.5.4, a matrix must have a nonzero determinant in order for it to be invertible; in this case, the determinant is zero if and only if the linear component and the plane are parallel, and so we handle this as a special case.

For each type of linear component, the first step is to find the determinant of the system, and if it is nonzero, to then compute the solution in order to find the region in which the solution lies. Once the region has been determined, calculations specific to that region are made in order to find the point $(\bar{u}, \bar{v}, \bar{t})$ on the boundary that represents the minimum.

Line to Triangle

For the line to triangle distance, the solution domain breaks up the domain into six regions. The pseudocode to determine the region is as follows:

```
float LineTriangleDistanceSquared(Line line, Triangle triangle)
{
    e0 = triangle.v[1] - triangle.v[0];
    e1 = triangle.v[2] - triangle.v[0];
    a00 =  Dot(e0, e0);
    a01 =  Dot(e0, e1);
    a02 = -Dot(e0, line.direction);
    a11 =  Dot(e1, e1);
    a12 = -Dot(e1, line.direction);
    a22 =  Dot(line.direction, line.direction);
    diff = triangle.v[0] - line.base;
    b0 =  Dot(e0, diff);
    b1 =  Dot(e1, diff);
    b2 = -Dot(line.direction, diff);
    c = Dot(diff, diff);

    // Cofactors to be used for determinant
    // and inversion of matrix A
    cof00 = a11 * a22 - a12 * a12;
    cof01 = a02 * a12 - a01 * a22;
    cof02 = a01 * a12 - a02 * a11;
```

```
det = a00 * cof00 - a01 * cof01 + a02 * cof02;

// Invert determinant and b if det is negative --
// Avoids having to deal with special cases later.
if (det < 0) {
    det = -det;
    b0 = -b0;
    b1 = -b1;
    b2 = -b2;
}

// Check if determinant is (nearly) 0
if (det < epsilon) {
    // Treat line and triangle as parallel. Compute
    // closest points by computing distance from
    // line to each triangle edge and taking minimum.
    Segment seg0 = {triangle.v[0], triangle.v[1] };
    dist0 = LineLineSegDistanceSquared(line, seg0);

    Segment seg1 = {triangle.v[0], triangle.v[1] };
    dist1 = LineLineSegDistanceSquared(line, seg1);

    Segment seg2 = {triangle.v[1], triangle.v[2] };
    dist2 = LineLineSegDistanceSquared(line, seg2);

    distance = MIN(dist0, MIN(dist1, dist2));

    return distance;
} else {
    // Determine the region in which solution lies by
    // computing u and v and checking their signs
    cof11 = a00 * a22 - a02 * a02;
    cof12 = a02 * a01 - a00 * a12;
    u = -(cof00 * b0 + cof01 * b1 + cof02 * b2);
    v = -(cof01 * b0 + cof11 * b1 + cof12 * b2);

    if (u + v <= det) {
        if (u < 0) {
            if (v < 0) {
                region 4
            } else {
                region 3
            }
        } else if (v < 0) {
```

```
                    region 5
                } else {
                    region 0
                }
            } else {
                if (u < 0) {
                    region 2
                } else if (v < 0) {
                    region 6
                } else {
                    region 1
                }
            }
        }
    }
}
```

The pseudocode for region 0 is

```
invDet = 1 / det;
u = u * invDet;
v = v * invDet;


cof22 = a00 * a11 - a01 * a01;
r = -(cof02 * b0 + cof12 * b1 + cof22 * b2) * invDet;
```

The code for the other regions is more complex. Consider the code for region 3—here, $\bar{u} = 0$. If we substitute this back into Equation 10.14, the original squared-distance formula, terms involving u drop out, and we have effectively a lower-dimension quadratic equation to solve:

$$Q_1(v, t) = a_{11}v^2 + a_{22}t^2 + 2a_{12}vt + 2b_1v + 2b_2t + c, \quad v, t \in [0, 1] \times (-\infty, \infty)$$

The region consists of an infinite strip bounded $v = 0$ and $v = 1$ lying in the (v, t) plane, and two half-planes, shown "looking down the t-axis" in Figure 10.41. The solution $(\bar{v}, \bar{t})$ to ∇Q_1 is computed; v may lie either in the infinite strip or on one of the two half-planes. If it lies in the infinite strip (i.e., $0 \leq \bar{v} \leq 1$, then the solution to Q is $(0, \bar{v}, \bar{t})$. Otherwise, it lies on one or the other half-plane, and the minimum will then be on the line at the intersection of the infinite strip and the half-planes (where $v = 0$ or $v = 1$). If $v = 0$, then the quadratic equation resulting from dropping out terms of both u and v of Equation 10.14 is

$$Q_2(t) = a_{22}t^2 + 2b_2t + c, \quad t \in (-\infty, \infty)$$

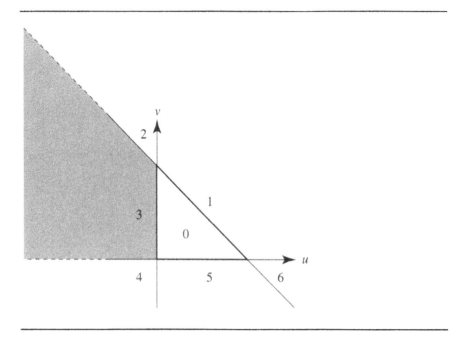

whose solution occurs when

$$\frac{dQ_2}{dt} = 0$$

so

$$t = \frac{-b_2}{a_{22}}$$

If $\bar{v} > 1$, then the quadratic to minimize is

$$Q_3 = a_{22}t^2 + 2(a_{12} + b_2)t + (a_{11} + 2b_1 + c)$$

so

$$t = -\frac{a_{12} + b_2}{a_{22}}.$$

The pseudocode for this is

```
u = 0;
v = a12 * b2 - a22 * b1;
if (t >= 0) {
    if (t <= det) {
        invDet = 1 / cof00;
        v *= invDet;
        t = (a12 * b1 - a22 * b2) * invDet;
    } else {
        v = 1;
        t = -(b2 + a12) / a22;
    }
} else {
    v = 0;
    t = -b2 / a22;
}
```

The analysis and associated code for regions 1 and 5 are similar to that for region 3. The analysis and code for regions 2, 4, and 6 are a bit simpler because we only have two half-planes against which to test: we have $(u = 0, v = 1)$, $(u = 0, v = 0)$, and $(u = 1, v = 0)$, respectively, for each of these regions.

Ray to Triangle and Segment to Triangle

The basic approach for the ray/triangle and segment/triangle distance problems is exactly analogous to that just presented for line/triangle distance. However, in the former case, instead of having 6 regions in the domain, we have 12 (the same 6 as for the line/triangle case, but doubled because the ray divides its infinite line into 2 regions—$t < 0$ and $t \geq 0$); in the latter case, we have 18 regions—three sets of the same 6 for $t < 0$, $0 \leq t \leq 1$, and $t > 1$.

10.9.2 LINEAR COMPONENT TO RECTANGLE

In this section we consider the problem of finding the distance between a linear component and a rectangle, as shown in Figure 10.42. The linear component is represented in the usual fashion, by a base point and direction vector: $\mathcal{L}(t) = P + t\vec{d}$. Typically, a rectangle is considered to be defined by four vertices V_0, V_1, V_2, and V_3. However, as for the problem of the linear component/triangle distance problem, we utilize an alternative representation, consisting of a vertex and two vectors defining

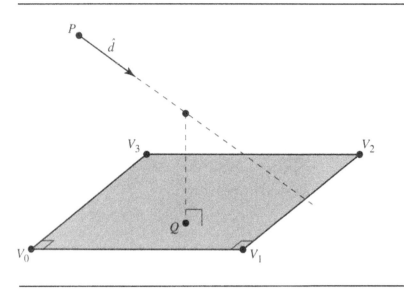

Figure 10.42   Distance between a line and a rectangle.

the edges incident on the vector. Arbitrarily, we choose V_0 as the "origin," giving us a rectangle $\{V, \vec{e}_0, \vec{e}_1\}$, where $V = V_0$, $\vec{e}_0 = V_1 - V_0$, and $\vec{e}_1 = V_3 - V_0$, as shown in Figure 10.13. This gives us a parametric rectangle as $\mathcal{R}(u, v) = V + u\vec{e}_0 + v\vec{e}_1$ with $0 \leq u, v \leq 1$.

Given this, our squared-distance function is

$$Q(u, v, t) = \|\mathcal{R}(u, v) - \mathcal{L}(t)\|.$$

Substituting in the formulas for the linear component and rectangle, we get

$$
\begin{aligned}
Q(u, v, t) = {} & (\vec{e}_0 \cdot \vec{e}_0)u^2 + (\vec{e}_1 \cdot \vec{e}_1)v^2 + (\vec{d} \cdot \vec{d})t^2 \\
& + (\vec{e}_0 \cdot \vec{e}_1)uv + (-\vec{e}_0 \cdot \vec{d})ut + (-\vec{e}_1 \cdot \vec{d})vt \\
& + 2(\vec{e}_0 \cdot (V - P))u + 2(\vec{e}_1 \cdot (V - P))v + 2((V - P) \cdot (V - P))t + c
\end{aligned}
$$

or, more compactly,

$$
\begin{aligned}
Q(u, v, t) = {} & a_{00}u^2 + a_{11}v^2 + a_{22}t^2 + a_{01}uv + a_{02}ut + a_{12}vt + 2b_0u \\
& + 2b_1v + 2b_2t + c
\end{aligned}
\tag{10.15}
$$

where

$$a_{00} = \vec{e}_0 \cdot \vec{e}_0$$

$$a_{01} = \vec{e}_0 \cdot \vec{e}_1$$

$$a_{11} = \vec{e}_1 \cdot \vec{e}_1$$

$$a_{12} = -\vec{e}_0 \cdot \vec{d}$$

$$a_{02} = -\vec{e}_0 \cdot \vec{d}$$

$$a_{12} = -\vec{e}_1 \cdot \vec{d}$$

$$a_{22} = \vec{d} \cdot \vec{d}$$

$$b_0 = \vec{e}_0 \cdot (V - P)$$

$$b_1 = \vec{e}_1 \cdot (V - P)$$

$$b_2 = (V - P) \cdot (V - P)$$

The domain of Q is $\mathbb{R}^3$ and is partitioned similarly to Figure 10.40, but instead defines either an infinite square column, a semi-infinite square column, or a cube, for the cases of lines, rays, and segments, respectively. The partitioning for the line segment case is shown in Figure 10.43. If the configuration of the rectangle and linear component are such that the point on the plane containing the rectangle that is nearest to the linear component actually lies within the rectangle, and the point on the linear segment nearest the rectangle is within the bounds (if any) of the linear segment, then the solution $(\bar{u}, \bar{v}, \bar{t})$ will lie within region 0 of the solution domain's cube; the distance between the linear segment and the rectangle will be $\|\mathcal{T}(\bar{u}, \bar{v}, \bar{t}) - \mathcal{L}(t)\|$. Otherwise, the minimum of $\nabla Q = (\bar{u}, \bar{v}, \bar{t})$ will be on a face separating the regions (and where it lies on a face may be along an edge or vertex of the boundaries between regions).

The first step in the algorithm is to find the values of u, v, and t that minimize the squared-distance function of Equation 10.15. Formally, we must find where the gradient $\nabla Q = 0$; this can be expressed as finding the solution to the system of equations

$$\begin{bmatrix} a_{00} & a_{01} & a_{02} \\ a_{10} & a_{11} & a_{12} \\ a_{20} & a_{21} & a_{22} \end{bmatrix} \begin{bmatrix} b_0 \\ b_1 \\ b_2 \end{bmatrix} = \begin{bmatrix} u \\ v \\ t \end{bmatrix}$$

which can be done by inverting the 3×3 matrix. As noted in Section 2.5.4, a matrix must have a nonzero determinant in order for it to be invertible; in this case, the determinant is zero if and only if the linear component and the plane are parallel, and so we handle this as a special case.

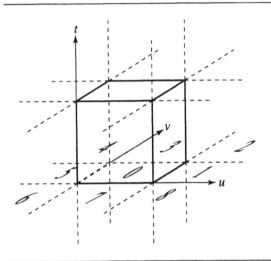

Figure 10.43   The partitioning of the solution domain for a line segment and rectangle.

For each type of linear component, the first step is to find the determinant of the system, and if it is nonzero, to then compute the solution in order to find the region in which the solution lies. Once the region has been determined, calculations specific to that region are made in order to find the point $(\bar{u}, \bar{v}, \bar{t})$ on the boundary that represents the minimum.

For the case of the line and rectangle distance, the domain is partitioned into an infinite square column, which defines nine regions. The pseudocode for finding the region in which the unconstrained solution lies is

```
float LineRectangleDistanceSquared(Line line, Rectangle rectangle)
{
    // Convert to parametric representation
    // Assumes rectangle vertices are ordered counterclockwise
    V = rectangle.V[0];
    e0 = rectangle.V[1] - V;
    e1 = rectangle.V[3] - V;

    a00 =  Dot(e0, e0);
    a01 =  Dot(e0, e1);
    a02 = -Dot(e0, line.direction);
    a11 =  Dot(e1, e1);
    a12 = -Dot(e1, line.direction);
    a22 =  Dot(line.direction, line.direction);
    diff = V - line.base;
```

```
b0 = Dot(e0, diff);
b1 = Dot(e1, diff);
b2 = Dot(line.direction, diff);
c = Dot(diff, diff);

// Cofactors to be used for determinant
// and inversion of matrix A
cof00 = a11 * a22 - a12 * a12;
cof01 = a02 * a12 - a01 * a22;
cof02 = a01 * a12 - a02 * a11;
det = a00 * cof00 + a01 * cof01 + a02 * cof02;

// Flip determinant and b, to avoid
// special cases later
if (det < 0) {
    det = -det;
    b0 = -b0;
    b1 = -b1;
    b2 = -b2;
}

// Check for (near) parallelism
if (det < epsilon) {
    // Line and rectangle are parallel.
    // Find the closest points by computing
    // the distance between the line to
    // the segment defining each edge and
    // taking the minimum.
    Segment seg0 = { rectangle[0], rectangle[1] };
    float dist0 = LineLineSegmentDistanceSquared(line, seg0);

    Segment seg1 = { rectangle[1], rectangle[2] };
    float dist1 = LineLineSegmentDistanceSquared(line, seg1);

    Segment seg2 = { rectangle[2], rectangle[3] };
    float dist2 = LineLineSegmentDistanceSquared(line, seg2);

    Segment seg3 = { rectangle[3], rectangle[0] };
    float dist3 = LineLineSegmentDistanceSquared(line, seg3);

    return (MIN(seg0, MIN(seg1, MIN(seg2, seg3))));
}

// Compute u, v
```

```
cof11 = a00 * a22 - a02 * a02;
cof12 = a02 * a01 - a00 * a12;
u = -(cof00 * b0 + cof01 * b1 + cof02 * b2);
v = -(cof01 * b0 + cof11 * b1 + cof12 * b2);

if (s < 0) {
    if (t < 0) {
        region 6;
    } else if (t <= det) {
        region 5;
    } else {
        region 4;
    }
} else if (s <= det) {
    if (t < 0) {
        region 7;
    } else if (t <= det) {
        region 0;
    } else {
        region 3;
    }
} else {
    if (t < 0) {
        region 8;
    } else if (t <= det) {
        region 1;
    } else {
        region 2;
    }
}
```

The code for the various regions is implemented in exactly the way that the line-to-triangle code is built.

Ray to Rectangle and Line Segment to Rectangle

The basic approach for the ray/rectangle and segment/rectangle distance problems is exactly analogous to that just presented for line/rectangle distance. However, in the former case, instead of having 9 regions in the domain, we have 18 (the same 9 as for the line/rectangle case, but doubled because the ray divides its infinite line into 2 regions—$t < 0$ and $t \geq 0$); in the latter case, we have 27 regions—three sets of the same 9 for $t < 0, 0 \leq t \leq 1$, and $t > 1$.

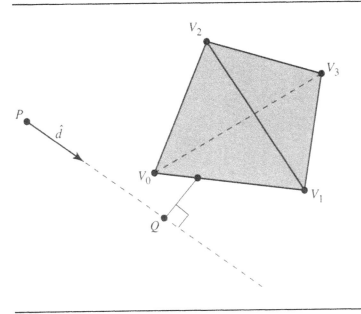

Figure 10.44   Distance between a line and a tetrahedron.

10.9.3 Linear Component to Tetrahedron

In this section we discuss the problem of computing the distance from a linear component to a tetrahedron, as shown in Figure 10.44. Let V_i, $0 \le i \le 3$, be the vertices of the tetrahedron. The linear component is $P + t\hat{d}$, where $\hat{d}$ is a unit-length vector and $t \in \mathbb{R}$ (line), $t \ge 0$ (ray), or $t \in [0, T]$ (segment). The construction can be modified slightly to handle $\hat{d}$ that is not unit length. The tetrahedron can be parameterized by $V_0 + s_1\vec{e}_1 + s_2\vec{e}_2 + s_3\vec{e}_3$, where $\vec{e}_i = V_i - V_0$, $s_i \ge 0$, and $s_1 + s_2 + s_3 \le 1$.

Distance

Translate the tetrahedron and line by subtracting P. The tetrahedron vertices are now $V_i = U_i - P$ for all i. The line becomes $s\hat{d}$. Project onto the plane containing the origin $\mathcal{O}$ and having normal $\hat{d}$; Figure 10.45(a) shows this projection (in 2D for clarity). The projected line is the single point $\mathcal{O}$. The projected tetrahedron vertices are $W_i = (I - \hat{d}\hat{d}^{\mathrm{T}})V_i$ for all i. The boundary of the projected solid tetrahedron is a convex polygon, either a triangle or a quadrilateral. If the convex polygon contains $\mathcal{O}$, the distance from the line to the tetrahedron is zero. Otherwise, the distance from the line to the tetrahedron is the distance from $\mathcal{O}$ to the convex polygon. The

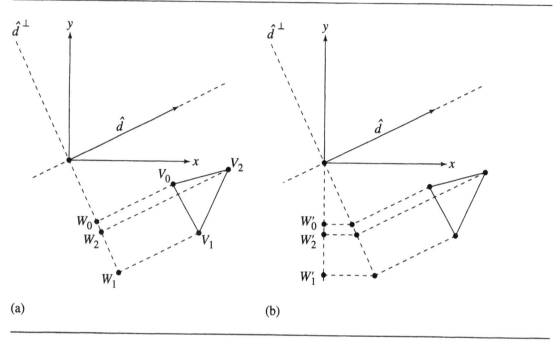

(a)   (b)

Figure 10.45   Projecting a tetrahedron (a) onto a plane perpendicular to $\hat{d}$ and then (b) into 2D.

projected values are in a plane in 3D and can be projected into 2D with the standard technique of eliminating the coordinate corresponding to the maximum absolute component of $\hat{d}$, as shown in Figure 10.45(b). The distance between a point and a convex polygon can be computed in 2D. This value must be adjusted to account for the 3D-to-2D projection. For example, if $\hat{d} = (d_0, d_1, d_2)$ with $|d_2| = \max_i\{|d_i|\}$ and r is the computed 2D distance, then the 3D distance is r/d_2.

Closest Points

The set of tetrahedron points closest to the line in many cases consists of a single point. In other cases, the set can consist of a line segment of points. For example, consider the tetrahedron with vertices $(0, 0, 0)$, $(1, 0, 0)$, $(0, 1, 0)$, and $(0, 0, 1)$. The line $(1/4, 1/4, 0) + t(0, 0, 1)$ intersects the tetrahedron for $t \in [0, 1/2]$, so the corresponding points are zero units of distance from the tetrahedron. The line $(-1, -1, 1/2) + t(0, 0, 1)$ is $\sqrt{2}$ units of distance from the tetrahedron. The closest points on the line are generated by $t \in [0, 1/2]$, and the closest points on the tetrahedron are $(0, 0, t)$ for the same interval of t values. The line $(1/2, -1/2, 0) + t(0, 0, 1)$ is $1/2$ units of distance from the tetrahedron. The closest points on the line are generated by $t \in [0, 1/2]$, and the closest points on the tetrahedron are $(1/2, 0, t)$ for the same interval of t values.

CASE 1   Let $\mathcal{O}$ be strictly inside the convex polygon. In this case, the line intersects the tetrahedron in an interval of points. Let $\mathrm{E} = [\vec{e}_1 \; \vec{e}_2 \; \vec{e}_3]$ be the matrix whose columns are the specified edge vectors of the tetrahedron. Let $\vec{s}$ be the 3×1 vector whose components are the s_i parameters. The line segment of intersection is $t\hat{d} + P = \mathrm{E}\vec{s} + V_0$ for $t \in [t_{\min}, t_{\max}]$. The problem now is to compute the t-interval. The edge vectors of the tetrahedron are linearly independent, so E is invertible. Multiplying the vector equation by the inverse and solving for the tetrahedron parameters yields

$$\vec{s} = \mathrm{E}^{-1}\left(t\hat{d} + P - V_0\right) = \vec{a}t + \vec{b}$$

where $\vec{a} = (a_1, a_2, a_3) = \mathrm{E}^{-1}\hat{d}$ and $\vec{b} = (b_1, b_2, b_3) = \mathrm{E}^{-1}(P - V_0)$. The parameters $\vec{s}$ must satisfy the inequality constraints for the tetrahedron. The parameter t is therefore constrained by the four inequalities:

$$a_1 t + b_1 \geq 0, \quad a_2 t + b_2 \geq 0, \quad a_3 t + b_3 \geq 0, \quad (a_1 + a_2 + a_3)t + (b_1 + b_2 + b_3) \leq 1$$

Each of these inequalities defines a semi-infinite interval of the form $[\bar{t}, \infty)$ or $(-\infty, \bar{t}]$. In this particular case, we know the intersection of the four intervals must be nonempty and of the form $[t_{\min}, t_{\max}]$.

The division required to compute E^{-1} can be avoided. Let us assume that the tetrahedron is oriented so that $\det(\mathrm{E}) > 0$. Multiply by the adjoint $\mathrm{E}^{\mathrm{adj}}$ to obtain

$$\det(\mathrm{E})\vec{s} = \mathrm{E}^{\mathrm{adj}}\left(t\hat{d} + P - V_0\right) = \vec{\alpha}t + \vec{\beta}$$

The four t-inequalities are of the same form as earlier, but where a_i refers to the components of $\vec{\alpha}$, b_i refers to the components of $\vec{\beta}$, and the last inequality becomes a comparison to $\det(\mathrm{E})$ instead of to 1. ∎

CASE 2   Let $\mathcal{O}$ be on the convex polygon boundary or outside the polygon. Let C be the closest polygon point (in 3D) to $\mathcal{O}$. The line $t\hat{d} + C$ intersects the tetrahedron with U_i vertices either in a single point or in an interval of points. The method in Case 1 may be used again, but now you need to be careful with the interval construction when using floating-point arithmetic. If the intersection is a single point, theoretically $t_{\min} = t_{\max}$, but numerically you might wind up with an empty intersection. It is not difficult to trap this and handle appropriately. Observe that Cases 1 and 2 are handled by the same code since in Case 1 you can choose $C = \mathcal{O}$. ∎

Ray and Tetrahedron

Use the line-tetrahedron algorithm for computing the closest line points with parameters $I = [t_{\min}, t_{\max}]$ (with possibly $t_{\min} = t_{\max}$). Define $J = I \cap [0, \infty)$. If $J \neq \emptyset$, the ray-tetrahedron distance is the same as the line-tetrahedron distance. The closest ray points are determined by J. If $J = \emptyset$, the ray origin P is closest to the tetrahedron.

Segment and Tetrahedron

Use the line-tetrahedron algorithm for computing the closest line points with parameters $[t_{\min}, t_{\max}]$ (with possibly $t_{\min} = t_{\max}$). Define $J = I \cap [0, T]$. If $J \neq \emptyset$, the segment-tetrahedron distance is the same as the line-tetrahedron distance. The closest segment points are determined by J. If $J = \emptyset$, the closest segment point is P when $t_{\max} < 0$ or $P + T\vec{d}$ when $t_{\min} > T$.

10.9.4   LINEAR COMPONENT TO ORIENTED BOUNDING BOX

In this section we discuss the problem of computing the distance between a linear component and an oriented bounding box (OBB). A linear component is defined as a base point and a direction vector:

$$\mathcal{L}(t) = P + t\vec{d}$$

An OBB is defined as a centerpoint C; three orthonormal orientation vectors $\hat{u}$, $\hat{v}$, and $\hat{w}$; and three half-extents h_u, h_v, and h_w, as shown in Figure 10.46.

The naive approach would compute the squared distance between the line and each of the six faces and take the minimum of these; however, this would be quite expensive because of the arbitrary orientation of the faces and also would fail to exploit the fact that each face is parallel or orthogonal to every other face.

The approach we take here is analogous to that taken for the problem of computing the distance of a point to an OBB, as described in Section 10.4.2.

The OBB's centerpoint C and $\hat{u}$, $\hat{v}$, and $\hat{w}$ define a frame. Observe that, relative to that frame, the OBB is an axis-aligned box centered at the origin, whose sides are each parallel to either the x-, y-, or z-axis. If we transform the line $\{P, \vec{d}\}$ into this frame, then we can exploit this axis-aligned, origin-centered nature of the OBB and compute the closest point, and the distance to it, more efficiently.

Given the OBB's center C and $\hat{u}$, $\hat{v}$, and $\hat{w}$, a point P's coordinates in that frame can be computed as

$$P' = [\, (P - C) \cdot \hat{u} \quad (P - C) \cdot \hat{v} \quad (P - C) \cdot \hat{w} \,]$$

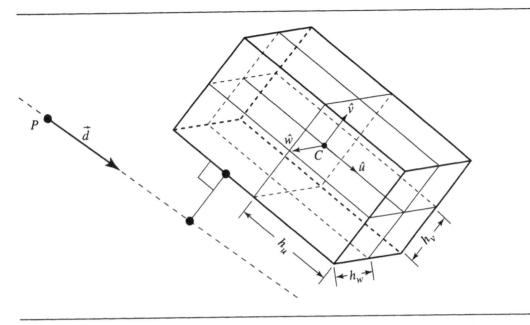

Figure 10.46   Distance between a line and an oriented bounding box.

That is, we simply project the vector between the P and C onto each of the OBB's basis vectors. Note that this is functionally equivalent to creating a transform T from global space into the local space of the OBB with matrix

$$T = \begin{bmatrix} \hat{u}^{\mathrm{T}} & \hat{v}^{\mathrm{T}} & \hat{w}^{\mathrm{T}} & \vec{0}^{\mathrm{T}} \\ & -C & & 1 \end{bmatrix}$$

and multiplying by P, but is more efficient. The same process may be applied to $\vec{d}$, the direction vector for the line.

Once inside the frame of the OBB, we can compute three things:

- The coordinates of the closest point on the OBB to the line.

- The parameter of the point on the line closest to the OBB.

- The squared distance between the OBB and the line.

(Note that, of course, if the line intersects the OBB, then the distance is 0, and the other two pieces of information are moot.)

The coordinates of the closest point on the OBB are found in a frame whose origin is [0   0   0] and whose basis vectors are orthonormal. Because of this, we

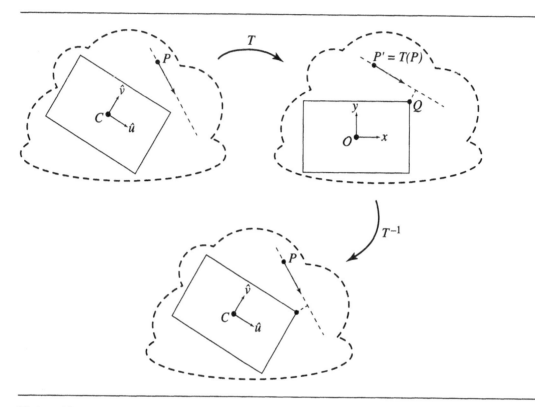

Figure 10.47   Schematic for line-OBB distance algorithm.

can view these coordinates as parameter values of the closest point on the OBB, in the untransformed frame. If we want the actual location of the closest point in that frame, we simply have to compute the following:

$$Q = C + Q'_x\hat{u} + Q'_y\hat{v} + Q'_z\hat{w}$$

Of course, the parameter of the point on the transformed line can simply be applied to the untransformed line, in order to find the actual point (if this is desired) in the untransformed frame. Figure 10.47 shows a schematic of this process (shown in 2D for clarity).

Once the line has been transformed into the OBB's local frame, we can exploit the fact that the faces are all parallel to the basis vectors of the frame. Certainly, it is more efficient to compute intersections and distances when the "target" is parallel to a basis vector, but we exploit this even further by breaking down the configurations into several cases, to which we apply an algorithm that computes only the minimum necessary for each case.

The configurations are categorized by looking at the (now-transformed) direction vector $\vec{d}'$ of the line $\mathcal{L}$. Specifically, we look for how many components of $\vec{d}'$ are zero—there may be none, one, two, or three. We discuss these cases in order of increasing complexity.

For the cases of zero, one, or two zero-components, we employ a bit of a "trick" in the implementation. We consider the values of the components of $\vec{d}'$: if a component is negative, we flip its sign and flip the sign of the corresponding component of P'. We then proceed with the rest of the algorithm, and then flip the corresponding components of the resulting nearest point on the OBB (this works because the OBB is symmetric about the origin in all three dimensions). This ensures that all the components of $\vec{d}'$ are nonnegative, which reduces the number of cases we have to consider.

Three Zero-Components

In this case, the line is simply a point, and the problem degenerates into finding the distance from a point to an axis-aligned box, the solution to which may be found in Section 10.4.2.

Two Zero-Components

In this case, the transformed line is perpendicular to two of the basis vectors and parallel to the third. Figure 10.48 shows a line that is perpendicular to the y- and z-axes of the OBB; the line may be above, within, or below the OBB.

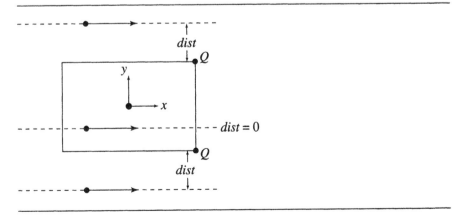

Figure 10.48   Case of two zero-components.

Here, the squared distance is simply the sum of the squared distances in y and z:

$$d_y^2 = \begin{cases} P_y'^2 + \text{extent}_y & P_y' < -\text{extent}_y \\ P_y'^2 - \text{extent}_y & P_y' > \text{extent}_y \\ 0 & \text{otherwise} \end{cases}$$

$$d_z^2 = \begin{cases} P_z'^2 + \text{extent}_z & P_z' < -\text{extent}_z \\ P_z'^2 - \text{extent}_z & P_z' > \text{extent}_z \\ 0 & \text{otherwise} \end{cases}$$

(Note that if the line intersects the box, the distance is 0.)

The closest point on the line is (arbitrarily, but consistently) chosen to correspond to the "positive" YZ face of the box:

$$t = \frac{\text{extent}_x - P_x'}{\vec{d'}}$$

The closest point on the box is (again arbitrarily, but consistently) chosen to be on the box's "positive" YZ face; the point will be within that face if the line intersects the box, and either along one of the edges or at a corner if it does not.

The pseudocode is

```
real CaseTwoZeroComponents_YZ(Line line, OBB box, real t)
{
    real distanceSquared = 0;

    // Parameter of closest point on the line
    t = (box.extents.x - line.origin.x) / line.direction.x;

    // Closest point on the box
    qPrime.x = box.extents.x;
    qPrime.x = line.origin.y;
    qPrime.x = line.origin.z;
    //
    // Compute distance squared and Y and Z components
    // of box's closest point
    //
    if (line.origin.y < - box.extents.y) {
        delta = line.origin.y + box.extents.y;
        distanceSquared += delta * delta;
        qPrime.y = -box.extents.y;
    } else if (line.origin.y > box.extents.y) {
        delta = line.origin.y - box.extents.y;
        distanceSquared += delta * delta;
```

```
        qPrime.y = box.extents.y;
    }

    if (line.origin.z < - box.extents.z) {
        delta = line.origin.z + box.extents.z;
        distanceSquared += delta * delta;
        qPrime.z = -box.extents.z;
    } else if (line.origin.z > box.extents.z) {
        delta = line.origin.z - box.extents.z;
        distanceSquared += delta * delta;
        qPrime.z = box.extents.z;
    }

    return distanceSquared;
}
```

One Zero-Component

In this case, the transformed line is perpendicular to only one of the basis vectors. Figure 10.49 shows a line that is perpendicular to the z-axis; the line may be above, within, or below the OBB. Note that in this case, if the line does not intersect the OBB, the closest point is always a corner.

The implementation of this can be highly optimized. Assume for the moment that the (transformed) line's direction vector $\vec{d}'$ has only positive components; in this case, if the line doesn't intersect the box, then the closest point will be either the upper-left or lower-right corner of the box, as can be seen in Figure 10.49. We can determine which of these cases is possible by looking at the angle between the vector $\vec{e}$ going from the upper-right corner to the line's origin and the line's direction vector $\vec{d}'$. The Kross function discussed in Section 7.1 can be applied to these two vectors in order to determine whether the angle between them is positive or negative; if $\text{Kross}(\vec{e}, \vec{d}') > 0$, then the line will intersect the "x-axis"; otherwise it will intersect the "y-axis." In the former case, the closest point on the box (if no intersection occurs) will be at the lower-right corner, and in the latter case, the closest point will be at the upper-left corner. Figure 10.50 demonstrates this. Once this has been determined, we need to determine whether or not the line intersects the box. Consider the case where the lower-right corner may be the closest point: If the angle between the line and a vector from the closest corner to the line's origin is positive, then the line will not intersect the box; if the angle is negative, the line will intersect the box. Taking the dot product of these vectors will not work, as the cosine function is symmetric about 0; however, we can use the Kross function on the "perp" of the line and the corner-to-line-origin vector, as shown in Figure 10.51. If the line intersects the box, then its distance is 0; otherwise, the distance squared is the distance between Q' and the transformed line.

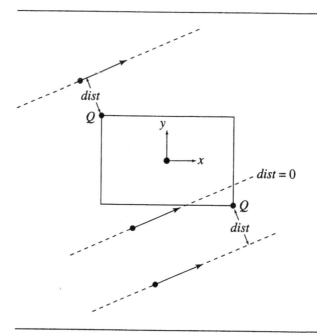

Figure 10.49 Case of one zero-component.

The pseudocode is

```
real CaseOneZeroComponent_Z(Line line, OBB box, real t0, Point qPrime)
{
    Vector3D ptMinusExtents = line.origin - box.extents;
    real prod0 = line.direction.y * ptMinusExtents.x;
    real prod1 = line.direction.x * ptMinusExtents.y;
    real distanceSquared = 0;
    qPrime.z = line.origin.z;

    if (prod0 >= prod1) {
        //
        // line intersects ''x-axis'' of OBB
        // Closest point is along bottom edge of right face of OBB
        //
        qPrime.x = box.extent.x;
        real tmp = line.origin.y + box.extents.y;
        delta = prod0 - line.direction.x * tmp;
        if (delta >= 0) {
            // There is no intersection, so compute distance
```

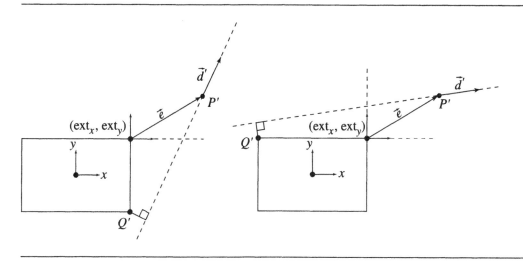

Figure 10.50   Determining where to look for the closest point on the box.

```
            invLSquared = 1 / (line.direction.x * line.direction.x +
                              line.direction.y + line.direction.y);
            distanceSquared += (delta * delta) * invLSquared;

            // If desired, compute the parameter of the line's closest
            //   point, and set the closest point on the box to be along
            //   the lower-right edge.
            qPrime.y = -box.extents.y;
            t0 = -(line.direction.x * ptMinusExtents.x * line.direction.y + tmp)
                   * invLSquared;
        } else {
            // Line intersects box. Distance is zero.
            inv = 1 / line.direction.x;
            qPrime.y = line.origin - (prod0 * inv);
            t0 = -ptMinusExtents.x * inv;
        }
    } else {
        //
        // line intersects the ''y-axis'' of OBB
        // Closest point is along top edge of left face of OBB
        // (or, equivalently, left edge of top face)
        // Code exactly parallels that above...

    }
```

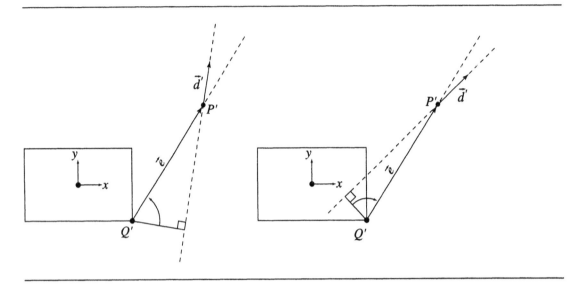

Figure 10.51   Determining whether the line intersects the box.

```
// Now, consider the z-direction
if (line.origin.z < -box.extents.z) {
    delta = line.origin.z + box.extents.z;
    distanceSquared += delta * delta;
    qPrime.z = -box.extents.z;
} else if (line.origin.z > box.extents.z) {
    delta = line.origin.z - box.extents.z;
    distanceSquared += delta * delta;
    qPrime.z = box.extents.z;
}

return distanceSquared;
}
```

No Zero-Components

In this case, the transformed line is not parallel to any of the basis vectors. We can, however, use the Kross operator as we did in the "one zero-component" case and also assume that all of the transformed line's components are positive; by doing so, we can determine which plane the line intersects first and exploit this knowledge in determining intersection with, or distance from, the faces of the box.

The pseudocode for this is

```
real CaseNoZeroComponents(Line line, OBB box, real t, Point qPrime)
{
    Vector3D ptMinusExtents = line.origin - box.extents;
    real dyEx = line.direction.y * ptMinusExtents.x;
    real dxEy = line.direction.x * ptMinusExtents.y;

    if (dyEx >= dxEy) {
        real dzEx = line.direction.z * ptMinusExtents.x;
        real dxEz = line.direction.x * ptMinusExtents.z;

        if (dzEx >= dxEz) {
            // line intersects x = box.extent.x plane
            distanceSquared = FaceX(line, box, ptMinusExtents, t, qPrime);
        } else {
            // line intersects z = box.extent.z plane
            distanceSquared = FaceZ(line, box, ptMinusExtents, t, qPrime);
        }
    } else {
        real dzEy = line.direction.z * ptMinusExtents.y;
        real dyEz = line.direction.y * ptMinusExtents.z;

        if (dzEy >= dyEz) {
            // line intersects y = box.extent.y plane
            distanceSquared = FaceY(line, box, ptMinusExtents, t, qPrime);
        } else {
            // line intersects z = box.extent.z plane
            distanceSquared = FaceZ(line, box, ptMinusExtents, t, qPrime);
        }
    }

    return distanceSquared;
}
```

Figure 10.52 shows each "positive" face, against which we test for intersection and distance. The line intersects the plane of the face (it may or may not intersect the face itself). Because all the components of the line's direction vector $\vec{d}$ are positive, it is not possible for the line to be closest to two of the four edges of the face (in the diagram, the potential "closest" edges are shown with thicker lines). Thus, we are only interested in six of the nine possible regions defined by the edges of the face.

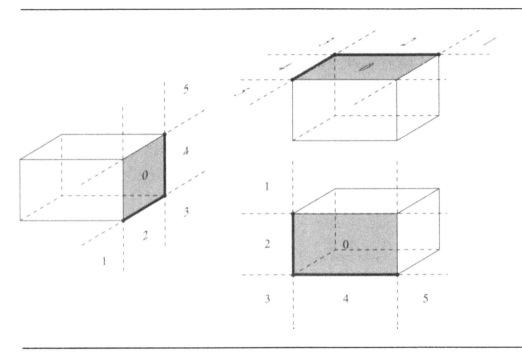

Figure 10.52   Each "positive" face of the OBB has two edges and three vertices that may be closest to the line.

The pseudocode for the face-testing routine for the "positive" X face is as follows:

```
real Face_X(Line line, OBB box, Vector3D ptMinusExtents, real t, Point3D qPrime)
{
    Point3D qPrime = line.origin;
    real    distanceSquared = 0;

    Vector3D ptPlusExtents = line.origin + box.extents;
    if (line.direction.x * ptPlusExtents.y >= line.direction.y * ptMinusExtents.x) {
        //
        //  region 0, 5, or 4
        //
        if (line.direction.x * pPe.z >= line.direction.z * ptMinusExtents.x) {
            //
            // region 0 - line intersects face
            //
            qPrime.x = box.extents.x;
            inverse = 1.0 / line.direction.x;
            qPrime.y -= line.direction.y * ptMinusExtents.x * inverse;
```

```
            qPrime.z -= line.direction.z * ptMinusExtents.x * inverse;
            t = -ptMinusExtents * inverse;
    } else {
        //
        //  region 4 or 5
        //
        lSqr = line.direction.x * line.direction.x
                + line.direction.z * line.direction.z;
        tmp = lSqr * ptPlusExtents.y - line.direction.y
              * (line.direction.x * ptMinusExtents.x + line.direction.z
                                 * ptPlusExtents.z);
        if (tmp <= 2 * lSqr * box.extents.y) {
            //
            //  region 4
            //
            tmp = ptPlusExtents.y - (tmp / lSqr);
            lSqr += line.direction.y * line.direction.y;
            delta = line.direction.x * ptMinusExtents.x + line.direction.y * tmp
                    + line.direction.z * ptPlusExtents.z;

            t = -delta / lSqr;
            distanceSquared += ptMinusExtents.x * ptMinusExtents.x
                             + tmp * tmp
                             + ptPlusExtents.z * ptPlusExtents.z
                             + delta * t;

            qPrime.x = box.extents.x;
            qPrime.y = t - box.extents.y;
            qPrime.z = -box.extents.z;
        } else {
            //
            //  region 5
            //
            lSqr += line.direction.y * lineDirection.y;
            delta = line.direction.x * ptMinusExtents.x
                    + line.direction.y * ptMinusExtents.y
                    + line.direction.z * ptPlusExtents.z;
            t = -delta / lSqr;
            distanceSquared += ptMinusExtents.x * ptMinusExtents.x
                             + ptMinusExtents.y * ptMinusExtents.y
                             + ptPlusExtents.z * ptPlusExtents.z
                             + delta * t;

            qPrime.x =  box.extents.x;
            qPrime.y =  box.extents.y;
```

```
                              qPrime.z = -box.extents.z;
                          }
                      }
              } else {
                  if (line.direction.x * ptPlusExtents.z >=  line.direction.z * ptMinusExtents.x)
                      //
                      //   region 1 or 2
                      //
                      lSqr = line.direction.x * line.direction.x + line.direction.y
                              * line.direction.y;
                      tmp = lSqr * ptPlusExtents.z - line.direction.z * (line.direction.x
                              * ptMinusExtents.x + line.direction.il * ptPlusExtents.y);
                      if (tmp <= 2 * lSqr * box.extents.z) {
                          //
                          //   region 2
                          //
                          tmp = ptPlusExtents.z - (tmp / lSqr);
                          lSqr += line.direction.z * line.direction.z;
                          delta = line.direction.x * ptMinusExtents.x + line.direction.y
                                  * ptPlusExtents.y + line.direction.z * tmp;
                          t = -delta / lSqr;
                          distanceSquared += ptMinusExtents.x * ptMinusExtents.x
                                          + ptMinuxExtents.y * ptMinusExtents.y
                                          + tmp * tmp
                                          + delta * t;

                          qPrime.x = box.extents.x;
                          qPrime.y = -box.extents.y;
                          qPrime.z = t - box.extents.z;
                      } else {
                          //
                          //   region 1
                          //
                          lSqr += line.direction.z * lineDirection.z;
                          delta = line.direction.x * ptMinusExtents.x
                                  + line.direction.y * ptMinusExtents.y
                                  + line.direction.z * ptPlusExtents.z;
                          t = -delta / lSqr;
                          distanceSquared += ptMinusExtents.x * ptMinusExtents.x
                                          + ptPlusExtents.y * ptPlusExtents.y
                                          + ptMinusExtents.z * ptMinusExtents.z
                                          + delta * t;

                          qPrime.x =  box.extents.x;
```

```
            qPrime.y = -box.extents.y;
            qPrime.z =  box.extents.z;
        }
    } else {
        lSqr = line.direction.x * line.direction.x +
                    line.direction.z * line.direction.z;
        tmp = lSqr * ptPlusExtents.y - line.direction.y * (line.direction.x
                * ptMinusExtents.x + line.direction.z * ptPlusExtents.z);
        if (tmp >= 0) {
            //
            //  region 4 or 5
            //
            if (tmp <= 2 * lSqr * box.extents.y) {
                //
                //  region 4. Code block same as previous region 4 code.
                //
            } else {
                //
                //  region 5. Code block same as previous region 5 code.
                //
            }
        }

        lSqr = line.direction.x * line.direction.x + line.direction.y
                * line.direction.y;
        tmp = lSqr * ptPlusExtents.z
            - line.direction.z * (line.direction.x * ptMinusExtents.x
                                + line.direction.y * ptPlusExtents.y);
        if (tmp >= 0) {
            //
            //  region 1 or 2
            //
            if (tmp <= 2 * lSqr * box.extents.z) {
                //
                //  Region 2. Code block same as previous region 2 code.
                //
            } else {
                //
                //  Region 1. Code block same as previous region 1 code.
                //
            }
        }
        return distanceSquared;
    }
```

```
            //
            //   region 3
            //
            lSqr += line.direction.y * line.direction.y;
            delta = line.direction.x * ptMinusExtents.x
                    + line.direction.y * ptPlusExtents.y
                    + line.direction.z * ptPlusExtents.z;
            t = -delta / lSqr;
            distanceSquared +=
                ptMinusExtents.x * ptMinusExtents.x
                + ptPlusExtents.y * ptPlusExtents.y
                + ptPlusExtents.z * ptPlusExtents.z
                + delta * t;
            qPrime.x =  box.extents.x;
            qPrime.y = -box.extents.y;
            qPrime.z = -box.extents.z;
        }
    }
}
```

Ray to OBB

In the case of a ray-OBB distance calculation, we first compute the distance of the
infinite line in which the ray lives to the OBB. If the parameter t of the closest point
on the ray is less than zero, then we have to compute the distance from the ray's point
of origin to the OBB.

The pseudocode is

```
real RayOBBDistanceSquared(Ray ray, OBB box)
{
    Line line;
    line.origin = ray.origin;
    line.direction = ray.direction;

    distanceSquared = LineOBBDistanceSquared(line, box, t);
    if (t < 0) {
        distanceSquared = PointOBBDistanceSquared(ray.origin, box);
    }

    return distanceSquared;
}
```

Line Segment to OBB

In the case of a line segment-OBB distance calculation, we first compute the distance of the infinite line in which the line segment lives to the OBB. If the parameter t of the closest point on the line segment is not within $[0, 1]$, then we need to find the distance from the point at the start of the line segment (if $t < 0$), or the distance from the point at the end of the line segment (if $t > 1$).

The pseudocode is

```
real LineSegmentOBBDistanceSquared(Segment seg, OBB box)
{
    Line line;
    line.origin = seg.start
    line.direction = seg.end - seg.start;

    distanceSquared = LineOBBDistanceSquared(line, box, t);
    if (t < 0) {
        distanceSquared = PointOBBDistanceSquared(seg.start, box);
    } else if (t > 1) {
        distanceSquared = PointOBBDistanceSquared(seg.end, box);
    }

    return distanceSquared;
}
```

10.10 LINE TO QUADRIC SURFACE

If the line intersects the quadric surface, then the distance between the two is zero. The intersection can be tested using the parametric form for the line, $X(t) = P + t\vec{d}$. The quadric surface is implicitly defined by $Q(X) = X^{\mathrm{T}}AX + B^{\mathrm{T}}X + c = 0$. Replacing the line equation into the quadratic equation produces the polynomial equation

$$(\vec{d}^{\mathrm{T}}A\vec{d})t^2 + \vec{d}^{\mathrm{T}}(2AP + B)t + (P^{\mathrm{T}}AP + B^{\mathrm{T}}P + c) = e_2t^2 + e_1t + e_0 = 0$$

This equation has real-valued solutions whenever $e_1^2 - 4e_0e_2 \geq 0$, in which case the distance between the line and the surface is zero.

If the equation has only complex-valued solutions, then the line and the surface do not intersect and the distance between them is positive. Imagine starting with a cylinder whose axis is the line and whose radius is small enough that it does not intersect the surface. As the radius is increased, eventually the cylinder will just touch the surface, typically at one point but possibly along an entire line. The distance between the surface and the line is the radius of this cylinder and corresponds to the distance between a surface point on the cylinder and the axis of the cylinder. If the line is represented as the intersection of two planes $\hat{n}_i \cdot X = c_i = \hat{n}_i \cdot P$ for $i = 0, 1$, where $\{\vec{d}, \hat{n}_0, \hat{n}_1\}$ is a set of mutually orthogonal vectors and $\|\hat{n}_i\| = 1$, then the squared distance from X to the cylinder axis is $F(X) = (\hat{n}_0 \cdot X - c_0)^2 + (\hat{n}_1 \cdot X - c_1)^2$. The problem is to find a point X on the quadric surface that minimizes $F(X)$. This is a constrained minimization problem that is solved using the method of Lagrange multipliers (see Section A.9.3), as is shown next.

Define

$$G(X, s) = (\hat{n}_0 \cdot X - c_0)^2 + (\hat{n}_1 \cdot X - c_1)^2 + s\,Q(X)$$

where s is the parameter introduced as the multiplier. The minimum of G occurs when $\nabla Q = \vec{0}$ and $\partial G/\partial s = 0$. The first equation is $2(\hat{n}_0 \cdot X - c_0)\hat{n}_0 + 2(\hat{n}_1 \cdot X - c_1)\hat{n}_1 + s\nabla Q = \vec{0}$, and the second equation just reproduces the constraint $Q = 0$. Dotting the first equation with $\vec{d}$ yields the condition

$$L(X) := \vec{d} \cdot \nabla Q(X) = 0$$

a linear equation in X. Geometrically, the condition $\vec{d} \cdot \nabla Q = 0$ means that when the minimum distance is positive, the line segment connecting the two closest points must be perpendicular to both the line and the quadratic curve. See Figure 6.23 for an illustration in the 2D setting. Now dot the first equation with $\hat{n}_0$ and with $\hat{n}_1$ to obtain two equations involving s, $2(\hat{n}_1 \cdot X - c_1) + s\hat{n}_0 \cdot \nabla Q = 0$ and $2(\hat{n}_0 \cdot X - c_0) + s\hat{n}_1 \cdot \nabla Q = 0$. In order for both linear equations to have a common solution, it is necessary that

$$M(X) := (\hat{n}_0 \cdot X - c_0)\hat{n}_1 \cdot \nabla Q - (\hat{n}_1 \cdot X - c_1)\hat{n}_0 \cdot \nabla Q = 0$$

a quadratic equation in X.

We have a system of three polynomial equations in the three unknown components of X. The two equations $Q = 0$ and $M = 0$ are quadratic, and the equation $L = 0$ is linear. Section A.2 shows how to solve such systems. Just as in the 2D problem for computing distance between a line and an ellipse, some care must be taken in solving the system. The equation $L = 0$ is degenerate when $A\vec{d} = \vec{0}$, in which case the equation becomes $\vec{d} \cdot B = 0$. Also notice that the equation $M = 0$ is rewritten as $\hat{n} \cdot (2AX + B) = 0$, where $\hat{n} = (\hat{n}_0 \cdot X - c_0)\hat{n}_1 - (\hat{n}_1 \cdot X - c_1)\hat{n}_0$, a vector orthogonal to $\vec{d}$. If $A\hat{n} = \vec{0}$, the equation $M = 0$ degenerates to $\hat{n} \cdot B = 0$. Either degeneracy can occur when the quadric surface contains a line, for example, a parabolic cylinder, hyperbolic cylinder, or a hyperboloid itself. An implementation must trap the degeneracies and switch to the appropriate code block for computing distance between lines.

An alternative approach to computing the distance between the line and the quadric surface is to use a numerical minimizer. If the line is $X(t) = P + t\vec{d}$ for $t \in \mathbb{R}$ and the distance between a point X and the quadric surface is $F(X)$, the distance between the line point $X(t)$ and the quadric surface is $G(t) = F(P + t\vec{d})$. A numerical minimizer can be implemented that searches the t-domain $\mathbb{R}$ for those values of t that produce the minimum for $G(t)$. The trade-offs to be considered are twofold. The approach that sets up a system of polynomial equations has potential numerical problems if variables are eliminated to produce a single polynomial equation of large degree. Both the elimination process and the root finding are susceptible to numerical errors due to nearly zero coefficients. The approach that sets up a function to minimize might be more stable numerically, but convergence to a minimum is subject to the problem of slowness if an initial guess is not close to the minimum point or the problem of the iterates trapped at a local minimum that is not a global minimum.

10.11 LINE TO POLYNOMIAL SURFACE

Let the line be represented by $\mathcal{L}(t) = P + t\vec{d}$ for $t \in \mathbb{R}$ and where $\|\vec{d}\| = 1$. Let the surface be represented parametrically by

$$X(r, s) = \sum_{i_0=0}^{n_0} \sum_{i_1=0}^{n_1} A_{i_0, i_1} r^{i_0} s^{i_1}$$

for $(r, s) \in [r_{\min}, r_{\max}] \times [s_{\min}, s_{\max}]$. The squared distance between a pair of points, one from the surface and one from the line, is

$$F(r, s, t) = \|X(r, s) - \mathcal{L}(t)\|^2$$

The squared distance between the surface and the line is $\min\{F(r, s, t) : (r, s, t) \in [r_{\min}, r_{\max}] \times [s_{\min}, s_{\max}] \times \mathbb{R}\}$. A numerical minimizer can be applied directly to F, but the usual warnings apply: beware of convergence to a local minimum that is not a global minimum. The standard calculus approach to finding the minimum is to construct the set of critical points, evaluate F at each point in that set, and select the minimum of the F values. The first-order derivatives of F are $F_r = 2(X - \mathcal{L}) \cdot X_r$, $F_s = 2(X - \mathcal{L}) \cdot X_s$, and $F_t = -(X - \mathcal{L}) \cdot \vec{d}$, where X_r and X_s are the first-order derivatives of X. Observe that the degree of X is $n_0 + n_1$ and the degree of X_r and X_s is $n_0 + n_1 - 1$. The critical points are defined below:

1. $(F_r, F_s, F_t)(r, s, t) = (0, 0, 0)$ for $(r, s, t) \in (r_{\min}, r_{\max}) \times (s_{\min}, s_{\max}) \times \mathbb{R}$

2. $(F_r, F_t)(r, s_{\min}, t) = (0, 0)$ for $(r, t) \in (r_{\min}, r_{\max}) \times \mathbb{R}$

3. $(F_r, F_t)(r, s_{\max}, t) = (0, 0)$ for $(r, t) \in (r_{\min}, r_{\max}) \times \mathbb{R}$

4. $(F_s, F_t)(r_{\min}, s, t) = (0, 0)$ for $(s, t) \in (s_{\min}, s_{\max}) \times \mathbb{R}$

5. $(F_s, F_t)(r_{\max}, s, t) = (0, 0)$ for $(s, t) \in (s_{\min}, s_{\max}) \times \mathbb{R}$

6. $F_t(r_{\min}, s_{\min}, t) = 0$ for $t \in \mathbb{R}$

7. $F_t(r_{\min}, s_{\max}, t) = 0$ for $t \in \mathbb{R}$

8. $F_t(r_{\max}, s_{\min}, t) = 0$ for $t \in \mathbb{R}$

9. $F_t(r_{\max}, s_{\max}, t) = 0$ for $t \in \mathbb{R}$

Item 1 in the list requires solving three equations in the three unknowns r, s, and t. Define $\vec{\Delta}(r, s) = X(r, s) - P$. The equation $F_t = 0$ may be solved for $t = \vec{d} \cdot \vec{\Delta}$. Replacing this in $F_r = 0$ and $F_s = 0$ yields the polynomial equations $(\vec{\Delta} - (\vec{d} \cdot \vec{\Delta})\vec{d}) \cdot X_r = 0$ and $(\vec{\Delta} - (\vec{d} \cdot \vec{\Delta})\vec{d}) \cdot X_s = 0$, the first of degree $2n_0 - 1$ in r and $2n_1$ in s, the second of degree $2n_0$ in r and $2n_1 - 1$ in s. Elimination theory (Wee and Goldman 1995a, 1995b) may be applied to reduce these to a single large-degree polynomial equation in r, $G(r) = 0$. For each root $\bar{r}$ of the equation, corresponding values of $\bar{s}$ are found that are roots to $(\vec{\Delta} - (\vec{d} \cdot \vec{\Delta})\vec{d}) \cdot X_r = 0$. For each such pair $(\bar{r}, \bar{s})$, the value $\bar{t}$ is computed and the $F(\bar{r}, \bar{s}, \bar{t})$ is evaluated. The minimum such F values is maintained throughout the process.

Item 2 requires solving two equations in the two unknowns r and t. The equation $F_t = 0$ again is solved for $t = \vec{d} \cdot \vec{\Delta}$, except that now $\vec{\Delta}$ varies only with r since $s = s_{\min}$. Replacing in $F_r = 0$ leads to a single polynomial equation in r of degree $2n_0 - 1$. For each root $\bar{r}$, $\bar{t}$ is computed, $F(\bar{r}, s_{\min}, \bar{t})$ is evaluated, and the minimum of F is updated to this new value if it happens to be smaller than the previously stored minimum. Items 3, 4, and 5 are handled similarly.

Item 6 is simple to handle. The single equation is solved for $\bar{t} = \vec{d} \cdot \vec{\Delta}$, and $F(r_{\min}, s_{\min}, \bar{t})$ is evaluated and used to update, if necessary, the currently stored minimum of F. Items 7, 8, and 9 are handled similarly.

10.12 GJK Algorithm

The GJK algorithm for computing distance between two convex polyhedra has the same theoretical foundation as its 2D equivalent for computing the distance between two convex polygons. The material in Section 6.10 was described for the n-dimensional problem in terms of simplices contained in the convex objects and applies when $n = 3$. The simplices, of course, are tetrahedra for this dimension. An implementation for a 3D collision detection system called SOLID (Software Library for Interference Detection) is built on top of the 3D GJK algorithm and is available at Van den Bergen (1997). The descriptions of the various algorithms used in the implementation are provided in Van den Bergen (1997, 1999, 2001a). Of great interest in this implementation is that special attention is paid to numerical issues that have plagued many other implementations of GJK.

10.13 MISCELLANEOUS

This section covers algorithms for handling some specific types of distance queries. In particular, the queries involve (1) distance between a line and a planar curve, (2) distance between two planar curves that do not lie in the same plane, (3) distance between moving objects, and (4) distance between two points on a surface. The latter query requires that the distance is calculated as the arc length of the shortest path between the points where the path itself must lie on the surface. The path is called a *geodesic path*, and the length is called *geodesic distance*.

10.13.1 DISTANCE BETWEEN LINE AND PLANAR CURVE

Two types of methods are presented for computing the distance between a line and a planar curve. The first method is based on a parametric representation of the curve. The second method is based on a representation of the curve as the solution set to a system of algebraic equations. In either case, the line is represented parametrically as $X(t) = P + t\hat{d}$, where $\|\hat{d}\| = 1$, and the plane of the curve is $\hat{n} \cdot X = c$, where $\|\hat{n}\| = 1$.

Parametric Representation

Let the curve be represented parametrically as $X(s)$ for some domain $[s_{\min}, s_{\max}]$. The squared distance between a pair of points, one from the curve and one from the line, is $F(s,t) = \|X(s) - (P + t\hat{d})\|^2$. Finding the minimum distance between line and curve requires computing a parameter pair $(s,t) \in [s_{\min}, s_{\max}] \times \mathbb{R}$ that minimizes F. A numerical minimizer can be applied directly to F, especially so if X is not continuously differentiable in s. If derivatives do exist and are continuous, then a calculus solution can be applied. Specifically, the minimum occurs when one of the following conditions holds:

i. $\nabla F(s,t) = \vec{0}$ for an $(s,t) \in (s_{\min}, s_{\max}) \times \mathbb{R}$

ii. $\partial F(s_{\min}, t)/\partial t = 0$ for some $t \in \mathbb{R}$

iii. $\partial F(s_{\max}, t)/\partial t = 0$ for some $t \in \mathbb{R}$

The simplest partial derivative equation to solve is $\partial F/\partial t = 0$. The solution is $t = \hat{d} \cdot (X(s) - P)$. If working with the full gradient, the t value can be replaced in the other derivative equation

$$0 = \frac{\partial F}{\partial s} = ((X(s) - P) - (\hat{d} \cdot (X(s) - P))\hat{d}) \cdot X'(s)$$

$$= X'(s)^{\mathrm{T}}(I - \hat{d}\hat{d}^{\mathrm{T}})(X - P) \tag{10.16}$$

The complexity of solving this equation is directly related to the complexity of the curve itself.

EXAMPLE   *Distance between a line and a circle.*   A circle in 3D is represented by a center C, a radius r, and a plane containing the circle, $\hat{n} \cdot (X - C) = 0$, where $\hat{n}$ is a unit-length normal to the plane. If $\hat{u}$ and $\hat{v}$ are also unit-length vectors so that $\hat{u}$, $\hat{v}$, and $\hat{n}$ form an orthonormal set, then the circle is parameterized as

$$X(s) = C + r(\cos(s)\hat{u} + \sin(s)\hat{v}) =: C + r\hat{w}(s)$$

for $s \in [0, 2\pi)$. The X values are equidistant from C since $\|X - C\| = r$ because $\|\hat{w}\| = 1$. They are also in the specified plane since $\hat{n} \cdot (X - C) = 0$ because $\hat{u}$ and $\hat{v}$ are perpendicular to $\hat{n}$.

Setting $\vec{\Delta} = C - P$, and after some algebraic steps, Equation 10.16 for this example becomes

$$a_{10} \cos s + a_{01} \sin s + a_{20} \cos^2 s + a_{11} \cos s \sin s + a_{02} \sin^2 s = 0$$

where $a_{10} = \vec{\Delta} \cdot \hat{v} - (\hat{d} \cdot \hat{v})(\hat{d} \cdot \vec{\Delta})$, $a_{01} = -\vec{\Delta} \cdot \hat{u} + (\hat{d} \cdot \hat{u})(\hat{d} \cdot \vec{\Delta})$, $a_{20} = -r(\hat{d} \cdot \hat{u})$ $(\hat{d} \cdot \hat{v})$, $a_{11} = r[(\hat{d} \cdot \hat{u})^2 - (\hat{d} \cdot \hat{v})^2]$, and $a_{02} = r(\hat{d} \cdot \hat{u})(\hat{d} \cdot \hat{v})$. A numerical root finder may be applied to this equation. Each root $\bar{s}$ is used to compute $\bar{t} = \hat{d} \cdot (X(\bar{s}) - P)$, and a corresponding squared distance $F(\bar{s}, \bar{t})$ is computed. The squared distance between the line and the circle is the smallest F value computed over all the roots. The amount of CPU time required to compute the distance in this manner is probably no less than the amount needed to minimize F directly using a numerical solver. In both cases, evaluation of the trigonometric functions is the main expense in time. ∎

Algebraic Representation

Let the curve be defined as the intersection of its containing plane and a surface defined implicitly by the polynomial equation $F(X) = 0$. It is assumed that ∇F and the plane normal $\hat{n}$ are never parallel—a reasonable assumption since the surface should transversely cut the plane to form the curve. The perpendicular distance from a point X to the line is the length of the line segment $S(X) = (X - P) - (\hat{d} \cdot (X - P))\hat{d}$. This segment is the projection of $X - P$ onto a plane orthogonal to $\hat{d}$. The problem is to compute a point X for which the squared distance $\|S(X)\|^2$ is minimized subject to the constraints $\hat{n} \cdot X = c$ and $F(X) = 0$. The method of Lagrange multipliers discussed in Section A.9.3 can be applied to solve this. Observe that

$$\|S\|^2 = (X - P)^{\mathrm{T}}(I - \hat{d}\hat{d}^{\mathrm{T}})(X - P) = (X - P)^{\mathrm{T}}A(X - P)$$

where $A = I - \hat{d}\hat{d}^T$. Define

$$G(X, u, v) = (X - P)^T A(X - P) + u(\hat{n} \cdot X - c) + vF(X)$$

The parameters u and v are the Lagrange multipliers. The function G has a minimum when $\partial G/\partial X = \vec{0}$, $\partial G/\partial u = 0$, and $\partial G/\partial v = 0$. The notation $\partial G/\partial X$ denotes the 3-tuple of first-order partial derivatives of G with respect to the three components of X. The last two equations are just a restatement of the constraints that define the object. By assumption, $\hat{n} \cdot \nabla F \neq \vec{0}$, so dotting the X derivative equation by this vector and dividing by 2 yields the scalar equation constraint

$$H(X) := \hat{n} \times \nabla F \cdot A(X - P) = 0$$

The candidate points X for minimizing the distance are solutions to the system of polynomial equations: $\hat{n} \cdot X = c$, $F(X) = 0$, and $H(X) = 0$.

EXAMPLE   *Distance between a line and a circle.*   Consider the same example discussed previously. Many choices may be made for F. For example, F can define a sphere of radius r centered at C. Or F can define a cylinder whose axis contains circle center C, has direction $\hat{n}$, and has radius r. The sphere provides a simpler equation, so we use it: $F(X) = \|X - C\|^2 - r^2$ and $\nabla F = 2(X - C)$. The function $H(X)$ is a quadratic polynomial. Elimination theory applied to the one linear and two quadratic equations results in a polynomial of large degree. Instead of solving all three, the planar coordinates can be used. Let $X = C + u\hat{u} + v\hat{v}$, where $\{\hat{u}, \hat{v}, \hat{n}\}$ is an orthonormal set. This representation of X automatically satisfies the plane equation $\hat{n} \cdot X = c$, where $c = \hat{n} \cdot C$. Replacing X into $F = 0$ and $H = 0$ produces two quadratic equations $f(u, v) = 0$ and $h(u, v) = 0$ in the two unknowns u and v. Elimination of v leads to a single quartic equation $g(u) = 0$. For each root $\bar{u}$, two values $\bar{v}$ are computed by solving the quadratic equation $f(\bar{u}, v) = 0$. The squared distance for each pair $(\bar{u}, \bar{v})$ is computed, and the minimum squared distance is selected from the set of squared distances. ▪

10.13.2 DISTANCE BETWEEN LINE AND PLANAR SOLID OBJECT

The previous method computed distance between a line and a curve. If the distance is required between a planar solid object whose boundary is a specified curve, the algorithm must be slightly modified. If the line intersects the plane at a point inside the solid object, then the distance is zero. If the line intersects the plane, but does not intersect the solid object, then the point in the solid object closest to the line must be a point on the object boundary. The argument is simple. If the closest point is an interior point, it must be obtained from the closest line point by a projection onto the plane of the object. A sufficiently small step along the line starting at the closest line point and in the direction toward the plane leads to a new line point, its projection being another interior point of the object, and this new pair of points attains smaller distance than the previous pair, a contradiction to the previous pair attaining minimum distance. Finally, if the line is parallel to the plane, then the closest points on the object to the line may be selected from the object boundary. Thus, the algorithm amounts to determining if the line intersects the object. If so, the distance is zero; if not, the distance is computed from line to object boundary.

10.13.3 DISTANCE BETWEEN PLANAR CURVES

If two planar curves lie on the same 3D plane $\hat{n} \cdot (X - C) = 0$, the distance between them can be calculated by using planar coordinates, effectively reducing the problem to one in two dimensions. That is, if $\hat{n}$ is unit length and if $\hat{u}$ and $\hat{v}$ are unit-length vectors such that $\{\hat{u}, \hat{v}, \hat{n}\}$ is an orthonormal set, then any point on the plane is represented by $X = C + r\hat{u} + s\hat{v} + t\hat{n}$ for some choice of scalars r, s, and t. Distance calculations are made within the plane by projecting out the normal component. The projected points are $C + r\hat{u} + s\hat{v}$. The two-dimensional distance algorithms are applied to points (r, s). In 3D, the point C corresponds to the origin $(0, 0)$ of the 2D system.

An application might require distance calculations between planar curves that do not lie in the same plane. In this case the problem requires calculations in the full three-dimensional space. We present two types of methods for handling such curves. One method applies if the planar curves are represented in some parametric form. The other method applies if the sets of points for the planar curves are represented as solution sets to systems of algebraic equations.

Parametric Representation

Let the curves be represented parametrically as $X(s)$ for some domain $[s_{\min}, s_{\max}]$ and $Y(t)$ for some domain $[t_{\min}, t_{\max}]$. The squared distance between a pair of points, one on each curve, is $F(s, t) = \|X(s) - Y(t)\|^2$. Finding the minimum distance between the curves requires computing a parameter pair $(s, t) \in [s_{\min}, s_{\max}] \times [t_{\min}, t_{\max}]$ that minimizes F. A numerical minimizer can be applied directly to F, especially if either X or Y is not continuously differentiable. If both curves are continuously differentiable, then a calculus solution can be applied. Specifically, the minimum occurs either at an interior point of the domain where $\nabla F = \vec{0}$ or at a boundary point of the domain. Each edge of the boundary provides a minimization problem in one less dimension. The set of points (s, t) for which F is evaluated and the minimum chosen from all such evaluations consists of these critical points:

1. $\nabla F(s, t) = \vec{0}$ for $(s, t) \in (s_{\min}, s_{\max}) \times (t_{\min}, t_{\max})$
2. $\partial F(s_{\min}, t)/\partial t = 0$ for $t \in (t_{\min}, t_{\max})$
3. $\partial F(s_{\max}, t)/\partial t = 0$ for $t \in (t_{\min}, t_{\max})$

4. $\partial F(s, t_{\min})/\partial s = 0$ for $s \in (s_{\min}, s_{\max})$

5. $\partial F(s, t_{\max})/\partial s = 0$ for $s \in (s_{\min}, s_{\max})$

6. $(s_{\min}, t_{\min}), (s_{\min}, t_{\max}), (s_{\max}, t_{\min}), (s_{\max}, t_{\max})$

The complexity of solving the partial derivative equations is directly related to the complexity of $F(s, t)$.

Algebraic Representation

Let the planes of the two curves be $\hat{n}_0 \cdot X = c_0$ and $\hat{n}_1 \cdot Y = c_1$, where X denotes any point on the first curve and Y denotes any point on the second curve. We assume that the normal vectors are unit length and that the two planes are distinct. This does allow for the curves to be on parallel planes. Suppose that the first curve is the intersection of its containing plane and a surface defined implicitly by the polynomial equation $P_0(X) = 0$. We can assume that $\hat{n}_0$ and ∇P_0 are not parallel since P_0 can be chosen so that the implicit surface intersects the plane transversely. Similarly let the second curve be the intersection of its containing plane and a surface defined implicitly by the polynomial equation $P_1(Y) = 0$, where $\hat{n}_1$ and ∇P_1 are not parallel. For each pair of points (X, Y), one from the first curve and one from the second curve, the squared distance is $\|X - Y\|^2$. The distance between the two curves is attained by a pair (X, Y) that minimizes $\|X - Y\|^2$ subject to the four algebraic constraints.

The minimization is accomplished by using the method of Lagrange multipliers discussed in Section A.9.3. Define

$$G(X, Y, s_0, t_0, s_1, t_1) = \|X - Y\|^2 + s_0\hat{n}_0 \cdot (X - C_0) + t_0 P_0(X)$$

$$+ s_1\hat{n}_1 \cdot (Y - C_1) + t_1 P_1(Y)$$

Observe that $G : \mathbb{R}^{10} \to \mathbb{R}$. The derivative $\partial G/\partial X$ denotes the 3-tuple of first-order partial derivatives with respect to the components of X. The derivative $\partial G/\partial Y$ is defined similarly. The minimum of G occurs when $\partial G/\partial X = \vec{0}$, $\partial G/\partial Y = \vec{0}$, $\partial G/\partial s_0 = 0$, $\partial G/\partial t_0 = 0$, $\partial G/\partial s_1 = 0$, and $\partial G/\partial t_1 = 0$. The last four derivative equations are just a restatement of the four constraints that define the two curves. The X and Y partial derivative equations are

$$\frac{\partial G}{\partial X} = 2(X - Y) + s_0\hat{n}_0 + t_0\nabla P_0(X) = \vec{0} \quad \text{and}$$

$$\frac{\partial G}{\partial Y} = 2(Y - X) + s_1\hat{n}_1 + t_1\nabla P_1(\vec{T}) = \vec{0}$$

Dotting these with $\hat{n}_0 \times \nabla P_0$ and $\hat{n}_1 \times \nabla P_1$, respectively, yields $\hat{n}_0 \times \nabla P_0(X) \cdot (X - Y) = 0$ and $\hat{n}_1 \times \nabla P_1(Y) \cdot (Y - X) = 0$. Combining these with the four constraints leads to six polynomial equations in the six unknown components of X and Y:

$$\hat{n}_0 \times X = c_0$$

$$\hat{n}_1 \times Y = c_1$$

$$P_0(X) = 0$$

$$P_1(Y) = 0$$

$$\hat{n}_0 \times \nabla P_0(X) \cdot (X - Y) = 0$$

$$\hat{n}_1 \times \nabla P_1(Y) \cdot (Y - X) = 0$$

As in the case of distance from line to planar curve, the variables may be eliminated directly from the equations to obtain a large-degree polynomial equation in a single variable. Roots for that equation are found, the remaining five components are constructed from the various intermediate polynomial equations, and all candidates X and Y are now known and F is evaluated at those points. The squared distance between the two curves is the minimum of all such F values.

Smaller-degree polynomial equations may instead be constructed by using the plane equations to eliminate two variables. That is, if $\{\hat{u}_i, \hat{v}_i, \hat{n}_i\}$ for $i = 0$ and $i = 1$ are two right-handed orthonormal sets, and if C_i are points on the planes, then $X = C_0 + u_0\hat{u}_0 + v_0\hat{v}_0$ and $Y = C_1 + u_1\hat{u}_1 + v_1\hat{v}_1$. Replacing these in the other four constraints leads to four polynomial equations in the four unknowns u_0, v_0, u_1, and v_1. The method of elimination applied to these equations yields smaller-degree polynomials than when applied in terms of the six components of X and Y.

EXAMPLE   *Distance between two circles in 3D.*   For circles in 3D, the polynomials P_0 and P_1 mentioned in the discussion are $P_0(X) = \|X - C_0\|^2 - r_0^2$ and $P_1(Y) = \|Y - C_1\|^2 - r_1^2$, where C_i are the circle centers and r_i are the circle radii. The implicit surfaces are spheres, and their intersection with the planes are circles. From the planar equations, we can represent $X = C_0 + u_0\hat{u}_0 + v_0\hat{v}_0$ and $Y = C_1 + u_1\hat{u}_1 + v_1\hat{v}_1$. The circles are defined by $u_i^2 + v_i^2 = r_i^2$ for $i = 0, 1$. Since $\nabla P_0(X) = 2(X - C_0) = 2r_0(u_0\hat{u}_0 + v_0\hat{v}_0)$, the cross product of normal and gradient is $\hat{n}_0 \times \nabla P_0 = 2r_0(u_0\hat{v}_0 - v_0\hat{u}_0)$. We have made use of the fact that $\{\hat{u}_0, \hat{v}_0, \hat{n}_0\}$ is a right-handed orthonormal set. Similarly, $\hat{n}_1 \cdot \nabla P_1 = 2r_1(u_1\hat{v}_1 - v_1\hat{u}_1)$. The circle equations and the two equations obtained from the method of Lagrange multipliers are

$$u_0^2 + v_0^2 = r_0^2$$

$$u_1^2 + v_1^2 = r_1^2$$

$$(u_0\hat{v}_0 - v_0\hat{u}_0) \cdot (C_0 - C_1 - u_1\hat{u}_1 - v_1\hat{v}_1) = 0$$

$$(u_1\hat{v}_1 - v_1\hat{u}_1) \cdot (C_1 - C_0 - u_0\hat{u}_0 - v_0\hat{v}_0) = 0$$

a system of four quadratic polynomial equations in the four unknowns u_0, v_0, u_1, and v_1.

Setting $\hat{d} = C_0 - C_1$, the last two equations are of the form

$$u_0(a_0 + a_1 u_1 + a_2 v_1) + v_0(a_3 + a_4 u_1 + a_5 v_1) = 0$$

$$u_1(b_0 + b_1 u_0 + b_2 v_0) + v_1(b_3 + b_4 u_0 + b_5 v_0) = 0$$

where

$$a_0 = \hat{v}_0 \cdot \hat{d}, \;\; a_1 = -\hat{v}_0 \cdot \hat{u}_1, \;\; a_2 = -\hat{v}_0 \cdot \hat{v}_1, \;\; a_3 = -\hat{u}_0 \cdot \hat{d}, \;\; a_4 = \hat{u}_0 \cdot \hat{u}_1, \;\; a_5 = \hat{u}_0 \cdot \hat{v}_1$$

$$b_0 = -\hat{v}_1 \cdot \hat{d}, \;\; b_1 = -\hat{v}_1 \cdot \hat{u}_0, \;\; b_2 = -\hat{v}_1 \cdot \hat{v}_0, \;\; b_3 = \hat{u}_1 \cdot \hat{d}, \;\; b_4 = \hat{u}_1 \cdot \hat{u}_0, \;\; b_5 = \hat{u}_1 \cdot \hat{v}_0$$

In matrix form we have

$$\begin{bmatrix} m_{00} & m_{01} \\ m_{10} & m_{11} \end{bmatrix} \begin{bmatrix} u_0 \\ v_0 \end{bmatrix} = \begin{bmatrix} a_0 + a_1 u_1 + a_2 v_1 & a_3 + a_4 u_1 + a_5 v_1 \\ b_1 u_1 + b_4 v_1 & b_2 u_1 + b_5 v_1 \end{bmatrix} \begin{bmatrix} u_0 \\ v_0 \end{bmatrix}$$

$$= \begin{bmatrix} 0 \\ -(b_0 u_1 + b_3 v_1) \end{bmatrix} = \begin{bmatrix} 0 \\ \lambda \end{bmatrix}$$

Let $\mathbf{M}$ denote the 2×2 matrix in the equation. Multiplying by the adjoint of $\mathbf{M}$ yields

$$\det(\mathbf{M}) \begin{bmatrix} u_0 \\ v_0 \end{bmatrix} = \begin{bmatrix} m_{11} & -m_{01} \\ -m_{10} & m_{00} \end{bmatrix} \begin{bmatrix} 0 \\ \lambda \end{bmatrix} = \begin{bmatrix} -m_{01}\lambda \\ m_{00}\lambda \end{bmatrix} \qquad (10.17)$$

Summing the squares of the vector components, using $u_0^2 + v_0^2 = r_0^2$, and subtracting to the left-hand side yields

$$r_0^2 \left(m_{00} m_{11} - m_{01} m_{10} \right)^2 - \left(m_{00}^2 + m_{01}^2 \right) \lambda^2 = 0 \qquad (10.18)$$

This is a quartic polynomial equation in u_1 and v_1.

Equation 10.18 can be reduced to a polynomial of degree 8 whose roots $v_1 \in [-1, 1]$ are the candidates to provide the global minimum of F. Formally computing the determinant and using $u_1^2 = r_1^2 - v_1^2$ leads to $m_{00} m_{11} - m_{01} m_{10} = p_0(v_1) + u_1 p_1(v_1)$, where $p_0(z) = \sum_{i=0}^{2} p_{0i} z^i$ and $p_1(z) = \sum_{i=0}^{1} p_{1i} z^i$. The coefficients are

$$p_{00} = r_1^2(a_1 b_2 - a_4 b_1), \qquad\qquad p_{10} = a_0 b_2 - a_3 b_1,$$

$$p_{01} = a_0 b_5 - a_3 b_4, \qquad\qquad p_{11} = a_1 b_5 - a_5 b_1 + a_2 b_1 - a_4 b_4,$$

$$p_{02} = a_2 b_5 - a_5 b_4 + a_4 b_1 - a_1 b_2$$

Similarly, $m_{00}^2 + m_{01}^2 = q_0(v_1) + u_1 q_1(v_1)$, where $q_0(z) = \sum_{i=0}^{2} q_{0i} z^i$ and $q_1(z) = \sum_{i=0}^{1} q_{1i} z^i$. The coefficients are

$$q_{00} = a_0^2 + a_3^2 + r_1^2(a_1^2 + a_4^2), \quad q_{10} = 2(a_0 a_1 + a_3 a_4),$$

$$q_{01} = 2(a_0 a_2 + a_3 a_5), \qquad\qquad q_{11} = 2(a_1 a_2 + a_4 a_5),$$

$$q_{02} = a_2^2 + a_5^2 - a_1^2 - a_4^2$$

Finally, $\lambda^2 = r_0(v_1) + u_1 r_1(v_1)$, where $r_0(z) = \sum_{i=0}^{2} r_{0i} z^i$ and $r_1(z) = \sum_{i=0}^{1} r_{1i} z$. The coefficients are

$$r_{00} = r_1^2 b_0^2, \quad r_{10} = 0,$$

$$r_{01} = 0, \qquad r_{11} = 2b_0 b_3,$$

$$r_{02} = b_3^2 - b_0^2$$

Replacing p, q, and r in Equation 10.18 and using the identity $u_1^2 = 1 - v_1^2$ yields

$$0 = r_0^2[p_0(v_1) + u_1 p_1(v_1)]^2 - [q_0(v_1) + u_1 q_1(v_1)][r_0(v_1) + u_1 r_1(v_1)]$$

$$= g_0(v_1) + u_1 g_1(v_1) \qquad\qquad (10.19)$$

where $g_0(z) = \sum_{i=0}^{4} g_{0i} z^i$ and $g_1(z) = \sum_{i=0}^{3} g_{1i} z^i$. The coefficients are

$$g_{00} = r_0^2(p_{00}^2 + r_1^2 p_{10}^2) - q_{00} r_{00}$$

$$g_{01} = 2r_0^2(p_{00}p_{01} + r_1^2 p_{10}p_{11}) - q_{01}r_{00} - q_{10}r_1^2 r_{11}$$

$$g_{02} = r_0^2(p_{01}^2 + 2p_{00}p_{02} - p_{10}^2 + r_1^2 p_{11}^2) - q_{02}r_{00} - q_{00}r_{02} - r_1^2 q_{11}r_{11}$$

$$g_{03} = 2r_0^2(p_{01}p_{02} - p_{10}p_{11}) - q_{01}r_{02} + q_{10}r_{11}$$

$$g_{04} = r_0^2(p_{02}^2 - p_{11}^2) - q_{02}r_{02} + q_{11}r_{11}$$

$$g_{10} = 2r_0^2 p_{00}p_{10} - q_{10}r_{00}$$

$$g_{11} = 2r_0^2(p_{01}p_{10} + p_{00}p_{11}) - q_{11}r_{00} - q_{00}r_{11}$$

$$g_{12} = 2r_0^2(p_{02}p_{10} + p_{01}p_{11}) - q_{10}r_{02} - q_{01}r_{11}$$

$$g_{13} = 2r_0^2 p_{02}p_{11} - q_{11}r_{02} - q_{02}r_{11}$$

We can eliminate the u_1 term by solving $g_0 = -u_1 g_1$, squaring, and subtracting to the left-hand side to obtain $0 = g_0^2 - (r_1^2 - v_1^2)g_1^2 = h(v_1)$, where $h(z) = \sum_{i=0}^{8} h_i z^i$. The coefficients are

$$h_0 = g_{00}^2 - r_1^2 g_{10}^2$$

$$h_1 = 2(g_{00}g_{01} - r_1^2 g_{10}g_{11})$$

$$h_2 = g_{01}^2 + g_{10}^2 + 2g_{00}g_{02} - r_1^2(g_{11}^2 + 2g_{10}g_{12})$$

$$h_3 = 2(g_{01}g_{02} + g_{00}g_{03} + g_{10}g_{11}) - 2r_1^2(g_{11}g_{12} + g_{10}g_{13})$$

$$h_4 = g_{02}^2 + g_{11}^2 + 2(g_{01}g_{03} + g_{00}g_{04} + g_{10}g_{12}) - r_1^2(g_{12}^2 + 2g_{11}g_{13})$$

$$h_5 = 2(g_{02}g_{03} + g_{01}g_{04} + g_{11}g_{12} + g_{10}g_{13} - r_1^2 g_{12}g_{13})$$

$$h_6 = g_{03}^2 + g_{12}^2 - r_1^2 g_{13}^2 + 2(g_{02}g_{04} + g_{11}g_{13})$$

$$h_7 = 2(g_{03}g_{04} + g_{12}g_{13})$$

$$h_8 = g_{04}^2 + g_{13}^2$$

To find the minimum squared distance, compute all the real-valued roots of $h(v_1) = 0$. For each root $\bar{v}_1 \in [-1, 1]$, compute $\bar{u}_1 = \pm\sqrt{1 - \bar{v}_1^2}$ and choose either (or both) of these that satisfy Equation 10.19. For each pair $(\bar{u}_1, \bar{v}_1)$ solve for $(\bar{u}_0, \bar{v}_0)$ in Equation 10.17. The main numerical issue to deal with is how close to zero is $\det(M)$.

Finally, evaluate the squared distance $\|X - Y\|^2$, where $X = C_0 + \bar{u}_0\hat{u}_0 + \bar{v}_0\hat{v}_0$ and $Y = C_1 + \bar{u}_1\hat{u}_1 + \bar{v}_1\hat{v}_1$. The minimum of all such squared distances is the squared distance between the circles. ▪

10.13.4 GEODESIC DISTANCE ON SURFACES

The following discussion can be found in textbooks on the differential geometry of curves and surfaces. The book by Kay (1988) is a particularly easy one to read. Given two points on a surface, we want to compute the shortest distance between the two points measured *on the surface*. A path of shortest distance connecting the two points is called a *geodesic curve*, and the arc length of that curve is called the *geodesic distance* between the points. For two points in a plane, the shortest path is the line segment connecting the points. On a surface, however, it is not necessary that the shortest path be unique. For example, two antipodal points on a sphere have infinitely many shortest paths connecting them, each path a half great circle on the sphere.

The method of construction for a geodesic curve that is discussed here is based on *relaxation*. Only the ideas are presented since the mathematical details are quite lengthy. An initial curve connecting the two points and lying on the surface is allowed to evolve over time. The evolution is based on a model of heat flow and has been studied extensively in the literature under the topic of *Euclidean curve shortening*. The ideas also apply to many other areas, particularly to computer vision and image processing (ter Haar Romeny 1994). The evolving curve is represented as $X(s, t)$, where s is the arc length parameter and t is the time of evolution. The end points of the curve are always the two input points, P and Q. In the plane, the idea is to allow the curve to evolve according to the linear heat equation $\vec{X}_t = \vec{X}_{ss}$, where $\vec{X}_t$ is the first-order partial derivative of X with respect to t and $\vec{X}_{ss}$ is the second-order partial derivative of X with respect to s. Although X is a point quantity, the derivatives are vector quantities; hence the use of vector caps on the derivatives. The limit of the curve as t becomes infinite will be the line segment connecting P and Q. Any initial curve $X(s, 0) = C(s)$ connecting the two points is viewed as a curve that is "stretched" from its natural state. As time increases, the curve is allowed to "relax" into its natural state, in this case the line segment connecting the points.

For a surface, the evolution is slightly more complicated:

$$\vec{X}_t = \vec{X}_{ss} - (\vec{X}_{ss} \cdot \hat{n})\hat{n}, \quad t > 0$$

$$X(s, 0) = C(s), \tag{10.20}$$

$$X(0, t) = P, \quad X(L(t), t) = Q$$

The vector $\hat{n}(s, t)$ is the surface normal at the associated point $X(s, t)$ on the surface. The evolving curve is required to stay on the surface. Any point $X(s, t)$ can only be moved tangentially to the surface. The movements are determined by the time derivative $\vec{X}_t$, so $\vec{X}_t$ must be a tangent vector to the surface. The right-hand side of the evolution equation has the diffusion term $\vec{X}_{ss}$, but observe that the correction term involving the normal vector simply projects out any contribution by $\vec{X}_{ss}$ in the normal direction, leaving only tangential components, as desired. The initial curve connecting the points is $C(s)$. The length of $X(s, t)$ is denoted by $L(t)$. The boundary conditions are the two constraints that the end points of the curve $X(s, t)$ must be the points P and Q. This problem is particularly complicated by the *time-varying* boundary condition $X(L(t), t) = Q$. Standard textbooks on partial differential equations tend to discuss only those problems for which the boundary conditions are time invariant.

The numerical method for solving the evolution equation, Equation 10.20, uses a central difference approximation for the s-derivatives and a forward difference approximation for the t-derivative. That is,

$$\vec{X}_{ss}(s, t) \doteq \frac{(X(s + h, t) - X(s, t)) + (X(s - h, t) - X(s, t))}{h^2}$$

and

$$\vec{X}_t(s, t) \doteq \frac{X(s, t + k) - X(s, t)}{k}$$

If $X(s, t)$ is known and the surface is defined implicitly by $F(X) = 0$, then the surface normal at that point is computed explicitly by $\hat{n}(s, t) = \nabla F(X(s, t)) / \|\nabla F(X(s, t))\|$. If the surface is defined parametrically by $X(u, v)$, then the surface normal is $\hat{n}(u, v) = \vec{X}_u \times \vec{X}_v / \|\vec{X}_u \times \vec{X}_v\|$. However, the evolution equation is unaware of the u and v parameters of the surface, so the normal must be estimated by other means. As long as the derivatives $\vec{X}_t$ and $\vec{X}_s$ are not parallel (the curve does not stretch only in the tangent direction during evolution), then the normal vector is estimated as $\hat{n}(s, t) \doteq \vec{X}_s(s, t) \times \vec{X}_t(s, t) / \|\vec{X}_s(s, t) \times \vec{X}_t(s, t)\|$. Replacing these approximations in the evolution equation leads to

$$X(s, t + k) = X(s, t) + \frac{k}{h^2} \left(I - \hat{n}\hat{n}^{\mathrm{T}} \right)$$

$$((X(s + h, t) - X(s, t)) + (X(s - h, t) - X(s, t))) \tag{10.21}$$

An initial curve $C(s)$ is chosen, and a set of equally spaced points s_i, $0 \le i \le M$, on this curve are selected. The number of chosen points is at the discretion of the application, but generally the larger the number, the more likely the approximation to the geodesic curve is a good one. A time step $k > 0$ and spatial step $h > 0$ are chosen. The ratio k/h^2 needs to be sufficiently small to guarantee numerical stability. How small that is depends on the surface and will require the standard techniques for determining stability. If $X(s_i, 0) = C(s_i)$ for all i, the curve samples at time $t = k$ are computed in the left-hand side $X(s_i, k)$ of Equation 10.21. Numerical errors can cause $X(s_i, k)$ to be off the surface. If the surface is defined implicitly by $F(X) = 0$, the defining equation potentially can be used to make a correction to $X(s_i, k)$ to place it back on the surface. If the surface is defined parametrically, the correction is a bit more difficult since it is not immediately clear how to select parameters u and v so that $X(u, v)$ is somehow the closest surface point to $X(s_i, k)$.

Equation 10.21 is iterated until some stopping criterion is met. There are many choices including (1) measuring the total variation between all sample points at times t and $t + k$ and stopping when the variation is sufficiently small or (2) computing the arc length of the polyline connecting the samples and stopping when the change in arc length between times t and $t + k$ is sufficiently small. In either case, the final polyline arc length is used as the approximation to the geodesic distance.

CHAPTER 11
INTERSECTION IN 3D

This chapter contains information on computing the intersection of geometric primitives in 3D. The simplest object combinations to analyze are those for which one of the objects is a linear component (line, ray, segment). These combinations are covered in the first four sections. The next four sections cover intersections of planar components (planes, triangles, polyhedra) with other objects: one another, polyhedra, quadric surfaces, and polynomial surfaces. Two sections cover the intersection of quadric surfaces with other quadric surfaces and polynomial surfaces with other polynomial surfaces. Included is a section covering the method of separating axes, a very powerful technique for dealing with intersections of convex objects. The last section covers a miscellany of intersection problems.

11.1 LINEAR COMPONENTS AND PLANAR COMPONENTS

This section covers the problems of computing the intersections of linear components and planar components in 3D. Linear components include rays, line segments, and lines. There are a variety of ways to define such geometric entities (see Section 9.1); for the purposes of this section, we use the coordinate-free parametric representation—a linear component $\mathcal{L}$ is defined using a point of origin P and a direction $\vec{d}$:

$$\mathcal{L}(t) = P + t\vec{d} \tag{11.1}$$

A ray $\mathcal{R}$ is most frequently defined using a normalized vector

$$\mathcal{R}(t) = P + t\hat{d}, \qquad 0 \le t \le \infty \tag{11.2}$$

while line $\mathcal{L}$ may or may not use a normalized vector:

$$\mathcal{L}(t) = P + t\vec{d}, \qquad -\infty \le t \le \infty \tag{11.3}$$

We assume a line segment S is represented by a pair of points $\{P_0, P_1\}$. We can again employ the same algorithm for ray/planar component intersection by converting the line segment into ray form:

$$S(t) = P_0 + t(P_1 - P_0)$$

That is, our direction vector $\vec{d}$ is defined by the difference of the two points. Note that, in general, $\|\vec{d}\| \ne 1$. However, not only is it unnecessary for the direction vector to be normalized, but it is also undesirable: note that $P_1 = P_0 + \vec{d}$, so if we compute the intersection for this "ray" and a planar component, then the point of intersection is in the line segment if and only if $0 \le t \le 1$.

11.1.1   LINEAR COMPONENTS AND PLANES

In this section, we discuss the problem of intersecting linear components and planes. A plane $\mathcal{P}$ is defined as $[\,a \quad b \quad c \quad d\,]$:

$$ax + by + cz + d = 0 \tag{11.4}$$

where $a^2 + b^2 + c^2 = 1$. Taken as a vector, $\hat{n} = [\,a \quad b \quad c\,]$ represents the normal to the plane, while $|d|$ represents the minimum distance from the plane to the origin $[\,0 \quad 0 \quad 0\,]$.

As shown in Figure 11.1, the intersection of the linear component $\mathcal{L}$ and $\mathcal{P}$ (if it exists) is at point $Q = P + t\vec{d}$, for some t. Since Q is a point on $\mathcal{P}$, it must also satisfy Equation 11.4.

We can then simply substitute Equation 11.1 into Equation 11.4:

$$a\left(P_x + d_x t\right) + b\left(P_y + d_y t\right) + c\left(P_z + d_z t\right) + d = 0$$

and solve for the parameter t:

$$t = \frac{-\left(a P_x + b P_y + c P_z + d\right)}{a d_x + b d_y + c d_z}$$

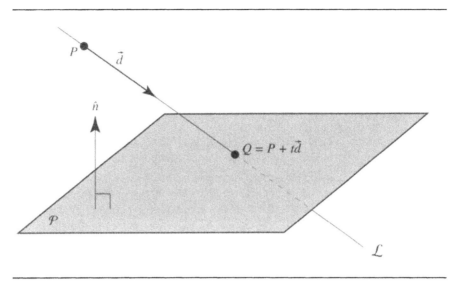

Figure 11.1   Intersection of a line and a plane.

It is useful to view this equation as operations on vectors:

$$t = \frac{-\left(\hat{n} \cdot P + d\right)}{\hat{n} \cdot \vec{d}}$$

Note that the denominator $\hat{n} \cdot \vec{d}$ represents the dot product of the plane's normal and the ray's direction; if this value is equal to 0, then the ray and the plane are parallel. If the ray is in the plane, then there are an infinite number of intersections, and if the ray is not in the plane, there are no intersections. Due to the approximate nature of the floating-point representation of real numbers and operations on them, lines and planes are rarely ever exactly parallel; thus, the comparison of the dot product should be made against some small number ϵ. The value for ϵ depends on the precision of the variables and on application-dependent issues. Calculating this value first will allow us to quickly reject such cases.

After computing the numerator, we then divide to get t. Computing the intersection point's coordinates requires simply substituting the computed value of t back into Equation 11.2:

$$Q = P + t\vec{d}$$

The pseudocode for line-plane intersection is

```
boolean LineIntersectPlane(
    Line3D   line,
    Plane    plane,
    float&   t,
    Point3D& intersection)
{
    // Check for (near) parallel line and plane
    denominator = Dot(line.direction, plane.normal)
    if (Abs(denominator) < epsilon) {
        // Check if line lies in the plane or not.
        // We do this, somewhat arbitrarily, by checking if
        // the origin of the line is in the plane. If it is,
        // set the parameter of the intersection to be 0. An
        // application may wish to handle this case differently...
        if (Abs(line.origin.x * plane.a + line.origin.y * plane.b +
                line.origin.z * plane.c + plane.d) < epsilon) {
            t = 0;
            return (true);
        } else {
            return false;
        }
    }

    // Nonparallel, so compute intersection
    t = -(plane.a * line.origin.x + plane.b * line.origin.y +
            plane.c * line.origin.z + plane.d);
    t = t / denominator;
    intersection = line.origin + t * line.direction;
    return true
}
```

Ray-Plane Intersection

A ray is only defined for $t \geq 0$, so we can simply check if the t value calculated by the line intersection routine is greater than or equal to 0, and accept or reject the intersection.

Line Segment–Plane Intersection

We assume a line segment is represented by a pair of points $\{P_0, P_1\}$. We can again employ a similar algorithm for line-plane intersection by converting the line segment into ray form:

$$\mathcal{R}(t) = P_0 + t(P_1 - P_0)$$

The segment is defined for $0 \leq t \leq 1$, and so we can simply compare the t-value computed to that range, and accept or reject the intersection.

11.1.2 LINEAR COMPONENTS AND TRIANGLES

In this section, we'll cover intersections of rays, lines, and line segments with triangles. In a subsequent section, we'll be covering the more general case of the intersection of linear components and polygons; it certainly would be possible to simply solve the line/triangle intersection problem as a special case of a three-vertex polygon, but we can exploit barycentric coordinates and come up with a more direct and efficient solution.

One approach is to intersect the linear component with the plane containing the triangle, and then determine whether or not the intersection point is *within* the triangle. The determination of containment can be done by simply projecting the triangle's vertices and the point of intersection onto one of the axis-aligned planes (choosing the plane that maximizes the area of the projected triangle), and then using a 2D point-in-triangle test (see Haines 1994 and Section 13.3.1). However, such an approach requires either computing the normal of the triangle every time an intersection test is done or storing the normal (and making sure it's recomputed if and when it changes).

An alternative is to use an approach due to Möller and Trumbore (1997). We'll again consider a linear component defined as an origin and direction vector (Equation 11.1). A triangle is defined simply as a sequence of vertices $\{V_0, V_1, V_2\}$ (see Figure 11.2).

To review, any point in a triangle can be defined in terms of its position relative to the triangle's vertices:

$$Q_{u,v,w} = w V_0 + u V_1 + v V_2 \tag{11.5}$$

where $u + v + w = 1$. The triple (u, v, w) is known as the *barycentric coordinates* of Q, although since $w = 1 - (u + v)$, frequently just the pair (u, v) is used (see Section 3.5).

As with the linear component–plane intersection, we can compute the linear component–triangle intersection by simply substituting Equation 11.2 into Equation 11.5:

$$P + t\hat{d} = (1 - (u + v))V_0 + u V_1 + v V_2$$

which can be expanded to

$$\begin{bmatrix} -\hat{d} & V_1 - V_0 & V_2 - V_0 \end{bmatrix} \begin{bmatrix} t \\ u \\ v \end{bmatrix} = \begin{bmatrix} P - V_0 \end{bmatrix}$$

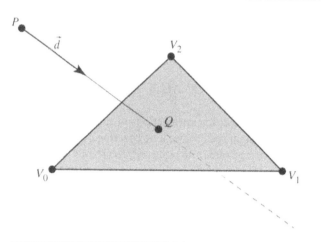

Figure 11.2   Intersection of a line and a triangle.

Recalling that each of these variables are vector-valued, you can see that this is a three-equation linear system, with three unknowns. There are any number of ways to solve this, but here we choose to use Cramer's rule (see Sections 2.7.4 and A.1).

By Cramer's rule, we have

$$\begin{bmatrix} t \\ u \\ v \end{bmatrix} = \frac{1}{|-\hat{d} \quad V_1 - V_0 \quad V_2 - V_0|} \begin{bmatrix} |P - V_0 \quad V_1 - V_0 \quad V_2 - V_0| \\ |-\hat{d} \quad P - V_0 \quad V_2 - V_0| \\ |-\hat{d} \quad V_1 - V_0 \quad P - V_0| \end{bmatrix}$$

$$= \frac{1}{(\hat{d} \times (V_2 - V_0)) \cdot (V_1 - V_0)} \begin{bmatrix} ((P - V_0) \times (V_1 - V_0)) \cdot (V_2 - V_0) \\ (\hat{d} \times (V_2 - V_0)) \cdot (P - V_0) \\ ((P - V_0) \times (V_1 - V_0)) \cdot \hat{d} \end{bmatrix}$$

This last rewriting is due to the fact that

$$| \vec{u} \quad \vec{v} \quad \vec{w} | = -(\vec{u} \times \vec{w}) \cdot \vec{v}$$

$$= -(\vec{w} \times \vec{v}) \cdot \vec{u}$$

and was done to expose the common subexpressions $\hat{d} \times (V_2 - V_0)$ and $(P - V_0) \times (V_1 - V_0)$.

Once we solve for t, u, and v, we can determine whether the intersection point is within the triangle (rather than somewhere else in the plane of the polygon) by inspecting their values: if $0 \le u \le 1$, $0 \le v \le 1$, and $u + v \le 1$, then the intersection is within the triangle; otherwise, it is in the plane of the polygon, but outside the triangle.

The pseudocode for this is

```
bool LineTriangleIntersect(
    Triangle3D tri,
    Line3D     line,
    Isect&     info,
    float      epsilon,
    Point3D&   intersection)
{
    // Does not cull back-facing triangles.
    Vector3D e1, e2, p, s, q;
    float t, u, v, tmp;
    e1 = tri.v1 - tri.v0;
    e2 = tri.v2 - tri.v0;
    p = Cross(line.direction, e2);
    tmp = Dot(p, e1);

    if (tmp > -epsilon && tmp < epsilon) {
        return false;
    }

    tmp = 1.0 / tmp;
    s = line.origin - tri.v0;

    u = tmp * Dot(s, p);
    if (u < 0.0 || u > 1.0) {
        return false;
    }

    q = Cross(s, e1);
    v = tmp * Dot(line.direction, q);

    if (v < 0.0 || v > 1.0) {
        return false;
    }

    if (u + v > 1.0) {
      return false;
    }

    t = tmp * Dot(e2, q);

    info.u = u;
    info.v = v;
    info.t = t;
```

```
    intersection = line.origin + t * line.direction;
    return true;
}
```

Ray-Triangle Intersection

A ray is only defined for $t \geq 0$, so we can simply check if the t value computed is nonnegative, and accept or reject the intersection.

Line Segment–Triangle Intersection

We assume a line segment is represented by a pair of points $\{P_0, P_1\}$. We can again employ a similar algorithm for line-triangle intersection by converting the line segment into line form. The segment is defined for $0 \leq t \leq 1$, and so we can simply compare the t-value to that range, and accept or reject the intersection.

11.1.3 LINEAR COMPONENTS AND POLYGONS

Computation of intersections between linear components and triangles was aided by our ability to specify the point of intersection in barycentric coordinates; the intersection was guaranteed (within floating-point error) to be in the plane of the triangle. Unfortunately, this trick cannot be directly exploited for polygons in general. For polygons that are not self-intersecting, it is theoretically possible to triangulate them, and then apply the linear component–triangle intersection algorithm on each triangle, but this is likely not efficient.

In the following sections, the polygons are assumed to be planar within floating-point error, non-self-intersecting, closed, and consisting of a single contour. Polygons are represented by a list of n vertices: $\{V_0, V_1, \ldots, V_{n-1}\}$. The plane of the polygon is implied by the vertices and represented in the usual fashion as a normal and distance from the origin: $ax + by + cz + d = 0$, where $a^2 + b^2 + c^2 = 1$.

Because we cannot (in general) exploit the "barycentric coordinates trick" we used for triangles, linear component–polygon intersection requires several steps:

1. Compute the plane equation for the polygon. This can be done by selecting an arbitrary vertex as a point on the plane and then computing the normal using the cross product of the vectors formed by that vertex and its neighbors; however, in general polygons are not exactly planar, so a more robust mechanism, such as Newell's method (Tampieri 1992) or the hyperplanar fitting of Section A.7.4 should be employed.

2. Compute the intersection of the linear component with the plane (see Section 11.1.1).

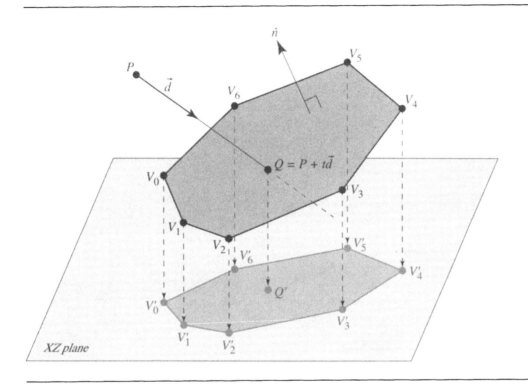

Figure 11.3   Intersection of a ray and a polygon.

3. If the linear component intersects the polygon's plane, determine whether the intersection point is within the boundaries of the polygon.

This last step corresponds to the inspection of the barycentric coordinates for the ray/triangle intersection, but for polygons we must employ a "trick." This trick consists of projecting the polygon's vertices and the intersection point Q onto one of the planes defined by the local frame (the XY, YZ, or XZ planes) and then determining whether the projected intersection point Q' lies within the projected polygon $\{V'_0, V'_1, \ldots, V'_{n-1}\}$ (see Figure 11.3).

As the projection we desire is orthographic, the projection step consists of choosing one coordinate to ignore and using the other two coordinates as (x, y) coordinates in a two-dimensional space. The coordinate to ignore should be the one that shows minimal variance across the vertices of the polygon; that is, if we compute a bounding box, the rejected coordinate should be the one that corresponds to the shortest side of the box. By doing this, numerical errors due to the projection are minimized, particularly when the polygon is very nearly coplanar with one of the orthogonal planes.

So, in the final step we simply have to solve a two-dimensional point-in-polygon problem, for which there are many algorithms (see Section 13.3).

We should note that a polygon may be defined as the intersection of a plane and a set of half-spaces; these half-spaces are those defined by considering each pair of vertices $\{V_i, V_{i+1}\}$ as two points on a plane perpendicular to the plane of the polygon. We could then determine if the intersection point of the line and the polygon's plane was on the same side of all of these half-spaces. This same sort of algorithm could be employed as the 2D point-in-polygon algorithm the other approach uses, and so the question arises, "Why project the points if we're going to use (basically) the same method?" The answer is efficiency—it's arguably faster to do it in (projected) 2D.

The pseudocode for this is

```
bool LinePolygonIntersection(
    Polygon3D poly,
    Line3D    line,
    float&    t,
    Point3D&  intersection)
{
    // lcp direction is assumed to be normalized
    // Also assumes polygon is planar
    Vector3D N, p, e1, e2;
    float numer, denom;
    e1 = poly.vertexPosition(1) - poly.vertexPosition(0);
    e2 = poly.vertexPosition(2) - poly.vertexPosition(1);
    N = Cross(e1, e2);
    N /= N.length();
    p = poly.vertexPosition(0);
    denom = Dot(line.direction, N);

    if (denom < 0) {
        numer = Dot(N, p - line.origin);
        t = numer / denom;
        if (t < 0) {
            return false;
        }
        p = line.origin + t * r.d;
        int projectionIndex = MaxAbsComponent(N);

        Point2D* 2dPoints;
        Point2D p2d;
        2dPoints = new Point2D[poly.numVertices];

        // Project Points into a 2D plane
        // by removing the coordinate that
        // was the fabs maximum in the normal
```

```
        //  return them in array 2dPoints.
        Project2D(poly.VertexArray, projectionIndex, 2dPoints,
                poly.numVertices);
        Project2D(p, projectionIndex, p2d, 1);

        // Choose your method of winding test
        // Sign of dotProducts etc...
        if (PointIn2DPolygon(p2d, 2dPoints)) {
            delete [] 2dPoints;
            intersection = line.origin + t * line.direction;
            return true;
        } else {
            delete [] 2dPoints;
            return false;
        }
    } else {
        // Back facing
        return false;
    }
}
```

Ray-Polygon Intersection

A ray is only defined for $t \geq 0$, so we can simply check if t is nonnegative, and accept or reject the intersection.

Line Segment–Polygon Intersection

We assume a line segment is represented by a pair of points $\{P_0, P_1\}$. We can again employ a similar algorithm for line-polygon intersection by converting the line segment into ray form. The segment is defined for $0 \leq t \leq 1$, and so we can simply check if t is in that range, and accept or reject the intersection.

11.1.4 LINEAR COMPONENT AND DISK

In this section we address the problem of intersecting a linear component with a disk (see Figure 11.4). The linear component is defined in the usual fashion:

$$\mathcal{L}(t) = P + t\vec{d}$$

and the disk is defined in the same fashion as the 3D circle (see Section 9.2.3):

$$P = C + r\hat{w}_\theta$$

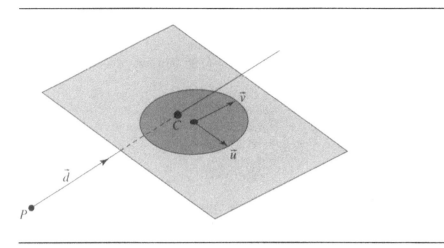

Figure 11.4   Intersection of a linear component and a disk.

where

$$\hat{w}_\theta = \cos\theta\,\hat{u} + \sin\theta\,\hat{v}$$

A disk is simply a 3D circle that also includes the planar region bounded by the perimeter of the circle: if a line goes through the "interior" of a circle, no intersection occurs, but if a line goes through a disk's interior, an intersection occurs. Alternatively, we can specify it simply as a centerpoint C, a plane normal $\hat{n}$, and a radius r; however, this loses any parametric information (of the intersection point, relative to the "axes" of the circle)—this may or may not be relevant to the application.

The algorithm is simply to intersect the linear component with the plane in which the disk lies, and then to compute the squared distance between the intersection and the center of the disk, and compare this against the squared radius. If the linear component lies within the plane of the disk, then an application may or may not wish to consider intersections. If intersections in this case are desired, a 3D generalization of the 2D linear component–circle intersection algorithm may be used; if the application is merely interested in whether or not an intersection occurred, then the distance (squared) from the linear component to the circle can be compared to the (squared) radius.

The pseudocode is

```
bool LineIntersectDisk(Line3D line, Disk3D disk, Point3D p)
{
    Plane3D plane;
    plane.normal = disk.normal;
```

```
plane.p = disk.center;
float t;
Point3D intersection

if (!LinePlaneIntersection(plane, line, t, p)) {
    return false;
}

if (DistanceSquared(p, disk.center) <= disk.radius * disk.radius) {
    return true;
} else {
    return false;
}
}
```

Ray-Disk Intersection

A ray is only defined for $t \geq 0$, so we can simply check if t is nonnegative, and accept or reject the intersection.

Line Segment–Disk Intersection

We assume a line segment is represented by a pair of points $\{P_0, P_1\}$. We can again employ a similar algorithm for line-disk intersection by converting the line segment into ray form. The segment is defined for $0 \leq t \leq 1$, and so we can simply check if t is in that range, and accept or reject the intersection.

11.2 LINEAR COMPONENTS AND POLYHEDRA

This section addresses the problem of intersecting linear components with polyhedra and polygonal meshes. The linear components ray, line, and line segment are defined by an origin point and a vector:

$$\mathcal{L}(t) = P + t\vec{d}$$

In the case of a line segment defined by two points P_0 and P_1, we let $\vec{d} = P_1 - P_0$. A polyhedron is defined as described in Section 9.3. A polygonal mesh, for the purposes of this section, is simply a polyhedron that is not necessarily closed. Figure 11.5 shows a ray intersecting with an octahedron, while Figure 11.6 shows a line segment intersecting with a triangle mesh. Note that polyhedra are not required to be regular, and polygonal meshes are not required to have all triangular faces.

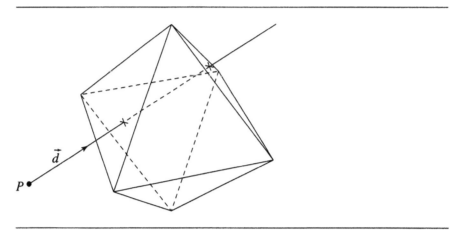

Figure 11.5   Intersection of a ray and a polyhedron (octahedron).

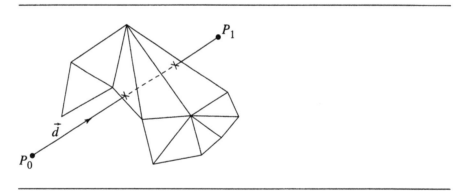

Figure 11.6   Intersection of a line segment and a polygonal (triangle) mesh.

As a polyhedron or polygonal mesh is simply a collection of polygons obeying specific rules regarding shared edges and vertices, the simplest approach is to test each face in succession for intersection (see Section 11.1.3). However, for polyhedra or polygonal meshes with a significant number of faces, this naive approach is extremely inefficient because it spends a lot of time computing intersections with faces that are nowhere near the linear component. In such cases, the application should employ a spatial-partitioning scheme, such as an octree or binary space-partitioning tree (see Foley et al. 1996 or Chapter 13). The cost of constructing such a spatial-partitioning scheme will be well worth incurring if there are a large number of faces, particularly if the polyhedron or polygonal mesh is to be intersected many times (as in ray tracing, for example).

Eric Haines (1991) describes an algorithm, based on the ideas of Roth (1981) and Kay and Kajiya (1986), for convex polyhedra that is significantly faster than the naive approach, an advantage due to the fact that he intersects the linear component with the planes containing each face (which is relatively cheap), rather than with the polygonal faces themselves (which can be quite expensive). The linear component is

$$\mathcal{L}(t) = P + t\hat{d}$$

and the planes of the faces are defined as

$$ax + by + cz + d = 0$$

Given these definitions, the distance from the linear component's origin P and its intersection with the plane $\mathcal{P}$ of a face of the polyhedron is

$$t_0 = \frac{-(\vec{n} \cdot P + d)}{\vec{n} \cdot \hat{d}} \tag{11.6}$$

where $\vec{n} = [\,a \quad b \quad c\,]$ is the plane normal of $\mathcal{P}$. If the denominator of Equation 11.6 is (near) zero, then the linear component is parallel to the plane; in this case the sign of the numerator indicates on which side of the plane the linear component's origin lies. Otherwise, the sign of the denominator indicates whether the linear component has intersected the front of the plane or the back: if it is positive, then the plane is intersected from the back (in terms of increasing t), and vice versa if the sign is negative.

The idea behind Haines's algorithm is this: the volume defined by a polyhedron can be understood to be the logical intersection of the half-spaces defined by the planes in which its faces lie. If we consider a linear component, its intersection with a polyhedron consists of a portion of it that is entirely contained within the half-spaces. The intersection of a linear component with each face's plane partitions the linear component into two regions—one that is "outside" the half-space defined by that plane and one that is "inside" the half-space. From these facts we can conclude that the portion of the linear component that intersects the entire polyhedron is the logical intersection of the portions (of the linear component) that are within the half-space defined by each face's plane. This is illustrated (in 2D, for clarity) in Figure 11.7.

Note that we've not listed the half-lines in order of increasing edge index, but rather in order of increasing intersection distance; this should make more evident the nature of their logical intersection. Any line that intersects a polyhedron will first intersect one or more "front faces" (if you consider the line "starting" at $t = -\infty$) and then some number of "back faces." The logical intersection is bounded by the last (farthest) front face and the first (nearest) back face.

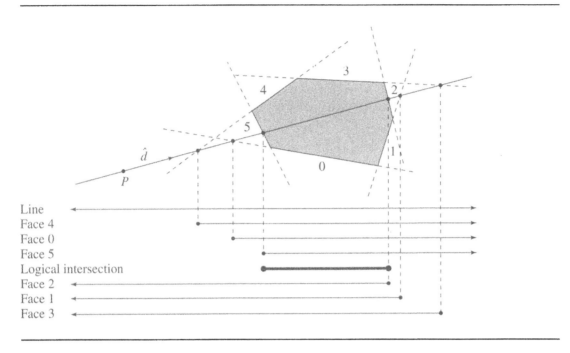

Figure 11.7   The logical intersection of half-lines defines the intersection of a line with a polyhedron.

Note that if the line does not intersect the polyhedron, as in Figure 11.8, then the line intersects a front face's plane *after* it has hit a back face's plane, and so the logical intersection doesn't exist.

This analysis leads to a simple algorithm. The only additional thing to note is that if we find a face-plane that is parallel to the line, and find that the line is to the outside of that plane, we can exit early from the algorithm, as no intersection with the polyhedron is possible in this case.

The pseudocode is as follows:

```
boolean LinePolyhedronIntersection(
    Line        line,
    Polyhedron  phd,
    float&      tNear,
    float&      tFar)
{
    tNear = -MAXFLOAT;
    tFar  =  MAXFLOAT;

    foreach face F in polyhedron {
        normal = { F.a, F.b, F.c };
```

```
            denominator = Dot(normal, line.direction);
            numerator   = Dot(normal, line.origin) + F.d;
            if (denominator  < epsilon) {
                //
                //  Face F is parallel to the line. Check
                //  if line is outside the half-space
                //  defined by the plane
                //
                if (numerator > 0) {
                    //
                    //  Line is outside face and therefore
                    //  outside the polyhedron.
                    //
                    return false;
                }
            } else {
                //
                //  Check if face is front- or back-facing
                //
                t = -numerator / denominator;
                if (denominator > 0) {
                    //  Back-facing plane. Update tFar.
                    if (t < tFar) {
                        tFar = t;
                    }
                } else {
                    //  Front-facing plane. Update tNear.
                    if (t > tNear) {
                        tNear = t;
                    }
                }

                //
                //  Check for invalid logical intersection
                //  of half-lines.
                //
                if (tNear > tFar) {
                    return false;
                }
            }
        }

    return true;
}
```

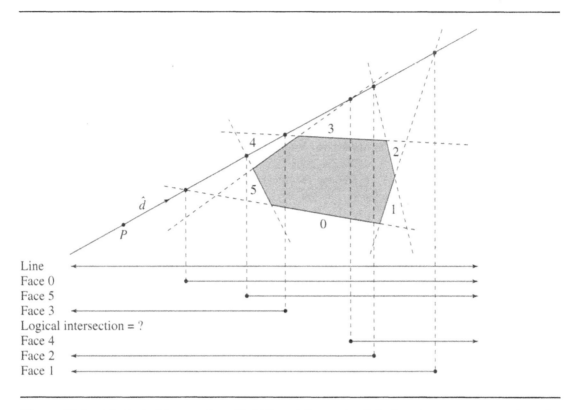

Figure 11.8   The logical intersection of half-lines fails to exist if the line does not intersect the polyhedron.

Ray or Segment and Polyhedron

In the case of a ray, it may be that the ray's origin is within the polyhedron itself. The previous algorithm for lines can be modified to handle rays by checking the value of t_{near} to see if it is less than 0, in which case the ray originates inside the half-space defined by the plane in question. If this is the case, then check if $t_{far} < \infty$: if it is, then t_{far} is the first valid intersection.

In the case of a line segment, we must check the computed values of t to see if they are in the range $0 \leq t \leq 1$.

11.3 LINEAR COMPONENTS AND QUADRIC SURFACES

Quadric surfaces include ellipsoids, cylinders, cones, hyperboloids, and paraboloids (see Section 9.4). A general method for intersecting linear components with quadric surfaces is covered in the next section; however, this method does not take advantage of the geometry of any particular quadric. Algorithms specific to particular quadrics are typically more efficient, and we cover a number of them in this section.

11.3.1 GENERAL QUADRIC SURFACES

The general implicit form of the equation for a quadric surface is

$$q(x, y, z) = ax^2 + 2bxy + 2cxz + 2dx + ey^2 + 2fyz + 2gy + hz^2 + 2iz + j = 0$$

$$(11.7)$$

This can be expressed in matrix notation as

$$
[x \quad y \quad z \quad 1]
\begin{bmatrix}
a & b & c & d \\
b & e & f & g \\
c & f & h & i \\
d & g & i & j
\end{bmatrix}
\begin{bmatrix}
x \\
y \\
z \\
1
\end{bmatrix} = 0
\qquad (11.8)
$$

If we let $X = [x \quad y \quad z \quad 1]$, we can more compactly represent a quadric as

$$XQX^{T} = 0 \qquad (11.9)$$

The intersection of a line $\mathcal{L}(t) = P + t\vec{d}$ with a quadric can be computed by substituting the line equation directly into Equation 11.9:

$$
\begin{aligned}
q(x, y, z) &= XQX^{T} \\
&= [P + t\vec{d}] \, Q \, [P + t\vec{d}]^{T} \\
&= (\vec{d}Q\vec{d}^{T})t^2 + (\vec{d}QP^{T} + PQ\vec{d}^{T})t + PQP^{T} \\
&= 0
\end{aligned}
$$

This is a quadratic equation of the form

$$at^2 + bt + c = 0$$

which can be solved in the usual fashion:

$$t = \frac{b \pm \sqrt{b^2 - 4ac}}{2a}$$

If there are two distinct real (nonimaginary) roots of this, then the quadric is intersected twice. If there are two real roots of the same value, then the line is touching, but not penetrating, the quadric. If the roots are imaginary (when the discriminant $b^2 - 4ac < 0$), then the line does not intersect the surface.

The normal for an implicitly defined surface $q(x, y, z) = 0$ at a point S on the surface is the gradient of q:

$$\vec{n}_S = \nabla q(S)$$

In terms of Equation 11.9, we have

$$\vec{n} = 2 \begin{bmatrix} 1 & 0 & 0 & 0 \\ 0 & 1 & 0 & 0 \\ 0 & 0 & 1 & 0 \\ 0 & 0 & 0 & 0 \end{bmatrix} QS^T$$

This last step may require some explanation: in general

$$\nabla f(x, y, z) = \left[\frac{\partial f(x, y, z)}{\partial x}, \frac{\partial f(x, y, z)}{\partial y}, \frac{\partial f(x, y, z)}{\partial z} \right]$$

That is, we simply compute the partial derivatives with respect to the basis vectors of the quadric's frame. Again referring back to the compact matrix notation, we have

$$\frac{\partial X}{\partial x} = [1 \quad 0 \quad 0 \quad 0]$$

$$\frac{\partial X}{\partial y} = [0 \quad 1 \quad 0 \quad 0]$$

$$\frac{\partial X}{\partial z} = [0 \quad 0 \quad 1 \quad 0]$$

For example,

$$\vec{n}_x = \frac{\partial f(x, y, z)}{\partial x}$$

$$= \frac{\partial X}{\partial x} QX^T + XQ\frac{\partial X^T}{\partial x}$$

$$= 2\frac{\partial X}{\partial x} QX^T$$

$$= 2[1 \quad 0 \quad 0 \quad 0]QX^T$$

The pseudocode is

```
int LineQuadricIntersection(Matrix4x4 Q, Line3D l, float t[2])
{
    float a, b, c;
    Matrix dTrans = transpose(l.d);
```

```
// * denotes matrix multiplication
a = dTrans * Q * l.d;
b = dTrans * Q * l.p + transpose(l.p) * Q * l.d;
c = transpose(l.p) * Q * l.p;

float discrm = b * b - 4 * a * c;
if (discrm < 0) {
    return 0;
}

if (discrm == 0) {
    t[0] = b / (2 * a);
    return 1;
} else {
    t[0] = (-b + sqrt(discrm)) / (2 * a);
    t[1] = (-b - sqrt(discrm)) / (2 * a);
}
return 2;
}
```

11.3.2 LINEAR COMPONENTS AND A SPHERE

For the purposes of this section, a sphere is represented by a center C and radius r, so that the implicit equation for the sphere is

$$f(X) = \|X - C\|^2 = r^2 \qquad (11.10)$$

The intersection of a linear component (defined by an origin P and direction vector $\hat{d}$) and a sphere can be computed by substituting the equation for a linear component (Equation 11.2) into Equation 11.10:

$$\|X - C\|^2 = r^2$$

$$\|P + t\hat{d} - C\|^2 = r^2$$

$$\|(P - C) + t\hat{d}\|^2 = r^2$$

$$(t\hat{d} + (P - C)) \cdot (t\hat{d} + (P - C)) - r^2 = 0$$

$$t^2(\hat{d} \cdot \hat{d}) + 2t(\hat{d} \cdot (P - C)) + (P - C) \cdot (P - C) - r^2 = 0$$

$$t^2 + 2t(\hat{d} \cdot (P - C)) + (P - C) \cdot (P - C) - r^2 = 0$$

This second-order equation is of the form

$$at^2 + bt + c = 0$$

and can be solved directly using the quadratic formula:[1]

$$t = -\hat{d} \cdot (P - C) \pm \sqrt{(\hat{d} \cdot (P - C))^2 - ((P - C) \cdot (P - C) - r^2)} \quad (11.11)$$

There are three possible conditions for line/sphere intersection, each of which can be identified by the value of the discriminant in Equation 11.11:

   i. No intersections: This condition exists if the discriminant is negative, in which case the roots are imaginary.

   ii. One intersection: This happens if the line is tangent to the sphere; in this case the discriminant is equal to zero.

   iii. Two intersections: This happens if the discriminant is greater than zero.

Figure 11.9 shows these three possible configurations, plus the situation in which the linear component is a ray and has its origin inside the sphere; in the latter case, there are two intersections, mathematically speaking, but only one of them is within the bounds of the ray.

The pseudocode is

```
int LineSphereIntersection(Sphere sphere, Line3d line, float t[2])
{
    float b, c, discrm;
    Vector3D pMinusC = l.origin - sphere.center;
    b = 2 * Dot(l.direction, pMinusC);
    c = Dot(pMinusC, pMinusC) - sphere.radius * sphere.radius;
    discrm = b * b - c;
    if (discrm > 0) {
        t[0] = -b + sqrt(discrm);
        t[1] = -b - sqrt(discrm);
        return 2;
    } else if (discrm == 0) {
        // The line is tangent to the sphere
```

---

1. Recall that a quadratic equation of the form $ax^2 + bx + c = 0$ has the two solutions $x = \frac{-b \pm \sqrt{b^2 - 4ac}}{2a}$.

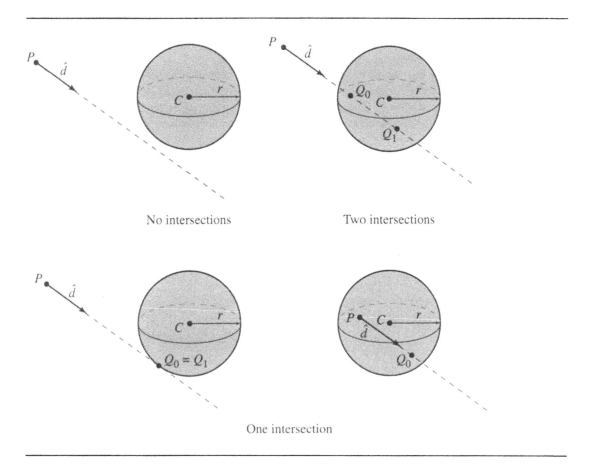

Figure 11.9   Possible ray-sphere intersections.

```
        t[0] = -b;
        return 1;
    } else {
        return 0;
    }
}
```

Ray or Line Segment and Sphere

In the case of a ray, the parametric value or values of the intersection (if the discriminant is nonnegative) must be checked for nonnegativity. An inexpensive test for the existence of an intersection is whether the ray's origin P is within the sphere, which is true if the term $(P - C) \cdot (P - C) - r^2$ is nonpositive. Further, in the case of a ray, only nonnegative solutions need be considered.

In the case of a line segment, the same sort of approach could be used. There are several inexpensive tests that can be done: First, if one of the end points of the segment is inside the sphere, and the other is not, then an intersection is guaranteed; second, if both end points are inside the sphere, then there is no intersection. Once we have done these two checks, then neither end point is inside the sphere. At this point, we could compute the intersection, checking that the roots (if they exist) are bounded between 0 and 1 (recall that a line segment's parametric representation is $\mathcal{R}(t) = P_0 + t(P_1 - P_0)$. A slightly more efficient approach was suggested by Paul Bourke (1992): note that the closest point on the line through $P_0 P_1$ to C is along a perpendicular from C to the line; in other words, if Q is the closest point on the line, then

$$(C - Q) \cdot (P_1 - P_0) = 0$$

If we substitute the equation of the line into this, we get

$$(C - P_0 - u(P_1 - P_0)) \cdot (P_1 - P_0) = 0$$

If we solve this, we get

$$u = \frac{(C - P_0) \cdot (P_1 - P_0)}{(P_1 - P_0) \cdot (P_1 - P_0)}$$

If $u < 0$ or $u > 1$, then the closest point is not within the bounds of the segment. If there is an intersection (or intersections), then $u \leq r$. If both these tests succeed, then we can compute the actual intersection as before.

11.3.3 LINEAR COMPONENTS AND AN ELLIPSOID

This section addresses the intersection of linear components and an ellipsoid, as shown in Figure 11.10.

The linear component $\mathcal{L}$ is represented in the usual fashion—as an origin point P and direction $\vec{d}$:

$$\mathcal{L}(t) = P + t\vec{d}$$

An ellipsoid is represented by a centerpoint C, a radius r, and three scaling factors—one associated with each basis vector. The implicit form of this is

$$k(x - C_x)^2 + l(y - C_y)^2 + m(z - C_z)^2 - r^2 = 0 \qquad (11.12)$$

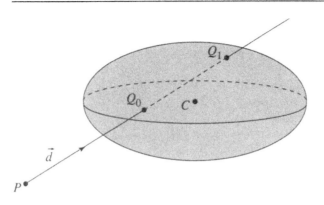

Figure 11.10   Intersection of a linear component and an ellipsoid.

If we substitute the (coordinate form of) the line equation into Equation 11.12, we get

$$k(P_x + td_x - C_x)^2 + l(P_y + td_y - C_y)^2 + m(P_z + td_z - C_z)^2 - r^2 = 0$$

This is a quadratic equation of the form

$$at^2 + bt + c = 0$$

where

$$a = kd_x^2 + ld_y^2 + md_z^2$$

$$b = 2k(P_x - C_x)d_x + 2l(P_y - C_y)d_y + 2m(P_z - C_z)d_z$$

$$c = k(P_x - C_x)^2 + l(P_y - C_y)^2 + m(P_z - C_z)^2 - r^2.$$

As with the sphere, the number of intersections depends on the value of the discriminant (see Section 11.3.2).

The pseudocode is

```
int LineEllipsoidIntersection(Ellipsoid e, line3D l, float t[2])
{
    float a, b, c, discrm;
    int numSoln = 0;
    a = e.k * l.d.x^2 + e.l * l.d.y^2 + e.m * l.d.z^2;
    b = 2 * e.k * (l.p.x - e.center.x) * l.d.x + 2 * e.l * (l.p.y -
            e.center.y) * l.d.y + 2 * e.m * (l.p.z - e.center.z) * l.d.z;
```

```
c = e.k * (1.p.x - e.center.x)^2 + e.1 * (1.p.y - e.center.y)^2 +
        e.m * (1.p.z - e.center.z)^2 - e.r^2;

discrm = b * b - 4 * a * c;

if (discrm > 0) {
    t[numSoln] = (-b + sqrt(discrm)) / (2 * a);
    numSoln++;
    t[numSoln] = (-b - sqrt(discrm)) / (2 * a);
    numSoln++;
} else if (discrm == 0) {
    t[0] = -b / (2 * a);
    numSoln++;
}

    return numSoln;
}
```

An alternative approach is based on the idea that an ellipsoid is simply a sphere that has been transformed by (nonuniform) scaling. If we invert this transformation, the ellipsoid turns back into a sphere; if this same inverted transformation is applied to the linear component, then we can simply find the intersection of the linear component with a sphere, and then transform the intersection point(s) (if any) back. To slightly simplify things, we can also translate the ellipsoid to the origin.

For an ellipsoid with scaling factors k, l, and m and center C, the matrix $\mathbf{M}$ that transforms the ellipsoid into a sphere is

$$\mathbf{M} = \begin{bmatrix} \frac{1}{k} & 0 & 0 & 0 \\ 0 & \frac{1}{l} & 0 & 0 \\ 0 & 0 & \frac{1}{m} & 0 \\ -C_x & -C_y & -C_z & 1 \end{bmatrix}$$

The linear component is then

$$\mathcal{L}'(t) = P\mathbf{M} + t\vec{d}\mathbf{M}$$

and the ellipsoid is then

$$x^2 + y^2 + z^2 - r^2 = 0$$

giving us an intersection equation

$$(P_x + td_x)^2 + (P_y + td_y)^2 + (P_z + td_z)^2 - r^2 = 0$$

which can be solved using the algorithm for linear component/sphere intersection (note, though, that a small efficiency can be gained when the sphere's center is the origin, which may be worth exploiting).

The pseudocode is

```
int LineEllipsoidIntersection(Ellipsoid e, line3D l, Point3D Intersection[2])
{
    float a, b, c, discrm;
    int numSoln;

    Line3D transformedl;
    Sphere s;
    Matrix4x4 M, MInv;
    M = e.TransformMatrix();
    transformedl.d = l.d * M;
    transformedl.p = l.p * M;
    s.radius = e.radius;
    float t[2];
    numSoln = lineSphereIntersection(s,transformedl,t)
    if (numSoln > 0) {
        MInv = M.Inverse();
    }
    for (i = 0 ; i < numSoln ; i++) {
        Intersection[i] = (transformedl.p + t[i] * transformedl.d ) * MInv;
    }
    return numSoln;
}
```

One final notational comment: you will frequently see an ellipsoid's equation given as

$$\left(\frac{x - C_x}{a}\right)^2 + \left(\frac{y - C_y}{b}\right)^2 + \left(\frac{z - C_z}{c}\right)^2 - r^2 = 0$$

which is equivalent to the one we used here, with $k = 1/a^2, l = 1/b^2$, and $m = 1/c^2$. If we use this other notation, then we can directly write down a parametric version of the ellipsoid:

$$x = C_x + ar\,\cos(\theta)\,\cos(\phi)$$

$$y = C_y + br\,\cos(\theta)\,\sin(\phi)$$

$$z = C_z + cr\,\sin(\theta)$$

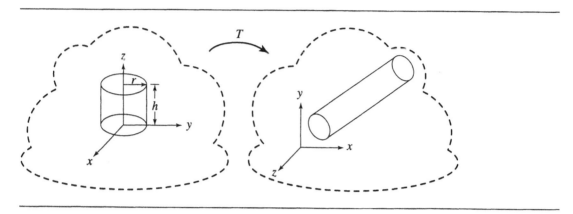

Figure 11.11   Parameterized standard cylinder representation.

11.3.4   LINEAR COMPONENTS AND CYLINDERS

Typically, a graphics library or application will implement one of three representations for cylinders:

- Pure standard representation: The object's base is at the origin, its axis is aligned with one of the local frame's basis vectors, and the radius and height are 1. Associated with the object is a transformation matrix **M** that translates and rotates the cylinder to the desired position and that scales its dimensions to give it arbitrary size and proportions (as well as allowing for elliptical cylinders).

- Parameterized standard representation: Similar to the "pure" representation, but the radius and height are parameters, and the axis may be any one of the three basis vectors of the local frame. Variations on this might allow for a specification of a height, a ratio of radius to height, and so on. See Figure 11.11.

- General representation: The cylinder is specified by a centerpoint C, an axis vector $\hat{a}$, radius r, and some scheme for specifying the extent of the cylinder (i.e., the location of the end caps). Extent specification varies from system to system, but a typical approach is to put one end cap at C and another at a distance from C (i.e., the height). See Figure 11.12.

We'll give an algorithm for computing the intersection of linear components with only a parameterized standard representation. An algorithm that can handle the completely general case could also be employed for the standard representations, and you could argue for that algorithm instead. You could also argue that if you have transformed a standard cylinder to its world-space location, then ray intersection, for example, wouldn't require you to transform the ray into the cylinder's local space, and then transform the intersection point(s) *back* into world space. All this may be

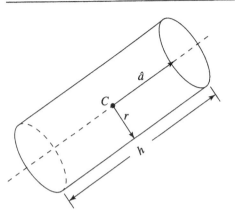

Figure 11.12   General cylinder representation.

true, but in nearly all 3D applications and libraries providing cylinders (and cones, etc.), geometric objects are organized by a scene graph, in which transformations are inherited down the tree. Because components like cylinders are located, sized, and oriented via a concatenation of transformations, you may as well transform the component from a standard position.

Parameterized Standard Representation

Here, we represent a cylinder as having its base at the origin, its axis aligned with the (local) z-axis, and a specified radius r and height h. In this case, the equation for the cylinder becomes

$$x^2 + y^2 = r^2, \qquad 0 \leq z \leq h \tag{11.13}$$

and the equations for the caps, which are on the $z = 0$ and $z = h$ planes, are

$$x^2 + y^2 \leq r^2, \qquad z = 0, z = h$$

In order to intersect a line $\mathcal{L}(t) = P + t\vec{d}$ with such a cylinder, we need to transform $\mathcal{L}$ by $\mathbf{M}^{-1}$ (that is, back into the local space of the standard cylinder),[2] compute the parameter t of the closest intersection point, and then plug t back into the line equation to compute the actual intersection point in the line's frame of reference.

---

2. To transform a parametric line equation $\mathcal{L}(t) = P + t\vec{d}$, we apply the inverse of the transformation to both the origin and the direction vector, remembering that the homogeneous coordinate of a vector is 0: $\mathcal{L}'(t) = P\mathbf{M}^{-1} + t\vec{d}\mathbf{M}^{-1}$.

The intersection with the sides is trivial: substitute the line equation into Equation 11.13, yielding

$$(P_x + td_x)^2 + (P_y + td_y)^2 - r^2 = 0$$

Expanding and collecting terms, we get

$$(d_x^2 + d_y^2)t^2 + 2(d_x P_x + d_y P_y)t + (P_x^2 + P_y^2) - r^2 = 0$$

As usual, this is a quadratic equation of the form

$$at^2 + bt + c = 0$$

which can be solved with the quadratic formula

$$t = \frac{b \pm \sqrt{b^2 - 4ac}}{2a}$$

Once we have computed t, we plug it back into the line equation to compute the point of intersection (again, in the local frame of reference for the cylinder). Note that the intersection(s), if they exist, are those of the line and the infinite cylinder. In order to compute only those intersections bounded by the end caps, we need to test the resulting intersection point(s) against $0 \le z \le h$.

Intersection with the end caps can be computed by computing the intersection of the line with the planes in which the end caps lie and then checking if $x^2 + y^2 \le r^2$. The closest intersection is then simply the closest of all the valid intersection points.

The pseudocode is

```
bool LineCylinderIntersection(Cylinder c, Line3D l, Point3D closestIntersection)
{
    Matrix4x4 transform, invTransform;
    float a, b, c, discrm;
    float t[4];
    bool valid[4];
    Line3D tline;
    Point3D ipoint[4];
    transform = c.transformMatrix();
    invTransform = transform.Inverse();
    tline.direction = l.direction * invTransform;
    tline.origin = l.origin * invTransform;

    a = (tline.direction.x + tline.direction.y) ^ 2;
    b = 2 * (tline.direction.x * tline.origin.x + tline.direction.y * tline.origin.y);
```

```
c = tline.origin.x^2 + tline.origin.y^2 - c.radius^2;

discrm = b*b - 4*a*c;

if (discrm > 0) {
    t[0] = (-b + sqrt(discrm) / (2 * a);
    t[1] = (-b - sqrt(discrm) / (2 * a);
    ipoint[0] = tline.origin + t[0] * tline.direction;
    if (ipoint[0].z < 0 || ipoint[0].z > c.height) {
        valid[0] = false;
    } else {
        valid[0] = true;
    }
    ipoint[1] = tline.origin + t[1] * tline.direction;
    if (ipoint[1].z < 0 || ipoint[1].z > c.height) {
        valid[1] = false;
    } else {
        valid[1] = true;
    }

    // Check end caps
    Plane3D p1,p2;
    p1.normal = [0,0,1];
    p2.normal = [0,0,-1];
    p1.point = [0,0,0];
    p2.point = [0,0,c.height];
    if (lineIntersectPlane(p1,tline,t[3])) {
        ipoint[3] = tline.origin + t[3] * tline.direction;
        float d = ipoint[3].x^2 + ipoint[3].y^2;
        if (d < = c.radius^2 ) {
            valid[3] = true;
        } else {
            valid[3] = false;
        }
    } else {
        valid[3] = false;
    }

    if (lineIntersectPlane(p2,tline,t[4])) {
        ipoint[4] = tline.origin + t[4] * tline.direction;
        float d = ipoint[4].x^2 + ipoint[4].y^2;
        if (d < = c.radius^2) {
            valid[4] = true;
```

```
            } else {
                valid[4] = false;
            }
        } else {
            valid[4] = false;
        }

        // Find smallest t of the valid intersection points
        float mint = infinity;
        int minIndex = 0;
        bool hit = false;
        for (i = 0; i < 4 ; i++) {
            if (valid[i]) {
                if (t[i] < mint) {
                    mint = t[i];
                    minIndex = i;
                    hit = true;
                }
            }
        }

        closestIntersection = transform*ipoint[minIndex];
        return hit;
    } else if (discrm == 0) {
        // Ray is tangent to side, no need to check caps
        t[0] = -b / (2 * a);
        ipoint[0] = tline.origin + t[0] * tline.direction;
        if (ipoint[0].z > c.z || ipoint[0].z < 0) {
            return 0;
        }

        closestIntersection = transform*ipoint[0];
        return true;
    }

    return false;
}
```

11.3.5 LINEAR COMPONENTS AND A CONE

As with the cylinder, a cone may be specified in some variation of a standard scheme or in a fully general scheme (see Figures 11.13 and 11.14).

```
float c2, c1, c0, discrm;

Vec3D delta = line.origin - cone.vertex;
c2 = line.direction.transpose() * M * line.direction;
c1 = line.direction.transpose() * M * delta;
c0 = delta.transpose() * M * delta;

discrm = c1 * c1 - c2 * c0;

if (discrm > 0) {
    float    t[3];
    Point3D ipoint[3];
    int      minIndex;
    bool     valid[3];

    if (fabs(c2) < zeroEpislon) {
        if (fabs(c1) < zeroEpislon) {
            valid[0] = false;
            valid[1] = false;
        } else {
            t[0] = -c0 / (2 * c1);
            ipoint[0] = line.origin + t[0] * line.direction;
        }
    } else {
        t[0] = (-c2 + sqrt(discrm)) / c0;
        t[1] = (-c2 - sqrt(discrm)) / c0;

        ipoint[0] = line.origin + t[0] * line.direction;
        ipoint[1] = line.origin + t[1] * line.direction;

        float  scalarProjection;

        if (scalarProjection = Dot(axis,ipoint[0] - cone.vertex) < 0) {
            valid[0] = false;
        } else {
            if (scalarProjection > cone.height) {
                valid[0] = false;
            } else {
                valid[0] = true;
            }
        }

        if (scalarProjection = Dot(axis,ipoint[1] - cone.vertex) < 0) {
            valid[1] = false;
```

```
                } else {
                    if (scalarProjection > cone.height) {
                        valid[1] = false;
                    } else {
                        valid[1] = true;
                    }
                }
            }
        }

        // Check for earlier intersection with cap
        Plane3D p1;
        p1.normal = axis;
        p1.origin = cone.vertex + cone.height * axis;

        if (lineIntersectPlane(p1, line, t[3])) {
            ipoint[3] = line.origin + t[3] * line.direction;
            if (distance(p1.origin, ipoint[3]) <= cone.radius) {
                valid[3] = true;
            } else {
                valid[3] = false;
            }
        } else {
            valid[3] = false;
        }

        // Now find earliest valid intersection
        bool hit = false;
        int minIndex = 0;
        float mint = infinity;

        for (i = 0 ; i < 3 ;i++) {
            if (valid[i]) {
                if (t[i] < mint) {
                    mint = t[i];
                    minIndex = i;
                    hit = true;
                }
            }
        }
        closestIntersection = ipoint[minIndex];
        return hit;
    } else if (discrm == 0) {
        // No need to check cap
        float scalarProjection;
```

```
    t[0] = -c1 / c2;
    ipoint[0] = line.origin + t[0] * line.direction;

    if (scalarProjection = dotProd(axis, ipoint[0] - cone.vertex) >= 0) {
        if (scalarProjection <= cone.height) {
            closestIntersection = ipoint[0];
            return true;
        }
    }
    }
    return false;
}
```

11.4 LINEAR COMPONENTS AND POLYNOMIAL SURFACES

A *polynomial surface* is a vector-valued function $X : D \subset \mathbb{R}^2 \to \mathbb{R}^3$, say, $X(s, t)$, whose domain is D and range is R. The components $X_i(s, t)$ of $X(s, t)$ are each a polynomial in the specified parameters

$$X_i(s, t) = \sum_{j=0}^{n_i} \sum_{k=0}^{m_i} a_{ijk} s^j t^k \tag{11.14}$$

where $n_i + m_i$ is the degree of the polynomial. The domain D is typically either $\mathbb{R}^2$ or $[0, 1]^2$. A *rational polynomial surface* is a vector-valued function $X(s, t)$ whose components $X_i(s, t)$ are ratios of polynomials

$$X_i(s, t) = \frac{\sum_{j=0}^{n_i} \sum_{k=0}^{m_i} a_{ijk} s^j t^k}{\sum_{j=0}^{p_i} \sum_{k=0}^{q_i} b_{ijk} s^j t^k}$$

where $n_i + m_i$ is the degree of the numerator polynomial and $p_i + q_i$ is the degree of the denominator polynomial.

A few common types of surfaces that occur in computer graphics are Bézier surfaces, B-spline surfaces, and nonuniform rational B-spline (NURBS) surfaces.

For the purposes of the following discussion, a linear component is defined in the usual fashion as an origin plus a direction vector

$$\mathcal{L}(t) = P + t\vec{d} \tag{11.15}$$

where $-\infty \leq t \leq \infty$ for a line, $0 \leq t \leq \infty$ for a ray, and for a segment $\{P_0, P_1\}$ we have $\vec{d} = P_1 - P_0$ and $0 \leq t \leq 1$.

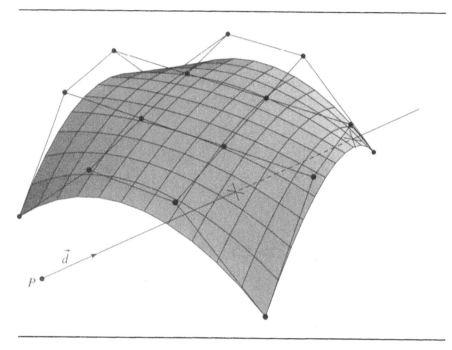

Figure 11.18   Intersection of a ray with a NURBS surface.

The two most common situations requiring the intersection of a polynomial surface and a linear component are in rendering—specifically, ray tracing—and in interactive applications in the process of *selection* or *picking*, in which the user uses a mouse or other pointing device to specify an object. In light of this observation, we'll concentrate on ray-surface intersection. An example is shown in Figure 11.18.

11.4.1 ALGEBRAIC SURFACES

Algebraic surfaces are those defined, in general, by an equation of the form

$$f(x, y, z) = 0 \tag{11.16}$$

where the function f is a polynomial; that is,

$$f(x, y, z) = \sum_{i=0}^{l} \sum_{j=0}^{m} \sum_{k=0}^{n} a_{ijk} x^i y^j z^k$$

whose degree is the sum of the degrees of the components: $d = l + m + n$.

If we rewrite Equation 11.15 in its component form

$$x = P_x + td_x$$

$$y = P_y + td_y$$

$$z = P_z + td_z$$

it can easily be seen that if we substitute this into Equation 11.16, we get another polynomial equation, of the form

$$g(t) = \sum_{i=0}^{d} a_i t^i$$

which can be solved using a standard method. Note that the maximum number of real roots of this equation is the same as the degree of the polynomial surface. In fact, for equations of degree four or less, easy analytic solutions are available. For higher-order equations, a numerical approach is necessary; Hanrahan (1983) used a method for first isolating the roots (Collins and Akritas 1976; Collins and Loos 1982), and then applied *regula falsi*.

11.4.2 FREE-FORM SURFACES

A free-form parametric surface is defined in general as shown in Equation 11.14. The intersection of a linear component with a polynomial Cartesian product patch is a polynomial equation of degree $2 \times M^2$, where M is the degree of the surface; for a bicubic patch, this means we get a polynomial intersection equation of degree 18. Taking a direct root-finding approach (such as Newton iteration) can result in a very slow algorithm that may fail to converge in some cases. In any case, predictable behavior results only when the initial guess is reasonably near the first root.

Kajiya (1982) presented an approach that has been adopted by later researchers and is worth outlining: a ray can be considered to be the intersection of two (nonparallel) planes. To intersect a ray with a patch, the surface equation is substituted into the plane equations; this gives us two equations defining the algebraic curves formed by the intersection of the patch with the two planes. The intersection of these two curves gives the (u, v) parameters of the point at which the ray intersects the patch. Kajiya then used Laguerre's method for root finding in order to solve the equations; he finds it superior to Newton's method in stability and the property that it converges on the nearest root irrespective of the original guess, and that it is cubically convergent. Others have also exploited this approach of considering the ray as the intersection of two planes (Sweeney and Bartels 1986; Martin et al. 2000). A full proof of the validity of this approach is found in Kajiya (1982).

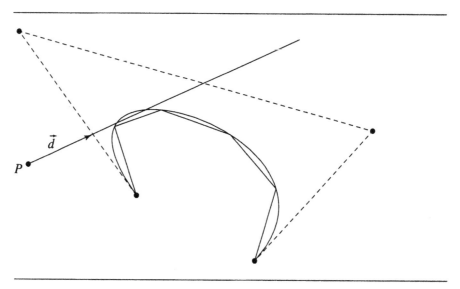

Figure 11.19   Failed intersection calculation due to insufficient surface tessellation (shown in cross section for clarity).

An alternative approach is to simply subdivide or *tessellate* the surface into polygons (either triangles or quads, typically), and then intersect the ray with each of these tessellants. This is very simple to program, but has several problems:

- It can be extremely inefficient if some sort of spatial-partitioning scheme is also not employed (e.g., bounding volume hierarchy).

- If the subdivision is not sufficiently fine, then there is a good chance that an intersection will be missed (see Figure 11.19).

- If the subdivision is too fine, then more (expensive) computation has been done than is necessary, but accuracy increases with subdivision granularity, and so there is an inherent incompatibility of goals.

Broadly stated, the direct evaluation approach can be quite slow, but very accurate, while the simple subdivision approach can be efficient, but may sacrifice accuracy while achieving that efficiency. Naturally, you may think of creating a hybrid of the two approaches, and this has, indeed, been done with good results.

Before describing these hybrid approaches, a few other interesting methods are worth mentioning. Nishita, Sederberg, and Kakimoto (1990) describe an approach they call "Bézier clipping"; the ray is considered to be the intersection of two orthogonal planes, and the Bézier surface is projected onto a plane perpendicular to the ray. The ray then is projected to a point, and the two planes are projected to two perpendicular lines; this forms an orthonormal basis. Distances between the (projected) control points and the "basis vectors" are computed, and the patch is "clipped" by use of the de Casteljau algorithm—portions of the surface that could not possibly contain the intersection are no longer considered. Once the size of the successively clipped patch reaches a specified size threshhold, the intersection is computed to be the center of the sufficiently small patch.

Fournier and Buchanan (1984) describe a method in which Chebyshev polynomials are used both to represent the polynomial surface and to create tight bounding boxes. The patch is approximated by adaptively subdividing it into a large number of bilinear patches. These bilinear patches are organized into a bounding box hierarchy to speed up ray intersections. The bounding box hierarchy is traversed to the leaf node intersecting the ray, and the intersection of the ray with the bilinear patch at that leaf is used as the (approximate) intersection of the ray with the surface.

Both of these methods were analyzed by Campagna, Slusallek, and Seidel (1997). Their results show what you might expect—the Bézier clipping approach was relatively slower than the Chebyshev boxing method (25–30%). They also noted that the Chebyshev boxing approach can only handle integral patches. As a result of these analyses, they developed their own bounding volume hierarchy approach that could handle rational patches and that was of comparable speed to the Chebyshev boxing approach.

Toth (1985) describes a ray intersection algorithm that is also based on Kajiya's approach; it also uses Newton iteration, but solves the problem of providing a good initial guess by the use of interval analysis techniques.

The general structure of the algorithm we'll present here has been utilized by Martin et al. (2000), Sweeney and Bartels (1986), and Campagna, Slusallek, and Seidel (1997). They all share a few basic ideas, which we'll now address.

Intersecting a Ray and a Parametric Polynomial Surface

Polynomial surfaces may be represented in your choice of basis. Here, we use the Bézier basis because any polynomial can be converted to this basis and because we can take advantage of some of the properties of the Bézier basis in our algorithm.

Our ray is defined in the usual fashion:

$$\mathcal{L}(t) = P + t\hat{d}$$

Following Kajiya (1982), we represent this ray as the intersection of two planes:

$$\mathcal{P}_0 : a_0 x + b_0 y + c_0 z + d_0 = 0$$

$$\mathcal{P}_1 : a_1 x + b_1 y + c_1 z + d_1 = 0$$

If we let

$$\vec{n}_0 = [\, a_0 \quad b_0 \quad c_0 \,]$$

$$\vec{n}_1 = [\, a_1 \quad b_1 \quad c_1 \,]$$

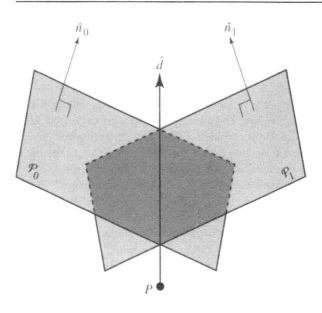

Figure 11.20   A ray represented as the intersection of two planes.

then (following Martin et al. 2000) we can define our planes as

$$\mathcal{P}_0 : \{P | \mathbf{P}_0 \cdot [\, P \quad 1\,] = 0\}$$
$$\mathcal{P}_1 : \{P | \mathbf{P}_1 \cdot [\, P \quad 1\,] = 0\}$$

where

$$\mathbf{P}_0 = [\, \vec{n}_0 \quad d_0\,]$$
$$\mathbf{P}_1 = [\, \vec{n}_1 \quad d_1\,]$$

See Figure 11.20.

There are an infinite number of planes that include $\mathcal{L}(t)$, all of which have $\vec{n}_0 \perp \hat{d}$; one convenient way to choose $\hat{n}_0$ is to set one of $n_x, n_y,$ or n_z to zero, and "perp" (see Section 4.4.4) the other two; the best solution is generally agreed to be to set the component of largest magnitude to zero:

$$\vec{n}_0 = \begin{cases} [\, d_y \quad -d_x \quad 0\,] & \text{if } |d_x| > |d_y| \text{ and } |d_x| > |d_z| \\ [\, 0 \quad d_z \quad -d_y\,] & \text{otherwise} \end{cases}$$

As it is computationally advantageous to have $\mathcal{P}_0$ and $\mathcal{P}_1$ orthogonal, we set

$$\vec{n}_1 = \vec{n}_0 \times \hat{d}$$

We can complete our plane equations by noting that both $\mathcal{P}_0$ and $\mathcal{P}_1$ must contain the ray origin P, and so we can set

$$d_0 = -\vec{n}_0 \cdot P$$
$$d_1 = -\vec{n}_1 \cdot P$$

Our (rational) Bézier surface is defined as

$$Q(u, v) = \frac{\sum_{i=0}^{n} \sum_{j=0}^{m} B_i^n(u) B_j^m(v) w_{ij} P_{ij}}{\sum_{i=0}^{n} \sum_{j=0}^{m} B_i^n(u) B_j^m(v) w_{ij}}$$

where P_{ij} are the Bézier control points and w_{ij} are the weights.

The intersection of a plane $\mathcal{P}_k$ and the Bézier patch can be represented by substitution:

$$S_k(u, v) = \sum_{i=0}^{n} \sum_{j=0}^{m} B_i^n(u) B_j^m(v) w_{ij} (P_{ij} \cdot [\,\vec{n}_k \quad d_k\,])$$

$$= [\,\vec{n}_k \quad d_k\,] \cdot [\,Q(u, v) \quad 1\,]$$

$$= 0$$

for $k \in \{0, 1\}$.

As any intersection point of the ray and the patch is on the ray, and the ray is on both planes $\mathcal{P}_0$ and $\mathcal{P}_1$, that intersection point must be on both planes; thus, the intersection point must satisfy both

$$[\,\vec{n}_0 \quad d_0\,] \cdot [\,Q(u, v) \quad 1\,] = 0$$
$$[\,\vec{n}_1 \quad d_1\,] \cdot [\,Q(u, v) \quad 1\,] = 0$$

Kajiya (1982) recommends Laguerre's method for solving this pair of implicit equations, while Martin et al. (2000) and Sweeney and Bartels (1986) use Newton iteration.

Suppose we have an initial guess of (u_0, v_0); Newton's method starts with these values and iteratively refines them

$$u_0 \to u_1 \to \cdots \to u_\lambda \to u_{\lambda+1} \to \cdots$$
$$v_0 \to v_1 \to \cdots \to v_\lambda \to v_{\lambda+1} \to \cdots$$

by repeatedly solving the 2×2 system

$$\begin{bmatrix} \frac{\partial S_0}{\partial u} & \frac{\partial S_0}{\partial v} \\ \frac{\partial S_1}{\partial u} & \frac{\partial S_1}{\partial v} \end{bmatrix} \begin{bmatrix} \delta u_{\lambda+1} \\ \delta v_{\lambda+1} \end{bmatrix} = \begin{bmatrix} S_0(u_\lambda, v_\lambda) \\ S_1(u_\lambda, v_\lambda) \end{bmatrix}$$

to produce

$$u_{\lambda+1} = u_\lambda - \delta u_{\lambda+1}$$

$$v_{\lambda+1} = v_\lambda - \delta v_{\lambda+1}$$

Once one or more of several conditions are met, the Newton iteration concludes, and the solution consists of the pair $(u_{\lambda+1}, v_{\lambda+1})$, or we conclude that the ray missed the patch. Both Martin et al. (2000) and Sweeney and Bartels (1986) use a simple "success" criterion—plug the $(u_{\lambda+1}, v_{\lambda+1})$ into S_0 and S_1, and compare the sum to some predetermined tolerance:

$$\|S_0(u_{\lambda+1}, v_{\lambda+1})\| + \|S_1(u_{\lambda+1}, v_{\lambda+1})\| < \epsilon$$

We conclude that the ray missed the surface if any one of several other conditions are encountered:

i. The iteration takes us outside the bounds of the surface:

$$u_{\lambda+1} < u_{\min} \text{ or } u_{\lambda+1} > u_{\max} \text{ or }$$

$$v_{\lambda+1} < v_{\min} \text{ or } v_{\lambda+1} > v_{\max}$$

ii. The iteration degrades, rather than improves, the solution:

$$\|S_0(u_{\lambda+1}, v_{\lambda+1})\| + \|S_1(u_{\lambda+1}, v_{\lambda+1})\| > \|S_0(u_\lambda, v_\lambda)\| + \|S_1(u_\lambda, v_\lambda)\|$$

iii. The number of iterations has exceeded some preset limit.

Use of Bounding Volumes

Two observations motivate the use of bounding volumes: first, Newton iteration can converge quadratically to a root; second, bounding volumes have proven to be generally useful in intersection tests because they allow for quick rejection and thus can help avoid many expensive intersection computations. These seemingly unrelated observations actually work together quite nicely if we can manage to make the bounding volumes do a double duty of providing us with our initial guesses for the Newton iteration.

The Chebyshev boxing described in Fournier and Buchanan (1984) was one example of this, but, as Campagna, Slusallek, and Seidel (1997) point out, the Chebyshev polynomials only allow for integral patches. Both Martin et al. (2000) and

Sweeney and Bartels (1986) use axis-aligned bounding boxes because they are simple to compute and efficient to intersect with a ray. Both approaches begin by taking a preprocessing step consisting of refining the surface, using the Oslo algorithm (Cohen, Lyche, and Riesenfeld 1980; Goldman and Lyche 1993). In the case of Martin et al. (2000), a heuristic is employed to estimate the number of additional knots to insert; this heuristic takes into account estimates of the curvature and arc length. These knots are then inserted, and each knot is increased in multiplicity up to the degree of the patch in each of the directions; this results in a (rational) Bézier patch between each pair of distinct knots. The $n \times m$ control mesh for each Bézier subpatch is then bounded with an axis-aligned bounding box. These bounding boxes are then organized into a hierarchical structure.

In the case of Sweeney and Bartels (1986), the Oslo algorithm is again used to refine the surface. Their refinement-level criteria are based on the (projected) size of the quadrilateral facets induced by the refinement, and whether the refined knots constitute "acceptably good starting guesses for the Newton iteration." They, too, build a hierarchy of bounding boxes, but their approach differs from that of Martin et al. (2000): they start by creating a bounding box around each refined vertex, each of which overlaps its neighbors by some globally specified factor. These overlapping bounding boxes are then combined into a hierarchy of bounding volumes.

In either case, the leaf nodes of the hierarchy contain parameter values for the regions of the surface they represent; in the method of Martin et al. (2000), the leaf nodes contain the minimum and maximum parameter values (in each direction) for the Bézier (sub)patches they represent, and in the method of Sweeney and Bartels (1986), the leaf nodes contain the parameter values associated with the refined vertex. In either case, the (u, v) parameter is used as the starting guess for the Newton iteration, once it is determined that the ray has intersected a leaf's bounding box.

Figure 11.21 shows the basic idea of the use of bounding volumes for a curve, for ease of illustration. The refined vertices are shown in solid black; once these are computed, the multiplicity of the knots is increased so that we get a Bézier (sub)curve between each pair of refined vertices. The control points for each (sub)curve then are used to define an axis-aligned bounding box, and the parameter values associated with the control points serve as the initial guess for the Newton iteration, once a ray has been determined to intersect a leaf's bounding box.

Figure 11.22 shows how the hierarchy of bounding boxes can be built up from the leaf nodes—adjacent pairs of subcurve bounding boxes are combined into a higher-level bounding box, and pairs of these are combined, and so on, until the hierarchy is capped with a single bounding box that encompasses the entire surface.

An alternative to using the Oslo algorithm for the refinement would be to use an adaptive subdivision algorithm. The usual trade-offs apply—an adaptive subdivision scheme will generally produce a "better" tessellation of the surface, in that the number of points of evaluation and their relative positioning will more accurately reflect the scale and curvature of the surface, but at a cost of efficiency (the preprocessing step will be slower). However, this cost may be more than made up for in the

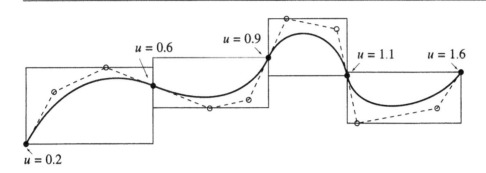

Figure 11.21   Leaf-node bounding boxes are constructed from the Bézier polygon between each pair of refined vertices.

actual intersection tests, as the bounding box hierarchy will tend to better reflect the geometry of the surface.

An outline for this algorithm is as follows:

1. Preprocess the surface:

    a. Refine or adaptively subdivide the surface until some flatness criteria are met. At each control point interpolating the surface, save the parameter values for that point.

    b. For each span of the refined surface, create an axis-aligned bounding box using the control points of the region. Associate with each box the parameters (in each direction) that the region represents.

    c. Recursively coalesce neighboring bounding boxes into a hierarchy.

2. Intersect:

    a. Intersect the ray with the bounding box hierarchy.

    b. When the ray intersects a leaf node, set initial guess for (u_0, v_0) using the parametric ranges stored with the bounding box. A good choice might be to use the midpoint of the range: $u_0 = (u_{min} + u_{max})/2$, and similarly for v_0.

    c. Repeatedly apply the Newton iteration step until convergence criterion is met or ray is determined to have missed the surface.

Martin et al. (2000) describe how this basic approach can be extended to handle trim curves: the orientation of each trim curve is analyzed to determine if it defines a hole or an island; then, each trim curve is placed in a node, and since trim curves can be nested, a hierarchy of nodes is created. Once a ray intersection is detected, the intersection is checked against the trimming hierarchy to see if it is to be culled or returned as a hit.

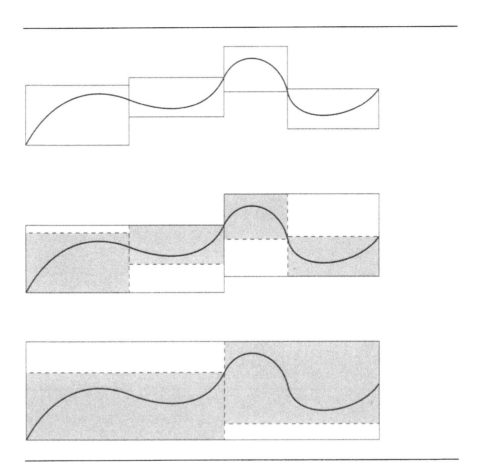

Figure 11.22   Adjacent bounding boxes are coalesced into a single box at the next level in the hierarchy.

11.5 PLANAR COMPONENTS

In this section, we discuss the problem of computing intersections of planar components—triangles and planes.

11.5.1 TWO PLANES

The intersection of two planes, if it exists (parallel planes don't intersect, but all others do), is a line $\mathcal{L}$ (see Figure 11.23). If we have two planes

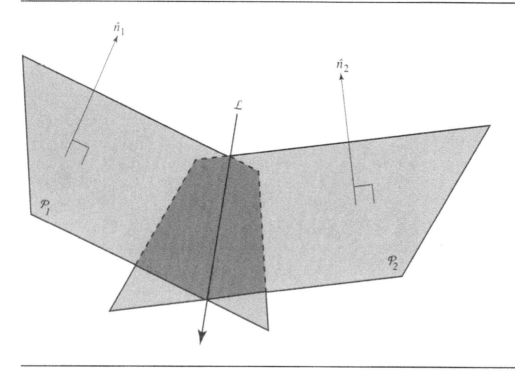

Figure 11.23   Intersection of two planes.

$$\mathcal{P}_1 : \vec{n}_1 \cdot P = s_1$$

$$\mathcal{P}_2 : \vec{n}_2 \cdot P = s_2$$

then that line has direction

$$\vec{n}_1 \times \vec{n}_2$$

To completely specify the intersection line, we need a point on that line. Suppose the point is a linear combination of $\vec{n}_1$ and $\vec{n}_2$, with these normal vectors considered as points:

$$P = a\vec{n}_1 + b\vec{n}_2$$

That point has to be on both planes, and so must satisfy both plane equations

$$\vec{n}_1 \cdot P = s_1$$

$$\vec{n}_2 \cdot P = s_2$$

yielding

$$a\|\vec{n}_1\|^2 + b\vec{n}_1 \cdot \vec{n}_2 = s_1$$

$$a\vec{n}_1 \cdot \vec{n}_2 + b\|\vec{n}_2\|^2 = s_2$$

Solving for a and b, we have

$$a = \frac{s_2 \vec{n}_1 \cdot \vec{n}_2 - s_1 \|\vec{n}_2\|^2}{(\vec{n}_1 \cdot \vec{n}_2)^2 - \|\vec{n}_1\|^2 \|\vec{n}_2\|^2}$$

$$b = \frac{s_1 \vec{n}_1 \cdot \vec{n}_2 - s_2 \|\vec{n}_1\|^2}{(\vec{n}_1 \cdot \vec{n}_2)^2 - \|\vec{n}_1\|^2 \|\vec{n}_2\|^2}$$

giving us the line equation

$$\mathcal{L} = P + t(\vec{n}_1 \times \vec{n}_2)$$

$$= (a\vec{n}_1 + b\vec{n}_2) + t(\vec{n}_1 \times \vec{n}_2)$$

Note that choosing the direction of the line to be $\vec{n}_2 \times \vec{n}_1$ instead will give you the same line, but with reversed direction.

The pseudocode is

```
bool IntersectionOf2Planes(Plane3D p1, Plane3D p2, Line3D line)
{
    Vector3D d = Cross(p1.normal,p2.normal)
    if (d.length() == 0) {
        return false;
    }

    line.direction = d;
    float s1, s2, a, b;
    s1 = p1.d; // d from the plane equation
    s2 = p2.d;
    float n1n2dot = Dot(p1.normal, p2.normal);
    float n1normsqr = Dot(p1.normal, p1.normal);
    float n2normsqr = Dot(p2.normal, p2.normal);
    a = (s2 * n1n2dot - s1 * n2normsqr) / (n1n2dot^2 - n1normsqr * n2normsqr);
    b = (s1 * n1n2dot - s2 * n2normsqr) / (n1n2dot^2 - n1normsqr * n2normsqr);
    line.p = a * p1.normal + b * p2.normal;
    return true;
}
```

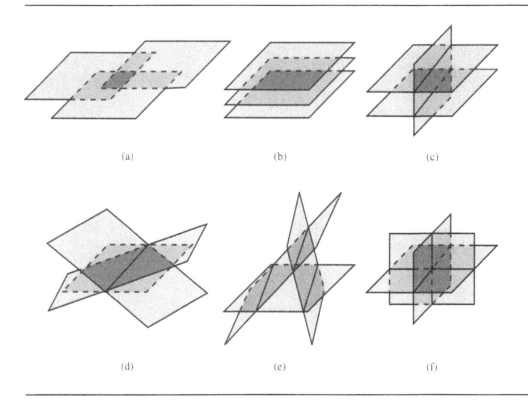

(a)   (b)   (c)

(d)   (e)   (f)

Figure 11.24   Possible configurations for three planes described in Table 11.1.

11.5.2 THREE PLANES

The problem of intersecting three planes is quite similar to that of intersecting two planes, but there are more cases to consider, and it is useful to distinguish between them. Given three planes

$$\mathcal{P}_0 : \{P_0, \vec{n}_0\}$$
$$\mathcal{P}_1 : \{P_1, \vec{n}_1\}$$
$$\mathcal{P}_2 : \{P_2, \vec{n}_2\}$$

there are six possible configurations, as shown in Figure 11.24. Following Dan Sunday's taxonomy (Sunday 2001c), we can describe each configuration in terms of intersection (or not) and the vector algebraic condition characterizing it (see Table 11.1).

A bit of explanation may be in order: if any planes $\mathcal{P}_i$ and $\mathcal{P}_j$ are parallel, then their normals are the same, which can be expressed as

Table 11.1   The six possible configurations of three planes can be distinguished by testing vector algebraic conditions.

Configuration	Intersection?	Condition
All planes parallel		$\vec{n}_i \times \vec{n}_j = 0, \forall i, j \in \{0, 1, 2\}$
Coincident (Figure 11.24a)	Plane	$\vec{n}_0 \cdot P_0 = \vec{n}_1 \cdot P_1 = \vec{n}_2 \cdot P_2$
Disjoint (Figure 11.24b)	None	$\vec{n}_0 \cdot P_0 \neq \vec{n}_1 \cdot P_1 \neq \vec{n}_2 \cdot P_2$
Only two planes parallel (Figure 11.24c) (or coincident)	Two parallel lines (or one line)	Only one $\vec{n}_i \times \vec{n}_j = 0, \forall i, j \in \{0, 1, 2\}$
No two planes parallel		$\vec{n}_i \times \vec{n}_j \neq 0, \forall i, j \in \{0, 1, 2\}, i \neq j$
Intersection lines parallel		$\vec{n}_0 \cdot (\vec{n}_1 \times \vec{n}_2) = 0$
Coincident (Figure 11.24d)	One line	Test point from one line
Disjoint (Figure 11.24e)	Three parallel lines	
Intersection lines nonparallel (Figure 11.24f)	Point	$\vec{n}_0 \cdot (\vec{n}_1 \times \vec{n}_2) \neq 0$

$$\vec{n}_i \times \vec{n}_j = 0$$

Further, if $\mathcal{P}_i$ and $\mathcal{P}_j$ are coincident, then any point on $\mathcal{P}_i$ will also be on $\mathcal{P}_j$, which can be expressed as

$$\vec{n}_i \cdot P_i = \vec{n}_j \cdot P_j$$

These conditions allow us to distinguish between the first three cases and to distinguish between them and the other cases.

If no two planes are parallel, then one of configurations (d), (e), or (f) holds. In order to distinguish (f) from the other two, we note that $\mathcal{P}_1$ and $\mathcal{P}_2$ must meet in a line, and that line must intersect $\mathcal{P}_0$ in a single point. As we saw in the problem of the intersection of two planes, the line of intersection has a direction vector equal to the cross product of the normals of those two planes; that is, $\vec{n}_1 \times \vec{n}_2$. If $\mathcal{P}_0$ is to intersect that line in a single point, then its normal $\vec{n}_0$ cannot be orthogonal to that line. Thus, the three planes intersect if and only if

$$\vec{n}_0 \cdot (\vec{n}_1 \times \vec{n}_2) \neq 0$$

This last equation should be recognized as the *scalar triple product* (see Section 3.3.2), which is the determinant of the 3×3 matrix of coefficients of the planes' normals.

Goldman (1990a) condenses the computation of the point of intersection to

$$P = ((P_0 \cdot \vec{n}_0)(\vec{n}_1 \times \vec{n}_2) + (P_1 \cdot \vec{n}_1)(\vec{n}_2 \times \vec{n}_0) + (P_2 \cdot \vec{n}_2)(\vec{n}_0 \times \vec{n}_1))/\vec{n}_0 \cdot (\vec{n}_1 \times \vec{n}_2)$$

If our planes instead are represented explicitly

$$\mathcal{P}_0 : a_0 x + b_0 y + c_0 z + d_0 = 0$$

$$\mathcal{P}_1 : a_1 x + b_1 y + c_1 z + d_1 = 0$$

$$\mathcal{P}_2 : a_2 x + b_2 y + c_2 z + d_2 = 0$$

then we can view the problem as solving three simultaneous linear equations. A technique such as Gaussian elimination or Cramer's rule (see Section 2.7.4) can be invoked to solve this. Bowyer and Woodwark (1983) condense this as follows: let

$$BC = b_1 c_2 - b_2 c_1$$

$$AC = a_1 c_2 - a_2 c_1$$

$$AB = a_1 b_2 - a_2 b_1$$

$$DC = d_1 c_2 - d_2 c_1$$

$$DB = d_1 b_2 - d_2 b_1$$

$$AD = a_1 d_2 - a_2 d_1$$

$$\text{invDet} = \frac{1}{a_0 BC - b_0 AC - c_0 AB}$$

$$X = (b_0 DC - d_0 BC - c_0 DB) * \text{invDet}$$

$$Y = (d_0 AC - a_0 DC - c_0 AD) * \text{invDet}$$

$$Z = (b_0 AD - a_0 DB - c_0 AB) * \text{invDet}$$

11.5.3   TRIANGLE AND PLANE

Suppose we have a plane $\mathcal{P}$ defined by a point P and normal $\hat{n}$, and a triangle $\mathcal{T}$ defined by its three vertices Q_0, Q_1, and Q_2, as shown in Figure 11.25. If the plane and triangle intersect, then one triangle vertex will be on the opposite side of the plane than the other two. If we compute the signed distance between each of Q_0, Q_1, and Q_2 and the plane $\mathcal{P}$ (see Section 10.3.1) and compare their signs, we can immediately determine if an intersection exists. Without loss of generality, assume that Q_0 is on the side of $\mathcal{P}$ opposite Q_1 and Q_2. Then, the two edges $Q_0 Q_1$ and $Q_0 Q_2$ must intersect $\mathcal{P}$ at some points I_0 and I_1, respectively. The line segment $I_0 I_1$ is then the intersection of $\mathcal{P}$ and $\mathcal{T}$ (see Section 11.1.1).

There are a number of "degenerate" cases that may arise, as shown in Figure 11.26. All of these involve one or more of the triangle's vertices being exactly on (or within ϵ of) the plane. In Figure 11.26(a), $\mathcal{P}$ and $\mathcal{T}$ are coplanar, and as such should probably not be considered an intersection, although the context of the application

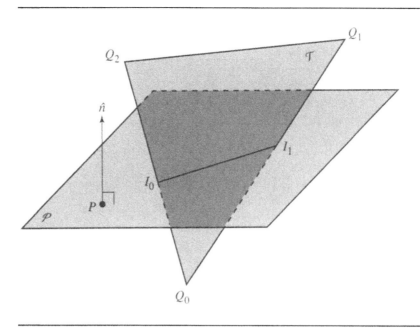

Figure 11.25   Plane-triangle intersection.

may have to deal with this situation specifically. The cases in Figures 11.26(b) and 11.26(c) can be handled in the same way, by considering that Q_i coinciding with the plane not be involved with any intersection. The case in Figure 11.26(d) is somewhat more interesting, as the "intersection" consists of a definite line segment, just as in a "normal" intersection; how this is handled depends on the semantics of the application.

The pseudocode is

```
bool IntersectionOfTriangleAndPlane(Plane3D pl,Triangle3D tri,
                                    Intersection isect)
{
    float dot1, dot2, dot3;
    dot1 = Dot(pl.normal, tri.p1 - pl.pointOnPlane);
    dot2 = Dot(pl.normal, tri.p2 - pl.pointOnPlane);
    dot3 = Dot(pl.normal, tri.p3 - pl.pointOnPlane);

    if (fabs(dot1) <= EPSILON) dot1 = 0.0;
    if (fabs(dot2) <= EPSILON) dot2 = 0.0;
    if (fabs(dot3) <= EPSILON) dot3 = 0.0;
```

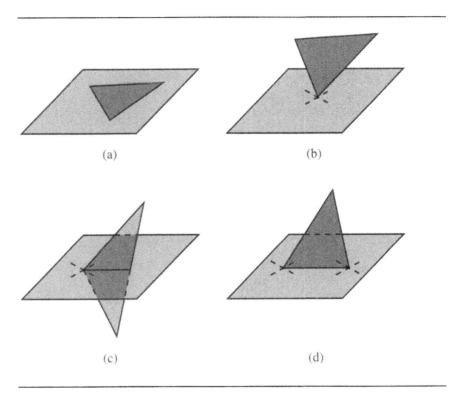

(a) (b)

(c) (d)

Figure 11.26   Plane-triangle intersection configurations.

```
if (dot1 > 0 && dot2 > 0 && dot3 > 0) {
    // all points above plane
    return false;
}

if (dot1 < 0 && dot2 < 0 && dot3 < 0) {
    // all points below plane
    return false;
}

if (fabs(dot1) + fabs(dot2) + fabs(dot3) == 0) {
    // coplanar case
    isect.type = plane;
    return true;
}
```

```
// Most common intersection

if ((dot1 > 0 && dot2 > 0 && dot3 < 0) ||
    (dot1 < 0 && dot2 < 0 && dot3 > 0) {
    isect.type = line;
    Line3D l1(tri.p1, tri.p3);
    Line3D l2(tri.p2, tri.p3);
    Point3D point1, point2;
    LineIntersectPlane(plane, l1, point1);
    LineIntersectPlane(plane, l2, point2);
    isect.line.d = point2 - point1;
    isect.line.p = point1;
    return true;
}

if ((dot2 > 0 && dot3 > 0 && dot1 < 0) ||
    (dot2 < 0 && dot3 < 0 && dot1 > 0) {
    isect.type = line;
    Line3D l1(tri.p2, tri.p1);
    Line3D l2(tri.p3, tri.p1);
    Point3D point1, point2;
    LineIntersectPlane(plane, l1, point1);
    LineIntersectPlane(plane, l2, point2);
    isect.line.d = point2 - point1;
    isect.line.p = point1;
    return true;
}

if ((dot1 > 0 && dot3 > 0 && dot2 < 0) ||
    (dot1 < 0 && dot3 < 0 && dot2 > 0) {
    isect.type = line;
    Line3D l1(tri.p1, tri.p2);
    Line3D l2(tri.p3, tri.p2);
    Point3D point1, point2;
    LineIntersectPlane(plane, l1, point1);
    LineIntersectPlane(plane, l2, point2);
    isect.line.d = point2 - point1;
    isect.line.p = point1;
    return true;
}

// Case b
if (dot1 == 0 && ((dot2 > 0 && dot3 > 0) || (dot2 < 0 && dot3 < 0))) {
    isect.type = point;
```

```
        isect.point = tri.p1;
        return true;
    }

    if (dot2 == 0 && ((dot1 > 0 && dot3 > 0) || (dot1 < 0 && dot3 < 0))) {
        isect.type = point;
        isect.point = tri.p2;
        return true;
    }

    if (dot3 == 0 && ((dot2 > 0 && dot1 > 0) || (dot2 < 0 && dot1 < 0))) {
        isect.type = point;
        isect.point = tri.p3;
        return true;
    }

    // Case c
    if (dot1 == 0 && ((dot2 > 0 && dot3 < 0) || (dot2 < 0 && dot3 > 0))) {
        isect.type = line;
        Line3D l1(tri.p3, tri.p2);
        Point3D point1;
        LineIntersectPlane(plane,l1, point1);
        isect.line.d = point1 - tri.p1;
        isect.line.p = tri.p1;
        return true;
    }

    if (dot2 == 0 && ((dot1 > 0 && dot3 < 0) || (dot1 < 0 && dot3 > 0))) {
        isect.type = line;
        Line3D l1(tri.p1, tri.p3);
        Point3D point1;
        LineIntersectPlane(plane,l1, point1);
        isect.line.d = point1 - tri.p2;
        isect.line.p = tri.p2;
        return true;
    }

    if (dot3 == 0 && ((dot1 > 0 && dot2 < 0) || (dot1 < 0 && dot2 > 0))) {
        isect.type = line;
        Line3D l1(tri.p1, tri.p2);
        Point3D point1;
        LineIntersectPlane(plane, l1, point1);
        isect.line.d = point1 - tri.p3;
        isect.line.p = tri.p3;
```

```
        return true;
    }

    // Case d
    if (dot1 == 0 && dot2 == 0) {
        isect.type = line;
        isect.line.d = tri.p2 - tri.p1;
        isect.line.p = tri.p1;
        return true;
    }

    if (dot2 == 0 && dot3 == 0) {
        isect.type = line;
        isect.line.d = tri.p3 - tri.p2;
        isect.line.p = tri.p2;
        return true;
    }

    if (dot1 == 0 && dot3 == 0) {
        isect.type = line;
        isect.line.d = tri.p3 - tri.p1;
        isect.line.p = tri.p1;
        return true;
    }

    return false;
}
```

11.5.4 TRIANGLE AND TRIANGLE

In this section we address the problem of intersecting two triangles. For the purposes of this section, we define our two triangles as sets of three vertices:

$$\mathcal{T}_0 : \{V_{0,0}, V_{0,1}, V_{0,2}\}$$

$$\mathcal{T}_1 : \{V_{1,0}, V_{1,1}, V_{1,2}\}$$

There are a number of different configurations that a triangle-triangle intersection method must handle (see Figure 11.27): the planes $\mathcal{P}_0$ and $\mathcal{P}_1$ may be parallel and noncoincident, parallel but coincident, or nonparallel, with $\mathcal{T}_0$ and $\mathcal{T}_1$ intersecting or not. Irrespective of the algorithm, the coincident-plane configuration must be handled as a special case (more on this later), as should cases where the triangles themselves are degenerate in some fashion (two or more vertices coincident).

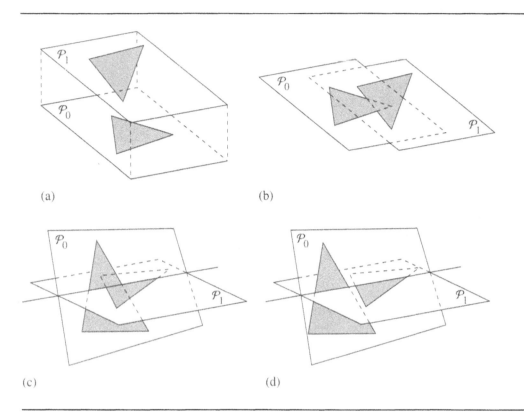

(a)   (b)

(c)   (d)

Figure 11.27   Triangle-triangle intersection configurations: (a) $\mathcal{P}_0 \| \mathcal{P}_1$, but $\mathcal{P}_0 \neq \mathcal{P}_1$; (b) $\mathcal{P}_0 = \mathcal{P}_1$; (c) $\mathcal{T}_0$ intersects $\mathcal{T}_1$; (d) $\mathcal{T}_0$ does not intersect $\mathcal{T}_1$.

The most obvious algorithm is to simply test if each edge of each polygon intersects the other triangle (face): when the first edge-face intersection is found, return true; if no edge-face intersections are found, return false. Given an efficient line segment–triangle intersection routine, this isn't too bad; however, several other algorithms are notably faster.

Möller and Haines describe the "interval overlap method" for determining if two triangles intersect (Möller and Haines 1999; Möller 1997); if there is an intersection, the line segment of the intersection is available fairly directly. The fundamental insight upon which their method is based is this: If we've already rejected pairs of triangles whose vertices are entirely on one side of each other's plane, then the line $\mathcal{L}$ at which the planes intersect will also intersect both triangles; the plane intersection line $\mathcal{L}$ is "clipped" by each triangle into two line segments ("intervals"). If these two line segments overlap, then the triangles intersect; otherwise, they do not. The line $\mathcal{L}$ is easily computed (see Section 11.5.1), giving us

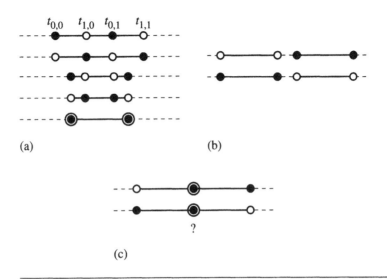

Figure 11.28   Triangle-triangle interval overlap configurations: (a) intersection; (b) no intersection; (c) ?.

$$\mathcal{L}(t) = P + t\vec{d}$$

Let $t_{0,0}$ and $t_{0,1}$ be the parameter values on $\mathcal{L}$ describing the segment intersected by $\mathcal{T}_0$, and $t_{1,0}$ and $t_{1,1}$ be the parameter values on $\mathcal{L}$ describing the segment intersected by $\mathcal{T}_1$. Figure 11.28 shows the possible relationships between the intervals. Clearly, we can easily reject nonintersecting triangles (although, as the figure illustrates, you must make a "policy" decision when the intervals abut exactly) and only compute the actual intersection once an intersection has been detected, and then only if we wish to know more than *whether* an intersection occurred.

Earlier, it was noted that we assumed the vertices of each triangle had been checked against the plane of the other, in order to do a quick reject on triangles that could not possibly intersect. The interval overlap method does this by checking the signed distance of each point from the other triangle's plane (see Section 10.3.1). This signed distance can now be put to use again: we know that one vertex of each triangle lies on the opposite side of $\mathcal{L}$ than the other two (rarely, one or two of the vertices of a triangle may actually be *on* $\mathcal{L}$ exactly, but this adds only a little bit of extra logic to the implementation). Without loss of generality, assume that $V_{0,0}$ and $V_{0,1}$ lie on one side of $\mathcal{L}$.

Now, it would be certainly possible to find the points on $\mathcal{L}$ where the edges $V_{0,0}V_{0,2}$ and $V_{0,1}V_{0,2}$ intersect it, by simply computing the intersection points of two 3D lines, but Möller and Haines employ a clever optimization:

1. Project the triangle vertices $V_{0,i}$ onto $\mathcal{L}$:

$$V'_{0,i} = \vec{d} \cdot (V_{0,i} - P), \qquad i \in \{0, 1, 2\}$$

2. Compute $t_{0,0}$ and $t_{0,1}$ as follows:

$$t_{0,i} = V'_{0,i} + (V'_{0,2} - V'_{0,i}) \frac{\mathrm{dist}_{V_{0,i}}}{\mathrm{dist}_{V_{0,i}} - \mathrm{dist}_{V_{0,2}}}, \qquad i \in \{0, 1\}$$

If the actual intersection line segment is desired, then we can find the overlapping interval by inspecting $t_{0,0}$, $t_{0,1}$, $t_{1,0}$, and $t_{1,1}$, and then plugging the parameter values back into the equation for $\mathcal{L}$.

An outline of the entire algorithm is as follows:

1. Determine if either $\mathcal{T}_0$ or $\mathcal{T}_1$ (or both) are degenerate, and handle in application-dependent fashion (this may mean exiting the intersection algorithm, or not).

2. Compute the plane equation of $\mathcal{T}_0$.

3. Compute the signed distances $\mathrm{dist}_{V_{1,i}}$, $i \in \{0, 1, 2\}$, of the vertices of $\mathcal{T}_1$.

4. Compare the signs of $\mathrm{dist}_{V_{1,i}}$, $i \in \{0, 1, 2\}$: if they are all the same, return *false*; otherwise, proceed to the next step.

5. Compute the plane equation of $\mathcal{T}_1$.

6. If the plane equations of $\mathcal{P}_0$ and $\mathcal{P}_1$ are the same (or rather, within ϵ), then compare the d values to see if the planes are coincident (within ϵ):

   - If coincident, then project the triangles onto the axis-aligned lane that is most nearly oriented with the triangles' plane, and perform a 2D triangle intersection test.[3]

   - Otherwise, the parallel planes are not coincident, so no possible intersection; exit the algorithm.

7. Compare the signs of $\mathrm{dist}_{V_{0,i}}$, $i \in \{0, 1, 2\}$: if they are all the same, return *false*; otherwise, proceed to the next step.

8. Compute intersection line.

9. Compute intervals.

   - If no interval overlap, triangles don't intersect. Return *false*.

   - Otherwise, if intersecting line segment is required, compute it. In any case, return *true*.

---

3. The method of separating axes (Section 7.7) can be used to determine whether or not an intersection exists. Generally speaking, the intersection of two 2D triangles will be one or more line segments (which may degenerate to a point); if this information is required (rather than merely determining whether or not an intersection exists), then we can compute the intersection of each edge of each triangle against the other triangle.

11.6 Planar Components and Polyhedra

In this section we discuss the intersection of planar components and polyhedra, which are a special type of polygonal mesh (or *polymesh*). A polygonal mesh is a collection of vertices, edges, and faces that satisfies the following conditions:

i. Each vertex must be shared by at least one edge. (No isolated vertices are allowed.)

ii. Each edge must be shared by at least one face. (No isolated edges or polylines allowed.)

iii. If two faces intersect, the vertex or edge of intersection must be a component in the mesh. (No interpenetration of faces is allowed. An edge of one face may not live in the interior of another face.)

Faces are convex polygons that live in 3D. Many applications support only triangular faces because of their simplicity in storage and their ease of use in operations applied to collections of the faces. It is possible to allow nonconvex polygon faces, but this only complicates the implementation and manipulation of the objects. If all the faces are triangles, the object is called a *triangle mesh*, or in short a *trimesh*.

A *polyhedron* (plural is *polyhedra*) is a polymesh that has additional constraints. The intuitive idea is that a polyhedron encloses a bounded region of space and that it has no unnecessary edge junctions. The simplest example is a *tetrahedron*, a polymesh that has four vertices, six edges, and four triangular faces. The additional constraints are

- The mesh is connected when viewed as a graph whose nodes are the faces and whose arcs are the edges shared by adjacent faces. Intuitively, a mesh is connected if you can reach a destination face from any source face by following a path of pairwise adjacent faces from the source to the destination.

- Each edge is shared by exactly two faces. This condition forces the mesh to be a closed and bounded surface.

11.6.1 Trimeshes

If the polyhedron's faces are all triangular, then the problem of intersecting the polyhedron with a plane or a triangle is relatively straightforward: we can simply apply the triangle-plane intersection algorithm (Section 11.5.3) or the triangle-triangle intersection algorithm (Section 11.5.4) to each triangular face of the polyhedron. Some efficiency may be gained by noting that a number of the operations involving the triangle mesh's vertices (e.g., checking which side of the plane a vertex is on) need be done only once.

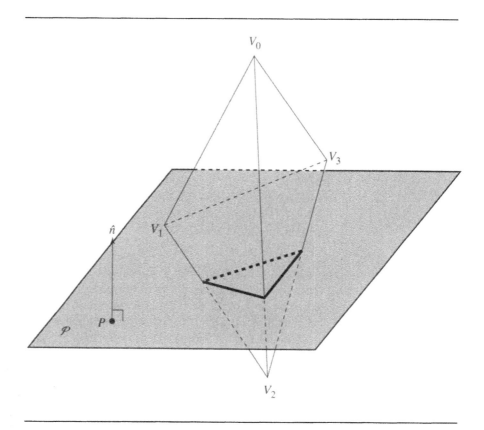

Figure 11.29   Intersection of a trimesh and a plane.

In general, the intersection of a triangle mesh and a plane or triangle will consist of a union of vertices, edges, and polylines (open or closed). Figure 11.29 shows a trimesh (a tetrahedron, in this case) intersecting a plane $\mathcal{P}$; the bold polyline shows the intersection, consisting of three line segments, which connect to form a polyline.

11.6.2   GENERAL POLYHEDRA

By our definition, a polyhedron may have faces with an arbitrary number of sides, subject only to the restriction that the faces be convex. If we wish to intersect such a polyhedron with a plane or triangle, then we're going to have to solve the problem of intersecting a polygon with a plane or with a triangle. If we then apply the same approach as just described for intersecting trimeshes with planes and triangles, then we'll have again a union of vertices, edges, and polylines.

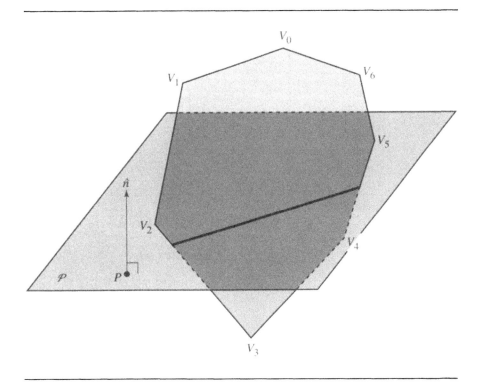

Figure 11.30   Intersection of a polygon and a plane.

Planes and Polygons

Figure 11.30 shows a convex polygon intersecting a plane $\mathcal{P}$. The edges $V_2 V_3$ and $V_4 V_5$ intersect the plane, and the intersection consists of a single line (shown in bold). The method for solving this is a simple generalization of the technique for intersecting a triangle and a plane (Section 11.5.3): If the plane and the plane containing the polygon are not parallel, then there is possibly an intersection. We compute the signed distance from each of $V_0, V_1, \ldots, V_{n-1}$, and if the signs differ, then we have an intersection. The edge $V_i V_{i+1}$ intersects the plane if the two vertices have different signs; there will be of course two such edges if there is an intersection; however, care must be taken if one or more vertices occur exactly in the plane.

Triangles and Polygons

Figure 11.31 shows a convex polygon $\mathcal{P}$ intersecting a triangle $\mathcal{T}$. Again we can first check if the plane of the polygon and the plane of the triangle are parallel, to determine if any intersection is possible. If an intersection is possible, then we can

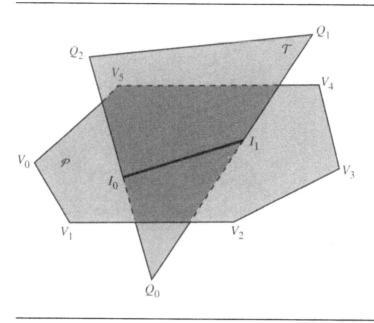

Figure 11.31   Intersection of a polygon and a triangle.

again compute the signed distances from the $\mathcal{P}$'s plane to the vertices of $\mathcal{T}$ in order to see if the triangle itself crosses the polygon's plane. However, the polygon and the plane may or may not intersect at this point; we have to check the edges of both the triangle and the polygon against the other to see if any edge penetrates the face of the other object. We can optimize this a little by noting that we only have to check edges $V_i V_{i+1}$ if the signs of the vertices differ. When checking the edge of the polygon against the triangle, we can easily use the method described in Section 11.1.2 to see if the edge intersects the interior of the triangle. However, to check whether an edge $Q_i Q_{i+1}$ intersects the interior of the polygon, we have to utilize the less efficient method of line segment/polygon intersection described in Section 11.1.3.

Planar Components and Polyhedra

In order to determine the intersection of a planar component and a polyhedron, we simply apply the triangle-polygon or plane-polygon intersection methods just described to each face of the polyhedron. Note again that some efficiency can be gained by computing the signed distances of all the vertices prior to testing each face, so that the same signed distance isn't recomputed as each face is tested.

11.7 PLANAR COMPONENTS AND QUADRIC SURFACES

In this section, we cover the intersection of planar components and quadric surfaces. We present several different solutions—one for the general case of a plane and any quadric, one for the case of a plane and the so-called "natural quadrics" (sphere, right circular cone, right circular cylinder), and one for the intersection of a triangle and a cone.

11.7.1 PLANE AND GENERAL QUADRIC SURFACE

In this section we address the problem of computing the intersection of a plane and a general quadric surface (Busboom and Schalkoff 1996). The solution presented holds for all quadric surfaces, but because it is general, it cannot take advantage of geometric characteristics of particular types of quadrics. Methods for handling some particular quadrics are covered in subsequent sections.

A general quadric surface can be described as

$$ax^2 + by^2 + cz^2 + 2fyz + 2gzx + 2hyx + 2px + 2qy + 2rz + d = 0 \quad (11.17)$$

The particular values of the coefficients $a, b, c, d, e, f, g, h, p, q$, and r determine the type of quadric (see Section 9.4).

For the purposes of this problem, we'll define a plane by specifying a point P on the plane and two orthogonal vectors $\vec{u}$ and $\vec{v}$ in the plane:

$$\mathcal{P}(t_u, t_v) = P + t_u \vec{u} + t_v \vec{v} \quad (11.18)$$

The intersection of the plane with the quadric surface is obtained by substituting Equation 11.18 into Equation 11.17. This yields a quadratic equation in terms of t_u and t_v:

$$At_u^2 + Bt_u t_v + Ct_v^2 + Dt_u + Et_v + F = 0 \quad (11.19)$$

The problem, then, consists in finding the coefficients A, B, C, D, E, and F.

Rather than writing out this very large algebraic expression, we'll take a slightly different approach: if we represent the sets of coefficients of Equations 11.17 and 11.19 as matrices, then we can express the transformation as a matrix. Let

$$\mathbf{C} = [\,A \quad B \quad C \quad D \quad E \quad F\,]^{\mathrm{T}}$$

and

$$\mathbf{Q} = [\,a \quad b \quad c \quad f \quad g \quad h \quad p \quad q \quad r \quad d\,]^{\mathrm{T}}$$

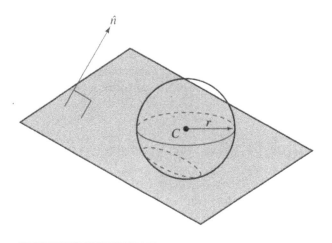

Figure 11.32   Intersection of a plane and a sphere.

Then, our transformation is the matrix **M** satisfying

$$C = MQ$$

which is

$$
M = \begin{bmatrix}
u_x^2 & u_y^2 & u_z^2 & 2u_yu_z & 2u_zu_x & 2u_xu_y & 0 & 0 & 0 & 0 \\
2u_xv_x & 2u_yv_y & 2u_zv_z & 2(u_yv_z + v_yu_z) & 2(u_zv_x + v_zu_x) & 2(u_xv_y + v_xv_y) & 0 & 0 & 0 & 0 \\
v_x^2 & v_y^2 & v_z^2 & 2v_yv_z & 2v_zv_x & 2v_xv_y & 0 & 0 & 0 & 0 \\
2P_xu_x & 2P_yu_y & 2P_zu_z & 2(P_yu_z + u_yP_z) & 2(P_zu_x + u_zP_x) & 2(P_xu_y + u_xP_y) & 2u_x & 2u_y & 2u_z & 0 \\
2P_xv_x & 2P_yv_y & 2P_zv_z & 2(P_yv_z + v_yP_z) & 2(P_zv_x + v_zP_x) & 2(P_xv_y + v_xP_y) & 2v_x & 2v_y & 2v_z & 0 \\
P_x^2 & P_y^2 & P_z^2 & 2P_yP_z & 2P_zP_x & 2P_xP_y & 2P_x & 2P_y & 2P_z & 1
\end{bmatrix}
$$

11.7.2 PLANE AND SPHERE

In this section we address the problem of computing the intersection of a plane and a sphere, as shown in Figure 11.32.

A sphere can be defined implicitly:

$$(x - C_x)^2 + (y - C_y)^2 + (z - C_z)^2 - r = 0 \qquad (11.20)$$

where C is the center of the sphere and r is the radius. If we define a plane parametrically, as we did in Section 9.2.1

$$\mathcal{P}(t_u, t_v) = P + t_u \vec{u} + t_v \vec{v}$$

we can substitute this equation into Equation 11.20, giving us a quadratic curve of the form

$$At_u^2 + Bt_u t_v + Ct_v^2 + Dt_u + Et_v + F = 0$$

If we do the substitution, expand, and collect terms, we have

$$A = u_x^2 + u_y^2 + u_z^2$$

$$B = 2(u_x v_x + u_y v_y + u_z v_z)$$

$$C = v_x^2 + v_y^2 + v_z^2$$

$$D = 2(P_x u_x + P_y u_y + P_x u_z) - 2(C_x v_x + C_y v_y + C_x v_z)$$

$$E = 2(P_x v_x + P_y v_y + P_x v_z) - 2(C_x v_x + C_y v_y + C_x v_z)$$

$$F = C_x^2 + C_y^2 + C_z^2 + P_x^2 + P_y^2 + PC_z^2 - 2(C_x P_x + C_y P_y + C_z P_z) - r$$

An alternative is to use a more direct geometric approach. Clearly, the intersection of a plane and a sphere, if it exists, is simply a circle lying in the plane. The plane's equation provides part of a 3D circle specification, so we need to find the circle's center and radius. The insight for the solution lies in observing that the center C of the sphere is located at some distance along a line that passes through the center of the circle Q of intersection and is normal to the plane $\mathcal{P}$, as can be seen more directly in cross section in Figure 11.33. If our plane $\mathcal{P}$ is given in the normalized coordinate-free version of the implicit form

$$P \cdot \hat{n} + d = 0$$

then the distance between the plane and the center of the sphere can be simply written as

$$b = \hat{n} \cdot Q + d$$

(see Section 10.3.1). If $|b| > r$, then there is no intersection; otherwise, the center of the circle of circle Q is simply

$$Q = C - b\hat{n}$$

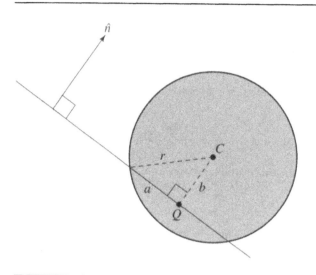

Figure 11.33   Cross-sectional view of sphere-plane intersection.

All that remains is for us to determine the radius of the circle of intersection. Again looking at Figure 11.33, we can easily see that

$$a^2 + b^2 = r^2$$

and so

$$a = \sqrt{r^2 - b^2}$$

is the radius.

If the plane just barely "grazes" the sphere, then $r^2 - b^2$ will be a very small number; in this case, the application may wish to consider that the intersection is actually just a point and act accordingly.

The pseudocode is

```
bool PlaneSphereIntersection(Plane3D plane, Sphere sphere, Intersection isect)
{
    Vec3D v1 = sphere.center - plane.pointOnPlane;
    // normal is unit length
    float b = fabs(dotProd(plane.normal,v1));
    if (b < r) {
        Point3D Q = sphere.center - b * plane.normal;
        float radius = sqrt(sphere.radius^2 + b^2);
```

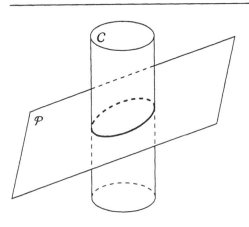

Figure 11.34   Intersection of a plane and a cylinder.

```
if (radius < epsilon) {
    // consider it as a point
    isect.point = Q;
    isect.type = point;
} else {
    isect.center = Q;
    isect.radius = radius;
    isect.type = circle;
}

        return true;
    }
    return false;
}
```

11.7.3 PLANE AND CYLINDER

In this section we address the problem of the intersection of a plane and a cylinder, as shown in Figure 11.34. There are actually quite a number of ways a cylinder and a plane can intersect, six of which are shown in Figure 11.35. Note that the intersections are shown for a finite cylinder. An infinite cylinder has fewer intersection configurations (we don't need to deal with the end caps); possible intersections are a circle, an ellipse, a single line, or a pair of lines. We give algorithms for intersection detection of a plane and an infinite cylinder and for a plane and a finite cylinder; the former

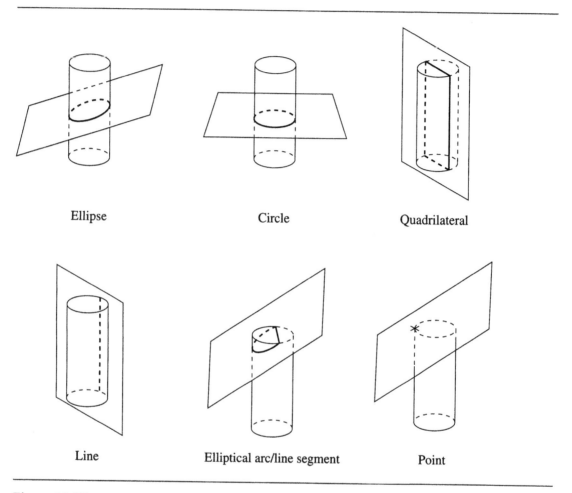

Figure 11.35   Some of the ways a plane and a cylinder can intersect.

is somewhat simpler. In a later section, we'll give an algorithm for computing the intersection of a plane and an infinite cylinder. These algorithms can be extended to a finite cylinder by "clipping" the extent of the conic intersection curve or lines by the planes containing the end caps.

Intersection Detection

For the intersection detection algorithm, we'll define a plane implicitly:

$$P \cdot \hat{n} + d = 0$$

(The coordinatized version is the usual $ax + by + cz + d = 0$, where $\hat{n} = [\, a \quad b \quad c \,]$ and $\sqrt{a^2 + b^2 + c^2} = 1$.) The cylinder is defined in "general position"—as a center-point C, axis $\hat{d}$, and half-height h (see Figure 11.12 in Section 11.3.4).

Infinite Cylinder

For the purposes of detecting an intersection, a plane $\mathcal{P}$ and an infinite cylinder C can be in one of several configurations:

1. If $\mathcal{P}$ is parallel to C's axis, then there will be an intersection if the distance between $\mathcal{P}$ and C is less than or equal to the radius of the cylinder.

2. If $\mathcal{P}$ is not parallel to C's axis, $\hat{d} \cdot \hat{n} = 1$, there will always be an intersection.

Finite Cylinder

For the purposes of detecting an intersection, a plane $\mathcal{P}$ and a cylinder C can be in one of several configurations:

1. $\mathcal{P}$ may be parallel to C's axis: $|\hat{d} \cdot \hat{n}| = 1$.

2. $\mathcal{P}$ may be perpendicular to C's axis: $\hat{d} \cdot \hat{n} = 0$.

3. $\mathcal{P}$ may be neither parallel nor perpendicular to C's axis. In this case, $\mathcal{P}$ may or may not intersect C.

Let's consider these cases one by one:

1. If $\mathcal{P}$ is parallel to C's axis, then there will be an intersection if the distance between $\mathcal{P}$ and C's axis is less than or equal to the radius of the cylinder (in which case the intersection will be a quadrilateral or a single line, respectively).

2. If $\mathcal{P}$ is perpendicular to C's axis, then there will be an intersection if the distance between $\mathcal{P}$ and C is less than or equal to the half-height of the cylinder (in which case the intersection will be a circle).

3. If $\mathcal{P}$ is neither parallel nor perpendicular to C's axis, then there are two cases to consider:

   a. The intersection of $\mathcal{P}$ and the axis of C is closer to the centerpoint of C than the half-height; in this case, there is definitely an intersection.

   b. $\mathcal{P}$ intersects the axis of C outside the end caps of the cylinder, in which case there may or may not be an intersection, depending on the relative location of the point of intersection and the angle between the plane and the axis.

In either case, the intersection will be either an ellipse, an elliptical arc and a straight line, or two elliptical arcs and two straight lines, depending on the relative orientation of the plane.

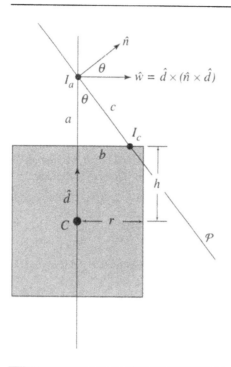

Figure 11.36   Edge-on view of plane-cylinder intersection.

All of the cases but the last are fairly trivial. Determining whether or not the plane is parallel or perpendicular to the cylinders's axis involves only a dot product. Computing the distance between the cylinder's centerpoint C and the plane is simple and inexpensive (see Section 10.3.1). Computing the intersection of the plane and the cylinder's axis is inexpensive as well (see Section 11.1.1). Only the last case has any expense associated with it, and so the tests should be done in the order discussed.

The last case is illustrated in Figure 11.36. The edge-on view is not simply a diagrammatic convenience—the method for determining whether or not an intersection exists is done in a plane perpendicular to $\mathcal{P}$ and going through C. The rest is basic trigonometry.

If I_a is the intersection of $\mathcal{P}$ and the axis of the cylinder, then if the point I_c is closer to the axis than r (the radius of the cylinder), we have an intersection. The plane $\mathcal{P}^\perp$ perpendicular to $\mathcal{P}$ and going through C is parallel to $\hat{d}$, and so its normal is

$$\hat{n} \times \hat{d}$$

We define a vector in $\mathcal{P}^{\perp}$ that is perpendicular to $\hat{d}$:

$$\hat{w} = \hat{d} \times (\hat{n} \times \hat{d})$$

The angle θ between $\hat{n}$ and $\hat{w}$ is

$$\cos(\theta) = \hat{n} \cdot \vec{w}$$

We also know the distance a:

$$a = \|I_a - C\| - h$$

By the definition of the cosine function, we know

$$\cos(\theta) = \frac{a}{c}$$

Substituting, we get

$$\hat{n} \cdot \vec{w} = \frac{\|I_a - C\| - h}{c}$$

and so

$$c = \frac{\|I_a - C\| - h}{\hat{n} \cdot \vec{w}}$$

Invoking the Pythagorean Theorem, we have

$$a^2 + b^2 = c^2$$

$$(\|I_a - C\| - h)^2 + b^2 = \left(\frac{\|I_a - C\| - h}{\hat{n} \cdot \vec{w}} \right)^2$$

$$b^2 = \left(\frac{\|I_a - C\| - h}{\hat{n} \cdot \vec{w}} \right)^2 - (\|I_a - C\| - h)^2$$

and so if $b^2 \leq r^2$, we have an intersection; otherwise, not.

Intersection with an Infinite Cylinder

The general plane-quadric intersection formulation given in Section 11.7 yields an implicit equation of a quadratic curve in terms of parameters of the plane. Such representations are not very convenient. In the case of the intersection of a plane and

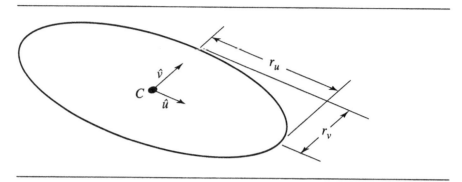

Figure 11.37   Ellipse in 3D.

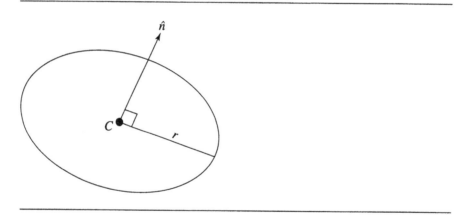

Figure 11.38   Circle in 3D.

a cylinder, we can get an ellipse or circle that ought to be described in a more direct geometric fashion; by this we mean that an ellipse should be defined by a centerpoint C, major and minor axes $\hat{u}$ and $\hat{v}$, and major and minor radii r_u and r_v, as shown in Figure 11.37, and a circle should be defined as a centerpoint C, normal to the plane $\hat{n}$, and radius r, as shown in Figure 11.38.

As seen in Figure 11.35, the intersection of a plane with an infinite cylinder can be a single line, two lines, a circle, or an ellipse. The first three of these are special cases that occur only when the plane and cylinder are at one of two special angles relative to one another, and so the ellipse may be considered to be the typical case.

That the general intersection between a cylinder and a plane is an ellipse was first shown by Germinal Pierre Dandelin (1794–1847). Consider a cylinder and a

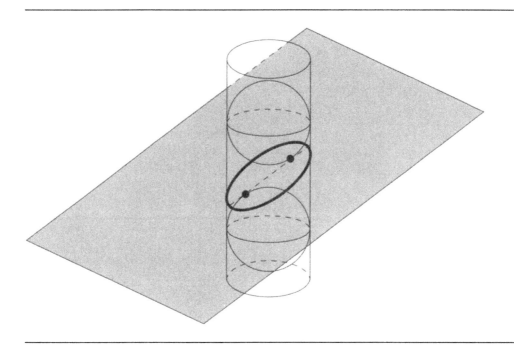

Figure 11.39   Dandelin's construction.

plane intersecting; take a sphere whose radius is the same as the cylinder, and drop it into the cylinder, and take a second sphere of the same radius, and push it up into the cylinder from underneath. These two spheres will contact the intersecting plane at two points, which are the two foci of the ellipse of intersection, as shown in Figure 11.39. In addition, the minimum distance along the cylinder between the circles at which the spheres are tangent to the cylinder is exactly twice the major radius of the ellipse of intersection. A sketch of the proof of this can be found in Miller and Goldman (1992), who describe how this fact can be used to find the intersecting ellipse in terms of the definition described earlier. We present that method here.

We assume the cylinder is represented by a base point B, axis $\hat{a}$, and radius r, and the plane is represented by a point P and normal $\hat{n}$, so the implicit equation is

$$(X - P) \cdot \hat{n} = 0 \tag{11.21}$$

The cylinder, intersecting plane, and two spheres are shown in cross section in Figure 11.40.

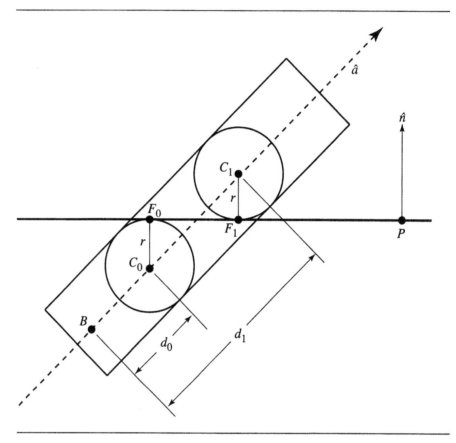

Figure 11.40   Cross section of a plane intersecting a cylinder, with the two spheres used to define the intersecting ellipse. After Miller and Goldman (1992).

Miller and Goldman begin by noting two facts:

- The two spheres' centers C_0 and C_1 must be located along the axis of the cylinder.
- The points of tangency are $C \pm r\hat{n}$ and constitute the foci of the ellipse of intersection.

As we know the radius of the spheres and the axis on which they lie, to complete their definition we can simply determine their distances d_0 and d_1 from some fixed point, such as B, the base of the cylinder:

$$C_0 = B + d_0\hat{a}$$

$$C_1 = B + d_1\hat{a}$$

The foci are then

$$F_0 = B + d_0\hat{a} + r\hat{n}$$
$$F_1 = B + d_1\hat{a} - r\hat{n}$$

(11.22)

To determine the distances, we substitute Equation 11.22 into Equation 11.21, and solve:

$$d_0 = \frac{(P - B) \cdot \hat{n} - r}{\hat{a} \cdot \hat{n}}$$

$$d_1 = \frac{(P - B) \cdot \hat{n} + r}{\hat{a} \cdot \hat{n}}$$

We would expect the center C of the ellipse of intersection to be on the axis $\hat{a}$ of the cylinder, and this can be shown by noting that C is precisely halfway between the foci F_0 and F_1:

$$C = \frac{F_0 + F_1}{2}$$

$$= \frac{B + d_0\hat{a} + r\hat{n} + B + d_1\hat{a} - r\hat{n}}{2}$$

$$= \frac{2B + (d_0 + d_1)\hat{a}}{2}$$

$$= B + \frac{d_0 + d_1}{2}\hat{a}$$

$$= B + \frac{\frac{(P-B)\cdot\hat{n}-r}{\hat{a}\cdot\hat{n}} + \frac{(P-B)\cdot\hat{n}+r}{\hat{a}\cdot\hat{n}}}{2}\hat{a}$$

$$= B + \frac{(P - B) \cdot \hat{n}}{\hat{a} \cdot \hat{n}}\hat{a}$$

The point C is the intersection of the plane and the cylinder axis $\hat{a}$. The direction of the major axis $\hat{u}$ is parallel to $F_0 - F_1$:

$$F_0 - F_1 = B + d_0\hat{a} + r\hat{n} - (B + d_1\hat{a} - r\hat{n})$$

$$= (d_0 + d_1)\hat{a} + 2r\hat{n}$$

$$= \frac{-2r}{\hat{a} \cdot \hat{n}}\hat{a} + 2r\hat{n}$$

Rearranging, we get

$$\frac{\hat{a} \cdot \hat{n}}{-2r}(F_0 - F_1) = \hat{a} - (\hat{a} \cdot \hat{n})\hat{n}$$

From this, Miller and Goldman observe that the direction of the major axis is the component of $\hat{a}$ perpendicular to $\hat{n}$. As stated earlier, the major axis is half the distance between the circles of tangency between the spheres and the cylinder, which is (as can be seen in Figure 11.40) $|d_1 - d_0|$, giving us

$$r_u = \frac{|d_1 - d_0|}{2}$$

$$= \frac{r}{|\hat{a} \cdot \hat{n}|}$$

The minor radius r_v is the same as r, the radius of the cylinder. To show this, we start with an observation: if we have an ellipse

$$\frac{x^2}{a^2} + \frac{y^2}{b^2} = 1$$

where $a > b$, it can be shown that the foci are at $\pm\sqrt{a^2 - b^2}$. So, if we define c to be the distance between the centerpoint C and the foci, the minor radius is

$$r_v = \sqrt{r_u^2 - c^2}$$

The distance between the foci is $2c$, and so the square of the distance is

$$4c^2 = |F_0 - F_1|^2$$

$$= 4r^2 \left(\frac{1}{(\hat{a} \cdot \hat{n})^2} - 1 \right)$$

Taking the square root of both sides, and substituting $\cos(\theta) = \hat{a} \cdot \hat{v}$, we get

$$2c = |F_0 - F_1|$$

$$= \sqrt{4r^2 \left(\frac{1}{\cos^2(\theta)} - 1 \right)}$$

$$= 2r \tan(\theta)$$

and so we have

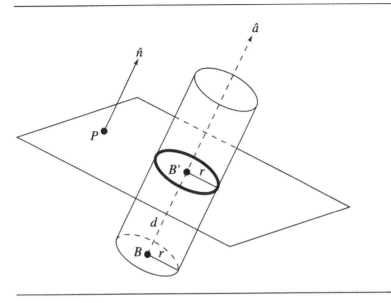

Figure 11.41   The intersection of a plane and a cylinder is a circle if the plane's normal is parallel to the cylinder's axis.

$$r_v = \sqrt{r_u^2 - c^2}$$

$$= \sqrt{\left(\frac{r}{|\hat{a} \cdot \hat{n}|}\right)^2 - \left(\frac{2r\tan(\theta)}{2}\right)^2}$$

$$= \sqrt{\left(\frac{r}{\cos(\theta)}\right)^2 - (r\tan(\theta))^2}$$

$$= \sqrt{r^2 \frac{1 - \sin^2(\theta)}{\cos^2(\theta)}}$$

$$= r$$

We mentioned earlier that the configurations in which the intersection was a circle or one or two lines are special cases, and we address these here. Clearly, if the plane normal $\hat{n}$ and the cylinder axis $\hat{a}$ are parallel, then the intersection is a circle, as shown in Figure 11.41.

If the plane normal $\hat{n}$ is perpendicular to the cylinder axis $\hat{a}$, then we find the distance d between the cylinder's base point B and the plane:

- If $|d| > r$, then there are no intersections.

- If $|d| = r$, then the intersection is one line $B' + t\hat{a}$, where B' is the projection of B onto the plane.

- If $|d| < r$, then the intersection consists of two lines:

$$B' \pm \sqrt{r^2 - d^2}(\hat{a} \times \hat{n}) + t\hat{a}$$

The pseudocode is

```
boolean PlaneCylinderIntersection(Plane plane, Cylinder cylinder)
{
    // Compute distance, projection of cylinder base point onto
    // plane, and angle between plane normal and cylinder axis
    d = PointPlaneDistance(cylinder.base, plane);
    bPrime = cylinder.base - d * plane.normal;
    cosTheta = Dot(cylinder.axis, plane.normal);

    // Check angle between plane and cylinder axis to
    // determine type of intersection

    if (cosTheta < abs(epsilon)) {
        // No intersection, or one or two lines. Check
        // which it is by looking at distance from cylinder
        // base point to plane
        if (abs(d) == cylinder.radius) {
            // Single line
            line.base = bPrime;
            line.direction = cylinder.axis;
            return true;
        }

        if (abs(d) > cylinder.radius) {
            // No intersection
            return false;
        }

        // abs(d) < cylinder.radius, so two intersection lines
        offset = Cross(cylinder.axis, plane.normal);
        e = sqrt(cylinder.radius * cylinder.radius - d * d);

        Line line1, line2;

        line1.base = bPrime - e * offset;
```

```
        line1.direction = cylinder.axis;
        line2.base = bPrime + e * offset;
        line2.direction = cylinder.axis;

        return true;
    }

    //  cosTheta != 0, so intersection is circle or ellipse
    if (abs(cosTheta) == 1) {
        //  Circle
        Circle circle;
        circle.center = bPrime;
        circle.normal = cylinder.axis;
        circle.radius = cylinder.radius;

        return true;
    }

    // abs(cosTheta) != 0 and abs(cosTheta) != 1, so ellipse
    Ellipse ellipse;
    ellipse.center = bPrime - (d / cosTheta) * cylinder.axis;
    ellipse.u = cylinder.axis - cosTheta * plane.normal;
    ellipse.v = Cross(plane.normal, ellipse.u);
    rU = cylinder.radius / abs(cosTheta);
    rV = cylinder.radius;

    return true;
}
```

11.7.4 PLANE AND CONE

In this section we address the problem of the intersection of a plane and a cone, as shown in Figure 11.42. There are actually quite a number of ways a cone and a plane can intersect, eight of which are shown in Figure 11.43. Note that the intersections are shown for a finite cone; an infinite cone has fewer intersection configurations because we don't need to deal with the end caps. We give algorithms for intersection detection of a plane and an infinite cone and for a plane and a finite cone; the former is somewhat simpler. In a later section, we'll give an algorithm for computing the intersection of a plane and an infinite cone. These algorithms can be extended to a finite cone by "clipping" the extent of the conic intersection curve or lines by the planes containing the end caps.

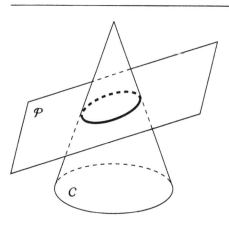

Figure 11.42   Intersection of a plane and a cone.

Intersection Detection

For the intersection detection algorithm, we'll define a plane implicitly:

$$P \cdot \hat{n} + d = 0$$

(The coordinatized version is the usual $ax + by + cz + d = 0$, where $\sqrt{a^2 + b^2 + c^2} = 1$.) The finite single cone is defined in "general position"—as a base point B, axis $\hat{d}$, and height h (see Figure 11.14 in Section 11.3.5). An infinite single cone is defined by a point A defining the apex of the cone, an axis $\hat{d}$, and a half-angle α (see Figure 11.44).

Infinite Cone

For the purposes of detecting an intersection, a plane $\mathcal{P}$ and an infinite cone C can be in one of several configurations:

1. If $\mathcal{P}$ is parallel to C's axis, $\hat{d} \cdot \hat{n} = 0$, then there will always be an intersection.

2. If $\mathcal{P}$ is perpendicular to C's axis, $|\hat{d} \cdot \hat{n}| = 1$, there will be an intersection if the (signed) distance from the cone's apex A to the plane is nonpositive (with respect to $\hat{d}$).

3. If $\mathcal{P}$ is neither perpendicular nor parallel to C's axis, then there may or may not be an intersection, depending on the distance from A to the intersection of the

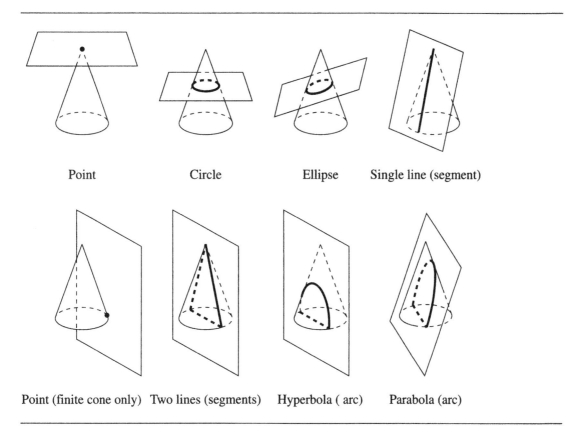

| Point | Circle | Ellipse | Single line (segment) |

| Point (finite cone only) | Two lines (segments) | Hyperbola (arc) | Parabola (arc) |

Figure 11.43   Some of the ways a plane and a cone can intersect.

cone's axis and the plane, and the relative angle between the cone's axis and the plane.

Figure 11.44 shows the intersection test for a cone with a plane, for the case where the cone's axis and the plane are neither perpendicular nor parallel. The plane $\mathcal{P}^\perp$ perpendicular to $\mathcal{P}$ and going through A is parallel to $\hat{d}$, and so its normal is

$$\hat{n} \times \hat{d}$$

We define a vector in $\mathcal{P}^\perp$ that is perpendicular to $\hat{d}$:

$$\hat{w} = \hat{d} \times (\hat{n} \times \hat{d})$$

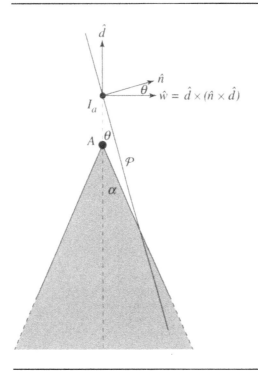

Figure 11.44   Intersection test for a plane and an infinite cone.

The angle θ between $\hat{n}$ and $\hat{w}$ is

$$\cos(\theta) = \hat{n} \cdot \vec{w}$$

If the intersection of the plane $\mathcal{P}$ and the axis of the cone is within the cone (i.e., the signed distance less than or equal to zero), then there is obviously an intersection. Otherwise, if $\theta \leq \alpha$, then there is an intersection.

Finite Cone

For the purposes of detecting an intersection, a plane $\mathcal{P}$ and a cone C can be in one of several configurations:

1. $\mathcal{P}$ may be parallel to C's axis: $|\hat{d} \cdot \hat{n}| = 1$.

2. $\mathcal{P}$ may be perpendicular to C's axis: $\hat{d} \cdot \hat{n} = 0$.

3. $\mathcal{P}$ may be neither parallel nor perpendicular to C's axis. In this case, $\mathcal{P}$ may or may not intersect C.

Let's consider these cases one by one:

1. If $\mathcal{P}$ is parallel to C's axis, then there will be an intersection if the distance between $\mathcal{P}$ and C's axis is less than or equal to the radius of the cone.

2. If $\mathcal{P}$ is perpendicular to C's axis, then there will be an intersection if the signed distance (relative to $\hat{d}$) from B to $\mathcal{P}$ is between 0 and h.

3. If $\mathcal{P}$ is neither parallel nor perpendicular to C's axis, then there are two cases to consider:

    a. The signed distance (relative to $\hat{d}$) from B to $\mathcal{P}$ is between 0 and h; in this case, there is definitely an intersection.

    b. $\mathcal{P}$ intersects the axis of C outside the apex or end cap of the cone, in which case there may or may not be an intersection, depending on the relative location of the point of intersection and the angle between the plane and the axis.

All of the cases but the last are fairly trivial. Determining whether or not the plane is parallel or perpendicular to the cone's axis involves only a dot product. Computing the distance between the cone's base point B and the plane is simple and inexpensive (see Section 10.3.1). Computing the intersection of the plane and the cone's axis is inexpensive as well (see Section 11.1.1). Only the last case has any expense associated with it, and so the tests should be done in the order discussed.

The last case is illustrated in Figure 11.45. The edge-on view is not simply a diagrammatic convenience—the method for determining whether or not an intersection exists is done in a plane perpendicular to $\mathcal{P}$ and going through B. The rest is basic trigonometry.

If I_a is the intersection of $\mathcal{P}$ and the axis of the cone, then if the point I_c is closer to the axis than r (the radius of the cone), we have an intersection. The plane $\mathcal{P}^\perp$ perpendicular to $\mathcal{P}$ and going through B is parallel to $\hat{d}$, and so its normal is

$$\hat{n} \times \hat{d}$$

We define a vector in $\mathcal{P}^\perp$ that is perpendicular to $\hat{d}$:

$$\hat{w} = \hat{d} \times (\hat{n} \times \hat{d})$$

The angle θ between $\hat{n}$ and $\hat{w}$ is

$$\cos(\theta) = \hat{n} \cdot \vec{w}$$

We also know the distance a:

$$a = \|I_a - B\| - h$$

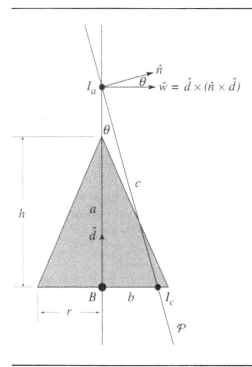

Figure 11.45   Edge-on view of plane-cone intersection.

By the definition of the cosine function, we know

$$\cos(\theta) = \frac{a}{c}$$

Substituting, we get

$$\hat{n} \cdot \vec{w} = \frac{\|I_a - B\| - h}{c}$$

and so

$$c = \frac{\|I_a - B\| - h}{\hat{n} \cdot \vec{w}}$$

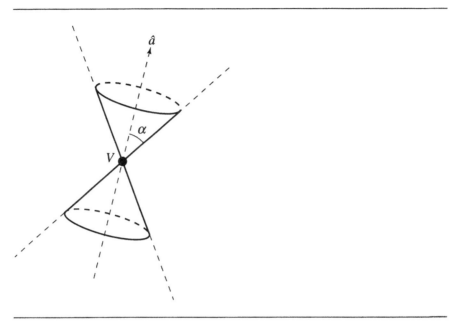

Figure 11.46 Infinite cone definition.

Invoking the Pythagorean Theorem, we have

$$a^2 + b^2 = c^2$$

$$(\|I_a - B\| - h)^2 + b^2 = \left(\frac{\|I_a - B\| - h}{\hat{n} \cdot \vec{w}} \right)^2$$

$$b^2 = \left(\frac{\|I_a - B\| - h}{\hat{n} \cdot \vec{w}} \right)^2 - (\|I_a - B\| - h)^2$$

and so if $b^2 \leq r^2$, we have an intersection; otherwise, not.

Intersection with an Infinite Cone

In this section, we address the problem of finding the intersection of a plane and an infinite cone. Here, we define a plane with a point P on the plane and a plane normal $\hat{n}$; a cone is defined by its vertex V, axis $\hat{a}$, and half-angle α, as shown in Figure 11.46.

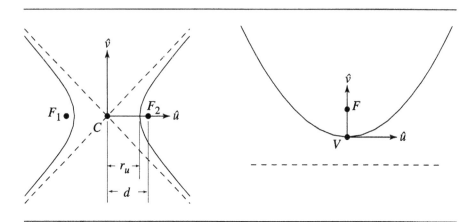

Figure 11.47   Geometric definitions for hyperbola and parabola.

As with the problem of intersecting a plane with an infinite cylinder (Section 11.7.3), we present an approach due to Miller and Goldman (1992). In that solution, they exploited Dandelin's construction—a nondegenerate intersection results in a curve with a special relationship to spheres internally tangent to the cylinder and tangent to the intersecting plane. For the problem of intersecting a plane and an infinite cone, a similar technique is applied. As pointed out previously (Figure 11.43), a plane and a cone can intersect in a point, one line, two lines, circle, ellipse, parabola, or hyperbola. The first three cases we call "degenerate," and the intersections are fairly trivial to compute. The last four cases are conic sections, and to these we can apply an analog to what was done with the plane-cylinder intersection.

The definitions of the ellipse and the circle were shown in Figures 11.37 and 11.38, respectively, in the discussion of the intersection of a plane and a cylinder. For the parabola and hyperbola, we have analogous geometric definitions: a parabola is defined by its vertex V_p, directrix and focus vectors $\hat{u}$ and $\hat{v}$, and focal length f (the distance between V_p and focus F); a hyperbola is defined by a centerpoint C, major and minor axes $\hat{u}$ and $\hat{v}$, and associated major and minor radii

$$r_u \text{ and } r_v = \sqrt{d^2 - r_u^2}$$

where d is the distance between C and the foci F_1 and F_2, as shown in Figure 11.47.

In the cases of nondegenerate intersection, either one or two spheres may be found that are both tangent to the cone in a circle (that is, they fit inside the cone) and tangent to the intersecting plane. If the plane and cone intersect in a parabolic curve, then there is one such sphere, and it touches the plane at the parabola's focus. If the plane and cone intersect in either an ellipse or hyperbola, then there are two such spheres, and they touch the plane at the intersecting curve's foci. As with the plane-cylinder intersection, the distance along the surface of the cone, between the two circles of tangency between the cone and spheres, is double the major radius of the intersecting curve. A sketch of a proof of this is found in Miller and Goldman (1992).

Configurations that result in degenerate intersections (point, one line, two lines) are trivially identifiable by a shared characteristic—they all result when the apex of the cone intersects the plane. Consider Figure 11.43: we can easily see this characteristic in the "Point," "Single line (segment)," and "Two lines (segments)" cases. It should be noted that, in an implementation, the test for the cone's apex being on the plane should not be exact—some ϵ should be applied; otherwise, the result instead will be a conic section with at least one parameter (e.g., major radius) being infinitesimally small, which is undesirable computationally.

Nondegenerate Plane-Cone Intersections

In order to distinguish between the intersections, we consider the angle between the cone's axis $\hat{a}$ and the plane's normal $\hat{n}$, and its relationship to the half-angle α defining the cone. We define the angle between the cone's axis and the plane's normal as θ. By the definition of the dot product, we then have $\cos(\theta) = \hat{a}$.

In order to exploit the tangent sphere properties, we first need to determine where the tangent spheres will be located, given the relative orientations of the cone and the plane. We do this by determining the conditions for the sphere(s) to be tangent to the cone, and the conditions for the sphere(s) to be tangent to the plane, and substituting one equation into the other to determine what conditions must hold for the sphere to be tangent to both. To simplify the situation, assume the following:

$$(V - P) \cdot \hat{n} < 0$$

$$\hat{a} \cdot \hat{n} \geq 0$$

If either of these assumptions is not already met, simply reverse $\hat{n}$ and/or $\hat{a}$.

Observing Figure 11.48, clearly the sphere $\{C, r\}$ is located along the line $V + t\hat{a}$; using the definition of the sine function, we have $h = \frac{r}{\sin(\alpha)}$, and so we then have

$$C = V + \frac{r}{\sin(\alpha)}\hat{a} \qquad (11.23)$$

Miller and Goldman note that r, if allowed to be negative, will generate the sphere on the other side of the cone.

For the sphere to be tangent to the plane, by definition we must have the sphere's center C at a distance r from the plane; that is,

$$\|(C - P) \cdot \hat{n}\| = |r|$$

or, squaring both sides,

$$((C - P) \cdot \hat{n})^2 = r^2 \qquad (11.24)$$

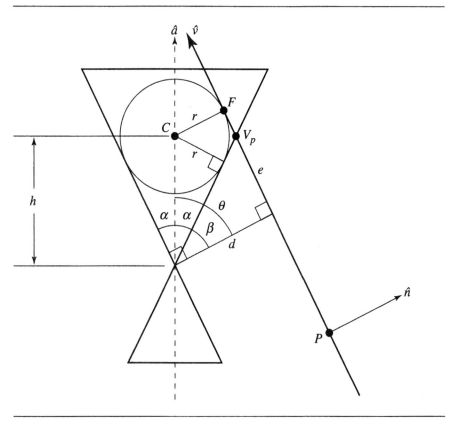

Figure 11.48   Parabolic curve intersection of plane and cone. After Miller and Goldman (1992).

If we substitute Equation 11.23 into Equation 11.24, we get

$$\left(\left((V - P) + \frac{r}{\sin(\alpha)}\hat{a}\right) \cdot \hat{n}\right)^2 = r^2$$

This is a quadratic equation in r, whose solutions are

$$r = \pm \frac{((V - P) \cdot \hat{n}) \sin(\alpha)}{\sin(\alpha) \mp \cos(\theta)} \tag{11.25}$$

The *intersection is a parabola* if the plane is parallel to a rule of the cone; that is, when $\theta + \alpha = \pi/2$, as shown in Figure 11.48. Note that only one of the solutions for r in Equation 11.25 is possible because when $\theta + \alpha = \pi/2$, we have $\cos(\theta) = \sin(\alpha)$, and one of the denominators of Equation 11.25 becomes 0. If we have $\cos(\theta) = \sin(\alpha)$, then Equation 11.25 becomes

$$r = -\frac{(V - P) \cdot \hat{n} \sin(\alpha)}{\sin(\alpha) + \cos(\theta)}$$

$$= -\frac{(V - P) \cdot \hat{n} \sin(\alpha)}{2 \sin(\alpha)}$$

$$= -\frac{(V - P) \cdot \hat{n}}{2}$$

The distance from the vertex of the cone to the plane is

$$d = -(V - P) \cdot \hat{n}$$

and so we have

$$r = \frac{d}{2} \tag{11.26}$$

To define the parabola, we need to find the focal length f, vertex V_p, and the bases $\hat{u}$ and $\hat{v}$. We compute f by determining F (the focus of the parabola) and finding its distance from the vertex V_p:

$$f = \| F - V_p \|$$

Points V_p and F lie in the plane containing V, $\hat{a}$, and $\hat{n}$, and $F - V_p \parallel \hat{v}$; therefore, $\hat{v}$ lies in this plane as well. As it also must be perpendicular to the plane normal $\hat{n}$, we have

$$\hat{v} = \frac{\hat{a} - (\hat{a} \cdot \hat{n})\hat{n}}{\| \hat{a} - (\hat{a} \cdot \hat{n})\hat{n} \|}$$

$$= \frac{\hat{a} - \cos(\theta)\hat{n}}{\| \hat{a} - \cos(\theta)\hat{n} \|}$$

which gives us the direction between V_p and F. To determine the positions of these points, we need to compute the value e. We start by noting that $\beta = \theta - \alpha = \pi/2 - 2\alpha$ and $\tan(\beta) = e/a$. Taken together, we have

$$e = d \tan(\beta)$$

$$= d \tan(\frac{\pi}{2} - 2\alpha)$$

$$= d \cot(2\alpha)$$

$$= d \cot(\pi - 2\theta)$$

$$= -d \cot(2\theta)$$

$$= d \left(\frac{\tan(\theta) - \cot(\theta)}{2} \right)$$

By observing Figure 11.48, we see that the plane intersects the cone's axis at a distance $2h$ from the cone's vertex, and so we have

$$\cos(\theta) = \frac{2h}{d}$$

or

$$h = \frac{d}{2 \cos(\theta)}$$

We can now compute the parabola's vertex and focus:

$$V_p = V + d\hat{n} + e\hat{v}$$

$$F = V + h\hat{a} + r\hat{v}$$

We could easily use these formula for computing f, the focal length. However, we can produce a more compact formula. Consider the triangle $\triangle FCV_p$: it is a right triangle with acute angle $\gamma = \pi/2 - \theta$, and one leg is clearly r. The other leg we denote as x. By trigonometry, we have

$$\tan(\gamma) = \frac{x}{r}$$

But we know that $r = d/2$ (Equation 11.26), so we can rewrite the above as

$$\tan(\pi/2 - \theta) = \frac{x}{\frac{d}{2}}$$

Recall from trigonometry these facts:

$$\cos(\frac{\pi}{2} - \alpha) = \sin(\alpha)$$

$$\sin(\frac{\pi}{2} - \alpha) = \cos(\alpha)$$

$$\tan(\alpha) = \frac{\sin(\alpha)}{\cos(\alpha)}$$

We can rewrite this as

$$\frac{1}{\tan(\theta)} = \frac{x}{\frac{d}{2}}$$

or

$$x = \frac{d}{2} \cot(\theta)$$

The pseudocode for this case is the following (Miller and Goldman 1992):

```
float d = Dot(plane.base - cone.vertex, plane.normal);
float cosTheta = Dot(plane.normal, cone.axis);
float sinTheta = Sqrt(1 - cosTheta * cosTheta);
float tanTheta = sinTheta / cosTheta;
float cotTheta = 1 / tanTheta;
float e = d/2 * (tanTheta - cotTheta);

// Parabola is {V, u, v, f}

Vector v = Normalize(cone.axis - cosTheta * plane.normal);
Vector u = Cross(v, plane.normal);
Point  V = cone.vertex + d * plane.normal + e * v;
float  f = d/2 * cotTheta;
```

A *circular intersection* occurs when the plane normal $\hat{n}$ is parallel to the cone axis $\hat{a}$; that is, if $|\hat{n} \cdot \hat{a}| < \epsilon$, as shown in Figure 11.49. Computing the circle is simple: clearly, the center of the circle C is

$$C = V - h\hat{a}$$

where h is the (signed) distance from the plane to V, the cone vertex. The circle's normal is of course just the plane's normal $\hat{n}$; the radius r can be computed with simple trigonometry:

$$r = \|h\| \tan(\alpha)$$

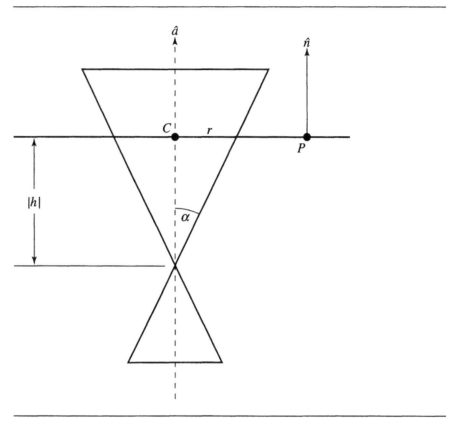

Figure 11.49   Circular curve intersection of plane and cone. After Miller and Goldman (1992).

The pseudocode is the following (Miller and Goldman1992):

```
//  Signed distance from cone's vertex to the plane
h = Dot(cone.vertex - plane.point, plane.normal);

circle.center = cone.vertex - h * plane.normal;
circle.normal = plane.normal;
circle.radius = Abs(h) * Tan(cone.alpha);
```

An elliptical intersection occurs when $\cos(\theta) \neq \sin(\alpha)$, but when the plane normal $\hat{n}$ and cone axis $\hat{a}$ are other than parallel, as shown in Figures 11.50 and 11.51. An *ellipse is the intersection* if $\cos(\theta) > \sin(\alpha)$, and a *hyperbola is the intersection* if $\cos(\theta) < \sin(\alpha)$. To define the ellipse or hyperbola, we first must determine the centerpoint C. By definition, this is a point halfway between the foci: $C = (F_0 + F_1)/2$.

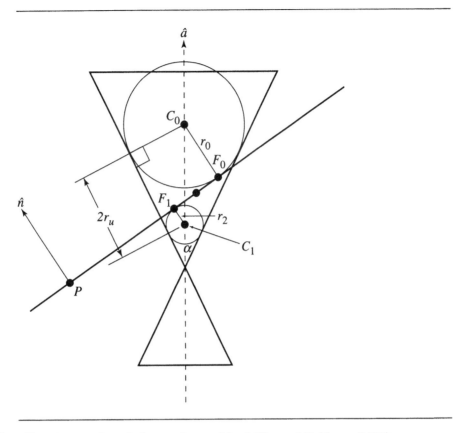

Figure 11.50   Ellipse intersection of plane and cone. After Miller and Goldman (1992).

We have

$$F_0 = V + \frac{r_0}{\sin(\alpha)} - r_0\hat{n}$$

$$F_1 = V + \frac{r_1}{\sin(\alpha)} - r_1\hat{n}$$

where r_0 and r_1 are the two radii indicated by Equation 11.25. In the case of the ellipse, the relationship between $\cos(\theta)$ and $\sin(\alpha)$ gives us positive values for r_0 and r_1, and the spheres lie on opposite sides of the plane, but on the same side of the cone; in the case of the hyperbola, the relationship between $\cos(\theta)$ and $\sin(\alpha)$ gives us a negative value for r_0 and a positive value for r_1, and the spheres lie on the same side of the plane, but on the opposite sides of the cone.

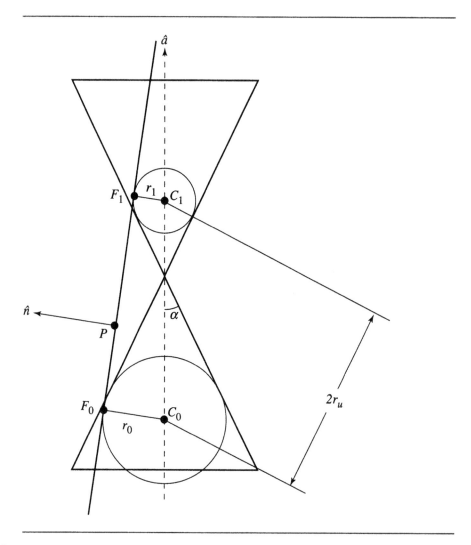

Figure 11.51   Hyperbola intersection of plane and cone. After Miller and Goldman (1992).

If we substitute the two versions of Equation 11.25 into the formula for the foci, and then substitute this into the formula for the center, we get (after some manipulation)

$$C = V + h \cos(\theta)\hat{a} - h \sin^2(\alpha)\hat{n}$$

where

$$t = (P - V) \cdot \hat{n}$$

$$b = \cos^2(\theta) - \sin^2(\alpha)$$

$$h = \frac{t}{b}$$

Next come the directrix and focus vectors $\hat{u}$ and $\hat{v}$. If we note that C, F_0, and F_1 all lie in the plane parallel to the family of planes containing $\hat{a}$ and $\hat{n}$, we see that

$$\hat{u} = \frac{\hat{a} - \cos(\theta)\hat{n}}{\|\hat{a} - \cos(\theta)\hat{n}\|}$$

and so

$$\hat{v} = \hat{n} \cdot \hat{u}$$

The major and minor radii computations are a bit more involved, and here we follow Miller and Goldman (1992) closely: recall that a characteristic of the tangent spheres for the cone-plane intersection is that the major radius is half the distance along a ruling between the circles of tangency between the spheres and the cone. For the ellipse, this gives us

$$r_u = \frac{1}{2}\left(\frac{r_0}{\tan(\alpha)} - \frac{r_1}{\tan(\alpha)}\right)$$

$$= h \sin(\alpha) \cos(\alpha)$$

and for the hyperbola

$$r_u = \frac{1}{2}\left(\frac{r_1}{\tan(\alpha)} - \frac{r_0}{\tan(\alpha)}\right)$$

$$= h \sin(\alpha) \cos(\alpha)$$

Note that in both cases, r_u is positive.

If we define d to be the (positive) distance between the center C and the foci, then the minor radius of the ellipse is

$$r_v = \sqrt{r_u^2 - d_u^2}$$

and for the hyperbola

$$r_v = \sqrt{d_u^2 - r_u^2}$$

Again, note that in both cases, r_v is positive.

The center C is halfway between the foci, so d is half the distance between the foci, and thus

$$d^2 = \frac{1}{4}(F_0 - F_2) \cdot (F_0 - F_2)$$

If we substitute the formulas for F_0 and F_1, and then substitute the formulas for $r_0 + r_1$ and $r_0 - r_1$, we get

$$r_v = t\frac{\sin(\alpha)}{\sqrt{b}}$$

The pseudocode is the following (Miller and Goldman 1992):

```
// Compute various angles
cosTheta = Dot(cone.axis, plane.normal);
cosThetaSqared = cosTheta * cosTheta;
sinAlpha = Sin(cone.alpha);
sinAlphaSquared = sinAlpha * sinAlpha;
cosAlpha = Sqrt(1 - sinAlphaSquared);

t = Dot(plane.point - cone.vertex, plane.normal);
b = cosThetaSquared - sinAlphaSquared;
h = t/b;

// Output is ellipse or hyperbola
center = cone.vertex + h * cosTheta * cone.axis
                     - h * sinAlphaSquared * plane.normal;
majorAxis = Normalize(cone.axis - cosTheta * plane.normal);
minorAxis = Cross(plane.normal, ellipse.u);
majorRadius = Abs(h) * sinAlpha * cosAlpha;
minorRadius = t * sinAlpha / Sqrt(Abs(b));
if (cosTheta > sinAlpha) {
    // Ellipse
    ellipse.center = center;
    ellipse.majorAxis = majorAxis;
    ellipse.minorAxis = minorAxis;
    ellipse.majorRadius = majorRadius;
    ellipse.minorRadius = minorRadius;

    return ellipse;
} else {
    // Hyperbola
    hyperbola.center = center;
    hyperbola.majorAxis = majorAxis;
```

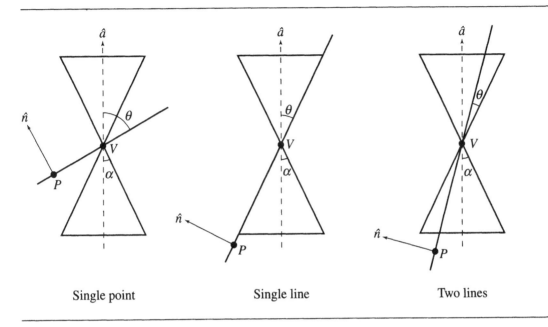

Single point   Single line   Two lines

Figure 11.52 Degenerate intersections of a plane and a cone. After Miller and Goldman (1992).

```
hyperbola.minorAxis = minorAxis;
hyperbola.majorRadius = majorRadius;
hyperbola.minorRadius = minorRadius;

return hyperbola;
}
```

Degenerate Plane-Cone Intersections

In order to distinguish between the three degenerate intersections, we consider the angle between the cone's axis $\hat{a}$ and the plane's normal $\hat{n}$, and its relationship to the half-angle α defining the cone. In each case, however, the plane contains the cone's vertex. The degenerate intersections are shown in Figure 11.52.

The *intersection is a point* if $\cos(\theta) > \sin(\alpha)$.

The *intersection is a single line* if $\cos(\theta) = \sin(\alpha)$. Clearly, the line passes through the cone vertex V, and so this can be the base point of the intersection line. Since the line lies in a plane parallel to the family of planes containing $\hat{v}$ and $\hat{a}$, its direction is

$$\frac{\hat{a} - \cos(\theta)\hat{n}}{\|\hat{a} - \cos(\theta)\hat{n}\|}$$

The *intersection is two lines* if $\cos(\theta) < \sin(\alpha)$. Again, the lines pass through the cone vertex V, and so this can be the base point of the lines. As Miller and Goldman point out, these lines can be considered to be the asymptotes of a degenerate hyperbola:

$$\hat{d} = \frac{\hat{u} \pm \frac{r_v}{r_u}\hat{v}}{\|\hat{u} \pm \frac{r_v}{r_u}\hat{v}\|}$$

From the previous section, we have

$$r_u = \frac{((P - V) \cdot \hat{n})\sin(\alpha)\cos(\theta)}{\sin^2(\alpha) - \cos^2(\theta)}$$

$$r_v = \frac{((P - V) \cdot \hat{n})\sin(\alpha)}{\sqrt{\sin^2(\alpha) - \cos^2(\theta)}}$$

and thus

$$\frac{r_v}{r_u} = \frac{\sqrt{\sin^2(\alpha) - \cos^2(\theta)}}{\cos(\theta)}$$

The pseudocode is the following (Miller and Goldman 1992):

```
// Assuming that Abs(Dist(cone.vertex, plane)) < epsilon...
if (Cos(theta) > Sin(alpha)) {
    // Intersection is a point
    intersectionPoint = cone.vertex;
} else if (Cos(theta) == Sin(alpha)) {
    // Intersection is a single line
    line.base = cone.vertex;
    line.direction = Normalize(cone.axis - Cos(theta) * plane.normal);
} else {
    // Intersection is two lines
    u = Normalize(cone.axis - Cos(theta) * plane.normal);
    v = Cross(plane.normal, u);
    sinAlpha = Sin(alpha);
    cosTheta = Cos(theta);
    rVOverRU = Sqrt(sinAlpha * sinAlpha - cosTheta * cosTheta)
               / (1 - sinAlpha * sinAlpha);
    line0.base = cone.vertex;
    line0.direction = Normalize(u + rVOverRU * v);
    line1.base = cone.vertex;
    line0.direction = Normalize(u - rVOverRU * v);
}
```

11.7.5 TRIANGLE AND CONE

Let the triangle have vertices P_i for $0 \le i \le 2$. The cone has vertex V, axis direction vector $\vec{a}$, and angle θ between axis and outer edge. In most applications, the cone is *acute*, that is, $\theta \in (0, \pi/2)$. This book assumes that, in fact, the cone is acute, so $\cos \theta > 0$. The cone consists of those points X for which the angle between $X - V$ and $\vec{a}$ is θ. Algebraically the condition is

$$\vec{a} \cdot \left(\frac{X - V}{\|X - V\|} \right) = \cos \theta$$

Figure 11.15 shows a 2D representation of the cone. The shaded portion indicates the *inside* of the cone, a region represented algebraically by replacing "=" in the above equation with "$\ge$".

To avoid the square root calculation $\|X - V\|$, the cone equation may be squared to obtain the quadratic equation

$$\left(\vec{a} \cdot (X - V) \right)^2 = (\cos^2 \theta) \|X - V\|^2$$

However, the set of points satisfying this equation is a *double cone*. The original cone is on the side of the plane $\vec{a} \cdot (X - V) = 0$ to which $\vec{a}$ points. The quadratic equation defines the original cone and its reflection through the plane. Specifically, if X is a solution to the quadratic equation, then its reflection through the vertex, $2V - X$, is also a solution. Figure 11.16 shows the double cone.

To eliminate the reflected cone, any solutions to the quadratic equation must also satisfy $\vec{a} \cdot (X - V) \ge 0$. Also, the quadratic equation can be written as a quadratic form, $(X - V)^{\mathrm{T}} \mathrm{M} (X - V) = 0$, where $\mathrm{M} = (\vec{a}\vec{a}^{\mathrm{T}} - \gamma^2 I)$ and $\gamma = \cos \theta$. Therefore, X is a point on the acute cone whenever

$$(X - V)^{\mathrm{T}} \mathrm{M} (X - V) = 0 \quad \text{and} \quad \vec{a} \cdot (X - V) \ge 0$$

Test Intersection

Testing if a triangle and cone intersect, and not having to compute points of intersection, is useful for a couple of graphics applications. For example, a spotlight illuminates only those triangles in a scene that are within the cone of the light. It is useful to know if the vertex colors of a triangle's vertices need to be modified due to the effects of the light. In most graphics applications, if some of the triangle is illuminated, then all the vertex colors are calculated. It is not important to know the subregion of the triangle that is in the cone (a result determined by a *find* query). Another example is for culling of triangles from a view frustum that is bounded by a cone for the purposes of rapid culling.

If a triangle intersects a cone, it must do so either at a vertex, an edge point, or an interior triangle point. The algorithm described here is designed to provide early exits using a testing order of vertex-in-cone, edge-intersects-cone, and triangle-intersects-cone. This order is a good one for an application where a lot of triangles tend to be fully inside the cone. Other orders may be used depending on how an application structures its world data.

To test if P_0 is inside the cone, it is enough to test if the point is on the cone side of the plane $\vec{a} \cdot (X - V) \geq 0$ and if the point is inside the double cone. Although the test can be structured as

```
D0 = triangle.P0 - cone.V;
AdD0 = Dot(cone.A, D0);
D0dD0 = Dot(D0, D0);
if (AdD0 >= 0 and AdD0 * AdD0 >= cone.CosSqr * D0dD0)
    triangle.P0 is inside cone;
```

if all the triangle vertices are outside the single cone, it will be important in the edge-cone intersection tests to know on which side of the plane $\vec{a} \cdot (X - V) = 0$ the vertices are. The vertex test is better structured as shown below. The term *outside cone* refers to the quantity being outside the single cone, not the double cone (a point could be outside the original single cone, but inside its reflection).

```
D0 = triangle.P0 - cone.V;
AdD0 = Dot(cone.A, D0);
if (AdD0 >= 0) {
    D0dD0 = Dot(D0, D0);
    if (AdD0 * AdD0 >= cone.CosSqr * D0dD0) {
        triangle.P0 is inside cone;
    } else {
        triangle.P0 is outside cone, but on cone side of plane;
    }
} else {
    triangle.P0 is outside cone, but on opposite side of plane;
}
```

All three vertices of the triangle are tested in this manner.

If all three vertices are outside the cone, the next step is to test if the edges of the triangle intersect the cone. Consider the edge $X(t) = P_0 + t\vec{e}_0$, where $\vec{e}_0 = P_1 - P_0$ and $t \in [0, 1]$. The edge intersects the single cone if $\vec{a} \cdot (X(t) - V) \geq 0$ and $(\vec{a} \cdot (X(t) - V))^2 - \gamma^2 \|X(t) - V\|^2 = 0$ for some $t \in [0, 1]$. The second condition is a quadratic equation, $Q(t) = c_2 t^2 + 2c_1 t + c_0 = 0$, where $c_2 = (\vec{a} \cdot \vec{e}_0)^2 - \gamma^2 \|\vec{e}_0\|^2$, $c_1 = (\vec{a} \cdot \vec{e}_0)(\vec{a} \cdot \vec{\Delta}_0) - \gamma^2 \vec{e}_0 \cdot \vec{\Delta}_0$, and $c_0 = (\vec{a} \cdot \vec{\Delta}_0)^2 - \gamma^2 \|\vec{\Delta}_0\|^2$, where $\vec{\Delta} = P_0 - V$. The domain of $Q(t)$ for which a root is sought depends on which side of the plane the vertices lie.

If both P_0 and P_1 are on the opposite side of the plane, then the edge cannot intersect the single cone. If both P_0 and P_1 are on the cone side of the plane, then the full edge must be considered, so we need to determine if $Q(t) = 0$ for some $t \in [0, 1]$. Moreover, the test should be fast since we do not need to know *where* the intersection occurs, just that there is one. Since the two vertices are outside the cone and occur when $t = 0$ and $t = 1$, we already know that $Q(0) < 0$ and $Q(1) < 0$. In order for the quadratic to have a root somewhere in $[0, 1]$, it is necessary that the graph be concave, since if it were convex, the graph would lie below the line segment connecting the points $(0, Q(0))$ and $(1, Q(1))$. This line segment never intersects the axis $Q = 0$. Thus, the concavity condition is $c_2 < 0$. Additionally, the t-value for the local maximum must occur in $[0, 1]$. This value is $\hat{t} = -c_1/c_2$. We could compute $\hat{t}$ directly by doing the division; however, the division can be avoided. The test $0 \leq \hat{t} \leq 1$ is equivalent to the test $0 \leq c_1 \leq -c_2$ since $c_2 < 0$. The final condition for there to be a root is that $Q(\hat{t}) \geq 0$. This happens when the discriminant for the quadratic is nonnegative: $c_1^2 - c_0 c_2 \geq 0$. In summary, when P_0 and P_1 are both on the cone side of the plane, the corresponding edge intersects the cone when

$$c_2 < 0 \quad \text{and} \quad 0 \leq c_1 \leq -c_2 \quad \text{and} \quad c_1^2 \geq c_0 c_2$$

If P_0 is on the cone side and P_1 is on the opposite side, the domain of Q can be reduced to $[0, \tilde{t}]$, where $P_0 + \tilde{t}\vec{e}_0$ is the point of intersection between the edge and the plane. The parameter value is $\tilde{t} = -(\vec{a} \cdot \vec{\Delta}_0)/(\vec{a} \cdot \vec{e}_0)$. If this point is V and it is the only intersection of the edge with the cone, at first glance the algorithm given here does not appear to handle this case because it assumes that $Q < 0$ at the end points of the edge segment corresponding to $[0, \tilde{t}]$. It appears that $Q(\tilde{t}) = 0$ and $c_2 \geq 0$ are consistent to allow an intersection. However, the geometry of the situation indicates the line containing the edge never intersects the cone. This can only happen if $Q(t) \leq 0$, so it must be the case that $c_2 < 0$ occurs. Now we analyze when Q has roots on the interval $[0, \tilde{t}]$. As before, $c_2 < 0$ is a necessary condition since $Q(0) < 0$ and $Q(\tilde{t}) < 0$. The t-value for the local maximum must be in the domain $0 \leq \hat{t} \leq \tilde{t}$. To avoid the divisions, this is rewritten as $0 \leq c_1$ and $c_2(\vec{a} \cdot \vec{\Delta}_0) \leq c_1(\vec{a} \cdot \vec{e}_0)$. The condition that the discriminant of the quadratic be nonnegative still holds. In summary, when P_0 is on the cone side and P_1 is on the opposite side, the corresponding edge intersects the cone when

$$c_2 < 0 \quad \text{and} \quad 0 \leq c_1 \quad \text{and} \quad c_2(\vec{a} \cdot \vec{\Delta}_0) \leq c_1(\vec{a} \cdot \vec{e}_0) \quad \text{and} \quad c_1^2 \geq c_0 c_2$$

Finally, if P_1 is on the cone side and P_0 is on the opposite side, the domain for Q is reduced to $[\tilde{t}, 1]$. Once again the graph must be concave, the discriminant of the quadratic must be nonnegative, and $\hat{t} \in [\tilde{t}, 1]$. The edge intersects the cone when

$$c_2 < 0 \quad \text{and} \quad c_1 \leq -c_2 \quad \text{and} \quad c_2(\vec{a} \cdot \vec{\Delta}_0) \leq c_1(\vec{a} \cdot \vec{e}_0) \quad \text{and} \quad c_1^2 \geq c_0 c_2$$

All three edges of the triangle are tested in this manner.

If all three edges are outside the cone, it is still possible that the triangle and cone intersect. If they do, the curve of intersection is an ellipse that is interior to the triangle. Moreover, the axis of the cone must intersect the triangle at the center of that ellipse. It is enough to show this intersection occurs by computing the intersection of the cone axis with the plane of the triangle and showing that point is inside the triangle. Of course this test does not need to be applied when all three vertices are on the opposite side of the plane—another early exit since it is known by this time on which side of the plane the vertices lie.

A triangle normal is $\vec{n} = \vec{e}_0 \times \vec{e}_1$. The point of intersection between cone axis $V + s\vec{a}$ and plane $\vec{n} \cdot (X - P_0) = 0$, if it exists, occurs when $s = (\vec{n} \cdot \vec{\Delta}_0)/(\vec{n} \cdot \vec{a})$. The point of intersection can be written in planar coordinates as

$$V + s\vec{a} = P_0 + t_0\vec{e}_0 + t_1\vec{e}_1$$

or

$$(\vec{n} \cdot \vec{\Delta}_0)\vec{a} - (\vec{n} \cdot \vec{a})\vec{\Delta}_0 = t_0(\vec{n} \cdot \vec{a})\vec{e}_0 + t_1(\vec{n} \cdot \vec{a})\vec{e}_1$$

Define $\vec{u} = (\vec{n} \cdot \vec{\Delta}_0)\vec{a} - (\vec{n} \cdot \vec{a})\vec{\Delta}_0$. To solve for t_0, cross the equation on the right with $\vec{e}_1$, then dot with $\vec{n}$. Similarly solve for t_1 by crossing on the right with $\vec{e}_0$ and dotting with $\vec{n}$. The result is

$$t_0(\vec{n} \cdot \vec{a})\|\vec{n}\|^2 = \vec{n} \cdot \vec{u} \times \vec{e}_1 \quad \text{and} \quad t_1(\vec{n} \cdot \vec{a})\|\vec{n}\|^2 = -\vec{n} \cdot \vec{u} \times \vec{e}_0$$

To be inside the triangle it is necessary that $t_0 \geq 0$, $t_1 \geq 0$, and $t_0 + t_1 \leq 1$. The comparisons can be performed without the divisions, but require two cases depending on the sign of $\vec{n} \cdot \vec{a}$. In the code, the quantities $\vec{n}$, $\vec{n} \cdot \vec{a}$, $\vec{n} \cdot \vec{\Delta}_0$, $\vec{u}$, and $\vec{n} \times \vec{u}$ are computed. If $\vec{n} \cdot \vec{a} \geq 0$, then the point is inside the triangle when $\vec{n} \times \vec{u} \cdot \vec{e}_0 \leq 0$, $\vec{n} \times \vec{u} \cdot \vec{e}_1 \geq 0$, and $\vec{n} \times \vec{u} \cdot \vec{e}_2 \leq (\vec{n} \cdot \vec{a})\|\vec{n}\|^2$. The inequalities in these three tests are reversed in the case $\vec{n} \cdot \vec{a} \leq 0$.

Find Intersection

The analysis in the previous section can be extended to actually partition the triangle into the component inside the cone and the component outside. The curve of separation will be a quadratic curve, possibly a line segment. If the triangle is represented as $X(s, t) = P_0 + s\vec{e}_0 + t\vec{e}_1$ for $s \geq 0$, $t \geq 0$, and $s + t \leq 1$, the points of intersetion of the single cone and triangle are determined by

$$\vec{a} \cdot (X(s, t) - V) \geq 0 \quad \text{and} \quad (\vec{a} \cdot (X(s, t) - V))^2 - \gamma^2\|X(s, t)\|^2 = 0$$

If any portion of the triangle satisfies the linear inequality, this trims down the triangle domain to a subset: the entire triangle, a subtriangle, or a subquadrilateral. On that subdomain the problem is to determine where the quadratic function is zero. Thus, the problem reduces to finding the intersection in 2D of a triangle or quadrilateral with a quadratic object. Locating the zeros amounts to actually finding the roots of $Q(t)$ for the edges of the triangle discussed in the previous section, and/or determining the ellipse of intersection if the cone passes through the triangle interior.

11.8 PLANAR COMPONENTS AND POLYNOMIAL SURFACES

In this section we cover the problem of intersecting a plane with a polynomial surface, an example of which can be seen in Figure 11.53.

A very general way to represent a polynomial surface is in rational parametric form

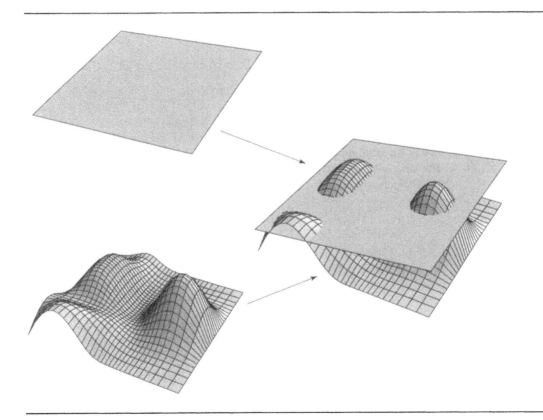

Figure 11.53   Intersection of a plane and a parametric surface.

$$x = \frac{x(s,t)}{w(s,t)}$$

$$y = \frac{y(s,t)}{w(s,t)} \tag{11.27}$$

$$z = \frac{z(s,t)}{w(s,t)}$$

where the polynomials $x(s,t)$, $y(s,t)$, and $z(s,t)$ may be in monomial, Bézier, B-spline, or other piecewise polynomial basis. Given this, two general methods may be employed to find the intersection of such a polynomial surface with a plane.

One method is to apply a series of transformations (rotation and translation) to map the intersecting plane into the XY plane. The same transformation applied to the polynomial surface results in

$$x' = \frac{x'(s,t)}{w'(s,t)}$$

$$y' = \frac{y'(s,t)}{w'(s,t)}$$

$$z' = \frac{z'(s,t)}{w'(s,t)}$$

The equation $z' = 0$ now represents the intersection in the parameter space of the rational polynomial surface.

The other method works the other way around—substitute the parametric equations of the polynomial surface into the plane equation

$$ax + by + cz + d = 0$$

If we substitute the expressions in Equation 11.27 into this plane equation, we get

$$ax(s,t) + by(s,t) + cz(s,t) + dw(s,t) = 0$$

the equation of the intersection curve in the parameter space of the surface.

We could also simply treat the plane–polynomial surface intersection problem as just an instance of the general surface-surface intersection problem (Section 11.10). Owing to the low degree of the plane, and the fact that the plane is of course flat, such an approach would probably be relatively reliable. However, we can more directly take advantage of the fact that one of the surfaces is a plane and derive a more efficient and robust algorithm for this special case. Two such algorithms are found in Boeing (1997) and Lee and Fredricks (1984). We present the latter here.

11.8.1 HERMITE CURVES

The intersection method we'll describe produces an (approximate) intersection curve using the Hermite form, and so we provide a brief review of this representation.

A Hermite curve is defined by its two end points P_0 and P_1 and two tangent vectors $\vec{d}_0$ and $\vec{d}_1$. The cubic Hermite basis functions are

$$a_0(t) = 2t^3 - 3t^2 + 1$$

$$a_1(t) = -2t^3 + 3t^2$$

$$b_0(t) = t^3 - 2t^2 + t$$

$$b_1(t) = t^3 - t^2$$

The basis functions are shown in Figure 11.54.

The curve is a linear combination of the points and tangents, using the (cubic) Hermite basis functions $a_0(t)$, $a_1(t)$, $b_0(t)$, and $b_1(t)$:

$$C(t) = a_0(t)P_0 + a_1(t)P_1 + b_0(t)\vec{d}_0 + b_1(t)\vec{d}_1$$

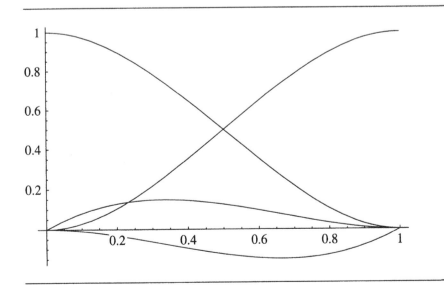

Figure 11.54   Hermite basis functions (cubic).

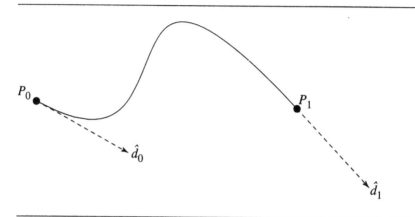

Figure 11.55   Cubic Hermite curve, specified by end points and tangents.

An example of such a curve is shown in Figure 11.55. (Note that the tangents are not drawn to scale for space reasons; $\vec{d}_0$ should be $\sqrt{10}$ times as long as drawn, and $\vec{d}_1$ should be 5 times as long as drawn.)

11.8.2   GEOMETRY DEFINITIONS

We're interested in the intersection of a plane P and a parametric surface S defined as $S(u, v)$. For convenience of discussion, we assume that the parameter domains are $0 \leq u, v \leq 1$. A surface may be viewed as the union of a number of subpatches, and this algorithm concentrates on the intersection of a subpatch with P; the complete intersection is found by finding the intersection curves for each subpatch and concatenating these curves into one or more intersection curves for the entire surface. A subpatch is denoted by its corners in parameter space (a, b, c, d), where (a, b) are the coordinates of the lower-left corner and (c, d) are the coordinates of the upper-right corner, as shown in Figure 11.56.

Let the intersection of the surface S and the plane P be $R(t)$, and let its preimage be $p(t) = [\, u(t) \quad v(t) \,]$. We wish to find a curve that approximately solves $R(t) = S(p(t))$. The algorithm consists of a two-stage recursive method that computes cubic Hermite approximations to (segments of) $R(t)$ and $p(t)$. Note that the Hermite curve segments, whose union comprises the intersection curves proper, is a curve defined in 3-space. The approximation criteria are as follows:

- For $p(t)$, an approximation is considered "sufficient" if its corresponding image in 3-space is in the plane P.

- For $R(t)$, an approximation is considered "sufficient" if it is within a specified tolerance of the 3-space image of the corresponding parameter space segment.

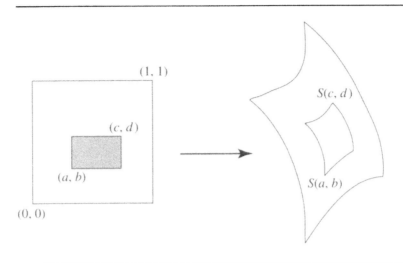

Figure 11.56 A subpatch in parameter space maps to a topologically rectangular region on the patch. After Lee and Fredricks (1984).

11.8.3 COMPUTING THE CURVES

Recalling that we're using a cubic Hermite curve, the tangent vector of $R(t)$ is

$$R'(t) = S_u(p(t))u'(t) + S_v(p(t))v'(t) \qquad (11.28)$$

where $S_u(p(t))$ and $S_v(p(t))$ are the partial derivatives with respect to u and v at parameter t, and u' and v' are the components of the tangent vector of p at parameter t.
   Because all points in $R(t)$ must lie in $\mathcal{P}$, it must be the case that

$$R'(t) \cdot \hat{n} = 0$$

where $\hat{n}$ is the unit normal to $\mathcal{P}$. Substituting Equation 11.28, we have

$$\big(S_u(p(t)) \cdot \hat{n}\big) + \big(S_v(p(t)) \cdot \hat{n}\big)$$

At a point $p(t)$, this equation gives us the tangents for $R(t)$. The (initial) estimates of the lengths are computed by estimating one of $u'(t)$ or $v'(t)$, and solving for the other one. The estimates are refined by making sure that the image of the midpoint of $p(t)$ is contained in $\mathcal{P}$.
   Figures 11.57 and 11.58 show the curves $R(t) = \{P_0, P_1, \vec{d}_0, \vec{d}_1\}$ and $p(t) = \{(u_0, v_0), (u_1, v_1), (u'_0, v'_0), u'_1, v'_1\}$, respectively (again, the tangent vectors are not drawn to scale).

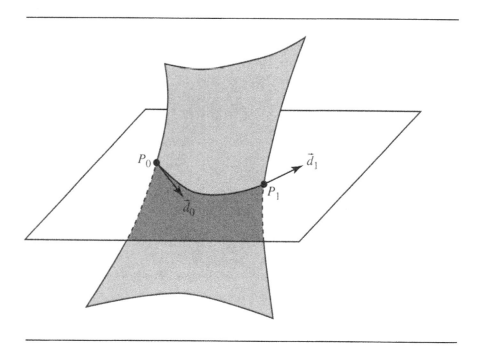

Figure 11.57   3-space intersection curve $R(t)$.

11.8.4 THE ALGORITHM

The algorithm consists of three parts, the first two recursive. The first part subdivides the surface S into subpatches, until either no intersections are found, or until a subpatch is found that intersects $\mathcal{P}$ exactly twice along its (the patch's) borders. Each subpatch so found is then passed, along with the 3D intersection points along each of the two intersecting borders, to the second recursive algorithm, which computes the intersection curve (segment).

The pseudocode is as follows:

```
Find(S, P, a, b, c, d) {
    // Compute intersections along borders, if any
    hits = ComputeIntersectionWithPlane(u0, v0, u1, v1, border0, border1);

    if (hits == 0) {
        return;
    }

    // Check for two hits, on different borders
    if (hits == 2 and border0 != border1) {
```

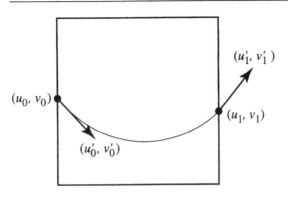

Figure 11.58   Parametric space intersection curve $p(t)$.

```
// Get the 3D points of the intersections
p0 = S(u0, v0);
p1 = S(u1, v1);

ComputeCurve(S, P, u0, v0, u1, v1, p0, p1);
} else {
    // Split the subpatch in half, alternating
    SplitSubPatch(S, a, b, c, d, parm, whichDirection);

    // Recursively solve each half
    if (whichDirection == uDir) {
        Find(S, P, a, b, parm, d);
        Find(S, P, parm, b, c, d);
    } else {
        Find(S, P, a, b, c, parm);
        Find(S, P, a, parm, c, d);
    }
}
}
```

The second part computes the intersection curve, recursively improving the approximation. As Lee and Fredricks (1984) note, the recursion is binary—that is, the curve is checked at its midpoint, and if it fails to meet the convergence criteria, it is split there and the algorithm recurses—but they suggest that it may be better to split the curve into more than two pieces.

The pseudocode is as follows:

```
ComputeCurve(S, P, u0, v0, u1, v1, p0, p1)
{
    Calculate:
        u0' = u'(u0, v0), v0' = v'(u0, v0) and
        u1' = u'(u1, v1), v1' = v'(u1, v1)
        as described in the text

    // Compute tangent vectors for R(t)
    d0 = sSubU(u0, v0) * u'(u0, v0) + sSubV(u0, v0) + v'(u0, v0);
    d1 = sSubU(u1, v1) * u'(u1, v1) + sSubV(u1, v1) + v'(u1, v1);

    Calculate midpoint (uMid, vMid) of
      parameter-space curve p: { (u0, v0), (u1, v1), (u0', v0'), (u1', v1') }

    // Calculate 3D image of p(uMid, vMid)
    pMid = S(uMid, vMid);
    recurse = false;

    // Check if we've met convergence criteria, both 2D and 3D
    if (pMid is not ''close enough'' to plane P) {
        // Intersect curve to find split point
        pMid = IntersectCurve(S, P, uMid, vMid);

        recurse = true;
    } else if (pMid is not ''close enough'' to 3D curve { p0, p1, d0, d1 } {
        recurse = true;
    }

    if (recurse) {
        // Recursively call function on split curve
        ComputeCurve(S, P, u0, v0, p0, uMid, vMid, pMid);
        ComputeCurve(S, P, uMid, vMid, pMid, u1, v1, p1);
    } else {
        // Found curve
        curve = { p0, p1, d0, d1 }
    }
}
```

A bit of explanation of the "IntersectCurve" function is in order: this computes the intersection of the plane $\mathcal{P}$ with an isoparametric curve $S(u_0, v)$ or $S(u, v_0)$ in a neighborhood of (*uMid*, *vMid*), returning a new (*uMid*, *vMid*).

The third part of the algorithm takes all the Hermite (sub)curves and joins them to produce the totality of the intersection curves proper. Note that the end points of the subcurves should exactly match, providing the intersections of adjacent boundaries of subpatches are intersected with the plane in a consistent fashion.

11.8.5 IMPLEMENTATION NOTES

As Lee and Fredricks point out, it is possible for a patch to intersect the plane, yet no border of the patch intersects. A reasonable approach for implementation is to compute a bounding volume for the patch (an axis-aligned or oriented bounding box) and test for intersections of the box with the plane. If no intersections are found, then the patch itself does not intersect the plane; otherwise, recursively split the patch and test the bounding boxes against the plane, until the bounding volumes no longer intersect the plane or a subpatch is found whose boundaries intersect the plane. If the patch is represented in Bézier or B-spline basis, the bounding and splitting can be quite efficiently done.

11.9 QUADRIC SURFACES

The intersection of two quadric surfaces can take one of several forms:

- A point—for example, two spheres touching at their poles
- A line—for example, two parallel cylinders, just touching along their sides
- A single curve—for example, two partially intersecting spheres meeting in a circle
- Two curves—for example, a plane and a double cone meeting in two parabolic curves
- A fourth-degree nonplanar space curve—for example, two cones intersecting

Generally speaking, the first four of these cases are relatively straightforward, as we saw in Section 11.7.3, for example, and will see in the next section, which covers the intersection of two ellipsoids: all of the curves are conic sections. Generation of parametric representations of these conic section curves is possible, and this is advantageous for many applications (e.g., rendering the intersection curve efficiently, etc.). Miller and Goldman (1995) describe geometric algorithms for detecting when two quadric surfaces intersect in a conic section, and for calculating such intersections when they exist.

It is also possible to represent the nonplanar space curves exactly and parametrically, as shown by Levin (1976, 1979, 1980) and Sarraga (1983). Miller (1987) presents an approach for the so-called natural quadrics—the sphere, cone, and cylinder—that is based entirely on geometric (rather than algebraic) techniques and that results in a parameterized curve representation.

11.9.1 GENERAL INTERSECTION

In this section we discuss general methods for intersecting quadric surfaces. There are two different types of representations for quadric surfaces: An algebraic one uses a general implicit equation in x, y, and z:

$$Ax^2 + By^2 + Cz^2 + 2Dxy + 2Eyz + 2Fxz + 2Gx + 2Hy + 2Jz + K = 0$$

The specific type of surface (sphere, cone, etc.) is encoded in the "patterns" of values of the coefficients (e.g., a sphere has $A = 1$, $B = 1$, $C = 1$, and $K = -1$).

Quadrics can also be represented in matrix form

$$PQP^{\mathrm{T}} = 0$$

where

$$P = [\,x \quad y \quad z \quad 1\,]$$

and

$$Q = \begin{bmatrix} A & D & F & G \\ D & B & E & H \\ F & E & C & J \\ G & H & J & K \end{bmatrix}$$

Linear combinations of two quadric surfaces $\mathbf{Q}_0$ and $\mathbf{Q}_1$:

$$\mathbf{Q} = \mathbf{Q}_0 - \lambda \mathbf{Q}_1$$

define a family of quadric surfaces called the *pencil* of surfaces. Where $\mathbf{Q}_0$ and $\mathbf{Q}_1$ intersect, every quadric in the pencil of the two surfaces intersects the two original quadrics in that same intersection curve.

The Algebraic Approach

Algebraic approaches exploit what Miller (1987) terms a "not intuitively obvious" characteristic—that at least one ruled surface[4] exists in the pencil. Ruled quadric surfaces are useful in intersection problems because they can be easily (and exactly) parameterized.

A ruled quadric can be represented either as a rational polynomial function or trigononometrically. The trigonometric representations describe quadrics in their

---

4. A *ruled surface* is one that can be viewed/defined as a set of straight lines, such as a cylinder or cone.

canonical positions and orientations, and so arbitrarily located and oriented surfaces are transformed into their canonical positions, where the intersections are calculated, and the intersections are transformed back by the inverse operation. A cylinder in canonical position can be represented trigonometrically as

$$x = r \cos(\theta)$$
$$y = r \sin(\theta) \tag{11.29}$$
$$z = s$$

while a cone with half-angle α is

$$x = s \tan(\alpha) \cos(\theta)$$
$$y = s \tan(\alpha) \sin(\theta) \tag{11.30}$$
$$z = s$$

Given two natural quadric surfaces Q_0 and Q_1, one surface is determined to play the role of the *parameterization surface*—the one in whose terms the intersection curve is described. The intersection curve is defined as

$$a(t)s^2 + b(t)s + c(t) = 0 \tag{11.31}$$

For any particular intersection, a, b, and c are computed as follows:

1. Transform one of the surfaces into the local coordinate space of the one chosen to be the parameterization surface.
2. Substitute either Equation 11.29 or Equation 11.30 (as appropriate) into the implicit equation of the transformed quadric.
3. Algebraically manipulate the result so it is in the form of Equation 11.31.

The substitution in step 2 above for cylinders yields

$a(t) = C$

$b(t) = 2Er \sin(t) + 2Fr \cos(t) + 2J$

$c(t) = Ar^2 \cos^2(t) + Br^2 \sin^2(t) + 2Dr^2 \sin(t) \cos(t) + 2Gr \cos(t) + 2Hr \sin(t) + K$

and for cones yields

$$a(t) = A \tan^2(\alpha) \cos^2(t) + B \tan^2(\alpha) \sin^2(t) + C + 2D \tan^2(\alpha) \sin(t) \cos t$$
$$\qquad + 2E \tan(\alpha) \sin(t) + 2F \tan(\alpha) \sin(t)$$
$$b(t) = 2G \tan(\alpha) \cos(t) + 2H \tan(\alpha) \sin(t) + 2J \tag{11.32}$$
$$c(t) = K$$

For any particular configuration of intersections, the range of the parameter t must be determined. To do this, we must determine the *critical points* of the curve—locations where the curve either turns back on itself, crosses itself, or goes to infinity. Algebraic analysis is used to find values of t that result in s going to infinity, and locations where the discriminant vanishes. The resulting partition of t-space defines where the curve is valid. We can then traverse the valid portions of t-space, substituting t into the appropriate version of Equation 11.32. We then find s by solving the quadratic equation (Equation 11.31). At this point we have pairs of values (s_i, t_i). These pairs can then be substituted into the appropriate parametric equation (for the cone or cylinder), yielding points of the form $[\,x \quad y \quad z\,]$. These points are then transformed into world space.

While this is all relatively straightforward, all is not rosy. The algebraic (implicit) equations for conics and quadrics are, as Miller points out, "extremely sensitive to small perturbations in the coefficients." The transformations common in graphics systems (including the transformation of one quadric into the space of the other to actually perform the intersection, as described above) will tend to perturb the coefficients. Further, the intersection points need to be (inversely) transformed once they are computed, and the coefficients are used to determine which object is used as the parameterization object. Finally, in actually computing results, we must employ a tolerance around zero, but this is quite difficult because of the difficulty of relating the tolerance to spatial distance. For these reasons, Miller recommends a geometric approach.

Recent work by Dupont, Lazard, and Petitjean (2001) has shown that some of the numerical disadvantages of Levin's approach can be significantly mitigated. First, we define some terms.

The *signature* of a quadric $\mathcal{P}$ with matrix $\mathbf{P}$ is an ordered pair (p, q), where p and q are the numbers of positive and negative eigenvalues of $\mathbf{P}$, respectively. Dupont et al. point out that if $\mathbf{P}$ has signature (p, q), then $-\mathbf{P}$ has signature (q, p), even though the quadric surfaces associated with $\mathbf{P}$ and $-\mathbf{P}$ are identical. Therefore, they define the signature as the pair (p, q) where $p \geq q$. The 3×3 upper-left submatrix of $\mathbf{P}$ is denoted $\mathbf{P}_u$ and called the *principal submatrix* of $\mathbf{P}$, and its determinant is called the *principal subdeterminant*. This principal subdeterminant is significant because it is zero for simple ruled quadrics.

A quadric's *canonical form* is given as

$$\sum_{i=1}^{p} a_i x_i^2 - \sum_{i=p+1}^{r} a_i x_i^2 + \xi = 0$$

or

$$\sum_{i=1}^{p} a_i x_i^2 - \sum_{i=p+1}^{r} a_i x_i^2 + x_{r+1} = 0$$

Table 11.2   Parametric representation of the canonical simple ruled quadrics. After Dupont, Lazard, and Petitjean (2001).

Quadric type	Canonical equation $(a_i > 0)$	Parameterization $(\mathbf{X} = [x_1, x_2, x_3], u, v \in \mathbb{R})$
Line	$a_1 x_1^2 + a_2 x_2^2 = 0$	$\mathbf{X}(u) = [0, 0, u]$
Plane	$x_1 = 0$	$\mathbf{X}(u, v) = [0, u, v]$
Double plane	$a_1 x_1^2 = 0$	$\mathbf{X}(u, v) = [0, u, v]$
Parallel planes	$a_1 x_1^2 = 1$	$\mathbf{X}(u, v) = [\frac{1}{\sqrt{a_1}}, u, v]$
		$\mathbf{X}(u, v) = [\frac{1}{-\sqrt{a_1}}, u, v]$
Intersecting planes	$a_1 x_1^2 - a_2 x_2^2 = 0$	$\mathbf{X}(u, v) = [\frac{u}{\sqrt{a_1}}, \frac{u}{\sqrt{a_2}}, v]$
		$\mathbf{X}(u, v) = [\frac{u}{\sqrt{a_1}}, -\frac{u}{\sqrt{a_2}}, v]$
Hyperbolic paraboloid	$a_1 x_1^2 - a_2 x_2^2 - x_3 = 0$	$\mathbf{X}(u, v) = [\frac{u+v}{2\sqrt{a_1}}, \frac{u-v}{2\sqrt{a_2}}, uv]$
Parabolic cylinder	$a_1 x_1^2 - x_2 = 0$	$\mathbf{X}(u, v) = [u, a_1 u^2, v]$
Hyperbolic cylinder	$a_1 x_1^2 - a_2 x_2^2 = 0$	$\mathbf{X}(u, v) = [\frac{1}{2\sqrt{a_1}}(u + \frac{1}{u}), \frac{1}{2\sqrt{a_2}}, (u + \frac{1}{u}), v]$

where $a_0 > 0$, $\forall i$, $\xi \in [0, 1]$, and $p \le r$. The canonical forms for the simple ruled quadrics are shown in Table 11.2.

Levin's method for intersecting two quadrics $\mathcal{P}$ and $\mathcal{Q}$ can be summarized as follows:

1. Find a ruled quadric in the pencil of $\mathcal{P}$ and $\mathcal{Q}$. This is done by determining the type of $\mathcal{Q}$ and of the quadrics $\mathcal{R}(\lambda) = \mathcal{P} - \lambda \mathcal{Q}$ such that λ is a solution of $\det(\mathcal{R}_u(\lambda))$.

2. Compute the orthogonal transformation $\mathbf{T}$ that takes $\mathcal{R}$ to canonical form. In that frame, $\mathcal{R}$ has a parametric form (as shown in Table 11.2). Compute $\mathbf{P}' = \mathbf{T}^{-1}\mathbf{P}\mathbf{T}$ of $\mathcal{P}$ in that frame, and consider

$$\mathbf{X}^{\mathsf{T}}\mathbf{P}' = a(u)v^2 + b(u)v + c(u) = 0$$

3. Solve the above equation for v in terms of u. Determine the domain of u over which these solutions are defined—this is the region in which the discriminant $b^2(u) - 4a(u)c(u) \ge 0$. Substitute v with its solutions in terms of u in $\mathbf{X}$, yielding a parameterization of $\mathcal{P} \cap \mathcal{Q} = \mathcal{P} \cap \mathcal{R}$ (in the frame where $\mathcal{R}$ is canonical).

4. Transform the parametric intersection formula back into world space as $\mathbf{T}\mathbf{X}(u)$.

Table 11.3   Parametric representation of the projective quadrics. After Dupont, Lazard, and
Petitjean (2001).

Signature	Canonical equation ($a_i > 0$)	Parameterization ($\mathbf{X} = [x_1, x_2, x_3, x_4] \in \mathbb{P}^3$)
(4,0)	$a_1 x_1^2 + a_2 x_2^2 + a_3 x_3^2 + a_4 x_4^2 = 0$	$\mathcal{Q} = \emptyset$
(3,1)	$a_1 x_1^2 + a_2 x_2^2 + a_3 x_3^2 + a_4 x_4^2 = 0$	$\det \mathcal{Q} < 0$
(3,0)	$a_1 x_1^2 + a_2 x_2^2 + a_3 x_3^2 = 0$	$\mathcal{Q}$ is a point
(2,2)	$a_1 x_1^2 + a_2 x_2^2 - a_3 x_3^2 - a_4 x_4^2 = 0$	$\mathbf{X}(u,v) = [\frac{ut+vw}{\sqrt{a_1}}, \frac{uw-vt}{\sqrt{a_2}}, \frac{ut-vw}{\sqrt{a_3}}, \frac{uw+vt}{\sqrt{a_4}}]$
(2,1)	$a_1 x_1^2 + a_2 x_2^2 - a_3 x_3^2 = 0$	$\mathbf{X}(u,v) = [\frac{u^2+v^2}{2\sqrt{a_1}}, \frac{u^2-v^2}{2\sqrt{a_2}}, \frac{uv}{\sqrt{a_3}}, wt]$
(2,0)	$a_1 x_1^2 + a_2 x_2^2 = 0$	$\mathbf{X}(u,v) = [0, 0, u, v], u, v \in \mathbb{P}^1$
(1,1)	$a_1 x_1^2 - a_2 x_2^2 = 0$	$\mathbf{X}(u,v) = [\frac{u}{\sqrt{a_1}}, \frac{u}{\sqrt{a_2}}, v, w],$
		$\mathbf{X}(u,v) = [\frac{u}{\sqrt{a_1}}, -\frac{u}{\sqrt{a_2}}, v, w], (u, v, w) \in \mathbb{P}^2$
(1,0)	$a_1 x_1^2 = 0$	$\mathbf{X}(u,v) = [0, u, v, w], (u, v, w) \in \mathbb{P}^2$

Dupont et al. (2001) point out three sources of potential numerical problems:

- In step 1, λ is the root of a cubic polynomial, potentially involving nested cubic and square roots.

- In step 2, the coefficients of $\mathbf{T}$ involve as many as four levels of nested roots.

- In step 3, we have a square root in the solution of the polynomial equation noted in step 2.

They propose several improvements to Levin's method to avoid these problems. First, they only consider the quadrics in $\mathbb{P}^3$—real projective 3-space. Levin's method works because there are sufficient canonical quadrics such that the substitution of step 3 results in a second-degree equation in one variable with a discriminant of degree four in another variable. Dupont et al. provide a set of parameterizations for projective space that share that property, with the exception of those of signature (3, 1) (ellipsoids, hyperboloids, and elliptic paraboloids). These are shown in Table 11.3.

This approach reduces the number of times the quadric $\mathcal{R}$ has to be searched for in the pencil; this search is required if and only if $\mathcal{P}$ and $\mathcal{Q}$ have signature (3, 1).

Another difference in their approach is based on a theorem: if two quadrics $\mathcal{P}$ and $\mathcal{Q}$ both have signature (3, 1) and intersect in more than two points, then there exists a rational number λ such that $\mathcal{P} - \lambda \mathcal{Q}$ does not have signature (3, 1). This ensures that $\mathcal{P}$ and $\mathcal{R}$ have rational coefficients, and that λ can be computed "most of the time" with normal floating-point arithmetic.

Finally, they use Gauss's reduction method for quadratic forms (Lam 1973) for transforming $\mathcal{R}$ into a canonical frame (in step 2). Compared to Levin's use of an orthogonal transformation in that step, the form of the solutions is "substantially" simplified.

Their algorithm is summarized as follows:

1. Find quadric $\mathcal{R}$ in the pencil of $\mathcal{P}$ and $\mathcal{Q}$ such that $\det \mathbf{R} \geq 0$ (or, find that the intersection is of dimension 0). This is done by checking $\det \mathbf{Q}$: if it is nonnegative, then let $\mathcal{R} = \mathcal{Q}$; otherwise, if there is a λ such that $\det(\mathbf{P} - \lambda \mathbf{Q}) \geq 0$, then set $\mathcal{R} - \mathcal{P} - \lambda \mathcal{Q}$. Otherwise, the intersection has dimension 0.

2. If $\mathcal{R}$'s signature is $(4, 0)$ or $(3, 0)$, then the intersection has dimension 0. Otherwise, compute transformation $\mathbf{T}$ taking $\mathcal{R}$ into canonical form. Then, compute $\mathbf{P}' = \mathbf{T}^{\mathrm{T}} \mathbf{PT}$.

3. Solve $\mathbf{X}^{\mathrm{T}} \mathbf{P}' \mathbf{X} = 0$, and determine the domains of $(u, v) \in \mathbb{P}^1$ that are valid. Substitute (w, t), wt, or w into $\mathbf{X}$ in terms of (u, v) (depending on the case). If a, b, and c all vanish for some values of (u, v), then replace (u, v) by those values in $\mathbf{X}$ and let $(w, t) \in \mathbb{P}^1$. This gives a parametric representation of the intersection of $\mathcal{P}$ and $\mathcal{Q}$ in $\mathcal{R}$'s frame.

4. Transform the solution back into world space as $\mathbf{TX}(u, v)$.

The result of this algorithm is an explicit parametric representation of the intersection of quadrics $\mathcal{P}$ and $\mathcal{Q}$; all the coefficients are in $\mathbb{Q}[\sqrt{a_1}, \sqrt{a_2}, \sqrt{a_3}, \sqrt{a_4}]$, where the a_i are the coefficients on the diagonal of $\mathbf{T}^{\mathrm{T}} \mathbf{RT}$.

The Geometric Approach

The geometric approach is so called because in it the quadric surfaces are instead represented by points, vectors, and scalars that are specific to each type of surface. For example, spheres are represented by a centerpoint and radius. In addition to the more advantageous numerical characteristics, this approach is more compatible with the definitions of such objects that you would want to use in a graphics library or application interface.

We have already seen a geometric approach in the problem of intersecting the sphere, cone, and cylinder with a plane (Section 11.7). As stated in the introduction to this section, intersections may be one of several types:

- A point—for example, two spheres touching at their poles

- A line—for example, two parallel cylinders, just touching along their sides

- A single curve—for example, two partially intersecting spheres meeting in a circle

- Two curves—for example, a plane and a double cone meeting in two parabolic curves

- A fourth-degree nonplanar space curve—for example, two cones intersecting

Natural Quadrics Intersecting in Planar Conic Sections

Any two natural quadrics, of course, intersect in one of these types. Miller and Gold-man (1995) note that the intersection of two natural quadrics can consist of either a conic section (which, of course, lies in some plane and which may be degenerate, consisting of a line, lines, or a point) or a fourth-degree nonplanar space curve. The configurations of two natural quadrics that result in a planar conic curve intersection are very special cases and few indeed, and their intersections can be computed by purely geometric means, using the geometric representation of the quadrics. The algorithms themselves are specific to the two types of quadrics involved and are similar in flavor to those for the intersection of a plane and a natural quadric (see Sections 11.7.2, 11.7.3, and 11.7.4).

As suggested earlier, the planar intersection calculations of the natural quadrics are similar in nature to the plane–natural quadric intersections presented earlier, and so in Table 11.4 we only show the conditions under which two natural quadrics intersect in a conic section (or degeneracy in the form of points or lines).

For those configurations of natural quadrics that do not result in a planar intersection, the result is a general fourth-degree space curve. These, too, can be computed using purely geometric means (Miller 1987), and each algorithm is type-specific. The papers (Miller and Goldman 1995; Miller 1987) covering the geometric algorithms for both the planar and nonplanar intersections, respectively, of the natural quadrics total 44 pages, and the presentation of the planar intersection is itself a summary of two much longer technical reports that provide the details (Miller and Goldman 1993a, 1993b). Even with this extensive coverage, including also the paper covering the plane–natural quadric intersection (Miller and Goldman 1992), only the natural quadrics' intersections are covered; you could, of course, make the argument that these are by far the most useful subset, but in any case, intersections of arbitarary quadric surfaces must either be treated with the approach of Levin (1976, 1979, 1980) or modifications thereof (Dupont, Lazard, and Petitjean 2001) or be treated as general surface-surface intersection (SSI) problems.

Nonplanar Quadric-Quadric Intersections

Because of the lengthy development and case-by-case treatment required for the geometric intersection of quadrics that result in nonplanar fourth-degree space curves, we present only a sketch of the approach and point the reader to Miller's exhaustive coverage (Miller 1987) for details and implementation.

The geometric approach shares with the algebraic approach the ideas of selecting one surface as the parameterization surface and transforming the other into its local space, and using the pencil of the two quadrics to parameterize the intersection curve. However, the representations for the objects differ: for the parameterization quadric, a coordinate-free parametric representation is used, while for the other surface, an object-type-specific version of the implicit equation is used. Because the parametric definition for the parameterization surface is based on geometrically meaningful

Table 11.4   Conditions under which natural quadric surfaces intersect in planar conic curves. After Miller and Goldman (1995).

Surface pair	Geometric conditions	Results
Sphere-sphere	All	Empty, one tangent point, or one circle
Sphere-cylinder	Center of sphere on axis of cylinder	Empty, one tangent circle, or two circles
Sphere-cone	Center of sphere on axis of cone	Empty, one tangent circle, one circle and a vertex, or two circles
Cylinder-cylinder	Parallel axes	Empty, one tangent line, or two lines
	Intersecting axes and equal radii	Two ellipses
Cylinder-cone	Coincident axes	Two circles
	Axes intersect in a point at distance $d = \frac{r}{\sin \alpha}$ from the vertex of the cone	Two ellipses (same or opposite halves of cone) or one ellipse and one tangent line
Cone-cone	Parallel axes, same half-angle	Ellipse, shared tangential ruling, or hyperbola
	Coincident axes	Two circles or single vertex
	Axes intersect at point I such that $d_1 \sin \alpha_1 = d_2 \sin \alpha_2$, where d_1 is the distance from vertex i to I	Various combinations of pairs of conics, or a tangent line plus a conic, or 1–4 lines if the vertices coincide

entities, the functions $a(t), b(t)$, and $c(t)$ in Equation 11.31 have a more direct geometric interpretation.

We can rewrite Equations 11.29 and 11.30 in coordinate-free terms. Define a cylinder as consisting of a base point B, radius r, and axis $\hat{w}$. As well, we need an additional two vectors $\hat{u}$ and $\hat{v}$ to parameterize the cylinder—these, together with $\hat{w}$ and B, form an orthonormal basis. Our equation is then

$$P(s, t) = B + r(\cos(t)\hat{u} + \sin(t)\hat{v}) + s\hat{w} \qquad (11.33)$$

A cone can be given a similar treatment:

$$P(s, t) = B + s(\tan(\alpha)(\cos(t)\hat{u} + \sin(t)\hat{v})) \qquad (11.34)$$

The object-type-specific implicit equations for the sphere, cone, and cylinder are as follows:

$$\text{Sphere:} \quad (P - B) \cdot (P - B) - r^2 = 0 \qquad (11.35)$$

$$\text{Cylinder:} \quad (P - B) \cdot (P - B) - ((P - B) \cdot \hat{w})^2 - r^2 = 0 \qquad (11.36)$$

$$\text{Cone:} \quad ((P - B) \cdot \hat{w})^2 - \cos^2(\alpha)(P - B) \cdot (P - B) = 0 \qquad (11.37)$$

The basic steps of Miller's method can be outlined as follows:

1. Choose one of the two (possibly) intersecting surfaces as the *parameterization surface*.

2. Substitute the parametric form of the parameterization surface (e.g., Equation 11.33 or 11.34) into the implicit equation for the other surface (i.e., one of Equations 11.35, 11.36, or 11.37).

3. Manipulate the resulting equation until it is in the form $a(t)s^2 + b(t)s + c(t) = 0$.

The resulting equation's functions a, b, and c will have, as Miller points out, "obvious geometric interpretations."

11.9.2 ELLIPSOIDS

This section describes how to compute information about intersections of ellipsoids. We cover the typical query: test for intersection without actually computing the intersection set. Additionally we show how to determine if one ellipsoid is properly contained in another. The latter method is based on the same idea shown in Section 7.5.3 for ellipses. The precise queries we answer for testing for intersection of two ellipsoids $\mathcal{E}_0$ and $\mathcal{E}_1$ are

- Do $\mathcal{E}_0$ and $\mathcal{E}_1$ intersect?

- Are $\mathcal{E}_0$ and $\mathcal{E}_1$ separated? That is, does there exist a plane for which the ellipsoids are on opposite sides?

- Is $\mathcal{E}_0$ properly contained in $\mathcal{E}_1$, or is $\mathcal{E}_1$ properly contained in $\mathcal{E}_0$?

Finding the set of intersection points is more complicated. A couple of methods are discussed. In this section, ellipsoid $\mathcal{E}_i$ is defined by the quadratic equation $Q_i(X) = X^T A_i X + B_i^T X + c_i = 0$, where A_i is a 3×3 positive definite matrix, B_i is a 3×1 vector, c_i is a scalar, and X_i is a 3×1 vector that represents an ellipsoid point. Because A is positive definite, $Q_i(X) < 0$ defines the inside of the ellipsoid and $Q_i(X) > 0$ defines the outside.

Testing for Intersections

The analysis is based on level surfaces of the quadratic functions. Section A.9.1 provides a discussion of level sets of functions. All level surfaces defined by $Q_0(x, y, z) = \lambda$ are ellipsoids, except for the minimum (negative) value λ for which the equation defines a single point, the center of every level surface ellipsoid. The ellipsoid defined by $Q_1(x, y, z) = 0$ is a surface that generally intersects many level surfaces of Q_0. The problem is to find the minimum Q_0-level value λ_0 and the maximum Q_0-level value λ_1 attained by any point (x, y, z) on the ellipsoid $\mathcal{E}_1$. If $\lambda_1 < 0$, $\mathcal{E}_1$ is properly contained in $\mathcal{E}_0$. If $\lambda_0 > 0$, then $\mathcal{E}_0$ and $\mathcal{E}_1$ are separated, or $\mathcal{E}_1$ contains $\mathcal{E}_0$. Otherwise, $0 \in [\lambda_0, \lambda_1]$ and the two ellipsoids intersect. Illustrations in two dimensions are shown in Figures 7.7, 7.8, and 7.9, but apply equally well to the three-dimensional case.

The problem can be formulated as a constrained optimization that is solved by the method of Lagrange multipliers (Section A.9.3). Optimize $Q_0(X)$ subject to the constraint $Q_1(X) = 0$. Define $F(X, t) = Q_0(X) + t Q_1(X)$. Differentiating with respect to the X-components yields $\vec{\nabla} F = \vec{\nabla} Q_0 + t \vec{\nabla} Q_1$. Differentiating with respect to t yields $\partial F / \partial t = Q_1$. Setting the t-derivative equal to zero reproduces the constraint $Q_1 = 0$. Setting the X-derivative equal to zero yields $\vec{\nabla} Q_0 + t \vec{\nabla} Q_1 = \vec{0}$ for some t. Geometrically this means the gradients are parallel.

Note that $\vec{\nabla} Q_i = 2 A_i X + B_i$, so

$$\vec{0} = \vec{\nabla} Q_0 + t \vec{\nabla} Q_1 = 2(A_0 + t A_1) X + (B_0 + t B_1)$$

Formally solving for X yields

$$X = -\frac{1}{2}(A_0 + t A_1)^{-1}(B_0 + t B_1) = \frac{1}{\delta(t)} Y(t)$$

where $A_0 + t A_1$ is a matrix of linear polynomials in t and $\delta(t)$ is its determinant, a cubic polynomial in t. The components of $Y(t)$ are cubic polynomials in t. Replacing this in $Q_1(X) = 0$ yields

$$Y(t)^T A_1 Y(t) + \delta(t) B_1^T Y(t) + \delta(t)^2 C_1 = 0$$

a sixth-degree polynomial in t. The roots can be computed, the corresponding values of X computed, and $Q_0(X)$ evaluated. The minimum and maximum values are stored as λ_0 and λ_1, and the earlier comparisons with zero are applied.

Finding Intersections

The quadratic equations for the ellipsoid can be written as quadratic polynomials in z whose coefficients are functions of x and y: $Q_0(x, y, z) = \alpha_0(x, y) + \alpha_1(x, y)z + \alpha_2(x, y)z^2$ and $Q_1(x, y, z) = \beta_0(x, y) + \beta_1(x, y)z + \beta_2(x, y)z^2$. Using the method of elimination discussed in Section A.2, the two equations have a common z-root if and only if the Bézout determinant is zero,

$$R(x, y) = (\alpha_2\beta_1 - \alpha_1\beta_2)(\alpha_1\beta_0 - \alpha_0\beta_1) - (\alpha_2\beta_0 - \alpha_0\beta_2)^2 = 0 \quad (11.38)$$

The polynomial $R(x, y)$ has degree at most 4. If (x, y) is a solution to $R(x, y) = 0$, the common z-root is

$$z = \frac{\alpha_2\beta_0 - \alpha_0\beta_2}{\alpha_1\beta_2 - \alpha_2\beta_1}$$

If Equation 11.38 has any solutions, there must be at least one solution (x, y) that is closest to the origin. This problem can be set up as a constrained minimization: Minimize $x^2 + y^2$ subject to the constraint $R(x, y) = 0$. Applying the method of Lagrange multipliers (see Section A.9.3), define $F(x, y, t) = x^2 + y^2 + t R(x, y)$. The derivatives are

$$(F_x, F_y, F_t) = (2x + t R_x, 2y + t R_y, R)$$

where the variable subscripts indicate partial derivatives with respect to those variables. The equation $F_t = 0$ just reproduces the constraint $R = 0$. The equations $F_x = 0$ and $F_y = 0$ yield $2x + t R_x = 0$ and $2y + t R_y = 0$. Eliminating t produces another polynomial equation

$$S(x, y) = y R_x - x R_y = 0. \quad (11.39)$$

The polynomial $S(x, y)$ also has degree at most 4.

We now have two polynomial equations in two unknowns, $R(x, y) = 0$ and $S(x, y) = 0$. Each polynomial can be written as polynomials in y whose coefficients are polynomials in x: $R(x, y) = \sum_{i=0}^{4} \alpha_i(x)y^i$ and $S(x, y) = \sum_{i=0}^{4} \beta_i(x)y^i$. The Bézout matrix for the two polynomials in y is the 4×4 matrix $\mathbf{M} = [\mathbf{M}_{ij}]$ with

$$\mathbf{M}_{ij} = \sum_{k=\max(4-j,4-i)}^{\min(4,7-i-j)} w_{k,7-i-j-k}$$

for $0 \le i \le 3$ and $0 \le j \le 3$, with $w_{i,j} = \alpha_i\beta_j - \alpha_j\beta_i$ for $0 \le i \le 4$ and $0 \le j \le 4$. In expanded form,

$$\mathbf{M} = \begin{bmatrix} w_{4,3} & w_{4,2} & w_{4,1} & w_{4,0} \\ w_{4,2} & w_{3,2}+w_{4,1} & w_{3,1}+w_{4,0} & w_{3,0} \\ w_{4,1} & w_{3,1}+w_{4,0} & w_{2,1}+w_{3,0} & w_{2,0} \\ w_{4,0} & w_{3,0} & w_{2,0} & w_{1,0} \end{bmatrix}$$

The degrees of α_i and β_i are at most $4 - i$. The degree of $w_{i,j}$ is at most $8 - i - j$. The Bézout determinant is $D(x) = \det(\mathbf{M}(x))$, a polynomial of degree at most 16 in x.

The roots of $D(x) = 0$ are computed. For each root $\bar{x}$, the coefficients of $f(y)$ are computed and the y-roots for $R(\bar{x}, y) = 0$ are computed. If $\bar{y}$ is such a root, the pair $(\bar{x}, \bar{y})$ is tested to make sure $S(\bar{x}, \bar{y}) = 0$. If so, we have found a point of intersection for the two ellipsoids. If the point is an isolated one, the two ellipsoids are tangent at that point. The point is isolated if $\nabla Q_0(\bar{x}, \bar{y})$ and $\nabla Q_1(\bar{x}, \bar{y})$ are parallel. A simple verification that the cross product of the gradient vectors is the zero vector will suffice. If the point is not isolated, the intersection set will consist of a closed curve. A differential equation solver can be used to traverse the curve:

$$\frac{dx}{dt} = R_y(x, y), \quad \frac{dy}{dt} = -R_x(x, y), \quad (x(0), y(0)) = (\bar{x}, \bar{y}) \qquad (11.40)$$

The vector (R_x, R_y) is normal to the level curve defined by $R = 0$, so the vector $(R_y, -R_x)$ is tangent to the level curve. The differential equations just specify to traverse the curve by following the tangent vector.

The main problem with the former algorithm is that numerically finding the roots of a degree 16 polynomial can be an ill-conditioned problem. An alternative is to use an iterative search by setting up a system of differential equations that allows you to walk along one ellipsoid in search of a point of intersection with the other ellipsoid. The search will either find a point or determine that there is none.

Start with a point X_0 on ellipsoid $\mathcal{E}_0$, so $Q_0(X_0) = 0$. If $Q_1(X_0) = 0$, we already have a point of intersection. If $Q_1(X_0) < 0$, then X_0 is inside the ellipsoid $\mathcal{E}_1$. The idea is to walk tangentially along the first ellipsoid while increasing the value of Q_1 to zero. In space, the direction of largest increase of Q_1 is $\vec{\nabla} Q_1$. This vector is normal to ellipsoid $\mathcal{E}_1$ but is usually not tangent to the ellipsoid $\mathcal{E}_0$. The vector must be projected onto the tangent space of $\mathcal{E}_0$ by subtracting the contribution by $\vec{\nabla} Q_0$. The path on $\mathcal{E}_0$ with the largest increase in Q_1 locally is determined by

$$\frac{dX}{dt} = \vec{\nabla} Q_1 - \frac{\vec{\nabla} Q_1 \cdot \vec{\nabla} Q_0}{\|\vec{\nabla} Q_0\|^2} \vec{\nabla} Q_0, \quad X(0) = X_0$$

In the event that $Q_1(X_0) > 0$, the tangent direction must be reversed so that Q_1 is decreased as rapidly as possible to zero. The differential equations for this case are

$$\frac{dX}{dt} = -\vec{\nabla} Q_1 + \frac{\vec{\nabla} Q_1 \cdot \vec{\nabla} Q_0}{\|\vec{\nabla} Q_0\|^2} \vec{\nabla} Q_0, \quad X(0) = X_0$$

Regardless of whether the ellipsoids intersect, eventually the traversal will lead to a point for which the gradients are parallel. In this case the right-hand side of the differential equation reduces to the zero vector. The length of the right-hand side vector can be used as a termination criterion in the numerical solver. Another concern is that the numerical solver will produce a new position from an old one and, because of numerical error, the new position might not be on the first ellipsoid. A correction can be made to adjust the new position so that it is on the first ellipsoid. The corrected value can be used to generate the next iterate in the solver.

Once a point $X_1 = X(T)$ at some time $T > 0$ for which $Q_1(X_1) = 0$, the 2D level curve traversal of Equation 11.40 can be applied. However, it is possible to traverse the curve of intersection directly in 3D. A tangent vector for the curve is perpendicular to both $\vec{\nabla} Q_0$ and $\vec{\nabla} Q_1$. The system of equations to solve is

$$\frac{dX}{dt} = \vec{\nabla} Q_0 \times \vec{\nabla} Q_1, \ \ X(0) = X_1$$

Regardless of which system of differential equations is used to traverse the intersection curve, some type of stopping criterion must be implemented that detects the traversal has reached the point X_0 at which the traversal originated.

11.10   POLYNOMIAL SURFACES

In this section, we briefly discuss the general problem of computing the intersection of two polynomial surfaces and point you to some of the wealth of literature addressing this difficult and important problem.

The problem of surface-surface intersections (SSIs) arises quite frequently in many computer graphics applications—modeling, finite-element mesh generation, tool path specification, scientific visualization, interference and feature detection, and so on. SSIs are obviously very significant in boundary-rep geometric modeling applications, and the intersection of algebraic and NURBS surfaces is considered to be a fundamental consideration in the integration of geometric and solid modeling systems. Figure 11.59 shows two B-spline surfaces intersecting in two closed loops and one open curve. Figure 11.60 shows the intersection curves in the parameter space of one of the surfaces.

A very large body of work, stretching back several decades, addresses the problems associated with SSI. Recent surveys can be found in Patrikalakis (1993), Pratt and Geisow (1986), and Hoffman (1989). SSI algorithms are typically classified into four categories: *subdivision methods*, *lattice evaluation*, *analytic methods*, and *marching methods*. Various hybrids involving several of these methods have been proposed as well.

11.10.1   SUBDIVISION METHODS

The core idea here is to (recursively) decompose the problem into smaller and simpler problems; a trivial example would be to recursively subdivide the surfaces into bilinear patches, which would then be intersected. Subdivision continues until some stated criteria are reached, at which point the individual curves are pieced together to form one or more contiguous curves. Typically, subdivision control is based on

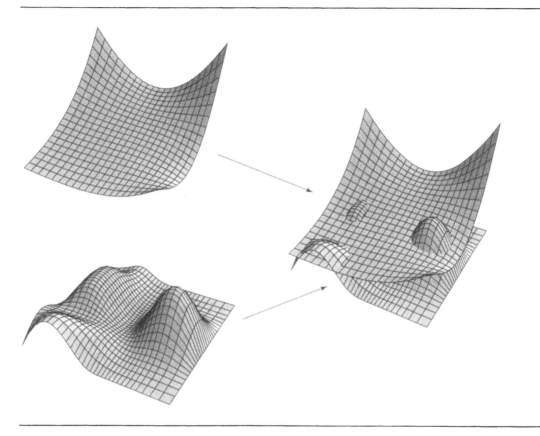

Figure 11.59   Intersection of two B-spline surfaces.

geometric properties of the control polygon—for example, variation-diminishing property, convex hull, and so on (Lane and Riesenfeld 1980; Lasser 1986). In the limit, subdivision methods converge on the actual intersection curve, but tend to produce very large amounts of data and run quite slowly. Attempts to reduce these problems by constraining the level of subdivision can improve the speed, but risk missing small features such as loops, or miss or incorrectly connect singularities.

11.10.2 LATTICE EVALUATION

In this approach, the surface intersection problem is reduced to a series of problems of lower geometric complexity, such as curve-surface intersections (Rossignac and Requicha 1987). Like the subdivision methods, lattice approaches tend to be slow and also exhibit problems with respect to missing loops and singularities.

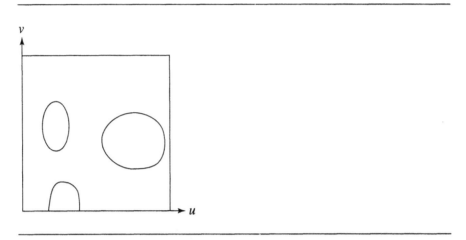

Figure 11.60   Intersection curves in one surface's parameter space.

11.10.3   ANALYTIC METHODS

The approach here is to attempt to find an explicit representation of the intersection curve. This has found success only in a limited area—generally cases in which the intersection curve is of low degree (Sederberg 1983; Sarraga 1983) and/or is limited to special cases or specific types of surfaces (Piegl 1989; Miller 1987; Miller and Goldman 1992, 1995) using a geometric (as opposed to strictly algebraic) approach.

11.10.4   MARCHING METHODS

Also known as *curve tracing*, the basic idea behind marching is this (Hoffman 1989, 206):

> At a point p on the intersection, a local approximation of the curve is constructed; for example, the curve tangent at p. By stepping along the approximation a specific distance, we obtain an estimate of the next curve point that we then refine using an iterative method.

Tracing/marching methods seem to be the most widely used (Barnhill and Kersey 1990; Farouki 1986; Bajaj et al. 1989). The reasons cited (Krishnan and Manocha 1997) are their (relative) ease of implementation and their generality (they can handle such things as offsets and blends, which are particularly important in CAD applications). Two major issues arise in this approach: first, the starting points for the intersection curves must be identified. Intersection curves, as we have seen, may be boundary segments or closed loops, and degeneracies such as singularities may be present. Boundary segment start points can be identified by curve-surface intersection methods (Sederberg and Nishita 1991). Detection of closed loops has proven more problematic; most approaches use Gauss maps for bounding and simply subdivide the surface until "sufficient conditions for the non-existence of loops are satisfied" (Krishnan and Manocha 1997).

The second major issue for tracing methods is this: once the start point(s) are identified, most algorithms use a variant of Newton's method to do the actual tracing. However, in practice the step size must be kept very small to avoid what is referred to as *component jumping*. The result is that this operation can be very slow. Relatively more recent work by Krishnan and Manocha (1997) has addressed these significant issues with a good deal of success.

11.11 THE METHOD OF SEPARATING AXES

The concept of separating axes in three dimensions is identical to that of two dimensions in Section 7.7. Two stationary convex objects do not intersect if there exists a line for which the projections of the objects onto that line do not intersect. The method applies to moving convex objects, and the geometric queries *test-intersection* and *find-intersection* can be formulated just as in two dimensions.

11.11.1 SEPARATION OF STATIONARY CONVEX POLYHEDRA

In two dimensions we concentrated our efforts on convex polygons. In three dimensions we focus on convex polyhedra, but particular attention must be given to the case when both polyhedra are really planar polygons. For a pair of convex polyhedra, only a finite set of direction vectors needs to be considered for separation tests. This is analogous to the two-dimensional problem with convex polygons, but we do not provide a proof of the claim in three dimensions. The intuition, however, is similar to that of convex polygons in two dimensions. If the two polyhedra are just touching with no interpenetration, the contact is one of face-face, face-edge, face-vertex, edge-edge, edge-vertex, or vertex-vertex. The set of potential directions that capture these types of contact includes the normal vectors to the faces of the polyhedra and vectors generated by a cross product of two edges, one from each polyhedron.

Let C_j for $j = 0, 1$ be the convex polyhedra with vertices $\{V_i^{(j)}\}_{i=0}^{N_j-1}$, edges $\{\vec{e}_i^{(j)}\}_{i=0}^{M_j-1}$, and faces $\{F_i^{(j)}\}_{i=0}^{L_j-1}$. Let the faces be planar convex polygons whose vertices are counterclockwise ordered as you view the face from outside the polyhedron. Outward-pointing normal vectors can be stored with each face as a way of storing the orientation. We assume that each face has queries that allow access to the face normal and to vertices on the face. We assume that each edge has a query that allows access to its vertices.

The pseudocode for testing for intersection of two convex polyhedra, both having positive volume (so $L_j \geq 4$), is similar to the direct implementation in 2D:

```
bool TestIntersection(ConvexPolyhedron C0, ConvexPolyhedron C1)
{
    // test faces of C0 for separation
    for (i = 0; i < C0.L; i++) {
        D = C0.F(i).normal;
        ComputeInterval(C0, D, min0, max0);
        ComputeInterval(C1, D, min1, max1);
        if (max1 < min0 || max0 < min1 )
            return false;
    }

    // test faces of C1 for separation
    for (j = 0; j < C1.L; j++) {
        D = C1.F(j).normal;
        ComputeInterval(C0, D, min0, max0);
        ComputeInterval(C1, D, min1, max1);
        if ( max1 < min0 || max0 < min1)
            return false;
    }

    // test cross products of pairs of edges
    for (i = 0; i < C0.M; i++) {
        for (j = 0; j < C1.M; j++) {
            D = Cross(C0.E(i), C1.E(j));
            ComputeInterval(C0, D, min0, max0);
            ComputeInterval(C1, D, min1, max1);
            if (max1 < min0 || max0 < min1)
                return false;
        }
    }

    return true;
}

void ComputeInterval(ConvexPolyhedron C, Point D, float& min, float& max)
{
    min = Dot(D, C.V(0));  max = min;
    for (i = 1; i < C.N; i++) {
        value = Dot(D, C.V(i));
        if (value < min) min = value; else max = value;
    }
}
```

The asymptotically better algorithm for finding the extreme points of a convex polygon in 2D does have a counterpart in 3D. Given n vertices, it is possible to find extreme points in $O(\log n)$ time (Kirkpatrick 1983; Dobkin and Kirkpatrick 1990). A well-written presentation of the algorithm is provided in O'Rourke (1998). However, for applications that have small n or those that have polyhedra with a lot of symmetry, typically oriented bounding boxes, the time spent implementing, testing, and debugging this algorithm is probably not justified, especially if the constant in the $O(\log n)$ algorithm is sufficiently large compared to the constant in the straightforward $O(n)$ algorithm.

The TestIntersection pseudocode listed earlier has problems when both convex polyhedra are convex polygons in the same plane. In this case the common normal vector is not a separating direction. The cross product of any pair of edges is again a normal vector to the plane, so it cannot separate the two polygons. In fact, coplanar convex polygons in 3D must be handled with the algorithm for convex polygons in 2D. All that we need in 3D are vectors that are in the plane of the polygons and are perpendicular to the appropriate edges. If $\vec{n}$ is a plane normal and if $\vec{e}$ is an edge vector for a polygon, then $\vec{n} \times \vec{e}$ is a potential separating direction. The pseudocode is

```
bool TestIntersection(ConvexPolygon C0, ConvexPolygon C1)
{
    // test normal of C0 for separation
    D = C0.normal;
    ComputeInterval(C0, D, min0, max0);
    ComputeInterval(C1, D, min1, max1);
    if (max1 < min0 || max0 < min1)
        return false;

    Point N0xN1 = Cross(C0.normal, C1.normal);
    if (N0xN1 != 0) {
        // polygons are not parallel
        // test normal of C1 for separation
        D = C1.normal;
        ComputeInterval(C0, D, min0, max0);
        ComputeInterval(C1, D, min1, max1);
        if (max1 < min0 || max0 < min1)
            return false;

        // test cross products of pairs of edges
        for (i = 0; i < C0.M; i++) {
            for (j = 0; j < C1.M; j++) {
                D = Cross(C0.E(i), C1.E(j));
                ComputeInterval(C0, D, min0, max0);
                ComputeInterval(C1, D, min1, max1);
```

```
                    if (max1 < min0 || max0 < min1)
                        return false;
                }
            }
        } else {
            // polygons are parallel (coplanar, C0.normal did not separate)
            // test edge normals for C0
            for (i = 0; i < C0.M; i++) {
                D = Cross(C0.normal, C0.E(i));
                ComputeInterval(C0, D, min0, max0);
                ComputeInterval(C1, D, min1, max1);
                if (max1 < min0 || max0 < min1)
                    return false;
            }

            // test edge normals for C1
            for (i1 = 0; i1 < 3; i1++) {
                D = Cross(C1.normal, C1.E(i));
                ComputeInterval(C0, D, min0, max0);
                ComputeInterval(C1, D, min1, max1);
                if (max1 < min0 || max0 < min1)
                    return false;
            }
        }

        return true;
}
```

In the presence of a floating-point arithmetic system, the comparison to the zero vector of the cross product of polygon normals should be modified to use relative error. The selected threshold epsilon is a threshold on the value of the squared sine of the angle between the two normal vectors, based on the identity $\vec{n}_0 \times \vec{n}_1 = \|\vec{n}_0\| \|\vec{n}_1\| \sin(\theta)$, where θ is the angle between the two vectors. The choice of epsilon is at the discretion of the application.

```
// comparison when the normals are unit length
Point N0xN1 = Cross(C0.normal, C1.normal);
float N0xN1SqrLen = Dot(N0xN1, N0xN1);
if (N0xN1SqrLen >= epsilon) {
    // polygons are (effectively) not parallel
} else {
    // polygons are (effectively) parallel
}
```

```
// comparison when the normals are not unit length
Point N0xN1 = Cross(C0.normal, C1.normal);
float N0xN1SqrLen = Dot(N0xN1, N0xN1);
float N0SqrLen = Dot(C0.normal, C0.normal);
float N1SqrLen = Dot(C1.normal, C1.normal);
if (N0xN1SqrLen >= epsilon * N0SqrLen * N1SqrLen) {
    // polygons are (effectively) not parallel
} else {
    // polygons are (effectively) parallel
}
```

11.11.2 SEPARATION OF MOVING CONVEX POLYHEDRA

The structure of this algorithm is similar to that of the two-dimensional problem. See Section 7.7 for the details. The pseudocode for testing for intersection of two convex polyhedra of positive volume is listed below.

```
bool TestIntersection(ConvexPolyhedron C0, Point W0, ConvexPolyhedron C1,
Point W1, float tmax, float& tfirst, float& tlast)
{
    W = W1 - W0;  // process as if C0 stationary, C1 moving
    tfirst = 0;  tlast = INFINITY;

    // test faces of C0 for separation
    for (i = 0; i < C0.L; i++) {
        D = C0.F(i).normal;
        ComputeInterval(C0, D, min0, max0);
        ComputeInterval(C1, D, min1, max1);
        speed = Dot(D, W);
        if (NoIntersect(tmax, speed, min0, max0, min1, max1, tfirst, tlast))
            return false;
    }

    // test faces of C1 for separation
    for (j = 0; j < C1.L; j++) {
        D = C1.F(j).normal;
        ComputeInterval(C0, D, min0, max0);
        ComputeInterval(C1, D, min1, max1);
        speed = Dot(D, W);
        if (NoIntersect(tmax, speed, min0, max0, min1, max1,
            tfirst, tlast))
            return false;
    }
```

```
// test cross products of pairs of edges
for (i = 0; i < C0.M; i++) {
    for (j = 0; j < C1.M; j++) {
        D = Cross(C0.E(i), C1.E(j));
        ComputeInterval(C0, D, min0, max0);
        ComputeInterval(C1, D, min1, max1);
        speed = Dot(D, W);
        if (NoIntersect(tmax, speed, min0, max0, min1, max1, tfirst, tlast) )
            return false;
    }
}

return true;
}
```

The function NoIntersect is exactly the one used in the two-dimensional problem. In the case of two convex polyhedra that are planar polygons, the full pseudocode
is not provided here but can be obtained by replacing each block of the form

```
if (max1 < min0 || max0 < min1)
    return false;
```

by a block of the form

```
speed = Dot(D, W);
if (NoIntersect(tmax, speed, min0, max0, min1, max1, tfirst, tlast))
    return false;
```

11.11.3 INTERSECTION SET FOR STATIONARY CONVEX POLYHEDRA

The find-intersection query for two stationary convex polyhedra is a special example
of Boolean operations on polyhedra. Section 13.6 provides a general discussion for
computing Boolean operations, in particular for computing the intersection of two
polyhedra.

11.11.4 CONTACT SET FOR MOVING CONVEX POLYHEDRA

Given two moving convex objects C_0 and C_1, initially not intersecting, with velocities
$\vec{w}_0$ and $\vec{w}_1$, if $T > 0$ is the first time of contact, the sets $C_0 + T\vec{w}_0 = \{X + T\vec{w}_0 : X \in C_0\}$ and $C_1 + T\vec{w}_1 = \{X + T\vec{w}_1 : X \in C_1\}$ are just touching with no interpenetration.
As indicated earlier for convex polyhedra, the contact is one of face-face, face-edge,
face-vertex, edge-edge, edge-vertex, or vertex-vertex. The analysis is slightly more

complicated than that of the 2D setting, but the ideas are the same—the relative orientation of the convex polyhedra to each other must be known to properly compute the contact set. We recommend reading Section 7.7 first to understand those ideas before finishing this section.

The TestIntersection function can be modified to keep track of which vertices, edges, or faces are projected to the end points of the projection interval. At the first time of contact, this information is used to determine how the two objects are oriented with respect to each other. If the contact is vertex-vertex, vertex-edge, or vertex-face, then the contact point is a single point, a vertex. If the contact is edge-edge, the contact is typically a single point, but can be an entire line segment. If the contact is edge-face, the contact set is a line segment. Finally, if the contact is face-face, the intersection set is a convex polygon. This is the most complicated scenario and requires a two-dimensional convex polygon intersector. Each end point of the projection interval is generated by either a vertex, an edge, or a face. Similar to the implementation for the two-dimensional problem, a two-character label can be associated with each polyhedron to indicate the projection type. The single character labels are V for a vertex projection, E for an edge projection, and F for a face projection. The nine two-character labels are VV, VE, VF, EV, EE, EF, FV, FE, and FF. The first letter corresponds to the minimum of the interval, and the second letter corresponds to the maximum of the interval. A convenient data structure for storing the labels, the projection interval, and the indices of the polyhedron components that project to the interval end points is exactly the one used in the two-dimensional problem:

```
Configuration
{
    float min, max;
    int index[2];
    char type[2];
}
```

The projection interval is [min, max]. As an example, if the projection type is VF, index[0] is the index of the vertex that projects to the minimum and index[1] is the index of the face that projects to the maximum.

Two configuration objects are delcared, Cfg0 for polyhedron C_0 and Cfg1 for polyhedron C_1. In the two-dimensional problem, the block of code for each potential separating direction $\vec{d}$ had the ComputeInterval calls replaced by ProjectNormal and ProjectGeneral. The function ProjectNormal knows that an edge normal is being used and only the other extreme projection must be calculated. The function ProjectGeneral determines the projection type at both interval extremes. The analogous functions must be implemented for the three-dimensional problem, but they apply to the separation tests involving face normals. The separation tests for cross products of pairs of edges require ProjectGeneral to replace both calls to ComputeGeneral since it is not guaranteed in these cases that only the edges project to interval extremes.

The pseudocode for the projection of a polyhedron onto a normal line for one of its own faces is listed below. The code was simpler in the two-dimensional problem because of the linear ordering of the vertices and edges. When the current minimum projection occurs twice, at that point you know that the value is the true minimum and that an edge must project to it. In the three-dimensional case, there is no linear ordering, so the code is more complicated. If the current minimum occurs three times, then the vertices must be part of a face that is an extreme face along the current direction under consideration. At this point you can return safely knowing that no other vertices need to be processed. The complication is that once you have found a third vertex that projects to the current minimum, you must determine which face contains those vertices. Also possible is that the current minimum occurs twice and is generated by an edge perpendicular to the current direction, but that edge is not necessarily an extreme one with respect to the direction. An early exit from the function when the current minimum occurs twice is not possible.

```
void ProjectNormal(ConvexPolyhedron C, Point D, int faceindex,
                   Configuration Cfg)
{
    // store the vertex indices that map to current minimum
    int minquantity, minindex[3];

    // project the face
    minquantity = 1;
    minindex[0] = C.IndexOf(C.F(faceindex).V(0));
    Cfg.min = Cfg.max = Dot(D,C.V(minindex[0]));
    Cfg.index[1] = faceindex;
    Cfg.type[1] = 'F';

    for (i = 0; i < C.N; i++) {
        value = Dot(D, C.V(i));
        if (value < Cfg.min) {
            minquantity = 1;
            minindex[0] = i;
            Cfg.min = value;
            Cfg.index[0] = i;
            Cfg.type[0] = 'V';
        } else if (value == Cfg.min && Cfg.min < Cfg.max) {
            minindex[minquantity++] = i;
            if (minquantity == 2) {
                if (C.ExistsEdge(minindex[0], minindex[1])) {
                    // edge is parallel to initial face
                    Cfg.index[0] = C.GetEdgeIndexFromVertices(minindex);
                    Cfg.type[0] = 'E';
                }
            }
        }
```

```
            // else:  two nonconnected vertices project to current
            // minimum, the first vertex is kept as the current extreme
        } else if ( minquantity == 3 ) {
            // Face is parallel to initial face.  This face must project
            // to the minimum and no other vertices can do so.  No need
            // to further process vertices.
            Cfg.index[0] = C.GetFaceIndexFromVertices(minindex);
            Cfg.type[0] = 'F';
            return;
        }
    }
  }
}
```

The pseudocode for general projection of a polyhedron onto the line is listed below.

```
void ProjectGeneral(ConvexPolyhedron C, Point D, Configuration Cfg)
{
    Cfg.min = Cfg.max = Dot(D, C.V(0));
    Cfg.index[0] = Cfg.index[1] = 0;

    for (i = 1; i < C.N; i++) {
        value = Dot(D, C.V(i));
        if (value < Cfg.min)  {
            Cfg.min = value;
            Cfg.index[0] = i;
        } else if (value > Cfg.max) {
            Cfg.max = value;
            Cfg.index[1] = i;
        }
    }

    Cfg.type[0] = Cfg.type[1] = 'V';
    for (i = 0; i < 2; i++)  {
        for each face F sharing C.V(Cfg.index[i])  {
            if (F.normal parallel to D) {
                Cfg.index[i] = C.GetIndexOfFace(F);
                Cfg.type[i] = 'F';
                break;
            }
        }

        if (Cfg.type[i] != 'F')  {
```

```
                        for each edge E sharing C.V(Cfg.index[i])  {
                            if (E perpendicular to D) {
                                Cfg.index[i] = C.GetIndexOfEdge(E);
                                Cfg.type[i] = 'E';
                                break;
                            }
                        }
                    }
                }
            }
```

The NoIntersect function that was modified in two dimensions to accept configuration objects instead of projection intervals is used exactly as is for the three-dimensional problem. With all such modifications, TestIntersection has the equivalent formulation:

```
bool TestIntersection(ConvexPolyhedron C0, Point W0, ConvexPolyhedron C1, Point W1,
    float tmax, float& tfirst, float& tlast)
{
    W = W1 - W0;  // process as if C0 stationary, C1 moving
    tfirst = 0;   tlast = INFINITY;

    // test faces of C0 for separation
    for (i = 0; i < C0.L; i++) {
        D = C0.F(i).normal;
        ProjectNormal(C0, D, i, Cfg0);
        ProjectGeneral(C1, D, Cfg1);
        speed = Dot(D, W);
        if (NoIntersect(tmax, speed, Cfg0, Cfg1, Curr0, Curr1, side, tfirst, tlast) )
            return false;
    }

    // test faces of C1 for separation
    for (j = 0; j < C1.L; j++) {
        D = C1.F(j).normal;
        ProjectNormal(C1, D, j, Cfg1);
        ProjectGeneral(C0, D, Cfg0);
        speed = Dot(D, W);
        if (NoIntersect(tmax, speed, Cfg0, Cfg1, Curr0, Curr1, side, tfirst, tlast))
            return false;
    }

    // test cross products of pairs of edges
    for (i = 0; i < C0.M; i++) {
```

```
        for (j = 0; j < C1.M; j++)  {
            D = Cross(C0.E(i), C1.E(j));
            ProjectGeneral(C0, D, Cfg0);
            ProjectGeneral(C1, D, Cfg1);
            speed = Dot(D, W);
            if (NoIntersect(tmax, speed, Cfg0, Cfg1, Curr0, Curr1, side, tfirst, t last))
                return false;
        }
    }

    return true;
}
```

The FindIntersection pseudocode has exactly the same implementation as TestIntersection, but with one additional block of code (after all the loops) that is reached if there will be an intersection. When the polyhedra intersect at time T, they are effectively moved with their respective velocities, and the contact set is calculated. The pseudocode is shown below. The intersection is a convex polyhedron and is returned in the last argument of the function. If the intersection set is nonempty, the return value is true. Otherwise, the original moving convex polyhedra do not intersect, and the function returns false.

```
bool FindIntersection(ConvexPolyhedron C0, Point W0, ConvexPolyhedron C1, Point W1,
    float tmax, float& tfirst, float& tlast, ConvexPolyhedron& I)
{
    W = W1 - W0;   // process as if C0 stationary, C1 moving
    tfirst = 0;   tlast = INFINITY;

    // test faces of C0 for separation
    for (i = 0; i < C0.L; i++) {
        D = C0.F(i).normal;
        ProjectNormal(C0, D, i,Cfg0);
        ProjectGeneral(C1, D, Cfg1);
        speed = Dot(D, W);
        if (NoIntersect(tmax, speed, Cfg0, Cfg1, Curr0, Curr1, side, tfirst, tlast))
            return false;
    }

    // test faces of C1 for separation
    for (j = 0; j < C1.L; j++) {
        D = C1.F(j).normal;
        ProjectNormal(C1, D, j, Cfg1);
        ProjectGeneral(C0, D, Cfg0);
        speed = Dot(D, W);
```

```
        if (NoIntersect(tmax, speed, Cfg0, Cfg1, Curr0, Curr1, side, tfirst, tlast))
            return false;
    }

    // test cross products of pairs of edges
    for (i = 0; i < C0.M; i++) {
        for (j = 0; j < C1.M; j++) {
            D = Cross(C0.E(i), C1.E(j));
            ProjectGeneral(C0, D, Cfg0);
            ProjectGeneral(C1, D, Cfg1);
            speed = Dot(D, W);
            if (NoIntersect(tmax, speed, Cfg0, Cfg1, Curr0, Curr1, side, tfirst, tlast))
                return false;
        }
    }

    // compute the contact set
    GetIntersection(C0, W0, C1, W1, Curr0, Curr1, side, tfirst, I);
    return true;
}
```

The intersection calculator pseudocode is shown below.

```
void GetIntersection(ConvexPolyhedron C0, Point W0, ConvexPolyhedron C1,
    Point W1, Configuration Cfg0, Configuration Cfg1, int side, float tfirst,
    ConvexPolyhedron I)
{
    if (side == 1) {
        // C0-max meets C1-min
        if (Cfg0.type[1] == 'V') {
            // vertex-{vertex/edge/face} intersection
            I.InsertVertex(C0.V(Cfg0.index[1]) + tfirst * W0);
        } else if (Cfg1.type[0] == 'V') {
            // {vertex/edge/face}-vertex intersection
            I.InsertVertex(C1.V(Cfg1.index[0]) + tfirst * W1);
        } else if (Cfg0.type[1] == 'E') {
            Segment E0Moved = C0.E(Cfg0.index[1]) + tfirst * W0;
            if (Cfg1.type[0] == 'E') {
                Segment E1Moved = C1.E(Cfg1.index[0]) + tfirst * W1;
                FindSegmentIntersection(E0Moved, E1Moved, I);
            } else {
                ConvexPolygon F1Moved = C1.F(Cfg1.index[0]) + tfirst * W1;
                FindSegmentPolygonIntersection(E0Moved, F1Moved, I);
            }
```

```
        } else if (Cfg1.type[0] == 'E') {
            Segment E1Moved = C1.E(Cfg1.index[0]) + tfirst * W1;
            if (Cfg0.type[1] == 'E')  {
                Segment E0Moved = C0.E(Cfg0.index[1]) + tfirst * W0;
                FindSegmentIntersection(E1Moved, E0Moved, I);
            } else {
                ConvexPolygon F0Moved = C0.F(Cfg0.index[1]) + tfirst * W0;
                FindSegmentPolygonIntersection(E1Moved, F0Moved, I);
            }
        } else {
            // Cfg0.type[1] == 'F' && Cfg1.type[0] == 'F'
            // face-face intersection
            ConvexPolygon F0Moved = C0.F(Cfg0.index[1]) + tfirst * W0;
            ConvexPolygon F1Moved = C1.F(Cfg1.index[0]) + tfirst * W1;
            FindPolygonIntersection(F0Moved, F1Moved, I);
        }
    } else if ( side == -1 ) {
        // C1-max meets C0-min
        if (Cfg1.type[1] == 'V') {
            // vertex-{vertex/edge/face} intersection
            I.InsertVertex(C1.V(Cfg1.index[1]) + tfirst * W1);
        } else if (Cfg0.type[0] == 'V')  {
            // {vertex/edge/face}-vertex intersection
            I.InsertVertex(C0.V(Cfg0.index[0]) + tfirst * W0);
        } else if (Cfg1.type[1] == 'E') {
            Segment E1Moved = C1.E(Cfg1.index[1]) + tfirst * W1;
            if (Cfg0.type[0] == 'E') {
                Segment E0Moved = C0.E(Cfg0.index[0]) + tfirst * W0;
                FindSegmentIntersection(E1Moved, E0Moved, I);
            } else  {
                ConvexPolygon F0Moved = C0.F(Cfg0.index[0]) + tfirst * W0;
                FindSegmentPolygonIntersection(E1Moved, F0Moved, I);
            }
        } else if (Cfg0.type[0] == 'E') {
            Segment E0Moved = C0.E(Cfg0.index[0]) + tfirst * W0;
            if (Cfg1.type[1] == 'E') {
                Segment E1Moved = C1.E(Cfg1.index[1]) + tfirst * W1;
                FindSegmentIntersection(E0Moved, E1Moved, I);
            } else {
                ConvexPolygon F1Moved = C1.F(Cfg1.index[1]) + tfirst * W1;
                FindSegmentPolygonIntersection(E0Moved, F1Moved, I);
            }
        } else {
            // Cfg1.type[1] == 'F' && Cfg0.type[0] == 'F'
```

```
              // face-face intersection
              ConvexPolygon F0Moved = C0.F(Cfg0.index[0]) + tfirst * W0;
              ConvexPolygon F1Moved = C1.F(Cfg1.index[1]) + tfirst * W1;
              FindPolygonIntersection(F0Moved, F1Moved, I);
          }
      } else {
          // polyhedra were initially intersecting
          ConvexPolyhedron C0Moved = C0 + tfirst * W0;
          ConvexPolyhedron C1Moved = C1 + tfirst * W1;
          FindPolyhedronIntersection(C0Moved, C1Moved, I);
      }
  }
```

The semantics of the functions for the moved convex objects are clear from the function names.

11.12   MISCELLANEOUS

This section covers a variety of intersection problems that do not fit directly into the previous categories of the chapter.

11.12.1   ORIENTED BOUNDING BOX AND ORTHOGONAL FRUSTUM

The separating axis method, discussed in Section 11.11, is used to determine if an oriented bounding box (OBB) intersects an orthogonal frustum. This is useful for accurate culling of an OBB bounding volume with respect to a view frustum.

The oriented bounding box is represented in symmetric form with center C; axis directions $\hat{a}_0$, $\hat{a}_1$, and $\hat{a}_2$; and extents e_0, e_1, and e_2. The axis directions form a right-handed orthonormal system. The extents are assumed to be positive. The eight vertices of the box are $C + \sum_{i=0}^{2} \sigma_i e_i \hat{a}_i$, where $|\sigma_i| = 1$ (eight choices on sign). The three normal vectors for the six box faces are $\hat{a}_i$ for $0 \le i \le 2$. The three edge direction vectors for the twelve box edges are the same set of vectors.

The orthogonal view frustum has origin E. Its coordinate axes are determined by left vector $\hat{l}$, up-vector $\hat{u}$, and direction vector $\hat{d}$. The vectors in that order form a right-handed orthonormal system. The extent of the frustum in the $\hat{d}$ direction is $[n, f]$, where $0 < n < f$. The view plane is assumed to be the near plane, $\hat{d} \cdot (X - E) = n$. The far plane is $\hat{d} \cdot (X - E) = f$. The four corners of the frustum in the near plane are $E \pm \ell\hat{l} \pm \mu\hat{u} + n\hat{d}$. The four corners of the frustum in the far plane are $E + (f/n)(\pm\ell\hat{l} \pm \mu\hat{u} + n\hat{d})$. The five normal vectors for the six frustum faces are $\hat{d}$ for the near and far faces, $\pm n\hat{l} - \ell\hat{d}$ for the left and right faces, and $\pm n\hat{u} - \ell\hat{d}$ for the top and bottom faces. The six edge direction vectors for the twelve frustum edges are $\hat{l}$ and $\hat{u}$ for the edges on the near and far faces, and $\pm \ell \hat{l} \pm \mu \hat{u} + n \hat{d}$. The normal and edge directions are not all unit length, but this is not necessary for the separation axis tests.

Separating Axis Test

Two convex polyhedra do not intersect if there exists a line with direction $\vec{m}$ such that the projections of the polyhedra onto the line do not intersect. In this case there must exist a plane with normal vector $\vec{m}$ that separates the two polyhedra. Given a line, it is straightforward to project the vertices of a polyhedron onto the line and compute the bounding interval $[\lambda_{\min}, \lambda_{\max}]$ for those projections. The two intervals obtained from the two polyhedra are easily compared for overlap.

The more difficult problem is selecting a finite set of line directions such that the intersection/nonintersection can be determined by separating axis tests using only vectors in that set. For convex polyhedra it turns out that the set consisting of face normals for the two polyhedra and vectors that are the cross product of edges, one edge from each polyhedron, is sufficient for the intersection testing. If polyhedron i has F_i faces and E_i edges, then the total number of vectors in the set is $F_0 + F_1 + E_0 E_1$. It is possible that some of the vectors formed by cross products of edges are zero, in which case they do not need to be tested. This happens, for example, with two axis-aligned bounding boxes. While the total number of vectors is $3 + 3 + 3 * 3 = 15$, the set has only three nonzero vectors.

The oriented bounding box has $F_0 = 3$ and $E_0 = 3$. The orthogonal view frustum has $F_1 = 5$ and $E_1 = 6$. The total number of vectors to test is 26. That set is

$$\{\hat{d}, \pm n \hat{l} - \ell \hat{d}, \pm n \hat{u} - \mu \hat{d}, \hat{a}_i, \hat{l} \times \hat{a}_i, \hat{u} \times \hat{a}_i, (\pm \ell \hat{l} \pm \mu \hat{u} + n \hat{d}) \times \hat{a}_i\}$$

The separating axes that are tested will all be of the form $E + \lambda \vec{m}$, where $\vec{m}$ is in the previously mentioned set. The projected vertices of the box have λ values $\vec{m} \cdot (C - E) + \sum_{i=0}^{2} \sigma_i e_i \hat{a}_i$, where $|\sigma_i| = 1$. Define $d = \vec{m} \cdot (C - E)$ and $R = \sum_{i=0}^{2} e_i |\vec{m} \cdot \hat{a}_i|$. The projection interval is $[d - R, d + R]$.

The projected vertices of the frustum have λ values $\kappa(\tau_0 \ell \vec{m} \cdot \hat{l} + \tau_1 \mu \vec{m} \cdot \hat{u} + n \vec{m} \cdot \hat{d})$, where $\kappa \in \{1, f/n\}$ and $|\tau_i| = 1$. Define $p = \ell |\vec{m} \cdot \hat{l}| + \mu |\vec{m} \cdot \hat{u}|$. The projection interval is $[m_0, m_1]$, where

$$m_0 = \begin{cases} \frac{f}{n}\left(n \vec{m} \cdot \hat{d} - p\right), & n \vec{m} \cdot \hat{d} - p < 0 \\ n \vec{m} \cdot \hat{d} - p, & n \vec{m} \cdot \hat{d} - p \geq 0 \end{cases}$$

and

$$m_1 = \begin{cases} \frac{f}{n}\left(n \vec{m} \cdot \hat{d} + p\right), & n \vec{m} \cdot \hat{d} + p > 0 \\ n \vec{m} \cdot \hat{d} + p, & n \vec{m} \cdot \hat{d} + p \leq 0 \end{cases}$$

Table 11.5   Coefficients for the separating axis test

$\vec{m}$	$\vec{m} \cdot \hat{l}$	$\vec{m} \cdot \hat{u}$	$\vec{m} \cdot \hat{d}$	$\vec{m} \cdot (C - E)$
$\hat{d}$	0	0	1	δ_2
$\pm n\hat{l} - \ell\hat{d}$	$\pm n$	0	$-\ell$	$\pm n\delta_0 - \ell\delta_2$
$\pm n\hat{u} - \mu\hat{d}$	0	$\pm n$	$-\mu$	$\pm n\delta_1 - \mu\delta_2$
$\hat{a}_i$	α_i	β_i	γ_i	$\alpha_i\delta_0 + \beta_i\delta_1 + \gamma_i\delta_2$
$\hat{l} \times \hat{a}_i$	0	$-\gamma_i$	β_i	$-\gamma_i\delta_1 + \beta_i\delta_2$
$\hat{u} \times \hat{a}_i$	γ_i	0	$-\alpha_i$	$\gamma_i\delta_0 - \alpha_i\delta_2$
$(\tau_0\ell\hat{l} + \tau_1\mu\hat{u} + n\hat{d}) \times \hat{a}_i$	$-n\beta_i + \tau_1\mu\gamma_i$	$n\alpha_i - \tau_0\ell\gamma_i$	$\tau_0\ell\beta_i - \tau_1\mu\alpha_i$	$[-n\beta_i + \tau_1\mu\gamma_i]\delta_0 + [n\alpha_i - \tau_0\ell\gamma_i]\delta_1 + [\tau_0\ell\beta_i - \tau_1\mu\alpha_i]\delta_2$

The box and frustum do not intersect if for some choice of $\vec{m}$ the two projection intervals $[m_0, m_1]$ and $[d - R, d + R]$ do not intersect. The intervals do not intersect if $d + R < m_0$ or $d - R > m_1$. An unoptimized implementation will compute d, R, m_0, and m_1 for each of the 26 cases and test the two inequalities. However, an optimized implementation will save intermediate results during each test and use them for later tests.

Caching Intermediate Results

Effectively the potential separating axis directions will all be manipulated in the coordinate system of the frustum. That is, each direction is written as $\vec{m} = x_0\hat{l} + x_1\hat{u} + x_2\hat{d}$, and the coefficients are used in the various tests. The difference $C - E$ must also be represented in the frustum coordinates, say, $C - E = \delta_0\hat{l} + \delta_1\hat{u} + \delta_2\hat{d}$. The coefficients are given in Table 11.5, where $0 \le i \le 2$ and $|\tau_j| = 1$ for $0 \le j \le 1$.

The quantities α_i, β_i, γ_i, and δ_i are computed only when needed to avoid unnecessary calculations. Some products are computed only when needed and saved for later use. These include products of n, ℓ, or μ with α_i, β_i, γ_i, or δ_i. Some terms that include sums or differences of the products are also computed only when needed and saved for later use. These include $n\alpha_i \pm \ell\gamma_i$, $n\beta_i \pm \mu\gamma_i$, $\ell\alpha_i \pm \mu\beta_i$, and $\ell\beta_i \pm \mu\alpha_i$.

11.12.2   LINEAR COMPONENT AND AXIS-ALIGNED BOUNDING BOX

An axis-aligned bounding box (AABB) is simply a rectangular parallelepiped whose faces are each perpendicular to one of the basis vectors. Such bounding boxes arise frequently in spatial subdivision problems, such as in ray tracing or collision de-

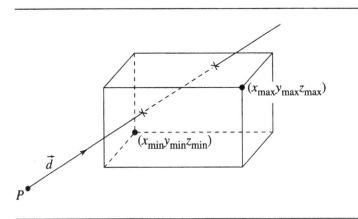

Figure 11.61   Intersection of a linear component with an axis-aligned bounding box.

tection. One common way to specify such a box is to provide two points $P_{min} = [\,x_{min}\quad y_{min}\quad z_{min}\,]$ and $P_{max} = [\,x_{max}\quad y_{max}\quad z_{max}\,]$, as shown in Figure 11.61.

This section considers the problem of finding the intersection of a linear component and an AABB. You might consider that a bounding box consists of six rectangular faces, and simply intersect the linear component with each rectangle. You might, in such an algorithm, exploit the fact that the rectangles' edges are all parallel to a basis vector, for the purpose of making the algorithm a bit more efficient.

An algorithm known as the "slabs method," originated by Kay and Kajiya (1986) and adapted by Haines (1989), can do a bit better, particularly if the linear component is a ray, which is the most likely use (as in ray tracing and picking algorithms). The basic idea is that intersection testing/calculation can be viewed as a clipping problem; the method is called the "slabs" method because you can think of the AABB as consisting of the intersection of three mutually perpendicular slabs of material, whose boundaries are defined by each pair of opposing faces (see Figure 11.62).

The basic clipping idea is illustrated in Figure 11.63, in which the ray $P + t\hat{d}$ is clipped against the YZ planes at x_{min} and x_{max}. We can see that the points of intersection, at parameter values t_0 and t_1, are calculated as

$$t_{0,x} = \frac{x_{min} - P_x}{d_x} \tag{11.41}$$

$$t_{1,x} = \frac{x_{max} - P_x}{d_x} \tag{11.42}$$

Note that if the ray originated on the other side of the slab and intersected it, then the nearest intersection would be t_1 instead of t_0.

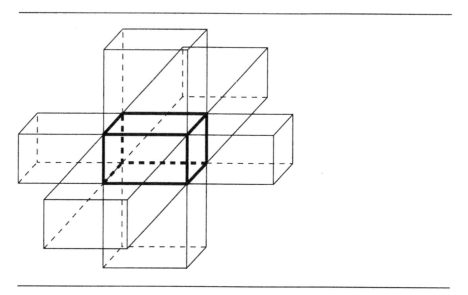

Figure 11.62   Axis-aligned box as the intersection of three "slabs."

The pseudocode for the algorithm is

```
boolean RayIntersectAABB(Point P, Vector d, AABB box, float& tIntersect)
{
    tNear = -INFINITY;
    tFar  =  INFINITY;

    foreach pair of planes {(XY_min, XY_max), (XZ_min, YZ_max), (YZ_min, YZ_max)} {
        // Example shown for YZ planes
        // Check for ray parallel to planes
        if (abs(d.x) < epsilon) {
            // Ray parallel to planes
            if (P.x < box.xMin || P.x > box.xMax) {
                return false;
            }
        }

        // Ray not parallel to planes, so find parameters of intersections
        t0 = (box.xMin - P.x) / d.x;
        t1 = (box.xMax - P.x) / d.x;

        // Check ordering
        if (t0 > t1) {
```

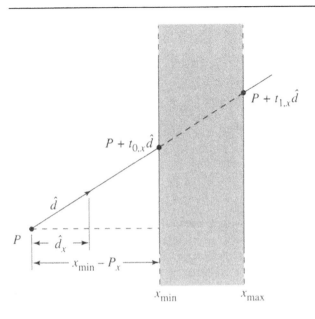

Figure 11.63   Clipping a line against a slab.

```
    // Swap them
    tmp = t1;
    t1 = t0;
    t0 = tmp;
}

// Compare with current values
if (t0 > tNear) {
    tNear = t0;
}
if (t1 < tFar) {
    tFar = t1;
}

// Check if ray misses entirely
if (tNear > tFar) {
    return false;
}
if (tFar < 0) {
    return false;
```

```
      }
   }

   // Box definitely intersected
   if (tNear > 0) {
      tIntersect = tNear;
   } else {
      tIntersect = tFar;
   }

   return true;
}
```

The reason this simple method works may not be readily apparent from the code, but should be apparent from Figure 11.64. The lower ray intersects the box because $t_{near} = t_{0,x} < t_{far} = t_{1,y}$ and $t_{near} > 0$. The upper ray misses because $t_{near} = t_{0,x} > t_{far} = t_{1,y}$.

11.12.3   LINEAR COMPONENT AND ORIENTED BOUNDING BOX

An oriented bounding box is simply a bounding parallelepiped whose faces and edges are not parallel to the basis vectors of the frame in which they're defined. One popular way to define them is to specify a (center) point C and orthonormal set of basis vectors $\{\hat{u}, \hat{v}, \hat{w}\}$, which determines location and orientation, and three scalars representing the half-width, half-height, and half-depth, as shown in Figure 11.65. Note that an AABB can be defined using exactly this scheme by choosing the box's basis vectors to be exactly those of the space the box is defined; however, AABBs are frequently computed by simply finding the maximum x, y, and z values of the geometric primitives they bound, making the AABB definition used in the previous section a bit more direct.

As an OBB is basically an AABB with a different orientation, you would expect that the same basic algorithm can be used for computing intersections, and that indeed is the case. Möller and Haines (1999) describe a version of the algorithm of the previous section that works for OBBs.

The distance calculation for oriented clipping is exactly analogous to that for slab clipping (see Equation 11.41):

$$t_{0,u} = \frac{\hat{u} \cdot (C - P) - h_u}{\hat{u} \cdot \hat{d}}$$

$$t_{1,u} = \frac{\hat{u} \cdot (C - P) + h_u}{\hat{u} \cdot \hat{d}}$$

as illustrated in Figure 11.66.

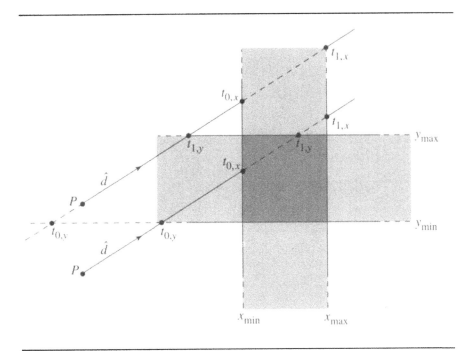

Figure 11.64   How slab clipping correctly computes ray-AABB intersection.

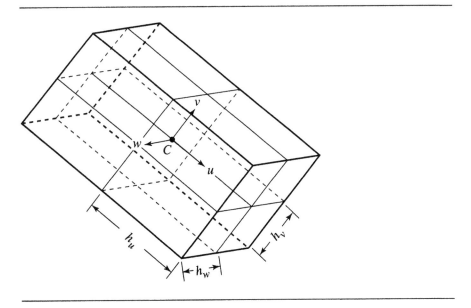

Figure 11.65   Specifying an oriented bounding box.

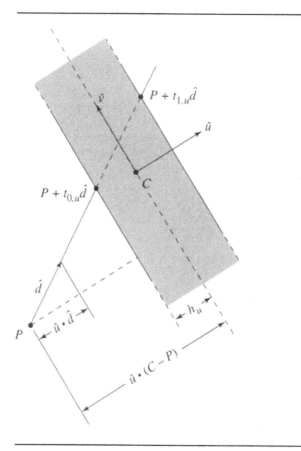

Figure 11.66   Clipping against an "oriented slab."

In the case of ray intersections, in most applications (ray tracing or interactive picking, for example) only the closest intersection is required; if both (potential) intersections are required, the following pseudocode can be modified to return both tNear and tFar:

```
boolean RayIntersectOBB(Point P, Vector d, OBB box, float& tIntersect)
{
    tNear = -INFINITY;
    tFar  =  INFINITY;

    foreach (i in {u, v, w}) {
        // Check for ray parallel to planes
```

```
    if (Abs(Dot(d, box.axis[i] < epsilon) {
        // Ray parallel to planes
        r = Dot(box.axis[i], box.C - P);
        if (-r - box.halfLength[i] > 0 || -r + box.halfLength[i] > 0) {
            // No intersection
            return false;
        }
    }

    r = Dot(box.axis[i], box.C - P);
    s = Dot(box.axis[i], d);

    // Ray not parallel to planes, so find parameters of intersections
    t0 = (r + box.halfLength[i]) / s;
    t1 = (r - box.halfLength[i]) / s;

    // Check ordering
    if (t0 > t1) {
        // Swap them
        tmp = t0;
        t0 = t1;
        t1 = tmp;
    }

    // Compare with current values
    if (t0 > tNear) {
        tNear = t0;
    }
    if (t1 < tFar) {
        tFar = t1;
    }

    // Check if ray misses entirely
    if (tNear > tFar) {
        return false;
    }
    if (tFar < 0) {
        return false;
    }
}

// Box definitely intersected
if (tNear > 0) {
```

```
                tIntersect = tNear;
        } else {
                tIntersect = tFar;
        }


        return true;
}
```

11.12.4   PLANE AND AXIS-ALIGNED BOUNDING BOX

This section discusses the problem of intersecting a plane and an axis-aligned bounding box. Unlike other intersection solutions we present, here we only *detect* whether an intersection has occurred. The reason is that AABBs are not geometric primitives in themselves, but rather are used to bound other primitives, generally in the context of quick rejection algorithms (as for rendering or collision detection): if no plane-AABB intersection exists, we needn't check the bounded primitive(s); if a plane-AABB intersection *does* exist, then we go on to find the true intersection between the bounded primitive(s) and the plane.

The simplest approach to the plane-AABB intersection problem is to simply note that an intersection exists if and only if there are corners of the AABB on either side of the plane. Note, however, that we may have to check *every* corner; this inefficiency may not seem so bad (checking which side of a plane a point is on is not extremely expensive), unless you consider that in a typical usage a huge number of AABBs may need to be checked for intersection.

In this problem, we define the AABB in the usual fashion, by a pair of points

$$P_{\min} = [\, x_{\min} \quad y_{\min} \quad z_{\min} \,]$$

$$P_{\max} = [\, x_{\max} \quad y_{\max} \quad z_{\max} \,]$$

and a plane in the coordinate-free version of the implicit form (see Section 9.2.1):

$$\vec{n} \cdot (P - P_0) = 0.$$

Figure 11.67 shows the intersection of a plane and an AABB.

Möller and Haines (1999) make the following observation: if we consider the diagonals of the AABB, the one aligned most closely with the plane normal will have at its end points the only pair of points that need be tested. This is a bit easier to see in a 2D version, as shown in Figure 11.68. Another optimization can be employed: once the most-aligned diagonal is found, if the minimal point is on the positive side of the plane, we can immediately conclude that the plane doesn't intersect the box because the maximal point will be on the positive side of the plane as well.

The pseudocode is

```
boolean PlaneIntersectAABB(Plane plane, AABB box)
{
    // Find points at end of diagonal
    // nearest plane normal
    foreach (dir in (x, y, z)) {
        if (plane.normal[dir] >= 0) {
            dMin[dir] = box.min[dir];
            dMax[dir] = box.max[dir];
        } else {
            dMin[dir] = box.max[dir];
            dMax[dir] = box.min[dir];
        }
    }

    // Check if minimal point on diagonal
    // is on positive side of plane
    if (Dot(plane.normal, dMin) + plane.d) >= 0) {
        return false;
    } else {
        return true;
    }
}
```

11.12.5 PLANE AND ORIENTED BOUNDING BOX

Here, we consider the problem of finding whether or not a plane and an oriented bounding box intersect, again stopping short of computing the actual intersection for the reasons previously given. Figure 11.69 illustrates this problem.

Möller and Haines (1999) suggest that because an OBB is simply an AABB in a transformed frame, we can simply transform the plane normal $\hat{n}$ into the frame defined by the OBB's center and basis vectors, and apply the same algorithm we used on the AABB. The transformed normal vector is

$$\hat{n}' = [\,\hat{u} \cdot \hat{n} \quad \hat{v} \cdot \hat{n} \quad \hat{w} \cdot \hat{n}\,]$$

This transformed normal can then be used in the plane-AABB intersection algorithm, which otherwise remains as is. However, recall that the AABB is defined by a pair of points, while the OBB is defined by a position, orientation frame, and half-width, half-height, and half-depth. Thus, to use the AABB algorithm, we'd have to find the minimal and maximal points of the OBB, in the frame defined by the OBB center and basis vectors, and *then* apply the AABB algorithm.

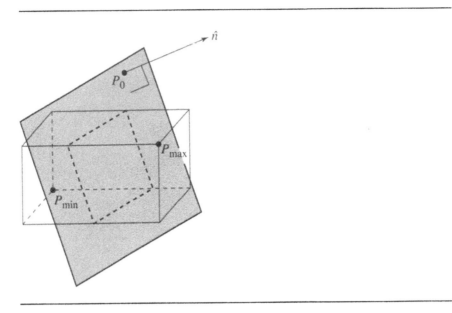

Figure 11.67   Intersection of a plane and an axis-aligned bounding box.

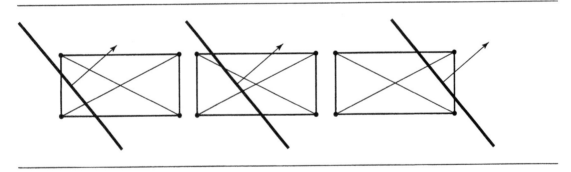

Figure 11.68   We only need to check the corners at the end of the diagonal most closely aligned with the normal to the plane.

Another method cited by Möller and Haines (1999) may be preferable. We project the diagonals of the OBB onto the plane normal, and then if the plane and either of the projected diagonals intersect, then the box and plane intersect. The trick employed is to not implement this literally, as this would not necessarily be as efficient as possible. Rather, consider Figure 11.70: We can't simply project the scaled basis vectors onto the plane normal; instead, we take the projected length of each scaled basis

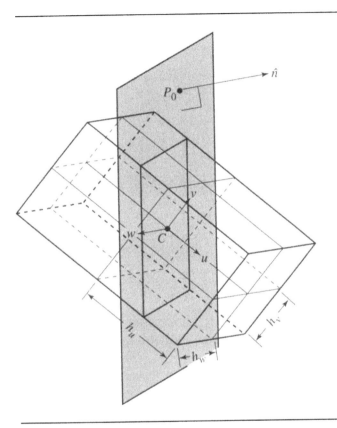

Figure 11.69   The intersection of a plane and an oriented bounding box.

vector, and sum them. This gives us the half-length of the longest projected diagonal:

$$d = \|h_u \hat{u} \cdot \hat{n}\| + \|h_v \hat{v} \cdot \hat{n}\|$$

Clearly, if the (unsigned) distance between C and the plane $\mathcal{P}$ is less than d, then the box and the plane do indeed intersect, and they do not otherwise. Of course, the comparison can be done with the squares of these values, saving a square root in the calculations.

11.12.6 AXIS-ALIGNED BOUNDING BOXES

The intersection of two axis-aligned bounding boxes is made relatively simple by the fact that the faces are perpendicular to their frame's basis vectors. Figure 11.71 shows

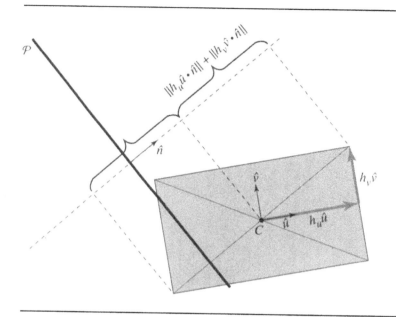

Figure 11.70   Projecting the diagonal of an OBB onto the plane normal.

two intersecting AABBs. The trick here is to create a test for *nonoverlapping* AABBs for each basis vector direction: if the AABBs fail to overlap in any direction, then they must not intersect at all; if the AABBs overlap in all directions, then they must intersect.

The pseudocode is

```
boolean AABBIntersectAABB(AABB a, AABB b)
{
    // Check if AABBs fail to overlap in any direction
    foreach (dir in {x, y, z}) {
        if (a.min[dir] > b.max[dir] || b.min[dir] > a.max[dir]) {
            return false;
        }
    }

    // AABBs overlapped in all directions, so they intersect
    return true;
}
```

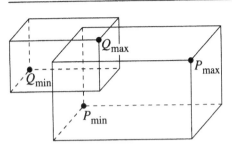

Figure 11.71   Intersection of two axis-aligned bounding boxes.

11.12.7 ORIENTED BOUNDING BOXES

In this section we discuss the problem of detecting the intersection of oriented bounding boxes. An OBB is defined in Section 11.12.3 by a centerpoint C, a right-handed orthonormal basis $\{\hat{u}, \hat{v}, \hat{w}\}$, and half-lengths $\{h_{\hat{u}}, h_{\hat{v}}, h_{\hat{w}}\}$. Because OBBs are used to bound other primitives for the purpose of speeding up intersection, picking, or (perhaps) rendering operations by culling out cases that definitely do not intersect, we only are concerned with finding out *if* there is an intersection; if the OBB's do intersect, then the primitives they bound may or may not, and we must then perform the object-specific tests on the bounded primitives.

The algorithm we present is due to Gottschalk, Lin, and Manocha (1996). The motivation is this: The naive approach would be to simply test every edge of each OBB against every face of the other, yielding 144 edge-face tests. Much more efficient is the use of the separating axis test, which is based on the following theorem: any two nonoverlapping polytopes can always be separated by a plane that is either parallel to a face of one of the polytopes or parallel to an edge of each. An illustration in 2D will help make this more clear; see Figure 11.72. The plane (line in 2D) that separates OBBs A and B is shown as a dotted line.

Each OBB has three face orientations and three edge directions. This gives us a total of 15 axes to test—3 faces from each of two boxes and 9 combinations of edges. If the OBBs don't overlap, then there will be at least one separating axis; if the OBBs do overlap, there will be none. Note that in general, if the OBBs are nonoverlapping, then a separating axis will be found (on average) in fewer than 15 tests.

The basic test is as follows:

1. Choose an axis to test.

2. Project the centers of the OBBs onto the axis.

3. Compute the radii of the intervals r_A and r_B.

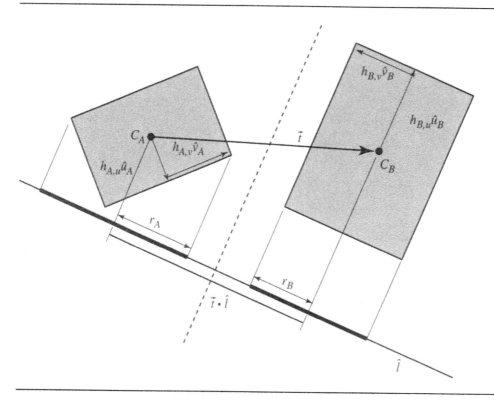

Figure 11.72 2D schematic for OBB intersection detection. After Gottschalk, Lin, and Manocha (1996).

4. If the sum of the radii is less than the distance between the projection of OBB centers C_A and C_B onto the chosen axis, then the intervals are nonoverlapping, and the OBBs are as well.

The "trick" employed here for efficiency is to treat the center C_A and orientation vectors $\{\hat{u}_A, \hat{v}_A, \hat{w}_A\}$ as an origin and basis, respectively, for a (coordinate) frame. Then, OBB B is considered in terms of a rotation and translation **T** relative to A; in this way, the three columns of **R** are just the three vectors $\{\hat{u}_B, \hat{v}_B, \hat{w}_B\}$.

The radii r_A and r_B of the projection can be obtained by scaling the bases of the OBBs by their associated half-dimensions, projecting each onto the separating axis, and summing:

$$r_A = \sum_{i \in \{u,v,w\}} h_{A,i} |a_{A,i} \cdot \hat{l}|$$

where $a_{A,i}$ is the axis of A associated with $\hat{u}$, $\hat{v}$, or $\hat{w}$, respectively, and similarly for r_B.

If we let $\vec{t} = C_B - C_A$, then the intervals are nonoverlapping if

$$|\vec{t} \cdot \hat{l}| > r_A + r_B$$

There are three basic cases to consider: when the axis to test is parallel to an edge of A, parallel to an edge of B, or a pairwise combination of an edge from each of A and B.

$\hat{l}$ Is Parallel to an Edge of A

This is the simplest case. Because we're using C_A and $\{\hat{u}_A, \hat{v}_A, \hat{w}_A,\}$ as a basis, the axes $\{\hat{a}_{A,u}, \hat{a}_{A,v}, \hat{a}_{A,w}\}$ are $[\,1 \quad 0 \quad 0\,]$, $[\,0 \quad 1 \quad 0\,]$, and $[\,0 \quad 0 \quad 1\,]$, respectively.

For example, if we're testing the axis parallel to $\hat{u}_A$, the projected distance between C_A and C_B is

$$|\vec{t} \cdot \hat{l}| = |\vec{t} \cdot a_{A,u}|$$

$$= |x_{\vec{t}}|$$

The projected radius of A is

$$r_A = \sum_{i \in \{u,v,w\}} h_{A,i} |a_{A,i} \cdot \hat{l}|$$

but since

$$\hat{l} = \hat{u}_A$$

we have

$$r_A = \sum_{i \in \{u,v,w\}} h_{A,i} |a_{A,i} \cdot a_{A,u}|$$

$$= h_{A,u}$$

The projected radius of B is

$$r_B = \sum_{i \in \{u,v,w\}} h_{B,i} |a_{B,i} \cdot \hat{l}|$$

but since

$$\hat{l} = \hat{u}_A$$

we have

$$r_B = \sum_{i \in \{u,v,w\}} h_{B,i} |a_{B,i} \cdot a_u|$$

$$= h_{B,u}|R_{00}| + h_{B,v}|R_{01}| + h_{B,w}|R_{02}|$$

The cases where $\hat{l} = \hat{v}_A$ and $\hat{l} = \hat{w}_A$ are analogous.

$\hat{l}$ Is Parallel to an Edge of B

This is almost as simple as the case where $\hat{l}$ is parallel to an edge of A. For example, if we're testing the axis parallel to $\hat{u}_B$, the projected distance between C_A and C_B is

$$|\vec{t} \cdot \hat{l}| = |\vec{t} \cdot a_{B,u}|$$

$$= |t_x R_{00} + t_y R_{10} + t_z R_{20}|$$

The projected radius of A is

$$r_A = \sum_{i \in \{u,v,w\}} h_{A,i} |a_{B,i} \cdot \hat{l}|$$

but since

$$\hat{l} = \hat{u}_B$$

we have

$$r_A = \sum_{i \in \{u,v,w\}} h_{A,i} |a_{A,i} \cdot a_{B,u}|$$

$$= h_{A,u}|R_{00}| + h_{A,v}|R_{10}| + h_{A,w}|R_{20}|$$

The projected radius of B is

$$r_B = \sum_{i \in \{u,v,w\}} h_{B,i} |a_{B,i} \cdot \hat{l}|$$

but since

$$\hat{l} = \hat{u}_B$$

we have

$$r_B = \sum_{i \in \{u,v,w\}} h_{B,i} |a_{B,i} \cdot a_u|$$

$$= h_{B,u}$$

The cases where $\hat{l} = \hat{v}_B$ and $\hat{l} = \hat{w}_B$ are analogous.

$\hat{l}$ Is a Combination of Edges from A and B

For testing axes that are combinations of edges from both OBBs, we use a vector that is the cross product of basis vectors of A and B.

For example, if we're testing the axis parallel to $\hat{u}_A \times \hat{v}_B$, the projected distance between C_A and C_B is

$$|\vec{t} \cdot \hat{l}| = |\vec{t} \cdot (a_{A,u} \times a_{B,v})|$$

$$= |\vec{t} \cdot [\, 0, -a_{B,v,z}, a_{B,v,y} \,]|$$

$$= |t_z \mathbf{R}_{11} - t_y \mathbf{R}_{21}|$$

The projected radius of A is

$$r_A = \sum_{i \in \{u,v,w\}} h_{A,i} |a_{A,i} \cdot \hat{l}|$$

but since

$$\hat{l} = (a_{A,u} \times a_{B,v})$$

we have

$$r_A = \sum_{i \in \{u,v,w\}} h_{A,i} |a_{A,i} \cdot (a_{A,u} \times a_{B,v})|$$

$$= \sum_{i \in \{u,v,w\}} h_{A,i} |a_{B,v} \cdot (a_{A,u} \times a_{A,i})|$$

$$= h_{A,v} |\mathbf{R}_{21}| + h_{A,w} |\mathbf{R}_{11}|$$

The projected radius of B is

$$r_B = \sum_{i \in \{u,v,w\}} h_{B,i} |a_{B,i} \cdot \hat{l}|$$

but since

$$\hat{l} = (a_{A,u} \times a_{B,v})$$

we have

$$r_B = \sum_{i \in \{u,v,w\}} h_{B,i} |a_{B,i} \cdot (a_{A,u} \times a_{B,v})|$$

$$= \sum_{i \in \{u,v,w\}} h_{B,i} |a_{A,v} \cdot (a_{B,i} \times a_{B,v})|$$

$$= h_{B,u} |\mathbf{R}_{02}| + h_{B,w} |\mathbf{R}_{00}|$$

11.12.8 SPHERE AND AXIS-ALIGNED BOUNDING BOX

In this section we address the problem of the intersection of an axis-aligned bounding box and a sphere. The AABB is defined by the two opposing corners with the least and greatest component values

$$P_{\min} = [\, x_{\min} \quad y_{\min} \quad z_{\min} \,]$$

$$P_{\max} = [\, x_{\max} \quad y_{\max} \quad z_{\max} \,]$$

while the sphere is simply defined by its center C and radius r, as shown in Figure 11.73.

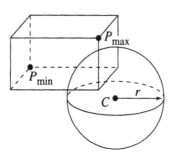

Figure 11.73   Intersection of an axis-aligned bounding box and a sphere.

An algorithm due to Arvo (1990) describes a rather clever way of determining whether or not a sphere intersects an AABB. The basic idea is to find the point on (or in) the AABB that is closest to the center of the sphere: if its squared distance is less than the sphere's squared radius, they intersect; otherwise, they do not. The clever aspect is the efficient way in which Arvo found to find this closest point. The closest point Q on (or in) the AABB minimizes the squared-distance function

$$\text{dist}^2(Q) = (C_x - Q_x)^2 + (C_y - Q_y)^2 + (C_z - Q_z)^2$$

subject to

$$P_{\min,x} \leq Q_x \leq Q_x$$

$$P_{\min,y} \leq Q_y \leq Q_y$$

$$P_{\min,z} \leq Q_z \leq Q_z$$

Arvo notes that we can find the minimum-distance point's components independently, which then can be combined to find the point itself.

The pseudocode is

```
boolean AABBIntersectSphere(AABB box, Sphere sphere)
{
    // Initial distance is 0
    float distSquared = 0;

    // Compute distance in each direction,
    // summing as we go.
    foreach (dir in {x, y, z}) {
        if (sphere.center[dir] < box.min[dir]) {
            distSquared += Square((sphere.c[dir] - box.min[dir]));
        } else if (sphere.center[dir] > box.max[dir]) {
            distSquared += Square((sphere.c[dir] - box.max[dir]));
        }
    }

    // Compare distance to radius squared
    if (distSquared <= sphere.radius * sphere.radius) {
        return true;
    } else {
        return false;
    }
}
```

Arvo also provides a version that handles "hollow" primitives, in which complete containment of one within the other means "no intersection," and a version that generalizes the above algorithm to ellipsoids (however, it should be noted that this only works for ellipsoids whose axes are parallel to its defining frame's basis vectors).

11.12.9 CYLINDERS

This section shows how to determine if two bounded cylinders intersect. The algorithm uses the method of separating axes as discussed in Section 11.11, although the construction is more complicated than what we encounter when separating convex polyhedra since the bounded cylinders are not polyhedra. The resulting algorithm is a fairly expensive one if you plan on using cylinders for bounding volumes in a real-time graphics engine. A better alternative to a cylinder is a *capsule*, the set of points a specified distance from a line segment. Two capsules intersect if and only if the distance between capsule line segments is smaller or equal to the sum of the capsule radii, a much cheaper test to perform.

In addition to using the method of separating axes that relies on projecting onto lines, the algorithm also requires separation by projection onto planes. The concept is similar to separating axes. If there exists a plane for which the regions of projection of the two convex objects onto that plane do not intersect, then the objects do not intersect. Just as with lines, it is sufficient to consider planes that contain the origin. Given a plane containing the origin and with unit-length normal $\hat{n}$, the projection of a convex set C onto the line is the set of points

$$R = \{Y : Y = X - (\hat{n} \cdot X)\hat{n} = (\mathbf{I} - \hat{n}\hat{n}^\mathsf{T})X, \quad X \in C\}$$

where $\mathbf{I}$ is the 3×3 identity matrix. The projection set is itself a convex set. Two convex sets C_0 and C_1 are separated if there exists a normal $\hat{n}$ such that the projection sets R_0 and R_1 do not intersect, $R_0 \cap R_1 = \emptyset$. The determination of this condition can involve one of many geometric methods, for example, by showing that the distance between the two sets is positive. It might be possible to analyze the projections in native 2D and attempt to find a separating line in 2D, but such a construction should work as well in 3D.

Representation of a Cylinder

A cylinder has a centerpoint C, unit-length axis direction $\hat{w}$, radius r, and height h. The end disks of the cylinder are located at $C \pm (h/2)\hat{w}$. Let $\hat{u}$ and $\hat{v}$ be any unit-length vectors so that $\{\hat{u}, \hat{v}, \hat{w}\}$ is a right-handed set of orthonormal vectors. That is, the vectors are unit length, mutually orthogonal, and $\hat{w} = \hat{u} \times \hat{v}$. Points on the cylinder surface are parameterized by

$$X(\theta, t) = C + (r \cos \theta)\hat{u} + (r \sin \theta)\hat{v} + t\hat{w}, \quad \theta \in [0, 2\pi), \ |t| \le h/2$$

The end disks are parameterized by

$$X(\theta, \rho) = C + (\rho \cos \theta)\hat{u} + (\rho \sin \theta)\hat{v} \pm (h/2)\hat{w}, \quad \theta \in [0, 2\pi), \ \rho \in [0, r]$$

The projections of a cylinder onto a line or plane are determined solely by the cylinder wall, not the end disks, so the second parameterization is not relevant for intersection testing.

The choice of $\hat{u}$ and $\hat{v}$ is arbitrary. Intersection queries between cylinders should be independent of this choice, but some of the algorithms are better handled if a choice is made. A quadratic equation that represents the cylinder wall is $(X - C)^{\mathrm{T}}(I - \hat{w}\hat{w}^{\mathrm{T}})(X - C) = r^2$. The boundedness of the cylinder is specified by $|\hat{w} \cdot (X - C)| \le h/2$. This representation is dependent only on C, $\hat{w}$, r, and h.

Projection of a Cylinder onto a Line

Let the line be $s\vec{d}$, where $\vec{d}$ is a nonzero vector. The projection of a cylinder point onto the line is

$$\lambda(\theta, t) = \vec{d} \cdot X(\theta, t) = \vec{d} \cdot C + (r \cos \theta)\vec{d} \cdot \hat{u} + (r \sin \theta)\vec{d} \cdot \hat{v} + t\vec{d} \cdot \hat{w}.$$

The interval of projection has end points determined by the extreme values of this expression. The maximum value occurs when all three terms involving the parameters are made as large as possible. The t-term has a maximum of $(h/2)|\vec{d} \cdot \hat{w}|$. The θ-terms, not including the radius, can be viewed as a dot product $(\cos \theta, \sin \theta) \cdot (\vec{d} \cdot \hat{u}, \vec{d} \cdot \hat{v})$. This is maximum when $(\cos \theta, \sin \theta)$ is in the same direction as $(\vec{d} \cdot \hat{u}, \vec{d} \cdot \hat{v})$. Therefore,

$$(\cos \theta, \sin \theta) = \frac{(\vec{d} \cdot \hat{u}, \vec{d} \cdot \hat{v})}{\sqrt{(\vec{d} \cdot \hat{u})^2 + (\vec{d} \cdot \hat{v})^2}}$$

and the maximum projection value is

$$\lambda_{\max} = \vec{d} \cdot C + r\sqrt{\|\vec{d}\|^2 - (\vec{d} \cdot \hat{w})^2} + (h/2)|\vec{d} \cdot \hat{w}|$$

where we have used the fact that $\vec{d} = (\vec{d} \cdot \hat{u})\hat{u} + (\vec{d} \cdot \hat{v})\hat{v} + (\vec{d} \cdot \hat{w})\hat{w}$, which implies $(\vec{d} \cdot \hat{u})^2 + (\vec{d} \cdot \hat{v})^2 + (\vec{d} \cdot \hat{w})^2 = \|\vec{d}\|^2$. The minimum projection value is similarly derived:

$$\lambda_{\min} = \vec{d} \cdot C - r\sqrt{\|\vec{d}\|^2 - (\vec{d} \cdot \hat{w})^2} - (h/2)|\vec{d} \cdot \hat{w}|$$

Projection of a Cylinder onto a Plane

Let the plane be $\hat{n} \cdot X = 0$, where $\hat{n}$ is a unit-length normal. The projection of a cylinder onto a plane has one of three geometric configurations:

1. A disk when $\hat{w}$ is parallel to $\hat{n}$
2. A rectangle when $\hat{w}$ is perpendicular to $\hat{n}$
3. A rectangle with hemielliptical caps

The projection matrix is $\mathbf{P} = \mathbf{I} - \hat{n}\hat{n}^{\mathrm{T}}$. In the first case, the center of the disk is $\mathbf{P}C$ and the radius is r. In the second case, the rectangle has center $\mathbf{P}C$ and has unit-length axis directions $\hat{w}$ and $\hat{w} \times \hat{n}$. The four corners of the rectangle are $\mathbf{P}C \pm r\hat{w} \times \hat{n} \pm (h/2)\hat{w}$.

The third case is only slightly more complicated. The centerpoint of the projection region is $\mathbf{P}C$. The axis of the projection region has non-unit-length direction $\mathbf{P}\hat{w}$. An axis of the cylinder that is in the plane and perpendicular to $\hat{n}$ has direction $\hat{u} = (\mathbf{P}\hat{w}) \times \hat{n}/\|(\mathbf{P}\hat{w}) \times \hat{n}\|$. The four points on the cylinder that map to the four corners of the rectangular portion of the projection are $C \pm r\hat{u} \pm (h/2)\hat{w}$. The four corners are $\mathbf{P}C \pm r\hat{u} \pm (h/2)\mathbf{P}\hat{w}$.

Let $\hat{v} = \hat{w} \times \hat{u}$. The end circles of the cylinder are $X(\theta) = C \pm r((\cos\theta)\hat{u} + (\sin\theta)\hat{v}) \pm (h/2)\hat{w}$. Let $Y = \mathbf{P}(X - C \pm (h/2)\hat{w})$; then $Y = r((\cos\theta)\hat{u} + (\sin\theta)\mathbf{P}\hat{v})$. Therefore, $\hat{u} \cdot Y = r\cos\theta$ and $\mathbf{P}\hat{v} \cdot Y = \|\mathbf{P}\hat{v}\|^2 r \sin\theta$. Combining these yields

$$1 = \frac{1}{r^2}\left((\hat{u} \cdot Y)^2 + \frac{1}{\|\mathbf{P}\hat{v}\|^4}(\mathbf{P}\hat{v} \cdot Y)^2\right)$$

$$= \frac{1}{r^2}Y^{\mathrm{T}}\left(\hat{u}\hat{u}^{\mathrm{T}} + \frac{1}{\|\mathbf{P}\hat{v}\|^2}\frac{\mathbf{P}\hat{v}}{\|\mathbf{P}\hat{v}\|}\frac{\mathbf{P}\hat{v}}{\|\mathbf{P}\hat{v}\|}^{\mathrm{T}}\right)Y$$

$$= (\mathbf{P}(X - C \pm (h/2)\hat{w}))^{\mathrm{T}}\left(\frac{1}{r^2}\hat{u}\hat{u}^{\mathrm{T}} + \frac{1}{r^2\|\mathbf{P}\hat{v}\|^2}\frac{\mathbf{P}\hat{v}}{\|\mathbf{P}\hat{v}\|}\frac{\mathbf{P}\hat{v}}{\|\mathbf{P}\hat{v}\|}^{\mathrm{T}}\right)(\mathbf{P}(X - C \pm (h/2)\hat{w}))$$

This is the equation for two ellipses with centers at $\mathbf{P}(C \pm (h/2)\hat{w})$, axes $\hat{u}$ and $\mathbf{P}\hat{v}/\|\mathbf{P}\hat{v}\|$, and axis half-lengths r and $r\|\mathbf{P}\hat{v}\|$.

Separating Line Tests for Two Cylinders

Given two cylinders with centers C_i, axis directions $\hat{w}_i$, radii r_i, and heights h_i, for $i = 0, 1$, the cylinders are separated if there exists a nonzero direction $\vec{d}$ such that either

$$\vec{d} \cdot C_0 - r_0\sqrt{\|\vec{d}\|^2 - (\vec{d} \cdot \hat{w}_0)^2} - (h_0/2)|\vec{d} \cdot \hat{w}_0| > \vec{d} \cdot C_1 + r_1\sqrt{\|\vec{d}\|^2 - (\vec{d} \cdot \hat{w}_1)^2} + (h_1/2)|\vec{d} \cdot \hat{w}_1|$$

or

$$\vec{d} \cdot C_0 + r_0 \sqrt{\|\vec{d}\|^2 - (\vec{d} \cdot \hat{w}_0)^2} + (h_0/2)|\vec{d} \cdot \hat{w}_0| < \vec{d} \cdot C_1 - r_1 \sqrt{\|\vec{d}\|^2 - (\vec{d} \cdot \hat{w}_1)^2} - (h_1/2)|\vec{d} \cdot \hat{w}_1|$$

Defining $\vec{\Delta} = C_1 - C_0$, these tests can be rewritten as a single expression, $f(\vec{d}) < 0$, where

$$f(\vec{d}) = r_0 \|\mathbf{P}_0 \vec{d}\| + r_1 \|\mathbf{P}_1 \vec{d}\| + (h_0/2)|\vec{d} \cdot \hat{w}_0| + (h_1/2)|\vec{d} \cdot \hat{w}_1| - |\vec{d} \cdot \vec{\Delta}|$$

and where $\mathbf{P}_i = \mathbf{I} - \hat{w}_i \hat{w}_i^{\mathrm{T}}$ for $i = 0, 1$.

If $\vec{\Delta} = 0$, then $f \geq 0$. This is geometrically obvious since two cylinders with the same center already intersect. The remainder of the discussion assumes $\vec{\Delta} \neq \vec{0}$. If $\vec{d}$ is perpendicular to $\vec{\Delta}$, then $f(\vec{d}) \geq 0$. This shows that any line perpendicular to the line containing the two cylinder centers can never be a separating axis. This is also clear geometrically. The line of sight $C_0 + s\vec{\Delta}$ intersects both cylinders at their centers. If you project the two cylinders onto the plane $\vec{\Delta} \cdot (X - C_0) = 0$, both regions of projection overlap. No matter which line you choose containing C_0 in this plane, the line intersects both projection regions.

If $\vec{d}$ is a separating direction, then $f(\vec{d}) < 0$. Observe that $f(t\vec{d}) = |t| f(\vec{d})$, so $f(t\vec{d}) < 0$ for any t. This is consistent with the geometry of the problem. Any nonzero multiple of a separating direction must itself be a separating direction. This allows us to restrict our attention to the unit sphere, $|\vec{d}| = 1$. Function f is continuous on the unit sphere, a compact set, so f must attain its minimum at some point on the sphere. This is a minimization problem in two dimensions, but the spherical geometry complicates the analysis somewhat. Different restrictions on the set of potential separating directions can be made that yield minimization problems in a line or a plane rather than on a sphere.

The analysis of f involves computing its derivatives, $\vec{\nabla}(f)$, and determining its critical points. These are points for which $\vec{\nabla}(f)$ is zero or undefined. The latter category is easy to specify. The gradient is undefined when any of the terms inside the five absolute value signs is zero. Thus, $\vec{\nabla}(f)$ is undefined at $\hat{w}_0$, $\hat{w}_1$, at vectors that are perpendicular to $\hat{w}_0$, at vectors that are perpendicular to $\hat{w}_1$, and at vectors that are perpendicular to $\vec{\Delta}$. We already argued that $f \geq 0$ for vectors perpendicular to $\vec{\Delta}$, so we can ignore this case.

Tests at $\hat{w}_0$, $\hat{w}_1$, and $\hat{w}_0 \times \hat{w}_1$

The cylinder axis directions themselves can be tested first for separation. The test function values are

$$f(\hat{w}_0) = r_1 \|\hat{w}_0 \times \hat{w}_1\| + (h_0/2) + (h_1/2)|\hat{w}_0 \cdot \hat{w}_1| - |\hat{w}_0 \cdot \vec{\Delta}|$$

and

$$f(\hat{w}_1) = r_0 \|\hat{w}_0 \times \hat{w}_1\| + (h_0/2)|\hat{w}_0 \cdot \hat{w}_1| + (h_1/2) - |\hat{w}_1 \cdot \vec{\Delta}|$$

If either function value is negative, the cylinders are separated. The square roots can be avoided. For example, the test $f(\hat{w}_0) < 0$ is equivalent to

$$r_1 \|\hat{w}_0 \times \hat{w}_1\| < |\hat{w}_0 \cdot \vec{\Delta}| - h_0/2 - (h_1/2)|\hat{w}_0 \cdot \hat{w}_1| =: \rho$$

The right-hand side is evaluated. If $\rho \leq 0$, then the inequality cannot be true since $\hat{w}_0 \times \hat{w}_1 \neq \vec{0}$ and the left-hand side is positive. Otherwise, $\rho > 0$ and it is now enough to test $r_1 \|\hat{w}_0 \times \hat{w}_1\|^2 < \rho^2$. A similar construction applies to $f(\hat{w}_1) < 0$.

One last test that does not require many more operations and might lead to a quick no-intersection test is

$$f(\hat{w}_0 \times \hat{w}_1) = (r_0 + r_1)\|\hat{w}_0 \times \hat{w}_1\| - |\hat{w}_0 \times \hat{w}_1 \cdot \vec{\Delta}| < 0$$

or equivalently

$$(r_0 + r_1)^2 \|\hat{w}_0 \times \hat{w}_1\|^2 < |\hat{w}_0 \times \hat{w}_1 \cdot \vec{\Delta}|^2$$

assuming of course that $\hat{w}_0 \times \hat{w}_1 \neq \vec{0}$. This vector is actually one for which the gradient of f is undefined.

If $\hat{w}_0$ and $\hat{w}_1$ are parallel, then $\hat{w}_0 \times \hat{w}_1 = \vec{0}$ and $|\hat{w}_0 \cdot \hat{w}_1| = 1$. The identity

$$(\vec{a} \times \vec{b}) \cdot (\vec{c} \times \vec{d}) = (\vec{a} \cdot \vec{c})(\vec{b} \cdot \vec{d}) - (\vec{a} \cdot \vec{d})(\vec{b} \cdot \vec{c})$$

can be used to show that $\|\hat{w}_0 \times \hat{w}_1\|^2 = 1 - (\hat{w}_0 \cdot \hat{w}_1)^2$. The test function for $\hat{w}_0$ evaluates to

$$f(\hat{w}_0) = (h_0 + h_1)/2 - |\hat{w}_0 \cdot \vec{\Delta}|$$

The two cylinders are separated if $(h_0 + h_1)/2 < |\hat{w}_0 \cdot \vec{\Delta}|$. If $f(\hat{w}_0) \geq 0$, the two cylinders are potentially separated by a direction that is perpendicular to $\hat{w}_0$. Geometrically it is enough to determine whether or not the circles of projection of the cylinders onto the plane $\hat{w}_0 \cdot X = \vec{0}$ intersect. These circles are disjoint if and only if the length of the projection of $\vec{\Delta}$ onto that plane is larger than the sum of the radii of the circles. The projection of $\vec{\Delta}$ is $\vec{\Delta} - (\hat{w}_0 \cdot \vec{\Delta})\hat{w}_0$, and its squared length is

$$\|\vec{\Delta} - (\hat{w}_0 \cdot \vec{\Delta})\hat{w}_0\|^2 = \|\vec{\Delta}\|^2 - (\hat{w}_0 \cdot \vec{\Delta})^2$$

The sum of the radii of the circles is the sum of the radii of the cylinders, $r_0 + r_1$, so the two cylinders are separated if $\|\vec{\Delta}\|^2 - (\hat{w}_0 \cdot \vec{\Delta})^2 > (r_0 + r_1)^2$.

For the remainder of this section we assume that $\hat{w}_0$ and $\hat{w}_1$ are not parallel.

Tests at Vectors Perpendicular to $\hat{w}_0$ or $\hat{w}_1$

Considering the domain of f to be the unit sphere, the set of vectors perpendicular to $\hat{w}_0$ is a great circle on the sphere. The gradient of f is undefined on this great circle. Define $\vec{d}(\theta) = (\cos\theta)\hat{u}_0 + (\sin\theta)\vec{v}_0$ and $F(\theta) = f(\vec{d}(\theta))$. If we can show that $F(\theta) < 0$ for some $\theta \in [0, 2\pi)$, then the corresponding direction is a separating line for the cylinders. However, F is a somewhat complicated function that does not lend itself to a simple analysis. Since $f(-\vec{d}) = f(\vec{d})$, we may restrict our attention to only half of the great circle. Rather than restricting f to a half circle, we can restrict it to a tangent line $\vec{d}(x) = x\hat{u}_0 + \hat{v}_0$ and define $F(x) = f(\vec{d}(x))$, so

$$F(x) = r_0\sqrt{x^2 + 1} + r_1\|(\mathbf{P}_1\hat{u}_0)x + (\mathbf{P}_1\hat{v}_0)\| + (h_1/2)|(\hat{w}_1 \cdot \hat{u}_0)x$$

$$+ (\hat{w}_1 \cdot \hat{v}_0)| - |(\vec{\Delta} \cdot \hat{u}_0)x + (\vec{\Delta} \cdot \hat{v}_0)|$$

$$= r_0\sqrt{x^2 + 1} + r_1\|\vec{a}_0 x + \vec{b}_0\| + (h_1/2)\|\vec{a}_1 x + \vec{b}_1\| - \|\vec{a}_2 x + \vec{b}_2\|$$

This function is more readily analyzed by breaking it up into four cases by replacing the last two absolute values with sign indicators,

$$G(x) = r_0\sqrt{x^2 + 1} + r_1\|\vec{a}_0 x + \vec{b}_0\| + \sigma_1(h_1/2)(\vec{a}_1 x + \vec{b}_1) - \sigma_2(\vec{a}_2 x + \vec{b}_2)$$

with $|\sigma_1| = |\sigma_2| = 1$. The minimum of G is calculated for each choice of (σ_1, σ_2) by computing $G'(x)$ and determining where it is zero or undefined. Any critical point x must first be tested to see if it is consistent with the choice of signs. That is, a critical point must be tested to make sure $\sigma_1(a_1 x + b_1) \geq 0$ and $\sigma_2(a_2 x + b_2) \geq 0$. If so, then $G(x)$ is evaluated and compared to zero. The derivative is

$$G'(x) = r_0\frac{x}{\sqrt{x^2 + 1}} + r_1\vec{a}_0 \cdot \frac{\vec{a}_0 x + \vec{b}_0}{\|\vec{a}_0 x + \vec{b}_0\|} + (\sigma_1 h_1/2)\vec{a}_1 - \sigma_2\vec{b}_2$$

The derivative is undefined when $\|\vec{a}_0 x + \vec{b}_0\| = 0$, but this case is actually generated when the original direction is parallel to $\hat{w}_0 \times \hat{w}_1$, discussed earlier. To algebraically solve $G'(x) = 0$, a few squaring operations can be applied. Note that $G'(x) = 0$ is of the form

$$L_0\sqrt{Q_0} + L_1\sqrt{Q_1} = c\sqrt{Q_0 Q_1}$$

where L_i are linear in x, Q_i are quadratic in x, and c is a constant. Squaring and rearranging terms yields

$$2L_0 L_1\sqrt{Q_0 Q_1} = c^2 Q_0 Q_1 - L_0^2 Q_0 - L_1^2 Q_1$$

Squaring again and rearranging terms yields

$$4L_0^2L_1^2Q_0Q_1 - (c^2Q_0Q_1 - L_0^2Q_0 - L_1^2Q_1)^2 = 0$$

The left-hand side is a polynomial in x of degree 8. The roots can be computed by numerical methods, tested for validity as shown earlier, and then G can be tested for negativity.

Yet one more alternative is to notice that attempting to locate a separating direction that is perpendicular to $\hat{w}_0$ is equivalent to projecting the two cylinders onto the plane $\hat{w}_0 \cdot X = 0$ and determining if the projections are disjoint. The first cylinder projects to a disk. The second cylinder projects to a disk, a rectangle, or a rectangle with hemielliptical caps depending on the relationship of $\hat{w}_1$ to $\hat{w}_0$. Separation can be determined by showing that (1) the projection of C_0 is not inside the projection of the second cylinder and (2) the distance from C_0 to the projection of the second cylinder is larger than r_0. If the second projection is a disk, the distance is just the length of the projection of $\vec{\Delta}$. If the second projection is a rectangle, then the problem amounts to computing the distance between a point and a rectangle in the plane. This test is an inexpensive one. If the second projection is a rectangle with hemielliptical caps, then the problem amounts to computing the minimum of the distances between a point and a rectangle and two ellipses, then comparing it to r_0. Calculating the distance between a point and an ellipse in the plane requires finding roots of a polynomial of degree 4. This alternative trades off, in the worst case, finding the roots to a polynomial of degree 8 for finding the roots of two polynomials of degree 4.

Tests for Directions at Which $\vec{\nabla}(f) = \vec{0}$

The symmetry $f(-\vec{d}) = f(\vec{d})$ implies that we only need to analyze f on a hemisphere; the other hemisphere values are determined automatically. Since $f \geq 0$ on the great circle of vectors that are perpendicular to $\vec{\Delta}$, we can restrict our attention to the hemisphere whose pole is $\hat{w} = \vec{\Delta}/\|\vec{\Delta}\|$. Rather than project onto the hemisphere, we can project onto the tangent plane at the pole. The mapping is $\vec{d} = x\hat{u} + y\hat{v} + \hat{w}$, where $\hat{u}$, $\hat{v}$, and $\hat{w}$ form a right-handed orthonormal set. Defining the rotation matrix $\mathbf{R} = [\hat{u}|\hat{v}|\hat{w}]$ and $\vec{\xi} = (x, y, 1)$, the function f reduces to

$$F(x, y) = r_0\|\mathbf{P}_0\mathbf{R}\vec{\xi}\| + r_1\|\mathbf{P}_1\mathbf{R}\vec{\xi}\| + (h_0/2)|\hat{w}_0 \cdot \mathbf{R}\vec{\xi}| + (h_1/2)|\hat{w}_1 \cdot \mathbf{R}\vec{\xi}| - \|\vec{\Delta}\|$$

for $(x, y) \in \mathbb{R}^2$. To determine if $F(x, y) < 0$ for some (x, y), it is enough to show that the minimum of F is negative. The point at which the minimum is attained occurs when the gradient of F is zero or undefined. $\vec{\nabla}(F)$ is undefined at points for which any of the first four absolute value terms is zero. In terms of points $\vec{d}$ on the unit sphere, the first term is zero at $\hat{w}_0$, the second term is zero at $\hat{w}_1$, the third term is zero at any vector perpendicular to $\hat{w}_0$, and the fourth term is zero at any vector perpendicular to $\hat{w}_1$. After all such points have been tested only to find that $F \geq 0$, the next phase of the separation test is to compute solutions to $\vec{\nabla}(F) = \vec{0}$ and test if any of those force $F < 0$.

If $\vec{d}$ is a separating direction, then $f(\vec{d}) < 0$. Observe that $f(t\vec{d}) = |t| f(\vec{d})$, so $f(t\vec{d}) < 0$ for any t. This is consistent with the geometry of the problem. Any nonzero multiple of a separating direction must itself be a separating direction. This allows us to restrict our attention to the unit sphere, $|\vec{d}| = 1$. Function f is continuous on the unit sphere, a compact set, so f must attain its minimum at some point on the sphere. This is a minimization problem in two dimensions, but the spherical geometry complicates the analysis somewhat. A different restriction on the set of potential separating directions can be made that yields a two-dimensional minimization in the plane rather than a two-dimensional minimization on a sphere.

First, some notation. The function $f(\vec{d})$ can be written as

$$f(\vec{d}) = r_0 \|\mathbf{A}_0^{\mathrm{T}} \vec{d}\| + r_1 \|\mathbf{A}_1^{\mathrm{T}} \vec{d}\| + (h_0/2)|\vec{d} \cdot \hat{w}_0| + (h_1/2)|\vec{d} \cdot \hat{w}_1| - |\vec{d} \cdot \vec{\Delta}|$$

where the matrices $\mathbf{A}_i = [\hat{u}_i | \hat{v}_i]$ are 3×2. Observe that $\mathbf{A}_i^{\mathrm{T}} \mathbf{A}_i = \mathbf{I}_2$, the 2×2 identity, and $\mathbf{A}_i \mathbf{A}_i^{\mathrm{T}} = \mathbf{I}_3 - \hat{w}_i \hat{w}_i^{\mathrm{T}}$, where $\mathbf{I}_3$ is the 3×3 identity matrix.

The symmetry $f(-\vec{d}) = f(\vec{d})$ implies that we only need to analyze f on a hemisphere; the other hemisphere values are determined automatically. The complicating factor in directly analyzing f turns out to be the presence of the absolute value terms $|\vec{d} \cdot \hat{w}_0|$, $|\vec{d} \cdot \hat{w}_1|$, and $|\vec{d} \cdot \vec{\Delta}|$. Instead we will look at functions where the absolute values are removed. To illustrate, consider

$$g_0(\vec{d}) = r_0 \|\mathbf{A}_0^{\mathrm{T}} \vec{d}\| + r_1 \|\mathbf{A}_1^{\mathrm{T}} \vec{d}\| - \vec{d} \cdot \vec{\phi}$$

where $\vec{\phi} = \vec{\Delta} - (h_0/2)\hat{w}_0 - (h_1/2)\hat{w}_1$. If the analysis of g_0 produces a direction $\vec{d}$ for which $g_0(\vec{d}) < 0$ *and* if $\vec{d} \cdot \hat{w}_0 \geq 0$, $\vec{d} \cdot \hat{w}_1 \geq 0$, and $\vec{d} \cdot \vec{\Delta} \geq 0$, then $f(\vec{d}) < 0$ and we have a separating direction. However, the inequality constraints might not be satisfied, even when $g_0(\vec{d}) < 0$, in which case $\vec{d}$ is rejected as a candidate for separation. The *companion* function is

$$g_1(\vec{d}) = r_0 \|\mathbf{A}_0^{\mathrm{T}} \vec{d}\| + r_1 \|\mathbf{A}_1^{\mathrm{T}} \vec{d}\| + \vec{d} \cdot \vec{\phi}$$

If the analysis of g_1 produces a direction $\vec{d}$ for which $g_1(\vec{d}) < 0$ *and* if $\vec{d} \cdot \hat{w}_0 \leq 0$, $\vec{d} \cdot \hat{w}_1 \leq 0$, and $\vec{d} \cdot \vec{\Delta} \leq 0$, then $f(\vec{d}) < 0$ and we have a separating direction. However, the inequality constraints might not be satisfied, even when $g_1(\vec{d}) < 0$, in which case $\vec{d}$ is rejected as a candidate for separation. There are four such pairs of functions to consider, exhausting all eight sign possibilities on the three absolute value terms.

Let us now analyze $g_0(\vec{d})$. If $\vec{\phi} = \vec{0}$, then clearly $g_0(\vec{d}) \geq 0$ for all directions, so no separation can occur. For the remainder of the argument, assume $\vec{\phi} \neq \vec{0}$. Any direction $\vec{d}$ for which $\vec{d} \cdot \vec{\phi} \leq 0$ cannot be a separating direction. This allows us to restrict our attention to a hemisphere of directions whose pole is $\hat{w} = \vec{\phi}/\|\vec{\phi}\|$. Moreover, we can avoid working on the hemisphere by projecting those points radially outward onto the tangent plane at the pole. That is, we need only analyze g_0 for directions $\vec{d} = x\hat{u} + y\hat{v} + \hat{w}$, where $\{\hat{u}, \hat{v}, \hat{w}\}$ forms a right-handed orthonormal set of vectors. Defining the rotation matrix $\mathbf{R} = [\hat{u}|\hat{v}|\hat{w}]$ whose columns are the indicated vectors, the restriction of g_0 to the plane is $F(x, y) = g_0(\vec{d}) = g_0(\mathbf{R}\vec{\xi})$, where $\vec{\xi} = (x, y, 1)$, so

$$F(x, y) = r_0\|\mathbf{A}_0^\mathrm{T}\mathbf{R}\vec{\xi}\| + r_1\|\mathbf{A}_1^\mathrm{T}\mathbf{R}\vec{\xi}\| - \|\vec{\phi}\| \tag{11.43}$$

In order to determine if $F(x, y) < 0$ for some (x, y), we will determine the minimum of F and test if it is negative. The minimum must occur at critical points, those points where $\vec{\nabla}F$ is zero or undefined. Any critical points that do not satisfy the inequality constraints for g_0 are rejected since F can be viewed as the restriction of g_0 to a convex subset of the plane defined by the inequality constraints. We only need to compute the minimum of F on this convex subset, so critical points outside that convex set are irrelevant. Analysis of the corresponding $F(x, y)$ for the companion function g_1 uses the projection $\vec{d} = x\hat{u} + y\hat{v} - \hat{w}$.

Analysis of $F(x, y)$

Using $\partial\mathbf{R}\vec{\xi}/\partial x = \hat{u}$ and $\partial\mathbf{R}\vec{\xi}/\partial y = \hat{v}$, the partial derivatives of F are

$$\frac{\partial F}{\partial x} = \hat{u} \cdot \left(r_0\mathbf{A}_0\frac{\mathbf{A}_0^\mathrm{T}\mathbf{R}\vec{\xi}}{\|\mathbf{A}_0^\mathrm{T}\mathbf{R}\vec{\xi}\|} + r_1\mathbf{A}_1\frac{\mathbf{A}_1^\mathrm{T}\mathbf{R}\vec{\xi}}{\|\mathbf{A}_1^\mathrm{T}\mathbf{R}\vec{\xi}\|} \right) \quad \text{and}$$

$$\frac{\partial F}{\partial y} = \hat{v} \cdot \left(r_0\mathbf{A}_0\frac{\mathbf{A}_0^\mathrm{T}\mathbf{R}\vec{\xi}}{\|\mathbf{A}_0^\mathrm{T}\mathbf{R}\vec{\xi}\|} + r_1\mathbf{A}_1\frac{\mathbf{A}_1^\mathrm{T}\mathbf{R}\vec{\xi}}{\|\mathbf{A}_1^\mathrm{T}\mathbf{R}\vec{\xi}\|} \right)$$

If we define $\mathbf{A} = [\hat{u}|\hat{v}]$, the equation $\vec{\nabla}F(x, y) = (0, 0)$ can be summarized by

$$\mathbf{A}^\mathrm{T}\left(r_0\mathbf{A}_0\frac{\mathbf{A}_0^\mathrm{T}\mathbf{R}\vec{\xi}}{\|\mathbf{A}_0^\mathrm{T}\mathbf{R}\vec{\xi}\|} + r_1\mathbf{A}_1\frac{\mathbf{A}_1^\mathrm{T}\mathbf{R}\vec{\xi}}{\|\mathbf{A}_1^\mathrm{T}\mathbf{R}\vec{\xi}\|} \right) = \vec{0}$$

Define the unit-length vectors $\hat{\eta}_i = \mathbf{A}_i^\mathrm{T}\mathbf{R}\vec{\xi}/\|\mathbf{A}_i^\mathrm{T}\mathbf{R}\vec{\xi}\|$ for $i = 0, 1$. Define the 2×2 matrices $\mathbf{B}_i = \mathbf{A}^\mathrm{T}\mathbf{A}_i$. The system of equations to be solved is

$$r_0\mathbf{B}_0\hat{\eta}_0 + r_1\mathbf{B}_1\hat{\eta}_1 = \vec{0}, \quad \|\hat{\eta}_0\|^2 = 1, \quad \text{and} \quad \|\hat{\eta}_1\|^2 = 1 \tag{11.44}$$

Given any solution $\hat{\eta}_0$ and $\hat{\eta}_1$ to these equations, it must be that $\hat{\eta}_i$ and $\mathbf{A}_i^\mathrm{T}\mathbf{R}\vec{\xi}$ point in the same direction. That is,

$$\hat{\eta}_0^\perp \cdot \mathbf{A}_0^T \mathbf{R} \vec{\xi} = 0, \quad \hat{\eta}_1^\perp \cdot \mathbf{A}_1^T \mathbf{R} \vec{\xi} = 0, \quad \hat{\eta}_0 \cdot \mathbf{A}_0^T \mathbf{R} \vec{\xi} > 0, \quad \text{and} \quad \hat{\eta}_1 \cdot \mathbf{A}_1^T \mathbf{R} \vec{\xi} > 0 \quad (11.45)$$

where $(a, b)^\perp = (b, -a)$. Each pair (x, y) that satisfies these conditions is a critical point for $F(x, y)$ with $\vec{\nabla} F(x, y) = (0, 0)$. The critical point can then be tested to see if $F(x, y) < 0$, in which case the cylinders are separated.

The outline of the algorithm for the analysis of $g0(\vec{d}(x, y)) = F(x, y)$ is

1. Using the notation $\mathbf{R}_i = [\hat{u}_i | \vec{v}_i | \hat{w}_i]$ for $i = 0, 1$, the various dot products of vectors required in the algorithm need to be computed. The 18 values are represented abstractly as $G_0 = \mathbf{R}^T \mathbf{R}_0 = [g_{ij}^{(0)}]$ and $G_1 = \mathbf{R}^T \mathbf{R}_1 = [g_{ij}^{(1)}]$.

2. Solve $r_0 \mathbf{B}_0 \hat{\eta}_0 + r_1 \mathbf{B}_1 \hat{\eta}_1 = \vec{0}$, $\|\hat{\eta}_0\|^2 = 1$, and $\|\hat{\eta}_1\|^2 = 1$ for $\hat{\eta}_0$ and $\hat{\eta}_1$. Note that there are multiple solution pairs, the obvious one being $(-\hat{\eta}_0, -\hat{\eta}_1)$ whenever $(\hat{\eta}_0, \hat{\eta}_1)$ is a solution. This negated pair leads to the same system of equations to extract (x, y) in step 4, so it can be ignored.

3. For each solution pair $(\hat{\eta}_0, \hat{\eta}_1)$, solve $\hat{\eta}_0^\perp \cdot \mathbf{A}_0^T \mathbf{R} \vec{\xi} = 0$ and $\hat{\eta}_1^\perp \cdot \mathbf{A}_1^T \mathbf{R} \vec{\xi} = 0$ for $\vec{\xi}$. This set of equations can also have multiple solutions.

4. For each solution $\vec{\xi}$, verify that $\hat{w}_0 \cdot \mathbf{R} \vec{\xi} \geq 0$, $\hat{w}_1 \cdot \mathbf{R} \vec{\xi}$, $\hat{\eta}_0 \cdot \mathbf{A}_0^T \mathbf{R} \vec{\xi} > 0$, and $\hat{\eta}_1 \cdot \mathbf{A}_1^T \mathbf{R} \vec{\xi} > 0$.

5. For each pair (x, y) from a valid $\vec{\xi}$ in the last step, test if $F(x, y) < 0$. If so, then $\vec{d} = \mathbf{R} \vec{\xi}$ is a separating direction for the cylinders, and the algorithm terminates.

The algorithm for the analysis of $g_1(x\hat{u} + y\vec{v} - \hat{w})$ is identical in the first three steps. The only difference in steps 4 and 5 is that $\vec{\xi} = (x, y, 1)$ for g_0 and $\vec{\xi} = (x, y, -1)$ for g_1.

Solving for $\hat{\eta}_i$

Note that

$$\mathbf{B}_i = \begin{bmatrix} \hat{u} \cdot \hat{u}_i & \hat{u} \cdot \vec{v}_i \\ \hat{v} \cdot \hat{u}_i & \hat{v} \cdot \vec{v}_i \end{bmatrix}$$

so

$$\det(\mathbf{B}_i) = (\hat{u} \cdot \hat{u}_i)(\hat{v} \cdot \vec{v}_i) - (\hat{u} \cdot \vec{v}_i)(\hat{v} \cdot \hat{u}_i) = (\hat{u} \times \hat{v}) \cdot (\hat{u}_i \times \vec{v}_i) = \hat{w} \cdot \hat{w}_i$$

If $\det(\mathbf{B}_0) = 0$ and $\det(\mathbf{B}_1) = 0$, then $\hat{w}$ must be perpendicular to both $\hat{w}_0$ and $\hat{w}_1$. Since $\hat{w} = \vec{\phi}/\|\vec{\phi}\|$, $\vec{\phi}$ is perpendicular to both $\hat{w}_0$ and $\hat{w}_1$. Observe that $\vec{\phi} = (C_1 - (h_1/2)\hat{w}_1) - (C_0 + (h_0/2)\hat{w}_0)$, a difference of two cylinder end points, one from each cylinder. The line segment connecting the two end points is therefore perpendicular to each cylinder. Draw yourself a picture to see that intersection/separation is determined solely by testing the direction $\vec{d} = \hat{w}$. Note that this direction does satisfy the inequality constraints since $\hat{w} \cdot \hat{w}_0 = 0$, $\hat{w} \cdot \hat{w}_1 = 0$, and $\hat{w} \cdot \vec{\Delta} = \hat{w} \cdot \vec{\phi} = \|\vec{\phi}\| > 0$. The two cylinders are separated if and only if $\|\vec{\phi}\|^2 > (r_0 + r_1)^2$.

If $\det(\mathbf{B}_0) \neq 0$ and $\det(\mathbf{B}_1) = 0$, then the columns of $\mathbf{B}_1$ are linearly dependent. Moreover, one of them must be nonzero. If not, then $0 = (\hat{u} \cdot \hat{u}_1)^2 + (\hat{v} \cdot \hat{u}_1)^2 = 1 - (\hat{w} \cdot \hat{u}_1)^2$, which implies $|\hat{w} \cdot \hat{u}_1| = 1$ and $\hat{u}_1$ is either $\hat{w}$ or $-\hat{w}$. Similarly $\vec{v}_1$ is either $\hat{w}$ or $-\hat{w}$. This cannot happen since $\hat{u}_1$ and $\vec{v}_1$ are orthogonal. Let $\vec{\psi}$ be a nonzero column of $\mathbf{B}_1$. The vector $\vec{\zeta} = \vec{\psi}^\perp$ satisfies the condition $\mathbf{B}_1^{\mathrm{T}} \vec{\zeta} = \vec{0}$; therefore,

$$0 = \vec{\zeta}^{\mathrm{T}} (r_0 \mathbf{B}_0 \hat{\eta}_0 + r_1 \mathbf{B}_1 \hat{\eta}_1) = r_0 (\mathbf{B}_0^{\mathrm{T}} \vec{\zeta}) \cdot \hat{\eta}_0$$

If $\mathbf{B}_0^{\mathrm{T}} \vec{\zeta} = (a, b)$, then $\hat{\eta}_0 = \pm(b, -a)/\sqrt{a^2 + b^2}$. The vector $\hat{\eta}_1$ is determined by $\|\hat{\eta}_1\| = 1$ and the linear equation

$$r_1 (\mathbf{B}_1^{\mathrm{T}} \vec{\psi}) \cdot \hat{\eta}_1 = -r_0 (\mathbf{B}_0^{\mathrm{T}} \vec{\psi}) \cdot \hat{\eta}_0$$

The $\hat{\eta}_1$ are therefore points of intersection, if any, between a circle and a line. The normalization of $\hat{\eta}_0$ can be avoided by defining $\vec{p}_0 = \|\mathbf{B}_0^{\mathrm{T}} \vec{\zeta}\| \hat{\eta}_0$ and $\vec{p}_1 = \|\mathbf{B}_0^{\mathrm{T}} \vec{\zeta}\| \hat{\eta}_1$. In this case $\vec{p}_0 = (\mathbf{B}_0^{\mathrm{T}} \vec{\zeta})^\perp$ and $r_1 (\mathbf{B}_1^{\mathrm{T}} \vec{\psi}) \cdot \vec{p}_1 = -r_0 (\mathbf{B}_0^{\mathrm{T}} \vec{\psi}) \cdot \vec{p}_0$. The extraction of (x, y) discussed later in fact does not require the normalizations. The intersection of line and circle does require solving a quadratic equation, so a square root has to be calculated (or the quadratic must be solved iteratively to avoid the cost of the square root). A similar construction applies if $\det(\mathbf{B}_0) = 0$ and $\det(\mathbf{B}_1) \neq 0$.

If $\det(\mathbf{B}_0) \neq 0$ and $\det(\mathbf{B}_1) \neq 0$, then $\mathbf{B}_0$ is invertible and

$$\hat{\eta}_0 = -(r_1/r_0) \mathbf{B}_0^{-1} \mathbf{B}_1 \hat{\eta}_1$$

with $\|\hat{\eta}_0\| = 1$ and $\|\hat{\eta}_1\| = 1$. The extraction of (x, y) discussed later does not require unit-length quantities for $\hat{\eta}_0$ and $\hat{\eta}_1$, so the three equations can be rewritten to avoid some divisions and normalizations. Rewrite the displayed equation as

$$r_0 \det(\mathbf{B}_0) \hat{\eta}_0 = -r_1 \operatorname{Adj}(\mathbf{B}_0) \mathbf{B}_1 \hat{\eta}_1$$

Define $\vec{p}_0 = r_0 \det(\mathbf{B}_0) \hat{\eta}_0$, $\vec{p}_1 = r_1 \hat{\eta}_1$, and $\mathbf{C} = \operatorname{Adj}(\mathbf{B}_0) \mathbf{B}_1$. The equations are now $\vec{p}_0 = -\mathbf{C} \vec{p}_1$, $\|\vec{p}_0\|^2 = r_0^2 \det(\mathbf{B}_0)^2$, and $\|\vec{p}_1\|^2 = r_1^2$.

The quadratic equations for $\vec{p}_1$ are $r_0^2 \det(\mathbf{B}_0)^2 = \vec{p}_1^{\mathrm{T}} \mathbf{C}^{\mathrm{T}} \mathbf{C} \vec{p}_1$ and $\|\vec{p}_1\|^2 = r_1^2$. Factor $\mathbf{C}^{\mathrm{T}} \mathbf{C} = \mathbf{Q} E \mathbf{Q}^{\mathrm{T}}$, where $E = \operatorname{Diag}(e_0, e_1)$ are eigenvalues and the columns of $\mathbf{Q}$ are eigenvectors. Let $\vec{\psi} = \mathbf{Q}^{\mathrm{T}} \vec{p}_1$. The equations become $\|\vec{\psi}\|^2 = r_1^2$ and $r_0^2 \det(\mathbf{B}_0)^2 = \vec{\psi}^{\mathrm{T}} E \vec{\psi}$. If $\vec{\psi} = (a, b)$, then $a^2 + b^2 = r_1^2$ and $e_0 a^2 + e_1 b^2 = r_0^2 \det(\mathbf{B}_0)^2$. These are two linear equations in the two unknowns a^2 and b^2. The formal solution is $a^2 = (e_1 r_1^2 - r_0^2 \det(\mathbf{B}_0)^2)/(e_1 - e_0)$ and $b^2 = (r_1^2 - e_0 r_0^2 \det(\mathbf{B}_0)^2)/(e_1 - e_0)$. Assuming both right-hand sides are nonnegative, you have four solutions (a, b), $(-a, b)$, $(a, -b)$, and

$(-a, -b)$, as expected (intersection of ellipse and circle). Only (a, b) and $(-a, b)$ need to be considered; the others generate no new information in the extraction of (x, y). Given a solution for $\vec{\psi}$, the corresponding nonnormalized vectors for extraction are $\vec{p}_1 = Q\vec{\psi}$ and $\vec{p}_0 = -C\vec{p}_1$.

Solving for (x, y)

The first two equations in Equation 11.45 can be written as two systems of equations in the unknowns x and y as

$$C \begin{bmatrix} x \\ y \end{bmatrix} = \vec{d}$$

where $\hat{\eta}_0 = (a_0, b_0)$, $\hat{\eta}_1 = (a_1, b_1)$, and

$$C = \begin{bmatrix} b_0 g_{00}^{(0)} - a_0 g_{01}^{(0)} & b_0 g_{10}^{(0)} - a_0 g_{11}^{(0)} \\ b_1 g_{00}^{(1)} - a_1 g_{01}^{(1)} & b_1 g_{10}^{(1)} - a_1 g_{11}^{(1)} \end{bmatrix}, \quad \vec{d} = \begin{bmatrix} a_0 g_{21}^{(0)} - b_0 g_{20}^{(0)} \\ a_1 g_{21}^{(1)} - b_1 g_{20}^{(1)} \end{bmatrix}$$

If C is invertible, then a unique solution is obtained for (x, y).

If C is not invertible, the problem is slightly more complicated. There are no solutions if $\text{Adj}(C)\vec{d} \neq \vec{0}$. Otherwise, the system only has one independent equation. Since $\hat{\eta}_0 \neq \vec{0}$ and since $A_0^T R$ has full rank (equal to 2), the 3×1 vector $R^T A_0 \hat{\eta}_0^\perp$ cannot be the zero vector. In fact, $\hat{\eta}_0^\perp$ is unit length, which implies $A_0 \hat{\eta}_0^\perp$ is unit length. Finally, since R is a rotation matrix, $R^T A_0 \hat{\eta}_0^\perp$ is a unit-length vector. The same argument shows that $R^T A_1 \hat{\eta}_1^\perp$ is a unit-length vector. Both of these conditions and the fact that the system has infinitely many solutions implies that $c_{00}^2 + c_{01}^2 \neq 0$ and $c_{10}^2 + c_{11}^2 \neq 0$.

If $c_{01} \neq 0$, then $y = (d_0 - c_{00}x)/c_{01}$. Replacing this in $A_0^T R \vec{\xi}$ yields

$$A_0^T R \vec{\xi} = \frac{(g_{00}^{(0)} g_{11}^{(0)} - g_{01}^{(0)} g_{10}^{(0)})x + (g_{11}^{(0)} g_{20}^{(0)} - g_{10}^{(0)} g_{21}^{(0)})}{a_0 g_{11}^{(0)} - b_0 g_{10}^{(0)}} =: (\alpha_0 x + \beta_0)\hat{\eta}_0$$

The numerator of α_0 is $\det(B_0)$. If $c_{01} = 0$ instead, then $c_{00} \neq 0$, and a similar expression is obtained for $A_0^T R \vec{\xi}$ in terms of y, namely, $\alpha_0' y + \beta_0'$, where the numerator of α_0' is also $\det(B_0)$. Similarly, if $c_{11} \neq 0$, then $y = (d_1 - c_{10}x)/c_{11}$ and

$$A_1^T R \vec{\xi} = \frac{(g_{00}^{(1)} g_{11}^{(1)} - g_{01}^{(1)} g_{10}^{(1)})x + (g_{11}^{(1)} g_{20}^{(1)} - g_{10}^{(1)} g_{21}^{(1)})}{a_1 g_{11}^{(1)} - b_1 g_{10}^{(1)}} =: (\alpha_1 x + \beta_1)\hat{\eta}_1$$

The numerator of α_1 is $\det(\mathbf{B}_1)$. If $c_{11} = 0$ instead, then $c_{10} \neq 0$, and a similar expression is obtained for $\mathbf{A}_1^T \mathbf{R} \vec{\xi}$ in terms of y, namely, $\alpha_1' y + \beta_1'$, where the numerator of α_1' is also $\det(\mathbf{B}_1)$.

In the case $c_{01} \neq 0$ and $c_{11} \neq 0$, then $F(x, y)$ reduces to

$$F(x, y) = r_0 |\alpha_0 x + \beta_0| + r_1 |\alpha_1 x + \beta_1| - |\vec{\phi}|$$

If $\alpha_0 \neq 0$ and $\alpha_1 \neq 0$, then the minimum of F is attained at either $x = -\beta_0/\alpha_0$ or $x = -\beta_1/\alpha_1$. Notice that the first x forces $\mathbf{A}_0^T \mathbf{R} \vec{\xi} = \vec{0}$, in which case the corresponding direction must have been $\vec{d} = \hat{w}_0$. The second x forces $\mathbf{A}_1^T \mathbf{R} \vec{\xi} = \vec{0}$, in which case the corresponding direction must have been $\vec{d} = \hat{w}_1$. Both of these directions were tested earlier, so this case can be ignored. If $\alpha_0 \neq 0$ and $\alpha_1 = 0$, then the minimum of F is attained at $x = -\beta_0/\alpha_0$. The corresponding direction must have been $\vec{d} = \hat{w}_0$, again handled earlier. The same argument applies to $\alpha_0 = 0$ and $\alpha_1 \neq 0$. The final case is $\alpha_0 = \alpha_1 = 0$, in which case $\det(\mathbf{B}_0) = \det(\mathbf{B}_1) = 0$, yet another case that was handled earlier. Therefore, these cases can be ignored in an implementation. A similar argument applies when $c_{00} \neq 0$ and $c_{10} \neq 0$, and $F(x, y)$ reduces to

$$F(x, y) = r_0 |\alpha_0' y + \beta_0'| + r_1 |\alpha_1' y + \beta_1'| - \|\vec{\phi}\|$$

All possibilities can be ignored in an implementation since they are handled by other separation tests. Finally, if there is a mixture of x and y terms,

$$F(x, y) = r_0 |\alpha_0 x + \beta_0| + r_1 |\alpha_1' y + \beta_1'| - \|\vec{\phi}\|$$

or

$$F(x, y) = r_0 |\alpha_0' y + \beta_0'| + r_1 |\alpha_1 x + \beta_1| - \|\vec{\phi}\|$$

then the minimization is applied in each dimension separately, but just as before, other separation tests cover these cases. The conclusion is that an implementation does not have to do anything when C is not invertible.

Fast Method to Test $F(x, y) < 0$

The two square roots, $\|\mathbf{A}_i^T \mathbf{R} \vec{\xi}\|$, in Equation 11.43 can be avoided. The test $F(x, y) < 0$ is equivalent to

$$r_0 \|\mathbf{A}_0^T \mathbf{R} \vec{\xi}\| + r_1 \|\mathbf{A}_1^T \mathbf{R} \vec{\xi}\| < \|\vec{\phi}\|$$

The inequality can be squared and rearranged to yield the test

$$2 r_0 r_1 \|\mathbf{A}_0^T \mathbf{R} \vec{\xi}\| \|\mathbf{A}_1^T \mathbf{R} \vec{\xi}\| < \|\vec{\phi}\|^2 - r_0^2 \|\mathbf{A}_0^T \mathbf{R} \vec{\xi}\|^2 - r_1^2 \|\mathbf{A}_1^T \mathbf{R} \vec{\xi}\|^2 =: \rho$$

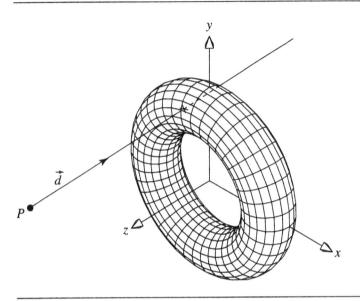

Figure 11.74   Intersection of a linear component and a torus.

If $\rho \leq 0$, then $F(x, y) \geq 0$ is forced, and no more work needs to be done. If $\rho > 0$, then squaring one more time yields the test

$$4r_0^2 r_1^2 \|\mathbf{A}_0^T \mathbf{R}\vec{\xi}\|^2 \|\mathbf{A}_1^T \mathbf{R}\vec{\xi}\|^2 < \rho^2$$

11.12.10 LINEAR COMPONENT AND TORUS

In this section we address the problem of intersecting a linear component with a torus (see Figure 11.74). A linear component is defined (as usual) as an origin point and a direction:

$$\mathcal{L}(t) = P + t\vec{d} \tag{11.46}$$

In the case of a line segment defined by two points P_0 and P_1, we let $\vec{d} = P_1 - P_0$.
A torus is defined implicitly:

$$(x^2 + y^2 + z^2 + R^2 - r^2)^2 - 4R^2(x^2 + y^2) = 0 \tag{11.47}$$

This defines a torus centered at the origin, and lying in the XY plane, with major radius R and minor radius r.

If we substitute Equation 11.46 into Equation 11.47, we get a quartic equation in t, of the form

$$c_4 t^4 + c_3 t^3 + c_2 t^2 + c_1 t + c_0 = 0 \qquad (11.48)$$

where

$$c_4 = (\vec{d} \cdot \vec{d})^2$$

$$c_3 = 4(P \cdot \vec{d})(\vec{d} \cdot \vec{d})$$

$$c_2 = 2(\vec{d} \cdot \vec{d})((P \cdot P) - (R^2 + r^2)) + 4(P \cdot \vec{d})^2 + 4R^2 \vec{d}_z^2$$

$$c_1 = 4(P \cdot \vec{d})((P \cdot P) - (R^2 + r^2)) + 8R^2 P_z \vec{d}_z$$

$$c_0 = ((P \cdot P) - (R^2 + r^2)) - 4R^2(r^2 - P_z^2)$$

This quartic equation can be solved using a root-finding method, such as found in Section A.5.

If the intersection is sought for purposes of ray tracing, then the desired intersection (there can be as many as four) will be the one closest to the ray origin P. In addition, the surface normal at that point will also be needed, as well as the "texture coordinates" and partial derivatives. The normal could be computed by computing the partial derivatives of Equation 11.48 with respect to x, y, and z; however, there is a more direct approach. Consider the "cross section" of a torus, as shown in Figure 11.75. Because the cross section is a circle, the normal $\vec{n}$ at any point X on the circle is simply the vector $(X - C)$. But C is easy to compute: the intersection point X is projected down onto the XY plane: $X' = [\, X_x \quad X_y \quad 0 \,]$; then C is just at a distance R from the origin $\mathcal{O} = [\, 0 \quad 0 \quad 0 \,]$, along the vector $(X' - \mathcal{O})$. Note that the vector $\vec{n} = X - C$ is not normalized unless $r = 1$.

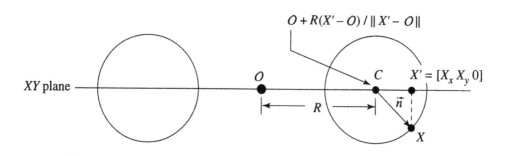

Figure 11.75   Computing the normal of a torus at a point (of intersection).

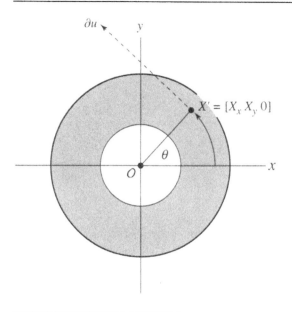

Figure 11.76   The u parameter of a point on a torus.

To compute texture coordinates, we'll define the u-direction to be counterclockwise (as we're looking down the z-axis), starting from the x-axis; the v-direction goes around the circumference of the "swept tube" of the torus, starting from the inside. Let's start with the u parameter. Consider the cross-sectional view (this time, cutting with the XZ plane) shown in Figure 11.76.

From this, we can easily see that a little trigonometry gives us the u parameter:

$$r_u = \|X' - \mathcal{O}\|$$

$$\cos(\theta) = \frac{X_x}{r_u}$$

$$\sin(\theta) = \frac{X_y}{r_u}$$

$$u = \begin{cases} \frac{\arccos(\theta)}{2\pi} & \text{if } \sin(\theta) \geq 0 \\ 1 - \frac{\arccos(\theta)}{2\pi} & \text{if } \sin(\theta) < 0 \end{cases}$$

For the v-direction, consider Figure 11.77. To get $\cos(\phi)$, we need the adjacent leg and hypotenuse of the triangle—these are $\|X' - \mathcal{O}\| - R$ and r, respectively. Note that if we want the parametric origin to be on the "inside" of the torus, we need to

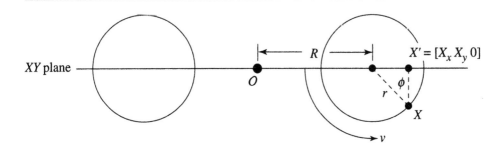

Figure 11.77   The v parameter of a point on a torus.

invert (i.e., negate) the cosine. To get $\sin(\phi)$, we need the length of the opposite leg of the triangle, which is simply X_z. So, we have

$$r_v = \|X' - \mathcal{O}\|$$

$$\cos(\phi) = \frac{-(r_v - R)}{r}$$

$$\sin(\phi) = \frac{X_z}{r_v}$$

$$u = \begin{cases} \frac{\arccos(\phi)}{2\pi} & \text{if } \sin(\phi) \geq 0 \\ 1 - \frac{\arccos(\phi)}{2\pi} & \text{if } \sin(\phi) < 0 \end{cases}$$

The partial derivatives are straightforward: as is obvious from observing Figure 11.76, we have

$$\partial u = (X' - \mathcal{O})^{\perp}$$

We *could* determine ∂v by a method similar to that used to compute the normal $\vec{n}$, but we can actually do this a little cheaper by simply noting that

$$\partial v = \vec{n} \times \partial u$$

Note that the partial derivatives are computed in the local space of the torus. They'll need to be transformed back into world space and normalized there.

CHAPTER 12

MISCELLANEOUS 3D PROBLEMS

This chapter includes a variety of problems involving 3D lines, planes, tetrahedra, and 3D circles. Most of these are commonly (or at least occasionally) encountered problems, while others, although less commonly encountered, serve to show how various techniques may be brought to bear on new problems.

12.1 PROJECTION OF A POINT ONTO A PLANE

In this section, we consider the projection of a point Q onto a plane $\mathcal{P}$, where $\mathcal{P}$ is defined as $ax + by + cz + d = 0$ (or $P \cdot \vec{n} + d = 0$), as shown in Figure 12.1. By definition, the line segment between Q and its projection Q' is parallel to the plane normal $\vec{n}$. Let the (signed) distance between the points be r; then we have

$$Q = Q' + \frac{r\vec{n}}{\|\vec{n}\|} \tag{12.1}$$

If we dot each side with $\vec{n}$, we get

$$Q \cdot \vec{n} = \left(Q' + \frac{r\vec{n}}{\|\vec{n}\|} \right) \cdot \vec{n}$$

$$= Q' \cdot \vec{n} + \frac{r\vec{n}}{\|\vec{n}\|} \cdot \vec{n} \tag{12.2}$$

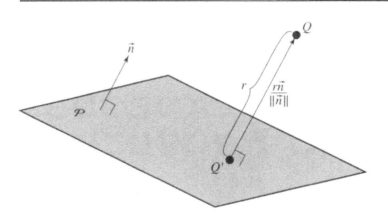

Figure 12.1   Projection of a point onto a plane.

But $Q' \cdot \vec{n} = -d$ because by definition Q' lies on $\mathcal{P}$ and $\vec{n} \cdot \vec{n} = \|\vec{n}\|^2$, so $\frac{r\vec{n}}{\|\vec{n}\|} \cdot \vec{n} = r\|\vec{n}\|$. If we substitute these into Equation 12.2 and solve for r, we get

$$r = \frac{Q \cdot \vec{n} + d}{\|\vec{n}\|} \tag{12.3}$$

We can then rearrange Equation 12.1 and substitute Equation 12.3:

$$Q' = Q - \frac{r\vec{n}}{\|\vec{n}\|}$$

$$= Q - \frac{\frac{Q \cdot \vec{n} + d}{\|\vec{n}\|}\vec{n}}{\|\vec{n}\|}$$

$$= Q - \frac{Q \cdot \vec{n} + d}{\|\vec{n}\|\|\vec{n}\|}\vec{n}$$

$$= Q - \frac{Q \cdot \vec{n} + d}{\vec{n} \cdot \vec{n}}\vec{n}$$

If the plane equation is normalized, we have $\|\hat{n}\| = 1$, and thus the division can be avoided:

$$Q' = Q - (Q \cdot \hat{n} + d)\,\hat{n}$$

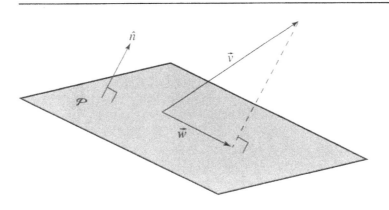

Figure 12.2   Projection of a vector onto a plane.

12.2 PROJECTION OF A VECTOR ONTO A PLANE

The projection of a vector $\vec{v}$ onto a plane $\mathcal{P} : P \cdot \hat{n} + d = 0$, as shown in Figure 12.2, is

$$\vec{w} = \vec{v} - (\vec{v} \cdot \hat{n})\hat{n} \tag{12.4}$$

or

$$\vec{w} = \vec{v} - \frac{\vec{v} \cdot \vec{n}}{\|\vec{n}\|^2}\vec{n}$$

if the plane normal is not unit length.

To see why this is so, consider Figure 12.3. Here, we see the projection of $\vec{v}$ onto $\hat{u}$. The vector $\vec{v}$ can be decomposed into $\vec{v} = \vec{v}_\perp + \vec{v}_\|$, components parallel and perpendicular, respectively, to $\hat{u}$. By the definition of the dot product, the length of $\vec{v}_\|$ is $\vec{v} \cdot \hat{u}$, and because the two components' sum is $\vec{v}$, we have

$$\vec{v}_\| = (\vec{v} \cdot \hat{u})\hat{u} \tag{12.5}$$

$$\vec{v}_\perp = \vec{v} - (\vec{v} \cdot \hat{u})\hat{u} \tag{12.6}$$

If we consider the vector $\hat{u}$ from Figure 12.3 to be the plane normal $\hat{n}$ from Figure 12.2, then we can see that $\vec{w} = \vec{v}_\perp$, and so Equation 12.4 follows from Equation 12.5 directly. The insight here is to realize that the projection of $\vec{v}$ onto $\mathcal{P}$ is the same for *any* plane perpendicular to $\hat{n}$, and so you can thus understand why the d component of the plane equation for $\mathcal{P}$ does not appear in the solution.

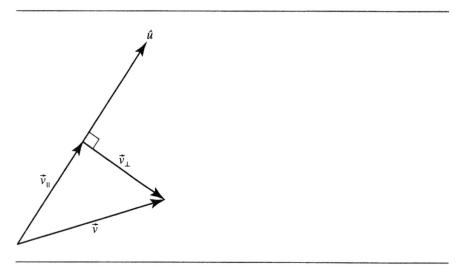

Figure 12.3   Projection of one vector onto another.

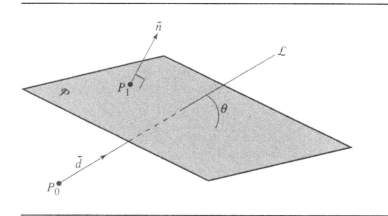

Figure 12.4   Angle between a line and a plane.

12.3 ANGLE BETWEEN A LINE AND A PLANE

The angle between a line $\mathcal{L}(t) = P_0 + t\vec{d}$ and a plane $\mathcal{P} : P_1 \cdot \vec{n} + d = 0$ can be computed in one of several ways, depending on whether the line, the plane, both, or neither are normalized (see Figure 12.4). The formula for ϕ, the angle between the plane normal and the line, is given in Table 12.1. The angle between the line and the plane itself is $\theta = \frac{\pi}{2} - \phi$.

Table 12.1 Formula for ϕ.

Plane	Line	
	Normalized	Nonnormalized
Normalized	$\phi = \arccos(\hat{n} \cdot \hat{d})$	$\phi = \arccos \frac{\hat{n} \cdot \vec{d}}{\|\vec{d}\|}$
Nonnormalized	$\phi = \arccos \frac{\vec{n} \cdot \hat{d}}{\|\vec{n}\|}$	$\phi = \arccos \frac{\vec{n} \cdot \vec{d}}{\|\vec{n}\| \|\vec{d}\|}$

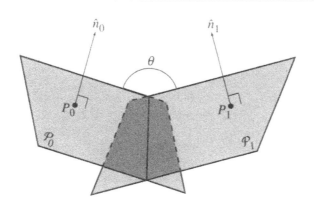

Figure 12.5 Angle between two planes.

12.4 ANGLE BETWEEN TWO PLANES

The angle between two planes $\mathcal{P}_0 : \{P_0, \vec{n}_0\}$ and $\mathcal{P}_1 : \{P_1, \vec{n}_1\}$ (see Figure 12.5) can easily be computed by the angle between their two normals. As with the angle between a line and a plane, the angle θ between the two planes can be computed in one of several ways, depending on whether $\mathcal{P}_0$, P_1, both, or neither are normalized (see Table 12.2).

12.5 PLANE NORMAL TO A LINE AND THROUGH A GIVEN POINT

Suppose we have a line $\mathcal{L}(t) = P + t\vec{d}$ and a point Q (see Figure 12.6). The plane normal to $\mathcal{L}$, going through Q, is

$$d_x x + d_y y + d_z z - (d_x Q_x + d_y Q_y + d_z Q_z) = 0$$

Table 12.2   Formula for θ.

$\mathcal{P}_0$	$\mathcal{P}_1$	
	Normalized	Nonnormalized
Normalized	$\theta = \arccos(\hat{n}_0 \cdot \hat{n}_1)$	$\theta = \arccos \frac{\hat{n}_0 \cdot \vec{n}_1}{\|\vec{n}_1\|}$
Nonnormalized	$\theta = \arccos \frac{\vec{n}_0 \cdot \hat{n}_1}{\|\vec{n}_0\|}$	$\theta = \arccos \frac{\vec{n}_0 \cdot \vec{n}_1}{\|\vec{n}_0\|\|\vec{n}_1\|}$

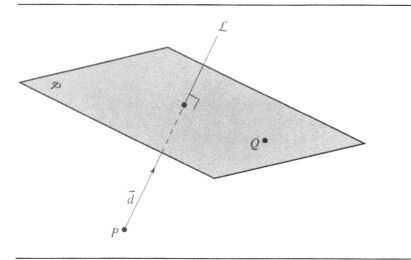

Figure 12.6   Plane normal to a line through a point.

The normal to $\mathcal{P}$ is obviously just the direction vector for $\mathcal{L}$. The d coefficient for $\mathcal{P}$ may not be quite so obvious. However, consider the "cross section" shown in Figure 12.7: if we draw the direction vector for $\mathcal{L}$ starting at the origin $\mathcal{O}$, and consider the vector $\overrightarrow{\mathcal{O}Q}$, it's clear that the d coefficient for $\mathcal{P}$ is the projection of $\overrightarrow{\mathcal{O}Q}$ onto $\vec{d}$, and so we have

$$d = -(\overrightarrow{\mathcal{O}Q} \cdot \vec{d})$$

which has the equivalent in component notation of

$$-(d_x Q_x + d_y Q_y + d_z Q_z)$$

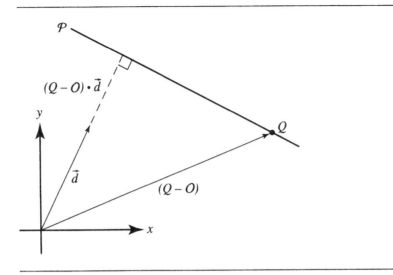

Figure 12.7   Computing the distance coefficient for the plane.

This equation holds true irrespective of whether or not $\mathcal{L}$ is normalized, and the equation for $\mathcal{P}$ is normalized if and only if $\|\vec{d}\| = 1$.

12.6 PLANE THROUGH THREE POINTS

Given three points P_0, P_1, and P_2, with none coincident and not all collinear, we can fairly directly derive the equation of the plane containing all three points (Figure 12.8). In fact, we can fairly directly derive any one of the several representations of a plane from the three points:

- Implicit: The implicit equation of a plane through three points satisfies

$$\begin{vmatrix} x - P_{0,x} & y - P_{0,y} & z - P_{0,z} \\ P_{1,x} - P_{0,x} & P_{1,y} - P_{0,y} & P_{1,z} - P_{0,z} \\ P_{2,x} - P_{0,x} & P_{2,y} - P_{0,y} & P_{2,z} - P_{0,z} \end{vmatrix} = 0$$

If we multiply this out, we get an equation of the form

$$ax + by + cz + d = 0$$

- Parametric:

$$\mathcal{P}(s, t) = P_0 + s(P_1 - P_0) + t(P_2 - P_0)$$

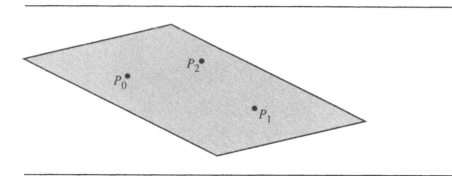

Figure 12.8   Three points defining a plane.

■ Explicit: This form requires that we specify a point on the surface, a normal, and a third parameter d (which represents the perpendicular distance to the origin). We have three such points from which to choose and can (as above) compute the normal as the cross product of the vectors between two pairs of points. Arbitrarily choosing P_0 as the point on the surface, and the normal $\vec{n}$ as $(P_1 - P_0) \times (P_2 - P_0)$, we have

$$P_0 \cdot \vec{n} + d = 0$$

Trivially, we have $d = -(P_0 \cdot \vec{n})$.

12.7 ANGLE BETWEEN TWO LINES

Given two lines $\mathcal{L}_0(t) = P_0 + t\vec{d}_0$ and $\mathcal{L}_1(t) = P_1 + t\vec{d}_1$, the angle between them can be computed by exploiting the relationship between the dot product and angle (see Section 3.3.1), so we have

$$\theta = \arccos \frac{\vec{d}_0 \cdot \vec{d}_1}{\|\vec{d}_0\| \|\vec{d}_1\|} \tag{12.7}$$

If both the line equations are normalized, this can be simplified to

$$\theta = \arccos(\hat{d}_0 \cdot \hat{d}_1)$$

A line's "direction" may or may not be significant to the problem domain, particularly if the line equation defines a line, rather than a ray or line segment. The angle computed above is between lines that "move" in the same direction. For example, if the lines are parallel and $\vec{d}_0$ and $\vec{d}_1$ point in the same direction, then $\theta = 0$; otherwise,

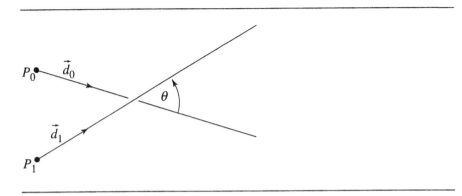

Figure 12.9   Angle between two lines in 3D.

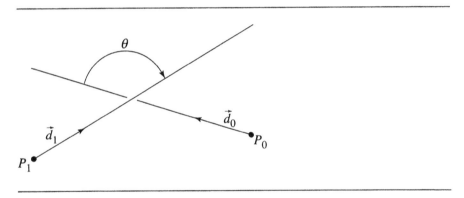

Figure 12.10   Angle between two lines in 3D, with one line reversed.

$\theta = \pi$ (180°). In Figure 12.9, $\theta \approx 46°$ as calculated using Equation 12.7, but if we reverse the direction of one of the lines, as in Figure 12.10, then $\theta \approx 134°$.

If the lines are not normalized, the pseudocode is

```
float Line3DLine3DAngle(Line l1, Line l2, boolean acuteAngleDesired)
{
    float denominator;

    denominator = Dot(l1.direction, l1.direction) *
                  Dot(l2.direction, l2.direction);
    if (denominator < epsilon) {
        //  One or both lines are degenerate,
        //  deal with in application-dependent fashion
```

```
    } else {
        float angle;

        angle = Acos(Dot(l1.direction, l2.direction) /
                     Sqrt(denominator);
        if (acuteAngleDesired && angle > Pi/2) {
            return Pi - angle;
        } else {
            return angle;
        }
    }
}
```

If both lines are normalized, the pseudocode is

```
float Line3DLine3DAngle(Line l1, Line l2, boolean acuteAngleDesired)
{
    float angle;

    angle = Acos(Dot(l1.direction, l2.direction));
    if (acuteAngleDesired && angle > Pi/2) {
        return Pi - angle;
    } else {
        return angle;
    }
}
```

CHAPTER 13

COMPUTATIONAL GEOMETRY TOPICS

The field of computational geometry is quite large and is one of the most rapidly advancing fields in recent times. This chapter is by no means comprehensive. The general topics covered are binary space-partitioning (BSP) trees in two and three dimensions, point-in-polygon and point-in-polyhedron tests, convex hulls of finite point sets, Delaunay triangulation in two and three dimensions, partitioning of polygons into convex pieces or triangles, containment of point sets by circles or oriented boxes in two dimensions and by spheres or oriented boxes in three dimensions, area calculations of polygons, and volume calculations of polyhedra.

The emphasis is, of course, on algorithms to implement the various ideas. However, attention is given to the issues of computation when done within a floating-point number system. Particular themes arising again and again are determining when points are collinear, coplanar, cocircular, or cospherical. This is easy to do when the underlying computational system is based on integer arithmetic, but quite problematic when floating-point arithmetic is used.

13.1 BINARY SPACE-PARTITIONING TREES IN 2D

The idea of partitioning space using a binary tree has its origins with Fuchs, Kedem, and Naylor (1979, 1980) and is very useful in many applications.

Consider a line in the plane with representation $\vec{n} \cdot X - c = 0$. The line partitions the plane into two half-planes. The half-plane on the side of the line to which $\vec{n}$ points is called the *positive side of the line*; the other side is called the *negative side of the line*. If X is on the positive side, then $\vec{n} \cdot X - c > 0$, hence the use of the phrase "positive

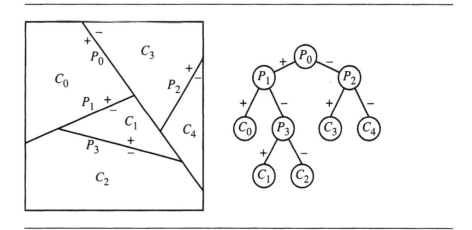

Figure 13.1   BSP tree partitioning of the plane.

side." If X is on the negative side, then $\vec{n} \cdot X - c < 0$. A point X on the line of course satisfies $\vec{n} \cdot X - c = 0$.

Each half-plane may be further subdivided by another line in the plane. The resulting positive and negative regions can themselves be subdivided. The resulting partitioning of the plane is represented by a binary tree, each node representing the splitting line. The left child of a node corresponds to the positive side of the splitting line that the node represents; the right child corresponds to the negative side. The leaf nodes of the tree represent the convex regions obtained by the partitioning. Figure 13.1 illustrates this. The square is intended to represent all of the plane. The partitioning lines are labeled with P, and the convex regions are labeled with C.

13.1.1   BSP TREE REPRESENTATION OF A POLYGON

A BSP tree represents a partitioning of the plane, but it can also be used to partition polygons into convex subpolygons. The decomposition can be used in various ways. The tree supports point-in-polygon queries, discussed later in this section. Other algorithms for point-in-polygon queries are discussed in Section 13.3. A BSP tree represents a general decomposition of a polygon into triangles—the idea explored in Section 13.9. Finally, BSP tree representations for polygons can be used to support Boolean operations on polygons—the idea explored in Section 13.5.

The simplest way to construct a BSP tree for a polygon is to create the nodes so that each represents a splitting line that contains an edge of the polygon. Other polygon edges are split at a node by using the splitting line. Any subedges that are on the positive side of a line are sent to the positive child, and the process is repeated. Any subedges that are on the negative side are sent to the negative child, and the process is repeated. It is possible that another polygon edge is fully on the splitting line. Such edges, called *coincident edges*, are also stored at the node representing the splitting line. In this construction, at least one edge of the polygon is contained by the splitting line. It is not necessary to require that the splitting lines contain polygon edges. We will revisit this idea later in the section. The pseudocode for construction of a BSP tree from a polygon is listed below. The input list for the top-level call is the collection of edges from the polygon, assumed to be nonempty.

```
BspTree ConstructTree(EdgeList L)
{
    T = new BspTree;

    // use an edge to determine the splitting line for the tree node
    T.line = GetLineFromEdge(L.first);  // Dot(N, X) - c = 0

    EdgeList posList, negList;  // initially empty lists
    for (each edge E of L) {
        // Determine how edge and line relate to each other.  If the edge
        // crosses the line, the subedges on the positive and negative
        // side of the line are returned.
        type = Classify(T.line, E, SubPos, SubNeg);

        if (type is CROSSES) {
            // Dot(N, X) - c < 0 for one vertex, Dot(N, X) - c > 0
            // for the other vertex
            posList.AddEdge(SubPos);
            negList.AddEdge(SubNeg);
        } else if (type is POSITIVE) {
            // Dot(N, X) - c >= 0 for both vertices, at least one positive
            posList.AddEdge(E);
        } else if (type is NEGATIVE) {
            // Dot(N, X) - c <= 0 for both vertices, at least one negative
            negList.AddEdge(E);
        } else {
            // type is COINCIDENT
            // Dot(N, X) - c = 0 for both vertices
            T.coincident.AddEdge(E);
        }
    }

    if (posList is not empty)
        T.posChild = ConstructTree(posList);
    else
        T.posChild = null;
```

Figure 13.2   A partitioning line for which two coincident edges have opposite direction normals.

```
if (negList is not empty)
    T.negChild = ConstructTree(negList);
else
    T.negChild = null;

return T;
}
```

The function GetLineFromEdge produces a line whose normal vector points to the outside region of the polygon at the specified edge. Other coincident edges may or may not have normals that point in the same direction as the line normal. Figure 13.2 shows such a situation.

The function Classify tries to find a point of intersection of the current edge and the node's line. If there is an intersection that is an interior point of the edge, the positive and negative subedges are returned. It is possible that one end point of the edge is on the line, but the other end point is not. In this case, the edge is classified as either a positive edge or a negative edge. Of course the edge can be fully on one side or the other without intersecting the line at all, in which case the edge is classified as either positive or negative. Finally, the edge can be entirely on the splitting line, in which case the edge is classified as coincident. The pseudocode for this function is

```
int Classify(Line L, Edge E, Edge SubPos, Edge SubNeg)
{
    d0 = Dot(L.normal, E.V(0) - L.origin);
    d1 = Dot(L.normal, E.V(1) - L.origin);
    if (d0 * d1 < 0) {
        // edge crosses line
        t = d0 / (d0 - d1);
        I = E.V(0) + t * (E.V(1) - E.V(0));
        if (d1 > 0) {
            SubNeg = Edge(E.V(0), I);
            SubPos = Edge(I, E.V(1));
```

```
        } else {
            SubPos = Edge(E.V(0), I);
            SubNeg = Edge(I, E.V(1));
        }

        return CROSSES;
    } else if (d0 > 0 or d1 > 0) {
        // edge on positive side of line
        return POSITIVE;
    } else if (d0 < 0 or d1 < 0) {
        // edge on negative side of line
        return NEGATIVE;
    } else {
        // edge is contained by the line
        return COINCIDENT;
    }
}
```

Because of floating-point round-off errors, it is possible that $d_0 d_1 < 0$, but t is nearly zero (or one) and may as well be treated as zero (or one). An implementation of Classify should include such handling to avoid the situation where two edges meet at a vertex; the first edge is used for the splitting line, and numerically the second edge appears to be crossing the line, thereby causing a split when there should be none.

EXAMPLE   Figure 13.3 shows an inverted L-shaped polygon that has 10 vertices and 10 edges. The vertices are indexed from 0 to 9. The edges are $\langle 9, 0 \rangle$ and $\langle i, i + 1 \rangle$ for $0 \le i \le 8$. We construct the BSP tree an edge at a time. At each step the splitting line is shown as dotted, the positive side region is shown in white, and the negative side region is shown in gray.

The first edge to be processed is $\langle 9, 0 \rangle$. Figure 13.4 shows the partitioning of the plane by a dotted line containing the edge and the root node (r) of the tree. The edge $\langle 9, 0 \rangle$ is part of that node (the edge defines the splitting line) and the positive (p) and negative (n) edges created by the splitting. In this case, all remaining edges are on the negative side of the line.

The next edge to be processed is $\langle 0, 1 \rangle$. Figure 13.5 shows the state of the BSP tree after the edge is processed.

The next edge to be processed is $\langle 1, 2 \rangle$. Figure 13.6 shows the state of the BSP tree after the edge is processed. The edge forces a split of both $\langle 4, 5 \rangle$ and $\langle 8, 9 \rangle$, causing the introduction of new vertices labeled as 10 and 11 in the figure.

The next edge to be processed is $\langle 10, 5 \rangle$. Figure 13.7 shows the state of the BSP tree after the edge is processed. The edge forces a split of $\langle 7, 8 \rangle$, causing the introduction of the new vertex labeled as 12 in the figure.

The next edge to be processed is $\langle 5, 6 \rangle$. Figure 13.8 shows the state of the BSP tree after the edge is processed. No new vertices are introduced by this step.

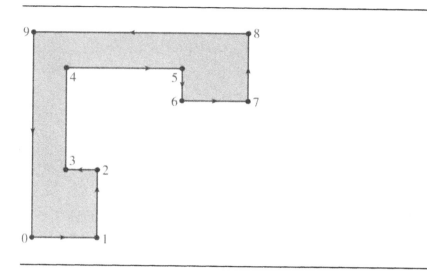

Figure 13.3   A sample polygon for construction of a BSP tree.

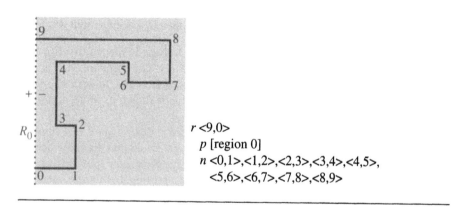

r <9,0>
p [region 0]
n <0,1>,<1,2>,<2,3>,<3,4>,<4,5>,
    <5,6>,<6,7>,<7,8>,<8,9>

Figure 13.4   Current state after processing edge $\langle 9, 0 \rangle$.

We leave it to you to verify that the remaining edges to be processed are $\langle 6, 7 \rangle$, $\langle 7, 12 \rangle$, $\langle 12, 8 \rangle$, $\langle 8, 11 \rangle$, $\langle 2, 3 \rangle$, $\langle 3, 4 \rangle$ (forcing a split of $\langle 11, 9 \rangle$ and introducing a new vertex labeled as 13), $\langle 4, 10 \rangle$, $\langle 11, 13 \rangle$, and $\langle 13, 9 \rangle$. The final state of the BSP tree is shown in Figure 13.9. The regions corresponding to the leaf nodes of the BSP tree are labeled in the figure. The new vertices in the partitioning are shown as black dots. The point 13 introduced in the split of $\langle 11, 9 \rangle$ is the leftmost one in the figure. ∎

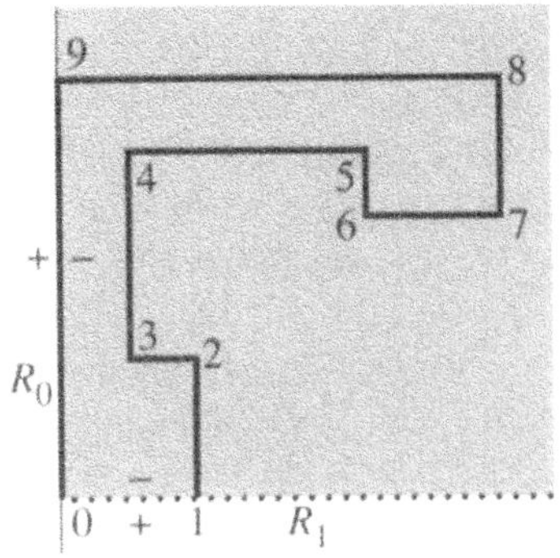

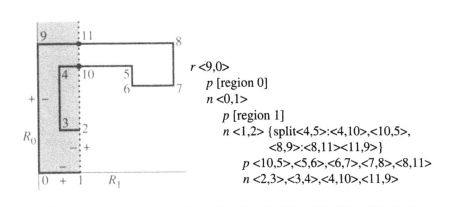

r <9,0>
  p [region 0]
  n <0,1>
    p [region 1]
    n <1,2>,<2,3>,<3,4>,<4,5>,
      <5,6>,<6,7>,<7,8>,<8,9>

Figure 13.5   Current state after processing edge ⟨0, 1⟩.

r <9,0>
  p [region 0]
  n <0,1>
    p [region 1]
    n <1,2> {split<4,5>:<4,10>,<10,5>,
      <8,9>:<8,11><11,9>}
      p <10,5>,<5,6>,<6,7>,<7,8>,<8,11>
      n <2,3>,<3,4>,<4,10>,<11,9>

Figure 13.6   Current state after processing edge ⟨1, 2⟩. This edge forces a split of ⟨4, 5⟩ to ⟨4, 10⟩ and ⟨10, 5⟩. It also forces a split of ⟨8, 9⟩ to ⟨8, 11⟩ and ⟨11, 9⟩.

EXAMPLE   Figure 13.10 shows a partitioning of space for a convex polygon and the corresponding BSP tree. The tree construction for the convex polygon requires no splitting of edges. However, the tree is just a linear list of nodes. Any tests for containment inside the polygon, in the worst case, require processing at every node of the tree. A better situation for minimizing the processing is to start with a binary tree that is balanced as much as possible. ▪

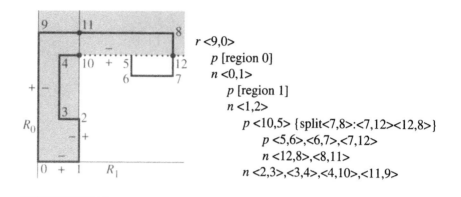

$r <9,0>$
  p [region 0]
  $n <0,1>$
    p [region 1]
    $n <1,2>$
      $p <10,5>$ {split$<7,8>$:$<7,12><12,8>$}
        $p <5,6>,<6,7>,<7,12>$
        $n <12,8>,<8,11>$
      $n <2,3>,<3,4>,<4,10>,<11,9>$

Figure 13.7   Current state after processing edge $\langle 10, 5 \rangle$. This edge forces a split of $\langle 7, 8 \rangle$ to $\langle 7, 12 \rangle$ and $\langle 12, 8 \rangle$.

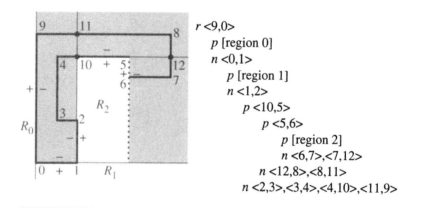

$r <9,0>$
  p [region 0]
  $n <0,1>$
    p [region 1]
    $n <1,2>$
      $p <10,5>$
        $p <5,6>$
          p [region 2]
          $n <6,7>,<7,12>$
        $n <12,8>,<8,11>$
      $n <2,3>,<3,4>,<4,10>,<11,9>$

Figure 13.8   Current state after processing edge $\langle 5, 6 \rangle$.

13.1.2 MINIMUM SPLITS VERSUS BALANCED TREES

As we saw in the example of a BSP tree for a convex polygon, the tree construction required no splitting, but the tree is very unbalanced since it is a linear list. The problem in the construction is that the splitting lines were selected to contain edges of the polygon. That constraint is not necessary for partitioning space by a polygon. An alternative is to choose splitting lines in a clever way to obtain minimum splitting and a balanced tree. For a convex polygon, it is always possible to build such a tree.

r <9,0>
  p [region 0]
  n <0,1>
    p [region 1]
    n <1,2>
      p <10,5>
        p <5,6>
          p [region 2]
          n <6,7>
            p [region 3]
            n <7,12>
              p [region 4]
              n [region 5]
        n <12,8>
          p [region 6]
          n <8,11>
            p [region 7]
            n [region 8]
      n <2,3>
        p <3,4>
          p <4,10>
            p [region 10]
            n <11,13>
              p [region 11]
              n [region 12]
          n <13,9>
            p [region 13]
            n [region 14]
        n [region 9]

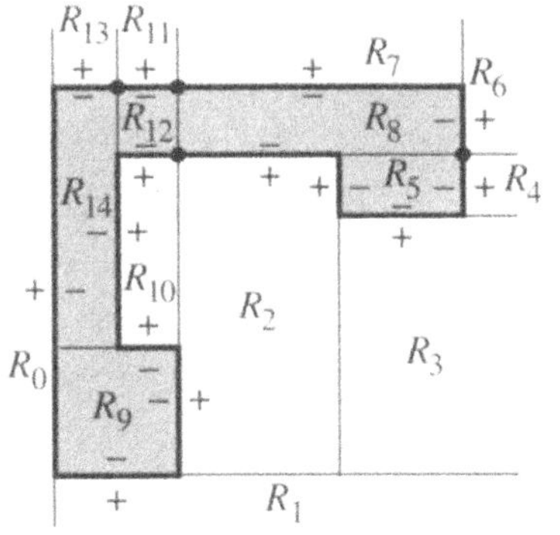

Figure 13.9   Final state after processing edge ⟨13, 9⟩.

For general polygons, it is not clear what the best strategy is for choosing the splitting lines.

For a convex polygon, a bisection method works very well. The idea is to choose a line that contains vertex V_0 and another vertex V_m that splits the vertices into two subsets of about the same number of elements. A routine to compute m was given in Section 7.7.2 for finding extreme points of convex polygons:

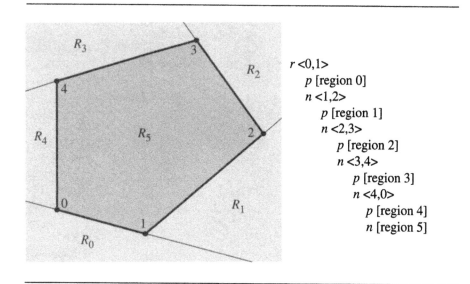

$r <0,1>$
   p [region 0]
   $n <1,2>$
      p [region 1]
      $n <2,3>$
         p [region 2]
         $n <3,4>$
            p [region 3]
            $n <4,0>$
               p [region 4]
               n [region 5]

Figure 13.10   Partition for a convex polygon and the corresponding BSP tree.

```
int GetMiddleIndex(int i0, int i1, int N)
{
    if (i0 < i1)
        return (i0 + i1) / 2;
    else
        return (i0 + i1 + N) / 2 (mod N);
}
```

The value N is the number of vertices. The initial call sets both i_0 and i_1 to zero. The condition when $i_0 < i_1$ has an obvious result—the returned index is the average of the input indices, certainly supporting the name of the function. For example, if the polygon has $N = 5$ vertices, inputs $i_0 = 0$ and $i_1 = 2$ lead to a returned index of 1. The other condition handles wraparound of the indices. If $i_0 = 2$ and $i_1 = 0$, the implied set of ordered indices is $\{2, 3, 4, 0\}$. The middle index is selected as 3 since $3 = (2 + 0 + 5)/2 \pmod 5$.

Because the splitting line passes through vertices and because the polygon is convex, no edges are split by this line. Because of the bisection, the tree will automatically be balanced. Figure 13.11 shows the partitioning and BSP tree for the convex polygon of the last example. Observe that the depth of this tree is smaller than that of the original construction.

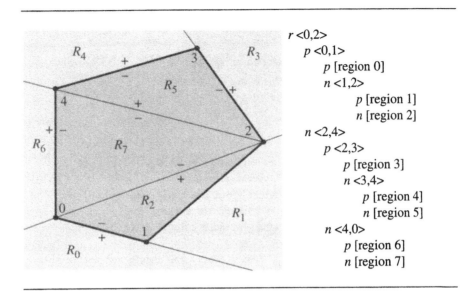

$$r <0,2>$$
$$p <0,1>$$
$$p \text{ [region 0]}$$
$$n <1,2>$$
$$p \text{ [region 1]}$$
$$n \text{ [region 2]}$$
$$n <2,4>$$
$$p <2,3>$$
$$p \text{ [region 3]}$$
$$n <3,4>$$
$$p \text{ [region 4]}$$
$$n \text{ [region 5]}$$
$$n <4,0>$$
$$p \text{ [region 6]}$$
$$n \text{ [region 7]}$$

Figure 13.11   Partition for a convex polygon and the corresponding balanced BSP tree.

13.1.3 POINT IN POLYGON USING BSP TREES

A BSP tree representation of a polygon naturally provides the ability to test if a point is inside, outside, or on the polygon. The point is processed at each node of the tree by testing which side of the splitting line it is on. If the processing reaches a leaf node, the point is in the corresponding convex region. If that region is inside (or outside) the polygon, then the point is inside (or outside) the polygon. At any node if the point is on an edge contained by the splitting line, then the point is, of course, on the polygon itself. The pseudocode is listed below. The return value of the function is +1 if the point is outside, −1 if the point is inside, or 0 if the point is on the polygon.

```
int PointLocation(BspTree T, Point P)
{
    // test point against splitting line
    type = Classify(T.line, P);
    if (type is POSITIVE) {
        if (T.posChild exists)
            return PointLocation(T.posChild, P);
        else
            return +1;
    } else if (type is NEGATIVE) {
        if (T.negChild exists)
            return PointLocation(T.negChild, P);
```

```
        else
            return -1;
    } else {
        // type is COINCIDENT
        for (each edge T.coincident[i]) {
            if (P on T.coincident[i])
                return 0;
        }

        // does not matter which subtree you use
        if (T.posChild exists)
            return PointLocation(T.posChild, P);
        else if (T.negChild exists)
            return PointLocation(T.negChild, P);
        else {
            // Theoretically you should not get to this block.  Numerical
            // errors might cause the block to be reached, most likely
            // because the test point is nearly an end point of a
            // coincident edge.  An implementation could throw an exception
            // or 'assert' in Debug mode, but still return a value in Release
            // mode.  For simplicity, let's just return 0 in hopes the test
            // point is nearly a coincident edge end point.
            return 0;
        }
    }
}
```

13.1.4 PARTITIONING A LINE SEGMENT BY A BSP TREE

Given a line segment in the plane, the segment is naturally partitioned by a BSP tree into subsegments that are contained by an outside region, contained by an inside region, or coincident to splitting lines. The line segment is processed at each node of the tree. If the segment is on the positive side of the line, possibly with one end point on the line, it is just sent to the positive-child subtree for further processing. If the node has no positive-child subtree, then the line segment is in an outside region. Similarly, if the segment is on the negative side of the line, it is further processed by the negative-child subtree unless that subtree does not exist, in which case the line segment is in an inside region. If the segment crosses the splitting line, it is partitioned into two pieces, one piece on the positive side of the line and one piece on the negative side. The positive piece is further processed by the positive-child subtree; the negative piece is further processed by the negative-child subtree. The final possibility is that the segment is coincident with the splitting line. The intersection of the segment with an edge generating the splitting line must be calculated. Any subsegments not contained by an edge must be further processed by both the positive-child and negative-child subtrees.

The end result of processing the line segment is a *partition*, a representation of the line segment as a union of contiguous subsegments. Each subsegment lives in an inside region, an outside region, or is on a polygon boundary. Those segments on the polygon boundary can be further classified based on the direction of the polygon edge and the direction of the line segment. This distinction is important when using BSP trees to support Boolean operations on polygons. Figure 13.2 shows a splitting line and two segments, E_0 and E_1, that are coincident to the line. E_0 and N are in the same direction, but E_1 and N are in opposite directions.

Figure 13.12 shows the polygon of Figure 13.3 and a line segment intersecting the polygon. The end points of the line segment are labeled as 0 and 1. The other labeled points, 2 through 6, are inserted into the partition as the segment is processed recursively through the tree. The right portion of the figure shows the BSP tree for the polygon. The segments are denoted by (i_0, i_1). Initially segment $(0, 1)$ is processed at the root node of the tree. The segment is not split by the line containing edge $\langle 9, 0 \rangle$, so region 0 does not contain any portion of the original segment. The segment $(0, 1)$ is sent to the negative child of the root and processed. The segment is split by the line containing edge $\langle 0, 1 \rangle$, the new point labeled 2. Segment $(0, 2)$ is on the positive side of the splitting line, but the root node has no positive child, so segment $(0, 2)$ is contained in region 1. Segment $(2, 1)$ is sent to the negative child and the process is repeated.

The final partition leads to positive segments $(0, 2)$, $(3, 5)$, and $(6, 1)$. The negative segments are $(2, 3)$, $(5, 4)$, and $(4, 6)$. Observe that the subsegments do not necessarily alternate between positive and negative. In the previous example, the subsegments $(5, 4)$ and $(4, 6)$ are adjacent, but both negative. An implementation of line segment partitioning can trap these cases and combine adjacent same-sign segments into single segments.

The pseudocode for line segment partitioning is listed below. The inputs are the tree, polygon, and line segment end points V_0 and V_1. The outputs are the four sets of subsegments. The Pos set contains those subsegments that are in positive regions, and the Neg set contains those subsegments that are in negative regions. The other two sets store subsegments that are contained by edges that are coincident to splitting lines. The CoSame set contains subsegments contained by edges where each subsegment is in the same direction as the edge. The CoDiff set contains subsegments contained by edges where each subsegment is in the opposite direction as the edge.

```
void GetPartition(BspTree T, Edge E, EdgeSet Pos, EdgeSet Neg,
    EdgeSet CoSame, EdgeSet CoDiff)
{
    type = Classify(T.line, E, SubPos, SubNeg);
    if (type is CROSSES) {
        GetPosPartition(T.posChild, SubPos, Pos, Neg, CoSame, CoDiff);
        GetNegPartition(T.negChild, SubNeg, Pos, Neg, CoSame, CoDiff);
    } else if (type is POSITIVE) {
```

```
                    GetPosPartition(T.posChild, E, Pos, Neg, CoSame, CoDiff);
          } else if (type is NEGATIVE) {
                    GetNegPartition(T.negChild, E, Pos, Neg, CoSame, CoDiff);
          } else {
                    // type is COINCIDENT
                    // construct segments of E intersecting coincident edges
                    A = {E};
                    for (each edge E' in T.coincident)
                        A = Intersection(A, E');

                    for (each segment S of A) {
                        if (S is in the same direction as T.line)
                            CoPos.Insert(S);
                        else
                            CoNeg.Insert(S);
                    }

                    // construct segments of E not intersecting coincident edges
                    B = {E} - A;
                    for (each segment S of B) {
                        GetPosPartition(T.posChild, S, Pos, Neg, CoSame, CoDiff);
                        GetNegPartition(T.negChild, S, Pos, Neg, CoSame, CoDiff);
                    }
          }
}

void GetPosPartition(BspTree T, Edge E, EdgeSet Pos, EdgeSet Neg,
        EdgeSet CoSame, EdgeSet CoDiff)
{
    if (T.posChild)
        GetPartition(T.posChild, E, Pos, Neg, CoSame, CoDiff);
    else
        Pos.Insert(E);
}

void GetNegPartition(BspTree T, Edge E, EdgeSet Pos, EdgeSet Neg,
        EdgeSet CoSame, EdgeSet CoDiff)
{
    if (T.negChild)
        GetPartition(T.negChild, E, Pos, Neg, CoSame, CoDiff);
    else
        Neg.Insert(E);
}
```

The function Classify is the same one used for BSP tree construction.

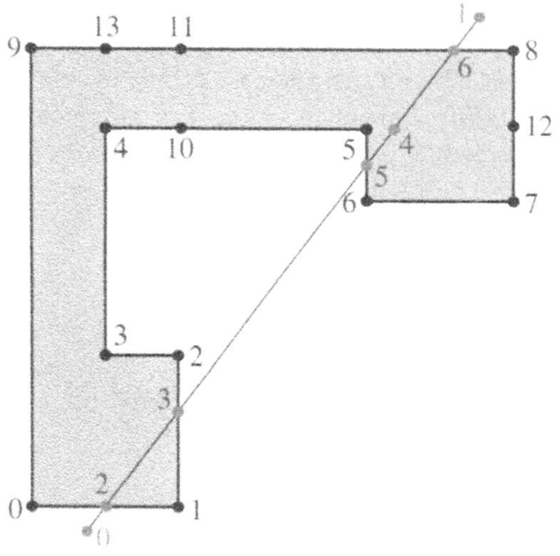

r <0,9> process (0,1)
  p [region 0] final = nothing
  n <0,1> process(0,1), add 2
    p [region 1] final = (0,2)
    n <1,2> process (2,1), add 3
      p <10,5> process (3,1), add 4
        p <5,6> process (3,4), add 5
          p [region 2] final = (3,5)
          n <6,7> process (5,4)
            p [region 3] final = nothing
            n <7,12> process (5,4)
              p [region 4] final = nothing
              n [region 5] final = (5,4)
        n <12,8> process (4,1)
          p [region 6] final = nothing
          n <8,11> process (4,1), add 6
            p [region 7] final = (6,1)
            n [region 8] final = (4,6)
    n <2,3> process (2,3)
      p <3,4>
        p <4,10>
          p [region 10]
          n <11,13>
            p [region 11]
            n [region 12]
      n <13,9>
        p [region 13]
        n [region 14]
    n [region 9] final = (2,3)

Figure 13.12   Partition of a line segment.

13.2 BINARY SPACE-PARTITIONING TREES IN 3D

We recommend reading Section 13.1 before reading this section to obtain intuition about binary space partitioning.

Consider a plane in space with representation $\vec{n} \cdot X - c = 0$. The plane partitions space into two half-spaces. The half-space on the side of the plane to which $\vec{n}$ points is called the *positive side of the plane*; the other side is called the *negative side of the plane*. If X is on the positive side, then $\vec{n} \cdot X - c > 0$, hence the use of the phrase "positive side." If X is on the negative side, then $\vec{n} \cdot X - c < 0$. A point X on the plane of course satisfies $\vec{n} \cdot X - c = 0$.

Each half-space may be further subdivided by another plane in space. The resulting positive and negative regions can themselves be subdivided. The resulting partitioning of the plane is represented by a binary tree, each node representing the splitting plane. The left child of a node corresponds to the positive side of the splitting plane that the node represents; the right child corresponds to the negative side. The leaf nodes of the tree represent the convex regions obtained by the partitioning.

13.2.1 BSP TREE REPRESENTATION OF A POLYHEDRON

Just as a 2D BSP tree is used to partition a polygon into convex subpolygons, a 3D BSP tree can be used to partition a polyhedron into convex subpolyhedra. The decomposition is useful for point-in-polyhedron queries and Boolean operations on polyhedra. The simplest construction uses polygon faces to determine the splitting planes. The recursive splitting is applied, just as in 2D, the only complication being that computing the intersection of a convex polygon and a plane is slightly more difficult than computing the intersection of a line segment and a line. The pseudocode for construction of a BSP tree from a polyhedron is listed below. As a reminder, we require that the polyhedron faces are convex polygons.

```
BspTree ConstructTree(FaceList L)
{
    T = new BspTree;

    // use a face to determine the splitting plane for the tree node
    T.plane = GetPlaneFromFace(L.first);   // Dot(N, X) - c = 0

    FaceList posList, negList;  // initially empty lists
    for (each face F of L) {
        // Determine how face and plane relate to each other.  If the face
        // crosses the plane, the subpolyhedra on the positive and
        // negative side of the plane are returned.
        type = Classify(T.plane, F, SubPos, SubNeg);

        if (type is CROSSES) {
            // Dot(N, X) - c < 0 for some vertices,
            // Dot(N, X) - c > 0 for some vertices
            posList.AddFace(SubPos);
            negList.AddFace(SubNeg);
        } else if (type is POSITIVE) {
            // Dot(N, X) - c >= 0 for all vertices, at least one positive
            posList.AddFace(F);
```

```
        } else if (type is NEGATIVE) {
            // Dot(N, X) - c <= 0 for all vertices, at least one negative
            negList.AddFace(F);
        } else {
            // type is COINCIDENT
            // Dot(N, X) - c = 0 for all vertices
            T.coincident.AddFace(F);
        }
    }

    if (posList is not empty)
        T.posChild = ConstructTree(posList);
    else
        T.posChild = null;

    if (negList is not empty)
        T.negChild = ConstructTree(negList);
    else
        T.negChild = null;

    return T;
}
```

The function GetPlaneFromFace produces a plane whose normal vector points to
the outside region of the polyhedron at the specified face. Other coincident faces may
or may not have normals that point in the same direction as the plane normal. This
is analogous to the situation shown in Figure 13.2 for the 2D polygon case.

The function Classify tries to find a line segment of intersection of the current
face and the node's plane. If there is an intersection that is an interior segment of the
face, the positive and negative subfaces are returned. If the face is only on the positive
side, with the possibility that some vertices or collinear edges are on the plane, then
the face is classified as a positive face. A similar classification is given for faces on the
negative side of the plane. The face can be entirely on the splitting plane, in which
case the face is classified as coincident. The pseudocode for this function is

```
int Classify(Plane P, Face F, Face SubPos, Face SubNeg)
{
    for (i = 0; i < F.vertexQuantity; i++)
        d[i] = Dot(P.normal, F.V(i) - P.origin);

    if (at least one d[i] > 0 and at least one d[i] < 0) {
        // face crosses plane
        SplitPolygon(F, P, d[], SubPos, SubNeg);
        return CROSSES;
```

```
        } else if (all d[i] >= 0 with at least one d[i] > 0)  {
            // All vertices of the face are on the positive side of the plane,
            // but not all vertices are on the plane.
            return POSITIVE;
        } else if (all d[i] <= 0 with at least one d[i] < 0)  {
            // All vertices of the face are on the negative side of the plane,
            // but not all vertices are on the plane.
            return NEGATIVE;
        } else {
            // All vertices of the face are on the plane.
            return COINCIDENT;
        }
    }
}
```

The function SplitPolygon determines those edges of F that intersect the plane (computable by the d[] values) and constructs the two subpolygons. The points of intersection of the edges with the plane are computed just like the point of intersection between edge and line was computed for the 2D problem. Floating-point round-off errors must be dealt with by an implementation when one or more of the d[i] are nearly zero. This is particularly important to avoid unnecessary splits.

13.2.2 MINIMUM SPLITS VERSUS BALANCED TREES

In the 2D problem, a convex polygon led to a BSP tree that was a linear list. A convex polyhedron also has a BSP tree that is a linear list since the faces of the polyhedron are always on the negative side of a plane of one of the faces. A balanced tree was constructed in the 2D case by selecting a splitting line connecting two nonadjacent vertices. The convexity of the polygon guaranteed that the splitting line did not split any edges of the polygon. The resulting tree was the best of both worlds: it was balanced and required no edge splitting.

The situation in 3D is not as simple. A splitting plane may be chosen that cuts the convex polyhedron in two pieces, but the plane in most cases will require splitting faces. The only situation where the splitting will not occur is if the plane intersects the polyhedron only at edges. That means the polyhedron must contain a polyline of edges that is coplanar—a situation that is not generic. Consequently, obtaining a balanced tree will require some splitting, the hope being that the number of splits is as small as possible. Selecting a heuristic that leads to a generic algorithm for minimum splitting is difficult at best. Greater success is more likely if an implementation uses a priori knowledge about its data sets. In any event, the quality of the algorithm used to build the tree is the key to the performance of a BSP tree system.

13.2.3 POINT IN POLYHEDRON USING BSP TREES

Computing the location of a point relative to a polyhedron is exactly the same algorithm as in the 2D problem. The point is compared against each node of the BSP tree.
If the point is on the positive side of a plane, and if the positive child exists, the point
is further processed by that subtree. If the positive child does not exist, the point is
outside the polyhedron. If the point is on the negative side of a plane, and if the negative child exists, the point is further processed by that subtree. If the negative child
does not exist, the point is inside the polyhedron. If the point is on the splitting plane
itself, it is either contained by a face, in which case the point is on the polyhedron
itself, or the point is not contained by a face and it is sent to any existing child subtree
for further processing. The pseudocode is shown below. The return value is $+1$ if the
point is outside, -1 if the point is inside, or 0 if the point is on the polyhedron.

```
int PointLocation(BspTree T, Point P)
{
    // test point against splitting plane
    type = Classify(T.plane, P);
    if (type is POSITIVE) {
        if (T.posChild exists)
            return PointLocation(T.posChild, P);
        else
            return +1;
    } else if (type is NEGATIVE) {
        if (T.negChild exists)
            return PointLocation(T.negChild, P);
        else
            return -1;
    } else {
        // type is COINCIDENT
        for (each face T.coincident[i]) {
            if (P on T.coincident[i])
                return 0;
        }

        // does not matter which subtree you use
        if (T.posChild exists)
            return PointLocation(T.posChild, P);
        else if (T.negChild exists)
            return PointLocation(T.negChild, P);
        else
            return 0;
    }
}
```

13.2.4   PARTITIONING A LINE SEGMENT BY A BSP TREE

Given a line segment in space, the segment is naturally partitioned by a BSP tree into subsegments that are contained by an outside region, contained by an inside region, or coincident to splitting planes. The line segment is processed at each node of the tree. If the segment is on the positive side of the plane, possibly with one end point on the plane, it is just sent to the positive-child subtree for further processing. If the node has no positive-child subtree, then the line segment is in an outside region. Similarly, if the segment is on the negative side of the plane, it is further processed by the negative-child subtree unless that subtree does not exist, in which case the line segment is in an inside region. If the segment crosses the splitting plane, it is partitioned into two pieces, one piece on the positive side of the line and one piece on the negative side. The positive piece is further processed by the positive-child subtree; the negative piece is further processed by the negative-child subtree. The final possibility is that the segment is coincident with the splitting plane. The intersection of the line segment with the faces contained by the splitting plane must be calculated. Observe that this is exactly the problem of finding the intersection of a line segment with a 2D polygon, a problem that can be solved using 2D BSP trees. However, since the faces are required to be convex polygons, the intersection of line segment and convex polygon can be implemented in a straightforward manner without having to create BSP trees for the faces. Any subsegments not contained by a face must be further processed by both the positive-child and negative-child subtrees.

The end result of processing the line segment is a *partition*—a representation of the line segment as a union of contiguous subsegments. Each subsegment lives in an inside region, an outside region, or is on a polygon boundary. The pseudocode for the partitioning is listed below.

```
void GetPartition(BspTree T, Edge E, EdgeSet Pos, EdgeSet Neg, EdgeSet Coin)
{
    type = Classify(T.plane, E, SubPos, SubNeg);
    if (type is CROSSES) {
        GetPosPartition(T.posChild, SubPos, Pos, Neg, Coin);
        GetNegPartition(T.negChild, SubNeg, Pos, Neg, Coin);
    } else if (type is POSITIVE) {
        GetPosPartition(T.posChild, E, Pos, Neg, Coin);
    } else if (type is NEGATIVE) {
        GetNegPartition(T.negChild, E, Pos, Neg, Coin);
    } else {
        // type is COINCIDENT
        // construct segments of E intersecting coincident faces
        A = {E};
        for (each face F in T.coincident)
            A = Intersection(A, F);
```

```
        for (each segment S of A)
            Coin.Insert(S);

        // construct segments of E not intersecting coincident faces
        B = {E} - A;
        for (each segment S of B) {
            GetPosPartition(T.posChild, S, Pos, Neg, Coin);
            GetNegPartition(T.negChild, S, Pos, Neg, Coin);
        }
    }
}

void GetPosPartition(BspTree T, Edge E, EdgeSet Pos, EdgeSet Neg, EdgeSet Coin)
{
    if (T.posChild)
        GetPartition(T.posChild, E, Pos, Neg, Coin);
    else
        Pos.Insert(E);
}

void GetNegPartition(BspTree T, Edge E, EdgeSet Pos, EdgeSet Neg, EdgeSet Coin)
{
    if (T.negChild)
        GetPartition(T.negChild, E, Pos, Neg, Coin);
    else
        Neg.Insert(E);
}
```

The function Classify in BSP tree construction splits a face, but the Classify function used in this routine has the simpler job of splitting only an edge.

The line segment does not necessarily have to represent a geometric entity consisting of a continuum of points at a given time. For example, in a collision detection system where a point abstractly represents an object moving through space that is partitioned by a BSP tree, the line segment can represent the predicted path of motion of the point over a specified time interval. If the object represented by the point is not allowed to pass through a "wall" (contained in a partitioning plane of the BSP tree) separating an inside region from an outside one, the line segment partitioning can be used to prevent the object from doing so. If the segment has to be split by partitioning planes, the shortest subsegment containing the initial point (at time zero) represents how far the object can move without a collision. The application can then move the object by that distance or, if desired, disallow any motion. Such an approach for collision detection is superior to one that samples the projected path to generate a lot of points, then processes each one by the BSP tree to see if it is contained by an inside or an outside region, then collectively analyzes the results to decide how far an object can move.

13.2.5 PARTITIONING A CONVEX POLYGON BY A BSP TREE

Partitioning a convex polygon by a 3D BSP tree is the direct analog of partitioning a line segment by a 2D BSP tree. The pseudocode is listed below. The input face F is assumed to be a convex polygon. The most complex part of the algorithm is handling the cases when the polygon is coincident to a splitting plane, in which case the problem is reduced to computing an intersection and a difference of polygons in a plane. Section 13.5 shows how to compute the intersection and difference of polygons.

```
void GetPartition(BspTree T, Face F, FaceSet Pos, FaceSet Neg,
    FaceSet CoPos, FaceSet CoNeg)
{
    type = Classify(T.plane, F, SubPos, SubNeg);
    if (type is CROSSES) {
        GetPosPartition(T.posChild, SubPos, Pos, Neg, CoPos, CoNeg);
        GetNegPartition(T.negChild, SubNeg, Pos, Neg, CoPos, CoNeg);
    } else if (type is POSITIVE) {
        GetPosPartition(T.posChild, F, Pos, Neg, Coin);
    } else if (type is NEGATIVE) {
        GetNegPartition(T.negChild, F, Pos, Neg, Coin);
    } else {
        // type is COINCIDENT
        // compute intersection of F with coincident faces
        A = {F};
        for (each face F' in T.coincident)
            A = Intersection(A, F');

        for (each face S of A) {
            if (S has normal in same direction as T.plane)
                CoPos.Insert(S);
            else
                CoNeg.Insert(S);
        }

        // construct complement of intersection of F with coincident faces
        B = {F} - A;
        for (each face S of B) {
            GetPosPartition(T.posChild, S, Pos, Neg, CoPos, CoNeg);
            GetNegPartition(T.negChild, S, Pos, Neg, CoPos, CoNeg);
```

```
            }
        }
    }

    void GetPosPartition(BspTree T, Face F, FaceSet Pos, FaceSet Neg,
        FaceSet CoPos, FaceSet CoNeg)
    {
        if (T.posChild)
            GetPartition(T.posChild, F, Pos, Neg, CoPos, CoNeg);
        else
            Pos.Insert(F);
    }

    void GetNegPartition(BspTree T, Face F, FaceSet Pos, FaceSet Neg,
        FaceSet CoPos, FaceSet CoNeg)
    {
        if (T.negChild)
            GetPartition(T.negChild, F, Pos, Neg, CoPos, CoNeg);
        else
            Neg.Insert(F);
    }
```

13.3 POINT IN POLYGON

A common query in graphics applications is to determine if a point is inside a polygon. Many approaches can be used to answer the query. A survey of these approaches is in the section "Point in Polygon Strategies" in Heckbert (1994). If the polygon is represented as a BSP tree, Section 13.1 discusses how to determine if a point is inside or outside the polygon. We discuss here a few methods that do not require preprocessing to create data structures that support fast queries. The last section discusses a method that does require preprocessing by decomposing the polygon into trapezoids.

13.3.1 POINT IN TRIANGLE

Consider a point P and a triangle with noncollinear vertices V_i for $0 \le i \le 2$. Let the triangle edges be $\vec{e}_0 = V_1 - V_0$, $\vec{e}_1 = V_2 - V_1$, and $\vec{e}_2 = V_0 - V_2$. Edge normals are $\vec{n}_i = \text{Perp}(\vec{e}_i)$, where $\text{Perp}(x, y) = (y, -x)$. The normals are outer-pointing if the vertices are counterclockwise ordered or inner-pointing if the vertices are clockwise ordered.

In the case of counterclockwise-ordered vertices, P is inside the triangle if it is on the negative side of each edge line $\vec{n}_i \cdot (X - V_i) = 0$. That is, P is inside the triangle when $\vec{n}_i \cdot (P - V_i) < 0$ for all i. The point is outside the triangle if $\vec{n}_i \cdot (P - V_i) > 0$

for at least one i. It is possible that P is on the triangle boundary itself, in which case $\vec{n}_i \cdot (P - V_i) \leq 0$ for all i with equality for at least one i. If an equality occurs once, the point is on an edge but not at a vertex. If an equality occurs twice, the point is a vertex. It is not possible for equality to occur three times. If the vertices are clockwise ordered, the inequalities on these tests are simply reversed. In an application where the vertex ordering is not consistent among all triangles, the test for point inside triangle that works regardless of order is

$$(\vec{n}_0 \cdot (V_2 - V_0))(\vec{n}_i \cdot (P - V_i)) > 0 \quad \text{for all } i$$

Of course, the first dot product effectively determines the vertex ordering.

The point can also be written in barycentric coordinates as $P = c_0 V_0 + c_1 V_1 + c_2 V_2$, where $c_0 + c_1 + c_2 = 1$. P is inside or on the triangle if $0 \leq c_i \leq 1$ for all i. If $c_j < 0$ for at least one j, the point is outside the triangle. The coefficient c_2 is computed in the following manner:

$$P - V_0 = (c_0 - 1)V_0 + c_1 V_1 + c_2 V_2 = (-c_1 - c_2)V_0 + c_1 V_1 + c_2 V_2$$

$$= c_1(V_1 - V_0) + c_2(V_2 - V_0)$$

so that $\vec{n}_0 \cdot (P - V_0) = c_2 \vec{n}_0 \cdot (V_2 - V_0)$. Similar constructions apply for c_0 and c_1 to obtain

$$c_0 = -\frac{\vec{n}_1 \cdot (P - V_1)}{\vec{n}_1 \cdot \vec{e}_0}, \quad c_1 = -\frac{\vec{n}_2 \cdot (P - V_2)}{\vec{n}_2 \cdot \vec{e}_1}, \quad c_2 = -\frac{\vec{n}_0 \cdot (P - V_0)}{\vec{n}_0 \cdot \vec{e}_2}$$

The exact representation of P is not important for testing if it is inside the triangle. The denominators of the fractions are all the same sign for a given triangle ordering, so the signs of the numerators are all that matter for the query. These signs are exactly what is considered in the test provided earlier in this section.

Although we assumed that the triangle vertices are noncollinear, applications might need to deal with the degenerate case of collinear vertices. More likely is that a triangle that is needlelike or has small area might be encountered in a data set. Such a triangle satisfies the noncollinear condition, but floating-point round-off errors can create problems.

Consider the case of three distinct vertices that are collinear, so the triangle is degenerate and is a line segment. One of the vertices must be an interior point to the edge connecting the other two vertices. For the sake of argument, suppose V_2 is that vertex. The normal vectors are mutually parallel, but $\vec{n}_0$ points in the opposite direction of $\vec{n}_1$ and $\vec{n}_2$. If P is not on the line of the vertices, then $\text{Sign}(\vec{n}_0 \cdot (P - V_0)) = -\text{Sign}(\vec{n}_1 \cdot (P - V_1))$ and $\text{Sign}(\vec{n}_1 \cdot (P - V_1)) = \text{Sign}(\vec{n}_2 \cdot (P - V_2))$. It is not possible for all three signs to be the same, so the point-in-triangle sign tests mentioned previously still produce the correct result, that P is outside the triangle (in this case, not on the line segment). If P is on the line of the vertices, then all three signs are zero—not enough information to determine if P is contained by the line segment. Further work must be done to resolve the problem. Specifically, P must be a linear combination of the segment end points, $P = (1 - t)V_0 + tV_1$ for some value t. If $t \in [0, 1]$, then P is contained by the line segment and P is "inside" the triangle. Otherwise it is outside. This type of analysis also occurs in the construction of the convex hull of a point set in 2D (Section 13.7).

If the triangle is needlelike, nearly collinear vertices, so to speak, floating-point round-off errors can make the situation look just like the collinear one. The same problem can occur if two of the vertices are nearly the same. In either case, an application has two options. The first is to preprocess the triangles to collapse nearly degenerate ones to line segments or points, then use point equality, point-in-segment, or point-in-triangle tests accordingly. This approach is recommended if a large number of containment queries will occur for the same collection of triangles. The second is to accept the triangles as is and test for the degeneracies and switch to the point equality or point-in-segment test as needed.

13.3.2 POINT IN CONVEX POLYGON

The sidedness tests used in the point-in-triangle query naturally extend to determining if a point is in a convex polygon. Let the convex polygon have counterclockwise-ordered, noncollinear vertices $\{V_i\}_{i=0}^{n-1}$ with the convention that $V_n = V_0$. If the vertices are collinear or the polygon is nearly degenerate in that it is needlelike, the potential numerical problems are handled in the same way as described in the point-in-triangle tests.

The edges of the polygon are $\vec{e}_i = V_{i+1} - V_i$, and outer-pointing edge normals are $\vec{n}_i = \text{Perp}(\vec{e}_i)$. The point P is inside the polygon when $\vec{n}_i \cdot (P - V_i) < 0$ for all i. The point is outside if $\vec{n}_i \cdot (P - V_i) > 0$ for some i. The point is on the polygon boundary itself if $\vec{n}_i \cdot (P - V_i) \leq 0$ for all i with equality occurring for at least one i. If equality occurs for exactly one i, then P is on an edge but is not a vertex. If equality occurs for two values of i, the point is a vertex. Equality cannot occur for three or more indices.

This algorithm is $O(n)$ since all n edges of the polygon must be tested to know that P is inside. The straightforward implementation for testing if a point is inside or on the polygon is

```
bool PointInPolygon(Point P, ConvexPolygon C)
{
    for (i0 = 0, i1 = C.N - 1; i < C.N; i0++) {
        if (Dot(Perp(C.V(i0) - C.V(i1)), P - C.V(i1)) > 0)
            return false;
    }
    return true;
}
```

When P is inside the polygon, the loop body is executed n times.

An Asymptotically Faster Method

Another algorithm uses the bisection method that was also used to build a balanced BSP tree for a convex polygon. To illustrate, consider a convex quadrilateral with counterclockwise-ordered vertices V_i for $0 \le i \le 3$. The polygon is treated as a union of two triangles, $\langle V_0, V_1, V_2 \rangle$ and $\langle V_0, V_2, V_3 \rangle$. The bisection implementation is

```
bool PointInConvexQuadrilateral(Point P, ConvexPolygon C)
{
    if (Dot(Perp(C.V(2) - C.V(0)), P - C.V(0)) > 0) {
        // P potentially in <V0, V1, V2>
        if (Dot(Perp(C.V(1) - C.V(0)), P - C.V(1)) > 0) return false;
        if (Dot(Perp(C.V(2) - C.V(1)), P - C.V(1)) > 0) return false;
    } else {
        // P potentially in <V0, V2, V3>
        if (Dot(Perp(C.V(3) - C.V(2)), P - C.V(3)) > 0) return false;
        if (Dot(Perp(C.V(0) - C.V(3)), P - C.V(3)) > 0) return false;
    }
    return true;
}
```

When P is inside the quadrilateral, three dot products are computed. The straightforward implementation computes four dot products. However, the straightforward implementation identifies some outside points with a single dot product (points outside the first edge), but the bisection for a quadrilateral requires a minimum of two dot products before rejection. For a general convex polygon, the bisection implementation is

```
int GetMiddleIndex(int i0, int i1, int N)
{
    if (i0 < i1)
        return (i0 + i1) / 2;
    else
        return (i0 + i1 + N) / 2 (mod N);
}
```

```
bool PointInSubpolygon(Point P, ConvexPolygon C, int i0, int i1)
{
    if (i1 - i0 is 1 modulo C.N)
        return Dot(Perp(C.V(i1) - C.V(i0)), P - C.V(i0)) <= 0;

    mid = GetMiddleIndex(i0, i1, C.N);
    if (Dot(Perp(C.V(mid) - C.V(i0)), P - C.V(i0)) > 0) {
        // P potentially in <V(i0), V(i0 + 1), ... ,V(mid - 1), V(mid)>
```

```
        return PointInSubpolygon(P, C, i0, mid);
    } else {
        // P potentially in <V(mid), V(mid + 1), ... ,V(i1 - 1), V(i1)>
        return PointInSubpolygon(P, C, mid, i1);
    }
}

bool PointInPolygon(Point P, ConvexPolygon C)
{
    return PointInSubpolygon(P, C, 0, 0);
}
```

The vertex indices are computed modulo C.N. Because of the bisection, the algorithm is $O(\log n)$ for a convex polygon with n vertices.

Another Asymptotically Faster Method

The method described in this subsection also requires $O(\log n)$ time to perform the point-in-convex-polygon query.

The polygon vertices V_i for $0 \le i < n$ are assumed to be stored in counterclockwise order. Extreme vertices in the x-direction are computed. This can be done in $O(\log n)$ time using the bisection method discussed in Section 7.7.2. The x-minimum vertex has index $i_{\min}$, and the x-maximum vertex has index $i_{\max}$. Observe that it is not necessary that $i_{\min} < i_{\max}$. As the vertices are counterclockwise traversed from $V_{i_{\min}}$ to $V_{i_{\max}}$, the corresponding edges have outer normal vectors whose y-components are negative or zero, the latter occurring at most twice if the polygon has vertical edges at either x-extreme. The corresponding vertices and edges are referred to as the *bottom half of the polygon*. Similarly, as the vertices are counterclockwise traversed from $V_{i_{\max}}$ to $V_{i_{\min}}$, the corresponding edges have outer normal vectors whose y-components are positive or zero. The corresponding vertices and edges are referred to as the *top half of the polygon*.

Let P be the point to be tested for containment. The index bisection method is used to determine which vertex V_t in the top half of the polygon has the smallest x-value larger or equal to the x-value of P. If the top half has vertical edges, the extreme indices found initially can be appropriately incremented or decremented to exclude those edges from this test without affecting the correctness of the algorithm. Similarly, index bisection can be used to determine which vertex V_b in the bottom half of the polygon has the largest x-value smaller or equal to the x-value of P. Both bisections are $O(\log n)$ in time.

The vertical line containing P intersects the two directed edges whose initial points are V_t and V_b. If P is between the two edges, then it is inside the polygon. Otherwise it is outside the polygon. Figure 13.13 illustrates the various concepts in this section.

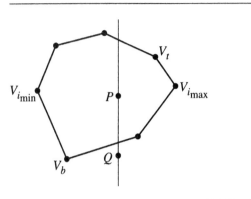

Figure 13.13   Point-in-convex-polygon test by determining two edges intersected by the vertical line through the test point. P is inside the polygon. Q is outside the polygon.

13.3.3   POINT IN GENERAL POLYGON

Perhaps the most used and effective algorithm for determining if P is inside a general polygon involves analyzing the intersections of the polygon and a ray whose origin is P and whose direction is $(1, 0)$. The idea is effectively the same one used in line segment partitioning by a BSP tree. As a ray is traversed starting from P, each time an edge is transversely crossed, a switch is made from inside to outside or vice versa. An implementation keeps track of the parity of the crossings. Odd parity means P is inside, even parity means it is outside. Figure 13.14 illustrates this.

To illustrate some technical difficulties, the figure includes polygon edges that are coincident to the ray for P_1 and polygon vertices that are on the ray. The problem at the polygon vertex 10 is that the ray transversely intersects the polygon boundary at that vertex, so the intersection should count as only one crossing. However, the two edges sharing the vertex are processed separately, each edge indicating that the crossing at the vertex is transverse. The result is that the vertex is counted twice as a crossing, incorrectly reversing the current parity for the intersection count. Vertex 2 has a slightly different problem. The ray is inside the polygon slightly to the left of the vertex and is inside the polygon slightly to the right. The crossing at vertex 2 should be ignored since the ray does not transversely cross the polygon boundary. Processing the edges separately leads to the correct result because both edges report a transverse crossing by the ray at the common vertex 2.

The problem with the coincident polygon edge $\langle 12, 13 \rangle$ is that it appears as if it is a single vertex, when viewed along the horizontal, that connects edges $\langle 11, 12 \rangle$ and $\langle 12, 13 \rangle$. If vertex 13 were to be relocated at vertex 12, the inside/outside count would not change—the crossing at vertex 12 is transverse to the polygon boundary. At first glance it appears we could just ignore the edge and call the crossing transverse, but

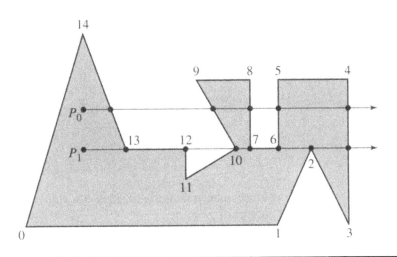

Figure 13.14   Point-in-polygon test by counting intersections of ray with polygon. The ray for point P_0 only crosses edges transversely. The number of crossings is odd (5), so the point is inside the polygon. The ray for point P_1 is more complex to analyze.

this is not correct. Consider the coincident edge $\langle 6, 7 \rangle$. If vertex 7 were to be relocated at vertex 6, the v-junction gets counted just like the one at vertex 2, so it is not a transverse crossing.

Preparata and Shamos (1985) mention how to deal with these configurations. The same idea is also mentioned by Haines (1989) and O'Rourke (1998). An edge is counted as a crossing of the ray with the polygon if one of the end points is strictly above the ray and the other end point is on or below the ray. Using this convention, coincident edges are not counted as crossing edges and can be ignored. Two edges above the ray that share a common vertex on the ray both count as crossings. If two edges below the ray share a common vertex on the ray, neither edge is counted. If one edge is above and one edge is below the ray, both sharing a vertex on the ray, the edge above is counted but the edge below is not. The pseudocode for this algorithm is listed below.

```
bool PointInPolygon(Point P, Polygon G)
{
    bool inside = false;
    for (i = 0, j = G.N - 1; i < G.N; j = i, i++)  {
        U0 = G.V(i);   U1 = G.V(j);

        if ((U0.y <= P.y and P.y < U1.y)    // U1 is above ray, U0 is on or below ray
            or
```

```
                    (U1.y <= P.y and P.y < U0.y)) // U0 is above ray, U1 is on or below ray
          {
              // Find x-intersection of edge with ray.  Only consider edge
              // crossings on the ray to the right of P.
              x = U0.x + (P.y -U0.y) * (U1.x - U0.x) / (U1.y - U0.y);
              if (x > P.x)
                  inside = not inside;
          }
      }
  }
  return inside;
}
```

A slight variation on the code is to compute x-P.x, combine the terms into a single fraction, and compare to zero:

```
dx = ((P.y - U0.y) * (U1.x - U0.x) - (P.x - U0.x) * (U1.y - U0.y)) /(U1.y - U0.y);
if (dx > 0)
   inside = not inside;
```

The numerator could be expanded to P.y * (U1.x - U0.x) -P.x * (U1.y - U0.y) + (U0.x * U1.y - U1.x * U0.y), but this requires 4 multiplications and 5 additions. The previous numerator requires only 2 multiplications and 5 additions. More important is that the floating-point division is an expensive operation. The division can be avoided by using

```
dy = U1.y - U0.y;
numer = ((P.y - U0.y) * (U1.x - U0.x) - (P.x - U0.x) * dy) * dy;
if (numer > 0)
    inside = not inside;
```

or, replacing the extra multiplication by a comparison to zero,

```
dy = U1.y - U0.y;
numer = (P.y - U0.y) * (U1.x - U0.x) - (P.x - U0.x) * dy;
if (dy > 0) {
    if (numer > 0) inside = not inside;
} else {
    if (numer < 0) inside = not inside;
}
```

A final variation takes advantage of knowing which vertex is above the ray, among other optimizations:

```
bool PointInPolygon(Point P, Polygon G)
{
    bool inside = false;
    for (i = 0, j = G.N-1; i < G.N; j = i, i++) {
        U0 = G.V(i);   U1 = G.V(j);

        if (P.y < U1.y) {
            // U1 above ray
            if (U0.y <= P.y) {
                // U0 on or below ray
                if ((P.y - U0.y) * (U1.x - U0.x) > (P.x - U0.x) * (U1.y - U0.y))
                    inside = not inside;
            }
        } else if (P.y < U0.y) {
            // U1 on or below ray, U0 above ray
            if ((P.y - U0.y) * (U1.x - U0.x) < (P.x - U0.x) * (U1.y - U0.y))
                inside = not inside;
        }
    }
    return inside;
}
```

The pseudocode properly classifies points that are strictly inside or strictly outside the polygon. However, points on the boundary sometimes are classified as inside, sometimes as outside. Figure 13.15 shows a triangle and two points P and Q on the boundary. The point P is classified as inside, the point Q is classified as outside. Such behavior may be desirable in an application when two polygons share an edge. A point can only be in one polygon or the other, but not both. In applications where any edge point is required to be classified as inside, the pseudocode can be modified to trap the case when the intersection of an edge with the ray occurs exactly at the test point.

Let us take a closer look at the classification issue. The reason that right edge points are classified as outside has to do with the choice of toggling a Boolean variable for inside/outside status. A different way of looking at the problem uses the line partitioning idea in Maynard and Tavernini (1984), an unpublished work that is summarized in Eberly (1999). The ideas in the work are of interest because they effectively provide constructions that are recursive in dimension. That is, an n-dimensional problem is reduced to solving $(n - 1)$-dimensional problems. Each point of intersection between an edge and a specified line is given a tag in $\{o, i, m, p\}$. The i tag, called the *inside* tag, is used if the intersection point occurs from a transverse intersection that is interior to the edge. The m tag, called the *minus* tag, is used if the intersection point is an end point of the edge, the other end point being on the negative side of the line. Similarly, the p tag, called the *plus* tag, is used if the intersection point is an

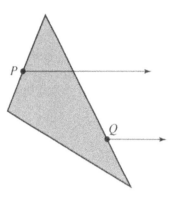

Figure 13.15   Points *P* on the "left" edges of the polygon are classified as inside. Points *Q* on the "right" edges of the polygon are classified as outside.

end point of the edge, the other end point being on the positive side of the line. The *o* tag, called the *outside* tag, is used for both end points if the edge is coincident with the line.

Each edge of the polygon is tested for intersection with the line. The first time a point of intersection occurs, the current tag must be modified. In particular, this happens when two or more edges share a vertex that lives on the line. The initial tag for any point is assumed to be *o*. If the point occurs again and an update tag is determined, conjunction with the old tag produces the new tag for the point. Table 13.1 provides the update information. The rows correspond to the old tag, the columns correspond to the update tag for the current edge, and the entry in the appropriate row and column is the new tag. For those with a background in group theory, you will notice that $\{o, i, m, p\}$ is just the Klein-4 group where the table indicates the group operator. The tag *o* is the identity element, and each element is its own inverse.

As an example, consider the polygon shown in Figure 13.14. The analysis is applied to the ray at P_1. The ray normal is chosen to be $(0, 1)$. Edge $\langle 1, 2 \rangle$ intersects the ray at vertex 2, and the edge is on the negative side of the ray, so the update tag for the intersection is *m*. The initial tag, by default, is *o*. The (o, m) entry in Table 13.1 is *m*, so the tag at vertex 2 is set to *m*. Edge $\langle 2, 3 \rangle$ also intersects the ray at vertex 2, and the update tag is *m* since the edge is on the negative side of the ray. The new tag is the table entry at (m, m), namely, *o*. Similar analysis leads to the final tags shown in Figure 13.16. Observe that the *i* tag at vertex 10 occurs because the two edges sharing that vertex have tags *m* and *p*, the table entry (m, p) being *i*.

The point tags are now used to label the intervals of the line partition, each interval having a tag from $\{o, i, m, p\}$. An interval with an *o* tag is outside the polygon. An interval with an *i* tag is inside the polygon. An interval with an *m* tag is coincident

Table 13.1   The tags for edge-line intersections are o, i, m, and p. The table is used to update the current tag at a point of intersection. The old tag is located in the row, the update tag for the current edge intersection is located in the column, and the new tag for the point of intersection is the corresponding entry in that row and column.

Old	Update			
	o	i	m	p
o	o	i	m	p
i	i	o	p	m
m	m	p	o	i
p	p	m	i	o

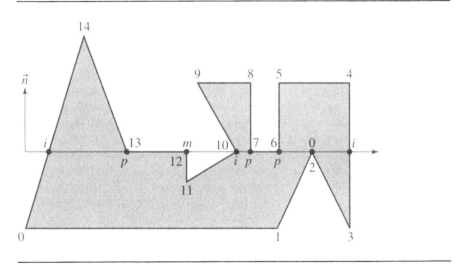

Figure 13.16   Point tags for the horizontal line containing P_1 in Figure 13.14.

with a polygon edge, and the interior of the polygon at that edge lies on the negative side of the line. An interval with a p tag is coincident with a polygon edge, and the interior of the polygon at that edge lies on the positive side of the line. The simple yet clever idea in Maynard and Tavernini (1984) is that the vertex tags are used to generate the interval tags using Table 13.1. The semi-infinite interval containing $+\infty$ is clearly outside the polygon and starts with a tag of o. The left end point of that interval is on the rightmost edge of the polygon, the point tag being i. The last interval tag is o and is used to select the row of Table 13.1. The point tag is i and is used to

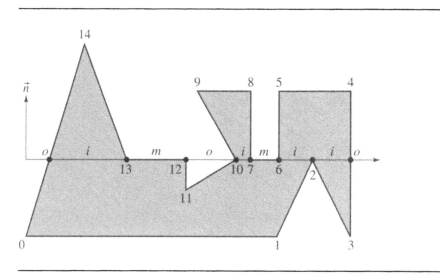

Figure 13.17   Interval tags for the horizontal line containing P_1 in Figure 13.14.

select the column of the table. The table entry (o, i) is i and becomes the tag for the next interval. Observe that this interval is, in fact, inside the polygon. The next point tag, at vertex 2, is o. The table entry (i, o) is i, so the interval immediately to the left of vertex 2 gets a tag of i (still inside the polygon). Figure 13.17 shows the tags for the other intervals. Classification of P_1 is now just a matter of determining which interval of the line partition contains the point and interpreting the label appropriately. If P_1 is in an *open* interval with tag o, the point is outside the polygon. Otherwise, P_1 is inside the polygon or on the polygon boundary. Although the tags can be constructed for all intervals of the line, we only need the tags for the ray, so point tags to the left of P_1 need not be computed.

13.3.4   FASTER POINT IN GENERAL POLYGON

Point-in-polygon tests that are sublinear are possible, but require some type of pre-processing of the polygon. A useful test is based on the horizontal decomposition of a polygon into trapezoids discussed in Section 13.9. The decomposition is $O(n \log n)$, but an intermediate data structure that is built for supporting the decomposition allows for a point-in-polygon test in $O(\log n)$ time. A brief summary of the data structure is given below. More details can be found in Section 13.9.

The y-values of the vertices, y_i for $0 \le i < n$, are used to split the polygon into horizontal strips. The sorted y-values, denoted y_{i_j} for $(i_0, \ldots, i_{n-1})$ (a permutation of $(0, \ldots, n-1)$), correspond to the horizontal lines that separate the strips. Each strip itself consists of a sequence of ordered trapezoids. The polygon is the union of all the trapezoids of all the strips. The sort of the y-values requires $O(n \log n)$ time, although any particular polygon might only have a very small number of distinct y-values. The trapezoids themselves are sorted by sorting the line segment left and right boundaries of the trapezoids within each strip. The boundaries never overlap, so the sort is well defined. This sort is also $O(n \log n)$ in time. The data structure uses binary search trees to allow dynamic construction. One tree is used to sort the horizontal strips, the other tree is used to sort the trapezoids within a strip. The point-in-polygon test amounts to searching the first binary tree to locate the strip containing the y-value of the input point, then searching the second binary tree to locate the trapezoid that contains the point, if it exists. If no trapezoid is found, the point must lie outside the polygon.

13.3.5 A GRID METHOD

This method is suggested by Haines in Heckbert (1994). An axis-aligned bounding box is constructed for the polygon. A grid is imposed on the box, and the polygon is rasterized into it. The grid cells are labeled based on their relationship to the polygon as fully inside, fully outside, or indeterminate. The indeterminate cells are assigned a list of edges that intersect the cell, and one corner of the cell is tagged as inside or outside accordingly.

The grid data structure supports a constant-time point-in-polygon test when the point occurs in a fully inside or fully outside cell. If the point occurs in an indeterminate cell, the line segment connecting the test point and the tagged corner is tested for intersection with all the edges in the cell's edge list. The parity of the number of intersections and knowing if the tagged corner is inside or outside tell you whether or not the test point is inside or outside. This is exactly the point-in-general-polygon test, but confined to the indeterminate cell. Because of the localization, the number of intersection calculations is far fewer than those used in the algorithm that counts intersections for all polygon edges. The containment test is $O(1)$, but you pay the price in $O(nm)$ memory for an $n \times m$ grid and in $O(nm)$ time to rasterize the polygon and classify the grid cells.

Haines notes that care must be taken when a polygon edge crosses (or nearly crosses) a grid corner. The corner is unclassifiable. Numerous options are given: deal with the numerical precision and topological problems, regrid a slightly modified bounding box (jittering, so to speak) in hopes that the problem goes away, or tag entire cell edges and use the horizontal or vertical segment connecting the test point and cell edge in the intersection counting with the edges in the cell's edge list. If you choose to cope with the numerical precision and topological problems, you might as well just use the point-in-general-polygon test and deal with the same problems, saving yourself the memory overhead and expensive preprocessing that goes with the grid method. Regridding the bounding box is also an expensive proposition, especially if the regridding must occur often (or worse, occurs for each test point).

The final suggestion is the most attractive in hopes that when a point falls inside an indeterminate cell the algorithm still requires a small amount of computation time.

Regardless of how you handle the problem, the grid method can be useful in applications such as ray tracing where the point-in-polygon test is the bottleneck, in which case you are willing to use a lot of memory and preprocessing time to obtain an $O(1)$ test. But if your application is more toward the real-time end of the spectrum and where memory is tight, the $O(n)$ point-in-general-polygon test is your best bet.

13.4 POINT IN POLYHEDRON

A common query in graphics applications is to determine if a point is inside a polyhedron. The ideas are similar to those in Section 13.3. If the polyhedron is represented as a BSP tree, Section 13.2.3 discusses how to determine if a point is inside or outside the polyhedron. We discuss methods here that do not assume any preprocessing of the polyhedron.

13.4.1 POINT IN TETRAHEDRON

Consider a point P and a tetrahedron with noncoplanar vertices V_i for $0 \le i \le 3$. To simplify the discussions, we assume that the vertices are ordered so that the 3×3 matrix $\mathbf{M}$ whose columns are $V_i - V_0$ for $0 \le i \le 2$, in that order, has a positive determinant. The canonical tetrahedron with this ordering is $V_0 = (0, 0, 0)$, $V_1 = (1, 0, 0)$, $V_2 = (0, 1, 0)$, and $V_3 = (0, 0, 1)$. Outer-pointing normal vectors for the triangular faces are $\vec{n}_0 = (V_1 - V_3) \times (V_2 - V_3)$, $\vec{n}_1 = (V_0 - V_2) \times (V_3 - V_2)$, $\vec{n}_2 = (V_3 - V_1) \times (V_0 - V_1)$, and $\vec{n}_3 = (V_2 - V_0) \times (V_1 - V_0)$. The face to which $\vec{n}_i$ is normal is the one opposite vertex V_i and contains the vertex V_{3-i}.

The point P is inside the tetrahedron if it is on the negative side of each face plane $\vec{n}_i \cdot (X - V_{3-i}) = 0$. That is, P is inside the tetrahedron when $\vec{n}_i \cdot (P - V_{3-i}) < 0$ for all i. The point is outside the tetrahedron if $\vec{n}_i \cdot (P - V_i) > 0$ for at least one i. It is possible that P is on the tetrahedron boundary itself, in which case $\vec{n}_i \cdot (P - V_i) \le 0$ for all i with equality for at least one i. If an equality occurs once, the point is on a face, but not on an edge or at a vertex. If two equalities occur, the point is on an edge, but not at a vertex. If three equalities occur, the point is at a vertex. It is not possible for equality to occur four times.

The point can also be written in barycentric coordinates as $P = \sum_{i=0}^{3} c_i V_i$, where $\sum_{i=0}^{3} c_i = 1$. P is inside the tetrahedron if $0 < c_i < 1$ for all i. The coefficient c_3 is computed in the following manner:

$$P - V_0 = (c_0 - 1)V_0 + \sum_{i=1}^{3} c_i V_i = \sum_{i=1}^{3} c_i (V_i - V_0)$$

so that $\vec{n}_3 \cdot (P - V_0) = c_3 \vec{n}_3 \cdot (V_3 - V_0)$. Similar constructions apply for c_0, c_1, and c_2 to obtain

$$c_0 = \frac{\vec{n}_0 \cdot (P - V_3)}{\vec{n}_0 \cdot (V_0 - V_3)} \quad c_1 = \frac{\vec{n}_1 \cdot (P - V_2)}{\vec{n}_1 \cdot (V_1 - V_2)}$$

$$c_2 = \frac{\vec{n}_2 \cdot (P - V_1)}{\vec{n}_2 \cdot (V_2 - V_1)} \quad c_3 = \frac{\vec{n}_3 \cdot (P - V_0)}{\vec{n}_3 \cdot (V_3 - V_0)}$$

The exact representation of P is not important for testing if it is inside the tetrahedron. The denominators of the fractions are all the same negative value. The point is inside the tetrahedron if all $c_i > 0$, in which case we need all numerators to be negative.

13.4.2 POINT IN CONVEX POLYHEDRON

The sidedness tests used in the point-in-tetrahedron query naturally extend to determining if a point is in a convex polyhedron. Let the faces be contained in the planes $\vec{n}_i \cdot (X - V_i) = 0$, where V_i is a vertex on the face and $\vec{n}_i$ is an outer normal vector to the face. The point P is inside the polyhedron when $\vec{n}_i \cdot (P - V_i) < 0$ for all i. The point is outside if $\vec{n}_i \cdot (P - V_i) > 0$ for some i. The point is on the polyhedron boundary itself if $\vec{n}_i \cdot (P - V_i) \leq 0$ for all i with equality occurring for at least one i. As in the case of the tetrahedron, if one equality occurs, the point is interior to a face. If two equalities occur, the point is interior to an edge. If three or more equalities occur, the point is a vertex. In this latter case, the number of equalities is the number of faces sharing that vertex.

The algorithm is $O(n)$, where n is the number of vertices, since the number of faces is also $O(n)$. The straightforward implementation is

```
bool PointInPolyhedron(Point P, ConvexPolyhedron C)
{
    for (i = 0; i < C.numberOfFaces; i++) {
        if (Dot(C.face(i).normal, P - C.face(i).vertex) > 0)
            return false;
    }
    return true;
}
```

An Asymptotically Faster Method

The index bisection method for convex polygons that supported an $O(\log n)$ query does not apply to convex polyhedrons because of the added complexity of the third dimension. However, a method similar to the one that bisected on the top half and bottom half of convex polygons does extend to three dimensions, but with some preprocessing that takes $O(n)$ time. As such, the method is useful when many point-in-convex-polyhedron queries must be answered.

The preprocessing consists of two steps. The first step is to iterate over the vertices to compute the axis-aligned bounding box of the polyhedron. This box is used for fast rejections. That is, if P is outside the bounding box, then it cannot be inside the polyhedron. The second step is to iterate over the faces of the polyhedron. Two xy-planar meshes of convex polygons are generated. Faces whose outer-pointing normals have a positive z-component are projected onto one planar mesh, called the *upper planar mesh*. Those with a negative z-component are projected onto the other planar mesh, called the *lower planar mesh*. Faces whose normals have a zero z-component are not relevant and can be ignored.

The two planar meshes consist of convex polygons (the polyhedron faces were convex). Given a test point P, the (x, y) portion of the point is tested for containment in the upper planar mesh. If it is outside the mesh, then P cannot be in the polyhedron. If it is inside the mesh, the convex polygon that contains the point must be computed. The (x, y) portion of P must necessarily be contained in the lower planar mesh. The convex polygon in that mesh that contains P is also computed. The line of constant (x, y) containing P intersects the polyhedral faces corresponding to the two planar convex polygons. We now only need to determine if P is on the line segment contained in the polyhedron—a simple task.

The technical issue is how to determine which convex polygon in a planar mesh contains a specified point. Each edge in the mesh is shared by either one or two polygons. Those edges shared by only one polygon form the *mesh boundary*—another polygon that is itself convex since the parallel projection of a convex polyhedron onto a plane is a convex polygon. The process of locating a point in a subdivision of the plane implied by the mesh is called the *planar point location problem*.

A simple algorithm for locating the containing convex polygon is to perform a *linear walk* over the mesh. An initial convex polygon is selected, and P is tested for containment in that polygon. If so, that polygon is the containing one and the algorithm terminates. If not, an edge of the current polygon is selected that intersects the ray from the polygon center (computed as the average of the polygon vertices) to P. The ray gives a general idea of which direction to walk to find P. If the ray passes through a vertex, select either edge sharing the vertex. Once the edge has been chosen, the next polygon to visit is the other one sharing the edge. The pseudocode is

```
int LinearWalk(Point P, int N, ConvexPolygon C[N])
{
    index = 0;
    for (i = 0; i < N; i++) {
        // at most N polygons to test
        if (P is contained in C[index])
            return index;
```

```
        Point K = C[index].center;  // ray origin
        Point D = P - K;  // ray direction
        for (each edge E of C[index]) {
            if (Ray(C, D) intersects E) {
                index = IndexOfAdjacent(C[index], E);
                break;
            }
        }
    }
    return -1;  // P not in mesh, return an invalid index
}
```

For n polygons in the mesh, this algorithm is $O(\sqrt{n})$. The order is based on intuition from a rectangular grid of size $m \times m$. This mesh has $n = m^2$ rectangles. A linear path, such as a row, column, or diagonal, contains $O(m) = O(\sqrt{n})$ rectangles.

The planar point location problem has an asymptotically faster solution (Kirkpatrick 1983). The method requires building a hierarchy of nested convex polygons and is based on the concept of independent sets of a graph. The essential result is that the planar mesh of n vertices can be preprocessed in $O(n)$ time and space so that point location queries take $O(\log n)$ time. The method is not further studied here, but is discussed in some detail by O'Rourke (1998).

13.4.3   POINT IN GENERAL POLYHEDRON

The point-in-polygon algorithm for a general polygon extends to three dimensions in an obvious way. The polyhedron must partition space into a bounded inside region and an unbounded outside region. A ray whose origin is the test point P and has direction $\hat{d} = (1, 0, 0)$ is intersected with the faces of the polyhedron. The number of intersections is calculated. Assuming that the ray only intersects the polyhedron at interior face points, the parity of the number of intersections characterizes inside from outside. If the parity is odd, the point is inside. Otherwise the parity is even and the point is outside.

However, the same problems arise as in the 2D case when the ray intersects the polyhedron at vertices or at interior edge points. In such a situation the parity might be incorrectly calculated. One way to handle the problem is based on using the vertex-edge-face table that represents the polyhedron. The algorithm performs an iteration over the faces of the polyhedron. Each processed face is tagged that it was visited. If the ray intersects a face at an interior edge point, the adjacent face that shares the edge is immediately tagged as visited so that when it is visited later in the iteration, it is not tested for intersection. Moreover, the parity will have to be adjusted based on the local configuration of the ray, the common edge, and the faces sharing that edge. Figure 13.18 shows the two relevant configurations. Determining the local configuration is

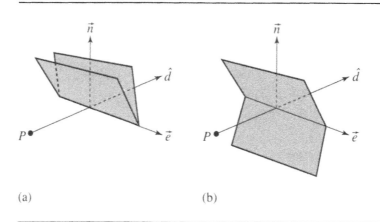

(a)   (b)

Figure 13.18   Two configurations for when the test ray $P + t\hat{d}$ intersects a shared edge $\vec{e}$ at an interior edge point. (a) The faces are on the same side of the plane formed by the edge and the ray. Parity is not changed. (b) The faces are on opposite sides. Parity is toggled.

a simple task of selecting two vertices, one from each face but not on the common edge, and computing on which side of the ray-edge plane they lie. The ray-intersects-edge situation in 3D is the analogy of the ray-intersects-vertex situation in 2D.

If the ray intersects a vertex V, the situation is more complicated and does not have a counterpart in the 2D setting. The problem is to decide if the ray penetrates the polyhedron at V or if it just grazes the vertex so that locally the ray remains in the same region. Specifically, let $V = P + t_0\hat{d}$ for some parameter t_0. For a suitably small $\epsilon > 0$, we need to determine if the two open line segments (line segments not including their end points) corresponding to parameter intervals $(t_0 - \epsilon, t_0)$ and $(t_0, t_0 + \epsilon)$ are both inside or both outside, in which case the current parity is not changed, or one is inside and one is outside, in which case the current parity is toggled. We can imagine a very "ruffled" vertex whose adjacent faces form a triangle strip that wanders aimlessly through space locally at the vertex, perhaps making the problem appear to be intractable. However, the saving fact is that a polyhedron is a manifold mesh (see Section 9.3.3). If a unit sphere is centered at V and the edges sharing V are rescaled to be unit length, the corresponding spherical points form a simple closed curve on the sphere, more precisely a piecewise-defined curve whose pieces are great circle arcs. The interior region bounded by that curve corresponds to the interior of the polyhedron at V. The ray direction itself can be normalized and corresponds to a point on the sphere. The ray interpenetrates the polyhedron at V if and only if the corresponding sphere point is inside the spherical polygon implied by the edges sharing V. (See Figure 13.19.) This is not quite the point-in-polygon

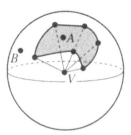

Figure 13.19   The spherical polygon implied by the edges sharing a vertex V that the test ray intersects. If the point A corresponds to the ray direction, the ray interpenetrates the polyhedron. If the point B corresponds to the ray direction, the ray does not interpenetrate the polyhedron.

test discussed earlier, but a similar algorithm to the one for planar polygons can be constructed for spherical polygons.

An alternative to the fine-scale handling is to use a randomized approach. The idea is to generate random directions until a ray is found that only intersects faces at interior points. The pseudocode is

```
bool PointInPolyhedron(Point P, ConvexPolyhedron C)
{
    parity = false;
    i = 0;

    while (i < C.numberOfFaces) {
        Point D = GenerateRandomUnitVector();
        for (i = 0; i < C.numberOfFaces; i++)  {
            if (Ray(P, D) intersects C.face(i))  {
                if (intersection point is interior to face))
                    parity = not parity;
                else  // bad ray, try a different one
                    break;
            }
        }
    }

    return parity;
}
```

Although it is expected that eventually the outer loop terminates, it is not clear how many iterations will occur until then. A variation is to replace the `while` loop by a `for` loop that runs at most a specified number of iterations. If a good ray is not found for all those iterations, a call can be made to a much slower algorithm, for example the algorithm in Paeth (1995), "Point in Polyhedron Testing Using Spherical Polygons." This method requires computing solid angles, operations that use inverse trigonometric function calls, hence the slower performance.

13.5 BOOLEAN OPERATIONS ON POLYGONS

A common question that arises in computer graphics is how to compute the intersection of two polygons A and B, a query that is one of a collection of queries generally known as *Boolean operations on polygons*. Each polygon is assumed to be non-self-intersecting in that no edge transversely crosses another edge, but edges meeting at vertices are allowed. Usually each polygon is assumed to enclose a connected, bounded region that possibly has holes. We do not require boundedness and allow edges to be line segments, rays, or lines. We also do not require connectedness. For example, two disjoint triangles may be considered to be part of a single polygon. The generality of the definition for polygon allows for operations other than intersection to be implemented in a fairly simple way.

The plane must be partitioned by the polygon into two disjoint regions, an *inside region* and an *outside region*. Each linear component of the (potentially unbounded) polygon has a normal vector associated with it. The region to which the normal is directed is labeled the "outside;" the opposite region is labeled as "inside." Equivalently, if the linear components are represented as having directions, as you traverse the component in the specified direction the inside region is to your left and the outside region is to your right. Figure 13.20 illustrates with three polygons, one bounded and convex, one bounded and not convex, and one unbounded.

Figure 13.20   Bounded and unbounded polygons that partition the plane into inside and outside regions. The inside region is gray. The unbounded polygon on the right is a half-space with a single line as the boundary of the region.

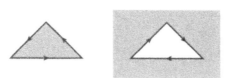

Figure 13.21   A polygon and its negation. The inside regions are gray. The edges are shown with the appropriate directions so that the inside is always to the left.

13.5.1 THE ABSTRACT OPERATIONS

The Boolean operations on polygons include the following operations.

Negation

This operation reverses the labeling of the inside and outside regions. The inside region becomes the outside region, and the outside region becomes the inside region. If the polygon is stored so that the normals for the edges are explicitly stored, then negation is implemented as a sign change on the normals. If the polygon is stored so that the edges are directed, then negation is implemented by reversing the directions of all edges. Figure 13.21 shows a polygon and its negation.

The remaining operations will be illustrated with the two polygons shown in Figure 13.22, an inverted L-shaped polygon and a pentagon. The edge directions are shown, indicating that the inside regions for both polygons are bounded.

Intersection

The intersection of two polygons is another polygon whose inside region is the intersection of the inside regions of the initial polygons. Figure 13.23 shows the intersection of two polygons. The polygon vertices and edges are black, and the intersection is gray. The intersection is a polygon according to our definition mentioned at the beginning of this section, and it consists of two components, each a simple polygon.

Union

The union of two polygons is another polygon whose inside region is the union of the inside regions of the initial polygons. Figure 13.24 shows the union of two polygons. The polygon vertices and edges are black, and the union is gray.

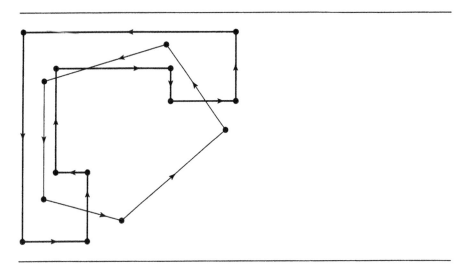

Figure 13.22   Two polygons whose inside regions are bounded.

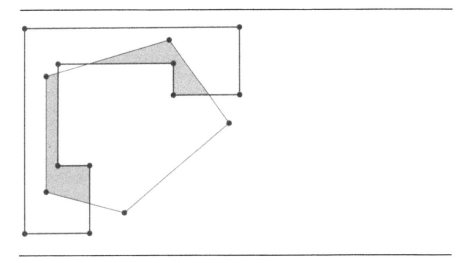

Figure 13.23   The intersection of two polygons shown in gray.

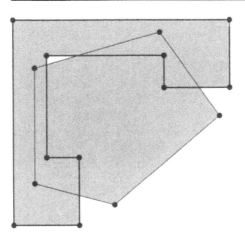

Figure 13.24   The union of two polygons shown in gray.

Difference

The difference of two polygons is another polygon whose inside region is the difference of the inside regions of the initial polygons. The order of the polygons is important. If A is the set of points for the inside of the first polygon and B is the set of points for the inside of the second polygon, then the difference $A \setminus B$ is the set of points that are in A, but not in B. Figure 13.25 shows the difference of the two polygons, the inverted L-shaped polygon minus the pentagon. The polygon vertices and edges are black, and the difference is gray.

Exclusive-Or

The exclusive-or of two polygons is another polygon whose inside region is the union of the two polygon differences. If A is the inside region for the first polygon and B is the inside region for the second polygon, then the inside region for the exclusive-or is the set $(A \setminus B) \cup (B \setminus A)$. Figure 13.26 shows the exclusive-or of the two polygons. The polygon vertices and edges are black, and the exclusive-or is gray.

13.5.2   THE TWO PRIMITIVE OPERATIONS

Although the Boolean operations can be implemented according to each of the set operations as defined, it is only necessary to implement negation and intersection. The other Boolean operations can be defined in terms of these two primitive operations.

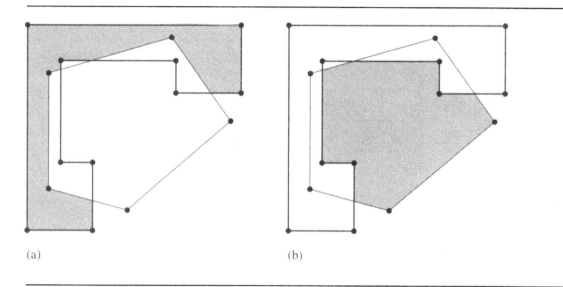

(a)   (b)

Figure 13.25   The difference of two polygons: (a) The inverted L-shaped polygon minus the pentagon. (b) The pentagon minus the inverted L-shaped polygon.

Negation

The negation of polygon P is denoted $\neg P$. This unary operator has precedence over any of the following binary operators.

Intersection

The intersection of polygons P and Q is denoted $P \cap Q$.

Union

The union of polygons P and Q is denoted $P \cup Q$ and can be computed using De Morgan's rules for sets by

$$P \cup Q = \neg(\neg P \cap \neg Q)$$

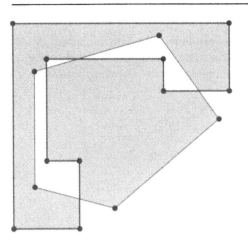

Figure 13.26   The exclusive-or of two polygons shown in gray. This polygon is the union of the two differences shown in Figure 13.25.

Difference

The difference of polygons P and Q, where Q is subtracted from P, is denoted $P \setminus Q$ and can be computed by

$$P \setminus Q = P \cap \neg Q$$

Exclusive-Or

The exclusive-or of polygons P and Q is denoted $P \oplus Q = (P \setminus Q) \cup (Q \setminus P)$ and can be computed by

$$P \oplus Q = \neg((\neg(P \cap \neg Q)) \cap (\neg(Q \cap \neg P)))$$

13.5.3 BOOLEAN OPERATIONS USING BSP TREES

Various approaches have been taken for computing Boolean operations on polygons. A popular method that is straightforward to implement uses BSP trees. The ideas extend in a natural way to three dimensions where the Boolean operations are applied to polyhedra (see Section 13.6). The two primitive operations are discussed below.

Negation

The polygon negation operation is simple to implement. Assuming the polygon data structure stores edges, as is the case in the discussion of BSP tree representations for polygons, negation is implemented by reversing the ordering for each edge.

```
Polygon Negation(Polygon P)
{
    Polygon negateP;
    negateP.vertices = P.vertices;
    for (each edge E of P) do
        negateP.Insert(Edge(E.V(1), E.V(0)));
    return negateP;
}
```

The BSP tree that represents the polygon is negated using the following pseudocode:

```
BspTree Negation(BspTree T)
{
    BspTree negateT = new BspTree;

    for (each edge E of T.coincident)
        negateT.coincident.Insert(Edge(E.V(1), E.V(0)));

    if (T.posChild)
        negateT.negChild = Negation(T.posChild);
    else
        negateT.negChild = null;

    if (T.negChild)
        negateT.posChild = Negation(T.negChild);
    else
        negateT.negChild = null;

    return negateT;
}
```

Intersection

The intersection of polygons can be computed in a straightforward manner. If A and B are polygons, each edge of A is intersected with B. Any portions of those edges that lie inside B are retained as part of the polygon of intersection. Similarly, each edge of

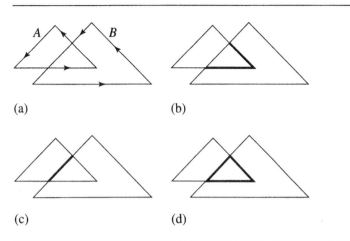

(a)   (b)

(c)   (d)

Figure 13.27   Intersection of two triangles: (a) The two triangles, A and B. (b) Edges of A intersected with inside of B. (c) Edges of B intersected with inside of A. (d) $A \cap B$ as the
collection of all intersected edges.

B is intersected with A, and any portions of those edges that lie inside A are retained
as part of the polygon of intersection. Figure 13.27 illustrates this. Although a simple
algorithm, the problem is that it is not as efficient as it could be. If polygon A has n
edges and polygon B has m edges, then the number of edge-edge intersection tests is
nm, so the algorithm has $O(nm)$ time complexity (quadratic in time). The use of BSP
trees reduces the number of comparisons since edges of A on one side of a splitting
line need not be compared to edges of B on the other side.

As illustrated in Figure 13.27, the edges of each polygon must be intersected with
the inside region of the other polygon. Any subedges that are inside become part of
the intersection of the two polygons.

The pseudocode is

```
Polygon Intersection(Polygon P, Polygon Q)
{
    Polygon intersectPQ;

    for (each edge E of P) {
        GetPartition(E, Q, inside, outside, coincidentSame, coincidentDiff);
        for (each S in (inside or coincidentSame))
            intersectPQ.Add(S);
    }

    for (each edge E of Q) {
```

```
                GetPartition(E, P, inside, outside, coincidentSame, coincidentDiff);
                for (each S in (inside or coincidentSame))
                    intersectPQ.Add(S);
        }

        return intersectPQ;
    }
```

The heart of the construction is partitioning an edge E of a polygon by intersecting it with the other polygon. The function GetPartition constructs four sets of segments of an edge E intersected with the specified polygon, at least one set being nonempty. Two sets correspond to segments inside the polygon or outside the polygon. The other two sets correspond to segments that are coincident with an edge of the polygon, one set storing those segments that are in the same direction as an edge (coincidentSame), the other set storing segments in the opposite direction (coincidentDiff). As discussed in Section 13.1.4, the partitioning is performed efficiently using a BSP tree representation of the polygon by the BSP tree function GetPartition.

The decision not to include coincident segments in the opposite direction of the corresponding polygon's edge has the consequence that intersection finding only computes intersections with positive area. For example, Figure 13.28 shows two polygons whose intersection is a line segment. The pseudocode for intersection shown earlier will report that the polygons do not intersect. You can, of course, include the other set of coincident edges if you want the intersector to return a line segment in this example. A slightly more complicated example is shown in Figure 13.29. The pseudocode, as listed, returns the triangle portion of the intersection but not the extra edge hanging off that triangle. If you modify the code to include all coincident segments, the intersector returns the triangle and the extra edge. Some applications might require the true set of intersection; others might only want the components of intersection with positive area. The implementation should handle this as needed.

The intersection operation as discussed here supports what are called *keyhole edges*, two edges that are collinear but have opposite direction. Keyhole edges are

(a)   (b)

Figure 13.28   (a) Two polygons that are reported not to intersect by the pseudocode. (b) The actual set intersection, a line segment.

Figure 13.29   (a) Two polygons and (b) their true set of intersection.

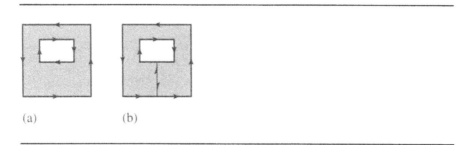

Figure 13.30   (a) Polygon with a hole requiring two lists of vertices/edges. (b) Keyhole version to allow a single list of vertices/edges.

Figure 13.31   Intersection of a rectangle and a keyhole polygon.

typically used to represent polygons with holes in terms of a single collection of vertices/edges. Figure 13.30 shows a polygon with a hole and a keyhole representation of it. However, be aware that the intersection of a polygon with a keyhole polygon might be theoretically a simple polygon, but constructed as a union of multiple simple polygons. Figure 13.31 illustrates the intersection of a rectangle with the keyhole polygon of the previous figure. The intersection set contains two adjacent but opposite direction edges that could be removed by a postprocessing step.

Other Boolean Operations

Using negation and intersection as the primitive operations, the remaining Boolean operations are implemented below.

```
Polygon Union(Polygon P, Polygon Q)
{
    return Negation(Intersection(Negation(P), Negation(Q)));
}

Polygon Difference(Polygon P, Polygon Q)
{
    return Intersection(P, Negation(Q));
}

Polygon ExclusiveOr(Polygon P, Polygon Q)
{
    return Union(Difference(P, Q), Difference(Q, P));
}
```

As mentioned earlier, the overhead of assembling the intersection from an edge list may lead to poor performance. An alternative would be to start with the edge lists and BSP trees from the original polygons and not create intermediate polygons, only the final polygon. A simple improvement for the exclusive-or operation is to use instead a binary operator `DisjointUnion` operation whose vertices are the union of the vertices of the two input polygons and whose edges are the union of the edges of the two input polygons. The two difference polygons have no edges in common, so a full-fledged `Union` operation does more work than it has to in this special case.

13.5.4 OTHER ALGORITHMS

The BSP tree-based algorithm is not the only possibility for implementing Boolean polygon operations, in particular intersection of polygons. All methods have one thing in common—they must find points of intersection between pairs of edges. The edges on which the intersection points occur must be split (in an abstract sense) into subedges. What varies among the methods is how the subedges are merged to form the intersection polygon.

We briefly mention some alternatives. The Weiler-Atherton (WA) algorithm (Weiler and Atherton 1977) is one whose implementation is requested frequently in the computer graphics newsgroups. A detailed description, including how the data structures are designed, is in Foley et al. (1996). However, the next two algorithms are, in our opinion, better choices for reasons shown below. An algorithm based on sweep lines (sorting vertices by one component) is attributed to Sechrest and

Greenberg (1981) and referred to here as the SG algorithm. A slightly modified SG algorithm is attributed to Vatti (1992) and referred to as the V algorithm. The latter algorithm allows the output of an intersection of polygons to be a collection of trapezoids rather than a general polygon, something that is useful for point-in-polygon tests. The flavor of the V algorithm is present in the horizontal decomposition of a polygon into trapezoids that is discussed in Section 13.9.

Performance in computing edge-edge intersections is important. The obvious algorithm that checks all possible pairs is certainly the most inefficient. The BSP algorithm avoids comparing all pairs of edges just by nature of the spatial sorting implied by the splitting lines. The WA algorithm checks all possible pairs. The SG and V algorithms provide the most efficient testing because of the horizontal sorting that occurs by using a sweep line approach.

The process of identifying subedges for the intersection polygon is a natural consequence of the BSP algorithm. Moreover, this algorithm inherently provides a convex decomposition of the intersection polygon. However, the general decomposition comes at the cost of more edge comparisons than in the SG and V algorithms. The subedge identification and merging in the WA algorithm is accomplished by doubling the edges. Each abstract polygon edge has two instantiations, one that is assigned to the inside of the polygon and one that is assigned to the outside. Labels on those edges are maintained that store this information. Intersection points for edge pairs are located, and the edges containing the point are split (all four of them). The edges are reconnected based on the labels to form nonintersecting contours, one of which corresponds to the intersection polygon. The subedge identification and merging in the SG and V algorithms is based on the partitioning of the polygon into horizontal strips, each strip containing a list of trapezoids in the strip. Again, the material in Section 13.9 gives greater detail on the partitioning.

The concern for any algorithm that computes the intersection of polygons is what types of polygons it will handle. All methods assume some consistent ordering of the polygon vertices, whether it be clockwise or counterclockwise. Does the method only handle convex polygons? Will it handle polygons with holes, or more generally, nested polygons? Will it allow polygons with self-intersecting edges? How does the method handle coincident edges? Some methods claim "correct" handling of coincident edges, but as seen in Figures 13.28 and 13.29, the choice of behavior for coincident edges is application-specific. An application might very well only want intersection polygons that have positive area. In theory, all the algorithms discussed here can handle nested polygons, but specific implementations might not.

Implementations of the various algorithms are available online. Klamer Schutte has one based on the WA algorithm, but with some modifications to the merge of subedges into the intersection polygon (Schutte 1995). This implementation requires clockwise ordering of vertices, does not support holes, and does not support self-intersecting polygons.

Michael Leonov has an implementation that is a modification of the one by Schutte, but allows for holes (Leonov 1997). The outer polygon must be counterclockwise ordered, and the inner polygons forming holes must be clockwise ordered.

Leonov also had, at one point, a very nice comparison of various implementations including an analysis of execution times to determine order of convergence and a chart indicating whether or not the implementations could handle various classes of polygons. Unfortunately as of the time of printing of this book, that page appears to no longer be available.

Alan Murtha has an implementation based on the V algorithm and appears to be well written and quite popular for downloading (Murtha 2000). Klaas Holwerda also has an implementation based on the V algorithm (Holwerda 2000).

Two implementations are available through the source code pages at Eberly (2001), one using the concept of polysolids and one using BSP trees.

13.6 BOOLEAN OPERATIONS ON POLYHEDRA

This topic is considered to be part of a general class of methods, collectively called computational solid geometry (CSG), that operate on 3D objects. The concepts for Boolean operations on polyhedra are identical to those for operations on polygons. We recommend reading Section 13.5 first to understand how Boolean operations apply to polygons. The polyhedra are assumed to partition space so that the abstract graph of regions is 2-colorable. Intuitively, each disjoint region is labeled as "inside" or "outside" the polyhedron. Generally, the inside regions are bounded (have finite volume), but the more general term "2-colorable" is used to allow both inside and outside regions to be unbounded. For example, a half-space is allowed in the Boolean operations. The outside region is labeled based on selecting a plane normal to point to that side of the plane. The inside region is on the other side. Polyhedra that provide a 2-coloring of space and for which the inside region is bounded have been referred to as *polysolids* in the context of CSG (Maynard and Tavernini 1984).

13.6.1 ABSTRACT OPERATIONS

The abstract operations include *negation of a polyhedron,* which reverses the labels on inside and outside regions; *intersection of two polyhedra,* the subpolyhedra that are contained by both input polyhedra; *union of two polyhedra,* the polyhedra that are contained by either input polyhedron; *difference of two polyhedra,* the polyhedra that are contained in the first input polyhedron, but not in the second; and *exclusive-or of two polyhedra,* the union of the differences of the two polyhedra. Just as in the two-dimensional setting, negation and intersection are primitive operations. The other operations are expressed in terms of them. Negation of a polyhedron P is denoted $\neg P$, and intersection of polyhedra P and Q is denoted $P \cap Q$. The union is $P \cup Q = \neg(\neg P \cap \neg Q)$, the difference is $P \setminus Q = P \cap \neg Q$, and the exclusive-or is $P \oplus Q = \neg((\neg(P \cap \neg Q)) \cap (\neg(Q \cap \neg P)))$. A minimal coding of Boolean operations involves implementing negation and intersection, then constructing the other operations according to these identities.

13.6.2 BOOLEAN OPERATIONS USING BSP TREES

The use of BSP trees is quite effective for implementing Boolean operations for polyhedra. The ideas can be found in Thibault and Naylor (1987); Naylor (1990); Naylor, Amanatides, and Thibault (1990); and Naylor (1992). The discussion in this section assumes that the polyhedra are stored in a vertex-edge-face table and that the face vertices are ordered so that the face normals correspond to a counterclockwise orientation of the vertices. The normals are assumed to point to the outside region.

Negation

The polyhedron negation is simple in that the vertex ordering for the faces is reversed and normals, if stored, have their directions reversed by multiplying by -1. The pseudocode is

```
Polyhedron Negation(Polyhedron P)
{
    Polyhedron negateP;
    negateP.vertices = P.vertices;
    negateP.edges = P.edges;
    for (each face F of P) {
        Face F';
        for (i = 0; i < F.numVertices; i++)
            F'.InsertIndex(F.numVertices - i - 1);
        negateP.faces.Insert(F');
    }
    return negateP;
}
```

The BSP tree that represents the polyhedron is negated using the following pseudocode:

```
BspTree Negation(BspTree T)
{
    BspTree negateT = new BspTree;

    for (each face F of T.coincident) {
        Face F';
        for (i = 0; i < F.numVertices; i++)
            F'.InsertIndex(F.numVertices - i - 1);
        negateT.coincident.Insert(F');
    }
```

```
if (T.posChild)
    negateT.negChild = Negation(T.posChild);
else
    negateT.negChild = null;

if (T.negChild)
    negateT.posChild = Negation(T.negChild);
else
    negateT.negChild = null;

    return negateT;
}
```

Intersection

The intersection of polyhedra is also computed in a straightforward manner. If *A* and *B* are polyhedra, each face of *A* is intersected with *B*. Any portions of those faces that lie inside *B* are retained as part of the polyhedron of intersection. Similarly, each face of *B* is intersected with *A*, and any portions of those faces that lie inside *A* are retained as part of the polyhedron of intersection. Just as in the two-dimensional setting, the $O(nm)$ algorithm that tests pairs of faces, each pair having one face from the *n* faces of *A* and one face from the *m* faces of *B*, is inefficient. The use of BSP trees reduces the number of comparisons because of the spatial sorting that is implied by the tree.

The pseudocode is listed below:

```
Polyhedron Intersection(Polyhedron P, Polyhedron Q)
{
    Polyhedron intersectPQ;

    for (each face F of P) {
        GetPartition(Q.bsptree, F, inside, outside, coinside, cooutside);
        for (each face S in (inside or coinside))
            intersectPQ.faces.Insert(S);
    }

    for (each face F of Q) {
        GetPartition(P.bsptree, F, inside, outside, coinside, cooutside);
        for (each face S in (inside or coinside))
            intersectPQ.faces.Insert(S):
    }
}
```

The heart of the construction is partitioning a face F of a polyhedron by intersecting it with the other polyhedron. The function that does this is GetPartition, the one discussed in Section 13.2.5.

Other Boolean Operations

The remainder of the Boolean operations use the identities discussed earlier.

```
Polyhedron Union(Polyhedron P, Polyhedron Q)
{
    return Negation(Intersection(Negation(P), Negation(Q)));
}


Polyhedron Difference(Polyhedron P, Polyhedron Q)
{
    return Intersection(P, Negation(Q));
}


Polyhedron ExclusiveOr(Polyhedron P, Polyhedron Q)
{
    return Union(Difference(P, Q), Difference(Q, P));
}
```

13.7 CONVEX HULLS

A set $S \subset \mathbb{R}^n$ is said to be *convex* if for any $X, Y \in S$, the line segment $(1-t)X + tY \in S$ for all $t \in [0, 1]$. This definition does not require the set to be bounded or to be closed. For example, all of $\mathbb{R}^2$ is convex. The half-plane in $\mathbb{R}^2$ defined by $x > 0$ is convex. Other examples of convex sets are circular disks and triangles. Of course, lines, rays, and line segments are all convex. Figure 13.32 shows two sets: the set in Figure 13.32(a) is convex, but the set in Figure 13.32(b) is not. In 3D, examples of convex sets are $\mathbb{R}^3$, half-spaces, spheres, ellipsoids, lines, rays, line segments, triangles, and tetrahedra.

The *convex hull* of a set S is the smallest convex set that contains S. Of particular interest in computer graphics is the convex hull of a finite set of points. This section focuses on the construction of convex hulls for point sets.

13.7.1 CONVEX HULLS IN 2D

Consider a finite point set S. If all points in the set are collinear, the convex hull is a line segment. The more interesting case is when at least three points are not collinear.

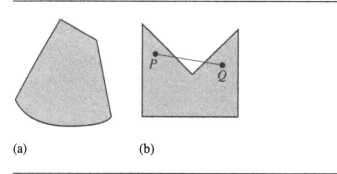

(a)   (b)

Figure 13.32   (a) Convex. (b) Not convex, since the line segment connecting P and Q is not entirely inside the original set.

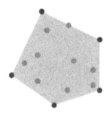

Figure 13.33   A point set and its convex hull. The points are in dark gray, except for those points that became hull vertices, marked in black. The hull is shown in light gray.

In this case the convex hull is a region bounded by a polygon that is denoted a *convex polygon*. Figure 13.33 shows a point set and its convex hull. The vertices of the convex hull are necessarily a subset of the original point set. Construction of the convex hull amounts to identifying the points in S that are the vertices of the convex polygon.

Numerous algorithms have been developed for computing the convex hull of point sets. A summary of these is found in O'Rourke (1998) and includes *gift wrapping, quickhull, Graham's algorithm, incremental construction,* and a *divide-and-conquer method*. We only discuss the last two algorithms in the list. Various computational geometry books make restrictions on the point sets in order to simplify the constructions and proofs. Typical assumptions include no duplicate points, no collinear points, and/or points have only integer coordinates to allow exact arithmetic. In practice, these restrictions are usually never satisfied, especially in the presence of a floating-point number system. We pay close attention to the pathological problems that can arise in order to provide a robust implementation.

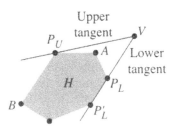

Figure 13.34   A convex hull H, a point V outside H, and the two tangents from V to the hull. The upper and lower tangent points are labeled as P_U and P_L, respectively.

Incremental Construction

The idea is simple. Given a set of points V_i, $0 \leq i < n$, each point is inserted into an already constructed convex hull of the previous points. The pseudocode is

```
ConvexPolygon IncrementalHull(int n, Point V[n])
{
    ConvexPolygon hull = {V[0]};
    for (i = 1; i < n; i++)
        Merge(V[i], hull);
    return hull;
}
```

The heart of the problem is how to construct the convex hull of a convex polygon H and a point V, the operation named Merge in the pseudocode. If V is inside H, the merge step does nothing. But if V is outside H, the merge step must find rays emanating from V that just touch the hull. These rays are called *tangents* to the hull (see Figure 13.34).

A tangent has the property that the hull is entirely on one side of the line with at most a vertex or an edge of points on the line. In Figure 13.34, the upper tangent intersects the current hull in a single point. The lower tangent intersects along an edge of the current hull. The points of tangency are the extreme points of all the hull vertices that are visible from V. The other hull vertices are occluded from V by the hull itself. In the figure, the lower tangent contains an edge with end points P_L and P'_L, but only P_L is visible to V.

The condition of visibility from V can be further exploited. The current hull edges inside the cone defined by the two tangents are visible to V. These edges are inside the new hull containing H and V. The new hull includes all the occluded edges of the current hull and new edges formed by the line segments from V to the tangent points. In the example of Figure 13.34, two edges are visible to V and can be discarded. The new edges are $\langle V, P_U \rangle$ and $\langle V, P_L \rangle$. Because the edge $\langle P'_L, P_L \rangle$ is entirely on the lower tangent, that edge can also be discarded and replaced by the new edge $\langle V, P'_L \rangle$. If this step is not performed, the final hull of the points will contain collinear edges. Such edges can be collapsed in a postprocessing phase.

Determining whether or not an edge is visible is just a matter of computing ordering of three points, the end points of the directed edge and the point V. In Figure 13.34, the directed edge $\langle P_L, A \rangle$ is visible to V. The triangle $\langle V, P_L, A \rangle$ is clockwise ordered. The directed edge $\langle P_U, B \rangle$ is not visible to V. The triangle $\langle V, P_U, B \rangle$ is counterclockwise ordered. Only P_L of the directed edge $\langle P'_L, P_L \rangle$ is visible to V. The triangle $\langle V, P'_L, P_L \rangle$ is degenerate (a line segment). The cases are quantified by a dot product test. Let $\langle Q_0, Q_1 \rangle$ be a directed hull edge and define $\vec{d} = Q_1 - Q_0$ and $\vec{n} = -\vec{d}^\perp$, an inner-pointing normal to the edge. The edge is visible to V whenever $\vec{n} \cdot (V - Q_0) < 0$ and not visible to V whenever $\vec{n} \cdot (V - Q_0) > 0$. If the dot product is zero, then only the closest end point of the edge is visible to V. End point Q_0 is closest if $\vec{d} \cdot (V - Q_0) < 0$; end point Q_1 is closest if $\vec{d} \cdot (V - Q_0) > \|\vec{d}\|^2$.

The order of the algorithm depends on the amount of work that must be done in the merge step. In the worst case, each input point to Merge is outside the current hull, and the tangent points are found by iterating over all hull vertices and testing the dot product conditions. The order is $O(n^2)$. Because of this, one hope is that the initial points are ordered in such a way that most of the time the input point is in the current hull. This is the idea of *randomized algorithms*, where the input points are randomly permuted in an attempt to generate a large partial hull from the first few input points. When this happens, many of the remaining points most likely will fall inside the current hull. Because the relationship between the next input point and the current hull is not known, a search over the hull vertices must be made to find the tangent points. A randomized algorithm is discussed in de Berg et al. (2000). The same idea occurs in Section 13.11 when finding the minimum-area circle containing a point set.

A nonrandomized approach that guarantees an $O(n \log n)$ algorithm actually sorts the points so that the next input point is outside the current hull! The sort of the points dominates the algorithm time. The points are sorted using the less-than operation: $(x_0, y_0) < (x_1, y_1)$ when $x_0 < x_1$ or when $x_0 = x_1$ and $y_0 < y_1$. The points are initially sorted in place for the discussion. In an implementation, the points are most likely sorted into separate storage so as not to change the original point set. After the sort, duplicate points can be eliminated. The sort and comparison can be implemented to use fuzzy floating-point arithmetic to handle those cases where floating-point round-off errors might cause two equal points (in theory) to be slightly different from each other.

The algorithm has information about the relationship between the next input and the current hull so that the tangent construction is only $O(n)$ over the total lifetime of the loop in the pseudocode. In particular, the last-inserted hull vertex is the starting point for the search for the points of tangency and may already be a tangent point itself. Although any single search might require visiting a significant number of points on the current hull, each such visited point will be interior to the merged hull and discarded. The average cost per discarded point is effectively constant time, so over the lifetime of the loop, the total time is $O(n)$.

The first point is the initial hull. As input points are processed, a flag, type, is maintained that indicates whether the hull is a single point (POINT), a line segment represented by two distinct points (LINEAR), or a convex polygon with positive area (PLANAR). Initially the flag is POINT since the initial point stored by the hull is the first input point. By keeping track of this flag, we effectively have a convex hull algorithm for a given dimensional space (in this case 2D) that is based on convex hull algorithms for the spaces of smaller dimension (in this case 1D). The pseudocode becomes

```
ConvexPolygon IncrementalHull(int n, Point V[n])
{
    Sort(n, V);
    RemoveDuplicates(n, V);  // n can decrease, V has contiguous elements
    ConvexPolygon hull;
    type = POINT;
    hull[0] = V[0];
    for (i = 1; i < n; i++) {
        switch (type) {
            case POINT:   type = LINEAR;  hull[1] = V[i];  break;
            case LINEAR:  MergeLinear(V[i], hull, type);   break;
            case PLANAR:  MergePlanar(V[i], hull);         break;
        }
    }
    return hull;
}
```

If the current hull has one point, the uniqueness of the points implies that V[i] is different from the one already in the hull. The point is added to the current hull to form a line segment and the type flag is changed accordingly.

If the current hull has two points (a line segment), the function MergeLinear determines whether or not the current input point is on the same line as the line segment. If it is on the same line, the current hull is updated and remains a line segment. If the input point is not on the same line, the current hull and input point form a triangle. In this case, the triangle is stored as the current hull and the type flag is changed accordingly. Moreover, we wish to store the hull as a set of counterclockwise-ordered points. This requires the collinearity test to do slightly more than just determine if the input point is on or off the line. If the hull is the line segment $\langle Q_0, Q_1 \rangle$ and the input point is P, Figure 13.35 shows the five possibilities for the relationship of P to the line segment.

The collinearity test uses a normal vector to the line containing the segment $\langle Q_0, Q_1 \rangle$. If $\vec{d} = Q_1 - Q_0$, then $\vec{n} = -\vec{d}^{\perp}$, a normal vector that points to the left as

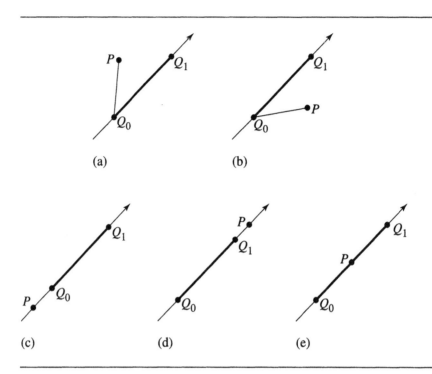

(a)   (b)

(c)   (d)   (e)

Figure 13.35   The five possibilities for the relationship of P to a line segment with end points Q_0 and Q_1: P is (a) to the left of the segment, (b) to the right of the segment, (c) on the line to the left of the segment, (d) on the line to the right of the segment, or (e) on the line and contained by the segment.

you traverse the segment from Q_0 to Q_1. Define $\vec{a} = P - Q_0$. The five possibilities, labeled according to Figure 13.35, are characterized mathematically by

a. $\vec{n} \cdot \vec{a} > 0$

b. $\vec{n} \cdot \vec{a} < 0$

c. $\vec{n} \cdot \vec{a} = 0$ and $\vec{d} \cdot \vec{a} < 0$

d. $\vec{n} \cdot \vec{a} = 0$ and $\vec{d} \cdot \vec{a} > \vec{d} \cdot \vec{d}$

e. $\vec{n} \cdot \vec{a} = 0$ and $0 \leq \vec{d} \cdot \vec{a} \leq \vec{d} \cdot \vec{d}$

The pseudocode uses an integer flag to distinguish between these cases, the values given in the order of the tests above as POSITIVE, NEGATIVE, COLLINEAR_LEFT, COLLINEAR_RIGHT, and COLLINEAR_CONTAIN.

```
int CollinearTest(Point P, Point Q0, Point Q1)
{
    Point D = Q1 - Q0, N = -Perp(D), A = P - Q0;

    float NdA = Dot(N, A);
    if (NdA > 0)
        return POSITIVE;
    if (NdA < 0)
        return NEGATIVE;

    float DdA = Dot(D, A);
    if (DdA < 0)
        return COLLINEAR_LEFT;
    if (DdA > Dot(D, D))
        return COLLINEAR_RIGHT;

    return COLLINEAR_CONTAIN;
}
```

Observe that the five possibilities match exactly those discussed for visibility of vertices and edges for the current hull from the input point V. The pseudocode for merging is listed below. If the hull becomes a triangle, the vertices are arranged in counterclockwise order.

```
void MergeLinear(Point P, ConvexPolygon& hull, int& type)
{
    switch (CollinearTest(P, hull[0], hull[1])) {
        case POSITIVE:
            type = PLANAR;
            hull = {P, hull[0], hull[1]};
            break;
        case NEGATIVE:
            type = PLANAR;
            hull = {P, hull[1], hull[0]};
            break;
        case COLLINEAR_LEFT:
            // collinear order <P, Q0, Q1>
            hull = {P, Q1};
            break;
        case COLLINEAR_RIGHT:
            // collinear order <Q0, Q1, P>
            hull = {Q0, P};
            break;
```

```
            case COLLINEAR_CONTAIN:
                // collinear order <Q0, P, Q1>, hull does not change
                break;
        }
    }
```

Although theoretically correct, `CollinearTest` suffers from the usual problems with floating-point round-off error. Points can be nearly collinear, but may as well be treated as if they were collinear. A robust application would instead use fuzzy arithmetic for the collinear test. Relative error tolerances should be used to avoid dependencies on the magnitude of the input points. One possibility is to use an error threshold $\varepsilon > 0$ on the cosine of the angle θ between $\vec{d}$ and $\vec{a}$. If $|\cos(\theta)| \leq \varepsilon$, then θ may as well be treated as zero. That is, if $|\vec{n} \cdot \vec{a}| = \|\vec{n}\| \|\vec{a}\| |\cos(\theta)| \leq \varepsilon \|\vec{n}\| \|\vec{a}\|$, then the three points are treated as collinear. The lengths of two vectors must be computed in this formulation, a performance issue. To avoid the square root calculations, the squared equation should be considered instead, $|\vec{n} \cdot \vec{a}|^2 \leq \varepsilon \|\vec{n}\|^2 \|\vec{a}\|^2$, where we are using ε as a tolerance on $|\cos(\theta)|^2$. A similar error threshold can be used for the case when the three points are collinear. The parametric interval of containment is $[0, \|\vec{d}\|^2]$, but can be expanded to $[-\varepsilon \|\vec{d}\|^2, (1 + \varepsilon) \|\vec{d}\|^2]$. The pseudocode to handle this is listed below where epsilon0 and epsilon1 are defined to be whatever the application writer deems appropriate.

```
int CollinearTest(Point P, Point Q0, Point Q1)
{
    Point D = Q1 - Q0, A = P - Q0;
    float NdA = D.x * A.y - D.y * A.x;  // N = -Perp(D) = (-D.y, D.x)
    float NdN = D.x * D.x + D.y * D.y;  // |N| = |D|
    float AdA = A.x * A.x + A.y * A.y;

    if (NdA * NdA > epsilon0 * NdN * AdA) {
        if (NdA > 0)
            return POSITIVE;
        if (NdA < 0)
            return NEGATIVE;
    }

    float DdA = Dot(D, A);
    if (DdA < -epsilon1 * NdN)
        return COLLINEAR_LEFT;
    if (DdA > (1 + epsilon1) * NdN)
        return COLLINEAR_RIGHT;

    return COLLINEAR_CONTAIN;
}
```

Once the current hull has three or more points, it is guaranteed to remain a convex polygon with positive area regardless of the values of any further input points.

The final function to discuss is MergePlanar. Once the first triangle, if any, is created by MergeLinear, the last inserted point that led to the triangle is always stored in hull[0]. This point is a good candidate for searching for the tangent points formed by the next input point and the current hull. The planar merge contains two loops, one to find the upper tangent point and one to find the lower tangent point. The loop bodies just test for visibility based on the results of CollinearTest applied to the input point and edges of the current hull. The pseudocode is

```
void MergePlanar(Point P, ConvexPolygon& hull)
{
    // find upper tangent point
    for (U = 0; i = 1; U < hull.N; U = i, i = (i + 1) mod hull.N) {
        test = CollinearTest(P, hull[U], hull[i]);

        if (test == NEGATIVE)  // edge visible, go to next edge
            continue;

        if (test == POSITIVE          // edge not visible,
        || test == COLLINEAR_LEFT) { // only edge end point is visible
            // upper found
            break;
        }

        // test == COLLINEAR_CONTAIN || test == COLLINEAR_RIGHT
        // Theoretically cannot occur when input points are distinct and
        // sorted, but can occur because of floating-point round-off
        // when P is very close to the current hull.  Assume P is on the
        // hull polygon--nothing to do.
        return;
    }

    // find lower tangent point
    for (L = 0; i = hull.N - 1; i >= 0; L = i, i--) {
        test = CollinearTest(P, hull[i], hull[L]);

        if (test == NEGATIVE)  // edge visible, go to next edge
            continue;

        if (test == POSITIVE           // edge not visible,
        || test == COLLINEAR_RIGHT) { // only edge end point is visible
            // lower found
            break;
        }
    }
```

```
        // test == COLLINEAR_CONTAIN || test == COLLINEAR_LEFT
        // Theoretically cannot occur when input points are distinct and
        // sorted, but can occur because of floating-point round-off
        // when P is very close to the current hull.  Assume P is on the
        // hull polygon--nothing to do.
        return;
    }


    // Both tangent points found.  Now do:
    // 1. Remove visible edges from current hull.
    // 2. Add new edges formed by P and tangent points.
}
```

The simplest algorithm for updating the hull in steps 1 and 2 indicated in the pseudocode is to create a temporary hull from the current hull and input point by iteration:

```
ConvexPolygon tmpHull;
tmpHull[0] = P;
for (i = 1; true; i++, U = (U + 1) mod hull.N) {
    tmpHull[i] = hull[U];
    if (U == L)
        break;
}
hull = tmpHull;
```

However, the iteration is $O(n)$, so the incremental algorithm becomes $O(n^2)$. To avoid this, it is important to maintain the hull as some type of linked structure so that the linked chain of visible edges can be disconnected at the tangent points, an $O(1)$ operation, *and deletion needs to be done in $O(1)$ time*. The chain should not be deleted one node at a time; otherwise you are back to $O(n)$ time. This requires an implementation that pays close attention to memory management. After the linked chain is removed, new links are added from the node representing P to the nodes representing the tangent points.

An important note about the architecture of the algorithm is in order. All of the problems due to floating-point round-off errors are encapsulated by the function CollinearTest. Any unexpected results from an application of the incremental hull algorithm can only be due to the implementation of CollinearTest, particularly in the choice of the relative error thresholds ε_0 and ε_1. The encapsulation makes it easy to debug any problems that arise in the application.

Divide-and-Conquer Method

A standard paradigm in computer science is *divide and conquer*. The idea is to take a problem, divide it into two smaller problems of the same type, solve the smaller problems, and merge the results to construct the solution to the original problem. If the problem has n inputs and T_n is the time it takes to solve the problem, the division into two smaller problems, each with half the inputs, leads to the recursion formula $T_n = 2T_{n/2} + M_n$. Each smaller problem has (approximately) $n/2$ inputs and takes $T_{n/2}$ time to solve (by definition of T_k). The quantity M_n represents the time it takes to merge the solution to the two smaller problems. If M_n takes linear time, $O(n)$, then it can be shown that the solution T_n is $O(n \log n)$. Recurrences of this form are discussed in detail in Cormen, Leiserson, and Rivest (1990). The divide-and-conquer method applied to convex hulls turns out to have a linear-time merge, so the convex hull algorithm for a set of n points takes $O(n \log n)$ time.

As in the incremental construction of the convex hull, the input points are sorted according to the same scheme: $(x_0, y_0) < (x_1, y_1)$ when $x_0 < x_1$ or when $x_0 = x_1$ and $y_0 < y_1$. We also make no assumptions about the structure of the point set. Just as in the incremental hull algorithm, the input points are sorted and duplicates are removed. The initial pseudocode is

```
ConvexPolygon DividAndConquerHull(int n, Point V[n])
{
    Sort(n, V);
    RemoveDuplicates(n, V);  // n can decrease, V has contiguous elements
    ConvexPolygon hull;
    GetHull(0, n - 1, V, hull);
    return hull;
}
```

The recursive construction occurs in GetHull. Its structure is shown below. The values i0 and i1 are the first and last indices of a subset of points whose convex hull must be computed.

```
void GetHull(int i0, int i1, Point V[], ConvexPolygon& hull)
{
    int quantity = i1 - i0 + 1;
    if (quantity > 1) {
        // middle index of input range
        int mid = (i0 + i1) / 2;

        // find hull of subsets (mid - i0 + 1 >= i1 - mid)
        ConvexPolygon LHull, RHull;
        GetHull(i0, mid, V, LHull);
```

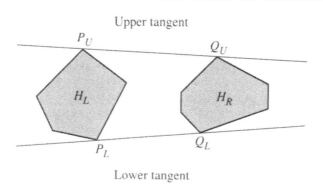

Figure 13.36   Two convex hulls H_L and H_R and their upper and lower tangents.

```
            GetHull(mid + 1, i1, V, RHull);

            // merge the convex hulls into a single convex hull
            Merge(LHull, RHull, hull);
        } else {
            // convex hull is a single point
            hull[0] = V[i0];
        }
    }
```

   The technical problem, of course, is how Merge computes the convex hull of two convex hulls. The idea is an extension of that for computing the convex hull of a single point, a convex set itself, and a convex polygon. In the latter case, the merge depended on finding upper and lower tangents to the hull and containing the single point; Figure 13.34 shows the typical situation. For two convex polygons, we still must find upper and lower tangents to both hulls; Figure 13.36 shows the typical situation. Unlike the incremental hull problem, we do not know one of the tangent points ahead of time. An exhaustive search over pairs of points, one from each polygon, results in an $O(n^2)$ merge. An $O(n)$ merge is readily available instead if we perform the following *walking algorithm* on the left hull H_L and the right hull H_R.
   The method is described for finding the lower tangent to the hulls. Find the point P_i on H_L with the largest x-component, a linear-time process. Find the point Q_j on H_R with the smallest x-component, also linear time. If the line containing P_i and Q_j is not tangent to H_L, traverse the vertices of H_L in the clockwise direction (decrement i) until the line is tangent to H_L. Now switch to H_R. If the line containing the current P_i and Q_j is not tangent to H_R, traverse the vertices of H_R in the counterclockwise direction (increment j) until the line is tangent to H_R. This traversal produces a new

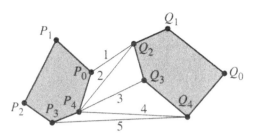

Figure 13.37   Two convex hulls H_L and H_R and the incremental search for the lower tangent.

line that might no longer be tangent to H_L. Alternately repeat the traversals until
the line is tangent to both hulls. Figure 13.37 shows a typical situation. The extreme
points are P_0 and Q_2. The initial segment, labeled 1, is $\langle P_0, Q_2 \rangle$. This segment is not
tangent to the left hull at P_0, so the left hull index is decremented (modulo 5), and
the new segment, labeled 2, is $\langle P_4, Q_2 \rangle$. This segment is tangent to the left hull at
P_4, but it is not tangent to the right hull at Q_2. The right hull index is incremented,
and the new segment, labeled 3, is $\langle P_4, Q_3 \rangle$. The segment is not tangent to the right
hull, so the right hull index is incremented again, and the new segment, labeled 4,
is $\langle P_4, Q_4 \rangle$. The segment is now tangent to the right hull, but not tangent to the left
hull. The left hull index is decremented, and the new segment, labeled 5, is $\langle P_3, Q_4 \rangle$.
This segment is tangent to both hulls and is the lower tangent to the hull. It is possible
that a tangent is collinear with a hull edge that shares the tangent point, but rather
than test for this in each merge and extend the tangent to include the collinear edge
if necessary, removal of collinear edges can be done as a postprocess on the convex
polygon returned by the hull construction.

The pseudocode for Merge is listed below. The case of small sets near the leaf nodes
of the implicit binary tree implied by the recursion are specially handled.

```
void Merge(ConvexPolygon LHull, ConvexPolygon RHull, ConvexPolygon& hull)
{
    if (LHull.n == 1 && RHull.n == 1) {
        // duplicate points were removed earlier, the hull is a line segment
        hull[0] = LHull[0];
        hull[1] = RHull[0];
        return;
    }
    if (LHull.n == 1 && RHull.n == 2) {
        // merge point and line segment, result in RHull
        MergeLinear(LHull[0], RHull);
        hull = RHull;
```

```
            return;
        }
        if (LHull.n == 2 && RHull.n == 1) {
            // merge point and line segment, result in LHull
            MergeLinear(RHull[0], LHull);
            hull = LHull;
            return;
        }
        if (LHull.n == 2 && RHull.n == 2) {
            // merge point and line segment, result in LHull
            MergeLinear(RHull[1], LHull);
            if (LHull.n == 2) {
                // RHull[1] was on line of LHull, merge next point
                MergeLinear(RHull[0], LHull);
                hull = LHull;
                return;
            }

            // RHull[1] and LHull form a triangle.  Remove RHull[1] so that
            // RHull is a single point.  LHull has been modified to be a
            // triangle.  Let the tangent search take care of the merge.
            RHull.Remove(1);
        }

        // find indices of extreme points with respect to x
        LMax = IndexOfMaximum{LHull[i].x};
        RMin = IndexOfMinimum{RHull[i].x};

        // get lower tangent to hulls, start search at extreme points
        LLIndex = LMax;  // lower left index
        LRIndex = RMin;  // lower right index
        GetTangent(LHull, RHull, LLIndex, LRIndex);

        // get upper tangent to hulls, start search at extreme points
        ULIndex = LMax;  // upper left index
        URIndex = RMin;  // upper right index
        GetTangent(RHull, LHull, URIndex, ULIndex);

        // construct the counterclockwise-ordered merged-hull vertices
        ConvexPolygon tmpHull;
        i = 0;
        for (each j between LRIndex and URIndex inclusive) {
            tmpHull[i] = hull[j];
            i++;
```

```
        }
        for (each j between ULIndex and LLIndex inclusive) {
            tmpHull[i] = hull[j];
            i++;
        }
        hull = tmpHull;
    }
```

The function MergeLinear has identical structure to the one used in the incremental hull construction, with the minor change in semantics that the input line segment polygon is modified to store the merged hull.

The tangent search uses the same concepts of visibility as in the incremental hull construction. As described earlier, the search flip-flops between the two input hulls. The input indices L and U are the starting ones for the search. On return, the indices correspond to the tangent points on the two hulls.

```
void GetTangent(ConvexPolygon LHull, ConvexPolygon RHull, int& L, int& R)
{
    // In theory the loop terminates in a finite number of steps, but the
    // upper bound for the loop variable is used to trap problems caused by
    // floating-point round-off errors that might lead to an infinite loop.

    for (int i = 0; i < LHull.n + RHull.n; i++) {
        // end points of potential tangent
        Point L1 = LHull[L];
        Point R0 = RHull[R];

        // walk clockwise along left hull to find tangency
        int Lm1 = (L - 1) mod LHull.n;
        Point L0 = LHull[Lm1];
        int test = CollinearTest(R0, L0, L1);
        if (test == NEGATIVE || test == COLLINEAR_LEFT) {
            L = Lm1;
            continue;
        }

        // walk counterclockwise along right hull to find tangency
        int Rp1 = (R + 1) mod RHull.n;
        Point R1 = RHull[Rp1];
        test = CollinearTest(L1, R0, R1);
        if (test == NEGATIVE || test == COLLINEAR_RIGHT) {
            R = Rp1;
            continue;
        }
```

```
            // tangent segment has been found
            break;
        }

        // Trap any problems due to floating-point round-off errors.
        assert(i < LHull.n + RHull.n);
    }
```

As each vertex is visited on one hull, the current edge on the other hull is tested for visibility using `CollinearTest`. When visible, the returned value is usually `NEGATIVE`. However, care must be taken when the initial extreme points on the hulls are on the same vertical line. Figure 13.38 shows a typical scenario. The initial candidate tangent is $\langle L_1, R_0 \rangle$, shown in Figure 13.38(a). In attempting to traverse the left hull, the output of `CollinearTest(R0,L0,L1)` is `COLLINEAR_RIGHT`. The left hull index remains unchanged, and a traversal is attempted on the right hull. The output of `CollinearTest(L1,R0,R1)` is also `COLLINEAR_RIGHT`. In this case the right hull index is incremented, effectively as if R_0 were slightly to the right of the common vertical line. Figure 13.38(b) shows the current state after the increment. The traversal switches back to the left hull. The output of `CollinearTest(R0,L0,L1)` is once again `COLLINEAR_RIGHT`, and the left hull index remains unchanged. The traversal switches to the right hull. The output of `CollinearTest(L1,R0,R1)` is `COLLINEAR_RIGHT`, and the right hull index is incremented, again as if R_0 were slightly to the right of the common vertical line. Figure 13.38(c) shows the current state after the increment. Switching back to the left hull, the output of `CollinearTest(R0,L0,L1)` is `NEGATIVE` since the edge $\langle R_0, R_1 \rangle$ is fully visible. The left hull index is decremented. Figure 13.38(d) shows the current state after the decrement. The loop is iterated one more time, but both calls to `CollinearTest` return `POSITIVE`, and $\langle L_1, R_0 \rangle$ in Figure 13.38(c) is tangent to the two hulls.

Once both tangents to the hulls are found, the construction of the merged hull is structured the same as for the incremental hull construction. The pseudocode shows the creation of a temporary convex polygon that contains subsets of indices from both hulls based on the tangent point locations, but just as in the incremental construction, a linked list structure can be used, and the detachment, attachment, and sublist deletion can all be performed in $O(1)$ time. However, the total time is still $O(n)$ because of the traversals over the two input hulls to find the extreme points.

13.7.2 CONVEX HULLS IN 3D

The ideas in 2D for constructing convex hulls of point sets using the incremental method or the divide-and-conquer method extend naturally to 3D. The incremental method has an easily implementable extension. The divide-and-conquer method is significantly more difficult to implement.

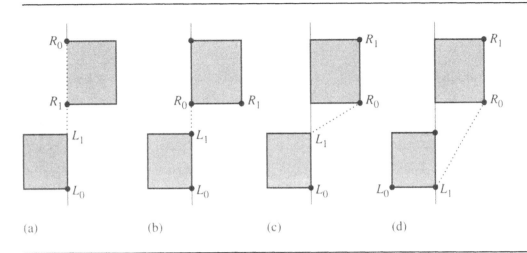

Figure 13.38   The extreme points used to initialize tangent search are on the same vertical line. The initial visibility tests both do not yield a NEGATIVE test, yet the initial segment connecting the extremes is not a tangent to the hulls. The current candidate for the tangent is shown as a dotted line.

Incremental Construction

The 3D algorithm is similar to the 2D algorithm. Each point is processed and merged with the convex hull of the previous points. The dimension of the hull is monitored to make sure that collinear points lead to a line segment hull and coplanar points lead to a planar convex polygon. The typical case is when the hull becomes a convex polyhedron.

The merge operation is slightly more complex than in the 2D case. Instead of two tangent lines, we obtain a *visibility cone* (not to be confused with the cone that is a quadric surface) whose vertex is the point to be merged and whose final edges form a closed polyline of current hull edges that separate the visible faces from the hidden ones. The closed polyline is sometimes called the *terminator*, a word used in astronomy to denote the boundary between the lit and unlit regions of an astronomical body. Figure 13.39 illustrates the typical situation. The visible faces must be removed from the current hull, and the faces of the visibility cone must be added. A simple algorithm for doing this involves traversing over all current faces, finding those faces with an edge on the terminator, and storing the edges in some data structure. During the traversal, visible faces are discarded and hidden faces are kept. Once all faces have been visited, the terminator is known as a closed polyline. The polyline is traversed, and faces formed by each edge with P are constructed and added to the merged hull data structure.

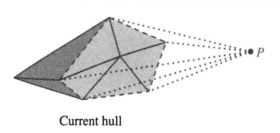

Current hull

Figure 13.39   The current hull and point to be merged. The visible faces are drawn in light gray. The hidden faces are drawn in dark gray. The polyline separating the two sets is dashed. The other edges of the visibility cone are dotted.

An algorithm for finding the terminator that is more efficient, but more complicated to implement, uses a linear search for a terminator edge. If a face lies on the plane $\hat{n} \cdot X + d = 0$, where $\hat{n}$ is a unit-length normal, the signed distance from P to the plane is $\delta = \hat{n} \cdot P + d$. If $\delta > 0$, the plane is visible to P (and so is the corresponding face). If $\delta \leq 0$, the plane is hidden, as is the corresponding face. In the case $\delta = 0$, the closest edge of the face is potentially visible to P, but that edge is part of another face for which $\delta \geq 0$. The face mesh for the current convex hull has a dual graph whose nodes represent the faces and whose arcs represent the edges of the faces. In particular, an arc between two nodes indicates that the corresponding faces are adjacent. Each node is assigned the signed distance from P to the face. Starting at a node in the graph with positive signed distance, a search is made to find a path of nodes whose distances are decreasing (more accurately, nonincreasing). The next node visited from the current node is the one whose signed distance is the smallest positive value of all adjacent nodes. Because the hull is convex, eventually a node must be reached that has at least one adjacent node with a nonpositive signed distance. The shared edge is on the terminator by definition. Once a first terminator edge is found, and assuming a data structure that maintains a list of adjacent edges for each vertex, the terminator can be traversed.

Observe that this approach is closely related to finding a zero-level curve of an image (the signed distances) defined on a graph of pixels. The intuition on the order of the algorithm follows from this. If the image were square with n pixels (number of faces in our problem), the linear search for the first point on the zero-level curve is $O(\sqrt{n})$. The traversal along the zero-level curve (the terminator in our problem) is also a linear search, again taking $O(\sqrt{n})$ time. The simple algorithm mentioned earlier visits all triangles, taking $O(n)$ time, an asymptotically slower method.

The pseudocode for the top-level call is

```
ConvexPolyhedron IncrementalHull(int n, Point V[n])
{
    Sort(n, V);
```

```
RemoveDuplicates(n, V);
ConvexPolyhedron hull;
type = POINT;
hull[0] = V[0];
for (i = 1; i < n; i++) {
    switch (type) {
        case POINT:   type = LINEAR;  hull[1] = V[i];  break;
        case LINEAR:  MergeLinear(V[i], hull,type);    break;
        case PLANAR:  MergePlanar(V[i], hull,type);    break;
        case SPATIAL: MergeSpatial(V[i], hull);        break;
    }
}
return hull;
}
```

The data structure for the convex polyhedron is most likely different for the spatial case than for the other cases. The natural storage for a linear hull is an array of two points, the end points of the line segment that is the hull. The natural storage for a planar hull is an array or list of ordered points. The natural storage for a spatial hull is more complicated. In its most abstract form, the data structure is a vertex-edge-face table that allows adding and removing each of the primitive components. In an application that is triangle based, the faces are stored as triangle fans. For 2D convex polygons, support can be added for collapsing collinear edges to a single edge. In 3D, the triangle fans can be collapsed into convex polygons, and the collinear edges of those convex polygons can be collapsed into single edges.

The function MergeLinear is nearly identical to the one for the 2D incremental hull. However, if the three input points (the next point to be merged and the end points of the current line segment hull) are not collinear, they lie on a plane and have no specific ordering (i.e., positive or negative as in the 2D case) until a normal vector is chosen for that plane. A normal vector should be chosen so that if the hull eventually becomes spatial, the first face is a convex polygon, and the normal can be used to reorder the vertices (if necessary) so that the polygon is counterclockwise ordered when viewed from outside the hull.

The function MergePlanar is slightly different from that of the 2D case. If the next input point is on the current plane, then the 2D merge algorithm is applied to update the current hull, a convex planar polygon, to another convex planar polygon. The merge is, of course, applied to points as 3D entities. If the next input point is not on the current plane, the hull becomes spatial, and MergeSpatial takes over for subsequent merges. If the data structure used to represent convex polyhedrons is a triangle mesh stored as a vertex-edge-triangle table, then the current hull, a convex planar polygon, must be fanned into triangles that are added to the table. The additional triangles formed by the next input point and the edges of the convex polygon are also added. The normal vector calculated earlier can be used at this time to make sure the triangles are added to be counterclockwise ordered when viewed from the outside of the spatial hull.

The function MergeSpatial performs the duties described earlier. By whatever means, the visible faces of the current hull are removed, and the new faces formed by the terminator and the next input point are added.

Divide-and-Conquer Method

The basic construction is similar to that in 2D. The input points are sorted along some axis. The set of points is divided into two sets, and the hulls are computed recursively on those sets. The resulting hulls are merged into a single hull with an algorithm that is $O(n)$ in time.

The idea is to wrap a plane about the two input hulls. The end result is a strip consisting of triangles and/or quadrilaterals that become the new faces of the merged hull. Figure 13.40 illustrates with two icosahedrons that are merged into a single convex polyhedron. The wrapping begins by finding a supporting plane for the two input hulls, a plane that is tangent to both hulls. For each hull the set of tangency is either a vertex, an edge, or a face. If the set is a face, we need only consider a single edge of the face, one visible to the other supporting set, to start the wrapping process. Because we need only consider vertices and edges, the new faces on the merged hull are either triangles or quadrilaterals.

Regardless of the type of supporting sets for the hulls, there must be vertices P_0 and Q_0, one from each hull, so that the line segment $\langle P_0, Q_0 \rangle$ is an edge of the merged hull. One half of the supporting plane containing that edge is "folded" along the line containing the edge until another hull vertex is encountered. If this vertex is on the first hull, call it P_1, then it must be adjacent to P_0. The triangle $\langle P_0, P_1, Q_0 \rangle$ is a face of the merged hull. Similarly, if the vertex is on the second hull, call it Q_1, then it must be adjacent to Q_0. The triangle $\langle Q_0, Q_1, P \rangle$ is a face of the merged hull. It is possible that both P_1 and Q_1 are encountered simultaneously, in which case the quadrilateral formed by the four points is a face of the merged hull. The plane is folded again on the line containing the next leading edge of the last found face. The process is repeated until the original folding edge is revisited. As described in O'Rourke (1998), the asymptotical analysis shows that the amortized cost for this search is $O(n)$.

Once the merged hull faces are constructed by the plane wrapping, the old faces that are no longer visible must be removed. In the 3D incremental hull construction, the merge is applied to a single point and a convex polyhedron. Recall that the terminator is the closed polyline of edges on the convex polyhedron that separates the visible faces from the hidden ones relative to the single point. As a graph whose nodes are the terminator vertices and whose arcs are the edges connecting consecutive vertices, the terminator is a simple cycle. The merge step in the incremental hull involved finding the terminator. The most efficient algorithm was to find an edge of the terminator, then traverse adjacent edges of the terminator that separate two faces, one of positive signed distance and one of nonpositive signed distance. This traversal succeeds because the terminator is a simple cycle. Figure 13.40 might lead you to believe that the terminators for the two input hulls are both simple cycles. As

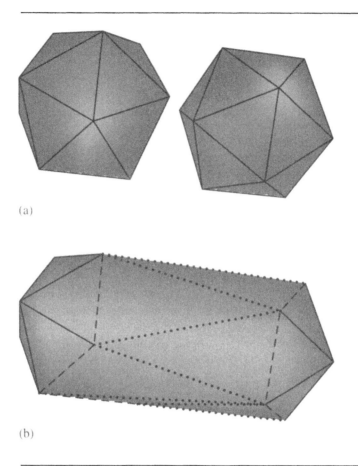

(a)

(b)

Figure 13.40   (a) Two icosahedrons. (b) The merged hull. The dashed lines indicate those edges that are part of faces of the original hulls. The dotted lines indicate those edges that are part of the newly added faces.

it turns out, this is not necessarily the case. A simple example to illustrate this involves merging a convex polyhedron and a line segment. The faces that are kept in the merged hull are those that are hidden to *all* points on the line segment. Equivalently, the discarded faces are those that are visible to *some* point on the line segment. Figure 13.41 shows an example where the convex polyhedron is a pyramid. The terminator for the pyramid consists of two triangles that share a single vertex. Because of this possibility, you should be careful not to assume that the terminators are simple cycles when attempting to delete the visible faces of each input hull. A correct method is to traverse all edges of the terminator and detach the visible faces from the hidden ones. It is true that the visible faces on an input hull are in the same connected component,

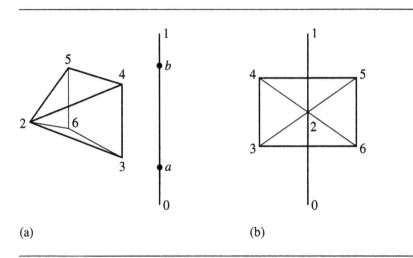

(a)   (b)

Figure 13.41   (a) A side view of the pyramid and line segment. (b) A view from behind the line
segment. The line segment $\langle 0, a \rangle$ can only see triangle $\langle 2, 3, 6 \rangle$ and quadrilateral
$\langle 3, 4, 5, 6 \rangle$. The line segment $\langle a, b \rangle$ can only see the quadrilateral. The line segment
$\langle b, 1 \rangle$ can only see triangle $\langle 2, 4, 5 \rangle$ and the quadrilateral. The faces that are hidden
in all cases are the triangles $\langle 2, 3, 4 \rangle$ and $\langle 2, 5, 6 \rangle$. The terminator consists of the
boundaries of these triangles, a sequence of line segments forming two cycles, not
a simple cycle.

so a depth-first search may be used to delete them one at a time. However, with extra
work, an $O(1)$ delete algorithm can be used as long as the application provides a
sophisticated memory manager along the lines that were mentioned for incremental
hull construction in 2D. The idea is to detach the visible faces from the hidden ones,
but allow the component of visible faces to exist until the full hull is constructed. At
that time, an iteration is made over the hull to construct a copy of it. The previous
copy and all the dangling components are part of temporary workspace in memory
that is deleted all at once.

13.7.3   CONVEX HULLS IN HIGHER DIMENSIONS

Convex hull algorithms in higher dimensions are more complex to implement, but
the ideas for incremental construction and divide-and-conquer construction extend
naturally. The asymptotic behavior is worse due to the result of Klee (1980) that
shows the convex hull of n points in dimension d can have at least the order of
$n^{\lfloor d/2 \rfloor}$ hyperfaces. In particular, in dimension $d = 4$ the number of hyperfaces can
be quadratic, so it is not possible to construct an $O(n \log n)$ algorithm.

Incremental Construction

A current hull is maintained whose dimension h starts at 0 (a point) and increases to some final value $h \leq d$, where d is the dimension of the full space. An origin and set of orthonormal basis vectors is maintained for the current hull. The initial point from the input set is saved as the origin A. Each time the insertion of an input point forces h to increase, a unit-length basis vector $\hat{d}_h$ is added that is orthogonal to all the previous basis vectors. At the cost of storing a second copy of the input points, something that occurred anyway in small dimensions to support sorting of the points without disturbing the original set, the origin and basis can be used to represent already processed points in that coordinate system. The advantage is that a convex hull finder for a specified dimension can be reused by hull finders in larger dimensions as long as the points are represented as arrays. The point coordinates for the specified dimension are stored in contiguous locations in the array, so the convex hull finder can access the coordinates safely within the array. Probably the most difficult technical challenge is maintaining data structures for the hull in each dimension. In 3D, a vertex-edge-triangle table can be used to store the hull (convex polygonal faces with more than three vertices are trifanned). In 4D, a vertex-edge-triangle-tetrahedron table is required. As the dimension increases, the complexity of the data structure increases.

A high-level outline for $d = 4$ is presented here, assuming distinct points and at least two of them, say, P_0 and P_1. The points are initially sorted. The initial point is stored as the origin $A = P_0$. The initial basis vector is $\hat{d}_1 = (P_1 - P_0)/\|P_1 - P_0\|$. The current hull dimension is $h = 1$. The merge functions are denoted Merge<h> for each dimension $h \leq 4$. The data structures representing the hull are denoted Hull<h>. Each point in the data structure is stored as a 4D array, but only the first h components are relevant. The initial linear hull therefore effectively stores only two scalars $s_i = \hat{d}_i \cdot P_i$, $0 \leq i \leq 1$, that represent the 4D points $P_i = A + s_i \hat{d}_i$ (so $s_0 = 0$).

The linear merge is shown below.

```
void Merge<1>(Point P, Hull<1> hull)
{
    // uses affine coordinate system {A; D1}
    B = P - A;
    t1 = Dot(D1, B);
    R = B - t1 * D1;  // project out D1 component
    if (|R| > 0) {
        // |R| is the length of R
        // dimension increases
        h = 2;
        D2 = R / |R|;  // affine coordinate system becomes {A; D1, D2}
        t2 = Dot(D2, B);
        ReformatAndInsert(hull, t1, t2); // P = A + t1 * D1 + t2 * D2
```

```
    } else {
        // hull is still linear
        Update(hull, t1);
    }
}
```

The ReformatAndInsert function for the hull is not complicated. The hull is a line segment, represented by a pair of points. The insertion of (t1,t2) requires creation of a triangle. The triangle can be stored as a triple of points. If the hull remains planar and more points are merged to form a convex polygon with more than three sides, the points can be maintained as an ordered list. The Hull<1> data structure represents the end points of the line segment with scalars s_0 and s_1. On the reformatting, these values become $(s_0, 0)$ and $(s_1, 0)$ to be in the same space as (t_1, t_2). All such 2-vectors are coordinates in the affine system with origin A and basis vectors $\hat{d}_1$ and $\hat{d}_2$.

The Update function finds the terminator of the hull, in this case one of the end points of the line segment that is the hull. Because of the sorting, exactly one of these end points must be visible to the input point P. The line segment is appropriately updated to replace the visible end point by P. The calculations are performed in a one-dimensionsal space. Since hull is represented in the Hull<1> format, only the first array entries are relevant and are all that the routine accesses.

The planar merge is shown below.

```
void Merge<2>(Point P, Hull<2> hull)
{
    // uses affine coordinate system {A; D1, D2}
    B = P - A;
    t1 = Dot(D1, B);
    t2 = Dot(D2, B);
    R = B - t1 * D1 - t2 * D2;   // project out D1, D2 components
    if (|R| > 0) {
        // dimension increases
        h = 3;
        D3 = R / |R|;  // affine coordinate system becomes {A; D1, D2, D3}
        t3 = Dot(D3, B);
        ReformatAndInsert(hull, t1, t2, t3);
        // P = A + t1 * D1 + t2 * D2 + t3 * D3
    } else {
        // hull is still planar
        Update(hull, t1, t2);
    }
}
```

The ReformatAndInsert function for the hull is nontrivial compared to the function for the previous dimension. The hull is a planar convex polygon that is represented as an ordered point list. If the hull representation in space is a vertex-edge-face table, then the current hull is added as a face to that table. The insertion of (t1,t2,t3) requires the addition of triangular faces to the merged hull, each face formed by this point and an edge of the convex polygon. If the hull is represented as a vertex-edge-triangle table, the convex polygon must be trifanned first. The triangles are added to the table. The triangular faces formed by the inserted point and the edges of the convex polygon are added to the table. The Hull<2> data structure represents points as (s_1, s_2). On the reformatting, these values become $(s_1, s_2, 0)$ to be in the same space as (t_1, t_2, t_3). All such 3-vectors are coordinates in the affine system with origin A and basis vectors $\hat{d}_1$, $\hat{d}_2$, and $\hat{d}_3$.

The Update function finds the terminator of the hull, in this case the two vertices that are tangent points to the hull and form the visibility cone whose vertex is the input point. The edges visible to P are removed, and new edges formed by P and the tangent points are added to the hull.

The spatial merge is shown below.

```
void Merge<3>(Point P, Hull<3> hull)
{
    // uses affine coordinate system {A; D1, D2, D3}
    B = P - A;
    t1 = Dot(D1, B);
    t2 = Dot(D2, B);
    t3 = Dot(D3, B);
    R = B - t1 * D1 - t2 * D2 - t3 * D3;
    // project out the D1, D2, D3 components
    if (|R| > 0) {
        // dimension increases
        h = 4;
        convert hull from Hull<3> format to Hull<4> format;
        D4 = R / |R|;
        // affine coordinate system becomes {A; D1, D2, D3, D4}
        t4 = Dot(D4,B);
        ReformatAndInsert(hull, t1, t2, t3, t4);
        // P = A + t1 * D1 + t2 * D2 + t3 * D3 + t4 * D4
    } else {
        // hull is still spatial
        Update(hull, t1, t2, t3);
    }
}
```

The ReformatAndInsert function for the hull is also nontrivial. The 3D hull is a spatial convex polyhedron that, for the sake of argument, is stored as a vertex-edge-triangle table. Also, for the sake of argument, assume that the 4D hull is stored as a vertex-edge-triangle-tetrahedron table. The convex polyhedron must be partitioned into tetrahedra first, a process slightly more complicated than triangle fanning. The tetrahedra are added to the table. The tetrahedral faces formed by the inserted point and the triangles of the convex polyhedron are added to the table. The `Hull<3>` data structure represents points as (s_1, s_2, s_3). On the reformatting, these values become $(s_1, s_2, s_3, 0)$ to be in the same space as (t_1, t_2, t_3, t_4). All such 4-vectors are coordinates in the affine system with origin A and basis vectors $\hat{d}_1$, $\hat{d}_2$, $\hat{d}_3$, and $\hat{d}_4$.

The `Update` function finds the terminator of the hull, in this case the simple, closed polyline that separates the visible faces from the hidden ones. The faces visible to P are removed, and new faces formed by P and the terminator edges are added to the hull.

Finally, the hyperspatial merge is shown below. Because the original space has dimension 4, there is no need to project out the basis components since the corresponding vector $\vec{r}$ (R in the pseudocode) will always be $\vec{0}$.

```
void Merge<4>(Point P, Hull<4> hull)
{
    // Uses affine coordinate system {A; D1, D2, D3}.
    // Hull remains hyperspatial.
    B = P - A;
    t1 = Dot(D1, B);
    t2 = Dot(D2, B);
    t3 = Dot(D3, B);
    t4 = Dot(D4, B);

    Update(hull, t1, t2, t3, t4);
}
```

The `Update` function finds the terminator of the hull, the collection of faces that separate the visible hyperfaces from the hidden ones. The hyperfaces visible to P are removed, and new hyperfaces formed by P and the terminator faces are added to the hull. Since the last routine works on 4-vectors, the affine coordinates are not necessary, and the points can be manipulated in the original coordinate system. If this choice is made in an implementation, then the block of code in `Merge<3>` for the increase in dimension to 4 can be appended with code to replace all the points (stored in affine coordinates) in the current hull with the original points. This requires storing the original indices of the input points, but this is something that is done in small-dimension implementations anyway because the indices for the input data set should be used to store connectivity information, not the indices of the sorted data set. Also if this choice is made, then `Merge<4>` just calls the update function.

If the general format of a merge function is preserved by doing the projection anyway, we can implement a single, generic merge function, as shown below.

```
void Merge<k>(Point P, Hull<k> hull)
{
    B = P - A;
    R = B;
    for (i = 1; i <= k; i++) {
```

```
        t[i] = Dot(D[i], B);
        R = R - t[i] * D[i];
    }

    if (|R| > 0)  {
        // dimension increases
        h = h + 1;
        convert hull from Hull<k> format to Hull<k + 1> format;
        D[k + 1] = R / |R|;
        t[k + 1] = Dot(D[k + 1], B);
        ReformatAndInsert<k + 1>(hull,t );  // t = (t[1],...,t[k + 1])
    } else {
        // hull remains the same dimension
        Update<k>(hull, t);  // t = (t[1],...,t[k])
    }
}
```

To keep the implementation simple, the Update<k> function can be written to just iterate over all hyperfaces and keep those that are hidden and remove those that are visible, all the while keeping track of each face that is shared by a visible hyperface and a hidden hyperface, then iterate over those faces and form the hyperfaces with P and add them to finalize the merged hull.

The floating-point issues in this approach are threefold. First, the computation of the affine coordinates t[i] will involve floating-point round-off errors. Second, the comparison of length of $\vec{r}$ to zero should be replaced by a comparison to a small, positive threshold. Even so, such a comparison is affected by the magnitude of the inputs. Third, the Update function tests for visibility of hyperfaces. Each test is effectively a $(k + 1) \times (k + 1)$ determinant calculation where the first row of the matrix has all 1 entries and the columns, not including the first row entries, are the points forming the hyperface and the input point. Floating-point round-off errors may cause incorrect classification when the determinant is theoretically nearly zero.

Divide-and-Conquer Method

The basic concept is the same as in small dimensions. The important function is Merge, which computes the convex hull of two other convex hulls. Although easy to describe, the implementation is quite difficult to build. A supporting hyperplane must be found for the two hulls. A hyperedge that is not part of either hull is used to fold the hyperplane until it encounters a vertex of either hull. That vertex and the hyperedge are used to form a hyperface of the merged hull. The wrapping continues until the original hyperedge is encountered. The hyperfaces visible to either of the input hulls must be removed. As in the 3D problem, the set of such hyperfaces on a single hull is connected, so a depth-first search suffices to find and remove them. The hidden hyperfaces on each input hull are, of course, kept for the merged hull.

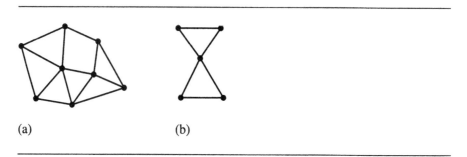

(a)   (b)

Figure 13.42   Triangulations of finite point sets: (a) with optional requirements; (b) without.

13.8 DELAUNAY TRIANGULATION

A *triangulation* of a finite set of points $S \subset \mathbb{R}^2$ is a set of triangles whose vertices are the points in S and whose edges connect pairs of points in S. Each point of S is required to occur in at least one triangle. The edges are only allowed to intersect at the vertices. An optional requirement is that the union of the triangles is the convex hull of S. Figure 13.42 shows triangulations of two point sets. The triangulation in Figure 13.42(a) includes the optional requirement, but the triangulation in Figure 13.42(b) does not. Similar terminology is used for constructing tetrahedra whose vertices are points in a finite set $S \subset \mathbb{R}^3$. The computational geometry researchers also refer to this as a triangulation, but some practitioners call this a *tetrahedralization*. For $S \subset \mathbb{R}^d$, an object whose vertices are in S is called a *simplex* (plural *simplices*), the generalization of triangle and tetrahedron to higher dimensions. We suppose that *simplexification* is as good a term as any for constructing the simplices whose vertices are in S.

A common desire in a triangulation is that there not be long, thin triangles. Consider the case of four points forming a convex quadrilateral. Figure 13.43 shows the two different choices for triangulation where the vertices are $(\pm 2, 0)$ and $(0, \pm 1)$. The goal is to select the triangulation that maximizes the minimum angle. The triangulation in Figure 13.43(b) has this property. The concept of maximizing the minimum angle produces a *Delaunay triangulation*. A better formal development is presented in computational geometry books and is based on understanding Voronoi diagrams for finite point sets and constructing the Delaunay triangulation from it. An important concept is that of a *circumcircle*, the circle containing the three vertices of a triangle. Although the angles of the triangles can be computed explicitly, the choice of one of the two triangulations is equivalently determined by containment of one point within the circumcircle of the other three points. In Figure 13.44, $(0, -1)$ is inside the circumcircle of triangle $\langle (2, 0), (0, 1), (-2, 0) \rangle$, but $(-2, 0)$ is outside the circumcircle of triangle $\langle (2, 0), (0, 1), (0, -1) \rangle$. The Delaunay triangulation has the property that the circumcircle of each triangle contains no other points of the input set. This property is used for incremental construction of the triangulation, the topic discussed

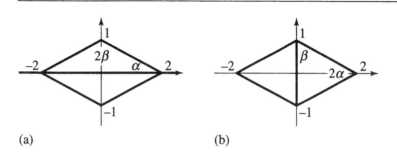

(a)   (b)

Figure 13.43   The two triangulations for a convex quadrilateral. The angle $\alpha \doteq 0.46$ radians and the angle $\beta \doteq 1.11$ radians. (a) The minimum angle of the top triangle is α (smaller than β). (b) The minimum angle is 2α radians (smaller than β); the triangles maximize the minimum angle.

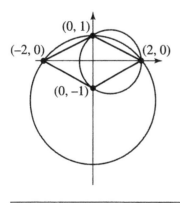

Figure 13.44   Two circumcircles for the triangles of Figure 13.43.

next. The original ideas of constructing the triangulation incrementally are found in Bowyer (1981) and Watson (1981).

13.8.1   INCREMENTAL CONSTRUCTION IN 2D

Given a finite set of points in $\mathbb{R}^2$, the triangulation begins by constructing a triangle large enough to contain the point set. As it turns out, it should be large enough to also contain the union of circumcircles for the final triangulation. The triangle is called a *supertriangle* for the point set. There are infinitely many supertriangles. For example, if you have one supertriangle, then any triangle containing it is also a supertriangle. A reasonably sized triangle that is easy to compute is one that contains a circle that contains the axis-aligned bounding rectangle of the points.

Each input point P is inserted into the triangulation. A triangle containing P must be found. An iteration over all triangles and point-in-triangle tests clearly allow you to find a triangle, but this can be a slow process when the input set has a large number of points. A better search uses a *linear walk* over the current triangles. This type of search was presented in Section 13.4.2 for a mesh of convex polygons. The idea, of course, specializes to the case when the polygons are all triangles. Two possible situations happen as shown in Figure 13.45. If P is interior to a triangle T, that triangle is split into three subtriangles, N_i for $0 \le i \le 2$. Before the split, the invariant of the algorithm is that each pair $\langle T, A_i \rangle$, where A_i is an adjacent triangle to T, satisfied the empty circumcircle condition. That is, the circumcircle of T did not contain the opposite vertex of A, and the circumcircle of A did not contain the opposite vertex of T. After the split, T will be removed, so the triangles A_i are now adjacent to the new triangles N_i. The circumcircle condition for the pairs $\langle N_i, A_i \rangle$ might not be satisfied, so the pairs need to be processed to make sure the condition is satisfied by a *swap of the shared edge*, the type of operation illustrated in Figure 13.43.

The pseudocode for the incremental construction is listed below:

```
void IncrementalDelaunay2D(int N, Point P[N])
{
    mesh.Insert(Supertriangle(N, P));  // mesh vertices V(0), V(1), V(2)

    for (i = 0; i < N; i++) {
        C = mesh.Container(P[i]);  // triangle or edge
        if (C is a triangle T) {
            // P[i] splits T into three subtriangles
            for (j = 0; j < 3; j++) {
                // insert subtriangle into mesh
                N = mesh.Insert(i, T.v(j), T.v(j + 1));

                // N and adjacent triangle might need edge swap
                A = T.adj(j);
                if (A is not null)
                    stack.push(N, A);
            }
            mesh.Remove(T);
        } else {
            // C is an edge E
            // P[i] splits each triangle sharing E into two subtriangles
            for (k = 0; k <= 1; k++) {
                T = E.adj(k);
```

```
                    if (T is not null) {
                        for (j = 0; j < 3; j++) {
                            if (T.edge(i) is not equal to E) {
                                // insert subtriangle into mesh
                                N = mesh.Insert(i, T.v(j), T.v(j + 1));

                                // N and adjacent triangle might need edge swap
                                A = T.adj(j);
                                if (A is not null)
                                    stack.push(N, A);
                            }
                        }
                        mesh.Remove(T);
                    }
                }
            }

            // Relevant triangles containing P[i] have been subdivided.  Now
            // process pairs of triangles that might need an edge swapped to
            // preserve the empty circumcircle constraint.
            while (stack is not empty) {
                stack.pop(T, A);

                // see Figure 13.45 to understand these indices
                compute i0, i1, i2, i3 with T.v(i1)= A.v(i2) and T.v(i2)= A.v(i1);

                if (T.v(i0) is in Circumcircle(A)) {
                    // swap must occur
                    N0 = mesh.Insert(T.v(i0), T.v(i1), A.v(i3));
                    B0 = A.adj(i1);
                    if (B0 is not null)
                        stack.push(N0, B0);   now <N0,B 0> might need swapping

                    N1 = mesh.Insert(T.v(i0), A.v(i3), A.v(i2));
                    B1 = A.adj(i3);
                    if (B1 is not null)
                        stack.push(N1, B1);   now <N1, B1> might need swapping
                }
            }
        }

        // remove any triangles that share a vertex from the supertriangle
        mesh.RemoveTrianglesSharing(V(0), V(1), V(2));
    }
```

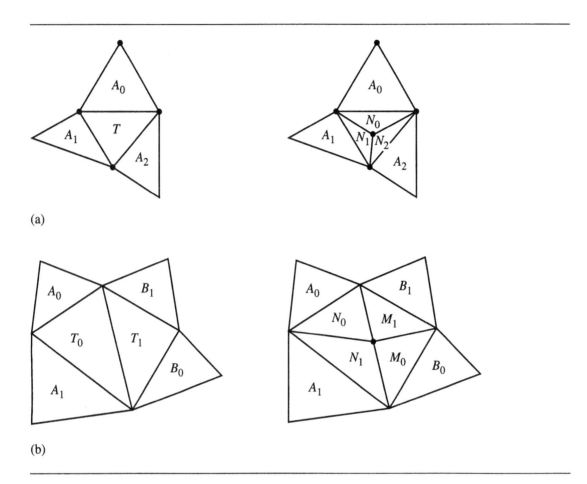

(a)

(b)

Figure 13.45   (a) The newly inserted point P, shown as an unlabeled black dot, is interior to a triangle, in which case the triangle is split into three subtriangles, or (b) it is on an edge of a triangle, in which case each triangle sharing the edge (if any) is split into two subtriangles.

The function Supertriangle computes the triangle described in the first paragraph of this section. The mesh object represents a triangle mesh stored as a vertex-edge-triangle table. The mesh operation Insert takes as input a triangle, either wholly or as three indices into the set of vertices managed by the mesh. It returns a reference to the actual triangle object inserted in the mesh so that the object can be used after the call. The mesh operation Remove just removes the specified triangle. The triangle object T is assumed to have an operation T.v(i) that allows you to access the index of the mesh vertex that the triangle shares. The indices are ordered so that the triangle vertices are counterclockwise ordered. The indexing is modulo 3, so T.v(0) and

T.v(3) are the same integer. The triangle object is also assumed to have an operation T.adj(i) that returns a reference to the adjacent triangle that shares the edge <T.v(i),T.v(i + 1)>. If there is no adjacent triangle to that edge, the reference is null. The edge object E is assumed to have an operation E.adj(i) that returns a reference to an adjacent triangle (at most two such triangles).

Figure 13.46 shows the various quantities used in the pseudocode in the loop where the stack of triangle pairs is processed. Theoretically, the loop can be infinite if a triangle pair has all vertices on a common circumcircle. Here is where the typical condition is specified by the computational geometers: no four points in the input set can be cocircular. However, an implementation must guard against this when floating-point arithmetic is used. It is possible that four points are not exactly cocircular, but floating-point round-off errors can make the triangle pair behave as if the points are cocircular. If such a pair is revisited in the loop, they might very well be swapped back to their original configuration, and the entire process starts over. To avoid the infinite loop, an implementation can evaluate *both* circumcircle tests, one for the current triangle configuration and one for the swapped configuration. If both tests indicate a swap should occur, then the swap should not be made. Be aware, though, that if the circumcircle test accepts two adjacent triangles as input, additional care must be taken to pass the triangles in the same order. Otherwise, the floating-point calculations involving the triangles might possibly cause the Boolean return value to differ. That is, if the function prototype is bool FirstInCircumcircleOfSecond(Triangle, Triangle), the calls FirstInCircumcircleOfSecond(T0,T1) and FirstInCircumcircleOfSecond(T1,T0) might return different values. One way to obtain a consistent ordering is as follows. The two vertices that are opposite the shared edge of the triangles have indices maintained by the mesh object. Pass the triangles so that the first triangle has the vertex of the smallest index between the two triangles.

Once all the points are inserted into the triangulation and all necessary edge swaps have occurred, any triangles that exist only because they share a vertex from the supertriangle must be removed. Another potential pitfall here is that *all* triangles might be removed. This is the case when the initial points all lie on the same line. If an application really needs the incremental algorithm to apply to such a set (interpolation based on a collection of data points is one such application), some type of preprocessing must occur to detect the collinearity. Probably the best bet is to use the relationship between the 2D Delaunay triangulation and the 3D convex hull that is described later in this section. The convex hull algorithms appear to be better suited for handling degeneracies due to the fact that the intrinsic dimensionality of the input point set is smaller than the dimension of the space in which the points lie.

13.8.2 INCREMENTAL CONSTRUCTION IN GENERAL DIMENSIONS

An attempt at extending the 2D edge swapping algorithm to 3D has a couple of technical issues to consider. The first involves the extension of the linear walk that was used to find a containing triangle. Each input point P is inserted into the current

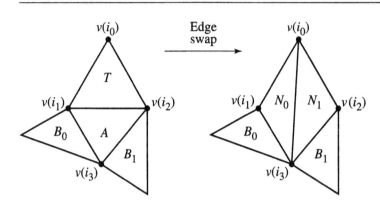

Figure 13.46   A triangle pair $\langle T, A \rangle$ that needs an edge swap. The index tracking is necessary so that the correct objects in the vertex-edge-triangle table of the mesh are manipulated. After the edge swap, up to two new pairs of triangles occur, $\langle N_0, B_0 \rangle$ and $\langle N_1, B_1 \rangle$, each pair possibly needing an edge swap. These are pushed onto the stack of pairs that need to be processed.

tetrahedral mesh. A tetrahedron containing P is found using the same type of walk that was used for the 2D problem. An initial tetrahedron is selected. If P is in that tetrahedron, the walk is complete. If not, construct a ray whose origin is the average of the current tetrahedron's vertices, call it C, and whose direction is $P - C$. A tetrahedron face that intersects the ray is located. The tetrahedron adjacent to the current one and that shares this face is the next candidate for containment of P. As it turns out, there are pathological data sets for which the walk can be quite long (Shewchuk 2000). A 3D Delaunay triangulation can have $O(n^2)$ tetrahedra. In the cited paper, it is shown that a line can stab $O(n^2)$ tetrahedra. In fact, for d dimensions, a line can stab on the order of $n^{\lceil d/2 \rceil}$ simplices.

The other technical issue is that the swapping mechanism does not have a counterpart in 3D. The edge swapping in 2D was intuitively based on maximizing a minimum angle, but that heuristic does not have a 3D counterpart (Joe 1991). The general method is based on Watson's algorithm (Watson 1981). The algorithm is described for a point set contained in $\mathbb{R}^d$ whose intrinsic dimensionality is d. That is, the point set does not lie in a linear space of dimension smaller than d. Unfortunately, an implementation must deal with degeneracy in dimension. A *very good* description of the practical problems that occur with implementing Watson's algorithm in 3D is presented in Field (1986). This paper is available online through the ACM Digital Library.

Because of the assumption of full dimensionality of the points, the elements of the triangulation are nondegenerate simplices, each having $d + 1$ points. The circumscribing hypersphere of a simplex will be called a *circumhypersphere*. The condition

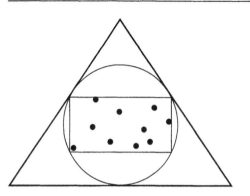

Figure 13.47   Supertriangle of the input point set.

for a Delaunay triangulation is that the circumhypersphere of a simplex does not contain any input points other than the vertices of that simplex (the *empty circumhypersphere constraint*). The algorithm is described in steps. Following the excellent presentation in Field (1986), the steps have associated figures that illustrate what is happening in two dimensions.

1. Construct a *supersimplex*, a simplex that is guaranteed to contain the input points as well as any circumhyperspheres in the final triangulation. A suitable choice is a simplex that contains a hypersphere that itself contains the axis-aligned bounding box of the input points (see Figure 13.47).

2. The supersimplex is added as the first simplex in a mesh of simplices. The mesh maintains the vertices and all the necessary connectivity between simplices. Moreover, the circumhypersphere for each simplex is stored to avoid having to recalculate centers and radii during the incremental updates.

3. Insert the other input points, one at a time, and process as described here.

    a. Determine which circumhyperspheres contain the given point. Here is where the direct appeal is made to satisfying the empty circumhypersphere condition. Before insertion, the empty condition is satisfied for all simplices. When the point is inserted, the simplices corresponding to the circumhyperspheres that violate the empty condition must be modified. The search for the containing hyperspheres is implemented as a search over simplices using the (attempted linear) walk described in earlier sections. But as pointed out in Shewchuk (2000), the worst-case asymptotic order for the stabbing is $O(n^{\lceil d/2 \rceil})$. Once the containing simplex (or simplices if the input point is on a shared boundary component) is found, a depth-first search can be performed to find other simplices whose circumhyperspheres contain the input point. A

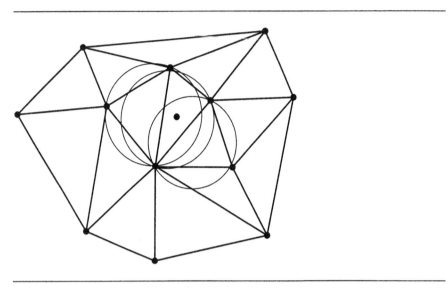

Figure 13.48   Circumcircles containing the next point to be inserted.

simpler method that just iterates over all current simplices will be easier to program, but potentially slower for the types of data sets seen in practice (see Figure 13.48).

b. The union of the simplices whose circumhyperspheres contain the input point form a d-dimensional polyhedron called the *insertion polyhedron*. Locate the boundary faces of that polyhedron (see Figure 13.49).

c. Create new simplices by connecting the input point to the boundary faces. Then remove the old simplices whose union was the insertion polyhedron (see Figure 13.50).

4. After all points are inserted, those simplices that share a vertex of the supersimplex are removed from the mesh. The resulting mesh is the Delaunay triangulation of the points (see Figure 13.51).

The 3D Delaunay triangulation can have *slivers*, tetrahedra that are nearly zero volume (needlelike or flat). Researchers in recent years have made attempts to develop methods to modify the final triangulation and obtain a good-quality one (Dey, Bajaj, and Sugihara 1991; Cheng et al. 2000).

If the input point set has intrinsic dimensionality smaller than the space in which the points live, probably a better approach is to use the relationship between the Delaunay triangulation in d dimensions and the convex hull in $d + 1$ dimensions as described in the next section. The convex hull algorithms appear to be better suited for handling degeneracies in dimension than the triangulation algorithms.

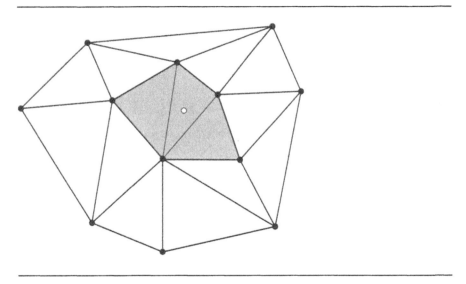

Figure 13.49   The insertion polygon for the next point to be inserted.

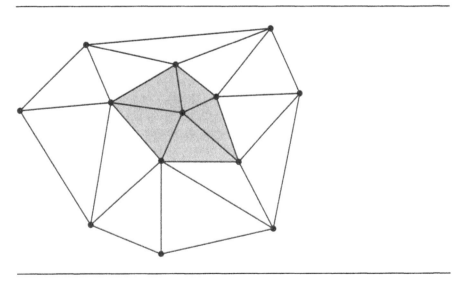

Figure 13.50   The modified insertion polygon that restores the empty circumcircle condition for the total mesh.

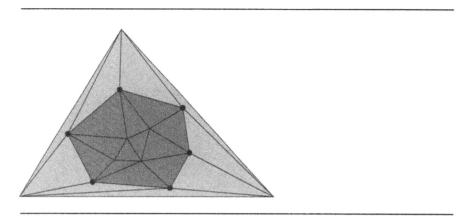

Figure 13.51   The final mesh triangles are dark gray. The removed triangles are shown in light gray.

13.8.3   CONSTRUCTION BY CONVEX HULL

The Delaunay triangulation of a finite point set $S \subset \mathbb{R}^d$ for any dimension d is obtainable from the convex hull of $S' = \{(X, \|X\|^2) : X \in S\} \subset \mathbb{R}^d \times \mathbb{R} = \mathbb{R}^{d+1}$, as shown in Edelsbrunner and Seidel (1986). In particular, let the convex hull be constructed so that its hyperfaces are $(d + 1)$-dimensional simplices. Each simplex has a normal vector in $\mathbb{R}^d \times \mathbb{R}$, say, $(\vec{N}, \lambda)$. The simplices for which $\lambda < 0$ form what is called the *lower hull*. The other simplices form the *upper hull*. The projections of the simplices of the lower hull onto $\mathbb{R}^d$ are themselves simplices (of dimension d) and are the Delaunay triangulation of S.

A simple illustration is shown in Figure 13.52 for a 2D triangulation obtained from a 3D convex hull. The five input points are $(0, 0)$, $(0, \pm 1)$, and $(1, \pm 1)$. Figure 13.52(b) shows the Delaunay triangulation. Figure 13.52(a) shows the convex hull of the lifted points $(0, 0, 0)$, $(0, \pm 1, 1)$, and $(1, \pm 1, 2)$. The lower hull consists of three triangles. The counterclockwise-ordered triangle $\langle(0, 0, 0), (0, 1, 1), (1, 1, 2)\rangle$ has normal vector $(1, 1, -1)$. The third component is negative, so this triangle is on the lower hull and is projected onto the xy-plane to obtain the counterclockwise-ordered Delaunay triangle $\langle(0, 0), (1, 1), (0, 1)\rangle$. Similarly, the triangles $\langle(0, 0, 0), (1, -1, 2), (0, -1, 1)\rangle$ and $\langle(0, 0, 0), (1, 1, 2), (1, -1, 2)\rangle$ have normals with a negative third component, so the xy-projections of these are part of the triangulation. The counterclockwise-ordered triangle $\langle(0, 1, 1), (0, 0, 0), (0, -1, 1)\rangle$ has normal vector $(-2, 0, 0)$. The third component is zero, so it is not part of the lower hull. The projection is a degenerate triangle and does not contribute to the triangulation. The upper hull consists of two triangles that are discarded.

This result is particularly useful from a numerical perspective. From experience, implementing a convex hull algorithm that is fully robust in the presence of floating-point numbers is easier than implementing a fully robust Delaunay triangulation algorithm.

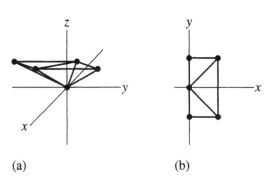

(a)   (b)

Figure 13.52   (a) Convex hull of 2D points lifted onto a paraboloid in 3D. (b) The corresponding
Delaunay triangulation, the projection of the lower hull onto the xy-plane.

13.9 POLYGON PARTITIONING

This section describes a few useful algorithms for partitioning a simple polygon into
triangles or into convex polygons. A key concept is that of visibility of other vertices
from a given vertex. Two vertices V_i and V_j are said to be *visible* to each other if the
open line segment connecting them is strictly inside the polygon. That is, there must
be a clear line of sight from one vertex to the other without any other portion of the
polygon blocking it, even if that portion is only a single vertex. When the two vertices
are visible to each other, the line segment connecting them is called a *diagonal* of the
polygon. Figure 13.53 illustrates the visibility between vertices. By the definition, the
edges of the polygon are not diagonals. However, in some applications it is useful
to allow them to be labeled as such. In the discussion we distinguish between types
of vertices. A vertex is said to be a *convex vertex* if the angle between the two edges
sharing the vertex is smaller than π radians, as measured inside the polygon. This
angle is called the *interior angle* at the vertex. If the two edges sharing the vertex are
on the same line, the vertex is a *collinear vertex*. In typical applications, these vertices
are not allowed in construction of a polygon or are removed after some operation
modifies a polygon. If the interior angle at a vertex is larger than π radians, the vertex
is said to be a *reflex vertex*.

13.9.1 VISIBILITY GRAPH OF A SIMPLE POLYGON

Given a simple polygon with ordered vertices V_0 through V_{n-1}, an undirected graph
can be constructed whose nodes represent the vertices and whose arcs represent the
diagonals of the polygon. The graph is called the *visibility graph* for the polygon.
In this graph, an arc connecting a vertex to itself is not allowed. If the graph is
represented as an adjacency matrix, the entry (i, j) is 1 if V_i and V_j are visible to

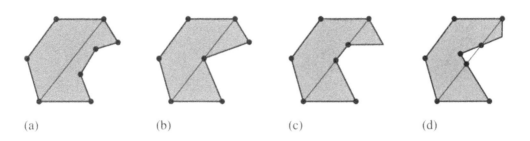

(a) (b) (c) (d)

Figure 13.53   (a) Two vertices that are visible to each other. The diagonal connecting them is shown. (b) Two vertices that are not visible to each other, blocked by a vertex between them. (c) Two vertices that are not visible to each other, blocked by a single edge. (d) Two vertices that are not visible to each other, blocked by a region outside the polygon.

each other, but 0 otherwise. Of course the matrix is symmetric since the graph is undirected. The matrix for a convex polygon consists of three zero diagonals, the main diagonal and its sub- and superdiagonal, but all other entries are one. For other simple polygons, the matrix can be complicated. In polygon partitions, it may be necessary to compute part, or all, of the visibility graph.

Visibility between V_{i-1} and V_{i+1}

For simplicity, assume that the vertex indices are computed modulo n, the number of vertices of the polygon. Let us start with the simplest case for visibility determination. Given a vertex V_{i-1}, we wish to determine if V_{i+1} is visible to it.

If V_i is a reflex vertex, then the line segment connecting V_{i-1} and V_{i+1} must be at least partially outside the polygon, so V_{i-1} and V_{i+1} are not visible to each other. It suffices to consider only those V_i that are convex vertices. For such a vertex, the line segment $\langle V_{i-1}, V_{i+1} \rangle$ is a diagonal as long as no edges on the polygon boundary intersect it. Geometrically equivalent is that no other vertices of the polygon lie in the triangle $\langle V_{i-1}, V_i, V_{i+1} \rangle$. If the polygon has r reflex vertices and $n - r$ convex vertices, the obvious implementation processes each of $n - r$ triangles and tries at most $n - 3$ point-in-triangle tests. The maximum number of tests occurs when in fact $\langle V_{i-1}, V_{i+1} \rangle$ is a diagonal. The order of the algorithm is $O((n - r)n) = O(n^2)$. A more efficient implementation avoids testing all other polygon vertices for triangle containment. If the polygon boundary intersects the segment $\langle V_{i-1}, V_{i+1} \rangle$, then the portion of the boundary inside the triangle must contain at least one reflex vertex. The idea is that the polygon boundary must enter the triangle and make a turn to exit the triangle later. The turning requires a reflex vertex. Therefore it is sufficient to test only for containment of reflex vertices by the triangle. The order of this algorithm

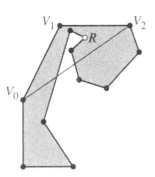

Figure 13.54   Illustration of why lack of visibility between V_0 and V_2 is equivalent to triangle $\langle V_0, V_1, V_2 \rangle$ containing a reflex vertex R.

is $O(nr)$, which is better than $O(n^2)$ when r is much smaller than n. Figure 13.54 illustrates this idea.

If $\langle V_{i-1}, V_{i+2} \rangle$ is a diagonal of the polygon, the vertices V_{i-1}, V_i, and V_{i+1} are said to form an *ear* of the polygon with V_i called the *ear tip*. One of the polygon triangulation methods discussed later uses a search for ears. In Figure 13.54, vertex V_0 is an ear tip, and the ear is the triangle formed by V_0 and its two neighboring vertices.

Visibility between Any Two Vertices

The test for $\langle V_i, V_j \rangle$, $|i - j| \geq 2$, being a diagonal is straightforward. The idea is to traverse the polygon edges and test if any of them intersects the segment $\langle V_i, V_j \rangle$. The edges adjacent to the specified segment need not be tested. The worst-case configuration is that the adjacent edge is collinear with the segment, in which case the next edge adjacent to the current adjacent edge has an end point on the segment. The intersection will be found by the intersection test with that edge.

If any edge of the polygon intersects the specified segment, then the segment is not a diagonal. However, if all edges (not counting the adjacent ones to the segment) do not intersect the segment, two situations are possible. One is that the segment is a diagonal. The other is that the segment is outside the polygon. The diagonal testing code must distinguish between these two. It is enough to determine the local behavior of the segment at only one end point, say, at V_i. The segment is a diagonal whenever it is contained in the cone with vertex V_i and edges with directions $V_{i\pm1} - V_i$. Figure 13.55 shows the containment condition for both convex and reflex vertices. The pseudocode for testing if $\langle V_{i_0}, V_{i_1} \rangle$ is a diagonal is listed below. The first two inputs are the simple polygon. The last two inputs are the indices of the end points of

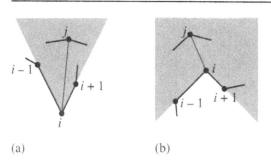

(a)   (b)

Figure 13.55   Cone containment (a) for a convex vertex and (b) for a reflex vertex.

the segment to be tested. It is assumed that $|i_0 - i_1| \geq 2$ where modulo n arithmetic is used for the indices.

```
bool IsDiagonal(int n, Point V[n], int i0, int i1)
{
    // Segment may be a diagonal or may be external to the polygon.  Need
    // to distinguish between the two.  The first two arguments of
    // SegmentInCone are the line segment.  The first and last two arguments
    // form the cone.

    iM = (i0 - 1) mod n;
    iP = (i0 + 1) mod n;
    if (not SegmentInCone(V[i0], V[i1], V[iM], V[iP]))
        return false;

    // test segment <V[i0], V[i1]> to see if it is a diagonal
    for (j0 = 0, j1 = n - 1; j0 < n; j1 = j0, j0++) {
        if (j0 != i0 && j0 != i1 && j1 != i0 && j1 != i1) {
            // The first two arguments of SegmentsIntersect form a line
            // segment.  The last two arguments form an edge to be tested
            // for intersection with the segment.

            if (SegmentsIntersect(V[i0], V[i1], V[j0], V[j1]))
                return false;
        }
    }
    return true;
}
```

The SegmentIntersect function can be implemented based on either computing an intersection point, if it exists, or on measuring the distance between the segments. Sections 6.6 and 7.1 cover these topics. The SegmentInCone function is shown in the pseudocode below:

```
float Kross(Point U, Point V)
{
    // Kross(U, V) = Cross((U,0), (V,0)).z
    return U.x * V.y - U.y * V.x;
}


bool SegmentInCone(Point V0, Point V1, Point VM, Point VP)
{
    // assert:  VM, V0, VP are not collinear

    Point diff = V1 - V0, edgeL = VM - V0, edgeR = VP - V0;
    if (Kross(edgeR, edgeL) > 0)  {
        // vertex is convex
        return (Kross(diff, edgeR) > 0 and Kross(diff, edgeL) < 0);
    } else {
        // vertex is reflex
        return (Kross(diff, edgeR) < 0 or Kross(diff, edgeL) > 0);
    }
}
```

Two facts about diagonals and ears are presented in Meister (1975). The first fact is that a polygon with at least four vertices has at least one diagonal. The second fact, referred to as Meister's Two Ears Theorem, is that a polygon with at least four vertices must have at least two nonoverlapping ears.

13.9.2 TRIANGULATION

Let a simple polygon have vertices V_i for $0 \le i < n$. A *triangulation* of the polygon is a partition of the polygon into triangles. Each triangle has vertices from the original polygon. If two triangles in the partition intersect, they may only do so at vertices or edges, not at interior points. Triangle edges that are introduced by the process are necessarily inside the polygon, so those edges must be diagonals. All of the diagonals used in the triangulation must be pairwise nonintersecting, by definition. It turns out that *any* triangulation of the polygon must use $n - 3$ diagonals and contains $n - 2$ triangles.

It is possible to have a smaller number of triangles whose union is the original polygon, but in this case T-junctions must occur. Equivalently this means that non-diagonal segments must be used to connect vertices. For example, the polygon with ordered vertices $V_0 = (0, 0)$, $V_1 = (1, -1)$, $V_2 = (1, 1)$, $V_3 = (-1, 1)$, $V_4 = (-1, -1)$ can be partitioned into three triangles, the index triples being $\{0, 1, 2\}$, $\{0, 2, 3\}$, and $\{0, 3, 4\}$. The diagonals used in the triangulation are $\{0, 2\}$ and $\{0, 3\}$. A partition with only two triangles is $\{0, 1, 2\}$ and $\{2, 3, 4\}$, but V_0 is a T-junction and the segment $\{2, 4\}$ is not a diagonal. T-junctions are usually not desirable in applications.

Triangulation by Ear Clipping

Because triangulation of a polygon involves the diagonals of the polygon, a divide-and-conquer algorithm may be used to construct the triangulation. The idea is to find a diagonal, split the polygon along the diagonal into two subpolygons, and recurse on each subpolygon. The pseudocode is shown below where the top-level call passes in a polygon stored as a linked list and an empty list of index triples. It is assumed that the polygon has at least three vertices.

```
void Triangulate(VertexList vlist, TriangleList tlist)
{
    n = vlist.size;
    if (n == 3) {
        tlist.Add(vlist(0), vlist(1), vlist(2));
        return;
    }

    for (i0 = 0; i0 < n; i0++) {
        for (i1 = 0; i1 < n; i1++) {
            if (IsDiagonal(vlist, i0, i1))  {
                Split(vlist,sublist0, sublist1);
                Triangulate(sublist0, tlist);
                Triangulate(sublist1, tlist);
                return;
            }
        }
    }
}
```

The double loop is $O(n^2)$ and the diagonal test is $O(n)$, so finding a diagonal in this way is $O(n^3)$. Using linked lists, the split operation is $O(1)$. Therefore, it takes $O(n^3)$ time before triangulation of the subpolygons. As a coarse analysis, if the subpolygons each have about $n/2$ vertices, then the recurrence formula for the time T_n it takes to solve the original problem is $T_n = 2T_{n/2} + O(n^3)$. Applying the master theorem in Cormen, Leiserson, and Rivest (1990) yields $T_n = O(n^3)$.

A variation that is slightly simpler to analyze uses *ear clipping*. Rather than search for any diagonal, it suffices to find an ear, add the corresponding triangle to the list, remove the ear from the polygon, and recurse on the reduced polygon. The pseudocode is

```
void Triangulate(VertexList vlist, TriangleList tlist)
{
    n = vlist.size;
    if (n == 3) {
        tlist.Add(vlist(0), vlist(1), vlist(2));
        return;
    }

    for (i0 = 0, i1 = 1, i2 = 2, i0 < n;
        i0++, i1 = (i1 + 1) mod n, i2 = (i2 + 1) mod n) {
        if (IsDiagonal(vlist, i0, i2))    {
            RemoveVertex(vlist, i1, sublist);
            Triangulate(sublist, tlist);
            return;
        }
    }
}
```

In this case, the outer loop and diagonal search combined are $O(n^2)$. The vertex removal is $O(1)$. The subpolygon has $n - 1$ vertices, so the recurrence formula for the execution time is $T_n = T_{n-1} + O(n^2)$. The solution to this recurrence is $T_n = O(n^3)$, the same order as the previous method.

The ear clipping algorithm can be further modified so that it is, in fact, an $O(n^2)$ algorithm. The idea is to make an initial pass over the polygon and keep track of which vertices are ear tips and which are not. The number of vertices to process is n and each ear test is $O(n)$, combined to yield $O(n^2)$. A second pass removes an ear, say, with ear tip located at vertex i. The earness, so to speak, of vertices $i - 1$ and $i + 1$ can change because of the removal. The earness of the other vertices does not change. Therefore, each ear removal requires only two updates to determine if the vertices $i - 1$ and $i + 1$ are ear tips for the reduced polygon. Each update involves a diagonal test, an $O(n)$ operation. The second pass is effectively an iteration over $O(n)$ ears, each update requiring $O(n)$ time for diagonal testing, so the combined pass is also $O(n^2)$. The pseudocode is

```
void Triangulate(VertexList vlist, TriangleList tlist)
{
    // dynamic list for polygon, to be reduced as ears are clipped
    VertexList vdynalist = vlist.Copy();  // copy entire list
    int vdynaquantity = vlist.Size();
```

```
// dynamic list for ear tips, reduced/updated as ears are clipped
VertexList node = vdynalist;
VertexList edynalist = empty;
for (i = 0; i < vdynaquantity; i++, node = node.Next())  {
    if (node is an ear of vlist) {
        VertexList tmp = node.CopySingle();  // copy only node (not links)
        if (edynalist is not empty)
            edynalist.InsertBefore(tmp);  // tmp inserted before edynalist
        else
            edynalist = tmp;  // first element in list
    }
}

// remove ears one at a time
while (true) {
    // add triangle to output list (three integer indices)
    tlist.Add(vdynalist.Previous().VertexIndex());
    tlist.Add(vdynalist.VertexIndex());
    tlist.Add(vdynalist.Next().VertexIndex());
    if (vdynaquantity == 3)
        return;  // last triangle was added, done triangulating

    // remove the ear tip from vertex list
    VertexList vprev = vdynalist.Previous();
    VertexList vnext = vdynalist.Next();
    vdynaquantity--;
    vdynalist.RemoveSelf();

    // Previous node to ear had a topological change.  Recompute its
    // earness.
    if (vprev is an ear of vlist)  {
        if (vprev.VertexIndex() != edynalist.Previous().VertexIndex()) {
            // removal of old ear caused vprev to be an ear
            edynalist.InsertBefore(vprev.CopySingle());
        }
    } else {
        if (vprev.VertexIndex() == edynalist.Previous().VertexIndex()) {
            // removal of old ear caused vprev not to be an ear
            edynalist.Previous().RemoveSelf();
        }
    }

    // Next node to ear had a topological change.  Recompute its earness.
    // Advance to next vertex/ear.
```

```
      if (vnext is an ear of vlist) {
         if (vnext.VertexIndex() != edynalist.Next().VertexIndex()) {
            // removal of old ear caused vnext to be an ear
            edynalist.InsertAfter(vnext.CopySingle());
         }
      } else {
         if (vnext.VertexIndex() == edynalist.Next().VertexIndex()) {
            // removal of old ear caused vnext not to be an ear
            edynalist.Next().RemoveSelf();
            vnext = vnext.Next();
         }
      }

      // get next vertex
      vdynalist = vnext;

      // get next ear and remove the old ear from list
      edynalist = edynalist.Next();
      edynalist.Previous().RemoveSelf();
   }
}
```

It is possible to triangulate a polygon with a better asymptotic order. Much research in the late 1980s and early 1990s addressed this topic. Chazelle (1991) showed that triangulation can be done in $O(n)$ time. However, the algorithm is complex, and it remains to be seen if it can be implemented in a practical setting. Asymptotically worse methods tend to be easier to implement.

13.9.3 TRIANGULATION BY HORIZONTAL DECOMPOSITION

This section describes an $O(n \log n)$ method based on decomposition into trapezoids whose parallel edge pairs are parallel to the x-axis (Chazelle 1991; Fournier and Montuno 1984). The decomposition, which requires $O(n \log n)$ time, can be further reduced in $O(n)$ time to a small number of monotone polygons. Each monotone polygon can be triangulated in $O(n)$ time. Faster algorithms that use randomization and are nearly linear are presented in Clarkson, Tarjan, and Van Wyk (1989) and Seidel (1991). The order of these algorithms is $O(n \log^* n)$, where $\log^* n$ is defined by iterated logarithms:

$$\log^{(i)}(n) = \begin{cases} n, & i = 0 \\ \log(\log^{(i-1)} n), & i > 0 \text{ and } \log^{(i-1)} n > 0 \\ \text{undefined}, & i > 0 \text{ and } \log^{(i-1)} n \le 0 \text{ or } \log^{(i-1)} n \text{ undefined} \end{cases}$$

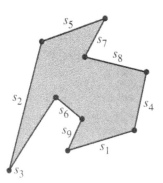

Figure 13.56   A simple polygon that is used to illustrate the horizontal decomposition into trapezoids. The edges are labeled randomly and are processed in that order in the figures
that follow.

The notation $\log^{(i)} n$ denotes an iterated function value, not the logarithm raised to
the ith power. The final definition is

$$\log^* n = \min\{i \geq 0 : \log^{(i)} n \leq 1\}$$

This is a very slowly growing function. For example, $\log^*(2) = 1$, $\log^*(4) = 2$,
$\log^*(16) = 3$, $\log^*(65536) = 4$, and $\log^*(2^{65536}) = 5$. In practical applications, effectively $\log^* n$ is a small constant. The randomized algorithms mentioned above are,
practically speaking, $O(n)$. A brief description of the algorithm is presented in Paeth
(1995), in the article "Fast Polygon Triangulation Based on Seidel's Algorithm." The
polygon example, shown in Figure 13.56, used to illustrate the ideas is taken from
Figure 1 in that article.

Horizontal Decomposition

The idea is to construct a set of horizontal strips by sorting the y-values of the polygon vertices. The y-values can be sorted directly with an array-based $O(n \log n)$ sort,
but by randomizing the edges and processing one at a time using a dynamic structure such as a binary search tree, the expected order is asymptotically better. Within
each strip, the subpolygons are decomposed into trapezoids, each strip managing a
dynamic structure such as a binary search tree to allow incremental sorting of the
trapezoids. It is convenient to think of the polygon as decomposing the entire plane.
This makes handling boundary conditions of the strips and trapezoid lists easier in
the implementation.

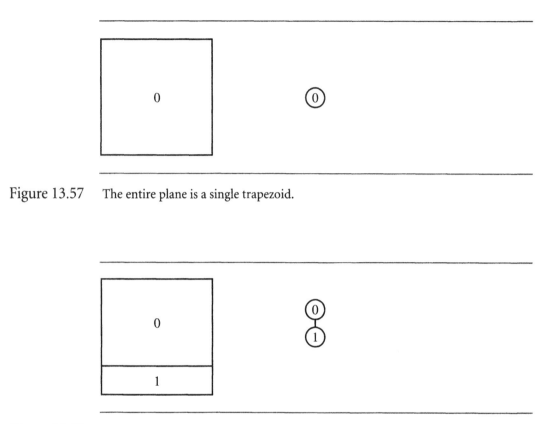

Figure 13.57   The entire plane is a single trapezoid.

Figure 13.58   Split by $s_1.y_0$.

We will describe the algorithm by example using the polygon in Figure 13.56. The polygon vertices are assumed to be counterclockwise ordered. We will give the pseudocode after the example. The entire xy-plane will be represented in this example as a rectangle. Initially, the first strip and first trapezoid T_0 are the entire plane, as illustrated in Figure 13.57. In each of the following figures, the geometric view of the decomposition is on the left and the corresponding graph of trapezoids is on the right.

An edges s_k has end points (x_0, y_0) and (x_1, y_1). The components are designated by $s_k.x_0$, $s_k.y_0$, $s_k.x_1$, and $s_k.y_1$. The first edge to be processed is s_1. The y-value $s_1.y$ requires the current strip to be partitioned into two strips, each strip containing a trapezoid that represents a half-plane (see Figure 13.58). The value $s_1.y_1$ causes another strip split, each strip containing an unbounded trapezoid (see Figure 13.59). The edge s_1 is inserted, so to speak, into the data structures. The insertion causes the single trapezoid of the middle strip to be partitioned into two trapezoids (see Figure 13.60).

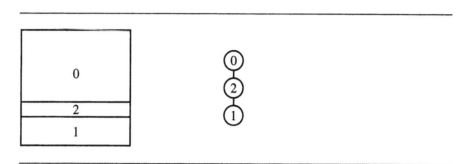

Figure 13.59   Split by $s_1.y_1$.

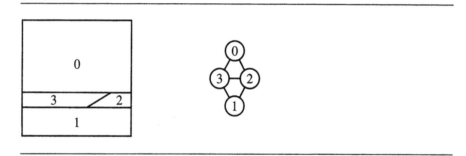

Figure 13.60   Insert s_1.

Edge s_2 is the next to be processed. The value $s_2.y_1$ forces a split (see Figure 13.61). The value $s_2.y_0$ forces a split (see Figure 13.62). Insertion of s_2 forces partitioning of trapezoids in the three strips that the edge spans (Figure 13.63).

Edge s_3 is the next to be processed. The value $s_3.y_1$ forces a split (see Figure 13.64). The value $s_3.y_0 = s_2.y_1$, which was already processed, so no splitting occurs. The insertion of s_3 forces partitioning of trapezoids in the strips that the edge spans (see Figure 13.65).

The remaining edges are processed in a similar manner. Edge s_9 is the final edge to be processed. Its insertion forces partitioning of trapezoids in the strips that the edge spans (see Figure 13.66). Observe that the plane has been partitioned into a finite number of strips and that each strip consists of a finite number of trapezoids. The data structure uses binary search trees, both for strips and for trapezoids within a strip. This data structure can be used for $O(\log n)$ point-in-polygon queries. Given a test point, its y-value is used to search the binary search tree for the strips to find the strip that contains that y-value. If the y-value is on a strip boundary, either strip sharing that boundary can be used. The binary search tree for the trapezoids stores the line equations for the left and right boundaries of the trapezoids. The x-value

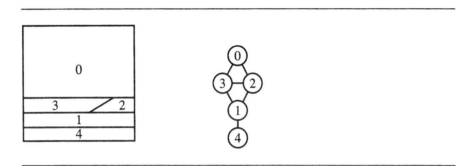

Figure 13.61   Split by $s_2.y_1$.

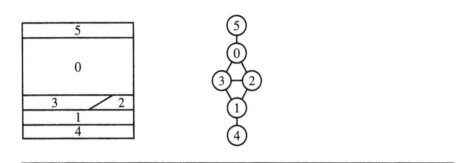

Figure 13.62   Split by $s_2.y_0$.

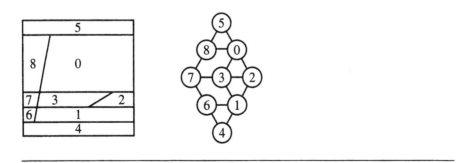

Figure 13.63   Insert s_2.

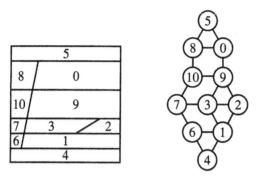

Figure 13.64   Split by $s_3.y_1$.

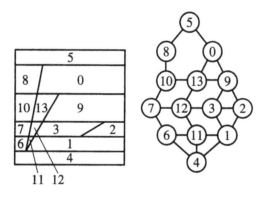

Figure 13.65   Insert s_3.

of the test point is compared against those lines to determine in which trapezoid the point lies. If the test input point is on a strip boundary, comparisons should use strict inequality whenever the trapezoid is an "outside" trapezoid. The inside/outside tag is easy to assign given the way that the polygon edges were used to partition the strips.

The pseudocode for the top-level call that constructs the strips and trapezoids is listed below. The Strip object supports a binary search tree data structure and additionally has three members, the minimum y-value of the strip min, the maximum y-value of the strip max, and a binary search tree of Trapezoid objects ttree. The Trapezoid object also supports a binary search tree data structure and additionally has three members, the polygon edge index corresponding to its left edge min, the polygon edge index corresponding to its right edge max, and a direction indicator classify

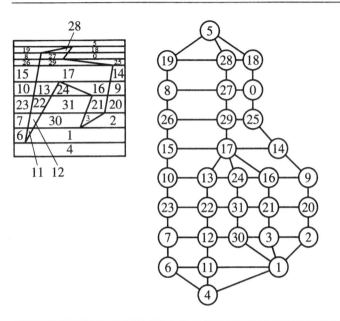

Figure 13.66   Insert s_9.

that is $+1$ if the interior of the polygon at the maximum edge is in the positive x-direction or -1 if the interior of the polygon at the minimum edge is in the negative x-direction.

```
void Decompose(int N, Point P[N])
{
    // randomly permute edges
    int index[N] = PermuteRange(0, N - 1);
    // prototypes: Strip(min, max, ttree), Trapezoid(min, max, classify)
    S = new Strip(-infinity, +infinity, new Trapezoid(-infinity, +infinity, -1));
    for (i0 = 0; i0 < N; i0++) {
        i1 = (i0 + 1) mod N;
        if (P[i0].y < P[i1].y)
            Insert(S,P[i0].y, P[i1].y, i, -1);  // interior in negative x-direction
        else if ( [i1].y < P[i0].y)
            Insert(S,P[i1].y, P[i0].y, i, +1);  // interior in positive x-direction

        // else ignore horizontal edges
    }
}
```

The strip insertion pseudocode is

```
void Insert(Strip S, float y0, float y1, int i, int classify)
{
    // binary search for strip containing y0, assumes S0 = [min, max)
    S0 = Locate(S, y0);
    if (y0 > S0.min) {
        // y0 interior to strip, split to N = [min, y0), S0 = [y0, max)
        N = new Strip(y0, max, S0.CopyOfTTree());
        S0.min = y0;
        S0.InsertBefore(N);  // insert N before S0 in search tree
    }

    // binary search for strip containing y1, assumes strip is min <= y < max
    S1 = Locate(S, y1);
    if (y1 > S1.min) {
        // y1 interior to strip, split to S1 = [min, y1), N = [y1, max)
        N = new Strip(y1, max, S1.CopyOfTTree());
        S1.max = y1;
        S1.InsertAfter(N);  // insert N after S1 in search tree
    }

    // add a trapezoid to each strip spanned by edge
    for (L = S0; L <= S1; L++)
        Insert(L.ttree, (L.min + L.max) / 2, i, classify);
}
```

The trapezoid insertion pseudocode is

```
void Insert(Trapezoid T, float mid, int i, int classify)
{
    // Locate correct place to insert new trapezoid by comparing x-values
    // along the mid line passing through the trapezoids.
    T0 = LocateMid(T, i);

    // Split T0 = {min,max} to N = {min,i} and T0 = {i,max}
    N = new Trapezoid(T0.min, i, classify);
    T0.min = i;
    T0.classify = -classify;
    T0.InsertBefore(N);  // insert N before T0 in search tree
}
```

The pseudocode supports construction of the point-in-polygon query data structure. To support triangulation, trapezoids that are vertically adjacent must be merged.

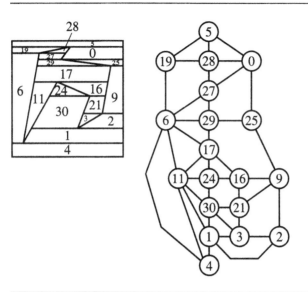

Figure 13.67   The plane after trapezoids are merged into maximally sized ones.

This requires adding to the Trapezoid object two list members that store links to trapezoids vertically adjacent at the strip minimum edge and at the strip maximum edge. The pseudocode must be modified accordingly to construct those links.

Monotone Polygon Construction

The next phase in the triangulation is to construct monotone polygons whose union is the original polygon. The first step in this process is to merge the trapezoids into maximally sized ones. Figure 13.67 shows the merged configuration for the plane. The figure shows the exterior trapezoids merged. However, for the purposes of triangulation, only the interior trapezoids are required. Figure 13.68 shows the merged trapezoids only for the polygon itself.

The second step is to add line segments connecting polygon vertices. These segments and the original polygon edges form a decomposition into monotone polygons where the monotonicity is relative to the y-direction. Suppose that the original polygon has no two vertices with the same y-value. Each trapezoid in the horizontal decomposition of that polygon contains exactly two vertices of the polygon, one on its top edge and one on its bottom edge. If the vertex is an edge-interior point, it must be a cusp. That is, the two edges that share the vertex are either both above or both below the horizontal line of the vertex. A cusp that opens downward occurs on the bottom edge of some trapezoid. A line segment is added from that cusp to the vertex

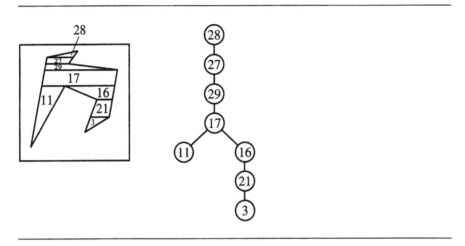

Figure 13.68   The sample polygon after trapezoids are merged into maximally sized ones.

Figure 13.69   The sample polygon as a union of monotone polygons. The two polygons are drawn in light gray and dark gray. The horizontal line segments from the trapezoidal decomposition are still shown.

on the trapezoid's top edge. Similarly, a cusp that opens upward occurs on the top edge of some trapezoid. A line segment is added from that cusp to the vertex on the trapezoid's bottom edge. It is possible that both end points of the newly added segment are cusps. Figure 13.69 shows the polygon of the ongoing example. Only one line segment needed to be added, from a downward opening cusp to a vertex on the trapezoid's top edge. The polygon consists of two monotone polygons.

The last paragraph had the assumption that no two vertices have the same y-value. This can, of course, happen in practice. The algorithm for adding line segments to form monotone polygons must be slightly modified to handle this case.

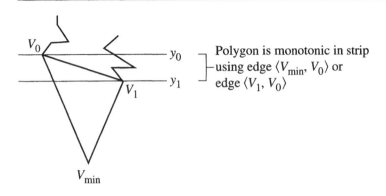

Figure 13.70   If the triangle at an extreme vertex is an ear, removing the ear yields another monotone polygon.

Monotone Polygon Triangulation

The polygons obtained in the decomposition of a simple polygon are monotone with respect to the y-axis. That is, any line in the x-direction intersects a y-monotone polygon in one point (an extreme point in the y-direction), in two points (the typical case), or along an entire edge of the polygon (edge is horizontal). The triangulation of a monotone polygon requires only $O(n)$ time to compute (Fournier and Montuno 1984). The method involves a greedy algorithm that removes triangles from the extreme ends of the polygon.

First, let us just try to remove a triangle from an extreme end of the polygon to see what issues arise. Let V_{min} and V_{max} be the extreme points of the polygon. The polygon has two monotonic chains referred to as the *left chain* and the *right chain*. Let $V_0 = (x_0, y_0)$ be the vertex on the left chain that is adjacent to V_{min}, and let $V_1 = (x_1, y_1)$ be the adjacent one on the right chain. For the sake of argument, assume $y_0 \geq y_1$. Otherwise, we can make the same argument with the roles of the chains reversed. If the triangle $\langle V_0, V_{min}, V_1 \rangle$ is an ear, that ear can be removed and added to the list of triangles in the triangulation. The edge $\langle V_{min}, V_0 \rangle$ of the left chain is removed and replaced by the edge $\langle V_1, V_0 \rangle$. The modified chain is still monotonic in the y-direction, so the process can be repeated on the new monotone polygon at its minimum vertex. Figure 13.70 provides an illustration.

The problem with this approach is that it requires determining whether or not the triangle at the minimum vertex is an ear. In fact, the minimum vertex might not be an ear tip. Figure 13.71 shows two types of failure that can occur. Failure to be an ear tip can occur simply because the next edge on the right chain $\langle V_0, W \rangle$ is inside the triangle $\langle V_0, V_{min}, V_1 \rangle$ (Figure 13.71(a)). The failure might also be a result of more complex behavior, for example, a chain of vertices in the strip $y_1 < y < y_0$ that are

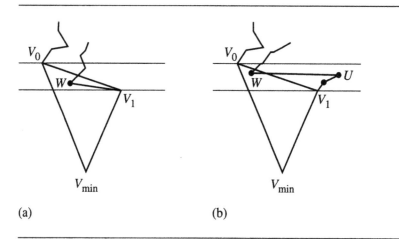

(a)   (b)

Figure 13.71   Failure of triangle $\langle V_0, V_{min}, V_1 \rangle$ to be an ear.

outside the mentioned triangle, but the next vertex W in that chain being inside the triangle (Figure 13.71(b)).

The configuration in Figure 13.71(a) is easy to handle. The triangle $\langle V_{min}, V_1, W \rangle$ is an ear and can be removed. The edge $\langle V_{min}, V_1 \rangle$ in the right chain is removed and replaced by $\langle V_{min}, W \rangle$. The right chain is still monotonic, so the reduced polygon is monotonic and the process can be repeated. The removal can occur even if W is not inside $\langle V_0, V_{min}, V_1 \rangle$ as long as V_1 is a convex vertex.

The configuration in Figure 13.71(b) is the more interesting one. A sequence of reflex vertices occur, called a *reflex chain*. In the figure, the predecessor U to W is the first vertex occurring after the reflex chain, so it is a convex vertex, and the very next edge with end point W makes the reflex chain invisible from V_0. All vertices in the reflex chain, however, are visible to W, so all triangles formed by W and the vertices in the reflex chain can be removed. The right chain reduces to a monotonic chain whose first three vertices are V_{min}, W, and U. The reduced polygon is still monotonic.

Even so, the configuration in Figure 13.71(b) is still not representative of other configurations. The vertex W might not be in the triangle $\langle V_0, V_{min}, V_1 \rangle$, yet the triangles formed by it and the reflex chain vertices can be removed. Worse is that not all of the reflex chain vertices are visible to W. Figure 13.72 illustrates this configuration. After all the valid triangles are removed, W will be the next vertex to be added to the reflex chain.

The final variation is that W might occur above the strip rather than inside it. In this case, the vertices in the reflex chain are all visible to V_0. It is sufficient to form all triangles containing V_0 and the reflex vertices and remove them. Observe that in this case, the triangle $\langle V_0, V_{min}, V_1 \rangle$ is an ear of the polygon, exactly the motivation originally for attempting to remove that triangle first. The valid triangles are removed

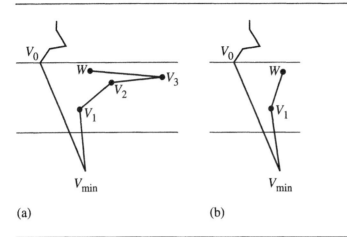

(a)   (b)

Figure 13.72   (a) Not all reflex chain vertices are visible to W. (b) Removal of the triangles leads to W being the next vertex to be added to the reflex chain.

starting with this one. Figure 13.73 illustrates this. The difference between the configurations in Figures 13.72 and 13.73 is the y-ordering of V_0 and W. To handle this, the vertices from both left and right chains must be sorted in a single list. Since the left and right chains are already sorted, the full sort requires a merge of two sorted lists, an operation that is performed in $O(n)$ time.

The pseudocode for triangulating a y-monotone polygon is listed below. The left and right chains are passed separately, each having the vertex with minimum y-value in the slot zero and each having the vertex with maximum y-value in the corresponding last slot.

```
void TriangulateMonotone(int NL, Point LChain[NL], int NR, Point RChain[NR],
                    TriangleList TList)
{
    // Each node in the list contains a vertex and an identifier of the
    // chain to which the vertex belongs.
    VertexList VList = MergeChains(NL, LChain, NR, RChain);

    // A list whose front corresponds to the y-minimum vertex and whose rear
    // corresponds to the y-maximum vertex.
    ReflexChain RList;

    // Initialize the chain with the first two vertices.  AddMax(VList) places
    // the specified list node at the end of the chain.  A side effect of the
    // operation is to provide RList with a 'whichChain' tag, L or R, about
```

```
// which of the left or right polygon chains the current reflex chain belongs.
RList.AddMax(VList);  VList = VList.Next();
RList.AddMax(VList);  VList = VList.Next();

// VList points to the third vertex in the list.
while (VList is not empty ) {
    // Max() is an accessor to the rear of the reflex chain that contains
    // the vertex of maximum y-value.
    if (VList.Previous() is equal to RList.Max()) {
        // VList.vertex is on the same chain as the reflex chain
        if (RList.Max() is a convex vertex) {
            TList.Add(RList.Max().Previous().vertex);
            TList.Add(RList.Max().vertex);
            TList.Add(VList.vertex);

            // Remove vertex from reflex chain and from vertex list.  These
            // are the same vertex.
            RList.RemoveMax();
            VList.Previous().RemoveSelf();
            if (RList is empty)
                VList = VList.Next();
        } else {
            // RList.Max() is a reflex vertex, no collinear allowed
            RList.AddMax(VList);
            VList = VList.Next();
        }
    } else {
        // VList.vertex is on the opposite chain to the reflex chain.
        // Min() is an accessor to the front of the reflex chain that
        // contains the vertex of minimum y-value.
        TList.Add(RList.Min().vertex);
        TList.Add(RList.Min().Next().vertex);
        TList.Add(VList.vertex);

        // Remove vertex from reflex chain and from vertex list.  These
        // are the same vertex.
        RList.RemoveMin();
        VList.Previous().RemoveSelf();
        if (RList is empty)
            VList = VList.Next();
    }
}
}
```

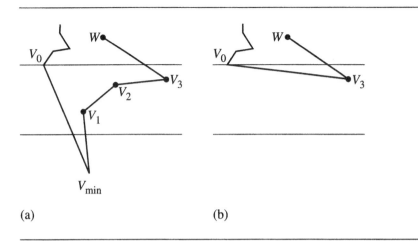

(a)   (b)

Figure 13.73   (a) W occurs above the current strip, V_0 is visible to all reflex chain vertices. (b) Removal of the triangles leads to a reduced monotone polygon, so the process can be repeated.

In summary, a simple polygon is triangulated by decomposing it into horizontal strips of trapezoids, merging the trapezoids into maximal pieces, connecting vertices between top and bottom trapezoid edges to form y-monotone polygons, then triangulating the monotone polygons.

A variation on this algorithm presented in O'Rourke (1998) finds *monotone mountains*. These are monotone polygons for which one of the monotone chains is a single line segment. Triangulating a monotone mountain is easier than triangulating a monotone polygon because it is easier to identify ears and remove them, one at a time. An implementation looks similar to the ear clipping presented earlier in this chapter.

13.9.4   CONVEX PARTITIONING

A polygon triangulation is a special case of partitioning the polygon into convex subpolygons, the number of subpolygons being $n - 2$ for n vertices. A more general problem is to partition the polygon into convex subpolygons, but minimize the number of such subpolygons. Clearly a triangulation does not do this. A square has two triangles in its triangulation, but is already convex, so the optimum number of convex pieces is one. Convex partitioning is useful for allowing artists to construct 3D polygonal models without concern for generating nonconvex faces. The models can be postprocessed to partition the faces so that all faces are convex. Moreover, generating the minimum number of convex faces is useful for a renderer whose primitives

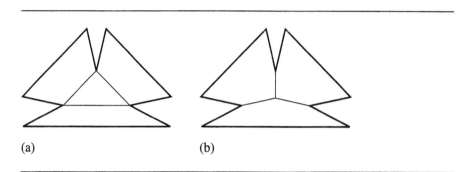

(a)   (b)

Figure 13.74   (a) Partition using only vertices. (b) Partition using an additional point interior to the polygon.

include convex polygons. By minimizing the number of input primitives, the setup costs for rasterizing the polygons is minimized.

A triangulation always uses diagonals of the polygon as edges of the triangles. Optimal convex partitioning might require additional points and segments to be specified in order to obtain the minimum number of subpolygons (see Figure 13.74). The convex partitioning methods mentioned in this section only use diagonals for the construction.

Chazelle showed that the minimum number μ of convex subpolygons in a partition is bounded by $\lceil r/2 \rceil + 1 \le \mu \le r + 1$, where r is the number of reflex vertices of the polygon. The bounds are tight since it is easy to construct two polygons, one whose optimum partition attains the lower bound and one whose optimum partition attains the upper bound. Algorithms that construct an optimum partition tend to run slowly (in asymptotic terms). Algorithms that partition rapidly tend not to obtain the optimum number of pieces. In this section we provide an example of each.

A Suboptimal But Fast Convex Partitioning

A fast and simple algorithm for producing a convex partitioning that is suboptimal is presented by Hertel and Mehlhorn (1983). However, it is known that the number of convex subpolygons is no larger than four times the optimal number. Given a convex partition involving diagonals, a diagonal incident to a vertex V is said to be *essential* for that vertex if removing the diagonal shared by two convex subpolygons leads to a union that is not convex (at V). Otherwise the diagonal is said to be *inessential*. A diagonal connecting two convex vertices is clearly inessential. It must be that for a diagonal to be essential for V, the vertex must be reflex. However, a reflex vertex can be an end point for an inessential diagonal (see Figure 13.75).

The algorithm is simple. Start by triangulating the polygon. Remove each inessential diagonal, one at a time. The triangulation has $O(n)$ diagonals, so the removal

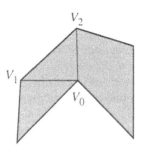

Figure 13.75   Vertex V_0 is reflex. The diagonal $\langle V_0, V_1 \rangle$ is inessential. The diagonal $\langle V_0, V_2 \rangle$ is essential for V_0.

phase is $O(n)$. In theory the triangulation can be done in $O(n)$ time, so this suboptimal partitioning can be done in $O(n)$ time. But as mentioned before, the triangulation algorithms implemented in practice are asymptotically slower, so the time for partitioning is dominated by the triangulation time.

An Optimal Convex Partitioning

An optimal partitioning algorithm by Keil and Snoeyink (1998) is described in this section. The algorithm uses only diagonals and has an asymptotic run time of $O(nr^2)$, where n is the number of polygon vertices and r is the number of reflex vertices. The algorithm is based on dynamic programming (Bellman 1987).

The simple polygon has counterclockwise-ordered vertices V_i for $0 \le i < n$. The diagonals are denoted by $d_{ij} = \langle V_i, V_j \rangle$ for $i < j$. The only diagonals that need to be considered are those that have at least one end point that is a reflex vertex. A diagonal with two convex vertex end points can clearly be removed to join two convex subpolygons into a single convex subpolygon. Thus, an optimal convex partitioning will never have diagonals with both end points being convex vertices. It is not necessary that a diagonal connecting two reflex vertices be part of the optimal partitioning.

Dynamic programming finds the optimal solution to a problem by combining optimal solutions to subproblems of the same form as the original. Given a diagonal d_{ik}, the subproblem involves the subpolygon P_{ik} whose vertices are $V_i, V_{i+1}, \ldots, V_k$. This polygon must itself be optimally partitioned into convex pieces. The *size* of this problem is the number of vertices in the polygon. The original polygon is $P_{0,n-1}$ and has size n. The subpolygon P_{ik} has size $k - i + 1$. The *weight* w_{ik} of the problem is the minimum number of diagonals in a convex partitioning of P_{ik}. The optimal partitioning involves computing the weight $w_{0,n-1}$ of the original polygon $P_{0,n-1}$. A convention is made that the edge $d_{0,n-1}$ is considered to be a diagonal. The optimization is done from the bottom up, so for initialization we need $w_{i,i+1} = -1$ for all i.

As indicated in Keil (1985), P_{ik} can have exponentially many decompositions that attain weight w_{ik}. However, by defining *equivalence classes* of decompositions, the decomposition of P_{ik} is simplified. Each decomposition of P_{ik} has an associated pair of vertex indices $[a, b]$, with possibly $a = b$, the vertices with indices a, i, k, b occurring in clockwise order in one of the convex polygons in the decomposition. Two decompositions are equivalent if they have the same weight and the same associated pair of indices. Additionally, some minimum decompositions are labeled as *narrowest pairs*, those whose convex regions in a small neighborhood of d_{ik} do not contain the convex region of any other minimum decomposition of P_{ik}. Keil (1985) observed that only narrowest pairs need to be considered when constructing solutions to the subproblem P_{ik}. Figure 13.76 shows an original polygon (upper left) and 11 minimum convex decompositions. The narrowest pairs are shaded in gray. As it turns out, the angular order of diagonals d_{ij_1} through d_{ij_k}, counterclockwise about a vertex V_i, is the same as the order of the vertices V_{j_1} through V_{j_k}, counterclockwise about the polygon. A consequence of this observation is that narrowest pairs for the subproblem P_{ik} can be tested for by just comparing indices of the associated pairs. Any associated pair $[a_0, b_0]$ of a potential decomposition is discarded whenever another associated pair $[a_1, b_1]$ with smaller indices is encountered; if $a_1 \leq a_0$, it must also be the case that $b_1 \leq b_0$. As narrowest pairs for the subproblem for P_{ik} are computed, they are pushed onto a stack so that the pairs from the bottom to the top of the stack are in counterclockwise order about vertices V_i and V_k. The stack for the polygon in Figure 13.76 will contain $[1, 3]$, $[3, 4]$, and $[6, 8]$, the last pair being the top of the stack. The diagonals d_{06} and d_{89} thereby form the narrowest pair that is furthest counterclockwise.

Another key idea involves *canonical triangulations* of the convex polygons in the decomposition. Each triangulation of a convex polygon is a triangle fan where the base vertex of the fan is a reflex vertex of that convex polygon. Figure 13.77 illustrates the canonical triangulations. The polygon of the figure is from Keil and Snoeyink (1998), but with the vertices labeled differently to meet the constraint in the paper that V_0 is a reflex vertex. The reflex vertex used as the base vertex of a fan has the smallest index of all reflex vertices in the convex polygon for which the fan is constructed. Keil and Snoeyink mention the following observations. In a canonical triangulation of the original polygon P, each diagonal d_{ik} with $i < k$ satisfies three conditions with respect to subpolygon P_{ik}:

1. The diagonals with end points in P_{ik} define a canonical triangulation of P_{ik}.

2. If V_i is a reflex vertex of P, then for the triangle $\langle V_i, V_j, V_k \rangle$ with $i < j < k$, either $j = k - 1$ or d_{jk} is a diagonal used in the convex decomposition.

3. If V_i is not a reflex vertex of P, then V_k is a reflex vertex. For the triangle $\langle V_i, V_j, V_k \rangle$ with $i < j < k$, either $j = i + 1$ or d_{ij} is a diagonal used in the convex decomposition.

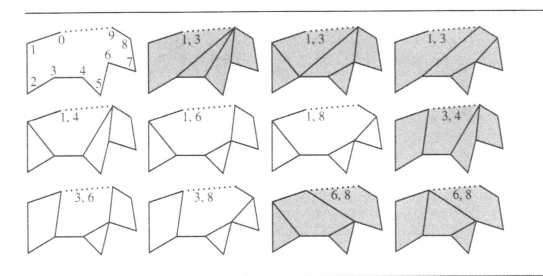

Figure 13.76 Original polygon (upper left) and 11 minimum convex decompositions, with the narrowest pairs shaded in gray. A dotted line indicates that the edge of the polygon is treated instead as a diagonal.

In Figure 13.77, consider subpolygon $P_{9,11}$ so that $i = 9$ and $k = 11$. The vertex V_9 is reflex, so condition 2 applies. Triangle $\langle V_9, V_{10}, V_{11}\rangle$ is in the canonical triangulation of P and has $j = 10 = k - 1$. In subpolygon $P_{16,23}$, $i = 16$ and $k = 23$. The vertex V_{16} is reflex, so condition 2 applies. Triangle $\langle V_{16}, V_{17}, V_{23}\rangle$ is in the canonical triangulation of P, but $j = 17 \neq 22 = k - 1$. However, $d_{17,23}$ is a diagonal used in the convex decomposition. Consider subpolygon $P_{5,9}$, so $i = 5$ and $k = 9$. The vertex V_5 is not a reflex vertex, but V_9 is. Triangle $\langle V_5, V_6, V_9\rangle$ is in the canonical triangulation of P and has $j = 6 = i + 1$.

The minimum convex decompositions of P_{ik} are constructed by considering which vertices V_j form a canonical triangle with diagonal d_{ik} and whether diagonals d_{ij} and d_{jk} either are part of the decompositions of P_{ij} and P_{jk} or are just part of the canonical triangulation. Putting this all together, the algorithm is to examine the canonical triangulations of the minimum decompositions of P_{ik} that have narrowest pairs. The algorithm associates with each subpolygon P_{ik} a stack S_{ik} that stores the narrowest pairs for P_{ik} in increasing order and a stack T_{ij} that stores these pairs in decreasing order. An invariant of the algorithm is that when analyzing P_{ik}, each subproblem P_{xy} smaller than P_{ij} has all its narrowest pairs stored in its corresponding stacks. Only one of the two stacks for a subproblem is used at a time, so both can be overlaid in the same memory. The data structure to use for S_{ik} is therefore a "double-ended stack." Operations on S_{ik} are applied at one end of the storage, whereas operations on T_{ik} are applied at the other end.

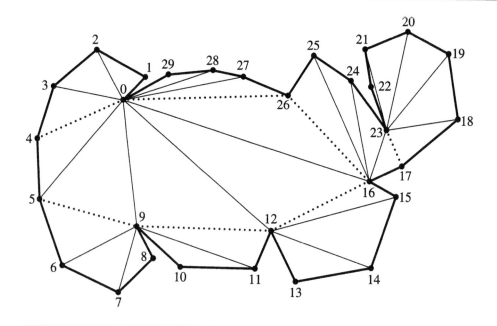

Figure 13.77 Canonical triangulations of the convex polygons in the minimum convex decomposition of a polygon. The original polygon has edges shown in a heavy line. The diagonals used in the decomposition are dotted. The diagonals used in the triangle fans for the canonical triangulations are shown in a light line.

Consider condition 2 above where V_i is a reflex vertex. The minimum decompositions of P_{ik} use the diagonal (or edge) d_{jk} for some j strictly between i and k, a decomposition of P_{jk}, and a decomposition of P_{ij} where the latter decomposition might or might not include d_{ij}. The dynamic programming recurrence is

$$w_{ik} = \min_{i < j < k,\, d_{ij} \text{ and } d_{jk} \text{ exist}} \begin{cases} w_{ij} + w_{jk} + 2, & \text{if } d_{ij} \text{ included in decomposition} \\ w_{ij} + w_{jk} + 1, & \text{otherwise} \end{cases}$$

For a single value of j, popping the T_{ij} stack will return the pairs in counterclockwise order. We seek the last pair $[s, t]$ such that d_{tj} and d_{jk} do not form a reflex angle at V_j. If there is no such pair, or if d_{is} and d_{ik} form a reflex angle at V_i, then d_{ij} is required in the convex decomposition of P_{ik} and has weight $w_{ij} + w_{ik} + 2$ and narrowest pair $[j, j]$. Otherwise a convex decomposition of P_{ik} has been found with weight $w_{ij} + w_{jk} + 1$ and narrowest pair $[s, j]$. The pairs on the stack S_{ik} for the selected j always have j as a second index. The stack is constructed by pushing each pair $[x, j]$ that achieves minimum weight onto the stack only if the stack top

$[x_0, j]$ satisfies $x_0 < x$. If $x_0 \geq x$, the stack top is a narrower pair than the candidate $[x, j]$, so it is not pushed. The diagonal d_{jk} is used in the decomposition, so either $j = k - 1$ (the diagonal is really a polygon edge) or at least one of V_j or V_k is a reflex vertex. This condition was referred to as "type A" in Keil and Snoeyink (1998), so the pseudocode function is given that name. The double-ended stack is referred to as S(i,j) or T(i,j) depending on which end the stack operations are applied. The diagonals are referred to as D(i,j). A pair of indices that is used for tracking narrowest pairs is (pair.first,pair.second).

```
void TypeA(int i, int j, int k)
{
    pair = null;
    while (T(i,j) is not empty) {
        tmpPair = T(i,j).Pop();
        if (D(tmpPair.second,j ) and D(j, k) are not reflex at j)
            pair = tmpPair;
    }

    if ((pair == null) or (D(i,pair.first) and D(i,k) are reflex at i)) {
        P(i, k) decomposition uses D(i,j );
        wtmp = w(i, j) + w(j, k) + 2;
        narrow = [j, j];
    } else {
        P(i, k) decomposition does not use D(i, j);
        wtmp = w(i, j) + w(j, k) + 1;
        narrow = [pair.first, j];
    }

    if (S(i, k) is empty) {
        w(i, k) = wtmp;
        S(i, k).Push(narrow);
    } else if (wtmp < w(i, k)) {
        S(i, k).PopAll();
        w(i, k) = wtmp;
        S(i, k).Push(narrow);
    } else if (wtmp == w(i, k)) {
        if (narrow.first > S(i, k).Top().first)
            S(i, k).Push(narrow);
    }
}
```

Condition 3 is the symmetric case of condition 2 except that checking the vertices V_i and V_k for reflexivity, in that order, means that V_i is convex and V_k is reflex. The cases where both are reflex vertices is caught by condition 2. This condition was referred to as "type B" in Keil and Snoeyink (1998), so the pseudocode function is given that name.

```
void TypeB(int i, int j, int k)
{
    pair = null;
    while (S(j,k) is not empty) {
        tmpPair = S(j, k).Pop();
        if (D(i, j) and D(j, tmpPair.first) are not reflex at j)
            pair = tmpPair;
    }

    if ((pair == null) or (D(pair.second, k) and D(i, k) are reflex at k)) {
        P(i, k) decomposition uses D(j, k);
        wtmp = w(i, j) + w(j, k) + 2;
        narrow = [j, j];
    } else {
        P(i, k) decomposition does not use D(j, k);
        wtmp = w(i, j) + w(j, k) + 1;
        narrow = [j, pair.second];
    }

    if (S(i, k) is empty) {
        w(i, k) = wtmp;
        S(i, k).Push(narrow);
    } else if (wtmp < w(i, k)) {
        S(i, k).PopAll();
        w(i, k) = wtmp;
        S(i, k).Push(narrow);
    } else if (wtmp == w(i, k)) {
        while (narrow.second <= S(i, k).Top().second )
            S(i, k).Push(narrow);
    }
}
```

The main function for the minimum convex decomposition (MCD) is listed below. The counterclockwise-ordered polygon vertices V[n] are passed to the function. The reflex vertices RV[r] are also passed in order to maintain the $O(nr^2)$ order of the algorithm. Precomputing the reflex vertices is an $O(n)$ process.

```
void MCD(int n, Point V[n], int r, Point RV[r])
{
    // size 2 problems
    for (i = 0, k = 1; k < n; i++, k++)
        w(i, k) = -1;
```

```
// size 3 problems
for (i = 0, k = 2; k < n; k++) {
    if (Visible(i, k)) {
        w(i, k) = 0;
        S(i, k).Push([i + 1, i + 1]);
    }
}

// size 4 and larger problems
for (size = 4; size <= n; size++) {
    for (m = 0; m < r; m++) {
        i = RV[m];   k = i + size - 1;
        if (k >= n) break;
        if (Visible(i, k)) {
            if (Reflex(k)) {
                for (j = i + 1; j <= k - 1; j++) {
                    if (Visible(i, j) and Visible(j, k))
                        TypeA(i, j, k);
                }
            } else {
                for (j = i + 1; j <= k - 2; j++) {
                    if (Reflex(j) and Visible(i, j) and Visible(j, k))
                        TypeA(i, j, k);
                }
                if (Visible(i, k - 1))
                    TypeA(i, k - 1, k);
            }
        }
    }

    for (m = r - 1; m >= 0; m--) {
        k = RV[m];   i = k - size + 1;
        if (i < 0) break;
        if ((not Reflex(i)) and Visible(i, k)) {
            if (Visible(i + 1, k))
                TypeB(i, i + 1, k);
            for (j = i + 2; j <= k - 1; j++) {
                if (Reflex(j) and Visible(i, j) and Visible(j, k))
                    TypeB(i, j, k);
            }
        }
    }
}
```

In the size 4 or larger block of code, the function is $O(nr^2)$ in time since TypeA or TypeB is called only for at least two reflex vertices or for one reflex vertex and one polygon edge. The work done in each call to TypeA or TypeB is $O(1)$ plus the number of pairs popped from the stacks. Since at most one pair is added to two stacks, at most $O(nr^2)$ elements can be popped. The memory requirements are also $O(nr^2)$ due to the space required for the stacks.

At first glance, the size 3 block of code appears to be $O(n^2)$ in time, $O(n)$ for the outer loop and $O(n)$ for each straightforward visiblity test that checks if $\langle V_i, V_{i+2}\rangle$ is a diagonal. This potentially offsets the $O(nr^2)$ time for the size 4 and larger block when r is much smaller than n. Since the size is 3, the visibility test is really checking if $\langle V_i, V_{i+2}\rangle$ is an ear. As shown at the beginning of this section, the ear test can be implemented by testing for containment of only the reflex vertices in the triangle $\langle V_i, V_{i+1}, V_{i+2}\rangle$. The size 2 block can therefore be implemented to take $O(nr)$ time.

Miscellaneous

Partitioning of a polygon can also be accomplished by using BSP trees. The BSP tree for a polygon is computed as shown in Section 13.1. The leaf nodes of the tree represent a convex partitioning of the plane. The positive/negative tags allow you to identify those leaf nodes that correspond to convex subpolygons of the original polygon. The union of these is the original polygon. This type of decomposition inserts points into the polygon, unlike the methods discussed in earlier sections that just use the original vertices. If a triangulation of the polygon is needed, the convex subpolygons can be fanned into triangles.

The problem of partitioning polyhedra into tetrahedra is the natural extension of partitioning a planar polygon. To date, the fastest algorithm to triangulate non-convex polyhedra is presented in Chazelle and Palios (1990). The asymptotic order is $O(n \log r + r^2 \log r)$, where n is the number of faces and r is the number of reflex edges. Another relevant paper is Hershberger and Snoeyink (1997), which decomposes a nonconvex polyhedron into convex pieces effectively by using BSP trees. Practically speaking, the BSP tree approach is easy to implement and has acceptable performance for the decomposition.

13.10   CIRCUMSCRIBED AND INSCRIBED BALLS

A triangle in two dimensions has two special circles associated with it, a *circumscribed circle* that contains the vertices of the triangle and an *inscribed circle* that is the largest-area circle contained in the triangle. Although the inscribed circle has the largest area of all circles contained in the triangle, the circumscribed circle is not necessarily the smallest-area circle containing the triangle. This is clearly the case when the triangle vertices are nearly collinear, in which case the circumscribed circle has an extremely large radius, but the minimum-area circle containing the triangle has a diameter

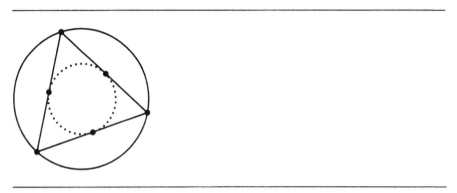

Figure 13.78   Circumscribed and inscribed circles for a triangle.

equal to the length of the longest edge. Figure 13.78 illustrates the circumscribed and inscribed circles for a triangle. The circumscribed circle is solid, and the inscribed circle is dotted. Our goal is to construct these circles for a specified triangle.

Similarly, a tetrahedron in three dimensions has two special spheres associated with it, a *circumscribed sphere* that contains the vertices of the tetrahedron and an *inscribed sphere* that is the largest-volume sphere contained in the tetrahedron. The circumscribed sphere is not necessarily the smallest-volume sphere containing the tetrahedron.

The ideas extend to higher dimensions. The generalization of triangle (2D) and tetrahedron (3D) to n dimensions is called a *simplex*. This object has $n + 1$ vertices, each vertex connected to every other vertex. If the vertices are V_i for $0 \le i \le n$, then the edges $\vec{e}_i = V_i - V_0$ are required to be linearly independent vectors. To illustrate what this constraint means, in 3D it prevents the case of four points being coplanar, in which case the tetrahedron is flat and has no volume. Two special hyperspheres (mathematical term) or balls (the vernacular) for a simplex are the *circumscribed ball* that contains the vertices of the simplex and the *inscribed ball* that is the largest-volume ball contained in the simplex.

The construction of the circumscribed and inscribed balls involves setting up systems of n linear equations in n unknowns. Because of the simplicity of the construction, there is no need to handle the 2D and 3D cases separately to provide intuition.

13.10.1 Circumscribed Ball

A circumscribed ball for the simplex is that ball passing through all the vertices of the simplex. The center of this ball, C, is equidistant from the vertices, say, of distance r. The constraints are

$$\|C - V_i\| = r, \quad 0 \le i \le n$$

Squaring the equations, expanding the dot products, and subtracting the squared equation for $i = 0$ yields $2(V_i - V_0) \cdot (C - V_0) - \|V_i - V_0\|^2$ for $1 \le i \le n$. This is a system of linear equations in the form $AX = B$, where the ith row of A is $V_i - V_0$ written as a $1 \times n$ vector, the ith row of B is $\|V_i - V_0\|^2/2$, and $X = C - V_0$ written as an $n \times 1$ vector. Since the edges sharing V_0 are linearly independent, A is an invertible matrix and the linear system has a unique solution $X = A^{-1}B$. Therefore, the center of the circumscribed ball is $C = V_0 + A^{-1}B$. Once the center has been calculated, the radius of the circumscribed ball is $r = \|C - V_0\|$.

Dimension 2

Define $V_i = (x_i, y_i)$ for $i = 0, 1, 2$. The triangle is assumed to be counterclockwise ordered. Define $X_i = x_i - x_0$ and $Y_i = y_i - y_0$. The area of the triangle is

$$A = \frac{1}{2} \det \begin{bmatrix} X_1 & Y_1 \\ X_2 & Y_2 \end{bmatrix}$$

and the center (x, y) and radius r are

$$x = x_0 + \frac{1}{4A}(Y_2 L_{10}^2 - Y_1 L_{20}^2)$$

$$y = y_0 + \frac{1}{4A}(X_1 L_{20}^2 - X_2 L_{10}^2)$$

$$r = \sqrt{(x - x_0)^2 + (y - y_0)^2}$$

where $L_{ij} = \|V_i - V_j\|$. It can be shown that $r = L_{10}L_{20}L_{12}/(4A)$, the product of the edge lengths divided by four times the area. It can also be shown (Blumenthal 1970) that the radius is a solution to the Cayley-Menger determinant equation

$$\det \begin{bmatrix} 0 & 1 & 1 & 1 & 1 \\ 1 & 0 & L_{10}^2 & L_{20}^2 & r^2 \\ 1 & L_{10}^2 & 0 & L_{21}^2 & r^2 \\ 1 & L_{20}^2 & L_{21}^2 & 0 & r^2 \\ 1 & r^2 & r^2 & r^2 & 0 \end{bmatrix} = 0$$

Dimension 3

Define $V_i = (x_i, y_i, z_i)$ for $i = 0, 1, 2, 3$. The tetrahedron $\langle V_0, V_1, V_2, V_3 \rangle$ is ordered so that it is isomorphic to the canonical one $\langle (0, 0, 0), (1, 0, 0), (0, 1, 0), (0, 0, 1) \rangle$. Define

$X_i = x_i - x_0$, $Y_i = y_i - y_0$, and $Z_i = z_i - z_0$. The volume of the tetrahedron is

$$V = \frac{1}{6} \det \begin{bmatrix} X_1 & Y_1 & Z_1 \\ X_2 & Y_2 & Z_2 \\ X_3 & Y_3 & Z_3 \end{bmatrix}$$

and the center (x, y, z) and radius r are

$$x = x_0 + \frac{1}{12V} \left(+(Y_2 Z_3 - Y_3 Z_2) L_{10}^2 - (Y_1 Z_3 - Y_3 Z_1) L_{20}^2 + (Y_1 Z_2 - Y_2 Z_1) L_{30}^2 \right)$$

$$y = y_0 + \frac{1}{12V} \left(-(X_2 Z_3 - X_3 Z_2) L_{10}^2 + (X_1 Z_3 - X_3 Z_1) L_{20}^2 - (X_1 Z_2 - X_2 Z_1) L_{30}^2 \right)$$

$$z = z_0 + \frac{1}{12V} \left(+(X_2 Y_3 - X_3 Y_2) L_{10}^2 - (X_1 Y_3 - X_3 Y_1) L_{20}^2 + (X_1 Y_2 - X_2 Y_1) L_{30}^2 \right)$$

$$r = \sqrt{(x - x_0)^2 + (y - y_0)^2 + (z - z_0)^2}$$

where $L_{ij} = \| V_i - V_j \|$. It can be shown (Blumenthal 1970) that the radius is a solution to the Cayley-Menger determinant equation

$$\det \begin{bmatrix} 0 & 1 & 1 & 1 & 1 & 1 \\ 1 & 0 & L_{10}^2 & L_{20}^2 & L_{30}^2 & r^2 \\ 1 & L_{10}^2 & 0 & L_{21}^2 & L_{31}^2 & r^2 \\ 1 & L_{20}^2 & L_{21}^2 & 0 & L_{32}^2 & r^2 \\ 1 & L_{30}^2 & L_{31}^2 & L_{32}^2 & 0 & r^2 \\ 1 & r^2 & r^2 & r^2 & r^2 & 0 \end{bmatrix} = 0$$

13.10.2 INSCRIBED BALL

An inscribed ball for the simplex is the ball of maximum volume contained in the simplex. Necessarily the ball is tangent to all faces of the simplex. The center of the ball, C, is equidistant from the faces, say, of distance r. The distance to each face is obtained as the length of the projection of $C - V$ onto the inner-pointing, unit-length normal vector to a face that contains V. The projections are

$$\hat{n}_i \cdot (C - V_i) = r, \quad 0 \le i \le n$$

where $\hat{n}_i$ is the inner-pointing, unit-length normal to the hyperface determined by the vertices $V_{i \bmod (n+1)}$, $V_{(i+1) \bmod (n+1)}$, $\ldots$, $V_{(i+n-1) \bmod (n+1)}$. This is a linear system of $n + 1$ equations in the $n + 1$ unknowns (C, r), where each equation is written as $(\hat{n}_i, -1) \cdot (C, r) = \hat{n}_i \cdot V_i$. Define the $(n + 1) \times (n + 1)$ matrix $\mathbf{A}$ to be that matrix whose ith row is the vector $(\hat{n}_i, -1)$ written as a $1 \times (n+1)$ vector. Define the $(n+1) \times 1$ vector B to be that vector whose ith row is $\hat{n}_i \cdot V_i$. The linear system is $A(C, r) = B$ and has solution $(C, r) = A^{-1}B$, where the left-hand side is thought of as an $(n+1) \times 1$ vector.

Dimension 2

Define $V_i = (x_i, y_i)$ for $i = 0, 1, 2$, and for notation's sake, let $V_3 = V_0$. The unit-length edge directions are $\hat{d}_i = (V_{i+1} - V_i)/L_i$ with $L_i = \|V_{i+1} - V_i\|$ for $0 \le i \le 2$. The inner-pointing unit-length normals are $\hat{n}_i = -\hat{d}_i^\perp$, where $(x, y)^\perp = (y, -x)$.

The radius and center of the inscribed circle can be constructed as shown previously. However, the solution has a nice symmetry about it if the center is written in barycentric coordinates as $C = t_0 V_0 + t_1 V_1 + t_2 V_2$, where $t_0 + t_1 + t_2 = 1$. In this form the equations $r = \hat{n}_i \cdot (C - V_i)$ become $r = t_2 L_2 \hat{d}_0 \cdot \hat{n}_2$, $r = t_0 L_0 \hat{d}_1 \cdot \hat{n}_0$, and $r = t_1 L_1 \hat{d}_2 \cdot \hat{n}_1$. The area A of the triangle is given by $2A = L_0 L_2 \hat{d}_0 \cdot \hat{n}_2 = L_1 L_0 \hat{d}_1 \cdot \hat{n}_0 = L_2 L_1 \hat{d}_2 \cdot \hat{n}_1$. Combining these with the previous equations yields $t_0 = RL_1/(2A)$, $t_1 = RL_2/(2A)$, and $t_2 = RL_0/(2A)$. Summing the t_i we have $1 = (L_0 + L_1 + L_2)r/(2A)$, in which case $r = 2A/(L_0 + L_1 + L_2)$. Again for the sake of notation, define $\ell_i = L_{(i-1)\bmod 3}$. The value ℓ_i is the length of the edge opposite vertex V_i. Define $L = L_0 + L_1 + L_2 = \ell_0 + \ell_1 + \ell_2$. In this form the radius and center are

$$ r = \frac{2A}{L}, \quad C = \sum_{i=0}^{2} \frac{\ell_i}{L} V_i $$

Dimension 3

Define $V_i = (x_i, y_i, z_i)$ for $i = 0, 1, 2, 3$. The tetrahedron $\langle V_0, V_1, V_2, V_3 \rangle$ is ordered so that it is isomorphic to the canonical one $\langle (0,0,0), (1,0,0), (0,1,0), (0,0,1) \rangle$. The inner-pointing normals for this configuration are $\vec{n}_0 = (V_1 - V_0) \times (V_2 - V_0)/(2A_0)$, where A_0 is the area of the face to which $\vec{n}_0$ is normal; $\vec{n}_1 = (V_3 - V_1) \times (V_2 - V_1)/(2A_1)$, where A_1 is the area of the face to which $\vec{n}_1$ is normal; $\vec{n}_2 = (V_3 - V_2) \times (V_0 - V_2)/(2A_2)$, where A_2 is the area of the face to which $\vec{n}_2$ is normal; and $\vec{n}_3 = (V_1 - V_3) \times (V_2 - V_3)/(2A_3)$, where A_3 is the area of the face to which $\vec{n}_3$ is normal.

As in dimension 2, the solution is nicely expressed when the center is represented in barycentric coordinates $C = \sum_{i=0}^{3} t_i V_i$ with $\sum_{i=0}^{3} t_i = 1$. The equations $r = \vec{n}_i \cdot (C - V_i)$ become $r = t_3 \vec{n}_0 \cdot (V_3 - V_0)$, $r = t_0 \vec{n}_1 \cdot (V_0 - V_1)$, $r = t_1 \vec{n}_2 \cdot (V_1 - V_2)$, and $r = t_2 \vec{n}_3 \cdot (V_2 - V_3)$. The volume of the tetrahedron is given by the following equations involving triple scalar products, $6V = [V_1 - V_0, V_2 - V_0, V_3 - V_0] = [V_0 - V_1, V_3 - V_1, V_2 - V_1] = [V_3 - V_2, V_0 - V_2, V_1 - V_2] = [V_2 - V_3, V_1 - V_3, V_0 - V_3]$. Combining these with the previous equations yields $t_0 = RA_1/(3V)$, $t_1 = RA_2/(3V)$, $t_2 = RA_3/(3V)$, and $t_3 = RA_0/(3V)$. Summing the t_i we have $1 = (A_0 + A_1 + A_2 + $

$A_3)r/(3V)$, in which case $r = 3V/(A_0 + A_1 + A_2 + A_3)$. Define $\alpha_i = A_{(i-1)\bmod 4}$. The value α_i is the area of the face opposite vertex V_i. Define $A = A_0 + A_1 + A_2 + A_3 = \alpha_0 + \alpha_1 + \alpha_2 + \alpha_3$. In this form the radius and center are

$$r = \frac{3V}{A}, \quad C = \sum_{i=0}^{3} \frac{\alpha_i}{A} V_i$$

Dimension n

The same construction using barycentric coordinates for C may be applied in general dimensions. The radius and center are

$$r = \frac{nV}{S}, \quad C = \sum_{i=0}^{n} \frac{\sigma_i}{S} V_i$$

where V is the volume of the simplex, σ_i is the surface area of the hyperface opposite vertex V_i, and $S = \sum_{i=0}^{n} \sigma_i$ is the total surface area of the simplex.

13.11 MINIMUM BOUNDS FOR POINT SETS

In this section, let the point set be $\{P_i\}_{i=0}^{n-1}$ with $n \geq 2$. In the discussions in this section, all points are assumed to be unique. However, an implementation must be prepared to handle sets that contain multiple copies of the same point or even two points that are nearly the same point (within some floating-point tolerance). This section covers the topics of minimum-area rectangles, circles, and ellipses in 2D and minimum-volume boxes, spheres, and ellipsoids in 3D.

13.11.1 MINIMUM-AREA RECTANGLE

It is evident that the only points that need to be considered are the vertices of the convex hull of the original point set. The problem is therefore reduced to finding the minimum-area rectangle that contains a convex polygon with ordered vertices P_i for $0 \leq i < N$. The rectangle is not required to be axis aligned with the coordinate system axes. It is the case that at least one of the edges of the convex polygon must be contained by an edge of the minimum-area rectangle. Given that this is so, an algorithm for computing the minimum-area rectangle need only compute the tightest-fitting bounding rectangles whose orientations are determined by the polygon edges.

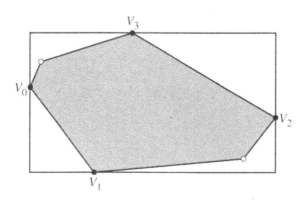

Figure 13.79   Purported minimum-area rectangle that has no coincident polygon edges.

Proof of Edge Containment

The proof of edge containment is by contradiction. Suppose that in fact no edge of the convex polygon is contained by an edge of the minimum-area rectangle. The rectangle must be supported by two, three, or four vertices of the convex polygon. Figure 13.79 illustrates the case of four supporting vertices. The supporting vertices are drawn in black and labeled V_0 through V_3. Other polygon vertices are white. For the sake of argument, rotate the convex polygon so that the axes of this rectangle are $(1, 0)$ and $(0, 1)$ as shown in the figure.

Define $\vec{u}_0(\theta) = (\cos\theta, \sin\theta)$ and $\vec{u}_1(\theta) = (-\sin\theta, \cos\theta)$. There exists a value $\varepsilon > 0$ such that the V_i are always the supporting vertices of the bounding rectangle with axes $\vec{u}_0(\theta)$ and $\vec{u}_1(\theta)$ for all angles θ satisfying the condition $|\theta| <= \varepsilon$. To compute the bounding rectangle area, the supporting vertices are projected onto the axis lines $V_0 + s\vec{u}_0(\theta)$ and $V_0 + t\vec{u}_1(\theta)$. The intervals of projection are $[0, s_1]$ and $[t_0, t_1]$, where $s_1 = \vec{u}_0(\theta) \cdot (V_2 - V_0), t_0 = \vec{u}_1(\theta) \cdot (V_1 - V_0)$, and $t_1 = \vec{u}_1(\theta) \cdot (V_3 - V_0)$.

Define $\vec{k}_0 = (x_0, y_0) = V_2 - V_0$ and $\vec{k}_1 = (x_1, y_1) = V_3 - V_1$. From Figure 13.79 it is clear that $x_0 > 0$ and $y_1 > 0$. The area of the rectangle for $|\theta| \leq \varepsilon$ is

$$A(\theta) = s_1(t_1 - t_0) = [\vec{k}_0 \cdot \vec{u}_0(\theta)][\vec{k}_1 \cdot \vec{u}_1(\theta)]$$

In particular, $A(0) = x_0 y_1 > 0$.

Since $A(\theta)$ is differentiable on its domain and since $A(0)$ is assumed to be the global minimum, it must be that $A'(0) = 0$. Generally,

$$A'(\theta) = [\vec{k}_0 \cdot \vec{u}_0(\theta)][\vec{k}_1 \cdot \vec{u}_1'(\theta)] + [\vec{k}_0 \cdot \vec{u}_0'(\theta)][\vec{k}_1 \cdot \vec{u}_1(\theta)]$$

$$= -[\vec{k}_0 \cdot \vec{u}_0(\theta)][\vec{k}_1 \cdot \vec{u}_0(\theta)] + [\vec{k}_0 \cdot \vec{u}_1(\theta)][\vec{k}_1 \cdot \vec{u}_1(\theta)]$$

Therefore, $0 = A'(0) = -x_0 x_1 + y_0 y_1$, or $x_0 x_1 = y_0 y_1$. Since $x_0 > 0$ and $y_1 > 0$, it must be that $\text{Sign}(x_1) = \text{Sign}(y_0)$. Moreover, since $A(0)$ is assumed to be the global minimum, it must be that $A''(0) \geq 0$. Generally,

$$
\begin{aligned}
A''(\theta) = &-[\vec{k}_0 \cdot \vec{u}_0(\theta)][\vec{k}_1 \cdot \vec{u}_0'(\theta)] - [\vec{k}_0 \cdot \vec{u}_0'(\theta)][\vec{k}_1 \cdot \vec{u}_0(\theta)] \\
&+ [\vec{k}_0 \cdot \vec{u}_1(\theta)][\vec{k}_1 \cdot \vec{u}_1'(\theta)] + [\vec{k}_0 \cdot \vec{u}_1'(\theta)][\vec{k}_1 \cdot \vec{u}_1(\theta)] \\
= &-[\vec{k}_0 \cdot \vec{u}_0(\theta)][\vec{k}_1 \cdot \vec{u}_1(\theta)] - [\vec{k}_0 \cdot \vec{u}_1(\theta)][\vec{k}_1 \cdot \vec{u}_0(\theta)] \\
&- [\vec{k}_0 \cdot \vec{u}_1(\theta)][\vec{k}_1 \cdot \vec{u}_0(\theta)] - [\vec{k}_0 \cdot \vec{u}_0(\theta)][\vec{k}_1 \cdot \vec{u}_1(\theta)] \\
= &-2 \left\{ [\vec{k}_0 \cdot \vec{u}_0(\theta)][\vec{k}_1 \cdot \vec{u}_1(\theta)] + [\vec{k}_0 \cdot \vec{u}_1(\theta)][\vec{k}_1 \cdot \vec{u}_0(\theta)] \right\}
\end{aligned}
$$

In particular, $A''(0) = -2(x_0 y_1 + x_1 y_0) \geq 0$. However, note that $x_0 y_1 > 0$ since $A(0) > 0$ and $x_1 y_0 > 0$ since $\text{Sign}(x_1) = \text{Sign}(y_0)$, which implies that $A''(0) < 0$, a contradiction.

An Implementation

Since the minimum-area rectangle must contain an edge, a simple implementation just iterates over the edges of the convex hull. For each edge, the corresponding smallest rectangle for the orientation defined by the edge is computed. The minimum area of all these rectangles is computed. The pseudocode for the algorithm is

```
ordered vertices P[0] through P[N - 1];
define P[N] = P[0];

minimumArea = infinity;
for (i = 1; i <= N; i++)  {
    U0 = P[i] - P[i - 1];
    U1 = (-U0.x, U0.y);
    s0 = t0 = s1 = t1 = 0;
    for (j = 1; j < N; j++) {
        D = P[j] - P[0];
        test = Dot(U0, D);
        if (test < s0) s0 = test; else if (test > s1) s1 = test;
        test = Dot(U1, D);
        if (test < t0) t0 = test; else if (test > t1) t1 = test;
    }
    area = (s1 - s0) * (t1 - t0);
    if (area < minimumArea)
        minimumArea = area;
}
```

This algorithm is $O(n^2)$ because of the double loops, each iterating over n items. A better algorithm is considered in the next section and is based on an idea called the *rotating calipers method*.

Rotating Calipers

The rotating calipers method is the idea used in the dissertation of Michael Shamos (1978), a work that is considered to be the origin of the area of computational geometry. The algorithm in that dissertation uses the method for computing the diameter of a convex polygon in $O(n)$ time. Godfreid Toussaint coined the phrase "rotating calipers" since the method resembles rotating a pair of calipers around the polygon. The method is quite useful in solving other problems. Among those are computing the minimum and maximum distances between two convex polygons, onion triangulations (useful for triangulating point sets that occur on various contour lines for a function $f(x, y)$), merging convex hulls, intersecting convex polygons, and computing the Minkowski sum/difference of two convex polygons (compare with the GJK algorithm discussed in Section 6.10 of this book). These and more algorithms are summarized at the rotating calipers home page (Pirzadeh 1999).

The application of rotating calipers to finding the minimum-area rectangle containing a convex polygon is quite simple. An initial edge of the polygon is selected. The edge direction and a perpendicular direction are used to find the smallest bounding rectangle with that orientation. The vertices and edge supporting the rectangle are tracked during the construction. The rectangle will be rotated an edge at a time. The edge starting at a supporting vertex forms an angle with the box edge containing the vertex. The box is rotated by the smallest angle of all supporting vertices. The new supporting edge is not necessarily adjacent to the previous supporting edge. The box size is updated in $O(1)$ time for the new orientation. The polygon has n edges to be visited, and the update is $O(1)$ for each rotation of the box, so the total algorithm is $O(n)$.

13.11.2   MINIMUM-VOLUME BOX

Just as in the 2D problem, it is evident that the only points that need to be considered are the vertices of the convex hull of the original point set. The problem is therefore reduced to finding the minimum-volume oriented box that contains a convex polyhedron. O'Rourke (1985) shows that one box face must contain a polyhedron face and another box face must contain a polyhedron edge *or* three box faces must each contain a polyhedron edge. The first case can be performed in $O(n^2)$ time, but the second case is performed in $O(n^3)$ time, so the total algorithm is $O(n^3)$. To date there appears to be no known algorithm with a smaller asymptotic run time. However, an approximation of the minimum-volume box can be efficiently computed (Barequet and Har-Peled 1999).

The box calculation based on a box face containing a polyhedron face uses the rotating calipers method. There are $O(n)$ polyhedron faces to process, each taking $O(n)$ time for a total of $O(n^2)$ time, as mentioned in the last paragraph. Given the polyhedron face, the projection of the polyhedron onto the plane of the face produces a convex polygon. If $\vec{n}$ is an outer normal vector to that face, the edges and faces of the polyhedron that project onto the polygon are the separators between the faces of the polygon whose normals $\vec{m}$ satisfy $\vec{n} \cdot \vec{m} > 0$ and those whose normals satisfy $\vec{n} \cdot \vec{m} < 0$. The projection of the box onto the plane is a rectangle. The rotating calipers method is applied to find the minimum-area rectangle containing the convex polygon. This equates to finding the minimum-volume box for the specifed polyhedron face.

The case of three edges supporting the box is handled in a straightforward manner by iterating over all combinations of three edges, a total of $O(n^3)$ possibilities. For each combination of three edges that are mutually orthogonal, a minimum-volume box of that orientation is constructed. The hope for reducing the asymptotic order is that somehow the combinations of three mutually orthogonal edges can be found during the $O(n^2)$ processing of polyhedron faces.

The minimum-volume box for the polyhedron is chosen as the minimum of all boxes constructed from faces and from edge combinations.

13.11.3 Minimum-Area Circle

An $O(n)$ method for finding *some* bounding circle is to compute the minimum-area axis-aligned rectangle that contains the points, then choose a circle that circumscribes the rectangle. In most cases this circle is not the minimum-area circle containing the points. In fact, sometimes the input points are all strictly interior to the circle. For example, this situation occurs for the points $\{(\pm 2, 0), (0, \pm 1)\}$. The bounding circle is centered at $(0, 0)$ and has radius $\sqrt{5}$. The maximum distance from the origin to an input point is 2. Many applications require a better fit than this.

A *support point* for a bounding circle is an input point that lies exactly on the circle. The minimum-area circle containing the points clearly must be supported by at least two input points; otherwise the purported circle could be shrunk in size until it does touch another input point. Even though the point set could have more than two input points, the minimum-area circle might only have two supporting points. For example, the points $\{(-1, 0), (0, 0), (1, 0)\}$ are collinear. The minimum-area circle containing them has center $(0, 0)$ and radius 1. The supporting points are $(\pm 1, 0)$. In other examples, the number of supporting points is three. It is possible for the number of input points exactly on the minimum-area circle to be four or more, but only three are necessary since three noncollinear points uniquely determine the circle (see Section 13.10).

Since at least two input points must be on the circle, it is tempting to assume that those two points must be the ones farthest apart. This is not the case based on the following counterexample. Let the input points be $\{(1, 0), (-1/2, \sqrt{3}/2), (-1/2, -\sqrt{3}/2), (-3/4, 0)\}$. The points form a convex quadrilateral. The first three points form an equilateral triangle, the common length of the sides being $\sqrt{3}$. The distance from $(1, 0)$ to $(-3/4, 0)$ is $7/4 > \sqrt{3}$. Therefore, $(1, 0)$ and $(-3/4, 0)$ form the most separated pair of input points. The minimum-area bounding circle is the one containing the equilateral triangle and has center $(0, 0)$ and radius 1. The circle containing $(1, 0)$, $(-1/2, \sqrt{3}/2)$, and $(-3/4, 0)$ has center $(1/8, \sqrt{3}/8)$ and radius $\sqrt{13}/4 < 1$, but $(-1/2, -\sqrt{3}/2)$ is not in that circle. The circle with antipodal points $(-3/4, 0)$ and $(1, 0)$ has center $(1/8, 0)$ and radius $7/8$, but $(-1/2, \pm\sqrt{3}/2)$ are not in that circle since the distance from those points to the circle center is approximately $1.068 > 7/8$.

An exhaustive approach will produce the answer, but is slow. All triples of points are analyzed. The minimum-area circle containing the three points is either the circumscribed circle or a circle for which two of the three points are antipodal. This is particularly the case when the three points are collinear. The bounding circle of minimum radius in this process is tracked during the analysis. At the end, we have the minimum-area circle for the input set. The algorithm is $O(n^3)$.

A more efficient approach is to *grow* a circle to contain the points. The initial circle is the one that contains the first two input points. Each additional point is tested for inclusion in that circle. If all are contained, with some possibly on the circle itself, the initial circle is the one of minimum area. We are not usually so lucky to have this happen. More likely is that one of the remaining points Q is outside the initial circle. If this happens, the initial circle was not large enough and must be grown to include Q. In fact, Q will be used as a supporting point for this new circle. A problem is that many point-in-circle tests were performed before Q was encountered (see Figure 13.80). When the initial circle is modified to a new circle, points in the initial circle might not be in the modified one. Effectively, the algorithm must start over, and all the points have to be tested for containment in the new circle.

If the initial circle is the minimum-area circle, that was determined by testing $n - 2 = O(n)$ points. If only m restarts are needed and m is effectively a small constant compared to n, then the algorithm is $O(n)$. However, if m is comparable in size to n, the asymptotic behavior is worse than $O(n)$. To see this, consider the points on a hemicircle, $P_i = (\cos\theta_i, \sin\theta_i)$, where $\theta_i = \pi i/(n-1)$ for $0 \le i < n$. The initial bounding circle is supported by P_0 and P_1. The next point P_2 is outside that circle, so the algorithm is restarted. The new circle is supported by P_0 and P_2. The point P_1 is inside this circle, but P_3 is not. At the ith iteration, the current bounding circle is supported by P_0 and P_i, points P_j for $0 < j < i$ are inside the circle, but P_{i+1} is not. That is, the algorithm must restart each time. The ith iteration requires i point-in-circle tests. The minimum-area circle is only known once you reach point P_{n-1}, and in fact all input points are on the circle. The total number of point-in-circle tests is $\sum_{i=1}^{n-1} = n(n-1)/2 = O(n^2)$. More complicated examples of this type even lead to $O(n^3)$ behavior, just like the exhaustive approach.

Taking a closer look at the hemicircle example, suppose that instead of processing the points in the order given, the points are randomly permuted, then processed. For the sake of argument, let P_0 always be a supporting point. If the second point in the permuted set is P_j, where j is nearly $n - 1$, the initial circle is quite large. In the

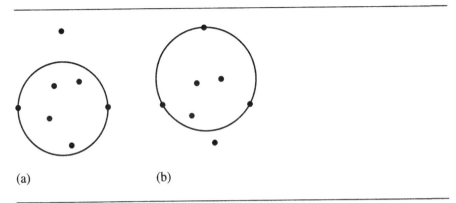

(a)   (b)

Figure 13.80   (a) Current bounding circle and a point that is outside the circle, causing the circle to grow. (b) The new bounding circle, but a point inside the old circle is now outside the new circle, causing a restart of the algorithm.

ordered case, it took j iterations to get to this circle. In the permuted case, we have saved a lot of time. Another point, P_k, processed in the permuted case that causes a restart hopefully will have index k that is larger than $j + 1$, again skipping a couple of iterations that were performed in the ordered case. The hope is that the number of restarts, m, is effectively a small constant compared to n, in which case the algorithm is $O(n)$.

The formalization of this approach is found in Welzl (1991) and is one of a class of algorithms called *randomized linear algorithms*. The permutation of the input data has *expected* time behavior of $O(n)$. This does not mean that all input data sets will run in this time. It is possible, although not highly probable, that the permutation of the input points leads to an ordering that does cause superlinear behavior. For example, the permutation for the hemicircle problem might turn out to be the identity, in which case that example runs in $O(n^2)$ time. Assuming uniform distribution of the permutations, the probability that the permutation is the identity in that example is $1/n!$, a very small number for large n. Of course, other permutations that result in only a couple of transpositions will cause similar slow construction of the circle, but as noted, the expected time is $O(n)$. The concept applies to higher dimensions, of which the 3D problem is discussed next. In d-dimensional space, the expected number of point-in-circle tests is $n(d + 1)!$. That is, the asymptotic constant is approximately $(d + 1)!$.

The recursive formulation of the algorithm is

```
Circle MinimumAreaCircle(PointSet Input, PointSet Support)
{
    if (Input is not empty) {
        P = GetRandomElementOf(Input);
        Input' = Input - {P};  // remove P from Input
```

```
            C = MinimumAreaCircle(Input', Support);
            if (P is inside C) {
                return C;
            } else {
                Support' = Support + {P}';   // add P to Support
                return MinimumAreaCircle(Input', Support');
            }
        } else {
            return CircleOf(Support);
        }
    }
}
```

A nonrecursive formulation is

```
Circle MinimumAreaCircle(int N, Point P[N])
{
    randomly permute P[0] through P[N - 1];
    C = ExactCircle1(P[0]);  // center P[0], radius 0
    Support = { P[0] };

    i = 1;
    while (i < N) {
        if (P[i] is not an element of Support) {
            if (P[i] is not contained by C)  {
                C = Update(P[i], Support);
                i = 0;  // restart the algorithm for the new circle
                continue;
            }
        }
        i++;
    }

    return C;
}
```

The Update function has the job of adding P[i] to the support set Support and removing other elements of Support that are no longer supporting points because of the addition of P. Beware: this function must be implemented with care when using floating-point arithmetic. The problem is that old supporting points are tested for containment in various combinations of the supporting points and P[i]. One of those combinations must theoretically contain all the old supporting points. However, numerical round-off errors can cause a situation where none of the combinations appears to contain all the points. Even with the introduction of a numerical epsilon for point-in-circle tests, you can still run into problems. One solution is to trap the case when no circle appears to contain all the support points and use the circle for which the offending point outside the circle is closest to that circle, compared to the same offending points for the other circles. The construction of the circles for the various combinations relies on the existence of functions that calculate the minimum-area circle of two points and of three points. An implementation must, of course, provide these.

Another potential problem with floating point is that the update call always assigns a new circle to the current minimum-area circle C. It is possible to encounter a situation, when using floating-point arithmetic, where the loop becomes infinite because of a cycle of two points in the support set that are alternately swapped out. The problem is that, in theory, the circle returned by the update has larger radius than the current circle C. However, numerical round-off errors cause the radius of the returned circle to be smaller, thus leading to the infinite loop. The solution is to replace the block containing the update by

```
Circle tmp = Update(P[i], Support);
if (tmp.radius > C.radius) {
    C = tmp;
    i = 0;
    continue;
}
```

Other concerns that an implementation must address include handling duplicate input points and points that are distinct but numerically nearly identical. The construction of circles containing three noncollinear points shows up in an implementation—the circumscribed-circle-about-triangle problem that uses a linear system solver to find the center and radius. The determinant of the system can be close to zero if three points are nearly collinear, so the implementation should handle this properly by detecting this and switching to computing the minimum-area circle containing two points (discarding the correct point from the nearly collinear points).

13.11.4 MINIMUM-VOLUME SPHERE

The problem of constructing the minimum-volume sphere that contains a set of input points is handled in the same manner as the 2D problem of finding a minimum-area circle containing a set of points. We recommend reading the previous section on the circle problem to understand the intuition and ideas.

A popular misconception among novice graphics programmers is that the smallest sphere containing the input points can be constructed by selecting the sphere center to be the average of the input points, then determining the input point farthest from the center to obtain the sphere radius. Although this is a viable and easily implementable algorithm for computing *a* bounding sphere, the resulting sphere is not necessarily the one of minimum volume.

The randomized algorithm in Welzl (1991) applies in general dimensions, so in 3D in particular. The recursive formulation is identical to the 2D formulation, but the function computes spheres instead of circles.

```
Sphere MinimumVolumeSphere(PointSet Input, PointSet Support)
{
    if (Input is not empty) {
        P = GetRandomElementOf(Input);
        Input' = Input - {P};  // remove P from Input
        S = MinimumVolumeSphere(Input', Support);
        if (P is inside S) {
            return S;
        } else {
            Support' = Support + {P}';  // add P to Support
            return MinimumVolumeSphere(Input', Support');
        }
    } else {
        return SphereOf(Support);
    }
}
```

The nonrecursive formulation is also similar to the one in two dimensions:

```
Sphere MinimumVolumeSphere(int N, Point P[N])
{
    randomly permute P[0] through P[N - 1];
    S = ExactCircle1(P[0]);  // center P[0], radius 0
    Support = { P[0] };

    i = 1;
    while (i < N) {
        if (P[i] is not an element of Support) {
            if (P[i] is not contained by S) {
                S = Update(P[i], Support);
                i = 0;  // restart the algorithm for the new sphere
                continue;
            }
        }
        i++;
    }

    return S;
}
```

The same numerical concerns that arise in the two-dimensional problem must be addressed in the three-dimensional one. See the end of Section 13.11.3 for what those concerns are and how to deal with them in an implementation.

13.11.5 MISCELLANEOUS

Other types of minimum-area or volume-bounding regions are sometimes called for in applications. Generally, the construction of such bounds can be quite challenging from the point of view of both algorithm development and implementation.

Minimum-Area Ellipse

As an example, consider the problem of finding the minimum-area ellipse that contains a set of points. An extension of the minimum-area circle algorithm is immediate (Gaertner and Schoenherr 1998). In the circle problem, the update of the supporting set required constructing the minimum circle for pairs and triples of support points. These are referred to as *small* problems whose solutions are used to determine the original *large* problem with n points. The small problems for the ellipse bounding involves computing minimum-area ellipses for three, four, or five points. For three noncollinear points P_i, $0 \le i \le 2$, the equation of the minimum-area ellipse that contains the points is $(X - C)^{\mathrm{T}} \mathbf{M}(X - C) = 2$, where

$$C = \frac{1}{3} \sum_{i=0}^{2} P_i$$

the average of the points, and $\mathbf{M}$ is the 2×2 matrix whose inverse is

$$\mathbf{M}^{-1} = \frac{1}{3} \sum_{i=0}^{2} (P_i - C)(P_i - C)^{\mathrm{T}}$$

For five points that form a convex polygon, the minimum-area ellipse is the exact fitting ellipse for the five points. The general quadratic equation that represents either an ellipse, hyperbola, or parabola is $x^2 + axy + by^2 + cx + dy + e = 0$. The five coefficients are computed by creating five linear equations from the general quadratic equation—a system that is easy to solve.

The harder problem is computing the minimum-area ellipse containing four points that form a convex quadrilateral. To see the complexity of the problem, consider the special case when the points are $(0, 0)$, $(1, 0)$, $(0, 1)$, and (u, v) with $u > 0$, $v > 0$, and $u + v > 1$. The quadratic equation that contains the four points as solutions is $x^2 + bxy + cy^2 - x - cy = 0$, where $c > 0$, $b^2 < 4c$, and $b = (1 - u)/v + c(1 - v)/u$. The independent variable is c, so there are infinitely many ellipses containing the four points. The problem is to construct the one with minimum area. The area as a function of c is

$$\text{Area}(c) = \frac{\pi c(1 - b + c)}{(4c - b^2)^{3/2}}$$

The minimum area occurs when c makes the derivative of area with respect to c zero, $\text{Area}'(c) = 0$. This leads to a cubic polynomial equation in c

$$P(c; u, v) = S(v)c^3 + T(u, v)c^2 - T(v, u)c - S(u) = 0$$

where $S(v) = v^3(v - 1)^2$ and $T(u, v) = uv^2(2v^2 + uv + u - 3v + 1)$. The maximum root for P provides the correct value of c. The minimum area occurs at $c = 1$ when $P(1; u, v) = 0$. This occurs when $u = v$ or $u^2 + uv + v^2 - u - v = 0$ (or $u + v = 1$ or $u = -v$). These curves decompose the valid (u, v) region into subregions where $c > 1$ or $c < 1$. Numerically, the largest root can be found in regions where $c < 1$ by applying Newton's method to $P(c) = 0$ with an initial guess of $c = 1$. In regions where $c > 1$, Newton's method can be applied to the inverted polynomial equation $P(1/c) = 0$ with an initial guess of $1/c = 1$.

Minimum-Area Ellipse for Fixed Center and Orientation

A special case of the minimum-area ellipse problem is to choose a center and orientation, then compute the ellipse axis lengths that produce the minimum-area ellipse with that center and orientation. Since the input points can be written in the coordinate system with the specified center as the origin and the specified orientation for the axes, we can analyze the problem when the center is the origin and the orientation is the identity matrix. The ellipse equation is $(x/a)^2 + (y/b)^2 = 1$, and the ellipse has area πab, which we want to minimize for the input set of points.

The constraints on the axis lengths are $a > 0$ and $b > 0$. Additional constraints come from requiring that each point (x_i, y_i) is inside the ellipse, $(x_i/a)^2 + (y_i/b)^2 \leq 1$. The problem is to minimize the quadratic function ab subject to all the inequality constraints. Let $u = 1/a^2$ and $v = 1/b^2$. The equivalent problem is to maximize $f(u, v) = uv$ subject to the linear inequality constraints $u \geq 0$, $v \geq 0$, and $x_i^2 u + y_i^2 v \leq 1$ for all i. This is a quadratic programming problem, so the general methods for such problems can be applied here (Pierre 1986). This type of programming arises in other computational geometry applications and is being investigated by various researchers (for example, Gaertner and Schoenherr 2000).

Although the general quadratic progamming methods apply here, the problem may be solved in a more geometric way. The domain of $f(u, v)$ is bounded by a convex polygon with edges $u = 0$, $v = 0$, and other edges in the first quadrant determined by the point-in-ellipse containment constraints. Not all the constraints necessarily contribute to the domain. The maximum of f must occur on the convex polygon boundary (not including $u = 0$ or $v = 0$), so a smart search of that polygon will produce the maximizing (u, v). This point can be a vertex or an interior edge point. The constraint line that produces the smallest v on the u-axis is located by a linear search. The other constraint lines are analyzed for intersection with this initial line to find the closest intersection to $(0, v)$. This search produces the first edge of the convex polygon. If f is maximized at an interior point or at the u-minimum end point, the problem is solved. Otherwise, the maximum of f on that edge occurs at the u-maximum end point. The process of sorting constraint lines relative to the constraint line that produced the u-maximum point is repeated. During the iterations, as constraint lines are processed and/or determined not to ever participate in the convex polygon boundary, they are marked as such to avoid processing them again.

Minimum-Volume Ellipsoid

The algorithm for computing the minimum-volume ellipsoid containing a set of 3D points is also similar to the one for minimum-volume spheres. The small problems for a sphere involved finding the minimum sphere containing two, three, or four points. For an ellipsoid, the small problems involve between four and nine points. For nine points that form a convex polyhedron, the ellipsoid is computed as the solution of nine linear equations in the nine unknown coefficients for a general quadric equation. For four points that form a convex polyhedron, an algebraic formula exists for the minimum-volume ellipsoid. The center is

$$C = \frac{1}{4} \sum_{i=0}^{3} P_i$$

the average of the points, and $\mathbf{M}$ is the 3×3 matrix whose inverse is

$$\mathbf{M}^{-1} = \frac{1}{4} \sum_{i=0}^{3} (P_i - C)(P_i - C)^{\mathrm{T}}$$

For the cases of $5 \le n \le 8$, computing the minimum-volume ellipsoid is quite difficult. The volume function depends on $9 - n$ variables (coefficients from the quadratic equation). The $9 - n$ derivatives with respect to the variables are computed and set to zero, each equation reducible to a polynomial equation. When $n = 8$, there is one polynomial equation to solve in one unknown, a very tractable problem. However, when $n = 5$, there are four polynomial equations in four unknowns. Variables can be reduced by elimination theory (Wee and Goldman 1995a, 1995b), but doing so is subject to a lot of numerical problems, and the resulting single-variable polynomial equation has an extremely large degree, so root finding itself will have a lot of numerical problems. The other alternative is to numerically solve the system of polynomial equations. It remains to be seen if anyone can produce a robust implementation of the minimum-volume ellipsoid algorithm.

Numerical Minimization Methods

Although perhaps unappealing to computational geometers, the minimum-area or minimum-volume bounding problems can be solved iteratively with numerical minimizers. In the case of circles, spheres, ellipses, or ellipsoids, the equations for these quadratic objects have unknown coefficients that are subject to inequality constraints based on point-in-object requirements. The area and volume formulas are derived based on the unknown coefficients as variables. The result is a function to be minimized subject to a set of inequality constraints, the topic of nonlinear programming. The attractiveness of such an approach in an industrial setting is that it is easy to set up and use existing robust nonlinear programming packages to solve the problem. The speed and accuracy that a purely geometric approach might have is traded for reduced development time, a viable trade-off in computer science that is typically not considered by researchers in an academic environment.

13.12   AREA AND VOLUME MEASUREMENTS

This section describes algorithms for computing areas of polygons, whether in 2D or 3D, and for computing volumes of polyhedra. Various algorithms are shown with algebraic, geometric, and analytic constructions.

13.12.1   AREA OF A 2D POLYGON

Consider a triangle $\langle V_0, V_1, V_2 \rangle$ whose vertices are counterclockwise ordered. Setting $V_i = (x_i, y_i)$, methods of basic algebra and trigonometry can be used to show that the area of the triangle is

$$\text{Area}(V_0, V_1, V_2) = \frac{1}{2} \det \begin{bmatrix} 1 & 1 & 1 \\ x_0 & x_1 & x_2 \\ y_0 & y_1 & y_2 \end{bmatrix} \tag{13.1}$$

Clearly, $\text{Area}(V_1, V_2, V_0) = \text{Area}(V_2, V_0, V_1) = \text{Area}(V_0, V_1, V_2)$ since it does not matter which vertex starts the counterclockwise ordering. However, if the order is clockwise, then $\text{Area}(V_0, V_2, V_1) = \text{Area}(V_2, V_1, V_0) = \text{Area}(V_1, V_0, V_2) = -\text{Area}(V_0, V_1, V_2)$, all negative numbers. Thus, for any set of three vertices U, V, and W, the function $\text{Area}(U, V, W)$ as defined by Equation 13.1 is referred to as the *signed area* of the triangle formed by the vertices. If the vertices are counterclockwise ordered, the signed area is positive. If the order is clockwise, the signed area is negative. If the vertices are collinear, the signed area is zero.

Area as an Algebraic Quantity

Let $V = (x, y)$ be an arbitrary point in the plane. The following algebraic identity is true:

$$\text{Area}(V_0, V_1, V_2) = \text{Area}(V, V_0, V_1) + \text{Area}(V, V_1, V_2) + \text{Area}(V, V_2, V_0) \quad (13.2)$$

The identity can be verified by expanding the determinants on the right-hand side of the equation and performing algebraic operations to show that the result is the same as the determinant on the left-hand side.

The formula for the area of a simple polygon $\mathcal{P}$ is inductive, the motivation being the geometric intuition for Equation 13.2. The area for counterclockwise-ordered vertices V_0 through V_{n-1} and for an arbitrary point V is

$$\text{Area}(\mathcal{P}) = \text{Area}(V, V_0, V_1) + \text{Area}(V, V_1, V_2) + \cdots + \text{Area}(V, V_{n-2}, V_{n-1})$$
$$+ \text{Area}(V, V_{n-1}, V_0) \quad (13.3)$$

The proof of the formula uses mathematical induction. Suppose that the formula is true for all simple polygons with n vertices. Now consider a polygon $\mathcal{P}'$ with $n + 1$ vertices. As mentioned in Section 13.9, a polygon must have at least one ear, a triangle that does not contain any other polygon vertices except the ones that form the triangle. Relabel the vertices of $\mathcal{P}'$ so that the ear $\mathcal{T}$ is the triangle $\langle V_{n-1}, V_n, V_0 \rangle$ and the polygon $\mathcal{P}$ obtained from $\mathcal{P}'$ by removing the ear is $\langle V_0, \ldots, V_{n-1} \rangle$. The area of $\mathcal{T}$ is

$$\text{Area}(\mathcal{T}) = \text{Area}(V, V_{n-1}, V_n) + \text{Area}(V, V_n, V_0) + \text{Area}(V, V_0, V_{n-1})$$

by Equation 13.2. The area of $\mathcal{P}$ is

$$\text{Area}(\mathcal{P}) = \text{Area}(V, V_0, V_1) + \text{Area}(V, V_1, V_2) + \cdots + \text{Area}(V, V_{n-2}, V_{n-1})$$
$$+ \text{Area}(V, V_{n-1}, V_0)$$

by the inductive hypothesis. The area of $\mathcal{P}'$ is the combined area $\text{Area}(\mathcal{P}') = \text{Area}(\mathcal{T}) + \text{Area}(\mathcal{P})$. When the two expressions are added together, the term $\text{Area}(V, V_0, V_{n-1})$ from $\text{Area}(\mathcal{T})$ cancels with the term $\text{Area}(V, V_{n-1}, V_0)$ from $\text{Area}(\mathcal{P})$. The final sum is

$$\text{Area}(\mathcal{P}') = \text{Area}(V, V_0, V_1) + \text{Area}(V, V_1, V_2) + \cdots + \text{Area}(V, V_{n-1}, V_n)$$
$$+ \text{Area}(V, V_n, V_0)$$

so the formula holds true for any $\mathcal{P}'$ with $n + 1$ vertices. By the principle of mathematical induction, the formula is true for all integers $n \geq 3$.

Using $V = (0, 0)$, $V_i = (x_i, y_i)$, and Equation 13.1 for each term $\text{Area}(\vec{0}, V_i, V_{i+1})$, an expansion of the right-hand side of Equation 13.3 leads to the formula that is implementable in a computer program

$$\text{Area}(\mathcal{P}) = \frac{1}{2} \sum_{i=0}^{n-1} (x_i y_{i+1} - x_{i+1} y_i) \tag{13.4}$$

where indexing is modulo n. That is, $x_n = x_0$ and $y_n = y_0$. Each term of the summation in Equation 13.4 requires two multiplications and one subtraction. A simple rearrangement of terms reduces this to one multiplication and one subtraction per term:

$$\sum_{i=0}^{n-1} (x_i y_{i+1} - x_{i+1} y_i) = \sum_{i=0}^{n-1} [x_i (y_{i+1} - y_{i-1}) + x_i y_{i-1} - x_{i+1} y_i]$$

$$= \sum_{i=0}^{n-1} x_i (y_{i+1} - y_{i-1}) + \sum_{i=0}^{n-1} (x_i y_{i-1} - x_{i+1} y_i)$$

$$= \sum_{i=0}^{n-1} x_i (y_{i+1} - y_{i-1}) + x_0 y_{-1} - x_n y_{n-1}$$

$$= \sum_{i=0}^{n-1} x_i (y_{i+1} - y_{i-1})$$

The last equality is valid since $x_n = x_0$ and $y_{-1} = y_{n-1}$ based on the assumption of indexing modulo n. The area is more efficiently calculated by a simple algebraic observation:

$$\text{Area}(\mathcal{P}) = \frac{1}{2} \sum_{i=0}^{n-1} x_i (y_{i+1} - y_{i-1}) \tag{13.5}$$

The FAQ for the Usenet newsgroup *comp.graphics.algorithms* attributes the formula to Dan Sunday (2001), but the formula has occurred earlier in Usenet, posted by Dave Rusin (1995) to the Usenet newsgroup *sci.math*. Given the simplicity of the observation, it probably was known even earlier than 1995.

If the polygon $\mathcal{P}$ is not simple and contains a hole that is itself a polygon, the area is computed as the difference of the area bounded by the outer polygon and the area bounded by the inner polygon. If your polygon data structure allows such a polygon to be stored in a single array so that the interior of the polygon is always to the left of

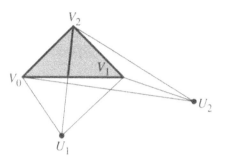

Figure 13.81   Points U_1 and U_2 chosen for computing Equation 13.2. Only one edge of the triangle is visible to the first point. Two edges of the triangle are visible to the second point.

each edge, then the inner polygon is clockwise ordered. In this case Equation 13.5 is still valid as shown without having to process the outer and inner polygons separately.

Area as a Geometric Quantity

Equation 13.2 has a geometric equivalent. Figure 13.81 shows a triangle and two candidate points for V. The triangles that are formed by V and the edges that are visible to it have negative signed areas. The other triangles have positive signed areas. Notice that regardless of the choice of V, the partial signed areas of the overlap of the triangles cancel, leaving only the area of the original triangle.

Area as an Analytic Quantity

The area of a 2D simple polygon $\mathcal{P}$ can also be derived using analytic methods from calculus. Let the vertices of the polygon be $V_i = (x_i, y_i)$ for $0 \le i \le n - 1$ and be counterclockwise ordered. The interior of the polygon is the simply connected region denoted R, so $\mathcal{P}$ is the boundary of region R. A formula for the area enclosed by the polygon is obtained by an application of Green's Theorem to a simply connected region R with boundary curve $\mathcal{P}$

$$\iint_R \vec{\nabla} \cdot F \, dx \, dy = \oint_{\mathcal{P}} F \cdot \vec{n} \, ds$$

where $F(x, y) = (F_1(x, y), F_2(x, y))$ is a differentiable vector field, $\vec{\nabla} \cdot F = \partial F_1 / \partial x + \partial F_2 / \partial y$ is the divergence of the vector field, and $\vec{n}$ is an outward-pointing normal vector to $\mathcal{P}$. This formula can be found in many standard texts on calculus (for example, Finney and Thomas 1996). If $\mathcal{P}$ is parameterized by $(x(t), y(t))$ for $t \in [a, b]$, a tangent vector is $\vec{t} = (x'(t), y'(t))$, where the prime indicates derivative with respect to t and an outer normal is $\vec{n} = (y'(t), -x'(t))$. The integral formula becomes

$$\iint_R \vec{\nabla} \cdot F \, dx \, dy = \int_a^b F(x(t), y(t)) \cdot (y'(t), -x'(t)) \, dt$$

The area formulation of Green's Theorem arises when we choose $F = (x, y)/2$. In this case $\vec{\nabla} \cdot F \equiv 1$ and the integral on the left represents the area of R, the value of which is determined by the integral on the right, an integral over the boundary $\mathcal{P}$ of R:

$$\text{Area}(R) = \frac{1}{2} \int_a^b x(t) y'(t) - y(t) x'(t) \, dt \tag{13.6}$$

Each edge of the polygon can be parameterized as $(x_i(t), y_i(t)) = V_i + t(V_{i+1} - V_i)$ for $t \in [0, 1]$. The integral over t becomes

$$\int_a^b x(t) y'(t) - y(t) x'(t) \, dt = \sum_{i=0}^{n-1} \int_0^1 x_i(t) y_i'(t) - y_i(t) x_i'(t) \, dt$$

$$= \sum_{i=0}^{n-1} \int_0^1 [x_i + t(x_{i+1} - x_i)][y_{i+1} - y_i]$$

$$- [y_i + t(y_{i+1} - y_i)][x_{i+1} - x_i] \, dt$$

$$= \sum_{i=0}^{n-1} [x_i + (x_{i+1} - x_i)/2][y_{i+1} - y_i]$$

$$- [y_i + (y_{i+1} - y_i)/2][x_{i+1} - x_i] \, dt$$

$$= \sum_{i=0}^{n-1} (x_i y_{i+1} - x_{i+1} y_i)$$

where $x_n = x_0$ and $y_n = y_0$. This is exactly Equation 13.4, obtained by algebraic means.

13.12.2   AREA OF A 3D POLYGON

Consider a 3D polygon $\mathcal{P}$ that encloses a simply connected region in the plane $\hat{n} \cdot X = c$, where $\hat{n}$ is unit length. Let the vertices be V_i for $0 \leq i \leq n - 1$, and assume that the vertices are counterclockwise ordered as you view the polygon from the side pointed to by $\hat{n}$. Equation 13.5 applies to the coordinates of the 3D polygon relative to the plane. If $\hat{u}$ and $\hat{w}$ are unit-length vectors such that $\hat{u}$, $\hat{w}$, and $\hat{n}$ are mutually perpendicular, then $V_i = x_i\hat{u} + y_i\hat{w} + c\hat{n}$ and the planar points are $(x_i, y_i) = (\hat{u} \cdot V_i, \hat{w} \cdot V_i)$ for all i. The area is

$$\text{Area}(\mathcal{P}) = \frac{1}{2} \sum_{i=0}^{n-1} (\hat{u} \cdot V_i)(\hat{w} \cdot (V_{i+1} - V_{i-1})) \tag{13.7}$$

This formula, although mathematically correct, requires more computing time to evaluate than necessary.

Area by Projection

A more efficient approach is to observe that if $\hat{n} = (n_0, n_1, n_2)$ is a unit-length normal and $n_2 \neq 0$, then the area of an object that lies in a plane with normal $\hat{n}$ is

$$\text{Area}(\text{object}) = \text{Area}(\text{Projection}_{xy}(\text{object}))/|n_2|$$

That is, the area of the projection of $\mathcal{P}$ onto the xy-plane is calculated and adjusted by the z-component of the normal. The result is a simple consequence of the surface area formula for the graph of a function. If the plane is $\hat{n} \cdot (x, y, z) = c$ and $n_2 \neq 0$, then $z = f(x, y) = (c - n_0 x - n_1 y)/n_2$. The surface area of the graph of a function f for (x, y) in a region R is

$$\iint_R \sqrt{1 + f_x^2 + f_y^2} \, dx \, dy$$

where $f_x = \partial f/\partial x$ and $f_y = \partial f/\partial y$ are the first-order partial derivatives of f. In the case of the plane mentioned earlier, $f_x = -n_0/n_2$, $f_y = -n_1/n_2$, and

$$\sqrt{1 + f_x^2 + f_y^2} = \sqrt{1 + \left(\frac{n_0}{n_2}\right)^2 + \left(\frac{n_1}{n_2}\right)^2}$$

$$= \sqrt{\frac{n_0^2 + n_1^2 + n_2^2}{n_2^2}}$$

$$= \frac{1}{|n_2|}$$

where the numerator of the fraction is 1 since $\hat{n}$ is assumed to be unit length. Therefore, $\iint_R \sqrt{1 + f_x^2 + f_y^2} \, dx \, dy = \iint_R 1/|n_2| dx dy = \text{Area}(R)/|n_2|$.

The area of a polygon in the plane with normal $\hat{n}$ can therefore be computed by calculating the area of the 2D polygon obtained by using only the (x, y) components of the polygon vertices, then dividing by the absolute value of the z-component of the plane normal. However, if n_2 is nearly zero, numerical problems might arise. Better is to use (x, y), (x, z), or (y, z) depending on which of $|n_2|$, $|n_1|$, or $|n_0|$ is largest, respectively. The final formula is

$$\text{Area}(\mathcal{P}) = \frac{1}{2} \begin{cases} \frac{1}{|n_2|} \sum_{i=0}^{n-1} x_i(y_{i+1} - y_{i-1}), & |n_2| = \max_i |n_i| \\ \frac{1}{|n_1|} \sum_{i=0}^{n-1} x_i(z_{i+1} - z_{i-1}), & |n_1| = \max_i |n_i| \\ \frac{1}{|n_0|} \sum_{i=0}^{n-1} y_i(z_{i+1} - z_{i-1}), & |n_0| = \max_i |n_i| \end{cases} \qquad (13.8)$$

Area by Stokes' Theorem

Another formula for the area appears in Arvo (1991) in an article entitled "Area of Planar Polygons and Volume of Polyhedra." That formula is

$$\text{Area}(R) = \frac{1}{2} \hat{n} \cdot \sum_{i=0}^{n-1} (P_i \times P_{i+1}) \qquad (13.9)$$

Given the counterclockwise ordering, the absolute values that appear in the actual formula are not necessary. They are useful if you have an ordered set of vertices, but you do not know if it is clockwise or counterclockwise. Replacing the formula $P_i = x_i U + y_i V + c\hat{n}$ in the triple scalar product yields $\hat{n} \cdot P_i \times P_{i+1} = x_i y_{i+1} - x_{i+1} y_i$, thereby showing the equivalence of the two formulas. However, $\hat{n}$ is factored outside the summation to reduce the n dot products to a single dot product. Each term $P_i \times P_{i+1}$ requires 6 multiplications and 3 additions. The sum of the n cross products requires $3(n-1)$ additions. The dot product with $\hat{n}$ requires 3 multiplications and 2 additions, and the final product by one-half requires 1 multiplication. The total calculation requires $6n + 4$ multiplications and $6n - 1$ additions. Clearly, Equation 13.8 is more efficient to compute than Equation 13.9.

The article in Arvo (1991) mentions that Equation 13.9 can be derived from Stokes' Theorem, which states

$$\iint_S \vec{\nabla} \times F \cdot \hat{n} \, d\sigma = \oint_C F \cdot d\vec{R}$$

where S is a manifold surface whose boundary is the bounded curve C. The vector field F is normal to S at each position. The curl of $F = (F_1(x, y, z), F_2(x, y, z), F_3(x, y, z))$ is

$$\vec{\nabla} \times F = \left(\frac{\partial F_3}{\partial y} - \frac{\partial F_2}{\partial z}, \frac{\partial F_1}{\partial z} - \frac{\partial F_3}{\partial x}, \frac{\partial F_2}{\partial x} - \frac{\partial F_1}{\partial y} \right)$$

the differential $d\vec{R} = (dx, dy, dz)$, but restricted to the curve C, and the differential $d\sigma$ represents an infinitesimal element of the surface S.

In the case of a polygon in 3D, S is the planar region bounded by the polygon, C is the polygon itself, $\hat{n}$ is a unit-length normal vector (the polygon vertices are counterclockwise ordered relative to $\hat{n}$), and $F = \hat{n} \times (x, y, z)/2$, in which case $\vec{\nabla} \times F = \hat{n}$. The area is

$$\text{Area}(S) = \iint_S d\sigma = \iint_S \hat{n} \cdot \hat{n} \, d\sigma = \oint_C \frac{1}{2}\hat{n} \times (x, y, z) \cdot (dx, dy, dz)$$

$$= \oint_C \frac{1}{2}\hat{n} \cdot (x, y, z) \times (dx, dy, dz)$$

If C is parameterized by $(x(t), y(t))$ for $t \in [a, b]$, the formula becomes

$$\text{Area}(S) = \frac{1}{2} \int_a^b \hat{n} \cdot (y(t)z'(t) - z(t)y'(t), z(t)x'(t) - x(t)z'(t), x(t)y'(t)$$

$$- y(t)x'(t)) \, dt$$

$$= \hat{n} \cdot \left(\frac{1}{2} \int_a^b y(t)z'(t) - z(t)y'(t) \, dt, \frac{1}{2} \int_a^b z(t)x'(t) - x(t)z'(t) \, dt, \right.$$

$$\left. \frac{1}{2} \int_a^b x(t)y'(t) - y(t)x'(t) \, dt \right)$$

Observe that each integral is of the form shown in Equation 13.6. Thus, the area of the polygon is a weighted sum of the areas of planar polygons obtained by projection of the original polygon onto the three coordinate planes, the weights being the components of the normal vector. Each of the integrals is given by Equation 13.5 with respect to the appropriate coordinates, so

$$\text{Area}(S) = \frac{1}{6}\hat{n} \cdot \left(\sum_{i=0}^{n-1} y_i(z_{i+1} - z_{i-1}), \sum_{i=0}^{n-1} z_i(x_{i+1} - x_{i-1}), \sum_{i=0}^{n-1} x_i(y_{i+1} - y_{i-1}) \right)$$

$$= \frac{1}{2}\hat{n} \cdot \sum_{i=0}^{n-1} P_i \times P_{i+1}$$

which is precisely Equation 13.9.

13.12.3 VOLUME OF A POLYHEDRON

The discussion of this section is the direct extension of the ideas for area of a polygon in 2D. Consider a tetrahedron $\langle V_0, V_1, V_2, V_3 \rangle$. Setting $V_i = (x_i, y_i, z_i)$, methods of basic algebra and trigonometry can be used to show that the *signed volume* of the tetrahedron is

$$\text{Volume}(V_0, V_1, V_2, V_3) = \frac{1}{6} \det \begin{bmatrix} 1 & 1 & 1 & 1 \\ x_0 & x_1 & x_2 & x_3 \\ y_0 & y_1 & y_2 & y_3 \\ z_0 & z_1 & z_2 & z_3 \end{bmatrix} \qquad (13.10)$$

Assuming the points are not all coplanar, half of the permutations produce a positive value and half produce the negative of that value.

Let $V = (x, y, z)$ be an arbitrary point in space. The following algebraic identity is true:

$$\begin{aligned} \text{Volume}(V_0, V_1, V_2, V_3) = \ & \text{Volume}(V, V_0, V_1, V_2) + \text{Volume}(V, V_1, V_2, V_3) \\ & + \text{Volume}(V, V_2, V_3, V_0) + \text{Volume}(V, V_3, V_0, V_1) \end{aligned} \qquad (13.11)$$

The identity can be verified by expanding the determinants on the right-hand side of the equation and performing algebraic operations to show that the result is the same as the determinant on the left-hand side. The geometric motivation is the same as in 2D. Some of the signed volume terms are positive; some are negative. Whenever two tetrahedra that share V overlap and have opposite sign volumes, there is cancellation.

The volume of a simple polyhedron P whose faces are all triangles can be computed by using the extension of Equation 13.3 to three dimensions. The faces are assumed to be counterclockwise oriented as viewed from the outside of the polyhedron. The point V is arbitrary; in practice it is chosen to be the zero vector $\vec{0}$.

$$\text{Volume}(P) = \sum_{\text{face } F} \text{Volume}(\vec{0}, F.V_0, F.V_1, F.V_2) \qquad (13.12)$$

The analytic construction using methods of calculus is presented below. Consider a polyhedron, denoted S, that encloses a simply connected region R in space. Let the n faces of the polyhedron be named S_i for $0 \le i < n$. Let each face S_i have unit-length outer normal $\hat{n}_i$ and vertices $P_{i,j}$ for $0 \le j < m(i)$, counterclockwise ordered when viewed from outside, where it is emphasized that the total number of vertices, $m(i)$, depends on the face i. A formula for the volume enclosed by the polyhedron is obtained by an application of the Divergence Theorem, the direct generalization of Green's Theorem from 2D to 3D, to a simply connected region R with boundary surface S

$$\iiint_R \vec{\nabla} \cdot F \, dx \, dy \, dz = \iint_S F \cdot \hat{n} \, d\sigma$$

where $F(x, y, z) = (F_1(x, y, z), F_2(x, y, z), F_3(x, y, z))$ is a differentiable vector field, $\vec{\nabla} \cdot F = \partial F_1/\partial x + \partial F_2/\partial y + \partial F_3/\partial z$ is the divergence of the vector field, $\hat{n}$ is an outward-pointing normal vector to the surface S, and $d\sigma$ represents an infinitesimal element of the surface. This formula can be found in many standard texts on calculus (for example, Finney and Thomas 1996).

The volume formulation of the Divergence Theorem arises when we choose $F = (x, y, z)/3$. In this case, $\vec{\nabla} \cdot F \equiv 1$ and

$$\text{Volume}(R) = \iiint_R dx\, dy\, dz = \frac{1}{3} \iint_S \hat{n} \cdot (x, y, z)\, d\sigma$$

Since the polyhedron is a disjoint union $S = \bigcup_{i=0}^{n-1} S_i$, the integral on the right becomes a sum of integrals, each integral related to a single polygonal face of the polyhedron

$$\iint_S \hat{n} \cdot (x, y, z)\, d\sigma = \sum_{i=0}^{n-1} \iint_{S_i} \hat{n}_i \cdot (x, y, z)\, d\sigma$$

where $\hat{n}_i$ is the unit-length outer normal to S_i. The plane of S_i is $\hat{n}_i \cdot (x, y, z) = c_i$ for some constant c_i. Any point on the polygon determines the constant, in particular $c = \hat{n}_i \cdot P_{0,i}$. The integral further reduces to

$$\sum_{i=0}^{n-1} \iint_{S_i} \hat{n}_i \cdot (x, y, z)\, d\sigma = \sum_{i=0}^{n-1} \iint_{S_i} c_i\, d\sigma = \sum_{i=0}^{n-1} c_i\, \text{Area}(S_i)$$

Substituting the formula from Equation 13.9, the volume formula is

$$\text{Volume}(R) = \frac{1}{6} \sum_{i=0}^{n-1} \left((\hat{n}_i \cdot P_{0,i}) \hat{n}_i \cdot \sum_{j=0}^{m(i)-1} (P_{i,j} \times P_{i,j+1}) \right) \qquad (13.13)$$

APPENDIX A

NUMERICAL METHODS

A.1 Solving Linear Systems

The general form of an $m \times n$ system of linear equations is

$$a_{1,1}x_1 + a_{1,2}x_2 + \cdots + a_{1,n}x_n = c_1$$
$$a_{2,1}x_1 + a_{2,2}x_2 + \cdots + a_{2,n}x_n = c_2$$
$$\vdots$$
$$a_{m,1}x_1 + a_{m,2}x_2 + \cdots + a_{m,n}x_n = c_n$$

Frequently, linear systems are written in matrix form:

$$\mathbf{A}\vec{x} = \vec{c}$$

$$\begin{bmatrix} a_{1,1} & a_{1,2} & \cdots & a_{1,n} \\ a_{2,1} & a_{2,2} & \cdots & a_{2,n} \\ & & \vdots & \\ a_{m,1} & a_{m,2} & \cdots & a_{m,n} \end{bmatrix} \begin{bmatrix} x_1 \\ x_2 \\ \vdots \\ x_n \end{bmatrix} = \begin{bmatrix} c_1 \\ c_2 \\ \vdots \\ c_n \end{bmatrix}$$

The matrix **A** is referred to as the *coefficient matrix*, and the matrix

$$
\begin{bmatrix}
a_{1,1} & a_{1,2} & \cdots & a_{1,n} & c_1 \\
a_{2,1} & a_{2,2} & \cdots & a_{2,n} & c_2 \\
& & \vdots & & \\
a_{m,1} & a_{m,2} & \cdots & a_{m,n} & c_n
\end{bmatrix}
$$

is known as the *augmented matrix*.

A.1.1 SPECIAL CASE: SOLVING A TRIANGULAR SYSTEM

In order to introduce a general method for solving square linear systems, let's look at a special case: that of a *triangular* system. Such a system is one in which $a_{i,j} = 0$ for $i > j$; it is called triangular because of its characteristic shape:

$$a_{1,1}x_1 + a_{1,2}x_2 + \cdots\cdots\cdots\cdots\cdots\cdots\cdots\cdots\cdots + a_{1,n}x_n = c_1$$

$$a_{2,2}x_2 + \cdots\cdots\cdots\cdots\cdots\cdots\cdots\cdots\cdots + a_{2,n}x_n = c_2$$

$$\vdots$$

$$a_{n-2,n-2}x_{n-2} + a_{n-2,n-1}x_{n-1} + a_{n-2,n}x_n = c_{n-2}$$

$$a_{n-1,n-1}x_{n-1} + a_{n-1,n}x_n = c_{n-1}$$

$$a_{n,n}x_n = c_n$$

We can solve this by a technique called *back substitution*. If we look at the last of the equations, we see that it has just one unknown (x_n), which we can solve trivially:

$$x_n = \frac{c_n}{a_{n,n}}$$

Now, since we have a solution for x_n, we can substitute it into the second-to-last equation and again trivially solve for x_{n-1}:

$$x_{n-1} = \frac{c_{n-1} - a_{n-1,n}\frac{c_n}{a_{n,n}}}{a_{n-1,n-1}}$$

and so on backward, until we have reached the first equation and solve for the first unknown, x_1. In general, x_k is computed by substituting the previously computed values of $x_n, x_{n-1}, \cdots, x_{k+1}$ in the kth equation:

$$x_k = \frac{c_k - \sum_{m=k+1}^{n} a_{k,m}x_m}{a_{k,k}}$$

A.1.2 GAUSSIAN ELIMINATION

Gaussian elimination is perhaps the most widely used method for solving general linear systems. It is based on the back-substitution technique we just covered: first, the system is converted step by step into triangular form, and then the previously described back-substitution technique is applied. In fact, we've already seen a (trivial) example of this algorithm in Section 2.4.2.

Gauss observed that a system of linear equations can be subjected to certain transformations and still have the same set of solutions. These modifications are

1. exchanging two rows

2. multiplying one row by a nonzero factor

3. replacing two rows with their sum

We saw transformations 2 and 3 in the earlier example, but you may be wondering what the point of exchanging rows might be. In the world of infinite-precision mathematics, it is irrelevant, but in the world of computer implementation, it is quite a beneficial transformation.

Consider a simple system of two equations in two unknowns, taken from Johnson and Riess (1982):

$$(1) \quad 0.0001x_1 + x_2 = 1$$
$$(2) \quad x_1 + x_2 = 2$$

If we want to eliminate the x_1 from (2), we'd need to multiply (1) by

$$-10000 \times (1): \quad -x_1 - 10000x_2 = -10000$$
$$1 \times (2): \quad x_1 + x_2 = 2$$
$$\text{Sum:} \quad -9999x_2 = -9998$$

yielding us a new system:

$$(1) \quad 0.0001x_1 + x_2 = 1$$
$$(2) \quad -9999x_2 = -9998$$

If we complete the solution by computing

$$x_2 = \frac{9998}{9999} \approx 0.99989999$$

and substitute this back into (1):

$$0.0001x_1 + x_2 = 1$$

$$0.0001x_1 + \frac{9998}{9999} = 1$$

$$0.0001x_1 = 1 - \frac{9998}{9999}$$

$$0.0001x_1 = \frac{1}{9999}$$

$$x_1 = \frac{10000}{9999}$$

$$x_1 \approx 1.00010001$$

One "problem" with this is that the above calculation is assuming infinite precision. Instead, consider what happens if we calculated with, say, six digits and stored only three. Then, if we again multiply (1) by $-10,000$, we would get

$$
\begin{array}{rrcr}
-10000 \times (1): & x_1 - 10000x_2 & = & -10000 \\
1 \times (2): & x_1 + x_2 & = & 2 \\
\hline
\text{Sum:} & -10000x_2 & = & -10000
\end{array}
$$

because of round-off, and $x_2 = 1$. If we substitute this back into (1), we'd get

$$0.0001x_1 + x_2 = 1$$

$$0.0001x_1 + 1 = 1$$

$$0.0001x_1 = 0$$

$$x_1 = 0$$

which is quite wrong. Of course, this example was contrived to show a worst-case scenario, but truncation and round-off errors will tend to compound themselves in each successive step.

Another precision-related problem can occur in the division step of the back substitution. Recall that the basic back-substitution step is

$$x_k = \frac{c_k - \sum_{m=k+1}^{n} a_{k,m} x_m}{a_{k,k}}$$

That is, the coefficient appears in the denominator. As division in a computer is most accurate when the divisor has as large an absolute value as possible, it would be best if the x_k with the largest coefficient (among all $x_{k,n}$) were the one subjected to the division.

Here's an example: Suppose we have the following system in three unknowns:

$$
\begin{aligned}
(1) \quad & x_1 - 3x_2 - 2x_3 = 6 \\
(2) \quad & 2x_1 - 4x_2 + 2x_3 = 18 \\
(3) \quad & -3x_1 + 8x_2 + 9x_3 = -9
\end{aligned}
$$

Thinking now of how this might be implemented in a computer program, we'd want to "rearrange" the system so that the largest coefficient of x_1 comes first

$$
\begin{aligned}
(1) \quad & -3x_1 + 8x_2 + 9x_3 = -9 \\
(2) \quad & 2x_1 - 4x_2 + 2x_3 = 18 \\
(3) \quad & x_1 - 3x_2 - 2x_3 = 6
\end{aligned}
$$

and then multiply (1) by 2 and (2) by 3 and add, yielding a new (2), and multiply (1) by 1 and (3) by 3 and add, yielding a new (3)

$$
\begin{aligned}
2 \times (1): \quad & -6x_1 + 16x_2 + 18x_3 = -18 \\
3 \times (2): \quad & 6x_1 - 12x_2 + 6x_3 = 54 \\
\hline
\text{Sum:} \quad & 4x_2 + 24x_3 = 36 \\
1 \times (1): \quad & -3x_1 + 8x_2 + 9x_3 = -9 \\
3 \times (3): \quad & 3x_1 - 9x_2 - 6x_3 = 18 \\
\hline
\text{Sum:} \quad & -1x_2 + 3x_3 = 9
\end{aligned}
$$

which gives us a new system:

$$
\begin{aligned}
(1) \quad & x_1 - 3x_2 + 2x_3 = 6 \\
(2) \quad & 4x_2 + 24x_3 = 36 \\
(3) \quad & -1x_2 + 3x_3 = 9
\end{aligned}
$$

We can then multiply (3) by 4 and add it to (2), yielding a new (3)

$$
\begin{aligned}
1 \times (2) \quad & 4x_2 + 24x_3 = 36 \\
4 \times (3) \quad & -4x_2 + 12x_3 = 36 \\
\hline
\text{Sum:} \quad & 36x_3 = 72
\end{aligned}
$$

which we can then solve by back substitution for $(1, -3, 2)$.

The pseudocode of the basic algorithm is

```
// j indexes columns (pivots)
for (j = 1 to n − 1) do
    // Pivot step
    find l such that a_{l,j} has the largest value among (a_{j,j}, a_{j+1,j}, ···, a_{n,j})
    exchange rows l and j

    // Elimination step
    // k indexes rows
    for (k = 1 to n) do
        // Form multiplier
        m = − a_{k,j}/a_{j,j}
        // Multiply row j by m and add to row k
        for (i = j + 1 to n) do
            a_{k,i} = a_{k,i} + m a_{k,j}
        // Multiply and add constant for row j
        c_k = c_k + m c_j

// Back substitute
x_n = c_n/a_{n,h}
for (k = n − 1 downto 1) do
    x_k = ( c_k − Σ_{m=k+1}^{n} a_{k,m} x_m ) / a_{k,k}
```

A.2 SYSTEMS OF POLYNOMIALS

The last section showed how to solve systems of linear equations. Given n equations in m unknowns, $\sum_{j=0}^{m} a_{ij} x_j = b_i$ for $0 \leq i < n$, let the system be represented in matrix form by $A\vec{x} = \vec{b}$, where $A = [a_{ij}]$ is $n \times m$, $\vec{x} = [x_j]$ is $m \times 1$, and $\vec{b} = [b_i]$ is $n \times 1$. The $n \times (m + 1)$ augmented matrix $[A|\vec{b}]$ is constructed and row-reduced to $[E|\vec{c}]$, a matrix that has the following properties:

- The first nonzero entry in each row is 1.
- If the first nonzero entry in row r is in column c, then all other entries in column c are 0.
- All zero rows occur last in the matrix.
- If the first nonzero entries in rows 1 through r occur in columns c_1 through c_r, then $c_1 < \ldots < c_r$.

If there is a row whose first m entries are zero, but the last entry is not zero, then the system of equations has no solution. If there is no such row, let $\rho = \text{rank}([E|\vec{c}])$

denote the number of nonzero rows of the augmented matrix. If $\rho = m$, the system has exactly one solution. In this case $\mathbf{E} = \mathbf{I}_m$, the $m \times m$ identity matrix, and the solution is $\vec{x} = \vec{c}$. If $\rho < m$, the system has infinitely many solutions, the solution set having dimension $m - \rho$. In this case, the zero rows can be omitted to obtain the $\rho \times (m + 1)$ matrix $[\mathbf{I}_\rho | \mathbf{F} | \vec{c}_+]$, where $\mathbf{I}_\rho$ is the $\rho \times \rho$ identity matrix, $\mathbf{F}$ is $\rho \times (m - \rho)$, and $\vec{c}_+$ consists of the first ρ entries of $\vec{c}$. Let $\vec{x}$ be partitioned into its first ρ components $\vec{x}_+$ and its remaining $m - \rho$ components $\vec{x}_-$. The general solution to the system is $\vec{x}_+ = \vec{c}_+ - \mathbf{F}\vec{x}_-$, where the $\vec{x}_-$ are the free parameters in the system.

Generic numerical linear system solvers for square systems ($n = m$) use row reduction methods so that (1) the order of time for the algorithm is small, in this case $O(n^3)$, and (2) the calculations are robust in the presence of a floating-point number system. It is possible to solve a linear system using cofactor expansions, but the order of time for the algorithm is $O(n!)$, which makes this an expensive method for large n. However, $n = 3$ for many computer graphics applications. The overhead for a generic row reduction solver normally uses more cycles than a simple cofactor expansion, and the matrix of coefficients for the application is usually not singular (or nearly singular) so that robustness is not an issue, so for this size system the cofactor expansion is a better choice.

Systems of polynomial equations also arise regularly in computer graphics applications. For example, determining the intersection points of two circles in 2D is equivalent to solving two quadratic equations in two unknowns. Determining if two ellipsoids in 3D intersect is equivalent to showing that a system of three quadratic equations in three unknowns does not have any real-valued solutions. Computing the intersection points between a line and a polynomial patch involves setting up and solving systems of polynomial equations. A method for solving such systems involves eliminating variables in much the same way that you do for linear systems. However, the formal calculations have a flavor of cofactor expansions rather than row reductions.

A.2.1 LINEAR EQUATIONS IN ONE FORMAL VARIABLE

To motivate the general idea, consider a single equation $a_0 + a_1 x = 0$ in the variable x. If $a_1 \neq 0$, there is a unique solution $x = -a_0/a_1$. If $a_1 = 0$ and $a_0 \neq 0$, there are no solutions. If $a_0 = a_1 = 0$, any x is a solution.

Now consider two equations in the same variable, $a_0 + a_1 x = 0$ and $b_0 + b_1 x = 0$, where $a_1 \neq 0$ and $b_1 \neq 0$. The first equation is multiplied by b_1, the second equation is multiplied by a_1, and the two equations are subtracted to obtain $a_0 b_1 - a_1 b_0 = 0$. This is a necessary condition that a value x be a solution to both equations. If the condition is satisfied, then solving the first equation yields $x = -a_0/a_1$. In terms of the row reduction method for linear systems discussed in the last section, $n = 2$, $m = 1$, and the augmented matrix with its reduction steps is

$$\begin{bmatrix} a_1 & -a_0 \\ b_1 & -b_0 \end{bmatrix} \sim \begin{bmatrix} a_1 b_1 & -a_0 b_1 \\ a_1 b_1 & -a_1 b_0 \end{bmatrix} \sim \begin{bmatrix} a_1 b_1 & -a_0 b_1 \\ 0 & a_0 b_1 - a_1 b_0 \end{bmatrix} \sim \begin{bmatrix} 1 & -a_0/a_1 \\ 0 & a_0 b_1 - a_1 b_0 \end{bmatrix}$$

The condition $a_0 b_1 - a_1 b_0 = 0$ is exactly the one mentioned in the previous section to guarantee that there is at least one solution.

The row reduction presented here is a formal construction. The existence of solutions and the solution x itself are obtained as functions of the parameters a_0, a_1, b_0, and b_1 of the system. These parameters are not necessarily known scalars and can themselves depend on other variables. Suppose that $a_0 = c_0 + c_1 y$ and $b_0 = d_0 + d_1 y$. The original two equations are $a_1 x + c_1 y + c_0 = 0$ and $b_1 x + d_1 y + d_0 = 0$, a system of two equations in two unknowns. The condition for existence of solutions is $0 = a_0 b_1 - a_1 b_0 = (c_0 + c_1 y) b_1 - a_1 (d_0 + d_1 y) = (b_1 c_0 - a_1 d_0) + (b_1 c_1 - a_1 d_1) y$. This condition is the result of starting with two equations in unknowns x and y and eliminating x to obtain a single equation for y. The y-equation has a unique solution as long as $b_1 c_1 - a_1 d_1 \neq 0$. Once y is computed, then $a_0 = c_0 + c_1 y$ is computed and $x = -a_0 / a_1$ is computed.

Let us modify the problem once more and additionally set $a_1 = e_0 + e_1 y$ and $b_1 = f_0 + f_1 y$. The two equations are

$$e_1 x y + e_0 x + c_1 y + c_0 = 0$$
$$f_1 x y + f_0 x + d_1 y + d_0 = 0$$

This is a system of two *quadratic* equations in two unknowns. The condition for existence of solutions is

$$0 = a_0 b_1 - a_1 b_0$$
$$= (c_0 + c_1 y)(f_0 + f_1 y) - (e_0 + e_1 y)(d_0 + d_1 y)$$
$$= (c_0 f_0 - e_0 d_0) + ((c_0 f_1 - e_0 d_1) + (c_1 f_0 - e_1 d_0))y + (c_1 f_1 - e_1 d_1)y^2$$

This equation has at most two real-valued solutions for y. Each solution leads to a value for $x = -a_0 / a_1 = -(c_0 + c_1 y)/(e_0 + e_1 y)$. The two equations define hyperbolas in the plane whose asymptotes are axis aligned. Geometrically the two hyperbolas can only intersect in at most two points.

Similar constructions arise when there are additional linear equations. For example, if $a_0 + a_1 x = 0$, $b_0 + b_1 x = 0$, and $c_0 + c_1 x = 0$, then solving pairwise leads to the conditions for existence: $a_0 b_1 - a_1 b_0 = 0$ and $a_0 c_1 - a_1 c_0 = 0$. If both are satisfied, then a solution is $x = -a_0 / a_1$. Allowing $a_0 = a_{00} + a_{10} y + a_{01} z$, $b_0 = b_{00} + b_{10} y + b_{01} z$, and $c_0 = c_{00} + c_{10} y + c_{01} z$ leads to three linear equations in three unknowns. The two conditions for existence are two linear equations in y and z, an elimination of the variable x. These two equations can be further reduced by eliminating y in the same manner. Note that in using this approach, there are many quantities of the form $AB - CD$. This is where our earlier comment comes in about the method having a "flavor of cofactor expansions." These terms are essentially determinants of 2×2 submatrices of the augmented matrix.

A.2.2   ANY-DEGREE EQUATIONS IN ONE FORMAL VARIABLE

Consider the polynomial equation in x, $f(x) = \sum_{i=0}^{n} a_i x^i = 0$. The roots to this equation can be found either by closed-form solutions when $n \leq 4$ or by numerical methods for any degree. If you have a second polynomial equation in the same variable, $g(x) = \sum_{j=0}^{m} b_j x^j = 0$, the problem is to determine conditions for existence of a solution, just like we did in the last section. The assumption is that $a_n \neq 0$ and $b_m \neq 0$. The last section handled the case when $n = m = 1$.

Case $n = 2$ and $m = 1$

The equations are $f(x) = a_2 x^2 + a_1 x + a_0 = 0$ and $g(x) = b_1 x + b_0 = 0$, where $a_2 \neq 0$ and $b_1 \neq 0$. It must also be the case that

$$0 = b_1 f(x) - a_2 x g(x) = (a_1 b_1 - a_2 b_0) x + a_0 b_1 =: c_1 x + c_0 \qquad (A.1)$$

where the coefficients c_0 and c_1 are defined by the last equality in the displayed equation. The two equations are now reduced to two linear equations, $b_1 x + b_0 = 0$ and $c_1 x + c_0 = 0$.

A bit more work must be done as compared to the last section. In that section the assumption was made that the leading coefficients were nonzero ($b_1 \neq 0$ and $c_1 \neq 0$). In the current construction, c_1 is derived from previously specified information, so we need to deal with the case when it is zero. If $c_1 = 0$, then $c_0 = 0$ is necessary for there to be a solution. Since $b_1 \neq 0$ by assumption, $c_0 = 0$ implies $a_0 = 0$. The condition $c_1 = 0$ implies $a_1 b_1 = a_2 b_0$. When $a_0 = 0$, a solution to the quadratic is $x = 0$. To also be a solution of $g(x) = 0$, we need $0 = g(0) = b_0$, which in turn implies $0 = a_2 b_0 = a_1 b_1$, or $a_1 = 0$ since $b_1 \neq 0$. In summary, this is the case $f(x) = a_2 x^2$ and $g(x) = b_1 x$. Also when $a_0 = 0$, another root of the quadratic is determined by $a_2 x + a_1 = 0$. This equation and $b_1 x + b_0 = 0$ are the case discussed in the last section and can be reduced appropriately.

We could also directly solve for $x = -b_0/b_1$, substitute into the quadratic, and multiply by b_1^2 to obtain the existence condition $a_2 b_0^2 - a_1 b_0 b_1 + a_0 b_1^2 = 0$.

Case $n = 2$ and $m = 2$

The equations are $f(x) = a_2 x^2 + a_1 x + a_0 = 0$ and $g(x) = b_2 x^2 + b_1 x + b_0 = 0$, where $a_2 \neq 0$ and $b_2 \neq 0$. It must also be the case that

$$0 = b_2 f(x) - a_2 g(x) = (a_1 b_2 - a_2 b_1) x + (a_0 b_2 - a_2 b_0) =: c_1 x + c_0 \quad (A.2)$$

The two quadratic equations are reduced to a single linear equation whose coefficients c_0 and c_1 are defined by the last equality in the displayed equation. If $c_1 = 0$, then for there to be solutions it is also necessary that $c_0 = 0$. In this case, consider that

$$0 = b_0 f(x) - a_0 g(x) = (a_2 b_0 - a_0 b_2) x^2 + (a_1 b_0 - a_0 b_1) x$$

$$= -c_0 x^2 + (a_1 b_0 - a_0 b_1) x = (a_1 b_0 - a_0 b_1) x$$

If $a_1 b_0 - a_0 b_1 \neq 0$, then the solution must be $x = 0$ and the consequences are $0 = f(0) = a_0$ and $0 = g(0) = b_0$. But this contradicts $a_1 b_0 - a_0 b_1 \neq 0$. Therefore, if $a_1 b_2 - a_2 b_1 = 0$ and $a_0 b_2 - a_2 b_0 = 0$, then $a_1 b_0 - a_0 b_1 = 0$ must follow. These three conditions imply that $(a_0, a_1, a_2) \times (b_0, b_1, b_2) = (0, 0, 0)$, so (b_0, b_1, b_2) is a multiple of (a_0, a_1, a_2) and the two quadratic equations were really only one equation. Now if $c_1 \neq 0$, we have reduced the problem to the case $n = 2$ and $m = 1$. This was discussed in the previous subsection.

A variation is to compute $a_2 g(x) - b_2 f(x) = (a_2 b_1 - a_1 b_2) x + (a_2 b_0 - a_0 b_2) = 0$ and $b_1 f(x) - a_1 g(x) = (a_2 b_1 - a_1 b_2) x^2 + (a_0 b_1 - a_1 b_0) = 0$. Solve for x in the first equation, $x = (a_0 b_2 - a_2 b_0)/(a_2 b_1 - a_1 b_2)$, and replace in the second equation and multiply by the denominator term to obtain

$$(a_2 b_1 - a_1 b_2)(a_1 b_0 - a_0 b_1) - (a_2 b_0 - a_0 b_2)^2 = 0$$

General Case $n \geq m$

The elimination process is recursive. Given that the elimination process has already been established for the cases with degrees smaller than n, we just need to reduce the current case $f(x)$ of degree n and $g(x)$ of degree $m \leq n$ to one with smaller degrees. It is assumed here that $a_n \neq 0$ and $b_m \neq 0$.

Define $h(x) = b_m f(x) - a_n x^{n-m} g(x)$. The conditions $f(x) = 0$ and $g(x) = 0$ imply that

$$0 = h(x)$$

$$= b_m f(x) - a_n x^{n-m} g(x)$$

$$= b_m \sum_{i=0}^{n} a_i x^i - a_n x^{n-m} \sum_{i=0}^{m} b_i x^i$$

$$= \sum_{i=0}^{n} a_i b_m x^i - \sum_{i=0}^{m} a_n b_i x^{n-m+i}$$

$$= \sum_{i=0}^{n-m-1} a_i b_m x^i + \sum_{i=n-m}^{n-1} (a_i b_m - a_n b_{i-(n-m)}) x^i$$

where it is understood that $\sum_{i=0}^{-1}(*) = 0$ (summations are zero whenever the upper index is smaller than the lower index). The polynomial $h(x)$ has degree at most $n - 1$.

Therefore, the polynomials $g(x)$ and $h(x)$ both have degrees smaller than n, so the smaller-degree algorithms already exist to solve them.

A.2.3 ANY-DEGREE EQUATIONS IN ANY FORMAL VARIABLES

A general system of polynomial equations can always be written formally as a system of polynomial equations in one of the variables. The conditions for existence, as constructed formally in the last section, are new polynomial equations in the remaining variables. Morever, these equations typically have higher degree than the original equations. As variables are eliminated, the degree of the reduced equations increases. Eventually the system is reduced to a single (high-degree) polynomial equation in one variable. Given solutions to this equation, they can be substituted into the previous conditions of existence to solve for other variables. This is similar to the back substitution that is used in linear system solvers.

Two Variables, One Quadratic Equation, One Linear Equation

The equations are $Q(x, y) = \alpha_{00} + \alpha_{10}x + \alpha_{01}y + \alpha_{20}x^2 + \alpha_{11}xy + \alpha_{02}y^2 = 0$ and $L(x, y) = \beta_{00} + \beta_{10}x + \beta_{01}y = 0$. These can be written formally as polynomials in x,

$$f(x) = (\alpha_{20})x^2 + (\alpha_{11}y + \alpha_{10})x + (\alpha_{02}y^2 + \alpha_{01}y + \alpha_{00}) = a_2x^2 + a_1x + a_0$$

and

$$g(x) = (\beta_{10})x + (\beta_{01}y + \beta_{00}) = b_1x + b_0$$

The condition for existence of $f(x) = 0$ and $g(x) = 0$ is $h(x) = h_0 + h_1x + h_2x^2 = 0$, where

$$h_0 = \alpha_{02}\beta_{00}^2 - \alpha_{01}\beta_{00}\beta_{01} + \alpha_{00}\beta_{01}^2$$

$$h_1 = \alpha_{10}\beta_{01}^2 + 2\alpha_{02}\beta_{00}\beta_{10} - \alpha_{11}\beta_{00}\beta_{01} - \alpha_{01}\beta_{01}\beta_{10}$$

$$h_2 = \alpha_{20}\beta_{01}^2 - \alpha_{11}\beta_{01}\beta_{10} + \alpha_{02}\beta_{10}^2$$

Given a root x to $h(x) = 0$, the formal value of y is obtained from $L(x, y) = 0$ as $y = -(\beta_{00} + \beta_{10}x)/\beta_{01}$.

EXAMPLE   Let $Q(x, y) = x^2 + xy + y^2 - 1$ and $L(x, y) = y - x + 1$. Solving $L(x, y) = 0$ yields $y = x - 1$. Replacing this in $Q(x, y) = 0$ leads to $3x^2 - 3x = 0$. The roots are $x_0 = 0$ and $x_1 = 1$. The corresponding y values are $y_0 = x_0 - 1 = -1$ and $y_1 = x_1 - 1 = 0$. The points $(0, -1)$ and $(1, 0)$ are the points of intersection between the quadratic curve defined by $Q(x, y) = 0$ and the line defined by $L(x, y) = 0$. ∎

Two Variables, Two Quadratic Equations

Consider two quadratic equations $F(x, y) = \alpha_{00} + \alpha_{10}x + \alpha_{01}y + \alpha_{20}x^2 + \alpha_{11}xy + \alpha_{02}y^2 = 0$ and $G(x, y) = \beta_{00} + \beta_{10}x + \beta_{01}y + \beta_{20}x^2 + \beta_{11}xy + \beta_{02}y^2 = 0$. These can be written formally as polynomials in x,

$$f(x) = (\alpha_{20})x^2 + (\alpha_{11}y + \alpha_{10})x + (\alpha_{02}y^2 + \alpha_{01}y + \alpha_{00}) = a_2x^2 + a_1x + a_0$$

and

$$g(x) = (\beta_{20})x^2 + (\beta_{11}y + \beta_{10})x + (\beta_{02}y^2 + \beta_{01}y + \beta_{00}) = b_2x^2 + b_1x + b_0$$

The condition for existence is

$$0 = (a_2b_1 - a_1b_2)(a_1b_0 - a_0b_1) - (a_2b_0 - a_0b_2)^2 = \sum_{i=0}^{4} h_iy^i =: h(y)$$

where

$$h_0 = d_{00}d_{10} - d_{20}^2$$

$$h_1 = d_{01}d_{10} + d_{00}d_{11} - 2d_{20}d_{21}$$

$$h_2 = d_{01}d_{11} + d_{00}d_{12} - d_{21}^2 - 2d_{20}d_{22}$$

$$h_3 = d_{01}d_{12} + d_{00}d_{13} - 2d_{21}d_{22}$$

$$h_4 = d_{01}d_{13} - d_{22}^2$$

with

$$d_{00} = \alpha_{22}\beta_{10} - \beta_{22}\alpha_{10}$$

$$d_{01} = \alpha_{22}\beta_{11} - \beta_{22}\alpha_{11}$$

$$d_{10} = \alpha_{10}\beta_{00} - \beta_{10}\alpha_{00}$$

$$d_{11} = \alpha_{11}\beta_{00} + \alpha_{10}\beta_{01} - \beta_{11}\alpha_{00} - \beta_{10}\alpha_{01}$$

$$d_{12} = \alpha_{11}\beta_{01} + \alpha_{10}\beta_{02} - \beta_{11}\alpha_{01} - \beta_{10}\alpha_{02}$$

$$d_{13} = \alpha_{11}\beta_{02} - \beta_{11}\alpha_{02}$$

$$d_{20} = \alpha_{22}\beta_{00} - \beta_{22}\alpha_{00}$$

$$d_{21} = \alpha_{22}\beta_{01} - \beta_{22}\alpha_{01}$$

$$d_{22} = \alpha_{22}\beta_{02} - \beta_{22}\alpha_{02}$$

The roots $h(y) = 0$ are computed. Each root $\bar{y}$ can be used to obtain $f(x) = F(x, \bar{y}) = 0$ and $g(x) = G(x, \bar{y}) = 0$. Two quadratic equations in one variable have a solution defined by Equation A.2, $x = (a_2 b_0 - a_0 b_2)/(a_1 b_2 - a_2 b_1)$, where $a_2 = \alpha_{20}$, $a_1 = \alpha_{11}\bar{y} + \alpha_{10}$, $a_0 = \alpha_{02}\bar{y}^2 + \alpha_{01}\bar{y} + \alpha_{00}$, $b_2 = \beta_{20}$, $b_1 = \beta_{11}\bar{y} + \beta_{10}$, and $b_0 = \beta_{02}\bar{y}^2 + \beta_{01}\bar{y} + \beta_{00}$.

EXAMPLE   Let $F(x, y) = x^2 + y^2 - 1$ and $G(x, y) = (x + y)^2 + 4(x - y)^2 - 4$. Then $h(y) = -36y^4 + 36y^2 - 1$, which has roots ± 0.169102 and ± 0.985599. The corresponding x values are defined by $x = (a_2 b_0 - a_0 b_2)/(a_1 b_2 - a_2 b_1) = 1/(6y)$, ± 0.985599 and ± 0.169102. ∎

Three Variables, One Quadratic Equation, Two Linear Equations

Let the three equations be $F(x, y, z) = \sum_{0 \le i+j+k \le 2} \alpha_{ijk} x^i y^j z^k$, $G(x, y, z) = \sum_{0 \le i+j+k \le 1} \beta_{ijk} x^i y^j z^k$, and $H(x, y, z) = \sum_{0 \le i+j+k \le 1} \gamma_{ijk} x^i y^j z^k$. As polynomial equations in x, these are written as $f(x) = a_2 x^2 + a_1 x + a_0 = 0$, $g(x) = b_1 x + b_0 = 0$, and $h(x) = c_1 x + c_0 = 0$, where

$$a_0 = \sum_{0 \le j+k \le 2} \alpha_{0jk} y^j z^k$$

$$a_1 = \sum_{0 \le j+k \le 1} \alpha_{1jk} y^j z^k$$

$$a_2 = \alpha_{200}$$

$$b_0 = \beta_{010} y + \beta_{001} z + \beta_{000}$$

$$b_1 = \beta_{100}$$

$$c_0 = \gamma_{010} y + \gamma_{001} z + \gamma_{000}$$

$$c_1 = \gamma_{100}$$

The condition for existence of x-solutions to $f = 0$ and $g = 0$ is

$$0 = a_2 b_0^2 - a_1 b_0 b_1 + a_0 b_1^2 = \sum_{0 \le i+j \le 2} d_{ij} y^i z^j =: D(y, z)$$

where

$$d_{20} = \alpha_{200}\beta_{010}^2 - \beta_{100}\alpha_{110}\beta_{010} + \beta_{100}^2\alpha_{020}$$

$$d_{11} = 2\alpha_{200}\beta_{010}\beta_{001} - \beta_{100}(\alpha_{110}\beta_{001} + \alpha_{101}\beta_{010}) + \beta_{100}^2\alpha_{011}$$

$$d_{02} = \alpha_{200}\beta_{001}^2 - \beta_{100}\alpha_{101}\beta_{001} + \beta_{100}^2\alpha_{002}$$

$$d_{10} = 2\alpha_{200}\beta_{010}\beta_{000} - \beta_{100}(\alpha_{110}\beta_{000} + \alpha_{100}\beta_{010}) + \beta_{100}^2\alpha_{010}$$

$$d_{01} = 2\alpha_{200}\beta_{001}\beta_{000} - \beta_{100}(\alpha_{101}\beta_{000} + \alpha_{100}\beta_{001}) + \beta_{100}^2\alpha_{001}$$

$$d_{00} = \alpha_{200}\beta_{000}^2 - \beta_{100}\alpha_{100}\beta_{000} + \beta_{100}^2\alpha_{000}$$

The condition for existence of x-solutions to $g = 0$ and $h = 0$ is

$$0 = b_0 c_1 - b_1 c_0 = e_{10}y + e_{01}z + e_{00} =: E(y, z)$$

where

$$e_{10} = \beta_{010}\gamma_{100} - \gamma_{010}\beta_{100}$$

$$e_{01} = \beta_{001}\gamma_{100} - \gamma_{001}\beta_{100}$$

$$e_{00} = \beta_{000}\gamma_{100} - \gamma_{000}\beta_{100}$$

We now have two equations in two unknowns, a quadratic equation $D(y, z) = 0$ and a linear equation $E(y, z) = 0$. This case was handled in an earlier section. For each solution $(\bar{y}, \bar{z})$, a corresponding x-value is computed from Equation A.1, $x = a_0 b_1/(a_2 b_0 - a_1 b_1)$.

EXAMPLE   Let $F(x, y, z) = x^2 + y^2 + z^2 - 1$, $G(x, y, z) = x + y + z$, and $H(x, y, z) = x + y - z$. The coefficient polynomials are $a_2 = 1$, $a_1 = 0$, $a_0 = y^2 + z^2 - 1$, $b_1 = 1$, $b_0 = y + z$, $c_1 = 1$, and $c_0 = y - z$. The intermediate polynomials are $D(y, z) = 2y^2 + 2yz + 2z^2 - 1$ and $E(y, z) = 2z$. The condition $E(y, z) = 0$ implies $\bar{z} = 0$. Replacing this in the other intermediate polynomial produces $0 = D(y, 0) = 2y^2 - 1$, so $\bar{y} = \pm 1/\sqrt{2}$. The corresponding x-values are determined by $x = a_0 b_1/(a_2 b_0 - a_1 b_1) = (y^2 + z^2 - 1)/(y + z)$, so $\bar{x} = \mp 1/\sqrt{2}$. There are two points of intersection, $(-1/\sqrt{2}, 1/\sqrt{2}, 0)$ and $(1/\sqrt{2}, -1/\sqrt{2}, 0)$. ∎

Three Variables, Two Quadratic Equations, One Linear Equation

Let the three equations be $F(x, y, z) = \sum_{0 \le i+j+k \le 2} \alpha_{ijk}x^i y^j z^k$, $G(x, y, z) = \sum_{0 \le i+j+k \le 2} \beta_{ijk}x^i y^j z^k$, and $H(x, y, z) = \sum_{0 \le i+j+k \le 1} \gamma_{ijk}x^i y^j z^k$. As polynomial equations in x, these are written as $f(x) = a_2 x^2 + a_1 x + a_0 = 0$, $g(x) = b_2 x^2 + b_1 x +$

$b_0 = 0$, and $h(x) = c_1 x + c_0 = 0$, where

$$a_0 = \sum_{0 \le j+k \le 2} \alpha_{0jk} y^j z^k$$

$$a_1 = \sum_{0 \le j+k \le 1} \alpha_{1jk} y^j z^k$$

$$a_2 = \alpha_{200}$$

$$b_0 = \sum_{0 \le j+k \le 2} \beta_{0jk} y^j z^k$$

$$b_1 = \sum_{0 \le j+k \le 1} \beta_{1jk} y^j z^k$$

$$b_2 = \beta_{200}$$

$$c_0 = \gamma_{010} y + \gamma_{001} z + \gamma_{000}$$

$$c_1 = \gamma_{100}$$

The condition for existence of x-solutions to $f = 0$ and $h = 0$ is

$$0 = a_2 c_0^2 - a_1 c_0 c_1 + a_0 c_1^2 = \sum_{0 \le i+j \le 2} d_{ij} y^i z^j =: D(y, z)$$

where

$$d_{20} = \alpha_{200} \gamma_{010}^2 - \gamma_{100} \alpha_{110} \gamma_{010} + \gamma_{100}^2 \alpha_{020}$$

$$d_{11} = 2\alpha_{200} \gamma_{010} \gamma_{001} - \gamma_{100}(\alpha_{110}\gamma_{001} + \alpha_{101}\gamma_{010}) + \gamma_{100}^2 \alpha_{011}$$

$$d_{02} = \alpha_{200} \gamma_{001}^2 - \gamma_{100} \alpha_{101} \gamma_{001} + \gamma_{100}^2 \alpha_{002}$$

$$d_{10} = 2\alpha_{200} \gamma_{010} \gamma_{000} - \gamma_{100}(\alpha_{110}\gamma_{000} + \alpha_{100}\gamma_{010}) + \gamma_{100}^2 \alpha_{010}$$

$$d_{01} = 2\alpha_{200} \gamma_{001} \gamma_{000} - \gamma_{100}(\alpha_{101}\gamma_{000} + \alpha_{100}\gamma_{001}) + \gamma_{100}^2 \alpha_{001}$$

$$d_{00} = \alpha_{200} \gamma_{000}^2 - \gamma_{100} \alpha_{100} \gamma_{000} + \gamma_{100}^2 \alpha_{000}$$

The condition for existence of x-solutions to $g = 0$ and $h = 0$ is

$$0 = b_2 c_0^2 - b_1 c_0 c_1 + b_0 c_1^2 = \sum_{0 \le i+j \le 2} e_{ij} y^i z^j =: E(y, z)$$

where

$$e_{20} = \beta_{200}\gamma_{010}^2 - \gamma_{100}\beta_{110}\gamma_{010} + \gamma_{100}^2\beta_{020}$$

$$e_{11} = 2\beta_{200}\gamma_{010}\gamma_{001} - \gamma_{100}(\beta_{110}\gamma_{001} + \beta_{101}\gamma_{010}) + \gamma_{100}^2\beta_{011}$$

$$e_{02} = \beta_{200}\gamma_{001}^2 - \gamma_{100}\beta_{101}\gamma_{001} + \gamma_{100}^2\beta_{002}$$

$$e_{10} = 2\beta_{200}\gamma_{010}\gamma_{000} - \gamma_{100}(\beta_{110}\gamma_{000} + \beta_{100}\gamma_{010}) + \gamma_{100}^2\beta_{010}$$

$$e_{01} = 2\beta_{200}\gamma_{001}\gamma_{000} - \gamma_{100}(\beta_{101}\gamma_{000} + \beta_{100}\gamma_{001}) + \gamma_{100}^2\beta_{001}$$

$$e_{00} = \beta_{200}\gamma_{000}^2 - \gamma_{100}\beta_{100}\gamma_{000} + \gamma_{100}^2\beta_{000}$$

We now have two equations in two unknowns, quadratic equations $D(y, z) = 0$ and $E(y, z) = 0$. This case was handled in an earlier section. For each solution $(\bar{y}, \bar{z})$, a corresponding x-value is computed from Equation A.1, $x = a_0b_1/(a_2b_0 - a_1b_1)$. The linear equation may be used instead to solve for x assuming that the coefficient of x is not zero.

EXAMPLE   Let $F(x, y, z) = x^2 + y^2 + z^2 - 1$ (a sphere), $G(x, y, z) = 4x^2 + 9y^2 + 36z^2 - 36$ (an ellipsoid), and $H(x, y, z) = x + y + z$ (a plane). The coefficient polynomials are $a_2 = 1$, $a_1 = 0$, $a_0 = y^2 + z^2 - 1$, $b_2 = 4$, $b_1 = 0$, $b_0 = 9y^2 + 36z^2 - 36$, $c_1 = 1$, and $c_0 = y + z$. The intermediate polynomials are $D(y, z) = 2y^2 + 2yz + 2z^2 - 1$ and $E(y, z) = 13y^2 + 8yz + 40z^2 - 36$. Now we are back to two quadratic equations in two unknowns, a problem solved earlier. The quartic polynomial obtained by eliminating y is $h(z) = -3556z^4 + 7012z^2 - 3481$. This polynomial has no real-valued solutions, so the polynomial system has no real-valued solutions. ∎

EXAMPLE   Let $F(x, y, z) = x^2 + y^2 + z^2 - 1$, $G(x, y, z) = x^2 + 16y^2 + 36z^2 - 4$, and $H(x, y, z) = x + y + 8z$. The coefficient polynomials are $a_2 = 1$, $a_1 = 0$, $a_0 = y^2 + z^2 - 1$, $b_2 = 1$, $b_1 = 0$, $b_0 = 16y^2 + 36z^2 - 4$, $c_1 = 1$, and $c_0 = y + 8z$. The intermediate polynomials are $D(y, z) = 2y^2 + 16yz + 65z^2 - 1$ and $E(y, z) = 17y^2 + 16yz + 100z^2 - 4$. The two quadratic equations $D(y, z) = 0$ and $E(y, z) = 0$ are reduced to a single quartic equation $0 = h(z) = -953425z^4 + 27810z^2 - 81$. The roots $\bar{z}$ are ±0.160893 and ±0.0572877. The $\bar{y}$-values are determined using Equation A.2, remembering that the current problem is in terms of y and z, not x and y. The equation is $\bar{y} = (-905\bar{z}^2 + 9)/(240\bar{z})$, so the $\bar{y}$-values corresponding to the $\bar{z}$-values are ∓0.373626 and ±0.438568. The $\bar{x}$-values are determined using Equation A.1, $\bar{x} = (\bar{y}^2 + \bar{z}^2 - 1)/(\bar{y} + 8\bar{z})$. The pair $(\bar{y}, \bar{z}) = (-0.373627, 0.160893)$ leads to $\bar{x} = -0.913520$, so the intersection point is $(\bar{x}, \bar{y}, \bar{z}) = (-0.913520, -0.373627, 0.160893)$. The other intersections are $(0.913520, 0.373627, -0.160893)$, $(-0.89687, 0.438568, 0.0572877)$, and $(0.89687, -0.438568, -0.0572877)$. As mentioned in the general discussion, we could have used the linear equation to solve for $\bar{x} = -(\bar{y} + 8\bar{z})$. ∎

Three Variables, Three Quadratic Equations

Let the three equations be $F(x, y, z) = \sum_{0 \le i+j+k \le 2} \alpha_{ijk} x^i y^j z^k$, $G(x, y, z) = \sum_{0 \le i+j+k \le 2} \beta_{ijk} x^i y^j z^k$, and $H(x, y, z) = \sum_{0 \le i+j+k \le 2} \gamma_{ijk} x^i y^j z^k$. As polynomial equations in x, these are written as $f(x) = a_2 x^2 + a_1 x + a_0 = 0$, $g(x) = b_2 x^2 + b_1 x + b_0 = 0$, and $h(x) = c_2 x^2 + c_1 x + c_0 = 0$, where

$$a_0 = \sum_{0 \le j+k \le 2} \alpha_{0jk} y^j z^k$$

$$a_1 = \sum_{0 \le j+k \le 1} \alpha_{1jk} y^j z^k$$

$$a_2 = \alpha_{200}$$

$$b_0 = \sum_{0 \le j+k \le 2} \beta_{0jk} y^j z^k$$

$$b_1 = \sum_{0 \le j+k \le 1} \beta_{1jk} y^j z^k$$

$$b_2 = \beta_{200}$$

$$c_0 = \sum_{0 \le j+k \le 2} \gamma_{0jk} y^j z^k$$

$$c_1 = \sum_{0 \le j+k \le 1} \gamma_{1jk} y^j z^k$$

$$c_2 = \gamma_{200}$$

The condition for existence of x-solutions to $f = 0$ and $g = 0$ is

$$0 = (a_2 b_1 - a_1 b_2)(a_1 b_0 - a_0 b_1) - (a_2 b_0 - a_0 b_2)^2 = \sum_{0 \le i+j \le 4} d_{ij} y^i z^k =: D(y, z)$$

The condition for existence of x-solutions to $f = 0$ and $h = 0$ is

$$0 = (a_2 c_1 - a_1 c_2)(a_1 c_0 - a_0 c_1) - (a_2 c_0 - a_0 c_2)^2 = \sum_{0 \le i+j \le 4} e_{ij} y^i z^k =: E(y, z)$$

The two polynomials $D(y, z)$ and $E(y, z)$ are fourth degree. The equations $D(y, z) = 0$ and $E(y, z) = 0$ can be written formally as polynomial equations in y, $d(y) = \sum_{i=0}^{4} d_i y^i$ and $e(y) = \sum_{i=0}^{4} e_i y^i$, where the coefficients are polynomials in z with degree($d_i(z)$) $= 4 - i$ and degree($e_i(z)$) $= 4 - i$. The construction for eliminating y results in a polynomial in z obtained by computing the determinant of the

Bézout matrix for d and e, the 4×4 matrix $\mathbf{M} = [m_{ij}]$ with

$$m_{ij} = \sum_{k=\max(4-j,4-i)}^{\min(4,7-i-j)} w_{k,7-i-j-k}$$

for $0 \le i \le 3$ and $0 \le j \le 3$, with $w_{i,j} = d_i e_j - d_j e_i$ for $0 \le i \le 4$ and $0 \le j \le 4$. In expanded form,

$$\mathbf{M} = \begin{bmatrix} w_{4,3} & w_{4,2} & w_{4,1} & w_{4,0} \\ w_{4,2} & w_{3,2} + w_{4,1} & w_{3,1} + w_{4,0} & w_{3,0} \\ w_{4,1} & w_{3,1} + w_{4,0} & w_{2,1} + w_{3,0} & w_{2,0} \\ w_{4,0} & w_{3,0} & w_{2,0} & w_{1,0} \end{bmatrix}$$

The degree of $w_{i,j}$ is $8 - i - j$. The Bézout determinant $\det(\mathbf{M}(z))$ is a polynomial of degree 16 in z. For each solution $\bar{z}$ to $\det(\mathbf{M}(z)) = 0$, we need to find corresponding values $\bar{x}$ and $\bar{y}$.

Using the Bézout method hides the intermediate polynomials that were conveniently used in the previous cases to compute the other variables. Let us find them explicitly. The elimination process may be applied directly to $d(y) = d_0 + d_1 y + d_2 y^2 + d_3 y^3 + d_4 y^4$ and $e(y) = e_0 + e_1 y + e_2 y^2 + e_3 y^3 + e_4 y^4$. Define $f(y) = e_4 d(y) - d_4 e(y) = f_0 + f_1 y + f_2 y^2 + f_3 y^3$. The coefficients are $f_i = e_4 d_i - e_i d_4$ for all i. Define $g(y) = f_3 d(y) - d_4 y f(y) = g_0 + g_1 y + g_2 y^2 + g_3 y^3$. The coefficients are $g_0 = f_3 d_0$, $g_1 = f_3 d_1 - f_0 d_4$, $g_2 = f_3 d_2 - f_1 d_4$, and $g_3 = f_3 d_3 - f_2 d_4$. Now $f(y)$ and $g(y)$ are cubic polynomials. The process is repeated. Define $h(y) = g_3 f(y) - f_3 g(y) = h_0 + h_1 y + h_2 y^2$, where $h_i = g_3 f_i - f_3 g_i$ for all i. Define $m(y) = h_2 f(y) - f_3 y h(y) = m_0 + m_1 y + m_2 y^2$, where $m_0 = h_2 f_0$, $m_1 = h_2 f_1 - h_0 f_3$, and $m_2 = h_2 f_2 - h_1 f_3$. Now $h(y)$ and $m(y)$ are quadratic polynomials. As we saw earlier, if the polynomials have a common solution, it must be $\bar{y} = (h_2 m_0 - h_0 m_2)/(h_1 m_2 - h_2 m_1)$. Because the d_i and e_i coefficients depend on $\bar{z}$, the values h_i and m_i depend on $\bar{z}$. Thus, given a value for $\bar{z}$, we compute a corresponding value $\bar{y}$. To compute $\bar{x}$ for a specified pair $(\bar{y}, \bar{z})$, $F(x, \bar{y}, \bar{z}) = a_2 x^2 + a_1 x + a_0 = 0$ and $G(x, \bar{y}, \bar{z}) = b_2 x^2 + b_1 x + b_0 = 0$ are two quadratic equations in the unknown x, so a common solution is $\bar{x} = (a_2 b_0 - a_0 b_2)/(a_1 b_2 - a_2 b_1)$.

EXAMPLE   Let $F(x, y, z) = (x - 1)^2 + y^2 + z^2 - 4$ (sphere), $G(x, y, z) = x^2 + 4y^2 - 4z$ (paraboloid), and $H(x, y, z) = x^2 + 4(y - 1)^2 + z^2 - 4$ (ellipsoid). The polynomial $d(y)$ with coefficients dependent on z that represents $D(y, z)$ has coefficients $d_0 = -9 + 40z - 10z^2 - 8z^3 - z^4$, $d_1 = 0$, $d_2 = -34 + 24z + 6z^2$, $d_3 = 0$, and $d_4 = -9$. The polynomial $e(y)$ with coefficients dependent on z that represents $E(y, z)$ has coefficients $e_0 = -9 - 4z^2$, $e_1 = 80$, $e_2 = 98$, $e_3 = 48$, and $e_4 = -9$. The w terms for the matrix $\mathbf{M}$ are

$$w_{1,0} = 720 - 3200z + 800z^2 + 640z^3 + 80z^4$$

$$w_{2,0} = -576 + 3704z - 898z^2 - 880z^3 - 122z^4$$

$$w_{3,0} = 432 - 1920z + 480z^2 + 384z^3 + 48z^4$$

$$w_{4,0} = 360z - 54z^2 - 72z^3 - 9z^4$$

$$w_{2,1} = -2720 + 1920z + 480z^2$$

$$w_{3,1} = 0$$

$$w_{3,2} = 1632 - 1152z - 288z^2$$

$$w_{4,1} = -720$$

$$w_{4,2} = 576 + 216z + 54z^2$$

$$w_{4,3} = -432$$

The determinant of $\mathbf{M}$ is degree 16 and has coefficients μ_i for $0 \leq i \leq 16$ given by

$\mu_0 =$	801868087296	$\mu_9 =$	2899639296
$\mu_1 =$	-4288520650752	$\mu_{10} =$	-105691392
$\mu_2 =$	4852953907200	$\mu_{11} =$	-211071744
$\mu_3 =$	-779593973760	$\mu_{12} =$	4082400
$\mu_4 =$	-1115385790464	$\mu_{13} =$	13856832
$\mu_5 =$	307850969088	$\mu_{14} =$	2624400
$\mu_6 =$	109063397376	$\mu_{15} =$	209952
$\mu_7 =$	-34894540800	$\mu_{16} =$	6561
$\mu_8 =$	-3305131776		

The real-valued roots to $\det(\mathbf{M})(z) = 0$ are 0.258255, 1.46202, 1.60199, and 1.63258. Observe that the coefficients of the polynomial are quite large. For numerical stability, for each z you should evaluate the determinant using Gaussian elimination rather than actually computing the μ_i as a preprocess.

The cubic polynomial $f(y)$ has coefficients that depend on z:

$$f_0 = -360z + 54z^2 + 72z^3 + 9z^4$$

$$f_1 = 720$$

$$f_2 = -576 - 216z - 54z^2$$

$$f_3 = 432$$

The cubic polynomial $g(y)$ has coefficients that depend on z:

$$g_0 = -3888 + 17280z - 4320z^2 - 3456z^3 + 432z^4$$

$$g_1 = -3240z + 486z^2 + 648z^3 + 81z^4$$

$$g_2 = -8208 + 10368z + 2592z^2$$

$$g_3 = -5184 - 1944z - 486z^2$$

The quadratic polynomial $h(y)$ has coefficients that depend on z:

$$h_0 = 1679616 - 5598720z + 2286144z^2 + 1189728z^3 - 26244z^4 - 52488z^5 - 4374z^6$$

$$h_1 = -3732480 - 559872z^2 - 279936z^3 - 34992z^4$$

$$h_2 = 6531840 - 2239488z - 139968z^2 + 209952z^3 + 26244z^4$$

The quadratic polynomial $m(y)$ has coefficients that depend on z:

$$m_0 = -2351462400z + 1158935040z^2 + 399748608z^3 - 185597568z^4$$
$$- 28343520z^5 + 15274008z^6 + 3779136z^7 + 236196z^8$$

$$m_1 = 3977330688 + 806215680z - 1088391168z^2 - 362797056z^3 + 30233088z^4$$
$$+ 22674816z^5 + 1889568z^6$$

$$m_2 = -2149908480 - 120932352z + 453496320z^2 - 37791360z^4 - 17006112z^5$$
$$- 1417176z^6$$

The $\bar{z}$-values are $\{0.258225, 1.46202, 1.60199, 1.63258\}$. The corresponding $\bar{y}$-values are computed from $\bar{y} = (h_2(\bar{z})m_0(\bar{z}) - h_0(\bar{z})m_2(\bar{z}))/(h_1(\bar{z})m_2(\bar{z}) - h_2(\bar{z})m_1(\bar{z}))$. The ordered set of such values is $\{0.137429, 0.336959, 1.18963, 1.14945\}$. The corresponding $\bar{x}$-values are computed from $\bar{x} = (a_2(\bar{y}, \bar{z})b_0(\bar{y}, \bar{z}) - a_0(\bar{y}, \bar{z})b_2(\bar{y}, \bar{z}))/(a_1(\bar{y}, \bar{z})b_2(\bar{y}, \bar{z}) - a_2(\bar{y}, \bar{z})b_1(\bar{y}, \bar{z}))$. The ordered set of such values is $\{-0.97854, 2.32248, 0.864348, 1.11596\}$. As it turns out, only the $(\bar{x}, \bar{y}, \bar{z})$ triples $(-0.97854, 0.137429, 0.258225)$ and $(1.11596, 1.14945, 1.53258)$ are true intersection points. The other two are extraneous solutions (the H-values are 7.18718 and -0.542698, respectively), an occurrence that is to be expected since the elimination process increases the degrees of the polynomials, thereby potentially introducing roots that are not related to the intersection problem. ∎

A.3 Matrix Decompositions

We present a collection of various matrix factorizations that arise in many computer graphics applications. An excellent reference for numerical methods relating to matrices is Golub and Van Loan (1993b). An excellent reference for matrix analysis is Horn and Johnson (1985).

A.3.1 Euler Angle Factorization

Rotations about the coordinate axes are easy to define and work with. Rotation about the x-axis by angle θ is

$$\mathbf{R}_x(\theta) = \begin{bmatrix} 1 & 0 & 0 \\ 0 & \cos\theta & -\sin\theta \\ 0 & \sin\theta & \cos\theta \end{bmatrix}$$

where $\theta > 0$ indicates a counterclockwise rotation in the plane $x = 0$. The observer is assumed to be positioned on the side of the plane with $x > 0$ and looking at the origin.

Rotation about the y-axis by angle θ is

$$\mathbf{R}_y(\theta) = \begin{bmatrix} \cos\theta & 0 & \sin\theta \\ 0 & 1 & 0 \\ -\sin\theta & 0 & \cos\theta \end{bmatrix}$$

where $\theta > 0$ indicates a counterclockwise rotation in the plane $y = 0$. The observer is assumed to be positioned on the side of the plane with $y > 0$ and looking at the origin.

Rotation about the z-axis by angle θ is

$$\mathbf{R}_z(\theta) = \begin{bmatrix} \cos\theta & -\sin\theta & 0 \\ \sin\theta & \cos\theta & 0 \\ 0 & 0 & 1 \end{bmatrix}$$

where $\theta > 0$ indicates a counterclockwise rotation in the plane $z = 0$. The observer is assumed to be positioned on the side of the plane with $z > 0$ and looking at the origin.

Rotation by an angle θ about an arbitrary axis containing the origin and having unit-length direction $\hat{u} = (u_x, u_y, u_z)$ is given by

$$\mathbf{R}_{\hat{u}}(\theta) = \mathbf{I} + (\sin\theta)\mathbf{S} + (1 - \cos\theta)\mathbf{S}^2$$

where I is the identity matrix,

$$S = \begin{bmatrix} 0 & -u_z & u_y \\ u_z & 0 & -u_x \\ -u_y & u_x & 0 \end{bmatrix}$$

and $\theta > 0$ indicates a counterclockwise rotation in the plane $\hat{u} \cdot (x, y, z) = 0$. The observer is assumed to be positioned on the side of the plane to which $\hat{u}$ points and is looking at the origin.

Factoring Rotation Matrices

A common problem is to factor a rotation matrix as a product of rotations about the coordinate axes. The form of the factorization depends on the needs of the application and what ordering is specified. For example, you might want to factor a rotation as $R = R_x(\theta_x)R_y(\theta_y)R_z(\theta_z)$ for some angles θ_x, θ_y, and θ_z. The ordering is xyz. Five other possibilities are xzy, yxz, yzx, zxy, and zyx. You might also envision factorizations such as xyx—these are not discussed here. The following discussion uses the notation $c_a = \cos(\theta_a)$ and $s_a = \sin(\theta_a)$ for $a = x, y, z$.

Factor as $R_x R_y R_z$

Setting $R = [r_{ij}]$ for $0 \le i \le 2$ and $0 \le j \le 2$, formally multiplying $R_x(\theta_x)R_y(\theta_y)$ $R_z(\theta_z)$, and equating yields

$$\begin{bmatrix} r_{00} & r_{01} & r_{02} \\ r_{10} & r_{11} & r_{12} \\ r_{20} & r_{21} & r_{22} \end{bmatrix} = \begin{bmatrix} c_y c_z & -c_y s_z & s_y \\ c_z s_x s_y + c_x s_z & c_x c_z - s_x s_y s_z & -c_y s_x \\ -c_x c_z s_y + s_x s_z & c_z s_x + c_x s_y s_z & c_x c_y \end{bmatrix}$$

From this we have $s_y = r_{02}$, so $\theta_y = \sin^{-1}(r_{02})$. If $\theta_y \in (-\pi/2, \pi/2)$, then $c_y \ne 0$ and $c_y(s_x, c_x) = (-r_{12}, r_{22})$, in which case $\theta_x = \text{atan2}(-r_{12}, r_{22})$. Similarly, $c_y(s_z, c_z) = (-r_{01}, r_{00})$, in which case $\theta_z = \text{atan2}(-r_{01}, r_{00})$.
  If $\theta_y = \pi/2$, then $s_y = 1$ and $c_y = 0$. In this case

$$\begin{bmatrix} r_{10} & r_{11} \\ r_{20} & r_{21} \end{bmatrix} = \begin{bmatrix} c_z s_x + c_x s_z & c_x c_z - s_x s_z \\ -c_x c_z + s_x s_z & c_z s_x + c_x s_z \end{bmatrix} = \begin{bmatrix} \sin(\theta_z + \theta_x) & \cos(\theta_z + \theta_x) \\ -\cos(\theta_z + \theta_x) & \sin(\theta_z + \theta_x) \end{bmatrix}$$

Therefore, $\theta_z + \theta_x = \text{atan2}(r_{10}, r_{11})$. There is one degree of freedom, so the factorization is not unique. One choice is $\theta_z = 0$ and $\theta_x = \text{atan2}(r_{10}, r_{11})$.

If $\theta_y = -\pi/2$, then $s_y = -1$ and $c_y = 0$. In this case

$$
\begin{bmatrix} r_{10} & r_{11} \\ r_{20} & r_{21} \end{bmatrix} = \begin{bmatrix} -c_z s_x + c_x s_z & c_x c_z + s_x s_z \\ c_x c_z + s_x s_z & c_z s_x - c_x s_z \end{bmatrix} = \begin{bmatrix} \sin(\theta_z - \theta_x) & \cos(\theta_z - \theta_x) \\ \cos(\theta_z - \theta_x) & -\sin(\theta_z - \theta_x) \end{bmatrix}
$$

Therefore, $\theta_z - \theta_x = \text{atan2}(r_{10}, r_{11})$. There is one degree of freedom, so the factorization is not unique. One choice is $\theta_z = 0$ and $\theta_x = -\text{atan2}(r_{10}, r_{11})$.

Pseudocode for the factorization is

```
thetaY = asin(r02);
if (thetaY < PI/2) {
    if (thetaY > -PI / 2) {
        thetaX = atan2(-r12, r22);
        thetaZ = atan2(-r01, r00);
    } else {
        // not a unique solution (thetaX - thetaZ constant)
        thetaX = -atan2(r10, r11);
        thetaZ = 0;
    }
} else {
    // not a unique solution (thetaX + thetaZ constant)
    thetaX = atan2(r10, r11);
    thetaZ = 0;
}
```

Factor as $\mathbf{R}_x \mathbf{R}_z \mathbf{R}_y$

Setting $\mathbf{R} = [r_{ij}]$ for $0 \le i \le 2$ and $0 \le j \le 2$, formally multiplying $\mathbf{R}_x(\theta_x)\mathbf{R}_z(\theta_z)$ $\mathbf{R}_y(\theta_y)$, and equating yields

$$
\begin{bmatrix} r_{00} & r_{01} & r_{02} \\ r_{10} & r_{11} & r_{12} \\ r_{20} & r_{21} & r_{22} \end{bmatrix} = \begin{bmatrix} c_y c_z & -s_z & c_z s_y \\ s_x s_y + c_x c_y s_z & c_x c_z & -c_y s_x + c_x s_y s_z \\ -c_x s_y + c_y s_x s_z & c_z s_x & c_x c_y + s_x s_y s_z \end{bmatrix}
$$

Analysis similar to the xyz case leads to the pseudocode

```
thetaZ = asin(-r01);
if (thetaZ < PI / 2) {
    if (thetaZ > -PI / 2) {
        thetaX = atan2(r21, r11);
        thetaY = atan2(r02, r00);
    } else {
        // not a unique solution (thetaX + thetaY constant)
        thetaX = atan2(-r20, r22);
```

```
        thetaY = 0;
    }
} else {
    // not a unique solution (thetaX - thetaY constant)
    thetaX = atan2(r20, r22);
    thetaY = 0;
}
```

Factor as $\mathbf{R}_y\mathbf{R}_x\mathbf{R}_z$

Setting $\mathbf{R} = [r_{ij}]$ for $0 \le i \le 2$ and $0 \le j \le 2$, formally multiplying $\mathbf{R}_y(\theta_y)\mathbf{R}_x(\theta_x)$ $\mathbf{R}_z(\theta_z)$, and equating yields

$$\begin{bmatrix} r_{00} & r_{01} & r_{02} \\ r_{10} & r_{11} & r_{12} \\ r_{20} & r_{21} & r_{22} \end{bmatrix} = \begin{bmatrix} c_y c_z + s_x s_y s_z & c_z s_x s_y - c_y s_z & c_x s_y \\ c_x s_z & c_x c_z & -s_x \\ -c_z s_y + c_y s_x s_z & c_y c_z s_x + s_y s_z & c_x c_y \end{bmatrix}$$

Analysis similar to the xyz case leads to the pseudocode

```
thetaX = asin(-r12);
if (thetaX < PI / 2) {
    if (thetaX > -PI / 2) {
        thetaY = atan2(r02, r22);
        thetaZ = atan2(r10, r11);
    } else {
        // not a unique solution (thetaY + thetaZ constant)
        thetaY = atan2(-r01, r00);
        thetaZ = 0;
    }
} else {
    // not a unique solution (thetaY - thetaZ constant)
    thetaY = atan2(r01, r00);
    thetaZ = 0;
}
```

Factor as $\mathbf{R}_y\mathbf{R}_z\mathbf{R}_x$

Setting $\mathbf{R} = [r_{ij}]$ for $0 \le i \le 2$ and $0 \le j \le 2$, formally multiplying $\mathbf{R}_y(\theta_y)\mathbf{R}_z(\theta_z)$ $\mathbf{R}_x(\theta_x)$, and equating yields

$$\begin{bmatrix} r_{00} & r_{01} & r_{02} \\ r_{10} & r_{11} & r_{12} \\ r_{20} & r_{21} & r_{22} \end{bmatrix} = \begin{bmatrix} c_y c_z & s_x s_y - c_x c_y s_z & c_x s_y + c_y s_x s_z \\ s_z & c_x c_z & -c_z s_x \\ -c_z s_y & c_y s_x + c_x s_y s_z & c_x c_y - s_x s_y s_z \end{bmatrix}$$

Analysis similar to the xyz case leads to the pseudocode

```
thetaZ = asin(r10);
if (thetaZ < PI / 2) {
    if (thetaZ > -PI / 2) {
        thetaY = atan2(-r20, r00);
        thetaX = atan2(-r12, r11);
    } else {
        // not a unique solution (thetaX - thetaY constant)
        thetaY = -atan2(r21, r22);
        thetaX = 0;
    }
} else {
    // not a unique solution (thetaX + thetaY constant)
    thetaY = atan2(r21, r22);
    thetaX = 0;
}
```

Factor as $\mathbf{R}_z\mathbf{R}_x\mathbf{R}_y$

Setting $\mathbf{R} = [r_{ij}]$ for $0 \leq i \leq 2$ and $0 \leq j \leq 2$, formally multiplying $\mathbf{R}_z(\theta_z)\mathbf{R}_x(\theta_x)$ $\mathbf{R}_y(\theta_y)$, and equating yields

$$
\begin{bmatrix} r_{00} & r_{01} & r_{02} \\ r_{10} & r_{11} & r_{12} \\ r_{20} & r_{21} & r_{22} \end{bmatrix} = \begin{bmatrix} c_yc_z - s_xs_ys_z & -c_xs_z & c_zs_y + c_ys_xs_z \\ c_zs_xs_y + c_ys_z & c_xc_z & -c_yc_zs_x + s_ys_z \\ -c_xs_y & s_x & c_xc_y \end{bmatrix}
$$

Analysis similar to the xyz case leads to the pseudocode

```
thetaX = asin(r21);
if (thetaX < PI / 2) {
    if (thetaX > -PI / 2) {
        thetaZ = atan2(-r01, r11);
        thetaY = atan2(-r20, r22);
    } else {
        // not a unique solution (thetaY - thetaZ constant)
        thetaZ = -atan2(r02, r00);
        thetaY = 0;
    }
} else {
    // not a unique solution (thetaY + thetaZ constant)
    thetaZ = atan2(r02, r00);
    thetaY = 0;
}
```

Factor as $\mathbf{R}_z\mathbf{R}_y\mathbf{R}_x$

Setting $\mathbf{R} = [r_{ij}]$ for $0 \le i \le 2$ and $0 \le j \le 2$, formally multiplying $\mathbf{R}_z(\theta_z)\mathbf{R}_y(\theta_y)$ $\mathbf{R}_x(\theta_x)$, and equating yields

$$
\begin{bmatrix} r_{00} & r_{01} & r_{02} \\ r_{10} & r_{11} & r_{12} \\ r_{20} & r_{21} & r_{22} \end{bmatrix} = \begin{bmatrix} c_y c_z & c_z s_x s_y - c_x s_z & c_x c_z s_y + s_x s_z \\ c_y s_z & c_x c_z + s_x s_y s_z & -c_z s_x + c_x s_y s_z \\ -s_y & c_y s_x & c_x c_y \end{bmatrix}
$$

Analysis similar to the xyz case leads to the pseudocode

```
thetaY = asin(-r20);
if (thetaY < PI / 2) {
    if (thetaY > -PI / 2) {
        thetaZ = atan2(r10, r00);
        thetaX = atan2(r21, r22);
    } else {
        // not a unique solution (thetaX + thetaZ constant)
        thetaZ = atan2(-r01, -r02);
        thetaX = 0;
    }
} else {
    // not a unique solution (thetaX - thetaZ constant)
    thetaZ = -atan2(r01, r02);
    thetaX = 0;
}
```

A.3.2   QR Decomposition

Given an invertible $n \times n$ matrix $\mathbf{A}$, we wish to decompose it into $\mathbf{A} = \mathbf{QR}$, where $\mathbf{Q}$ is an orthogonal matrix and $\mathbf{R}$ is upper triangular. The factorization is just an application of the Gram-Schmidt orthonormalization algorithm applied to the columns of $\mathbf{A}$. Let those columns be denoted as $\vec{a}_i$ for $1 \le i \le n$. The columns are linearly independent since $\mathbf{A}$ is assumed to be invertible. The Gram-Schmidt process constructs from this set of vectors an orthonormal set $\hat{q}_i$, $1 \le i \le n$. That is, each vector is unit length, and the vectors are mutually perpendicular.

The first step is simple; just normalize $\hat{q}_1$ by

$$
\hat{q}_1 = \frac{\vec{a}_1}{\|\vec{a}_1\|}
$$

We can project $\vec{a}_2$ onto the orthogonal complement of $\hat{q}_1$ and represent $\vec{a}_2 = c_1 \hat{q}_1 + \vec{p}_2$, where $\hat{q}_1 \cdot \vec{p}_2 = 0$. Dotting this equation with $\hat{q}_1$ leads to $c_1 = \hat{q}_1 \cdot \vec{a}_2$. Rewritten, we have $\vec{p}_2 = \vec{a}_2 - (\hat{q}_1 \cdot \vec{a}_2)\hat{q}_1$. The vectors $\hat{q}_1$ and $\vec{p}_2$ are perpendicular by the construction, but $\vec{p}_2$ is not necessarily unit length. Thus, define $\hat{q}_2$ to be the normalized $\vec{p}_2$:

$$\hat{q}_2 = \frac{\vec{a}_2 - (\hat{q}_1 \cdot \vec{a}_2)\hat{q}_1}{\|\vec{a}_2 - (\hat{q}_1 \cdot \vec{a}_2)\hat{q}_1\|}$$

A similar construction is applied to $\vec{a}_3$. We can project $\vec{a}_3$ onto the orthogonal complement of the space spanned by $\hat{q}_1$ and $\hat{q}_2$ and represent $\vec{a}_3 = c_1\hat{q}_1 + c_2\hat{q}_2 + \vec{p}_3$, where $\hat{q}_1 \cdot \vec{p}_3 = 0$ and $\hat{q}_2 \cdot \vec{p}_3 = 0$. Dotting this equation with the $\hat{q}_i$ leads to $c_i = \hat{q}_i \cdot \vec{a}_3$. Rewritten, we have $\vec{p}_3 = \vec{a}_3 - (\hat{q}_1 \cdot \vec{a}_3)\hat{q}_1 - (\hat{q}_2 \cdot \vec{a}_3)\hat{q}_2$. The next vector in the orthonormal set is the normalized $\vec{p}_3$:

$$\hat{q}_3 = \frac{\vec{a}_3 - (\hat{q}_1 \cdot \vec{a}_3)\hat{q}_1 - (\hat{q}_2 \cdot \vec{a}_3)\hat{q}_2}{\|\vec{a}_3 - (\hat{q}_1 \cdot \vec{a}_3)\hat{q}_1 - (\hat{q}_2 \cdot \vec{a}_3)\hat{q}_2\|}$$

In general for $i \geq 2$,

$$\hat{q}_i = \frac{\vec{a}_i - \sum_{j=1}^{i-1}(\hat{q}_j \cdot \vec{a}_i)\hat{q}_j}{\|\vec{a}_i - \sum_{j=1}^{i-1}(\hat{q}_j \cdot \vec{a}_i)\hat{q}_j\|}$$

Let $\mathbf{Q}$ be the $n \times n$ matrix whose columns are the vectors $\hat{q}_i$. The upper triangular matrix in the factorization is

$$\mathbf{R} = \begin{bmatrix} \hat{q}_1 \cdot \vec{a}_1 & \hat{q}_1 \cdot \vec{a}_2 & \cdots & \hat{q}_1 \cdot \vec{a}_n \\ 0 & \hat{q}_2 \cdot \vec{a}_2 & \cdots & \hat{q}_2 \cdot \vec{a}_n \\ \vdots & \vdots & & \vdots \\ 0 & 0 & \cdots & \hat{q}_n \cdot \vec{a}_n \end{bmatrix}$$

A.3.3 EIGENDECOMPOSITION

Given an $n \times n$ matrix $\mathbf{A}$, an *eigensystem* is of the form $\mathbf{A}\vec{x} = \lambda\vec{x}$ or $(\mathbf{A} - \lambda\mathbf{I})\vec{x} = \vec{0}$. It is required that there be solutions $\vec{x} \neq \vec{0}$. For this to happen, the matrix $\mathbf{A} - \lambda\mathbf{I}$ must be noninvertible. This is the case when $\det(\mathbf{A} - \lambda\mathbf{I}) = 0$, a polynomial in λ of degree n called the *characteristic polynomial* for $\mathbf{A}$. For each root λ, the matrix $\mathbf{A} - \lambda\mathbf{I}$ is computed, and the system $(\mathbf{A} - \lambda\mathbf{I})\vec{x} = \vec{0}$ is solved for nonzero solutions. While standard linear algebra textbooks show numerous examples for doing this symbolically, most applications require a robust numerical method for doing so. In particular, if $n \geq 5$, there are no closed formulas for roots to polynomials, so numerical methods must be applied. A good reference on solving eigensystems is Press et al. (1988).

Most of the applications in graphics that require eigensystems have symmetric matrices. The numerical methods are quite good for these since there is guaranteed a full basis of eigenvectors. The standard approach is to apply orthogonal transformations, called *Householder transformations,* to reduce A to a tridiagonal matrix. The QR algorithm is applied iteratively to reduce the tridiagonal matrix to a diagonal one. Press et al. (1998) advise using a QL algorithm with implicit shifting to be as robust as possible. For $n = 3$, the problem can be solved by simply computing the roots of $\det(A - \lambda I) = 0$. The numerical issues many times can be avoided since the end result is some visual presentation of data where the numerical error is not as important as for applications that require high precision.

Solving the eigensystem for an $n \times n$ symmetric matrix A implies a factorization for A. Let λ_1 through λ_m be the distinct eigenvalues for A. The dimension of the eigenspace for λ_i is $d_i \geq 1$ and $\sum_{i=1}^{m} d_i = n$. That is, we can choose an orthonormal set of vectors $\hat{q}_i$, $1 \leq i \leq n$, that is the union of orthonormal sets for each of the eigenspaces. Because these vectors are themselves eigenvectors, $A\hat{q}_i = \lambda_{i'}\hat{q}_i$, where $\lambda_{i'}$ is the eigenvalue corresponding to the eigenspace in which $\hat{q}_i$ lives. Define the diagonal matrix $\Lambda = \text{Diag}\{\lambda_{1'}, \ldots, \lambda_{n'}\}$. Define Q to be the matrix whose columns are the $\hat{q}_i$. The eigenequations are jointly written as $AQ = Q\Lambda$, or $A = Q\Lambda Q^T$. This last equation is called an *eigendecomposition* of A.

A.3.4   POLAR DECOMPOSITION

Suppose an object has been transformed by translations, rotations, and nonuniform scalings through a sequence of homogeneous matrix operations. The total transformation is just the product of the individual transformations. A common question asked by many practitioners is how to extract from the total transformation its translation, rotation, and nonuniform scales. The question is ill-posed, but the motivation for asking it is as follows. Suppose that the homogeneous transformations are of the block form

$$H_i = \left[\begin{array}{c|c} R_i S_i & \vec{t}_i \\ \hline \vec{0}^T & 1 \end{array}\right]$$

where $\vec{t}_i$ is a 3×1 translation vector; $\vec{0}^T$ is a 1×3 zero vector; S_i is the nonuniform scaling matrix, a 3×3 diagonal matrix whose diagonal entries are positive; and R_i is a 3×3 rotation matrix. Suppose that n such transformations are applied to an object and the final transformation is $H = H_n H_{n-1} \cdots H_2 H_1$. What the question is aimed at is factoring

$$H = \left[\begin{array}{c|c} RS & \vec{t} \\ \hline \vec{0}^T & 1 \end{array}\right]$$

Clearly the translation vector is an easy term to select! However, the scaling and rotation are problematic. Consider just the product of two such homogeneous transformations

$$\begin{bmatrix} RS & \vec{t} \\ \hline \vec{0}^T & 1 \end{bmatrix} = \begin{bmatrix} R_2S_2 & \vec{t}_2 \\ \hline \vec{0}^T & 1 \end{bmatrix} \begin{bmatrix} R_1S_1 & \vec{t}_1 \\ \hline \vec{0}^T & 1 \end{bmatrix} = \begin{bmatrix} R_2S_2R_1S_1 & R_2S_2\vec{t}_1 + \vec{t}_2 \\ \hline \vec{0}^T & 1 \end{bmatrix}$$

The total translation is $\vec{t} = R_2S_2\vec{t}_1 + \vec{t}_2$. The total scale-rotation component is $R_2S_2R_1S_1$. In the special case that both S_1 and S_2 represent uniform scales, that is, $S_i = \sigma_i I$ for $i = 1, 2$ and where I is the identity matrix, we can determine R and S uniquely by

$$R_2S_2R_1S_1 = R_2\sigma_2 IR_1\sigma_1 I = R_2\sigma_2 R_1\sigma_1 = R_2R_1(\sigma_2\sigma_1)$$

The ability to commute σ_2 and R_1 is just a property of scalar multiplication of a matrix. The final selection is $S = \sigma_2\sigma_1 I$, another uniform scaling, and $R = R_2R_1$, a rotation since it is the product of two rotations. In this special case of two homogeneous terms, if S_2 is a uniform scale matrix, then $S = S_2\sigma_1$ and $R = R_2R_1$. But the complication is when S_2 is nonuniform. Generally, if D_1 is a diagonal matrix for which at least two diagonal entries are different, and if R_1 is a rotation matrix, it is not possible to find a diagonal matrix D_2 for which $R_1D_1 = D_2R_2$ with R_2 a rotation matrix. Generally, if the transformation system of a graphics engine allows nonuniform scaling, the complication arises.

The intuitive problem is that the nonuniform scales are applied along specific axes, so the orientation of those axes is an important issue. In 2D consider transforming the circle $x^2 + y^2 = 1$ by rotations and nonuniform scaling. Figure A.1 illustrates the problem. Observe that if we allow scaling along a different set of coordinate axes, in this case the axes $(1, 1)/\sqrt{2}$ and $(-1, 1)/\sqrt{2}$, we can force the circle in the bottom sequence to stretch to the final ellipse in the top sequence. The scale 2 must be applied along the direction $(1, 1)/\sqrt{2}$.

This motivates what is called the *polar decomposition*. A nonuniform scale in a particular coordinate system is obtained by rotating that system to the standard coordinate system, applying the scaling in the standard system, then rotating back to the original system. If R represents the rotation from the specified coordinate system to the standard coordinate system and if D is the diagonal nonuniform scaling matrix in the standard coordinate system, then the scaling in the specified coordinate system is $S = R^TDR$. This just states mathematically what we said in words. The matrix S is necessarily symmetric.

Given a matrix A, the polar decomposition is $A = QS$, where Q is an orthogonal matrix and S is a symmetric matrix. In the application mentioned previously, the matrix of interest is $A = R_2S_2R_1S_1$. It is generally not possible to factor $A = RS$, where R is a rotation and S is diagonal. The polar decomposition is always possible. The

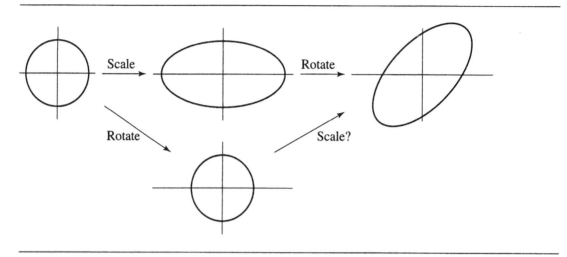

Figure A.1   The top sequence shows a nonuniform scale $(x, y) \rightarrow (2x, y)$ applied first, a counterclockwise rotation by $\pi/4$ second. The bottom sequence shows a rotation by any angle (the circle is invariant under rotations), but clearly there is no nonuniform scaling along coordinate axes that can force the circle to become the ellipse of the top sequence.

symmetric matrix S represents scaling in some coordinate system. If that coordinate system is the standard one (directions $(1, 0, 0)$, $(0, 1, 0)$, $(0, 0, 1)$), then S is diagonal. Observe that $A^T A = S^T Q^T Q S = S^T S = S^2$, where the second equality is true since Q is orthogonal and the third equality is true since S is symmetric. The matrix $A^T A$ is positive semidefinite since $\vec{x}^T B \vec{x} = \vec{x}^T A^T A \vec{x} = \|A\vec{x}\|^2 \geq 0$. Therefore, $S^2 = A^T A$ must have a positive semidefinite square root (Horn and Johnson 1985). The square root can be constructed by an eigendecomposition $S^2 = R^T D R$, where R is orthogonal and D is diagonal with nonnegative diagonal entries. A square root is $S = R^T D^{1/2} R$, where $D^{1/2}$ is the diagonal matrix whose diagonal entries are the square roots of the diagonal entries of D. If S is invertible (the scalings are all positive), Q is obtained by $Q = A S^{-1}$. If S is not invertible, then A itself is not invertible. The polar decomposition for such a matrix can be obtained by singular value decomposition, which is discussed in the next section. In typical graphics applications, A is in fact invertible.

Construction of S as shown in the previous paragraph is certainly a valid way of obtaining the decomposition. If a standard numerical eigensystem solver is used, the construction is iterative. An alternative method that is also iterative is presented in Heckbert (1994) by Ken Shoemake and constructs Q first. Once Q is known, $S = Q^T A$. The initial iterate is $Q_0 = A$. The next iterates are generated by $Q_{i+1} = (Q_i + Q_i^{-T})/2$. The iteration terminates when the change between consecutive iterates is sufficiently small.

A.3.5 SINGULAR VALUE DECOMPOSITION

An eigendecomposition naturally factors a symmetric matrix A into $A = R^T D R$, where R is orthogonal and D is diagonal. For a nonsymmetric matrix, this type of factorization is not always possible. What is possible is a factorization called the *singular value decomposition*. Any matrix A can be factored into $A = LSR^T$, where L and R are both orthogonal matrices and where S is diagonal with nonnegative diagonal entries (for a proof, see Horn and Johnson 1985). The diagonal entries of S are the eigenvalues of AA^T, the columns of L are eigenvectors of AA^T, and the columns of R are eigenvectors of $A^T A$ arranged in the same order relative to the eigenvalues as that for the columns of L. As a result, an eigendecomposition of AA^T and $A^T A$ will lead to the singular value decomposition. But as it turns out, there are more efficient numerical methods for the decomposition, for example, in Golub and Van Loan (1993).

A.4 REPRESENTATIONS OF 3D ROTATIONS

This section discusses three different schemes for representing 3D rotations—matrix, axis-angle, and quaternion—and how to convert between schemes.

A.4.1 MATRIX REPRESENTATION

A 2D rotation is a tranformation of the form

$$\begin{bmatrix} x_1 \\ y_1 \end{bmatrix} = \begin{bmatrix} \cos(\theta) & -\sin(\theta) \\ \sin(\theta) & \cos(\theta) \end{bmatrix} \begin{bmatrix} x_0 \\ y_0 \end{bmatrix}$$

where θ is the angle of rotation. A 3D rotation is a 2D rotation that is applied within a specified plane that contains the origin. Such a rotation can be represented by a 3×3 *rotation matrix* $R = [\hat{r}_0\ \hat{r}_1\ \hat{r}_2]$ whose columns $\hat{r}_0$, $\hat{r}_1$, and $\hat{r}_2$ form a right-handed orthonormal set. That is, $\|\hat{r}_0\| = \|\hat{r}_1\| = \|\hat{r}_2\| = 1$, $\hat{r}_0 \cdot \hat{r}_1 = \hat{r}_0 \cdot \hat{r}_2 = \hat{r}_1 \cdot \hat{r}_2 = 0$, and $\hat{r}_0 \cdot \hat{r}_1 \times \hat{r}_2 = 1$. The columns of the matrix correspond to the final rotated values of the standard basis vectors $(1, 0, 0)$, $(0, 1, 0)$, and $(0, 0, 1)$, in that order. Given a 3×1 vector $\vec{x} = [x_j]$ and 3×3 rotation matrix $R = [r_{ij}]$, the rotated vector is

$$R\vec{x} = \left[\sum_{j=0}^{2} r_{ij} x_j \right] \tag{A.3}$$

A.4.2 AXIS-ANGLE REPRESENTATION

If the plane of rotation has unit-length normal $\hat{w}$, then the *axis-angle representation* of the rotation is the pair $\langle \hat{w}, \theta \rangle$. The direction of rotation is chosen so that as you look down on the plane from the side to which $\hat{w}$ points, the rotation is counterclockwise about the origin for $\theta > 0$. This is the same convention used for a 2D rotation.

Axis-Angle to Matrix

If $\hat{u}$, $\hat{v}$, and $\hat{w}$ form a right-handed orthonormal set, then any point can be represented as $\vec{x} = u_0\hat{u} + v_0\hat{v} + w_0\hat{w}$; see Section 9.2.2 on coordinate frames relative to a plane. Rotation of $\vec{x}$ about the axis $\hat{w}$ by the angle θ produces $\mathbf{R}\vec{x} = u_1\hat{u} + v_1\hat{v} + w_1\hat{w}$. Clearly from the geometry, $w_1 = w_0 = \hat{w} \cdot \vec{x}$. The other two components are changed as if a 2D rotation has been applied to them, so $u_1 = \cos(\theta)u_0 - \sin(\theta)v_0$ and $v_1 = \sin(\theta)u_0 + \cos(\theta)v_0$. Using the right-handedness of the orthonormal set, it is easily shown that

$$\hat{w} \times \vec{x} = u_0\hat{w} \times \hat{u} + v_0\hat{w} \times \hat{v} + w_0\hat{w} \times \hat{w} = -v_0\hat{u} + u_0\hat{v}$$

and

$$\hat{w} \times (\hat{w} \times \vec{x}) = -v_0\hat{w} \times \hat{u} + u_0\hat{w} \times \hat{v} = -u_0\hat{u} - v_0\hat{w}$$

Combining these in the form shown and using the relationship between u_0, v_0, u_1, and v_1 produces

$$(\sin\theta)\hat{w} \times \vec{x} + (1 - \cos\theta)\hat{w} \times (\hat{w} \times \vec{x}) = (-v_0\sin\theta - u_0(1 - \cos\theta))\hat{u}$$
$$+ (u_0\sin\theta - v_0(1 - \cos\theta))\hat{v}$$
$$= (u_1 - u_0)\hat{u} + (v_1 - v_0)\hat{v}$$
$$= \mathbf{R}\vec{x} - \vec{x}$$

Therefore, the rotation of $\vec{x}$ given the axis $\hat{w}$ and angle θ is

$$\mathbf{R}\vec{x} = \vec{x} + (\sin\theta)\hat{w} \times \vec{x} + (1 - \cos\theta)\hat{w} \times (\hat{w} \times \vec{x}) \qquad \text{(A.4)}$$

This can also be written in matrix form by defining the following, where $\hat{w} = (a, b, c)$,

$$S = \begin{bmatrix} 0 & -c & b \\ c & 0 & -a \\ -b & a & 0 \end{bmatrix}$$

in which case

$$R = I + (\sin \theta)S + (1 - \cos \theta)S^2$$

and consequently $R\vec{x} = \vec{x} + (\sin \theta)S\vec{x} + (1 - \cos \theta)S^2\vec{x}$.

Matrix to Axis-Angle

The inverse problem is to start with the rotation matrix and extract an angle and unit-length axis. There are multiple solutions since $-\hat{w}$ is a valid axis whenever $\hat{w}$ is and $\theta + 2\pi k$ is a valid solution whenever θ is. First, the *trace* of a matrix is defined to be the sum of the diagonal terms. Some algebra will show that $\cos \theta = (\mathrm{Trace}(R) - 1)/2$, in which case

$$\theta = \cos^{-1}((\mathrm{Trace}(R) - 1)/2) \in [0, \pi] \tag{A.5}$$

Also, it is easily shown that

$$R - R^T = (2 \sin \theta)S \tag{A.6}$$

where S is a skew-symmetric matrix. The constructions below are based on the cases $\theta = 0$, $\theta \in (0, \pi)$, and $\theta = \pi$.

If $\theta = 0$, then any unit-length direction vector for the axis is valid since there is no rotation. If $\theta \in (0, \pi)$, Equation A.6 allows direct extraction of the axis, $\vec{d} = (r_{21} - r_{12}, r_{02} - r_{20}, r_{10} - r_{01})$ and $\hat{w} = \vec{d}/\|\vec{d}\|$. If $\theta = \pi$, Equation A.6 does not help with constructing the axis since $R - R^T = 0$. In this case note that

$$R = I + 2S^2 = \begin{bmatrix} 1 - 2(w_1^2 + w_2^2) & 2w_0 w_1 & 2w_0 w_2 \\ 2w_0 w_1 & 1 - 2(w_0^2 + w_2^2) & 2w_1 w_2 \\ 2w_0 w_2 & 2w_1 w_2 & 1 - 2(w_0^2 + w_1^2) \end{bmatrix}$$

where $\hat{w} = (w_0, w_1, w_2)$. The idea is to extract the maximum component of the axis from the diagonal entries of the rotation matrix. If r_{00} is maximum, then w_0 must be the largest component in magnitude. Compute $4w_0^2 = r_{00} - r_{11} - r_{22} + 1$ and select $w_0 = \sqrt{r_{00} - r_{11} - r_{22} + 1}/2$. Consequently, $w_1 = r_{01}/(2w_0)$ and $w_2 = r_{02}/(2w_0)$. If r_{11} is maximum, then compute $4w_1^2 = r_{11} - r_{00} - r_{22} + 1$ and select $w_1 = \sqrt{r_{11} - r_{00} - r_{22} + 1}/2$. Consequently, $w_0 = r_{01}/(2w_1)$ and $w_2 = r_{12}/(2w_1)$. Finally, if r_{22} is maximum, then compute $4w_2^2 = r_{22} - r_{00} - r_{11} + 1$ and select $w_2 = \sqrt{r_{22} - r_{00} - r_{11} + 1}/2$. Consequently, $w_0 = r_{02}/(2w_2)$ and $w_1 = r_{12}/(2w_2)$.

A.4.3 QUATERNION REPRESENTATION

A third representation involves *unit quaternions*. Only a summary is provided here. Details of the relationship between rotations and quaternions can be found in Shoemake (1987) and Eberly (2000). A unit quaternion is denoted by $q = w + xi + yj + zk$, where w, x, y, and z are real numbers and where the 4-tuple (w, x, y, z) is unit length. The set of unit quaternions is just the unit hypersphere in $\mathbb{R}^4$. The products of i, j, and k are defined by $i^2 = j^2 = k^2 = -1$, $ij = -ji = k$, $jk = -kj = i$, and $ki = -ik = j$. Observe that the products are *not commutative*. The product of two unit quaternions $q_n = w_n + x_n i + y_n j + z_n k$ for $n = 0, 1$ is defined by distributing the product over the sums, keeping in mind that the order of operands is important:

$$
\begin{aligned}
q_0 q_1 = \; & (w_0 w_1 - x_0 x_1 - y_0 y_1 - z_0 z_1) \\
& + (w_0 x_1 + x_0 w_1 + y_0 z_1 - z_0 y_1)i \\
& + (w_0 y_1 - x_0 z_1 + y_0 w_1 + z_0 x_1)j \\
& + (w_0 z_1 + x_0 y_1 - y_0 x_1 + z_0 w_1)k
\end{aligned}
$$

The conjugate of q is defined by

$$
q^* = w - xi - yj - zk
$$

Observe that $qq^* = q^*q = 1$ where the right-hand side 1 is the w-term of the quaternion, the x-, y-, and z-terms all being 0.

Axis-Angle to Quaternion

If $\hat{a} = (x_0, y_0, z_0)$ is the unit-length axis of rotation and if θ is the angle of rotation, a quaternion $q = w + xi + yj + zk$ that represents the rotation satisfies $w = \cos(\theta/2)$, $x = x_0 \sin(\theta/2)$, $y = y_0 \sin(\theta/2)$, and $z = z_0 \sin(\theta/2)$.

If a vector $\vec{v} = (v_0, v_1, v_2)$ is represented as the quaternion $v = v_0 i + v_1 j + v_2 k$, and if q represents a rotation, then the rotated vector $\vec{u}$ is represented by quaternion $u = u_0 i + u_1 j + u_2 k$, where

$$
u = qvq^* \tag{A.7}
$$

It can be shown that the w-term of u must really be 0.

Quaternion to Axis-Angle

Let $q = w + xi + yj + zk$ be a unit quaternion. If $\|w\| = 1$, then the angle is $\theta = 0$ and any unit-length direction vector for the axis will do since there is no rotation.

If $\|w\| < 1$, the angle is obtained as $\theta = 2 \cos^{-1}(w)$, and the axis is computed as $\hat{u} = (x, y, z)/\sqrt{1 - w^2}$.

Quaternion to Matrix

Using the identities $2 \sin^2(\theta/2) = 1 - \cos(\theta)$ and $\sin(\theta) = 2 \sin(\theta/2) \cos(\theta/2)$, it is easily shown that $2wx = (\sin \theta)w_0$, $2wy = (\sin \theta)w_1$, $2wz = (\sin \theta)w_2$, $2x^2 = (1 - \cos \theta)w_0^2$, $2xy = (1 - \cos \theta)w_0 w_1$, $2xz = (1 - \cos \theta)w_0 w_2$, $2y^2 = (1 - \cos \theta)w_1^2$, $2yz = (1 - \cos \theta)w_1 w_2$, and $2z^2 = (1 - \cos \theta)w_2^2$. The right-hand sides of all these equations are terms in the expression $\mathbf{R} = \mathbf{I} + (\sin \theta)\mathbf{S} + (1 - \cos \theta)\mathbf{S}^2$. Replacing them yields

$$
\mathbf{R} = \begin{bmatrix}
1 - 2y^2 - 2z^2 & 2xy + 2wz & 2xz - 2wy \\
2xy - 2wz & 1 - 2x^2 - 2z^2 & 2yz - 2wx \\
2xz + 2wy & 2yz - 2wx & 1 - 2x^2 - 2y^2
\end{bmatrix}
\tag{A.8}
$$

Matrix to Quaternion

Earlier it was mentioned that $\cos \theta = (\text{Trace}(\mathbf{R}) - 1)/2$. Using the identity $2 \cos^2(\theta/2) = 1 + \cos \theta$ yields $w^2 = \cos^2(\theta/2) = (\text{Trace}(\mathbf{R}) + 1)/4$ or $|w| = \sqrt{\text{Trace}(\mathbf{R}) + 1}/2$. If $\text{Trace}(\mathbf{R}) > 0$, then $|w| > 1/2$, so without loss of generality choose w to be the positive square root, $w = \sqrt{\text{Trace}(\mathbf{R}) + 1}/2$. The identity $\mathbf{R} - \mathbf{R}^\mathsf{T} = (2 \sin \theta)\mathbf{S}$ also yielded $(r_{21} - r_{12}, r_{02} - r_{20}, r_{10} - r_{01}) = 2 \sin \theta (w_0, w_1, w_2)$. Finally, identities derived earlier were $2xw = w_0 \sin \theta$, $2yw = w_1 \sin \theta$, and $2zw = w_2 \sin \theta$. Combining these leads to $x = (r_{21} - r_{12})/(4w)$, $y = (r_{20} - r_{02})/(4w)$, and $z = (r_{10} - r_{01})/(4w)$.

   If $\text{Trace}(\mathbf{R}) \leq 0$, then $|w| \leq 1/2$. The idea is to first extract the largest one of x, y, or z from the diagonal terms of the rotation $\mathbf{R}$ in Equation A.8. If r_{00} is the maximum diagonal term, then x is larger in magnitude than y or z. Some algebra shows that $4x^2 = r_{00} - r_{11} - r_{22} + 1$, from which is chosen $x = \sqrt{r_{00} - r_{11} - r_{22} + 1}/2$. Consequently, $w = (r_{12} - r_{21})/(4x)$, $y = (r_{01} + r_{10})/(4x)$, and $z = (r_{02} + r_{20})/(4x)$. If r_{11} is the maximum diagonal term, then compute $4y^2 = r_{11} - r_{00} - r_{22} + 1$ and choose $y = \sqrt{r_{11} - r_{00} - r_{22} + 1}/2$. Consequently, $w = (r_{20} - r_{02})/(4y)$, $x = (r_{01} + r_{10})/(4y)$, and $z = (r_{12} + r_{21})/(4y)$. Finally, if r_{22} is the maximum diagonal term, then compute $4z^2 = r_{22} - r_{00} - r_{11} + 1$ and choose $z = \sqrt{r_{22} - r_{00} - r_{11} + 1}/2$. Consequently, $w = (r_{01} - r_{10})/(4z)$, $x = (r_{02} + r_{20})/(4z)$, and $y = (r_{12} + r_{21})/(4z)$.

A.4.4 PERFORMANCE ISSUES

A question asked quite often is, "What is the best representation to use for rotations?" As with most computer science topics, there is no answer to this question, only trade-

Table A.1   Comparison of memory usage.

Representation	Floats	Comments
Rotation matrix	9	
Axis-angle	4	No precompute of $\sin \theta$ or $1 - \cos \theta$
Axis-angle	6	Precompute of $\sin \theta$ and $1 - \cos \theta$
Quaternion	4	

offs to consider. In the discussion, the rotation matrix is $\mathbf{R}$, the quaternion is q, and the axis-angle pair is $(\hat{a}, \theta)$. Various high-level operations are compared by a count of low-level operations including multiplication (M), addition or subtraction (A), division (D), and expensive math library function evaluations (F). In an actual implementation, comparisons (C) should also be counted because they can be even more expensive than multiplications and/or additions. Summary tables are provided to allow you to quickly compare the performance.

Memory Usage

A rotation matrix requires 9 floats, a quaternion requires 4 floats, and an axis-angle pair requires 4 floats, so clearly the rotation matrix will use more memory. Storing only the angle in the axis-angle formulation is clearly not helpful when transforming is required since you need to know the values of $\sin \theta$ and $1 - \cos \theta$. Evaluating the trigonometric functions is quite expensive. It is better to precompute both quantities and store them, so in fact an axis-angle pair will require 6 floats, making the quaternion representation the cheapest in memory usage. Table A.1 is a summary of the memory usage. The axis-angle count includes 3 floats for the axis, 1 float for the angle θ, and 2 floats for $\sin \theta$ and $1 - \cos \theta$. Without the precomputation of the trigonometric functions, any operation requiring the function values will be quite expensive.

Conversion Time

Applications using rotations invariably have to convert from one representation to another, so it is useful to have measurements of costs for the conversions. The entities involved are a rotation matrix $\mathbf{R}$, an axis-angle pair $(\hat{a}, \theta)$, and a quaternion q. It is assumed that the angle of rotation is in $(0, \pi)$.

Axis-Angle to Matrix

Evaluation of $\sigma = \sin(\theta)$ and $\gamma = \cos(\theta)$ requires two function calls. The term $1 - \gamma$ requires 1 addition. The skew-symmetric matrix S obtained from $\hat{a}$ requires no computation. The matrix S^2 requires 6 unique multiplications and 3 additions; sign changes are not counted. The term $(1 - \gamma)S^2$ requires 6 unique multiplications. The term σS requires 3 unique multiplications. Finally, the combination $R = I + \sigma S + (1 - \gamma)S^2$ uses 9 additions. The total cost is $13A + 15M + 2F$.

Matrix to Axis-Angle

The extraction $\theta = \cos^{-1}((\text{Trace}(R) - 1)/2)$ requires 3 additions, 1 multiplication, and 1 function call. The vector $\vec{d} = (r_{21} - r_{12}, r_{02} - r_{20}, r_{10} - r_{01})$ requires 3 additions. The normalized vector $\hat{a} = \vec{d}/|\vec{d}|$ requires 6 multiplications, 2 additions, 1 division, and 1 function call. The total cost is $8A + 7M + 1D + 2F$.

Axis-Angle to Quaternion

Extracting $\theta = 2\cos^{-1}(w)$ requires 1 function call and 1 multiplication. Constructing $\hat{a} = (x, y, z)/\sqrt{1 - w^2}$ requires 4 multiplications, 1 addition, 1 division, and 1 function call. The total cost is $1A + 5M + 1D + 2F$.

Quaternion to Axis-Angle

Evaluation of $\theta/2$ uses 1 multiplication. Evaluation of $\sigma = \sin(\theta/2)$ and $w = \cos(\theta/2)$ requires 2 function calls. The products $(x, y, z) = \sigma\hat{a}$ require 3 multiplications. The total cost is $4M + 2F$.

Quaternion to Matrix

The conversion requires 12 multiplications. The terms $t_x = 2x$, $t_y = 2y$, and $t_z = 2z$ are computed. From these the following terms are computed: $t_{wx} = wt_x$, $t_{wy} = wt_y$, $t_{wz} = wt_z$, $t_{xx} = t_x x$, $t_{xy} = xt_y$, $t_{xz} = xt_z$, $t_{yy} = t_y y$, $t_{yz} = yt_z$, and $t_{zz} = t_z z$. The rotation matrix entries require 12 additions: $r_{00} = 1 - t_{yy} - t_{zz}$, $r_{01} = t_{xy} - t_{wz}$, $r_{02} = t_{xz} + t_{wy}$, $r_{10} = t_{xy} + t_{wz}$, $r_{11} = 1 - t_{xx} - t_{zz}$, $r_{12} = t_{yz} - t_{wx}$, $r_{20} = t_{xz} - t_{wy}$, $r_{21} = t_{yz} + t_{wx}$, and $r_{22} = 1 - t_{xx} - t_{yy}$. The total cost is $12A + 12M$.

Matrix to Quaternion

The conversion depends on the sign of the trace of R. Computing the trace $\tau = \text{Trace}(R)$ requires 2 additions. Suppose that $\tau > 0$ (this comparison is $1C$ in cost). The calculation $w = \sqrt{\tau + 1}/2$ requires 1 addition, 1 multiplication, and 1 function call. The expression $\lambda = 1/(4w)$ requires 1 multiplication and 1 division. The terms

Table A.2   Comparison of operation counts for converting between representations of rotations.

Conversion	A	M	D	F	C
Axis-angle to matrix	13	15		2	
Matrix to axis-angle	8	7	1	2	
Axis-angle to quaternion	1	5	1	2	
Quaternion to axis-angle		4		2	
Quaternion to matrix	12	12			
Matrix to quaternion ($\tau > 0$)	6	5	1	1	1
Matrix to quaternion ($\tau \leq 0$)	6	5	1	1	3

$x = \lambda(r_{21} - r_{12})$, $y = \lambda(r_{02} - r_{20})$, and $z = \lambda(r_{10} - r_{01})$ require 3 additions and 3 multiplications. The total cost is $6A + 5M + 1D + 1F + 1C$.

If $\tau \leq 0$, the maximum of the diagonal entries of the rotation matrix must be found. This requires two comparisons; call this cost $2C$. For the sake of argument, suppose that r_{00} is the maximum. The calculation $x = \sqrt{r_{00} - r_{11} - r_{22} + 1}/2$ requires 3 additions, 1 multiplication, and 1 function call. The expression $\lambda = 1/(4x)$ requires 1 multiplication and 1 division. The terms $w = \lambda(r_{21} - r_{12})$, $y = \lambda(r_{10} + r_{01})$, and $z = \lambda(r_{20} + r_{02})$ require 3 additions and 3 multiplications. The total cost is $6A + 5M + 1D + 1F + 3C$.

Table A.2 is a summary of the costs of converting among the various rotation representations.

Transformation Time

The transformation of $\vec{v}$ by a rotation matrix is the product $\vec{u} = R\vec{v}$ and requires 9 multiplications and 6 additions for a total of 15 operations.

If $\vec{v} = (v_0, v_1, v_2)$ and if $v = v_0 i + v_1 j + v_2 k$ is the corresponding quaternion with zero w-component, then the rotate vector $\vec{u} = (u_0, u_1, u_2)$ is computed as $u = u_0 i + u_1 j + u_2 k = qvq^*$. Applying the general formula for quaternion multiplication directly, the product $p = qv$ requires 16 multiplications and 12 additions. The product pq^* also uses the same number of operations. The total operation count is 56. However, since v has no w-term, p only requires 12 multiplications and 8 additions— one term is theoretically zero, so no need to compute it. We also know that u has no w-term, so the product pq^* only requires 12 multiplications and 9 additions. Using these optimizations, the total operation count is 41. Observe that conversion from quaternion q to rotation matrix R requires 12 multiplications and 12 additions. Transforming $\vec{v}$ by R takes 15 operations. Therefore, the process of converting to rotation and multiplying uses 39 operations, 2 less than calculating qvq^*. Purists who

Table A.3   Comparison of operation counts for transforming one vector.

Representation	A	M	Comments
Rotation matrix	6	9	
Axis-angle	12	18	
Quaternion	24	32	Using generic quaternion multiplies
Quaternion	17	24	Using specialized quaternion multiplies
Quaternion	18	21	Convert to matrix, then multiply

implement quaternion libraries and only use quaternions will sadly lose a lot of cycles when transforming large sets of vertices.

The formula for transforming $\vec{v}$ using an axis-angle pair is

$$\mathbf{R}\vec{v} = \vec{v} + (\sin\theta)\hat{a} \times \vec{v} + (1 - \cos\theta)\hat{a} \times (\hat{a} \times \vec{v})$$

As indicated earlier, $\sin\theta$ and $1 - \cos\theta$ should be precomputed and stored in addition to the axis and angle, a total of 6 floats. The cross product $\hat{a} \times \hat{v}$ uses 6 multiplications and 3 additions. So does $\hat{a} \times (\hat{a} \times \hat{v})$, assuming the cross product in the parentheses was computed first and stored in temporary memory. Multiplying the cross products by a scalar requires 6 multiplications. Adding three vectors requires 6 additions. Therefore, we need to use 18 multiplications and 12 additions, for a total of 30 operations.

Therefore, the rotational formulation yields the fastest transforming. The quaternion formulation yields the slowest transforming for a single vector. But keep in mind that a batch transform of n vectors requires converting the quaternion to a rotation matrix only once at a cost of 24 operations. The total operations for transforming by quaternion are $24 + 15n$. The axis-angle formulation uses $30n$, so the quaternion transformation is faster for two or more vectors. Table A.3 is a summary of the operation counts for transforming a single vector. Table A.4 is a summary of the operation counts for transforming n vectors.

Composition

The product of two rotation matrices requires 27 multiplications and 18 additions, for a total cost of $18A + 27M$.

The product of two quaternions requires 16 multiplications and 12 additions, for a total cost of $12A + 16M$, clearly outperforming matrix multiplication. Moreover, renormalizing a quaternion to adjust for floating-point errors is cheaper than renormalizing a rotation matrix using Gram-Schmidt orthonormalization.

Table A.4   Comparison of operation counts for transforming n vectors.

Representation	A	M	Comments
Rotation matrix	$6n$	$9n$	
Axis-angle	$12n$	$18n$	
Quaternion	$24n$	$32n$	Using generic quaternion multiplies
Quaternion	$17n$	$24n$	Using specialized quaternion multiplies
Quaternion	$12 + 6n$	$12 + 9n$	Convert to matrix, then multiply

Table A.5   Comparison of operation counts for composition.

Representation	A	M	D	F
Rotation matrix	18	27		
Quaternion	12	16		
Axis-angle (convert to matrix)	52	64	1	6
Axis-angle (convert to quaternion)	14	30	2	6

Composition of two axis-angle pairs is unthinkable in an application that requires computational efficiency. One way to do the composition is to convert to matrices, multiply the matrices, then extract the axis-angle pair. The two conversions from axis-angle to matrix cost $26A + 30M + 4F$, the matrix product costs $18A + 27M$, and the conversion from matrix to axis-angle costs $8A + 7M + 1D + 2F$. The total cost is $52A + 64M + 1D + 6F$.

Another way to do the composition of two axis-angle pairs is to convert to quaternions, multiply the quaternions, then extract the axis-angle pair. The two conversions from axis-angle to quaternion cost $2A + 10M + 2D + 4F$, the quaternion product costs $12A + 16M$, and the conversion from quaternion to axis-angle costs $4M + 2F$. The total cost is $14A + 30M + 2D + 6F$. Table A.5 is a summary of the operation counts for composing two rotations.

Interpolation

This section discusses how to interpolate rotations for each of the three representation schemes.

Table A.6   Operation counts for quaternion interpolation.

Term	A	M	D	F
$a_0 = p \cdot q$	3	4		
$\theta = \cos^{-1}(a_0)$				1
$1 - t$	1			
$(1-t)\theta$		1		
$t\theta$		1		
$\sin(\theta)$				1
$\sin((1-t)\theta)$				1
$\sin(t\theta)$				1
$a_1 = 1/\sin(\theta)$			1	
$a_2 = a_1 \sin((1-t)\theta)$		1		
$a_3 = a_1 \sin(t\theta)$		1		
$a_2 p + a_3 q$	4	8		
Total	8	16	1	4

Quaternion Interpolation

Quaternions are quite amenable to interpolation. The standard operation that is used is *spherical linear interpolation*, affectionately known as *slerp*. Given quaternions p and q with acute angle θ between them, slerp is defined as $s(t; p, q) = p(p^*q)^t$ for $t \in [0, 1]$. Note that $s(0; p, q) = p$ and $s(1; p, q) = q$. An equivalent definition of slerp that is more amenable to calculation is

$$s(t; p, q) = \frac{\sin((1-t)\theta)p + \sin(t\theta)q}{\sin(\theta)}$$

If p and q are thought of as points on a unit circle, the formula above is a parameterization of the shortest arc between them. If a particle travels on that curve according to the parameterization, it does so with constant speed. Thus, any uniform sampling of t in $[0, 1]$ produces equally spaced points on the arc.

We assume that only p, q, and t are specified. Moreover, since q and $-q$ represent the same rotation, you can replace q by $-q$ if necessary to guarantee that the angle between p and q treated as 4-tuples is acute. That is, $p \cdot q \geq 0$. As 4-tuples, p and q are unit length. The dot product is therefore $p \cdot q = \cos(\theta)$. Table A.6 shows the operation counts. Any term shown on the left that includes an already computed term has only its *additional* operations counted to avoid double-counting operations.

Rotation Matrix Interpolation

The absence of a meaningful interpolation formula that directly applies to rotation matrices is used as an argument for the superiority of quaternions over rotation matrices. However, rotations can be interpolated directly in a way equivalent to what slerp produces. If P and Q are rotations corresponding to quaternions p and q, the slerp of the matrices is

$$S(t; \mathbf{P}, \mathbf{Q}) = \mathbf{P}(\mathbf{P}^\mathrm{T}\mathbf{Q})^t$$

the same formula that defines slerp for quaternions. The technical problem is to define what is meant by $\mathbf{R}^t$ for a rotation $\mathbf{R}$ and real-valued t. If the rotation has axis $\hat{a}$ and angle θ, then $\mathbf{R}^t$ has the same rotation axis, but the angle of rotation is $t\theta$. The procedure for computing the slerp of the rotation matrices is

1. Compute $\mathbf{R} = \mathbf{P}^\mathrm{T}\mathbf{Q}$.

2. Extract an axis $\hat{a}$ and an angle θ from $\mathbf{R}$.

3. Compute $\mathbf{R}^t$ by converting the axis-angle pair $\hat{a}, t\theta$.

4. Compute $S(t; \mathbf{P}, \mathbf{Q}) = \mathbf{P}\mathbf{R}^t$.

This algorithm requires an axis-angle extraction that involves an inverse trigonometric function call and a square root operation, a couple of trigonometric evaluations (for $t\theta$), and a conversion back to a rotation matrix. This is quite a bit more expensive than computing the slerp for quaternions, which requires three trigonometric function calls. The quaternion interpolation is therefore more efficient, but a purist wishing to avoid quaternions in an application has, indeed, a method for interpolating rotation matrices.

Table A.7 shows the operation counts and uses the same format and rules as the table for quaternion interpolation. Both the quaternion and rotation matrix interpolation use 1 division and 4 function evaluations. However, the number of additions and multiplications in the rotation matrix interpolation is excessive compared to that of quaternion interpolation.

Axis-Angle Interpolation

There is no obvious and natural way to produce the same interpolation that occurs with quaternions and rotation matrices. The only choice is to convert to one of the other representations, interpolate in that form, then convert the interpolated result back to axis-angle form. A very expensive proposition, just as in composition of rotations.

Table A.7   Operation counts for rotation matrix interpolation.

Term	A	M	D	F
$\mathbf{R} = \mathbf{P}^{\mathrm{T}}\mathbf{Q}$	18	27		
$a_0 = 0.5(\mathrm{Trace}(\mathbf{R}) - 1)$	4	1		
$\theta = \cos^{-1}(a_0)$				1
$\vec{d} = (r_{21} - r_{12}, r_{02} - r_{20}, r_{10} - r_{01})$	3			
$a_1 = 1/|\vec{d}|$	2	3	1	1
$\hat{a} = a_1\vec{d}$		3		
$t\theta$		1		
$a_2 = \sin(t\theta)$				1
$a_3 = 1 - \cos(t\theta)$	1			1
Matrix $\mathbf{S}$, no cost				
$\mathbf{S}^2$	3	6		
$\mathbf{R}^t = \mathbf{I} + a_2\mathbf{S} + a_3\mathbf{S}^2$	9	9		
$\mathbf{PR}^t$	18	27		
Total	58	77	1	4

A.5 ROOT FINDING

Given a continuous function $\vec{F} : D \subset \mathbb{R}^n \to \mathbb{R}^n$, the problem is to find an $\vec{x}$ (or find a set of points) for which $\vec{F}(\vec{x}) = 0$.

A.5.1 METHODS IN ONE DIMENSION

Given a continuous function $f : [a, b] \to \mathbb{R}$, the first question is whether or not $f(r) = 0$ for some $r \in [a, b]$. If $f(a)f(b) < 0$, then there is at least one root. However, there may be multiple roots. If a root r is computed, other analyses are required to locate others. For example, if f is a polynomial and r is a root, the function can be factored as $f(t) = (t - r)^p g(t)$, where $p \geq 1$ and g is a polynomial with degree$(g) =$ degree$(f) - p$. The root-finding process is now continued with function g on $[a, b]$.

If $f(a)f(b) > 0$, there is no guarantee that f has a root on $[a, b]$. For problems of this type, a root-bounding preprocessing step can be used. The interval is partitioned into $t_i = a + i(b - a)/n$ for $0 \leq i \leq n$. If $f(t_i)f(t_{i+1}) < 0$ for some i, then that subinterval is bisected to locate a root. A reasonable choice of n will be related to what information the application knows about its function f.

Finally, it might be necessary to find roots of $f : \mathbb{R} \to \mathbb{R}$ where the domain of f is not a bounded interval. Roots of f can be sought in the interval $[-1, 1]$. Any root t of f outside this interval can be computed as $t = 1/r$, where $r \in [-1, 1]$ is a root of $g(r) = f(1/r)$.

Bisection

Bisection is the process of finding a root to a continuous function $f : [a, b] \to \mathbb{R}$ by bracketing a root with an interval, then successively bisecting the interval to narrow in on the root. Suppose that initially $f(a)f(b) < 0$. Since f is continuous, there must be a root $r \in (a, b)$. The midpoint of the interval is $m = (a + b)/2$. The function value $f(m)$ is computed and compared to the function values at the end points. If $f(a)f(m) < 0$, then the subinterval (a, m) brackets a root and the bisection process is repeated on that subinterval. If $f(m)f(b) < 0$, then the subinterval (m, b) brackets a root and the bisection process is repeated instead on that subinterval. If $f(m) = 0$ or is zero within a specified tolerance, the process terminates. A stopping condition might also be based on the length of the current subinterval—that is, if the length becomes small enough, terminate the algorithm. If a root exists on $[a, b]$, bisection is guaranteed to find it. However, the rate of convergence is slow.

Newton's Method

Given a differentiable function $f : \mathbb{R} \to \mathbb{R}$, an initial guess is chosen about where f is zero, $(x_0, f(x_0))$. The tangent line to the graph at this point is used to update the estimate to a (hopefully) better one. The tangent line is $y - f(x_0) = f'(x_0)(x - x_0)$ and intersects the x-axis at $(0, x_1)$, so $-f(x_0) = f'(x_0)(x_1 - x_0)$. Assuming $f'(x_0) \neq 0$, solving for x_1 yields

$$x_1 = x_0 - \frac{f(x_0)}{f'(x_0)}$$

The next point in the iteration is $(x_1, f(x_1))$, and the process is repeated until a stopping condition is met, typically one based on closeness of the function value to zero. Unlike bisection, the iterations are not guaranteed to converge, but if there is convergence, it is at a faster rate. Success depends a lot on the initial guess for x_0.

Polynomial Roots

A polynomial of degree n is $f(t) = \sum_{i=0}^{n} a_i t^i$, where $a_n \neq 0$. While standard root finders may be applied to polynomials, a better approach takes advantage of the nature of such functions. For $2 \leq n \leq 4$, there are closed-form equations for the roots of the polynomial. Direct application of the formulas is possible, but numerical problems tend to occur, particularly when the polynomial has a root of multiplicity larger than 1. For example, the roots of a quadratic $f(t) = at^2 + b^t + c$ are $t = (-b \pm \sqrt{b^2 - 4ac})/(2a)$. If $b^2 - 4ac = 0$, the quadratic has a double root $t = -b/(2a)$. However, numerical round-off errors might cause $b^2 - 4ac = -\epsilon < 0$ for very small ϵ. Another condition that leads to numerical problems is if a is nearly zero. If so, it is possible to solve $g(t) = t^2 f(1/t) = ct^2 + bt + a = 0$ and get $t = (-b \pm \sqrt{b^2 - 4ac})/(2c)$. But the problem still exists if c is also nearly zero. Similar problems occur with the formulas for cubic and quartic polynomials.

An approach based on iteration schemes is to attempt to bracket the roots in a way that each bracketing interval contains exactly one root. For each such interval, bisection can be applied to find the root. A hybrid scheme is also possible that mixes bisection steps with Newton steps; the bisection step is used only when the Newton step generates an iterate outside the current bracketing interval. The hope is that the Newton iterates converge quickly to the root, but if they appear not to, bisection attempts to generate better initial guesses for the Newton iteration.

Bounding Roots by Derivative Sequences

A simple approach to the bracketing problem is to partition $\mathbb{R}$ into intervals, the polynomial $f(t)$ being monotone on each interval. If it can be determined where the derivative of the polynomial is zero, this set provides the partition. If d_i and d_{i+1} are consecutive values for which $f'(d_i) = f'(d_{i+1}) = 0$, then either $f'(t) > 0$ on (d_i, d_{i+1}) or $f'(t) < 0$ on (d_i, d_{i+1}). In either case, f can have at most one root on the interval. The existence of this root is guaranteed by the condition $f(d_i)f(d_{i+1}) < 0$ or $f(d_i) = 0$ or $f(d_{i+1}) = 0$.

Solving $f'(t) = 0$ requires the same techniques as solving $f(t) = 0$. The difference is that degree(f') = degree(f) $- 1$. A recursive implementation is warranted for this problem, the base case being the constant polynomial that is either never zero or identically zero on the real line.

If $f'(t) \neq 0$ for $t \in (-\infty, d_0)$, it is possible that f has a root on the semi-infinite interval $(-\infty, d_0]$. Bisection does not help locate a root because the interval is unbounded. However, it is possible to determine the largest bounded interval that contains the roots of a polynomial. The construction relies on the concepts of *spectral radius* and *norm of a matrix* (see Horn and Johnson 1985). Given a square matrix A, the spectral radius, denoted $\rho(A)$, is the maximum of the absolute values of the eigenvalues for the matrix. A matrix norm of A, denoted $\|A\|$, is a scalar-valued function that must satisfy the five conditions: $\|A\| \geq 0$, $\|A\| = 0$ if and only if $A = 0$, $\|cA\| = |c|\|A\|$ for any scalar c, $\|A + B\| \leq \|A\| + \|B\|$, and $\|AB\| \leq \|A\|\|B\|$. The relationship between the spectral radius and any matrix norm is $\rho(A) \leq \|A\|$. Given $f(t) = \sum_{i=0}^{n} a_i t^i$, where $a_n = 1$, the *companion matrix* is

$$\mathbf{A} = \begin{bmatrix} -a_{n-1} & -a_{n-2} & \cdots & -a_1 & -a_0 \\ 1 & 0 & \cdots & 0 & 0 \\ 0 & 1 & \cdots & 0 & 0 \\ \vdots & \vdots & \ddots & \vdots & \vdots \\ 0 & 0 & \cdots & 1 & 0 \end{bmatrix}$$

The characteristic polynomial is $f(t) = \det(\mathbf{A} - t\mathbf{I})$, so the roots of f are the eigenvalues of $\mathbf{A}$. The spectral norm therefore provides a bound for the roots. Since there are lots of matrix norms to choose from, there are many possible bounds. One such bound is Cauchy's bound:

$$|t| \le \max\{|a_0|, 1 + |a_1|, \ldots, 1 + |a_{n-1}|\} = 1 + \max\{|a_0|, \ldots, |a_{n-1}|\}$$

Another bound that can be obtained is the Carmichael and Mason bound:

$$|t| \le \sqrt{1 + \sum_{i=0}^{n-1} |a_i|^2}$$

If $a_0 \ne 0$, then $f(0) \ne 0$, so the roots of f are bounded away from zero. It is possible to construct lower bounds by using $g(t) = [t^n f(1/t)]/a_0$. The roots of $g(t)$ are the reciprocal roots of $f(t)$. Cauchy's bound applied to $g(t)$, then taking reciprocals, is

$$|t| \ge \frac{|a_0|}{1 + \max\{1, |a_1|, \ldots, |a_{n-1}|\}}$$

The Carmichael and Mason bound is

$$|t| \ge \frac{|a_0|}{\sqrt{1 + \sum_{i=0}^{n-1} |a_i|^2}}$$

These bounds are used in the recursive call to determine where $f(t)$ is monotone. The polynomial can be factored $f(t) = t^p g(t)$, where $p \ge 0$ and g is a polynomial for which $g(0) \ne 0$. If $p = 0$, then $f = g$ and f is processed for $0 < a \le |t| \le b$, where a and b are bounds computed from the previously mentioned inequalities. If $p > 0$, then g is processed on the intervals obtained by using the bounds from the same inequalities.

Bounding Roots by Sturm Sequences

Consider a polynomial $f(t)$ defined on interval $[a, b]$. A Sturm sequence for f is a set of polynomials $f_i(t)$, $0 \le i \le m$, such that degree(f_{i+1}) > degree(f_i) and the number of distinct real roots for f in $[a, b]$ is $N = s(a) - s(b)$, where $s(a)$ is the number of sign changes of $f_0(a), \ldots, f_m(a)$ and $s(b)$ is the number of sign changes of

Table A.8   Signs of the Sturm polynomials for $t^3 + 3t^2 - 1$ at various t values.

t	Sign $f_0(t)$	Sign $f_1(t)$	Sign $f_2(t)$	Sign $f_3(t)$	Sign changes
$-\infty$	$-$	$+$	$-$	$+$	3
-3	$-$	$+$	$-$	$+$	3
-2	$+$	0	$-$	$+$	2
-1	$+$	$-$	$-$	$+$	2
0	$-$	0	$+$	$+$	1
$+1$	$+$	$+$	$+$	$+$	0
$+\infty$	$+$	$+$	$+$	$+$	0

Table A.9   Signs of the Sturm polynomials for $(t - 1)^3$ at various t values.

t	Sign $f_0(t)$	Sign $f_1(t)$	Sign $f_2(t)$	Sign changes
$-\infty$	$-$	$+$	0	1
0	$-$	$+$	0	1
$+\infty$	$+$	$+$	0	0

$f_1(b), \ldots, f_m(b)$. The total number of real-valued roots of f on $\mathbb{R}$ is $s(-\infty) - s(\infty)$. It is not always the case that $m = \text{degree}(f)$.

The classic Sturm sequence is $f_0(t) = f(t)$, $f_1(t) = f'(t)$, and $f_i(t) = -$ Remainder (f_{i-2}/f_{i-1}) for $i \geq 2$. The polynomials are generated by this method until the remainder term is a constant. An instructive example from the article by D. G. Hook and P. R. McAree in Glassner (1990) is $f(t) = t^3 + 3t^2 - 1$. The Sturm sequence is $f_0(t) = t^3 + 3t^2 - 1$, $f_1(t) = 3t^2 + 6t$, $f_2(t) = 2t + 1$, and $f_3 = 9/4$. Table A.8 lists the signs of the Sturm polynomials for various t values. Letting $N(a, b)$ denote the number of real-valued roots on the interval (a, b), the table shows that $N(-\infty, -3) = 0$, $N(-3, -2) = 1$, $N(-2, -1) = 0$, $N(-1, 0) = 1$, $N(0, 1) = 1$, and $N(1, \infty) = 0$. Moreover, the number of negative real roots is $N(-\infty, 0) = 2$, the number of positive real roots is $N(0, \infty) = 1$, and the total number of real roots is $N(-\infty, \infty) = 3$.

The next example shows that the number of polynomials in the Sturm sequence is not necessarily the degree$(f) + 1$. The function $f(t) = (t - 1)^3$ has a Sturm sequence $f_0(t) = (t - 1)^3$, $f_1(t) = 3(t - 1)^2$, and $f_2(t) \equiv 0$ since f_1 exactly divides f_0 with no remainder. Table A.9 lists sign changes for f at various t values. The total number of real roots is $N(-\infty, \infty) = 1$.

A.5.2   METHODS IN MANY DIMENSIONS

This section discusses the extension of bisection and Newton's method to many dimensions.

Bisection

The bisection method for one dimension can be extended to multiple dimensions. Let $(f, g) : [a, b] \times [c, d] \to \mathbb{R}^2$. The problem is to find a point $(x, y) \in [a, b] \times [c, d]$ for which $(f(x, y), g(x, y)) = (0, 0)$. A quadtree decomposition of $[a, b] \times [c, d]$ can be used for the root search. Starting with the initial rectangle, f and g are evaluated at the four vertices.

- If either f or g has the same sign at the four vertices, the algorithm stops processing that region.

- If both f and g have a sign change at the vertices, they are evaluated at the centerpoint of the region. If the values at the center are close enough to zero, that point is returned as a root and the search is terminated in that region.

- If the center value is not close enough to zero, the region is subdivided into four subregions by using the original four vertices, the midpoints of the four edges, and the centerpoint. The algorithm is recursively applied to those four subregions.

It is possible that when a region is not processed further because f or g has the same sign at all four vertices, the region really does contain a root. The issue is the same as for one dimension—the initial rectangle needs to be partitioned to locate subrectangles on which a root is bound. The bisection method can be applied to each subrectangle that contains at least one root.

For three dimensions, an octree decomposition is applied in a similar way. For n dimensions, a 2^n-tree decomposition is used.

Newton's Method

Given differentiable $F : \mathbb{R}^n \to \mathbb{R}^n$, the equation $F(\vec{x}) = \vec{0}$ can be solved by the extension of Newton's method in one dimension. The iteration scheme that directly generalizes the method is to select an initial guess $(\vec{x}_0, F(\vec{x}_0))$ and generate the next iterate by

$$\vec{x}_1 = \vec{x}_0 - (DF(\vec{x}_0))^{-1} F(\vec{x}_0)$$

The quantity $DF(\vec{x})$ is the matrix of partial derivatives of F, called the Jacobian matrix, and has entries $\partial F_i / \partial x_j$, where F_i is the ith component of F and x_j

is the jth component of $\vec{x}$. Each iterate requires a matrix inversion. While the obvious extension, it is not always the best to use. There are variations on the method that work much better in practice, some of those using what are called *splitting methods* that avoid having to invert a matrix and usually have better convergence behavior.

A.5.3   STABLE SOLUTION TO QUADRATIC EQUATIONS

The general form of the quadratic is

$$ax^2 + bx + c = 0$$

and the solution is

$$\lambda = \frac{-b \pm \sqrt{b^2 - 4ac}}{2a}$$

However, simply solving this problem in the "obvious" way can result in numerical problems when implemented on a computer. We can see this if we rearrange the standard solution (Casselman 2001):

$$\{x_0, x_1\} = \frac{-b \pm \sqrt{b^2 - 4ac}}{2a}$$

$$= \left(\frac{b}{2a}\right)\left(-1 \pm \sqrt{1 - \frac{4ac}{b^2}}\right)$$

If the quantity $\frac{4ac}{b^2}$ is very small, then one of these involves the subtraction of two nearly equal-sized positive numbers—this can result in a large rounding error.

However, if we rewrite the quadratic equation by factoring out a

$$ax^2 + bx + c = a(x^2 + \frac{b}{a}x + \frac{c}{a})$$

$$= a(x - x_0)(x - x_1)$$

then we see that the product of the two roots is $\frac{c}{a}$. We can avoid the problem noted above by doing the operations in this order:

$$A \leftarrow \frac{b}{2a}$$

$$B \leftarrow \frac{4ac}{b^2}$$

$$\leftarrow \frac{c}{aA^2}$$

$$C \leftarrow -1 - \sqrt{1-B}$$

$$x_0 \leftarrow AC$$

$$x_1 \leftarrow \frac{AB}{C}$$

A.6 Minimization

The generic problem is to find a global minimum for a function $f : D \subset \mathbb{R}^n \to \mathbb{R}$. The function is constrained to be at least continuous, and D is assumed to be a compact set. If the function is continuously differentiable, this fact can help in locating a minimum, but there are methods that do not require derivatives in finding one.

A.6.1 Methods in One Dimension

Consider $f : [t_{\min}, t_{\max}] \to \mathbb{R}$. If f is differentiable, then the global minimum must occur either at a point where $f' = 0$ or at one of the end points. This standard approach is what is used in computing distance between a point and a line segment (see Section 6.1.3 on distance methods). The squared-distance function is quadratic and is defined on a compact interval. The minimum of that function occurs at an interior point of the interval (closest point is interior to line segment) or at an end point. Solving the problem $f'(t) = 0$ may be complicated in itself. This is a root-finding problem that is described in Section A.5.

Brent's Method

Continuous functions that are not necessarily differentiable must attain a minimum on a compact interval. A method to find the minimum that does not require derivatives or does not require determining where the derivative is zero when the function is differentiable is very desirable. One such method is called *Brent's method* and uses inverse parabolic interpolation in an iterative fashion.

The idea is to *bracket* the minimum by three points $(t_0, f(t_0))$, $(t_m, f(t_m))$, and $(t_1, f(t_1))$ for $t_{\min} \le t_0 < t_m < t_1 \le t_{\max}$, where $f(t_m) < f(t_0)$ and $f(t_m) < f(t_1)$. This means the function must decrease for some values of $t \in [t_0, t_m]$ and must increase for some values of $t \in [t_m, t_1]$. This guarantees that f has a local minimum somewhere in $[t_0, t_1]$. Brent's method attempts to narrow in on the local minimum, much like the bisection method narrows in on the root of a function (see Section A.5).

The following is a variation of what is described for Brent's method in Press et al. (1988). The three bracketing points are fit with a parabola, $p(t)$. The vertex of the parabola is guaranteed to lie within (t_0, t_1). Let $f_0 = f(t_0)$, $f_m = f(t_m)$, and $f_1 = f(t_1)$. The vertex of the parabola occurs at $t_v \in (t_0, t_1)$ and can be shown to be

$$t_v = t_m - \frac{1}{2} \frac{(t_1 - t_0)^2(f_0 - f_m) - (t_0 - t_m)^2(f_1 - f_m)}{(t_1 - t_m)(f_0 - f_m) - (t_0 - t_m)(f_1 - f_m)}$$

The function is evaluated there, $f_v = f(t_v)$. If $t_v < t_m$, then the new bracket is (t_0, f_0), (t_v, f_v), and (t_m, f_m). If $t_v > t_m$, then the new bracket is (t_m, f_m), (t_v, f_v), and (t_1, f_1). If $t_v = t_m$, the bracket cannot be updated in a simple way. Moreover, it is not sufficient to terminate the iteration here, as it is simple to construct an example where the three samples form an isosceles triangle whose vertex on the axis of symmetry is the parabola vertex, but the global minimum is far away from that vertex. One simple heuristic is to use the midpoint of one of the half-intervals, say, $t_b = (t_0 + t_m)/2$, evaluate $f_b = f(t_b)$, and compare to f_m. If $f_b > f_m$, then the new bracket is (t_b, f_b), (t_m, f_m), and (t_1, f_1). If $f_b < f_m$, then the new bracket is (t_0, f_0), (t_b, f_b), and (t_m, f_m). If $f_b = f_m$, the other half-interval can be bisected and the same tests repeated. If that also produces the pathological equality case, try a random sample from $[t_0, t_1]$. Once the new bracket is known, the method can be repeated until some stopping criterion is met.

Brent's method can be modified to support derivative information. A description of that also occurs in Press et al. (1988).

A.6.2 METHODS IN MANY DIMENSIONS

Consider $f : D \subset \mathbb{R}^n \to \mathbb{R}$, where D is a compact set. Typically in graphics applications, D is a polyhedron or even a Cartesian product of intervals. If f is differentiable, then the global minimum must occur either at a point where $\vec{\nabla} f = \vec{0}$ or on the boundary of D. In the latter case if D is a polyhedron, then the restriction of f to each face of D produces the same type of minimization problem, but in one less dimension. For example, this happens for many of the distance methods described in Chapter 10 on geometrical methods. Solving the problem $\vec{\nabla} f = \vec{0}$ is a root-finding problem and itself may be a difficult problem to solve.

Steepest Descent Search

This is a simple approach to searching for a minimum of a differentiable function. From calculus it is known that the direction in which f has its greatest rate of decrease is $-\vec{\nabla} f$. Given an initial guess $\vec{x}$ for the minimum point, the function $\phi(t) = f(\vec{x} - t\vec{\nabla} f(\vec{x}))$ is minimized using a one-dimensional algorithm. If t' is the parameter at which the minimum occurs, then $\vec{x} \leftarrow \vec{x} - t'\vec{\nabla} f(\vec{x})$ and the algorithm is repeated until a stopping condition is met. The condition is typically a measure of how different the last starting position is from the newly computed position.

The problem with this method is that it can be very slow. The pathological case is the minimization of a paraboloid $f(x, y) = (x/a)^2 + y^2$, where a is a very large number. The level sets are ellipses that are very elongated in the x-direction. For points not on the x-axis, the negative of the gradient vector tends to be nearly parallel to the y-axis. The search path will zigzag back and forth across the x-axis, taking its time getting to the origin where the global minimum occurs. A better approach is not to use the gradient vector but to use something called the conjugate direction. For the paraboloid, no matter where the initial guess is, only two iterations using conjugate directions will always end up at the origin. These directions in a sense encode shape information about the level curves of the function.

Conjugate Gradient Search

This method attempts to choose a better set of directions than steepest descent for a minimization search. The main ideas are discussed in Press et al. (1988), but a brief summary is given here. Two sequences of directions are built, a sequence of gradient directions $\vec{g}_i$ and a sequence of conjugate directions $\vec{h}_i$. The one-dimensional minimizations are along lines corresponding to the conjugate directions. The following pseudocode uses the Polak and Ribiere formulation as mentioned in Press et al. (1988). The function to be minimized is $E(\vec{x})$. The function MinimizeOn minimizes the function along the line using a one-dimensional minimizer. It returns the location x of the minimum and the function value fval at that minimum.

```
x = initial guess;
g = -gradient(E)(x);
h = g;
while (not done) {
    line.origin = x;
    line.direction = h;
    MinimizeOn(line, x, fval);
    if (stopping condition met)
        return <x, fval>;

    gNext = -gradient(E)(x);
```

```
    c = Dot(gNext - g, gNext) / Dot(g, g);
    g = gNext;
    h = g + c * h;
}
```

The stopping condition can be based on consecutive values of fval and/or on consecutive values of x. The condition in Press et al. (1988) is based on consecutive function values, f_0 and f_1, and a small tolerance value $\tau > 0$,

$$2|f_1 - f_0| \leq \tau(|f_0| + |f_1| + \epsilon)$$

for a small value $\epsilon > 0$ that supports the case when the function minimum is zero.

Powell's Direction Set Method

If f is continuous but not differentiable, then it attains a minimum on D. The search for the minimum simply cannot use derivative information. A method to find a minimum that does not require derivatives is *Powell's direction set method*. This method solves minimization problems along linear paths in the domain. The current candidate for the point at which the minimum occurs is updated to the minimum point on the current line under consideration. The next line is chosen to contain the current point and has a direction selected from a maintained set of direction vectors. Once all the directions have been processed, a new set of directions is computed. This is typically all but one of the previous set, but with the first direction removed and the new direction set to the current position minus the old position before the line minimizations were processed. The minimizations along the lines use something such as Brent's method since f restricted to the line is a one-dimensional function. The fact that D is compact guarantees that the intersection of the line with D is a compact set. Moreover, if D is convex (which in most applications it is), then the intersection is a connected interval so that Brent's method can be applied to that interval (rather than applying it to each connected component of the intersection of the line with D). The pseudocode for Powell's method is

```
// F(x) is the function to be minimized
n = dimension of domain;
directionSet = {d[0],..., d[n - 1]};  // usually the standard axis directions
x = xInitial = initial guess for minimum point;
while (not done) {
    for (each direction d) {
        line.origin = x;
        line.direction = d;
        MinimizeOn(line, x, fval);
    }
```

```
    conjugateDirection = x - xInitial;
    if (Length(conjugateDirection) is small)
        return <x, fval>;  // minimum found

    for (i = 0; i <= n - 2; i++)
        d[i] = d[i + 1];
    d[n - 1] = conjugateDirection;
}
```

The function MinimizeOn is the same one mentioned in the previous subsection on the conjugate gradient search.

A.6.3 MINIMIZING A QUADRATIC FORM

Let A be an $n \times n$ symmetric matrix. The function $Q : \mathbb{R}^n \to \mathbb{R}$ defined by $Q(\hat{v}) = \hat{v}^T A \hat{v}$ for $\|\hat{v}\| = 1$ is called a *quadratic form*. Since Q is defined on the unit sphere in $\mathbb{R}^n$, a compact set, and since Q is continuous, it must have a maximum and a minimum on this set.

Let $\hat{v} = \sum_{i=1}^{n} c_i v_i$, where $A\hat{v}_i = \lambda_i \hat{v}_i$, $\lambda_1 \le \cdots \le \lambda_n$, and $\sum_{i=1}^{n} c_i^2 = 1$. That is, the λ_i are the eigenvalues of A, and the $\hat{v}_i$ are the corresponding eigenvectors. Expanding the quadratic yields

$$Q(\hat{v}) = \left(\sum_{i=1}^{n} c_i \hat{v}_i^T \right) A \left(\sum_{j=1}^{n} c_j \hat{v}_j \right) = \sum_{i=1}^{n} \sum_{j=1}^{n} c_i c_j \hat{v}_i^T A \hat{v}_j = \sum_{k=1}^{n} \lambda_k c_k^2$$

The rightmost summation is a convex combination of the eigenvalues of A, so its minimum is λ_n and occurs when $c_1 = 1$ and all other $c_i = 0$. Consequently, $\min Q(\hat{v}) = \lambda_1 = Q(\hat{v}_1)$.

A.6.4 MINIMIZING A RESTRICTED QUADRATIC FORM

In some applications it is desirable to find the minimum of a quadratic form defined on the unit hypersphere S^{n-1}, but restricted to the intersection of this hypersphere with a hyperplane $\hat{n} \cdot X = 0$ for some special normal vector $\hat{n}$. Let A be an $n \times n$ symmetric matrix. Let $\hat{n} \in \mathbb{R}^n$ be a unit-length vector. Let $\hat{n}^\perp$ denote the orthogonal complement of $\hat{n}$. Define $Q : \{\hat{n}\}^\perp \to \mathbb{R}$ by $Q(\hat{v}) = \hat{v}^T A \hat{v}$, where $\|\hat{v}\| = 1$. Now Q is defined on the unit sphere in the $(n-1)$-dimensional space $\hat{n}^\perp$, so it must have a maximum and a minimum.

Let $\hat{v}_1$ through $\hat{v}_{n-1}$ be an orthonormal basis for $\hat{n}^\perp$. Let $\hat{v} = \sum_{i=1}^{n-1} c_i \hat{v}_i$, where $\sum_{i=1}^{n} c_i^2 = 1$. Let $A\hat{v}_i = \sum_{j=1}^{n-1} \alpha_{ji} \hat{v}_j + \alpha_{ni} \hat{n}$, where $\alpha_{ji} = \hat{v}_j^T A \hat{v}_i$ for $1 \le i \le n-1$

and $1 \leq j \leq n - 1$, and where $\alpha_{ni} = \hat{n}^t \mathbf{A} \hat{v}_i$ for $1 \leq i \leq n - 1$. Expanding the quadratic form yields

$$Q(\hat{v}) = \left(\sum_{i=1}^{n-1} c_i \hat{v}_i^t \right) \mathbf{A} \left(\sum_{j=1}^{n-1} c_j \hat{v}_j \right) = \sum_{i=1}^{n-1} \sum_{j=1}^{n-1} c_i c_j \alpha_{ij} = \vec{c}^{\mathrm{T}} \bar{\mathbf{A}} \vec{c} =: P(\vec{c})$$

where quadratic form $P : \mathbb{R}^{n-1} \to \mathbb{R}$ satisfies the conditions for the minimization in the last section. Thus, $\min Q(\hat{v}) = \min P(\vec{c})$, which occurs for $\vec{c}$ and λ such that $\bar{\mathbf{A}} \vec{c} = \lambda \vec{c}$ and λ is the minimum eigenvalue of $\bar{\mathbf{A}}$. The following calculations lead to a matrix formulation for determining the minimum value:

$$\sum_{j=1}^{n-1} \alpha_{ij} c_j = \lambda c_i$$

$$\sum_{j=1}^{n-1} c_j \hat{v}_i = \lambda c_i \hat{v}_i$$

$$\sum_{i=1}^{n-1} \sum_{j=1}^{n-1} \alpha_{ij} c_j \hat{v}_i = \lambda \sum_{i=1}^{n-1} c_i \hat{v}_i$$

$$\sum_{j=1}^{n-1} \left(\sum_{i=1}^{n-1} \alpha_{ij} \hat{v}_i \right) c_j = \lambda \hat{v}$$

$$\sum_{j=1}^{n-1} \left(A \hat{v}_j - \alpha_{nj} \hat{n} \right) c_j = \lambda \hat{v}$$

$$A \left(\sum_{j=1}^{n-1} c_j \hat{v}_j \right) - \left(\sum_{j=1}^{n-1} \alpha_{nj} c_j \right) \hat{n} = \lambda \hat{v}$$

$$A \hat{v} - \left(\hat{n}^t A \hat{v} \right) \hat{n} = \lambda \hat{v}$$

$$(\mathbf{I} - \hat{n} \hat{n}^t) A \hat{v} = \lambda \hat{v}$$

Therefore, $\min Q(\hat{v}) = \lambda_1 = Q(\hat{v}_1)$, where λ_1 is the minimum positive eigenvalue corresponding to the eigenvector $\hat{v}_1$ of $(\mathbf{I} - \hat{n} \hat{n}^{\mathrm{T}}) A$. Note that $n - 1$ of the eigenvectors are in $\hat{n}^\perp$. The remaining eigenvector is $\hat{v}_n = \mathbf{A}^{\mathrm{adj}} \hat{n}$, where $\mathbf{A} \mathbf{A}^{\mathrm{adj}} = (\det \mathbf{A}) \mathbf{I}$ and $\lambda_n = 0$.

A.7   LEAST SQUARES FITTING

Least squares fitting is the process of selecting a parameterized equation that represents a discrete set of points in a continuous manner. The parameters are estimated by minimizing a nonnegative function of the parameters. This section discusses fitting by lines, planes, circles, spheres, quadratic curves, and quadric surfaces.

A.7.1   LINEAR FITTING OF POINTS $(x, f(x))$

This is the usual introduction to least squares fit by a line when the data represents measurements where the y-component is assumed to be functionally dependent on the x-component. Given a set of samples $\{(x_i, y_i)\}_{i=1}^{m}$, determine a and b so that the line $y = ax + b$ best fits the samples in the sense that the sum of the squared errors between the y_i and the line values $ax_i + b$ is minimized. Note that the error is measured only in the y-direction.

Define $E(a, b) = \sum_{i=1}^{m}[(ax_i + b) - y_i]^2$. This function is nonnegative, and its graph is a paraboloid whose vertex occurs when the gradient satisfies $\vec{\nabla} E = (0, 0)$. This leads to a system of two linear equations in a and b that can be easily solved. Precisely,

$$(0, 0) = \vec{\nabla} E = 2 \sum_{i=1}^{m}[(ax_i + b) - y_i](x_i, 1)$$

and so

$$\begin{bmatrix} \sum_{i=1}^{m} x_i^2 & \sum_{i=1}^{m} x_i \\ \sum_{i=1}^{m} x_i & \sum_{i=1}^{m} 1 \end{bmatrix} \begin{bmatrix} a \\ b \end{bmatrix} = \begin{bmatrix} \sum_{i=1}^{m} x_i y_i \\ \sum_{i=1}^{m} y_i \end{bmatrix}$$

The solution provides the least squares solution $y = ax + b$.

A.7.2   LINEAR FITTING OF POINTS USING ORTHOGONAL REGRESSION

It is also possible to fit a line using least squares where the errors are measured *orthogonally* to the proposed line rather than measured vertically. The following argument holds for sample points and lines in n dimensions. Let the line be $\mathcal{L}(t) = t\hat{d} + A$, where $\hat{d}$ is unit length. Define X_i to be the sample points; then

$$X_i = A + d_i \hat{d} + p_i \hat{d}_i^{\perp}$$

where $d_i = \hat{d} \cdot (X_i - A)$ and $\hat{d}_i^{\perp}$ is some unit-length vector perpendicular to $\hat{d}$ with appropriate coefficient p_i. Define $\vec{y}_i = X_i - A$. The vector from X_i to its projection onto the line is

$$\vec{y}_i - d_i \hat{d} = p_i \hat{d}_i^{\perp}$$

The squared length of this vector is $p_i^2 = (\vec{y}_i - d_i \hat{d})^2$. The energy function for the least squares minimization is $E(A, \hat{d}) = \sum_{i=1}^{m} p_i^2$. Two alternate forms for this function are

$$E(A, \hat{d}) = \sum_{i=1}^{m} \left(\vec{y}_i^t \left[I - \hat{d}\hat{d}^t \right] \vec{y}_i \right)$$

and

$$E(A, \hat{d}) = \hat{d}^t \left(\sum_{i=1}^{m} \left[(\vec{y}_i \cdot \vec{y}_i) I - \vec{y}_i \vec{y}_i^t \right] \right) \hat{d} = \hat{d}^t M(A) \hat{d}$$

Using the first form of E in the previous equation, take the derivative with respect to A to get

$$\frac{\partial E}{\partial A} = -2 \left[I - \hat{d}\hat{d}^t \right] \sum_{i=1}^{m} \vec{y}_i$$

This partial derivative is zero whenever $\sum_{i=1}^{m} \vec{y}_i = 0$, in which case $A = (1/m) \sum_{i=1}^{m} X_i$, the average of the sample points.

Given A, the matrix $M(A)$ is determined in the second form of the energy function. The quantity $\hat{d}^t M(A) \hat{d}$ is a quadratic form whose minimum is the smallest eigenvalue of $M(A)$. This can be found by standard eigensystem solvers. A corresponding unit-length eigenvector $\hat{d}$ completes our construction of the least squares line.

For $n = 2$, if $A = (a, b)$, then matrix $M(A)$ is given by

$$M(A) = \left(\sum_{i=1}^{m} (x_i - a)^2 + \sum_{i=1}^{n} (y_i - b)^2 \right) \begin{bmatrix} 1 & 0 \\ 0 & 1 \end{bmatrix}$$
$$- \begin{bmatrix} \sum_{i=1}^{m} (x_i - a)^2 & \sum_{i=1}^{m} (x_i - a)(y_i - b) \\ \sum_{i=1}^{m} (x_i - a)(y_i - b) & \sum_{i=1}^{m} (y_i - b)^2 \end{bmatrix}$$

For $n = 3$, if $A = (a, b, c)$, then matrix $\mathbf{M}(A)$ is given by

$$\mathbf{M}(A) = \delta \begin{bmatrix} 1 & 0 & 0 \\ 0 & 1 & 0 \\ 0 & 0 & 1 \end{bmatrix}$$

$$- \begin{bmatrix} \sum_{i=1}^{m}(x_i - a)^2 & \sum_{i=1}^{m}(x_i - a)(y_i - b) & \sum_{i=1}^{m}(x_i - a)(z_i - c) \\ \sum_{i=1}^{m}(x_i - a)(y_i - b) & \sum_{i=1}^{m}(y_i - b)^2 & \sum_{i=1}^{m}(y_i - b)(z_i - c) \\ \sum_{i=1}^{m}(x_i - a)(z_i - c) & \sum_{i=1}^{m}(y_i - b)(z_i - c) & \sum_{i=1}^{m}(z_i - c)^2 \end{bmatrix}$$

where

$$\delta = \sum_{i=1}^{m}(x_i - a)^2 + \sum_{i=1}^{m}(y_i - b)^2 + \sum_{i=1}^{m}(z_i - c)^2$$

A.7.3 PLANAR FITTING OF POINTS $(x, y, f(x, y))$

The assumption is that the z-component of the data is functionally dependent on the x- and y-components. Given a set of samples $\{(x_i, y_i, z_i)\}_{i=1}^{m}$, determine a, b, and c so that the plane $z = ax + by + c$ best fits the samples in the sense that the sum of the squared errors between the z_i and the plane values $ax_i + by_i + c$ is minimized. Note that the error is measured only in the z-direction.

Define $E(a, b, c) = \sum_{i=1}^{m}[(ax_i + by_i + c) - z_i]^2$. This function is nonnegative, and its graph is a hyperparaboloid whose vertex occurs when the gradient satisfies $\vec{\nabla} E = (0, 0, 0)$. This leads to a system of three linear equations in a, b, and c that can be easily solved. Precisely,

$$(0, 0, 0) = \vec{\nabla} E = 2 \sum_{i=1}^{m}[(ax_i + by_i + c) - z_i](x_i, y_i, 1)$$

and so

$$\begin{bmatrix} \sum_{i=1}^{m} x_i^2 & \sum_{i=1}^{m} x_i y_i & \sum_{i=1}^{m} x_i \\ \sum_{i=1}^{m} x_i y_i & \sum_{i=1}^{m} y_i^2 & \sum_{i=1}^{m} y_i \\ \sum_{i=1}^{m} x_i & \sum_{i=1}^{m} y_i & \sum_{i=1}^{m} 1 \end{bmatrix} \begin{bmatrix} a \\ b \\ c \end{bmatrix} = \begin{bmatrix} \sum_{i=1}^{m} x_i z_i \\ \sum_{i=1}^{m} y_i z_i \\ \sum_{i=1}^{m} z_i \end{bmatrix}$$

The solution provides the least squares solution $z = ax + by + c$.

A.7.4 HYPERPLANAR FITTING OF POINTS USING ORTHOGONAL REGRESSION

It is also possible to fit a plane using least squares where the errors are measured *orthogonally* to the proposed plane rather than measured vertically. The following argument holds for sample points and hyperplanes in n dimensions. Let the hyperplane be $\hat{n} \cdot (X - A) = 0$, where $\hat{n}$ is a unit-length normal to the hyperplane and A is a point on the hyperplane. Define X_i to be the sample points; then

$$X_i = A + \lambda_i \hat{n} + p_i \hat{n}_i^\perp$$

where $\lambda_i = \hat{n} \cdot (X_i - A)$ and $\hat{n}_i^\perp$ is some unit-length vector perpendicular to $\hat{n}$ with appropriate coefficient p_i. Define $\vec{y}_i = X_i - A$. The vector from X_i to its projection onto the hyperplane is $\lambda_i \hat{n}$. The squared length of this vector is $\lambda_i^2 = (\hat{n} \cdot \vec{y}_i)^2$. The energy function for the least squares minimization is $E(A, \hat{n}) = \sum_{i=1}^m \lambda_i^2$. Two alternate forms for this function are

$$E(A, \hat{n}) = \sum_{i=1}^m \left(\vec{y}_i^t \left[\hat{n}\hat{n}^t \right] \vec{y}_i \right)$$

and

$$E(A, \hat{n}) = \hat{n}^t \left(\sum_{i=1}^m \vec{y}_i \vec{y}_i^t \right) \hat{n} = \hat{n}^t \mathbf{M}(A) \hat{n}$$

Using the first form of E in the previous equation, take the derivative with respect to A to get

$$\frac{\partial E}{\partial A} = -2 \left[\hat{n}\hat{n}^t \right] \sum_{i=1}^m \vec{y}_i$$

This partial derivative is zero whenever $\sum_{i=1}^m \vec{y}_i = 0$, in which case $A = (1/m) \sum_{i=1}^m X_i$ (the average of the sample points).

Given A, the matrix $\mathbf{M}(A)$ is determined in the second form of the energy function. The quantity $\hat{n}^t \mathbf{M}(A) \hat{n}$ is a quadratic form whose minimum is the smallest eigenvalue of $\mathbf{M}(A)$. This can be found by standard eigensystem solvers. A corresponding unit-length eigenvector $\hat{n}$ completes our construction of the least squares hyperplane.

For $n = 3$, if $A = (a, b, c)$, then matrix $\mathbf{M}(A)$ is given by

$$\mathbf{M}(A) = \begin{bmatrix} \sum_{i=1}^m (x_i - a)^2 & \sum_{i=1}^m (x_i - a)(y_i - b) & \sum_{i=1}^m (x_i - a)(z_i - c) \\ \sum_{i=1}^m (x_i - a)(y_i - b) & \sum_{i=1}^m (y_i - b)^2 & \sum_{i=1}^m (y_i - b)(z_i - c) \\ \sum_{i=1}^m (x_i - a)(z_i - c) & \sum_{i=1}^m (y_i - b)(z_i - c) & \sum_{i=1}^m (z_i - c)^2 \end{bmatrix}$$

A.7.5 FITTING A CIRCLE TO 2D POINTS

Given a set of points $\{(x_i, y_i)\}_{i=1}^{m}$, $m \geq 3$, fit them with a circle $(x-a)^2 + (y-b)^2 = r^2$, where (a, b) is the circle center and r is the circle radius. An assumption of this algorithm is that not all the points are collinear. The energy function to be minimized is

$$E(a, b, r) = \sum_{i=1}^{m}(L_i - r)^2$$

where $L_i = \sqrt{(x_i - a)^2 + (y_i - b)^2}$. Take the partial derivative with respect to r to obtain

$$\frac{\partial E}{\partial r} = -2 \sum_{i=1}^{m}(L_i - r)$$

Setting equal to zero yields

$$r = \frac{1}{m}\sum_{i=1}^{m} L_i$$

Take the partial derivative with respect to a to obtain

$$\frac{\partial E}{\partial a} = 2\sum_{i=1}^{m}(L_i - r)\frac{\partial L_i}{\partial a} = -2\sum_{i=1}^{m}\left((x_i - a) + r\frac{\partial L_i}{\partial a}\right)$$

and take the partial derivative with respect to b to obtain

$$\frac{\partial E}{\partial b} = 2\sum_{i=1}^{m}(L_i - r)\frac{\partial L_i}{\partial b} = -2\sum_{i=1}^{m}\left((y_i - b) + r\frac{\partial L_i}{\partial b}\right)$$

Setting these two derivatives equal to zero yields

$$a = \frac{1}{m}\sum_{i=1}^{m}x_i + r\frac{1}{m}\sum_{i=1}^{m}\frac{\partial L_i}{\partial a} \quad \text{and} \quad b = \frac{1}{m}\sum_{i=1}^{m}y_i + r\frac{1}{m}\sum_{i=1}^{m}\frac{\partial L_i}{\partial b}$$

Replacing r by its equivalent from $\partial E/\partial r = 0$ and using $\partial L_i/\partial a = (a - x_i)/L_i$ and $\partial L_i/\partial b = (b - y_i)/L_i$ leads to two nonlinear equations in a and b:

$$a = \bar{x} + \bar{L}\bar{L}_a =: F(a, b), \quad b = \bar{y} + \bar{L}\bar{L}_b =: G(a, b)$$

where

$$\bar{x} = \frac{1}{m}\sum_{i=1}^{m} x_i, \quad \bar{y} = \frac{1}{m}\sum_{i=1}^{m} y_i, \quad \bar{L} = \frac{1}{m}\sum_{i=1}^{m} L_i, \quad \bar{L}_a = \frac{1}{m}\sum_{i=1}^{m} \frac{a - x_i}{L_i},$$

$$\bar{L}_b = \frac{1}{m}\sum_{i=1}^{m} \frac{b - y_i}{L_i}$$

Fixed point iteration can be applied to solving these equations: $a_0 = \bar{x}$, $b_0 = \bar{y}$, and $a_{i+1} = F(a_i, b_i)$ and $b_{i+1} = G(a_i, b_i)$ for $i \geq 0$.

A.7.6 FITTING A SPHERE TO 3D POINTS

Given a set of points $\{(x_i, y_i, z_i)\}_{i=1}^{m}$, $m \geq 4$, fit them with a sphere $(x - a)^2 + (y - b)^2 + (z - c)^2 = r^2$, where (a, b, c) is the sphere center and r is the sphere radius. An assumption of this algorithm is that not all the points are coplanar. The energy function to be minimized is

$$E(a, b, c, r) = \sum_{i=1}^{m}(L_i - r)^2$$

where $L_i = \sqrt{(x_i - a)^2 + (y_i - b)^2 + (z_i - c)}$. Take the partial derivative with respect to r to obtain

$$\frac{\partial E}{\partial r} = -2\sum_{i=1}^{m}(L_i - r)$$

Setting equal to zero yields

$$r = \frac{1}{m}\sum_{i=1}^{m} L_i$$

Take the partial derivative with respect to a to obtain

$$\frac{\partial E}{\partial a} = 2\sum_{i=1}^{m}(L_i - r)\frac{\partial L_i}{\partial a} = -2\sum_{i=1}^{m}\left((x_i - a) + r\frac{\partial L_i}{\partial a}\right)$$

take the partial derivative with respect to b to obtain

$$\frac{\partial E}{\partial b} = 2\sum_{i=1}^{m}(L_i - r)\frac{\partial L_i}{\partial b} = -2\sum_{i=1}^{m}\left((y_i - b) + r\frac{\partial L_i}{\partial b}\right)$$

and take the partial derivative with respect to c to obtain

$$\frac{\partial E}{\partial c} = 2\sum_{i=1}^{m}(L_i - r)\frac{\partial L_i}{\partial c} = -2\sum_{i=1}^{m}\left((z_i - c) + r\frac{\partial L_i}{\partial c}\right)$$

Setting these three derivatives equal to zero yields

$$a = \frac{1}{m}\sum_{i=1}^{m}x_i + r\frac{1}{m}\sum_{i=1}^{m}\frac{\partial L_i}{\partial a}, \quad b = \frac{1}{m}\sum_{i=1}^{m}y_i + r\frac{1}{m}\sum_{i=1}^{m}\frac{\partial L_i}{\partial b}, \quad \text{and}$$

$$c = \frac{1}{m}\sum_{i=1}^{m}z_i + r\frac{1}{m}\sum_{i=1}^{m}\frac{\partial L_i}{\partial c}$$

Replacing r by its equivalent from $\partial E/\partial r = 0$ and using $\partial L_i/\partial a = (a - x_i)/L_i$, $\partial L_i/\partial b = (b - y_i)/L_i$, and $\partial L_i/\partial c = (c - z_i)/L_i$ leads to three nonlinear equations in a, b, and c:

$$a = \bar{x} + \bar{L}\bar{L}_a =: F(a,b,c), \quad b = \bar{y} + \bar{L}\bar{L}_b =: G(a,b,c), \quad c = \bar{z} + \bar{L}\bar{L}_c =: H(a,b,c)$$

where

$$\bar{x} = \frac{1}{m}\sum_{i=1}^{m}x_i, \quad \bar{y} = \frac{1}{m}\sum_{i=1}^{m}y_i, \quad \bar{z} = \frac{1}{m}\sum_{i=1}^{m}z_i$$

$$\bar{L} = \frac{1}{m}\sum_{i=1}^{m}L_i, \quad \bar{L}_a = \frac{1}{m}\sum_{i=1}^{m}\frac{a - x_i}{L_i}, \quad \bar{L}_b = \frac{1}{m}\sum_{i=1}^{m}\frac{b - y_i}{L_i}, \quad \bar{L}_c = \frac{1}{m}\sum_{i=1}^{m}\frac{c - z_i}{L_i}$$

Fixed point iteration can be applied to solving these equations: $a_0 = \bar{x}$, $b_0 = \bar{y}$, $c_0 = \bar{z}$, and $a_{i+1} = F(a_i, b_i, c_i)$, $b_{i+1} = G(a_i, b_i, c_i)$, and $c_{i+1} = H(a_i, b_i, c_i)$ for $i \geq 0$.

A.7.7 FITTING A QUADRATIC CURVE TO 2D POINTS

Given a set of points $\{(x_i, y_i)\}_{i=0}^{n}$, a quadratic curve of the form $Q(x, y) = c_0 + c_1 x + c_2 y + c_3 x^2 + c_4 y^2 + c_5 xy = 0$ is sought to fit the points. Given values c_i that provide the fit, any scalar multiple provides the same fit. To eliminate this degree of freedom, require that $\hat{c} = (c_0, \ldots, c_5)$ have unit length. Define the vector variable $\vec{v} = (1, x, y, x^2, y^2, xy)$. The quadratic equation is restated as $Q(\vec{v}) = \hat{c} \cdot \vec{v} = 0$ and is a linear equation in the space of $\vec{v}$. Define $\vec{v}_i = (1, x_i, y_i, x_i^2, y_i^2, x_i y_i)$ for the ith data point. While generally $Q(\vec{v}_i)$ is not zero, the idea is to minimize the sum of squares

$$E(\hat{c}) = \left(\sum_{i=0}^{n}\hat{c}\cdot\vec{v}_i\right)^2 = \hat{c}^{\mathrm{T}}\mathbf{M}\hat{c}$$

where $\mathbf{M} = \sum_{i=0}^{n} \vec{v}_i \vec{v}_i^{\mathrm{T}}$ and subject to the constraint $\|\hat{c}\| = 1$. Now the problem is in the standard format for minimizing a quadratic form, a topic discussed in Section A.6. The minimum value is the smallest eigenvalue of $\mathbf{M}$, and $\hat{c}$ is a corresponding unit-length eigenvector. The minimum itself can be used as a measure of how good the fit is (0 means the fit is exact).

If there is reason to believe the input points are nearly circular, a minor modification can be used in the construction. The circle is of the form $Q(x, y) = c_0 + c_1 x + c_2 y + c_3(x^2 + y^2) = 0$. The same construction can be applied where $\vec{v} = (1, x, y, x^2 + y^2)$ and $E(\hat{c}) = \hat{c}^{\mathrm{T}} \mathbf{M} \hat{c}$ subject to $|\hat{c}| = 1$.

A.7.8   FITTING A QUADRIC SURFACE TO 3D POINTS

Given a set of points $\{(x_i, y_i, z_i)\}_{i=0}^{n}$, a quadric surface of the form $Q(x, y, z) = c_0 + c_1 x + c_2 y + c_3 z + c_4 x^2 + c_5 y^2 + c_6 z^2 + c_7 xy + c_8 xz + c_9 yz = 0$ is sought to fit the points. Just like the previous section, $\hat{c} = (c_i)$ is required to be unit length and $\vec{v} = (1, x, y, z, x^2, y^2, z^2, xy, xz, yz)$. The quadratic form to minimize is $E(\hat{c}) = \hat{c}^{\mathrm{T}} \mathbf{M} \hat{c}$, where $\mathbf{M} = \sum_{i=0}^{2} \vec{v}_i \vec{v}_i^{\mathrm{T}}$. The minimum value is the smallest eigenvalue of $\mathbf{M}$, and $\hat{c}$ is a corresponding unit-length eigenvector. The minimum itself can be used as a measure of how good the fit is (0 means the fit is exact).

If there is reason to believe the input points are nearly spherical, a minor modification can be used in the construction. The circle is of the form $Q(x, y, z) = c_0 + c_1 x + c_2 y + c_3 z + c_4(x^2 + y^2 + z^2) = 0$. The same construction can be applied where $\vec{v} = (1, x, y, z, x^2 + y^2 + z^2)$ and $E(\hat{c}) = \hat{c}^{\mathrm{T}} \mathbf{M} \hat{c}$ subject to $\|\hat{c}\| = 1$.

A.8   SUBDIVISION OF CURVES

Sometimes it is desirable to have a polyline approximation to a curve $X(t)$ for $t \in [t_{\min}, t_{\max}]$. The methods discussed here apply to any dimension curve. A *subdivision* of the curve is a set of points corresponding to an increasing sequence of parameters $\{t_i\}_{i=0}^{n} \subset [t_{\min}, t_{\max}]$ for a specified n. Usually the end points of the curve are required to be in the subdivision, in which case $t_0 = t_{\min}$ and $t_n = t_{\max}$. The subdivision points are $X_i = X(t_i)$ for $0 \le i \le n$. A few useful subdivision methods are presented in this section.

A.8.1   SUBDIVISION BY UNIFORM SAMPLING

The simplest way to subdivide is to uniformly sample $[t_{\min}, t_{\max}]$. The parameter values are $t_i = t_{\min} + (t_{\max} - t_{\min})i/n$ for $0 \le i \le n$. This type of sampling is simple to implement, but it ignores any intrinsic variation of the curve. Consequently, the polyline generated by this subdivision is not always a good approximation. The pseudocode for the subdivision is

```
Input:   Curve X(t) with t in [tmin, tmax]
         n, the number of subdivision points is n + 1
Output: subdivision {P[0],...,P[n]}

void Subdivide(int n, Point P[n + 1])
{
    for (int i = 0; i <= n; i++) {
        float t = tmin + (tmax - tmin) * i / n;
        P[i] = X(t);
    }
}
```

A.8.2   SUBDIVISION BY ARC LENGTH

This method selects a set of points on the curve that are uniformly spaced along the curve. The spacing between a pair of points is a distance measurement made along the curve itself. The distance in this case is called *arc length*. For example, if the curve is the semicircle $x^2 + y^2 = 1$ for $y \geq 0$, the distance between the end points $(1, 0)$ and $(-1, 0)$ is 2 units when measured in the plane. As points on the semicircle, the distance between the end points is π units, the arc length of the semicircle. The points $X_i = (\cos(\pi i/n), \sin(\pi i/n))$ for $0 \leq i \leq n$ are a subdivision of the semicircle. The distance $\|X_{i+1} - X_i\|$ measured in the plane varies with i. However, the arc length between the consecutive pairs of points is π/n, a constant. The points are uniformly spaced with respect to arc length.

Let L be the total length of the curve. Let $t \in [t_{\min}, t_{\max}]$ be the curve parameter, and let $s \in [0, L]$ be the arc length parameter. The subdivision is constructed by finding those points located at $s_i = Li/n$ for $0 \leq i \leq n$. The technical problem is to determine t_i that corresponds to s_i. The process of computing t from a specified s is called *reparameterization by arc length*. This is accomplished by a numerical inversion of the integral equation relating s to t. Define Speed$(t) = \|\vec{X}'(t)\|$ and Length$(t) = \int_{t_{\min}}^{t} \|\vec{X}'(\tau)\| \, d\tau$. The problem is now to solve Length$(t) - s = 0$ for the specifed s, a root-finding task. From the definition of arc length, the root must be unique. An application of Newton's method will suffice (see Section A.5). Evaluation of Length(t) does require a numerical integration. Various algorithms for numerical integration are provided in Press et al. (1988). The pseudocode for computing t from s is

```
Input: The curve X(t), domain [tmin, tmax], and total length L are available
       globally.  The Length and Speed calls implicitly use these values.  The
       value of s must be in [0, L].
Output:  The value of t corresponding to s.

float GetParameterFromArcLength(float s)
```

```
{
    // Choose an initial guess based on relative location of s in [0,L].
    float ratio = s / L;
    float t = (1 - ratio) * tmin + ratio * tmax;

    for (int i = 0; i < imax; i++) {
        float diff = Length(t) - s;
        if (|diff| < epsilon)
            return t;

        t -= diff / Speed(t);
    }

    // Newton's method failed to converge.  Return your best guess.
    return t;
}
```

An application must choose the maximum number of iterations imax and a tolerance epsilon for how close to zero the root is.

The pseudocode for the subdivision is

```
Input: The curve X(t), domain [tmin, tmax], and total length L are available
    globally. The number of subdivision points is n + 1.
Output: subdivision {P[0],..., P[n]}

void Subdivide (int n, Point P[n + 1])
{
    for (int i = 0; i <= n; i++) {
        float s = L * i / n;
        float t = GetParameterFromArcLength(s);
        P[i] = X(t);
    }
}
```

A.8.3 SUBDIVISION BY MIDPOINT DISTANCE

This scheme produces a nonuniform sampling by recursively bisecting the parameter space. The bisection is actually performed, and the resulting curve point corresponding to the midpoint parameter is analyzed. If A and B are the end points of the segment and if C is the computed point in the bisection step, then the distance d_0 from C to the segment is computed. If $d_1 = \|B - A\|$, then B is added to the tessellation if $d_0/d_1 > \varepsilon$ for an application-specified maximum relative error of $\varepsilon > 0$. The pseudocode is given below. Rather than maintaining a doubly linked list to handle the insertion of points on subdivision, the code maintains a singly linked list of ordered points.

```
Input: The curve X(t) and domain [tmin, tmax] are available globally.
       m, the maximum level of subdivision
       epsilon, the maximum relative error
       sub {}, an empty list
Output: n >= 1 and subdivision {p[0],..., p[n]}

void Subdivide (int level, float t0, Point X0, float t1, Point X1, List sub)
{
    if (level > 0) {
        tm = (t0 + t1) / 2;
        Xm = X(tm);
        d0 = length of segment <X0, X1>
        d1 = distance from Xm to segment <X0, X1>;

        if (d1 / d0 > epsilon) {
            Subdivide(level - 1, t0, X0, tm, Xm, sub);
            Subdivide(level - 1, tm, Xm, t1, X1, sub);
            return;
        }
    }

    sub.Append(X1);
}

Initial call:
    List sub = { X(tmin) };
    Subdivide(maxlevel, tmin, X(tmin), tmax, X(tmax), sub);
```

The calculations of d_0 and d_1 require expensive square roots. The division d_0/d_1 is also somewhat expensive. An implementation would use squared distances d_0^2 and d_1^2 and make the comparison $d_1^2 > \varepsilon^2 d_0^2$ to reduce the computational costs.

A.8.4 SUBDIVISION BY VARIATION

The subdivision itself can be designed to reflect the variation in the curve. A straightforward subdivision by uniform sampling does not capture places where the curve is nearly linear or highly varying. If the goal is to get an extremely accurate distance measurement, a better method is to recursively subdivide where the subdivision step is applied based on variation between the curve and the current line segment of interest. The recursion terminates when all the variations are smaller than a prescribed tolerance.

The variation metric can be one of many quantities. The one described here is based on an integral of squared distance between the curve and the line segment. Let $[t_0, t_1]$ be the current subinterval under consideration. The curve end points on this interval are $X_i = X(t_i)$ for $i = 0, 1$. The line segment of approximation is

$$\mathcal{L}(t) = X_0 + \frac{t - t_0}{t_1 - t_0} \left(X_1 - X_0 \right)$$

The variation is defined by the integral

$$V([t_0, t_1]) = \int_{t_0}^{t_1} \| X(t) - \mathcal{L}(t) \|^2 dt$$

The difference between the curve and the line segment is a polynomial

$$X(t) - \mathcal{L}(t) = \sum_{i=0}^{n} B_i t^i$$

where $B_0 = A_0 - (t_1 X_0 - t_0 X_1)/(t_1 - t_0)$, $B_1 = A_1 - (X_1 - X_0)/(t_1 - t_0)$, and $B_i = A_i$ for $2 \leq i \leq n$. The squared length is a polynomial of degree $2n$:

$$\| X(t) - \mathcal{L}(t) \|^2 = \sum_{i=0}^{n} B_i t^i \sum_{j=0}^{n} B_j t^j = \sum_{k=0}^{2n} \left(\sum_{m=\max\{0,k-n\}}^{k} B_{k-m} \cdot B_m \right) t^k$$

so the variation is

$$V([t_0, t_1]) = \sum_{k=0}^{2n} \left(\sum_{m=\max\{0,k-n\}}^{k} B_{k-m} \cdot B_m \right) \frac{t_1^{k+1} - t_0^{k+1}}{k + 1}$$

The pseudocode for the subdivision is

```
Input: The curve X(t) and domain [tmin, tmax] are available globally.
       maxlevel, the maximum level of subdivision;
       minvariation, the variation tolerance;
       sub {}, an empty list;
Output: n >= 1 and subdivision {p[0],..., p[n]};

void Subdivide(int level, float t0, Point X0, float t1, Point X1, List sub)
{
    if (level > 0) {
```

```
        var = Variation(t0, X0, t1, X1);
        if (var > minvariation) {
            tm = (t0 + t1) / 2;
            xmid = X(tm);
            Subdivide(level - 1, t0, X0, tm, Xm, sub);
            Subdivide(level - 1, tm, Xm, t1, X1, sub);
            return;
        }
    }

    sub.Append(X1);
}

Initial call:
    List sub = { X(tmin) };
    Subdivide(maxlevel, tmin, X(tmin), tmax, X(tmax), sub);
```

The `maxlevel` parameter avoids deep recursive calls when a small `minvariation` is specified. However, if `level` reaches zero, the variation for the current interval is not necessarily within the specified tolerance. Since the variation does not provide error bounds for the distance calculation, this is not a problem.

A.9 TOPICS FROM CALCULUS

This section reviews several topics from calculus that can be useful in solving a number of problems discussed in this book, particularly distance and intersection.

A.9.1 LEVEL SETS

Political maps show boundaries of states and countries, and some amount of geographical features (rivers, oceans, etc.), but these are often shown indicatively. Topographic maps, on the other hand, are useful because they explicitly show the elevation of the land. This is done by the use of *contours*—curves representing the cross section of the land at a particular altitude. By observing the altitude markings associated with particular contours, as well as their topology, the map user can easily distinguish inclines, peaks, and valleys. Further, the steepness of a slope can easily be discerned, by the relative distance between adjacent contours—the closer together they are, the steeper the slope.

A contour map can be considered to be a way of visualizing a function of two variables $f(x, y) = z$, where x and y are the latitude and longitude and z is the height (altitude). If we intersect the function f with a horizontal plane

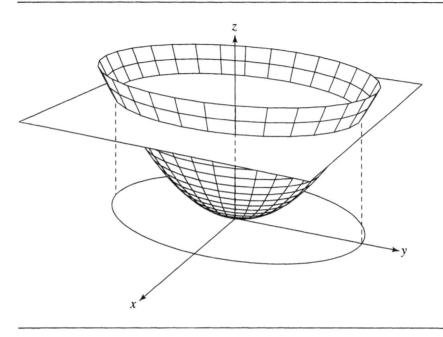

Figure A.2   Intersection of a function $f(x, y) = z$ and plane $z = 0.8$ yields a level curve, shown projected on the xy-plane.

$$z = h$$

and project the resulting curve onto the xy-plane, then we get what is referred to as a *level curve* (see Figure A.2). This level curve has the equation

$$f(x, y) = a$$

If we have the paraboloid

$$f(x, y) = \frac{2x^2}{3} + y^2$$

(see Figure A.3), then the level curves have equations of the form

$$\frac{2x^2}{3} + y^2 = h$$

For $h > 0$, these are ellipses; for $h = 0$, it is a point; and for $h < 0$, there are no curves. A number of the projected level curves are shown in Figure A.4.

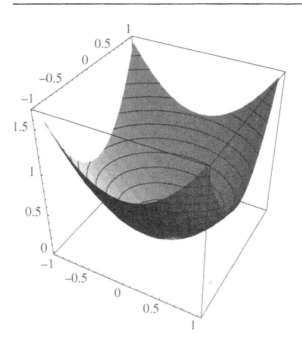

Figure A.3   Level curves for $f(x, y) = \frac{2x^2}{3} + y^2$.

Level curves of a function $f(x, y)$ and the gradient of the function $\nabla f(x, y)$ have an important geometric relationship. Suppose we have any point (in f's domain, of course) x_0, y_0 and that $f(x_0, y_0) = c$ for some constant c. We know that $f(x, y) = c$ defines some level curve for f, and that $f(x_0, y_0)$ is a point on that curve. The maximum rate of increase for f at (x_0, y_0) is in the direction of $\nabla f(x_0, y_0)$ and the minimum in the direction of $-\nabla f(x_0, y_0)$. Intuitively, it seems, then, that the gradient must be perpendicular to the level curve at $f(x_0, y_0)$, and this indeed turns out to be the case. An outline of the proof follows (Anton 1980).

Assume we have a level curve

$$f(x, y) = c \qquad (A.9)$$

through (x_0, y_0). We can represent this curve parametrically, as

$$x = x(t)$$

$$y = y(t)$$

which has a nonzero tangent vector at (x_0, y_0)

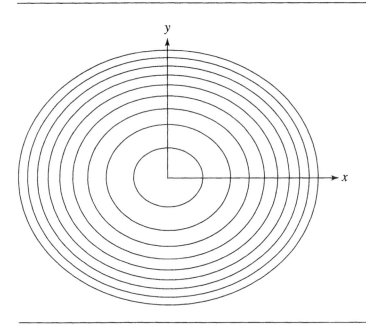

Figure A.4　Level curves for $f(x, y) = \frac{2x^2}{3} + y^2$, projected onto the xy-plane.

$$x'(t_0)\mathbf{i} + y'(t_0)\mathbf{j} \neq 0$$

where t_0 is the value of the parameter at the point (x_0, y_0).

If we differentiate Equation A.9 with respect to t and apply the chain rule, we get

$$f_x(x(t), y(t))x'(t) + f_y(x(t), y(t))y'(t) = 0$$

Using the facts that $x(t_0) = x_0$ and $y(t_0) = y_0$, and substituting $t = t_0$, we get

$$f_x(x_0, y_0)x'(t_0) + f_y(x_0, y_0)y'(t_0) = 0$$

which can be rewritten as

$$\nabla f(x_0, y_0) \cdot (x'(t_0)\mathbf{i} + y'(t_0)\mathbf{j}) = 0$$

That is, $\nabla f(x_0, y_0)$ is perpendicular to the tangent vector of the level curve at (x_0, y_0).

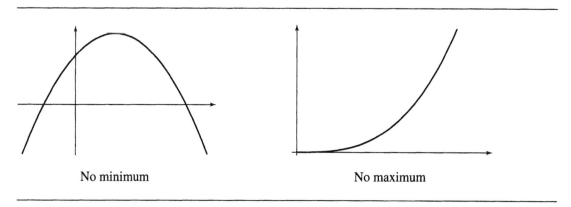

No minimum   No maximum

Figure A.5   Two functions lacking either a minimum or maximum value.

A.9.2   MINIMA AND MAXIMA OF FUNCTIONS

This section addresses the problem of finding the minimum and maximum values of a function, in both one and two variables. Such problems arise often in the context of *optimization* problems—informally, situations in which we want to find the "best" (or perhaps "worst") solution.

Functions of One Variable

Given a function f, we might wish to know various facts about minimum or maximum values (the *extrema*), such as

- Does $f(x)$ have a minimum (maximum) value?
- If $f(x)$ has a minimum (maximum), what is it, and where does it occur?
- Does $f(x)$ have a minimum (maximum) within an interval $[a, b]$ or $[a, b)$?

Figure A.5 shows two functions, one of which has no minimum value over its domain, and the other no maximum value.

We begin with some relevant definitions

DEFINITION   A number M is called an *absolute maximum value* for a function f with domain D if
A.1

  i. $f(x) \leq M, \forall x \in D$.

  ii. $\exists x \in D \mid f(x) = M$. ∎

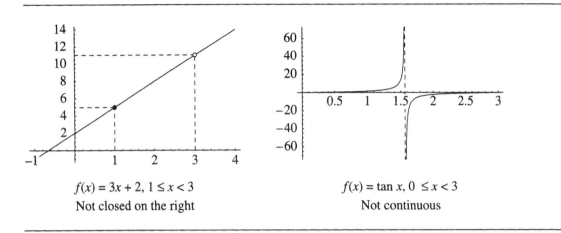

$f(x) = 3x + 2, \, 1 \le x < 3$

Not closed on the right

$f(x) = \tan x, \, 0 \le x < 3$

Not continuous

Figure A.6   Two functions that violate the assumptions of the Extreme Value Theorem.

DEFINITION
A.2

A number M is called an *absolute minimum value* for a function f with domain D if

i. $f(x) \ge M, \forall x \in D$.

ii. $\exists x \in D | f(x) = M$. ■

Often, we are interested in extrema in some restricted portion of the domain of f.

THEOREM A.1

Extreme Value Theorem—One-Variable Form: Let $f(x)$ be continuous on the closed interval $[a, b]$; then, there are numbers $x_0, x_1 \in [a, b]$ such that $f(x) \le f(x_0)$ and $f(x) \ge f(x_1), \forall x \in [a, b]$. ■

Note that the two conditions—that f be continuous and that the interval be closed—are both essential for guaranteeing the existence of relative extrema. Two examples, each of which violates one of the conditions, respectively, are $\tan(x), \forall x \in [0, 3]$, and $f(x) = 3x + 2, \forall x \in [2, 6)$. The tangent function fails to be continuous at the value 1.5, and the line function fails because it is not closed on the right (there is no "largest value less than 11"); graphs of these functions are shown in Figure A.6.

The Extreme Value Theorem merely defines the conditions under which extrema exist—it does nothing directly to help *find* them. For this, we must turn to the concept of critical points.

DEFINITION
A.3

For function f, a *critical point* is any point $x \in D$ such that either

i. the first derivative is $0 - f'(x) = 0$ or

ii. the first derivative does not exist

The critical points where $f'(x) = 0$ are known as *stationary points*. ■

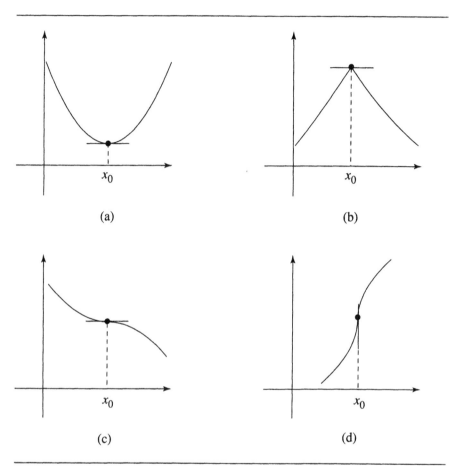

Figure A.7   A variety of functions, showing critical points—(a) and (b) are stationary points; (c) and (d) are inflection points.

Figure A.7 shows a variety of critical points. Those in Figure A.7(a), A.7(b), and A.7(c) are stationary points; the critical points in Figure A.7(c) and A.7(d) are also called *inflection points*. Critical points are significant because they are key to determining the extrema, as the following theorem states.

THEOREM A.2   If a function f has an extremum on an interval (a, b), then the extremum occurs at a critical point of f. ∎

A proof of this theorem can be found in Anton (1980). This theorem can be used to locate an extremum of f on closed intervals as well: the extremum occurs either within the interval or at one of the boundaries. Figure A.8 shows intervals of functions at which the maximum occurs at the right end, within the interval at a

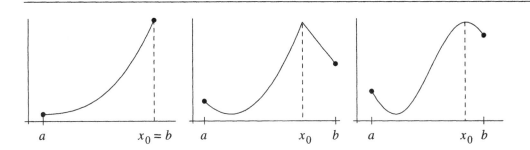

a $x_0 = b$ a x_0 b a x_0 b

Figure A.8   The maximum of a function may occur at the boundary of an interval or within the interval.

point at which f is not differentiable, and within the interval at a point at which f is differentiable. Thus, an effective procedure to find the extrema of a (continuous) function f on a closed interval $[a, b]$ is

1. Find the critical points in the open interval (a, b).

2. Evaluate f at the interval boundaries a and b.

3. Compare the values of the critical points and the interval boundaries. The smallest among them is the minimum, and the largest is the maximum.

An example should demonstrate this. Consider the equation

$$f(x) = x^3 + 6x^2 - 7x + 19 \qquad (A.10)$$

We wish to find the extrema on the interval $[-8, 3]$ (see Figure A.9). First, we must verify that the function is continuous in order for the Extreme Value Theorem to apply, but this function is a polynomial and so we know it is continuous. Our theorem tells us that if there is an extremum in the open interval, it must occur at a critical point, and as critical points (in this case) must occur where the derivative is zero, we must solve $f'(x)$ to find these points.

The derivative of f is

$$f'(x) = 3x^2 + 12x - 7 \qquad (A.11)$$

whose roots are $\{\{x \to \frac{-6-\sqrt{57}}{3}\}, \{x \to \frac{-6+\sqrt{57}}{3}\}\} \approx \{-4.51661, 0.516611\}$ (see Figure A.10). The values of f at the end points are $f(-8) = -53$, $f(3) = 79$. The minimum therefore occurs at the left boundary $f(-8) = -53$, and the maximum occurs at the critical point $f(\frac{-6-\sqrt{57}}{3}) \approx f(-4.51661) \approx 80.8771$.

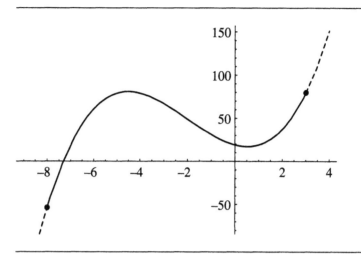

Figure A.9 $f(x) = x^3 + 6x^2 - 7x + 19, \forall x \in [-8, 3]$.

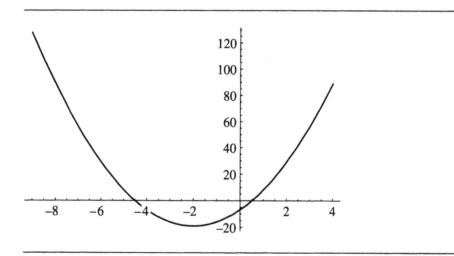

Figure A.10 $f'(x) = 3x^2 + 12x - 7, \forall x \in [-8, 3]$.

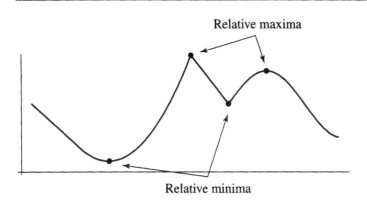

Figure A.11   Relative extrema.

Relative Extrema

The Extreme Value Theorem applies only when the interval is closed and when the function is continuous. So, there are cases in which it cannot be applied. The graphs of many functions contain intervals that contain what we may informally refer to as "hills" and "valleys"—these are called *relative extrema*; an example is shown in Figure A.11. These characteristics are defined formally as follows

DEFINITION A.4   A function f has a *relative maximum* at x_0 if

$$\exists (a, b) \mid f(x_0) \geq f(x), \forall x \in (a, b) \quad \blacksquare$$

DEFINITION A.5   A function f has a *relative minimum* at x_0 if

$$\exists (a, b) \mid f(x_0) \leq f(x), \forall x \in (a, b) \quad \blacksquare$$

Three theorems allow us to identify relative extrema.

THEOREM A.3   *Relative Extreme Value Theorem:* If a function f has a relative extremum at a point x_0, then x_0 is a critical point for f. $\blacksquare$

Note that this does *not* work the other way—a critical point may or may not be an extremum at all; Figure A.7(c) has a critical point that is not a relative extremum.

THEOREM A.4   *First Derivative Test:* If a function f is continuous at a critical point x_0, then

    i. If $f'(x) > 0$ within an (open) interval extending left from x_0 and $f'(x) < 0$ within that interval, extending right from x_0, then $f(x_0)$ is a relative maximum.

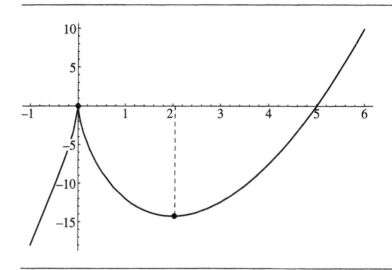

Figure A.12   Relative extrema of $f(x) = 3x^{\frac{5}{3}} - 15x^{\frac{2}{3}}$.

ii. If $f'(x) < 0$ within an (open) interval extending left from x_0 and $f'(x) > 0$ within that interval, extending right from x_0, then $f(x_0)$ is a relative minimum.

iii. If $f'(x)$ has the same sign within an (open) interval both to the left and right of x_0, then $f(x_0)$ is not a relative extremum. ∎

Informally, the relative extrema of such functions occur at critical points where the derivative changes sign.

An example from Anton (1980) shows how this theorem can be used to find the relative extrema of the function

$$f(x) = 3x^{\frac{5}{3}} - 15x^{\frac{2}{3}}$$

We take the derivative of f to find the critical points:

$$f'(x) = 5x^{\frac{2}{3}} - 10x^{-\frac{1}{3}}$$

$$= 5x^{-\frac{1}{3}}(x - 2)$$

The critical points, then, are $x = 0$ (where the derivative does not exist), and $x = 2$ (see Figure A.12).

The third theorem is the following

THEOREM A.5   *Second Derivative Test:* If f is twice differentiable at a stationary point x_0, then

i. If $f''(x_0) > 0$, then $f(x_0)$ is a relative minimum.

ii. If $f''(x_0) < 0$, then $f(x_0)$ is a relative maximum. ∎

The intuition for this theorem is as follows: The graph of the function at a critical point where the second derivative is negative is "concave up." The graph of the function at a critical point where the second derivative is positive is "concave down."

An example shows how this works. We wish to find the local extrema of

$$f(x) = x^4 - 3x^2 + 3$$

We take the first derivative to find the critical points:

$$f'(x) = 4x^3 - 6x$$

which are

$$\{\{x \to -1.22474\}, \{x \to 0\}, \{x \to 1.22474\}\}$$

The second derivative is

$$f''(x) = 12x^2 - 6$$

If we plug in the stationary points of f' into f'' we get

$$f''(-1.22474) = 12 > 0$$
$$f''(0) = -6 < 0$$
$$f''(1.22474) = 12 > 0$$

and so we can conclude that there is a relative maximum at $x = 0$ and relative minima at $x \approx -1.22474$ and $x \approx 1.22474$.

Functions of More than One Variable

In the previous subsection, we presented techniques for finding the extrema of functions of one variable; here, we describe analogous techniques for functions of two variables. Single-variable functions are conveniently visualized as curves in the plane, and in an analogous fashion, two-variable functions can be visualized as surfaces in 3D space. As surfaces are the 3D analogs of curves, so too we have techniques for optimization that extend those used for curves.

As with the graphs of single-variable functions, the "hills and valleys" of the graphs of two-variable functions are the relative extrema (see Figure A.13). This is formalized with the following definitions.

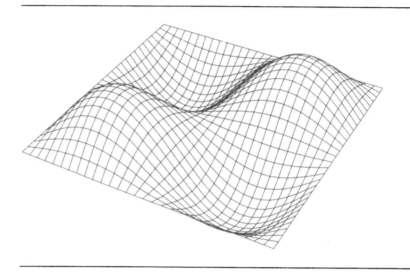

Figure A.13   Relative extrema of a function of two variables are the hills and valleys of its graph.

DEFINITION
A.6
A function f of two variables has a *relative maximum* at a point (x_0, y_0) if there is a circle with center (x_0, y_0) such that $f(x_0, y_0) \geq f(x, y), \forall x$ inside the circle. ∎

DEFINITION
A.7
A function f of two variables has a *relative minimum* at a point (x_0, y_0) if there is a circle with center (x_0, y_0) such that $f(x_0, y_0) \leq f(x, y), \forall x$ inside the circle. ∎

This idea of the circle can be understood to be the natural generalization of the linear interval of the domain of a single-variable function.

Definitions for *absolute extrema* are the following.

DEFINITION
A.8
A function f of two variables with domains D_1 and D_2 has an *absolute maximum* at a point (x_0, y_0) if $f(x_0, y_0) \geq f(x, y), \forall (x, y) \in D_1 \times D_2$. ∎

DEFINITION
A.9
A function f of two variables with domains D_1 and D_2 has an *absolute minimum* at a point (x_0, y_0) if $f(x_0, y_0) \leq f(x, y), \forall (x, y) \in D_1 \times D_2$. ∎

For a one-variable function, a relative extremum exists where the first derivative is zero; on the graph, this is depicted by the tangent being horizontal. For two-variable functions, the analogous condition is that we have a relative extremum at a point where the partial derivatives with respect to x and y are both zero (provided they exist); graphically, this can be seen in that the traces of the graph of $z = f(x, y)$ on the planes $x = x_0$ and $y = y_0$ have horizontal tangent lines at (x_0, y_0) (Figure A.14). Thus, we have

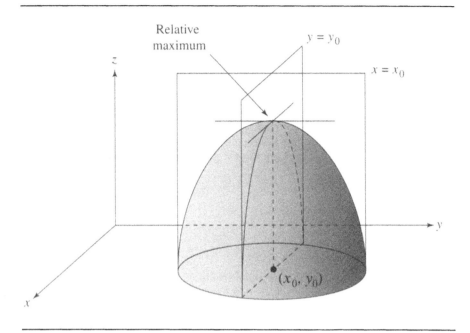

Figure A.14   The relative maximum of a function $z = f(x, y)$. After Anton (1980).

$$\frac{\partial f}{\partial x}(x_0, y_0) = 0$$

and

$$\frac{\partial f}{\partial y}(x_0, y_0) = 0$$

This is formalized in the following theorem.

THEOREM A.6   If a two-variable function f has a relative extremum at (x_0, y_0), and if the first partial derivatives of f both exist at that point, then

$$\frac{\partial f}{\partial x}(x_0, y_0) = 0$$

and

$$\frac{\partial f}{\partial y}(x_0, y_0) = 0 \quad \blacksquare$$

Just as with one-variable functions, points in the domain of a function $f(x, y)$ with partial first derivatives equal to zero are called *critical points*, and so the theorem echoes the analogous one for one-variable functions in stating that the relative extrema of functions occur at critical points.

Recall that for a one-variable function, the first derivative being zero does not guarantee that the point is a relative extremum; the example was an inflection point in the graph of the function. Similarly, for two-variable functions, the partial derivatives being both zero do not guarantee you have a relative extremum. Figure A.15 shows the graph of the function $f(x, y) = x^2 - y^2$. At the point $(0, 0)$, the traces of the function in both the *XZ* and *YZ* planes have horizontal tangent lines because

$$\frac{\partial f}{\partial x}(x_0, y_0) = 0$$

$$\frac{\partial f}{\partial y}(x_0, y_0) = 0$$

Observe that *any* circle centered at $(0, 0)$ will have points that have a z-value greater than 0 and points that have a z-value less than zero, and so $(0, 0)$, in spite of being a critical point, is not an extremum. Not surprisingly, such points are called *saddle points*.

We can use the first partial derivatives to locate relative extrema and saddle points of functions. For example, given the function

$$f(x, y) = 3 - x^2 - y^2$$

we take the partial derivatives

$$\frac{\partial f}{\partial x} = -2x$$

$$\frac{\partial f}{\partial y} = -2y$$

and set them to zero. This yields $x = 0$ and $y = 0$, and so $(0, 0)$ is the only critical point. Evaluating the function at this critical point, we get $f(0, 0) = 3$; for all points (x, y) other than $(0, 0)$, we have $f(x, y) < 3$ because $f(x, y) = 3 - x^2 - y^2 = 3 - (x^2 + y^2)$. Thus, $(0, 0)$ is a relative maximum for f.

For single-variable functions, we have a second derivative test (Theorem A.5) that we can apply for more complex functions. For two-variable functions, we have an analogous theorem.

THEOREM A.7   *Second Partials Test:* Suppose we have a function f with a critical point at (x_0, y_0), and which has continuous second partial derivatives in some circle around that point. If we let

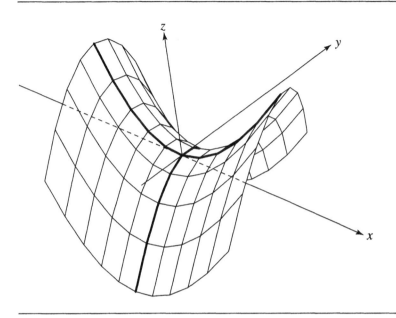

Figure A.15   A "saddle function"—the point $(0, 0)$ is not an extremum, in spite of the first partial
derivatives being zero.

$$D = \frac{\partial^2 f}{\partial x^2}(x_0, y_0)\frac{\partial^2 f}{\partial y^2}(x_0, y_0) - (\frac{\partial^2 f}{\partial y \partial x}(x_0, y_0))^2$$

then the following hold:

i. If $D > 0$ and $\frac{\partial^2 f}{\partial x^2}(x_0, y_0) > 0$, then f has a relative minimum at (x_0, y_0).

ii. If $D > 0$ and $\frac{\partial^2 f}{\partial x^2}(x_0, y_0) < 0$, then f has a relative maximum at (x_0, y_0).

iii. If $D < 0$, then f has a saddle point at (x_0, y_0).

iv. If $D = 0$, then there are no conclusions to be drawn. ■

As an example, consider the function

$$f(x, y) = 2y^2 x - yx^2 + 4xy$$

We begin by finding the first partials:

Table A.10   Second partials of $f(x, y) = 2y^2x - yx^2 + 4xy$ at critical points.

Critical point (x_0, y_0)	$\frac{\partial^2 f}{\partial x^2}(x_0, y_0)$	$\frac{\partial^2 f}{\partial y^2}(x_0, y_0)$	$\frac{\partial^2 f}{\partial y \partial x}(x_0, y_0)$	$D = \frac{\partial^2 f}{\partial x^2}\frac{\partial^2 f}{\partial y^2} - (\frac{\partial^2 f}{\partial y \partial x})^2$
$(0, -2)$	4	0	-4	-16
$(0, 0)$	0	0	-4	-16
$(\frac{4}{3}, -\frac{2}{3})$	$\frac{4}{3}$	$\frac{16}{3}$	$-\frac{4}{3}$	$\frac{16}{3}$
$(4, 0)$	0	16	-4	-16

$$\frac{\partial f}{\partial x} = 4y - 2xy + 2y^2$$

$$\frac{\partial f}{\partial y} = 4x - x^2 + 4xy$$

If we take the right-hand sides of these and solve them simultaneously for x and y, we get

$$\{\{x \to 0, y \to -2\}, \{x \to 0, y \to 0\}, \{x \to \frac{4}{3}, y \to -\frac{2}{3}\}, \{x \to 4, y \to 0\}\}$$

The second partial derivatives are

$$\frac{\partial^2 f}{\partial x^2}(x, y) = 4y - 2xy + 2y^2$$

$$\frac{\partial^2 f}{\partial y^2}(x, y) = 4x - x^2 + 4xy$$

$$\frac{\partial^2 f}{\partial y \partial x}(x, y) = 4 - 2x + 4y$$

For convenient analysis, see Table A.10 We have $D < 0$ at $(0, -2)$, $(0, 0)$, and $(4, 0)$, and so these are saddle points; $D > 0$ and $\frac{\partial^2 f}{\partial x} > 0$ at $(\frac{4}{3}, -\frac{2}{3})$, and so this is a relative minimum. The surface is shown in Figure A.16, and its contour plot is shown in Figure A.17.

A.9.3   LAGRANGE MULTIPLIERS

Geometric problems frequently involve finding minima or maxima of an equation; schemes for solving these problems are discussed in Section A.9.2. In this section we

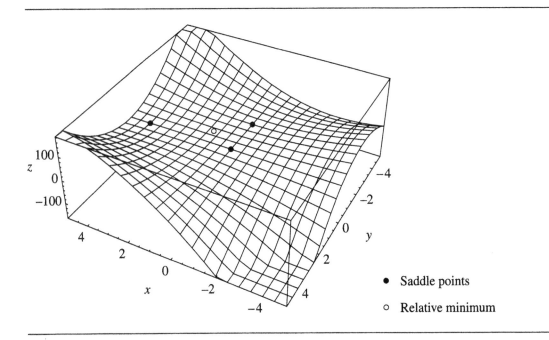

Figure A.16   Graph of $2y^2x - yx^2 + 4xy$, showing saddle points and relative minimum.

cover a particular type of these problems, which involve finding minima or maxima subject to a constraint. The canonical forms for these problems are the following.

Two-Variable Extremum Problem with One Constraint: Maximize or minimize the function

$$f(x, y)$$

subject to the constraint

$$g(x, y) = 0$$

Three-Variable Extremum Problem with One Constraint: Maximize or minimize the function

$$f(x, y, z)$$

subject to the constraint

$$g(x, y, z) = 0$$

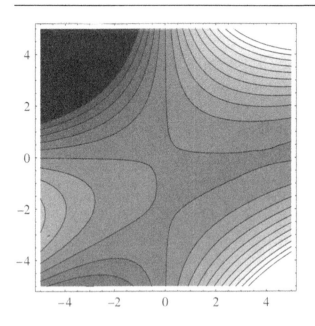

Figure A.17   Contour plot of $2y^2x - yx^2 + 4xy$.

Constrained extremum problems can be thought of as a restriction on the domain of $f(x, y)$.

Note that the extremum may be at one end or the other of the interval, or anywhere in between. Now, we need an analogous definition for functions of two variables. First, a couple of definitions.

DEFINITION A.10   A closed set is one that contains all of its boundary points; for example, on a closed curve. ▪

DEFINITION A.11   A bounded set is one whose members can be enclosed by a disk. ▪

We are now able to proceed.

THEOREM A.8   *Extreme Value Theorem—Two-Variable Form:* Let D be a closed and bounded set, and let $f(x, y)$ be continuous on it; then, there are points $(x_0, y_0), (x_1, y_1) \in D$ such that $f(x, y) \leq f(x_0, y_0)$ and $f(x, y) \geq f(x_1, y_1), \forall (x, y) \in D$. ▪

The constraint equation can be solved for one of the variables in terms of the rest, and the result substituted into the extremum equation. Then, the techniques described in Section A.9.2 can be applied (also, we have to plug in the boundary points as well, in case they are the extrema). However, this may not be feasible—the constraint equation can be too complex. In such cases, the method of Lagrange multipliers can be applied.

THEOREM A.9   *Constrained-Extremum Principle—Two-Variable Form:* Let f and g be two-variable functions with continuous first partial derivatives on some set D containing the curve $g(x, y) = 0$, with $\nabla g \neq 0$ at any point on that curve. Suppose that f has a constrained extremum on the constraint curve; then this extremum occurs at the point (x_0, y_0), and the gradients of f and g are parallel at that point:

$$\nabla f(x_0, y_0) = \lambda \nabla g(x_0, y_0), \qquad \lambda \in \mathbb{R}$$

The number λ is called a *Lagrange multiplier*. ∎

This may not necessarily seem obvious at first, so here's a less formal explanation. From Section A.9.1, we know that the gradient of f is perpendicular to the tangent vector of f:

$$\nabla f(x_0, y_0) \cdot (x'(t_0)\mathbf{i} + y'(t_0)\mathbf{j}) = 0$$

If we assume that (x_0, y_0) is indeed an extremum, then it lies on the constraint curve $g(x, y) = 0$.

But of course, $\nabla g(x_0, y_0)$ is also perpendicular to $g(x, y)$ at (x_0, y_0) because it is the level curve for function g. Thus, $\nabla f(x_0, y_0)$ and $\nabla g(x_0, y_0)$ are both perpendicular to the constraint curve at (x_0, y_0), and therefore both of their tangent vectors are parallel. Put more directly, the curves are tangent at the extrema.

A simple example can illustrate this. Suppose we have an ellipse with the equation

$$\mathcal{E} : 15x^2 + 7y^2 + 11xy = 30$$

and wish to find the point on the ellipse closest to the origin $(0, 0)$. That is, we wish to *minimize* the distance function $\sqrt{x^2 + y^2}$, subject to the constraint that $(x, y) \in \mathcal{E}$. The set $\mathcal{E}$ is closed and bounded, so by Theorem A.8 we know that there is some point $P \in \mathcal{E}$ such that $f(P) \leq f(Q), \forall Q \in \mathcal{E}$.

We want to minimize

$$f(x, y) = x^2 + y^2$$

(we use the squared distance to avoid an otherwise unneccessary square root call) subject to the constraint

$$g(x, y) = 17x^2 + 8y^2 + 12xy = 100$$

By Theorem A.9, we must have

$$\nabla f = \lambda \nabla g$$

which yields a pair of equations

$$2x = \lambda(34x + 12y)$$

$$2y = \lambda(12x + 16y)$$

There are two cases to consider.

CASE 1   Assume that $34x + 12y \neq 0$ and $12x + 16y \neq 0$. We need to solve the equations for λ and equate them:

$$\frac{2x}{34x + 12y} = \frac{2y}{12x + 16y}$$

$$2x(12x + 16y) = 2y(34x + 12y)$$

$$12x^2 + 16xy = 34xy + 12y^2$$

$$2x^2 - 3xy - 2y^2 = 0$$

This yields the system

$$17x^2 + 12xy + 8y^2 = 100$$

$$2x^2 - 3xy - 2y^2 = 0$$

which has solutions $(2, 1)$, $(2, -4)$, $(-2, -1)$, $(-2, 4)$. We then plug these into the equation:

$$f(2, 1) = 5$$

$$f(-2, -1) = 5$$

$$f(2, -4) = 20$$

$$f(-2, 4) = 20 \quad \blacksquare$$

CASE 2   Either $34x + 12y = 0$ or $12x + 16y = 0$, but in either of these cases, $x = y = 0$, which doesn't satisfy the ellipse equation.

The geometric intuition can be assisted by looking at the plots of the functions involved. Figure A.18 shows the ellipse $17x^2 + 8y^2 + 12xy = 100$. The objective function $x^2 + y^2$ is shown in Figure A.19, and various level curves for it in Figure A.20.

If we plot both the ellipse and the level curves together, then we can see the point of mutual tangency at $(2, 1)$ and $(-2, -1)$ (the minimizing solutions), and at $(2, -4)$ and $(-2, 4)$ (the maximizing solutions)—see Figure A.21. $\blacksquare$

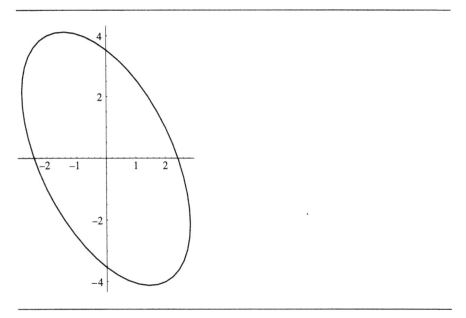

Figure A.18   Plot of the ellipse $17x^2 + 8y^2 + 12xy = 100$.

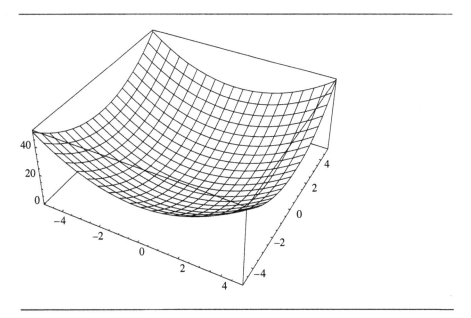

Figure A.19   Plot of the function $x^2 + y^2$.

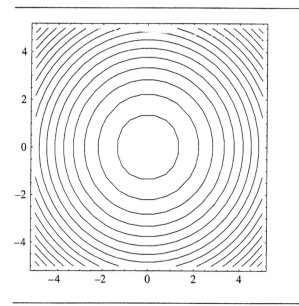

Figure A.20   Level curves for $x^2 + y^2$.

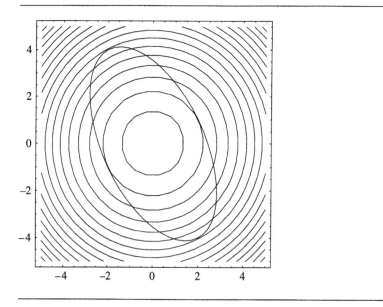

Figure A.21   The constraint curve and the ellipse are tangent at the minima.

Three-Variable Extrema Problems

Lagrange multipliers can also be applied to the problem of finding the extrema of functions in three variables, subject to one or two constraints.

Single Constraint

In the case of a single constraint, we wish to maximize or minimize $f(x, y, z)$ subject to a constraint $g(x, y, z) = 0$. The graph of a three-variable function of the form $g(x, y, z) = 0$ is a surface S in 3-space. The geometric intuition here is that we are looking for the maximum or minimum of $f(x, y, z)$ as (x, y, z) varies over the surface S. The function $f(x, y, z)$ has a constrained relative maximum at some point (x_0, y_0, z_0) if that point is the center of a sphere, with

$$f(x_0, y_0, z_0) \geq f(x, y, z)$$

for all points on S that are within this sphere. If the maximum value of f is $f(x_0, y_0, z_0) = c$, then the level surface $f(x, y, z) = c$ is tangent to the level surface g, and so their gradient vectors at that point are parallel:

$$\nabla f(x_0, y_0, z_0) = \lambda \nabla g(x_0, y_0, z_0)$$

To solve a problem of this type, we must do the following:

1. Find all values of x, y, z that satisfy

$$\nabla f(x_0, y_0, z_0) = \lambda \nabla g(x_0, y_0, z_0)$$

and

$$g(x_0, y_0, z_0) = k$$

This is done by solving, as before, a set of simultaneous equations.

2. Evaluate the function f at all the points from step 1 to determine which is (are) the maximum value and which is (are) the minimum value.

An example should help illustrate this.

Find the point on the sphere $x^2 + y^2 + z^2 = 36$ that is closest to the point $(1, 2, 2)$. That is, we wish to find the point (x_0, y_0, z_0) that minimizes the distance (squared) function $f(x, y, z) = (x - 1)^2 + (y - 2)^2 + (z - 2)^2$, subject to the constraint that the point lies on the sphere $g(x, y, z) = x^2 + y^2 + z^2 = 36$. Equating $\nabla f(x, y, z) = \lambda \nabla g(x, y, z)$ for this problem we have

$$2(x - 1)\mathbf{i} + 2(y - 2)\mathbf{j} + 2(z - 2)\mathbf{k} = \lambda(2x\mathbf{i} + 2y\mathbf{j} + 2z\mathbf{k})$$

which gives us this system:

$$2(x - 1) = 2x\lambda$$
$$2(y - 2) = 2y\lambda \qquad \text{(A.12)}$$
$$2(z - 2) = 2z\lambda$$

As the sphere is centered at the origin, and none of the components of the point are 0, the nearest point cannot have any components that are 0, and so there are no special cases to consider as in the previous example. We can then rewrite System A.12 as

$$\frac{x - 1}{x} = \lambda$$
$$\frac{y - 2}{y} = \lambda \qquad \text{(A.13)}$$
$$\frac{z - 2}{z} = \lambda$$

The first two equations give us

$$\frac{x - 1}{x} = \frac{y - 2}{y}$$
$$xy - y = xy - 2x \qquad \text{(A.14)}$$
$$y = 2x$$

while the first and third give us

$$\frac{x - 1}{x} = \frac{z - 2}{z}$$
$$xz - z = xz - 2x \qquad \text{(A.15)}$$
$$z = 2x$$

Substituting these results back into the constraint equation (that is, the sphere equation), we get

$$9x^2 = 36$$

or

$$x = \pm 2$$

If we substitute these back into Equations A.14 and A.15, we get the two points $(2, 4, 4)$ and $(-2, -4, -4)$. Plugging these values back into f, we have $f(2, 4, 4) = 9$

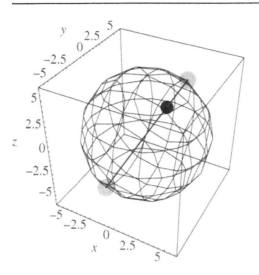

Figure A.22 The closest and farthest point to $(1, 2, 2)$ on the sphere $x^2 + y^2 + z^2 = 36$.

and $f(-2, -4, -4) = 81$, and so we can conclude that the closest point is $(2, 4, 4)$; see Figure A.22.

An alternative way of looking at this is that we're solving a system of four equations in four variables

$$\frac{\partial f}{\partial x}(x_0, y_0, z_0) = \lambda \frac{\partial g}{\partial x}(x_0, y_0, z_0)$$

$$\frac{\partial f}{\partial y}(x_0, y_0, z_0) = \lambda \frac{\partial g}{\partial y}(x_0, y_0, z_0)$$

$$\frac{\partial f}{\partial z}(x_0, y_0, z_0) = \lambda \frac{\partial g}{\partial z}(x_0, y_0, z_0)$$

$$g(x_0, y_0, z_0) = 0$$

or

$$2(-1 + x) = 2x\lambda$$

$$2(-2 + y) = 2y\lambda$$

$$2(-2 + z) = 2z\lambda$$

$$x^2 + y^2 + z^2 - 36 = 0$$

which can be solved using standard techniques. This gives us the (same) results directly, including the actual values of the Lagrange multipliers: $\{\{\lambda \rightarrow \frac{1}{2}, x \rightarrow 2, y \rightarrow 4, z \rightarrow 4\}, \{\lambda \rightarrow \frac{3}{2}, x \rightarrow -2, y \rightarrow -4, z \rightarrow -4\}\}$.

Two Constraints

If we have a function of three variables, we can have two constraints.

THEOREM A.10 *Constrained Extremum Principle—Three-Variable Form with Two Constraints:* If there is an extremum for $f(x, y, z)$ on the constraint curve determined by the intersection of the implicit surfaces defined by $g_1(x, y, z) = 0$ and $g_2(x, y, z) = 0$, then it occurs at a point (x_0, y_0, z_0) satisfying all of

$$\nabla f(x_0, y_0, z_0) = \lambda_1 \nabla g_1(x_0, y_0, z_0)$$

$$\nabla f(x_0, y_0, z_0) = \lambda_2 \nabla g_2(x_0, y_0, z_0)$$

$$g_1(x_0, y_0, z_0) = 0$$

$$g_2(x_0, y_0, z_0) = 0$$

That is, the gradient of f must be parallel to the gradients of both g_1 and g_2. ∎

Again, an example can help illuminate this: find the extreme values of $f(x, y, z) = x + 2y + 3z = 0$, subject to the constraints $g_1(x, y, z) = x - y + z = 1$ and $g_2(x, y, z) = x^2 + y^2 = 1$. Geometrically speaking, the two constraints represent a plane and a cylinder, respectively; these intersect in an ellipse. The function f is another plane, and so we're looking to find the extrema of this plane on the ellipse. Figure A.23 shows constraint functions g_1 and g_2, which intersect in an ellipse.

Theorem A.10 states that the extrema can be found by solving a system of equations. For this example, our equations can be stated as

$$\frac{\partial f}{\partial x} = \lambda_1 \frac{\partial g_1}{\partial x} + \lambda_2 \frac{\partial g_2}{\partial x}$$

$$\frac{\partial f}{\partial y} = \lambda_1 \frac{\partial g_1}{\partial y} + \lambda_2 \frac{\partial g_2}{\partial y}$$

$$\frac{\partial f}{\partial z} = \lambda_1 \frac{\partial g_1}{\partial z} + \lambda_2 \frac{\partial g_2}{\partial z}$$

$$g_1 = x - y + z - 1$$

$$g_2 = x^2 + y^2 - 1$$

which is

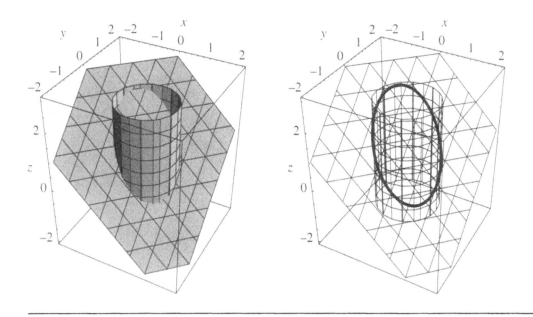

Figure A.23 Constraint equations $g_1(x, y, z) = x - y + z = 1$ and $g_2(x, y, z) = x^2 + y^2 = 1$.

$$1 = 2\,x\,\lambda_1 + 2\,x\,\lambda_2$$

$$2 = 2\,y\,\lambda_1 + 2\,y\,\lambda_2$$

$$3 = 2\,z\,\lambda_1$$

$$x^2 + y^2 + z^2 - 36 = 0$$

$$x^2 + y^2 - 1 = 0$$

and which can be solved using standard techniques to yield

$$\left\{ \lambda_1 \to 3, \quad \lambda_2 \to \frac{-\sqrt{29}}{2}, \quad x \to \frac{2}{\sqrt{29}}, \quad y \to \frac{-5}{\sqrt{29}}, \quad z \to \frac{29 - 7\sqrt{29}}{29} \right\},$$

$$\left\{ \lambda_1 \to 3, \quad \lambda_2 \to \frac{\sqrt{29}}{2}, \quad x \to \frac{-2}{\sqrt{29}}, \quad y \to \frac{5}{\sqrt{29}}, \quad z \to \frac{29 + 7\sqrt{29}}{29} \right\}$$

These points—the minimum and maximum—are shown on the constraint curve determined by the intersection of the implicit surfaces defined by $g_1 = 0$ and $g_2 = 0$ in Figure A.24.

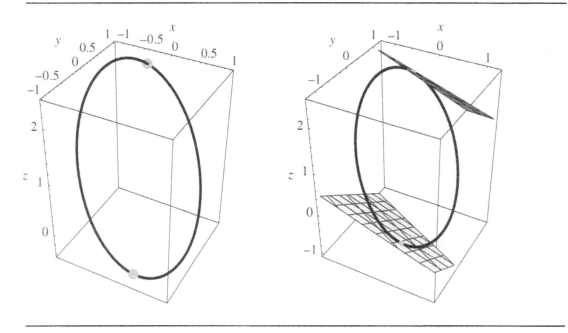

Figure A.24   Extrema of f shown as points on the constraint curve determined by the intersection of implicit surfaces defined by $g_1 = 0$ and $g_2 = 0$, and the level sets of f at those extrema.

APPENDIX B

TRIGONOMETRY

B.1 INTRODUCTION

This appendix serves as a review of some fundamental trigonometry that you may find useful, as well as a handy reference for commonly used definitions and relationships of trigonometric functions.

B.1.1 TERMINOLOGY

Trigonometry is generally concerned with angles between lines (or more properly, half-lines or rays) in the plane. By convention, the ray from which an angle is measured is termed the *initial side*, and the ray to which the angle θ is measured is termed the *terminal side*. Angles are considered *positive* if measured in a counterclockwise direction and *negative* if measured in a clockwise direction.

The end point of the two rays in question is termed the *vertex*. An angle whose vertex is at the origin and whose initial side lies along the positive x-axis is in *standard position* (see Figure B.1).

B.1.2 ANGLES

The angle θ between two rays is measured in either degrees or radians. Degrees are more common in informal or popular usage, and radians are more common in technical usage. If we consider a ray that is swept starting from the initial side, and continuing until the terminal side again coincides with the initial side, the end point

923

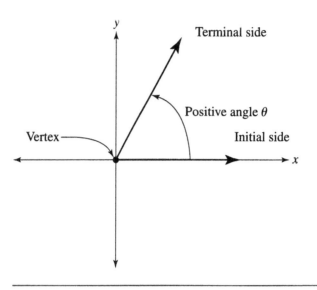

Figure B.1   Standard terminology for angles.

of the ray describes a complete circle. The angle corresponding to this circle is defined as being either 360 degrees or 2π radians:

$$1° = \frac{\pi}{180} \text{ radians}$$

$$\approx 0.017453 \text{ radians}$$

and

$$1 \text{ radian} = \frac{180°}{\pi}$$

$$\approx 57.2958°$$

$$\approx 57°17'44.8''$$

Generally, if no units are given, an angle measure is considered to be in radians.

The definition of radians is not arbitrary—there is a reason why a full circle is equivalent to 2π radians. First, we must define *arc length*: if we trace the path of a point moving from A to B on a circle, then the distance traveled by that point is some arc of the circle, and its length is the arc length, conventionally notated as s (see Figure B.2).

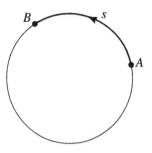

Figure B.2   Definition of arc length.

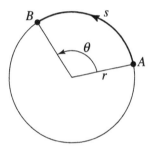

Figure B.3   Definition of radians.

Define

$$\theta = \frac{s}{r}$$

to be the radian measure of angle θ (Figure B.3), and consider the unit circle (where $r = 1$). Recall that the definition of π is the ratio of the circumference of a circle to its diameter (i.e., $2r$); the result is that there must be 2π radians in a full circle.

B.1.3   CONVERSION EXAMPLES

Problem: Convert 129° to radians.
Solution: By definition

$$1° = \frac{\pi}{180} \text{ radians}$$

We can simply do a little arithmetic:

$$129° = \frac{\pi}{180} \cdot 129 \text{ radians}$$

$$= \frac{129}{180}\pi \text{ radians}$$

$$\approx 2.2514728 \text{ radians}$$

Problem: Convert 5 radians to degrees.
Solution: By definition

$$1 \text{ radian} = \left(\frac{180}{\pi}\right)°$$

We can again simply do some arithmetic:

$$5 \text{ radians} = \left(5 \cdot \frac{180}{\pi}\right)°$$

$$= \left(\frac{900}{\pi}\right)°$$

$$\approx 286.47914°$$

B.2 TRIGONOMETRIC FUNCTIONS

The standard trigonometric functions *sine, cosine, tangent, cosecant, secant,* and *cotangent* may for (positive, acute) angle θ be defined in terms of ratios of the lengths of the sides of a right triangle (see Figure B.4):

$$\sin \theta = \frac{\text{side opposite } \theta}{\text{hypotenuse}} = \frac{y}{r}$$

$$\cos \theta = \frac{\text{side adjacent to } \theta}{\text{hypotenuse}} = \frac{x}{r}$$

$$\tan \theta = \frac{\text{side opposite } \theta}{\text{side adjacent to } \theta} = \frac{y}{x}$$

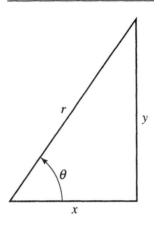

Figure B.4   The ratios of sides of a right triangle can be used to define trig functions.

$$\csc \theta = \frac{\text{hypotenuse}}{\text{side opposite } \theta} = \frac{r}{y}$$

$$\sec \theta = \frac{\text{hypotenuse}}{\text{side adjacent to } \theta} = \frac{r}{x}$$

$$\cot \theta = \frac{\text{side adjacent to } \theta}{\text{side opposite } \theta} = \frac{x}{y}$$

Inspection of the above definitions reveals the following:

$$\csc \theta = \frac{1}{\sin \theta}$$

$$\sec \theta = \frac{1}{\cos \theta}$$

$$\cot \theta = \frac{1}{\tan \theta}$$

$$\tan \theta = \frac{\sin \theta}{\cos \theta}$$

$$\cot \theta = \frac{\cos \theta}{\sin \theta}$$

A convenient mnemonic for remembering these is the phrase *soh cah toa*, for "*s*ine equals *o*pposite over *h*ypotenuse, *c*osine equals *a*djacent over *h*ypotenuse, *t*angent

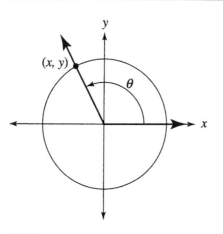

Figure B.5   Generalized definition for trigonometric functions.

equals *opposite* over *adjacent*"; csc, sec, and cot can be recalled simply as "1 over" the appropriate one of the three basic functions.

Note, however, that the above definitions only are valid for acute angles in standard position. A more complete and formal set of definitions can be created by considering the following: for an arbitrary pair of rays sharing a common vertex, define a coordinate system transform such that the angle is in standard position; then construct a unit circle, centered at the origin, and mark the point at which the terminal side intersects the circle (Figure B.5).

With this, we have the following definitions:

$$\sin \theta = y = \frac{y}{1} = \frac{y}{r}$$

$$\cos \theta = x = \frac{x}{1} = \frac{x}{r}$$

$$\tan \theta = \qquad \frac{y}{x}$$

$$\csc \theta = \frac{1}{y} \quad = \frac{r}{y}$$

$$\sec \theta = \frac{1}{x} \quad = \frac{r}{x}$$

$$\cot \theta = \qquad \frac{x}{y}$$

Table B.1   Trigonometric function values for some commonly used angles.

		$\sin\theta$	$\cos\theta$	$\tan\theta$	$\csc\theta$	$\sec\theta$	$\cot\theta$
$0 =$	$0°$	0	1	0	—	1	—
$\pi/12 =$	$15°$	$\frac{1}{4}(\sqrt{6}-\sqrt{2})$	$\frac{1}{4}(\sqrt{6}+\sqrt{2})$	$2-\sqrt{3}$	$\frac{4}{\sqrt{6}-\sqrt{2}}$	$\frac{4}{\sqrt{6}+\sqrt{2}}$	$2+\sqrt{3}$
$\pi/6 =$	$30°$	$1/2$	$\sqrt{3}/2$	$1/\sqrt{3}$	2	$2/\sqrt{3}$	$\sqrt{3}$
$\pi/4 =$	$45°$	$1/\sqrt{2}$	$1/\sqrt{2}$	1	$\sqrt{2}$	$\sqrt{2}$	1
$\pi/3 =$	$60°$	$\sqrt{3}/2$	$1/2$	$\sqrt{3}$	$2/\sqrt{3}$	2	$1\sqrt{3}$
$5\pi/12 =$	$75°$	$\frac{1}{4}(\sqrt{6}+\sqrt{2})$	$\frac{1}{4}(\sqrt{6}-\sqrt{2})$	$2+\sqrt{3}$	$\frac{4}{\sqrt{6}+\sqrt{2}}$	$\frac{4}{\sqrt{6}-\sqrt{2}}$	$2-\sqrt{3}$
$\pi/2 =$	$90°$	1	0	—	1	—	0
$7\pi/12 =$	$105°$	$\frac{1}{4}(\sqrt{6}+\sqrt{2})$	$-\frac{1}{4}(\sqrt{6}-\sqrt{2})$	$-2-\sqrt{3}$	$\frac{4}{\sqrt{6}+\sqrt{2}}$	$-\frac{4}{\sqrt{6}-\sqrt{2}}$	$-2+\sqrt{3}$
$2\pi/3 =$	$120°$	$\sqrt{3}/2$	$-1/2$	$-\sqrt{3}$	$2/\sqrt{3}$	-2	$-1/\sqrt{3}$
$3\pi/4 =$	$135°$	$1/\sqrt{2}$	$-1/\sqrt{2}$	-1	$\sqrt{2}$	$-\sqrt{2}$	-1
$5\pi/6 =$	$150°$	$1/2$	$-\sqrt{3}/2$	$-1/\sqrt{3}$	2	$-2/\sqrt{3}$	$-\sqrt{3}$
$11\pi/12 =$	$165°$	$\frac{1}{4}(\sqrt{6}-\sqrt{2})$	$-\frac{1}{4}(\sqrt{6}+\sqrt{2})$	$-2-\sqrt{3}$	$\frac{4}{\sqrt{6}-\sqrt{2}}$	$-\frac{4}{\sqrt{6}+\sqrt{2}}$	$-2-\sqrt{3}$
$\pi =$	$180°$	0	-1	0	—	-1	—
$3\pi/2 =$	$270°$	-1	0	—	-1	—	0
$2\pi =$	$360°$	0	1	0	—	1	—

Note that the radius, which equals 1, corresponds to a hypotenuse of length 1 for acute angles, and thus the final column can be observed to be equivalent to the earlier definition. Note also that for angles that cause x or y to be zero, trigonometric functions that divide by x or y, respectively, become undefined (see Table B.1).

An interesting and useful observation can be deduced from the equations above: if we have an angle in standard position, then its terminal side intersects the unit circle at the point $(x, y) = (\cos\theta, \sin\theta)$. Further, all of the fundamental trigonometric functions have a geometrical interpretation, as shown in Figure B.6.

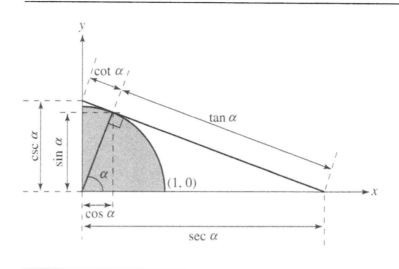

Figure B.6   Geometrical interpretation of trigonometric functions.

B.2.1 DEFINITIONS IN TERMS OF EXPONENTIALS

Interestingly, the basic trigonometric functions can be defined exactly in terms of e

$$\sin \alpha = \frac{e^{i\alpha} - e^{-i\alpha}}{2i}$$

$$\cos \alpha = \frac{e^{i\alpha} + e^{-i\alpha}}{2}$$

$$\tan \alpha = -i\frac{e^{i\alpha} - e^{-i\alpha}}{e^{i\alpha} + e^{-i\alpha}}$$

$$= -i\frac{e^{2i\alpha} - 1}{e^{2i\alpha} + 1}$$

where $i = \sqrt{-1}$.

The value of e itself can be defined in terms of trigonometric functions:

$$e^{i\alpha} = \cos \alpha + i \sin \alpha$$

Table B.2 Domains and ranges of trigonometric functions.

	Domain	*Range*
sin	$-\infty < x < \infty$	$-1 \leq y \leq 1$
cos	$-\infty < x < \infty$	$-1 \leq y \leq 1$
tan	$-\infty < x < \infty, x \neq \frac{\pi}{2} + n\pi$	$-\infty < y < \infty$
sec	$-\infty < x < \infty, x \neq \frac{\pi}{2} + n\pi$	$|y| \geq 1$
csc	$-\infty < x < \infty, x \neq n\pi$	$|y| \geq 1$
cot	$-\infty < x < \infty, x \neq n\pi$	$-\infty < y < \infty$

B.2.2 DOMAINS AND RANGES

Table B.2 shows the ranges and domains of the fundamental trigonometric functions. As can be observed in Figure B.7, generally the domains are infinite, with only some discrete special values excluded in all but the sin and cos functions.

B.2.3 GRAPHS OF TRIGONOMETRIC FUNCTIONS

Figure B.7 shows a portion of the graphs of each of the fundamental trigonometric functions.

B.2.4 DERIVATIVES OF TRIGONOMETRIC FUNCTIONS

The derivative of a function f, notated as f', is defined as

$$f'(x) = \lim_{n \to 0} \frac{f(x+h) - f(x)}{h}$$

We can find the derivative of the trigonometric functions by substituting each function into this definition and using the trigonometric addition formulas along with some simple manipulations to simplify them. For example,

$$\frac{d}{dx}(\sin x) = \lim_{n \to 0} \frac{\sin(x+h) - \sin x}{h}$$

$$= \lim_{n \to 0} \frac{\sin x \cos h + \cos x \sin h - \sin x}{h}$$

$$= \lim_{n \to 0} \left[\sin x \left(\frac{\cos h - 1}{h} \right) + \cos x \left(\frac{\sin h}{h} \right) \right]$$

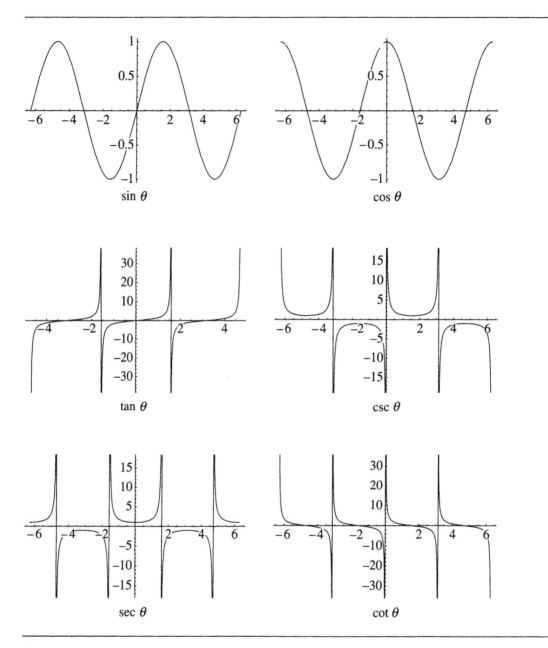

Figure B.7   Graphs of the fundamental trigonometric functions.

The sin x and cos x terms are constants with respect to h, so

$$\lim_{n \to 0} \sin x = \sin x$$

$$\lim_{n \to 0} \cos x = \cos x$$

and thus

$$\frac{d}{dx}(\sin x) = \sin x \cdot \lim_{n \to 0}\left(\frac{\cos h - 1}{h}\right) + \cos x \cdot \lim_{n \to 0}\left(\frac{\sin h}{h}\right)$$

It can be shown that

$$\lim_{n \to 0} \frac{\cos h - 1}{h} = 0$$

$$\lim_{n \to 0} \frac{\sin h}{h} = 1$$

and so

$$\frac{d}{dx}[\sin x] = \cos x$$

The derivative for cos x can be computed similarly, resulting in

$$\frac{d}{dx}[\cos x] = -\sin x$$

The remaining trigonometric functions can be defined as simple fractions involving sin and cos (see Section B.2.1). We can simply invoke the *quotient rule* from calculus and compute

$$\frac{d}{dx}[\tan x] = \sec^2 x$$

$$\frac{d}{dx}[\cot x] = -\csc^2 x$$

$$\frac{d}{dx}[\sec x] = \sec x \tan x$$

$$\frac{d}{dx}[\csc x] = -\csc x \cot x$$

B.2.5   INTEGRATION

$$\int \sin u \, du = -\cos u + C$$

$$\int \cos u \, du = \sin u + C$$

$$\int \tan u \, du = \ln |\sec u| + C$$

$$\int \cot u \, du = -\ln |\sin u| + C$$

$$\int \sec u \, du = \ln |\sec u + \tan u| + C$$

$$= \ln \left| \tan \left(\frac{1}{4}\pi + \frac{1}{2}u \right) \right| + C$$

$$\int \csc u \, du = \ln |\csc u - \cot u| + C$$

$$= \ln \left| \tan \frac{1}{2}u \right| + C$$

B.3   TRIGONOMETRIC IDENTITIES AND LAWS

Consider Figure B.4, and apply the Pythagorean Theorem. The following relationship holds:

$$x^2 + y^2 = r^2$$

If we apply a little arithmetic manipulation and the definitions of the sin and cos functions, we get

$$x^2 + y^2 = r^2$$

$$\frac{x^2 + y^2}{r^2} = 1 \quad \text{Dividing both sides by } r^2$$

$$\sin^2 \theta + \cos^2 \theta = 1 \quad \text{Using the definition of sin and cos}$$

The next set of fundamental identities involves the negation of an angle. Consider an angle θ and the definitions found in Section B.2.1. If we consider an angle $-\theta$, we can see that the terminal side of such an angle intercepts the unit circle at the same x-coordinate as does the terminal side of θ, but the y-coordinate is negated (observe Figure B.5). We can then, using the definitions given in Section B.2.1, define

$$\sin(-\theta) = \frac{-y}{r}$$

$$= -\frac{y}{r}$$

$$= -\sin\theta$$

and

$$\cos(-\theta) = \frac{x}{r}$$

$$= \cos\theta$$

and

$$\tan(-\theta) = \frac{-y}{r}$$

$$= -\frac{y}{r}$$

$$= -\tan(\theta)$$

B.3.1 PERIODICITY

The graphs of the trigonometric functions shown in Figure B.7 make it appear that the trigonometric functions are periodic, and inspection of the definitions given in Section B.2.1 reveals that the trigonometric function values for all angles sharing a common terminal side are the same. Thus, it is true by definition and the observation that a circle comprises 2π radians that

$$\sin\theta = \sin(\theta \pm 2n\pi)$$

$$\cos\theta = \cos(\theta \pm 2n\pi)$$

$$\csc\theta = \csc(\theta \pm 2n\pi)$$

$$\sec\theta = \sec(\theta \pm 2n\pi)$$

for all $n = \ldots, -2, -1, 0, 1, 2, \ldots$. However, the tangent and cotangent functions have a period of π:

$$\tan \theta = \tan(\theta \pm n\pi)$$

$$\cot \theta = \cot(\theta \pm n\pi)$$

for all $n = \ldots, -2, -1, 0, 1, 2, \ldots$.

B.3.2 LAWS

This section discusses three laws that define relationships between general triangles' edges, angles, and trigonometric functions.

Law of Sines

The *law of sines* is one of the fundamental trigonometric relationships, and it relates to general triangles, not only right triangles (see Figure B.8). Informally put, the law of sines states that for any triangle, the ratios of each side to the angle opposite are all equal

$$\frac{a}{\sin \alpha} = \frac{b}{\sin \beta} = \frac{c}{\sin \gamma} = 2r$$

where r is the *circumradius* (the radius of the circle passing through the triangle's vertices).

The following proof is due to Ronald Goldman (1987):

$$2\,\mathrm{Area}(\triangle ABC) = \|(A - B) \times (C - B)\| = ca \sin \beta$$

$$2\,\mathrm{Area}(\triangle BCA) = \|(B - C) \times (A - C)\| = ab \sin \gamma$$

$$2\,\mathrm{Area}(\triangle CAB) = \|(C - A) \times (B - A)\| = bc \sin \alpha$$

$$\therefore ca \sin \beta = ab \sin \gamma = bc \sin \alpha$$

$$\therefore \frac{a}{\sin \alpha} = \frac{b}{\sin \beta} = \frac{c}{\sin \gamma}$$

The relationship to the circumradius can also be easily proved. Consider again our triangle $\triangle ABC$; choose any vertex, and draw a line from it, through the *circumcenter* (the center of the circle that passes through a triangle's vertices), and intersecting the circle at a point D (Figure B.9).

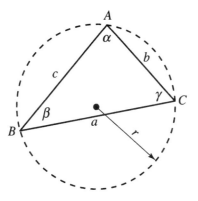

Figure B.8   The law of sines.

We know that $\angle ADC$ is a right angle because it subtends a semicircle. By definition of the sine function, we then have

$$\sin \delta = \frac{b}{AD}$$

But of course $\delta = \beta$ because they both subtend the same arc $\overset{\frown}{AC}$. Thus,

$$\sin \delta = \sin \beta$$

Substituting, we get

$$\sin \beta = \frac{b}{AD}$$

But since AD passes through the circumcenter, $AD = 2r$, and so we have

$$\sin \beta = \frac{b}{2r}$$

Rearranging, we have

$$2r = \frac{b}{\sin \beta}$$

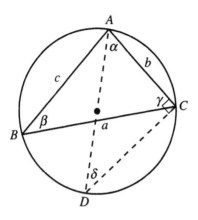

Figure B.9   Proof of the law of sines.

Combined with the previous proof, we can then conclude

$$\frac{a}{\sin \alpha} = \frac{b}{\sin \beta} = \frac{c}{\sin \gamma} = 2r$$

The Law of Cosines

The *law of cosines* is another frequently useful relationship and may be viewed as a generalization of the Pythagorean Theorem to all triangles.

For any triangle with sides a, b, and c, if θ is the angle opposite side c, then

$$c^2 = a^2 + b^2 - 2ab \cos \theta$$

The proof is again due to Goldman (1987):

$$c^2 = \|B - A\|^2$$
$$= (B - A) \cdot (B - A)$$
$$= [(B - C) + (C - A)] \cdot [(B - C) + (C - A)]$$
$$= (B - C) \cdot (B - C) + (C - A) \cdot (C - A) - 2(A - C)(B - C)$$
$$= \|B - C\|^2 + \|C - A\|^2 - 2\|A - C\|\|B - C\| \cos C$$
$$= a^2 + b^2 - 2ab \cos C$$

Law of Tangents

The *law of tangents* states that in any triangle, the ratio of the difference between two sides to their sum is the same as the ratio of the tangent of half the difference of the opposite angles to the tangent of half their sum. Again, referring to Figure B.8, we have

$$\frac{a+b}{a-b} = \frac{\tan\frac{\alpha+\beta}{2}}{\tan\frac{\alpha-\beta}{2}}$$

The proof, due to the "Math Forum" Web site *(http://forum.swarthmore.edu/dr.math)*, is as follows. Consider the addition and subtraction formulas for the sine function:

$$\sin(t+u) = \sin(t)\cos(u) + \cos(t)\sin(u)$$

$$\sin(t-u) = \sin(t)\cos(u) - \cos(t)\sin(u)$$

Adding and subtracting, respectively, each of these with themselves gives

$$\sin(t+u) + \sin(t-u) = 2\sin(t)\cos(u)$$

$$\sin(t-u) + \sin(t-u) = 2\cos(t)\sin(u)$$

If we let $t = (\alpha+\beta)/2$ and $u = (\alpha-\beta)/2$, then $t+u = \alpha$ and $t-u = \beta$, giving us

$$\sin(\alpha) + \sin(\beta) = 2\sin((\alpha+\beta)/2)\cos((\alpha-\beta)/2)$$

$$\sin(\alpha) + \sin(\beta) = 2\cos((\alpha+\beta)/2)\sin((\alpha-\beta)/2)$$

We can then take the ratio of these two equations, giving us

$$\frac{\tan((\alpha+\beta)/2)}{\tan((\alpha-\beta)/2)} = \frac{\sin((\alpha+\beta)/2)\cos((\alpha-\beta)/2)}{\cos((\alpha+\beta)/2)\sin((\alpha-\beta)/2)}$$

$$= \frac{2\sin((\alpha+\beta)/2)\cos((\alpha-\beta)/2)}{2\cos((\alpha+\beta)/2)\sin((\alpha-\beta)/2)}$$

$$= \frac{\sin(\alpha) + \sin(\beta)}{\sin(\alpha) - \sin(\beta)}$$

which, by the law of sines, is equal to

$$\frac{a+b}{a-b}$$

B.3.3 FORMULAS

This section presents a number of fundamental formulas that are occasionally useful in solving geometric problems.

Mollweide's Formula

If you are solving a problem consisting of computing vertices and/or edges of a triangle, given (sufficient) other information about the triangle, relationships such as the laws of sines, cosines, and tangents can be used to find the solution. Mollweide's and Newton's formulas can be used to verify such solutions because they both involve all three vertices and all three edges of the triangle.

$$\frac{b - c}{a} = \frac{\sin \frac{B-C}{2}}{\cos \frac{A}{2}}$$

Newton's Formula

$$\frac{b + c}{a} = \frac{\cos \frac{B-C}{2}}{\sin \frac{A}{2}}$$

Area Formula

For right triangles, the area formula $A = 1/2$ base $\times$ height is easy to compute; however, for a general triangle it is not so convenient. A more general formula may be used instead:

$$A = \frac{bc \sin \alpha}{2} = \frac{ac \sin \beta}{2} = \frac{ab \sin \gamma}{2}$$

Addition and Subtraction Formulas

You frequently run into problems that require the use of trigonometric functions of the sum or difference of two angles, where you already have values for the trigonometric functions for each angle individually. These are given below:

$$\sin(\alpha + \beta) = \sin \alpha \cos \beta + \cos \alpha \sin \beta$$

$$\sin(\alpha - \beta) = \sin \alpha \cos \beta - \cos \alpha \sin \beta$$

$$\cos(\alpha + \beta) = \cos \alpha \cos \beta - \sin \alpha \sin \beta$$

$$\cos(\alpha - \beta) = \cos \alpha \cos \beta + \sin \alpha \sin \beta$$

$$\tan(\alpha + \beta) = \frac{\tan \alpha + \tan \beta}{1 - \tan \alpha \tan \beta}$$

$$\tan(\alpha - \beta) = \frac{\tan \alpha - \tan \beta}{1 + \tan \alpha \tan \beta}$$

$$\cot(\alpha + \beta) = \frac{\cot \alpha \cot \beta - 1}{\cot \alpha + \cot \beta}$$

$$\cot(\alpha - \beta) = \frac{\cot \alpha \cot \beta + 1}{\cot \alpha - \cot \beta}$$

You also run into problems that require the use of sums of trigonometric functions of two angles:

$$\sin \alpha + \sin \beta = 2 \sin \frac{\alpha + \beta}{2} \cos \frac{\alpha - \beta}{2}$$

$$\sin \alpha - \sin \beta = 2 \cos \frac{\alpha + \beta}{2} \sin \frac{\alpha - \beta}{2}$$

$$\cos \alpha + \cos \beta = 2 \cos \frac{\alpha + \beta}{2} \cos \frac{\alpha - \beta}{2}$$

$$\cos \alpha - \cos \beta = -2 \sin \frac{\alpha + \beta}{2} \sin \frac{\alpha - \beta}{2}$$

$$\tan \alpha + \tan \beta = \frac{\sin (\alpha + \beta)}{\cos \alpha \cos \beta}$$

$$\tan \alpha - \tan \beta = \frac{\sin (\alpha - \beta)}{\cos \alpha \cos \beta}$$

Product Formulas

$$\sin \alpha \sin \beta = \cos \frac{\alpha - \beta}{2} - \cos \frac{\alpha + \beta}{2}$$

$$\sin \alpha \cos \beta = \sin \frac{\alpha + \beta}{2} + \sin \frac{\alpha - \beta}{2}$$

$$\cos \alpha \cos \beta = \cos \frac{\alpha - \beta}{2} + \cos \frac{\alpha + \beta}{2}$$

$$\cos \alpha \cos \beta = \cos \frac{\alpha + \beta}{2} - \cos \frac{\alpha - \beta}{2}$$

Double-Angle Formulas

$$\sin 2\alpha = 2 \sin \alpha \cos \alpha$$

$$= \frac{2 \tan \alpha}{1 + \tan^2 \alpha}$$

$$\cos 2\alpha = \cos^2 \alpha - \sin^2 \alpha$$

$$= 2 \cos^2 \alpha - 1$$

$$= 1 - 2 \sin^2 \alpha$$

$$= \frac{1 - \tan^2 \alpha}{1 + \tan^2 \alpha}$$

$$\tan 2\alpha = \frac{2 \tan \alpha}{1 - \tan^2 \alpha}$$

$$\cot 2\alpha = \frac{\cot^2 \alpha - 1}{2 \cot \alpha}$$

Triple-Angle Formulas

$$\sin 3\alpha = 3 \sin \alpha - 4 \sin^3 \alpha$$

$$\cos 3\alpha = 4 \cos^3 \alpha - 3 \cos \alpha$$

$$\tan 3\alpha = \frac{3 \tan \alpha - \tan^3 \alpha}{1 - 3 \tan^2 \alpha}$$

Quadruple-Angle Formulas

$$\sin 4\alpha = 4 \sin \alpha \cos \alpha - 8 \sin^3 \alpha \cos \alpha$$

$$\cos 4\alpha = 8 \cos^4 \alpha - 8 \cos^2 \alpha + 1$$

$$\tan 4\alpha = \frac{4 \tan \alpha - 4 \tan^3 \alpha}{1 - 6 \tan^2 \alpha + \tan^4 \alpha}$$

General Multiple-Angle Formulas

There are two different approaches to defining these. The first is based on a series involving powers of the functions

$$\sin n\alpha = n \sin \alpha \cos^{n-1} \alpha - \binom{n}{3} \sin^3 \alpha \cos^{n-3} \alpha + \binom{n}{5} \sin^5 \alpha \cos^{n-5} \alpha - \ldots$$

$$\cos n\alpha = \cos^n \alpha - \binom{n}{2} \sin^2 \alpha \cos^{n-2} \alpha + \binom{n}{4} \sin^4 \alpha \cos^{n-4} \alpha - \ldots$$

and the second is defined in terms of combinations of lesser multiples:

$$\sin n\alpha = 2 \sin (n-1)\alpha \cos \alpha - \sin (n-2)\alpha$$

$$\cos n\alpha = 2 \cos (n-1)\alpha \cos \alpha - \cos (n-2)\alpha$$

$$\tan n\alpha = \frac{\tan (n-1)\alpha + \tan \alpha}{1 - \tan (n-1)\alpha \tan \alpha}$$

Selected Exponential Formulas

$$\sin^2 \alpha = \frac{1 - \cos 2\alpha}{2}$$

$$\sin^3 \alpha = \frac{3 \sin \alpha - \sin 3\alpha}{4}$$

$$\sin^4 \alpha = \frac{3 - 4 \cos 2\alpha + \cos 4\alpha}{8}$$

$$\cos^2 \alpha = \frac{1 + \cos 2\alpha}{2}$$

$$\cos^3 \alpha = \frac{3 \cos \alpha + \cos 3\alpha}{4}$$

$$\cos^4 \alpha = \frac{3 + 4 \cos 2\alpha + \cos 4\alpha}{8}$$

$$\tan^2 \alpha = \frac{1 - \cos 2\alpha}{1 + \cos 2\alpha}$$

General Exponential Formulas

$$\sin^{2n}\alpha = \binom{2n}{n}\frac{1}{2^{2n}} + \frac{1}{2^{2n-1}}\sum_{k=1}^{n}(-1)^k\binom{2n}{n-k}\cos 2k\alpha$$

$$\sin^{2n-1}\alpha = \frac{1}{2^{2n-2}}\sum_{k=1}^{n}(-1)^k\binom{2n-1}{n-k}\sin(2k-1)\alpha$$

$$\cos^{2n}\alpha = \binom{2n}{n}\frac{1}{2^{2n}} + \frac{1}{2^{2n-1}}\sum_{k=1}^{n}\binom{2n}{n-k}\cos 2k\alpha$$

$$\cos^{2n-1}\alpha = \frac{1}{2^{2n-2}}\sum_{k=1}^{n}\binom{2n-1}{n-k}\sin(2k-1)\alpha$$

Half-Angle Formulas

$$\sin\frac{\alpha}{2} = \pm\sqrt{\frac{1-\cos\alpha}{2}}$$

$$\cos\frac{\alpha}{2} = \pm\sqrt{\frac{1+\cos\alpha}{2}}$$

$$\tan\frac{\alpha}{2} = \frac{\sin\alpha}{1+\cos\alpha}$$

$$= \frac{1-\cos\alpha}{\sin\alpha}$$

$$= \pm\sqrt{\frac{1-\cos\alpha}{1+\cos\alpha}}$$

$$\cot\frac{\alpha}{2} = \frac{\sin\alpha}{1-\cos\alpha}$$

$$= \pm\sqrt{\frac{1+\cos\alpha}{1-\cos\alpha}}$$

B.4 INVERSE TRIGONOMETRIC FUNCTIONS

You may intuit that, since the trigonometric functions *are* functions, they of course have inverses. Computation of values of inverse trigonometric functions are frequently useful in computer graphics; for example, you may come upon a problem in which the expression

$$a = \tan b$$

appears. Of course, if we have *a* but need *b*, we need to instead take the inverse of the tangent function:

$$b = \tan^{-1} a$$

The inverses of the fundamental trigonometric functions have names consisting of the fundamental name with the prefix *arc*: arcsine, arccosine, and so on. There are two common sets of mathematical notations for this:

- arcsin, arccos, arctan, etc.
- $\sin^{-1}$, $\cos^{-1}$, $\tan^{-1}$, etc.

B.4.1 DEFINING ARCSIN AND ARCCOS IN TERMS OF ARCTAN

Interestingly, arcsin and arccos may be defined with formulas involving only inverse tangents:

$$\arcsin x = \arctan \frac{x}{\sqrt{1 - x^2}}$$

$$\arccos x = \frac{\pi}{2} - \arctan \frac{x}{\sqrt{1 - x^2}}$$

B.4.2 DOMAINS AND RANGES

The domains of the inverse trigonometric functions are generally more restricted than their counterparts. The graphs of these functions show this; see Table B.3 for the exact values.

Table B.3   Domains and ranges of inverse trigonometric functions.

	Domain	*Range*
$\sin^{-1}$	$-1 \le x \le 1$	$-\frac{\pi}{2} \le y \le \frac{\pi}{2}$
$\cos^{-1}$	$-1 \le x \le 1$	$0 \le y \le \pi$
$\tan^{-1}$	$-\infty < x < \infty$	$-\frac{\pi}{2} \le y \le \frac{\pi}{2}$
$\sec^{-1}$	$\|x\| \ge 1$	$0 \le y \le \pi, \, y \ne \frac{\pi}{2}$
$\csc^{-1}$	$\|x\| \ge 1$	$-\frac{\pi}{2} \le y \le \frac{\pi}{2}, \, y \ne 0$
$\cot^{-1}$	$-\infty < x < \infty$	$0 < y < \pi$

B.4.3   GRAPHS

Figure B.10 shows a portion of the graphs of each of the fundamental inverse trigono-metric functions.

B.4.4   DERIVATIVES

$$\frac{d}{dx}\left[\sin^{-1}x\right] = \frac{1}{\sqrt{1-x^2}}$$

$$\frac{d}{dx}\left[\cos^{-1}x\right] = -\frac{1}{\sqrt{1-x^2}}$$

$$\frac{d}{dx}\left[\tan^{-1}x\right] = \frac{1}{1+x^2}$$

$$\frac{d}{dx}\left[\cot^{-1}x\right] = -\frac{1}{1+x^2}$$

$$\frac{d}{dx}\left[\sec^{-1}x\right] = \frac{1}{|x|\sqrt{x^2-1}}$$

$$\frac{d}{dx}\left[\csc^{-1}x\right] = -\frac{1}{|x|\sqrt{x^2-1}}$$

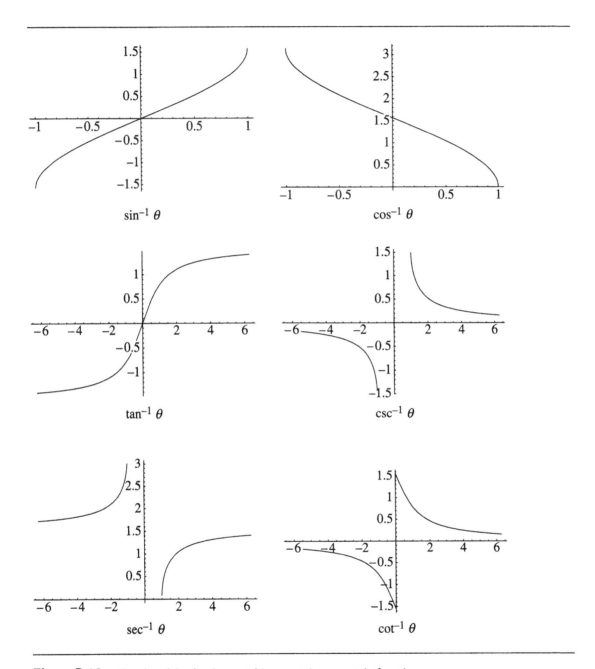

Figure B.10   Graphs of the fundamental inverse trigonometric functions.

B.4.5 INTEGRATION

$$\int \sin^{-1} u \; du = u \sin^{-1} u + \sqrt{1 - u^2} + C$$

$$\int \cos^{-1} u \; du = u \cos^{-1} u + \sqrt{1 - u^2} + C$$

$$\int \tan^{-1} u \; du = u \tan^{-1} u - \ln \sqrt{1 + u^2} + C$$

$$\int \cot^{-1} u \; du = u \cot^{-1} u + \ln \sqrt{1 + u^2} + C$$

$$\int \sec^{-1} u \; du = u \sec^{-1} u - \ln \left| u + \sqrt{u^2 - 1} \right| + C$$

$$\int \csc^{-1} u \; du = u \csc^{-1} u + \ln \left| u + \sqrt{u^2 - 1} \right| + C$$

B.5 FURTHER READING

The Web site of Wolfram Research, Inc. (*http://functions.wolfram.com/Elementary Functions*) contains literally hundreds of pages of information regarding trigonometric functions. Textbooks on trigonometry abound: a recent search on *www.amazon .com* for books whose subject contained the word "trigonometry" yielded 682 entries.

APPENDIX C

BASIC FORMULAS FOR GEOMETRIC PRIMITIVES

C.1 INTRODUCTION

This appendix contains some useful formulas for various properties of common geometric objects.

C.2 TRIANGLES

C.2.1 SYMBOLS

- a, b, c: sides
- α, β, γ: angles
- h: altitude
- m: median
- s: bisector
- $2p = a + b + c$: perimeter
- A: area
- R: circumradius (radius of circle passing through all three vertices)
- C_R: circumcenter (center of circle passing through all three vertices)

- r: inradius (radius of circle tangent to all three sides)
- C_r: incenter (center of circle tangent to all three sides)
- C_g: center of gravity (intersection of the medians)
- C_{alt}: intersection of the altitudes
- V_1, V_2, V_3: vertices

C.2.2 DEFINITIONS

Perimeter and Area

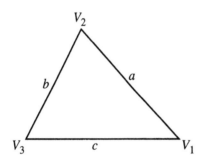

$$2p = a + b + c$$
$$= \|V_1 - V_2\| + \|V_2 - V_3\| + \|V_3 - V_1\|$$

$$A = \frac{\|V_1 \times V_2 + V_2 \times V_3 + V_3 \times V_1\|}{2}$$

Intersection of Medians: Center of Gravity

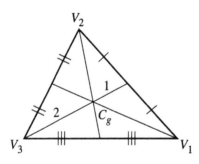

$$C_g = \frac{V_1 + V_2 + V_3}{3}$$

Intersection of Angle Bisectors: Inradius and Incenter

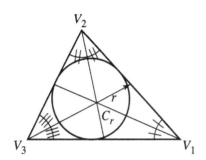

$$r = \frac{2A}{2p}$$

$$C_r = \frac{\|V_2 - V_3\|V_1 + \|V_3 - V_1\|V_2 + \|V_1 - V_2\|V_3}{2p}$$

Intersection of Perpendicular Bisectors: Circumradius and Circumcenter

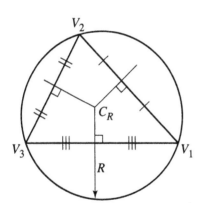

$$d_{ca} = (V_3 - V_1) \cdot (V_2 - V_1)$$

$$d_{ba} = (V_3 - V_2) \cdot (V_1 - V_2)$$

$$d_{cb} = (V_1 - V_3) \cdot (V_2 - V_3)$$

$$n_1 = d_{ba}d_{cb}$$

$$n_2 = d_{cb}d_{ca}$$

$$n_3 = d_{ca}d_{ba}$$

$$R = \frac{\sqrt{(d_{ca} + d_{ba})(d_{ba} + d_{cb})(d_{cb} + d_{ca}) / (n_1 + n_2 + n_3)}}{2}$$

$$C_R = \frac{(n_2 + n_3) V_1 + (n_3 + n_1) V_2 + (n_1 + n_2) V_3}{2(n_1 + n_2 + n_3)}$$

Intersection of Altitudes

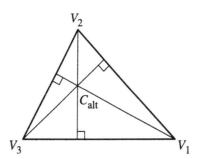

$$C_{\text{alt}} = \frac{n_1 V_1 + n_2 V_2 + n_3 V_3}{n_1 + n_2 + n_3}$$

C.2.3 RIGHT TRIANGLES

Here are some frequently useful right triangles:

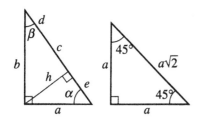

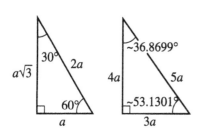

$$c^2 = a^2 + b^2$$

$$A = ab/2$$

$$h = ab/c$$

$$d = a^2/c$$

$$e = b^2/c$$

$$R = c/2$$

$$r = \frac{a + b - c}{2}$$

C.2.4 EQUILATERAL TRIANGLE

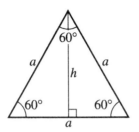

$$A = \frac{a^2\sqrt{3}}{4} = \frac{h^2}{\sqrt{3}}$$

$$h = \frac{a\sqrt{3}}{2}$$

$$R = \frac{a}{\sqrt{3}}$$

$$r = \frac{a}{2\sqrt{3}}$$

C.2.5 GENERAL TRIANGLE

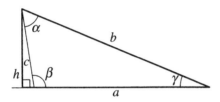

$$A = \frac{ah}{2}$$

$$= bc \sin \alpha$$

$$= \sqrt{p(p-a)(p-b)(p-c)}$$

$$h_a = c \sin \beta$$

$$= \frac{2\sqrt{p(p-a)(p-b)(p-c)}}{a}$$

$$m_a = \frac{1}{2}\sqrt{2b^2 + 2c^2 - a^2}$$

$$s_a = \sqrt{bc[1 - (\frac{a}{b+c})^2]}$$

$$R = \frac{abc}{4A}$$

$$r = \frac{2A}{a+b+c}$$

$$= \frac{A}{p}$$

C.3 QUADRILATERALS

C.3.1 SQUARE

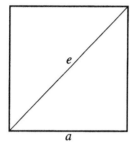

$$A = a^2$$

$$= \frac{e^2}{2}$$

$$R = \frac{a}{\sqrt{2}}$$

$$e = a\sqrt{2}$$

$$r = \frac{a}{2}$$

C.3.2 RECTANGLE

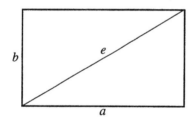

$$A = ab$$

$$R = \frac{e}{2}$$

$$e = \sqrt{a^2 + b^2}$$

C.3.3 PARALLELOGRAM

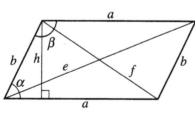

$$A = ah$$

$$= a^2 \sin \alpha$$

$$h = b \sin \alpha$$

$$e^2 + f^2 = 2(a^2 + b^2)$$

$$e = \sqrt{a^2 + b^2 + 2ab \cos \alpha}$$

$$e = \sqrt{a^2 + b^2 - 2ab \cos \alpha}$$

C.3.4   RHOMBUS

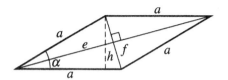

$$A = ah$$
$$= a^2 \sin \alpha$$
$$h = \frac{1}{2}ef$$
$$e^2 + f^2 = 4a^2$$
$$e = 2a \cos \frac{\alpha}{2}$$
$$f = 2a \sin \frac{\alpha}{2}$$

C.3.5   TRAPEZOID

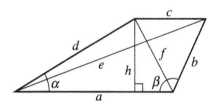

$$A = \frac{(a+c)h}{2}$$
$$h = d \sin \alpha$$
$$= b \sin \beta$$
$$e = \sqrt{a^2 + b^2 - 2ab \cos \beta}$$
$$f = \sqrt{a^2 + d^2 - 2ad \cos \alpha}$$

C.3.6   GENERAL QUADRILATERAL

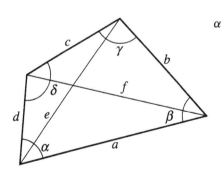

$$\alpha + \beta + \delta + \gamma = 360°$$
$$\theta = 90 \Leftrightarrow a^2 + c^2 = b^2 + d^2$$
$$A = \frac{1}{2}ef \sin \theta$$
$$= \frac{1}{4}(b^2 + d^2 - a^2 - c^2) \tan \theta$$
$$= \frac{1}{4}\sqrt{4e^2 f^2 - (b^2 + d^2 - a^2 - c^2)^2}$$

C.4 CIRCLES

C.4.1 SYMBOLS

- r: radius
- d: diameter
- c: circumference
- s: length of arc

C.4.2 FULL CIRCLE

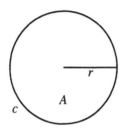

$$c = 2\pi r$$
$$= \pi d$$
$$A = \pi r^2$$
$$= \frac{\pi d^2}{4}$$

C.4.3 SECTOR OF A CIRCLE

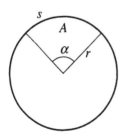

$$s = \alpha r$$
$$A = \frac{sr}{2}$$
$$= \frac{\alpha r^2}{2}$$

C.4.4 SEGMENT OF A CIRCLE

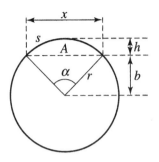

$$x = 2r \sin \frac{\alpha}{2}$$

$$h = r(1 - \cos \frac{\alpha}{2})$$

$$h(2r - h) = (\frac{x}{2})^2$$

$$= \frac{\alpha r^2}{2}$$

$$A = \frac{r^2}{2}(\alpha - \sin \alpha)$$

$$= \frac{1}{2}(rx - bx)$$

C.5 POLYHEDRA

C.5.1 SYMBOLS

- a, b, c: edges
- d: diagonal
- B: area of base
- S: surface area
- V: volume

C.5.2 BOX

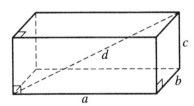

$$d = \sqrt{a^2 + b^2 + c^2}$$

$$S = 2(ab + bc + ac)$$

$$V = abc$$

C.5.3   PRISM

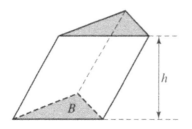

$$V = Bh$$

C.5.4   PYRAMID

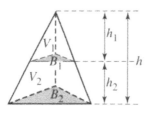

$$V = \frac{1}{3}Bh$$

$$\frac{V_1}{V} = \left(\frac{B_1}{B}\right)^{\frac{3}{2}}$$

$$= \left(\frac{h_1}{h}\right)^3$$

$$V_1 = \frac{h_1^3 B}{3h^2}$$

$$V_2 = \frac{h_2}{3}\left(B + \sqrt{BB_1} + B_1\right)$$

C.6   CYLINDER

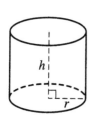

$$B = \pi r^2$$
$$A = 2\pi rh$$
$$S = 2\pi r(r + h)$$
$$V = \pi r^2 h$$

C.7 CONE

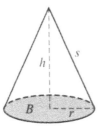

$$s = \sqrt{r^2 + h^2}$$

$$A = \pi r s$$

$$S = \pi r (r + s)$$

$$V = \frac{1}{3} \pi r^2 h$$

C.8 SPHERES

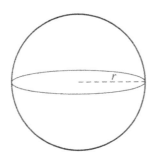

$$S = 4 \pi r^2$$

$$V = \frac{4}{3} \pi r^3$$

C.8.1 SEGMENTS

One Base

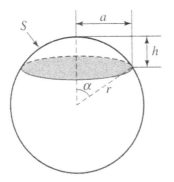

$$a = r \sin \alpha$$

$$a^2 = h(2r - h)$$

$$h = r(1 - \cos \alpha)$$

$$S = 2 \pi r h$$

$$V = \frac{\pi}{3} h^2 (3r - h)$$

$$= \frac{\pi}{6} h (3a^2 + h^2)$$

Two Bases

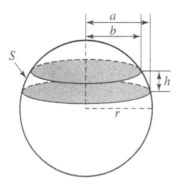

$$S = 2\pi r h$$

$$V = \frac{\pi}{6}h(3a^2 + 3b^2 + h^2)$$

C.8.2   SECTOR

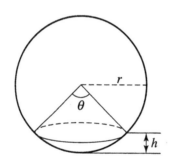

$$V = \frac{2\pi r^2 h}{3}$$

$$= \frac{\pi r^3}{3}\left(2 - 3\cos\frac{\theta}{2} + \cos^3\frac{\theta}{2}\right)$$

C.9   TORUS

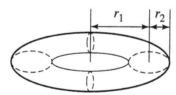

$$S = 4\pi^2 r_1 r_2$$

$$V = 2\pi^2 r_1 r_2{}^2$$

REFERENCES

Agnew, Jeanne, and Robert C. Knapp. 1978. *Linear Algebra with Applications*. Brooks/ Cole Publishing Company, Monterey, CA.

Anton, Howard. 1980. *Calculus with Analytic Geometry*. John Wiley and Sons, New York.

Arvo, James. 1990. A simple method for box-sphere intersection testing. In Andrew Glassner, editor, *Graphics Gems*, Academic Press, New York, pages 335–339.

Arvo, James, editor. 1991. *Graphics Gems II*. Academic Press, San Diego.

Bajaj, C. L., C. M. Hoffman, J. E. H. Hopcroft, and R. E. Lynch. 1989. Tracing surface intersections. *Computer Aided Geometric Design*, 5:285–307.

Barequet, Gill, and Sariel Har-Peled. 1999. Efficiently approximating the minimum-volume bounding box of a point set in three dimensions. *Proc. 10th ACM-SIAM Sympos. Discrete Algorithms*, pages 82–91.

Barnhill, Robert E., and S. N. Kersey. 1990. A marching method for parametric surface/surface intersection. *Computer Aided Geometric Design*, 7:257–280.

Bartels, Richard H., John C. Beatty, and Brian A. Barsky. 1987. *An Introduction to Splines for Use in Computer Graphics and Geometric Modeling*. Morgan Kaufmann Publishers, San Francisco.

Bellman, R. E. 1987. *Dynamic Programming*. Princeton University Press, Princeton, NJ.

Blumenthal, Leonard M. 1970. *Theory and Applications of Distance Geometry*. Chelsea House Publishers, Broomall, PA.

Boeing Information & Support Services. 1997. DT_NURBS spline geometry subprogram library: Theory document, version 3.5. Carderock Division, Naval Surface Warfare Center.

Bourke, Paul. 1992. Intersection of a line and a sphere (or circle). *astronomy.swin.edu .au/pbourke/geometry/sphereline*.

Bowyer. A. 1981. Computing dirichlet tessellations. *The Computer Journal*, 24(2): 162–166.

Bowyer, Adrian, and John Woodwark. 1983. *A Programmer's Geometry*. Butterworth's, London.

Busboom, Axel, and Robert J. Schalkoff. 1996. Active stereo vision and direct surface parameter estimation: Curve-to-curve image plane mappings. *IEEE Proceedings on Vision, Image, and Signal Processing*, 143(2), April. Web version: *ece.clemson.edu/iaal/vsip1rw/vsip1rw.htm*.

Bykat, A. 1978. Convex hull of a finite set of points in two dimensions. *Information Processing Letters*, 7:296–298.

Cameron, S. 1997. Enhancing GJK: Computing minimum and penetration distances between convex polyhedra. *Proc. IEEE Int. Conf. on Robotics and Automation*, pages 3112–3117.

Cameron, S., and R. K. Culley. 1986. Determining the minimum translational distance between convex polyhedra. *Proc. IEEE Int. Conf. on Robotics and Automation*, pages 591–596.

Campagna, Swen, Philipp Slusallek, and Hans-Peter Seidel. 1997. Ray tracing of spline surfaces: Bézier clipping, Chebyshev boxing, and bounding volume hierarchy—a critical comparison with new results. *The Visual Computer*, 13.

Casselman, Bill. 2001. Mathematics 309—conic sections and their applications. *www.math.ubc.ca/people/faculty/cass/courses/m309-01a/text/ch4.pdf*.

Chasen, Sylvan H. 1978. *Geometric Principles and Procedures for Computer Graphics Applications*. Prentice Hall, Englewood Cliffs, NJ.

Chazelle, B. 1991. Triangulating a simple polygon in linear time. *Disc. Comp. Geom.*, 6:485–524.

Chazelle, B., and J. Incerpi. 1984. Triangulation and shape complexity. *ACM Transactions on Graphics*, 3:135–152.

Chazelle, B., and L. Palios. 1990. Triangulating a nonconvex polyhedron. *Discrete and Computational Geometry*, 5:505–526.

Cheng, S.-W., T. K. Dey, H. Edelsbrunner, M. A. Facello, and S.-H. Teng. 2000. Sliver exudation. *Journal of the ACM*, 47(5):883–904.

Clarkson, K., R. E. Tarjan, and C. J. Van Wyk. 1989. A fast Las Vegas algorithm for triangulating a simple polygon. *Disc. Comp. Geom.*, 4:387–421.

Cohen, Elaine, Tom Lyche, and Richard Riesenfeld. 1980. Discrete B-splines and subdivision techniques in computer-aided geometric design and computer graphics. *Computer Graphics and Image Processing*, 14:87–111.

Cohen, Elaine, Richard F. Riesenfeld, and Gershon Elber. 2001. *Geometric Modeling with Splines: An Introduction*. A. K. Peters, Natick, MA.

Cohen, J. D., M. C. Lin, D. Manocha, and M. K. Ponamgi. 1995. I–Collide: An interactive and exact collision detection system for large-scale environments. *Proc. ACM Symposium on Interactive 3D Graphics*, pages 189–196.

Collins, G. E., and A. G. Akritas. 1976. Polynomial real root isolation using Descartes' rule of signs. *ACM Symposium on Symbolic and Algebraic Computation*, pages 272–276.

Collins, G. E., and R. Loos. 1982. Real zeros of polynomials. *Computing, Suppl.*, 4:83–94.

Cormen, Thomas H., Charles E. Leiserson, and Ronald L. Rivest. 1990. *Introduction to Algorithms*. The MIT Press, Cambridge, MA.

Crawford, Diane, editor. 2002. Game engines in scientific research (seven articles). *Communications of the ACM*, 45(1), January.

Dahmen, W., C. A. Micchelli, and H.-P. Seidel. 1992. Blossoming begets B-spline bases built better by B-patches. *Mathematics of Computation*, 1(1):97–115, July.

de Berg, Mark (editor), Marc van Kreveld, Mark Overmars, and O. Schwarzkopf. 2000. *Computational Geometry: Algorithms and Applications* (2nd edition). Springer, Berlin.

DeRose, Tony D. 1989. A coordinate-free approach to geometric programming. *Math for SIGGRAPH: Course Notes 23, SIGGRAPH '89*, pages 55–115, July.

DeRose, Tony D. 1992. *Three-Dimensional Computer Graphics: A Coordinate-Free Approach*. Unpublished manuscript, University of Washington.

Dey, Tamal K., Chandrajit L. Bajaj, and Kokicki Sugihara. 1991. On good triangulations in three dimensions. *Proceedings of the First Symposium on Solid Modeling Foundations and CAD/CAM Applications*, pages 431–441.

Dobkin, D. P., and D. G. Kirkpatrick. 1990. Determining the separation of preprocessed polyhedra—A unified approach. *Proc. 17th Internat. Colloq. Automata Lang. Program, Lecture Notes in Computer Science*, volume 443, pages 400–413. Springer-Verlag.

Dupont, Laurent, Sylvain Lazard, and Sylvain Petitjean. 2001. Towards the robust intersection of implicit quadrics. In *Workshop on Uncertainty in Geometric Computations, The University of Scheffield (England)*. Kluwer.

Eberly, David H. 1999. Polysolids and boolean operations. *www.magic-software.com/Documentation/psolid.pdf*.

Eberly, David H. 2000. *3D Game Engine Design*. Morgan Kaufmann, San Francisco.

Eberly, David H. 2001. Polysolid and BSP-based Boolean polygon operations. *www.magic-software.com/ConstructivePlanarGeometry.html*.

Edelsbrunner, H., and R. Seidel. 1986. Voronoi diagrams and arrangements. *Disc. Comp. Geom.*, 1:25–44.

Farin, Gerald. 1990. *Curves and Surfaces in Computer Aided Geometric Design: A Practical Guide*. Academic Press, Boston.

Farin, Gerald. 1995. *NURB Curves and Surfaces, From Projective Geometry to Practical Use*. A. K. Peters, Wellesley, MA.

Farouki, R. T. 1986. The characterization of parametric surface sections. *Computer Vision, Graphics, and Image Processing*, 33:209–236.

Field, D. A. 1986. Implementing Watson's algorithm in three dimensions. *Proceedings of the Second Annual ACM SIGACT/SIGGRAPH Symposium on Computational Geometry*, pages 246–259.

Finney, Ross L., and George B. Thomas. 1996. *Calculus and Analytic Geometry*, 9th edition. Addison-Wesley Publishing Company, Reading, MA.

Foley, James D., Andries van Dam, Steven K. Feiner, and John F. Hughes. 1996. *Computer Graphics: Principles and Practices*. Addison-Wesley Publishing Company, Reading, MA.

Fournier, Alain, and John Buchanan. 1984. Chebyshev polynomials for boxing and intersections of parametric curves and surfaces. *Computer Graphics Forum: Proceedings of Eurographics '94*, volume 13(3), pages 127–142.

Fournier, A., and D. Y. Montuno. 1984. Triangulating simple polygons and equivalent problems. *ACM Transactions on Graphics*, 3:153–174.

Fuchs, Henry, Zvi Kedem, and Bruce Naylor. 1979. Predetermining visibility priority in 3-d scenes. *Proceedings of SIGGRAPH*, pages 175–181.

Fuchs, Henry, Zvi Kedem, and Bruce Naylor. 1980. On visible surface generation by a priori tree structures. *Proceedings of SIGGRAPH*, pages 124–133.

Gaertner, Bernd, and Sven Schoenherr. 1998. Exact primitives for smallest enclosing ellipses. *Information Processing Letters*, 68:33–38.

Gaertner, Bernd, and Sven Schoenherr. 2000. An efficient, exact, and generic quadratic programming solver for geometric optimization. *Proc. 16th Annual ACM Symposium on Computational Geometry (SCG)*, pages 110–118.

Georgiades, Príamos. 1992. Signed distance from point to plane. In David Kirk, editor, *Graphics Gems III*, Academic Press, New York, pages 223–224.

Gilbert, E. G., and C.-P. Foo. 1990. Computing the distance between general convex objects in three-dimensional space. *IEEE Transactions on Robotics and Automation*, 6(1):53–61.

Gilbert, E. G., D. W. Johnson, and S. S. Keerthi. 1988. A fast procedure for computing the distance between complex objects in three-dimensional space. *IEEE Journal of Robotics and Automation*, 4(2):193–203.

Glaeser, Georg. 1994. *Fast Algorithms for 3D-Graphics*. Springer-Verlag, New York.

Glassner, Andrew S., editor. 1989. *An Introduction to Ray Tracing*. Academic Press, Berkeley.

Glassner, Andrew S., editor. 1990. *Graphics Gems*. Academic Press, San Diego.

Goldman, Ronald N. 1985. Illicit expressions in vector algebra. *ACM Transactions on Graphics*, 4(3):223–243, July.

Goldman, Ronald N. 1987. Vector geometry: A coordinate-free approach. *Geometry for Computer Graphics and Computer Aided Design: Course Notes 19, SIGGRAPH '87*, pages 1–172, June.

Goldman, Ronald N. 1990a. Intersection of three planes. In Andrew Glassner, editor, *Graphics Gems*, Academic Press, San Diego, page 305.

Goldman, Ronald N. 1990b. Matrices and transformations. In Andrew Glassner, editor, *Graphics Gems*, Academic Press, San Diego, pages 472–475.

Goldman, Ronald N. 1990c. Triangles. In Andrew Glassner, editor, *Graphics Gems*, Academic Press, San Diego, pages 20–23.

Goldman, Ronald N. 1991. More matrices and transformations: Shear and pseudo-perspective. In James Arvo, editor, *Graphics Gems II*, Academic Press, San Diego, pages 338–341.

Goldman, Ronald N., and Tom Lyche, editors. 1993. *Knot Insertion and Deletion Algorithms for B–Spline Curves and Surfaces*. Society for Industrial and Applied Mathematics, Philadelphia.

Golub, Gene H., and Charles F. Van Loan. 1993. *Matrix Computations,* 2nd edition. The Johns Hopkins University Press, Baltimore, MD.

Gottschalk, Stefan, Ming Lin, and Dinesh Manocha. 1996. OBBTree: A hierarchical structure for rapid interference detection. *Computer Graphics (SIGGRAPH '96 Proceedings)*, pages 171–180, August.

Haines, Eric. 1987. Abnormal normals. *Ray Tracing News*, 0, September.

Haines, Eric. 1989. Essential ray tracing algorithms. In Andrew Glassner, editor, *An Introduction to Ray Tracing*, Academic Press, San Diego, pages 33–77.

Haines, Eric. 1991. Fast ray–convex polyhedron intersection. In James Arvo, editor, *Graphics Gems II*, Academic Press, San Diego, pages 247–250.

Haines, Eric. 1994. Point in polygon strategies. In Paul S. Heckbert, editor, *Graphics Gems IV*, Academic Press, San Diego, pages 24–46.

Hanrahan, Pat. 1983. Ray tracing algebraic surfaces. *Computer Graphics (SIGGRAPH '83 Proceedings)*, ACM, July, pages 83–90.

Hart, John. 1994. Distance to an ellipsoid. In Paul S. Heckbert, editor, *Graphics Gems IV*, Academic Press, New York, pages 113–119.

Heckbert, Paul S., editor. 1994. *Graphics Gems IV*. Academic Press, San Diego.

Hecker, Chris. 1997. Physics, part 4: The third dimension. *Game Developer*, pages 15–26, June.

Hershberger, John E., and Jack S. Snoeyink. 1988. Erased decompositions of lines and convex decompositions of polyhedra. *Computational Geometry, Theory and Applications*, 9(3):129–143.

Hertel, S., and K. Mehlhorn. 1983. Fast triangulation of simple polygons. *Proc. 4th Internat. Conf. Found. Comput. Theory*, volume 158 of *Lecture Notes in Computer Science*, pages 207–218.

Hill, F. S., Jr. 1994. The pleasures of 'perp dot' products. In Paul S. Heckbert, editor, *Graphics Gems IV*, Academic Press, New York, pages 139–148.

Hoffman, C. M. 1989. *Geometric and Solid Modeling*. Morgan Kaufmann, San Francisco.

Holwerda, Klaas. 2000. Boolean, version 6. *www.xs4all.nl/ kholwerd/bool.html*.

Horn, Roger A., and Charles R. Johnson. 1985. *Matrix Analysis*. Cambridge University Press, Cambridge, England.

Huber, Ernst H. 1998. Intersecting general parametric surfaces using bounding volumes. In Mike Soss, editor, *Proceedings of the 10th Canadian Conference on Computational Geometry*, Montréal, Québec, School of Computer Science, McGill University, pages 52–53.

Joe, Barry. 1991. Delaunay versus max-min solid angle triangulations for three-dimensional mesh generation. *International Journal for Numerical Methods in Engineering*, 31:987–997.

Johnson, L., and R. Riess. 1982. *Numerical Analysis*. Addison-Wesley Publishing Company, Reading, MA.

Kajiya, James T. 1982. Ray tracing parametric surfaces. *Computer Graphics (SIGGRAPH '82 Proceedings)*, ACM, volume 16(3), pages 245–254 .

Kay, D. D. 1988. *Schaum's Outline of Theory and Problems of Tensor Calculus*. McGraw-Hill, New York.

Kay, Timothy L., and James T. Kajiya. 1986. Ray tracing complex scenes. *Computer Graphics (SIGGRAPH '86 Proceedings)*, ACM, pages 269–278.

Keil, J. M. 1985. Decomposing a polygon into simpler components. *SIAM J. Comput.*, 14:799–817.

Keil, J. M., and J. Snoeyink. 1998. On the time bound for convex decomposition of simple polygons. *Proceedings of the 10th Canadian Conference on Computational Geometry*, pages 54–55.

Kirk, David, editor. 1992. *Graphics Gems III*. Academic Press, San Diego.

Kirkpatrick, D. G. 1983. Optimal search in planar subdivisions. *SIAM J. Comp.*, 12:28–35.

Klee, V. 1980. On the complexity of d-dimensional Voronoi diagrams. *Archiv. Mathem.*, 34:75–80.

Krishnan, Shankar, and Dinesh Manocha. 1997. An efficient surface intersection algorithm based on lower dimensional formulation. *ACM Transactions on Graphics*, 16(1).

Lam, T. 1973. *The Algebraic Theory of Quadratic Forms*. W.A. Benjamin, Reading, MA.

Lane, Jeffrey, and Robert F. Riesenfeld. 1980. A theoretical development for the computer generation and display of piecewise polynomial surfaces. *IEEE Transactions on Pattern Analysis and Machine Intelligence*, 2(1):150–159.

Lasser, D. 1986. Intersection of parametric surfaces in the Bernstein-Bézier representation. *Computer-Aided Design*, 18(4):186–192.

Lee, Randy B., and David A. Fredricks. 1984. Special feature: Intersection of parametric surfaces and a plane. *IEEE Computer Graphics and Applications*, 4(8):48–51, August.

Leonov, Michael. 1997. poly_boolean. *woland.it.nsc.ru/ leonov/clipdoc.html*.

Levin, Joshua. 1976. A parametric algorithm for drawing pictures of solid objects composed of quadric surfaces. *Communications of the ACM*, 19(11):553–563, October.

Levin, Joshua. 1979. Mathematical models for determining the intersection of quadric surfaces. *Computer Graphics and Image Processing*, 11(1):73–87.

Levin, Joshua. 1980. *QUISP: A Computer Processor for the Design and Display of Quadric-Surface Bodies*. Ph.D. dissertation, Rensselaer Polytechnic Institute, Troy, NY.

Levine, Ron. 2000. Collisions of moving objects. GD algorithms list at *sourceforge.net*, November.

Lin, M. C., and J. F. Canny. 1991. A fast algorithm for incremental distance computation. *Proc. IEEE Int. Conf. on Robotics and Automation*, pages 1008–1014.

Martin, William, Elaine Cohen, Russell Fish, and Peter Shirley. 2000. Practical ray tracing of trimmed NURBS surfaces. *Journal of Graphics Tools*, 5(1):27–52.

Maynard, Hugh, and Lucio Tavernini. 1984. Boolean operations on polysolids. Unpublished work. (See a summary of the work in [Eberly 1997].)

Meister, G. H. 1975. Polygons have ears. *Amer. Math. Monthly*, 82:648–651.

Miller, James R. 1987. Geometric approaches to nonplanar quadric surface intersection curves. *ACM Transactions on Graphics*, 6(4), October.

Miller, James R. 1999a. Applications of vector geometry for robustness and speed. *IEEE Computer Graphics and Applications*, 19(4):68–73, July.

Miller, James R. 1999b. Vector geometry for computer graphics. *IEEE Computer Graphics and Applications*, 19(3):66–73, May.

Miller, James R., and Ronald N. Goldman. 1992. Using tangent balls to find plane sections of natural quadrics. *IEEE Computer Graphics and Applications*, 16(2):68–82, March.

Miller, James R., and Ronald N. Goldman. 1993a. Detecting and calculating conic sections in the intersection of two natural quadric surfaces, Part I: Theoretical analysis. Technical Report TR-93-1, Department of Computer Science, University of Kansas.

Miller, James R., and Ronald N. Goldman. 1993b. Detecting and calculating conic sections in the intersection of two natural quadric surfaces, Part II: Geometric constructions for detection and calculation. Technical Report TR-93-2, Department of Computer Science, University of Kansas.

Miller, James R., and Ronald Goldman. 1995. Geometric algorithms for detecting and calculating all conic sections in the intersection of any two natural quadric surfaces. *Computer Vision, Graphics, and Image Processing*, 57(1):55–66, January.

Mirtich, B. 1997. V-clip: Fast and robust polyhedral collision detection. *ACM Transactions on Graphics*, 17(3):177–208.

Möller, Tomas. 1997. A fast triangle-triangle intersection test. *Journal of Graphics Tools*, 2(2):25–30.

Möller, Tomas, and Eric Haines. 1999. *Real-Time Rendering*. A.K. Peters, Ltd., Natick, MA.

Möller, Tomas, and Ben Trumbore. 1997. Fast, minimum storage ray-triangle intersection. *Journal of Graphics Tools*, 2(1):21–28.

Murtha, Alan. 2000. gpc (general polygon clipper library), version 2.31. *www.cs.man. ac.uk/aig/staff/alan/software/index.html*.

Naylor, B. 1990. SCULPT: An interactive solid modeling tool. *Proceedings of Graphics Interface '90*, pages 138–148, May.

Naylor, B. 1992. Interactive solid geometry via partitioning trees. *Proceedings of Graphics Interface '92*, pages 11–18, May.

Naylor, B., J. Amanatides, and W. Thibault. 1990. Merging BSP trees yields polyhedral set operations. *Proceedings of SIGGRAPH*, pages 115–124.

Newman, W., and R. Sproull. 1979. *Principles of Interactive Computer Graphics*, 2nd edition. McGraw-Hill, New York.

Nishita, Tomoyuki, Thomas W. Sederberg, and Masanori Kakimoto. 1990. Ray tracing trimmed rational surface patches. *Computer Graphics (SIGGRAPH '90 Proceedings)*, ACM, volume 24 (4), pages 337–345.

O'Rourke, J. 1985. Finding minimal enclosing boxes. *Internat. J. Comput. Inform. Sci.*, 14:183–199, June.

O'Rourke, Joseph. 1998. *Computational Geometry in C*, 2nd edition. Cambridge University Press, Cambridge, England.

Paeth, Alan W., editor. 1995. *Graphics Gems V*. Academic Press, San Diego.

Patrikalakis, N. M. 1993. Surface-to-surface intersections. *IEEE Computer Graphics and Applications*, 13(1):89–95.

Piegl, Les. 1989. Geometric method of intersecting natural quadrics represented in trimmed surface form. *Computer-Aided Design*, 13(1):89–95.

Piegl, Les, and Wayne Tiller. 1995. *The NURBS Book*. Springer-Verlag, Berlin.

Pierre, Donald A. 1986. *Optimization Theory with Applications*. Dover Publications, New York.

Pirzadeh, Hormoz. 1999. Rotating calipers home page. *www.cs.mcgill.ca/~orm/rotcal.html*.

Pratt, M. J., and A. D. Geisow. 1986. Surface/surface intersection problems. In J. A. Gregory, editor, *The Mathematics of Surfaces*, volume 6, Clarendon Press, Oxford, pages 117–142.

Preparata, Franco P., and Michael Ian Shamos. 1985. *Computational Geometry: An Introduction*. Springer-Verlag, New York.

Press, W. H., B. P. Flannery, S. A. Teukolsky, and W. T. Vetterling. 1988. *Numerical Recipes in C: The Art of Scientific Computing*. Cambridge University Press, Cambridge, England.

Rade, Lennart, and Bertil Westergren. 1995. *Mathematics Handbook for Science and Engineering*. Birkhauser, Boston.

Rogers, David F. 2001. *An Introduction to NURBS with Historical Perspective*. Morgan Kaufmann Publishers, San Francisco.

Rogers, David F., and J. A. Adams. 1990. *Mathematical Elements for Computer Graphics*, 2nd edition. McGraw-Hill, New York.

Rossignac, J. R., and A. A. G. Requicha. 1987. Piecewise-circular curves for geometric modeling. *IBM Journal on Research and Development*, 31(3):39–45.

Roth, Scott. 1981. Ray casting for modeling solids. *Computer Graphics and Image Processing*, 18(2):109–144.

Rusin, Dave. 1995. General formula for the area of a polygon. *www.math.niu.edu/~rusin/known-math/95/greens*.

Salomon, David. 1999. *Computer Graphics and Geometric Modeling*. Springer-Verlag, New York.

Sarraga, R. F. 1983. Algebraic methods for intersection of quadric surfaces in GM-SOLID. *Computer Vision, Graphics, and Image Processing*, 22(2):222–238, May.

Schneider, Philip J. 1990. A Bézier curve-based root finder. In Andrew Glassner, editor, *Graphics Gems*, Academic Press, San Diego, pages 408–415.

Schutte, Klamer. 1995. An edge labeling approach to concave polygon clipping. *www.ph.tn.tudelft.nl/People/klamer/clip.ps.gz*.

Sechrest, S., and D. Greenberg. 1981. A visible polygon reconstruction algorithm. *Comput. Graph.*, 15(3):17–26.

Sederberg, Thomas W. 1983. *Implicit and Parametric Curves and Surfaces*. Ph.D. thesis, Purdue University.

Sederberg, Thomas W. 1984. Ray tracing of Steiner patches. *Computer Graphics (SIGGRAPH '84 Proceedings)*, ACM, volume 18 (3), pages 159–164.

Sederberg, Thomas W., and Tomoyuki Nishita. 1991. Geometric Hermite approximation of surface patch intersection curves. *Computer Aided Geometric Design*, 8:97–114.

Seidel, R. 1991. A simple and fast incremental randomized algorithm for computing trapezoidal decompositions and for triangulating polygons. *Computational Geometry: Theory and Applications*, 1(1):51–64.

Shamos, Michael I. 1978. *Computational Geometry*. Ph.D. dissertation, Yale University.

Shewchuk, Jonathan Richard. 2000. Stabbing Delaunay tetrahedralizations. *www.cs.cmu.edu/ jrs/papers/stab.ps*.

Shoemake, Ken. 1987. Animating rotation with quaternion calculus. *ACM SIGGRAPH Course Notes 10: Computer Animation: 3-D Motion, Specification, and Control*.

Sunday, Dan. 2001a. Area of triangles and polygons (2d and 3d). *www.softsurfer.com*.

Sunday, Dan. 2001b. Distance between lines, segments, and the closest point of approach. *www.softsurfer.com*.

Sunday, Dan. 2001c. Intersection of line, segment, and plane in 2d and 3d. *www.softsurfer.com*.

Sweeney, Michael A. J., and Richard H. Bartels. 1986. Ray tracing free-form B-spline surfaces. *IEEE Computer Graphics and Applications*, 6(2):41–49, February.

Tampieri, Filippo. 1992. Newell's method for computing the plane equation of a polygon. In David Kirk, editor, *Graphics Gems III*, Academic Press, San Diego, pages 231–232.

ter Haar Romeny, B. M., editor. 1994. *Geometry-Driven Diffusion in Computer Vision*. Computational Imaging and Vision Series. Kluwer Academic Publishers, Dordrecht, the Netherlands.

Thibault, William C., and Bruce F. Naylor. 1987. Set operations on polyhedra using binary space partitioning trees. *Proceedings of the 14th Annual Conference on Computer Graphics*, pages 153–162.

Toth, Daniel L. 1995. On ray tracing parametric surfaces. *Computer Graphics (SIGGRAPH '85 Proceedings)*, ACM, volume 19 (3), pages 171–179.

van den Bergen, Gino. 1997. Efficient collision detection of complex deformable models using AABB trees. *Journal of Graphics Tools*, 2(4):1–13.

van den Bergen, Gino. 1999. A fast and robust GJK implementation for collision detection of convex objects. *Journal of Graphics Tools*, 4(2):7–25.

van den Bergen, Gino. 2001a. Proximity queries and penetration depth computation on 3d game objects. *Game Developers Conference Proceedings*, pages 821–837.

van den Bergen, Gino. 2001b. SOLID: Software library for interference detection. *www.win.tue.nl/ gino/solid/*.

Vatti, B. R. 1992. A generic solution to polygon clipping. *Communications of the ACM*, 35(7):56–63.

Watson, D. 1981. Computing the n–dimensional Delaunay tessellation with applications to Voronoi polytopes. *The Computer Journal*, 24(2):167–172.

Wee, Chionh Eng, and Ronald N. Goldman. 1995a. Elimination and resultants part 1: Elimination and bivariate resultants. *IEEE Computer Graphics and Applications*, January, pages 69–77.

Wee, Chionh Eng, and Ronald N. Goldman. 1995b. Elimination and resultants part 2: Multivariate resultants. *IEEE Computer Graphics and Applications*, March, pages 60–69.

Weiler, K., and P. Atherton. 1977. Hidden surface removal using polygon area sorting. *Proceedings of SIGGRAPH*, volume 11, pages 214–222.

Weisstein, Eric. 1999. Torus. *mathworld.wolfram.com/Torus.html*.

Welzl, Emo. 1991. Smallest enclosing disks (balls and ellipsoids). *Lecture Notes in Computer Science, New Results and New Trends in Computer Science*, 555:359–370.

Wikipedia. 2002. Field. *www.wikipedia.com/wiki/Field*.

Yamaguchi, Fujio. 1988. *Curves and Surfaces in Computer Aided Geometric Design*. Springer-Verlag, Berlin.

INDEX

About the Authors

Philip Schneider leads a modeling and dynamic simulation software group at Walt Disney Feature Animation. Prior to that, his work at Apple and Digital Equipment Corporation in 3D graphics ranged from low-level interfaces to graphics libraries and interactive applications. He holds an M.S. in Computer Science from the University of Washington.

David Eberly is President of Magic Software, Inc. and is the architect of the real-time 3D game engine Wild Magic. Previously, he was Director of Engineering at Numerical Design, Ltd., the company responsible for the real-time 3D game engine NetImmerse. He holds a Ph.D. in Computer Science from the University of North Carolina at Chapel Hill and a Ph.D. in Mathematics from the University of Colorado at Boulder.